Editor-in-Chief
Asa S. Knowles

Chancellor, Northeastern University

THE
INTERNATIONAL
ENCYCLOPEDIA
OF HIGHER
EDUCATION

Volume 4
D-F

Jossey-Bass Publishers
San Francisco • Washington • London • 1978

THE INTERNATIONAL ENCYCLOPEDIA OF HIGHER EDUCATION
Volume 4
Asa S. Knowles, Editor-in-Chief

Copyright © 1977 by: Jossey-Bass, Inc., Publishers
433 California Street
San Francisco, California 94104
&
Jossey-Bass Limited
28 Banner Street
London EC1Y 8QE

Library of Congress Cataloging in Publication Data

Main entry under title:

The international encyclopedia of higher education.

    Includes index.
    1. Education, Higher—Dictionaries. I. Knowles,
Asa Smallidge, 1909–
LB15.157   378'.003   77-73647
ISBN 0-87589-323-6 (set)
ISBN 0-87589-327-9 (v. 4)

Manufactured in the United States of America
    Composition by Chapman's Phototypesetting
    Printing by Hamilton Printing Company
    Binding by Payne Edition Bindery

COVER DESIGN BY WILLI BAUM

FIRST EDITION
    First printing: December 1977
    Second printing: November 1978

Code 7726

THE
INTERNATIONAL
ENCYCLOPEDIA
OF HIGHER
EDUCATION

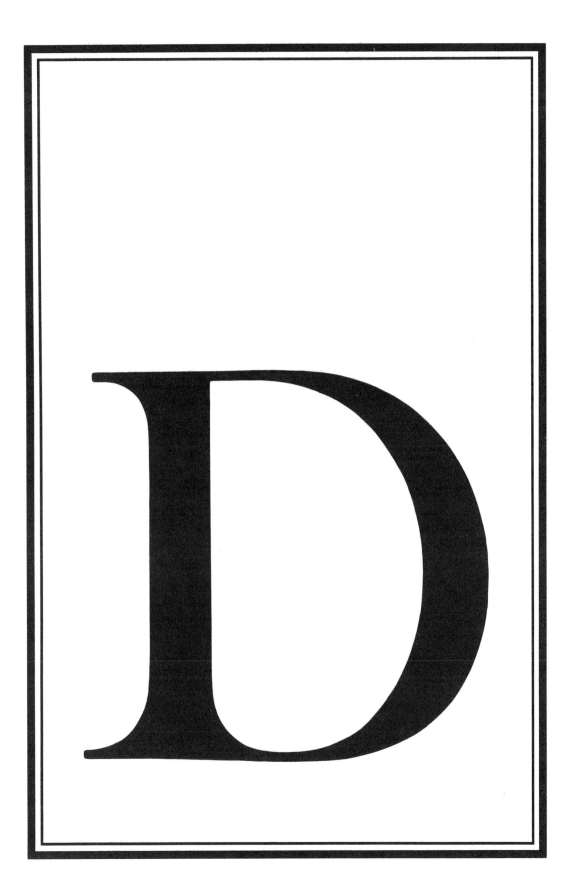

DAHOMEY

See Benin, People's Republic of.

DAIRY SCIENCE (Field of Study)

Dairy science deals with all aspects of the arts, sciences, and crafts involved in the production, collection, processing, and distribution of milk and milk products. It embraces the applied agricultural and technological sciences, plus the more basic sciences of chemistry, biochemistry, microbiology, physics, mathematics, genetics, physiology, and endocrinology. Dairy farming is an integral part of animal agriculture, fitting especially into an intensive type of agriculture where the dairy cow has demonstrated her efficiency of production over other farm animals.

Dairy science normally includes two branches: (1) dairy production (dairy husbandry) and (2) dairy technology (dairy manufacturing, dairy industry). Dairy production includes studies in dairy cattle selection, breeding, feeding, and management; physiology and biochemistry of lactation; growth and development; dairy cattle diseases and maintenance of herd health; housing; milk hygiene; and efficiency and costs of milk production. Dairy technology, covering all aspects of milk after it has been produced on the farm, includes studies on milk collection and transport, milk processing, manufacture of dairy products, distribution and marketing, dairy engineering, and quality control.

In recent years in the United States and some of the other highly developed countries, the trend has been toward the merger of dairy production, or dairy husbandry, into animal science. In some countries dairy science, dairy technology, and dairy manufacturing have been combined with other food processing into food science departments; but most countries prefer to keep dairy science and technology as a distinct discipline. Under some circumstances the name *dairy husbandry* is still used, especially in the developing areas, even though the trend has been to replace *dairy husbandry* with *dairy science*.

The most obvious closely related field to dairy production is animal science (where animal science is defined as the study of animals other than dairy cattle). And the most closely allied field to dairy technology is food science.

In curricula where the emphasis is on dairy production, about 40 to 60 percent of the courses are in the physical, biological, physiological, and social sciences, including the communication arts; the remainder are in the various applied subjects in dairy science and other related agricultural sciences. Special emphasis is given to soil science, crop science, crop protection (entomology and plant pathology), agricultural economics, farm management, and agribusiness. In curricula where the emphasis is on dairy technology, the subjects taken include mathematics, physics, chemistry (including biochemistry), microbiology, and technology as well as subjects in economics and the social and management sciences.

Because of the great diversity of student interest and vocational goals, curricula in dairy science at most educational institutions in the United States, and also in other countries, gradually have become more flexible. Beyond the college requirements for graduation for the baccalaureate degree, the student has a broad choice of electives that will best meet his needs. For example, students who plan to go to graduate school to prepare for careers in teaching or research or as extension service agents may take a larger proportion of basic science subjects. Those who plan to go into dairy production positions on dairy farms may elect a larger proportion of subjects in the related agricultural sciences, animal science, veterinary medicine, communication arts, agricultural economics, and agribusiness. Students interested in management positions in the dairy industry usually select a larger proportion of subjects in economics and the social, management, and business sciences.

The degree of flexibility in the dairy science curriculum varies widely among institutions in all countries. A more rigid curriculum, largely composed of required subjects with only limited electives, still prevails in some countries.

The field now known as dairy science has a long history. As far back as history records, man has possessed cattle and has used milk and products made from milk. In the oldest parts of the Bible, many references are made to cattle, milk, butter, and cheese. The cow has served man through the ages as a source of food, as a beast of burden, as an object of worship, as a source of sacrificial offering, and as

an object of mythology. Dairying has been described in the ancient countries of India and Egypt. The Greeks, in 1000 to 450 B.C., used butter and cheese. The Romans, in 750 B.C. to 475 A.D., also used dairy products, and cheese became an important article of commerce for them. Knowledge of the use of milk and its products eventually spread over Europe. From the third or fourth century A.D., the monasteries were the chief sources of information on dairying. In 1717 the first dairy school was organized in Germany, and many other European countries soon followed Germany's lead. Early in the development of the dairy industry, Holland and Switzerland became centers of the industry, a position which they have retained to modern times.

North America is indebted to the United Kingdom and other European countries for its breeds of dairy cattle, for most of the early knowledge of dairying, for the early practices in the use of milk, and for methods of manufacturing products from it. The first cattle were brought to America by Columbus on his second voyage, but there was relatively little growth and development of a dairy industry until about 1850. Before that time, dairying was largely a home or domestic activity, and little progress was made in milk production and processing, although improved breeds were imported from the United Kingdom and other European countries by the early part of the nineteenth century. Since 1850, with the beginning of the factory system— and especially since 1925, with the application of many scientific discoveries and inventions—more progress has been made in the dairy industry than in all recorded history up to that time.

Many factors have played significant roles in the development of the dairy industry in the United States; chief among them have been education and research in dairying and agriculture—particularly in the agricultural schools and colleges that train and educate large numbers of men and women. Many graduates of these schools become teachers of agriculture in secondary schools; others become extension education agents, who help carry knowledge to the public. In addition, dairy cattle breed associations, state dairymen's associations, state dairy councils, the National Dairy Council, the American Dairy Association, and cooperative milk marketing organizations all carry on educational programs on the nutritive value of dairy products. Similar organizations provide educational functions in other countries where dairying is an important industry.

The first agricultural college in the United States was established in Michigan in 1855, but the growth and development of agricultural schools began after the passage of the Land-Grant Act in 1862. In the early years these land-grant colleges primarily were teaching institutions where the art of dairying and other agricultural subjects were taught. After a few years it became apparent that research was needed to produce new knowledge, so in 1887 the Hatch Act provided government funds for the establishment of an experiment station in each of the states, under the direction of the colleges of agriculture. The colleges became organized into subject matter departments, such as dairy husbandry, for teaching and research. Along with other agricultural sciences, the science of dairying developed rapidly and gradually replaced the art of dairying as a subject.

Almost from their beginning, agricultural colleges provided farmers with information on dairy production, handling of milk, and other agricultural subjects. In order to extend more effectively new knowledge gained through research, the Smith-Lever Act (passed by the Congress in 1914) established the Extension Service, to be implemented in each of the states through the colleges of agriculture. Thus, the threefold functions of teaching, research, and extension came into being and established what has become widely known as the land-grant philosophy of service to the people.

Higher education in dairy science and the other agricultural and technological sciences has been changing rapidly for many years, especially in the more highly developed temperate regions. Major studies of courses and curricula have resulted in significant changes, in keeping with a dynamic, modern agricultural society. Goals have been redefined, and new courses and curricula have been geared increasingly to modern farming and to trends in science and technology and in business and industries that serve agriculture. Curricula have been developed that cut across the traditional areas of animal science, dairy science, and poultry science. New subjects, such as international dairy and animal science, have been added in some universities. Greater emphasis has been given to the international perspectives of subjects in dairy science.

Modern dairy industries use the systems approach to the production of milk as it moves through the channels of processing, marketing, and distribution to the consumer. The systems approach has taken over most of the essential functions that once were the concern of the individual farmer. Fewer dairy farmers, with larger farms and herds, are now producing more milk per cow, per man, and per acre than ever before in history. In the developed countries dairy industries are making use of highly automated processing units with a high production capacity. These trends demand different approaches and relate directly to educational programs necessary to produce the kinds of people for progressive leadership to serve the dairy industry and agriculture in the future.

The high costs in labor, feed, and machinery have increased the necessity for attaining efficiency of milk production. Disposal of waste from dairy farms has become a major problem in the intensive dairy regions. These and similar problems have stimulated greater emphasis on agribusiness, agricultural economics, and engineering subjects in the curriculum.

Characteristics and backgrounds of students enrolling in agriculture for major work in dairy science have been changing. A lower percentage (sometimes less than 25 percent) enter college with farm backgrounds and practical experience than was true a few years ago. Instructional and training programs have been changed to reflect an appreciation of the diverse backgrounds of entering students.

In the developing countries the percentage of farm boys and girls that ever attend college is very small. Coupled with this is the fact that agriculture, including dairying, is a low-status profession and therefore often does not attract the highest-quality students. Students in agricultural colleges in developing countries usually are taught by teachers who did not have farm backgrounds and practical experience and who are generally not involved in research. It is from this background of experience that many students go abroad for advanced studies.

In many of the land-grant universities in the United States, the foreign student population represents about one third of the graduate students studying agricultural subjects. With this proportion of graduate students from abroad, a majority from developing countries, the host university has a challenge and responsibility to give them the kind of training and experience that will enable them to be of greatest service in their home countries. Flexibility in selection of subjects makes it possible for the student to get a course of study suitable to his needs.

An innovation relating to the thesis research of foreign graduate students has been in effect since the early 1960s at a number of universities in the United States and at some universities in other countries. After careful planning for adequate supervision, foreign students are sent back to their home country, or one of similar environment, for their thesis research, so that they can work on problems that are relevant to their own country.

Quite adequate education and training in dairy science are provided in the more highly developed countries of North Amer-

ica, Europe, the United Kingdom, Australia, New Zealand, and Japan, and to a lesser degree in some of the developing countries. Curricula and levels of training vary widely among countries, depending upon the needs of government and industry and upon the country's stage of development. The greatest need often may be for informal training. In most of the developing countries the major needs are for courses of the diploma type covering milk production and dairy technology and containing considerable amounts of practical work.

Systems of regional training courses have been developed for dealing with large numbers of students. Further specialized training is available for a select few of the outstanding students. Examples of this system are courses organized by the Food and Agriculture Organization (FAO) and financed by the government of Denmark.

Until quite recently, with the notable exception of India, there were virtually no dairy training facilities in any of the developing areas of the world. However, since about 1950 various international and national agencies have recognized the need and have given assistance in the form of funds, expert staff, and equipment to start dairy education programs. Local dairy centers, schools, and colleges have been developed with foreign financial assistance to train students for service in the dairy industry, both in production and in dairy technology. The courses may extend over a period of weeks, months, or years, depending upon the syllabus being followed, the needs of the country for trained manpower, and the educational background of the students. Frequently, such centers have expatriate international dairy experts on the teaching staff for varying periods of time. Examples of these centers are the Naivasha Dairy School (Kenya), Guildford Dairy Institute at Egerton College (Kenya), and the Dairy Training and Research Institute at College, Laguna (Philippines).

In the more highly developed countries and in a few of the developing countries, education and training in dairy science are available at several levels: (1) two- or three-year diploma or nondegree courses in agricultural and technical institutes; (2) baccalaureate degree (B.S.) level in colleges of agriculture; and (3) graduate or postgraduate level, for the M.S. and Ph.D., in the universities. At the undergraduate level, students may take a concentration in dairy science subjects, but very often the degree awarded is a B.S. in agriculture. At the graduate level, students may major in a discipline such as dairy science, dairy nutrition, dairy physiology, or genetics. Graduate work is the time for specialization for careers in teaching, research, and extension; in industry; as dairy scientists in nutrition, genetics and breeding, and physiology; or in production and management.

In many areas of the world one of the greatest nutritional problems is a lack of animal protein in the diets of the people. The high-producing dairy cow is an unparalleled converter of materials which are not suitable for human consumption into the palatable and nutritive human food product milk. Preparation of students through education and training for leadership has never been more important. Dairy cattle and other animals, and their products, will continue to play a significant role in meeting the challenge to feed the people of a world that seems determined to double its population before the year 2000.

KENNETH L. TURK

Major International and National Organizations

INTERNATIONAL

Commonwealth Bureau of Dairy Science and Technology
Bureau de la science et de la technologie de la laiterie du Commonwealth
Shinfield
Reading, Berks. RG2 9AT, England

Dairy Society International (DSI)
Société internationale laitière
3008 McKinley Street NW
Washington, D.C. 20015 USA

Food and Agriculture Organization of the United Nations (FAO)
Animal Production and Health Division
via delle Terme di Caracalla
00100 Rome, Italy
This organization sponsors international conferences on dairy education and is a good source of information on dairy education internationally.

International Dairy Committee (IDC)
Comité international laitier
Giggs Hill Green, Thames Ditton
Surrey, England

International Dairy Federation (IDF)
Fédération internationale de la laiterie (FIL)
41 square Vergote
1040 Brussels, Belgium

NATIONAL

Australia:
    Australian Society of Dairy Technology
    Box 20
    Highett 3190, Victoria

Belgium:
    Société nationale de laiterie
    49 avenue Charles Verhaegen
    Crainhem

Denmark:
    Dansk mejeristforening
    Vindegade 74
    5000 Odense

India:
    Indian Dairy Science Association
    Honsur Road, Advgodi P.O.
    Bangalore 30, Mysore State

United Kingdom:
    Society of Dairy Technology
    17 Devonshire Street
    London W1, England

United States:
    American Dairy Science Association
    113 North Neil Street
    Champaign, Illinois 61820

Principal Information Sources

GENERAL

Guides to the literature in the field include:

Bush, E. A. R. *Agriculture: An Annotated Bibliography.* (2 vols.) London: Macdonald, 1974. A comprehensive annotated bibliography which covers dairying, milk production and products, and dairy practice. Includes bibliographies, abstracts, periodicals, dictionaries, and general reference works.

Catalogue of IDF Publications. (2 vols.) Brussels: International Dairy Federation, 1969–1970.

Information Sources on the Animal Feed Industry. UNIDO Guides to Information Sources, No. 13. Vienna: United Nations Industrial Development Organization, 1975. Includes professional and research organizations, information sources, directories, handbooks, dictionaries, bibliographies, and periodicals.

Schulz, M. E., and Sydow, G. (Eds.) *Manuale Lactis: Periodisch erscheinendes Handbuch der milchwirtschaftlichen Weltliteratur, geordnet nach dem System der Bibliotheca Lactis.* (10 vols.) Nuremberg, Federal Republic of Germany: Verlag Hans Carl, 1952–1975. International bibliography of dairy literature.

Introductions and overviews to the field include:

Alexander, G., and Williams, O. B. (Eds.) *The Pastoral Industries of Australia: Practice and Technology of Sheep and Cattle Production.* Sydney: University of Sydney Press, 1973.

Becker, R. B. *Dairy Cattle Breeds: Origin and Development.* Gainesville: University of Florida Press, 1973.

Cole, H. H., and Magnar, R. (Eds.) *Animal Agriculture: The Biology of Domestic Animals and Their Use by Man.* San Francisco: W. H. Freeman, 1974.

Foley, R. C., Bath, D. L., Dickinson, F. N., and Tucker, H. A. *Dairy Cattle: Principles, Practices, Problems, Profits.* Philadelphia: Lea & Febiger, 1972.

McDowell, R. E. *Improvement of Livestock Production in Warm Climates.* San Francisco: W. H. Freeman, 1972.

Schmidt, G. H., and Van Vleck, L. D. *Principles of Dairy Science.* San Francisco: W. H. Freeman, 1974.

Works dealing with education in the field of dairy science include:

Kosikowski, F. V., and Marsden, A. W. *Contemporary Views on World Dairy Education.* Ithaca: New York State College of Agriculture and Life Science, Department of Food Science, 1965. Presented at the first international meeting on dairy education, Paris, 1964.

"Proceedings: Conference on Undergraduate Education in Dairy Science." *Journal of Dairy Research*, 1966, *49*, 525–600. This conference was held at the University of Nebraska, Lincoln, August 10–11, 1965.

Report on the Third Food and Agriculture Organization's Ad Hoc Meeting on Dairy Education. Rome: FAO, 1974. Conference held in Rome, January 23–26, 1974. Contains suggestions for the integration and development of the FAO regional dairy training centers into the International Scheme for the Coordination of Dairy Development (ISCDD).

The International Dairy Federation has produced several documents dealing with dairy education. They are: *Higher and Secondary Education,* IDF Document 22 (1964), by Dr. Surkov (USSR); *Problems of Dairy Science Education,* IDF Document 28 (1965), by G. Hoppe and F. Kiermeier (FRG); *Textbooks & Manuals Used in Dairy Education,* IDF report X/Doc 16 (1966), by various authors; and *Visual and Audio/Visual Media Used for Dairy Training,* IDF report F/Doc 41 (1975), by various authors.

Also see *Journal of Dairy Science* for occasional articles dealing with education in dairy science.

CURRENT BIBLIOGRAPHIES

Biological and Agricultural Index: Cumulative Subject Index to Periodicals in the Fields of Biology, Agriculture and Related Sciences. New York: Wilson, 1916–. Formerly *Agricultural Index.* Lists English-language sources.

Commonwealth Bureau of Animal Breeding and Genetics. *Animal Breeding Abstracts: A Monthly Abstract of World Literature.* Farnham Royal, Bucks, England: Commonwealth Agricultural Bureaux, 1933–.

Commonwealth Bureau of Pastures and Field Crops. *Herbage Abstracts.* Farnham Royal, Bucks, England: Commonwealth Agricultural Bureaux, 1931–.

Dairy Science Abstracts. Reading, England: Commonwealth Bureau of Dairy Science and Technology, 1939–. Published monthly; international in scope.

Nutrition Abstracts and Reviews. Farnham Royal, Bucks, England: Commonwealth Agricultural Bureaux, 1931–. Abstracts world literature on animal and human nutrition.

United States Department of Agriculture, National Agricultural Library. *Bibliography of Agriculture.* Scottsdale, Arizona: Oryx Press, 1942–. Monthly; international in scope.

PERIODICALS

American Dairy Review, Australian Journal of Dairy Technology, Belgique laitière, Dairy Industries (UK), *Deutsche Milchwirtschaft* (FRG), *Deutsche Molkereizeitung* (FRG), *IDF News* (Belgium), *Indian Dairyman, Indian Journal of Dairy Science, International Dairy Federation Annual Bulletin* (Belgium), *Japanese Journal of Dairy Science, Journal of Dairy Research* (UK), *Journal of Dairy Science* (US), *Journal of Milk and Food Technology* (US), *Journal of the Society of Dairy Technology* (UK), *Kieler milchwirtschaftliche For-*

schungsberichte (FRG), *Le lait* (France), *Meijeritieteellinen aikakauskirja/Finnish Journal of Dairy Science, Milchwissenschaft/Milk Science International* (FRG), *Milk Industry* (UK), *Modern Dairy* (Canada), *Molochnaya promyshlennost* (USSR), *Mondo del latte* (Spain), *Netherlands Milk and Dairy Journal/Nederlands melk en zuiveltijdschrift, New Zealand Journal of Dairy Science, Österreichische Milchwirtschaft, Philippine Journal of Animal Science, Revista española de lechería, Revue laitière française, Schweizerische Milchzeitung, Scienza e tecnica lattiero-casearia* (Italy), *South African Journal of Dairy Technology, Svenska mejeritidningen, Technique laitière* (France), *World Animal Review* (Italy).

For a more complete listing of journals in the field see:

1000 Selected Journals in Agriculture and Related Subjects. Beltsville, Maryland: U.S. Department of Agriculture, National Agricultural Library, 1973. An international listing.

Ulrich's International Periodicals Directory. New York: Bowker, biennial. See "Dairying and Dairy Products."

ENCYCLOPEDIAS, DICTIONARIES, HANDBOOKS

An International Encyclopedia of Dairy Science and Technology. London: Hill, 1965.

Casalis, J., Mann, E. J., and Schulz, M. E. *Dairy Dictionary/Dictionnaire laitier/Milchwirtschaftliches Wörterbuch.* Edited under the auspices of the International Dairy Federation. Nuremberg, Federal Republic of Germany: Verlag Hans Carl, 1963.

Coletti, A. *Handbook for Dairymen.* Ames: Iowa State University Press, 1963.

Dairy Dictionary. Edited under the auspices of the International Dairy Federation. Kempten, Federal Republic of Germany: Volkswirtschaftlicher Verlag, 1963.

Davis, J. G. *Dictionary of Dairying.* (2nd ed.) London: Hill, 1955.

Frandsen, J. H. (Ed.) *Dairy Handbook and Directory.* Amherst, Massachusetts: J. H. Frandsen, 1958.

Krüger, W., and Penner, E. *Fachwörterbuch für die Milchwirtschaft.* Leipzig, German Democratic Republic: VEB Fachbuchverlag, 1969. In German, English, Russian, Bulgarian, Hungarian, Polish, Romanian, and Czechoslovakian.

Schulz, M. E., and Voss, E. *Das grosse Molkerei-Lexikon.* (4th ed., 2 vols.) Kempten, Federal Republic of Germany: Volkswirtschaftlicher Verlag, 1965.

DIRECTORIES

Index of Agricultural Research Institutions in Europe Concerned with Animal Production and Their Principal Lines of Investigation. Rome: Food and Agriculture Organization, 1953.

International Dairy Federation. *Census of Dairy Research Institutes.* Brussels: International Dairy Federation, 1970. Document F-Doc 6.

Webb, H. R. *Directory of Australian Grassland and Animal Production Research Centers.* St. Lucia, Brisbane: University of Queensland Press, 1970.

RESEARCH CENTERS AND INSTITUTES

Austria:
Institut und Lehrkanzel für Milchwirtschaft und Mikrobiologie der Hochschule für Bodenkultur
Gregor Mendelstrasse 33
A 1180 Vienna 18

Canada:
Department of Dairy Science
Ontario Agricultural College
University of Guelph, Ontario

Czechoslovakia:
Dairy Research Institute
Jindrisska str. 5
Prague 1

Denmark:
Government Research Institute for the Dairy Industry
3400 Hillerød

Federal Republic of Germany:
Bundesanstalt für Milchforschung
Kiel Hermann Weigmannstrasse 1-27

Finland:
Department of Dairy Science
Helsinki University
Helsinki

France:
Station centrale de recherches laitières
Centre national de recherches zootechniques
Domaine de Vilvert 78
Jouy-en-Josas

India:
National Dairy Research Institute
Karnal (Haryana)

Israel:
Volcani Institute of Agricultural Research
Division of Dairy Research
P.O. Box 6
Bet Dagan

Japan:
National Institute for Animal Industry
Ministry of Agriculture and Forestry
959, Aaba-cho, Chiba-shi
Tokyo

Netherlands:
  Netherlands Institute for Dairy Research
  Kernhemseweg 2
  Ede

Poland:
  Dairy Industry Institute
  Hoza Street 66/68
  Warsaw

South Africa:
  Animal Husbandry and Dairy Research
    Institute
  Private Bag 117
  Pretoria

Soviet Union:
  All Union Dairy Research Institute
  35 Lusinovskaja Str.
  Moscow M93

Sweden:
  Food Research Institute
  Faculty of Technology
  University of Lund
  Alnarp

Switzerland:
  Eidgenössische Forschungsanstalt für
    Milchwirtschaft
  3097 Liebefeld
  Bern

United Kingdom:
  National Institute for Research in
    Dairying
  University of Reading
  Reading, England

United States:
  American Dairy Science Association
  113 N. Neil Street
  Champaign, Illinois 61820

DANCE (Field of Study)

Dance is a form of expression that incorporates varying degrees of body action and rest for ritualistic, fitness, recreational, educational, cathartic, and esthetic purposes. On the one hand, dance is considered the mother of the arts by numerous authorities; yet, on the other, it is the last of the art fields to gain recognition as a separate field of study in higher education. Early programs in dance were mainly concentrations or minors within the major field of physical education. Between 1930

and 1960 such concentrations typically incorporated dance as a valuable contributor to physical development, to grace and social development, and to creative development. Only as programs changed from concentrations to dance majors have they warranted recognition as true fields of study.

From 1900 to 1910 the ballet-based dance of M. B. Gilbert in Harvard's summer school for teachers provided inspiration for the earliest courses in dance in higher education. This "esthetic" form was adopted by physical educators, who from 1920 to 1940 taught first an "interpretive" or Duncan-inspired form of dance and a "natural" rhythmic form that led into educational or creative dance. Two early educators had considerable influence on programs of dance education: Gertrude Colby at Teachers College, Columbia University; and Margaret H'Doubler, who developed in 1926 at the University of Wisconsin a major program for preparing dance teachers. By 1940 there were other modern dance programs—for example, at Smith College, Wellesley College, Sargent College at Boston University, and Boston-Bouvé at Northeastern University (Massachusetts); Barnard College and Vassar College (New York); Bennington College (Vermont); and Mills College (California).

Beyond the professional influences of such early "modern dancers" as Ruth St. Denis, Ted Shawn, Martha Graham, Doris Humphrey, and Hanya Holm (American promoter of German "absolute dance") on dance in higher education, Margaret H'Doubler's view of educational dance as an integrator of personality and of dance as a "process" rather than an end in itself made modern dance superior to ballet in serving higher educational aims of "self-realization" and "human relations." This philosophy continues to serve the general educational aims of nonmajors in dance. Moreover, the 1960s and early 1970s brought renewed influences from outside professionals to implement a philosophy espoused by critic George Beiswanger in

1938—of presenting "dance as an integrated art movement." Resurgences of professional group tours to universities (a precedent set by Shawn's male group); college appointments of professional artists-in-residence; scheduling of university-sponsored summer dance courses (in Oakland, California; New London, Connecticut; Long Beach, California; Kansas City, Missouri; Colorado Springs, Colorado; Washington, D.C.; and the Berkshires in Massachusetts); and a new awareness and acceptance of dance by the American public have emphasized the dedication requisite for dance specialists. Curricular revisions in dance major programs occurred as dance administrators recognized the need for implementing the philosophy expounded in the 1930s by Gertrude Lippincott and in 1960 by Hanya Holm—that there was "a need to teach the subject matter of dance," not merely the "process." In 1975 state certification of dance teachers was possible in California, Michigan, Missouri, Maryland, Texas, Utah, and Wisconsin.

Dance as a major field of undergraduate study, and even graduate study leading to a master's degree, did not materialize, however, until the 1960s. Undergraduate branches of the field are principally performance, teaching, and choreography. The more diversified graduate branches of the field include in-depth concentrations in two or three of the following: dance education; technical training (ballet, modern, jazz, and other social and ethnic forms); philosophy; performance, production, and choreographic experience; history; criticism of dance as an art form; remedial and kinesiological analysis of dance movement; creative rhythms for children; dance for theater; retention and reconstruction of dance through "written dance" (notation); dance therapy; and dance ethnology. Of approximately twenty universal systems of dance notation, those of Rudolf von Laban—Labanotation (Dance Notation Bureau in New York City)—and Rudolf Benesch—(American Institute of Choreol-

ogy in New York City)—are the most widely used. Effort/Shape (E/S) movement analysis, Rudolf von Laban's quality analysis of movement, is gaining rapid acceptance by dance therapists as an analytical tool for making personality assessments, by researchers for comparing cultural differences, by teachers for developing body image awareness, and by choreographers for stylistic analysis and to promote improvisational creativity. The Waschmann-Eshkol system is used in Israel, as is Benesch among a great number of American ballet dancers and choreographers (though less frequently taught in universities than Labanotation and E/S, which have their widest acceptance among North American contemporary dance exponents and dance therapists, respectively).

Two of the newest branches of graduate study are dance ethnology, the study of dance as a way of understanding society and of revealing a culture; and dance therapy, the adaptation of developmental and creative dance experiences to surmount specific emotional, physical, or mental maladaptive behaviors. As late as the 1960s there were no programs in dance therapy, but by the mid 1970s about ten state-sanctioned master's programs were either approved or in the offing, and at least one undergraduate program existed in Canada. The American Dance Therapy Association and authorities within the field firmly believe that dance therapy degrees should begin on the graduate level.

Of the approximately 180 United States universities and colleges that list one or more baccalaureate degree programs with a major in dance, 50 percent include them under a department of dance, or a related art field (less than 10 percent), and the remainder under the physical education department. Master's degrees are almost never offered where no baccalaureate exists. About sixty master's degree programs are available; the majority are in dance or related art departments, but about a dozen universities that advertise a physical education–dance baccalaureate list their master's degree in dance within a fine or applied art field. Fewer than ten United States physical education schools or divisions offer doctoral degrees with principal study in dance; even fewer schools offer such degrees in a comparative or related arts program; and only one known Ph.D. or Ed.D. degree program in dance exists within a performing arts department.

Internationally, few universities outside of the United States and Canada provide professional dance preparation with sufficient academic course work to transfer acceptable baccalaureate equivalencies toward graduate study in the United States, where nearly all of the advanced degree programs are offered in the dance field. Indian, Hungarian, and Israeli applicants to United States graduate degree programs in dance have encountered such problems. GITIS, a theater institute for dance in Moscow, offers a *candidat* degree in dance, and Ochanomizu Women's University in Tokyo offers a Ph.D. degree in dance in a comparative arts program, one of the few schools in the world that does. Nonuniversity-based professional dance training is prevalent in France, Italy, Switzerland, Virgin Islands, Panama, Honduras, Puerto Rico, Guatemala, Haiti, Lebanon, Spain, Japan, Egypt, Venezuela, and Argentina. Israel offers at least one conservatory type of professional undergraduate university degree program in dance. Dance major and minor programs in Brazil, Australia, New Zealand, and Ghana are under physical education auspices. Undergraduate course work—not degrees—in dance therapy is available in the Federal Republic of Germany, Israel, Canada, Australia, Norway, and Sweden. Norway and Sweden offer university-based professional training in teaching and choreography.

Innovations in the visual arts since 1960 have pointed up the relationship between dance and the general field of the fine and creative (applied) arts. For example, dance played a key part in the development of "happenings" and was involved in some electronic music experimentations. These and "living theater" have influenced the evolving dance and related arts degree programs in United States universities and in professional dance in Europe. In physical education, dance has influenced gymnastic program innovations by incorporating dance technique for warm-ups, rhythm, and choreography for balance beam and free exercise routines. A yet-to-be incorporated specialization in any field of higher education is "ice dancing," a competitive event at the 1976 Winter Olympics.

A research drawback and hindrance to the academic acceptance of dance as an autonomous field of study will persist, however, as long as international systems of classification fail to include a category for dance among the fine and applied arts. Much of this emerging field's body of knowledge remains invisible to those outside of the specialty. Dissertation and private researchers in the field must file their titles obscurely among one of a dozen related fields of study for lack of a particular category for dance in the Dewey Decimal and Library of Congress systems and the *Dissertation Abstracts International* listings. The 1974–75 thirteen-volume publication of the *Dictionary Catalogue of the Dance Collection* is evidence of the scope of researchable topics within this performing art. ERIC incorporates dance in its *Thesaurus of Descriptors,* and the United States Department of HEW includes it as a category of fine and applied arts.

Levels and Programs of Study

The initial preparation of performing dancers usually starts well before the college level. Early professional technical training may take place almost entirely in facilities separate from public schools. Worldwide, the increased incidence of first-level, nondegree dance programs is evident in three types of setups: in a separate school of ballet, modern dance, or indigenous dance; in a similar type of school affiliated with a college; or in a curriculum of dance offered at a college or university, with minimal or no course credit given.

Well-developed programs of all three types are offered in such areas as Cairo; Tokyo; Taiwan; and Bahia, Brazil. Some countries, such as Sweden, offer government-approved professional programs for dancers and teachers. A majority of the conservatory programs offer their land's indigenous form of dance, such as Spanish, Manipuri, Bayanihan, Kabuki, and Javanese, which other countries refer to as ethnic forms. Professional schools like the Juilliard School and the Boston Conservatory of Music offer certificates of professional competency.

Only recently in the United States is there evidence of interest on the part of private studio programs in gaining approval from private trade and technical accrediting organizations for competency in teacher preparation.

Unlike conservatory-type university dance programs offered outside of the United States, North American programs may lead to an A.A. or A.F.A. degree, and to a B.F.A. when liberal arts course work is taken beyond the minimum certificate requirements. These programs concentrate on dance technique, body alignment, and character training, and on various types of dance performances. All variations of this course work, plus dance history, composition, notation, and repertory, can be found in the available four-year baccalaureate degree programs. Teacher preparation programs require a block of courses in educational (general and special) theory and principles, developmental psychology, observation and practice teaching of dance in local schools, and kinesiology.

For college teaching, an M.A., M.M., M.Ed., or M.F.A. is usually combined with professional dance experience. Programs require in-depth concentration in dance research, history, notation, therapy, ethnology, or teaching and curriculum development.

PATRICIA A. ROWE

Major International and National Organizations

INTERNATIONAL

Imperial Society of Teachers of Dancing
70 Gloucester Place
London W1, England
  Maintains reference library and information center in dance; members and overseas branches in thirty-five countries.

International Dance Teachers' Association
76 Bennett Road
Brighton, Sussex BN2 5JL, England

North American Ballet Association (NABA)
% Henry Holth, Houston Ballet
2018 W. Gray
Houston, Texas 77019 USA
  Members are professional ballet companies in Canada and the United States.

Royal Academy of Dancing
48 Vicarage Crescent
Battersea
London SW11, England

NATIONAL

United Kingdom:
    Art of Movement Centre
    Goldsmiths' College, New Cross
    London SE14 6NW, England

    British Ballet Organization
    39 Lonsdale Road
    London SW13 9OP, England

    Cecchetti Society
    70 Gloucester Place
    London W1, England

    Contemporary Dance Trust
    17 Dukes Road
    London WC1, England

United States:
    American Dance Guild
    245 West 52nd Street
    New York, New York 10006

    American Dance Therapy Association
    1000 Century Plaza, Suite 216 E
    Columbia, Maryland 21044

    Association of American Dance
      Companies
    250 West 57th Street
    New York, New York 10019

Ballet Society
New York State Theatre
Lincoln Center for the Performing Arts
1865 Broadway
New York, New York 10023

Cecchetti Council of America (CCA)
1556 First National Bank Building
Detroit, Michigan 48226
    Association of ballet teachers and ballet dancers.

Committee on Research in Dance (CORD)
Department of Dance and Dance Education
New York University
New York, New York 10003
    Association of dance teachers; administrators of dance departments in colleges, universities, and professional institutions; and researchers of dance.

Dance Notation Bureau
19 Union Square West
New York, New York 10003

National Association for Regional Ballet
1564 Broadway
New York, New York 10036
    Conducts educational dance activities in the United States and Canada.

National Dance Association
1201 16th Street NW
Washington, D.C. 20036
    An association of the American Alliance for Health, Physical Education, and Recreation (AAHPER).

The following directories are helpful in locating additional dance organizations:

Directory of Associations in Canada. Toronto, Ontario: University of Toronto Press, 1975.
Directory of British Associations and Associations in Ireland. (4th ed.) Beckenham, Kent, England: CBD Research, 1974–75.
Directory of European Associations. Part 1: *National Industrial, Trade and Professional Associations.* Beckenham, Kent, England: CBD Research; Detroit: Gale Research, 1971.
Encyclopedia of Associations. (9th ed.) Detroit: Gale Research, 1975. With quarterly supplements; United States organizations only.

Principal Information Sources

GENERAL

Guides to the literature include:

Beaumont, C. W. *Bibliography of Dancing.* New York: Blom, 1963. Reprint of a 1929 edition based on items in the British museum.

Forrester, F. S. *Ballet in England: A Bibliography and Survey, c. 1700–June 1966.* London: Library Association, 1968. Guide to books, periodicals, and articles.
Laban, J. de. "Selected Reference Materials for Dance." *Theatre Documentation,* Nov. 1, 1971, *4,* 21–30.
Leslie, S. *A Bibliography of the Dance Collection of Doris Niles and Serge Leslie.* (2 vols.) London: Beaumont, 1966–1968. Covers mainly ballet literature.
Magriel, P. D. (Comp.) *A Bibliography of Dancing: A List of Books and Articles.* New York: Blom, 1966. Reprint of 1936 ed. A major source.
New York [City] Public Library. Dance Collection. *Dictionary Catalog of the Dance Collection: A List of Authors, Titles and Subjects of Multi-Media Materials in the Dance Collection of the Performing Arts Research Center of the New York Public Library.* Boston: Hall, 1974.
Schoolcraft, R. N. (Ed.) *Performing Arts Books in Print: An Annotated Bibliography.* New York: Drama Book Specialists, 1973.
Tanzbibliographie. Verzeichnis der in deutscher Sprache veröffentlichten Schriften und Aufsätze zum Bühnen, Gesellschafts, Kinder-, Volks- und Turniertanz sowie zur Tanzwissenschaft, Tanzmusik und zum Jazz. Leipzig, German Democratic Republic: VEB bibliographisches Institut, 1966–. Classified bibliography on books and periodical articles in German on all types of dance.

Overviews and introductions to the field include:

Bowers, F. *Theatre in the East: A Survey of Asian Dance and Drama.* London: Nelson, 1956.
Denby, E. *Looking at the Dance.* New York: Horizon Press, 1968. New edition of the 1949 classic work on the dance.
Garaudy, R. *Danser sa vie.* Paris: Editions du Seuil, 1973.
Hayes, E. R. *Introduction to the Teaching of Dance.* New York: Ronald Press, 1964.
Kerensky, O. *The World of Ballet.* New York: Coward-McCann, 1970.
Martin, J. J. *Book of the Dance* New York: Tudor, 1963. Includes a history of classic ballet and modern dance.
Nadel, C., and Nadel, M. *The Dance Experience.* New York: Praeger, 1970.
Preston, Dunlop, V. *A Handbook for Modern Educational Dance.* New York: International Publications Service, 1963.
Pridden, D. *The Art of the Dance in French Literature from Théophile Gautier to Paul Valéry.* London: Black, 1952.
Redfern, H. B. *Concepts in Modern Educational Dance.* New York: British Book Centre, 1976.

Sweigard, L. E. *Human Movement Potential: Its Ideokinetic Facilitation.* New York: Dodd, Mead, 1974.

Todd, M. *The Thinking Body: A Study of the Balancing Forces of Dynamic Man.* Newton Center, Massachusetts: Charles T. Branford, 1937.

Wethered, A. *Movement and Drama in Therapy: The Therapeutic Use of Movement, Drama and Music.* Boston: Plays, Inc., 1973.

Education and career sources include:

Haberman, M., and Meisel, T. G. (Eds.) *Dance: An Art in Academe.* New York: Teachers College Press, Columbia University, 1970.

Hawkins, A. M. *Modern Dance in Higher Education.* New York: Teachers College Press, Columbia University, 1954. Study concerned with developing a concept of modern dance as education; identifying specific contributions of modern dance to the goals of education; and determining principles that should guide the teaching of modern dance.

Hawkins, A. M. (Ed.) *Dance, A Projection for the Future.* San Francisco: Impulse Publications, 1968.

Kraus, R. B. *History of the Dance in Art and Education.* Englewood Cliffs, New Jersey: Prentice-Hall, 1969.

"Professional Preparation and Certification for Dance: Guidelines Recommended by the American Alliance for Health, Physical Education and Recreation, Dance Division Curriculum Committee." *Journal of Health, Physical Education, Recreation,* February 1970, *41,* 32–35.

Terry, W. *Careers for the 70s: Dance.* New York: Crowell, 1971.

Histories of the field include:

Cohen, S. J. *Dance as a Theatre Art: Source Readings in Dance History from 1581 to the Present.* New York: Dodd, Mead, 1974.

Kinney, T., and Kinney, M. *Dance: Its Place in Art and Life.* New York: Tudor, 1935.

Kirstein, L. *Dance: A Short History of Classic Theatrical Dancing.* Westport, Connecticut: Greenwood Press, 1969. Reprint of 1935 edition.

Kirstein, L. *Movement and Metaphor: Four Centuries of Ballet.* New York: Praeger, 1971.

Kraus, R. *History of the Dance: In Art and Education.* Englewood Cliffs, New Jersey: Prentice-Hall, 1969.

Lloyd, M. *The Borzoi Book of Modern Dance.* New York: Dance Horizons, 1970. History of the development of modern dance in the United States.

Maynard, O. *American Modern Dancers: The Pioneers.* Boston: Little, Brown, 1965.

Moore, L. *Artists of the Dance.* New York: Dance Horizons, 1938.

Sachs, C. *World History of the Dance.* New York: Norton, 1973. Originally published in German.

Sharp, C. J., and Oppé, A. P. *The Dance: An Historical Survey of Dancing in Europe.* Totawa, New Jersey: Rowman & Littlefield, 1972. Reprint of 1924 edition.

Sorrell, W. *The Dance Through the Ages.* New York: Grosset & Dunlap, 1967.

Willis, J. *Dance World.* New York: Crown, 1965–. Annual comprehensive pictorial and statistical record of the dance season in the United States.

CURRENT BIBLIOGRAPHIES

Belknap, S. H. (Comp.) *Guide to Dance Periodicals: An Analytical Index of Articles and Illustrations.* Gainesville: University of Florida Press, 1948–1959; Metuchen, New Jersey: Scarecrow Press, 1959–1963.

Belknap, S. H. (Comp.) *Guide to the Performing Arts.* Metuchen, New Jersey: Scarecrow Press, 1960–. Published annually.

Bulletin signalétique. Part 523: *Histoire et science de la littérature.* Paris: Centre national de la recherche scientifique, 1961–.

CORD Dance Research Annual. New York: Committee on Research in Dance, Department of Dance and Dance Education, New York University, 1967–. Published annually.

Education Index. New York: Wilson, 1929–.

Humanities Index. New York: Wilson, 1975–. Formerly *Social Sciences and Humanities Index.*

Music Index. New York: Wilson, 1949–.

PERIODICALS

A sampling of journals in the field includes *American Dance Guild Newsletter, Arabesque* (Belgium), *Art et danse* (France), *Ballet Dancer* (US), *Ballet Review* (US), *Balletto* (Italy), *Dance* (UK), *Dance* (US), *Dance/America, Dance and Dancers* (UK), *Dance Magazine* (US), *Dance Perspectives* (US), *Dance Research Journal* (US), *Dance Scope* (US), *Dance Teacher* (UK), *The Dancing Times* (UK), *Dans* (Sweden), *Danses* (Belgium), *La danza* (Italy), *Focus on Dance* (US), *Marg* (India), *Modern Dance and Dancer* (UK), *Les saisons de la danse* (France), *Square Dancing* (US), *Tanecni listy* (Czechoslovakia), *Tanzarchiv* (FRG), *Tanz und Gymnastik* (Switzerland), *Viltis* (US), *Washington International Arts Letter* (US).

Dance Index (US, 1942–1948) and *Impulse* (US, 1948–1968) are both invaluable, though no longer published. The former is indexed in:

Kirstein, L., and others. (Eds.) *Dance Index 1942 thru 1948.* (7 vols.) New York: Arco, 1970. Reprint of 1948 edition.

For additional titles see:

Ulrich's International Periodicals Directory. New York: Bowker, biennial.

ENCYCLOPEDIAS, DICTIONARIES, HANDBOOKS

Balanchine, G. *Balanchine's Complete Stories of the Great Ballets.* Garden City, New York: Doubleday, 1954.

Baril, J. *Dictionnaire de la danse.* Paris: Editions du Seuil, 1964.

Baum, E. L. *Dictionary of Dance Terms.* Boston: B. Humphereys, 1932.

Beaumont, C. W. *Complete Book of Ballets.* London: Putnam's, 1949. Reprinted in 1951, with additions.
Supplement. London: Putnam's, 1945 (reprinted 1952).
Ballets of Today. 2nd Supplement. London: Putnam's, 1954.
Ballets Past and Present. 3rd Supplement. London: Putnam's, 1955.

Beaumont, C. W. (Comp.) *A French-English Dictionary of Technical Terms Used in Classical Ballet.* (Rev. ed.) London: The Author, 1968.

Charmet, R. *Follett Larousse Concise Encyclopedia of Ballet.* Chicago: Follett, 1974.

Chujoy, A., and Manchester, P. W. (Comps. and Eds.) *The Dance Encyclopedia.* (Rev. ed.) New York: Simon & Schuster, 1967. A standard work.

Cohen, S. J. (Ed.) *Dictionary of Modern Ballet.* New York: Tudor, 1959.

DeMille, A. *The Book of the Dance.* New York: Golden Press, 1963. An encyclopedic work on the development of the dance in many countries and all periods.

Enciclopedia dello spettacolo. (9 vols.) Rome: Casa editrice le maschere, 1954–1962. The definitive encyclopedia of staged entertainment, including dance and ballet.

Grant, G. *Technical Manual and Dictionary of Classical Ballet.* (2nd rev. ed.) New York: Dover, 1967.

Kersley, L., and Sinclair, J. *A Dictionary of Ballet Terms.* (2nd enl. ed.) London: Black, 1964.

Love, P. *Modern Dance Terminology.* New York: Kamin, 1953.

Mara, T. *The Language of Ballet: An Informal Dictionary.* Cleveland, Ohio: World, 1966.

O'Moore, M. *ABC's of Dance Terminology.* Washington, D.C.: Dance Masters of America, 1949.

Raffe, W. G. (Comp.) *Dictionary of the Dance.* New York: Barnes & Noble, 1975.

Terry, W. *The Ballet Companion: A Popular Guide for the Ballet Goer.* New York: Dodd, Mead, 1968. Covers training, dress, design, choreography, history; includes a glossary of terms.

Wilson, G. B. L. *A Dictionary of Ballet.* (Rev. ed.) London: Black, 1974.

Zorn, F. A. *Grammar of the Art of Dancing.* New York: Dance Horizons, 1975.

DIRECTORIES

Commonwealth Universities Yearbook. London: Association of Commonwealth Universities; 1914–. Published annually; for degree programs in dance in Commonwealth countries see "Dance."

Dance Directory: Programs of Professional Preparation in American Colleges and Universities. (9th ed.) Washington, D.C.: American Alliance for Health, Physical Education and Recreation, 1976.

Spiesman, E. (Ed.) *Directory of College and University Dance Programs.* New York: Dance Magazine, 1976.

The World of Learning. London: Europa, 1947–. Published annually. For many countries lists schools of art and music separately, including dance programs.

RESEARCH CENTERS, INSTITUTES, INFORMATION CENTERS

Committee on Research in Dance
Department of Dance and Dance Education
New York University
New York, New York 10003 USA

Research Center for Dance
Gertrude Kurath, Director
1126 Spring Street
Ann Arbor, Michigan 48103 USA
Emphasis on the anthropology of dance.

For listings of research studies see:

International Federation of Libraries and Museums. *Performing Arts Libraries and Museums of the World.* (2nd ed.) Paris: Editions du Centre national de la recherche scientifique, 1967. Lists important collections in the arts, including dance.

Research in Dance: Vol. 2. Washington, D.C.: American Alliance for Health, Physical Education and Recreation, 1973. Lists research studies in the United States, including projects and published articles in all areas of dance.

DANISH INSTITUTE FOR EDUCATIONAL RESEARCH (Danmarks paedagogiske institut)

Founded in 1954 in Copenhagen, the Danish Institute for Educational Research is directly responsible to the Danish Ministry of Education. The institute conducts research in education at the primary, secondary, higher, and adult levels. Maintaining a national or international focus, research in higher education is carried out in the following areas: educational planning, curricula and instruction, and methodology of research in higher education.

In addition to research activities, the institute assists the Ministry of Education in planning and coordinating educational experiments, provides facilities for students of educational psychology to work as trainees, and constructs and distributes tests and similar materials that are not publicly available. The institute has its own television studio for educational productions and analysis.

The institute is divided into a statistical department, a department of experimental education, and a department of educational planning and methods. Funded by the Danish government, it is governed by a director, a board of research directors and university professors, and a council of forty representatives of educational organizations and institutions. The staff includes seventeen research professionals, eighteen part-time technicians, two paid consultants, three administrative personnel, two secretaries, and seventeen part-time student aides.

The institute publishes reports of its activities and provides general information of interest to educators.

28 Hermodsgade
DK-2200 Copenhagen N, Denmark

DANISH NATIONAL ARCHIVES

See Archives: Northern Europe, National Archives of.

DAR ES SALAAM UNIVERSITY STUDENTS' ORGANIZATION, Tanzania

The Dar es Salaam University Students' Organization (DUSO) was established in Tanzania in 1970 under an act of parliament. DUSO aims to create a sense of public responsibility and service in the students of the university, promote respect for learning and the desirable aspects of cultural development, and maintain worthy traditions of academic life. Every student admitted to the university as an undergraduate becomes a member of DUSO. There is an annual subscription of thirty-five Tanzanian shillings per member.

DUSO encourages the organization of politically conscious cadres to combat underdevelopment and gives moral support to oppressed peoples throughout the world. DUSO sponsors seminars, panel discussions, films, and visits to *ujamaa* (collective) villages.

Publications include *University Echo* and *Campus Review.*

P. O. Box 35080
Dar es Salaam, Tanzania

DATA PROCESSING

See Computers, Role of in Higher Education: Computers in Administration; Statistics in Higher Education.

DATA PROCESSING TRAINING

See Business and Office Technologies (field of study).

DAVIS REPORT

See Learning Society, The (Higher Education Report), Canada.

DAY CARE CENTERS

See Women and Higher Education: Day Care Centers.

DEAF, HIGHER EDUCATION FOR THE

Hearing loss often greatly affects a person's educational needs, but not necessarily his potential for learning. Deafness is a complex syndrome, involving such factors as the time of onset, kind and degree of hearing loss, effectiveness of auditory amplification, and personal adjustment to the handicap. Although there are specific definitions of deafness for medical, psychological, educational, or legal purposes, the Conference of Executives of American Schools for the Deaf states that deaf persons are "those in whom the sense of hearing is non-functional for the ordinary purposes of life" ("Report of Conference Committee on Nomenclature," 1938, p. 3). A 1974 census of hearing-impaired persons in the United States listed as deaf those persons who cannot hear and understand speech—approximately .9 percent of the noninstitutionalized civilian population (Schein and Delk, 1974, p. 16). (Persons whose sense of hearing is defective but functional with or without a hearing aid are known as *hard of hearing* and are not the subject of this article.) Persons who are born deaf are known as *congenitally deaf* individuals; persons who were born with normal hearing and subsequently lost it due to an illness or an accident are called *adventitiously deaf* persons. Schein and Delk (1974) distinguish three categories of deaf persons: (1) those who have experienced a *prelingual* hearing loss—one that occurred before three years of age; (2) those who have experienced a *prevocational* hearing loss—one that occurred before nineteen years of age; (3) those whose hearing loss occurred after nineteen years of age. These distinctions are most useful, since the educational impact of deafness is significantly reduced for persons who have experienced the complexities of language and have developed speech.

The Conference of Executives of American Schools for the Deaf has estimated the educational impact of degrees of deafness by relating hearing threshold levels to the special types of classroom settings that hearing-impaired students require: (1) students with mild deafness, whose hearing threshold levels range from 26 to 54 deci-

bels, most frequently achieve *full integration* into a normal school environment and can receive all their instruction with hearing classmates, as long as they are provided with supplementary assistance from a specialist; (2) students with moderate or severe deafness, whose hearing threshold levels range from 55 to 89 decibels, most frequently achieve *partial integration* into a normal school environment, receiving some instruction with hearing classmates and some with deaf classmates; (3) students with profound deafness, whose hearing threshold levels exceed 89 decibels, most frequently require a *self-contained* educational setting where all instruction is taken with deaf and/or hearing-impaired classmates, whether within a normal school, a special day school, or a special residential school. The educational needs of deaf students vary when physical, psychological, personal, or social problems exist in addition to hearing impairment. In addition, the appropriateness of a given educational setting or methodology can change as an individual progresses from one age level to another, or attains higher functional levels of proficiency in language and communication, education, and personal and social development (Conference of Executives, 1975, pp. 4, 2).

Instructional Problems

To perform adequately within the higher education setting, the deaf person must demonstrate academic readiness, adequacy of language skills, and the ability to communicate meaningfully within the classroom setting. In addition, he may have difficulty achieving acceptance and developing a positive self-image within the social milieu of the institution. These are challenges that face any young person, but they loom larger to the student who is deaf. Data from a "Special Edition for Hearing Impaired Students" of the 1973 Stanford Achievement Test—developed at Gallaudet College in Washington, D.C., and administered in 1974 to a stratified random sample of nearly seven thousand American hearing-impaired students—indicate that academic readiness for postsecondary education does not come easily for severely hearing-impaired students, even with special assistance and a commendable Intelligence Quotient. Results from the Reading Comprehension and Mathematics Computation subtests show linear increases in grade equivalent scores with the age of the hearing-impaired students, but their mean scores fall three to five grades below the mean grade equivalent scores of their normally hearing peers in the age range from eight to nineteen years. Another challenge calls for the deaf student to demonstrate adequacy of language—especially vocabulary, syntax, usage, and idioms. This, of course, is related to the student's readiness for college; since the deaf student does not experience language in an oral environment as hearing persons do, his linguistic sophistication may not be sufficient for a classroom setting in which speech is the principal medium of communication. The deaf student who enters a postsecondary education program may therefore have difficulty accommodating the wide range of communication that is required both in and out of the classroom. He must employ speech, which he may use with varying degrees of clarity, and he must speech-read (lip-read) the complex and often technical communication of the instructor. Although some deaf students can cope with this problem alone, most require supporting services.

Speech and communication may pose problems for the deaf student on a social level, too. The higher education environment is one in which exchanges with peers not only account for important learning experiences but also provide the context for social life. The deaf student is challenged, therefore, to relate to other students in a meaningful and sensitive way; but he may find that his ability to communicate, particularly in informal settings, is not sufficient, even when the deaf student finds interest and cooperation among hearing peers. Finally, like all students, the

deaf student must develop a self-image that gives him assurance that he can reach the goals he has established for himself. This image, moreover, must permit him to feel that he is capable not only of relating to hearing people but of competing with them in his chosen field.

These are the primary obstacles that deaf persons face as they proceed into postsecondary programs. The problems are not insurmountable, but they constitute tangible concerns that usually have to be accommodated, on the academic level, by program adaptations, special services, and instructors who have understanding attitudes toward the deaf learner. The deaf student has a much better opportunity of succeeding in pursuit of higher education if he has access to services that permit him to function more effectively. Provision of an interpreter in the classroom and note taking by another student are generally considered to be minimum support needed by most deaf students in postsecondary programs. For some deaf students to succeed, preparatory instruction will be necessary to remedy academic deficiencies; if the college has a number of deaf students, a separate class might be established, for example, to assist with language development. It is not uncommon for colleges to provide tutorial assistance for deaf students, since students learning through an interpreter often need clarification of classroom presentation and help with assignments. Opportunities for continued auditory training and speech therapy are also essential for severely hearing-impaired students enrolled in higher education programs.

Like all other students, deaf students need access to educational and career counseling. The counselor should be a professional who is familiar with the adjustment problems deaf students face as they mature academically and socially. It is also necessary for the academic counselor to be acquainted with the achievements and potential of deaf persons and with the career opportunities that are open to them.

An institution that accepts deaf students should help them select programs that will lead to useful careers and should support deaf students in their search for appropriate positions by emphasizing the abilities of deaf candidates and explaining how they can minimize their handicap in employment situations. In general, it is essential that a variety of programs and services exist so that the deaf college student can select a learning environment suited to his abilities and his special needs.

Study Programs

The need for as well as the feasibility of higher education for deaf persons emerged from early efforts to educate deaf children at elementary school levels. The first public school for the deaf in the United States was established at Hartford, Connecticut, in 1817 by Thomas Hopkins Gallaudet. The New York Institute for the Deaf opened in 1818, and the Pennsylvania Institute for the Deaf and Dumb opened in 1820. The first state school for the deaf opened at Danville, Kentucky, in 1823. By 1863 the United States had twenty-two public schools for the deaf in operation. This development was paralleled by the growth of private and denominational schools, some of which were nonresidential. The Horace Mann School, opened in Boston, Massachusetts, in 1869, was the first nonresidential school for the deaf.

The idea of a college program for deaf students was at first controversial; some educators and policymakers doubted that deaf young people could achieve at an advanced academic level, while others predicted that the college environment would promote intermarriage among deaf persons and would thus perpetuate deafness. But as schools became more accessible to deaf children, the need for more advanced educational opportunities became apparent. This need was met by a bold development—an enabling act, passed by the United States Congress in 1864, that authorized the granting of college degrees

by the Columbia Institution for the Deaf and Dumb, later officially named Gallaudet College. The institution's College Department was opened in 1871; in its early days it enrolled approximately one hundred students for a curriculum that emphasized Latin, Greek, French, German, the English language, natural sciences, mathematics, history, metaphysics, and political science. In 1891 the college opened a center for training teachers of the deaf.

For over ninety years Gallaudet College was the only college in the world for deaf persons. In most countries hearing-impaired persons had only limited access to typical college or university degree programs, and the numbers of deaf graduates were small or nonexistent. A new momentum developed in the 1960s, however, that resulted in increasing options worldwide for deaf students interested in higher education. Innovative programs with a commitment to assisting handicapped persons emerged in several countries, and the numbers of deaf persons holding university degrees have increased proportionately.

Vocational and academic programs. Countries that emphasize oral education—such as France, the Federal Republic of Germany, and the Scandinavian countries—do not have special programs for deaf students at the postsecondary level. Oral education aims to eliminate the need for special accommodations, such as sign language, by giving intensive early training in language, speech, speech-reading, and use of residual hearing. It is therefore assumed that the oral (linguistically competent) deaf child can proceed successfully as an adolescent into any program available to hearing people. Most educational programs for the deaf in African and Middle Eastern countries have been modeled after European educational systems; they assume the termination of formal education—supplemented, perhaps, by limited vocational training—at age seventeen or eighteen. A few deaf students from African countries have received degrees from Gallaudet College in the United States. Central and South

American and Asian countries offer no special programs or services to deaf students who wish to pursue postsecondary programs, although these countries do provide some financial assistance for students to attend college in another country.

In the United States a public law passed in 1965 established the National Technical Institute for the Deaf (NTID) as an integral part of the Rochester Institute of Technology in Rochester, New York. With the assistance of federal funds, community colleges and other technical institutes began to develop programs that accommodated the instructional needs of deaf young people. Among these institutions were Delgado College in New Orleans, Louisiana; Technical Vocational Institute of St. Paul in St. Paul, Minnesota; and Seattle Community College in Seattle, Washington. In addition, the California State University at Northridge established a leadership training program in the form of a master's degree for deaf persons and also admits deaf undergraduates. By 1975 the number of college-level programs for deaf persons had grown substantially. The Annual Survey of Hearing Impaired Children and Youth in the United States during the 1974–75 academic year reported 2864 students attending 43 postsecondary programs. These figures do not include students attending graduate schools nor do they include students in postsecondary programs that provide no services for hearing-impaired students. Of the 2864 students, 53 percent were enrolled at Gallaudet College or the National Technical Institute for the Deaf (Rawlings and others, 1975). The above data describe an emerging pattern in American postsecondary education of the deaf characterized by endeavors to neutralize distracting problems caused by deafness and to create an environment similar to that of any other college campus. Gallaudet College offers a strong emphasis on the liberal arts, uses simultaneous communication (a combined system of speech, English syntax, signs, and finger spelling) as the medium of instruction in all

classes, employs a significant percentage (25–30 percent) of deaf instructors, and encourages extracurricular organizations and sports teams. The student body is large enough to permit free communication, socialization, and peer interaction. The NTID offers a wide variety of technical programs requiring from one to four years for completion and terminating in certificates, associate degrees, or bachelor's degrees. It offers special classes for the deaf, employs some deaf instructors, uses simultaneous communication, and provides opportunities for deaf students to take courses and to socialize with the hearing students of the Rochester Institute of Technology. Both Gallaudet College and the NTID are supported in large part by federal appropriations. Some postsecondary institutions provide special services for deaf students within a regular college setting. These services are often minimal, consisting only of an interpreter and a note taker in the classroom. Qualified deaf students may also be admitted to many colleges and universities on the same basis as hearing students.

Between 1971 and 1975 five colleges in Canada established programs for hearing-impaired students. These colleges, and their approximate fall 1975 enrollments in the programs for hearing-impaired students, are Alberta College in Edmonton, Alberta (30 students); George Brown College in Toronto, Ontario (65 students); Red River Community College in Winnipeg, Manitoba (20 students); Vancouver City College in Vancouver, British Columbia (20 students); and Vanier College in Montreal, Quebec (5 students). In addition, 65 Canadians were enrolled at Gallaudet College in 1975. Each of the Canadian programs has a counselor-coordinator who advises the deaf students in planning their curriculum and makes arrangements for preparatory studies, tutorial services, and interpreters.

Since 1965 Great Britain has developed technical colleges, established the Open University, and enlarged its colleges of further education to meet the growing need for and increasing interest in post-secondary instruction. Efforts have been made to make higher education at each of these types of institutions more accessible to handicapped persons. The Open University especially has attempted to recruit deaf students, since its combination of tele-vised instruction and individual tutoring is well suited to deaf persons who are competent speech readers. By 1975 the Open University had awarded degrees to a half-dozen hearing-impaired persons in as many years of operation and had increased its enrollment of deaf students to approxi-mately one hundred.

In Japan the deaf child proceeds through a prefectorial school for the deaf, such as the Kushiro School for the Deaf, the Kyoto School for the Deaf, or the Japan Oral School for the Deaf. In his secondary school program he receives some vocational in-struction that will enable him to seek em-ployment if he does not wish to continue his education. An additional year of tutor-ing in speech and speech reading, counsel-ing, assistance with social development, and vocational training is available at three National Centers of Speech and Hearing Disorders. Further academic education is available at junior colleges associated with the schools for the deaf; these colleges pro-vide courses of study in such fields as art and design, dental technology, and print-ing. Tokyo University of Education has a teacher certification and/or bachelor's de-gree program that had, by 1975, graduated approximately one hundred deaf teachers of the deaf, thirty of whom received de-grees plus certification and seventy of whom received teacher certification only. These academic programs illustrate a trend in Japan in the latter half of the twentieth century toward greater professional oppor-tunities for deaf persons.

Deaf children in the Soviet Union begin their education in a kindergarten at age three and continue there until they are seven, at which point they are enrolled in an eight-year special secondary school. At the end of eight years the deaf student

may work in an industrial or agricultural enterprise while continuing his secondary education or taking remedial instruction in night school or correspondence school; he may pursue a training course at his place of his employment; or he may enroll in a polytechnical or trade school. Poly-technical and trade schools provide the bulk of postsecondary educational oppor-tunities for the deaf in the Soviet Union; at the beginning of 1975 more than 750 deaf students were enrolled in polytechni-cal schools and higher educational institu-tions in the Russian Soviet Federal Socialist Republic. The Ministry for Higher and Specialized Secondary Education and the Ministry for Public Health have approved more than 300 trades and professions for the deaf. The largest postsecondary edu-cational center for the deaf is the Lenin-grad Rehabilitation Center (LRC) of the All-Russian Society of the Deaf. The center has an auditory-speech laboratory, a poly-technical school, a trade school, and an industrial training enterprise. The poly-technical school trains students for highly skilled technical and clerical jobs such as artist-decorator (five-year course), accoun-tant (four-and-a-half-year course), and spe-cialist in physical education (four-year course). From 1971 through 1974 a total of 550 deaf students completed postsec-ondary programs at the LRC: 270 became administrators of clubs for the deaf, artist-decorators, or legal experts; 280 were trained with specialties in sewing, account-ing, or physical education. A significant feature of the above programs is that through them the student can gain techni-cal competence and at the same time obtain his ten-year school diploma, which is a prerequisite for admittance to higher edu-cational institutions. The deaf compete with hearing adults for university places; however, few gain admission or obtain degrees.

Opportunities for advanced study. It is possi-ble for a deaf student who has a commend-able record at the undergraduate level to enroll in a postgraduate or professional program. The instructional problems that deaf students encounter on the advanced level are similar to those that deaf undergraduates face—comprehending the substantive content of most advanced programs and managing clear communication and exchanges of information with other graduate students. Advanced study under these conditions is difficult, but significant numbers of deaf students in the United States have succeeded in graduate programs leading to the master's degree or the doctorate. Graduate schools in a few American universities have established special programs to accommodate deaf students. The California State University at Northridge has a leadership training program leading to a master's degree that enrolled approximately forty deaf students in 1975. New York University's Deafness Research and Training Center enrolled thirty hearing-impaired students in 1975; twenty-one were pursuing a master's degree, one a law degree, and eight a doctorate. Gallaudet College had thirty-three deaf master's degree students and one deaf doctoral student enrolled in 1975. The numbers of deaf students pursuing advanced degrees at other institutions are small, and the supplementary services available to deaf students are varied. Usually the student must provide his own interpreter or note taker. In general, provisions for advanced study for deaf persons with bachelor's degrees were increasing but still limited in the last quarter of the twentieth century. Special programs for deaf students were few in number, were widely scattered across the country, and had limited offerings. The master's degree had become much more accessible to American deaf students, providing them with new opportunities to enter professional fields, but the number of deaf persons holding the doctorate was relatively small. In other countries advanced study had been successfully attempted by very few deaf persons.

Opportunities for any level of postsecondary education for hearing-impaired persons must always be seen in the context of educational opportunity as it exists in each country. When access to higher education is limited for all people, it is especially limited for hearing-impaired persons who need special services. Deaf persons in settings where college or university education is available to only a small percentage of the population do well to enter a trade or vocational school. The rather bleak international picture in 1975 was partially offset by a growing interest in broadening the opportunities of deaf persons to obtain an education beyond the secondary level.

Bibliography

Conference of Executives of American Schools for the Deaf. *Report on Definitions.* Washington, D.C.: Conference of Executives, 1975.

Craig, W. N., and Craig, H. B. *Directory of Services and Programs.* Washington, D.C.: American Annals of the Deaf, 1974.

Davis, H., and Silverman, S. R. (Eds.) *Hearing and Deafness.* (3rd ed.) New York: Holt, Rinehart and Winston, 1970.

Doctor, V. (Ed.) *Communication with the Deaf.* Washington, D.C.: American Annals of the Deaf, 1969.

Mykelbust, R. *Psychology of Deafness.* New York: Grune & Stratton, 1960.

Rawlings, B., Trybus, R. J., Delgado, G. L., and Stuckless, E. R. *A Guide to College/Career Programs for Deaf Students.* (Rev. ed.) Washington, D.C.: Gallaudet College, 1975.

"Report of Conference Committee on Nomenclature." *American Annals of the Deaf,* 1938, *83* (1), 1–3.

Ries, P., and Voneiff, P. "Demographic Profiles of Hearing Impaired Students." *Deafness Annual,* 1975, *4,* 30–31.

Schein, D., and Delk, M. T., Jr. *The Deaf Population in the United States.* Silver Spring, Maryland: National Association of the Deaf, 1974.

Sussman, A. E. "The Comprehensive Counseling Needs of Deaf Persons," *Hearing and Speech News,* 1970, *38,* 12–13, 22–24.

EDWARD C. MERRILL, JR.

See also: Blind, Higher Education for the; Handicapped, Higher Education for the Physically; Special Education.

DEBATING SOCIETY
See College Unions.

**DECISION, PLANNING AND
BUDGETING—UNIVERSITY
OF COPENHAGEN**
See Organisation for Economic Co-operation and Development.

DEDICATIONS
See Ceremonies.

DEGREE MILLS
See Diploma Mills.

DEGREES, DIPLOMAS, AND CERTIFICATES

The academic degree is a title conferred on an individual, usually by a college or university, as recognition of the completion of a course of study or for attainments in research or in a profession. Traditionally, there are three stages in higher education, represented in English-speaking countries by the degrees of bachelor, master, and doctor. The names of degrees vary, however, as do the requirements for their attainment, the time required for their completion, and the valuation placed on them. These differences create the two major problems associated with degree granting: equivalences among nations, and credentialism within certain countries—especially the United States.

History of Academic Degrees

The formal certification of graduates has a long history, with the continuous practice of granting degrees dating from the Middle Ages. Al-Azhar (established as a school in 970) in Egypt and al-Qarawiyin (founded in 859) in Morocco awarded the *ijazah,* which was a license or diploma. Without the *ijazah,* no scholar could practice his profession.

Development of the master's and doctor's degrees. In the medieval European universities, the faculties were organized as guilds and could establish their own standards for membership. Degrees granted to medieval scholars were analogous, therefore, to the trade permits granted apprentices on completion of a satisfactory service and training period. The university student, after a period of study, was given an oral examination to test his intellectual and moral fitness to perform his profession, that of teacher. If he were successful, he was presented to the chancellor of the university and, through him, granted permission to teach by the ecclesiastical authorities. He was then given the degree of master—that is, teacher—the only degree then given.

The first doctorates, given in theology, were awarded by the University of Paris sometime after 1150, while the Doctor of Grammar and Doctor of Philosophy were first conferred at Paris in the mid thirteenth century. But it was at the University of Bologna that doctorates were first conferred by a chartered university. Bologna was granted a charter by Frederick I in 1158. By virtue of the charter, all graduates of Bologna could teach or practice their specialization without further examination. The degree was a permanent license, recognized by all other schools and universities. The first degrees granted by "authority" were Doctor of Laws *(legis doctor)* degrees conferred soon after 1158. During the twelfth century, Bologna conferred, in addition to the Doctor of Laws degree, those of Doctor of Canon Law, Doctor of Both Laws *(juris utriusque doctor),* Doctor of Theology, and Doctor of Medicine. (The modern Doctor of Philosophy and its derivatives did not originate until nineteenth-century Germany, as discussed below.)

Little distinction appears to have been made between the titles of master and doctor until sometime in the fifteenth century. The title of doctor specifically indicated a teacher, however, while master might also designate a practitioner in one of the guilds or crafts. By the end of the fifteenth century, the graduates of the lower faculties (grammar, arts) were generally called master, while those of the higher faculties (theology, law, and medicine) were given the title of doctor.

Development of the bachelor's degree. Although the bachelor's degree is the first degree in most English-speaking countries, historically it developed after the master's degree. In his progress toward the mastership, the medieval student was given permission, during his three to four years of study in the trivium (grammar, rhetoric, and logic), to teach beginning students. At that point he was called "bachelor" or novice, meaning both a candidate for the master's degree and a student teacher. The bachelor's degree was thus established as a first degree, a position it maintained in the English universities when the English scholars were called back from Paris by King Henry II in 1167–68 and took up residence at Oxford. When Cambridge was founded nearly one hundred years later, the custom of granting the bachelor's as the first degree continued. The degree of *theologiae baccalaureus* appeared at Paris during the early part of the thirteenth century.

Modern Academic Degrees

In most nations the three stages in higher education are each marked by a degree. While the majority of students do not go beyond the first degree, those who do go on to advanced studies generally move through the stages in order. Thus, the bachelor's degree (in English-speaking countries) precedes the master's, and the master's precedes the doctorate. There are, however, exceptions to this norm of academic progress. In many countries the master's degree is not a prerequisite for admission to a doctoral program, and the first degree is sometimes not a prerequisite for graduate study. And honorary degrees are awarded without regard to previously earned degrees.

In several countries academic awards (although not necessarily degrees) are given prior to the traditional first degree for completing a two-year program. Some two-year programs are terminal, while others are intermediate, a step on the way to the first degree. Their awards are variously termed certificates, diplomas, or associate degrees.

Two-year programs. Most two-year programs are vocationally oriented. In the United States, the associate degree awarded for two-year programs may be in arts or in science, but it is also likely to be in business, in applied science, in secretarial science, in engineering, or in a large number of other technical and vocational specialties. Associate degrees are usually awarded by junior or community colleges or technical institutes. The general associate degree, in arts or science, is commonly seen as an intermediate or transfer degree; it is assumed that the student, at some point, will enroll in a four-year college and finish the work for the bachelor's degree. The technical and vocational degrees, however, are usually terminal degrees. The associate degree is also awarded in the Philippines and in Thailand; in Thailand it is an intermediate degree, while in the Philippines it is a terminal degree.

Similar programs and distinctions exist in several countries in various parts of the world. In the Republic of China, junior college graduates are awarded a diploma. Both public and private junior colleges offer cooperative educational programs in industry and business as part of the course requirements. In the Republic of Korea, two-year programs leading to a certificate train students for technical occupations; there are also two-year programs in colleges of education for training primary school teachers. In Venezuela *certificados de estudios* (certificates of studies) are given students who have completed short courses in technological institutions of university level. A teaching diploma can be gained in Portugal after two years of study in a teacher-training college at secondary level and one year of teaching practice. A *brevet d'aptitude pédagogique* (certificate of teaching ability) is given in Luxembourg after a two-year course (and examination) at the pedagogical institute; the *brevet* allows holders to teach in primary school.

In the Middle East teacher training institutes in Jordan, Saudi Arabia, and Iraq award two-year teaching diplomas. In Jordan programs are offered in general education, psychology, and pedagogy in both public and private institutions. A two-year program to prepare specialists in social work for government and private organizations is offered by Jordan's Institute of Social Work. A diploma is awarded in this course as well.

There are several two-year programs offered in the health sciences, leading either to diplomas or certificates, or, in the United States, to an associate degree. In Kenya a diploma in advanced nursing is awarded after two years; in Papua New Guinea, diplomas are given in health science (and in other fields, such as public administration, police studies, and library science), while a certificate is conferred in the nursing program.

Among the educational systems that have nonterminal two-year programs are Nepal, Morocco, Belgium, and France. In Nepal an intermediate certificate is given after the first two-year phase of higher education in the English system, the *uttar madhyama* after two years in the Sanskrit system. In Belgium the *candidature/kandidaat* is given after two (or three) years of study. It signifies the end of a period of broadly based studies that are required both for further study and for specialization. In France the *diplôme d'études universitaires générales* (DEUG: university diploma of general studies) is given after the first two-year course at a university. The programs leading to this diploma are multi-disciplinary. The diploma may be, but is not primarily, a terminal qualification. The *diplôme universitaire de technologie* (DUT: university diploma of technology) is awarded after two years in a university institute of technology. While this is usually a terminal degree, in some cases the holder of a DUT may proceed to the second stage of higher education.

The evolution of two-year degree-granting programs underlines a major shift in the idea of the purpose of higher education and in the student body. With the limited exception of those qualifications that are awarded as a stepping stone to an academic degree, most two-year programs are specifically designed to train students for work. The nature of the programs in each country tends, more than university programs generally do, to define the economic and social needs of the country. The weight of academic tradition that determines university academic programs has little apparent influence on most two-year programs, and they thus respond more directly to perceived needs in the society. This flexibility, however, can result in proliferation and, since programs have in the past been easier to begin than to end, there are no doubt many two-year programs that no longer serve a need.

The development of degree programs in technical and vocational education can also reflect the growth of credentialism. The degree-granting course of study has in some, perhaps many, cases taken the place of the apprenticeship system, reflecting (especially in the United States) the increasing emphasis on credentials as defined by the educational system.

First degrees. Generally, completion of the first degree takes three to six years of study and requires the passage of examinations, either in course, at the end of the period of study, or both. In some nations a thesis is also required, especially for an honors degree. The first degree occasionally serves as a license to practice a profession, although procedures for granting licenses vary greatly from country to country.

The bachelor's remains the significant first degree in universities in Great Britain (with the exception of arts faculties in Scotland, where the Master of Arts is the first degree), Commonwealth Nations and the United States. The degree usually requires three to four years of study: in some cases a pass or ordinary degree may be attained in three years, while an honors degree requires four. Many Middle Eastern countries also award the bachelor's as a first degree, usually after three to five years. Among these are Saudi Arabia, Syria, Kuwait, and Libya.

In most countries of continental Europe the bachelor's, or *baccalauréat*, is not a higher education degree. Rather, in France (and in countries whose educational systems were established in periods of French domination), it signifies the completion of secondary education and is generally required for access to higher education, although those not holding it may gain university admission through a special entrance examination. In Algeria, for example, the *baccalauréate* gives access to all institutions of higher education, even though some faculties require that it show a specialization in science for entrance into medical or engineering training, or in mathematics for entrance into a polytechnic school.

In Spain the *bachillerato unificado y polivalente* (BUP: baccalaureate is given after a three-year course, usually completed by the age of seventeen. The qualification *bachiller* allows the student entrance to intermediate-level professional training and to the *curso de orientación universitaria* (COU: university orientation course), which is the usual mode of access to higher education in Spain. The *bachillerato* is also the title given to the secondary school–leaving certificate in several Latin American countries.

In the Netherlands the usual first qualification is that of *kandidaat*, given after three (sometimes two) years of study. This qualification is intermediate only, representing work in basic studies and not conferring the right to exercise a profession. That right is given only with the *doctorandus* degree, which requires two to four more years of study. There is, however, a *baccalaureus* degree awarded after three and a half years of study at a technical university. This is a terminal degree, unlike the *kandidaat*. In 1976 there were plans for granting the *baccalaureus* degree to graduates of higher vocational colleges.

In those educational systems awarding the bachelor's or baccalaureate as a first degree, the time required to complete the degree is fairly consistent, usually from three to six years. Time requirements are often related to the field of study, however. The bachelor's in medicine takes an average of six years of study in countries that grant it. A first degree in the humanities, by contrast, may take as little as three years. In systems following the British pattern, the student may take an ordinary or pass degree in three years. If he wishes an honors degree, the additional, more specialized study requires a fourth year.

In addition to the bachelor's, there is a variety of other titles for first degrees and of time required to complete them. Most common among these are the diploma and the licentiate. Some systems, however, award the master's as a first degree (Scotland), and in rare instances a doctorate is a first degree. In addition, several nations have specific designations for professional qualifications gained after study in technical institutions. The relationship between the degree and the right to pursue a profession varies from country to country and among disciplines. In some cases, the degree is equivalent to a license to practice a profession; in others, further study and further state examinations are required.

In the Federal Republic of Germany students at technical universities may receive the degree of *Diplom-Ingenieur* after four to six years of study, while students in nontechnical universities receive the *Diplom* after successfully passing either the state examination *(Staatsexamen)* or an examination set by their university *(Diplomprüfung)*. Those who wish to practice medicine, pharmacy, or law, or to teach in academic secondary schools must pass the *Staatsexamen*. Success in it can lead, in some subjects, directly to the doctorate *(Doktor)*. However, in the physical and biological sciences, and in technology *(Doktor-Ingenieur)*, the doctorate requires two years of study past the diploma.

In the Soviet Union the first phase of higher education, a five-year program designed to set the subject of study in its social and economic contexts and provide both theoretical and practical perspective, leads to the diploma of higher education. The diploma, which has in its title the specific field of study, permits the holder to exercise his chosen profession and go on to advanced studies.

In Italy there is only one academic degree, that of doctor *(dottore)*. Students who complete four to six years of academic study and pass a final examination *(esame di laurea)* are given the *laurea* diploma and the title of doctor. There are a few shorter nondegree courses available, either diploma courses or specialized courses for vocational training *(corsi a fini speciali)*. In order to practice a profession, candidates holding the degree must also pass a state examination *(esame di stato)*.

In Chile, and in several other Latin American countries, the licentiate *(licenciatura)* or a professional title is the first degree. This degree usually requires four to six years of study, depending on the specialty, and is generally a professional qualification as well as a degree.

The *licence* had traditionally been the first degree in France; training for the *licence* was the central concern of the French system of higher education. However, with the reform of French university diplomas, begun in 1973 and completed in 1976, the position of the *licence* was altered. The reformed system has three consecutive two-year diplomas. The first diploma, the *diplôme d'études universitaires générales,* gives students a two-year period of training after *lycée,* designed to aid them in finding employment. The courses are intended to emphasize the application of academic subjects to professional activities, a corrective to the importance formerly given by the universities to the traditional *licence* courses as preparation for teaching. Since only 10 percent of French university students were entering the teaching profession in the mid 1970s, such a reform was

seen as necessary. Attempts were made to abandon the *licence* degree entirely or to turn it into a two-year degree. However, the opposition from both students and teachers was so strong that it had to be retained as a three-year diploma. (The *licence de lettres,* the arts degree, takes three years; for the *licence de science,* the student must complete the first two certificates of higher study of a *maîtrise,* or master's.) It was hoped by the reformers that more emphasis would be placed on teaching professional subjects in preparing students for the *licence.* The *licence* remains the prerequisite for those who wish to take the competitive recruitment examination for secondary school teaching, the *certificat d'aptitude au professorat de l'enseignement secondaire* (CAPES: certificate for secondary school teaching.)

In Switzerland the *licence* (French-speaking cantons) or *Lizentiat* (German-speaking cantons) is the first degree in arts, law, and science faculties, granted after a minimum of six semesters. Examinations and a short thesis are required for the degree. The master's degree is not generally required for entrance to a doctoral program.

Second degrees. The second degree corresponds to the master's degree as it is granted in the United States and several other countries. At this stage, students generally do more highly specialized work in an academic field and undertake research, if the degree is other than a professional degree, although the level of research is generally less than that for the doctorate. The second degree usually requires one to two years of study beyond the first. Historically, the master's degree was a first degree, and the title is retained for the first degree in a few instances. For example, the art faculties of universities in Scotland (with the exception of the University of Stirling) award a master's as a first degree.

In Denmark the qualifications of *kandidat* (candidate—the first degree) and *magister* (master) coexist. The degree of *kandidatus magisterii* is granted after a minimum of five years of study to students intending to teach in secondary schools. There is also a Master of Arts *(magister artium)* degree, which requires a final examination *(magister-konferens)* in addition to the five or more years of study. The *magister artium* is a research degree and is a step toward the *doktorgrad*, the research doctorate, which is very seldom awarded.

At the Universities of Oxford and Cambridge in England, the Master of Arts degree can be gained simply by having one's name "kept on the books" for five years after taking a first degree. On graduation from an Oxford or a Cambridge college, the student pays the college secretary a fee for this service; in five years he becomes a Master of Arts with a vote in convocation. Some American institutions followed this practice in earlier centuries, but have since abandoned it. In other British universities, however, and in those in the United States and several other nations, the master's degree requires one to two years of study beyond the bachelor's and usually involves written or oral examinations. A thesis has traditionally been required, although with the gradual devaluation of the master's degree (especially in the United States) this requirement has often been dropped.

As is also true of the bachelor's degree, the titles of master's degrees have multiplied, reflecting the increasing specialization of higher education. Thus, in addition to the Master of Arts and the Master of Science, there are the Master of Arts in Teaching (M.A.T.), the Master of Business Administration (M.B.A.), the Master of Education (M.Ed.), the Master of Forestry (M.F.), the Master of Mechanical Engineering (M.M.E.), and several others. Some, as the titles suggest, are professional degrees; others are academic.

The valuation placed on these degrees again varies among nations and among disciplines. In some fields, such as fine arts and city planning, the master's is the highest degree generally awarded and thus has the weight accorded the doctorate in other fields. The generalized Master of Arts in the humanities, on the other hand, has become, at least in the United States, a relatively unimportant degree. It is sought after most often by secondary school teachers whose professional advancement is dependent on work beyond the bachelor's degree. In Great Britain, however, the master's degree retains more of its original value, since the importance of the doctorate is not as strongly felt as it is in the United States. Although the proportion of Doctors of Philosophy teaching in British universities has been growing since the 1960s, there has not developed the disproportionate emphasis on the doctorate found in American higher education.

The doctorate. The doctoral degree, in a variety of forms, is commonly the highest degree. The Doctor of Philosophy degree, as granted in the United States and in several other nations, is a modern development. Until well into the nineteenth century, the Bachelor of Arts was the highest degree awarded in American universities. Gradually, the great prestige of German universities, famed for their development of scientific methods, began to draw American students there to study for the doctorate in philosophy (Ph.D.). As the possession of a German doctorate became more frequent among professors, steps were taken to create similar programs in the United States. The first American doctorate in philosophy was awarded by Yale University in 1861, but it was the founding of Johns Hopkins University (in Baltimore, Maryland) that marked the first attempt to create an institution to rival the German universities. By the 1970s several hundred American institutions were awarding the doctorate.

In addition to earned doctorates, honorary doctorates are regularly granted by universities. These honorary degrees require no academic work or academic background and are given as a recognition of professional attainment or of public and community service. There are two forms of earned doctorate, research and professional, and the significance attached to each varies with the academic traditions of the country. In some countries the research doctorate, a Doctor of Philosophy (Ph.D.) degree, requires course work, oral or written examinations (or both), and a thesis representing original research. In others an original piece of research, deemed a contribution to knowledge by scholars in the field, is the sole requirement. In some cases, the thesis must be published in order for the degree to be awarded. This is true of the rarely given *doktorgrad* in Denmark.

Professional doctorates vary in their requirements, although most require vocationally or professionally oriented course work, proven expertise in the field, examinations, and, in some cases, research. The most frequently awarded professional degree in the United States is the Doctor of Education (Ed.D.), first awarded at Harvard in 1920. Subsequently, a number of similarly named professional or practitioner's doctorates appeared, including the Doctor of Clinical Psychology (D.C.P.), the Doctor of Social Science (D.S.S.), the Doctor of Physical Education (D.P.E.), and the Doctor of Social Work (D.S.W.). Doctoral degrees in law and medicine occupy a middle ground between the research and professional doctorates. The graduate in medicine in a British university generally receives first the degrees of Bachelor of Medicine (M.B.) and Bachelor of Surgery (B.Sur.). To receive the doctorate in medicine (M.D.), he must write and defend a thesis and take further examinations. In the United States the M.D. requires schooling and practical training beyond the bachelor's, but the Bachelor of Medicine degree is not granted.

There are no set times for gaining the doctorate, although some universities set a maximum time to prevent students from extending their work indefinitely. There is a wide range in the time taken among countries and among fields, as well as in the requirements. In some countries the master's degree is a prerequisite; in others a student may enter a doctoral program with only a first degree.

In Egypt, for example, the research doctorate requires two to three years of study beyond the master's. To be accepted into a doctoral program, a student must have a general rating of "good" and a master's degree. A dissertation, representing original research, is required.

In the Sudan the degree of Doctor of Philosophy can be reached at the university through individual research and the presentation of a thesis. In addition, the university awards higher doctorates (Doctor of Laws, Doctor of Letters, Doctor of Science) in recognition of published work that is seen as contributing significantly to knowledge in a particular field.

Within Scandinavian and European universities there is also a range of requirements and of time needed to complete the degree. In Sweden the *doktorsexamen* requires four years of research beyond the *kandidat* level. Doctoral candidates must also defend a thesis that has been published. To obtain the *doktorgrad,* the highest degree awarded in Norway, a graduate must submit a dissertation to a committee of specialists; each individual has a specially appointed committee. The candidate must also give two public lectures. There are similar research requirements in Finland.

In some European countries, notably France, the Federal Republic of Germany, and Eastern European countries, there are two levels of doctorate, the higher being required of those who wish to teach at university level. Thus, the culmination of the third two-year cycle of higher education in France is the awarding of either the *doctorat d'université* or the *doctorat du troisième cycle.* Study carried on beyond the six-year period, including the preparation of a thesis, leads, depending on the field, to the highest degrees of *docteur ingénieur,* or *doctorat d'état* in pharmacy, law, economic sciences, science, and the humanities. In the latter two fields, preparation of the thesis can be a very lengthy process, with a literary thesis generally taking five years. The *doctorat d'université*, given after one to two years of study, does not qualify an individual for university teaching. Access to university teaching depends on proven ability in research.

In the German Democratic Republic there are two doctorates. The first, the *Doktor eines Wissenschaftszweiges* (doctorate in a specialized field) requires three to four years of study beyond the first degree *(Diplom)* and the successful presentation and defense of a thesis. If a student continues for four more years of highly specialized research, he may be awarded the *Doktor der Wissenschaften* (Doctor of Science). This degree is given in philosophy, natural sciences, law, medicine, agriculture, education, economics, and technology. The preparation and defense of a further thesis are also required.

In the Federal Republic of Germany, the doctorate may be obtained by success in the state examinations, which must be taken to qualify in medicine, pharmacy, law, and secondary school teaching. However, if a person wishes to teach in an institution of higher education, he must obtain the further qualification of the *Habilitation*. To qualify he must already hold the doctorate, and he must pass an examination and present a thesis, *Habilitationschrift*. In most cases, the candidate spends three years doing research while also serving as a *wissenschaftlicher Assistent* (assistant in higher education).

The titles of doctorates, like those of degrees at other levels, have multiplied in the twentieth century. It is difficult at all levels to determine the equivalent value of a degree from country to country, but perhaps especially difficult at the doctoral level. While most nonprofessional doctorates require some research, there can be, for example, a vast difference between the research done for a doctorate in certain United States universities and that done for the *doctorat d'état* in France or the very rarely attained *doktorgrad* in Denmark. The value placed on the degree by society may also vary, with degrees from certain elite universities having greater prestige than those of others.

Because of the many differences among national systems of education, the determination of equivalencies among degrees is extremely difficult. As Guiton and Halls point out in their introduction to the *World Guide to Higher Education* (1976, p. ix), the development of both higher education and educational exchange among nations is hampered by isolationist policies and confusing inconsistencies of practice among nations. Their volume, from which much information has been drawn for this article, attempts to deal with this problem by providing information concerning degree titles and requirements at all levels of higher education for all nations.

Authority to Grant Degrees

The history of the authorized degree begins with the chartering of the University of Bologna by Frederick I. The source for authorization varies somewhat from country to country. In some cases, it is reserved to a national body, such as a ministry of education, in others to state or regional offices. There are also instances in which degree-granting authorities are established for various kinds of institutions. In England each university has been granted a royal charter, which gives it the right to award degrees. For the polytechnics, however, degree-granting authority is vested in the Council for National Academic Awards (CNAA). Like the universities, the CNAA can award degrees in the humanities, sciences, social sciences, and technology, as well as diplomas in several areas. It is also empowered to grant higher degrees.

Under the reorganization of higher education in France, universities are autonomous in administrative, budgetary, and financial matters. Each university has an administrative council (composed of university teachers, students, and representatives from outside the university); the council awards either national diplomas regulated by the Ministry of Education or its own diplomas. National diplomas can be awarded only by public institutions.

Another pattern is found in Argentina. There a council of rectors of the national universities (each of which is administratively autonomous) acts as a body for university planning; examines problems that are common to all; sets administrative procedures and entrance requirements; and clarifies, with the universities, recommendations for the validity of degrees and qualifications. In the twenty-five private universities, degree-granting authority is given by the state, which must approve an institution's statutes, courses, and programs. While each private university is autonomous, their degrees, to be nationally valid, must be recognized by the central government.

In Israel, universities are generally independent institutions, although with few exceptions (such as Bar-Ilan University) they are mainly financed by the state. The Council of Higher Education (two thirds of whose members are recommended by the minister for education and culture) advises, coordinates, and accredits institutions of higher education.

In the United States colleges and universities are authorized by state charter or legislation to grant degrees. Their degree-granting power is limited in the case of two-year institutions, which may grant an associate but not a baccalaureate degree, and may be limited in the case of other colleges to master's or lower degrees. In some states granting of the doctorate in public institutions is reserved to the state universities, with other public institutions limited to the bachelor's and master's degrees. For most nonpublic institutions, the degree-granting power is limited largely by their ability to sustain a graduate program. For example, colleges and universities are frequently denied power to confer degrees in medicine and other health pro-

fessions unless they have specific faculties and facilities in these fields.

Generally, degree-granting institutions in the United States are autonomous in academic matters. Except among training colleges for religious orders and the service academies of the federal government, governance is by external boards that delegate control over the internal affairs of the institution to the administration and faculty. The language used in awarding degrees reflects the order of authority. At a commencement ceremony, the presiding officer (the university president or dean) grants degrees by virtue of the authority vested in the board of trustees of the institution by the state and in the president by the board of trustees.

The federal government has chartered seven federal installations, and Congress has authorized them to grant academic degrees comparable to those offered by nonfederal institutions. The four military service academies and the Merchant Marine Academy are authorized to grant only the bachelor's degree, while the United States Naval Postgraduate School and the United States Air Force Institute of Technology can offer bachelor's, master's, and doctor's degrees. The Merchant Marine Academy is operated by the United States Maritime Administration; the others are branches of the military services.

The receipt of a professional degree does not always carry with it the authority to practice the profession. Although the degree and the license to practice are sometimes awarded simultaneously, as discussed above, the license to practice often requires further examinations, supervised either by the state or by professional bodies, particularly in areas where public protection is involved, as in medicine, dentistry, law, architecture, and engineering. In such cases, receipt of the degree serves as a screening device for the licensing examination, in that only graduates of approved or accredited institutions may sit for the examination. In the United States, for example, professional licenses are generally awarded by state agencies composed largely of members of the profession. Thus, state boards of medical examiners evaluate graduates of approved medical schools, while state committees of bar examiners evaluate candidates for admission to the practice of the law.

Degree Trends

Because of the many differences among national systems of education, the determination of equivalencies is extremely difficult. An equally significant problem in some nations is that of the value placed on degrees for their own sake.

Credentialism. With the spread of higher education and the trend toward homogenization of education created by modern technology, the disease of credentialism—of valuing degrees for their own sake—is spreading. Positions such as that of salesperson for a large company, for which a high school diploma might have sufficed in the 1930s and 1940s, may well have required at least a bachelor's degree in the 1970s. As Bender and Davis (1972, p. 2) comment: "Society has contributed to the complex problem of credentialism by perpetuating a system of status symbols and rewards for advanced degrees in lieu of demonstrated mastery or competency. . . . Degrees, rather than proficiency evaluations, have become the basis for career entry in many fields, along with the related prestige and status from society in general."

One risk of credentialism is the expansion of so-called "degree mills"—paper institutions that sell degrees to the unwary or unscrupulous for little, if any, educational training or achievement. While laws have been passed in many American states against such institutions, their proprietors frequently manage to vanish under attack only to reappear in another state. Because there is no uniformity among state laws and because of the nonjurisdictional posture of the federal government, degree mills can resurrect themselves easily (Bender and Davis, 1972, p. 5).

Credentialism can also lead to shoddy degrees as well as fraudulent ones. With the spread of the demand for degrees, institutions have come into existence (often only briefly) that award degrees easily, and even some long-established institutions have simplified degree-granting programs. For example, in the mid 1970s observers of higher education in the United States expressed concern over "grade-inflation." Following the often chaotic demands in the 1960s for the revaluation of higher education, some faculty and students contended that the emphasis on grades was contradictory to the value of learning for its own sake. One result was the granting of more high grades to more students. While the deemphasis on grades should have been a very positive development, it sometimes resulted in a deemphasis on knowledge, and thus degrees were sometimes awarded without any rigorous attainment. Credentialism did not lie behind the demands of those who genuinely wanted to see education focus on values rather than on grades. Unfortunately, however, that argument was picked up by less intellectually committed individuals and used by some as a way to ease the path toward commercially useful degrees.

Another quite opposite pressure of credentialism is the increased emphasis on the need for graduate degrees. Students feel under pressure to gain higher or professional degrees in order to compete in a period of high unemployment. Their sense of urgency sometimes communicates itself to the college or university granting the first degree, with, on occasion, grade inflation being the result.

The increasing demand for degrees has led proprietary institutions, as well as some research firms and other nonuniversity institutions, to apply for the authority to grant degrees. For example, a large and prestigious American hospital, Massachusetts General Hospital in Boston, has petitioned the state for the authority to grant degrees to a variety of medical and technical personnel. The degrees granted by nonuniversity institutions represent genuine academic and professional accomplishment in many cases. In some instances, however, such degrees have not been equivalent to university degrees, with a devaluation of all degrees being the net result.

Clearly, the lack in countries such as the United States of any common standards for each degree level leads to the risk of abuse. In many smaller nations, the paucity or proximity of institutions of higher education ensures some control over the meaning of a degree. State examinations and the use of outside examiners ensure a similar regulation of degree quality in many other nations. The increasing emphasis on the degree and the extension of the degree-granting authority to institutions other than universities add to the difficulty of evaluating degrees and determining equivalences among degrees, both within a single large nation such as the United States and among nations.

Expansion and innovation. Two other significant trends that may have important effects on the value of degrees are the expansion of higher education and the development of innovative degree programs, in which a great percentage of the work for the degree is done outside the institution.

In many nations, since World War II, there has been a sharp increase in the number of degree-granting institutions and the number of persons seeking degrees. Although this trend seemed to be slowing or even reversing in the mid 1970s, the numbers pursuing some form of higher education were still extremely high. In the United States, in 1971, more than twelve million persons in the labor market, aged seventy or under, possessed academic degrees awarded by United States institutions. This figure was eight times the number possessing such degrees in 1930. Between 1930 and 1970 the annual rate of increase in the degree-holding population was 5.3 percent (Adkins, 1975, p. xix). Clearly, the large numbers involved in seeking and in granting degrees complicate the problem

of monitoring the quality and significance of those degrees.

In addition, a number of innovative programs have developed, especially in the United States, in response to a variety of educational needs and beliefs. The vast range in innovative programs prohibits generalization about format and requirements. It can be said, however, that the designers of most nontraditional programs see them as a way to respond to the needs of student populations who are not served by traditional university programs. Such innovative programs also reflect a tendency toward shortening the time required for the first degree. Thus, several programs are designed to acknowledge the previous professional and life experience of the student and to give him credit for this experience insofar as it is relevant to the degree he is seeking. In this way, an adult student can attain a bachelor's degree in less than the usual four years. Life experience credits are offered by a growing number of institutions in the United States and have been especially useful to many women who wish to obtain a degree later in life, after responsibilities of home and children are lessened. A recognition that the management of a household can provide significant training for outside employment and an acceptance of volunteer work as similarly relevant have led some institutions to grant such credits to qualified students.

Work experience credits are also being granted, again shortening the time required for the degree. Thus, in such experimental programs as that of the College of Public and Community Service of the University of Massachusetts, it would be possible for a student to receive a bachelor's degree in as little as one year, although most students take longer than that. This college emphasizes, as the title suggests, preparation of students for work in various community and public service agencies and branches of government. A large proportion of the students have prior experience in such fields, on either a paid or a volunteer basis. This experience can count toward degree requirements, if the student is able to prove his current competency in the field. The program is entirely competency-based and combines liberal arts with professional training. Students are required to demonstrate their competency in a range of academic, professional, writing, and speaking skills, either in courses or by the submission of papers.

In many areas of the United States, "universities without walls" have developed. This phrase has been used to describe a wide variety of programs, a few of which are questionable in their academic or professional value. The designation originally meant using the community and community institutions as sites for learning rather than confining education to educational institutions. Thus, students would work under the supervision of a college or university faculty member but would spend much of their time working in a wide variety of institutions, such as museums, day care centers, or mental health facilities. Academic credit could be given for a variety of experiences, from European travel to work with disadvantaged groups. The university without walls concept stresses self-directed learning and imaginative experimentation. Several conventional universities have adopted the idea on a limited scale and combine traditional academic programs with the opportunity for the student to complete part of his program by work outside the institution. Thus, students may gain academic credit for activities ranging from helping a local history society catalog its collection to organizing after-school programs for disadvantaged children.

The university without walls concept reflects a conviction, seen also in other nations (as in the reorganization of French higher education), that higher education must be more directly related to the society outside the educational institution. This conviction is also reflected in the world-wide expansion of programs in cooperative education, alternating periods of work with periods of study. Thus, the traditional academic degree is coming often to represent training that is social and professional as well as academic.

Bibliography

Adkins, D. L. *The Great American Degree Machine.* New York: Carnegie Commission on Higher Education, 1975.

Bartholomew, C. A. *Epithetology.* Red Bank, N.J.: The Commercial Press, 1948.

Bender, L. W., and Davis, J. A. *Danger: Will External Degrees Reincarnate Bogus Degree Mills?* Tallahassee: Center for State and Regional Leadership, University of Florida, 1972.

Guiton, J., and Halls, W. D. *World Guide to Higher Education: A Comparative Survey of Systems, Degrees and Qualifications.* Paris: UNESCO, 1976.

CAROL GREEN

DELEGATION OF INTERNATIONAL UNIVERSITY RELATIONS
(Délégation aux relations universitaires internationales), France

The *Délégation aux relations universitaires internationales* (Delegation of International University Relations) coordinates the international activities of the French secretary of state to the universities and encourages the internationalization of university study in French universities and *grandes écoles* (higher professional schools). Directed by a delegate general who is under the authority of the secretary of state to the universities, the delegation approves and finances university projects of international cooperation. Maintaining close ties with the *Conférence des présidents des universités françaises* (Conference of Presidents of French Universities) and *Conférence des directeurs des grandes écoles* (Conference of Directors of *Grandes Ecoles*) as well as with individual universities, the delegation represents the secretary of state to the universities at all public functions and in international cultural organizations.

173 boulevard Saint-Germain
Paris VI, France

P. TABATONI

DEMANDS, STUDENT
See Unrest, Campus.

DEMOCRATIC CAMBODIA*

Population: 5,000,000 (1977 estimate). Student enrollment in primary school: 446,000; secondary school (academic, vocational, technical): 84,000; higher education: 10,800 (1971–72). Language of instruction: Khmer and French. Academic calendar: generally September/October to June/July. Percentage of gross national product (GNP) expended on all education: 6.5%; higher education: .25%. Percentage of national budget expended on all education: 12.5%; higher education: .4%. [Figures are for 1972 unless otherwise indicated.]

In the fifteenth century education in Cambodia was offered in the *wat*, a Buddhist temple, where young boys received instruction in the Khmer language, Buddhist scriptures *(sutras)*, and manual arts. This education, the manifestation of a culture in which social life was centered in the temple, was characteristic of Cambodia until the French introduced Western concepts in the mid nineteenth century.

In 1863 Cambodia became a protectorate of France; three years later the king of Cambodia founded a school to teach the French language to the children of the royal family. Between the founding of this first French school and 1893, several other French primary schools were built in Phnom Penh, the capital city, and in provincial capitals. In 1893 secondary education was initiated when the *Collège du protectorat* was established for civil servants. Secondary education expanded in 1903 with the founding of the Practical School

*Previously the Khmer Republic.

of Industry. In 1917 the governor general of French Indochina initiated a plan to incorporate Cambodian education into the French educational system, which was becoming available in all of the colonized Indochinese countries. According to the plan, Cambodian students would receive the secondary school *baccalauréat* after thirteen years of study and could thus enter universities in France or higher institutions elsewhere in Indochina.

Between 1910 and 1940 the temple schools, which remained active throughout the French rule, were modernized, and European teaching methods were introduced. In the late 1940s embryonic institutions of higher education were introduced. In 1946 a school for health officers, based on a minimum of ten years of previous schooling, was established; and in 1949 the National Institute of Juridical, Political, and Economic Studies was opened.

After independence in 1953–54, several higher institutions were founded. Between 1956 and 1960 the Royal School of Medicine (affiliated with the faculty of medicine of the University of Paris), the Royal School of Administration, the National Pedagogical School, the National School of Commerce, the Buddhist University, and the faculties of letters and of science and technology were started. By 1964 the Royal Khmer University was organized; it was composed of the faculty of law and economics, which had its origins in the 1949 National Institute; a faculty of medicine, derived from the former medical school; a faculty of letters; a faculty of science and technology; and the National Pedagogical Institute. In 1965 the Technical University was founded.

As the Cambodian agricultural and industrial sectors grew, the government encouraged the establishment of more universities, which would produce technicians, engineers, and teachers to meet the needs of development. By 1972 there were about 7500 students attending nine universities. There were about thirty different faculties. In April 1975 the Khmer Rouge movement assumed power in Cambodia; since then, scant data have been available, although it appears that the new regime plans fundamental changes in the structure of society, which will undoubtedly be reflected in educational policy.

National Educational Policy

Cambodia's educational policy has emphasized the eradication of illiteracy—which is high, especially among women—and the extension of educational facilities to areas outside major cities and towns, including the mountain regions and the central part of the country. A national conference of educators, students, and economists, held in late 1973, recommended changes in the aims of higher education. The new goals emphasized research that would aid economic growth and develop natural resources.

Legal Basis of Educational System

Education in Cambodia is based on orders and decrees promulgated since the early years of the twentieth century. The Royal Orders of 1911, 1912, and 1915 made education compulsory for young boys. They could attend either temple schools or French schools. In 1917 these decrees were superseded by the plan of the governor general to incorporate Cambodia into the new French-model educational system devised for Indochina. In 1962 *Kret* (Decree) 664-CE established a National Educational Planning Office. In 1965 a law was passed making it an obligation of all citizens between the ages of ten and fifty to know how to read, write, and calculate in the Khmer language; in the same year *Kret* 198-CE established a Higher Council of Royal Universities, which was designed to coordinate programs of study and advise on development of higher education. In 1967 Ministerial Decree 847 made primary schools free, coeducational, and open to all children regardless of religion, nationality, or race. After a change in government in 1970, a new constitution for the republic was established. It reaf-firmed compulsory education and created the highest educational authority in the country, the National Board of Education and Culture. Four years later a government *kret* made the Directorate General of Education the chief administrative unit within the Ministry of National Education, Youth, and Sport, which had been organized in 1973. Since the assumption of power by the Khmer Rouge new decrees and laws are anticipated.

Types of Institutions

By 1974 there were officially nine institutions of higher education labeled "university" in Cambodia. These included six within the capital city: the University of Phnom Penh, formerly the Royal University; the University of Fine Arts; the University of Agronomical Sciences; the Technical University; the Buddhist University; and the Popular University. The three outside the capital were the University of Kampong Cham, the University of Takeo-Kampot, and the University of Battambang. It is believed that all universities were closed in 1975.

Relationship with Secondary Education and Admission Requirements

Secondary education in Cambodia consists (1974) of a four-year first cycle and a three-year second cycle. The first stage is designed to impart literacy and provide basic scientific knowledge as well as an appreciation of the national culture. The second stage prepares students for higher study in an academic or technical program.

At the end of the second year of the final stage, students must pass an examination for the first part of the second-cycle diploma, the *baccalauréat;* at the end of the third year, they take another examination to complete the *baccalauréat,* which is required for entry into the universities.

Primary schools consist of two three-year stages. The system of lower schools includes temple primary schools, staffed by monks who have attended teacher training courses.

Since 1967 the national language, Khmer, has been introduced gradually grade by grade to replace the French language as the medium of instruction. However, the French language retains an important position in the school curriculum; English has been introduced as a second major modern language. Compulsory education is a goal, but it has been hampered by the Vietnam war and lack of financial resources.

Programs and Degrees

The University of Phnom Penh maintains faculties of education; law and economic science; pharmacy, paramedical science, and medicine; humanities and letters; science; and commercial science. The Buddhist University includes faculties of languages, history, and religion and philosophy, whereas the University of Fine Arts has faculties of music, choreography, archeology, and architecture. The University of Agronomical Sciences trains agronomists and specialists in fisheries, stock raising, rural engineering, and forestry.

The Technical University trains engineers and skilled technicians in its faculty of arts and crafts, which offers programs in general and motor mechanics and building design. The Popular University trains middle-level technical and professional personnel, while the provincial universities—the University of Battambang, the University of Kampong Cham, and the University of Takeo-Kampot (heavily damaged by war in 1970)—emphasize engineering and food technology. The Khmer-Soviet Friendship Higher Technical Institute offers programs in electronics, construction engineering, agricultural hydraulics, textiles, and mining (1974).

Administration and Control and Teaching Staff

Until 1975 the ultimate educational authority in Cambodia was the National Board of Education and Culture, whose membership included political leaders and members of cultural, humanitarian,

and social organizations. The primary administrative body for education was the Ministry of National Education, Youth, and Sport, established in 1973. Educational policy developed by the ministry was considered by the government council of ministers and approved by the National Board of Education and Culture.

Within the ministry the foremost subunit was the Directorate General of Education, which administered primary, secondary, and technical education. The directorate general also controlled the National Institute of Educational Documentation, Research, Study, and Training; and the National Institute for Khmerization of Language. Apart from this main subunit, three other branches of the ministry were concerned with higher education. The Directorate of Higher Education, designed to oversee higher study, coordinate university functions, and examine problems within tertiary-level institutions, was the most important. The Higher Council of Universities, directed by the minister of education and composed of the university rectors and the directors of the various divisions of the Ministry of Education, resolved political, technical, and administrative problems in the entire educational system. The National Educational Planning Office was in charge of educational planning and also conducted research.

The universities were administered by a rector who was responsible to the Ministry of Education but had the freedom to make decisions on internal matters. The governing councils of the universities formulated curricular content and educational policy.

The takeover by the Khmer Rouge on April 17, 1975, is expected to result in a reorganization of the educational system, probably along the lines of Chinese higher education, which aligns education closely with rural development and emphasizes a practical rather than a theoretical approach.

Teaching staff at higher education institutions in Cambodia were recruited through competitive examination and appointed by governmental decree of the cabinet council and the president of the republic. The minister of national education specified the assignment of staff and ordered transfers and promotions.

Current Problems and Trends

The Khmer Rouge government, in attempting to reconstruct the economy and social structure after the conclusion of warfare, is also drawing up a plan for postwar reconstruction and development of the educational system. The present regime faces the tasks of reorganizing both formal and nonformal education to meet the demand for trained manpower necessary to national development. Practical aspects of all levels of education will undoubtedly be emphasized. Rural schools and provincial universities will also receive more attention than they were accorded under the previous government.

One of the chief problems that has confronted educators in Cambodia has been an overabundance of students enrolled in the secondary academic program that prepares students for university study, while the technical program has not been training enough prospective employees to meet anticipated middle-level manpower needs. The present regime will no doubt emphasize middle-level manpower for rural development.

International Cooperation

In 1971 the largest number of the students studying abroad were enrolled in higher institutions in France. The United States was host to less than one quarter of these Cambodian students, while the United Kingdom enrolled about one eighth. Other countries enrolling a small number of Cambodians were Australia, Canada, Czechoslovakia, the Federal Republic of Germany, Hungary, India, Japan, New Zealand, Romania, Switzerland, and Yugoslavia.

For one month each year since 1967, the United Nations Children's Fund (UNICEF) has aided in the training of principals of primary schools and other administrative personnel in the first-level system.

In 1970 the then Khmer Republic became a member of the Regional Institute of Higher Education and Development (RIHED), which conducts research studies and holds conferences and seminars on higher education and development in the Southeast Asian region. In 1971 Cambodia joined the regional intergovernmental body known as the Southeast Asian Ministers of Education Organization (SEAMEO), which emphasizes nonformal, primary, and secondary level education. Until 1975 the country actively participated in the affairs of the two regional bodies. Future direction in international cooperation, especially in education, remains to be seen.

[Prepared with the assistance of Amnuay Tapingkae, Director, Regional Institute of Higher Education and Development, Singapore.]

Bibliography

Dim, M. "Educational Administration in the Khmer Republic." *Bulletin of the UNESCO Regional Office for Education in Asia*, June 1974, *15*, 85–100.

Dremuk, R. *Report of the Training Workshop on the Evaluation of Asian Educational Credentials*. Washington, D.C.: National Association for Foreign Student Affairs, 1968.

Hayden, H., and others. *Higher Education and Development in Southeast Asia*. Vol. 1: *Director's Report*; Vol. 2: *Country Profiles*. Paris: UNESCO, 1967.

Huon, T. K. *Role of the Universities in Development Planning: Khmer Republic Case*. Singapore: Regional Institute of Higher Education and Development, 1974.

See also: Religious Influences in Higher Education: Buddhism.

DEMOGRAPHY AND POPULATION STUDIES
(Field of Study)

Demography has been defined as "the study of components of population variation and change." Population studies, on the other hand, "are concerned not only with population variables but also with relationships between population changes and other variables—social, economic, political, biological, genetic, geographical" (Hauser and Duncan, 1959, p. 2). Population studies go back to Plato, who said in *The Laws* that although the city-state needs enough people for production and defense, too many will make effective rule and civil order impossible. Plato and Aristotle in Greece, as well as Confucius in China, had population policy recommendations, including incentives for fertility or for infertility. Demography began much later—with John Graunt, who in 1661 published his conclusions derived from the bills of mortality and christenings. He found that male births were more numerous than female and that mortality was higher in the city than in the countryside.

In spite of the differences between them, demography and population studies are generally considered one field of study, centered in a knowledge of demographic techniques: how to measure and compare mortality, fertility, migration, and population distribution. Beyond this, population study is interdisciplinary. Like sociology, it is concerned with the social causes and effects of population change—for example, the decline in fertility when work outside the home provides women with an alternative to motherhood. Population studies also overlap with economics, in analyses of the relationship between population growth and economic growth and in the economic theory of fertility (the costs and benefits of children under various conditions). Other branches of the field are the politics and geography of population, historical demography, the demography of isolated groups, and the mathematics of population.

The first academic with a major interest in population was the English economist Thomas Robert Malthus (1766–1834), who viewed population as a dependent variable, determined largely by the means of subsistence. Charles Darwin's theory of the survival of the fittest developed from Darwin's acceptance of Malthus's belief that

only so many of a species could survive, since—without natural or social checks—population increases more rapidly than means of subsistence. Throughout the nineteenth century, population was studied chiefly by economists in England; by the middle of the twentieth century, however, population studies came to be centered in the United States. Louis Henry in France and Peter Laslett in England developed historical demography; and by the 1960s ecology, the environment, and population analysis had become important studies in the United States.

All large United States universities offer some instruction in population, most commonly in sociology, economics, and biology departments. Introductory undergraduate courses cover elementary demographic techniques, world population, and whatever theory is available for explaining it. They deal with birth, death, and migration; the problem of increasing population; environmental pollution; and overrapid urbanization, especially in poor countries. At the graduate level a Ph.D. in demography is offered by departments of sociology at Duke University, Brown University, and the Universities of Michigan, Wisconsin, California, Texas, and Chicago, among others. Smaller numbers of demographers come from departments of economics, especially from Princeton University. At Harvard, Johns Hopkins, Michigan, and North Carolina, population activists—both scholars and administrators—take master's and doctor's degrees in schools of public health.

A number of universities in western Europe (Sweden, France, Belgium, the United Kingdom, and Italy) offer instruction in population. Elsewhere, population studies are pursued at universities in Montreal, London (Ontario), Calgary, Canberra, Warsaw, Tokyo, and Budapest.

Most scholars want population study to be an international rather than a United States discipline. Consequently, foundations and the government in the United States have sponsored large numbers of

Asian, African, and Latin American students in United States graduate departments; many of these students—from India, Indonesia, Mexico, and the Philippines—have subsequently founded centers of research and learning in their own countries.

In the Soviet Union and the People's Republic of China, population has had difficulty gaining academic recognition, because of the polemics of Marx against Malthus. But a major group of Soviet scholars acknowledge the relationship between population and development, and population study is now going on in the Soviet Union.

A number of international centers exist, including the *Centro latinoamericano de demografía* (CELADE) in Santiago, Chile; the International Institute for Population Studies (IIPS) in Bombay; and others in Cairo and in Africa—all associated with the United Nations. The International Institute for Applied Systems Analysis (IIASA) in Vienna includes work on spatial aspects of population, and the European Centre for Population Studies, in The Hague, has been in operation since 1953.

The community of demographers is represented by the International Union for the Scientific Study of Population (IUSSP) in Liège, Belgium; the Population Association of America (PAA), which also has international membership; and national associations in Canada and the Federal Republic of Germany.

Some twenty centers of population research exist in nineteen United States universities, each small (fewer than five faculty) and in part funded by federal and foundation grants and contracts. Other research institutions are located in Paris, London, Rome, Montreal, Moscow, Louvain, Canberra, Mexico City, Manila, Djakarta, and Budapest. Europe's senior institution is the *Institut national d'études démographiques* (INED), in Paris. The United Kingdom's senior institution is the Population Investigation Committee in the London School of Economics.

[Notes: **P. M. Hauser** and **O. D. Duncan**

(Eds.), *The Study of Population* (Chicago: University of Chicago Press, 1959.]

NATHAN KEYFITZ

Levels and Programs of Study

Programs in demography and population studies generally require a first university degree or equivalent, usually in the same or a related field and lead to a master's degree (M.A. or M.Sc.), the doctorate, or their equivalents. Programs deal with the theory of human population growth and the measurement of human populations and consist of study, seminar or group discussions, and original research work as substantiated by the presentation of a scholarly thesis or dissertation. Principal subject matter areas within which courses and research projects tend to fall include the theory of population growth and change; techniques of population projection; and methods of measuring population size and characteristics (census taking), fertility, mortality, and morbidity in human populations. Background studies include courses in sociology, economics, family planning, anthropology, mathematics, and statistics.

[This section was based on UNESCO's *International Standard Classification of Education (ISCED)* (Paris: UNESCO, 1976).]

Major International and National Organizations

INTERNATIONAL

There are many agencies and organizations interested and working in the demography and population field internationally, among them national government agencies and organizations, the United Nations and its specialized agencies, other intergovernmental organizations, nongovernmental international organizations, and private organizations. Those with important research and training programs are listed below.

The following are United Nations organizations:

United Nations Environment Programme
   (UNEP)
P.O. Box 30552
Nairobi, Kenya

United Nations Fund for Population
Activities (UNFPA)
485 Lexington Avenue
New York, New York 10017 USA

United Nations Industrial Development
Organization (UNIDO)
P.O. Box 707
A-1011 Vienna, Austria

United Nations Population Division
Department of Economic and Social Affairs
UN Building
New York, New York 10017 USA

The following are United Nations specialized agencies:

Food and Agriculture Organization of the
United Nations (FAO)
via delle Terme di Caracalla
00100 Rome, Italy

International Bank for Reconstruction and
Development (IBRD)
1818 H Street NW
Washington, D.C. 20433 USA

International Labour Organisation (ILO)
1211 Geneva 22, Switzerland

United Nations Educational, Scientific and
Cultural Organization (UNESCO)
7 place de Fontenoy
75700 Paris, France

World Health Organization (WHO)
1211 Geneva 27, Switzerland

The following are international organizations:

Council of Europe
67006 Strasbourg, France

Intergovernmental Committee for European
Migration (ICEM)
P.O. Box 100
CH-1211 Geneva 19, Switzerland

Organisation for Economic Co-operation
and Development (OECD)
2 rue André Pascal
75016 Paris, France

Organization of American States (OAS)
17th and Constitution Avenue NW
Washington, D.C. 20006 USA

Swedish International Development Authority
(SIDA)
105 25 Stockholm, Sweden

The following are nongovernmental international organizations:

Committee for International Coordination of
National Research in Demography
Comité international de coordination des
recherches nationales en démographie
(CICRED)
27 rue du Commandeur
Paris XIVe, France

European Centre for Population Studies
Pauwenlaan 17
The Hague, Netherlands

International Planned Parenthood
Federation (IPPF)
18/20 Lower Regent Street
London SW1Y 4PW, England

International Statistical Institute (ISI)
Prinses Beatrixlaan 428
Voorburg, Netherlands

International Union for the Scientific Study
of Population (IUSSP)
rue Forgeur 5
4000 Liège, Belgium

The Population Council
245 Park Avenue
New York, New York 10017 USA

World Fertility Survey
(International Statistical Institute)
35-37 Grosvenor Gardens
London SW1W OBS, England

For a more detailed listing of agencies and
organizations—including national governmental organizations of international significance, private organizations, and individuals
working in the population and demography
field—refer to the following:

Buck, E., and Rodel, D. (Eds.) *Directory of IEC
Assistance and Services.* Honolulu: East-West
Communication Institute, East-West Center,
1973.

Directory of Demographic Research Centres. Paris:
Committee for International Coordination
of National Research in Demography, 1974.

Directory of Members' Scientific Activities. Liège,
Belgium: International Union for the Scientific Study of Population, 1975.

Hankinson, R. (Comp.) *Agencies and Organizations Working in the International Population
Assistance Field.* Paris: Development Centre of
the Organisation for Economic Co-operation
and Development, 1973.

*International Directory of Population Information
and Library Resources.* Chapel Hill: University of North Carolina, Carolina Population
Center, 1972.

*Research, Teaching and Training in Demography:
A Directory of Institutions in the ECAFE Region.* New York: United Nations, 1972.

NATIONAL

The best source for national organizations in demography and population studies is:

International Directory of Population Information and Library Resources. Chapel Hill: University of North Carolina, Carolina Population Center, 1972.

A listing of government agencies and organizations in developed countries of the world, with descriptions of their interests and population assistance, is given in the above-mentioned *Agencies and Organizations Working in the International Population Assistance Field.*

Principal Information Sources

GENERAL

Guides to the literature of demography and population include:

Bibliographie démographique 1945–62. Paris: Institut national de la statistique et des études économiques, 1963.

Dechesne, J. L. *Bibliography of IUSSP Conference Proceedings.* Liège, Belgium: International Union for the Scientific Study of Population, 1974.

Eldridge, H. T. *The Materials of Demography.* Westport, Connecticut: Greenwood, 1975. Reprint of 1959 edition.

Golini, A. *Bibliografia delle opere demografiche in lingua italiana (1930–65).* Rome: Università di Roma, Istituto di demografia, 1966.

Golini, A., and Caselli, G. *Bibliografia delle opere demografiche italiane, 1966–1972.* Rome: Università di Roma, Istituto di demografia, 1973.

Hankinson, R. *Population and Development: A Summary Information Guide.* Paris: Development Centre of the Organisation for Economic Co-operation and Development, 1972.

Konoshima, S., and others. *Sources of Information on Population/Family Planning: A Handbook for Asia.* Honolulu: East-West Communication Institute, 1975. Lists sixty-four information sources divided into two groups: (1) national agencies in Asia which offer services to users in other Asian countries; and (2) regional, international, and other specialized information organizations and centers, located throughout the world, which respond to requests from Asia for information and materials. Each profile describes the organization's general activities, its information and materials services, its resource base, and the subject and geographical coverage of its information and materials services.

Legeard, C. *Guide de recherches documentaires en démographie.* Paris: Gauthier-Villars, 1966.

Population, Population and Family Education, and Family Planning: A Bibliography. Bangkok, Thailand: UNESCO Regional Office for Education in Asia, 1973.

"A Sourcebook on Population." *Population Bulletin.* November 1969, *25*, 1–51.

For introductions and overviews to the field see:

Bogue, D. J. *Principles of Demography.* New York: Wiley, 1969.

Borrie, W. D. *The Place of Demography in the Development of the Social Sciences.* Liège, Belgium: International Population Conference, International Union for the Scientific Study of Population, 1973.

Borrie, W. D. *Population, Environment, and Society.* Auckland, New Zealand: Auckland University Press, 1973.

Bose, A., and others. *Studies in Demography.* Chapel Hill: University of North Carolina Press, 1971.

Coale, A. J. *The Growth and Structure of Human Populations.* Princeton, New Jersey: Princeton University Press, 1972.

Hauser, P. M., and Duncan, O. D. (Eds.) *The Study of Population.* Chicago: University of Chicago Press, 1959. Older study of the state of the art.

Heer, D. M. *Society and Population.* (2nd ed.) Englewood Cliffs, New Jersey: Prentice-Hall, 1975.

International Social Science Journal, 1974, *26*(2), entire issure. Devoted to population policy and concerns; includes "Towards a Broader Definition of Population Education," by S. Viederman, pp. 315–327.

Keyfitz, N. *Introduction to the Mathematics of Population.* Reading, Massachusetts: Addison-Wesley, 1968.

Peterson, W. *Population.* (3rd ed.) New York: Macmillan, 1974.

Szabady, E. (Ed.) *World View of Population Problems.* Budapest: Demographic Committee of the Hungarian Academy of Sciences and Demographic Research Institute, 1968.

In the area of population education, the following are important:

Burleson, N. D. "Population Education: Problems and Perspectives." *Educational Documentation and Information,* 1974, *193* (4th quarter), entire issue. The result of UNESCO's activity during the 1974 World Population Year, the entire issue is on population education; includes an annotated bibliography of materials on population education globally at all levels.

Jayasuriya, J. E. *Population Education: Its Goals and Its Nature.* Bangkok, Thailand: UNESCO Regional Office for Education in Asia, 1974.

Lorimer, F. *The University Teaching of Social Sciences: Demography.* Paris: UNESCO, 1957. A survey on the status of the teaching of demography in twenty-nine countries; includes bibliographical references at the end of each area and country survey.

Population Education in Asia: A Source Book. Bangkok, Thailand: UNESCO, Regional Office for Education in Asia, 1975. See especially Section 2, "Orientation to Population Education."

For surveys of the history of population see:

Carr-Saunders, A. *World Population: Past Growth and Future Trends.* New York: Barnes & Noble, 1965.

Glass, D. V., and Eversley, D. C. C. (Eds.) *Population in History—Essays in Historical Demography.* Chicago: Aldine, 1965.

Hollingsworth, T. H. *Historical Demography.* Ithaca, New York: Cornell University Press, 1969.

Lorimer, F. "The Development of Demography." In P. M. Hauser and O. D. Duncan (Eds.), *The Study of Population.* Chicago: University of Chicago Press, 1959.

Sanchez-Albornoz, N. *The Population of Latin America: A History.* (Translated by W. A. R. Richardson.) Berkeley: University of California Press, 1974.

CURRENT BIBLIOGRAPHIES

Current Publications in Population/Family Planning. New York: Population Council, 1969–1975. Beginning in 1976 absorbed by *Studies in Family Planning.*

European Demographic Information Bulletin. The Hague: European Centre for Population Studies, 1970–.

Population. Paris: Institut national d'études démographiques, 1946–. See the bibliographical section at the end of each issue.

Population Index. Princeton, New Jersey: Office of Population Research, Princeton University, 1935–.

Population Sciences, Index of Biomedical Research. Bethesda, Maryland: National Institute of Child Health and Human Development, Center for Population Research, 1973–. Published monthly.

PERIODICALS

The following journals of demography and population are an international sampling: *Annales de démographie historique* (France), *Boletín demográfico* (Chile), *Boletín de población* (Spanish ed. of *Population Bulletin*, US), *Canadian Stud-*

ies in Population, CICRED (France), *Demográfia* (Hungary), *Demografia y economía* (Mexico), *Demographie* (Czechoslovakia), *Demographie* (FRG), *Demography* (US), *Demography India, Demosta* (Czechoslovakia), *Egyptian Population and Family Planning Review, Family Planning Perspectives* (US), *Genus* (Italy), *In'gu murje nonjip/Journal of Population Studies* (Republic of Korea), *International Migration* (Netherlands), *International Migration Review* (US), *IPPF Medical Bulletin* (UK), *IUSSP Newsletter* (Belgium), *IUSSP Papers* (Belgium), *Journal of Population Problems* (Japan), *Metropolitan Life Insurance Company. Statistical Bulletin* (US), *Population* (France), *Population* (USSR), *Population and Development Review* (US), *Population Bulletin* (US), *Population Index* (US), *Population Newsletter* (United Nations, US), *Population Review* (US), *Population Studies* (UK), *Studia demograficzne* (Poland), *Zeitschrift für Bevölkerungswissenschaft* (FRG).

For a more extensive listing of journals refer to:

Population Index. Princeton, New Jersey: Office of Population Research, Princeton University, 1935–. Each annual cumulated volume contains a list of current bibliographies and periodicals relevant to the field.

Ulrich's International Periodicals Directory. New York: Bowker, biennial.

ENCYCLOPEDIAS, DICTIONARIES, HANDBOOKS

Cubas, L. *Demografic Dictionary.* Turin, Italy: International Centre for Advanced Technical and Vocational Training, International Labour Office, 1975.

Demographic Yearbook. New York: United Nations Statistical Office, annual. The standard international compendium and source book for world demographic information.

Multilingual Demographic Dictionary. New York: Prepared by the Demographic Dictionary Committee of the International Union for the Scientific Study of Population, 1958–. The most important multilingual dictionary, with separate editions in French, Spanish, Italian, German, Arabic, Czechoslovakian, Finnish, Polish, Portuguese, Russian, Serbo-Croatian, Swedish, and Hebrew. The first part of the latest revision (which will appear in parts by subject) is: E. Grebenik and A. Hill, *International Demographic Terminology: Fertility, Family Planning, and Nuptiality* (Liège, Belgium: International Union for the Scientific Study of Population, 1975).

DIRECTORIES

Buck, E., and Rodel, D. (Eds.) *Directory of IEC Assistance and Services.* (Rev. ed.) Honolulu: East-West Communication Institute, East-

West Center, 1973. Source of information on fifty-three organizations and institutions that provide assistance and services for population and family planning IEC (information, education, and communications) programs in developing countries.

Directory of Selected Training Facilities in Family Planning and Allied Subjects. (2nd ed.) London: International Planned Parenthood Federation, 1968. Information on training programs worldwide in demography and population.

International Directory of Population Information and Library Resources. Chapel Hill: University of North Carolina, Carolina Population Center, 1972. Describes the program orientation, publications, library holdings and services, and information activities of each of 250 population-related organizations throughout the world. Part 2 (supplement): 1975 address list, compiled and edited by K. J. Gleiter; identifies 975 organizations internationally, selected for their activities, publications, and information resources.

"Population Programs and Organizations." *Population Bulletin* (Population Reference Bureau), November 1969, *25*, 1–51. Lists graduate-level university population centers in the United States, nonuniversity population libraries open to outside researchers, the major private United States and international organizations in population and family planning, and population programs of the United States government.

Research, Teaching and Training in Demography: A Directory of Institutions in the ECAFE Region. New York: United Nations, 1972. Lists the population activities of over two hundred institutions in nineteen countries in the Asian region. Updated by *Supplement No. 1,* 1974, and *Supplement No. 2,* 1974.

RESEARCH CENTERS, INSTITUTES, INFORMATION CENTERS

There are six United Nations–sponsored demographic training and research institutes in Africa, Asia, Latin America, and Europe:

Cairo Demographic Centre (CDC)
6 Willcocks Street
Zamalek, Cairo, Egypt

Centre démographique ONU–Roumanie
(CEDOR)
39 boulevard Ana Ipatescu
Bucharest, Romania

Institut de formation et de recherches
démographiques (IFORD)
B. P. 1556
Yaoundé, Cameroon

International Institute for Population Studies
Govandi Station Road
Deonar, Bombay 400088, India

Centro latinoamericano de demografía
(CELADE)
José Manuel Infante 9
Casilla 91
Santiago, Chile

Regional Institute for Population Studies
(RIPS)
P.O. Box 96
Legon, Ghana

There are many other institutions with population centers that offer training and research in demography and population studies; many of these centers are connected to universities in the United States. The following is a representative list:

Carolina Population Center (CPC)
University of North Carolina
University Square
Chapel Hill, North Carolina 27514

Center for Population Studies
Harvard University
9 Bow Street
Cambridge, Massachusetts 02138

Community and Family Study Center
University of Chicago
East 60th Street
Chicago, Illinois 60637

Department of Population Dynamics
Johns Hopkins University
School of Hygiene and Public Health
622 North Washington Street
Baltimore, Maryland 21205

East-West Population Institute
East-West Center
1777 East-West Road
Honolulu, Hawaii 96822

Office of Population Research
Princeton University
21 Prospect Avenue
Princeton, New Jersey 08540

Population Studies and Training Center
Brown University
Providence, Rhode Island 02912

Population Studies Center
University of Michigan
1225 South University
Ann Arbor, Michigan 48103

Population Studies Center
University of Pennsylvania
3718 Locust Walk
Philadelphia, Pennsylvania 19174

More complete listings of centers and institutes in the field are found in the following directories:

Directory of Demographic Research Centers. Paris: Committee for International Coordination of National Research in Demography, 1974.

Directory of Members' Scientific Activities. Liège, Belgium: International Union for the Scientific Study of Population, 1975.

Directory of Population Study Centers; U.S. and Canada. Washington, D.C.: Population Association of America, 1971.

International Directory of Population Information and Library Resources. Chapel Hill: University of North Carolina, Carolina Population Center, 1972.

Research, Teaching and Training in Demography: A Directory of Institutions in the ECAFE Region. New York: United Nations, 1972.

The following organization has as its goal an international cooperative network of population documentation, information, and library centers for the exchange, dissemination, and communication of population information:

Association for Population Family Planning
    Libraries and Information
    Centers–International
165 South Second Avenue
Clarion, Pennsylvania 16214 USA

DENMARK, KINGDOM OF

Population: 5,095,000 (1975 estimate). Student enrollment in primary and secondary school: 776,000 (1973); higher education: 87,000 (1973). Language of instruction: Danish. Academic calendar: September to June. Percentage of gross national product (GNP) expended on all education: 7% (1975 estimate).

Higher education began in Denmark with the founding of the University of Copenhagen in 1479 by King Christian I. Modeled on other Western European universities, it did not achieve major stature until after the Reformation, when it became more closely allied with Lutheran interests and secured new endowments. The Age of Enlightenment provided fresh impetus to the growth of education, and in 1788 the university was granted a new charter, which provided for the expansion of its faculties and teaching staff and the initiation of final examinations. During this period the Royal Danish Academy of Art (1754) was also established.

In the nineteenth century higher education facilities expanded throughout Denmark. The Technical University of Denmark opened in 1829, and four other institutions of higher learning date from this period: the Royal Veterinary and Agricultural College (1856), the Royal Danish Conservatory (1867), the Royal College of Dentistry (1888), and the Royal Danish School of Pharmacy (1892).

In the twentieth century the increasing number of students and the growing demand for scientific and technical education have had a profound effect on the shape of higher education in Denmark. Early in the century the need for a second university to relieve some of the pressure at the University of Copenhagen resulted in the formation of a committee under the Ministry of Education to study the problem. At the same time, the city council in Århus was developing its own plans for a local university, which resulted in an institution called "University Education in Jutland," which opened its doors in 1928 with municipal support. During the next five years private, local funding gave way to state funding; and in 1934 the name was officially changed to Århus University. In 1964 a third university, the University of Odense, was founded and began operations in September 1966. Six years later the University Center of Roskilde was added to the roster of universities. In 1974 the University Center at Ålborg was founded, and the University Center of Ribe-Esbjerg is projected for the late 1970s.

In the meantime, technical education was receiving unprecedented attention. Primarily an agricultural country, Denmark in the nineteenth century had little concern for the development of technicians. Except for the founding of the Technical University of Denmark, the development of technical education lagged behind that of academic education. In 1956 a Technical Commission under the egis of the prime minister was appointed to study the situation. In its report in 1959, the commission recommended the development of already existing civil and technical engineering training facilities as well as the introduction of new engineering education. The Danish Academy of Engineering *(Danmarks ingeniørakademi)*, founded in 1957, and the Technical University of Denmark provided advanced engineering education. At the recommendation of the Technical Commission, several new technical colleges opened. Although the first such facility to train technical engineers on a postsecondary level had opened in Odense in 1905, it was not until the 1960s that these technical colleges achieved any real growth.

Since the 1960s a reform of Danish higher education has been in progress. Centers which offer both traditional university subjects and nonacademic education are largely products of this reform. Technical and professional training has been under close scrutiny. Attempts have been made to shorten the duration of study in some disciplines. In engineering, programs have been initiated which require less time than is needed for traditional civil engineering degrees. In pharmaceutical training, the traditional eighteen-month apprenticeship requirement prior to academic study has been abolished in favor of a shorter trainee period. Dental, veterinary, agricultural, and commercial education has been expanded.

The tendency of higher education since the 1960s has been away from elitist academic training toward more scientific professional training that will reach a larger segment of the population.

National Educational Policy

The aim of education in Denmark is not only to impart knowledge but also to give a liberal education and to influence character building. The duties of the schools are to develop and strengthen the student's appreciation of ethical and Christian values; to impart a respect for the ideas of others and an appreciation of human life and nature; and to develop an affinity with the other Nordic peoples.

Legal Basis for Education

Major recent legislation regulating higher education in Denmark includes Act 271 of June 4, 1970, which recognized four universities—in Copenhagen, Århus, and Odense, and the Danish Technical University—as state institutions under the Ministry of Education. Article 14 of the act defined the responsibilities of the ministry in relation to these institutions, while other articles defined the conditions of service for teachers and the general administration and function of the university. An act of May 1970 created university centers—multidisciplinary centers intended to develop alongside the universities. The Management of Institutions for Higher Education Act of June 13, 1973, delineates the power of the Ministry of Education in regard to all institutions of higher education.

Types of Institutions

University-level education is available at the University of Copenhagen (1479), the University of Århus (1928), the University of Odense (1964), and the Technical University of Denmark (1829). It is also offered at university centers—experimental institutions initiated by the act of May 1970. These experimental institutions use project-based teaching methods and offer nonuniversity programs alongside of university-level programs. Such centers are, or will be, located at Odense, Roskilde, Ålborg, and Ribe-Esbjerg. Certain specialized schools also offer university-level education in specific fields. Institutions of this type include the Engineering Academy of Denmark, the Royal Veterinary and Agricultural College, the Royal Danish School of Pharmacy, and the Royal Danish College of Educational Studies. Dental schools also fall into this category.

The remainder of the specialized schools in Denmark are considered nonuniversity higher education. These schools include the Royal Danish Institute of Physical Education, the Royal Danish Academy of Fine Arts, the Århus School of Architecture, the Royal Danish School of Librarianship, the School of Social Work, the Nursing School, and the School of Midwifery. Teacher training colleges, domestic science training colleges, academies of music, colleges of physiotherapy and occupational therapy, and colleges of technology are also non-university higher education institutions.

Relationship with Secondary Education

Education in Denmark is compulsory for students between the ages of seven and sixteen. Prior to 1969 the legal school-leaving age was fourteen, after grade 7, but a 1969 act of parliament made an eighth grade mandatory for 1972–73, and a ninth grade was required for 1974.

Although private schools operated by religious, national, or special-interest groups exist, the majority of Danish children attend publicly funded primary and secondary schools. (Private schools receive 85 percent of their funding from the state, which controls their examinations.)

The first seven grades offer basic education. At the end of the seventh grade, the student may go on to a general division school—a three-year nonacademic program leading to a leaving certificate (either a technical leaving certificate earned at the end of the ninth year or an advanced technical certificate awarded at the end of the tenth year); or he may continue into the *réalskole*, a three-year lower secondary school. At the end of the ninth year at the *réalskole*, the student confronts still another option. He may take a state qualifying examination for entry to a *gymnasieskole* (higher secondary education), or he may continue into the tenth grade, which is optional and vocationally oriented and leads to the *réaleksamen* (examination). A *brevis* (certificate) is awarded on passing the examination, and the student may then take a further examination for entrance into the *gymnasieskole*.

After the first year the *gymnasieskole* is divided into two streams—Latin and mathematics; both lead to the *studentereksamen* (secondary school-leaving examination).

There is also a nonformal educational system composed of a variety of schools which do not have fixed curricula and do not offer certificates but which provide secondary-level courses. Among these are folk high schools, continuation schools, and evening schools. Folk high schools are private self-governing institutions offering subjects of human and social appeal and of general interest to the individual regardless of his education, occupation, or social status. The duration of the courses varies from school to school and from year to year at each school. The shortest courses last one week, and the longest last forty weeks. The folk high school is not part of the general educational system and does not admit directly to schools of any kind. Continuation schools, a specifically Danish form of education, emphasize the direct teaching of practical subjects. These schools are private self-governing establishments receiving state grants. Courses usually last for ten months, and students may receive a leaving certificate. Evening schools for adults offer cultural, social, general, and vocational subjects. Attendance is two evenings per week, and teachers at these schools have limited formal training.

Admission Requirements

Admission to the universities requires the *studentereksamen*. For students who have not completed the *réalskole* or *gymnasieskole*, there are special courses leading to a higher preparatory examination (*højere forberedelseseksamen*), which also admits students to the university. Admission to technical or professional studies also requires special entrance examinations, certificates, and often some previous practical training for entry. In instances where there are more qualified applicants than places, students are selected on the basis of grades. As part of an endeavor to liberalize admission to universities and enable persons to enroll who do not fulfill the general entrance requirements, special dispensation may be granted. Applications are dealt with by a special committee of teachers and students under the authority of the governing board. The criteria for dispensation are a certain level of education, relevant to the desired area of study, or proof of maturity, knowledge, and experience justifying the assumption that the applicant can complete a university course in normal time.

Some nonuniversity institutions of higher education, such as the Institute of Physical Education, the School of Librarianship, and teacher training institutes, also require the *studentereksamen* or higher preparatory examination. Others have lower admission requirements. Although they offer advanced-level courses, credit is not transferable to university-level institutions. Colleges of technology, social work, journalism, and commercial studies, among others, fall into this category, and admission requirements vary from school to school.

Administration and Control

The Ministry of Education is the highest administrative authority for universities, institutes of higher education, teacher training colleges, technical colleges, technical institutes of engineering, and vocational schools. This power is imparted to the ministry through the Management of Institutions for Higher Education Act of June 13, 1973. Some institutions of higher education are under the authority of other ministries. The academies of music, the Royal Danish Academy of Fine Arts, and the Royal Danish School of Librarianship report to the Ministry of Culture. The Ministry of Agriculture is in charge of the Royal Veterinary and Agricultural College, while the Ministry of the Interior supervises health-related training. The Shipping Department of the Ministry for Economic Affairs and Commerce is responsible for schools of navigation.

Each institution under the Ministry of Education is governed by statutes which have to be approved by the minister, who also has authority in policy planning, ad-

missions, hiring of teachers and research fellows, and expulsion of students.

The administrative structure of all the universities is basically comparable. The chief administrative officer is the *rektor,* who represents the university externally and is responsible for the daily management of the institution. The *rektor* is elected from among the full-time faculty for a two- or three-year term, with eligibility for re-election by the members of the councils and members of the governing board who are not on these councils. The *prorektor* assists the *rektor* and acts in his absence. The *prorektor* is elected in the same manner as the *rektor* but for a two-year term. A *kurator* is appointed by the Crown and is in charge of financial administration.

The governing board *(konsistorium)* of the institution consists of thirty-two members, including the *rektor* as chairman, the *prorektor,* the *dekaner* (deans), and the *kurator.* In addition, the board has representation from full- and part-time teaching staff, technical and administrative staff, and students. The ratio of teachers, technical-administrative personnel, and students is 2:1:1. The governing board is responsible for matters concerning the institution as a whole and the relationship between two or more subject groups within a field. This body also draws up proposals for rules of procedure and establishes and abolishes departments.

Each faculty has an elected dean *(dekan),* a faculty council *(fakultetsråd),* and a departmental council *(fagråd).* The functions of these two councils are to undertake research and training, decide appointments or dismissals of academic staff, and award licentiate and doctoral degrees. The faculty council is concerned with the entire faculty, while the departmental councils serve each group of subjects. Teachers, technical-administrative personnel, and students are represented on these councils in a 2:1:1 ratio. Each department also has a central study committee and a number of departmental study committees which handle matters concerning study programs, examination arrangements, and the awarding of grades. They also plan and supervise teaching and appoint teaching assistants.

Programs and Degrees

The University of Copenhagen and the University of Århus have faculties of theology, law and economics, medicine, mathematics and natural sciences, and philosophy (arts or the humanities). The University of Odense, which is planned to expand as a university center offering a variety of post-secondary programs, has faculties of humanities, medicine, and natural sciences. The Technical University of Denmark has departments of chemical engineering, mechanical engineering, civil engineering, electrical engineering, and general science. *Candidatus* is the first degree awarded by the universities. The length of study varies according to the program, with seven to eight years required for medicine, four and a half to five and a half years for engineering and dentistry, and five years for pharmacy. Most other faculties require six years of study. The *licentiatgrad* (advanced postgraduate degree) may be earned by students with the *candidatus* after two to three additional years in postgraduate research and study under the guidance of a specially appointed tutor. A thesis and additional examination may also be required. The doctoral degree, indicating a very high level of scholarship, is also awarded in Denmark but is rare. A candidate for a doctorate must publish original research in the form of a thesis and must defend his thesis in public lectures before authorities in the field.

Some specialized schools award the first and the advanced degrees, but the majority of them award diplomas and certificates. A certificate is granted after two to four years of study in such programs as teacher training, building construction, physical education, music, librarianship, social work, nursing, and physical therapy. The technical colleges award the title of *teknikumingeniør* after four years of study. *Danmarks ingeniørakademi* awards the title of *akademiingeniør* after three and a half to four years of study.

Financing of Higher Education and Student Financial Aid

Higher education is wholly supported by the Danish government. In 1974, 13 percent of the national budget was spent on education, and one third of that amount went to higher education.

There are no tuition fees charged by institutions of higher education in Denmark. There are, however, fees for examinations, matriculation, laboratory materials, and living accommodations. Students approved by the University Scholarship Committee may receive scholarships or loans from the Education Fund. Private scholarships and grants are also awarded.

Teaching Staff

The full-time teaching staff at Danish institutions of higher education include *professor* (professor); *afdelingsleder* (head of section), whose duties are to teach and conduct research; and *amanuensis* (assistant), whose duties are also to teach and conduct research but at a less sophisticated level than the *afdelingsleder*. In addition, there are *lektor* (lecturer) positions, which are usually part time. The *lektor*, who conducts upper-level courses, may be a head of section or an assistant, or his main focus of interest may be outside the university. Lower-level courses are taught by *undervisningsassistenter* (part-time teaching assistants).

Appointments to the academic staff are made on the basis of academic qualifications and the quality of the applicant's previous research work. Apart from professorships, salary contracts for academic positions are generally made between professional academic organizations and the government.

Research Activities

Freedom of research both for universities and individual scholars is guaranteed by the Management of Institutions for

Higher Education Act of 1973. Research and instruction are closely related at universities. Prior to 1970 professors were expected to devote as much as 30 percent of their time to research responsibilities. As a result of Act 271 of June 1970, research responsibility was shifted to departmental or institute councils elected by the faculty and by student representatives.

Major research work that is not covered by permanent annual grants is supported by the Danish State Research Foundation, the Danish Government Fund for Scientific and Industrial Research, and private funds.

Denmark encourages visits by foreign research workers through the Rask-Ørsted Foundation, which finances exchange programs. Research projects must be submitted and accepted in advance by the foundation. Visits are usually limited to one year but may be extended to three years.

Current Problems and Trends

In the academic year 1972–73, approximately eighty thousand students (28 percent of the relevant age group) were enrolled in higher education. Despite the growing number of students entering higher education, less than half of them graduate. Theology, engineering, natural sciences, and veterinary and agricultural sciences have the highest number of graduates, but only half of the students in humanities, economics, and medicine complete their course. A program is under investigation to alleviate the student dropout problem by reducing the average duration of study. If it succeeds in solving this problem, this program will create another serious situation—graduate unemployment. Denmark is turning out more trained graduates now than there are suitable jobs, and with additional graduates the condition can only worsen.

Relationship with Industry

The technical schools of higher education in Denmark have a close relationship with industry; students in most courses are required to work six to twelve months in industry prior to graduation. Technical engineering schools require students to have practical work experience before applying for admission.

International Cooperation

Schools in Denmark participate in numerous exchange programs. Each year foreign teachers are employed by the government to teach English at public primary and lower secondary schools. The University of Copenhagen sponsors a semester of undergraduate work for students at two American institutions of higher education: Washburn University of Topeka (Kansas) and Whittier College (California). Denmark has also established a program whereby students between the ages of eighteen and thirty can come to Denmark for an academic year to study Scandinavian culture, live in Danish homes, and attend Danish schools.

Teachers in Denmark's universities are encouraged to go abroad to study and teach, and those who go often continue to receive all or part of their Danish salaries. Research fellows are also allowed to continue their studies in other countries while on fellowship. Various foundations frequently defray the cost of travel.

[Information supplied by Ministry of Education, Copenhagen.]

Educational Associations

Akademikernes centralorganisation
Association of Graduates from Institutions for
	Higher Education
Gothersgade 131
1123 Copenhagen, Denmark

Danske studerendes faellesråd
National Union of Danish Students
Knabrostraede 3
1210 Copenhagen Denmark

Bibliography

Access to Institutions of Higher Education. Copenhagen: Ministry of Education, 1970.
The Admission and Academic Placement of Students from Nordic Countries. A Workshop Report. Washington, D.C.: National Association for Foreign Student Affairs and American Association of College Registrars and Admissions Officers, 1974.

Classification of Educational Systems: Belgium, Denmark, United States. Paris: Organisation for Economic Co-operation and Development, 1972.

Denmark: An Official Handbook. Copenhagen: Press and Information Department, Royal Ministry of Foreign Affairs, 1970.

Educational Classification, Conversion Key. Copenhagen: Royal Ministry of Education, 1971.

Educational Goals and Long-Term Planning. Copenhagen: Royal Ministry of Education, 1970.

Josepsson, B. *Educational Systems: A Comparative Study of Educational Legislation in Scandinavia.* Reykjavik, Iceland: Royal Ministry of Education, 1974.

The Management of Institutions for Higher Education Act, N. 362 of June 13th, 1973. Copenhagen: Royal Ministry of Education, 1973.

Problems of Long-Term Economic Planning in Denmark, 1970–1985: Education. Copenhagen: Royal Ministry of Education, 1972.

Study in Denmark. New York: Institute of International Education, 1969.

Wastage in Higher Education. Copenhagen: Royal Ministry of Education, International Relations Division, 1969.

See also: Academic Dress and Insignia; Adult Education: Role of Labor and Industry; Agriculture in Higher Education: History of Agricultural Education; Aid to Other Nations: Bilateral Participation in Higher Education; Faeroe Islands; Graduate and Professional Education: General History and Contemporary Survey; Greenland; Internationalization of Higher Education; Nonacademic Personnel Administration; Research: Financing and Control of Research; Science Policies: Highly Industrialized Nations: Western Europe.

DENTAL AUXILIARIES
(Field of Study)

Dental auxiliaries provide assistance to dentists so that the dentists can deliver oral health care more efficiently. Many different types of dental auxiliaries are employed throughout the world, but all may be classified into four categories by means of two criteria.

The first criterion is a determination of whether the auxiliaries are directly providing a complete or partial unit of a treatment procedure to patients. If they are, they are classified as operating dental aux-iliaries. If they are not, they are classified as nonoperating auxiliaries. There are two types of nonoperating auxiliaries. One type, known as a dental assistant, provides a wide range of services, including assistance to the dentist at chairside, oral health education, and preparation of operatories, as well as greeting patients and scheduling appointments. The other type is the dental laboratory technician, who fabricates inlays, crowns, bridges, partial dentures, and full dentures on models prepared from impressions taken by dentists.

The second criterion for classifying auxiliaries is based on the kind of supervision that the dentist provides for the operating dental auxiliary. Direct supervision means that the supervising dentist authorizes the treatment procedure, is always present in the dental facility when the auxiliary is functioning, and evaluates the treatment before dismissal of the patient. Examples of this type of auxiliary are (1) the dental auxiliary who is trained at the New Cross Hospital, London, to provide dental care for children in school dental clinics under the direct supervision of dentists employed by local authorities and (2) expanded-function dental assistants and dental hygienists in the United States, who in some states are permitted to insert and finish restorations in teeth under the dentist's supervision. Auxiliaries under general supervision may perform treatment services without the dentists, who are present at all times and who assume responsibility for the activities of the auxiliaries. Examples of this type of operating auxiliary are dental hygienists, who provide specific preventive services; and the New Zealand dental nurse, who provides dental care for children in school dental clinics operated by the government but without direct supervision. In those areas of the world with very few dentists to treat large populations, the operating dental auxiliary, who is officially classified as working under the general supervision of a dentist, does for all practical purposes perform in an unsupervised status.

Although the first dental school was

established in 1840, formal educational programs for dental auxiliaries were not provided until 1913—largely because apprenticeship training was firmly established very early, making it extremely difficult for formal programs to compete. Indeed, even in the United States, which is widely recognized as one of the most dentally sophisticated countries, apprenticeship training of dental hygienists in dental offices is still recognized by the state of Alabama, and most dental assistants and dental laboratory technicians are trained as apprentices in dental offices and commercial dental laboratories.

The first formal educational program for dental auxiliaries was a school for dental hygienists founded in 1913 by Dr. A. C. Fones in Bridgeport, Connecticut. The dental hygienist was conceived as an operating auxiliary working under the direct or general supervision of a dentist. The functions of the dental hygienist include making preliminary oral examinations, removing calcareous deposits and stains from the surfaces of the teeth, and providing additional services and information about the prevention of oral disease. Until World War II, dental hygienists were employed only in the United States. They were trained and used in the Royal Air Force in the United Kingdom during the war, and postwar civilian training was rapidly accepted in Canada, Japan, and the United Kingdom. During the 1965–1975 decade, twenty-three other countries began training some form of operating auxiliary.

The first school for operating dental auxiliaries who performed restorative services on decayed teeth was founded in 1921 at Wellington, New Zealand. These auxiliaries, known as New Zealand dental nurses, work in government-operated school dental clinics under the indirect supervision of dental officers and provide most of the routine dental care required by the children of New Zealand. During the 1965–1975 decade, the New Zealand dental nurse concept was initiated in several parts of the world, including, for example, the province of Saskatchewan in Canada, England, Jamaica, Australia, Malaysia, and Singapore.

A program to train a new type of operating auxiliary, the preventive dentistry technician, has been initiated in Puerto Rico. These auxiliaries are trained in a few weeks to apply dental caries preventive measures, such as the topical application of fluorides to teeth, and are assigned to various populations of school children. It is proposed that these auxiliaries be prepared for other functions through a longer educational program, which is being developed.

Formal educational programs for the training of nonoperating auxiliaries—the dental assistant and the dental laboratory technician—did not get under way to any significant degree until the early 1960s. Except for the United States, where there are now over 270 accredited dental assistant training programs, the number of these programs worldwide is quite small but increasing. The two factors that contributed the greatest stimulus for the development of dental assistant training programs in the United States were the rapid nationwide growth of the community college system, which accepted dental assisting and dental hygiene as part of its educational concept, and the simultaneous initiation of federally supported Dental Assistant Utilization (DAU) programs, which enabled dental students to work with chairside dental assistants.

The dental auxiliary training program that has been most neglected throughout the world involves the preparation of dental laboratory technicians. Establishment of accredited programs has been slow in the United States. From the early 1950s to 1976, only thirty-four programs were recognized. Yet it is this technician who permits the dentist to avoid spending time on mechanical laboratory work and who influences, to a considerable degree, the quality of the inlays, crowns, bridges, partial dentures, and full dentures which dentists provide for their patients. In some provinces in Canada, dental laboratory technicians have sought and obtained enactment of laws which allow them to be independent operating dental auxiliaries and provide denture services directly to the public.

Because so many different classifications of dental auxiliaries are utilized in a variety of dental care delivery systems throughout the world, it is difficult to predict the future course of dental auxiliary education. However, throughout the world there is rising concern over the problems of oral disease in entire populations and a concomitant concern over the cost of the solutions to these problems. Therefore, regardless of the type of dental care delivery system considered best suited to each country, dental auxiliaries will play an increasingly important role in that system, and dental auxiliary education will be an expanding field throughout the world for the foreseeable future.

JOHN W. HEIN

Levels and Programs of Study

Programs for dental auxiliaries generally require as a minimum prerequisite a secondary education, although mature students, especially those with relevant work experience, may sometimes be admitted with lower educational qualifications. Programs consist of classroom, hospital, and laboratory instruction and deal with the technology of dental care, dental laboratory technology, and dental hygiene technology. The usual award for successful completion is a certificate or diploma, an associate degree, a bachelor's degree (B.S.), or their equivalents. Graduates may enter careers as dental hygienists, dental assistants, or dental laboratory technicians.

Principal course content usually includes dental assistant subjects (such as dental anatomy and physiology, oral pathology, dental materials, preventive dentistry, dental instrument care, and dental hygiene), dental surgery assistant subjects (such as anatomy and physiology, anesthetics, bacteriology and sterilization, dental radiography, periodontology, orthodontics, re-storative dentistry, and prosthetics and mechanics), dental laboratory technology subjects (such as oral anatomy, investments and casting procedures, impression materials, dental waxes, synthetic resin materials, amalgams, dental ceramics, and dental metallurgy), dental hygiene subjects (such as dental health education, oral therapeutics, and clinical and community dental services), and operating dental auxiliary subjects (such as curative dental procedures, treatment of teeth affected by dental decay, and tooth extraction). Background courses often included are dental terminology, oral histology, sterilization and disinfection procedures, general chemistry, microbiology, general physics, radiology, mathematics, nutrition, psychology, sociology, dental law and ethics, and elementary principles of nursing (including first aid).

[This section was based on UNESCO's *International Standard Classification of Education (ISCED)* (Paris: UNESCO, 1976).]

Major International and National Organizations

INTERNATIONAL

International Dental Federation
Fédération dentaire internationale (FDI)
64 Wimpole Street
London W1M 8AL, England

World Health Organization (WHO)
Oral Health Unit
1211 Geneva 27, Switzerland

NATIONAL

A sampling of national organizations in the field includes:

Austria:
    Bundesinning der österreichischen
       Zahntechniker
    Bauernmarkt 13
    Vienna I

Canada:
    Canadian Dental Hygienists Association
    234 St. George Street
    Toronto 5, Ontario

    Ontario Dental Hygienists Association
    Box 264
    Maxville, Ontario

Denmark:
Dansk tandlaegeforening
14 Oslo Plads
2100 Copenhagen

Federal Republic of Germany:
Verband deutscher Zahntechniker
Innungen (VDZI)
1 Gustav Freytag Strasse 36
6000 Frankfurt/Main

Japan:
Japanese Dental Hygienists Association
% Japan Dental Association
1-20 Kudan-kita, 4-chome
Chiyoda-ku, Tokyo 102

Nigeria:
Nigeria Dental Hygienists Association
% Federal Ministry of Health
Principal Federal School of
Dental Hygiene
1 Broad Street
Lagos

Sweden:
Swedish Dental Hygienists Association
Becksjubarvägen 45-47
13100 Nacka

United Kingdom:
Associated Dental Technicians
203 Kings Cross Road
London WC1, England

Association of British Dental
Surgery Assistants
3 Market Place
Blackpool, Lancaster, England

British Dental Hygienists Association
Eastman Dental Hospital
Gray's Inn Road
London WC1X 8LD, England

United States:
American Dental Assistants Association
211 East Chicago Avenue
Chicago, Illinois 60611

American Dental Hygienists Association
211 East Chicago Avenue
Chicago, Illinois 60611

National Association of Dental
Laboratories
3801 Mt. Vernon Avenue
Alexandria, Virginia 22305

For a more complete listing of national and international dental organizations see:

International Dental Journal, 1976, *26*(1), 96–97. Provides a listing, with addresses, of the members of International Dental Federation.

National and International Dental Organizations of the World. Chicago: American Dental Association, 1976.

Principal Information Sources

GENERAL

The following are general guides containing sources on dental auxiliaries:

Basic Dental Reference Works. Chicago: American Dental Association, Bureau of Library Services, 1975.

Blake, J. B., and Roos, C. (Eds.) *Medical Reference Works 1679–1966: A Selected Bibliography.* Chicago: Medical Library Association, 1967. *Supplement I* (1967–1968), compiled by M. V. Clark, 1970; *Supplement II* (1969–1972), compiled by J. S. Richmond, 1973; *Supplement III* (1973–1974), compiled by J. S. Richmond, 1975.

Books and Package Libraries for Dentists. Chicago: American Dental Association, Bureau of Library Services, 1976. English-language books published 1972–1975. For pre-1972 and foreign titles, write to the ADA. Updated regularly.

Richards, N. D., and Cohen, L. K. (Eds.) *Social Sciences and Dentistry: A Critical Bibliography.* Leiden, Netherlands: A. W. Sijthoff, 1971.

Spencer, E. M. "Dentistry." In L. T. Morton (Ed.), *Use of Medical Literature.* Hamden, Connecticut: Archon; London: Butterworth, 1974.

Overviews to the field include:

Castano, F., and Alden, B. *Handbook of Expanded Dental Auxiliary Practice.* Philadelphia: Lippincott, 1973.

"Reports by the Council for Dental Education." *Journal of the American Dental Association,* 1974, *88,* 1039–1061. Includes sections on the education and utilization of dental auxiliaries and on new educational standards for dental auxiliaries.

Hamburg, J. (Ed.) *Review of Allied Health Education: 1.* Lexington: University Press of Kentucky, 1974.

Park, V. R., and others. *A Textbook for Dental Assistants.* (2nd ed.) Philadelphia: Saunders, 1975.

"Report of the Inter-Agency Committee on Dental Auxiliaries." *Journal of the American Dental Association,* 1972, *84,* 1025–1087. Examines the history and philosophy of dental auxiliary education in the United States and provides information concerning its future.

"Symposium on the Expanding Role of the Auxiliary in Dentistry." *Dental Clinics of North America,* 1974, *18*(4). Limited to the United States.

World Health Organization. "Report of the Committee of Experts on Dental Auxiliaries." *Boletín de información dental*, 1972, *32*, 67–92.

Comparative education sources for the field include:

Dunning, J. M. "Deployment and Control of Dental Auxiliaries in New Zealand and Australia." *Journal of the American Dental Association*, 1972, *85*, 618–626.

Garza, S. J. *Dental Auxiliary Utilization and Education in Latin America*. Washington, D.C.: Pan American Health Organization (PAHO), PA Sanitary Bureau, Regional Office of WHO, 1970. Results of two research studies conducted by PAHO.

Index to Dental Literature. Chicago: American Dental Association, Bureau of Library Services, 1923–. Lists articles on programs of study in foreign countries; see listings under "Dental Assistants—Education," "Dental Hygienists—Education," and "Dental Technicians—Education."

Ishikawa, T. "The Present Education Conditions of Operative Dentistry and Dental Hygiene in North America and Europe." *Shikwa gakuho*, 1974, *74*(8), 1299–1304.

Leatherman, G. H. "An International Survey of Auxiliary Dental Personnel." *Journal of the American Dental Hygienists Association*, 1971, *45*(3), 45–51.

Lucaccini, L. F., and Handley, J. *Research in the Use of Expanded Function Auxiliaries*. Washington, D.C.: U.S. Department of Health, Education and Welfare, 1974. Report on a symposium, 1974; pages 42–54 are devoted to a discussion of the curricula of several important auxiliary programs.

Myers, S. E. "WHO and Dental Auxiliaries Around the World." *Journal of the American Dental Hygienists Association*, 1970, *44*, 32–39. Overview of WHO's role in training and utilization of auxiliary personnel in developed and developing countries.

Ward, M. A. "Dental Hygiene in the Continent of Europe." *Journal of the American Dental Hygienists Association*, 1971, *45*, 107–113. Excellent discussion of historical background of dental hygiene in Europe and of dental hygiene curricula in Europe.

Histories of the field include:

Hein, J. "The Dilemma in Dental Education." In J. Hamburg (Ed.), *Review of Allied Health Education: 1*. Lexington: University Press of Kentucky, 1974. Hein's chapter offers a history of the field in the United States as well as a section on the New Zealand dental nurse.

Helgeson, B. "1924–74: American Dental Assistants—Commemorative 50th Anniversary." *Journal of the American Dental Association*, 1974, *89*(3), 539–544.

Motley, W. E. *Ethics, Jurisprudence and History for the Dental Hygienist*. (2nd ed.) Philadelphia: Lea & Febiger, 1976.

CURRENT BIBLIOGRAPHIES

Books for the Dentist. Palo Alto, California: Stacey, annual.

Dental Abstracts. Chicago: American Dental Association, 1956–. A selection of world dental literature.

Excerpta Medica. Amsterdam: Excerpta Medica Foundation, 1947–. See the dentistry section.

Index Medicus. Bethesda, Maryland: National Library of Medicine, 1960–.

Index to Dental Literature. Chicago: American Dental Association, 1923–.

Indice de la literatura dental periódica en castellano y portugués. Buenos Aires: Asociación odontología argentina, 1952–. Published annually; Spanish and Portuguese literature.

National Library of Medicine. Current Catalog. Washington, D.C.: U.S. Public Health Service, 1966–. Offers a listing of published books, manuals, and periodicals under the following headings: "Dental Assistants," "Dental Hygienists," "Dental Technologists." United States and foreign titles; issued monthly and cumulated annually.

PERIODICALS

A sampling of the important international journals for the field includes *British Dental Surgical Assistant, Canadian Dental Hygienist/Hygieniste dentaire du Canada, Dental Assistant* (US), *Dental cadmos: Revista mensile di odontoiatria e tecnica dentaria* (Italy), *Dental Health* (UK), *Dental Hygiene* (US), *Dental-Labor* (FRG), *Dental laboratorie bladet* (Denmark), *Dental Technician* (UK), *Journal das auxiliares odontológicas* (Portugal), *NADL Journal* (US), *Quintessenz Journal: Zeitschrift für die Zahnarzthelferin* (FRG).

For additional listings of journals dealing with dental auxiliaries and related areas consult:

Dental Journals Published Outside the United States. Chicago: American Dental Association, Bureau of Library Services, annual.

Schmidt, H. J. *Index der Zahnärztlichen Zeitschriften der Welt*. Munich, Federal Republic of Germany: Verlag Neuer Merkur GmbH, 1970.

Selected List of Dental Journals Published in the United States. Chicago: American Dental Association, Bureau of Library Services, annual.

Ulrich's International Periodicals Directory. New York: Bowker, biennial.

ENCYCLOPEDIAS, DICTIONARIES, HANDBOOKS

Some helpful educational directories include:

Allied Health Education Programs in Junior Colleges. Washington, D.C.: American Association of Community and Junior Colleges and U.S. Department of Health, Education .and Welfare, annual.

Basic Fact Sheets. London: Fédération dentaire internationale, 1974. See Appendix 2: "World Situation Regarding Dental Manpower"; and Appendix 4: "Survey of Auxiliary Personnel Throughout the World."

Dental Auxiliary Education: Annual Report. Chicago: American Dental Association, annual. Includes lists of programs in the United States, admission policies and data, and summary of information obtained for the Annual Survey of Dental Auxiliary Education programs.

Dental Hygiene Schools in Europe 1971. Chicago: American Dental Hygienists Association, n.d. One-page information sheet.

Directory of Dental Auxiliary Programs in Latin America. Washington, D.C.: Pan American Health Organization, 1968.

[Bibliography prepared by Deborah Tobin.]

DENTISTRY AND DENTAL SPECIALTIES (Field of Study)

The *Fédération dentaire internationale* (FDI) defines dentistry as the science and art of preventing, diagnosing, and treating diseases and malformations of and injuries to the teeth, mouth, and jaws, and of replacing lost teeth and associated structures. This definition is accepted by the seventy-five member associations of the FDI from sixty-eight countries. Efforts to treat or overcome tooth decay and gum disease occupy most of the professional time of dentists throughout the world. However, a variety of other conditions—including malocclusion (abnormality in the coming together of the teeth), traumatic injuries to the face and jaws, benign and malignant tumors, and oral infections—also command the dentist's attention. Since highly efficient measures to prevent the major diseases of the oral cavity are still unavailable, loss of teeth due to disease occurs

throughout life for most people. Consequently, a considerable portion of dental education must be devoted to the development of skills related to the preparation of prosthetic appliances (bridges, partial and full dentures) to restore masticatory functions and esthetics. In addition, because oral disease can affect the general health and because disease of other parts of the body often influences the health of oral structures, the education of fully trained, general dental practitioners must include sufficient instruction in the basic and applied medical sciences.

The first school for the training of dental practitioners was the Baltimore College of Dental Surgery, founded in 1840. The first dental school associated with a university was the dental school at Harvard University, founded in 1867. In the mid 1970s all dental schools in the United States and in most other countries are affiliated with institutions of higher education—usually as separate entities, with programs varying in length from four to six academic years, but sometimes as a subspecialty of medicine. In this case the student first completes medical school and then undertakes two years of dental training; graduates of these programs are often known as stomatologists.

Specialization in various branches of dentistry has occurred to the greatest extent in the United States. Currently the following specialties are recognized by the American Dental Association: dental public health, endodontics (preservation of nonvital teeth), oral pathology, oral surgery, orthodontics (treatment of malocclusion), pedodontics (dentistry for children), periodontics (treatment of diseases of the gums), and prosthodontics (replacement of lost teeth). Postdoctoral programs preparing dentists for practice in these specialties range from two to five academic years. They take place not only in dental schools but in teaching hospitals, clinics, dental institutes, and institutions of higher education which have a medical or public health component.

Among the recent developments in dental education in the United States, Canada, Australia, Japan, and some countries in Europe are programs that give dental students experience in managing teams of dental auxiliaries. Some of these auxiliaries are trained to perform functions previously reserved for dentists; for example, the insertion and carving of restorative materials.

There has also been a reaction against the high proportion of dental graduates entering into specialty training. One proposed solution to this problem is to cut back on the opportunities for specialty training and increase the number of post-doctoral general dentistry internships and residencies for the training of "family dentists." Another proposal is to recognize general dental practice as a specialty and thus to reduce the attractiveness of specialty practice. A third suggestion is to lengthen undergraduate dental education by including much of what is presently taught in specialty training programs.

There is also a trend for dentists who are seeking to enter the specialty of maxillofacial surgery to earn a medical degree in addition to undertaking specialty training in oral surgery, because the medical degree enables the maxillofacial surgeon to operate more freely in the hospital environment.

Another growing trend is the emphasis on continuing education; for example, several states in the United States have instituted requirements that must be met if dental licensure or membership in dental organizations is to be maintained. Considerable uncertainty still exists, however, about the particular courses that should be required in order to ensure that practitioners will maintain a high level of clinical competence in keeping with modern treatment procedures.

This description of dental education and the practice of dentistry and its specialties relates primarily to countries with advanced socioeconomic status, which can support dentist-to-population ratios between 1 to 800 and 1 to 2000, or to practices devoted to serving the upper classes of developing nations. Dental schools in most countries are oriented toward educating dentists for these types of practices. In many localities, however, the dentist-to-population ratio is only 1 to 10,000, or even as small as 1 to 100,000. Since oral disease is just as prevalent in these localities, dental education might better fulfill its international responsibilities by providing dental health service personnel to meet the current needs of total populations, especially in the developing countries.

JOHN W. HEIN

Levels and Programs of Study

Programs in dentistry generally require as a minimum prerequisite a secondary-level education and lead to the following awards: dental practitioner certificate or diploma, bachelor's degree in dentistry, the degree of Doctor of Dental Science, a Doctor of Dental Science with a higher degree or certificate of specialization, or their equivalents. Programs deal with the principles and practices of dental care and consist of classroom, laboratory, and clinical instruction and, on advanced levels, study, case histories, practice, and conferences dealing with various aspects of specialization.

Programs that lead to awards not equivalent to a first university degree deal primarily with the practical applications of dental care. Students completing these programs are qualified, in some countries, to practice dentistry as a dental practitioner. Principal course content usually includes such subjects as oral anatomy and physiology, oral pathology, local anesthesia, oral surgical procedures, dental X-ray technology, and oral hygiene. Background courses usually include biology, chemistry, physics, dental ethics, and practice management.

Programs that lead to a first university-level degree provide a broad background in the social sciences and related subjects. Principal course content usually includes subjects such as general dentistry, oral anatomy and physiology, oral pathology, general and local anesthesia, oral surgical procedures, endodontics, orthodontics, pedodontics, prosthodontics, periodontics, dental jurisprudence, dental ethics, and practice management. Background courses often included are histology, hematology, immunology, serology, pharmacology, biochemistry, microbiology, radiobiology, and medicine.

Programs that lead to a postgraduate university degree deal with the principles and practices of operative (therapeutic) dentistry, oral surgery, periodontics, pedodontics, endodontics, prosthodontics, or orthodontics. Depending on the course of study, emphasis is given to original research work as substantiated by the presentation of a scholarly thesis or dissertation or to the clinical and practical aspects necessary for obtaining a Doctor of Dental Science degree. Principal subject matter areas within which courses and research projects tend to fall include crown and bridge prosthodontics, denture prosthodontics, endodontics, orthodontics, pedodontics, periodontics, operative dentistry, oral diagnosis, oral surgery and anesthesia, preventive medicine, and radiology. Subject areas within which background studies tend to fall include dental anatomy and physiology, pharmacology, principles of medicine, jurisprudence, and practice management.

[This section was based on UNESCO's *International Standard Classification of Education (ISCED)* (Paris: UNESCO, 1976).]

Major International and National Organizations

INTERNATIONAL—GENERAL

International Dental Federation
Fédération dentaire internationale (FDI)
64 Wimpole Street
London W1M 8AL, England

Latin American Association of Dental Schools
Asociación latinoamericana de facultades de odontología (ALAFO)
9a Calle 1–42, Zona 1
Guatemala City, Guatemala

World Health Organization (WHO)
Oral Health Unit
1211 Geneva 27, Switzerland

INTERNATIONAL—SPECIALIST

European Association of Dental Educators
Professor E. D. Farmer
P.O. Box 147
Liverpool L69 38X, England

International Association for Dental
  Research (IADR)
Association internationale de recherches dentaires
211 East Chicago Avenue
Chicago, Illinois 60611 USA

International Association of Dental
  Students (IADS)
Association internationale des étudiants dentaires (AIED)
Dental Secretary, Medical Protection Society
50 Hallam Street
London WI, England

International Association of Dentistry for
  Children (IADC)
Société internationale de pédodontie
Eastman Dental Hospital, Gray's Inn Road
London WI, England

International Association of
  Dento-Maxillofacial Radiology
School of Dentistry
Fack S-400, 33 Göteborg, Sweden

International Association of Oral
  Surgeons (IAOS)
Association internationale des chirurgiens de la bouche
Knabostraede 3
DK-1210 Copenhagen K, Denmark

NATIONAL

The following is a sampling of national dental organizations:

Argentina:
    Confederación odontológica de la República Argentina
    Junín 959
    Buenos Aires

Australia:
    Australian Dental Association
    116 Pacific Highway
    North Sydney, New South Wales 2060

Brazil:
    Associação brasileira de odontologia
    Rua Alvaro Alvim, 33-37, Salas 514
    Rio de Janeiro

Canada:
   Canadian Dental Association
   234 St. George Street
   Toronto, Ontario M5R ZP2

Czechoslovakia:
   Československá stomatologická
      společnost
   Karlovo nám. 32
   12111 Prague 2

Federal Republic of Germany:
   Bundesverband der deutschen
      Zahnärzte e.V.
   Universitätsstrasse 73
   5 Cologne 41

France:
   Association dentaire française
   Commission des affaires internationales
   29–31 rue des Grandes Arcades
   67 Strasbourg

Hong Kong:
   Hong Kong Dental Association
   G.P.O. Box 14412

India:
   Indian Dental Association
   15 Purasavalkam High Road
   Madras 600007

Iran:
   Iranian Dental Association
   82 Hafez Avenue
   Tehran

Israel:
   Israel Dental Association
   49 Bar-Kochba Street
   63427 Tel Aviv

Japan:
   Japan Dental Association
   1-20 Kudan-kita, 4-chome
   Chiyoda-ku, Tokyo 102

Mexico:
   Asociación dental mexicana
   Ezequiel Montes No. 92
   Mexico 4, D.F.

Philippines:
   Philippine Dental Association
   P.O. Box 1142
   Manila

Soviet Union:
   Vsesoiuznoe nauchoe meditsinskoe
      obschestvo stomatologvo
   All-Union Scientific Medical Association
      of Stomatologists
   Timur Frunze Street 16
   Moscow 119840 GSP-3

Sweden:
   Svenska tandläkare sällskapet
   Nybrogatan 53
   S 114 50 Stockholm

Switzerland:
   Société suisse d'odonto-stomatologie
   Hirschengraben 11
   CH 3011 Bern

United Kingdom:
   British Dental Association
   64 Wimpole Street
   London W1M 8AL, England

United States:
   American Dental Association (ADA)
   211 East Chicago Avenue
   Chicago, Illinois 60611

For a more complete list of dental associations see:

International Dental Journal, 1976, *26*(1), 96–97.
   Provides a listing, with addresses, of the
   members of the International Dental Federation.
*National and International Dental Organizations
   of the World.* Chicago: American Dental Association, 1976.

Principal Information Sources

GENERAL

Guides to the literature of the field include:

Basic Dental Reference Works. Chicago: Amer-
   ican Dental Association, 1975.
Blake, J. B., and Roos, C. (Eds.) *Medical Reference Works 1679–1966: A Selected Bibliography.* Chicago: Medical Library Association,
   1967. *Supplement I* (1967–1968), compiled by
   M. V. Clark, 1970; *Supplement II* (1969–
   1972), compiled by J. S. Richmond, 1973;
   Supplement III (1973–1974), compiled by
   J. S. Richmond, 1975.
Books and Package Libraries for Dentists. Chicago:
   American Dental Association, Bureau of
   Library Services, 1976. English-language
   books published 1972–1975; for pre-1972
   and foreign titles, write to the ADA. Up-
   dated regularly.
Richards, N. D., and Cohen, L. K. (Eds.) *Social
   Sciences and Dentistry: A Critical Bibliography.*
   Leiden, Netherlands: A. W. Sijthoff, 1971.
   Presents the world's literature on dentistry
   and social science from 1955 to 1970.
Spencer, E. M. "Dentistry." In L. T. Morton
   (Ed.), *Use of Medical Literature.* Hamden,
   Connecticut: Archon; London: Butterworth,
   1974.

Overviews and introductions include:

Commission on the Survey of Dentistry in the United States. *The Survey of Dentistry: The Final Report.* Washington, D.C.: American Council on Education, 1961.

Morris, A. L., and Bohannan, H. M. (Eds.) *The Dental Specialties in General Practice.* Philadelphia: Saunders, 1969. A general introduction to various branches of the field.

Sources concerning education and training in the field include:

Carnegie Commission on Higher Education. *Higher Education and the Nation's Health: Policies for Medical and Dental Education.* New York: McGraw-Hill, 1970.

Dental Health Education. Technical Report Series No. 449. Geneva: World Health Organization, 1970.

Dental Postgraduate Study in the United Kingdom and the Republic of Ireland. London: General Dental Council, 1970.

Ennis, J. *The Story of the Fédération dentaire internationale, 1900–1962.* London: Fédération dentaire internationale, 1967. Presents a history of the field with respect to international activity in dentistry.

Handbook of Regulations of Dental Practice. London: Fédération dentaire internationale, 1970. Regulations and information for 101 countries.

International Dental Journal. Leiden, Netherlands: A. W. Sijthoff, 1950–.

Journal of the American Dental Association. Chicago: American Dental Association, 1913–. Features news on international dentistry and occasionally special articles.

"Undergraduate Dental Education in Europe." *WHO Chronicle,* 1970, *24,* 506–511.

Histories of the field include:

Guerini, V. *A History of Dentistry.* Boston: Milford House, 1909. A classic work.

Lindsay, L. *Short History of Dentistry.* London: Bale, 1933.

Lufkin, A. W. *A History of Dentistry.* (2nd ed.) Philadelphia: Lea & Febiger, 1948.

Histories of the specialties include:

Koch, C. R. E. *History of Dental Surgery.* Fort Wayne, Indiana: National Art Publishing Co., 1910.

Wienberger, B. W. *Orthodontics: An Historical Review of Its Origin and Evolution.* St. Louis, Missouri: Mosby, 1926.

Wienberger, B. W. *An Introduction to the History of Dentistry with Medical and Dental Chronology and Bibliographic Data.* St. Louis, Missouri: Mosby, 1948.

CURRENT BIBLIOGRAPHIES

Dental Abstracts. Chicago: American Dental Association, 1956–. Abstracts the world literature in dentistry; from these abstracts are published volumes in various specialties: *Advances in Orthodontics, Advances in Pedodontics, Advances in Oral Surgery, Advances in Periodontics, Advances in Prosthodontics, Advances in Caries Research, Advances in Socio-Dental Research.*

Deutsche Zahn-, Mund- und Kieferheilkunde. Leipzig, German Democratic Republic: Johann Ambrosius Barth, 1934–. Provides abstracts from the world's dental literature.

Excerpta Medica. Amsterdam: Excerpta Medica Foundation, 1947–. See the dentistry section.

Index Medicus. Bethesda, Maryland: National Library of Medicine, 1960–.

Index to Dental Literature. Chicago: American Dental Association, 1923–.

Indice de la literatura dental periódica en castellano y portugués. Buenos Aires: Asociación odontológica argentina, 1952–. Published annually. Covers dental literature in Spanish and Portuguese.

Journal of the American Dental Association. Chicago: ADA, 1913–. Additions to the Bureau of Library Services collection are listed monthly in the journal.

National Library of Medicine. Current Catalog. Washington, D.C.: U.S. Public Health Service, 1966–.

Oral Research Abstracts. Chicago: American Dental Association, 1966–.

PERIODICALS

A sampling of dentistry journals internationally includes *Acta Odontologica Scandinavica* (Sweden), *Australian Dental Journal, Boletín de información dental* (Spain), *British Dental Journal, Caries Research* (Switzerland), *Le chirurgien dentiste de France* (France), *Community Dentistry and Oral Epidemiology* (Denmark), *Dental Journal of Malaysia, Hellenic Stomatological Annals* (Greece), *IADR Abstracts* (US), *International Dental Journal* (Netherlands), *International Journal of Forensic Dentistry* (UK), *International Journal of Oral Surgery* (Denmark), *Israel Journal of Dental Medicine, Journal of the Academy of General Dentistry* (US), *Journal of the American Dental Association, Journal of the Canadian Dental Association, Journal of the Dental Association of South Africa, Journal of Dental Education* (US), *Journal of Dental Research* (US), *Journal of the Indian Dental Association, Journal of the International Association of Dentistry for*

Children (UK), *Journal of the Japan Dental Association, Journal of the Philippine Dental Association, Nederlands tandartsenblad, New Zealand Dental Journal, Odonto-stomatologica & implanto protesi* (Italy), *Proceedings of the Finnish Dental Association, Revista de ALAFO* (Guatemala), *Revista de la Asociación odontológica argentina, Revista de la Federación odontológica colombiana* (Colombia), *Revue du SESDA* (Senegal), *Schweizerische Monatsschrift für Zahnheilkunde, Stomatologiia* (USSR), *Tandläkar tidningen* (Sweden), *Zahnärztliche Mitteilungen* (FRG).

For additional listings of dental journals consult:

Dental Journals Published Outside the United States. Chicago: American Dental Association, Bureau of Library Services, annual.

Schmidt, H. J. *Index der Zahnärztlichen Zeitschriften der Welt.* Munich, Federal Republic of Germany: Verlag Neuer Merkur GmbH, 1970.

Selected List of Dental Journals Published in the United States. Chicago: American Dental Association, Bureau of Library Services, annual.

Ulrich's International Periodicals Directory. New York: Bowker, biennial.

ENCYCLOPEDIAS, DICTIONARIES, HANDBOOKS

Boucher, C. O. (Ed.) *Current Clinical Dental Terminology: A Glossary of Accepted Terms in All Disciplines of Dentistry.* (2nd ed.) St. Louis, Missouri: Mosby, 1974.

Chaves, M. M. *Odontología sanitaria.* Washington, D.C.: Pan American Health Organization, 1962.

Dictionnaire français de médecine et de biologie. Paris: Masson, 1972.

Fairpo, J. E. H. *Heinemann Modern Dictionary for Dental Students.* (2nd ed.) London: Heinemann, 1974.

Finn, S. B., and others. (Eds.) *Year Book of Dentistry.* Chicago: Year Book Medical Publishers, 1975.

International Dental Federation. *Lexicon of English Dental Terms; with Their Equivalents in Español, Deutsch, Français and Italiano.* Leiden, Netherlands: A. W. Sijthoff, 1966.

Morrey, L. W., and Nelsen, R. J. *Dental Science Handbook.* Washington, D.C.: U.S. Government Printing Office, 1970.

Slack, G. L. *Dental Public Health.* Bristol, England: Wright, 1974.

DIRECTORIES

American Dental Directory. Chicago: American Dental Association, 1975.

Archer, W. H. (Ed.) *Oral Surgery Directory of the World.* (4th ed.) Pittsburgh: The Editor,

1971. Source of information on graduate and postgraduate training programs in the United States; bibliography of textbooks; lists societies in the United States and names of oral surgeons around the world.

Basic Fact Sheets. London: Fédération dentaire internationale, 1974. Provides information on education, licensing, and manpower in ninety-three countries; updated every three years.

Dental Schools Outside the United States. Chicago: American Dental Association, 1974.

Directory of Latin American Schools of Dentistry, Medicine, Nursing, Midwifery, Public Health, Veterinary Medicine. Washington, D.C.: Pan American Health Organization, 1971.

Medical Research Index: A Guide to World Medical Research. Guernsey, Channel Islands: Francis Hodgson, 1971. Includes a guide to institutions involved with dental research.

Oliver, W. H. M. (Ed.) *Orthodontic Directory of the World.* (27th ed.) Nashville, Tennessee: American Association of Orthodontists, 1974. Lists orthodontic schools and societies around the world; provides information on training and qualifications for specialization.

Prosthodontics Worldwide. Chicago: American Prosthodontic Society and American Dental Association, 1972.

World Directory of Dental Schools 1963. Geneva: World Health Organization, 1967.

[Bibliography prepared with the assistance of Donald A. Washburn.]

DEVELOPING NATIONS AND BILATERAL AID
See Aid to Other Nations.

DEVELOPMENT, COLLEGE AND UNIVERSITY

The phrase *college and university development*, which began to be liberally used in the United States in the mid 1940s, designates programs organized by colleges and universities to create an understanding of their missions, services, and accomplishments and thereby to generate goodwill and voluntary financial support to sustain and advance their educational objectives. The precise dimensions of these programs vary among colleges and universities. The term *college and university development* and the program it attempts to define for implementation purposes would not exist were it not for philanthropy, a human instinct as old as civilization itself.

Historical Overview

Evidence of philanthropy in higher education exists as early as the fourth century B.C. during the reign of Alexander the Great, who extended his empire to include Egypt and the Near East and who founded, by gift, Alexandria University in northern Egypt. Voluntary gift support to establish and help finance institutions of higher education first becomes well documented during the Middle Ages with the establishment of the medieval universities. At the University of Bologna, founded in A.D. 1088, twenty-three professorial chairs were endowed by the state to provide salaries adequate to keep teachers at Bologna. The university also had a treasure chest or *archo* from which scholarships were awarded to needy students (Rashdall, 1936). At the University of Paris, founded in 1130, students banded together to hire a communal house, called a *hospicium,* at a fixed rent. Eventually these houses were endowed by gifts from individuals and became colleges within the university (Daly, 1961). In 1258 Robert de Sorbon endowed a college which marked the beginning of the Sorbonne, and in 1266 five hundred pounds were contributed to it by the archdeacon of Tournai in Flanders (Thorndike, 1949). This practice of establishing colleges spread throughout Europe and attained great popularity, particularly in England, where it became the dominant feature of university life at Oxford and Cambridge. In 1584 Emmanuel College was founded at Cambridge by Sir Walter Mildmay, chancellor of the exchequer in the government of Elizabeth I. His philanthropic act was to have a profound effect upon all of what is now higher education in the United States. The Reverend John Harvard, an early graduate of Emmanuel College, came to the Massachusetts Bay Colony, died two years later, and left his library of 400

books and half of his small estate to a struggling college that had been established in 1636. In gratitude, the college adopted its benefactor's name and became Harvard College. Several institutions were thereafter founded, each by personal, devoted, persistent efforts and private gifts, often in small amounts, with great sacrifice from varied sources (Marts, 1953). So began the long, close, and successful relationship between philanthropy and institutions of higher education in what was to become, in 1776, the United States of America. Perhaps no form of philanthropy deserves more careful study because it is unique and unapproached elsewhere in the world. Private higher education in the United States, in particular, owes a considerable portion of its present growth and development to philanthropists past and present, who deemed giving to colleges and universities an opportunity to invest in the welfare of mankind.

Voluntary gift support. Highly organized efforts utilizing individuals who devote full time to obtaining philanthropic support for colleges and universities remain predominantly a United States phenomenon. However, this practice has growing international importance and implications. Increasing numbers of educational institutions throughout the world are beginning to seek voluntary gift support, often using the United States practice as a working model to encourage greater activity and higher achievement.

There are approximately 3100 postsecondary institutions of education in the United States. In its report *Voluntary Support of Education: 1974–1975* (1976), the Council for Financial Aid to Education (CFAE) estimates that institutions of higher education in the United States received voluntary gift support totaling $2,160,000,000 in fiscal year 1975. The definition of voluntary support used for the report excludes support received from federal, state, and local governments and income from invested funds; it includes gifts from non-alumni donors ($516,000,000), foundations

($497,000,000), alumni ($486,000,000), business corporations ($357,000,000), religious denominations ($112,000,000), and miscellaneous gift sources such as trade associations and service clubs ($192,000,000). These figures estimated by CFAE are based on responses to a questionnaire by 986 colleges and universities that reported receipt of voluntary support totaling $1,670,000,000. Of the 986 respondents, sixty-nine major private (not tax-supported) colleges and universities received $649,000,000, representing 39 percent of the total reported voluntary gift support of $1,670,000,000 and 30 percent of the total estimated voluntary support of $2,160,000,000. According to the American Association of Fund-Raising Counsel, Inc. *(Giving USA,* 1976), eighteen large gifts to United States colleges and universities in 1975 included a $23,000,000 business corporation gift; nine foundation gifts, each in excess of $2,000,000, to nine institutions (total of $47,500,000); and eight individual gifts, each in excess of $2,000,000 (total of $101,000,000). Five United States universities commenced programs in 1975 and 1976 to obtain gifts of more than $100,000,000 per institution over a period of time. The total voluntary gift support sought by these five institutions exceeds $967,000,000 ("Capital Campaigns," 1976).

To some, the term *development* is synonymous with *fund raising*—the obtaining of voluntary gift support. Although the obtaining of resources is a major function of any development program, the term *college and university development* suggests also the establishment of understanding, sympathy, and interest among the public of the institution and its goals. J. W. Leslie (1969, p. 3) uses the phrase *institutional advancement program* to refer to these goals of development programs. He states: "The advancement program is an umbrella concept typically including public relations activities, alumni programs, fund raising, publications production, and, in some institutions, state and federal liaison, student recruitment, university press operation, central printing and mailing services—to mention a few."

The Development Office

While it is recognized that terms other than *development,* such as *resources, advancement, external affairs,* or *public affairs,* are used by many colleges and universities in the United States to designate those functions inclusive of fund raising, the present discussion will use the term *development* almost solely as it relates to voluntary gift support, the by-product of fund raising.

Staff. The manager of the development office, given the title vice-president for development, director of development, executive officer for development, executive assistant to the president, or another appropriate designation, need not be a graduate of the institution but must demonstrate genuine loyalty to it and to education, executive managerial ability and experience, talent for organization and teamwork, a good sense of public relations, skill at written and verbal communication, personal appeal, knowledge of fund raising, energy necessary to take creative and innovative initiative, willingness to attain goals without requiring public credit or praise, and empathy. Staff members reporting to the development officer must have many of these same talents and qualities but may often be specialists in particular areas of fund raising—such as alumni, foundations, or corporations—rather than generalists knowledgeable in all fund-raising areas. The size of the staff will vary, depending primarily on the size of the institution; its educational programs, financial needs, and capabilities; and the types of fund-raising programs to be conducted based upon the philosophy and continuing mission of the institution's president and governing board. Due to the precision and professionalism required for success in fund raising, secretarial and clerical personnel also must be of high caliber.

Relationships with administration officers.

The chief development officer must have a close working relationship with the chief executive of the institution, with immediate access to him and to other members of the central administrative staff. The president is the key person in an institution's fund-raising program, not only because there are times when only he can successfully close the appeal for a large gift but because he personifies the institution and can use his presence and influence to stimulate the entire development operation. Most often the development officer will suggest appropriate presidential efforts in a development campaign.

As the highest policymaking body of the institution, the governing board must provide leadership and support to fund raising, both in giving to and in working for the institution. All members of the board must extend themselves so that they will be convincing and effective in appealing to others for support. If their degree of generosity is not impressive, it is not realistic to expect impressive generosity from others. Indeed, the fund-raising ability of a college can often be rated by the involvement, influence, and power of its governing board.

Effective relationships should also be maintained between the development office and the faculty and students. Funds are most often generated by an institution's educational programs and goals. Thus, faculty and students should understand the institution's financial needs and the ways programs are financed and maintained. They should become involved in helping to meet financial objectives, either through financial support or by serving on committees, assisting in publicity, helping in solicitation, speaking at fund-raising meetings, and otherwise transmitting and generating enthusiasm for the institution. Involvement of students will help them become more responsible alumni, particularly as they will understand that tuition and fees most often do not cover the full costs of an educational program.

Policies. Policies pertinent to the efficiency and effectiveness of a development office should be clearly defined and disseminated by the president to the college or university community. Clear and concise development office policies include final authority, subject to presidential or governing board approval, for determining potential sources of support to be approached, and for what purpose, to avoid an embarrassing multiplicity of appeals or appeals for nonpriority needs; authority to approve, or to recommend changes in, the content of all written communications seeking voluntary gift support; knowledge of all voluntary gift support received by the institution; and responsibility for accepting and recording gifts and ensuring that they are properly acknowledged.

Less clear is the development office's involvement in the planning of academic programs and facilities and other institutional projects based on voluntary gift support requirements. As the development office has the responsibility for obtaining voluntary gift support for specific projects, it must understand these projects and have some authority in determining whether or not they should be undertaken.

Budget and costs. The budget of the development office must be a direct outgrowth of the plan for fund-raising activities, based on a realistic estimate of the costs of the planned fund raising. The following items should be part of a development office budget (which includes direct costs of raising funds but excludes indirect costs such as services rendered by the administrative officials and maintenance of space for personnel): (1) salaries—administrative, secretarial, clerical, part time—and benefits; (2) consulting—professional fund-raising counsel services; (3) office expenses—equipment and furnishings, maintenance, postage, telephone and telegraph, supplies, computer services, photocopying; (4) organizational expenses—travel, professional memberships, on- and off-campus conferences, subscriptions, and books; (5) promotion and publicity—promotional literature, advertising, radio and television, honorariums, films, slides, charts, awards, plaques, citations; and (6) contingencies and special services.

Fund-raising costs will vary for primarily the same reasons that the size of a development staff will vary—the size of an institution; its educational programs, financial needs, and capabilities; and the types of fund-raising programs to be conducted. Generally, the smaller the fund-raising goal, the higher the cost. As Leslie reports (1969, pp. 26, 32), institutions raising $1,000,000 or more in voluntary gifts per year do so at a cost of less than 20 percent on the dollar, whereas institutions raising $200,000 or less per year do so at a median cost of over 60 percent on the dollar. He states that: "Obviously some financial support objectives require greater expenditures of resources in terms of funds and staffs than do others. . . . For certain objectives, expending almost as much as or more than gift income may be justified in the short run. On the other hand, while advancement programs with high cost dollars might be deemed effective by the institution in accomplishing specific short-term objectives, by no means could they be considered efficient over a long period." Thus, the president, along with the governing board and the chief development officer, must continually measure the effectiveness as well as the efficiency of any institution's voluntary gift support effort. In essence, they must monitor results versus expenditures.

Forms of Fund Raising

An institution should give careful attention to identifying potential sources of voluntary financial support, often termed "gift categories." The most common categories, excluding government, are alumni, nonalumni friends of the institution, foundations, and business corporations, with parents, faculty, students, community organizations, service clubs, and labor and trade associations as other categories or subcategories. Most voluntary gift support to colleges and universities comes

from individuals, and of this, more is from nonalumni than alumni.

A total development effort encompasses three planned forms of fund raising, in which due emphasis is provided to each: annual giving, capital giving, and deferred giving.

Annual giving. Annual appeals by a college or university to alumni and friends for financial support is termed annual giving. Annual giving is often the foundation of an institution's regular ongoing development programs. It provides funds to help balance the operating budget and to be used at the discretion of the institution for whatever purpose it deems appropriate. Because many colleges and universities have made definite provisions in their operating budgets for unrestricted sums raised through annual giving, it becomes increasingly important to obtain these funds from such programs. In the conduct of annual giving programs it is possible to set forth each year certain areas of need for promotional emphasis: scholarships; faculty salaries; equipment; selected educational programs; library resources; and plant maintenance, remodeling, or construction.

Annual giving is usually thought of in terms of alumni solicitation, but an annual giving program often seeks gifts from students, parents, other nonalumni, and business corporations. Alumni support is vital, of course, if the institution is to receive support from other sources.

An institution's annual giving program is determined by the size, age, and geographical distribution of its public, as well as by its philosophy, history, and traditions. All colleges and universities will use some volunteer workers who are organized, trained, and directed by volunteer leaders and the development office staff. Most institutions solicit alumni either primarily along graduation-class lines, with teams of class agents, or on a geographical basis with regional committees. The class agent approach takes its strength from the affiliation of alumni with their own classmates and involves each class choosing a chairperson to recruit members of the class to solicit other classmates, often on a regional basis. The regional committee approach uses volunteer chairpersons who recruit alumni from any graduating classes in their particular geographical area to solicit other local alumni.

Broad-based participation is the objective of annual giving programs and is the basic prerequisite to an effective and successful program. Since the amount of each gift is usually small, the success of such programs depends on large numbers of donors to achieve significant sums. Once individuals are giving on a regular basis, the size of their gifts can be increased relatively easily; but the process begins by gaining as many annual gifts as possible, regardless of their amount.

Capital giving. Capital gift campaigns are intensive drives that seek substantial donations for specific capital purposes, like the purposes of construction, land acquisition, or additions to endowment funds. Just as annual giving is basic to an institution's regular ongoing programs, so capital giving is basic to an institution's progress. Capital gifts to an institution, which may be in the form of outright grants or of financial commitments payable over a number of years (often termed "pledges") are usually considered restricted funds in that they are donated for specific projects. Capital giving campaigns often inspire annual givers to increase their donations and encourage long-time nondonors to contribute. Brakeley, John Price Jones, Inc., a recognized leader in the area of professional fundraising counsel, notes:

Apart from the purely economic or financial factors—the dollar goals and the objectives they represent—there are sound philosophical as well as practical reasons for a capital campaign. For example: (1) Creation of an atmosphere of excitement and drama which affects leadership, workers and prospective contributors, and which has a carry-over value. (2) Elevation of giving standards, leading to new platforms for giving in subsequent annual fund efforts. (3) Disclosure of new trustee and other leadership material, as well as new sources of support for annual funds and subsequent capital campaigns. (4) Seeding of future bequest possibilities. (5) Spotlighting of institutional missions, aims and dreams, accompanied by a growing pride on the part of old friends and new in what the institution has achieved. (6) Stretching of institutional manpower resources, trustees, administrators, staff people, the entire "family"—to accomplish objectives possible only under the pressure of a campaign. In nearly every capital campaign there is a tensing of the spiritual "muscles" of an institution, which enables it to surge forward at an unprecedented rate [*Philanthropic Papers, 1971*].

The interrelationships between annual and capital giving make coordination between them essential. Coordination can be accomplished by conducting concurrent programs and asking all prospects, in distinct ways, to support both; by maintaining the annual giving program among all prospects while launching the capital campaign among a select group of these prospects; or by combining the programs and asking all prospects to designate their gifts in whole or in part for unrestricted operating needs and in part for restricted capital uses.

Deferred giving. Deferred giving is a program whereby individuals agree to make gifts at a future time. It involves the irrevocable transfer of money or property by an individual by will at death, or at a particular time during his lifetime, in exchange for life income either for himself or for others. Deferred giving is often more appropriately termed *planned giving*, since it involves the application of sound personal financial and estate planning concepts to a donor's lifetime and testamentary giving. Successful planned giving programs require careful coordination among the development staff, legal counsels for both the institution and the donor, and other institutional officers such as the treasurer, finance officer, or business officer.

Basically, deferred or planned gifts fall

into two categories. The first is a bequest, a legacy of personal property, such as cash, which is left to the institution by the will of one or more individuals, either as a set amount or as a percentage of a residual amount. The second is a retained life interest gift: property or funds given with certain stipulations during the lifetime of the donor. Property may be given to a college or university with the provision that the title will be transferred to the institution only after the donor's death or the death of designated others, thus allowing the donor the full use of property which will ultimately be owned by the institution. Funds may be transferred with the agreement that income from them will be paid to the donor or to designated others for as long as they live. Three main types of retained life interest giving are (1) charitable gifts annuities, (2) pooled income funds, and (3) charitable remainder annuity trusts and unitrusts.

With charitable gifts annuities, the donor transfers money or property to an institution in return for a promise of a fixed income for life. The income payments, made monthly, quarterly, semi-annually, or annually, are determined by the donor's age at the time he enters into the annuity contract. The donor may also direct that the annuity be paid to another (amount determined by the other's age) or to a survivor beneficiary (annuity is then less because it is paid for two lives).

In a pooled income fund, the institution accepts gifts of cash or property from a number of donors, commingles the gifts in a pooled fund, and manages the investment of the pooled funds in a diversified portfolio. Ordinary income earned by the participating units in the pooled fund is paid each quarter to the donor or to other beneficiaries.

In a charitable remainder annuity trust or a charitable remainder unitrust, the money or property is transferred to a trustee (in many instances the institution) and is segregated from all other funds. This deferred-giving plan is the most flexible,

since it enables the donor to personally design a life income plan. The annuity trust provides for fixed annual dollar payments to beneficiaries of at least 5 percent of the value of the gift property at the time the trust is created. The unitrust provides for variable dollar payments based upon a fixed percentage of at least 5 percent of the annually redetermined market value of the assets (principal and any earned income) in trust. In both the annuity trust and the unitrust, principal may be used to supplement the required payments if the income of the trust is insufficient to meet the previously established rate. Variations in the unitrust agreement may provide that only income can be used for payments and that any insufficiency will be made up in subsequent years.

The major advantage to the donor of these kinds of planned giving is the preferential tax treatment of the gift under United States income, estate, and gift tax regulations. Other forms of deferred gifts, such as life insurance trusts, provide similar tax benefits.

Organizational Sources of Support

In addition to the vital donations from individuals, three of the most important sources of organizational support are foundations, corporations, and foreign governments and international organizations.

Foundations. In recent years, voluntary gift support to American higher education from foundations has ranked second only to individual donations, and several American foundations—particularly the Ford Foundation, the Rockefeller Foundation, and the Carnegie Corporation of New York—have provided major support for international educational development. For example, through its international division the Ford Foundation provided $134,000,000 from the mid 1950s through its fiscal year 1974 to selected universities in the developing countries (*Current Interests of the Ford Foundation,* 1975). During fiscal year 1975 the Carnegie Corporation of New York reported grants to African universities in Botswana, Lesotho, Swaziland, Ghana, Kenya, and Nigeria, among others (*Annual Report*, 1976).

Successful fund raising from foundations requires careful planning and thorough research. Many educational institutions, particularly large ones, usually designate one or more development staff members as foundation liaison officers to stimulate and coordinate their solicitation of foundations. These staff members may undertake research to identify particular foundations that may be interested in special projects of the institution. They may also draft applications or proposals that delineate the major features of the project—its purposes, importance, unique characteristics, and intended results; its relation to the history and needs of the institution; the duties and qualifications of project personnel; financial information about budgets and provisions for continued funding beyond the grant period; and plans for evaluation through assessment of results and progress reports.

Foundation criteria used in assessing proposals vary widely, although they most often include the merit of the project compared to that of others competing for support; the project's compatibility with foundation policy, emphasis, and focus; the feasibility of the endeavor; benefit to the community or the society in general; the need for support, prospects for future support by others, and the possibility for self-support; and the project's merit compared to other projects competing for support.

Throughout the process of seeking foundation grants, the development officer's role is to provide staff assistance and direction for the program seeking voluntary gift support from foundations. This direction often can prevent conflicting approaches to several officials by a representative of the institution who may know the officials rather than an approach to the foundation person designated as the "contact" person by the same or another institution representative. It can also ensure that gifts are promptly acknowledged and that reports describing their use and results are properly submitted.

Corporations. Beginning in the late 1940s and early 1950s, several American business leaders became outspoken advocates of voluntary corporate support to colleges and universities, if for no other reason than the fact that business corporations recruit most of their staff executives and technical personnel from these institutions. Since the 1950s corporate support has become a significant factor in philanthropy for higher education. Gift support has not only increased in amount but has also become more varied in its purposes. Many, if not most, corporate grants are based on corporate self-interest, with specific motives and criteria ranging from direct business benefits for the company and the cultivation of goodwill to a wish to promote the general welfare of the community in which the company is located and society at large. The motives and criteria of corporate giving include the following: location of principal employment centers and principal markets of the corporation as well as geographical relationship to the institution, that is, grants to institutions in areas where corporate offices, branches, or plants are located or in the areas considered principal markets of the corporation; principal sources of personnel, or grants to institutions where company recruits personnel; direct business benefits, or grants to institutions doing substantial sponsored research, or having a relationship with the corporate product; interest in the future and general responsibility toward improvement of society, or grants made to further educational opportunities of minorities, support of the arts, or for the general welfare of the community and nation; public relations, or grants made in terms of public relations value of goodwill, favorable image, and prestige indicating business' role as a corporate citizen.

Since competition for corporate gifts is severe, such funds must be sought in a systematic manner. To approach a corporation successfully, it is important to know its policies, interests, and past giving records and thus to do continuous and accurate research on the corporation and on personnel within the corporation, particularly its executives. Information is also useful about the number of institutional alumni employed by the firm and its pattern of recruitment of graduates; alumni who are executives or directors of the company; relationships among members of the institution's governing board and corporate officers; number of employees who are enrolled in programs at the institution, faculty members who consult with the company; corporation executives who serve on institution advisory councils, or who have been lecturers, speakers, or participants in institution events; institutional programs of particular interest to the company; and special relationships, such as provider of supplies to the institution. After completing research on such factors, the institution prepares a case that is well defined and documented as to why support is deserved. The case is often written by the development officer and presented personally or by mail to the appropriate corporate officer by the president, a member of the governing board, or a member of a volunteer committee on corporate contributions.

Four other forms of voluntary support are also utilized by corporations: (1) matching gifts—first adopted by the General Electric Company in 1955—whereby the firm matches a gift by an employee, who is an alumnus of an institution, to that college or university; (2) matching tuition fees and grants based on employee tenure—whereby corporations will make a gift based on the tuition paid by employees who are enrolled in courses at the institution or based on the length of service of its employees who are alumni; (3) service contract grants (sometimes obtained by an institution establishing an organization of business corporations, termed a "business and industry council" or "corporate associates council"), in which a corporation makes a gift based upon specified services received from the

institution, such as consultation, placement, special training programs, and publications; and (4) gifts in kind, such as new or surplus equipment, produced or acquired by the corporation, or real estate it no longer needs.

Foreign governments and international organizations. International investment is a vital feature of the worldwide financial scene and a feature of increasing significance and influence in international college and university development.

A dramatic example of international financial support and, specifically, international philanthropy is the establishment, in 1972, of the United Nations University. Functioning under the joint sponsorship of the United Nations and UNESCO, the United Nations University requires a projected endowment fund of $500,000,000, to be met by voluntary gift support from governments, United Nations agencies, foundations, and individuals. The government of Japan has pledged $100,000,000 toward this amount; Venezuela will contribute $10,000,000; and Senegal, Sweden, Norway, Libya, and Ghana have already made contributions.

The tremendous growth of multinational corporations and the billions of petrodollars which governments of the Middle East are directing toward modernization are some indications that fund raising, particularly as it affects United States higher education, is emerging as multinational in scope. In the United States colleges and universities seeking international capital are signing contracts with Middle Eastern governments to "sell" their expertise to assist in the development of new schools; health centers; and agricultural, transportation, and communication systems. Even more significant, foreign governments are underwriting new professorships and programs, among them, a $1,000,000 endowed professorship in petroleum engineering at the University of Southern California from Iran; a similar grant for the King Faisal professorship in Islamic and Arab studies at the same institution from Saudi Arabia; and an equal grant for a professorship in multinational management to George Washington University from Iran (Van Dyne, 1976).

In June 1972, Willy Brandt, the chancellor of the Federal Republic of Germany, announced at a Harvard University commencement that West Germany would donate $47,500,000 over fifteen years to the United States to establish and run an independent educational foundation specializing in European problems, to be known as the German Marshall Fund of the United States. He also announced that Harvard would receive $900,000 from this fund to establish an endowment to promote European study projects. *Philanthropic Digest* (published by Brakeley, John Price Jones, Inc.) summarizes news and donations to education, health, religion, welfare, and the arts. Some other examples it has provided of foreign voluntary support for United States colleges and universities include a $1,000,000 grant to Harvard University from the Mitsubishi Group of Industries in Japan to establish an endowed chair in Japanese legal studies; a $1,000,000 grant from the government of Japan to each of ten United States universities to establish professorships in Japanese studies; a $1,000,000 grant from the Mitsui Group of Japan to the Massachusetts Institute of Technology for a professorship in problems of contemporary technology; a $2,000,000 grant by the Sumitomo Group of Japan to Yale University to finance Japanese studies; a $100,000 grant from His Majesty Qaboos Bin Sa'id to Johns Hopkins University for Arabic and Islamic Studies; a $200,000 grant from the Sultanate of Oman and the United Arab Emirates to Georgetown University for the Center for Contemporary Arab Studies; a $2,000,000 grant from the Krupp Foundation (Federal Republic of Germany) to Harvard University, one half for an endowed chair in European studies and one half for endowed graduate fellowships; and another $1,000,000 grant to Harvard University, this from the government

of Greece to endow a professorship in modern Greek studies.

Colleges and universities in many nations are becoming increasingly aware of the fund-raising potential of foreign governments and organizations. From a United States point of view, the competitive advantage obviously belongs to well-established colleges and universities that have high visibility and prestige, outstanding research capabilities, and international recognition and relationships. However, many institutions can, should, and are attempting to define a case for international financial support.

Components of Successful Fund Raising

The most essential requirement of raising voluntary gift support is the effort that is required to obtain it. Certain fundamentals comprise critical components of this effort.

Survey. Often called a self-examination or a feasibility study, the survey determines the needs of the institution, the validity of its financial goals, and the feasibility of reaching them. The survey, prepared by the staff of an institution or by an independent professional fund-raising counsel, provides the guidelines for a development campaign. Financial needs are determined by the educational philosophy and objectives of the institution and its past, present, and future characteristics. These needs typically far exceed the institution's potential, and thus priorities must be set on the basis of institutional capabilities. The survey involves the gathering of facts from the institution's records and from trustees, faculty, administrative staff, students, parents, community leaders, business corporation and foundation executives, and others. Facts are gathered by confidential personal interview or questionnaire to evaluate the institution's image among its publics, identify potential campaign leaders, determine the probability of enlisting sufficient volunteers, estimate the giving potential of various constituencies, and evaluate whether or not the institution is ready for and capable of succeeding in the campaign.

Professional fund-raising counsel. Not all institutions need professional fund-raising counsel, but all should consider the possibility, since professional counsel can bring outside experience of campaign successes and failures and can make objective recommendations and evaluations to the institution without conflict of interest. Professional fund-raising counsel falls into three general categories: (1) the twenty-eight fund-raising counseling firms belonging to the American Association of Fund-Raising Counsel, Inc. (AAFRC), New York, which maintains a code of fair practice and ethical guidelines now accepted as a standard for professional fund-raising counsel; (2) other professional counseling firms not members of AAFRC but operating under the same guidelines; and (3) individuals or independent counselors with no affiliation with professional firms, only a few of whom have wide experience and reputation for success.

An institution's chief development officer, president, and governing board must decide whether to use professional counsel for consultation services or campaign direction and staffing. Payment should be based on a specified fee determined in advance, not on a commission or percentage of the funds raised, a practice contrary to established codes of ethics. Professional counsel should be engaged early, often prior to the survey. If the decision is made to select professional counsel, the choice can be facilitated by contacting the AAFRC. The services rendered and the fee charged will be considered in relation to the institution to be served and its total fund-raising program.

The case and campaign literature. The case is the combination of reasons advanced by the institution in justification of its appeal for gifts, with emphasis on its services, past, present, and potential. The case tells what kind of a job an institution is doing, why its services and mission are valuable, why it should be supported, and what funds it

needs to operate properly. If it is strong enough, the case transforms the institution into a cause, demonstrating the institution's service to society and its suitability for voluntary gift support on this basis rather than on grounds of need alone. A case is usually initiated by the president; authorized by the governing board; prepared by the development officer or professional counsel in collaboration with faculty, staff, and students; reviewed by representatives of the institution's publics; approved by the administration and the board; and utilized by the entire institution as its basis for seeking voluntary support.

The case statement is the basic printed document for a development campaign. It should be clear, concise, and attractive, but not extravagant. In *Designs for Fund Raisers* (1966, p. 43) Harold Seymour, a pioneer and acknowledged leader in fund raising, says that if the statement "has simplicity, good taste, and logical order, the eloquence should be allowed to find its way in, as beauty does the beholder." Besides the case statement, other publicity materials are required, including the campaign announcement; the major brochure describing the campaign and its goals; facts pamphlets; progress report flyers; volunteer workers' handbooks; gift and memorial opportunity brochures; tax benefits brochures; deferred giving brochures.

Prospect lists. Identifying individuals and organizations for possible support is the first step in list building or prospecting. Researching these prospects on the list comes next, then screening or evaluating them for rating purposes. Rating determines those who may have interests compatible with the needs of an institution and who may have the financial capacity to provide significant pace-setting gifts early in the campaign. Rating also permits the construction of gift tables, which are projections of the numbers and amounts of gifts necessary to attain the goal. A typical table might project that 10 percent of the donors will provide from 70 to 90 percent of the goal and that the largest gift must provide 10 to 25 percent of the goal.

Accurate, complete, and constantly maintained prospect lists enhance the probability of reaching the fund-raising goal economically and efficiently. Many references are available—directories, bulletins, digests, newspapers, registers, subscription services—that provide information on individuals, business corporations, and foundations for building these lists. Typical references in the United States are the *Dun & Bradstreet Million Dollar Directory* (Dun & Bradstreet, Inc., 99 Church Street, New York, New York 10007); *Fortune Double 500 Directory* (Time, Inc., 541 North Fairbanks Court, Chicago, Illinois 60611); *The Foundation Directory* (The Foundation Center, 888 7th Avenue, New York, New York 10019); *The New York Times* (New York Times Company, 229 West 43rd Street, New York, New York 10036); *Philanthropic Digest* (Brakeley, John Price Jones, Inc., 6 East 43rd Street, New York, New York 10017); *Standard & Poor's Register of Corporations, Directors and Executives* (Standard & Poor's Corporation, 345 Hudson Street, New York, New York 10014); *Wall Street Journal* (Dow, Jones & Co., Inc., 22 Courtland Street, New York, New York 10017); *Who's Who in America* (Marquis Who's Who, Inc., 200 East Ohio Street, Chicago, Illinois 60611).

The Foundation Center (888 7th Avenue, New York, New York 10019), or one of its satellite offices in selected major United States cities, provides relatively complete information on foundations, including annual reports, newspaper clippings, and tax information returns such as tax form 990-A, which contains complete financial data plus grant listings. Public libraries and selected United States national professional and fund-raising organizations are also sources of valuable information for college and university development purposes. Such organizations include American Association of Fund-Raising Counsel, Inc. (500 Fifth Avenue, New York, New York 10036); American Council on Education (One Dupont Circle

NW, Washington, D.C. 20036); Association of American Colleges (1818 R Street NW, Washington, D.C. 20009); Council for the Advancement and Support of Education (One Dupont Circle NW, Washington, D.C. 20036); Council for Financial Aid to Education (680 Fifth Avenue, New York, New York 10019); and National Society of Fund Raisers, Inc. (130 East 40th Street, New York, New York 10016).

Volunteer leadership and solicitors. The quality, dedication, and training of volunteers and volunteer leadership are intimately related to the success of the development program. Volunteers both make their own gifts and devote their efforts to fund raising. The most important selection within a volunteer group is its chairperson, who should be well respected and able to inspire, motivate, and lead others. A member of the institution's governing board can usually be recruited for this position. Other volunteer leaders can then be enlisted to head various subcommittees or geographical campaigns, as needed.

The manpower needs for a campaign are usually based on a 1:5 ratio of volunteer solicitors to prospects. Thus, a campaign aimed at soliciting five hundred prospects would require one hundred solicitors, twenty team captains (five solicitors per captain), four vice-chairpersons, and the chairperson, for a total group of 125.

Solicitation of prospects takes three basic forms: face-to-face; telephone; and mail, through personal letters or direct-mail appeals. Face-to-face solicitation is by far the most effective in terms of more financial support from more donors, but since the 1960s, particularly in annual alumni giving programs, the telephone has been increasingly used and accepted as a medium for solicitation. Less effective than the face-to-face personal call, the telephone is still far superior to even the best letter. Meetings with individual prospects can be complemented with functions to which prospects are invited and at which the president can advocate the institution's case and needs. His style, dedication, enthusiasm, and patience provide the central force in convincing prospects to make major gifts to the institution. All the prior planning, researching, and publicity will produce few gifts without solicitation. Thus, volunteer solicitations can well be called the most important aspect of a campaign. The most serious error in fund raising is one of omission—not asking for a gift. No prospect should ever not give because he was not asked to give.

Acknowledgments and reports. Prompt and appreciative acknowledgment of gifts, through printed cards or personal letters is an integral part of a total fund-raising program. In its *Bulletin on Public Relations and Development for Colleges and Universities* (1966, pp. 1–3), public relations and development consultants Gonser, Gerber, Tinker, & Stuhr detail appropriate acknowledgment of gifts and communications with donors. Careful determination should be given to who makes the acknowledgment; the general community should be notified about donations; and donors should be kept fully informed about the uses of their gifts and the progress of projects they have supported. Reporting as well to volunteers, the governing board, the administrative staff, and faculty also is essential to raising voluntary support.

Designated gift and memorial opportunities. Specific gift and memorial opportunities should be diverse as to type and amount. Memorial gifts, perpetuating the name of the donor, often include buildings, classrooms, laboratories, equipment, and library acquisitions. Gifts for endowment may be designated for a variety of specific purposes, such as faculty salaries, loans, fellowships, and scholarships, and endowed chairs or named professorships. Endowed chairs are usually underwritten by a capital fund in endowment, the income of which pays the salary (and, in some cases, secretarial, office, and professional expenses) of an outstanding scholar in a particular field. Endowed amounts must be determined by the institution's salary structure and in-

flation factors, but currently in the United States chairs are most often endowed with a capital sum of $1,000,000, which earns an annual income of $50,000, assuming a 5 percent interest rate. Chairs may be rotating, enabling many distinguished scholars to come to an institution during a given period.

Endowed or named professorships also are underwritten by a capital fund in endowment. The endowment, however, can be substantially less than that of an endowed chair. It is used to supplement the salary provided an outstanding professor already teaching at the institution or to supplement the currently approved salary range to facilitate the recruitment of an outstanding scholar.

Should donors wish to endow a named professorship or a chair without providing the entire capital fund during their lifetime, they may provide the necessary annual income to the institution, together with irrevocable provisions in their wills for the necessary capital endowment funds.

Awards and major gift organizations. Awards are appropriate to recognize the contributions of major donors and volunteers. They usually utilize the institution's seal, emblem, or motto and include chairs, plaques, certificates, neckties, etchings, silver trays, statues, or bowls.

Major gift societies, often called associate programs, serve to raise funds (usually unrestricted) for an institution and to relate an institution and its goals to persons of influence and affluence. Membership criteria can be a gift of a certain amount made as part of an annual giving program, a pledge to a capital giving program paid at a particular predetermined annual level, or a deferred (usually irrevocable) gift. These societies provide a special means for recognizing major contributors, encouraging continued close identification with the institution, and obtaining help in advancing the institution in significant ways, such as locating other top priority prospects. Most major gift societies provide donor recognition and increase the probability of favorable responses from future sources of voluntary gift support.

Conclusion

College and university development plays a vital role in advancing the quality of educational life. It is much more than obtaining voluntary gift support from various sources: it depends on the dedication and expertise of volunteers as well as professionals in assuring investment in higher education; and its accomplishment is measured not only by institutional financial support but by general encouragement of higher education at large.

Bibliography

The Advancement of Understanding and Support of Higher Education. Washington, D.C.: American College Public Relations Association, 1958.

Andrews, F. E. *Philanthropy in the United States: History and Structure.* New York: The Foundation Center, 1974.

Bulletin on Public Relations and Development for Colleges and Universities. Chicago: Gonser, Gerber, Tinker, & Stuhr, 1966.

"Capital Campaigns: A Progress Report." *Chronicle of Higher Education,* May 17, 1976, p. 9.

Carnegie Corporation of New York. *Annual Report, 1975.* New York: Carnegie Corporation of New York, 1976.

Chambers, M. M. *Higher Education: Who Pays? Who Gains?* Danville, Illinois: Interstate, 1968.

Current Interests of the Ford Foundation 1976 and 1977. New York: Ford Foundation, 1975.

Curti, M. *American Philanthropy Abroad: A History.* New Brunswick, New Jersey: Rutgers University Press, 1963.

Curti, M., and Nash, R. *Philanthropy in the Shaping of American Higher Education.* New Brunswick, New Jersey: Rutgers University Press, 1965.

Cutlip, S. M. *Fund Raising in the United States, Its Role in America's Philanthropy.* New Brunswick, New Jersey: Rutgers University Press, 1965.

Daly, L. J. *The Medieval University.* London: Oxford University Press, 1961.

Detmold, J. H. *Papers in Educational Fund Raising.* Washington, D.C.: American Alumni Council, 1972.

Ferner, D. C. *Program for Priority Prospects.*

New York: Frantzreb and Pray Associates, 1968.

Giving USA—1976 Annual Report. New York: American Association of Fund Raising Counsel, 1976.

Knowles, A. S. (Ed.) *Handbook of College and University Administration.* (2 vols.) New York: McGraw-Hill, 1970.

Leslie, J. W. *Focus on Understanding and Support: A Study in College Management.* Washington, D.C.: American College Public Relations Association, 1969.

Marts, A. C. *Philanthropy's Role in Civilization.* New York: Harper & Row, 1953.

Marts, A. C. *Man's Concern for His Fellow-Man.* New York: Marts and Lundy, 1961.

Marts, A. C. *The Generosity of Americans: Its Source—Its Achievements.* Englewood Cliffs, New Jersey: Prentice-Hall, 1966.

Mirkin, H. R. *The Complete Fund Raising Guide.* New York: Public Service Materials Center, 1972.

Philanthropic Foundations in the United States. New York: The Foundation Center, 1969.

Philanthropic Papers. New York: Brakeley, John Price Jones, 1963–present.

The President's Role in Development. Washington, D.C.: Association of American Colleges, 1975.

Rashdall, H. *The Universities of Europe in the Middle Ages.* Oxford: Clarendon Press, 1936.

Seymour, H. J. *Designs for Fund-Raising.* New York: McGraw-Hill, 1966.

Stewart, E. T., Jr. *The "How To" of Educational Fund Raising.* Washington, D.C.: American Alumni Council, 1956.

Taft, J. R. *Understanding Foundations.* New York: McGraw-Hill, 1967.

Thorndike, L. *University Records and Life in the Middle Ages.* New York: Columbia University Press, 1949.

Van Dyne, L. "U.S. Universities Try Mideast Grantsmanship." *Chronicle of Higher Education,* May 17, 1976, pp. 3–4.

Voluntary Support of Education 1974–1975. New York: Council for Financial Aid to Education, 1976.

EUGENE M. REPPUCCI, JR.

See also: Alumni Affairs; Financing of Higher Education: Financing of Institutions and Systems; Philanthropy and Foundations; Public Relations.

DEVELOPMENT OF HIGHER EDUCATION 1950–67

See Organisation for Economic Co-operation and Development.

DEVELOPMENT OF
PROFESSIONAL ADMINISTRATORS

The administration of higher education can be defined as the fulfillment of responsibilities pertaining to the efficient and effective operation of colleges, universities, systems of higher education, or some segment of a system. Educational administration has become increasingly complex and specialized as institutions of higher learning have burgeoned in the second half of the twentieth century. Particularly after World War II colleges and universities in Western countries experienced considerable change in organization and scope, great expansion in enrollments, and large increases in the resources available for development and operations. In the United States, for example, the number of institutions grew tremendously with the establishment of numerous two-year colleges, the enlargement of many small state schools into universities, and the creation of complex university systems encompassing a variety of two-year, four-year, and technical institutions. With such growth, functions became differentiated, student populations grew more heterogeneous, and the need for a revised approach to higher education administration became clear.

The needs and problems of educational administration have also changed as colleges and universities have become more involved with government: rising costs have made institutions of higher learning more dependent on government funding, and new programs such as affirmative action entail increased attention to government regulations. These developments have imposed new responsibilities on higher education management. They have also led to greater professionalism and more specialized training among educational administrators. In fact, the increased complexity of university operations has served to make administrative functions in higher education more and more similar to those of management in the business sector (Institute for Educational Management, 1974).

The need for professional trained administrators, then, is a relatively recent phenomenon, a direct result of expanding educational systems. In the past, administrators received no specialized training; they were recruited from among those faculty who through departmental and committee work indicated a facility for and interest in administrative matters. Such faculty members, whose formal training was limited, of course, to their academic disciplines, gained their management skills and expertise only through on-the-job training. But this slow, informal system proved inadequate to the specialized, diversified, and heterogeneous needs of higher education in the post–World War II world. Individuals specially trained in finance, student personnel and student aid, computer technology, junior college administration, institutional research, or public relations were now necessary to sound higher education administration.

Types of Administration

The training of professional administrators has generally developed according to the different management functions at any institution of higher education. Such functions initially can be grouped according to the three broad categories of higher education programs identified by standard management and financial analytic procedure in the United States. *Primary programs* include instruction, research, public service, and student aid. *Support programs* include academic support (libraries, computer services, computer and audiovisual services); student services (counseling, recreation, social activities, health, financial aid management); institutional support (executive, academic, fiscal, and logistical management); and plant operation. *Separate operations* include auxiliary enterprises (housing, food service, intercollegiate sports); teaching hospitals; and independent research or other centers managed on behalf of government agencies (National Association of College and University Business Officers, 1974).

Educational administrative functions can also be broken down according to two distinct tracks: academic and support management. The education, career preparation, and training differ for these two types of administrators.

Academic management. Academic management includes such positions as department chairpersons, deans of colleges and their assistants, directors of research centers and public service programs, vice-presidents, and chief administrative officers (presidents, chancellors, or rectors). Some larger universities have in addition instituted two new kinds of academic management positions: an academic planning officer and an academic budget officer. Academic planning had its origin in the planning of instructional facilities but has become increasingly concerned with the scope and enrollment of programs, the relationship of enrollment to prospective professional employment, and the cost of program operation. Concern with program costs and priorities has in turn led to the creation of the position of budget officer, a position often held by a person with background in academic management.

The very establishment of these new positions indicates how higher education has needed administrative expertise in finance and planning that is not normally attainable through academic training alone. In fact, out of concern that chief administrative officers may not be adequately prepared by academic experience to serve as effective managers, boards of trustees at some United States colleges and universities have appointed presidents from outside academic ranks—from business, the public school system, or the military. Such selections, breaking as they do with tradition, often result in an increase in management efficiency but a decrease in faculty leadership. Faculty members have sometimes viewed as suspect persons specifically trained as academic managers, preferring instead individuals recruited from the ranks of an academic discipline or professional field of study.

Support management. Support management includes positions like librarians, computer systems directors, audiovisual staff, museum directors, student personnel administrators, business officers, hospital and clinic administrators, physical plant officers, public affairs managers, directors of auxiliary enterprises, athletic coaches, and other managers of specialized services such as student health and recreation programs. Administrators in these support areas tend to be specifically prepared for their positions by both education and experience. In the United States, for instance, where there is an extensive array of postsecondary professional education programs, scarcely a single support activity exists for which there is no professional education. The similarity of so many support activities in higher education to support activities in business, industry, and government probably explains this particular availability of educational opportunities in the United States. In nations where the infrastructure of professional education and professional practice is less extensive, the preparation and recruitment of support staff personnel may present more of a problem. In those European nations where universities use municipal facilities and services, this problem is diminished, but universities with sizable campuses in nonurban settings often find it difficult to hire adequately prepared support personnel.

It must be noted, however, that even when support personnel with sufficient professional background are available, colleges and universities have generally found it desirable to provide additional in-service training in order to familiarize the support managers with the peculiar aspects of college and university operations. For example, financial accounting in a college or university is quite different from financial accounting in business or government. Inasmuch as all support programs must be operated to serve the purposes of higher education, personnel need to become familiar with the policies, traditions, and values of the institution in which they are employed.

Types of Training for Professional Administrators

The demand for professionally trained administrators—academic as well as support—has been recognized in two general forms of training: short-term training (workshops, seminars, conferences) and formal courses of study in higher education administration.

Short-term training programs. Short-term training programs are varied and diverse. In Great Britain, for example, the need for organized administrative training was recognized toward the end of the 1960s, with the result that training activity has come to play "an important role in developing a professional group of administrators with a corporate identity, a sense of common purpose and a concern about standards" (Kitchen, 1976, p. 6). The Committee of Vice-Chancellors and Principals of the Administrative Training Committee (ATC) has made such opportunities as the following available in Great Britain: introductory courses (three days in duration) in university management for newly recruited administrators; short appreciation courses for younger administrators intended to improve communication between generalists and specialists; middle management courses for more senior staff; internal training arrangements within each university; and varied other training activities, such as seminars, arranged on an ad hoc basis (Kitchen, 1976).

In-service training has also been promoted in the United Kingdom by the Trust for the Development of Education Overseas, a body that arranges for academic planning and management advisers from the United Kingdom, Canada, the United States, and other countries to visit universities in Africa and the South Pacific. Other administrative training efforts include the Inter-University Council of East Africa, which has sponsored short-study courses for middle-level administrative staff. Sim-

ilar arrangements have been discussed by universities in West Africa, and the Australian Vice-Chancellor's Committee sponsors an annual university administrative staff training course.

In the United States, the American Council on Education (ACE) offers a variety of short training courses for newly appointed presidents, academic deans, and department chairpersons. Similar training efforts are offered by other agencies and departments of higher education in many universities (Irwin, 1975). The Institute for Education Management at Harvard University (Cambridge, Massachusetts), for example, yearly offers a six-week training program for educational administrators. The management division of the Academy for Educational Development (in New York and Washington, D.C.) conducts seminars and colloquia for top administrators to further managerial expertise, and Stanford University in California offers summer workshops for administrators seeking to upgrade themselves (Phillips, 1966). These are only a few of the most notable short-term programs available. The ACE, together with the Academy for Educational Development, publishes an annual *Guide to Professional Opportunities for College and University Administrators* that details the many training programs available in the United States which promote greater professionalism in educational administration.

Internships. A very significant type of training designed to train top academic administrators is the internship. Some internship efforts have been extremely effective in training specially selected persons who exhibit administrative leadership. The intern, according to Phillips, is in effect granted a "sabbatical leave during which he serves with a 'mentor' who is an experienced administrator" (1966, p. 150). Outstanding among United States opportunities is the Academic Administration Internship Program of the American Council on Education. This program, initiated during the 1960s through a Ford Foundation grant, identifies promising individuals and trains them for top administrative positions through one-year internships at a host institution. The interns observe and participate in academic management during the one-year period. The Center for the Study of Higher Education at the University of Michigan (in Ann Arbor, Michigan) also operates another effective internship program. Such internships provide educational managers the experience unavailable through formal graduate study alone.

Formal study in higher education. In addition to short-term training programs, and internships, the need for professional administrators is being met by a growing number of departments of higher education that provide graduate-level instruction in educational administration. Higher education as a field of study was first recognized in a course offered by G. Stanley Hall, first president of Clark University (in Worcester, Massachusetts), in 1893. In 1908 Dean James gave a course in educational organization at the University of Minnesota. But it was not until 1920, when higher education began a post–World War I expansion, that course work in the field really got under way (Ewing and Stickler, 1964). Among the first United States institutions to offer courses in educational administration were the University of Chicago (in Chicago, Illinois), Ohio State University (in Columbus, Ohio), and Teachers College of Columbia University (in New York). One of the first full programs in higher education was established at Syracuse University in Syracuse, New York.

In more recent years professional training opportunities remain available at these institutions as well as at many others. For instance, promising administrators are selected for study at the Center for the Study of Higher Education at the University of Michigan (in Ann Arbor, Michigan). The Kellogg Foundation supports study in educational management, as does the Leadership Training Project at the North Central Association of Colleges and Secondary Schools (Phillips, 1966, p. 152). An interesting regional approach has been undertaken by the Institute of Higher Education at the University of Georgia (in Athens, Georgia). The institute offers a variety of training opportunities, including a doctoral program in higher education.

Many opportunities for postdoctoral study in educational management are also available. Dressel and Mayhew (1974) point out that postdoctoral fellowships have certain advantages over doctoral programs in that they provide freedom from degree requirements and the status of an earned degree as well as offering greater involvement in university affairs.

Professional Associations

Higher education, then, has been attempting to meet its need for professionally trained administrators through a variety of programs ranging from in-service training courses of relatively short duration to formal graduate degree programs in educational management. The increased professionalism in higher education administration is reflected in the growing number of professional associations for higher education administrators. In the United States, for example, support managers have their own professional associations. Often the college or university pays the annual dues for membership, and private foundations frequently provide supplementary grants. These associations organize a number of in-service training programs as well as offering information services to assist support managers in the performance of their activities. One of the most effective of these associations is the National Association of College and University Business Officers (NACUBO) in Washington, D.C. There are also professional associations of librarians; officers of admissions, student aid, student personnel, public affairs, planning, and purchasing; registrars, plant managers, and legal advisers.

Continuing professional education for university administrators is indispensable at a time when colleges and universities throughout the world are experiencing significant changes in enrollments, financing, and social objectives. Shifts in enrollments, particularly in the United States and Europe, have created new problems of reduced institutional income. And new social expectations reflected in such programs as affirmative action have forced colleges and universities, through various associations and with the assistance of private foundations, to give increased attention to in-service training. The problems of higher education clearly demand well-trained administrators familiar with finance, business, and management procedures. The new directions in higher education demand administrative specialists in student personnel, public relations, long-range planning, and computer technology. With adequate training opportunities, the need will be met for expertise and excellence of administrative leadership.

Bibliography

"Courses for Administrators in Three Countries." *A.C.U. Bulletin of Current Documentation,* October 1975, No. 20, 14–15.

Dressel, P. L., and Mayhew, L. B. *Higher Education as a Field of Study.* San Francisco, California: Jossey-Bass, 1974.

Ewing, J. C., and Stickler, H. W. "Progress in the Development of Higher Education as a Field of Professional Graduate Study and Research." *Journal of Teacher Education,* 1964, *15*(4), 397–403.

Institute for Educational Management. *A Management Development Program for College and University Administrators.* Cambridge, Massachusetts: IEM at Harvard University, 1974.

Irwin, J. T. (Ed.) *A Guide to Professional Development Opportunities for College and University Administrators.* Washington, D.C.: Academy for Educational Development and American Council on Education, 1975.

Kitchen, K. E. "The Training of University Administrators in Britain." *A.C.U. Bulletin of Current Documentation,* October 1976, No. 25, pp. 2–6.

National Association of College and University Business Officers. *College and University Business Administration.* (3rd ed.) Washington, D.C.: NACUBO, 1974.

Phillips, E. L., Jr. "Toward More Effective Administration in Higher Education." *Educational Record,* Spring 1966, *47*(2), 148–162.

"Something for Everyone." *A.C.U. Bulletin of Current Documentation,* June 1975, No. 19, 8–9.

Udagama, P. "Educational Administrator— Disoriented or Committed?" *Bulletin of the UNESCO Regional Office for Education in Asia,* June 1974, No. 15, pp. 244–249.

JOHN D. MILLETT

See also: Evaluation of Administrators.

DIPLOMA MILLS

A diploma mill (or degree mill as it is called in the United Kingdom and the United States) is an institution that offers for sale certificates purporting to confer an academic qualification. This "qualification," which is not recognized by any government or university authority, does not require the completion of any serious course of study—or, indeed, any course of study at all.

There are in the world a very large number of institutions whose diplomas do not enjoy official recognition. Some offer study courses of genuine academic value, and in such cases it would be injurious and improper to describe them as diploma mills. Provided they do not claim or mislead their students into thinking that their certificates have other or greater value than they in fact possess, such institutions are in no sense fraudulent. Other institutions, however, are of such low academic standard that the studies they require of their clients are hardly more than a formality. Since diploma mills proper may also insist on the completion of a piece of "scientific work" or of a test paper (making it clear that these will not call for effort or the acquisition of new knowledge), the borderline between legitimate and fraudulent enterprises is evidently fluid, if not indistinguishable. The distinction tends to be mainly a practical one: the operator of a diploma mill, more concerned with selling his product than with dispensing instruction, usually charges a considerable sum for the certificates he issues, whereas an institution offering courses of instruction usually claims an amount large enough only to cover administrative expenses.

The primary focus of diploma mills is the sale of certificates which require no serious academic work and may be obtained simply by paying an appropriate sum of money. Such institutions illustrate both the socioethical and the legal-practical aspects of the problem. The fact that some people find diploma mills repugnant and reprehensible (as they may find other aspects of human behavior) is not necessarily a sufficient reason for national or international bodies to suppress them. The crucial question is: What actual harm do degree mills cause? If their sole effect is to transfer money from the pockets of the vain to the pockets of the unscrupulous, the justification for national and/or international action may appear insufficient. More generally, the need for countermeasures would be assessed differently by those persons and regimes who think the law is made to protect fools than by those who hold to the principle of *caveat emptor*.

As regards the legal-practical aspects, it is very difficult to suppress diploma mills by legislation, though in some countries the law does indeed make their operation hazardous. What is of course possible is to confer legal protection on those academic qualifications that the government accepts as valid, and this has been done by most European states and in many countries outside Europe. Again, even where there is no specific definition of a degree or diploma, there is nearly always legal protection against false representations or pretenses. However, between the state-recognized qualification and the patently bogus certificate, there is a large gray area that the law cannot—or at any rate usually does not—regulate. Even where legal provision exists, its implementation often poses serious problems. Operators of diploma mills frequently employ "accommodation" addresses and change these rapidly. They tend to base their activities in countries where the legal situation is permissive (for example, the United States and the United Kingdom) but to advertise and attract clients from outside the national frontiers, especially from countries where academic titles confer high social prestige and where domestic legislation regarding degrees and diplomas is exhaustive and strict—as in Austria and the Federal Republic of Germany. Diploma mills often seek legal advice and conduct their operations within the letter of the law, if not its spirit. Should their customers break the law—for example, by using a fictitious title to increase the sale of their services—years may pass before someone suspects that the title is indeed bogus and decides to press charges; even then it may be quite difficult to prove that "Dr." Smith's qualification is worthless and that he has used it knowingly to mislead the public. In any case there may well be no possibility of taking legal action against the diploma mill that sold him his credentials.

The Council of Europe became interested in the problem of diploma mills in the context of its work on the international equivalence of academic qualifications. To establish such equivalence even within the limited and, educationally speaking, relatively homogeneous area of Western Europe is a formidably difficult task, particularly when one takes into account the need (and desire) to respect university autonomy and to encourage innovation in curricula and course structures.

Diploma mills constitute such a complication. At the least they involve national or university authorities responsible for recognizing the equivalence of foreign qualifications in considerable time-consuming work. There have been cases of persons holding qualifications from reputable academic institutions who experienced difficulty in having these authorized credentials recognized because they were issued by institutions with names very similar to those of known diploma mills.

At this point the harm caused by diploma mills becomes more obvious. If employers, confronted by an applicant with a genuine foreign degree, are reluctant to accept it for fear that it might be bogus, then the applicant certainly suffers harm. If—as has happened—the owner of a spurious degree in psychology is appointed head of a psychology clinic, the harm can be quite great. In the main, clients of diploma mills are motivated by reasons of snobbery, with negligible effects upon their fellow men or society. However, incidents of abuse of false diplomas are not rare, and their consequences can be serious.

The Council of Europe's working party of equivalence has recommended specific state protection for academic diplomas, titles, and degrees, which would also cover the right to confer such qualifications; at the moment such protection does not exist among a number of member countries—Republic of Ireland, Malta, Sweden, and the United Kingdom. However, even if it were instituted (in 1975 the United Kingdom was considering appropriate action in this sense, but possibly with respect to first degrees only, since it is doubtful whether the Crown-granted privilege to confer degrees extends to doctorates), the problem of diploma mills would not be resolved. It is noteworthy that diploma mills in Europe are implanted in large numbers not only in Great Britain but also in such countries as Belgium, France, Italy, and Switzerland, where diplomas are legally protected. Legislation making it a criminal offense for institutions other than those officially authorized to issue qualifications or for persons to use such unauthorized qualifications is conceivable but would be difficult to draft and to enforce, mainly because the term *qualifications* is so difficult to define. Private schools and colleges must presumably remain free to introduce new final qualifications (for instance, the title of *gradué*), and to have them recognized by public authority. Legislation would need to be uniformly stringent and applied over a wide geographical area, embracing at least North America and Europe, if it were to have much practical effect.

While experts do not place much hope in the legislative approach, they do see a possibility of ameliorating the situation considerably through a concerted effort to improve information and have offered the following recommendations: (1) Publish lists of authentic (officially recognized) institutions of higher education and of the diplomas, titles, and degrees they award. (2) Disseminate at national and international levels information enabling the public to identify bogus diplomas and advising them of existing regulations. (3) Increase the exchange of information on diploma mills, circulating lists of these as well as copies of their publicity material and certificates among government agencies and universities. (4) Take steps to prohibit advertising of bogus degrees and diplomas. (This action would squarely confront the question of how to define such degrees and diplomas; at the moment there is some measure of international agreement on the criteria of serious academic study, but a legal definition does not exist.) (5) Inform employers and the public of cases where persons have invented and printed their own diplomas; one such case involved a number of overseas students who created a false Belgian diploma of *ingénieur industriel.* This was doubly ingenious: not only could it be confused with the authentic title of *ingénieur technique,* but it reflected knowledge of Belgian plans to introduce a diploma having the same title.

It is significant that these recommendations do not include the one that at first sight would seem the most effective and helpful—namely, that some *official* body, national or international, promulgate the names and addresses of known diploma mills. It is not the policy of the United States Department of Health, Education and Welfare, or of most European ministries of education or their equivalent, to issue such a list. In the first place, it could hardly ever be complete, and diploma mills not included would inadvertently capitalize, at least in the short run, on their omission. Second, given the ease with which names and even addresses can be changed, it would not long remain up to date. Third, in view of the problems of definition, the publisher might run the risk of being sued for libel. Finally, as W. J. Dey, secretary to the University Entrance Requirements Department of the University of London and a world authority on the subject, has pointed out, the list of bogus institutions would have to give information not only about existing diploma mills and their whereabouts but also about all institutions known over the last thirty to forty years. Otherwise, "a bogus degree awarded twenty-five years ago may still be presented somewhere, and, if an institution is not named on current lists under the name it (then) used, an enquirer might think that the degree was genuine because the name did not appear in the list." Obviously, such a comprehensive listing would be essentially impossible to obtain.

For these same reasons, international organizations concerned with the subject have also been unwilling to publish lists of diploma mills. Though conscious that its list would be imperfect and incomplete, the Council of Europe nonetheless decided to disseminate one in 1974. Since then the list has been updated and improved (notably, by the omission of institutions which, though their certificates are not officially recognized, do offer genuine courses of study by qualified instructors), and revised versions are issued from time to time. Future editions may also indicate reputable institutions with which certain diploma mills might be confused.

HUGH L. BEESLEY

DIPLOMAS
See Degrees, Diplomas, and Certificates.

DISABILITY EDUCATION
See Blind, Higher Education for the; Deaf, Higher Education for the; Handicapped, Higher Education for the Physically.

DISABLED VETERANS AND HIGHER EDUCATION BENEFITS
See Veterans Education Benefits.

DISSENT AND DISRUPTION (Higher Education Report), United States

Dissent and Disruption: Proposals for Consideration by the Campus (New York: McGraw-Hill, June 1971), a report of the Carnegie Commission on Higher Education, considers campus unrest and proposes measures by which a university community can prepare itself to deal reasonably and democratically with expressions of dissatisfaction. The following findings and recommendations are reported.

Each campus should adopt a bill of rights and responsibilities, reflecting four basic principles: (1) Campus members have the same rights and responsibilities that all citizens have. (2) Additional responsibilities of campus members are engendered by the nature of the academic process. (3) Institutions also have rights and responsibilities. (4) All campus members have the right to due process procedures. The report presents a detailed working model of such a bill, which can be adapted to the particular circumstances of diverse institutions.

In addition to the implementation of a bill of rights, each campus should make advance preparations to prevent and handle emergency situations. Specifically, campuses should have well-publicized methods for dealing with grievances, and decisions in grievance cases should be based on consultation with all involved persons. A crisis should be dealt with by the campus president in consultation with faculty and student representatives. In addition, each campus should develop a contingency plan for handling nonviolent disruptions as well as violent actions and establish a clear policy on the use of the campus security force or outside law enforcement authorities in emergency situations. Each campus also should establish procedures for determining violations of campus regulations and for assessing penalties. Campus authorities must determine whether violations of campus law should be handled by the campus or by the outside courts. Campuses might consider the use of ombudsmen, hearing officers, and campus attorneys when handling more serious violations of campus law.

Upholding the distinction between lawful dissent, which must be protected, and illegal disruption, which must be eliminated, the commission urges the academic community to address itself to the full recognition of the rights and responsibilities of its members. The report includes examples and documents chosen to aid in this process.

DISTANCE EDUCATION
See Independent Study.

DIVERSIFICATION OF TERTIARY EDUCATION (Higher Education Report), Multinational

Diversification of Tertiary Education (Strasbourg, France: Council of Europe, Council for Cultural Co-operation, 1974) is the report of a working party set up under the auspices of the Committee for Higher Education and Research of the Council of Europe's Council for Cultural Co-operation, with R. Crausaz as chairman. The report considers the establishment of new tertiary programs and more effective distribution of resources available for tertiary study.

The report offers a theoretical definition of diversification of tertiary education, including its goals, resources, and impact. Diversified tertiary education, the report states, should contribute to the growth of knowledge and culture, cultivate the individual, and provide vocational training which enables a student to adapt to changes in a field.

The working party assessed the results of experiments in tertiary education in the Federal Republic of Germany, France, Norway, Switzerland, and the United Kingdom. It determined that tertiary study should be an active force in society, not merely a sector of society adjusted to societal demands. Obstacles to diversification should be analyzed and the development

of national experiments should be monitored by a group of two or three experts. The working party proposed that the Committee for Higher Education and Research organize a study on diversification experiments in other member states of the Council of Europe.

DJIBOUTI, REPUBLIC OF
See Afars and Issas; independent June 1977.

DOCUMENTATION AND INFORMATION CENTERS IN HIGHER EDUCATION

The following discussion of documentation and information centers and services will demonstrate the variety of patterns followed by different countries in organizing their educational information services in higher education, as well as show some of the regional and international arrangements for the provision of information on higher education. The examples of specific documentation centers and information services used throughout are only a representative selection chosen to illustrate a particular feature or pattern.

This discussion is based on an international survey conducted by the author. A questionnaire was sent to major international, regional, and national organizations involved in higher education. Among the organizations solicited were government units variously described as "office," "bureau," "department," or "division," and separate institutions called "center," "institute," "council," "association," "library," or "foundation." University libraries, national libraries, and large general or public libraries in most countries were not sent questionnaires. Those organizations eventually included in the directory were chosen on the basis of their activities in three areas: the collection of information pertaining to higher education; the dissemination of this information through response to local or mail inquiries, publications, exhibitions, seminars, and conferences; and investigation or research about higher education.

It is difficult to determine what constitutes, on the one hand, a documentation center and, on the other hand, a library. Documentation centers may concentrate on an efficient data-processing and information-retrieval system and be distinguished by the large proportion of data in the form of pieces of paper in filing cabinets, whereas libraries may be mainly concerned with the acquisition and provision of literature, in book or bound form; a further distinction may be the active information service offered by the former, as opposed to the passive repository function of the latter. In some parts of the world, however, these distinctions appear to be gradually disappearing. Many special or technical libraries, for example, fulfill the functions both of a library and a documentation center. In some cases a library unit may be an important part of a documentation center. In other cases a center may have an important information dissemination role, although it has no library. Not only is there often considerable overlap of functions between libraries, particularly technical or special libraries, and other information systems, such as documentation centers, information services/centers, clearinghouses, and information analysis centers, but, as Weisman (1972, p. 15) points out, there is also much duplication of functions among information systems themselves.

The field of higher education has a dual nature. First, there is a recognizable field of study itself, the study of higher education, which is, at least in the United States, recognized as a discipline (Dressel and Mayhew, 1974, pp. 3–4). The field includes, among other disciplines, history, philosophy, economics and financing, administration, planning, students and faculty, and curricula and teaching. Teacher training, adult education, and vocational and technical education could also be included at the postsecondary or tertiary level. Secondly, higher education can be viewed in a much broader sense as being involved with all aspects of knowledge at the tertiary level, including all the fields of study of the curriculum. The author attempted to restrict his survey and discussion to the narrower definition.

National Centers

In many countries there is as yet no center concerned with gathering and diffusing information about education at the national level. And only a small proportion of those countries with national educational documentation centers have specialized centers or services that provide resources and information solely on the higher education level. There is evidence, however, that an increasingly larger number of nations are beginning to recognize the importance of communication and information for progress in higher education. Universities, research institutes, and governments, particularly in developing countries, are giving higher priority to the establishment of documentation and information centers for the gathering, processing, production, and dissemination of educational information.

The place assigned to documentation and information centers in higher education varies considerably from country to country. In a large number of nations, documentation centers are set up within the Ministry of Education and are subordinate to it. Usually these centers gather information and offer services on all levels of education. Examples of this arrangement include the Central Bureau of Education in Pakistan, the Center of Educational Documentation and Information in Cuba, and the Educational Documentation Center in Jordan. These centers serve as principal educational documentation centers for their respective countries. The centers in Cuba and Pakistan receive copies of official documents relating to education issued by government offices, which enhance their position as educational depositories for their countries.

In some countries a separate office has been established under the Ministry of Education to deal with the tertiary or higher level of the educational system. The Republic of China, for example, has created the Department of Higher Education; Argentina has a Department of University Affairs; Venezuela has established a Center for Information and Documentation in Higher Education, which is part of the Office of University Planning; Papua New Guinea has an Office of Higher Education; and, Algeria has established the Office for Pedagogical Documentation within its separate Ministry of Higher Education and Scientific Research. The centers in Venezuela, Papua New Guinea, and Algeria were all established in the 1970s, which indicates a trend toward the separation of tertiary education from the lower levels through the establishment of specialized units.

In another group of countries, the principal educational documentation and information service is part of a national educational research institute. Usually the institute is concerned with all levels of education. Examples of this pattern are found in France, with its prestigious National Institute of Pedagogical Research and Documentation; Brazil, with its National Institute for Educational Research; Spain, with its National Institute of Educational Sciences; and Czechoslovakia, with its two Institutes of Educational Information (the larger one in Prague, the much smaller one in Bratislava). In all these examples, the respective Ministry of Education serves as the parent organization for the institutes.

Paralleling the development of separate departments of higher education within Ministries of Education is the creation of separate research institutes for higher education. Poland, for example, has created a Documentation Center and Library within the Research Institute of Science Policy and Higher Education; Ireland has a National Institute for Higher Education; and the Soviet Union has consolidated higher education activities within the National Research Institute for Higher Education.

Still another pattern is found in those countries with central or national libraries of education. The libraries have usually assumed the role of the principal educational documentation and information center for all levels of education in their countries. Examples of countries with national education libraries include Belgium, Denmark, Hungary, Israel, Italy, Norway, Romania, and Sweden. As of 1976, no country had established a separate national library devoted solely to the tertiary level of education.

In certain countries documentation centers have been established by universities, in some cases directly under the rector's office and in other cases under the faculty of education or attached to a research institute or library. Under such a system each university in a country may have its own documentation services and therefore act not as a national but as an institutional documentation center. This seems to be the situation in Chile and Ecuador. Some centers attached to research institutes may be of more than local interest, however, as seems true of the Research Institute for Higher Education at Hiroshima University in Japan and the Center for Research into Higher Education at the Catholic University of Nijmegen in the Netherlands.

In small countries or countries with limited resources, the national university or its library has often assumed the role of a documentation and information center for the country. The University of Malawi Library, for example, serves in this capacity in that country, as does the University of Benin in Togo. Antilles-Guiana University Center, with the assistance of foreign universities, is developing a documentation collection to serve French Guiana, Martinique, and Guadeloupe.

In large or wealthy countries with highly developed systems of higher education, nongovernmental agencies often either supplement the activities of government offices or take the initiative in higher education. In these countries one is likely to find university associations, councils, or rectors' conferences providing important documentation and information services. The West German Rectors Conference, for example, as the central representative body of institutions with university status in the Federal Republic of Germany, informally serves as the principal information service in higher education for that country. A similar role is exercised by the Association of Universities and Colleges of Canada and the Association of Indian Universities. The Australian Vice-Chancellors' Committee has assumed an important function in that country as an information clearinghouse for all Australian universities and holds copies of government publications of interest to universities. The Supreme Council of Universities in Egypt is planning to expand its library into a national center for documentation and information in university education and to establish an international exchange of information and publications to serve local, regional, and international organizations interested in promoting higher education.

Still other examples of private initiative's exerting an important influence in the area of higher education information may be seen in the United Kingdom, with the Society for Research into Higher Education, and in the United States, where such organizations as the American Association of University Women, the American Council on Education, and the National Association of State Universities and Land-Grant Colleges maintain their own information resources in higher education. In addition to organizations of a more general nature, there are in the United States numerous institutions with resources in specialized areas of higher education. For example, the American College Testing Program, the Foundation Center, the National Association for Foreign Student Affairs, and the National Center for the Study of Collective Bargaining in Higher Education all emphasize the collection of information in their special areas of interest.

Through the survey the attempt has been made to identify and describe institutions concerned mainly with educational documentation and information as such, whether for all levels of schooling or for the tertiary level alone. There are other centers, however, that are not primarily concerned with educational information but which nonetheless play an important role in higher education information in their countries. The Iranian Documentation Center, for example, serves as a national documentation center in many fields. Its activities in education are important enough to warrant its consideration as an educational documentation center. Although the Commonwealth Caribbean Resource Center is primarily concerned with documentation on the culture and folklore of the Caribbean, it also serves as an education documentation center for the West Indies.

International and Regional Centers

Besides national educational documentation and information centers—that is, centers which, although they may have regional and even international influence or contacts, are established by government and nongovernment organizations to serve the needs of a particular country—numerous regional and international libraries and documentation centers are concerned with higher education. Among the more than twenty-one international and twenty regional organizations involved in higher education documentation and information, one of the most important is the Library and Documentation Center of the International Association of Universities, which has one of the most extensive libraries on higher education internationally. Its collection of over 7000 books; 3000 reports, documents, and pamphlets; and 265 current periodicals is probably unique in higher education. Intended chiefly to provide the secretariat with an authoritative basis for its role as a central source of information, the center is also used extensively by official academic and governmental visitors for research.

Another international organization with major documentation and information services is the Association of Commonwealth Universities. Its documentation service includes the *ACU Bulletin of Current Documentation,* a *Select Bibliography* (included as an appendix in the *Commonwealth Universities Yearbook*), the *Accessions List* of the Reference Library's most important acquisitions, bibliographical searches on particular subjects, and an emergency airmail purchase service of books or reports published in the United Kingdom and needed more quickly than a foreign university's bookstore can provide. Although the documentation services are primarily for senior offices of member universities, students and visitors may use the Reference Library, which includes an extensive collection on higher education.

UNESCO conducts an important program of activities with regard to educational documentation and information throughout the world. Dissemination of information on all levels of education is chiefly carried out by the Education Clearing House at UNESCO headquarters in Paris, by the International Institute for Educational Planning (IIEP), by the International Bureau of Education Documentation Center (IBEDOC), and by documentation centers in the regional offices for education in Africa, Asia, and Latin America. The European Center for Higher Education *(Centre européen pour l'enseignement supérieur:* CEPES) in Bucharest, Romania, was established as a center of documentation, information, and liaison to provide services to national authorities in the European region (including Canada, the United States, and all European countries) who are concerned with higher education. CEPES has also established contacts with universities and other higher bodies. Although its activities and services are limited to the European area, it is the single UNESCO center working exclusively in the field of higher education.

The UNESCO center in Romania is one example of a number of important regional centers throughout the world that concentrate their activities solely in higher education. On the African continent the Documentation Center of the Association of

African Universities collects information on member universities, which is then published in the *Directory of African Universities,* a bulletin and newsletter, an acquisitions list, and various reports and surveys. The Documentation Center was started in 1972 with a grant from the Ford Foundation of $65,000 (over a two-year period), followed by a second, and final, grant of $50,000. The future of the center appears bleak, however, unless additional funds can be found.

In Asia the Regional Institute of Higher Education and Development (RIHED) in Singapore serves as both a regional and a national information center for matters relating to higher education in Southeast Asia. Its active publishing program is supported by an important library on higher education, which includes government documents from member nations.

Latin America has several organizations of consequence that provide higher education information services. The Union of Universities of Latin America and the Federation of Private Universities of Central America and Panama both have large library collections of reports, documents, and pamphlets. Their services are used by a large public, including educational institutions, teachers, administrators and planners, and researchers from Latin America and other regions.

Functions of Centers

As pointed out in an earlier international survey of education clearinghouses and documentation centers, educational documentation centers generally have three principal functions: the collection of information; the diffusion or dissemination of this information; and investigative or research activity *(Education Clearing Houses and Documentation Centres,* 1957, pp. 9–11). Although not all documentation and information centers fulfill these three functions, and some centers may have additional functions (for example, in training or the handling of teaching materials), the extent to which a center fulfills these three essential functions is an indication of the degree to which it meets the definition of a well-developed information service.

Collection of information. Since the documentation function implies a library and trained staff or access to special libraries, most centers devote a considerable amount of staff time to the first function. Documentary collections generally consist of three categories of materials: books; unbound or nonbook materials, such as reports, documents, and pamphlets; and periodical subscriptions. The Educational Documentation Center in Jordan is typical of a general collection on all levels of education, having 5500 books, over 8000 unbound items, and 230 periodical titles. Approximately 10 percent of its total collection is on the higher education level. Less typical is the collection of the National Institute of Pedagogical Research and Documentation in France, which is unusually large for an educational research institute, consisting of over 1,000,000 books and unbound items and over 1840 current periodicals, with some 30 percent in higher education. In central or national education libraries, the collections are understandably large, in most cases exceeding 150,000 books and other items and 500 current periodicals; the Central Library of the Ministry of National Education in Belgium contains over 500,000 volumes and 1800 periodical titles. Although the percentage on higher education would be difficult to determine for these libraries, an approximate figure would be between 20 to 30 percent.

The collections of government offices, research institutes, and professional associations concerned only with higher education are much smaller than those of a more general nature, and usually average between 1000 to 5000 in the book and unbound categories and fewer than 100 periodical titles. The West German Rectors Conference Library and that of the Association of Universities and Colleges of Canada are exceptions to the general rule

of small, specialized higher education collections.

Diffusion of information. The second function of a documentation center, that of diffusion or dissemination, has several elements. It involves, first of all, responding to inquiries either directly or through the mail. Most documentation centers regard this as a normal part of their duties and are willing to answer foreign inquiries as well. Dissemination of information is also accomplished through a program of publications, exhibitions, and seminars and conferences. Most centers produce at least a bibliographical bulletin or library acquisitions list. A large number publish one or more periodicals that carry educational abstracts, essays, studies, book reviews, and information on national developments in education. Some centers publish studies and surveys, and a few have rather extensive publishing activities. The West German Rectors Conference, for example, issues five periodical publications covering general news and bibliographical information. The Association of Universities and Colleges of Canada has a similarly active publication program, including a large number of monographs. Research institutes that function as national educational documentation centers usually publish the results of their own research and therefore often have vigorous publishing programs. In some cases documentation centers collaborate in the publications of the organization to which they are attached. The Zalman Aranne Central Education Library in Israel, for instance, has collaborated with the Hebrew University of Jerusalem's school of education to publish several monographs. Centers also often are represented in an official publication of their Ministry of Education.

Investigation. The third function of a documentation center is investigation or research. Most documentation centers either encourage researchers to use their resources or employ researchers on their own staffs. A number of centers are specifically concerned with accomplishing research or fostering research in higher education. Examples include the Society for Research into Higher Education in England, the Center for Research into Higher Education in the Netherlands, the Research Institute of Science Policy and Higher Education in Poland, and the Research Institute for Higher Education in Japan. Other centers, although involved with research on all levels of education, accomplish important results on the tertiary level. This is the case with the National Institute of Pedagogical Research and Documentation in France, the National Institute of Educational Sciences in Spain, and the Institute for Pedagogical and Psychological Research in Romania.

Clientele of Centers

Institutions are created in response to a need. Documentation and information centers are no exception. Centers throughout the world reveal considerable variety in the needs they are expected to satisfy and the purposes for which they were established. These needs and purposes can sometimes be revealed by considering the audiences which the centers are intended to serve. Each Ministry of Education or corresponding official agency requires information on which to base decisions involving the system of higher education within the country. The major purpose of most educational documentation centers is to serve the educational authorities (including administrators and legislators) responsible for the administration of higher education in a country. Many centers, however, have a larger audience outside of their official one. This clientele may consist of educational institutions, teachers, researchers, students, parents or even the general public. The National Center for the Study of Collective Bargaining in Higher Education in the United States, for example, serves as an information clearinghouse on collective bargaining and counts among its users, educational institutions, researchers, faculty members, lawyers, administrators, legislators, and

students of education. The National Association for Foreign Student Affairs in the United States disseminates information on international higher education to educational institutions, public and private educational agencies, professional associations, national and international corporations and foundations, and community groups.

A number of national centers surveyed indicated that they were used by an international clientele. In most cases this included visiting scholars from other countries or members of international organizations located in the same city or country. The library of the Central Bureau of Education in Islamabad, Pakistan, for example, is used by personnel of other nations and international organizations and agencies, which one would expect with a national center located in a capital city. The services of the National Council of Peruvian Universities are used by visitors from UNESCO and the Union of Universities of Latin America. The National Institute of Pedagogical Research and Documentation in France includes among its clients teachers and education science institutes throughout the world.

Staffing of Centers

The extent and quality of services provided by documentation centers vary considerably and depend to a large degree on the material and financial resources available and on the professional qualities of the staff. As regards staff, several observations can be made. In those countries where the principal educational documentation services are part of a national educational research institute, the total number of staff can approach one hundred; the National Institute of Educational Sciences in Spain and the National Institute of Pedagogical Research and Documentation in France have more than a hundred staff members. In countries with a central library of education, the average staff size is around fifty, although in at least three countries (Norway, Sweden, and Israel) the staff of the central education library is considerably smaller, averaging ten.

In countries with separate departments of higher education, research institutes for the study of higher education, or higher education associations, councils, or conferences, the staff size of the library of documentation centers understandably tends to be smaller than in those organizations concerned with all levels of education. The average staff size is close to ten in all three categories of higher education organizations. There are exceptions to this average, for example, in the case of the Research Institute for Higher Education in Japan, which employs fifty-one persons, and the Center for Information and Documentation in Higher Education, which is part of the National Council of Universities in Venezuela and has a staff of fifty-five.

One of the difficulties in determining the staff size of documentation centers lies in the fact that some organizations fail to specify the number of their staff involved in documentation and information activities and those working with the other activities of the organization. For example, the Office of State Universities in Thailand has a staff of two hundred, not all of whom would be assigned to documentation duties. Although its library collection is relatively large, the organization is also involved in training and administration activities, which normally require numerous personnel. Closer examination of the staff in the Research Institute for Higher Education in Japan, for example, reveals that a more realistic number than the fifty-one given is seven full-time staff members, which is closer to the average for that type of center. The other forty-four researchers probably are employed either on a part-time or on a temporary basis.

A second difficulty regarding staff is that, although nearly all organizations distinguish between the number of professional and nonprofessional staff, what constitutes professional duties is not uniform. Thus, it is difficult to determine how many trained librarians or documentalists

occupy posts in various educational services. It would appear, however, that many centers, particularly those in developing countries, lack trained personnel and are overstaffed with clerical help.

Funding of Centers

Data are limited on funding of centers, but the approximate amount of money devoted to a documentation center can be roughly inferred from the number of staff, the size of its collection, and the number of its publications. Many of the organizations are parts of government ministries or other departments and have to rely on sums allotted to them in the budget of the departmental, ministerial, or university body to which they are subordinate. The greater part of a documentation center's budget undoubtedly would be set aside for staff salaries, with lesser amounts for acquisition of materials, printing and reproduction of documents, and other expenses. In many cases, the physical facilities to house the center are provided by the parent organization, and often the two are located on the same premises. One study published in 1957 has suggested that between $10,000 and $50,000 is required to operate a national documentation center in education, and that a staff of ten persons would be sufficient (*Education Clearing Houses and Documentation Centres,* 1957, pp. 12–13). In the mid 1970s it would cost considerably more to operate such a center. A center specializing in higher education, however, should be able to function with a staff of five to ten and a budget of $20,000 to $50,000 (not including staff salaries). The minimum staff for a center normally would include a professional educator as director, a trained librarian or documentalist, and several clerical or bibliographical assistants. Additional staff would depend on the function of a center's program that is emphasized. The collection or documentation function normally includes books, reports, documents, pamphlets, and periodical subscriptions, necessary shelving and file cabinets, and documentation or library staff; the diffusion or dissemination function includes the editorial and, possibly, the printing staff and equipment; and the investigation or research function includes researchers, perhaps comparative educationalists, and office equipment.

Conclusions

Not only are nations showing an increased interest in improving communication in higher education within their boundaries, but their interest is turning outward to other countries as well. It is evident that many centers are not content with their international contacts and are becoming more interested in providing information that other countries request and in using information that they obtain from abroad. Most institutions express a willingness to extend their contact with other nations, either by answering foreign inquiries or by expanding their exchange of information and publications. Increased contact through the exchange of information and publications is one of the best ways to transfer experience and enrich higher education programs in many nations.

On both the national and the international level, the establishment and expansion of centers of educational information seem desirable, and even essential, to the future of higher education, and perhaps ultimately to the future of international relations. Communication is a fundamental element of all university life. One of the obstacles to effective cooperation within a country and between countries is lack of sufficient information on the activities and interests of other scholars, universities, and governments, coupled with the lack of satisfactory channels of communication. Documentation and information centers and services are designed to meet this need for information by providing a system of communication.

Bibliography

Bristow, T. "A Survey of Education Libraries and Documentation Centres in Europe." *Comparative Education*, June 1975, *11*(2).

"Development of Educational Documentation and Information in Arab Countries." *Educational Documentation and Information*, 1973, No. 186, pp. 9–11.
"Development of Educational Documentation in South America." *Educational Documentation and Information*, 1972, No. 183, pp. 9–17.
Directory of Educational Documentation and Information Services. Paris: UNESCO, 1975.
"The Documentation Centre for Education in Europe." *Educational Documentation and Information*, 1971, No. 179, pp. 9–14.
Dressel, P. L., and Mayhew, L. B. *Higher Education as a Field of Study: The Emergence of a Profession.* San Francisco: Jossey-Bass, 1974.
Education Clearing Houses and Documentation Centres: A Preliminary International Survey. Paris: UNESCO, 1957.
International Guide to Educational Documentation. (2nd ed.) Paris: UNESCO, 1971.
Majault, J. *Education Documentation Centres in Western Europe: A Comparative Study.* Paris: UNESCO, 1963.
Situación de los servicios de documentación e información pedagógica en América latina. Santiago, Chile: UNESCO Regional Office for Education in Latin America and the Caribbean, 1971.
Weisman, H. M. *Information Systems, Services, and Centers.* New York: Wiley, 1972.

GARY KRASKE

See also: International Directory of Documentation and Information Centers in Higher Education.

DOMESTIC ELECTRICITY
See Electricity, Industrial and Domestic (field of study).

DOMINICA

Population: 75,000. Student enrollment in primary school: 20,777 (10,346 females); secondary school: 2086 (1113 females); postsecondary education: 158 (68 females); higher education (abroad): 137 (39 females). Language of instruction: English. [Figures are for 1974.]

Dominica, one of the Windward Islands in the Caribbean, is a state in an associated relationship with the United Kingdom. Although university education is not available in Dominica, teacher training programs and technical training in a technical college are offered. The programs last two years and lead to a professional certificate (for teachers) and a certificate with designation of the field of study in the technical college.

Dominica is a supporting territory of the University of the West Indies, where a majority of Dominican students receive their higher education. The main campus of UWI is located in Mona, Jamaica, with branch campuses located in Cave Hill, Barbados, and St. Augustine, Trinidad. A resident tutor of the Department of Extra-Mural Studies of UWI is located in Dominica, which is also a site of one of the university centers of UWI. In 1974 the government awarded forty-four scholarships for study at UWI, eighteen for study in Great Britain, eleven for study in Canada, one for study in the United States, and nine for study in various other countries. The rest of the students were privately sponsored.

[Information supplied by Department of Education, Dominica.]

See also: Caribbean: Regional Analysis.

DOMINICAN REPUBLIC, THE

Population: 4,432,000. Student enrollment in primary school: 836,942; secondary school (academic, vocational, technical): 206,554; higher education (university): 30,000. Language of instruction: Spanish. Academic calendar: August/September to June/July, two semesters. Percentage of gross national product (GNP) expended on all education: 3%. Percentage of national budget expended on all education: 19%; higher education: approximately 5%. [Figures are for 1974. Source: Ministry of Education.]

Higher education in the Dominican Republic dates back to 1538, when Pope Paul III, through his Bull *In Apostulatus Culmine,* created *Universitas Santi Dominici,* thus founding the first university in the Americas (*Origen y evolución*, 1974, p. 3). It remained the only university in the country until 1962, surviving foreign intervention, revolution, internal chaos, and closure for long periods. The history of the university—which is closely interwoven with that of the country, since every major political change had an impact on the university—can be divided into three distinctive periods: (1) the Spanish colonial period, from the establishment of the university in 1538 until the declaration of independence in 1821; (2) the republican period, from 1821 until the end of the Trujillo era in 1961; and (3) the reformation period, since 1961.

The legacy of the Spanish period is still in evidence in the social structure and the educational system of the country. The national language and the cultural traditions of the Dominican Republic are Spanish. No indigenous culture has arisen on the island. The Spanish brought with them a rigid two-class social system, which is still prevalent despite the slow growth of a middle class.

After an initial period of economic and intellectual flowering, the colony entered a period of decline in the seventeenth century. In 1801 the country was overrun by Haitian conquerors, and the university was closed until 1815, when it was reopened through the efforts of José Núñez de Cáceres, who in 1821 declared the Dominican Republic independent. The first republic was short-lived, however; and in 1822 Haitian troups reoccupied the country, remaining in power until 1844. As during the first occupation, the university was forced to close while most of its students were drafted into military service. When the nation regained its independence in 1844, establishment of the university as a symbol of the country's cultural tradition became important. That same year a chair in Latin was established, a seminary opened in 1848, and the *Colegio San Buenaventura* was started in 1852. The establishment of these institutions signified a new beginning for the university, which was formally reestablished in 1859 but was again closed shortly thereafter, when the country was annexed to Spain in 1861 and had to fight for its independence.

After restoration of the republic in 1865, it took seventeen years until the Professional Institute was established on the foundations of the university. This institute became the University of Santo Domingo in 1914, during the presidency of Ramón Báez, who later served as rector of the university.

During the intervention by the United States, from 1916 to 1924, the university again entered a period of decline, which continued during the thirty years of Rafael Trujillo's dictatorship (1930–1961), when more emphasis was given to the physical plant than to academic achievement. After the overthrow of Trujillo in 1961, the university was renamed the *Universidad autónoma de Santo Domingo* (UASD: Autonomous University of Santo Domingo). The period since 1961 has been characterized by political changes and periods of unrest, leading in 1965 to a revolution and another intervention by the United States.

A movement for the renovation of the university resulted in internal reforms in 1966, when students and faculty gained increased participation in decision making. However, continued instability led to a departure from the university of some of the more conservative professors, who in 1966 established a private university, *Universidad nacional Pedro Henríquez Ureña*, with assistance from the business community and foundations in the United States. Another private university, the *Universidad católica madre y maestra,* had been founded in 1962 by the conference of Dominican bishops.

The colonial past is still in evidence in the Dominican Republic. Although the universities offer education of a high standard to some 30,000 students and primary education is free and compulsory, access to education is limited by factors such as social class and place of residence. Reforms instituted by the government since 1970, with the assistance of UNESCO and the

International Bank for Reconstruction, aim at alleviating the discrepancy between educational opportunity in the urban and rural areas and at expanding needed opportunities for intermediate-level training. This expansion—heralded in the educational reform for the secondary level of 1971, but severely restricted by financial problems and a lack of teachers—is projected to make it possible and desirable for greater numbers of students to attend school longer. When instituting the reform in 1971, the National Council of Education cited figures indicating that only 50 percent of all students entering first grade in the country successfully completed fourth grade *(Ordenanza,* 1970, p. 2).

Legal Basis of Educational System

The institutions of higher education in the Dominican Republic are established by law, and their right to award degrees is sanctioned by the government. UASD was granted its autonomous status and continued state support in Law 5778 of December 31, 1961; the private *Universidad católica madre y maestra* was recognized by Law 6150 of December 31, 1962; and the *Universidad nacional Pedro Henríquez Ureña* received its legal status by Law 1090 of March 21, 1967. The *Universidad central del este* was recognized in Presidential Decree 1205 of July 2, 1971. All private institutions of higher education are regulated by Law 236 of December 20, 1967, as to structure and right to award degrees.

Types of Institutions

Higher education in the Dominican Republic is offered only at the university level. It is available in one public university, UASD, which is composed of seven faculties: humanities, sciences, economic and social sciences, juridical sciences, engineering and architecture, medicine, agronomy and veterinary sciences, and in three private universities: (1) *Universidad nacional Pedro Henríquez Ureña*, with nine faculties: humanities, sciences, law and politics, engineering and technology, economic and social sciences, medical sciences, agronomy and veterinary study, sciences of education, architecture and arts; (2) *Universidad católica madre y maestra,* which offers fourteen programs leading to degree level, five at the level of technician, and one at postgraduate level; (3) the *Universidad Central del este,* founded in 1970 and inaugurated by Decree 1205 on July 2, 1971, with six faculties: medicine, engineering, sciences, economics and social sciences, law, and pedagogy. In 1974 it enrolled 38 percent of its 1700 students in preuniversity courses, and 38 percent of its students were foreigners, with about 85 percent of those enrolled in the medical faculty. The *Instituto tecnológico de Santo Domingo* (Technological Institute of Santo Domingo), which opened in 1972 as the country's only postgraduate institution, offers courses both at the degree and postgraduate levels.

Relationship with Secondary Education and Admission Requirements

Secondary education in the Dominican Republic lasts four years, based upon eight years of primary school, and is compulsory between the ages of seven to fourteen. In 1970 a reform was instituted by the government to restructure the first two levels of education. This reform, inplemented gradually, started with the 1970–71 school year and is expected to be effective in the whole country by 1978. It consolidates the school system into two levels: a six-year primary school and a six-year secondary school *(educación media).* The *educación media* is divided into a four-year general course *(ciclo común),* which is uniform for all students and leads to the *certificado oficial de suficiencia.* The *certificado* is necessary for access to the two-year higher cycle and also prepares students for intermediate positions in public administration or private enterprise. The higher cycle offers specialization in one of three fields: academic, technical, or teacher training studies. All three areas of specialization prepare students for higher education. Because of financial problems and lack of trained

teachers, the restructured system has not been implemented as widely as expected.

In the traditional system the secondary school certificate, *bachillerato,* is given in one of three fields: *ciencias físicas y naturales* (physical and natural sciences), *filosofía y letras* (philosophy and letters), and *matemáticas* (mathematics). The *bachillerato* is retained as the leaving certificate for two sections of the restructured schools: *bachillerato en ciencias y letras* for academic study and *bachillerato técnico* for technical studies in industrial, commercial, agricultural, or home economics programs. Graduates of the teacher training course receive the title *maestro primario* (primary teacher), qualifying them for teaching in the primary schools.

The leaving certificate from the secondary school, the *bachillerato* is a prerequisite for admission to higher education. In all higher institutions, except UASD, applicants must also pass an entrance examination.

Administration and Control

The supervision of education in the Dominican Republic is the responsibility of the Secretary of State for Education and Fine Arts and the National Council of Education. The state has assumed full financial responsibility for the Autonomous University of Santo Domingo (UASD) and also subsidizes the other institutions of higher learning, which must be recognized by the state before they can grant degrees. Recognition requires programs of study and standards equivalent to those at UASD.

UASD is unique in its concept of cogovernance, or one-third student representation on all academic bodies. The chief officer of all the universities is the rector, who at UASD is elected by the university assembly for two years, renewable for a second term. The rector has to be Dominican and a professor in active service with at least three years of teaching experience. At the National University Pedro Henríquez Ureña, the teaching experience required is five years and the rector is appointed for four years, renewable indefinitely by the establishing foundation.

The highest administrative authority at UASD is the university assembly, consisting of the rector as chairman, the two vice-rectors, the secretary general, the directors of all academic units, all professors, and student representatives. Among the duties of the assembly are election of the rector and vice-rectors, creation and revocation of administrative positions, creation and dissolution of faculties, approval and reform of statutes, and approval of the rector's annual report. The university council (composed of the rector as chairman, the two vice-rectors, the deans, one delegate of the academic organizations, and one-third student representation), among other responsibilities, is in charge of the budget; appoints professors after recommendation of the faculty assemblies; establishes academic standards; regulates admissions, examinations, and degrees; and approves the organization of new schools, departments, and institutes.

The basic units within the universities are the faculties, divided into schools, departments, or institutes. Each faculty is headed by a dean, who is assisted by a faculty assembly (consisting of the dean as chairman, the vice-dean as secretary, professors of the faculty in active service, and one-third student representation). The faculty assembly elects the dean (who has to fulfill the same qualifications as the rector), establishes a faculty budget for submission to the university council, and makes proposals to the university council regarding teaching staff and organization of the faculty. Technical councils within the faculties elaborate on and submit recommendations for programs, degrees, and internal faculty matters to the faculty assembly for consideration; they also suggest nominees for positions as directors of the schools, departments, and institutes.

The governing body of the private universities is generally the founding authority, such as the *Fundación universitaria dominicana* in the case of the National University

Pedro Henríquez Ureña. The internal structure of the private universities, although not as multilayered, is similar to that of UASD, generally consisting of a rector; university (academic) council; general assembly; faculties headed by a dean; and directors of schools, departments, and institutes. The council assists the rector in his administrative capacity, submits the annual budget, and suggests internal administrative and academic changes to the governing body. There is no student representation on the governing bodies of the private universities.

Programs and Degrees

Students at the universities are required to complete a *curso básico* (basic course) prior to entering the professional programs.

The universities generally offer programs at only two levels, the intermediate and professional. The intermediate level lasts two to three years and culminates with the award of the Certificate of Higher Study. Graduates of this short-cycle program work as technicians. Professional study leading to a professional title such as engineer, architect, or *licenciado* (which is awarded in fields such as business, humanities, sciences, education, and law) generally takes four to five years; medicine may take up to seven years. Engineering graduates have to work one year after graduation to be licensed as engineers by the government.

Most students go abroad for graduate study, mainly to the United States. The only postgraduate programs at UASD are in medicine and lead to a postgraduate certificate. The *Universidad católica madre y maestra* offers a postgraduate program in public administration and awards the title *magister* to successful graduates. The Technological Institute of Santo Domingo, which opened in 1972 as the only postgraduate institution in the Dominican Republic, offers programs in industrial engineering, agricultural economy, and business administration. It also offers four-year undergraduate programs leading to academic titles in engineering, economics, business administration, accounting, social sciences, and medicine. The medical title awarded, *médico general* (or general physician), requires six years of study. Enrollment at the institution is still low.

Financing

According to law, the Autonomous University of Santo Domingo receives most of its financing from the government, which commits 5 percent of the national budget to this purpose. Additional sources of income are fees and donations. The private universities also receive small government subsidies, but they derive their main income from student fees and donations from industry and private parties.

Foreign assistance has also been received, especially by the *Universidad católica madre y maestra*, which established its engineering faculty with assistance from UNESCO and has received financial support from international sources such as the Agency for International Development (AID) and the Ford Foundation in the United States.

Student Financial Aid

Education at UASD is free, and students pay only a nominal yearly registration fee. During the Trujillo period scholarships were available; but the reformation movement in the 1960s opposed these scholarships, charging that they were awarded only to the rich and for services performed for the government. As a result, student financial assistance was changed from scholarships to educational credits *(créditos educativos),* which can consist of a monthly allowance, credits for free meals, and credits and waivers for registration fees. The educational credits are awarded on the basis of economic need and study results. Credits and waivers of the registration fees are also given to members of cultural associations at the university, students on work brigades, and students who achieve more than 85 percent success on their examinations.

Although educational credits are avail-

able only to a small number of students, UASD, through the services of the Department of Student Welfare, provides other types of student assistance, such as low-cost meals, transportation and health services, and a student discount shop.

The private universities charge monthly fees, generally on a sliding scale depending on the parents' income. The *Universidad católica madre y maestra* has arranged for loans for students who lack the financial means for study.

Student Social Background and Access to Education

Due to the specific socioeconomic background of the population (which consists mainly of two classes with a small middle class), most students tend to be urban and financially well off. Fewer educational opportunities are available to the rural population (some 60 percent of the total population). Many rural schools offer education only through the fourth grade, and illiteracy is high. The level of teacher training, especially among teachers in the rural areas, has been of concern to the government, which, in connection with the 1970 educational reform, has specifically addressed itself to upgrading teacher training.

Students in the Dominican Republic are politically active. Their participation in the reform movement since 1961, through strikes and demonstrations, led to the granting in 1966 of one-third student representation on all decision-making bodies at UASD. This political participation has at the same time led to internal instability at UASD. Students in the private universities are less active politically and do not take part in decision making.

Teaching Staff

The teaching and research staff at the University of Santo Domingo are divided into the following categories: ordinary professors and assistants, and temporary professors and assistants. Ordinary professors perform both teaching and research functions; temporary professors generally do not undertake research. Assistants are divided into two ranks, monitor and assistant to the professor. Appointments are made after a competitive examination.

The ranks of the academic staff are full professor *(profesor titular),* associate professor *(profesor adjunto),* and lecturer *(profesor adscrito).* The academic career is started with appointment as *profesor adscrito* after a competitive examination. The duties of this rank include both theoretical and practical teaching, supervision and coordination of assistants, and participation in research activities. Evaluation of performance is once a year by the technical councils, which make their recommendations to the university council for continued appointment. Promotion to the following rank is by competitive examination after recommendation by the technical councils *(Estatuto,* 1973, pp. 43–44).

The ranks and conditions of employment are similar at the other universities.

About 85 percent of the professors are employed part time and paid by the hour. They derive their main income from outside activities; however, a teaching appointment at one of the universities is considered prestigious; therefore, candidates are not lacking.

Current Problems and Trends

The universities in the Dominican Republic offer education of a high quality but limit themselves mainly to the first degree, or title. Students desiring graduate degrees have to go abroad. This, in addition to the part-time nature of most of the professorial appointments, contributes to a low level of research at the institutions of higher education. A postgraduate institution, the Technological Institute of Santo Domingo, opened in 1972 but has not expanded rapidly.

The programs at the universities lead to the traditional professional titles: engineer, architect, medical doctor, lawyer. There is less emphasis on technology and science. Few intermediate personnel are available in the country. The difference between a technician certificate and a pro-

fessional title is generally just one year of study, and the rewards of the full degree are much greater.

The lack of diversification at the secondary level is being addressed in the 1970 government reform, which aims at an expansion of vocational offerings; however, due to restraints such as financing and poor teacher preparation, the new programs have been extended only to a small number of the public schools. Financial assistance in the form of loans received through the World Bank is expected to help expand the new programs, which are intended to make education more relevant to the students who previously did not consider education beyond primary school due to financial and social restraints. Technological progress in the country requires diversified training of the population at many levels.

International Cooperation

Most students get their professional title in the Dominican Republic but go abroad for graduate study, generally to the United States. The universities also have arrangements for cooperation with universities abroad; for instance, the *Universidad nacional Pedro Henríquez Ureña* cooperates with the State University of New York at Oswego and has received research assistance from the Federal Republic of Germany. The *Universidad católica madre y maestra* has received assistance from UNESCO, which organized the university's engineering department and provided teaching staff and laboratory equipment; the Agency for International Development (AID); and the Ford Foundation in the United States. Further assistance from UNESCO and loans from the World Bank have mainly benefited the two lower levels of education.

[Information submitted by the Secretary of State for Education, Fine Arts and Culture and the Dominican National Commission for UNESCO.]

Bibliography

Adams, D., and Bjork, R. M. *Education in Developing Areas.* New York: McKay, 1968.

Estatuto orgánico 1966. Santo Domingo: Universidad autónoma de Santo Domingo, 1973.

Gobierno, estructura académica, carreras ofrecidas 1970–1971. Santo Domingo: Universidad nacional Pedro Henríquez Ureña, 1970.

Ley orgánica de educación y leyes que la modifican. Santo Domingo: Secretaría de estado de educación, bellas artes y culto, 1971.

Ordenanza número 1/1970. Santo Domingo: Secretaría de estado de educación, bellas artes y culto, 1970.

Origen y evolución de la Universidad autónoma de Santo Domingo. Santo Domingo: UASD, Departamento de extensión cultural y acción social, 1974.

Parker, P. "Change and Challenge in Caribbean Higher Education." Unpublished doctoral thesis, Florida State University, Tallahassee, 1971.

Wiarda, H. J. *The Dominican Republic: Nation in Transition.* New York: Praeger, 1969.

Williams, E. *From Columbus to Castro: The History of the Caribbean 1942–1969.* London: André Deutsch, 1970.

See also: Archives: Mediterranean, the Vatican, and Latin America, National Archives of.

DRAFTING AND DESIGN
(Field of Study)

The term *drafting* has been used in engineering and technology to denote the skills needed to communicate accurately the size and shape of objects and/or systems. Around 1960 drafting in most educational institutions became known as *graphics*. Graphics encompasses the activities of drafting, but it also employs the principles of drawing to analyze a design concept. Hence, one may find similar curricula leading to specialization in "drafting and design" or in "graphics and design," but the term *graphics* generally denotes a broader concern.

Pictures have been used for thousands of years to communicate technical thinking. The construction of the Egyptian pyramids, for example, followed the recorded plans which are believed to have been made on papyrus. Records are available of the plans made by Leonardo da Vinci of such inventions as the flying apparatus and the great crossbow. But a standard system of drawing, without the use of extensive verbal explanations, was not developed until the latter part of the eighteenth century, when Gaspard Monge, a mathematician at the military school in Mézières, France, developed the science of descriptive geometry. The new science, which was developed to eliminate the laborious mathematical computations necessary to design fortifications, provided a graphic solution in the form of drawings to communicate design ideas. These drawings were based on a series of interrelated views of a line, plane, or solid object which identify two perpendicular dimensions and which were developed by a method called *orthographic projection*. A draftsman employs such instruments as a pencil, compass, 30°–60°–90° and 45°–45°–90° triangles, french (irregular) curves, and circle and ellipse templates to produce orthographic drawings. Although modifications have been made through the years, the principles of orthographic projection have not changed for centuries.

Claude Crozet—who had studied at the *Ecole polytechnique* in France, where Gaspard Monge was a professor—became the first professor of engineering at the United States Military Academy in 1816; there he introduced the methods developed by Monge. Although the academy had had a drawing design department since 1803, engineering drawing skills were not taught until after 1820. Later, other schools of engineering recognized the value of the orthographic projection system of drawing objects and began to include it in their curricula. The first known textbook on engineering drawing as a discipline was written by Thomas E. French of Ohio State University and published in 1911.

Early technical institutes called their curriculum or courses "drafting and design" because they emphasized the drafting of objects that were already designed. But when departments of engineering education began to emphasize science and research, instructors of drafting and of engineering drawing felt that they must follow suit or watch their discipline be dropped from engineering education. They therefore began to teach graphical calculus, empirical equations solved graphically, pictorial drawings of solid geometric figures, and other graphical mathematics. The name of the discipline was changed to "engineering graphics" or "graphic science" to reflect these changes. However, the discipline's prestige began to fade because many engineering educators considered it unnecessary for professional expertise.

After years of trial and error, design processes were developed which enabled graphics (formerly drafting) to be reunited with design. The definition of *design* as a plan or idea expressed in visible form was the basis for the drafting and design curriculum, which emphasized the training of skills to express ideas graphically. After the development of the design processes, however, the term denoted the application of knowledge to create new systems and/or objects.

A graphics course in the "graphics and design" curriculum usually includes the development of drafting skills, orthographic projections, pictorial drawings, dimensioning methods, and conventional practices used to clearly describe an object, a system, or other ideas. The aspects of such a course which relate to design may include the development of a design process, the study of human factors to be considered in design, methods of making maximum use of one's creative abilities, production processes, and methods of presenting design ideas.

In the 1970s technical schools offer associate degrees and bachelor's degrees in graphics and design. Although the curriculum may be called "graphics and design" or "drafting and design," it is often found as a specialization in another major area of study, such as mechanical engineering technology. Other curricula in this area, leading to the associate degree, can include drafting, design, architectural drafting, drafting and tool design, and structural design. These programs also generally include courses in graphics, design, mathematics, physics, and basic courses in engineering.

Schools that offer the bachelor's degree in graphics and design specializations generally require courses in the liberal arts, business, and other professional studies. Although graduate programs are not yet available, holders of bachelor's degrees can continue in a more general curriculum, such as mechanical engineering technology, structural technology, or electrical engineering technology. Opportunities available to graduates of the engineering technology programs seem to be equal to those for graduates of engineering programs of comparable length.

Drafting and design is found in various engineering and/or technology curricula throughout the world. A few countries—such as Australia, Iran, and Israel—offer this discipline as a major area of study. Generally, however, drafting and design programs are part of a degree-granting curriculum in institutions of higher education where engineering or technology is taught. Since there is much exchange of technical information as well as manufactured products and processes, the basic standards for the study of drafting and design are the same despite slight variations in the name of the discipline.

BORAH L. KREIMER

Levels and Programs of Study

Programs in drafting and design generally require as a minimum prerequisite a secondary education and lead to a certificate or diploma or to an associate's or bachelor's degree. Programs consist primarily of classroom and practice sessions dealing with the principles and practices of drawing blueprints (for buildings, machinery, and other subjects) and plans (for layouts of streets, public works, and community development). The programs may last from one to three or more years.

Principal course content usually includes mechanical drawing and engineering drawing; the use of equipment such as the pantograph and other drawing instruments; mathematics, including plane geometry, trigonometry, and algebra; basic engineering subjects such as applied mechanics, engineering graphics, theory of structures, and electrical circuitry; and usually some related subjects such as surveying, principles of architecture, town planning, and photogrammetry.

[This section was based on UNESCO's *International Standard Classification of Education (ISCED): Three Stage Classification System, 1974* (Paris: UNESCO, 1974).]

Major International and National Organizations

INTERNATIONAL

World Congress for Engineering Graphics
%Amarillo College
Amarillo, Texas 79105 USA
This organization is being established at the date of publication of this encyclopedia.

NATIONAL

United Kingdom:
 Institution of Engineering Designers
 1 Earle's Lane
 London EC1, England

United States:
 American Institute for Design and
 Drafting
 3119 Price Road
 Bartlesville, Oklahoma 74003

 Engineering Design Graphics Division
 American Society for Engineering
 Education
 One Dupont Circle
 Washington, D.C. 20036

Principal Information Sources

GENERAL

Guides to the literature of drafting and design include:

Siddall, J. N. *Mechanical Design Reference Sources.* Toronto, Ontario: University of Toronto Press, 1967.

General introductions to the field are provided by:

Beakley, G. C. *Introduction to Engineering Design and Graphics.* New York: Macmillan, 1973.
French, T. E., and Vierck, C. J. *Engineering Drawing and Graphic Technology.* (11th ed.) New York: McGraw-Hill, 1972.
Giesecke, F. E., Mitchell, A., Spencer, H. C., and Hill, I. L. *Technical Drawing.* (6th ed.) New York: Macmillan, 1974.
Hill, P. H. *The Science of Engineering Design.* New York: Holt, Rinehart and Winston, 1970.

Some additional textbooks and manuals are:

American Institute of Steel Construction. *Structural Steel Detailing.* (2nd ed.) New York: American Institute of Steel Construction, 1971.
Baer, C. J. *Electrical and Electronics Drawing.* (3rd ed.) New York: McGraw-Hill, 1973.
Coleman, R. M. *Technical Drafting: Aerospace/Electrical-Electronics/Structural.* Corte Madera, California: Rinehart, 1971.
McKelvey, K. K. *Drawing for the Structural Concrete Engineer.* London: Cement and Concrete Association, 1974.
Prestressed Concrete Institute. *Architectural Precast Concrete Drafting Handbook.* Englewood Cliffs, New Jersey: Prentice-Hall, 1975.
Raskhodoff, N. M. *Electronic Drafting and Design.* Englewood Cliffs, New Jersey: Prentice-Hall, 1972.
Weidhaas, E. R. *Architectural Drafting and Construction.* Boston: Allyn & Bacon, 1974.

A historical account of the field is offered by:

Booker, P. J. *A History of Engineering Drawing.* London: Chatto and Windus, 1963.

For a discussion of design in engineering education see:

Glenister, S. H. *The Teaching of Technical Drawing.* London: Harrap, 1966.
Teare, B. R. "Design." In N. A. Hall (Ed.), *Britannica Review of Developments in Engineering Education.* Chicago: Encyclopaedia Britannica, 1970.

Works that deal with drafting and design as a career include:

DeLong, F. J. *Aim for a Job in Drafting.* New York: Richards Rosen Press, 1968.
Hollyhock, W. S. *Engineering Draughtsmanship as a Career.* London: Museum Press, 1964.

CURRENT BIBLIOGRAPHIES

The following abstracting and indexing services are important sources of current information in the field:

Applied Science and Technology Index. New York: Wilson, 1913–.
British Technology Index. London: Library Association, 1962–.
Engineering Index. New York: Engineering Index, Inc., 1884–.

PERIODICALS

Important journals in the field include *Design and Components in Engineering* (UK), *Design Engineering* (Canada), *Engineering Designer* (UK), *Engineering Design Graphics Journal* (US), *Engineering Design Service* (UK), *Engineering Education* (US), *Engineering Materials and Design* (UK), *Machine Design* (US).

For additional titles see:

Ulrich's International Periodicals Directory. New York: Bowker, biennial.

ENCYCLOPEDIAS, HANDBOOKS, DICTIONARIES

General engineering reference sources which include information on drafting, design, or mechanical drawing include:

Arnell, A. *Standard Graphical Symbols.* New York: McGraw-Hill, 1963.

Jones, F. D., and Schubert, P. B. *Engineering Encyclopedia.* New York: Industrial Press, 1963. A condensed encyclopedia and mechanical dictionary.

McGraw-Hill Encyclopedia of Science and Technology. New York: McGraw-Hill, 1971.

Potter, J. H. *Handbook of the Engineering Sciences.* (2 vols.) New York: Van Nostrand Reinhold, 1967.

DIRECTORIES

Directory of Engineering College Research and Graduate Study. Washington, D.C.: American Society for Engineering Education, annual. Supplement to the journal *Engineering Education;* lists research and graduate programs available at institutions in the United States, Puerto Rico, and Canada.

DRAMATIC ARTS
See Theater Arts (field of study).

DRAWING AND PAINTING
(Field of Study)

Two of the oldest and most closely related forms of expression in the visual arts are drawing and painting. Although formal definitions of these two modes vary considerably, it has always been difficult to determine exactly where, especially in particular works of art, drawing leaves off and painting begins, or vice versa. The *New Encyclopaedia Britannica* (Vol. 5, pp. 992–993) defines drawing as the "primary linear rendition of objects in the visible world, as well as of concepts, thoughts, attitudes, emotions, and fantasies given visual form, of symbols and even of abstract forms . . . techniques that are characterized by an emphasis on form or shape rather than mass and colour, as in painting. . . . Furthermore, because of the immediacy of its statement, drawing expresses the draftsman's personality spontaneously in the flow of the line; it is, in fact, the most personal of all artistic statements." The same reference (Vol. 13, p. 869) defines painting as "the expression of ideas and emotions, with the creation of certain aesthetic qualities, in a two-dimensional visual language . . . in order to represent real or supernatural phenomena, to interpret a narrative theme, or to create wholly abstract visual relationships."

Many drawings, however, go well beyond representing or outlining an object by lines, and some drawings emphasize "mass and color" as well as "form and shape"; yet these works are not generally considered to be paintings. For example, some artists (including many Orientals) "draw" with a brush, and some artists produce masses of color by holding their pencils in a near-flat position as they create blended or solid tonal effects on paper, or even canvas, plaster, or plastic surfaces. Pastels, moreover, are produced in pencil-like sticks and are often used like pencils to "draw" lines of color. They are also often used while held flat upon the surface of paper or canvas. But whether they are used up-ended or flat, the finished results are called paintings, not drawings. Two other new media also create definitional problems: "paint sticks," oil paints in seal-wrapped, stick form, with which one "draws" upon canvas, paper, or other surfaces; and "oil crayons," a stick-shaped, oil-based (rather than gum arabic or other binder) medium with which one also "draws" or rubs color on various surfaces. Consequently, higher education courses and professional exhibitions ostensibly limited to drawing sometimes include painting, and vice versa. One also finds drawings and/or paintings which include collage and three-dimensional, even sculptural, elements such as plaster, wood, plastic, metal, sand, and stones, as well as some which incorporate craft elements and processes such as embedded or attached jewels, stitchery, and macramé.

The basic nature of drawing and/or painting has not changed much over the years. Despite certain changes in ingredients, tools, and techniques as civilizations have alternately become more or less sophisticated, most artists who draw still prefer conventional pencils, charcoal sticks, metal- or quill-point pens, and wax-based crayons or chalks, and a few use mechanically propelled lead pencils or felt-tip or ball-point pens. Most artists who paint still use brushes identical to those used centuries ago. Although some painters prefer acrylic paints and acrylic fiber brushes to more conventional paints and brushes, there is an increasing trend away from acrylic painting and felt-tip or ball-point pen drawing back to the more conventional—and, indeed, more permanent and versatile—media of oil, watercolor, and, to a lesser extent, tempera and gouache painting. (Tempera and gouache are opaque, water-based paints; the former sometimes incorporates whole-egg admixtures, and the latter may be purchased in a premixed form or may be made by adding opaque, such as Chinese, white to transparent watercolor paints.)

Drawing and painting courses and degree programs developed mainly in the twentieth century. Postsecondary education which does not lead to college degrees or diplomas, however, can be traced back to at least 1100 B.C. For example, the progeny of Chinese ruling-class members of the Early Chou period (1122–721 B.C.) were taught calligraphy, a brush-writing technique that combines drawing and painting. Considering their artistic sophistication, even prehistoric cave artists and the painters and draftsmen of early Egyptian and other ancient civilizations may be said to have received the artistic (and probably even the liberal arts) equivalent of higher education in the 1970s. The master-apprentice teaching method of these prehistoric and ancient cultures is still utilized and has been introduced in degree-granting higher education programs.

The teaching of drawing preceded that of painting as a formal subject; for example, as early as the fourth century B.C., Aristotle indicated, in his treatise on the ideal city-state, that students "may be taught drawing . . . because it makes them judges of the beauty of the human form. To be always seeking after the useful does not become free and exalted souls." From the sixth to the thirteenth century, there were a few "centres of drawing": "the scriptoria of the monasteries of Corbie and Reims in France, as well as those of Canterbury and Winchester in England, and also a few places in southern Germany, where various strongly delineatory (graphically illustrated) styles of book illustration were cultivated" (*Encyclopedia of Education*, Vol. 5., p. 1007).

The first academies of art were founded in the late sixteenth and early seventeenth centuries. In the early eighteenth century, a number of art schools based upon the French Academy model were established in England, culminating in 1768 with the Royal Academy, a group of never more than forty mutually elected artists (presumably art school graduates) who were felt to deserve this honor. But just as the French Revolution had "brought down" the French Academy in 1793, and re-formed it as the *Commune des arts* under the leadership of the painter Jacques Louis David, so too in England the industrial revolution led to the creation of government-supported art schools; by 1864 ninety of these schools provided college-level instruction in the arts. Similar institutions were founded in many European cities, particularly in Germany, Austria, and the Netherlands. But the "fine arts" and "applied arts" were taught in separate institutions and, in some cases, still are.

In the late nineteenth century, the art critic John Ruskin and the poet and craftsman William Morris, both of whom sought to devise means of humanizing the industrial revolution, were instrumental in reviving public and professional interest in hand-crafted objects and in creating a number of English schools (most notably the London Central School of Arts and Crafts, established in 1896) in which both the fine and the applied arts were taught. This idea spread to Germany, where, in a considerably enlarged and more sophisticated form, it gave rise to the *Bauhaus,* which was established in 1919 by the architect Walter Gropius. He believed that "all students, whether they intended to become fine artists or applied artists, should receive basically the same training. He stated also that no one should be admitted to an art school without first having learned a trade in a workshop or trade school. . . . The *Bauhaus* ideal was to unite all arts and crafts to create a new architecture that comprised a living environment; to break down the false separation between the applied arts and the fine arts, between art and utility; and to train artists in the creative possibilities of machine design" (*Encyclopaedia Britannica,* Vol. 1, p. 95).

Gropius and his many influential colleagues and students (such as László Moholy-Nagy, Josef Albers, and Gyorgy Kepes) argued for including—and even featuring—the arts in programs of higher education. Largely as a result of their efforts and accomplishments, the subsequent decades of the twentieth century saw drawing and painting—as well as the related and sometimes combined arts of photography, printmaking, sculpture, and the crafts—become slowly but steadily an accepted part of the curricula of higher education.

Drawing and painting as studio-practice subjects are now offered as undergraduate courses, course sequences, minors, majors, and degree programs in institutions of higher education throughout most of the world, leading to such degrees as the Bachelor of Fine Arts (B.F.A.), Bachelor of Arts (B.A.), Bachelor of Science (B.S.), Bachelor of Education (B.Ed.), and a variety of certificates and diplomas, including the British Diploma of Art and Design (D.A.D.). A smaller number of colleges, universities,

professional art schools, and academies—particularly in the United States, but also in England, India, Japan, and South Africa—offer graduate programs in drawing and painting, some of which lead to advanced degrees such as the Master of Fine Arts (M.F.A.), Master of Arts (M.A.), Master of Science (M.S.), Master of Education (M.Ed.), and, in rare cases (probably only in the United States), to the Doctor of Fine Arts (D.F.A.), Doctor of Arts (D.A.), Doctor of Philosophy (Ph.D.), Doctor of Education (Ed.D.), and various diplomas or certificates.

The teaching of drawing and painting in institutions of higher learning throughout most of the world has been enhanced but also made more uniform (to the occasional detriment of regional uniqueness) by the establishment of professional organizations such as the International Society for Education Through Art (INSEA). Founded in the late 1940s by the British art critic Sir Herbert Read and a group of his professional colleagues in the United States, Germany, France, Italy, the Netherlands, Yugoslavia, and Japan, INSEA promoted creativity in the teaching of drawing and painting in elementary and secondary schools, teachers colleges, universities, and art schools in most of the developed countries. National organizations, such as the National Art Education Association in the United States and similar professional groups in the Netherlands, France, and Japan, contributed to the dissemination of similarly "creative" philosophies of teaching drawing and painting. These organizations have become less one-sided and have recommended, as alternatives to "pure" creativity, such teaching-learning techniques as interpreting the works of early master artists; expressing oneself through concept formations; and providing step-by-step directions on watercolor, oil, and acrylic painting, as well as a variety of drawing media.

Colleges, universities, professional art schools, and academies throughout the world attract many students to their courses and programs in the studio arts of drawing and painting. Studio work in drawing and painting usually is augmented by art historical studies, as well as by studio experiences in printmaking, photography, sculpture, and the crafts; and in most institutions liberal arts courses are also required of degree, diploma, or certificate candidates. Institutions of higher education also have realized the importance of inviting artists to teach their studio courses in drawing or painting, and in many instances they have waived their usual "earned advanced degree" requirement for widely acclaimed professional artists who are able to teach drawing and painting courses at the undergraduate or graduate level.

[Notes: *Encyclopedia of Education* (New York: Macmillan, 1971). *The New Encyclopaedia Britannica* (Chicago: Encyclopaedia Britannica, 1974).]

HOWARD CONANT

Levels and Programs of Study

Programs in drawing and painting usually require as a minimum prerequisite a secondary education and/or demonstrated skill or talent in drawing or painting and lead to the following awards: certificate or diploma, bachelor's degree (B.A., B.F.A.), master's degree (M.A., M.F.A.), the doctorate (Ph.D., D.F.A.), or their equivalents. Programs are designed to provide professional training and develop skill in drawing and painting for professional, cultural, or recreational purposes and consist of lectures, seminars, group discussions, demonstrations, and studio practice sessions.

Programs that lead to an award not equivalent to a first university degree emphasize the practical applications of drawing and painting. Programs normally are given on a full- or part-time basis in a college of art and last the equivalent of from one to three years, full time. The chief aim of the program is the development of skill in drawing and painting, but related prescribed courses may be included in design, freehand drawing, history of art, lettering or calligraphy, theory of color, and silk-screen printing.

Programs that lead to a first university degree are designed to provide a broad background and basic professional training in drawing and painting, with emphasis on both theory and practice. Programs usually last from three to five years in a university or a college of art. They consist of a number of prescribed courses in subjects designed to provide a core or foundation in drawing and painting (such subjects as basic drawing, design, freehand drawing, history of art, lettering, theory of color, calligraphy, and silk screen printing) as well as a number of liberal arts courses such as the literature of the indigenous language, history, social science, foreign languages, philosophy, and some elective courses, possibly in some specific field of emphasis.

Programs that lead to a postgraduate university degree are designed to prepare specialists in drawing or painting. Through study, seminars, studio work, and independent research, students acquire a comprehensive knowledge of some specialty within the broad areas of drawing and painting, such as the theory of color, basic forms, analysis of the visual arts, life drawing, and lettering. Programs usually last between one and three years, full time, in a university or college of art and may consist of a certain number of prescribed courses, the achievement of a professional standard in the particular art form, demonstrated facility in one or more foreign languages, and the preparation of a thesis or dissertation based on original research into a particular problem within the major subject.

[This section was based on UNESCO's *International Standard Classification of Education (ISCED)* (Paris: UNESCO, 1976).]

Major International and National Organizations

INTERNATIONAL

International Association of Art—Painting, Sculpture, Graphic Art (IAA)
Association internationale des arts plastiques
UNESCO House
1 rue Miollis
75015 Paris, France

International Association of Art Critics
Association internationale des critiques d'art
Palais du Louvre, Pavillon de Marsan
107 rue de Rivoli
75001 Paris, France

International Society for Education Through
    Art (INSEA)
106 rue du Point du Jour
92100 Boulogne-sur-Seine, France

NATIONAL

Australia:
    Australia Council
    168 Walker Street
    Box 302
    North Sydney, New South Wales, 2060

Austria:
    Künstlerhaus
    Karlsplatz 5
    Vienna 1

Belgium:
    Association des artistes professionnels
        de Belgique
    461 avenue Louise
    Brussels

Brazil:
    Sindicato des compositores, artísticos,
        musicais e plásticos do estado de
        São Paulo
    São Paulo

Canada:
    Canadian Council
    151 Sparks Street
    P.O. Box 1047
    Ottawa, Ontario

Cuba:
    Centro regional de la UNESCO en el
        Hemisferio occidental
    Calle 5 No. 306, Apartado 1358
    Havana

Denmark:
    Malende kunstneres sammenslutning
    Nørregade 33
    Copenhagen

France:
    Société des artistes indépendants
    Grand Palais des Champs-Elysées
    avenue Winston Churchill, Porte H
    Paris 8e

    Société nationale des beaux-arts
    11 rue Berryer
    Paris 8e

Israel:
    Association of Painters and Sculptors
    9 Alharizi Street
    Tel Aviv

Italy:
    Comitato nazionale delle arti plastiche
    Largo Villa Massimo 2
    Rome

Mexico:
    Instituto nacional de bellas artes
    Palacio de bellas artes
    Mexico 1, D.F.

Netherlands:
    Pulchri Studio (Society of Painters,
        Sculptors, Engravers)
    Large Voorhout 15
    The Hague

People's Republic of China:
    All China Association of Fine
        Arts Workers
    Peking

Republic of China:
    China Art Association
    13 Section 2, Shanghai Road
    Taipei

Soviet Union:
    Union of USSR Artists
    Gogolouski bul 10, Moscow

Spain:
    Asociación national de pintores y
        escultores de España
    Infantas 30
    Madrid

United Kingdom:
    Arts Council of Great Britain
    105 Piccadilly
    London W1, England

    Federation of British Artists
    17 Carlton House Terrace
    London SW, England

United States:
    American Federation of Arts
    41 East 65th Street
    New York, New York 10021

    College Art Association of America
    16 East 52nd Street
    New York, New York 10022

    National Art Education Association
    1916 Association Drive
    Reston, Virginia 22091

    National Association of Schools of Art
    11250 Roger Bacon Drive
    Reston, Virginia 22090

For additional international and national
organizations see:

International Directory of Arts. (2 vols.) Berlin,
    Federal Republic of Germany: Art Adress

Verlag Müller GMBH, 1952/53–. Published biennially.

The World of Learning. London: Europa, 1947–. Published annually.

Principal Information Sources

GENERAL

Guides to the literature in the field include:

Carrick, N. *How to Find Out About the Arts: A Guide to Sources of Information.* Elmsford, New York: Pergamon Press, 1965.

Chamberlin, M. W. *Guide to Art Reference Books.* Chicago: American Library Association, 1959. A standard reference work in the field. See pages 152–223 for sections on drawing and painting.

Dove, J. *Fine Arts.* London: Clive Bingley, 1966. A selective bibliographical essay in the fine arts. See pages 31–39 for section on painting.

Goldman, B. *Reading and Writing in the Arts: A Handbook.* Detroit: Wayne State University Press, 1972.

Gould, B. E. *A Basic Guide to Literature on the History of Painting in the Occidental Tradition: A Thesis Submitted for the Fellowship of the Library Association.* (4 vols.) London: Library Association, 1966.

Keaveney, S. S. *American Painting: A Guide to Information Sources.* Art and Architecture: An Information Guide Series. Detroit: Gale Research, 1974.

Lucas, E. L. *Art Books: A Basic Bibliography on the Fine Arts.* Greenwich, Connecticut: New York Graphic Society, 1968. An unannotated listing. See pages 71–95 for sections on drawing and painting.

McColvin, E. R. *Painting, A Guide to the Best Books . . .* London: Grafton, 1934.

Rogers, A. R. *The Humanities: A Selective Guide to Reference Sources.* Littleton, Colorado: Libraries Unlimited, 1974.

Some important introductions and histories are:

Barr, A. H. *What Is Modern Painting?* New York: Museum of Modern Art, 1949.

Gaunt, W. *A Guide to the Understanding of Painting.* New York: Abrams, 1968.

Great Centuries of Painting. New York: Skira, 1952–.

Haftmann, W. *Painting in the 20th Century.* (2nd ed., 2 vols.) New York: Praeger, 1965.

Kulturmann, V. *The New Painting.* (Translated by G. Orn.) New York: Praeger, 1970.

Newton, E. *An Introduction to European Painting.* Essex, England: Longman, 1949.

Newton, E. *Painting and Sculpture.* Middlesex, England: Penguin, 1950.

Popham, A. E. *A Handbook of the Drawings and Watercolors in the Department of Prints and Drawings, British Museum.* London: British Museum, Department of Prints and Drawings, 1944.

Read, H. *A Concise History of Modern Painting.* New York: Praeger, 1959.

Robb, D. M. *The Harper History of Painting: The Occidental Tradition.* New York: Harper & Row, 1951.

Rose, B. *Readings in American Art: 1900–1975.* New York: Praeger, 1975.

Sirén, O. *Chinese Painting: Leading Masters and Principles.* (7 vols.) New York: Ronald Press, 1956–1958.

Some works dealing with comparative education, research, and national education are:

Adlers, M. "Painting and Teaching." *Art Education,* June 1972, *25,* 5–7.

Art Education: An International Survey. Paris: UNESCO, 1972. Countries included are Argentina, Australia, Czechoslovakia, France, Federal Republic of Germany, India, Italy, Japan, Nigeria, United Kingdom, United States, and the Soviet Union.

Artistic Education. New York: Istituto italiano di cultura, 1969. Detailed information on study facilities on all levels in Italy.

Art/1975: The Journal of the Professional Artist. Paris: International Association of Art, 1975. Entire issue No. 70 is devoted to "UNESCO Project: The Education of Artists. A Report on Experimental and Advanced Programmes for the Education of Painters-Sculptors, Craftsmen, Graphic Designers, Industrial Designers."

Ascot, R. "Art Education in Canada." *Studio International,* October 1972, *184*(948), 139–140.

Bryce, M. *Fine Arts Education in the Soviet Union.* Washington, D.C.: U.S. Office of Education, 1963.

Conant, H. *Art Education.* New York: Center for Applied Research in Education, 1964.

Fuller, N. L. *A Beginning Painting Course for Undergraduate College Students.* New York: Columbia University Press, 1970.

"International Education Year: Summary Report of the Second International Conference on the Professional Training of the Artist, Belgrade, Yugoslavia, 18–24 May, 1970." *Art: The Journal of the Professional Artist,* 1971/72, *64/65,* 10–13.

"The Professional Training of the Artist, International Conference, London, 8–14 June, 1965." *Information Bulletin: International Association of Art,* April 1966, *57/58,* 3–24.

Rothenstein, M. "Contrasts: English and American Art Students." *Studio International,* December 1972, *184,* 248–249.

Journals that often include articles on art education are *Art Education: Journal of the National Art Association* (US), *Art Journal* (US), and *Studies in Art Education* (US).

CURRENT BIBLIOGRAPHIES

Art Bibliographies: Current Titles. Santa Barbara, California: ABC-Clio, 1972–.

Art Bibliographies: Modern. Santa Barbara, California: ABC-Clio, 1973–. Annual bibliography of books and journal articles on twentieth-century art. Formerly *LOMA: Literature on Modern Art;* published 1969–1972.

Art Index. New York: Wilson, 1933–.

Education Index. New York: Wilson, 1929–.

PERIODICALS

Some of the many important periodical publications that cover the areas of drawing and painting and art education are *African Arts* (US), *American Art Journal, Antike Kunst* (Switzerland), *Apollo* (UK), *Art Bulletin* (US), *Art Education* (US), *Artforum* (US), *Art International* (Switzerland), *Art Journal (College Art Journal)* (US), *Art: The Journal of the Professional Artist* (France), *Art News* (US), *Art Quarterly* (US), *Arts Canada, Bollettino d'arte* (Italy), *Burlington Magazine* (UK), *Canadian Art, Marsyas* (US), *Master Drawings* (US), *Oud-Holland* (Netherlands), *Pantheon* (FRG), *Studies in Art Education* (US), *Studio International* (UK).

For additional titles see:

Chicago Art Institute, Ryerson Library. *Index to Art Periodicals.* (11 vols.) Boston: Hall, 1962.

Ulrich's International Periodicals Directory. New York: Bowker, biennial.

ENCYCLOPEDIAS AND DICTIONARIES

Berckelaers, F. L. (Ed.) *A Dictionary of Abstract Painting, Preceded by a History of Abstract Painting by Michel Seuphor.* New York: Tudor, 1957.

Conant, H. (Ed.) *Lincoln Library of the Arts.* (2 vols.) Columbus, Ohio: Frontier Press, 1973.

Encyclopedia of World Art. (15 vols.) New York: McGraw-Hill, 1959–1968.

Gaunt, W. *Everyman's Dictionary of Pictorial Art.* (2 vols.) New York: Dutton, 1962.

Kindler's Malerei Lexikon. (6 vols.) Zurich: Kindler, 1964–1971. Best all-round dictionary of painting.

Lake, C., and Maillarde, R. (Eds.) *Dictionary of Modern Painting.* (3rd. ed.) New York: Tudor, 1955.

Mayer, R. *A Dictionary of Art Terms and Techniques.* New York: Crowell, 1969.

Myers, B. S. (Ed.) *Encyclopedia of Painting: Painters and Painting of the World from Prehistoric Times to the Present Day.* New York: Crown, 1955.

Pope, A. *The Language of Drawing and Painting.* Cambridge, Massachusetts: Harvard University Press, 1949.

Taubes, F. *The Painter's Dictionary of Materials and Methods.* New York: Watson-Guptill, 1971.

HANDBOOKS

Blake, V. *The Art and Craft of Drawing: A Study Both of the Practice of Drawing and Its Aesthetic Theory as Understood Among Different Peoples at Different Epochs . . .* London: Oxford University Press, 1927. A standard work.

Cooke, H. L. *Drawing Techniques of the Masters.* (Rev. ed.) New York: Watson-Guptill, 1972.

DeTolnay, C. *History and Technique of Old Master Drawings: A Handbook.* New York: Bittner, 1943.

Doerner, M. *Materials of the Artist and Their Use in Painting, with Notes on the Techniques of the Old Masters.* (Rev. ed., E. Newhaus, trans.) New York: Harcourt Brace Jovanovich, 1949.

Mayer, R. *The Painter's Craft: An Introduction to the Artist's Materials.* (2nd ed.) New York: Van Nostrand, 1966.

Mendelowitz, D. M. *Drawing.* New York: Holt, Rinehart and Winston, 1967.

Nicolaides, K. *The Natural Way to Draw a Working Plan for Art Study.* Boston: Houghton Mifflin, 1941.

DIRECTORIES

American Art Directory. New York: Bowker, 1898–. Annual listing of art museums, universities, college art departments, and art schools in the United States as well as several in Europe.

International Directory of Arts. (2 vols.) Berlin, Federal Republic of Germany: Art Adress Verlag Müller GMBH, 1952/53–. Published biennially. A worldwide listing of people and institutions affiliated with the arts. Volume 1 contains names and addresses of museums, art galleries, schools, colleges, artists, collectors, and art associations. Volume 2 contains names and addresses of art and antique dealers, galleries, art publishers, art periodicals, art booksellers, restorers, experts, and dealers. The standard directory of the arts.

Kay, E. *International Who's Who in Art and Antiques.* Cambridge, England: Melrose Press, 1972. Complete international listing of art associations and art schools.

The World of Learning. London: Europa, 1947–. Annual listing of colleges, universities, institutions, learned societies, and research institutes and centers throughout the world.

Directories to museums of the world include:

Hudson, K., and Nicholls, A. (Eds.) *The Directory of World Museums.* New York: Columbia University Press, 1975. A comprehensive international directory which also includes a bibliography of national and regional museum directories and articles.

Kloster, G. B. *Handbook of Museums/Handbuch der Museen.* (2 vols.) Vol. 1: *Federal Republic of Germany.* Vol. 2: *German Democratic Republic, Austria, and Switzerland.* New York: Bowker; Pullach/Munich, Federal Republic of Germany: Verlag Dokumentation, 1971. A comprehensive listing of museums and collections in German-speaking countries; includes art museums and galleries and offers information on collections in libraries and archives and collections of slides and tapes.

Museums of the World/Museen der Welt: A Directory of 17,500 Museums in 150 Countries, Including a Subject Index. (2nd ed.) New York: Bowker, 1975.

The Official Museum Directory, 1975. Washington, D.C.: American Association of Museums; New York: National Register Publishing Co., 1975. Includes the United States and Canada.

[Bibliography prepared by Nancy Cottrill.]

DROPOUT

See Attrition: Wastage in Higher Education.

DUE PROCESS AND GRIEVANCE PROCEDURES

According to Jacob Diemert, American academic due process derives from the clause in the Fourteenth Amendment to the Constitution of the United States, which holds that "nor shall any State deprive any person of life, liberty, or property, without due process of law." He delineates two forms of due process: *substantive* due process, which in an educational context limits the content of rules and other academic regulations that seek to control, regulate, or prescribe conduct; and *procedural* due process, which limits procedures adopted

in making decisions. As applied to universities and schools, procedural due process is most relevant in disciplinary proceedings, both of students and faculty members. The concept has frequently been resented by administrators, who tend to consider it a limitation on their right to make educational decisions (Diemert, 1971, pp. 32–33).

Grievances in higher education are normally defined as complaints brought by faculty members that their rights, under an existing contractual agreement, have been violated. In the absence of a collective bargaining agreement, the grievance generally refers to an alleged violation of published institutional regulations or well-established practices and to unfair or inequitable treatment of the individual as a result. Grievance procedures, both formal and informal, have evolved as an integral part of the governance system of colleges and universities to regulate relationships between faculty members and administrators. Most grievance systems are logical extensions of efforts by these institutions to deal with the concept of academic due process (Carr and Van Eyck, 1973, p. 216).

History of Academic Due Process and Grievance Procedures

As a "system of procedures designed to produce the best possible judgments in those personnel problems of higher education which may yield a serious adverse decision about a teacher" (Joughin, 1969, p. 269), academic due process has been a major concern and a major outgrowth of the American Association of University Professors (AAUP). Shortly after its founding in 1915, the AAUP issued a "Declaration of Principles" from its Committee on Academic Freedom and Tenure, which proposed procedures for dismissal and for judicial hearings before dismissal. In this document the association first identified basic elements of due process: (1) charges should be in writing and "formulated with reasonable definiteness"; (2) there should be a fair trial before a "special or permanent judicial committee chosen by the faculty senate or council, or by the faculty at large"; (3) the teacher should have "full opportunity to present evidence," with adequate provision for expert testimony if his competence is at issue (Joughin, 1969, p. 266).

Since 1915 the AAUP has been consistently concerned with due process and grievance procedures; and most of its policies, published in the *AAUP Bulletin* and subsequently compiled in its periodic *AAUP Policy Documents and Reports,* bear on these topics. The three particularly relevant policy statements now in effect and reproduced in the 1977 edition of this volume are the 1958 "Statement on Procedural Standards in Faculty Dismissal Proceedings," the 1971 "Procedural Standards in the Retention or Non-Retention of Faculty Appointments," and the 1976 "Recommended Institutional Regulations on Academic Freedom and Tenure."

Typical grievance procedures under these standards call for a hearing by a faculty committee, with the grievant having the right of counsel. Testimony, evidence, and briefs are allowable, and the faculty committee makes its findings and then transmits its decision to both the administration and the grievant in writing. It is expected that the governing body will normally accept the faculty committee's decision when it is transmitted to that body through the administration. Should this not be the case, the decision is returned to the faculty committee for further review, with specific objections stated. It is only after the governing body studies the faculty committee's reconsideration that a final decision on the grievance is made.

Much academic tradition and practice regarding due process and grievances has been based on the concept of collegiality or "shared authority," which gives recognition to the composition of the college or university as a community of scholars. The normal expectation of a faculty member is considerable participation in educational matters, especially in the evaluation of the profes-

sional performance of colleagues. This involvement in evaluation is based on the assumption that academic personnel decisions are best made by faculty because of their academic competence and expertise. It follows logically then that academic administrators, who in many instances are former faculty members themselves, are expected to share this authority and accept, for the most part, the decisions of relevant academic committees.

Despite these AAUP standards and the 1954 statement on "Academic Due Process" by the American Civil Liberties Union, the degree of shared authority, faculty participation, and due process varies with the institution. In those colleges and universities with long traditions of shared authority and collegiality, there is a tendency for the faculty to exert considerable influence on personnel decisions such as faculty appointments, retention, promotion, and tenure; and these decisions are generally supported by the administration. Faculty can also influence the choice of chairmen or deans through their participation on search committees (Rehmus, 1972, p. 91). Grievances in such a setting are treated on an informal basis by either an appeal to a faculty committee or an academic administrator. Usually the mechanism is simple and direct, and a grievance is resolved in a relatively uncomplicated manner. John Ellis illustrates the advantage of such an informal system before recourse to formal grievance hearings from his experience at one such collegial institution, the University of California at Santa Cruz:

Formal adversary hearings are bitter experiences for everybody, and . . . whatever their outcome—either for or against the faculty member vis-à-vis his department chairman or dean—the atmosphere they leave behind is very poisonous for everyone. Whatever chances there were for a reasonable working relationship are finally destroyed when an individual hauls another before a tribunal and accuses him publicly of malpractice, prejudice, discrimination, or dishonesty. In a sense, such a hearing is the end of the road; if the hearing is necessary, it must happen, but the cost is great [1974, p. 67].

Grievance systems in industry began to develop largely after the passage of the National Labor Relations Act of 1935, but beyond informal procedures, few formal grievance systems were in existence in higher education before the early 1960s, and most systems have been codified since 1965. With the growth in the number of public institutions of higher education covered by collective bargaining laws for public employees, cutbacks in the resources devoted to higher education, and declining student enrollments, many faculty members have faced employment insecurity and have begun to organize to meet threat to their livelihood through collective bargaining. In seeking to emulate employer and employee relationships in the private sector, they have questioned the concept of collegiality and the advantages of shared authority. As a defense against new managerial types of administrators who are charged with making education decisions in a cost-benefit framework, formal grievance procedures are becoming an integral part of collective bargaining agreements.

These grievance systems tend to be very detailed, and the resolution of troublesome issues is not only complicated but extremely adversarial. One of the first grievance procedures included in a collective bargaining agreement at a four-year college or university, however, was startling in its simplicity. In the 1971 agreement between the Bryant College of Business Administration of Providence, Rhode Island, and the American Federation of Teachers, it consisted of only a short paragraph outlining the arbitration of grievances:

> Any dispute, claim or grievance arising out of or relating to the interpretation or application of this agreement may be submitted to a binding arbitration by either party under the Voluntary Labor Arbitration Rules of the American Arbitration Association. The parties further agree that there shall be no suspension of work when such dispute arises and while it is in process of adjustment or arbitration during the life of this contract.

This agreement was in sharp contrast to the many existing procedures in both unionized and nonunionized colleges and universities, which are often extremely detailed and frequently run four or five pages in length.

Differences Between Industrial and Academic Grievance Procedures

Grievance mechanisms for governing relationships between faculty and administration borrow heavily from the private sector but contain unique features peculiar to the decision-making processes of higher education. One important difference between private sector and higher education mechanisms is found in the identification of the adversaries in personnel decisions. In industry, the employee can clearly identify management during grievance procedures, but higher education procedures often involve a process where a faculty member protests adverse decisions made by colleagues in the same department or the same bargaining unit (Weisberger, 1976, p. 11). In higher education, the line between employee and management is quite indistinct.

Second, unlike customary practices of the private sector, university grievance systems often exclude certain personnel decisions from arbitral review. Many of these grievance mechanisms allow the arbitrator to review only the procedures or the rules of the institution, and almost always, by mutual agreement, preclude academic judgment by an arbitrator (Benewitz, 1973, p. 155). Typical language limiting the authority of the arbitrator is exemplified in the Northeastern University Faculty Grievance Procedure of 1973:

> The decision of the arbitrator, within the scope of his jurisdiction, shall be final and binding on the parties to the dispute and the University. However, the arbitrator shall be without power to, (1) Make a decision which requires the commission of an act prohibited by law, (2) Substitute his judgment on the professional qualifications of a faculty member for the judgment of the relevant academic committee, or (3) Add to, subtract from, or modify provisions of the Faculty Handbook where provisions exist which cover the case in hand.

At Northeastern University, where no union and therefore no collective bargaining agreement exists, the university procedures contain a list of grievable issues that is considerably more expansive than many of those found in the procedures of colleges and universities which do have collective bargaining agreements:

A "grievance" is defined as a complaint by a faculty member that he (1) Has been discriminated against on the basis of age, sex, race, religion, national origin, or marital status, (2) Has been denied academic freedom, (3) Has been dismissed without just cause, (4) Has been denied due process in consideration for tenure, renewal of contract, or promotion, (5) Has been subject to a violation, misinterpretation or inequitable application of provisions of the Faculty Handbook, or (6) Has otherwise been treated unfairly or inequitably.

This statement that a grievance can be pursued when a faculty member feels he or she has otherwise been treated unfairly or inequitably allows a faculty member who could not file a complaint under the standard list of grievance to fit any grievance under this catch-all phrase.

The grievance system adopted in 1973 at Northeastern differs substantially from earlier procedures developed by the Northeastern faculty senate. The earlier procedures called for the appointment of a grievance committee of five members, three of which were to be members of the faculty senate. This committee heard and acted on grievances and appeals (including questions of tenure) made by individual faculty members. The committee then made its recommendations on these matters directly to the president of the university. This was typical of grievance mechanisms found in many nonunionized colleges and universities.

The present Northeastern procedure provides for initial informal attempts to resolve a grievance. Should these initial attempts fail, the grievance is then submitted to arbitration and the administration is bound by the decision of the arbitrator. This procedure is unique in that it represents the voluntary acceptance, by a nonunion, private university, of a binding system of channeling internal conflicts to a third party external to the university.

Despite the similarities to grievance mechanisms found in unionized colleges and universities, the Northeastern procedure has a number of provisions other than that already noted which are quite unique. The introduction of a special mediation committee, comprised of faculty members, for each grievance represents an effort to provide faculty support and guidance in helping to resolve grievances. Still another Northeastern variation from typical collective bargaining agreements found in institutions of higher education is the treatment of the arbitration costs. Normally, where a contract exists, the costs of arbitration are split equally between the parties involved. However, recognizing the absence of a union, so that a grievant has no access to union resources to support the arbitration, the agreement stipulates that the grievant, if successful, pays nothing for the costs of the arbitration and the administration bears the costs in an amount not to exceed $1000. On the other hand, if the administration is upheld, the maximum payment required of the grievant is $200 and the administration is liable for the remainder of such costs, not to exceed $800. Each party is liable for its own expenses, services, and fees.

In the absence of union representation, the presence of a faculty member at various steps of the procedure can be enormously helpful in providing an atmosphere of restraint and an ambience wherein helpful suggestions are offered for the resolution of a grievance. Yet, many times, faculty members cannot dissuade a colleague from a grievance that may be frivolous or has little chance for a successful outcome. In a situation where the faculty is unionized, the union might not support a grievance of little merit but would support a serious grievance with financial and legal resources.

It is interesting to note that, despite the nonunion context, the Northeastern University grievance mechanism more closely resembles those procedures normally found in a unionized college or university and yet, at the same time, preserves some structure of the system characteristic of educational institutions not covered by collective bargaining agreements.

Summary

It is quite likely that, with further growth of faculty unionism, especially in public institutions, the grievance mechanism will more and more tend to resemble its industrial counterpart. With the institution of grievance procedures, it is safe to assume that both faculty and administration will rely more on legal processes and that there will be an increasing tendency to systematize deliberations and be acutely alert to due process. The comfortable model of resolving conflicts in the collegial setting will no longer prevail.

Bibliography

American Association of University Professors. "Council Position on Collective Bargaining." *AAUP Bulletin,* 1971, *57,* 511.

American Association of University Professors. *AAUP Policy Documents and Reports.* 1977 edition. Washington, D.C.: American Association of University Professors, 1977.

Benewitz, M. C. "Grievance and Arbitration Procedures." In T. N. Tice (Ed.), *Faculty Bargaining in the Seventies.* Ann Arbor, Michigan: Institute for Continuing Legal Education, 1973.

Carr, R. K., and Van Eyck, D. V. *Collective Bargaining Comes to the Campus.* Washington, D.C.: American Council on Education, 1973.

Diemert, J. C. "Due Process and You." In *New England Proceedings.* Burlington, Massachusetts: New England Association of Schools and Colleges, 1971.

Ellis, J. M. "Grievance Procedures: Real and Ideal." In R. H. Peairs (Ed.), *New Directions for Higher Education 7: Avoiding Conflict in Faculty Personnel Practices.* San Francisco: Jossey-Bass, 1974.

Joughin, L. *Academic Freedom and Tenure: A Handbook of the American Association of University Professors.* 1969 edition. Madison: University of Wisconsin Press, 1969.

Rehmus, C. M. "Alternatives to Bargaining and Traditional Governance." In T. N. Tice (Ed.), *Faculty Power: Collective Bargaining on Campus.* Ann Arbor, Michigan: Institute for Continuing Legal Education, 1972.

Weisberger, J. *Faculty Grievance Arbitration in Higher Education: Living with Collective Bargaining.* Institute of Public Employment Monograph 5. Ithaca, New York: Cornell University, 1976.

SIDNEY HERMAN

See also: Legal Aspects of Higher Education; Legal Status of Faculty Unionization in Higher Education.

DUFF REPORT

See University Government in Canada (Higher Education Report).

E

EARLY CHILDHOOD EDUCATION, TEACHER TRAINING FOR
(Field of Study)

Historically, the major purpose of early childhood education has been to provide care, nutrition, and education for needy children. These services were provided mainly by church groups or private organizations. Since around 1925, however, the demand for preschool experiences for middle-class children has increased dramatically. Moreover, since the early 1960s preschool enrollments for disadvantaged children have grown even more rapidly, to permit early educational intervention in the lives of these children. These services are now increasingly provided by public organizations. In general, however, the purpose of preschool education remains the same: the provision of welfare, health, and educational services for young children.

Traditionally, in early childhood education, emphasis has been placed upon the social and emotional aspects of child growth and development. Only since the 1960s, as an outgrowth of Head Start activities in the United States, have cognitive aspects been stressed in the training of teachers for preschool education. The Head Start type of experiment is also being tried in the United Kingdom, the Netherlands, and the Federal Republic of Germany.

The fields of social work and nursing are closely allied to teacher training for early childhood education. Other allied fields include child psychology, developmental psychology, basic educational skills instruction (such as reading, arithmetic, music, and art), and such socially related fields as home and family relations and the school and the community.

The origin of early childhood education is most commonly traced to such educators as Jean Jacques Rousseau (1712–1778), Johann Heinrich Pestalozzi (1746–1827), and Friedrich Froebel (1782–1852). These men saw the need to provide disadvantaged and poor children with some early education. Following these early pioneers is the work of such childhood educators as Maria Montessori (1870–1952) in Italy and Ovide Decroly (1871–1932) in Belgium.

The training of teachers for work in early childhood education is quite similar in North and South America and in Western and Eastern Europe. In the rest of the world relatively little has been done in the area of early childhood education because of the pressing needs of primary and secondary education.

Teachers of early childhood education are usually classified by the type of preschool in which they work. Children entering preschool can range from two to six years of age. The program types range from care-giving to highly structured, cognitively oriented programs.

In England and Wales early childhood education centers are called *nursery schools* (located in separate buildings) or *nursery classes* (attached to a primary school). England and Wales also have many privately operated preschool groups. The largest of these groups, the Play Groups Movement, employs qualified nursery teachers or nursery class teachers but also encourages parental participation. Many volunteers, primarily middle-class mothers, work actively in the Play Groups Movement. This movement is the middle class's answer to the problem of finding space for its young children when the public sector does not, cannot, or will not respond to a demand.

The Soviet Union has a very extensive, highly centralized, well-equipped, and well-staffed system of preschools. These schools are available to very large numbers of children, especially in the urban areas—where, typically, 85 to 90 percent of the children from ages three to seven attend preschools. The Soviet Union has perhaps the most highly developed national preschool curriculum of any in the world. The Laboratory for the Study of the Preschool Child, in Moscow, and several other research institutes are constantly developing new teaching techniques and revising old ones. A modern trend is to combine the nurseries with the kindergarten in what are called *nursery kindergarten* facilities.

In Israel compensatory programs have been designed to enrich the lives of the young children, to ensure them a broad range of experiences, and to help them make up for perceived deficits in language, self-image, knowledge of technology, and awareness of the cultural heritage. The programs undertaken by Sarah and Moshe Smilansky in Israel, for example, were relatively structured cognitive-oriented programs and emphasized such matters as celebration of the Jewish customs and holidays and the establishment of Hebrew as the common language.

In Sweden preschools are called *playschools* or *day nurseries*. In France they are called *nursery schools;* in the Federal Republic of Germany, *kindergartens*. In the United States schools for five-year-old children are usually called *kindergartens,* and schools that take younger children are called *nursery schools.*

After studying preschool teacher training programs in nine countries, Austin (1972) concluded that "the course work taken by students preparing to be preschool teachers is quite similar across the nine nations." All of the programs emphasize physical, intellectual, emotional, and social growth–in such courses as psychology and development of young children; sociological history; and philosophy, theory, and method of preschool education. Geography, mathematics, natural science, hygiene, the language of the country, music, art, home and family life, and a variety of similar subjects also are part of the curriculum. Many countries are now including courses in ecology which cut across formerly separate subject areas. All countries also have their students participate in practice-teaching experiences for varying periods of time; many teachers (both those being trained and those doing the training) believe that such experiences are potentially the most beneficial part of the training. In all countries in-service course work and graduate study are increasingly being offered by schools and colleges of education.

In a twelve-nation study of child care, N. and H. Robinson (1975–76) indicate that some countries provide alternate education routes for preschool teachers. In the Soviet Union, for example, a preschool teacher may qualify after eight years of compulsory schooling plus a specialized vocational course lasting three and a half years. More complete training—a five-year course—is offered to those who have finished ten years of regular schooling; these teachers, who are in the minority in most schools, are much more likely to advance through the administrative hierarchy after some years. Poland also offers two levels of training, a two-year post–high school vocational course and a three-year program of teacher training in a university-affiliated academy. In Hungary a two-year post–high school course in a teachers college has been required since 1959, but teachers without such qualifications can take a three-year correspondence course, which will yield a degree.

By and large, it appears that the more centralized the preschool system, the more centralized the systems of education through which teachers are trained. Some countries have highly specific curricula which are uniform within the country, whatever the institution attended. This is, for example, the case in the socialist countries and in Sweden; it is far from true in the United Kingdom, Israel, Switzerland, or the United States.

All countries apparently require some practice teaching in the course of training—sometimes during the entire period of training but more often late in the course of study. In fact, student helpers constitute a valuable source of help in many countries, particularly in Sweden and the Soviet Union, where they are utilized quite openly as aides to experienced teachers.

Training of early childhood educators starts at a very young age in Italy (age fourteen) and lasts on the average about three years. Canada and the Federal Republic of Germany have the lowest requirements for teacher training: in Canada, one year beyond the junior or senior year in high school; in Germany, a two-year program in a vocational school. France requires four years of training with a secondary school education, two years with a *baccalauréat*, and an examination. Most programs in these countries take place in teacher training colleges or colleges of education; in the Federal Republic of Germany, however, prospective preschool teachers are trained in a special secondary technical school.

Most countries, for various reasons, make some use of teacher aides or assistants as well as parent volunteers. Some educators believe that the job of the teachers has become unmanageable and that the use of aides can help. Others believe that it is a good way to stimulate parental involvement and to increase school-community rapport. Still others see it as a way of helping disadvantaged adults get a start in a career development program; an aide may be promoted to assistant teacher and perhaps ultimately to head teacher. This last concept is only in its infancy in some countries. France does have women who help with the children, but their role is much more that of a domestic than a teacher aide. In Sweden and England and Wales the use of aides is well established.

[*Notes:* **G. R. Austin,** *Early Childhood Education: An International Perspective* (New York: Academic Press, 1976); the countries treated in this study are the Netherlands, Sweden, France, Canada, the United States, Italy, Belgium, England and Wales, and the Federal Republic of Germany. **N. Robinson** and **H. Robinson,** *Early Child Care* (New York: Gordon and Breach, 1975–76); a series of monographs on child care in the following countries: Cuba, France, the United Kingdom, Hungary, India, the Soviet Union, Israel, Poland, Sweden, Switzerland, the United States, and Yugoslavia.]

GILBERT R. AUSTIN

Levels and Programs of Study

Programs for teacher training in early childhood education generally require as a prerequisite a secondary education, though mature applicants with relevant experience may be admitted with lower educational qualifications. For short programs, especially those designed to improve the qualifications of teachers, work experience may be given greater weight than educational qualifications. Study at the graduate level usually requires the holding of an initial teaching qualification, demonstrated potential for study at that level, and, in some programs, experience in teaching or administration at an appropriate level. Usual awards for successful completion are a certificate or diploma, a teaching certificate or bachelor's degree, a master's degree, a doctorate, or their equivalents.

Programs leading to degrees not equivalent to the first university degree are designed to train students to teach preschool or kindergarten classes and consist of lectures and practice teaching. Various facets of the role of the preschool teacher are studied, with emphasis on teaching practice rather than on the theory of education. The programs, generally full time for one to three years, are usually given in a teachers college, normal school, or college. Principal course content usually includes the philosophy, history, psychology, and sociology of education; courses specifically related to the teaching and directing of children at preschool and kindergarten ages; audiovisual aids; school administration; and sometimes general academic subjects. In addition, time is devoted to observing experienced teachers and to supervised practice teaching.

Work leading to the first university degree is designed to train teachers for preschool or kindergarten level and consists of lectures, group discussion, and practice teaching. These programs emphasize the theory of education and the theoretical and general principles of the subjects studied. The programs, full or part time for the equivalent of one year's full-time study, are usually given in a teachers college or a university. They consist primarily of courses in pedagogy (teacher training) and related subjects, such as the theory of education and educational administration. Usually included are courses in the history, philosophy, psychology, and sociology of education; the theory and practice of teaching in general and the teaching of preschool children in particular; and general courses that will assist in the understanding and guidance of preschool and kindergarten children. In addition, time is de-

voted to observing experienced teachers and to supervised practice teaching.

Programs that lead to a postgraduate university degree are designed to prepare specialists in the theory and practice of dealing with young children and of teaching in the preschool or kindergarten level. Programs, full time for one to three years, consist of a number of prescribed courses, demonstrated facility in one or more foreign languages, and the preparation of a thesis or dissertation involving original research into a particular problem within the major subject. Through seminars, directed reading, and independent research, the student acquires a comprehensive grasp of one field within the general area of kindergarten education, such as reading instruction and child psychology, and may also study related subjects or other areas of education. Attention is paid to psychology, sociology, and the theory of curriculum development.

[This section was based on UNESCO's *International Standard Classification of Education (ISCED): Three Stage Classification System, 1974* (Paris: UNESCO, 1974).]

Major International and National Organizations

INTERNATIONAL

Council of Europe
Council for Cultural Co-operation
avenue de l'Europe
67 Strasbourg, France

International Association for Child Psychiatry
   and Allied Professions (IACP)
Yale Child Study Center
333 Cedar Street
New Haven, Connecticut 06510 USA

International Union for Child Welfare (IUCW)
1 rue de Varembé
P.O. Box 41
1211 Geneva 20, Switzerland

Organisation for Economic Co-operation and
   Development (OECD)
Château de la Muette
2 rue André Pascal
75775 Paris, France

United Nations Children's Fund (UNICEF)
United Nations
New York, New York 10017 USA

United Nations Educational, Scientific and Cultural Organization (UNESCO)
place de Fontenoy
75007 Paris, France

World Organization for Early Childhood Education
Organisation mondiale pour l'éducation préscolaire (OMEP)
69 rue de la Tombe-Issoire
75014 Paris, France

The largest international organization concerned essentially with the education of young children who are not yet liable for compulsory education. There are national committees in thirty-six countries, preparatory committees in six countries, and cooperating groups in four countries.

NATIONAL

United States:

Association for Childhood Education International
3615 Wisconsin Avenue NW
Washington, D.C. 20016

National Association for the Education of Young Children
1834 Connecticut Avenue NW
Washington, D.C. 20009

A list of the thirty-six national committees and ten preparatory and cooperating groups of the World Organization for Early Childhood Education is found in the bulletin of the International Bureau of Education, *Educational Documentation and Information*, 1974, *192*, 111–116.

Principal Information Sources

GENERAL

Recent bibliographies which serve as guides to the literature of early childhood education can be found in:

An Annotated Bibliography on Early Childhood. Ann Arbor: University of Michigan Press, 1970.
Compensatory Early Childhood Education: A Selective Working Bibliography. The Hague: Bernard van Leer Foundation, 1971.
Early Childhood Education: An ERIC Bibliography. New York: Macmillan, 1973.
Early Childhood Education Research: A Select Annotated Bibliography of Recent Research. London: Nursery School Association of Great Britain and Northern Ireland, 1972.
Huu Dong, N., and others (under the direction of M. Thomine-Desmazures). *Enfants et jeunes ruraux: Bibliographie signalétique.* Paris: Institut national de la recherche agronomique. Laboratoire de sociologie rurale, 1969.

Kessen, W. (Ed.) *Childhood in China.* New Haven, Connecticut: Yale University Press, 1975.
Kochan-Doderlein, H. von, Erler, H. M., Kolb, E., Riedel, H., and Schirm, H. (Institut für Frühpädagogik–Munich). *Bibliographie zur Frühpädagogik.* Pullach/Munich, Federal Republic of Germany: Verlag Dokumentation, 1972.
Mandl, P. E. *A Working Bibliography on the Child in Developing Communities.* Geneva: United Nations Research Institute for Social Development, 1968.
Mialaret, G. "Early Childhood Education." *Educational Documentation and Information*, 1974, *192*, entire issue.
"Selected and Classified References on Comparative Preschool Education." *Western European Education*, 1974, *6*, 67–76.

Overviews and introductions to the profession of early childhood education include:

Almy, M. *The Early Childhood Educator at Work.* New York: McGraw-Hill, 1974.
Beyer, E. *Teaching Young Children.* New York: Pegasus, 1968.
Brown, C. *For Beginning-to-Be-Teachers of Beginning-to-Be-Students.* Nashville, Tennessee: Demonstration and Research College of Early Education, George Peabody College for Teachers, 1971.
Butler, A. *Early Childhood Education: Planning and Administering Programs.* New York: D. Van Nostrand, 1974.
Evans, E. D. *Contemporary Influences in Early Childhood Education.* (2nd ed.) New York: Holt, Rinehart and Winston, 1975.
Frost, J. L. (Ed.) *Revisiting Early Childhood Education.* New York: Holt, Rinehart and Winston, 1973.
Spodek, B. *Early Childhood Education.* Englewood Cliffs, New Jersey: Prentice-Hall, 1973.

On the training of early childhood educators see:

Colvin, R. W., and Zaffiro, E. M. *Preschool Education: A Handbook for the Training of Early Childhood Educators.* New York: Springer-Verlag, 1974.
Compte rendu du colloque international de Leyde sur la formation des éducatrices préscolaires. Strasbourg, France: Council of Europe, Council for Cultural Co-operation, 1974.
L'éducatrice di scuola materna/The Nursery School Teacher. Brescia, Italy: Ministero della pubblica istruzione, Centro didattico nazionale per la scuola materna, 1973. Overall study of the functions, personality, and training of the nursery school teacher.
World Organization for Early Childhood Education. *La formation du personnel pour les institu-*

tions destinées aux enfants d'âge préscolaire. Brussels: Comité belge de l'OMEP, n.d.

Comparative education sources are offered by the following:

Chauncey, H. (Ed.) *Soviet Preschool Education.* (2 vols.) New York: Holt, Rinehart and Winston, 1969.

Crosher, J. A. *Pre-School Education in Australia: A Review of Recent Developments.* Hawthorn, Victoria: Australian Council for Educational Research, 1971.

Curriculum in Early Childhood Education: Report of a Seminar on Curriculum in Compensatory Early Childhood Education Held in Jerusalem, 1972. The Hague: Bernard van Leer Foundation, 1974.

Hawes, H. W. R. *Planning the Primary School Curriculum in Developing Countries.* Paris: UNESCO International Institute for Educational Planning, 1972. One of seventeen booklets in an IIEP series.

Leiner, M., and Ubell, R. *Children Are the Revolution.* New York: Viking, 1974. Preschool education in Cuba.

Nursery Education. DES Reports on Education, No. 81. London: Department of Education and Science, 1975.

Sidel, R. *Women and Child Care in China: A Firsthand Report.* New York: Holt, Rinehart and Winston, 1973.

Historical perspectives on the field include:

Braun, S. J., and Edwards, E. P. (Ed.) *History and Theory of Early Childhood Education.* Worthington, Ohio: Charles A. Jones, 1972.

DeMause, L. (Ed.) *The History of Childhood.* New York: Psychohistory Press, 1974.

Feshbach, N. D., Goodlad, J. I., and Lombard, A. *Early Schooling in England and Israel.* New York: McGraw-Hill, 1973.

Goodlad, J. I., Klein, M. F., and Novotney, J. M. *Early Schooling in the United States,* New York: McGraw-Hill, 1973.

Snyder, A. *Dauntless Women in Childhood Education, 1856–1931.* Washington, D.C.: Association for Childhood Education International, 1972. A history of children's education in the United States.

Whitbread, M. *The Evolution of the Nursery-Infant School: A History of Infant and Nursery Education in Britain, 1800–1970.* London: Routledge and Kegan Paul, 1972.

CURRENT BIBLIOGRAPHIES

Australian Education Index. Hawthorn, Victoria: Australian Council for Educational Research, 1957–.

Bibliographie Pädagogik. Wiesbaden, Federal Republic of Germany: Verlag J. Beltz, 1966–.

British Education Index. London: Library Association, 1954–. Primarily covers selected British periodicals.

Canadian Education Index. Toronto, Ontario: Canadian Education Association, 1965–. Index to education articles published in Canada.

Child Development Abstracts and Bibliography. Chicago: Society for Research in Child Development, 1927–. Abstracts 140 journals and about 100 books dealing with child development.

Current Contents—Behavioral, Social and Educational Sciences. Philadelphia: Institute for Scientific Information, 1969–. Gives tables of contents of more than 700 foreign and domestic journals in education.

Current Index to Journals in Education (CIJE). New York: CCM Information Corp., 1969–. Covers some 500 journals in education.

Education Index. New York: Wilson, 1929–. Indexes references from significant American and some British publications.

PERIODICALS

Important journals in the field include *Australian Pre-School Quarterly, Child Development* (US), *Childhood Education* (US), *Children Today* (US), *Child Study Journal* (US), *Child Welfare* (US), *Doskolnoye vospitaniye* (USSR), *Early Child Development and Care* (UK), *Educating Children: Early and Middle Years* (US), *History of Childhood Quarterly* (US), *International Child Welfare Review* (Switzerland), *International Journal of Early Childhood* (Ireland), *International Monograph Series on Early Child Care* (US), *Japanese Journal of Child Psychiatry, Journal of Child Psychology and Psychiatry and Allied Disciplines* (US), *Merrill Palmer Quarterly of Behavior and Development* (US), *Monographs of the Society for Research in Child Development* (US), *Praxis der Kinderpsychologie und Kinderpsychiatrie* (FRG), *Review of Child Development Research* (US), *Revue de neuropsychiatrie infantile et d'hygiene mentale de l'enfance* (France), *UNICEF News, The World's Children* (UK), *Young Children* (US), and *Zeitschrift für Entwicklungspsychologie und pädagogische Psychologie* (FRG).

For a more comprehensive list of early childhood journals see the latest volume of:

Child Development Abstracts and Bibliography. Chicago: Society for Research in Child Development, 1927–.

ENCYCLOPEDIAS, DICTIONARIES, HANDBOOKS

Anthony, E. J., and Koupernik, C. *International Yearbook for Child Psychiatry and Allied Disciplines.* New York: Wiley, 1970–1973.

Dolch, J. *Grundbegriffe der pädagogischen Fach-*

sprache. (5th ed.) Aufl. mit viersprachigen Register. Munich, Federal Republic of Germany: Ehrenwirth, 1965. Includes equivalent terms in English, French, and Italian.

Encyclopedia of Education. New York: Macmillan, 1971.

Good, C. V. *Dictionary of Education.* (3rd ed.) New York: McGraw-Hill, 1973.

Lafon, R. *Vocabulaire de psychopedagogie et de psychiatrie de l'enfant.* (2nd ed.) Paris: Presses universitaires de France, 1969.

Lexikon der Pädagogik. Hrsg. vom Willmann-Institut München. Freiburg, Federal Republic of Germany: Herder, 1970.

DIRECTORIES

LaCrosse, E. R. *Early Childhood Education Directory: A Selected Guide to 2000 Preschool Educational Centers.* New York: Bowker, 1971. A selected representative list of early childhood education facilities in the United States.

World Organization for Early Childhood Education. *La formation et la condition professionnelle du personnel enseignant préscolaire.* Rome: Comité italien de l'OMEP, 1971. A survey, conducted in collaboration with UNESCO, giving information from forty countries on nursery school teachers' training and conditions of service.

RESEARCH CENTERS, INSTITUTES, INFORMATION CENTERS

Educational Research Information Center (ERIC)
Clearinghouse on Early Childhood Education
University of Illinois, College of Education
805 West Pennsylvania Avenue
Urbana, Illinois 61801 USA

A specialized information center, part of a national system sponsored by the United States Office of Education, which indexes and abstracts publications on early childhood education.

The following is a selected listing of the numerous early childhood research centers and institutes:

Faculty of Education
University of Tokyo
Hongo, Bunkyo-ku
Tokyo, Japan

Istituto di psicologia
CNR, via dei Monti Tiburtini, 509
Rome, Italy

International Center for the Study of the Family
via Giotto 36
Milan, Italy 20145

Laboratory for the Study of the Preschool Child
Scientific Research Institute of Pre-School Education
Klimentovsky perevlok I, Moscow USSR

Yale Child Study Center
333 Cedar Street
New Haven, Connecticut 06510 USA

For a worldwide listing of educational documentation centers, education libraries and museums, and research centers and institutes, consult:

International Guide to Educational Documentation. (2nd ed.) Paris: UNESCO, 1971.

EASTERN EUROPEAN SCIENCE POLICIES

See Science Policies: Industrialized Planned Economies: Eastern European Socialist Countries.

EASTERN EUROPEAN SOCIALIST COUNTRIES: REGIONAL ANALYSIS

The Eastern European socialist countries covered in this overview of higher education are Albania, Bulgaria, Czechoslovakia, German Democratic Republic, Hungary, Poland, Romania, the Soviet Union, and Yugoslavia. Since the educational systems of these countries differ considerably, generalizations about the region should be viewed as a broad tendency that may not necessarily be reflected in any individual case. One characteristic common to all these countries is the dynamic growth in higher education institutions and enrollments achieved under socialism. Except for the Soviet Union, which became a socialist republic in 1917, all the countries in the region acquired socialist governments after World War II. Under their former governments, some of these countries had little or no facilities for higher education. Where it existed, higher education was highly elite, essentially inaccessible to young people from the working class and the peasantry. For example, in 1939 there were no higher education institutions at all in Albania; in Hungary only 3 to 4 percent of the entire student body belonged to the working class or peasantry; in Poland 14.5 percent of the first-year students came from working class or peasant backgrounds. In 1917 almost 75 percent of the Soviet population was illiterate, and among the national minorities, illiteracy extended to almost all of the population; by 1923, 50 percent of the total enrollment in Soviet institutions of higher education stemmed from the working and peasant classes.

A fundamental principle underlying the educational system in all the Eastern European socialist countries is that the social structure of students must correspond more or less with the social structure of the country as a whole. In national planning, education is considered a very important element of economic growth and social development. Education at all levels is free, and the operating costs of higher education institutions are covered by the budgets·of the central and regional governments. In financing higher education, the state strives to employ graduates according to their attained qualifications. To achieve this goal, the government controls enrollments, setting limits on admissions at the various higher education institutions and in specific fields of study. Thus, in 1965, as national needs for highly skilled professionals began to level off, so did the rate of expansion in higher education, as shown in Table 1. Nevertheless, the total number of students in higher schools of learning continued to increase, as shown in Table 2. Differences in the rate of growth reflect differences in each country's rate of development, specific demographic situation, and level of saturation with college trained staff.

Academic Levels and Studies

As in many other parts of the world, higher education in the Eastern European socialist countries falls into three categories, defined by UNESCO as levels A, B, and C. Level A includes programs of a practical orientation, designed to prepare students for vocations, such as highly skilled technicians, nurses, or production supervisors; completion of a level A program leads to a diploma that is lower in rank than a first university degree. Level-B programs lead to a first university degree, such as a bachelor's, *licence,* or equivalent qualification, as well as to a first professional degree awarded after completion of studies in such fields as medicine, engineering, or law. Level-C programs are of a high professional or scholarly nature, requiring a first university degree or equivalent qualification for admission and independent research for completion; it leads to a postgraduate university degree that is roughly equivalent to a master's or doctorate. Students in higher education normally follow academic or vocational programs. However, the emphasis placed on these two types of education is not homogenous throughout the region. The Soviet Union, for example, is striving for purely academic studies in all higher schools of education. Poland is also restricting studies that have immediate vocational applications, although such programs are still prevalent in extramural education, called "studies for working people." In the German Democratic Republic and Yugoslavia, on the other hand, both vocational and academic studies have had a long tradition that shows no sign of changing. In Hungary vocational higher education is expanding, while in Czechoslovakia and Romania higher education is strictly academic.

Because of national differences in the organization of higher education and lack of consistency in reporting educational statistics, detailed data on fields of study for the region as a whole are not readily comparable. Nevertheless, one can observe some general trends. One is the high percentage of students in engineering throughout the area, a phenomenon that is connected with the dynamic development of industry and the shift from an agricultural to an industrial economic structure. However, the pressing need for highly qualified technical staff appears to be abating, and

Table 1: Average Rate of Growth in the Number of Students in the Years 1950–1970

Country	1950–60	1950–55	1955–60	1960–70	1960–65	1965–70
Albania	—	—	—	14.3	13.8	14.8
Bulgaria	5.8	3.4	8.1	5.0	10.4	0.1
Czechoslovakia	7.6	9.9	5.4	3.4	9.1	0.2
German Democratic Republic[a]	—	—	—	3.1	1.3	5.0
Hungary	3.2	6.9	0.4	6.1	16.1	3.0
Poland	—	—	—	6.9	10.8	3.2
Romania	3.1	8.0	1.5	7.8	12.7	3.1
Soviet Union	6.7	8.4	5.1	6.7	10.1	3.5
Yugoslavia	8.8	3.0	15.0	6.4	5.6	7.1
Europe	—	—	—	7.3	9.5	5.2
World	—	—	—	8.8	9.6	7.9

Source: Enseignement supérieur (1975).

[a]Covers only universities and equivalent institutions; does not include higher technical schools of a professional profile.

Table 2: Student Population as a Percentage of the Total Population in the 20–24 Age Group

Country	1960		1965		1970	
	Male	Female	Male	Female	Male	Female
Albania	7.5	1.5	12.6	3.7	20.0	10.0
Bulgaria	12.5	8.5	19.0	15.0	13.8	14.7
Czechoslovakia	14.3	7.5	17.0	10.7	12.7	8.0
German Democratic Republic	10.8	3.7	13.7	4.9	19.0	10.9
Hungary	9.0	4.2	15.3	9.9	11.4	8.8
Poland	10.9	7.3	18.7	16.3	14.3	13.4
Romania	6.1	3.0	11.8	7.8	11.0	8.6
Soviet Union	12.5	9.5	32.5	26.5	25.1	24.8
Yugoslavia	12.0	5.1	17.3	8.8	18.2	12.3
Europe	11.1	6.5	20.1	13.4	20.0	15.5
World	8.3	4.2	12.0	6.9	14.1	9.1

Source: Enseignement supérieur (1975).

trends are emerging that reflect the ever changing priorities in the social and economic lives of the Eastern European socialist countries. For example, efforts are under way to reduce the number of majors and specializations in higher education and provide graduates with knowledge and skills of a more durable and universal character. The shift toward academic studies applies mainly to level-B and level-C students; level-A graduates are still expected to perform technical work immediately on completion of their studies.

The rapid development of higher education in the region brought with it a crucial need for university faculty and research scientists, and formal postgraduate programs were instituted throughout the region. Although most graduate students are enrolled in full-time programs, extramural postgraduate studies are also available, usually leading to the lesser level-C degree of candidate of science. In Poland doctoral degrees are presented to individuals not enrolled in a formal postgraduate program, provided they pass all the required examinations and present an individual research thesis. The majority of graduates earning the higher doctoral degree take positions in higher schools of education.

Studies for Working People

The opportunity for higher education afforded working people in the Eastern European socialist countries is an important regional innovation. Called "studies for working people" or "in-service studies," this type of higher education fulfills a necessary function in the educational politics of socialist countries. It is an important element in the democratization of higher education, enabling working people to receive a diploma from a higher school of education and, at the same time, professional and social advancement. To qualify for these studies, students must have completed a vocational or general secondary school and be employed in a permanent occupation.

Studies for working people were instituted almost immediately after the advent of socialism in each of the Eastern European countries—1917 in the Soviet Union and after World War II in the others. In the first years after their establishment, in-service studies were essentially workshops for the education of administrative personnel in schools, political organizations, and industry. Students were recruited mainly from the working class to train for political and social functions in the new governments. In-service studies provided a way for workers to acquire higher qualifications without leaving their active political or professional posts. With the subsequent expansion of formal higher education, in-service studies became a secondary method of acquiring trained personnel—the preferred approach being to staff the necessary social, political, and industrial functions with university graduates. Initially, studies were conducted in the evenings at the various universities, with students attending classes after their normal working day. Evening courses were soon superseded by extramural studies, which have since become the more prevalent form of worker higher education. Table 3 shows the distribution of students in extramural education over a nearly twenty-year period throughout the region.

The organizational forms for extramural studies vary from country to country. In general, students attend required classes at the university or some other higher school of education. Classes take the form of meetings that are held once every two weeks, once a month for two to three days, or once every three months for three to four days. Most often, extramural studies take one year longer to complete than analogous full-time educational programs. In the Soviet Union there is an independent academy for working students. In Yugoslavia, the institution directing studies for working people refunds the cost of a student's higher education. In the other Eastern European countries, these studies are financed by the university budget and, like the higher educational system as a whole, are free.

Along with evening and extramural

**Table 3: Students in Evening and Extramural Higher Education
as a Percentage of the Total Student Body**

Country	1955	1960	1965	1968	1970	1972–73
Albania	—	47.8	45.3	—	56.1	—
Bulgaria	15.3	28.1	32.6	—	26.0	26.6
Czechoslovakia	—	28.4	24.5	24.9	19.5	16.5
German Democratic Republic	19.6	32.0	31.1	29.2	27.1	25.5
Hungary	—	34.1	45.7	—	33.2	34.8
Poland	23.9	32.8	39.6	36.6	36.6	37.0
Romania	22.6	21.5	26.2	31.2	29.5	28.8
Soviet Union	38.5	51.7	59.0	54.4	51.4	48.4
Yugoslavia	45.6	53.4	76.3	71.1	68.3	78.8

Source: Tymowski and Januszkiewicz (1976).

studies, a form of cooperative education—so-called sandwich studies—is being developed in several countries, primarily Romania, Poland, and the Soviet Union. The significant feature of these studies is that vocational activities and intramural studies are deliberately interlaced in the curriculum. In Poland, for example, sandwich studies are provided in alternating semesters; students are employed in a company one semester and enrolled in academic programs on campus during the other.

Research Institutes

Higher education in socialist countries is systematically investigated by special research agencies. The oldest, established in 1962, is the Research Institute of Science Policy and Higher Education in Warsaw; directly under the Ministry of Science, Higher Education, and Technology, this center coordinates all the country's research in higher education. Similar bodies in other countries are the National Research Institute of Higher Education Problems in the Soviet Union; the Pedagogical Research Center of Higher Education in Budapest; the Research Institute of Engineering Studies at the Technical University of Prague; the Chair of Higher Educational

Pedagogics at the Comenius University of Bratislava, Czechoslovakia; the Research Institute of Higher Education at Humboldt University in Berlin; and the science research center of the Board of Science, Technical Progression, and Higher Education in Bulgaria. All these research institutes are bound together in close cooperative work, often in the form of bilateral contracts. They conduct cooperative research on higher education, organizing bilateral and multilateral workshops and seminars. Those in Poland, the German Democratic Republic, and the Soviet Union coordinate research on higher education for the entire country. Their work reinforces the research conducted at higher schools of education, mainly in the departments of pedagogics, educational economics, and sociology. The research institutes also maintain international contacts, especially with UNESCO and its European Centre for Higher Education in Bucharest.

Regional Characteristics

While the Eastern European socialist countries maintain quite separate educational establishments, the principles underlying their different systems stem from a common ideology based on fundamental

Marxist pedagogics, which declare that a human being develops his personality and is capable of learning throughout his entire active intellectual life. Thus, higher schools of education throughout the region are structured to create conditions for the development of individual talents and creative skills.

Each national system sees the basic functions of higher education institutions as the development of scientific research; the application of research to the economic and social needs of the country; the education of personnel to fill the country's economic and social needs, including the education of scholarly personnel; the shaping of attitudes toward activism and commitment; and the strengthening of patriotic and international attitudes among graduates.

Since national objectives call for full democratization of education, access to higher education is available to members of all strata and social groups on the basis of open competition. Youth of worker-peasant families, however, are often given preferential treatment. Each government attempts to structure the student community in accordance with the class structure of society at large, and each has some system of material aid to students in the form of stipends, dormitories, medical services, and free tuition at every level. As higher education is one of the most important factors in the socioeconomic development of these socialist countries, all government development plans include a special section devoted to the direction, rate of development, and current obligations of schools of higher education.

While higher education institutions in the region are laic in character, there are some active theological academies and faculties, such as the Academy of Catholic Theology and the Academy of Christian Theology in Poland and the faculties of theology in the various German Democratic Republic universities—all of which are financed by the state. Private universities also exist (the Catholic University of Lublin, Poland, for example), but they generally

take on the character of a state institution.

Since 1965 there has been rapid development of postgraduate studies throughout the region, particularly in engineering, medicine, and teacher education. Periodic postexperience improvement programs are also provided for the purposes of updating professional knowledge, enhancing professional competence, and enabling professionals to master new areas of study and qualify for new jobs.

Until 1974 the politics of development of higher education was coordinated at yearly conferences of ministers of higher education in socialist countries. The participating countries are Bulgaria, Czechoslovakia, the German Democratic Republic, the Democratic Republic of Vietnam, Cuba, Mongolia, Hungary, Poland, Romania, and the Soviet Union. At the ninth conference, held in Cuba in 1974, it was decided to hold meetings at two-year intervals, with the tenth conference taking place in the fall of 1976 in Moscow. The activities coordinated by the Conference of Ministers include educational research plans, communist training for students, modernization of didactical processes, development of postgraduate studies, computerization, and development of student self-government.

Bibliography

Dabrowska, E. *Szkolnictwo Socjalistycznej Federacyjnej Republiki Jugoslawii na tle potrzeb rozwojowych kraju.* Wrocław, Poland: Ossolineum wydawnictwo Polskiej akademii nauk, 1975.
Education in the Socialist Republic of Romania. Bucharest: Ministry of Education, 1973.
Enseignement supérieur: Tendances internationales, 1960–1970. Paris: UNESCO, 1975.
Filipovic, M. *L'enseignement supérieur en Yougoslavie.* Belgrade: 1970.
Higher Education in Europe: Problems and Prospects, Statistical Study. Paris: UNESCO, 1973.
Ilku, P. "Glavnyie zadači vysšego obrazovania v Vengerskoi Narodnoi Respublikie." *Sovremennaia vysšaia škola,* 1973, *3.*
Januszkiewicz, F. *Education in Poland.* Warsaw: Interpress, 1973.
Jelutin, W. P. (Ed.) *Vysšaia škola SSSR za 50 let.* Moscow: Izdatelstvo "Vyshaya Shkola," 1967.

Ladanyi, A. "Važneišyie statističeskie pokaza-
tieli vysšego obrazovania v VNR." *Sovremennaia vysšaia škola,* 1972, *2*.

*Loi de l'enseignement dans la République socialiste
de Roumanie.* Bucharest: Didactic and Peda-
gogic, 1971.

Manulescu, K. "Aktualynie voprosy vysšego
obrazovania v Socialističeskoi Respublikie
Rumynii," *Sovremennaia vysšaia škola,* 1975, *2*.

Pančev, I. "Razvitie i problemy zaočnogo obrazovania v vysšych učebnych zavedeniach
Narodnoi Respublikie Bolgarii." *Sovremennaia vysšaia škola,* 1973, *3*.

Planification de l'éducation en Roumanie. Paris:
UNESCO, 1975.

Schultz, H. J. "Nekotory e voprosy razvitia
vysšego obrazovania GDR v usloviach tech-
niceskogo progressa." *Sovremennaia vysšaia
škola,* 1975, *3*.

*Statističeskii ežegodnik stran členov Sovieta Ekono-
mičeskoi Vzaimopomošči.* Moscow: Council for
Mutual Economic Aid, 1974.

Todoriev, N. "Sistema vysšego obrazovania v
Narodnoi Respublikie Bolgarii." *Sovremennaia vysšaia škola,* 1975, *1*.

Tomich, V. *Education in Yugoslavia and the
New Reform.* Washington, D.C.: U.S. Department of Health, Education and Welfare,
1973.

Tymowski J., and Januszkiewicz, F. *Post Sec-
ondary Education of Persons Already Gainfully
Employed in European Socialist Countries.*
Paris: UNESCO, 1976.

"Vysšaia škola socialističeskich stran: 30 let
razvitia u usloviach mira." *Sovremennaia
vysšaia škola,* 1975, *3*.

FRANCISZEK JANUSZKIEWICZ

See also: Albania, People's Socialist Republic
of; Bulgaria, People's Republic of; German
Democratic Republic; Hungarian People's
Republic; Polish People's Republic; Romania,
Socialist Republic of; Union of Soviet Socialist
Republics; Yugoslavia, Socialist Federal Re-
public of.

EAST-WEST CENTER

The East-West Center, officially designated the Center for Cultural and Technical Interchange Between East and West,
was established in Hawaii by the United
States Congress in 1960 as a national educational institution with multinational
programs. The center's mandate, in the
words of the federal legislation by which
it was created (Public Law 86–472), is "to
promote better relations and understanding between the United States and the
nations of Asia and the Pacific through
cooperative study, training and research."

Organization and Purpose

Thus, from its inception, the East-West
Center has differed from others in the
educational field because its programs are
required to be: (1) international in scope,
(2) cooperative in nature and process, and
(3) productive of better multinational relations and understanding through cultural
and technical interchange. In 1975 the
center was chartered by a special act of
the Hawaii State Legislature as a public
educational nonprofit corporation, with a
governing board of distinguished individuals from the United States, Asia, and
the Pacific area. Members include five
persons appointed by the United States secretary of state and five persons appointed
by the governor of Hawaii. Ex officio members of the corporation's board of governors include the governor of Hawaii and
the assistant secretary of state for educational and cultural affairs. The president
of the University of Hawaii serves as a nonvoting member. The appointed and ex
officio members elect an additional five
governors. The corporation governing
board makes an annual agreement with the
Department of State for congressional
funding of center programs. Other support comes in the form of contracts with
government agencies, private foundations,
and international organizations. The center also makes arrangements for joint funding with Asian and Pacific governments
and other sources.

Each year about fifteen hundred scholars, public officials, middle- and upper-
level managers, and graduate students
come to the center to exchange ideas and
experiences in programs concerned with
seeking alternative approaches and solutions to important world problems of mutual concern to people in both the East and
the West. Participants and staff are drawn
from the United States and more than sixty

countries and territories, ranging from Korea to Iran on the Asian continent and from Japan to Australia to Easter Island in the Pacific. For each participant selected from the United States, two are selected from the Asian-Pacific area. Some participants from other areas of the world also come to the center if nonappropriated funding is available.

Located in Honolulu, Hawaii, on twenty-one acres of land adjacent to the Manoa campus of the University of Hawaii, the center campus includes buildings for program activities and offices, administrative services, and residence halls for participants. Through cooperative relationships with the University of Hawaii, many center staff members hold joint appointments with the university; staff members also have access to university libraries, the computer center, and athletic facilities. University degree programs also are made available to center participants who come to Hawaii for that purpose.

The professional staff of the center includes men and women of more than a dozen nationalities, diverse academic backgrounds, and wide practical experience. The staff provides the framework, content, and continuity for the widespread multinational participation in center programs and for cooperative relationships with universities and other institutions in Asia, the Pacific, and the United States.

Programs

The programs of the center are conducted by five problem-oriented institutes, organized in 1970, in which international, interdisciplinary teams of staff work with each other and participants on mutual concerns. Each program is designed to have an academic staff of from fifteen to twenty people from different disciplines, nations, cultures, and professions. Working with participants and cooperating with other institutions on the American mainland and in Asia, each program works to produce new knowledge on a given problem and ways of applying this new knowl-

edge to policy, education, curricula, and other educational materials. The most important product, perhaps, is the participant in the program, who gains an international, solution-oriented perspective.

The East-West Communication Institute seeks new knowledge about the processes of communication and fosters the reduction of barriers to understanding by improving communication and sharing of knowledge between peoples of different cultures.

The East-West Culture Learning Institute focuses on developing new knowledge about the differences and similarities between cultures, how people learn their own culture, how those of one culture learn a second culture and language, and what persons learn about their own culture when they make the effort to function in a second culture.

The East-West Food Institute generates and disseminates knowledge and viewpoints concerning the world food system and the human, economic, and technical problems of food use, distribution, and production.

The East-West Population Institute contributes to the understanding and solution of population problems through cooperative investigation of the population process and structure, the causes and effects of demographic behavior, and the development of national and international population policy.

The East-West Technology and Development Institute aims at increasing understanding of the development process as a whole, with particular emphasis on the roles and interactions of peoples, institutions, policies, and technological change as development proceeds and on the effects of technology on the processes of economic, social, and cultural change in both East and West.

The center aspires to be a learning institution rather than a teaching institution. Consequently, it emphasizes the cooperative generation and exchange of knowledge; does not offer credit courses or confer degrees; attempts to ensure that problem issues addressed in its programs are of concern both to the East and to the West; develops intellectual products useful to educators and policymakers; and conducts its projects with multiprofessional, multinational, and multidisciplinary participation.

Insofar as possible, center programs are designed as two-way processes of communication, in which no one side, East or West, is always the teacher or always the learner. Thus, although the center is in the United States, Easterners are included among the teachers and Westerners among the learners. Continuing links with agencies and institutions in Asia, the Pacific, and the United States are strengthened by the center's policy of designing, conducting, and evaluating its projects in cooperation with other organizations, universities, and agencies.

Participants

Each year the center also awards a limited number of open grants for graduate study and research by scholars and professionals in problem areas not encompassed by the center's formal programs.

All participants are encouraged to develop their capacity for critical judgment and to engage in sustained and independent search for the truth. Since both pursuits require freedom of inquiry and freedom of expression, the charter of the new corporation states that the corporation shall uphold and preserve academic freedom in all of the programs and activities of the East-West Center, shall neither conduct nor support any classified activity or research, and shall make the results of its activities and research available to the public.

The basic units of work in the center's multidisciplinary programs are projects designed to integrate the efforts of both staff and participants. Project participants fall into three broad categories. The first category consists of visiting research associates and fellows, who are primarily engaged in cooperative research in specific center projects. The second category consists of professionals from middle- and upper-management echelons of government, business, and education. Professionals come for a variety of center-sponsored seminars, workshops, and other activities, in which research is outlined, curricula and other products are developed, and planning and policy are discussed. Individual internships also are arranged for professional development of potential leaders in management and research. The third category consists of degree students, mostly at the graduate level, who receive scholarships for study at the University of Hawaii while also engaged in center projects, and joint doctoral interns from other universities, who are offered research opportunities in center programs after completing doctoral course requirements at their home institutions.

EVERETT KLEINJANS

ECONOMIC COMMITTEE FOR LATIN AMERICA
See Organization of American States.

ECONOMIC COUNCIL OF CANADA (Conseil économique du Canada)

The Economic Council of Canada (*Conseil économique du Canada*), created in 1963 by an act of the Parliament of Canada, is an economic research and policy advisory agency. Although it is neither an institution of higher education nor formally affiliated with any such institutions, the Economic Council interfaces, informally and indirectly, with higher education. Consensus reports and research studies of the council are used widely as course material and references in universities and colleges, both inside and outside Canada. Council researchers often give lectures or seminars at institutions of higher education, and professors of economics frequently are contracted to undertake specific research assignments for the council.

There are twenty-eight members of the council, all appointed by the federal cabinet. Of these, twenty-five are appointed for three-year terms, on a part-time basis, from various elements of the private sector across the country. Three members—the chairperson, vice-chairperson, and director—are professional economists appointed for seven-year terms on a full-time basis. The council is financed out of annual grants by Parliament. Expenditures are audited by the auditor general of Canada.

The council's research and analysis provide a broad economic blueprint for Canada. Through participation by representatives of labor, business, agriculture, and other interests, the council tries to influence public policy on important national issues. In an attempt to gain widespread public agreement about national objectives, the council publishes consensus reports and background research studies.

The research program includes ongoing and short-term projects such as an annual report on the performance of the economy, an econometric model of the economy, and studies of social indicators and financial markets. The council also undertakes special studies, either on its own initiative or at the request of the government. Examples of the former are studies on commercial policy and labor markets. Three special study areas have been referred to the council by the government—income policy, competition policy, and the construction cycle. In 1973 and 1974 the council sponsored national economic conferences.

333 River Road
Vanier, Ontario, Canada

WILLIAM E. HAVILAND

ECONOMIC IMPACT OF COLLEGES AND UNIVERSITIES

See Urban University.

ECONOMICS (Field of Study)

The term *economics* is derived from the Greek *oikonomike*, which means "the man-agement of a household or state"; and when economists speak of an economy, they are referring to the ways in which a community manages its resources. More specifically, economics is a social science concerned principally with the way a society chooses to employ its limited resources to produce goods and services for present and future consumption. Economics is also concerned with economic growth and development, income and wealth distribution, and personal economic wealth. Economists analyze the ways that different types of economic systems organize their limited human and physical resources to meet the individual's wants for such things as food, clothing, shelter, and other goods, and society's collective wants for such things as police and fire protection, education, transportation, and health.

Economics can trace its beginnings to the ancient Greeks and the writings of Aristotle, Plato, the Stoics, and the Epicureans. Contributions to economics have been made through the centuries. A major breakthrough into modern economics occurred in 1776 with the publication of *Inquiry into the Nature and Causes of the Wealth of Nations* by Adam Smith, followed by writings of John Stuart Mill, David Ricardo, and Thomas Robert Malthus. These men are considered the classical economists. In 1890 Alfred Marshall published his *Principles of Economics* and became the foremost exponent of neoclassical economics. Although many other individuals and groups—for instance, the German Historical School, the Austrian School, and Karl Marx—made some contributions to economics, the modern theory of income and employment (that is, modern macroeconomic theory) is the result of work done by John Maynard Keynes, *The General Theory of Employment, Interest and Money*, published in 1936.

As a social science, economics is closely related to other social and behavioral sciences—history, political science, psychology, and sociology. In many aspects of economics, economists use the tools and framework of these related fields. Statistics and mathematics also are major analytical tools for economists.

There are various branches or divisions of economics; the following listing includes the major categories: (1) economic theory—study of the theoretical framework from which microeconomic and macroeconomic problems are analyzed; (2) economic history—the study of history, with major focus on economic factors; (3) history of economic thought—study of the chronological development of economic ideas, generally through the theories of noted economists; (4) economic systems—comparative study of the economic functioning of different economic systems, such as capitalism, socialism, and communism; (5) economic statistics—study of various statistical techniques, as applied to economic phenomena; (6) agricultural economics—application of economic theory and concepts to the agricultural sector and its special problems; (7) econometrics—a field of study that uses the combined knowledge of economics, statistics, and mathematics as a tool to analyze complex economic problems; (8) economic growth and development—study of the factors that lead to growth and development; (9) industrial organization—study of the theoretical framework of the performance of real markets; (10) international economics—study of the theory of international trade and its role in resource allocation, including foreign exchange and the balance-of-payments mechanism; (11) mathematical economics—application of mathematical analysis to economics; (12) monetary and fiscal theory—study of the effect of money and government fiscal policy on the economy; (13) labor and manpower economics—study of the special problems of the labor market and the labor force, and the institutions and policies dealing with them; (14) public finance—study of the principles of taxation, tax incidence, and government expenditures, and their effect on the total economy; (15) regional and urban economics—study

of theories concerning the impact of the location of firms, industries, and people on the modern city.

In recent years there have been a number of significant developments in economics. Most notably, economists have made increased use of sophisticated mathematical and statistical tools, such as the computer; as a result, they have been able to analyze many complex problems that previously appeared impossible. Moreover, to a greater degree than previously, economists have focused on the study of applied economics, in contrast to theoretical economics. Also, more economists are specializing in one or more of the related branches of economics.

Although economics originated mainly in Western Europe, it has become a genuinely international discipline in the sense that economists from various countries generally draw on and, depending on their inclination, try to contribute to the same analytic structure; to a notable degree, they also make use of similar empirical methodologies and share empirical findings. There are, of course, differences among countries in emphasis and approach. At one time such differences were marked indeed, as exemplified by the empirical stress of the German Historical School, on the one hand, and the strong a priori tradition in England, on the other. But as time has passed, such differences have tended to diminish rather than increase.

The trend toward internationalization, if it may be called that, has been especially strong since World War II. This trend reflects both the evolving nature of the discipline, especially the increased use of mathematics and quantitative data, and the changing international environment, which to a greater degree than previously has posed problems of common concern to economists in different countries. Advances in technology of travel and communication have also contributed to internationalization by facilitating contacts and exchanges. In addition, after World War II many international organizations concerned with the promotion of such contacts and exchanges were established. Among these organizations the International Economic Association is probably the best known, but there are numerous others.

Although economics transcends national boundaries, economics as a discipline had for a long time only a relatively limited existence in communist countries. But Marxism-Leninism never entirely excluded the discipline of economics, and the process of internationalization has been marked even there. Thus, analytic principles and tools and research methodologies familiar elsewhere have come to be accepted in communist countries as well, and economists from those countries participate with colleagues from other societies in diverse international exchanges.

MORRIS A. HOROWITZ

Levels and Programs of Study

Programs in economics generally require as a prerequisite a secondary education and lead to the following awards: certificate or diploma, bachelor's degree, master's degree (M.A., M.Sc.), the doctorate (Ph.D.), or their equivalents. Programs consist of instruction, group or seminar discussion, and, for advanced degrees, study and original research work as substantiated by the presentation of a scholarly thesis or dissertation.

Programs that lead to an award not equivalent to a first university degree deal with the fundamental principles of economics and the functioning of economic institutions and are typically given in technological or similar institutions. Short courses of less than one year are often sponsored by employers, employers' associations, or trade unions. Principal course content usually includes basic concepts and terminology of economics, economic activities and institutions, analysis of economic problems, standards of living, problems of the consumer, operations of business, business costs and prices, competition and monopoly, corporations, antitrust laws, public

utilities, government and business, money and credit, effects of inflation and deflation, monetary standards, natural resources and the farm problems of the worker, labor-management relations, international economic relations, government and taxation, and business cycles.

Programs that lead to a first university degree deal with the theoretical and institutional bases of modern economic systems, their histories, and their operating principles. Principal course content usually includes principles of economics, economic theory, history of economic thought, economic history, economic organization and planning, economic development in historical perspective, public finance, labor economics, money and banking, industrial organization, urban economics, national accounts, international and interregional exchange, monetary policy, international payments, marketing, and econometrics. Usual background courses include statistical methods, mathematics, and study of social and political institutions.

Programs that lead to a postgraduate university degree deal with economic theories, economic institutions, and economic policies. Principal course content and areas of research usually include advanced economic theory, history of economic doctrines, economic history, international trade and payments, monetary theory and policy, the business cycle, transportation economics, public finance, labor economics, welfare economics, marketing, econometrics, problems of economic development, and consumption economics. Background studies usually include courses in business administration, sociology, political science, psychology, mathematics, and statistics.

[This section was based on UNESCO's *International Standard Classification of Education (ISCED): Three Stage Classification System, 1974* (Paris: UNESCO, 1974).]

Levels and Programs of Study in Socialist Countries

In the socialist countries students of economics are required to take four to five years of work in universities or institutes after they have successfully completed a secondary education and passed an entrance examination. Programs consist of lectures, seminars, and examinations. The student must defend a thesis before completing undergraduate work. Course work in economics usually includes political economy of capitalism and socialism; economic history; history of economic thought; planning; economic geography; econometrics and application of computers; accounting; statistics; management; and, according to the student's specialty, economics of industry, agriculture, transportation, construction, or finance; world economics; or foreign trade. The number of hours for lectures and seminars varies from 50 to 60 (for branches of economics) to 120 to 150 (for planning) and 200 to 250 (for political economy). Background courses include philosophy, mathematics, and principles of technology.

A student at the postgraduate degree level takes entrance examinations and then works (usually for three years) under the supervision of a professor. The student must take a candidate examination (in three main areas in the field and two languages) and successfully defend a dissertation before he is awarded a degree of candidate of economics. To receive a doctorate in economics, a student must defend a dissertation of much higher scientific value.

Graduates from universities may teach economics in universities and institutes, or they may work as economists in management offices on all levels, from national economy to enterprise. Usually they work in planning, accounting, statistics, trade, financing, and supply.

Since economics is also important for engineers, undergraduates in technological institutes take short courses in economics—namely, political economy (up to 80-100 hours) and the economics of such industries as metallurgy, machine building, or chemicals (up to 50-60 hours). Refresher courses in economics are also offered to graduates after several years of work. Special institutions or faculties give short advanced courses in planning, econometrics, management, and marketing.

[This section was provided by T. Khachaturov, Chairman of the Presidium, Association of the Soviet Economic Scientific Institutions, Moscow.]

Major International and National Organizations

INTERNATIONAL

The following are nongovernmental organizations:

Afro-Asian Organization for Economic Co-operation
Organisation afro-asiatique de coopération économique
Cairo Chamber of Commerce Building
Midan, el-Falaky
Cairo, Egypt

Association of European Institutes of Economic Research
Association d'instituts européens de conjuncture économique
Adenauerallee 170
53 Bonn, Federal Republic of Germany

Econometric Society
Box 1264
Yale Station
New Haven, Connecticut 06520 USA

European Scientific Association of Applied Economics
Association scientifique européenne d'économie appliquée
University of Geneva
Centre d'économétrie
6 rue de Saussure
Geneva, Switzerland

International Association for Research in Income and Wealth
Box 2020
Yale Station
New Haven, Connecticut 06520 USA

International Association of Agricultural Economists
600 South Michigan Avenue
Chicago, Illinois 60605 USA

International Association of Students in Business and Economics
Association internationale des étudiants en sciences économiques et commerciales
45 avenue Legrand
B1050 Brussels, Belgium

International Confederation of Associations
of Graduates in Economic and Commercial
Sciences
Confédération internationale des associations
de diplômes en sciences économiques et
commerciales (CIADEC)
BP 504
CH-2001 Neuchâtel, Switzerland

International Economic Association (IEA)
Association internationale des sciences
économiques
54 boulevard Raspail
Paris 6e, France

International Economic History Association
Association internationale d'histoire
économique
Rindermarkt 6
8001 Zurich, Switzerland

The following are intergovernmental international organizations:

European Economic Community (EEC)
200 rue de la Loi
1040 Brussels, Belgium

Inter-American Economic and Social Council
General Secretariat, Organization of American
States (OAS)
17th and Constitution Avenue
Washington, D.C. 20006 USA

International Bank for Reconstruction and
Development (IBRD)
1818 H Street NW
Washington, D.C. 20433 USA

International Monetary Fund (IMF)
19th and H Streets NW
Washington, D.C. 20431 USA

Organisation for Economic Co-operation and
Development
2 rue André Pascal
75775 Paris, France

United Nations Economic and Social Council
New York, New York 10017 USA
Includes four semiautonomous regional eco-
nomic commissions:

Economic Commission for Africa (ECA)
P.O. Box 3001
Addis Ababa, Ethiopia

United Nations Economic Commission for
Asia and the Far East (ECAFE)
Sala Santitham
Rajadamnern Avenue
Bangkok, Thailand

United Nations Economic Commission for
Europe (ECE)
Palais des Nations
CH-1211 Geneva, Switzerland

United Nations Economic Commission for
Latin America (ECLA)
P. O. Box 179-D
Santiago, Chile

For a comprehensive list of international
organizations important in economics see:

Yearbook of International Organizations. Brussels: Union of International Associations,
biennial.

NATIONAL

Australia:
Economic Society of Australia and
New Zealand
% University of Melbourne
Parkville, Victoria 3052

Canada:
Canadian Economics Association
100 Saint George Street
Toronto 5, Ontario

Federal Republic of Germany:
Bundesverband deutscher Verwaltungs-
und Wirtschafts-Akademien
Postfach 8002 03
D-5000 Cologne 80

France:
Institut national de la statistique et des
études économiques
23 quai Branly
75 Paris 7e

Société d'économie et de sciences sociales
66 avenue de Saxe
F-75005 Paris

Japan:
Kokusai keizai gakkai
Society of International Economics
seiko biru 7-2-1, Minami-Aoyama
Minato-ku
Tokyo 107

United Kingdom:
Economics Association
101 Hatton Garden
London EC1, England

Royal Economics Society
Marshall Library
Sidgwick Avenue
Cambridge CB3 9DB, England

United States:
American Economic Association
Suite 809, Oxford House
1313 21st Avenue, South
Nashville, Tennessee 37212

Joint Council on Economic Education
(JCEE)
1212 Avenue of the Americas
New York, New York 10036

For additional listings see:

Minerva, Wissenschaftliche Gesellschaften. Berlin, Federal Republic of Germany: de Gruyter, 1972.

World Guide to Scientific Associations. New York: Bowker; Pullach/Munich, Federal Republic of Germany: Verlag Dokumentation, 1974.

The World of Learning. London: Europa, annual. Provides details of learned societies; international in scope.

For American organizations see:

Encyclopedia of Associations. (9th ed.) Detroit: Gale Research, 1975.

Principal Information Sources

GENERAL

General guides to the literature in economics include:

Fletcher, J. (Ed.) *The Use of Economics Literature.* Hamden, Connecticut: Archon, 1971.

Guide des sources d'information économique en Europe. Paris: Les éditions d'organisation, 1974.

Maltby, A. *Economics and Commerce: The Sources of Information and Their Organization.* London: Bingley, 1968.

Melnyk, P. *Economics: Bibliographic Guide to Reference Books and Information Resources.* Littleton, Colorado: Libraries Unlimited, 1971.

Parsons, S. *How to Find Out About Economics.* Oxford, England: Pergamon Press, 1972.

White, C., and others. (Eds.) *Sources of Information in the Social Sciences.* (2nd ed.) Chicago: American Library Association, 1973.

Among the general histories of economic thought are:

Blaug, M. *Economic Theory in Retrospect.* (2nd ed.) Homewood, Illinois: Irwin, 1968.

Dobb, M. *Theories of Value and Distribution Since Adam Smith.* Cambridge, England: Cambridge University Press, 1973.

Nove, A., and Nuti, D. M. (Eds.) *Socialist Economics.* Middlesex, England: Penguin, 1972.

Schumpeter, J. A. *History of Economic Analysis.* New York: Oxford University Press, 1954.

Whittaker, E. *A History of Economic Ideas.* New York: Longmans, Green and Co., 1943.

Introductory texts to the field include:

Boulding, K. A. *Economic Analysis.* (3rd ed.) New York: Harper & Row, 1955.

Lipsey, R. G., and Steiner, P. *Economics.* (2nd ed.) New York: Harper & Row, 1969.

Paish, F. W., and Culyer, A. J. *Benham's Economics.* New York: Beekman, 1973.

Samuelson, P. A. *Economics: An Introductory Analysis.* (9th ed.) New York: McGraw-Hill, 1973.

Additional texts on aspects of economics include:

Baumol, W. J. *Economic Theory and Operations Analysis.* (3rd ed.) Englewood Cliffs, New Jersey: Prentice-Hall, 1961.

Branson, W. H. *Macroeconomic Theory and Policy.* New York: Harper & Row, 1972.

Dernburg, T., and McDougall, D. M. *Macroeconomics: The Measurement, Analysis, and Control of Aggregate Economic Activity.* (4th ed.) New York: McGraw-Hill, 1972.

Ferguson, C. E., and Gould, J. P. *Microeconomic Theory.* (4th ed.) Homewood, Illinois: Irwin, 1975.

Stigler, G. J. *The Theory of Price.* (3rd ed.) London: Macmillan, 1966.

CURRENT BIBLIOGRAPHIES

Sources of current economic writings are found in the following:

Documentation économique. Paris: Presses universitaires de France, 1947–.

Economic Abstracts. The Hague: Library of the Economic Information Service, 1953–.

Economic Books: Current Selections. Clifton, New Jersey: Augustus M. Kelley, 1974–.

Economics Selections: An International Bibliography. Pittsburgh: University of Pittsburgh, Department of Economics, 1954–.

Ekonomisk dokumentation. Stockholm: Stockholm School of Economics Library, 1969–.

Index of Economic Journals. Homewood, Illinois: Irwin, 1961–. Now titled *Index of Economic Articles.*

International Bibliography of Economics. Chicago: Aldine, 1962–.

Journal of Economic Literature. Kingsport, Tennessee: American Economic Association, 1969–.

Keizogaku, B. K. *Quarterly Bibliography of Economics.* Tokyo: Yuhikaku, 1956–.

Public Affairs Information Service Bulletin. New York: Public Affairs Information Service, 1915–.

Schweizerische Bibliographie für Statistik und Volkswirtschaft. Bern, Switzerland: Schweizerische Gesellschaft für Statistik und Volkswirtschaft, 1938–.

PERIODICALS

Among the most important economics journals internationally are *American Economic Review, Canadian Journal of Economics, Econometrica* (US), *Economia internazionale* (Italy), *Economica* (Argentina), *Economic History Review* (UK), *Economic Journal* (UK), *Economic Record* (Australia), *Indian Journal of Economics, International Economic Review* (US), *Journal of Development Economics* (Netherlands), *Journal of Econometrics* (Netherlands), *Journal of Economic Education*

(US), *Journal of Economic History* (US), *Journal of Economic Literature* (US), *Journal of Economic Theory* (US), *Journal of Financial Economics* (Netherlands), *Journal of Mathematical Economics* (Netherlands), *Journal of Monetary Economics* (Netherlands), *Journal of Political Economy* (US), *Journal of Public Economics* (Netherlands), *Oxford Economic Papers* (US), *Pakistan Development Review*, *Problems of Economics* (US), *Quarterly Journal of Economics* (US), *Review of Economics and Statistics* (US), *Review of Economic Studies* (UK), *Revue des sciences économiques* (Belgium), *Revue économique* (France), *Rivista di politica economica* (Italy), *Weltwirtschaftliches Archiv/Review of World Economics* (FRG), *Zeitschrift für Nationaloekonomie/Journal of Economics* (Austria and US).

For a more complete listing of journals in economics consult:

Economic Abstracts. The Hague: Library of the Economic Information Service, 1953–. International selection of economic periodicals.
Ulrich's International Periodicals Directory. New York: Bowker, biennial.

ENCYCLOPEDIAS, DICTIONARIES, HANDBOOKS

Clifford-Vaughan, F., and Clifford-Vaughan, m. (Eds.) *A Glossary of Economics Including Soviet Terminology in English/American-French-German-Russian*. Amsterdam: Elsevier, 1966.
Gould, J., and Kolb, W. L. (Eds.) *Dictionary of the Social Sciences*. New York: Free Press, 1964.
Higgs, H. (Ed.) *Palgrave's Dictionary of Political Economy*. London: Macmillan, 1923–1926.
McGraw-Hill Dictionary of Modern Economics. (2nd ed.) New York: McGraw-Hill, 1973.
Paenson, I. *Systematic Glossary English/French/Spanish/Russian of Selected Economic and Social Terms*. New York: Macmillan, 1963.
Romeuf, J. (Ed.) *Dictionnaire des sciences économiques*. Paris: Presses universitaires de France, 1956–1958.
Seligman, E. R. A. (Ed.) *Encyclopedia of the Social Sciences*. New York: Macmillan, 1930–1935.
Sills, D. L. (Ed.) *International Encyclopedia of the Social Sciences*. New York: Macmillan, 1968.
Sloan, H. S., and Zurcher, A. J. *Dictionary of Economics*. (5th ed.) New York: Barnes & Noble, 1971.

DIRECTORIES

The following guides contain information on educational facilities in economics throughout the world:

American Universities and Colleges. (11th ed.) Washington, D.C.: American Council on Education, 1973.
Commonwealth Universities Yearbook. London: As-

sociation of Commonwealth Universities, annual.
International Handbook of Universities. (5th ed.) Paris: International Association of Universities, 1971.
World Guide to Universities. Pullach/Munich, Federal Republic of Germany: Verlag Dokumentation, 1972.
The World of Learning. London: Europa, annual.

RESEARCH CENTERS, INSTITUTES, INFORMATION CENTERS

For an international directory of research centers and institutes in economics consult:

Minerva, Forschungsinstitute. Berlin, Federal Republic of Germany: de Gruyter, 1972.
World Index of Social Science Institutions. Paris: UNESCO, 1970–.

About seven hundred scientific research institutes, universities, and facilities of economics are listed in:

List of Institutions in the Field of Applied Economics in E.C.E. Countries. Geneva: United Nations Economic Commission for Europe, 1966.

Some important economics libraries are:

Bibliothèque de l'Institut national de la statistique et des études économiques (Paris)
British Library of Political and Economic Science (London School of Economics)
Dag Hammarskjöld Library (United Nations, New York)
Goldsmith's Library (University of London)
Harvard University Libraries, Baker Library (Cambridge, Massachusetts)
Hitotsubashi University Library (Tokyo)
Institute for World Economics (Kiel, Federal Republic of Germany)
Joint Bank-Fund Library of the World Bank and International Monetary Fund (Washington, D.C.)
Library of Congress (Washington, D.C.)
New York Public Library (New York)
United Nations Library (Geneva)
Yale University Libraries (New Haven, Connecticut)

ECONOMICS OF HIGHER EDUCATION

Traditionally, the factors influencing education in the community have been examined from the sociodemographic point of view. It has been established, for example, that education promotes such social goals as the creation of better citizens and the possibility of social mobility by facilitating occupational change. It is also well-known that a higher birthrate will generate, after a time lag, a higher demand for school places.

Since the late 1950s, however, education has been increasingly looked on from the (complementary) economic viewpoint. This involves comparing the costs and benefits associated with particular educational activities. In the process of comparison, economists also assess the producers' (societies') and consumers' (students') reactions to changing incentives and rewards. Furthermore, one could study people's behavior as producers and consumers of a good called education. According to this approach, then, education has an economic impact on the individual and on society as a whole. At the same time, the country's economic conditions influence the demand for education by individuals. Although these factors—the economic effects of higher education and the factors affecting demand for higher education—will be discussed separately, it should be obvious that they are, in practice, closely related. In this sense, it would be wise to think in terms of associations rather than causes and effects.

Social Importance of Education

There are two ways of assessing the importance of education in a society. One is by looking at the number of students enrolled (by educational level) and noting growth trends over time. Another is by looking at the amount of resources a country devotes to education.

Growth of enrollments. While primary education accounts for the major share of total school enrollment in all countries, a UNESCO study (1972) reveals that higher education levels grow faster than those of other levels. This growth is seen especially in less developed countries. In 1970 a little over 71 percent of all students enrolled worldwide were in primary education; only 5.4 percent were enrolled in higher education. In the same year, the percentage of students in higher education in developed countries was 8.8 percent; in less developed countries, 2.2 percent. However, between 1965 and 1970, higher education enrollments rose 8.4 percent in less developed countries, as compared to 7.5 percent in developed countries. The worldwide growth rate for primary education was 2.8 percent; for secondary education, it was 3.8 percent.

Resources allocated to education. The monetary corollary of the figures in the 1972 study is that developed countries today devote about 8 percent of their national income, or as much as 20 percent of their budget, to education (UNESCO, 1972); less developed countries spend about half as much. About 20 percent of the total resources a country spends on education is used for higher education. This statistic does not vary much with degree of economic development. Whereas advanced countries have a higher relative enrollment in the tertiary sector, less developed countries have relatively higher direct student costs in this sector, so the net result is a fairly stable budgeting pattern worldwide, regardless of national differences in higher education enrollments or economic development. For example, the share of higher education in the total recurring educational expenditure in the United States is 29 percent, whereas the corresponding statistic is 24 percent in Chile, 23 percent in India, and 20 percent in France (UNESCO, 1970, Table 2.20).

These figures underestimate the true amount of resources devoted to education, since they refer to the direct component only; that is, they do not take into account the output lost while students are at school. Students' forgone earnings are a resource cost and form a significant proportion of the social costs of education. This factor is particularly important at the higher education level in advanced countries, and even at the primary level in poor countries, where children help in agricultural production. Taking into account this *in-*

direct cost, the amount of resources devoted to education could be easily doubled (Psacharopoulos, 1973, p. 14).

Income Value

The provision of education has economic effects on the individual, the society as a whole, the country's rate of growth, and the way that income is distributed in a society. The relationship among these factors may be seen by examining them in turn.

Individual returns. It is a statistical fact that people with more education earn more than people with less education. For example, in the United States a college degree means on the average an extra annual income of nearly $5000, relative to someone without such a degree. In 1972, for example, the mean income of persons with an elementary education was $5467; a high school graduate received an average of $8148; and the average salary for the college graduate was $12,938 (United States Bureau of the Census, 1972).

Of course, this extra income was obtained at some cost. That cost includes a sacrifice of $8000 or more in potential earnings during the four years of stay in college and direct expenses of at least $2000 per year for tuition and books. The yield of this venture to the individual is 12.5 percent = 5000/4(8000 + 2000). In other words, the typical United States college graduate makes 12.5 percent per year on the money he has invested in his college education. This rate of return, naturally, differs for different countries; statistics from earlier studies indicate an international average return to the individual of 17.5 percent (Psacharopoulos, 1973, p. 5).

Benefits to society. The social effects of education are not as easily quantifiable as the individual effects. As a first approximation, one can assume that the annual social benefit generated by one college graduate is equal to the before-tax earnings differential between college graduates and secondary school graduates. This benefit could then be compared to the true social cost of a college place (approximately

$4000—the difference between the social and private direct cost of education arising because of public subsidization of education in most countries). The result of this illustrative cost-benefit analysis is a social yield of 10 percent = 5000/4(8000 + 4000). In other words, society as a whole enjoys a 10 percent return on its resources devoted to the education of one college graduate. Again, the rate varies nationally, the average being 11.3 percent (Psacharopoulos, 1973, p. 5). (In this example, the before- and after-tax earnings were assumed to be the same, to stress the point that it is really the direct public subsidy of higher education that produces a lower social rate of return.)

One can, of course, question the validity of the above calculation on the grounds that the social contribution of one college graduate might be greater or smaller than his wages. There exist econometric techniques according to which one can base profitability calculations of this kind on the true marginal product of labor rather than on the observed wages (Psacharopoulos, 1970).

Effects on national growth. The economic effects reported above refer to one typical college graduate. Taking into account the human capital created in an economy as a whole by graduates at all educational levels, it is possible to estimate the contribution of education to a country's output or rate of economic growth. This can be accomplished by multiplying an estimate of the total human investment by the social rate of return on this form of investment (Schultz, 1961). Calculations of this kind performed for the United States show that investment in education as a whole contributes about 18 percent to the country's rate of output growth, or slightly more than the international average (Psacharopoulos, 1973, p. 119). The share of higher education is about one fourth of this figure in the United States, as compared with one seventh worldwide; the rest comes from primary and secondary education.

Income distribution. Since education has a strong impact on individual earnings, it must also affect the way income is distributed in a society. It seems reasonable to assume that if more higher education were provided, income distribution would become more equal. However, recent studies show that the relationship between education and income distribution is not so straightforward. In fact, it has been claimed that the lower-income groups subsidize (through taxes) the education of the rich. (For the controversy on this issue, see Hansen and Weisbrod, 1969; and Hight and Pollock, 1973). Another line of argument against education as an equalizer stems from the claims that income should be redistributed by more direct means, such as taxes and subsidies, rather than indirectly via the provision of education (Jencks, 1972). Jencks' work, however, has been subject to wide criticism regarding the methodology by which he arrived at his conclusions (Rivlin, 1973).

Economic development and profitability. Lastly, it should be mentioned that the economic effects of education vary for each level of education and according to a country's degree of economic development. It is now widely accepted that the lower levels of education (primary and secondary) are more profitable, both privately and socially, than higher education, because the direct and indirect costs of education are lower at the early stages of schooling. A typical example of the application of the so-called "law of diminishing returns" in education is the evidence of the profitability of masters and doctoral programs in the United States and Great Britain, where returns on the order of 1 to 3 percent have been found (Bailey and Schotta, 1972). By a similar reasoning, the returns on all levels of education are higher in less developed countries, because the human capital base in these countries is still low and the completion of education carries a high premium (Psacharopoulos, 1973, p. 9).

Factors Affecting Demand

The traditional approach in explaining the growth of education has been the so-called "social demand" model. According to this model, parents and students express their demand for school places; politicians then provide these places—subject, of course, to their budgetary constraints. The economic approach, however, construes the demand for education (that is, for higher education) as a function of income and price. As the country's per capita income grows, more education is demanded in exactly the same way as, in a growing economy, consumers demand more meat and less grain. In other words, the growth of higher education can be explained by the concept of the income elasticity of demand.

Relative costs and benefits. Another reason that education is increasingly demanded is because it is cheaper relative to other goods. Since higher education is almost universally subsidized by the state and philanthropy, individuals aspire to a higher level of education than they would if they themselves had to pay the full cost. In this sense, the observed social demand for education is shaped by two economic factors. It is affected, first, by the increasing income of the consumer (because of economic growth), and second, by the subsidization policy of the state and philanthropy.

Another way one can apply the concept of price to demand for higher education is by looking at the relative salaries of graduates and nongraduates. Economic theory predicts that the higher the wages of graduates relative to nongraduates, the higher the demand for college enrollment. This proposition also applies in reverse— namely, when the relative salaries of graduates are depressed, the demand for higher education will slacken. In fact, this last phenomenon has been widely observed in Europe and in America in the first half of the 1970s. Simple economics suggest that the educational explosion of the 1960s is responsible for the decline in the relative salaries of graduates and, therefore, for the eventual decline in the rate of growth of college enrollment. This proposition has been documented even within professional fields, such as engineering (Freeman, 1971, p. 61). Similarly, there will be a sustained demand for higher education, so long as the individual's rate of return from college education exceeds the yield of alternative forms of investment.

Employment opportunities. That people respond to economic rewards may be seen in the case of the brain drain. Although there are many push-or-pull factors that have been mentioned in the literature on this phenomenon (Adams, 1968), the economic factors seem to be at least somewhat instrumental. One reason that graduates in less developed countries emigrate to the United States and Canada is the higher salaries obtainable in those countries (Psacharopoulos, 1973, Chapter 9). In turn, the enticement of possible employment at a higher salary abroad boosts the supply of graduates in developing countries. For example, the Philippines might produce fewer doctors if graduates from that country had fewer opportunities of emigrating to the United States.

Hiring policies. Two further economic factors should be mentioned to account for the expansion of higher education in less developed countries. The proliferation of manpower plans around the world since the late 1950s is one cause. These plans were (and some still are) produced on the basis of sectoral output targets that can only be achieved if specific numbers of graduates in different fields are available in the economy. The resulting recommendations for more university graduates were implemented by several governments via the creation of new (and very expensive) universities. The philosophy behind these plans has been mostly fallacious, as it assumes low substitution possibilities of labor with different educational qualifications (Ahamad and Blaug, 1973, Chapters 1 and 12).

Another reason for the popularity of higher education in less developed countries (and partly also in advanced ones) is the fact that, in the absence of profit maximizing guidelines, organizations usually hire on the basis of degrees (Psacharopoulos and Williams, 1973). This inevitably

generates a demand for paper qualifications at all levels and especially for higher degrees.

Limitations of an Economic Perspective

The cornerstone of economics as it is applied to education is that the higher earnings of graduates (relative to nongraduates) represent a true increment in productivity. This assumption has, however, often come under attack. Some economists maintain that there is no necessary correspondence between wages and the marginal product of labor. More recently, the so-called "screening hypothesis" has been advanced, which says that employers offer higher wages to graduates, not because they are more productive but because the degree is a good signal of the ability and probable performance of the employee (Arrow, 1973; Taubman and Wales, 1973). The implication is that educational credentials simply provide information about the ability of the individual and that, since a cheaper ability test could do the same thing, education is not socially profitable (although it continues to be privately profitable). Existing evidence, however, does not appear to support the screening hypothesis (Layard and Psacharopoulos, 1974).

Finally, an economic approach to education necessarily emphasizes monetary benefits and rewards because these are measurable entities. However, the true social effects of education include externalities that can hardly be measured. (For an effort to do so, see Weisbrod, 1964.) Therefore, the conclusions drawn from applying economics to education must be qualified by reference to the nonpecuniary and external effects. These qualifications usually reinforce the position, presented above, that higher education is socially valuable in an economic sense. The true economic effect of higher education is actually greater than the estimated pecuniary social rate of return because of the consumption benefits the individual derives over his lifetime and because of the beneficial effect he has on others.

Bibliography

Adams, W. "Introduction." In W. Adams (Ed.), *The Brain Drain*. London: Macmillan, 1968.

Ahamad, B., and Blaug, M. *The Practice of Manpower Forecasting*. Amsterdam: Elsevier, 1973.

Arrow, K. "Higher Education as a Filter." *Journal of Public Economics*, July 1973, *2*, 193–216.

Bailey, D., and Schotta, G. "Private and Social Rates of Return to Education of Academicians." *American Economic Review*, March 1972, *62*, 19–31.

Blaug, M. (Ed.) *Economics of Education: 1*. Middlesex, England: Penguin, 1968.

Blaug, M. (Ed.) *Economics of Education: 2*. Middlesex, England: Penguin, 1969.

Blaug, M. *Economics of Education: A Selected Annotated Bibliography*. Oxford, England: Pergamon Press, 1970.

Blaug, M. *An Introduction to the Economics of Education*. London: Allen Lane, 1970.

Freeman, R. *The Market for College Trained Manpower*. Cambridge, Massachusetts: Harvard University Press, 1971.

Gordon, M. (Ed.) *Higher Education and the Labour Market*. New York: McGraw-Hill, 1974.

Hansen, W. L., and Weisbrod, B. "The Distribution of Costs and Direct Benefits of Public Higher Education: The Case of California." *Journal of Human Resources*, 1969, *9*(2), 176–191.

Hight, J. E., and Pollock, R. "The Distribution of Transfers Among Income Classes Resulting from Higher Education Expenditures: A Comparison of California, Florida and Hawaii." *Journal of Human Resources*, 1973, *8*(3), 318–330.

Jencks, C. *Inequality*. New York: Basic Books, 1972.

Layard, R., and Psacharopoulos, G. "The Screening Hypothesis and the Returns to Education." *Journal of Political Economy*, 1974, *82*(5), 985–998.

Lipsey, R. *An Introduction to Positive Economics*. London: Weidenfeld and Nicolson, 1970.

Parnes, H. *Forecasting Educational Needs for Economic and Social Development*. Paris: Organisation for Economic Co-operation and Development, 1962.

Psacharopoulos, G. "Estimating Shadow Rates of Return to Investment in Education." *Journal of Human Resources*, 1970, *5*, 34–50.

Psacharopoulos, G. *Returns to Education: An International Comparison*. Amsterdam: Elsevier, 1973.

Psacharopoulos, G., and Williams, G. "Public Sector Earnings and Educational Planning." *International Labour Review*, 1973, *108*, 43–57.

Rivlin, A. "Forensic Social Science." *Harvard Educational Review*, 1973, *43*(1), 61–75.

Schultz, T. W. "Education and Economic Growth." In N. B. Henry (Ed.), *Social Forces Influencing American Education*. Chicago: University of Chicago Press, 1961.

Taubman, P., and Wales, T. "Higher Education, Mental Ability and Screening." *Journal of Political Economy*, 1973, *81*, 28–55.

UNESCO. *Statistical Yearbook*. Paris: UNESCO, 1970.

UNESCO. *Statistical Yearbook*. Paris: UNESCO, 1972.

United States Bureau of the Census. *Statistical Abstract of the United States*. Washington, D.C.: Bureau of the Census, 1972.

Weisbrod, W. *External Benefits of Public Education: An Economic Analysis*. Princeton, New Jersey: Industrial Relations Section, Princeton University, 1964.

GEORGE PSACHAROPOULOS

See also: Accountability; Financial Affairs: Cost Analysis.

ECUADOR, REPUBLIC OF

Population: 6,500,845. Student enrollment in primary school: 1,234,217; secondary school (academic, vocational, technical): 334,465; higher education—university: 136,695; higher education—nonuniversity: 8000 (estimate); higher education—total: 144,000 (estimate). Student enrollment in higher education as percentage of age group (18–22): 30% (estimate). Language of instruction: Spanish. Academic calendar: Pacific coast, May to end of January; rest of Ecuador, October to end of June. Percentage of gross national product (GNP) expended on all education: 3.07%; higher education: .72%. Percentage of national budget expended on all education: 22.3%; higher education: 5.2%. [Population figure is from Censo nacional de población (1974); enrollment figures are from Consejo nacional de educación superior (1975); budget figures are from Junta nacional de planificación (1974).]

Among the factors that are influencing the structure of postsecondary education in Ecuador in the 1970s can be mentioned (1) the rapid annual growth rate of 3.5 percent (one of the highest in the world); (2) the large proportion of rural population

(58.7 percent); (3) a process of moderate industrialization, which was begun in the late 1950s and brought large population increases to Quito and Guayaquil; and (4) an inequitable distribution of wealth, which is concentrated in a small upper class. Although Ecuador's middle class is statistically growing, its sociological impact is insignificant. The lower classes, which comprise some 50 percent of the population, are denied cultural and economic benefits and political participation.

Ecuador has been an independent republic since 1822; however, its political history has been quite unsettled, partly because it still has not achieved economic independence. Three steps may be noted in its history, which are reflected in the development of its higher education system: (1) the colonial period, (2) the period of the republic, and (3) the twentieth century.

Three universities were established in Quito during the colonial period: the University of Saint Fulgencio, founded by the Augustine Fathers in 1586; the University of Saint Gregory, founded by the Jesuits in 1622; and the University of Saint Thomas Aquinas, founded by the Dominicans in 1688. The Catholic church dominated university life during the colonial period and was the institution that contributed most to the development of education and culture in the country. The church universities fostered the growth of the humanistic and ecclesiastical disciplines. The University of Saint Gregory achieved the greatest fame during this period and included among its enrollees students from other regions of Spanish America. King Charles III of Spain in 1769 suppressed and then reestablished these universities into the first single official university in the country.

The public university, in addition to offering humanistic and ecclesiastical studies, established chairs in algebra, geometry, civil history, Spanish and New World jurisprudence, public law, political economy, and medicine. The university was open only to Spaniards and *criollos* (descendants of Spanish parentage); the few *mestizos*

(persons of mixed parentage) who attended (such as Eugenio de Santa Cruz y Espejo, writer, journalist, doctor, scientific researcher, and ideological precursor of political independence) succeeded in doing so only by legal subterfuge.

The first university during the period of the republic was the Central University of Ecuador, opened in 1826 under the name Central University of Southern Colombia. The state established the University of Guayaquil in 1867, the University of Cuenca in 1868, and the University of Loja and the National Polytechnic School in Quito in 1869. During the republican period the universities did not show much development of academic quality or level of scholarship as compared to that of the colonial period. A notable exception to this rule was the National Polytechnic School, intended exclusively to train professors of science and technology, civil engineers, architects, machinists, and mining engineers. Serious research in geography, geology, botany, and natural resources was conducted at this school. It also had the most important astronomical observatory in Latin America and achieved a privileged academic level. Administered by the German Jesuits, the National Polytechnic School was soon dissolved for political reasons.

In the early twentieth century the university in Ecuador was influenced by two factors: one internal, the "liberal revolution of 1895"; and the other external, the "revolution of Córdoba" (Argentina) in 1918. The liberal revolution effected changes in the administrative structure of the university, permitted academic freedom (largely by reducing the influence of the church), and improved the quality of education. The rector of the university was to be elected by the National Congress and the vice-rector by the Council of Professors. Greater emphasis was placed on the study of the sciences and also on the training of professionals in accordance with the needs for the country's development. The Córdoba revolution in 1918 and the examples of university reform movements in other Latin American countries produced the first Ecuadorian university reform, leading to student participation in collegiate organizations, university autonomy with respect to the national government, the selection of professors by competitive examination, and the beginning of the struggle for the right of students to challenge professors.

At the beginning of 1940 the university was clearly oriented toward greater political participation. Students reflected the economic and social conflicts of the country. Their philosophy of participation and their criticism and interpretation of the national situation at all levels became the basis for the restructuring of the Ecuadorian university. The 1950s reflected the results of the population explosion. They were years of accelerated construction of new campuses and of rapid quantitative growth. The 1960s were a period of instability. Four universities were closed by the government; the Central University of Ecuador was invaded by the army; professors who were suspected of communist tendencies were deprived of their chairs; and, due to the passing of various laws dealing with higher education, the university suffered a crisis from which it still has not recovered.

In the 1970s the Central University of Ecuador, and to varying degrees the other state universities, initiated the second university reform. One of the principles contained in this reform deals with the democratization of education. From 1969 to 1970 its application was seen in the elimination of entrance examinations for state universities. The right of challenge was incorporated into official university statutes, and students were given more participation in university administration, with the aim of achieving cogovernance (*Estatuto universitario*, 1973, p. 15). Students became divided into antagonistic factions grasping for power. According to some, the university entered into a period of introspection (Hurtado, 1974, p. 42); according to others, it began restructuring, focusing on the true

needs of the country (*Estatuto universitario*, 1973, p. 15).

The polytechnic schools have been somewhat exempt from these problems, because of the small number of students enrolled, the strict selection process of the candidates, their technological orientation, their search for excellence, and the greater stability of their governing boards. The Catholic universities, created as of 1946, also have been relatively free of problems because of their more elitist nature, their more authoritative administrative organization, and possibly because of their greater academic demands.

Legal Basis of Educational System

The 1926 Law of Higher Education established technical-administrative autonomy of the universities. Although the Ministry of Public Education sanctions the statutes for each university and resolves in the last instance the recommendations of the University Councils, absolute autonomy was established by the law of 1938. According to the political constitution of the state (1945, Article 143): "The universities are autonomous in accordance with the law, and will, in a special way, tend to the study and resolution of national problems and to the dispersal of culture among the lower classes. To guarantee this autonomy, the State will seek the creation of the University Patrimony."

In 1966 the national government promulgated a Law of Higher Education, which was well received by the universities, since they had drafted it. This law established the creation of a National Council of Higher Education, composed of administrators, professors, students, and a delegate from the Ministry of Public Education. The council was created to coordinate, plan, and unify university activities; to set the prerequisites for the creation of new universities; to distribute government funds among the state universities; and to approve the internal regulations of each university.

A law was passed in 1970 favoring the

internal restructuring of the universities, which were then in crisis because of official intervention. This law was rejected by the universities, primarily because it gave greater representation to the government on the National Council of Higher Education, while excluding students, and broadened the powers of that organization so that it could eliminate university and academic faculties, dismiss rectors and vice-rectors, and intervene more directly in the life of each university. When the political circumstances of the country changed, the universities asked the national government to reestablish the 1966 law. The government announced that it would pass a new law instead. However, since a new law has not been passed, the universities continue to be ruled by the law of 1966. None of these laws has even attempted to set the basis for a structural reform of the Ecuadorian university.

Types of Institutions

The most common type of postsecondary education is the university, comparable to the North American college and/or university. There are seventeen universities in Ecuador; twelve are state universities, and five are private, although four of these are connected with the Catholic church.

The Central University of Ecuador (CU) in Quito, with 42,773 students enrolled in 1974–75, is the largest and most important university. Following CU in importance are two state-controlled universities—the University of Guayaquil and the University of Cuenca—and the Pontifical Catholic University of Ecuador in Quito. The Private Technical University of Loja is the smallest, with an enrollment of 1095 students.

By law the national polytechnic schools in Quito and Guayaquil are equivalent to universities. Their purpose is to prepare students for careers in technological fields and to foster scientific research, especially applied research.

The higher normal institutes, which have been created recently, offer two-year programs in education to secondary school graduates. The junior colleges, also offering two-year programs, are oriented toward the training of middle-level administrators. This type of institution is, however, not very common and is usually associated with the so-called American colleges (high schools under the tutelage of the American Embassy). Their degrees are not recognized by the university.

The armed forces maintain some institutions in different branches of engineering for the training of their members. The programs last from two to six years. The most important of these institutions is the Military Geographical Institute, which offers programs in geography, cartography, and similar disciplines. Some of these programs are organized like postgraduate programs and require a large amount of research.

The churches, particularly the Catholic church, maintain seminaries for the training of their members, both clergy and lay members. The seminaries are oriented toward the philosophical, theological, biblical, and pastoral disciplines, with programs lasting from four to six years. Some of these institutes are associated with the Catholic universities, and others form the schools of theology at some of the Catholic universities.

The Institute of Higher National Studies, supported by the central government, offers one-year courses for high-ranking military personnel and selected civilians, generally university graduates. Its orientation is toward in-depth studies of segments of the national realm in the political, social, economic, and religious fields, and the theory of national security.

The Institute of Anthropological Studies in Otavalo is dedicated to ethnological and archeological research and also to social anthropology. It maintains ties with the universities, since it offers practical training and direction and assistance to university students who are preparing their theses.

It is difficult to classify some postsecondary institutions. In certain technical schools the boundaries between the secondary and higher levels are not clearly defined. These institutions are gradually moving toward establishing middle-level education to train technicians.

Relationship with Secondary Education

Secondary education is not mandatory in Ecuador. In 1971–72, 74.22 percent of the student population between the ages of thirteen and eighteen did not have access to it *(Boletín estadístico,* 1973). Nevertheless, between the 1962–63 and 1972–73 school years, enrollments at the secondary level tripled.

Secondary education lasts for six years and is divided into two cycles of three years. It consists of a basic level for general studies and a diversified level for more specialized studies leading to university entrance. A student at the diversified level selects from three alternatives: (1) modern humanities, with an emphasis on philosophical and social studies or on the exact sciences and biology; (2) educational programs, which lead to a teaching career at the primary level; (3) technical disciplines such as agronomy, accounting and management, industrial arts, arts, and bilingual secretarial studies. This type of organizational structure was introduced in 1969, and some schools are still in the process of converting to the new system.

The average age for completion of secondary school is eighteen, at which time the student receives the *bachillerato,* specifying his area of specialization.

Admission Requirements

The only academic requirement for admission in state universities is the *bachillerato.* There are also certain nonacademic requirements: the student must be at least eighteen years of age, possess the necessary health certificates, and have all military obligations fulfilled. Because of the lack of other academic requirements, the first year at the university consists of a course of preparation and orientation, which is part of the total curriculum. Each college indi-

cates the type of *bachillerato* necessary for admission.

The polytechnic schools and Catholic universities, besides requiring the *bachillerato,* have courses to prepare the student for university admission. These courses, which culminate in a final selective examination, may be either outside of the normal curriculum or integrated into it.

Administration and Control

The relationship of the universities with the Ministry of Public Education is legally established through the National Council of Higher Education and is minimal because of absolute university autonomy. Although the Catholic universities maintain ties with the church, the church has not organized any overall governing body for planning, liaison, or administrative control of these universities. The only cooperation between universities on a national level occurs mainly at the meetings of the rectors and in the university councils. There are also some informal sessions between institutions, but these have not led to any general cooperation or mutual planning. The general comptrollership of the nation attempts to control state funds that have been designated for the official state universities, although these universities plan their own budgets.

The organizational structure of the universities is traditional, consisting of a group of faculties divided into departments, schools, and institutes. There is no standard definition for department, school, or institute. In practice, the faculty is an almost autonomous unit, with administrative and academic policies of its own. The second university reform advocated by the Central University of Ecuador has structural reform as one of its objectives; however, this reform involves only a unification of existing titles and the coordination of colleges through collegiate agencies *(Estatuto universitario,* 1973, p. 75).

The administrative structure of the universities is essentially as follows: university assembly; university council; rector; vice-rector; faculty council; directive council; dean; director of a school, department, or institute.

The university assembly is composed of the full and associate professors and student representatives. Its major function is to elect the rector, the vice-rector, and the faculty member who will represent it on the university council. In addition the council is composed of the deans of the faculties, a professor representing the academic and teaching centers and institutes of the university, a student representative from each faculty, a representative from the university administration, the secretary general, and the secretary of administration and personnel. The major function of the university council is to direct the academic, research, and methodological activities of the university. It also sets up various commissions for academic and research matters.

The rector and the vice-rector must be Ecuadorian, over forty years of age, and university professors with at least five years of experience in teaching. Their terms are for four years with the possibility of reelection.

The dean and directors of each faculty, together with the relevant councils, have responsibility for the academic and teaching direction of the faculty and its dependent organizations. The faculty council consists of senior and associate professors and also has student representation equal to half of the number of voting professors. The principal function of the council is to elect the dean and the assistant dean.

The directive council—which is made up of the dean, the assistant dean, the directors of the respective schools, two faculty members, and student representatives corresponding to half of the instructors on the council—handles the direct administration of each faculty and determines academic policies, programs, and examinations.

The administrative structure of the Catholic universities follows the same organization; however, there is a representative of the church on the higher governing board, and student representation is significantly less at all levels.

Programs and Degrees

In the universities and polytechnics the following titles are granted: technologist in various specialties after two or three years of study, according to the type of career; *licenciado,* after four years of study, written and sometimes oral final examinations, and the writing of a minor research thesis (a student who has finished the four years of study but not the thesis requirement is called an *egresado* and does not receive a degree or a diploma); doctor, after six years of study, written and sometimes oral final examinations, some seminars, and a major research thesis. The equivalent to the doctoral degree for the technical careers is the title of engineer with mention of appropriate specialization. Some universities distinguish between the titles of attorney and Doctor of Jurisprudence, according to whether the student has completed a thesis and depending on the fields he has completed.

In the higher institutes of education, the student receives the title of teacher of primary education *(maestro para la enseñanza primaria)* at the end of two years. The *licenciado* in the science of education is required for teaching at the secondary level.

In Ecuador no program exists for training university professors. In the mid 1970s two-year postgraduate courses are being initiated to the level of master's and Ph.D. degrees. Courses previously referred to as postgraduate have been short-term specialized courses offered after the doctorate and generally accompanied by a diploma attesting that the student has completed the course. They have not led to a special title or degree.

The university council and the directive councils are responsible for maintaining academic standards and for the accreditation of a title, which must be registered with the Ministry of Public Education and with the respective professional society having national jurisdiction—for example, the Society of Engineers or the Medical Society.

Financing

The public universities, the polytechnic, and other institutions on the postsecondary level established by the government are financed by the state. More than 50 percent of the budget of the Catholic universities is contributed by the state. According to the Law of Higher Education of 1966, no less than 10 percent of the total annual increment in the general budget of the state is to be used for higher education. The distribution of this amount is made in a proportion of 80 percent based on the number of students at each university, and 20 percent according to the needs of each institution. In addition, each public university depends upon additional funds from income taxes and petroleum export taxes.

Part of the financing of the Catholic universities is through student tuition. These universities also depend upon aid from private citizens and international Catholic organizations, although this financing is not really significant except at the Private Technical University of Loja.

Student Financial Aid

Financial aid to students is minimal, since the state universities and the polytechnics are practically free. Each university maintains a limited number of scholarships. In 1973 the state created the Ecuadorian Institute for Educational Credit and Scholarships. This institute lends money to university students of limited economic means and sufficient intellectual capacity for study in the universities of Ecuador and for postgraduate studies abroad. The loans are for food and lodging, tuition, books, and the cost of preparing the thesis. The funds come from an allotment of .2 sucres for each barrel of oil produced, based on 1973 prices, and are awarded to 1.5 percent of the university population of the country. The institute also administers the scholarships offered by the various ministries and national institutions for study within the country. At the university level these scholarships are inadequate, since they are available to scarcely .2 percent of the university population. International scholarships offered by friendly governments and international institutions are also administered by the institute. These scholarships ordinarily are for postgraduate studies (brief specialization courses), rarely for university studies. They are granted to the universities and to various official institutions in the country. In some universities the scholarship carries with it a work obligation in administrative branches or in the ministry that offered the scholarship.

Student Social Background and Access to Higher Education

The social origins of the students are the upper and middle classes, with scant participation from the lower class and minority groups such as Indians and blacks. Thus, in 1968–69 the children of craftsmen and workers represented only 7.2 percent of the university population at the Central University, and this percentage dropped to 7.1 percent in the next academic year. Although the law does not discriminate in theory, the reality of it is quite different. University enrollment represents approximately 2.09 percent of the total population.

Women accounted for 31.8 percent of the total enrollment in 1972–73, and they tended to be concentrated in the Central University of Ecuador, the University of Guayaquil, and the Catholic University of Quito, which have a combined total of 79.5 percent of the total female enrollment in the country. The growth index of female enrollments is astounding; in 1972–73 female enrollments increased 927.9 percent over the previous year (*Estadísticas universitarias*, 1975).

Since 1944, when the government approved the statutes of the National Federation of Students (NFS), student activities have been directed toward political participation. Since 1960 the NFS has been controlled by Marxist students of diverse leanings. Since its inception it has attempted to be the "social conscience" of the nation. Other student movements associated with political parties of the country have usually lacked importance and strength. In the Catholic universities and the polytechnics student movements are less politicized. The NFS, through its subsidiaries, is beginning to exercise greater influence in these institutions. Student movements also have charge of the so-called university extension, which is usually organized into courses for workers and minority groups.

Teaching Staff

Members of the teaching staff of the universities are classified as senior professors (*principales*), associates (*agregados*), assistants (*auxiliares*), teaching aides (*ayudantes de cátedra*), and lecturers (*ad honorem*). Appointments to the first two categories require academic degrees. The assistants must at least be *egresados,* and the teaching aides must be in the last three years of university study. All are chosen by competition, and the system for advancement is to serve two years as an assistant before becoming an associate, and four years as an associate prior to appointment as full professor. The lecturers are either retirees who have distinguished themselves in their teaching career or professors of exceptional merit. The years required for promotion are less when the applicant has published research work of special merit.

Depending upon the time devoted to teaching, professors are classified as full time (minimum of thirty hours per week devoted to the university), half time (fifteen hours per week), and part time (six hours). The number of professors on full time does not reach 20 percent of the total teaching staff—largely because of inadequate government planning for human resources development; economic restrictions imposed by budgetary insufficiencies or inflation of the administrative bureaucracy; and the general law of the country, which permits university professors to hold more lucrative outside appointments. Salaries

are low and cannot compete with those of private business and industry.

In the Catholic universities professors are appointed in a more informal way, and until recently the social prestige of the candidate and his Catholic ideology were of greater importance than his teaching credentials. The polytechnics have paid the most attention to the training and background of their teaching staff and also offer the best salaries. Salary scales are set by the governing bodies of the universities.

Academic freedom, set forth in the laws of higher education, is a fundamental part of university autonomy. In general, it has been well guarded, and although there is no organization expressly charged with supervising it, the associations of professors defend it. In the Catholic universities there was a tendency, which is disappearing, to curtail academic freedom on points of ethical philosophy and religious pluralism. The right of challenge to the professor, established by some state universities, is indirectly a threat to academic freedom, in spite of the fact that university statutes have carefully regulated it.

Research Activities

Research activities are focusing on the study of the national situation and on cooperation with national and local governments on development projects. The polytechnics undertake sophisticated technological research, sometimes geared to development problems. The funds for research come in part from the university budget, in part from contracts with public bodies, and in part from international sources. There is still no systematic serious research on postsecondary education.

Current Problems and Trends

Among educational problems in Ecuador can be mentioned the population explosion, the lack of qualified personnel for teaching and research, the obsolete structure of the universities, the flight of professionals, the inadequate financing, and the lack of coordination and planning for universities on the national level. The great increase in university enrollments is a result of the high rate of population growth in the country and the disproportionately large population below the age of fifteen; the removal of entrance examinations in the state universities; the fact that the university is almost the only means to achieve social status and higher salaries; and the exodus from the rural areas to the cities. The brain drain represents economic losses for both the university and the country. Ecuadorian universities graduated 172 medical doctors in 1966–67, but of the 17,000 Ecuadorians who emigrated to the United States in 1968–69, 142 were doctors and 148 were technicians with the highest university degree. Although all of these problems were being widely discussed, no reforms have been initiated to alleviate them.

Educational innovations include the creation of higher-level normal schools in 1975 to better prepare primary teachers (on an experimental basis) and the creation of new technical schools of secondary education to develop middle-level personnel. Other changes are in the area of teaching practice and social service—for instance, the "rural conscription" (a work period of one year in the rural or outlying areas) for doctors and dentists. This innovation has been successful and is coordinated and financed by the Ministry of Public Health. Some public institutions, when offering economic aid to scholarship recipients at the universities, reserve the right to indicate the degree thesis that the candidate (for the highest degree) must work on, so that the theses respond more to specific projects, such as in the area of electrification and the construction of means of communication.

Relationship with Industry

The impact of industrialization and the rapid growth of private and multinational enterprises have had the effect of promoting interest in new careers such as business administration, auditing, accounting, and various types of engineering; however, financial assistance from industry has not increased appreciably.

International Cooperation

At the government level international cooperation is centralized by the Ministry of Foreign Affairs, the National Council for Planning, and the Ecuadorian Institute for Educational Credit and Scholarships. These organizations carry out the projects of multinational and bilateral cooperation with other nations or with international organizations such as the Organization of American States (OAS), UNESCO, and other United Nations agencies. Some universities have initiated cooperation of this type on their own. For example, the Coastal Polytechnic has trained many of its teachers through the programs of the Latin American Scholarship Program of American Universities (LASPAU) in the United States. Other sources of aid are the Ford Foundation and programs administered under the Fulbright-Hays Act of 1961 of the United States. The Konrad Adenauer Foundation in Bonn, in the Federal Republic of Germany, also has extended assistance to education in Ecuador.

SIMÓN ESPINOSA

Bibliography

Aguirre, M. A. *La reforma universitaria y sus problemas.* Quito: Instituto de investigaciones económicas de la Universidad central, n.d.

Boletín estadístico del Ministerio de educación 1970–71. Quito: Ministerio de educación pública, 1973.

Chaves, A. P. *El problema universitario en el Ecuador.* Quito: Instituto de altos estudios nacionales, 1973.

Cueva, A. *El proceso de dominación política en el Ecuador.* Quito: Instituto ecuatoriano de planificación para el desarrollo, 1969.

Estadísticas universitarias no. 11. 1972–73. Quito: Instituto de investigaciones económicas y financieras. Editorial universitaria, 1975.

Estatuto universitario. Universidad central del Ecuador. Quito: Editorial universitaria, 1973.

Hurtado, O. *Dos mundos superpuestos: Ensayo*

diagnóstico de la realidad ecuatoriana. Quito: Ediciones crítica, 1972.

Hurtado, O. "Visión histórica de la universidad ecuatoriana." *Estudios sociales,* 1974, *11* (4), 30–45.

Investigaciones educativas, 1972–73. Loja: Universidad nacional de Loja, n.d.

Malo, H. "La estructura académica de la universidad." *Revista de la universidad católica,* 1975, *1* (1), 103–117.

Moncayo, C. *Marco socio-cultural de referencia para la planificación de la Universidad católica de Quito.* Quito: Oficina de planificación de la Universidad católica, 1975.

Moncayo de Monge, G. *La Universidad de Quito: Su trayectoria en tres siglos.* Quito: Editorial universitaria, 1944.

Plan de desarrollo de la educación, 1973–1977. Quito: Ministerio de educación pública, n.d.

See also: Archives: Mediterranean, the Vatican, and Latin America, National Archives of; Science Policies: Advanced Developing Countries: Andean Common Market Countries; South America: Regional Analysis.

EDUCATION BENEFITS, VETERANS

See Veterans Education Benefits.

EDUCATION COMMISSION OF THE STATES, United States

The Education Commission of the States (ECS) is a nonprofit organization headquartered in Denver, Colorado. Formed in 1966 by interstate compact, the commission provides a partnership between educational and political leaders for the improvement of education in the United States and assists states in working with the federal government. Forty-five states, Puerto Rico, and the Virgin Islands are members.

Each state has seven commissioners, usually the governor, two members of the state legislature, and four persons selected by the governor. This group of more than three hundred meets annually to authorize studies, suggest policy alternatives, analyze

educational innovations, and provide communications among the states on educational matters. The chairperson is always a governor. The commission, primarily an advisory body, has no power to enforce its recommendations.

The commission works closely with the State Higher Education Executive Officers Organization and sponsors state, regional, and national forums on education topics of concern to the states. Topics related to postsecondary education include financing and budgeting; statewide coordination, governance, and structure; collective bargaining; and residency and reciprocity. The commission has developed state legislation which establishes guidelines for the approval of new postsecondary educational institutions and authorization to grant degrees.

In the postsecondary field ECS has grants from the Kellogg Foundation and the Lilly Endowment for an in-service education program and a project in evaluation and improvement of statewide planning. In addition to foundation grants, ECS is funded by fees from member states and by federal grants.

ECS publishes *ECS Bulletin,* monthly; *Higher Education in the States,* monthly; *Compact,* bimonthly; and *State Leaders Directory* and *Directory of Professional Personnel: State Higher Education Agencies,* annually. Bibliographies, reports, and special newsletters on specific topics or projects are published occasionally.

300 Lincoln Tower
1860 Lincoln Street
Denver, Colorado 80203 USA

EDUCATION CONSULTANTS

See Consultants, Use of.

EDUCATION, HIGHER

See Higher Education (field of study).

EDUCATION IN THE COUNTRIES OF THE COMMON MARKET (Higher Education Report), Multinational

Education in the Countries of the Common Market (Paris: Institut pédagogique national, 1965) is a report of the European Study Commission for the Development of Education and Research, organized by the European Community Institute for University Studies, under the chairmanship of R. Poignant. The report examines the development of education in the six original countries of the Common Market through the use of a quantitative comparison of higher education statistics in the six countries, the United States, the United Kingdom, and the Soviet Union.

The study describes the development of general education at the primary and secondary levels and the development of professional and technical education at the secondary and tertiary levels. It also considers financial, human, and material resources devoted to education in the various countries. The report's conclusions about higher education are drawn from facts uncovered by the quantitative comparison of enrollments, finances, degrees, faculties, fields of study, hours of study, and types of institutions.

The commission found that the Common Market countries are making relatively slow progress in the formation of high-level technical and scientific manpower compared to the rate of development of manpower in the Soviet Union, the United Kingdom, and the United States. The commission felt that this situation in the six countries was likely to become worse between 1965 and 1975. The shortage of manpower training programs, the study indicates, is accompanied by a lack of democratic access to higher education.

The report stresses that change is needed in general secondary education, where resistance to democratic reform by graduates of established systems of education and by certain groups of specialized teachers exists. It concludes that an active policy of recruitment and training of teaching personnel, accompanied by the renewal and perfection of teaching methods, could allow the necessary quantitative expansion and at the same time ensure the traditional quality of education in the six Common Market countries.

EDUCATION PROJECT OF PLAN EUROPE 2000

Plan Europe 2000 was conceived in 1970 as a conceptual approach to the problems of living in the twenty-first century and as an investigation of the measures necessary to prepare for that time. Sponsored by the *Fondation Européenne de la Culture* (European Cultural Foundation), the plan involved four projects in all: on education, industry, urbanization, and agriculture and the environment. Although each project was developed separately, the investigators worked in close collaboration, directing their efforts toward the synthesization of the projects' findings.

The education project, developed within the overall context of the plan, had four particular concerns: (1) to study education in a Europe which was moving toward economic and political unity but which remained open and closely linked to other parts of the world, particularly the United States, Japan, and the developing countries; (2) to consider education not as an isolated system but in relation to its rapidly changing sociocultural context; (3) to approach the study of education from an interdisciplinary point of view; and (4) to accomplish these objectives from the long-term perspective of the year 2000, taking into account the major constraints and unyielding trends which would not change significantly within the intervening years.

The special concerns guiding the project arose from the awareness that the educational systems of Europe were no longer keeping pace with the rapid changes in society, nor were they able to guide society's development. Previously, reform had been piecemeal and sporadic, hampered by obsolete teaching methods, assessment tools, and curricula as well as by the inequality of educational opportunity and the passive role of students.

Consequently, the project's investigation of possible educational systems for the future was conducted from the perspective of several anticipated developments: (1) Equality of opportunity is vital to the progress of education in Europe. Implying the absence of any discrimination on grounds of sex, race, social background, religion, or nationality, equality of opportunity would also guarantee the implementation of measures through which any natural, socioeconomic, or cultural inferiority would be compensated for—as far as possible—by the educational system itself. (2) Lifelong education principles and methods must respond to the need for scientific and technological progress as well as to the needs of the individual. (3) Full and active participation of the individual in his educational process is considered desirable. Such participation assumes the strengthening of the student's capacity to "to learn to learn," rather than to memorize facts and of his power to take responsibility for the content and patterns of education most appropriate to his own abilities and interests. (4) An adequate system of orientation and guidance is needed to make the individual aware of his true potentialities, informing him of available educational possibilities and corresponding career prospects and advising him on the correction of personal deficiencies. (5) An open, diversified, and flexible structure will provide freedom of choice of educational patterns, fields, and establishments, ensuring high mobility of students and teachers among different patterns and eliminating irreversible choices and "blind alleys" in the educational system.

As the education project progressed, five basic themes were developed: (1) basic factors of educational development—studies that describe the present European situation and identify specific factors that have led to it; (2) prospectives—studies that attempt a description of man's likely environment in the twenty-first century; (3) new educational systems—studies that consider the likely structure and content of education in the year 2000 and the factors which will affect it (for example, costs, or the relationship between education and the division of labor in the economy); (4) strategies for action—studies that identify, analyze, and recommend alternative strategies in key areas such as curriculum development, educational technology, and teacher training; and (5) final synthesis—studies that identify the main findings and orientations arising from these themes and present them as an integrated whole, showing interrelationships among the desirable, the possible, and the probable, among education and other social subsystems, and between education and society in general.

Work on the project was completed early in 1975, and most of the findings have already been published.

Scheduled for publication in 1976 and 1977 are a redefinition of the youth-education-employment relationship for subgroups within the 16–25 age group; an investigation of educational measures to cope with youth unemployment; a study of the "left-asides" and those who leave school at age fifteen and do not receive any further education or training; a survey of the literature on university dropouts; an analysis of the changing attitudes and expectations of young people about their education and work; a series of maps showing the regional distribution of postsecondary institutions within Europe; case studies in six European regions of the relationship between regional development and postsecondary education; a study of the role of adult education in regional development; and policy guidelines for permanent education.

The European Cultural Foundation,

the sponsor of the plan, has allowed for a permanent follow-up of these efforts by establishing the Institute of Education in Paris. This institute, which has on its staff many of those originally connected with the project, will continue the various policy studies which the education project began. The institute's completed reports include *Educational Leave; Recent Student Flows in Twelve European Countries, the United States of America, and Japan; The Mobility of Undergraduate Students;* and *The Impact of New Structures of Higher Education on the Equalization Opportunity.*

LADISLAV CERYCH

See also: Institute of Education, France.

EDUCATION RESEARCH UNIT, Australia

The Education Research Unit was founded in 1968 at the Australian National University, in Canberra, to study education and society from a multidisciplinary perspective. Research is carried out on the secondary and higher education levels. Focusing on problems of the Australian universities, higher education research at the unit is concerned with the following areas: administration, especially governance; economics of higher education; educational planning; and university students and faculty. In addition, comparative studies have been made of students' attitudes in India and Australia and of community colleges in North America and Australia.

Financed by university funds, the unit's staff includes eight research professionals, seven research assistants and/or graduate students, and three secretarial and clerical personnel.

The unit issues the Education Research Unit Occasional Report Series, published by the Australian National University Press.

Institute of Advanced Studies
Australian National University
Canberra City, A.C.T. 2600, Australia

EDUCATION SCIENCE AND TEACHER TRAINING (Field of Study)

Education science includes the body of knowledge and skills surrounding the processes of learning and teaching. During the past several decades this field has grown substantially in comprehensiveness and complexity as the peoples of the world, and especially their governments, have come to understand the vital importance of education in all aspects of national development. Education has become a major tool for social and economic growth, as well as for the establishment of national and international peace and stability. Developing nations in particular are using education as a means to establish an independent identity and an economic base.

One phenomenon found in all parts of the world is the rapid increase in adult or continuing education. The explosion of human knowledge, the increase in leisure time, and the growing number of people who continue to learn throughout life have combined to foster this development. This division of the field has been marked by experimentation and innovation in regard to the location, structure, and content of education. In this branch, we see a much greater involvement of practitioners in the process, particularly as the need increases for in-service training in areas where changes in practice are most in evidence. Effort has been made to develop processes that are effective with older and more experienced learners.

As education has become more complex and extended, a need has arisen to assist persons to choose and order their learning. Consequently, counselor education has developed as a division of education. Counselor education has expanded to include activities that help the learner to deal effectively with learning problems, to understand himself better, and to hasten the individualization of learning and teaching in order to make the process both more satisfying and more effective. This branch of education science draws heavily upon psychology, statistics and measurement, and the dynamics of group activity.

An important division of education science is early childhood education. In the more highly developed countries, the age at which children start school has been extended downward. In the socialist nations, governments have used this practice to allow mothers to serve as productive members of the labor force while their children receive early education. In the West, the emerging desire on the part of women to be afforded full access to careers—along with the social concern that children, particularly urban children, be provided with a full and rich cultural environment—has pushed the age of schooling downward. Although the age at which schooling commences may differ from country to country, the emphases are commonly placed upon the teaching of reading, writing, and numbers; the development of positive learning attitudes and habits; and the adjustment of the child to an institutional environment.

Secondary education provides students with an understanding of specialized subject matter and prepares them for college or university study, vocational careers, and their future roles as citizens. Secondary education age levels, structures, and curricula vary widely among the countries of the world, depending upon differing philosophies and value systems.

Concomitant with the increase in the comprehensiveness and structure of the educational enterprise is the need to plan, organize, supervise, manage, and evaluate the educational process. These activities comprise a branch of education science known as education administration. This division draws from both the broad field of education and the field of business administration. The study of education administration is carried on largely at advanced levels and has been greatly affected by advances in technology, especially data processing and computer science.

The decades of the 1950s and 1960s have been marked by a worldwide increase in higher education. There has been a rapid increase in the numbers of students involved in the educational process and in the length of the higher education experience. While there has been a diminution of the purely classical type of education, the growth of professional schools has been tremendous. Traditional subject matter has been made more practical and more closely related to industrial and professional practices. There has developed a closer relationship between theoretical base and actual practice. In fields such as medicine, engineering, and law this trend is most observable. Although pure science and research continue, we find a growing emphasis upon the application of scientific knowledge. In the more highly industrialized countries, this trend has existed for some time; in the socialist nations and in developing countries, applied science becomes a matter of national policy.

As the need for knowledge and skills has increased, there has arisen a necessity to hasten and improve the transmission process. Instructional technology has attempted to contribute to this effort. The traditional classroom lecture and textbook have been augmented by the use of a rapidly expanding number of audiovisual learning and teaching devices: films, tape recorders, television, radio, and the computer. These devices are often used in combination to increase the capacity of a nation to extend educational programs to remote places and so to people who were formerly excluded from educational opportunities. This field is still in the developmental stage in even the more highly developed countries. Some educators fear the wider application of audiovisual techniques, possibly as a threat to their positions or as a result of a lack of awareness of the potential of this technique. In recent years educational technology has become a division for serious study, research, and experimentation.

The internationalization of athletics through such events as the Olympic Games and the popularity of competition among the athletes of the world have combined with the concept of good health as a national resource to hasten the development of physical education as a field of education science. In more highly developed nations, the increase in leisure time and the earlier retirement of persons from the work force have led to a need to increase knowledge and understanding in the area of recreation. As a result, physical education has grown rapidly, and serious study and research in this field are being carried on by an increasing number of specialists. This division draws largely from the areas of physiology, kinesiology, the fine arts, psychology, and education science.

Several factors have combined to create a division of education science known as special education. Whereas in past years societies have more or less ignored those who were unable to cope with the educational process, nations have now developed a concern for their handicapped populations. As industrialism has grown, these people have become public charges or, at best, have remained unproductive members of a labor force. In a more humane spirit, nations now strive to provide the means through which more of their citizens become able to enjoy fulfilling life experiences. The chief disabilities that must be dealt with are physical impairments, intellectual limitations, and emotional disturbances. Special education as a branch of education science draws its substance from medicine, psychology, sociology, and education science as such. Concerted efforts have resulted in a deeper and broader understanding of the problems associated with special education. A number of promising therapies have been developed that offer great hope for the future. Special education is an important element within the field of education science.

Teacher education is another significant and important part of education science. From humble beginnings, this field has grown to command an increasing share of resources. It no longer deals solely with training the young in communication skills. A more fitting definition is that teacher education includes all studies and experiences that are necessary to prepare a person to teach, to organize learning experiences, to administer educational institutions, or to provide supportive services for the learning process at all levels. In the West, a number of institutions, public and private, are engaged in teacher education. In the socialist nations, as well as in the developing countries, teacher education is considered so vital to national progress that it is strictly directed by the state.

A number of disciplines are allied to education science. The science of psychology has increased our understanding of human behavior, the learning process, and the methods of assisting persons with learning disabilities. Sociology and anthropology have added to knowledge of the cultural bases of society and the dynamics of organizations as well as the role and function of social institutions. Political science has helped us to view educational institutions as integral parts of government and increased our ability to utilize political power as an educational tool. Economics and business administration have contributed skills and knowledge in the areas of planning and management of resources. As teachers have become better organized and more militant, there has arisen a need to become more skilled in labor management practices. Administration has become a major concern for educators. Social science research skills—including statistics, measurements, computer-based technology, data processing, and the synthesis and analysis of data—have become increasingly important to education science. Finally, history and philosophy contribute much to education science as we continue to view education in its historical perspective and to establish values and theoretical bases for practice.

Education science has experienced a long and interesting development. It has been a primary concern of civilization for as long as man has inhabited this planet.

Since the days of the ancient Greeks, philosophers have pondered the values that surround education. There has existed a polarity between the role of education in developing the potential of the individual and the use of education as a means of enhancing the welfare of the state. This divergence continues and has tended to result in educational productivity. The artistic genius of the Greeks and Romans and the moral-ethical fervor of the Hebraic-Christian culture led to the explosive creativity of the Middle Ages. These same years saw the growth of medieval universities in Europe and the deep involvement of the Catholic church in the education of children. The universities continue to exert a strong influence on higher education around the world. The Roman church has been joined by other denominations to form parochial schools as an educational force. To augment parochial schools, a large number of colleges and universities supported by religious orders as well as a number of church-related colleges and universities have arisen, so that religious bodies still remain active participants in the educational enterprise at all levels.

As political states emerged in the seventeenth and eighteenth centuries, a polarity also developed between the well-established church-dominated educational structure and state-controlled systems. Gradually the states have prevailed, and their control over the educational process has grown to the point where in many parts of the world it is dominant. In the West, the structure is heterogeneous. Public, church-related, and nonsectarian private institutions share responsibility for education. However, in developing nations and in socialist countries education from preschool through university level is carefully controlled by the central government and is an important aspect of national policy.

The twentieth century has been marked by the rapid development of education science. This development has been both vertical and horizontal. At all levels the number of educational institutions has dramatically increased. Perhaps the most significant development has been a broadening of the dimensions of education. There has been a vast lateral expansion of education into new and developing areas. Today virtually every aspect of daily living is enriched by education, in one form or another. This trend will increase as our technology becomes more sophisticated and complex. As new fields emerge, they seek educational support, including theory, methodology, and a research component. Education has also taken on an international aspect. This is attested to by the growth of international educational organizations. The United Nations has placed great emphasis upon UNESCO as its major educational agency. At all levels, professionals have attempted to organize on an international basis to enhance understanding and to share in the development of new and more effective systems of education. In the forefront of this effort have been teacher organizations, colleges and universities, and national governments. International conferences, study tours, and student or faculty exchange programs have laid the groundwork of an effort to make education a major tool in the fostering of international understanding. Once rivalries can be reduced and economic resources can be more equitably distributed, the potential of education sciences can be greatly widened. The result will be an ever greater sharing of both scientific and cultural knowledge. The world will then pass from the stage where education is merely a tool of national policy. Education will become an instrument for international sharing and may provide a basis for peace and progress.

The twentieth century finds the field of education science in a situation where a wide divergence exists between theory and practice. In the West we find educational structures that can produce the necessary transmission of knowledge that is supportive of a complex industrial society and at the same time can provide opportunity for individual fulfillment and enrichment. In societies that are in a developmental stage, or moving from outside domination to a state of national identity, or still trying to sustain some form of collectivism, we see more emphasis upon conformity and an adherence to the values that support the needs of the state. Education science, the product of a long history and development, is still engaged in a struggle between the polarities that marked its earliest beginnings.

FRANK E. MARSH, JR.

Levels and Programs of Study

Programs in education science generally require as a minimum prerequisite a secondary education, though mature students with related work experience may be admitted with lower educational qualifications, particularly to programs for teachers of vocational subjects or adult education. Programs lead to the following awards: teaching certificate approved by an educational authority, bachelor's degree, master's degree (M.Ed.), the doctorate (D.Ed. or Ph.D.), a higher diploma (for example, *diplôme d'études supérieures*), or their requivalents.

Programs that lead to awards not equivalent to a first university degree deal with the principles and practice of school teaching, as well as the training of instructors, extension workers, and personnel for out-of-school and adult education, both formal and nonformal. The programs, designed particularly to prepare students for teaching in the regular school system at the first level and at the first stage of the second level of education, stress the techniques of teaching (teaching methods), including lesson planning and preparation, classroom management, methods for developing group activities, organization and administration of the school system, along with sessions of practice teaching and observation of experienced teachers. Courses in the technology of education, including programed learning, are often included. Programs for the training of instructors, extension workers, and others to be engaged

in out-of-school activities place more emphasis on knowledge of the basic subject matter to be taught and on special techniques such as organization and guidance of discussion groups, demonstration, communication, and the use of audiovisual media, radio forums, and village development committees. Important kinds of programs included are general teacher training; programs emphasizing particular subject matters such as science, mathematics, social studies, and physical education; programs emphasizing particular vocational subjects, including fine arts, metal trades, woodworking, mechanical repair trades, and printing trades; programs emphasizing techniques for teaching preschool children; programs concerned particularly with teaching in adult education, both in school and out of school; and programs concerned with teaching handicapped children. In most programs some time is spent on general academic subjects such as mathematics, history, philosophy, psychology, geography, and social studies. Programs may be taken full time or part time, day or evening, and many are given during school vacations (particularly those designed to improve the qualifications of employed teachers). Refresher courses are common.

Programs that lead to a first university degree deal with the theory and history of education, practice teaching, and the observation of experienced teachers. Programs for school teaching are intended primarily to prepare students to teach at the second stage of the second level of education, although some include preparation for teaching at the first stage of the second level or for third-level nonuniversity teaching. At this level the heaviest enrollment is likely to be in programs for subject matter specialists; that is, those who expect to teach one or two special subjects. Along with courses in educational theory and teaching methods, these programs often include courses in educational administration, and teacher supervision. Important kinds of programs included are general programs (that is, not specialized by subject matter or by type of student to be taught); programs for teachers with a subject matter specialty, either in a nonvocational subject (for example, history, languages, natural sciences, mathematics, geography, physical education) or in a vocational subject both in and out of school (for example, fine arts, home economics, woodworking, metalworking, welding, commercial subjects, or agriculture); programs for teaching preschool or kindergarten; programs for teaching in adult education both in school and out of school; programs for teaching handicapped and gifted children; programs for teaching teacher trainees; and programs for higher-level staff for extension and other types of out-of-school education of adults and young people. Programs may be full time or part time, day or evening. Many part-time programs are for improving the qualifications of teachers; others are for personnel in extension, adult education, and other nonformal teaching. Many programs are provided during school vacations, particularly those for teachers and those providing partial qualification in areas of teacher shortage (that is, a prospective teacher can gain full qualification by study in successive vacation periods and is encouraged to take employment as a teacher in the intervals).

Programs that lead to a postgraduate university degree deal with the theoretical and practical aspects of teaching, the principles of education, comparative education, curricula, and educational psychology, with emphasis given to the theoretical principles of the subjects. Original research work, as substantiated by the presentation and defense of a scholarly thesis, is usually an important element. Programs at this level are usually concerned with one specialized area of education, but practical aspects—such as practice teaching and other observation of and participation in educational processes—are important in some cases. Important kinds of programs are general teacher training programs (less

common here than at lower levels), specialized programs directed toward certain groups (for example, early childhood teaching or adult education teaching), teaching of teacher trainees, and specialized programs on problems of teaching particular subjects (such as languages, science, or mathematics). The programs tend to be more highly specialized because they are designed for university graduates, most of whom are qualified teachers and many of whom have had some years of teaching or related working experience. The objective of these programs is to develop high-level specialists in particular aspects of education, including teaching and related activities such as supervision and inspection of teaching, educational counseling, educational planning, and the economics of education. Background courses are not so important here as at other educational levels, but many programs include courses in related specialties such as administration, psychology, educational guidance, and statistics. Most of these programs are full time, but many are taken in school vacation periods or as part-time activities by employed teachers. Other examples of part-time programs are refresher courses and special courses to introduce new methods and techniques.

[This section was based on UNESCO's *International Standard Classification of Education (ISCED)* (Paris: UNESCO, 1976).]

Major International and National Organizations

INTERNATIONAL

Asian Institute for Teacher Educators
University of the Philippines
Quezon City, Philippines

Association francophone d'éducation comparée
1 avenue Léon Journault
92310 Sèvres, France

Commonwealth Secretariat
Marlborough House, Pall Mall
London SW1Y 5HX, England

Comparative Education Society in Europe
University of London Institute of Education
Malet Street
London WC1E 7HS, England

Council of Europe
Council for Cultural Co-operation
avenue de l'Europe
67006 Strasbourg, France

The following sections regularly conduct research and publish information on teacher education in the member countries: Committee on Higher Education and Research, Committee on General and Technical Education, Documentation Centre for Education in Europe.

European Association of Teachers
122 rue André Pascal
Geneva, Switzerland

Inter-American Education Association
1150 Avenue of the Americas, Room 401
New York, New York 10036 USA

International Association for Education and
   Vocational Information
20 rue de l' Estrapade
75005 Paris, France

International Council on Education for
   Teaching
One Dupont Circle
Washington, D.C. 20036 USA
   Conducts research in all areas related to teacher education; publishes a journal, conference proceedings, and occasional papers.

International Federation of Secondary
   Teachers
Fédération internationale des professeurs de
   l'enseignement secondaire officiel (FIPESO)
120 rue du Président Roosevelt
78100 Saint-Germain-en-Laye, France

International Federation of Teachers'
   Associations
Fédération internationale des associations
   d'instituteurs (FIAI)
3 rue de La Rochefoucauld
75009 Paris, France

International Schools Association
Palais Wilson
1211 Geneva 14, Switzerland

Organisation for Economic Co-operation and
   Development (OECD)
2 rue André Pascal
75775 Paris, France

The following sections are concerned with education: Directorate for Social Affairs, Manpower and Education; Education Committee.

Organization of American States (OAS)
Departamento de asuntos educativos
Pan American Union Building
Washington, D.C. 20006 USA

World Confederation of Organizations of the
   Teaching Profession (WCOTP)
3-5 Chemin du Moulin
1110 Morges, Switzerland

One of the most important international educational organizations is UNESCO (United Nations Educational, Scientific and Cultural Organization), which has four regional offices for education.

UNESCO
7 place de Fontenoy
75700 Paris, France

Regional Centre for Education in Africa
P.O. Box 3311
Dakar, Senegal

Regional Office for Education in the Arab
   Countries
P.O. Box 5244
Bir Hassan
Beirut, Lebanon

Regional Office for Education in Asia
P.O. Box 1425
Bangkok 11, Thailand

Regional Office for Education in Latin America
   and the Caribbean
Enrique Delpiano 2058
Casilla 3187
Santiago, Chile

Other educational organizations affiliated with UNESCO are:

International Bureau of Education (IBE)
Palais Wilson
1211 Geneva 14, Switzerland

International Institute for Educational
   Planning (IIEP)
7-9 rue Eugène Delacroix
75016 Paris, France

UNESCO Institute for Education
70 Feldbrunnenstrasse
2 Hamburg 13, Federal Republic of Germany

NATIONAL

A representative list of nonspecialized educational organizations includes:

Brazil:
      Associação de educação católica do Brasil
      Rua Martins Ferreira 23
      20000 Rio de Janeiro

Canada:
      Canadian Education Association
      252 Bloor Street West
      Toronto, Ontario M5S 1U5

Chile:
   Sociedad de escuelas normales de Chile
   Catedral 2395
   Santiago

Denmark:
   Dansk forening for hjem og skole
   V. Vedsted
   Copenhagen

   Gymasieskolernes tysklaererforening
   Torkel Badens Vej 10
   Hellerup

Federal Republic of Germany:
   Bundesverband der Lehrer an
      beruflichen Schulen
   Mozartstrasse 30
   Bonn

Finland:
   Kasvatusopillinen yhdistys
   Museokatu 18
   Helsinki

   Suomen ammattikoulujen opettajaliitto
   Töölöntullinkatu 8
   Helsinki

France:
   Association des certifiés
   3 rue de la Parfumerie 92
   Asnières

   Institut national de recherche et de
      documentation pédagogiques
   29 rue d'Ulm
   Paris 5

   Syndicat national des professeurs des
      écoles normales
   10 rue de Solférino
   Paris 7e

Ghana:
   Ghana National Association of Teachers
   P.O. Box 209
   Accra

India:
   Indian Association of Teacher Educators
   N.I.E. Campus, 2nd Floor
   Mehrauli Road
   New Delhi 16

   National Council of Educational
      Research and Training
   Sri Aurobindo Marg
   New Delhi 110016

Italy:
   Associazione nazionale insegnanti lingue
      straniere (ANILS)
   via Val Maira 20
   Rome 00141

Japan:
   Nihon kyoiku gakkai
   University of Tokyo, Faculty of Education
   Tokyo

Mexico:
   Sociedad de educación
   Sección educacional
   Edificio del Banco del Londres y México
   Desp. 7/8
   Mexico, D.F.

New Zealand:
   New Zealand Educational Institute
   Box 466
   Wellington

   New Zealand Post Primary Teachers'
      Association
   P.O. Box 2119
   Wellington

   New Zealand Teachers' Colleges
      Association
   North Shore Teachers College,
      Northcote
   Auckland 9

Norway:
   Landslaget for Norsk laererutdanning
   Postnoks 6062, Etterstad
   Oslo 6

Pakistan:
   All-Pakistan Educational Conference
   Saeeda Manzil, Nazimabad
   Karachi

   Teachers' Subordinate Education Service
      Association
   A. V. Section, Men's Branch
   Government Central Model School
   Lower Mall
   Lahore

Poland:
   Poland Teachers' Union
   ul. Spasowskiego 6-8
   00-389 Warsaw 30

Soviet Union:
   Academy of Pedagogical Sciences of the
      U.S.S.R.
   Bolshaya Polyanka 58
   113095 Moscow M-95

Sweden:
   Svenska barnavardslärares förening
   (% Mrs. Karin Uddstromer, Källvägen
      27)
   Bergsbrunna
   Uppsala 18

Switzerland:
Conférence des directeurs des écoles
normales de Suisse
% Directeur de l'Ecole normale de
Lausanne
place de l'Ours
Lausanne 1000

Union suisse pour l'enseignement
professionnel
Spitalackerstrasse 60
Bern 3000

United Kingdom:
Association of Teachers in Technical
Institutions
Hamilton House, Mabledon Place
London WC1, England

National Association of Schoolmasters
(NAS)
Swan Court, Waterhouse Street
Hemel Hempstead
London, England

United States:
American Association of Colleges for
Teacher Education
One Dupont Circle
Washington, D.C. 20036

American Council on Education
Council on Cooperation in Teacher
Education
One Dupont Circle
Washington, D.C. 20036

American Council on Education
Commission on Teacher Education
One Dupont Circle
Washington, D.C. 20036

Association of Teacher Educators (ATE)
1201 16th Street NW
Washington, D.C. 20036

National Council for the Accreditation of
Teacher Education
1750 Pennsylvania Avenue NW
Washington, D.C. 20036

National Education Association
1201 16th Street NW
Washington, D.C. 20036

Venezuela:
Colegio de profesores de Venezuela
avenida los Samanes N46
Caracas

Additional organizations may be found in
the following directories:

International Guide to Educational Documentation.
(2nd ed.) Paris: UNESCO, 1971.

Minerva, Wissenschaftliche Gesellschaften. Berlin,
Federal Republic of Germany: de Gruyter,
1972.
Teachers' Associations. (2nd rev. ed.) Paris:
UNESCO, 1971. A brief list of international
organizations (pp. 17–21) followed by a
country arrangement; includes all types of
teacher associations.
The World of Learning. London: Europa, 1947–.
Published annually.

Principal Information Sources

GENERAL

General guides and guides to resources in
teacher education include:

*Bibliography of Publications Issued by UNESCO or
Under Its Auspices: The First Twenty-Five Years:
1946–1971.* Paris: UNESCO, 1973. See
"Teacher Training," pp. 115–118.
Burke, A. J., and Burke, M. A. *Documentation
in Education.* New York: Teachers College
Press, Columbia University, 1967. An intro-
duction to the basic skills of literature search
in the field of education; lists basic reference
sources.
*Documents on Teacher Training and In Service
Training.* Bangkok, Thailand: UNESCO
Regional Office for Education in Asia, 1969.
Includes listing of documents available at
the regional office. Areas covered are Asia,
Africa, Latin America and the Caribbean,
North America, Australia, Europe, Near
East, New Zealand, and the Soviet Union.
*International Guide to Educational Documentation,
1955–1960.* Paris: UNESCO, 1963.
*International Guide to Educational Documentation,
1960–1965.* Paris: UNESCO, 1971. An ex-
tensive guide to the principal sources of
documentation on education worldwide;
country-by-country annotated bibliographies of the major educational publications
in ninety-five states and countries.
Marks, B. S. *New York University List of Books in
Education.* New York: Citation Press, 1968.
An annotated list of over 2800 books, pamphlets, and yearbooks.
Natalis, E. *A Quarter of a Century of Educational
Literature.* Gembloux, Belgium: J. Duculot,
1971. An international listing of books in
twenty-four languages, covering the period
1945–1970.
Richmond, W. K. *The Literature of Education:
A Critical Bibliography, 1945–1970.* London:
Methuen, 1972. A listing of some of the key
works published in all areas of education;
strong British emphasis.

"Technical and Vocational Education." *Educational Documentation and Information,* 1973, *186,* entire issue. Includes "Training of Technical and Vocational Teachers and Instructors," pp. 73–85.

"Trends and Innovations in Teacher Education." *Educational Documentation and Information,* 1975, *195,* entire issue.

Woodbury, M. *A Guide to Educational Resources.* Stanford, California: Stanford Center for Research and Development in Teaching, 1974.

Educational bibliographies for limited geographical areas include:

Baron, G. *Bibliographical Guide to the English Educational System.* (3rd ed.) Bristol, England: Western Printing Services, 1965.

Bibliography of Publications Issued by UNESCO or Under Its Auspices: The First Twenty-Five Years, 1946–1971. Paris: UNESCO, 1973. Includes items on all aspects of educational theory and practice.

Educational Development in Africa. Washington, D.C.: African Bibliographic Center, 1973.

Fraser, S. E., and Fraser, B. J. *Scandinavian Education: A Bibliography of English-Language Materials.* White Plains, New York: International Arts and Sciences Press, 1973.

Fraser, S. E., and Hsu, K. *Chinese Education and Society: A Bibliographic Guide. The Cultural Revolution and Its Aftermath.* White Plains, New York: International Arts and Sciences Press, 1972.

Hanson, J. W., and Gibson, G. *African Education and Development Since 1960: A Select and Annotated Bibliography.* East Lansing: Institute for International Studies in Education and African Studies Center, Michigan State University, 1966.

McNeill, M. *Guidelines to Problems of Education in Brazil: A Review and Selected Bibliography.* New York: Teachers College Press, Columbia University, 1970.

Martin, L. A. *Education in Kenya Before Independence: An Annotated Bibliography.* Syracuse, New York: Syracuse University, Maxwell Graduate School of Citizenship and Public Affairs, 1969.

Neff, K. L. *Selected Bibliography on Education in Southeast Asia.* Washington, D.C.: U.S. Department of Health, Education and Welfare, 1963.

Passin, H. *Japanese Education: A Bibliography of Materials in the English Language.* New York: Teachers College Press, Columbia University, 1970.

Roth, H. *A Bibliography of New Zealand Education.* Wellington, New Zealand: Council for Educational Research, 1964.

Overviews and introductions to the field include:

Bereday, G. Z. F., and Lauwerys, J. A. (Eds.) *The Yearbook of Education 1963: The Education and Training of Teachers.* New York: Harcourt Brace Jovanovich, 1963. Section 2, "Organization of Teacher Training: Area Studies," includes area studies in Europe, the United States, Australia, Canada, the Federal Republic of Germany, Lebanon, India, Turkey, South Africa, Latin America, Spain, Czarist Russia, and others.

Cantor, L. M., and Roberts, I. F. *Further Education in England and Wales.* London: Routledge and Kegan Paul, 1969.

Combs, A. W. *The Professional Education of Teachers: A Human Approach to Teacher Preparation.* (2nd ed.) Boston: Allyn & Bacon, 1974.

DeYoung, C. A., and Wynn, R. *American Education.* (7th ed.) New York: McGraw-Hill, 1972. An introductory text surveying the current concerns in each of the main areas of the field.

Evans, R. N., and Terry, D. R. (Eds.) *Changing the Role of Vocational Teacher Education.* Bloomington, Illinois: McKnight and McKnight, 1971. Based on a four-day institute concerned with the state of the art in vocational teacher education in the United States.

Garcia Hoz, V. *Principios de pedagogía sistemática.* (4th ed.) Madrid: Ediciones Rialp, 1968. An overview of major educational topics.

Hughes, J. M. *Education in America.* (3rd ed.) New York: Harper & Row, 1970. An overview of the field, with emphasis on the practical concerns of teachers.

Ilina, T. A. *Pedagogika.* Moscow: Izdatelstvo "Prosveshchenie," 1969. An introduction to education from the communist viewpoint, with special reference to the Soviet Union.

Kneller, G. F. (Ed.) *Foundations of Education.* New York: Wiley, 1971. A collection of basic essays grouped under the following headings: Historical Foundations, Social Foundations, Philosophic Foundations, Scientific Foundations, and Structural Foundations.

Majault, J. *Teacher Training.* Strasbourg, France. Council of Europe, Council for Cultural Co-operation, 1965. A survey of programs of elementary and secondary school teachers' preparation in Western European countries. French version is entitled *La formation du personnel enseignement.*

Myers, D. *Educating Teachers: Critiques and Proposals.* Toronto, Ontario: Institute for Studies in Education, 1974.

Nicolin, F. (Ed.) *Pädagogik als Wissenschaft.* Darmstadt, Federal Republic of Germany:

Wissenschaftliche Buchgesellschaft, 1969. Classic essays written between 1806 and 1966 concerned with the nature of education.

Planchard, E. *La pédagogie scolaire contemporaine.* Louvain, Belgium: Editions Nauwelaerts, 1968. A detailed overview of the field and the problems of the teacher.

Razick, T. A. *Systems Approach to Teacher Training and Curriculum Development: The Case of Developing Countries.* Paris: International Institute for Educational Planning, 1972.

Somers, G. G., and Little, K. J. (Eds.) *Vocational Education: Today and Tomorrow.* Madison: Center for Studies in Vocational and Technical Education, University of Wisconsin, 1971. Includes considerable emphasis on vocational and technical teacher education and qualifications in the United States.

The Teacher and Educational Change. (2 vols.) Paris: Organisation for Economic Co-operation and Development, 1974. Volume 1, *The Teacher and Educational Change: A New Role, General Report,* looks at the changing role of the teacher in various countries and seeks solutions and policies for the improved quality of teaching in a rapidly changing social structure. Volume 2, *Recent Trends in Teacher Recruitment,* presents quantitative and statistical data which mainly update the information in the 1971 OECD study cited below. All aspects of teaching are considered.

Training, Recruitment and Utilization of Teachers in Primary and Secondary Education. Paris: Organisation for Economic Co-operation and Development, 1971. Based on a series of country surveys; stresses the need for closer links between the qualitative and quantitative aspects of teacher training and recruitment. This study in part is updated by the second volume of the 1974 OECD study cited above.

Comparative education sources include:

Beck, C. E. (Ed.) *Perspectives on World Education.* Dubuque, Iowa: W. C. Brown, 1970. Original essays from scholars in other countries.

Bereday, G. Z. F. *Comparative Method in Education.* New York: Holt, Rinehart and Winston, 1964. An introduction to the field of comparative education for the nonspecialist; deals with general theory, practical methods, problems of preparation for the field, and an overview of teaching and research centers and major types of bibliographical sources.

Bristow, T., and Holmes, B. *Comparative Education Through the Literature: A Bibliographic Guide.* Hamden, Connecticut: Archon, 1968. A selective bibliography directed to librarians who are building up a section, university

lecturers developing courses in comparative education, and beginning students seeking a basis on which more advanced studies can be built.

Gezi, K. I. *Education in Comparative and International Perspectives.* New York: Holt, Rinehart and Winston, 1971. A collection of essays on comparative education and educational problems in other countries.

International Commission on the Development of Education. *Learning to Be: The World of Education Today and Tomorrow,* Paris: UNESCO, 1972. Describes the state of education around the world; defines a global conception for the future; and makes practical recommendations to serve as guidelines for action by UNESCO, governments, and the international community.

Mallinson, V. *Introduction to the Study of Comparative Education.* (4th ed.) Atlantic Highlands, New Jersey: Humanities Press, 1975.

Noah, H. J., and Eckstein, M. J. *Toward a Science of Comparative Education.* New York: Macmillan, 1969.

World Survey of Education: Handbook of Educational Organizations and Statistics. (5 vols.) Paris: UNESCO, 1955–1971. A compendium of facts about the educational systems of other countries. Vol. 1: *Handbook of Educational Organization and Statistics;* Vol. 2: *Primary Education;* Vol. 3: *Secondary Education.* Vol. 4: *Higher Education;* Vol. 5: *Educational Policy, Legislation, and Administration.*

Historical views are offered in:

Bereday, G. Z. F., and Lauwerys, J. A. (Eds.) *The Yearbook of Education 1963: The Education and Training of Teachers.* New York: Harcourt Brace Jovanovich, 1963.

Borrowman, M. L. *Teacher Education in America: A Documentary History.* New York: Teachers College Press, Columbia University, 1965.

Bowen, J. *A History of Western Education.* (3 vols.) New York: St. Martin's, 1972–. A comprehensive history beginning with Mesopotamia and Egypt and ending in a summation of the modern period of Western education.

Castle, E. B. *The Teacher.* London: Oxford University Press, 1970. The history of the teacher from ancient times to the twentieth century.

Good, H. G., and Teller, J. D. *A History of Western Education.* (3rd ed.) New York: Macmillan, 1969.

Monroe, W. S. *Teacher-Learning Theory and Teacher Education, 1890–1950.* Urbana: University of Illinois Press, 1952. A classic review of the historical progression of teaching and teacher education in the United States.

Myers, E. D. *Education in the Perspective of History.* New York: Harper & Row, 1960.

Strong, M. E. "Vocational Education: Training of Teachers." *Encyclopedia of Education*, 1971, *9*, 480–486. United States summary only.

Taylor, William. *Society and the Education of Teachers.* London: Faber & Faber, 1969.

Teacher Training in Britain. London: Central Office of Information, Reference Division, 1974. Reviews provisions for teacher training in England, Scotland, Wales, and Northern Ireland against a historical background.

Ulrich, R. *Three Thousand Years of Educational Wisdom: Selections from Great Documents.* (2nd ed.) Cambridge, Massachusetts: Harvard University Press, 1954. A collection of Eastern and Western classics of educational thought.

General sources on education and training in the field throughout the world include:

Commonwealth Conference on Teacher Education, Nairobi, 1973. *Teacher Education in a Changing Society.* London: Commonwealth Secretariat, 1974. The second section of papers notes information country by country on the current situation in teacher training.

Crisis and Change in Teachers' Education: International Perspectives on Theory and Practice. Washington, D.C.: International Council on Education for Teaching, 1971.

Dodd, W. A. *Teacher Education in the Developing Countries of the Commonwealth: A Survey of Recent Trends.* London: Commonwealth Secretariat, 1970.

Education in Rural Areas. London: Commonwealth Secretariat, 1970.

"Future Prospects for Teacher Education." *UNESCO Chronicle*, April 1971, *17*(4), 131–137.

Klassen, F. H., and Collier, J. L. *Innovation Now! International Perspectives on Innovation in Teacher Education.* Washington, D.C.: International Council on Education for Teaching, 1972.

Klassen, F. H., and Imig, D. G. (Eds.) *National and Community Needs—The Challenge for Teacher Education: International Perspectives on Theory and Practice.* Washington, D.C.: International Council on Education for Teaching, 1973.

Klassen, F. H., Imig, D. G., and Collier, J. L. *Innovation in Teacher Education: An International Perspective.* Washington, D.C.: International Council on Education for Teaching, 1972.

New Patterns of Teacher Education and Tasks: Country Experience. Paris: Organisation for Economic Co-operation and Development, 1974. Each volume in the series deals with a specific country or group of countries and reports on OECD activities on problems posed by the new patterns of teacher education at primary and secondary levels. Countries studied are Sweden, Belgium, France, the United Kingdom, and the United States. Includes bibliographies and references to major sources.

New Patterns of Teacher Education and Tasks: General Analysis. Paris: Organisation for Economic Co-operation and Development, 1974. Summary of papers and discussions of a meeting of experts, held March 28–29, 1974, at Château de la Muette, Paris. Divided into two main sections: "Initial and Continuing Training of Teachers: New Trends and Concepts" and "New Patterns of Teacher Tasks and Their Implications." Teaching is taken in the broadest sense, and the work is international in scope. Contains excellent bibliographical notes and references.

Second International Conference on the Further Education of Teachers, Bratislava, 1970. *Conference Proceedings.* Bratislava, Czechoslovakia: Comenius University, Institute for Teacher Education, 1970.

Teacher Education: A Selected List of References for A.I.D. Technicians. Washington, D.C.: Office of Education and Human Resources, Agency for International Development, 1972. Entries include publications of AID as well as other international organizations; entries cover teacher training in developing countries in the late 1950s and 1960s. Useful for historical perspective.

Technical and Vocational Teacher Education and Training. Paris: UNESCO, 1973. Summary of a study conducted by UNESCO and the International Labour Organisation, based on questionnaires sent to thirty-seven countries (primarily developing). Purpose is to analyze problems in the education and training of teachers and to suggest various guidelines. Contains an extensive bibliography, including documents from UNESCO and other international organizations.

Training, Recruitment and Utilisation of Teachers: Country Case Studies—Primary and Secondary Education. Paris: Organisation for Economic Co-operation and Development, Directorate for Scientific Affairs, 1968–1969. Series of surveys prepared by member countries, including France and Ireland (1969); Denmark, Italy, and Luxembourg (1968); Austria, Greece, and Sweden (1968); Germany, Belgium, and the United Kingdom (1969); Netherlands and Portugal (1968); Switzerland and Yugoslavia (1968). Surveys in English or French.

Warren, H. *Vocational and Technical Education:*

A Comparative Study of Present Practice and Future Trends in Ten Countries. Paris: UNESCO, 1967. Deals with the provisions for and the practice of technical education in Czechoslovakia, France, Federal Republic of Germany, Italy, Netherlands, Sweden, Soviet Union, United Kingdom, United States, and Yugoslavia. Vocational teacher training is discussed on pages 164–168.

Yates, A. (Ed.) *Current Problems of Teacher Education.* Hamburg, Federal Republic of Germany: UNESCO Institute for Education, 1970. Report of meeting of experts (from thirteen countries), held in Hamburg, January 20–23, 1969. Bibliography, pp. 186–192.

Sources on training in North and South Africa include:

Bolibaugh, B. *Educational Development in Guinea, Mali, Senegal, and the Ivory Coast.* Washington, D.C.: Institute of International Studies, 1972. (ERIC document number Ed 069 581.)

Commonwealth Conference on Teacher Education, Nairobi, 1973. *Teacher Education in a Changing Society.* London: Commonwealth Secretariat, 1974. Includes a section on Ghana (pp. 219–231), Lesotho (pp. 250–252), Malawi (pp. 253–255), Mauritius (pp. 270–271), Nigeria (pp. 282–284), Sierra Leone (pp. 287–290), and Zambia (pp. 307–311).

Haidara, B. A. "An Example of an African Higher Teacher-Training College: Bamako." *Prospects,* Autumn 1973, *3*(3), 383–390.

Kajubi, W. S. "Teacher Education in East Africa." *International Review of Education,* 1971, *17*(2), 197–210.

Najman, D. *L'éducation en Afrique: Que faire?* Aubenas, France: Editions Deux Mille, 1972.

Practical Guide to In-Service Teacher Training in Africa—Establishment, Execution and Control of Training Programmes. Paris: UNESCO, 1970.

Sources on training in Asia and Oceania include:

Asian Institute for Teacher Educators. *Integration and Modernization of Teacher-Education Curriculum.* Final report of the Second Subregional Workshop on Teacher Education, Bangkok, November, 1971. Quezon City: University of the Philippines, 1972.

Asian Institute for Teacher Educators. *Research and Development in Teacher Education in Asia.* Final report of a working group meeting, Baguio City, January 11–20, 1972. Quezon City: University of the Philippines, 1972.

Australian Commission on Advanced Education. *Teachers Education 1973–1975: Report of the Special Committee on Teacher Education.* Canberra: Australian Government Publishing Service, 1973.

Bady, P. "L'école et la révolution." *Projet,* April 1974, *84*, 401–423. Relates recent changes in the Chinese colleges of education, especially teacher retraining.

Country Reports: New Zealand. Paris: Organisation for Economic Co-operation and Development, 1974.

Further Education of Teachers in Service in Asia: A Regional Survey. Bangkok, Thailand: UNESCO Regional Office for Education in Asia, 1973.

Klassen, F. H., Imig, D. G., and Collier, J. L. (Eds.) *Innovation in Teacher Education: An International Perspective.* Washington, D.C.: International Council on Education for Teaching, 1972.

Lee, Y. D. *Educational Innovation in the Republic of Korea.* Paris: UNESCO, 1974.

Takakura, S. "Innovative Trends in Teacher Training and Retraining in Japan." In *New Patterns of Teacher Education in Canada and Japan.* Paris: Organisation for Economic Co-operation and Development, 1975, pp. 51–88.

Sources on training in Western Europe include:

Breuse, E. "Belgium: Experiments in Continuing Teacher Training." *Country Experience: Belgium, France, United Kingdom.* Paris: Organisation for Economic Co-operation and Development, 1974. Pp. 5–27.

Continued Reform of Teacher Education. Stockholm: Swedish Committee on Teacher Education, 1972.

Ferreria, G. T. "A reforma do sistema educativo." *Revista portuguêsa de pedagogia,* 1973, pp. 227–233.

Geissler, G. *Eingliederung der Lehrerbildung in die Universität (Das Hamburger Beispiel).* Weinheim, Federal Republic of Germany: Beltz, 1973.

Olsen, T. P. "The Work of Teachers Centres in Denmark." In *In-Service Training of Teachers: Report of a WCOTP European Seminar, Berlin: April 1971.* Morges, Switzerland: World Confederation of Organizations of the Teaching Profession, 1971. Pp. 37–41.

Seidenfaden, F. "Probleme der Lehrerbildung im Siegel norwegischer Erfahrungen." *Pädagogische Rundschau,* February 1974, *2*, 89–177.

Sources on training for Eastern Europe and the Soviet Union include:

Atutov, P. R., and Stavrosky, A. E. "The Training of Teachers for Polytechnical Education." In S. G. Shapovalenko (Ed.), *Polytechnical Education in the USSR*. Paris: UNESCO, 1963. Pp. 235–249.

Bakos, L. "Innovations in Teachers' Education in Bulgaria, Czechoslovakia, Rumania and the Union of Soviet Socialist Republics." In F. H. Klassen and J. L. Collier, *Innovation Now! International Perspectives on Innovation in Teacher Education*. Washington, D.C.: International Council on Education for Teaching, 1972.

Frankovic, D. "Teacher Training in Socialist Countries." *International Review of Education,* 1970, *16*(3), 350–356.

Krneta, L. "Education and In-Service Training for Teachers in Yugoslavia." In F. H. Klassen and J. L. Collier, *Innovation Now! International Perspectives on Innovation in Teacher Education*. Washington, D.C.: International Council on Education for Teachers, 1972. Pp. 118–120.

Ogorodnikov, I. T., and Il'ina, T. A. "Professional Preparation of Teachers in the Light of Recent Advances in Educational Theory and Teaching Techniques: Educational Development in the USSR." In A. Yates (Ed.), *Current Problems of Teacher Education*. Hamburg, Federal Republic of Germany: UNESCO Institute for Education, 1970. Pp. 133–155.

Rosen, V. "Vergleichende Lehrerbildung in der Bundesrepublik Deutschland und der Deutschen Demokratischen Republik." Unpublished master's thesis, Faculté des lettres, Département d'allemand, Université de Paris-Nanterre, 1971.

Sources on training in the Middle East include:

"ICdad al-muCallimin lil-marhala al-'ibtida'iyya qabla al'bidma wa baCdaha (Teacher Training Before and After Recruitment)." *An-Nasra at-tarbawiyya,* December 1971, *5*, 70–76.

Mihriz, Z. *Teachers in Egypt*. Cairo: Markaz at-tawtio at-tarawiy, 1969.

Yosuf, A. *Teacher Training in the Yemen Arab Republic*. Beirut, Lebanon: Regional Centre for Educational Planning and Administration, 1972.

Yosuf, A. "La formation du maître arabe à la lumière du rapport Faure." *L'éducation nouvelle,* December 1973, *1*(1), entire issue.

Sources on training in Latin America and the Caribbean include:

"Approaches to Educational Reform in Latin America." In *Crisis and Change in Teacher Education*. Washington, D.C.: International Council on Education for Teaching, 1971. Pp. 21–34.

"Bibliografía especializada: Formación docente." *Informaciones y documentos CENDIE,* April–June 1974, *13*, 60–69.

Crisis and Change in Teacher Education. International Perspectives on Theory and Practice. Washington, D.C.: International Council on Education for Teaching, 1971. Particular emphasis on the Western hemisphere.

de Cáceres, R. D. *La formación permanente del profesorado de enseñanza primaria y media general en América latina*. Santiago, Chile: Oficina regional de educación de la UNESCO para América latina y el Caribe, 1972.

del Camino, I., and Muñoz, J. "La enseñanza normal y la enseñanza superior en México, 1972." *Revista del Centro de estudios educativos,* 1974, *4*(3), 151–176.

D'Oyley, V. R., and Wilson, S. *Instrumentation to Improve Teacher Education in Jamaica*. Washington, D.C.: ERIC Document Reproduction Service, 1972. (ERIC document number ED 068 454.)

Escuela de formación de profesores de enseñanza media: Documento de trabajo. Guatemala: Universidad de San Carlos de Guatemala, Facultad de humanidades, 1973.

McAnany, E. G., and others. *The El Salvador Educational Reform: Some Effects of the First Teacher Retraining Course*. Stanford: California Institute for Communication Research, Stanford University, 1969.

Oliveros, A. *La formación de los profesores en América latina*. Salamanca, Spain: n.p., 1974.

Planes y programas de las escuelas normales latinoamericanas. Washington, D.C.: Pan American Union, n.d.

"Teachers' Education in the Contemporary Caribbean: Four Perspectives." In *Crisis and Change in Teacher Education*. Washington, D.C.: International Council on Education for Teaching, 1971. Pp. 35–48.

Sources on training for North America include:

Bigelow, D. N. (Ed.) *The Liberal Arts and Teacher Education: A Confrontation*. Lincoln: University of Nebraska Press, 1971.

Burns, R. W., and Klingstedt, J. L. (Eds.) *Competency-Based Education*. Englewood Cliffs, New Jersey: Educational Technology Publications, 1973.

Channon, G. *Innovations in Teacher Education in Canada*. Ottawa, Ontario: Canadian Teachers' Federation, 1971.

Landrum, R., and Zinsser, C. *A Model for the Preparation of Undergraduates for Primary Education in a Liberal Arts Setting*. New Haven,

Connecticut: Institution for Social and Policy Studies, Yale University, 1974.

Snow, R. E. *A Model Teacher Training System: An Overview.* Stanford, California: Stanford University, Center for Research and Development in Teaching, 1972.

Wees, W. R. *Teaching Teachers Teaching.* Toronto, Ontario: Canadian Education Association, 1974.

Useful sources on vocational teacher training in individual countries may be found in *Educational Documentation and Information,* nos. 186 and 195. Studies on the United States can be readily obtained through the ERIC system.

CURRENT BIBLIOGRAPHIES

Abstracts of Instructional and Research Materials in Vocational and Technical Education (AIM/ARM). Columbus, Ohio: Center for Vocational Education, 1974–. Published monthly. Emphasis is on the United States, but international items are included on a selective basis.

American Dissertations on Foreign Education: A Bibliography with Abstracts. Troy, New York: Whitston, 1971–. Each volume in this series lists dissertations written about education in a particular country. The following volumes have appeared: Vol. 1: *Canada;* Vol. 2: *India;* Vol. 3: *Japan;* Vol. 4: *Africa;* Vol. 5: *Scandinavia;* Vol. 6: *China;* Vol. 7: *Korea.*

Australian Education Index. Hawthorn, Victoria: Australian Council for Educational Research, 1957–.

Bibliografia brasileira de educação. Rio de Janeiro: Centro brasileira de pesquisas educacionais, 1952–.

British Education Index. London: Library Association, 1954–.

CIRF Abstracts. Geneva: CIRF Publications, International Labour Organisation, 1961–. Contains fairly detailed abstracts of books, articles, and legal writings concerned with vocational training in the broadest sense; international in scope; of particular interest for teacher education is section eleven, "Instructors and Teachers." Additional abstracts on teacher education may be located through the subject index under "Instructors"; "Teachers"; and "Training Officers."

Current Index to Journals in Education (CIJE). New York: CCM Information Corporation, 1969–.

Educational Administration Abstracts. Columbus, Ohio: University Council for Educational Administration, 1966–.

Education Index. New York: Wilson, 1929–.

Journal of Teacher Education. Washington, D.C.: National Education Association, National Commission on Teacher Education and Professional Standards, 1950–. Each issue features a "Report from the ERIC Clearinghouse on Teacher Education," an alerting mechanism for the materials in the ERIC files.

Sociology of Education Abstracts. Liverpool, England: Information for Education, 1965–.

T & D Abstracts. Geneva: CIRF Publications, 1975–.

PERIODICALS

A representative list of journals in the field would include *African Journal of Educational Research* (Nigeria), *Australian Journal of Education, British Journal of Teacher Education, Bulletin d'information du Centre de documentation pour l'éducation en Europe* (France), *Bulletin of the UNESCO Regional Office for Education in Asia* (Thailand), *Cahiers pédagogiques* (France), *Comparative Education* (UK), *Comparative Education Review* (US), *Dansk paedagogisk tidsskrift* (Denmark), *Educación hoy* (Colombia), *Educational Documentation and Information* (Switzerland), *Educational Record* (US), *Educational Review* (UK), *Educational Studies: A Filipino Teacher* (Philippines), *Education and Culture* (France), *Education Canada* (Canada), *Education for Teaching* (UK), *L'éducation nouvelle* (Lebanon), *Education Quarterly* (India), *Education Quarterly* (Philippines), *Forum for the Discussion of New Trends in Education* (UK), *Harvard Educational Review* (US), *Information bulletin* (France), *Interchange* (Canada), *International Review of Education* (FRG), *International Review of Education* (UNESCO), *Journal of Educational Research* (US), *Journal of Industrial Teacher Education* (US), *Journal of Teacher Education* (US), *Malaysian Journal of Education, NIE Journal* (India), *Pedagogía* (Puerto Rico), *Pédagogie* (France), *Pedagogisk forskning/Scandinavian Journal of Educational Research* (Norway), *Prospects* (France), *Revista brasileira de estudos pedagógicos* (Brazil), *Sovetskaja pedagogika* (USSR), *Teacher Education* (Canada), *Teacher Education* (India), *Teacher Education* (US), *Teacher Education in New Countries* (UK), *Teacher Education News and Notes* (US), *The Teacher Today: Journal of the Singapore Teachers' Training College, Times Education Supplement* (UK), *Trends in Teacher Education* (Philippines), *UNESCO Chronicle* (France), *Vergleichende Pädagogik* (GDR).

Additional periodicals may be found in the following directories:

Educational Periodicals/Revues pédagogiques/Revistas pedagógicas. (2nd ed.) Paris: UNESCO,

1963. Arranged in two major sections: (1) journals from all countries except the United States, with topical headings under each country; (2) United States journals. Dated but still useful.

Index to Asian Educational Periodicals, 1960–1970. Bangkok, Thailand: UNESCO Regional Office for Education in Asia, 1974. Indexes journals available in the regional office containing articles in French or English.

Ulrich's International Periodicals Directory. New York: Bowker, biennial.

ENCYCLOPEDIAS, DICTIONARIES, HANDBOOKS

The Encyclopedia of Education. (10 vols.) New York: Macmillan, 1971. More than 1000 articles on educational subjects, with bibliographies appended.

Encyclopedia of Educational Research. New York: American Educational Research Association, 1969. Concise articles on all educational topics.

Foulquié, P. *Dictionnaire de la langue pédagogique.* Paris: Presses universitaire de France, 1971.

Good, C. V. *Dictionary of Education.* (3rd ed.) New York: McGraw-Hill, 1973.

Lexikon der Pädagogik. Fribourg, Federal Republic of Germany: Herder, 1970.

A Russian-Chinese-English Glossary of Education. New York: Teachers College Press, Columbia University, 1970.

The UNESCO IBE Education Thesaurus. (2nd ed.) Paris: UNESCO, 1975.

DIRECTORIES

Ash, L. *Subject Collections.* New York: Bowker, 1974. A guide to special book collections in university, college, public, and special libraries and museums in the United States and Canada.

Commonwealth Universities Yearbook. London: Association of Commonwealth Universities, 1914–. Published annually. A good source of current information; its general index includes references to universities offering programs in particular subjects.

Directory of Teacher-Training Colleges. Paris: UNESCO, 1970.

Education Authorities Directory and Annual. London: School Government Publishing Co., annual. Lists programs in the United Kingdom.

Educator's World. Philadelphia: North American Publishing, 1972. A standard guide to American-Canadian educational associations, conventions, foundations, publications, and research centers.

Handbook of Colleges and Departments of Education and Other Institutions for the Training of Teachers in England and Wales. (11th ed.) London:

Country Press, 1973. Descriptive and statistical information for the training of teachers in England and Wales.

International Handbook of Universities and Other Institutions of Higher Education. Paris: International Association of Universities, 1971. Provides information about universities and colleges in 108 countries and territories, excluding those in the British Commonwealth and the United States.

Minerva: Jahrbuch der gelehrten Welt. Abteilung Universitäten und Fachhochschulen. Berlin, Federal Republic of Germany: de Gruyter, 1966–1970. Descriptions of universities in the language used at the university described. Its subject index, in German, includes a section on "Pädagogik, Psychologie."

Peterson's Annual Guides to Graduate Study, 1976. Princeton, New Jersey: Peterson's Guides, 1975. Directories to various subject fields, with descriptions of selected programs. Covers the United States and Canada.

Technical and Vocational Education and Training. Paris: UNESCO, 1973. Includes a list of sixty institutes and universities which train teachers for technical and vocational education.

World Guide to Libraries. (4th ed.) New York: Bowker; Pullach/ Munich, Federal Republic of Germany: Verlag Dokumentation, 1974. Includes a subject index indicating which libraries have substantial holdings in particular subjects, including education.

World Guide to Universities. New York: Bowker; Pullach/Munich, Federal Republic of Germany: Verlag Dokumentation, 1972. Lists universities offering programs in education.

The World of Learning. London: Europa, 1947–. Published annually. A comprehensive country-by-country listing of learned societies, research institutes, libraries, archives, museums, and universities.

For a list of schools offering accredited programs in teacher education in the United States, write to the National Council for the Accreditation of Teacher Education, 1750 Pennsylvania Avenue NW, Washington, D.C. 20006. A guide for foreign students, *Teacher Education in the United States,* is available from the Institute of International Education (IIE), 809 United Nations Plaza, New York, New York 10017. An additional list of institutions offering degree programs in the field may be found in IIE's *Handbook on U.S. Study for Foreign Nationals* (5th ed.), 1970.

RESEARCH CENTERS, INSTITUTES, INFORMATION CENTERS

Probably the most extensive educational information center in the United States, if not in the world, is ERIC (Educational Resources Information Center), which acquires, reviews, and indexes journal articles announced in *CIJE (Current Index to Journals in Education);* prepares bibliographical citations and abstracts of research documents announced in *Resources in Education;* and disseminates these documents through a document reproduction service. *Research in Education,* an index of educational documents, is also helpful. The major organization in the United States responsible for disseminating information on teacher education is the ERIC Clearinghouse on Teacher Education. Its coverage is international, and its holdings can be searched through a computer search service. The work performed by ERIC is shared among its following sixteen clearinghouses:

Career Education
Northern Illinois University
DeKalb, Illinois 60115

Counseling and Personnel Services
University of Michigan
Ann Arbor, Michigan 48104

Disadvantaged
Teachers College, Columbia University
New York, New York 10027

Early Childhood Education
University of California at Los Angeles
Los Angeles, California 90024

Educational Management
University of Oregon
Eugene, Oregon 97403

Handicapped and Gifted Children
Council for Exceptional Children
Reston, Virginia 22091

Higher Education
George Washington University
Washington, D.C. 20006

Information Resources
Stanford University
Stanford, California 94305

Junior Colleges
University of California at Los Angeles
Los Angeles, California 90024

Languages and Linguistics
Center for Applied Linguistics
Arlington, Virginia 22209

Reading and Communication Skills
National Council of Teachers of English
Urbana, Illinois 61801

Rural Education and Small Schools
New Mexico State University
Las Cruces, New Mexico 88001

Science, Mathematics, and Environmental
  Education
Ohio State University
Columbus, Ohio 43221

Social Studies/Social Science Education
Social Science Education Consortium, Inc.
Boulder, Colorado 80302

Teacher Education
American Association of Colleges for Teacher
  Education
Washington, D.C. 20005

Tests, Measurement, and Evaluation
Educational Testing Service
Princeton, New Jersey 08540

Another important information center is:

Southeast Asian Ministers of Education
  Organization (SEAMEO)
Center for Educational Innovation and
  Technology
INNOTECH Center, 39 Newton Road
Singapore, 11

For other important research and information centers consult:

International Guide to Educational Documentation. (2nd ed.) Paris: UNESCO, 1971.
Minerva, Forschungsinstitute. Berlin, Federal Republic of Germany: de Gruyter, 1972.
The World of Learning. London: Europa, 1947–. Published annually.

For listings of international and national organizations which conduct research and provide information in the field consult the following:

Directory of Educational Documentation and Information Services. Paris: UNESCO, 1975. An international guide to information centers.
Directory of Educational Research Institutions in the Asian Region. (2nd ed.) Bangkok, Thailand: UNESCO Regional Office for Education in Asia, 1970.
Educator's World: The Standard Guide to American-Canadian Educational Associations, Conventions, Foundations, Publications, Research Centers. Philadelphia: North American Publishing, 1972.
Information Bulletin, 2/1974. Strasbourg, France: Council of Europe, Documentation Center for Education in Europe, 1974.
International Conference on Public Education, 29th Session, Geneva, 1966. *The Organization of Educational Research: Comparative Education Study.* Geneva: International Bureau of Education; Paris: UNESCO, 1966.
International Guide to Educational Documentation. (2nd ed.) Paris: UNESCO, 1971. A guide to research centers, institutes, and information

centers worldwide; somewhat dated, but still useful.

Resources for R & D: 18 Institutional Capability Statements of Eighteen Contractors. Washington, D.C.: Council for Educational Development and Research, 1975.

[Information on teacher education was obtained from the bibliography prepared by Margaret Morris and Jane Sanchez. Information on education science was obtained from the bibliography prepared by Kristine Anderson.]

See also: Adult Education, Teacher Training for; Counselor Education; Early Childhood Education, Teacher Training for; Educational Administration; Higher Education; Instructional Technology; Physical Education; Special Education.

EDUCATIONAL ADMINISTRATION
(Field of Study)

Educational administration, in general, is concerned with the management of state and local school systems and with local school attendance units. Identified with the executive branch of government, educational administration is treated usually as a field of study in itself and not as a part of public administration. A more sophisticated definition of educational administration is: "A social process concerned with creating, maintaining, stimulating, controlling and unifying, formally and informally, the organized human and material energy within a unified system designed to accomplish predetermined (educational) objectives" (Knezevich, 1969, p. 11). Educational administration is concerned, therefore, with directing and managing human energy in order to accomplish educational objectives which have been formulated by governmental authority and expressed in written policies.

In some countries—notably Canada, England, and the United States—the educational system is decentralized; in most other countries (for instance, France, Spain, the Soviet Union, and the developing nations) education as a function of government is

centralized, and national ministries of education are common. Indeed, the Soviet Union's entire educational system is government owned and controlled. In many of the nation-states where education is centralized, education and society are interdependent, and education is used consciously to achieve the ends of government. Whether a nation's system of education is centralized or decentralized, however, does not necessarily relate directly to the political ideology of the controlling party. Democratic nations, as well as those with more authoritarian governments, may have a relatively centralized system of education.

In some nations following a democratic philosophy, the determination of what is wanted in and from education is the responsibility of the citizenry, expressed through its elected representatives. How to obtain these goals is the responsibility of the educator, and especially the administrator, who is usually appointed by elected representatives. Persons selected to assume administrative responsibilities in the field of education may be called principal or head of a separate school, superintendent or head of a school system, commissioner or head of a state educational system, minister or head of a national system of education.

In some nations school administrators serve chiefly as agents to transmit government policies throughout the respective schools or school systems over which they preside. In other countries, especially the United States, school administrators are expected to serve as professional educational leaders. Thus, school administrators in various countries range from those who are appointed by the political party in power to those selected for teaching skills, management competence, or other leadership abilities.

Horace Mann of Massachusetts and Henry Barnard of Connecticut are considered among the first educational administrators in the United States. Each served during the nineteenth century as the chief administrative officer of emerging state boards or state departments of education. It remained for Elwood P. Cubberley of Stanford University and others in the 1930s and later to write materials which could be incorporated into student programs for the training of administrators (Cubberley, 1929). In the United States training in educational administration has been provided at most large state universities in formal graduate course work and in various internship programs through a degree not found in most other nations. In many cases these programs lead to a doctoral degree.

In many nations educational administration is considered synonomous with management. In some nations the concept of "planning" seems an essential, if not basic, component of educational administration. In the United States programs to prepare educational administrators are comprehensive and generally include several areas of knowledge which could be considered auxiliary fields of study or a responsibility of other units of government in many nations. These areas are (1) organization and administrative theory; (2) politics of education; (3) curricular programs; (4) school law, finance, and business management; (5) school plant administration; (6) counseling and guidance services; (7) supervision and personnel management; (8) program evaluation procedures; and (9) coordinate activities, including transportation, school lunch programs, and extracurricular activities.

Preparation programs for school administrators in the United States include considerable discussion of administrative theory. Decision-making skills are primary components of new courses designed to improve leadership capabilities. Furthermore, administrative and organizational models have become widespread. In addition, modern management programs have been infused into the overall preparation programs for educational administrators. Foremost among these concepts and programs are (1) accountability and evaluation models; (2) management by objectives; and

(3) planning, programing, and budgeting systems. The latter are considered more than new approaches to budgeting, since they represent an attempt to facilitate decision making relating to the allocation of resources among various units of the educational enterprise and in consideration of various educational purposes and objectives.

Curriculum is a substantive area in which the administrator must be especially competent. Traditionally, the educational program has been considered an organized means of providing classroom instruction in various subjects. An activity program—controlled, in part, by student organizations—has been considered extracurricular. The trend, however, is to consider all aspects of the pupil's experience as an integrated program which acknowledges the importance of all of life's activities. The modern educational administrator is required to know the nature and scope of modern curricula and procedures needed for effecting change. One of the responsibilities of the administrator is to initiate programs of curriculum reconstruction and to justify such programs to the governing board to which he reports.

The educational administrator is required to know the financial needs of various programs and understand the tax structure and/or other financial report systems of the state and community. With respect to local school and/or district management, the school administrator must know how to make a budget, maintain custody of funds, expend funds appropriately, keep financial accounts, and make financial reports. In addition, training has always included an introduction to the vast field of public school law. Above all, the educational administrator should be mindful that profits derived from an investment in schools are educational, not financial.

Since 1950 educational administrators in some nations have become highly involved in school plant administration. Creating and building a school plant to meet educational needs are matters of hard, painstaking work, which largely must be done before the pressures requiring more space become so great that constructive planning procedures give way to expediency.

Another area of concern to the educational administrator is learning theory. The administrator who is knowledgeable about theories of learning and theories of intelligence, and who understands the need for appropriate guidance and counseling programs, will effect better leadership than those who perceive themselves only as managers of an educational enterprise. School administrators are also required to be effective in the field of personnel management. Salary schedules, merit-rating programs, retirement programs, and tenure are all significant parts of the administrator's responsibility. Finally, a most important part of an administrator's responsibility is the ability to evaluate the educational program—that is, to determine whether the program meets appropriate educational standards.

The educational administrator must have at his command a substantial body of facts about his government, his profession, and his administrative role. The history and philosophy of education and the theories of public and educational administration afford substance to the administrator's background. The successful administrator recognizes his relationship to the policy-making group to which he is responsible and to the teaching corps for which he is responsible.

"Democratic administration" has been a primary concern of the twentieth century. Teachers and other professional personnel have wanted to be involved in school administration, both in planning and in executing school programs. The public also wishes to be represented in the determination of policies, in the development of programs, and, in some cases, in the actual administration of the educational enterprise. Democratic administration is founded on the educator's willingness to accept professional responsibility for the accomplishment of philosophical and ed-

ucational objectives which have been determined in consultation with all concerned persons or their representatives. The preparation of administrators who will be mature, secure, and skilled enough to meet the demands of democratic administration may exceed the capacity of traditional training programs. There is a divergence of opinion concerning the values of the more traditional training programs and those of new models and systems. Undoubtedly both programs have elements of merit, and new programs may do well to combine the strengths of each.

[*Notes.* **E. P. Cubberley,** *Public School Administration* (Boston: Houghton Mifflin, 1929). **S. J. Knezevich,** *Administration of Public Education* (New York: Harper & Row, 1969).]

F. ROBERT PAULSEN

Levels and Programs of Study

Programs in educational administration generally require as a prerequisite a first university degree, usually in teacher training, demonstrated potential for study at the higher level, and some experience in educational administration. The usual award for successful completion of the program is a master's degree, a sixth-year certificate, or their equivalents. A doctor's degree (Ed.D.) may be awarded after a period of study lasting for at least two or three years if research has played an important role and a thesis or dissertation is presented. Through seminars, directed reading, visits, supervised internship, and independent research, a student seeks to acquire a comprehensive understanding of educational administration. A program in a specialty of this kind usually includes study of related subjects in the humanities, social and behavioral sciences, law, fine and applied arts, mathematics, and statistics.

[This section was based on UNESCO's *International Standard Classification of Education (ISCED): Three Stage Classification System, 1974* (Paris: UNESCO, 1974).]

Major International and National Organizations

INTERNATIONAL

Commonwealth Council for Educational
    Administration (CCEA)
University of New England
Armidale, New South Wales, Australia
    Encourages research, arranges conferences,
stimulates publications, and accredits courses
for practitioners in the field.

University Council for Educational
    Administration (UCEA)
29 West Woodruff Avenue
Columbus, Ohio 43210 USA

Organization of departments of educational
administration in United States and Canadian
universities. Promotes training of school administrators and conducts research through
interuniversity cooperation.

Since 1966 a series of International Intervisitation Programs for professors of educational administration and senior administrators
from major English-language countries and
Commonwealth countries have been held. The
first, sponsored by UCEA, was held in 1966 at
the Universities of Michigan and Alberta. The
second was organized in 1970 at the University
of New England in Australia. The most recent
was held in 1974 in London and other sites
in Great Britain.

In addition to the two organizations representing the English-language countries, other
international organizations are involved in the
training of educational planners and administrators. The United Nations Economic and
Social Council, through its semiautonomous regional economic commissions, is particularly
active in sponsoring institutes which offer training in educational planning and administration. The following is a list of the other principal
international and regional organizations in the
field:

Arab States Centre for Educational Planning
    and Administration
P.O. Box 5244
Beirut, Lebanon
    Provides training for Arab educators in the
field of educational planning and administration; sponsored by UNESCO and the Lebanese
government.

Asian Institute of Educational Planning and
    Administration
Indraprastha Estate
New Delhi 1, India

Conducts training courses for senior educational planners and administrators of Asian
member and associated member states of
UNESCO; sponsored by UNESCO and the government of India.

International Institute for Educational
    Planning
Institut international de planification de
    l'éducation (IIPE)
7-9 rue Eugène-Delacroix
75016 Paris, France
    Serves as world center for advanced train-
ing and research in education planning;
prepares future teachers and researchers of
educational planning.

Organisation for Economic Co-operation
    and Development (OECD)
2 rue André Pascal
Paris 16e, France
    Conducts training courses and seminars on
educational planning and development.

UNESCO
Department of Educational Planning and
    Administration
place de Fontenoy
Paris 7e, France
    Activities conducted in five major areas: (1)
supports institutes for educational planning,
(2) organizes conferences on educational planning, (3) sponsors educational planning advisory missions, (4) provides experts and fellowships in educational planning and allied fields,
and (5) provides documentation and advisory
and analytical services on educational planning.

UNESCO Regional Group for Educational
    Planning and Administration in Africa
P.O. Box 3311
Dakar, Senegal
    Organizes regional, subregional, or national
training courses in educational planning for
African education officers.

United Nations Asian Institute for Economic
    Development and Planning
Henry Dunant Street
Bangkok, Thailand
    Conducts courses in educational planning
for officials of countries in Asia and the
Far East.

United Nations Economic Commission for
    Africa:
African Institute for Economic Development
    and Planning
Boîte Postale 3186
Dakar, Senegal
    Autonomous institution whose course in

economic development and planning includes elements of educational planning.

United Nations Economic Commission for Latin America:
Latin American Institute for Economic and Social Planning
avenida José Miguel Infante 9
Casilla 1567
Santiago, Chile
Organizes an annual course for medium-level officials of Latin American educational planning or educational administrative services.

NATIONAL

There are numerous associations of both primary and secondary school principals throughout the world, but few national associations of educational administrators or professors except in the following countries:

Canada:
    Canadian Association of School Administrators
    Association canadienne des administrateurs scolaires
    Suite N843
    252 Bloor Street West
    Toronto, Ontario M5S 1V5

United Kingdom:
    British Educational Administration Society
    Cardiff University College, Faculty of Education
    Senghennydd Road
    Cardiff, Wales 24AG

United States:
    American Association of School Administrators (AASA)
    1801 North Moore Street
    Arlington, Virginia 22209

    National Conference of Professors of Educational Administration (NCPEA)
    College of Education
    University of Texas
    Austin, Texas
    Professional organization of professors in universities and colleges who are identified with the preparation of school administrators.

For other lists of national organizations see:

Educational Planning: A Directory of Training and Research Institutions. (2nd ed.) Paris: International Institute for Educational Planning, 1968. Includes a list of training and research groups throughout the world interested in educational planning.
Stone, F. D. *Voluntary Organizations in Educa-*

tional Administration, A Report. Report compiled in June 1974, available from Franklin D. Stone, College of Education, University of Iowa, Iowa City, Iowa. An extensive listing of educational administration organizations in Australia, Canada, Great Britain, New Zealand, and the United States.
Teachers' Associations. (2nd ed.) Paris: UNESCO, 1971. Lists national organizations concerned with administration.

Principal Information Sources

GENERAL

Guides to the literature include:

"Educational Administration: Bibliography." *EducAfrica,* 1974, *1* (2), 107–114.
Gosden, P. H. J. H. *Educational Administration in England and Wales: A Bibliographic Guide.* Leeds, England: University of Leeds Institute of Education, 1967.

Overviews and introductions to the field of educational administration include:

Birley, D. *The Education Officer and His World.* London: Routledge and Kegan Paul, 1970.
Campbell, R. F., and others. *Introduction to Educational Administration.* (4th ed.) Boston: Allyn & Bacon, 1971.
Culbertson, J., and others. *Social Science Content for Preparing Educational Leaders.* Columbus, Ohio: Merrill, 1973.
Hack, W. G., and others. *Educational Administration: Selected Readings.* (2nd rev. ed.) Boston: Allyn & Bacon, 1971.
Halpin, A. W. (Ed.) *Administrative Theory in Education.* New York: Macmillan, 1967.
Lewis, L. J., and Loveridge, A. J. *The Management of Education.* London: Pall Mall Press, 1965. For teachers and administrators in developing countries.
Monahan, W. G. *Theoretical Dimensions of Educational Administration.* New York: Macmillan, 1975.
The Role, Function, Recruitment and Training of District Education Officers. New Delhi: Asian Institute of Educational Planning and Administration, 1970.
Swift, W. H. *Educational Administration in Canada: A Memorial to A. W. Reeves.* Toronto, Ontario: Macmillan, 1970.
Walker, W. G. (Ed.) *Theory and Practice in Educational Administration.* St. Lucia, Brisbane: University of Queensland, 1970; New York: Crane, Russak, 1970.
Walker, W. G. *School, College, and University: The Administration of Education in Australia.* New York: Crane, Russak, 1973.
Walker, W. G, and others. (Eds.) *Explorations*

in Educational Administration. New York: Crane, Russak, 1972.

Comparative education sources include the following:

Baron, G., Cooper, D. H., and Walker, W. G. (Eds.) *Educational Administration: International Perspectives.* Chicago: Rand McNally, 1969. Contains essays on the preparation of educational administrators in Australia, Canada, New Zealand, the United Kingdom, the United States, and internationally.

Commonwealth Regional Seminar/Workshop on Administration and Supervision in Education. Georgetown, 1974. *Final Report.* London: Commonwealth Secretariat, 1974.

Educational Planning: A World Survey of Problems and Prospects. Paris: UNESCO, 1970.

Enns, F. "The Promise of International Cooperation in the Preparation of Educational Administrators." In G. Baron, D. H. Cooper, and W. G. Walker (Eds.), *Educational Administration: International Perspectives.* Chicago: Rand McNally, 1969. Pp. 300–320.

Hughes, M. *Administering Education: International Challenge.* Atlantic Highlands, New Jersey: Humanities Press, 1975.

International Intervisitation Program 1970. Armidale, New South Wales, Australia: Commonwealth Council for Educational Administration, University of New England, 1970.

International Intervisitation Programme on Education Administration, 6th–27th July 1974. Armidale, New South Wales, Australia: Commonwealth Council for Educational Administration, University of New England, 1974.

Ponsioen, J. A. (Ed.) *Educational Innovations in Africa: Policies and Administration.* The Hague: Institute of Social Studies, 1972.

Reller, T., and Morphet, E. L. (Eds.) *Comparative Educational Administration.* Englewood Cliffs, New Jersey: Prentice-Hall, 1962.

Rudman, H. C. *The School and State in the USSR.* New York: Macmillan; London: Collier-Macmillan, 1967.

Thomas, A. R. "The Preparation of Educational Administrators in Canadian Universities: Laying On of the Hands." *Journal of Educational Administration,* May 1975, *13* (1), 35–60.

Walker, W. G. "Innovation in the Commonwealth: The International Intervisitation Program, Australia, 1970." *Journal of Educational Administration,* May 1971, *9,* 3–9.

On the training of educational administrators see:

Cronin, J. M., and Horoschak, P. P. *Innovative Strategies in Field Experiences for Preparing Ed-*

ucational Administrators. ERIC/CEM-UCEA Series on Administrator Preparation, No. 8. Columbus, Ohio: University Council for Educational Administration, 1973.

Culbertson, J. A., and Hencley, S. P. (Eds.) *Preparing Administrators: New Perspectives.* Columbus, Ohio: University Council for Educational Administration, 1962.

Cunningham, K. S., and Radford, W. C. *Training the Administrator: A Study with Special Reference to Education.* Hawthorn, Victoria: Australian Council for Educational Research, 1963.

Glasser, R. *Training for Management (An Outline of Requirements).* Paris: International Institute for Educational Planning, 1970.

Henderson, A. D. *Training University Administrators: A Programme Guide.* Paris: UNESCO, 1970.

"A Latin American Experience in the Field of Training of Educational Planners and Administrators." Paper prepared for participants in the seminar on the Training of Specialists in Educational Administration and Planning: Evaluation and Prospects. Paris: UNESCO, July 2–11, 1973.

Lutz, F. W., and Ferrante, R. *Emergent Practices in the Continuing Education of School Administrators.* ERIC/CEM-UCEA Series on Administrator Preparation. Columbus, Ohio: University Council for Educational Administration, 1972.

March, J. G. "Analytical Skills and the University Training of Educational Administrators." *Journal of Educational Administration,* May 1974, *12* (1), 17–44.

Miklos, E. "Preparation Programs for Educational Administrators in Canada." Paper presented at annual conference of the Canadian Society for the Study of Education, 1973.

Ogunniyi, O. "The Training of Educational Administrators in Africa." *EducAfrica,* 1974, *1* (2), 39–58.

Stout, R. T. *New Approches to Recruitment and Selection of Educational Administrators.* ERIC/CEM-UCEA Series on Administrator Preparation, No. 5. Columbus, Ohio: University Council for Educational Administration, 1973.

Willower, D. J., and Culbertson, J. A. (Eds.) *The Professorship in Educational Administration.* Columbus, Ohio: University Council for Educational Administration, 1964.

Wynn, R. *Unconventional Methods and Materials for Preparing Educational Administrators.* ERIC/CEM-UCEA Series on Administrator Preparation, No. 2. Columbus, Ohio: University Council for Educational Administration, 1972.

Historical perspectives on the field include:

Cubberley, E. P., and Elliott, E. C. (Eds.) *State and County School Administration*. Vol. 2: *Source Book*. New York: Macmillan, 1922.

Gosden, P. H. J. H. *The Development of Educational Administration in England and Wales*. Oxford, England: Blackwell, 1966.

Moehlman, A. B. *School Administration: Its Development, Principles, and Function in the United States*. (2nd ed.) Westport, Connecticut: Greenwood Press, 1951.

CURRENT BIBLIOGRAPHIES

There are numerous general education abstracting and indexing services which list articles on educational administration. The following is the only specialized current bibliography entirely devoted to the field. It features short abstracts of articles relevant to the field of educational administration from one hundred English-language journals:

Educational Administration Abstracts. Columbus, Ohio: University Council for Educational Administration, 1966–. Published quarterly.

PERIODICALS

The following journals are important to the practice of educational administration: *Administrator's Notebook* (US), *American School and University*, *American School Board Journal*, *Cahiers africains d'administration publique* (Morocco), *Canadian Administrator*, *Educational Administration and History* (UK), *Educational Administration Bulletin* (UK), *Educational Administration Quarterly* (US), *Education et gestion* (France), *Journal of Educational Administration* (Australia), *National Association for Women Deans, Administrators and Counselors. Journal* (US), *National Association of Secondary-School Principals. Bulletin* (US), *National Elementary Principal* (US), *Oregon University: Center for the Advanced Study of Educational Administration. Research and Development Perspectives* (US), *Public Administration Review* (US), *School Administrator* (US), *Skolfoerfattningar* (Sweden).

For a more extensive listing of journals carrying articles on educational administration see:

Educational Administration Abstracts. Columbus, Ohio: University Council for Educational Administration, 1966–. Published quarterly.

ENCYCLOPEDIAS, DICTIONARIES, HANDBOOKS

Good, C. V. *Dictionary of Education*. (3rd ed.) New York: McGraw-Hill, 1973.

Knowles, A. S. *Handbook of College and University Administration*. New York: McGraw-Hill, 1970.

Prentice-Hall Editorial Staff. *Handbook of Successful School Administration*. Englewood Cliffs, New Jersey: Prentice-Hall, 1974.

School Systems: A Guide. (2nd ed.) Strasbourg, France: Council of Europe, 1970.

Stoops, E., Rafferty, M., and Johnson, R. E. *Handbook of Educational Administration: A Guide for the Practitioner*. Boston: Allyn & Bacon, 1975.

Walker, W. G. *A Glossary of Educational Terms: Usage in Five English Speaking Countries*. St. Lucia, Brisbane: University of Queensland Press, n.d.

World Survey of Education: Vol. 5: *Educational Policy, Legislation and Administration*. Paris: UNESCO, 1971.

DIRECTORIES

Peterson's Annual Guides to Graduate Study. Princeton, New Jersey: Peterson's Guides, annual. Includes a directory of institutions in the United States offering programs in educational administration.

Study Abroad. Paris: UNESCO, biennial. Lists programs in educational administration and planning offered by international organizations and national institutions.

Universities and Colleges of Canada. Ottawa, Ontario: Association of Universities and Colleges of Canada, annual.

RESEARCH CENTERS, INSTITUTES, INFORMATION CENTERS

Center for Educational Policy and Management
1472 Kincaid Street
University of Oregon
Eugene, Oregon 97403 USA
Integral unit of the College of Education; conducts research in the field of educational administration and trains research workers and administrators; maintains library on educational administration and school organization.

Midwest Administration Center
University of Chicago
5835 South Kimbark Avenue
Chicago, Illinois 60637 USA
Integral unit of the Graduate School of Education. Conducts research in educational administration; holds conferences, seminars, and workshops for school administrators and school board members.

University Council for Educational Administration (UCEA)
29 West Woodruff Avenue
Columbus, Ohio 43210 USA
Important research center and seminal organization in educational administration.

EDUCATIONAL ASSESSMENT CENTER, United States

The Educational Assessment Center was established in 1972 at the University of Washington, Seattle, with the merger of the university's student ratings organization, founded in 1924; the bureau of testing, begun in 1946; and the bureau of institutional research, founded in 1959. The center conducts research in higher education, focusing on local, national, and regional problems in the following areas: administration, especially academic policies; educational planning, university students and faculty; curricula and instruction; educational technology; methodology of research in higher education; and reform in higher education. Specifically, studies have been made on general evaluation theory and practice, college science teacher training, and the development of vocational interest inventory tests. The center also conducts ongoing studies of grade distribution and affirmative action. In addition to research activities, the center develops evaluation tools such as tests and measurements; trains university teachers, administrators, and researchers; and holds conferences and seminars.

The center is supported by the university, a National Science Foundation grant, and contractual research and consulting services. The staff includes four research professionals, four research assistants and/or graduate students, nine technicians, two administrative personnel, and ten secretarial and clerical personnel. The staff has access to computer and optical scanning equipment, testing facilities, student ratings of instruction forms, a small library of unpublished materials, and microfilm and microfiche readers.

The center publishes a newsletter, *Currents in University Education,* which comes out quarterly.

University of Washington
448 Schmitz Building, PB-30
1400 NE Campus Parkway
Seattle, Washington 98195 USA

EDUCATIONAL FACILITIES LABORATORIES, United States

The Educational Facilities Laboratories (EFL) was established in the United States by the Ford Foundation in 1958 to conduct research on advancements in design, construction, and utilization of educational facilities. EFL seeks to improve function and economy in design, construction, and use of educational material—buildings, equipment, furniture—and the general surroundings. Studies related to higher education include the following: generating revenue from college facilities, educational change and architectural consequences, environmental education, student housing, and career education facilities. EFL provides a consultant service to schools, colleges, and other nonprofit educational agencies, but it does not make grants for capital outlay.

Originally funded exclusively by the Ford Foundation, EFL became a publicly supported, nonprofit organization in 1971. Funding is received from nonprofit agencies, both governmental and philanthropic.

In addition to research reports, EFL publishes two quarterly newsletters—*Planning for Higher Education* and *Schoolhouse.*
850 Third Avenue
New York, New York 10022 USA

EDUCATIONAL REFORM IN PROGRESS (Higher Education Report), Spain

Educational Reform in Progress (Madrid: Ministry of Education and Science Publications Service, 1972), a report prepared by the Spanish Ministry of Education and Science, describes the ongoing implementation in Spain of the 1970 general educational reform law. The law, scheduled to be fully implemented by 1978, constitutes a reform of the traditional Napoleonic system formed in the nineteenth century into a modern system composed of obligatory preschool education for two- to five-year-old children, basic education for the six to thirteen age group, and technical and higher education for students aged thirteen and above. The report discusses the structure of the new educational system and its development under the law and considers the administration of the system, personnel policy, financing, planning, quality control, students, special education, and adult education.

At the higher education level, the report describes progress toward the division of university and technical school study into three degree programs leading to bachelor's, master's, and doctoral awards as called for in the law. Progress in the creation, transformation, and equipping of centers of education is assessed. The report also discusses the control of the centers' educational costs and the establishment of nonstate centers. The development of the structure and administration of the universities during the period of implementation of the law is also examined.

The report discusses the development of a new national science policy and the promotion of scientific research. In addition, it reviews the status of the national scientific and technical information service, libraries, archives, and museums.

EDUCATIONAL RESEARCH AND DEVELOPMENT UNIT
(Afdeling onderzoek en ontwikkeling van onderwijs), Netherlands

The Educational Research and Development Unit was founded at the State University of Utrecht to conduct research and development projects in teaching and learning at the university level. Maintaining a local or national focus, research at the unit is concerned with the following areas: educational technology, curricula and instruction, and reform in higher education. The unit offers a number of short courses to train university teachers, administrators, and researchers in constructing and im-

plementing educational programs. Training workshops for students interested in educational innovation at the university level are also offered. In addition to research and teaching activities, the unit designs curricula and provides a documentation service. Members of the unit act as consultants to specialists in university faculties and departments and serve on educational committees.

Funded by the State University of Utrecht, the unit has a staff of twelve research professionals, two research assistants and/or graduate students, two administrative personnel, and five secretaries. The staff has access to a specialized library of books, reports, and journals of higher education; a computer terminal, connected with various data bases in the United States and Sweden, for on-line documentation service; a microfiche reader and printer; and video and sound recording equipment.

The unit's publication, *O&O—Memo,* is issued six times a year and contains information about the unit's activities and publications as well as an article on a subject of general interest in the field of education. The unit also publishes the *Mededelingen* (Communications) series, reports of research and development projects and instruments that have been developed for educational fact finding.

Maliebaan 5
Utrecht, Netherlands

EDUCATIONAL RESEARCH CENTER
(Bureau onderzoek van onderwijs), Netherlands

The Educational Research Center was established at the State University of Leiden, in the Netherlands, to conduct educational research in higher education and to advise the faculty and board of governors of the university on educational matters. Research, focusing on local and national problems, is concerned with the following areas: economics of higher education, university students and faculty, educational technology, curricula and instruction, methodology of research in higher education, and reform in higher education. In addition to research activities, the center designs curricula; develops evaluation tools such as tests and measurements; trains university teachers, administrators, and researchers; holds conferences and seminars; and provides a documentation service.

Funded by the university and by foundation grants, the center's staff includes six research professionals, two research assistants and/or graduate students, one technician, and three secretaries. The staff has access to a library, a computer, and audiovisual aids.

The center publishes a series of reports and research memoranda. With few exceptions, all publications are in Dutch. A list of publications is available on request.

Rijksuniversiteit Leiden
Boerhaavelaan 2
Leiden, Netherlands

EDUCATIONAL RESEARCH CENTER
(Onderwijs research centrum), Netherlands

The Educational Research Center was founded in 1969 at Tilburg University to assist the university in its efforts to develop new educational systems and to provide solutions to problems of educational innovation. Higher education research at the center, with a local or national focus, is conducted in educational technology and curricula and instruction. The center has conducted, for example, studies of self-paced study systems, computer-assisted instruction, and multimedia educational innovations. In addition to research activities, the center designs curricula, develops evaluation tools such as tests and measurements, provides in-service teacher training, holds conferences and seminars, and provides a documentation service.

Funded by Tilburg University, the cen-

ter includes six research professionals, three research assistants and/or graduate students, and one secretary.

The center publishes research reports.
Katholieke hogeschool te Tilburg
Hogeschoollaan 225
Tilburg, Netherlands

EDUCATIONAL RESEARCH INSTITUTE
(Instituto de investigaciones educativas), Venezuela

Founded in 1970, the Educational Research Institute at the Simón Bolívar University, Caracas, Venezuela, studies problems in higher education in Venezuela. The institute is divided into three units: basic research, educational technology, and institutional research. Contracting with the Venezuelan Ministry of Education and other universities or educational institutions, the basic research unit conducts higher education studies on the national level. The educational technology unit conducts an ongoing program of faculty improvement, with emphasis on the development and evaluation of teaching techniques. The institutional research unit, a permanent self-study office, helps the university's planning office evaluate curricula and other educational programs and practices. It also studies the relation between the socioeconomic status of a student's parents and his educational achievement.

In addition to research activities, the institute conducts postgraduate courses to train university teachers, administrators, and researchers. Members of the staff use the computer facilities of the Simón Bolívar University.

The institute receives financial support from university funds and contractual research services. The staff includes four research professionals and one secretary.

Universidad Simón Bolívar
Apartado Postal 80659
Caracas 108, Venezuela

EDUCATIONAL RESOURCES

1. ADMINISTRATION
2. LEARNING RESOURCES CENTERS
3. RADIO AND TELEVISION AS
   INSTRUCTIONAL MEDIA

1. ADMINISTRATION

Educational institutions of all levels are centers where the resources of teaching and learning are available. The library is part of these resources and has been traditionally print oriented; books have long been considered a primary source of instructional information. With the advent of film, audio sources, and television, the preeminence of the printed word is undergoing reassessment. As a logical corollary to this scrutiny, the spoken word in the classroom has gained attention.

Although there may be controversy in some educational quarters about the importance of print as against nonprint sources, this article focuses on the significance of all media in the educational setting. A definition is proposed in support of learning resources that appears to transcend the traditional bounds of print and nonprint media and that discusses not learning resources per se, but the much larger and all-inclusive domain of instructional technology.

During the early 1970s, efforts were under way to define instructional technology. One of the most viable models that emerged was that conceptualized by Silber (1970, p. 21): "The Development (Research, Design, Production, Evaluation, Support-Supply, Utilization) of Instructional System Components (Messages, Men, Materials, Devices, Techniques, Settings), and the Management of that development (Organization, Personnel), in a systematic manner with the goal of solving instructional problems."

Organizing Learning Resources

At one end of the management spectrum, the model facilitates a highly integrated approach to dealing with curriculum and learning. At the other end, more often contingent on philosophical grounds rather than economic or any other constraints, this same model reflects an approach to media that construes audiovisual techniques, equipment, and materials as teaching aids, part of a support service ancillary to the principal concerns of the classroom. The essential difference between the two approaches is the educator's regard for systematic preplanning in curriculum development and course design.

In discussing the organization of learning resources, this article considers functional models predicated on the more integrated approach. Such a view allows a clearer look at all elements involved in a media support service as well as their interrelationships with the curriculum. Library organizations are excluded from this discussion because, in both young and old institutions, they have a fairly well-established and accepted history of efficacious development and service.

The set of goals for a service organization responsible for supporting the media and instructional development needs of institutions of higher learning may be summarized as follows: (1) to facilitate more effective teaching and learning through applications of instructional technology; (2) to apply research findings from behavioral science, education, and subject matter disciplines to the instructional process; (3) to maintain contact with all activities concerning instructional technology and innovative approaches to learning; (4) to provide an environment for more adequate implementation of instructional technology; (5) to assist institutional management in establishing plans, policies, and facilities concerned with instructional technology; and (6) to develop academic programs, courses, and workshops relating to media and the learning process. One additional goal is appropriate, depending on the relationship of the institution to the community in which it is situated: (7) to provide the immediate community with general media assistance and services.

Basically, six operational groups are readily identified for assignment to the various functions designed to achieve these goals.

Campus media services. The campus media services group distributes equipment and materials to the classroom; provides film rental service, preview areas, and maintenance of the institutional film library; locates sources and arranges for instructional materials purchases; collects information on media and the learning process; and provides audiotape and videotape duplication service.

Learning resources study center. The learning resources study center group provides students with individualized learning systems featuring individual or small-group viewing and listening carrels equipped with programed texts, films, audiotapes, videotapes, language laboratory materials, and music recordings.

Media workshops. The media workshops group makes available to faculty and students special facilities and staff for learning to use audiovisual and video equipment and to produce audiovisual materials.

Analysis and design. The analysis and design group provides staff support to faculty for developing more effective course materials; conducts workshop sessions in instructional systems design (how to develop programed instruction, learning packages, "personalized system of instruction," and interactive lectures); consults with faculty on improving teaching skills; and evaluates the effectiveness of media units.

Media production. The media production group produces video, audio, and filmed units in accordance with instructional designs and prepared scripts; collaborates in prescribing media for programed units; and provides a graphics and photography production service.

Engineering and maintenance. The engineering and maintenance group provides technical support for television and audio-studio productions; operates closed-circuit television broadcast systems; and maintains and repairs inventory of audiovisual and video equipment.

Each of these groups can vary in size, from the proverbial "one-man operation" to a staff rivaling the size of the teaching faculty. Obviously, the constraining factor here is economic and, in some areas, the availability of specialists. Moreover, resources can be allocated in any strength to different groups, depending on the immediate and projected needs of the institution, without sacrificing the integrity of the overall integrated approach.

Global Examples of Instructional Technology

The concept of a center for learning resources support services in institutions of higher learning has taken hold predominantly in universities and colleges in the United States, some Western European countries, a few Commonwealth nations, and, in the Orient, Japan. Where, in some of these nations, the government plays an extraordinary role in the daily affairs of instructors, the focal point of centralization may even be located primarily in an official agency, as, for example, the National Board of Education in Sweden.

Some notable examples of centralized media support organizations advocating and practicing an integrated approach to the application of learning resources are the Center for Instructional Development at Syracuse University in New York; the organization at Michigan State University, Lansing, which coordinates the Instructional Media Center, Learning Service, and Evaluation Service through the provost's office; the Division of Instructional Communications at Western Michigan University, Kalamazoo; the Center for Educational Technology at the University of Sussex, England; the Instructional Services Center at the University of South Carolina, Columbia; the Office of Instructional Resources at the University of Illinois at Champaign-Urbana; the Center for Science of Learning at Keio University, Tokyo; the Media Resources Center at Iowa State University, Ames; the Instructional Resources Center at San Jose State

University, California; the Division of Instructional Research and Services at Florida State University, Tallahassee; and the Office of Educational Resources at Northeastern University, Boston.

In many other countries, learning resources in a systematic framework are often a response to specialized but related needs. Outstanding examples of such efforts, related to teacher training and organized around a systems approach toward a competency-based curriculum, can be found at the Teacher Training School in Bouaké, Ivorian Educational Television Ministry, Ivory Coast, and at teacher training colleges for elementary, intermediate, and higher education at Bakht er Ruda and Omdurman, Sudan.

As Kulkarni (1969) points out in his article summarizing India's trial efforts to update curriculum through television, radio, and films, it was the advent of programed learning alone that led educators to advocate more systematic use of instructional technology in developing courses.

Open University programs characterize, intrinsically, an integrated and centrally organized approach to the use of instructional technology. The British Open University and a number of such programs in the United States (Empire State College, New York; Rutgers University, New Jersey; The University of Mid-America, regionally supported in Iowa, Kansas, Missouri, and Nebraska) are quite outstanding products of the systematic use of learning resources. In Colombia the University of Antioquia has been developing the Open University system to provide higher education to the general public. Instructional technology is applied by their school of education toward individualizing instruction by means of radio, programed materials, and audio cassette. The Free University of Iran based its modified approach on the British Open University model, with a highly sophisticated approach to using instructional technology.

Finally, the two-year community college has lately gained considerable support and widespread implementation in the United States. Because these institutions customarily practice open admissions, they need a particularly flexible and effective curriculum. For this reason, most of these institutions establish highly organized and integrated learning resources centers.

Instructional Technology and the University

To facilitate discussion of the administrative concerns of a learning resources center, a hypothetical organizational structure is now proposed. This model is consistent with the objectives and functional groupings enumerated earlier.

Two divisions are assigned responsibility for the six functional groups. Although they operate with considerable autonomy in carrying out their respective missions, providing media service on the one hand and collaborating with content specialists on the other, both divisions are the active complements of an integrated approach to the institution's need for instructional technology. For example, media workshops can provide faculty with the skills requisite to improved classroom performance; the graphics and photo service responds to basic service requests (apart from those associated with systems development projects); the learning resources study center administers individualized units developed through design and production efforts; and engineering and maintenance support the electronic repair requirements of the one division's production studios and the portable video inventory of campus media services in the other division.

The administrative policy and operations guidelines of this organization are conveyed through each of the division heads. Counsel with the dean or director of the organization forms an integral part of the overall management system. The dean or director reports directly to the vice-president of academic affairs or provost and represents the principal liaison between the administration (with respect to institutional goals, policy and constraints) and learning resources (with respect to

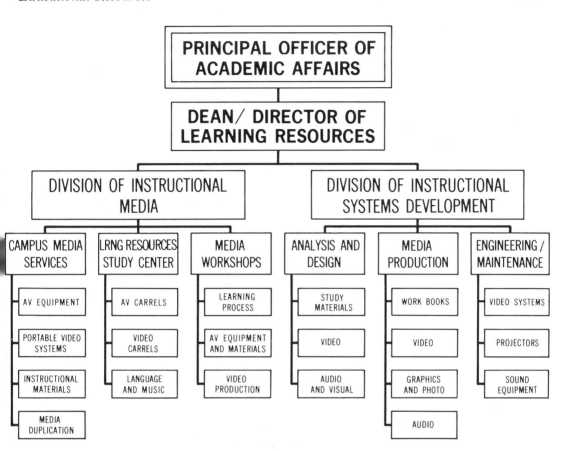

its assigned functions and commitments). Overall, the office of the dean or director is charged with responsibility for promoting collaborative, balanced, and more systematic applications of instructional technology throughout the institution.

Space for the system. In many universities and colleges, physical space is at a premium. The pressure on maintaining and increasing classroom availability simply outweighs all other considerations. However, a learning resources support service, similar to one presented in the organization chart above, must be assigned the following basic space allocations: equipment storage and distribution area; technical repair shop; audiovisual materials library; television, sound, and motion picture studios; instructional development conference area; individualized study carrel area (space may be preempted from the central library area); graphics and photography work areas; and offices for professional staff.

For an operation that involved approximately fifty staff members in an institution of 20,000 full-time students, the total space allocation for these facilities would approach 10,000 square feet (1000 square meters). If a new campus is being planned or building modifications are possible, attention to space design should address not only current media needs but also provisions for maximum flexibility for both technical facilities and classroom areas. The application of media and instructional design is apt to bring about basic changes in the size of student groups assembled for classroom instruction.

Learning resources: an academic service. It is critical that the learning resources support service be identified as closely as possible with academic interests, much as the library has been identified at most institutions of higher learning. Learning resources centers are often the focal point on campus of innovative efforts in teaching and learning. If these organizations are too distinctly removed, they run the risk of discouraging many faculty members from becoming involved in what may be misconstrued as projects dealing exclusively with mechanical and electronic devices. In fact, the key professionals in a learning resources organization should be encouraged to cultivate images as educators rather than as media specialists. One way to facilitate this association is to appoint such professionals jointly to academic departments.

The organizational structure itself, however, may remain an administrative branch of the institution rather than a part of any distinct college or academic department. The provisions of centralization are best served in this context.

Instructional technology as an organ of change. In their chapter on organized support services, MacKenzie, Eraut, and Jones. (1970, p. 183) proposed the following as the most desirable evolutionary pattern for learning resources in institutions of higher learning: "Once the institution as a whole begins to be concerned with innovation . . . a media unit no longer needs to play the role of change agent for the institution in default of anyone else, and it can adopt the more comfortable posture of a partner in the change process rather than forcing itself into the stance of promoter." Although the transition from change agent to active partner is no doubt important in institutions flourishing in the developed countries, such evolution is questionable in less fortunate areas. In fact, sustaining an image as the vanguard for change, albeit as an indigenous agency, may better serve the operational interests of a learning resources support service surrounded by adverse socioeconomic conditions.

The degree to which an instructional media organization can facilitate change is obviously contingent, in large part, on the availability of funds for physical facilities, equipment, materials, support staff (media and electronic technicians), and learning specialists (instructional technologists, educational psychologists, evaluation experts, curriculum developers). Many governments, keenly aware of the benefits that invariably accrue from the increased applications of instructional technology, have provided their institutions of higher learning with ample financial support. Initial investments are high and continued support is frequently burdensome, but the end product—far more effective teaching and learning—is regarded in many communities as an invaluable commodity.

Foundations, such as the Ford and Rockefeller Foundations, have also been directly instrumental in promoting interest in, and accelerated use of, instructional technology where the national economies could not possibly finance the initiation of media programs. Maintaining these programs, once foundation money is exhausted, can present formidable burdens to such economies. However, if the emphasis is not primarily on the use of expensive and sophisticated electronic systems like television, but rather on instructional expertise among staff members in the techniques of instructional development (as in India, where programed learning was vigorously promoted as an instructional methodology), the viability of media development programs can frequently be extended beyond the period supported by major funding.

Problems and issues. It is debatable whether or not centralization of learning resources represents the most desirable organizational, inventory, and facilities approach. Certainly, decentralization of such resources produces a high level of convenience for faculty and their academic departments. However, the lack of staff efficiency, coupled with wasteful duplication of equipment, materials, and facilities, has been found by most large institutions to be too high a price to pay for their faculty's convenience. Further, as pointed out by MacKenzie, Eraut, and Jones (1970, p. 190), centralization may actually be a transitional necessity for allowing media and innovative methods to "nurture" until interest becomes widely based at the institution.

Because the library has academic credibility on most campuses, using it as an organizing unit is an issue presently under debate. Although a firm and valid case may be made for the substantial similarities of library and learning resources support functions (see, for example, Case, Hamreus, Wallington, and Myers, 1972), other points of view stress the unsuitability of this context for administering an innovative agency because of the library's traditionally passive role in academic affairs. The library, however, is still an excellent campus site for implementing the individualized carrel activity requiring media.

Finally, we must confront the humanistic questions provoked by the increased use of instructional technology. If the technology is being used to replace teachers where they are otherwise available, then the humanists' opposition deserves careful consideration. If, however, instructional technology is a tool that either facilitates learning in spite of unavailable teachers or makes the teacher's role more effective through classroom support or adjunct learning packages, then the fears are groundless.

Bibliography

Brown, J. W., and Norberg, K. D. *Administering Educational Media: Instructional Technology and Library Services.* (2nd ed.) New York: McGraw-Hill, 1972.

Case, R. N., Hamreus, D. G., Wallington, J., and Myers, D. C. "Reactions . . ." *Audiovisual Instruction*, 1972, *17*(1), 36–43.

Chapman, A. S., and Unwin, D. "Educational Technology at Large." *Educational Technology*, 1969, *9*(11), 7–9.

Donnelly, E. J. "Audiovisual Media Services." In A. S. Knowles (Ed.), *Handbook of College and University Administration: Academic.* New York: McGraw-Hill, 1970.

Frailey, L. E., and Vargas, E. A. "Academic Tradition and Instructional Technology." *Journal of Higher Education*, 1975, *45*(1), 1–15.

Gilbert, J. E., and Hulbert, T. E. "Instructional Services." In A. S. Knowles (Ed.), *Handbook*

of *College and University Administration: Academic.* New York: McGraw-Hill, 1970.

Grady, W. F. "Media International." *Audiovisual Instruction*, 1976, *21*(2), 4.

Kent, A. "Programmed Learning Services." In A. S. Knowles (Ed.), *Handbook of College and University Administration: Academic.* New York: McGraw-Hill, 1970.

Kulkarni, S. S. "Educational Technology in India." *Educational Technology*, 1969, *9*(11), 28–32.

Lowery, M. A. "School Library Manpower Project Launches Phase II." *Audiovisual Instruction*, 1972, *16*(1), 26–28.

MacKenzie, N., Eraut, M., and Jones, H. C. *Teaching and Learning—An Introduction to New Methods and Resources in Higher Education.* Paris: UNESCO, 1970.

Razik, T. A. *Systems Approach to Teacher Training and Curriculum Development: The Case of Developing Countries.* Paris: UNESCO, 1972.

Seaman, S. K. "Administration of a Learning Resources Center." *Educational Broadcasting*, September/October 1975, pp. 25–27.

Silber, K. H. "What Field Are We In Anyhow?" *Audiovisual Instruction*, 1970, *6*(5), 21–24.

Thornton, J. W., Jr., and Brown, J. W. *New Media and College Teaching.* Washington, D.C.: National Education Association, 1968.

ALVIN KENT

2. LEARNING RESOURCES CENTERS

The learning resources center is a new and important tool of higher education. It enables students to see, hear, and experience learning activities in a variety of ways. It can provide access to information in a variety of media and to instruction organized in a variety of strategic patterns. Learners vary in the way they learn, the rate at which they learn, and the amount they learn. These variations can frequently be accommodated through the range of materials, information, equipment, and planning capabilities of the learning resources center and the people who staff it. The goal of the resources center structure in any institution of higher education should be the facilitation of learning.

Learning Resources Centers Activities

The range and diversity of college and university resources centers are considerable. Many centers, perhaps most, are managed by one person working with a faculty. A very few demand the attention of several hundred people. In all, the functions are remarkably similar.

In virtually all learning resources centers and at a wide variety of levels of sophistication, the activities divide into three basic functions: the information function, the production function, and the instructional design function. The information function is generally divided into two main categories, the collection of instructional materials and the provision of access to appropriate types of equipment. The production function provides for the manufacture of otherwise unavailable instructional materials. The instructional design function refines instructional programs, develops strategic approaches to instruction, and organizes instruction in a systematic way.

Information function. Information services should consist of an instructional materials center, a department of audiovisual services, and an independent learning facility. The instructional materials center should house the major resource collections of the institution. It will house, variously, books, a film library, a videotape library, a slide library, and various collections of audio and other types of materials. Discrimination will not be made among media. All appropriate materials should be made available to students and staff on request. This center will be serviced by librarians and media specialists specially trained in the handling of books and the new media. Materials should be made available on an open stack basis to ensure easy access by students. Appropriate equipment should be available to permit access to all microform materials and other types of nonprint materials. The major difference between the learning resources center and the conventional library is the comprehensive variety of media.

An independent learning facility is frequently located in the same area as the resources center. In contrast to the instructional materials center, which houses a cataloged and accessible collection of materials in a variety of media, independent learning facilities are designed to provide spaces for specific learning tasks using a variety of media. Independent learning facilities can function as an important part of the existing course structure of an institution. Where facts, perceptual motor skills, and, to a lesser extent, attitudes are to be learned, the independent learning facility can provide an ideal vehicle. Each student position should contain a slide projector and an audiocassette playback machine. Other carrels, as required, should contain super 8 mm motion picture projectors, filmstrip projectors, videocassette playback equipment, and appropriate microfilm projection equipment.

Typically, programs available in these carrels will have been produced by the production capabilities described below. (The instructional materials center, on the other hand, is designed primarily for access to commercially available materials.) Programs in the independent learning facility are usually geared to ongoing courses. Such programs can cover factual and motor skilled problems. When this type of program is available, faculty can be spared these teaching responsibilities, and students can enjoy the pleasure of dealing with problems at their own pace.

Production function. The second major function of the learning resources center is the production function. Higher education frequently demands specially prepared materials. Further, institutions that are remote from the source of materials frequently must rely totally on materials they themselves produce. Ordinarily, production functions are divided into television production, motion picture production, audio production, graphics, and still photography. Within these areas there is also a great deal of interaction. For example, graphic and still photography capabilities are frequently called on to support both motion picture and television production efforts.

Since the mid 1960s, the miniaturization

and simplification of television recording, playback, and monitoring equipment has brought television as an instructional tool within the range of virtually every institution of higher education. These efforts, largely Japanese, have had a potent effect on the way television is used in higher education. The videocassette has done for television what the audiocassette did for the world of recorded sound. The simplification and low cost of portable video equipment now makes it possible to record in the classroom or instructional setting, play back, erase, and rerecord—all within a short period of time in a single facility. For field observation, for clinical study, for image magnification, for documentation, and for the recording of perceptual motor skills, the low-cost half-inch or videocassette equipment is unsurpassed. This new and portable equipment has also reduced the necessity of relying on studio facilities for the production of instructional materials. The acceptability of comparatively low light levels permits the use of portable video recording equipment in a wide range of previously impossible settings. In 1976 it was further expected that the inexpensive video disc system would soon permit the widespread distribution of video programing at a cost even lower than that of videocassette technology.

At a minimum, television production facilities should include the capability of recording and playing back the videocassette format or the half-inch videotape format. Increasing levels of sophistication call for studio capabilities and color video potential. For larger institutions where television is an important part of the capabilities of the learning resources center, studio facilities should be provided. The advantages of studio production over field production are mainly in terms of control and lighting. A better-quality product can be obtained through the use of studio-quality equipment. Experimental processes can be carefully controlled and videotape recorded. Visiting faculty presentations can also be preserved on videotape. In addition, of course, materials can be prepared with extreme care in the studio for subsequent use by students in the instructional materials center or independent learning facility. Further, the television studio can serve the needs of the learning resources center staff for audio recording, motion picture photography, and, if necessary, for still photography.

Television then, is ideal when low-cost, quickly produced, video images are required. Videotape can be erased and reused many times.

The capability of producing motion pictures is enjoyed by a number of learning resources centers. Color motion picture film provides a high definition image, can be readily duplicated and disseminated widely, and enjoys, at least in the 16mm format, worldwide standardization. Although the production of motion pictures is an expensive process, motion picture photography is especially useful for difficult field photography away from commercial power sources and in extreme climatic conditions. Further, when large groups of people are to screen information at a single time, motion picture photography is particularly suitable. In the late 1940s and early 1950s, for example, the Audio Visual Center at Syracuse University produced instructional motion pictures in a number of Mediterranean countries. Completed films were then shown in village squares on basic topics, such as health, animal husbandry, and agriculture.

A less costly alternative to 16mm motion picture production is the now standardized super 8mm format. The cost of camera equipment is many times less, the cost of film less, and the cost of production less. The disadvantages of super 8mm production include reduced quality, difficulty in handling super 8mm film materials, and the limited numbers of laboratories capable of duplicating and processing super 8mm film. Further, black and white emulsions readily available in 16mm formats are most difficult to obtain in super 8mm. For remote institutions, the advantages of local

processing of black and white motion picture footage may be extremely important.
It should be noted that motion picture systems generally require less engineering
and technical support than do television
systems of comparable complexity. For this
reason, they may be more useful for institutions in remote areas.

One of the cheapest and most useful
pieces of instructional production technology is the audiocassette. Developed in
the Netherlands and half the size of a package of cigarettes, the audiocassette can
accept up to two hours of audio material.
Teamed up in the independent learning
facility with two-by-two-inch slides, the
combination makes a powerful instructional tool.

With the use of the audiocassette, the
possibility for foreign-language instruction
is obvious. A language facility should be
located in the audio department of the
learning resources center, where it can
be maintained more efficiently than in a
language department. Further, as part of
the learning resources center, the language
laboratory could open for longer hours
during the week and therefore be more
accessible to students.

The audio department should be responsible for all audio recording, editing,
and duplication. One of the most important
capacities of the audiocassette is the ease
with which it can be duplicated at high
speed. Low-cost, high-speed duplicators
can provide duplicate audiocassettes for
large numbers of students in a comparatively short period of time. The usefulness
of the audiocassette among illiterate populations is obvious.

A graphics and still photography service
is essential in any learning resources center
production facility. The use of television
is crippled without access to good graphics.
The motion picture production capabilities
of any institution are similarly handicapped
without a graphic capability. A still photography area is essential for the production of two-by-two-inch slides as well as for
black and white photography for exhibits,

displays, and faculty needs. Graphics and
still photography are frequently grouped
together because they are so closely related.

Perhaps the most important function of
the graphics department is the capability
of translating faculty needs into graphic
form for use in the classroom. Because
of the need for design work of this type,
the graphics department must employ
both designers and technicians. In most
graphics departments, both original art
and technical-mechanical drawing skills
are needed for the preparation of materials. Usually, two very different types
of graphics specialists meet these rather
different job requirements. It is of considerable importance, therefore, to match
the person to the job description.

The photography laboratory should
adjoin the graphics laboratory and should
be capable of processing and printing all
types of black and white materials as well
as processing color transparencies. Generally, it is unnecessary and too expensive
to equip a laboratory for the printing and
enlargement of color photographs. However, in areas inaccessible to color printing
laboratories, these capabilities may be
appropriate.

Instructional development function. The
third and final component of the learning
resources center is, in many ways, the most
important. The instructional development
function (or instructional design function,
as it is sometimes called) is, or should be,
the strategic heart of the learning resources
center. This is the department in which
planning and organization are applied to
the instructional process. The basic concept of instructional development is that of
a systematic approach to the instructional
process.

Fairly new in concept, the theory of
instructional development suggests the
application of the scientific method to the
art of teaching. Thaddeous Crabster, the
project architect for Lincoln Center in New
York, once told the author that "acoustics
is an art to which acousticians bring a scientific approach." Similarly, one might say

that teaching is an art to which the instructional developer brings a scientific approach. The relationship between the instructional developer and the faculty member is one of collaboration on a professional level. The faculty member represents subject matter expertise; the instructional developer represents expertise in the area of design and the application of technology. Typically, an instructional developer asks a faculty member to identify the objectives of a course of study. He might ask what a student must be able to do as a result of a learning experience. For the faculty member, this is frequently a difficult task, but one that is at the very heart of teaching effectiveness. Once identified, behavioral objectives can be used as a basis for planning. The instructional developer can help establish an instructional strategy with the faculty member—a task requiring tact and discretion. In most countries, it is assumed that college faculty are masters of the teaching process, which, of course, is not always the case. The teamwork between faculty member and instructional developer in determining instructional strategies, instructional systems, and instructional hierarchies can be a profitable endeavor. An important by-product of this process is the systematic analysis at each step in the instructional process of the behavioral objectives of the course. In many colleges and universities, this process is infrequently pursued, and in some situations not at all.

It is often desirable for the instructional development area of the learning resources center to maintain a measurement and evaluation capability. This capability permits and encourages a more accurate assessment of the activities of the center. Instructional innovations and experimental techniques can be more intelligently integrated into a college or university curriculum when they can be quantified and evaluated.

Use and Placement of the Center

The appropriate use of the disparate functions of the resources center can greatly

enrich the way students learn. The learning resources center, by permitting the student to interact with the tools of education, encourages him to be active rather than passive, to be a participator instead of just a spectator. The student can pace his own learning within a system that provides an infinitely patient environment where he can expose himself to repetition that would bore or tire a teacher. The use of programed instruction and educational systems is one of the many powerful tools in the learning resources center. The center's media collection should include a variety of materials in each subject to expose the student to a wide range of stimuli and ideas that encourage him to generalize his knowledge. Learning with understanding is more permanent and more transferable than rote learning.

At the college level, student differences are far more important than student similarities. One of the most useful characteristics of a learning resources center is the way in which the environment and associated materials complement each other to meet the needs of students working independently.

Uppermost in the minds of most higher education planners is the need to provide a series of environments in which students and faculty can interact in a productive relationship with the tools important to their teaching and learning tasks. From a practical point of view, some resources are unique and are best placed within the learning resources centers. Just as surely, others can be placed throughout a campus within academic departments or in student living areas.

Some production activities, such as television production, are fairly complex and should be undertaken in a central facility only. On the other hand, overhead transparency production of a simplified type, as well as two-by-two-inch slide duplication, can be very well undertaken in satellite locations on a given campus.

Further, many learning resource center facilities are heavily used by the community that the institution serves. In fact, the opening of learning resources center facilities to nonstudent populations near higher education institutions is frequently an important way in which college and community relationships can be furthered.

The learning resources center has been described as a central facility serving the needs of a single college or university. It is a center given over to the facilitation of learning, largely through the use of instructional resources and instructional technology. As such, it constitutes a dynamic core through which instruction can be facilitated and the process of learning enriched on any college or university campus.

Bibliography

Carnegie Commission on Higher Education. *The Fourth Revolution: Instructional Technology in Higher Education.* New York: McGraw-Hill, 1972.

Ford Foundation. *An Inquiry into the Uses of Institutional Technology.* New York: Ford Foundation, 1973.

Green, A. C. (Ed.) *Educational Facilities with New Media.* Washington, D.C. and Troy, New York: Association for Educational Communications and Technology, and Rensselaer Polytechnic Institute, 1969.

Lewis, P. "New Dimensions in Educational Technology for Multi-Media Centers." *Library Trends,* 1971, *19*(4), 399–534.

Merrill, I. R., and Drob, H. A. *Criteria for Planning the University Learning Resources Center.* San Francisco: Office of the Vice-President of Academic Affairs and Personnel, University of California, 1974.

Pearson, N. P., and Butler, L. *Instructional Materials Centers: Selected Readings.* Minneapolis: Burgess: 1969.

Thornton, J. W., and Brown, J. W. *New Media and College Teaching.* Washington, D.C.: Association for Educational Communications and Technology, 1968.

Ward, P. L., and Beacon, R. *The School Media Center: A Book of Readings.* Metuchan, New Jersey: Scarecrow Press, 1973.

DAVID M. CROSSMAN

See also: Independent Study; Instruction, Individualized.

3. RADIO AND TELEVISION AS INSTRUCTIONAL MEDIA

Broadcasting as a force in education serves a threefold purpose: the maintenance, extension, and transmission of a culture. The Royal Charter, which prescribes the terms under which the British Broadcasting Corporation (BBC) has operated since 1926, and the instruments of government of many other public service broadcasting organizations throughout the world call for a service of information, education, and entertainment. The educational obligation is commonly discharged through programs for the general public that have a cultural value and through programs designed specifically to serve the purposes of either the various institutions that constitute the national system of education or of the adult engaged in serious study at home.

A typical service, such as that of the BBC, provides a wide range of program series for adults designed to extend knowledge in science and the arts; to increase social awareness; to enable people to understand themselves better; and to communicate more effectively in their own and other languages. Programs are also designed to enable people to acquire practical skills and to bring social workers, teachers, doctors, engineers, and administrators up to date in their fields.

Characteristics and Origins of Educational Radio and Television

The Organizing Committee of the Third World Conference on Educational Radio and Television, held in Paris in 1967, identified five main characteristics that distinguish programs called "educational" in the full sense from those that are broadly "educative": (1) they must contribute to the systematic growth of knowledge; (2) they must form part of a continuous provision and be so planned that their effect is progressive; (3) they must be accompanied by supporting documents; (4) they must evoke an active response from the audience, whether they are received individually or collectively, under supervision or by home listeners and viewers; and (5) the impact of the programs must be monitored and checked (*Proceedings of the Third EBU International Conference,* 1967).

Educational broadcasting had its first major development, beginning in the 1920s, in the form of school radio, which was supplemented but not supplanted by television in the 1940s. In the United States school broadcasting services were run by school boards, universities, and community councils, each operating in a restricted area with comparatively modest resources. Elsewhere, services were built up by broadcasting organizations having autonomous powers. They were financed and equipped to work on a national scale, and established various types of relationships with educational authorities.

Most countries now have educational broadcasting services in both radio and television and at many levels. Those of the BBC and of the *Nippon hoso kyokai* (NHK), the corresponding Japanese organization, are the most extensive. In a realm of activity that profits from a fruitful international cross-fertilization, they are matched in range and professional skill by those of many smaller countries. In El Salvador, for example, a national instructional television (ITV) system for grades 7 to 9 was instituted as part of a general program of educational reform begun in 1968. The success of television teaching was suggested by a 1972 study that showed that ITV learning gains were significantly greater than the non-ITV gains in almost all cases (Mayo, Hornik, and McAnany, 1975, p. 123).

Developments in School and Adult Educational Broadcasting

School broadcasting originally offered services for curriculum enrichment. The urgency of the needs created by the postwar expansion of education led everywhere to a shift toward more direct teaching, a trend powerfully reinforced by television. A seminally important advance was made when television was first used to provide a complete substitute for normal schooling, with support from print and group activities. In Italy, where a legislative raising of the school age outran the national capacity to provide school buildings and qualified teachers, the national broadcasting organi-

zation, *Radiotelevisione italiana* (RAI), decided in 1958 to provide courses covering the whole curriculum of the junior secondary school. These programs were aimed at children assembled in private homes or in public centers staffed by teachers unqualified for secondary work (UNESCO, 1967, Vol. 3).

For many years NHK in Japan had been offering broadcast assistance to students who had left school early and were pursuing their secondary studies in established regional correspondence high schools. Finally, NHK set up its own school and provided its students with radio and television courses, with full supporting literature, tuition, and a modicum of face-to-face teaching (UNESCO, 1967, Vol. 1).

It was thus at the school level that ideas were developed for the use of radio and television for rigorous educational purposes, as resource material, as a basis for further teaching, and as part of a complete multimedia service. It was at that level also that research findings first established the validity of radio and television as modes of instruction and that appropriate methods of presentation and program forms were first explored in depth.

The progress of educational broadcasting for adults has followed a path much like that of school broadcasting. It began with lightly systematized series of radio programs designed to widen the horizons of self-selected groups of listeners. While still including such series, broadcasting for adults now offers both radio and television courses of a more demanding character and vital components of multimedia teaching systems up to university level. The techniques of integrated multimedia teaching pioneered by the Japanese correspondence high school, for example, are successfully being used for adults by the Munich *Telekolleg,* which prepares students to enter higher technical education, and by the Polish Television Agricultural High School. They are also used at full university level by a number of Australian and French universities, working in collaboration.

University-level multimedia teaching. An

immense stimulus in this field has been afforded by the success of the British Open University, and the Open University model is being adapted by institutions in the United States and elsewhere. For example, the regional University of Mid-America (UMA) in Lincoln, Nebraska, is planned both as a model for the regionalization of postsecondary education and as a model for the use of technology in making college courses available to people in their homes. At UMA new systems are being designed for the presentation and delivery of multimedia courses to students in Nebraska, Missouri, Kansas, and Iowa. Courses are to be designed by teams, comprising content specialists, instructional designers, professional writers, and media experts. A range of instructional materials will be used, from high-quality television segments to printed references and workbooks. In order to provide more than a passive learning experience, the delivery system is planned to include, in Nebraska, regional resource centers to be located within driving distance of all of the state's residents. These centers will be staffed by trained counselors and supplied with instructional resources. In addition, professors of the televised courses will visit the centers regularly to give learners an opportunity to ask questions or to seek additional advice (Wall, 1974, pp. 14–15).

There are several other examples in the United States of multimedia teaching at the college and university level. In one of the earliest such programs, Chicago City College's TV College, over 100,000 students took courses for credit between 1956 and 1974. The majority of students in the TV College used the television courses as only a part of a more conventional educational program. (By 1974 only slightly more than four hundred students had earned their Associate of Arts degree entirely by study on television, of whom approximately three hundred were inmates in correctional institutions.) However, the single-course completion rate is high, with an average of 70 to 75 percent of home viewers finishing their courses (Zigerell, 1974, pp. 34–36).

In Southern California a consortium of twenty-three community colleges was formed in 1970 to provide college-credit television courses. Each course is taught by a teacher from one of the colleges of the consortium. On every campus a regular instructor for each television course administers examinations (prepared by the television teacher) and maintains office hours during which television students may either telephone or come in with questions (Gross, 1973, p. 16).

KOCE-TV, in Orange County, California, was originally designed by the Coast Community College District as a black and white ITV facility at which community college students could prepare for telecommunications careers. However, the recognition of the large potential audience for televised teaching in the area led to a change in the plan. In 1972, consequently, KOCE-TV went on the air as an all-color "communiversity." In the spring of 1974, approximately 1400 people registered for television college courses, the most popular of which was a three-credit psychology course, "As Man Behaves." Filming for the course was done by the station's own cinematographers, all of whom are young filmmakers. Students registered for the courses at one of the county's two community colleges. At one campus, they were assigned a "facilitator" who would guide and supervise on a one-to-one basis; at the other, weekend seminars were held for television students. Over 80 percent of those enrolled participated in at least one seminar (Gerdts, 1975, pp. 23–24).

In public (educational) television, many courses for college credits have been broadcast by stations in various parts of the United States. Viewers watch the programs, then do additional work within structures at a nearby college or university. Stations involved in such work, among many others, include WTTW in Chicago and WGBH in Boston. During the 1960s, the Boston station produced a broadcast college-level course using faculty from such institutions as Tufts, Brandeis, Northeastern, Boston University, Massachusetts Institute of Technology, and Harvard.

Learning by radio and television. There is no longer any doubt that the broadcast as instruction is a fully effective means for the basic presentation of most subjects, although it requires further effort or reading by the individual home student. Broadcast instruction may be incomplete without the dialectic process of the face-to-face seminar or tutorial. Nevertheless, within its own limits of one-way communication, it can carry the main teaching burden as surely as can a live teacher. Theoretically, and without any regard for the special advantages of either medium, there is no reason why a radio lecture or a televised scientific demonstration should have more or less impact than a live presentation using the same resources.

The factors that contribute to the success of instructional programs are not identical with those that may be appropriate in mass-audience broadcasts. It has been shown experimentally that neither color nor professional polish in the photography of television programs makes any contribution to the learning process in adequately motivated groups, unless these features are integral and necessary to the presentation of the subject. The more intent an audience is on learning, the less tolerant it is of digression and poor material (Gage, 1965; Reid and McLennan, 1967).

The first concern of students committed to the task of learning in any medium is making satisfactory progress. For such students, the most important characteristics of radio and television programs are the correct level of discourse for the audience, clarity, cogency, firmness of structure, a just judgment of pace, and relevant illustration.

Comparisons of Radio and Television as Instructional Media

Radio and television as instructional media have some factors in common. Both are addressed to a remote audience unknown personally by the producers. That audience must therefore be carefully defined, and its needs and capacities assessed through study of an adequate sample before the programs are produced and through subsequent feedback. Both forms are ephemeral and need the support of printed material to advise the audience of the character and function of the program and to apprise them of any necessary vocabulary or apparatus of concepts beforehand. Printed material is also needed to provide a record to be studied and a basis for the students' written responses to the presentation.

Because radio and television are one-way communications, they cannot be packed too tightly with new material. Radio and television are capable, however, of holding and presenting an assemblage of heterogeneous material. A television program, for example, may profitably include the laboratory demonstration of a scientific principle, a filmed illustration of its industrial applications, and a discussion of its social significance.

Little research has been done on the comparative efficacy of the two media in specific educational contexts, so common sense and empirical experiences must be the main guides. The choice of medium will often depend mainly on availability and cost. Television may cost up to eight times as much as radio per unit hour. In addition, television air time is limited and in many countries controlled by authorities not primarily concerned with education. Finally, in many areas of the world the ownership of television receivers is far from widely diffused.

Advantages of educational broadcasting. The primary importance of both media lies in the power of broadcasting to distribute the best teaching to the largest possible audience. Because of its centralized production, broadcasting can afford to spend large sums on teaching programs. It can use the best authorities, the best expositors, and the widest range of illustrative material, and it can serve as a rapid means for the diffusion of new knowledge and ideas. The audiodisc and audiocassette are now within financial reach of many teaching systems, but in spite of rapid technological advances the cost of distributing film or videotape is very high. Thus, broadcasting will probably remain for many years the cheapest way of disseminating audiovisual material.

Developments in recording techniques have removed many of the disabilities of "off-air" reception. Local recording in either medium escapes the restrictions of transmission times and allows the broadcasts to be used more than once. If the costs of the blank tape and storage can be met, broadcasting can become the source of semipermanent teaching material. These advantages are of particular importance to multimedia open learning systems, not least in countries where the ownership of receivers is not widely diffused and where group reception provides an opportunity for discussion and tutorial reinforcement of the educational message.

In countries where both media are widely accessible, television obviously has greater appeal to the mass audience than radio and greater opportunities as an informally educative agency. For an adequately motivated student audience, radio has an equivalent strength in the teaching of languages, music, literature, philosophy, and any other subject where such illustration as is required can be supplied in printed form or in the form of "radiovision," a specially prepared filmstrip synchronized with a radio program in live or recorded form for use by the individual student.

Educational radio in developing countries. Radio is still by far the more important of the media in developing countries. In most of these countries, television receivers are still a luxury, and the future of television as an instrument of social development lies in its planned use with communal groups, as in India. In that context, satellite distribution may well play an important part.

Radio continues to be valuable in literacy campaigns and social education. Radio "farm forums" have proven to be important instruments not only in instruction in agriculture techniques but in village democracy as well. In Algeria and Japan communal listening by women's groups has played a part in bringing them into the mainstream of national life. At another level, radio has become an important component of schemes for upgrading the qualifications of teachers serving in Kenya and in the UNESCO/UNWRAA scheme for teacher training in Palestinian refugee camps *(Audio-Visual Aids,* 1965).

A very interesting experiment in rural educational radio began in Senegal in 1968. *Dissóó* (meaning both dialog and concerted study) was designed to allow farmers from the highly populated area of the groundnut-growing basin to air their opinions and their grievances with government agricultural policy by means of recorded interviews with radio teams. The response was overwhelming, leading to the formation of new policies and, with UNESCO aid, to the expansion and reorganization of *Dissóó* to assure its continuity.

Although the programs were originally aimed only at the villagers of the groundnut basin, programs with greater diversity in theme were gradually offered to a much wider public. In 1974 residents of ten thousand of the thirteen thousand villages in Senegal listened to *Dissóó*, and in many villages listener groups were organized to facilitate discussion. The promoters of rural educational radio note, however, that approximately three fourths of the time on the air in three weekly programs was still devoted to direct presentation of villagers' views by tapes made in the villages and by the reading of letters sent to the studios.

The programs presented by *Dissóó* not only helped farmers to improve their farming techniques but also allowed them a wider perspective. As one peasant farmer commented, the programs made him aware that Senegal "is all one village" (Clerc, 1974).

The uses of television. The "live" teaching of many subjects calls for an extension of the student's visual experience and awareness. Television, aided by its powers of magnification, can offer a close view of a scientific demonstration to any number of students. It can facilitate the teaching of science and mathematics with animated diagrams, and it can bring the social sciences alive by filmed interviews and case studies of men and women in action in distant places. It can also bring to students a vivid knowledge of classroom situations.

In using television for instruction, however, the efficacy of sequences of pictures alone as vehicles for carrying ideas has to be considered. Because thinking is crammed with verbal elements, the more closely the response of the audience to a television program is controlled by its words, the more complete the process of communication is likely to be.

Closed-circuit television. Since the early 1950s, the powers of television have been exploited by university closed-circuit systems. Medical schools and science departments can use television not only as a way of showing a large group of students the details of an operation but also relay the demonstration to "overspill" gatherings, record it for future use, and offer it to other universities (MacLean, 1968, p. 10).

Universities with several campuses can also benefit from closed-circuit television, as is seen by its use by the City University of New York (CUNY). CUNY is a public institution comprising ten senior colleges, eight community colleges, a graduate center, an affiliated medical school, and two urban centers. Development of a closed-circuit two-way television system (CUMBIN: City University Mutual Benefit Instructional Network) was seen as a means of permitting the university to offer specialized courses, especially in advanced technology, to students at several locations without having to duplicate instructional costs. Consequently, a pilot system was established at four campuses in 1968. Each campus was equipped with a studio classroom and two receiving classrooms. Students in the receiving classrooms could communicate directly with the television instructor by means of telephone handsets. Despite some technical problems, CUMBIN expanded between 1968 and 1971 from three graduate courses (in physics and chemistry) to over thirty hours of weekly programing, extending to such subjects as Judaic studies and oceanography (Freund and Mailman, 1971).

It is, nonetheless, in distance teaching schemes designed to extend the range of higher education to wider groups that both radio and television have found their greatest opportunity for formal instruction. Finally, the experience of most educational broadcasting suggests that radio and television work best in the field of formal education, not merely when they are used with print, tutorial, and face-to-face teaching, but when a systems approach leads to a full integration of all the media, and when the producers of the radio and television components of the course are involved in the planning from the inception. This integration can best be achieved, as in the Open University, by placing the detailed planning of each course in the hands of a course team composed of representatives of all those who contribute to the finished product. This team is then given responsibility for both the academic content and the teaching methods (including the broadcast presentation) so that both are worked out concurrently and cooperatively.

Bibliography

Audio-Visual Aids in Higher Scientific Education. London: H. M. Stationery Office, 1965.

British Broadcasting Corporation. *The Further Education Annual Programme.* London: BBC, annual.

Clerc, J. P. "Rural Educational Broadcasting in Senegal." *Prospects,* 1974, *4*(4), 574–578.

Council of Europe. *European Research on Audio-Visual Aids.* Strasbourg, France: Council of Europe, 1967.

DeKorte, D. A. *Television in Education and Training.* Eindhoven, Netherlands: Philips, 1967.

De Vera, J. M. *Educational Television in Japan.* Rutland, Vermont: Tuttle, 1967.

Diamond, R. M. (Ed.) *A Guide to Instructional Television.* New York: McGraw-Hill, 1964.

Freund, S., and Mailman, J. C. "CUMBIN: City University Mutual Benefit Instructional Network." *Educational Television,* 1971, *3*(7), 20–22.

Gage, N. L. *Handbook of Research on Teaching.* Chicago: Rand McNally, 1965.

Gerdts, D. D. "KOCE-TV: A Communiversity." *Educational Broadcasting,* 1975, *8*(1), 23–26.

Gross, L. S. "The Southern California Consortium for Community College Television." *Educational and Industrial Television,* January 1973, pp. 16–20.

Hancock, A. *Planning for ETV: A Handbook of Educational Television.* Essex, England: Longman, 1971.

Lewis, P. *Educational Television Guidebook.* New York: McGraw-Hill, 1961.

MacKenzie, N., Postgate, R., and Scupham, J. *Open Learning.* Paris: UNESCO/Ford Foundation, 1975.

MacLean, R. *Television in Education.* London: Methuen, 1968.

Mayo, J. K., Hornik, R. C., and McAnany, E. G. "Instructional Television in El Salvador's Educational Reform." *Prospects,* 1975, *5*(1), 120–126.

Multi-Media Systems in Adult Education: Twelve Project Descriptions in Nine Countries. ERIC Report ED 067 817. Bethesda, Maryland: Educational Resources Information Center, 1971.

Proceedings of the Third European Broadcasting Union International Conference on Educational Radio and Television. Paris: Office de radiodiffusion télévision française, 1967.

Reid, J. C., and McLennan, D. W. *Research on Instructional Television and Film.* Washington, D.C.: U.S. Government Printing Office, 1967.

Schramm, W. *Mass Media and National Development.* Paris: UNESCO, 1964.

Schramm, W. *The New Media: Memo to Educational Planners.* Paris: UNESCO, 1967.

Scupham, J. *Broadcasting and the Community.* London: Watts, 1967.

Trenaman, J. I. *Communication and Comprehension.* Essex, England: Longman, 1967.

UNESCO, *New Educational Media in Action: Case Studies for Planners.* Vol. 1; *Japan's Broadcast-Correspondence High School;* Vol. 2: *Chicago's Television College;* Vol. 3: *The Centro di Telescuola of Italy.* Paris: UNESCO, 1967.

Wall, M. "Technology takes college to the students." *College Management,* 1974, *9*(8), 14–15.

Zigerell, J. L. "The Trouble with Open Learn-ing and What to Do About It." *Public Telecommunications Review,* 1974, *2*(4), 33–37.

JOHN SCUPHAM

See also: Open University.

EDUCATIONAL RESOURCES INFORMATION CENTER, United States

The Educational Resources Information Center (ERIC) was originated in 1966 by the United States Office of Education as a system for providing ready access to educational literature. At the time ERIC was first discussed, the literature of education was largely uncontrolled; research reports submitted to the Office of Education received an initial scattered distribution and then disappeared, and reports from other sources generally were equally inaccessible. ERIC was intended to correct this chaotic condition and to provide a foundation for activities concerning information analysis and the dissemination of information on current developments.

Because of the decentralized nature of American education, education's many specializations, and the existence of numerous professional organizations, ERIC's designers opted for a network of "clearinghouses" located across the country in "host" organizations that were already strong in the field of education in which they would operate. Originally contracts with clearinghouses gave them responsibility for acquiring and selecting all documents in their area and for processing these documents— cataloging, indexing, and abstracting. Well-qualified clearinghouse staff with expertise in specialized subjects manage ERIC document selection functions. Decentralization worked out well for information analysis and user service activities. However, in order to generate products that would include the output of all network components, some form of centralization was needed. ERIC's final design, therefore, included decentralized clearinghouse operations integrated around a central computerized facility, which serves as a switching center for the network. The data recorded by each of the clearinghouses are sent to the facility to form a central data base from which publications and indexes are produced. Similar arrangements are used to supply the public with copies of reports added to the system. ERIC decided to make documents available from a central source rather than merely to inform users of their existence. It was therefore necessary to provide a document reproduction service whereby any noncopyrighted document announced could be obtained. In other words, ERIC was developed as a complete document announcement and retrieval service.

Users pay for reports that they request, and persons wanting ERIC magnetic tapes are required to meet order-processing, tape, and duplication costs. The federal government limits its investments in both areas by generating a fundamental data base and then permitting the private sector to market it at prices as advantageous to the public as possible. In support of this strategy and because central facility operations depend on use of advanced technologies (computerized photocomposition and microreprographic technology), these functions were located in the commercial sector.

ERIC therefore emerged as a network with four levels. The first or government level is represented by the National Institute of Education and ERIC (the funder, policy setter, and monitor). The second or nonprofit level is made up of sixteen clearinghouses located at universities or professional societies. The third or commercial level consists of the centralized facilities for managing the data base, putting out published products, making microfiche, and reproducing documents. Fourth, and last, are the users who receive the benefit of these activities.

The ERIC clearinghouses have responsibility within the network for acquiring the significant educational literature within their particular areas, selecting the highest-quality and most relevant material, processing the selected items for input to the data base, and providing information analysis products and various user services based on the data base. The exact number of clearinghouses has fluctuated over time in response to the shifting needs of the educational community. There are currently sixteen clearinghouses. These are listed below, with brief notes describing those that are the most closely associated with higher education:

ERIC Clearinghouse in Career Education
Northern Illinois University,
    College of Education
DeKalb, Illinois 60115

ERIC Clearinghouse on Counseling and
    Personnel Services
University of Michigan
School of Education Building, Room 2108
Ann Arbor, Michigan 48104

ERIC Clearinghouse on Urban Education
Columbia University, Teachers College
Information Retrieval Center on
    the Disadvantaged
Box 40, 525 West 120th Street
New York, New York 10027

ERIC Clearinghouse on Early
    Childhood Education
University of Illinois, College of Education
Urbana, Illinois 61801

ERIC Clearinghouse on
    Educational Management
University of Oregon
Eugene, Oregon 97403

ERIC Clearinghouse on Handicapped
    and Gifted Children
Council for Exceptional Children
1920 Association Drive
Reston, Virginia 22091

ERIC Clearinghouse on Higher Education
George Washington University
One Dupont Circle, Suite 630
Washington, D.C. 20036

Various subjects relating to college and university students, college and university conditions and problems, college and university programs. Curricular and instructional problems and programs, faculty, institutional research, federal programs, professional education (medical, law, etc.), graduate education, university extension programs, teaching-learning, planning, governance, finance, evaluation, interinstitutional arrangements, and management of higher educational institutions. Publications include *ERIC/Higher Education Research Currents*, eight issues per year; and *ERIC/Higher Education Reports*, ten issues per year.

ERIC Clearinghouse on Information Resources
Stanford University, School of Education
Center for Research and Development
   in Teaching
Stanford, California 94305

ERIC Clearinghouse for Junior Colleges
University of California
Powell Library, Room 96
Los Angeles, California 90024
   Development, administration, and evaluation of public and private community junior colleges; junior college students, staff, curricula, programs, libraries, and community services.

ERIC Clearinghouse on Languages
   and Linguistics
Modern Language Association of America
62 Fifth Avenue
New York, New York 10011

ERIC Clearinghouse for Reading and
   Communication Skills
National Council of Teachers of English
111 Kenyon Road
Urbana, Illinois 61801

ERIC Clearinghouse on Rural Education
   and Small Schools
New Mexico State University
Las Cruces, New Mexico 88003

ERIC Clearinghouse on Science, Mathematics,
   and Environmental Education
Ohio State University
1800 Cannon Drive, 400 Lincoln Tower
Columbus, Ohio 43210

ERIC Clearinghouse for Social Studies/Social
   Science Education
855 Broadway
Boulder, Colorado 80302

ERIC Clearinghouse on Teacher Education
American Association of Colleges for
   Teacher Education
One Dupont Circle, Suite 616
Washington, D.C. 20036
   School personnel at all levels; all issues from selection through preservice and in-service preparation and training to retirement; curricula; educational theory and philosophy; general education not specifically covered by Educational Management Clearinghouse; Title XI NDEA institutes not covered by subject spe-

cialty in other ERIC clearinghouses; all aspects of physical education.

ERIC Clearinghouse on Tests, Measurement,
   and Evaluation
Educational Testing Service
Princeton, New Jersey 08540

   ERIC publications include *Current Index to Journals in Education* (monthly journal announcements) and *Resources in Education* (monthly report announcements). Lists are available upon request from each individual ERIC clearinghouse.
National Institute of Education
Washington, D.C. 20208 USA

EDUCATIONAL STANDARDS IN JAPAN (Higher Education Report)

Educational Standards in Japan, a 1970 "White Paper on Education" (Tokyo: Ministry of Education, 1971), is a descriptive study of educational standards in Japan as compared with other selected countries; namely, France, the Federal Republic of Germany, the Soviet Union, the United Kingdom, and the United States. It reviews educational structures and presents comparative data on preschool education, compulsory education, upper secondary education, higher education, and opportunities for education and training outside of formal schools. The focus on both quantitative and qualitative aspects of education clarifies present standards and indicates future needs in Japanese education.

   The study considers educational content and teaching methods, staff and facilities, and allocation and sources of educational expenditures. Education in Japan, the study finds, is expanding rapidly. However, improvement is needed in areas such as individualizing educational experiences, equalizing educational conditions among geographical regions and between public and private schools, and reversing the decreasing level of educational expenditure as a percentage of national income.

   The paper concludes with an overview of educational reforms in developed countries and educational plans in developing countries. Citing the inadequacy of educational expansion in relation to social development and social change, it describes the qualitative measures for reform advanced by the Central Council for Education in Japan. Those dealing with higher education include diversification in qualifications and in curricula and selection procedures, and flexibility in patterns of school attendance and certification. The paper supports planning and research within a framework concerned with educational priorities and focused on the establishment of opportunities for lifelong education. International cooperation is advocated, as is educational assistance to developing countries.

EDUCATIONAL TECHNOLOGY
See Instructional Technology.

EDUCATIONAL TESTING SERVICE, United States

The Educational Testing Service (ETS)— a nonprofit organization founded by the American Council on Education, Carnegie Foundation for the Advancement of Teaching, and College Entrance Examination Board—was chartered in December 1947 under the education law of the state of New York. Its main offices are on a 400-acre site on the outskirts of Princeton, New Jersey. Other offices are located in Atlanta, Georgia; Austin, Texas; Berkeley and Los Angeles, California; Washington, D.C.; Evanston, Illinois; and San Juan, Puerto Rico. ETS employs about two thousand permanent staff members, of whom more than five hundred are on the professional staff. The primary aim of all its activities is to serve education through measurement, research, and related services.

ETS initiates, conducts, or improves practical programs of measurement and related services, conducts research on measurement theory and practice and on teaching and learning, creates or improves appropriate measures for use in assessment and evaluation, provides information and professional counsel to educators, and develops and conducts instructional programs for educators and others concerned with educational and social issues. Much of this work has been done in the area of higher education. For example, ETS conducts more than one hundred testing programs at various educational levels. Most of these programs are at the college and university level, conducted for outside sponsors such as the College Board, Graduate Record Examinations Board, Law School Admission Council, and Graduate Business Admission Council. To make these tests available abroad for students who wish to enter institutions in the United States, 115 centers are set up in many countries.

Of particular interest to students whose native language is not English is the Test of English as a Foreign Language, a testing program jointly sponsored by ETS, College Board, and Graduate Record Examinations Board. Colleges use this test to evaluate, for admissions or placement purposes, the English proficiency of foreign students.

A program somewhat different in purpose has taken a number of ETS staff members to more than fifty countries throughout the world. This is a program for ACTION-Peace Corps in which ETS trains persons in their own countries to conduct language proficiency interviews.

Research is conducted for each testing program to ensure that the measures are appropriate and valid and to provide information to students and to schools and colleges. In addition, ETS carries out an extensive program of research in higher education, in areas such as institutional research, student characteristics, teacher behavior, academic practices, and nontraditional study (with an assembly of about 150 colleges conducting research on matters related to experiential learning). While most of this research is focused on the United States scene for postsecondary ed ucation, many of the findings have implications for institutions abroad.

At the request of a number of countries, ETS has assisted in developing or adapting and translating tests—including *Examen para estudios post-graduados* (Examination for Postgraduate Studies), *Prueba de Admisión para estudios graduados* (Test of Admission for Graduate Studies), *Teste de aptidão acadêmica para posgraduação* (Academic Aptitude Test for Postgraduate Studies), and *Pedagogía y conocimientos generales* (Teaching and General Knowledge). The Admission Test for Graduate Study in Business has been translated into French, and the Preliminary Scholastic Aptitude Test into German.

Members of the ETS staff frequently serve abroad for the United States government, or private foundations, as consultants to colleges and universities, measurement centers, and ministries of education on a wide range of subjects. The length of time for such consultations may range from several days to several years. Many of these consultations take the form of workshops where instruction is given to teachers in some aspect of testing. Others are consultations with university administrators on their measurement needs and practices. From 1964 to 1974, more than sixty-five members of the staff engaged in such missions on more than one hundred visits. Other consulting is done when educators from foreign countries visit ETS to discuss their particular problems.

Since 1957 ETS has sponsored a five-week summer training program in test development for foreign scholars. More than three hundred educators from more than fifty countries have attended these sessions. In addition to the group programs, a number of foreign educators have come to ETS for training sessions extending over one week or more.

A major international activity of ETS has been a move to organize measurement centers throughout the world into an association that will be called the International Association for Educational Assessment. Representatives of member agencies, many of them university based, have met in Arnhem, the Netherlands, and, in the spring of 1975, in Geneva, Switzerland.

ETS publishes *Findings,* quarterly; *ETS Developments,* quarterly; and *ETS Annual Report.*

Princeton, New Jersey, 08540 USA

EGYPT, ARAB REPUBLIC OF

Population: 37,000,000 (1974 estimate). Student enrollment in primary school: 3,900,000; secondary school (academic, vocational, technical): 1,500,000; higher education: 241,690 (university: 199,074; nonuniversity: 42,616). Student enrollment in higher education as percentage of age group (18–22): 7.7%. Language of instruction: Arabic and English. Academic calendar: September to June (two semesters). Percentage of gross national product (GNP) expended on education: 5%. [Except where otherwise indicated, figures are for 1972.]

Since the revolution of 1952, the government of Egypt has been working to implement a system of education that will meet national manpower needs, a system capable of producing leaders as well as the required labor force in the various fields of production and services.

Egypt was an established leader in the field of education as early as A.D. 970, the founding date of al-Azhar University, one of the most renowned institutions of higher learning in the Arab world for the study of Islamic religion, law, and philosophy. Al-Azhar was at the head of a traditional educational system which developed soon after the spread of Islam throughout Egypt in the seventh century A.D. The traditional school system consisted of the *kuttab*, which provided basic religious training, and the mosque, which offered a more advanced religious education.

The first secular schools were established in Egypt after the invasion of the French in 1798. The Egyptian ruler Mehemet Ali (1805–1848) was responsible for starting numerous schools based on the French model. During his rule Western influences further increased with the opening of many foreign schools by Catholic and Protestant missionaries. Also at this time, many Egyptian students were being sent to Europe by the government for advanced study.

In 1882 the British occupation of Egypt began. During the period of British rule (1882–1922), a dual system of education developed, consisting of traditional *kuttabs* for the masses and modern secular schools for the elite; "neither . . . provided the kind of training that was functional in terms of development" (Szyliowicz, 1973, p. 132). The British used the modern schools primarily to train manpower for low and middle positions in the government and discouraged others from furthering their education. Those fortunate enough to complete the highly demanding school program normally sought the prestigious government positions. The populace had little access to education, and the British remained indifferent to Egyptian demands for additional educational facilities.

Students seeking a secular higher education at this time were forced to study abroad. The government provided a small number of scholarships for this purpose; however, the majority of students received financial support from their families. By the early 1900s Egyptian intellectuals were demanding that the British establish an Egyptian university; however, funds were denied. Due entirely to the efforts and financial contributions of private Egyptian citizens, the nucleus of the Egyptian University was finally formed in 1908.

In 1922 the British protectorate ended, although British influence, especially in education, continued for some time. The Egyptian government inherited severe problems from the British in the area of education and for the next few decades experimented with various reforms in an effort to alleviate some of the problems. The government attempted to modify the traditional *kuttab* schools, which continued to use virtually the same curricula and teaching methods as had been used in the seventh century; at the same time, the gov-

ernment initiated changes in the schools established under the British. Both of these attempts were largely unsuccessful. The government achieved its greatest success in expanding the school system, and numerous new schools were opened.

The Egyptian University was formally established in 1925, incorporating the several existing institutions, including those founded in 1908. In 1940 its name was changed to Fuad I University and finally to the University of Cairo in 1953. In 1942 a second university, the University of Alexandria, was established, followed by the University of Ain Shams in 1950.

The revolution of 1952 marked a turning point in the history of Egypt and in the area of education. President Gamal Abdel Nasser, dedicated to the goal of modernization, implemented a series of reforms designed to bring education to the forefront of the national development effort. Under Nasser attempts were made for the first time to relate educational policy to developmental requirements. School facilities at all levels increased substantially, with the goal of providing every child with a primary education by 1975. The curricula in all the schools were Arabicized, and emphasis was placed on the fields of science and technology.

One of the most significant reforms implemented during Nasser's presidency was the transformation of al-Azhar in 1961 from a medieval to a modern institution. Under Nasser Egypt's fourth university, the University of Assiut, was officially opened in 1957. Because of expanded enrollments at the primary and secondary levels, university enrollment increased proportionately. The government took measures to ensure easier access to the universities in 1962 by making all public education free and by providing additional fellowships and grants for students in financial need. Nonuniversity higher education also expanded as a number of higher institutes were established after 1957.

Expansion at the higher education level continued in the 1970s. By 1975 five new universities had been established, including a technical university.

Legal Basis of Educational System

Among the major legal decisions affecting higher education are Presidential Decree 103 (1961), which deals with the reorganization of al-Azhar; Decree 1665 (1961), which established the Ministry of Higher Education; and Decree 49 (1972), concerning the organization of the universities. Another significant legal decision, Decree 70 (1975), established Helwan University; this decree also turned all higher institutes into colleges and affiliated them to the closest university.

Types of Institutions

In addition to al-Azhar, university education is available at the nine state universities and at the American University of Cairo, a private institution.

Egypt's first state university, the University of Cairo, is the largest higher education institution in the country, with an enrollment of more than 60,000 students in 1972. The university consists of twelve faculties, including art, law, economics and political science, commerce, medicine, science, pharmacy, veterinary medicine, engineering, dentistry, agriculture, and Arabic and Islamic studies. Six institutes—for cancer research, statistical studies, archeology, African studies, mass communication, and nursing—are also attached to the university. A branch of the University of Cairo has been operating in Khartoum, Sudan, since 1955.

The University of Alexandria, which was established in 1942 by incorporating three former faculties of the University of Cairo, now consists of nine faculties: agriculture, arts, commerce, dentistry, engineering, law, medicine, pharmacy, and sciences. The university also has institutes of public health and nursing and operates a branch campus in Beirut, Lebanon. Ain Shams University has faculties of engineering, commerce, medicine, law, education, agriculture, arts, and veterinary medicine; it also operates a

college for women, which offers courses in the arts and sciences. The University of Assiut has faculties of science, pharmacy, veterinary medicine, engineering, agriculture, medicine, commerce, arts, and two faculties of education.

Mansoura University (1972)—with faculties of law, commerce, science, medicine, and pharmacy—was established from former faculties of the University of Cairo. The University of Tanta (1972) was established from former faculties of the University of Alexandria; originally consisting of faculties of education, science, and medicine, it now has, in addition, faculties of commerce, pharmacy, dentistry, and agriculture. The University of Zagazig (1974) was established from former faculties of the University of Ain Shams; it offers programs in five faculties: commerce, science, agriculture, veterinary medicine, and education.

In 1975 two additional universities, founded at Menia and Helwan, evolved from existing higher education institutions. The former University of Assiut faculty of education at Menia was the basis for the new university of Menia. All of the higher technical institutes in the Cairo-Helwan area were to be incorporated as faculties of the new university at Helwan. Both universities were in embryonic stages of development in 1975, and plans call for their gradual expansion to include other areas of study as required.

Al-Azhar University, one of the oldest universities in the world, is best known for its faculty of Islamic law and jurisprudence and its faculty of theology, which attract thousands of students from throughout the Islamic world. However, since its reorganization in 1961, which brought it into the state university system, the university has provided a wider range of programs in medicine, engineering, science, agriculture, education, and commerce. The university also operates a college for women, which has sections for medicine, science, commerce, and arts, and an institute of language and translation.

The American University in Cairo, founded in 1919, provides a liberal arts education for approximately 6000 students. Courses are offered in several departments, including Arabic studies, economics and political science, and materials engineering and physical sciences.

Aside from the universities, higher education is available in a number of higher institutes, which provide four- or five-year programs leading to the same degrees offered at the universities. Among them are the higher institutes for commerce, agriculture, fine arts, teachers, industrial training, artistic education, musical education, applied arts, physical training, home economics, social work, languages, and tourism and hotels. The al-Tabbin Metallurgical Institute for Higher Studies, established through a cooperative agreement with the Soviet Union, provides courses on the graduate level only. The institute was initially established to provide trained manpower for an iron and steel complex being constructed in Egypt (*Higher Education in Egypt—1974*, 1975). According to Presidential Decree 70 (1975), these higher institutes were to be affiliated to universities.

Training for industrial technicians is provided in two-year industrial institutes affiliated with the Ministry of Higher Education. Included in this category are the institutes for automobile technicians, land reclamation technicians, chemical technicians, and telephone technicians. Two-year training programs in areas such as taxation, accounting, and management-secretarial work are offered at the secondary commercial institutes, which are also affiliated with the Ministry of Higher Education.

The Ministry of Health runs several institutes for health technicians; they offer two-year programs for X-ray technicians, laboratory technicians, and medical assistants. A small number of private one-year institutes provide programs in areas such as secretarial studies.

In addition to the education faculties at the universities and the higher institutes, which prepare teachers for areas such as physical education or home economics, teacher training is provided in a number of colleges on the upper secondary level. These colleges offer a five-year program, for graduates of the preparatory level, to train teachers for the country's primary schools. Graduates of the general secondary school may complete the teacher training program in three years.

An adult education and literacy campaign was started in 1964 and is continuing under the direction and support of the Ministry of Education, with the cooperation of UNESCO. Literacy training is provided in a system of special schools operated by the ministry. Both day and evening classes are offered. Rural cultural centers, which are located in larger villages, conduct classes in reading and writing. Special literacy programs are also provided by the Arab Socialist Union (ASU), by trade unions, and by sports clubs. In 1965 a law was passed which made it mandatory for all businesses having more than fifty illiterate employees to provide them with literacy training (Smith and others, 1970).

Relationship with Secondary Education

The general system of education in Egypt consists of six years of compulsory primary school followed by a three-year preparatory level and a three-year secondary level. At the end of the primary and preparatory levels, students must pass a final examination in order to proceed to the next level. The preparatory and secondary programs are divided into vocational and academic streams. The vocational programs generally lead to employment, and the academic programs prepare students for higher education. The academic secondary certificate is awarded after successful completion of the academic secondary program and a national examination.

Parallel to the general system of education are the religious primary and secondary schools, which operate under the auspices of the Ministry of Waqfs (Islamic Affairs). Students enrolled in these schools generally seek admission to al-Azhar upon completion of their studies. Since 1961 the curriculum of these schools has expanded to include academic and vocational subjects as well as religious subjects.

Admission Requirements

Admission to a faculty at the universities is, for the most part, determined by the national examination for the general secondary certificate. Those students who score highest on the examination have priority to enter the faculties of medicine, engineering, science, pharmacy, dentistry, veterinary medicine, and economics (*Higher Education in Egypt—1974,* 1974).

The number of students to be admitted to each faculty is determined by the Supreme Council of Universities at the end of each academic year. The council also establishes the regulations for admission. In most cases, students are placed in a particular faculty through the placement office of the Ministry of Higher Education. Al-Azhar University sets the admission requirements for its faculties of Islamic law and jurisprudence, Muslim theology, and Arabic language, and also for the higher institute for Islamic and Arabic studies.

In 1974 more than 110,000 students passed the national examination for the secondary certificate; half were accepted into the universities, and the other half entered the higher institutes. Special provision is made in the admission process for students whose parents have served on the university faculty for a number of years, for outstanding athletes, and for brothers or sons of war victims.

Secondary school graduates who are unable to gain admission to the university are allowed to study as "external" students in the faculties which have no attendance requirements: arts, commerce, and law. Under this system, which was initiated in 1953, students are not allowed to attend classes but may study at home, take the same examinations as regularly enrolled students, and earn the same degrees. If a student receives a final grade of "good" on any one year's examinations, his status

is changed to that of a regularly enrolled student (*Higher Education in Egypt—1974,* 1975).

Administration and Control

Most higher education institutions in Egypt operate under the supervision of the Ministry of Higher Education. The exceptions are the institutes for health technicians, which are affiliated with the Ministry of Health, and several faculties at al-Azhar University, which operate under the sole authority of the university's own governing board.

According to Presidential Decree 1665 (1961), the Ministry of Higher Education is responsible for establishing policies for all levels and types of higher education in light of national development goals, and for the development and implementation of plans and programs required for the application of such policies. The ministry is also charged with expanding higher education and taking the necessary steps to avoid duplication of facilities; providing equal higher education facilities throughout the state; and establishing standards for faculty and teaching staff. The ministry also studies the manpower needs of other ministries and business concerns to ensure an adequate supply of graduates, and it oversees cultural and educational projects carried out in cooperation with other countries. The government's program for educational scholarships is also a responsibility of the ministry.

The planning and coordination of university education is the responsibility of the Supreme Council of Universities. Among other duties, the council defines general education and research policies in the universities in relation to national goals for social, economic, cultural, and scientific development. The council is also charged with the coordination of studies, degrees, faculties, departments, and teaching staff among the universities; and it advises the government on the distribution of funds among the universities. In addition, the council responds to any matters presented to it by the Ministry of Higher Education or any of the universities, and also evaluates foreign degrees, reviews the academic record of candidates for appointments as assistant professors and professors through specialized committees, and determines university admission policies. The Supreme Council of Universities is supervised by the minister of higher education. Members of the council include the presidents and deputy presidents of each university; a dean from each university, selected by the university councils; and five authorities in the areas of university education or public affairs.

According to the law on the university organization (Presidential Decree 49 of 1972), each university has a council, a president, deputy presidents, and a secretary general. The chief executive officer, the president, is appointed by a presidential decree on the recommendation of the minister of higher education from among those who have held chairs at one of the universities. The university president—who is assisted by two deputy presidents appointed in the same manner—is responsible for implementing all university laws and statutes and for carrying out all decisions of the university council. The secretary general handles all administrative and financial affairs under the supervision of the president and his assistants. He is also appointed by a presidential decree on the recommendation of the university president and the minister of higher education.

The chief administrative body at the university is the university council, which consists of the president, as chairman; the two deputy presidents; the secretary general; the deans of faculties and institutes; a representative of the Ministry of Higher Education; and two experts from outside the university, appointed by the university council. Among other duties, the university council is responsible for establishing curricula and programs of study; for the granting of scholarships and financial aid; and for the coordination of university research. The council also confers academic degrees and appoints teaching staff.

The universities are divided into faculties, which are administered by deans, assistant deans, and faculty councils. The deans and assistant deans are appointed by the minister of higher education on the recommendation of the president. Only those holding chairs are considered for selection as deans or assistant deans. The faculty council is composed of the dean and his assistants and the department heads. The dean or the senior assistant dean serves as chairman. Two outside experts are selected by the council and appointed by the Ministry of Higher Education to serve on the faculty council. The faculty council is responsible for determining admission, degree, and examination requirements and for proposing curricula and programs of study to the university council for approval. Each faculty is divided into departments, and the senior professor serves as head of each department.

Programs and Degrees

The first degree awarded at the universities is the bachelor's degree, which requires four years of study beyond the secondary level for most fields of study. Pharmacy, dentistry, engineering, and veterinary medicine require five years; and medicine requires six years. Students who complete the six-year medical program are allowed to practice medicine only after completing an additional year of training. In several fields students may earn a diploma after two years of additional specialized work beyond the bachelor's degree. However, with the exception of medicine, the diploma is not a prerequisite for admission to an advanced degree program (*Higher Education in Egypt–1974*, 1975).

The next higher degree awarded by most faculties is the master's degree, which requires two to three years of study beyond the bachelor's degree. Candidates in the master's program generally attend classes for one year and spend the remaining year writing a thesis, which they must defend. Usually only those students who hold the bachelor's degree with an overall rating of "good" are admitted to the master's program.

The highest degree awarded by most faculties is the doctorate, which takes two to three years of study beyond the master's degree. Students who hold the master's degree with an overall rating of "good" may be admitted to the doctoral program. Doctoral candidates are required to conduct original research and write a thesis. An oral examination is required in some doctoral programs. In clinical medicine the thesis is a prerequisite for sitting for the doctoral examination.

Many of the nonuniversity higher education institutes award the bachelor's degree after four or five years of study beyond the secondary level. The higher institutes for commerce, teachers, and general studies offer a four-year program leading to the bachelor's degree, while the industrial higher institutes offer five-year programs.

The institutes for technical training (affiliated with the Ministry of Higher Education) and the institutes for health technicians (affiliated with the Ministry of Health) award diplomas below the first degree level after two years of specialized study beyond the secondary level.

Financing and Student Financial Aid

Most higher education institutions are financed by the government. No tuition fees are charged at the state universities and higher institutes. The universities receive their operating funds from the government in the form of annual grants. Each university has its own budget, which is prepared by the university council and submitted to the Supreme Council of Universities for approval.

The universities provide grants to outstanding students who score more than 80 percent in the general secondary certificate examination. The continuation of the grants is determined by the academic record of the student. In addition, scholarships are awarded by the Ministry of Higher

Education, upon the recommendation of the faculty and university councils, for outstanding postgraduate students to continue their studies abroad. Between 1973 and 1975 the government awarded 763 scholarships for postgraduate study, mainly in the United States, the United Kingdom, the Federal Republic of Germany, France, and Switzerland. The Egyptian government also offers a substantial number of scholarships to students from other countries, mostly Arab and African countries, to study in Egypt. The government also accepts scholarships offered by other countries through cultural exchange programs.

A foundation established in 1961 offers financial assistance to university students. The foundation grants interest-free loans to needy students, who need not repay the loans until they have graduated and secured employment.

Student Social Background and Access to Education

Higher education facilities have expanded considerably in recent years, allowing greater numbers of students an opportunity to further their education. At the university level, enrollment increased more than 50 percent between 1968 and 1972 (*Higher Education in Egypt—1974*, 1975). Approximately 27 percent of those enrolled in higher education are female. The continuous expansion of educational facilities and the absence of fees in all public schools have equalized educational opportunities in both urban and rural areas and for all classes of society.

Perhaps the most limiting factor in regard to access for educational advancement is the rigorous examination system, which forces numerous students to terminate their education at the primary or preparatory level.

Teaching Staff

The academic staff at Egyptian universities are classified as demonstrators, assistant lecturers, lecturers, assistant professors, and professors. All permanent staff are required to hold a doctoral degree.

Demonstrators are selected from among university graduates by the president on the recommendation of the department involved and with the approval of the faculty council. Demonstrators usually hold only a bachelor's degree when appointed; but they are expected to continue their education and obtain a doctoral degree, after which time they may be considered for appointment to the permanent staff of the university. When they obtain a master's degree, they are appointed assistant lecturers. Lecturers, assistant professors, and professors are appointed by the minister of higher education on the recommendation of the university council, the faculty council, and the particular department.

For an assistant lecturer to be appointed to the position of lecturer, a period of several years must elapse between achievement of the master's degree and his appointment. Lecturers are required to serve at least five years, during which time they are required to conduct original research before being considered for the position of assistant professor. Assistant professors must serve for a period of five years, during which time they must publish original research to be eligible for promotion to the position of professor.

The salaries of the academic staff are determined by the government and are considered high in comparison with salaries for other civil service positions.

Members of the teaching staff may be transferred from one chair to another, from one department to another, to other faculties within the university, or to other universities with the approval of the concerned university council. Teaching staff also may be assigned to other universities abroad for a period of three to four years or may serve for the same period in a position outside the university—for example, in government departments, international agencies, and nongovernment organizations. Some teaching staff, by special per-

mission, hold part-time positions outside the university in addition to their work in the university.

Research Activities

Since the early 1970s research has assumed an important role in the university. Presidential Decree 49 (1972) established a separate budget for university research. Funds are also provided by donations from business firms and individuals. Members of the university teaching staff are encouraged to undertake research, and original research is a prerequisite for academic promotion. Teaching staff are particularly encouraged to participate in applied research projects in cooperation with commercial or industrial institutions. Joint research projects have been carried out by university staff and industry, and industrial concerns have contributed funds to university research activities.

All research undertaken in the university is supervised and coordinated by a special committee of the university council, which takes steps to prevent duplication and to facilitate interdisciplinary or interdepartmental cooperation.

Research is also a function of various specialized institutes throughout the country. Some of these institutes are affiliated with the universities, while others are attached to various ministries. The largest of these is the National Research Center. Although an independent institution, the center assists in the development of research in the universities; and the universities, in turn, are involved in the promotion of research work in the center.

Current Problems and Trends

In 1974 Egypt's national library, Dar-ul-Kutub, moved into new quarters in the Bulaq section of Cairo. As a national research resource, the new library complex will facilitate the research work of scholars interested in the role of Egyptian, Arab, and foreign cultures in ancient and modern Egyptian history. Among other activities,

Dar-ul-Kutub coordinates exchanges for many government agencies and organizations with approximately 700 other similar centers throughout the world.

Audiovisual centers equipped with slides, films, tapes, and television are being formed to augment existing facilities used by the various faculties and institutes.

Since the review of all educational policy in the early 1970s, the government has emphasized the expansion of technical education to prepare the manpower required for national development. Plans call for a reform of the lower educational levels for the purpose of channeling more students into technical-vocational education leading to employment; however, equal emphasis will continue to be placed on technical and academic programs that lead to higher education.

International Cooperation

Egypt pursues an active policy of international cooperation in the area of education. In the academic year 1971–72 more than 11,000 Egyptian university graduates were teaching abroad, primarily in Arab countries; and more than 900 Egyptian university professors were seconded to foreign, mainly Arab, institutions. In addition, more than 15,000 foreign students were enrolled in Egyptian universities (14,000 from other Arab countries), while more than 4300 Egyptian students were studying abroad.

A. H. SOROUR

Educational Associations

Egyptian Association of University Women
26 Saleh Salem
Alexandria, Arab Republic of Egypt

General Union of Students
Arab Socialist Union Building, El
  Tahrir Square
Cairo, Arab Republic of Egypt

Bibliography

AFME Report. Washington, D.C.: American Friends of the Middle East, quarterly.

Arminjon, P. *L'enseignement, la doctrine et la vie dans les universités musulmanes d'Egypte*. Paris: Félix Alcan, 1907.

Al-Azhar fi 12 'aman. Cairo: National Printing and Publishing Establishment, 1964.

Budair, A. A. F. *Al-amir Ahmad Fu'ad wa nash'at al-jami'a al-misriya*. Cairo: University of Cairo Press, 1950.

Dodge, B. *Al-Azhar: A Millennium of Muslim Learning*. Washington, D.C.: Middle East Institute, 1961. Memorial edition, 1974.

Economic Supplement of al-Ahram. *Dalil al-dirasat al-'ulya bil-jami'at al-misriya*. Cairo: Al-Ahram, October 1974.

Egyptian National Institute of Planning. *Takhtit al-quwa al-'amila fil-jumhuriya al-'Arabiya al-Muttahida*. Cairo: Egyptian National Institute, 1966 (Vol. 1), 1971 (Vol. 2).

Hassan, M. M. *Tatwir khutat at-tá-aleem al-'ali waljami'i*. Cairo: University of Cairo Press, 1974.

Higher Education in Egypt—1974. Washington, D.C.: American Friends of the Middle East, 1975.

'Inan, M. *Tarikh al-jami' al-Azhar*. Cairo: Committee on Authorship, Translation and Publication, 1958.

Isma'il, H. M. "Formation of the Teaching Staff at Cairo University." In V. G. Onushkin (Ed.), *Planning the Development of Universities—III*. Paris: UNESCO, 1974.

Matveyev, A., Adamson, C., and Boze, S. K. *Arab Republic of Egypt: The Feasibility of Establishing Technical Universities in the Arab Republic of Egypt*. Paris: UNESCO, 1972.

The Middle East and North Africa, 1973–1974. London: Europa, 1973.

Qubain, F. I. *Education and Science in the Arab World*. Baltimore: Johns Hopkins University Press, 1966.

el-Sa'id, S. M. *The Expansion of Higher Education in the United Arab Republic*. Cairo: University of Cairo Press, 1960.

Smith, H. H., and others. *Area Handbook for the United Arab Republic (Egypt)*. Washington, D.C.: U.S. Government Printing Office, 1970.

Sorour, A. H. "University of Cairo." In T. M. Yesufu (Ed.), *Creating the African University*. Ibadan, Nigeria: Oxford University Press, 1973.

Statistical Handbook. Cairo: Central Agency for Public Mobilisation and Statistics, 1973.

Supreme Council of Universities of the UAR. *Mudhakkira fi sha'n al-malamih al-ra'isiya lil-syassa al-muqtaraha lil-ta'lim al-jami'i*. Cairo: University of Cairo Press, 1967.

Supreme Council of Universities of the UAR. *Mu'tamarat al-ta'lim al-jami'i wal-'ali: al-taqrir*. Cairo: Ain Shams University Press, 1967.

Supreme Council of Universities of the UAR.

Dalil a'da' hay'at al-tadris wal-mu'idin bi-jami'at al-jumhuriya al-'Arabiya al-Muttahida. Cairo: University of Cairo Press, 1970.

Supreme Council of Universities of the UAR. *Dalil al-jami'at fil-jumhuriya al-'Arabiya al-Muttahida.* Cairo: University of Cairo Press, 1970.

Szyliowicz, J. S. *Education and Modernization in the Middle East.* Ithaca, New York: Cornell University Press, 1973.

United Arab Republic, Ministry of Higher Education. *Al-ta'lim al-'ali fi 12 sana.* Cairo: Ministry, 1964.

Wagner, E. H. *The United Arab Republic: A Study of the Educational System of the United Arab Republic and Guide to the Academic Placement of Students from the United Arab Republic in United States Educational Institutions.* Washington, D.C.: American Association of Collegiate Registrars and Admissions Officers (AACRAO), 1970.

Who's Who in the Arab World, 1974–1975. (4th ed.) Beirut, Lebanon: Publitec Publications, 1974.

See also: Arab World: Regional Analysis; Archives: Africa and Asia, National Archives of; Health Services, Worldwide University; History of Higher Education; Religious Influences in Higher Education: Islam; Science Policies: Less Developed Countries: Arab World.

EISENHOWER, DWIGHT D., LIBRARY

See Archives: United States, National Archives of.

ELDERY, PROGRAMS FOR THE

See Adult Education: Elderly, Programs for the.

ELECTRICAL AND ELECTRONICS ENGINEERING (Field of Study)

Electrical and electronics engineering deals with useful technical applications of electrical and magnetic phenomena. This discipline consists primarily of the application of mathematics and physics to the design and analysis of real physical entities (for example, electric motors, generators, amplifiers, radio receivers, and computers) and of small- and large-scale physical systems (for example, controlled energy systems, telecommunication systems, and computer-controlled manufacturing processes) where these physical entities, interconnected and interacting in various ways, are used as components of the systems. (The distinction between a "component" and a "system" is somewhat arbitrary. To the designer of a complete communication system, for example, a radio transmitter is a component; on the other hand, to the designer of the transmitter itself, an amplifier is a component and the transmitter is the system.) The systems to which the field addresses itself also include abstract entities (for example, computation schemes, conceptual models, and information structures) which form the basis of actual physical devices used for information processing and transmission.

Electrical engineering was originally divided into two major branches, one stressing high-energy-level applications (power engineering) and the other concentrating on low-energy-level applications (telecommunication engineering). Since the early years in electrical engineering's development, however, entirely new subdivisions— such as instrumentation, automatic control, applied electronics, computers, and information systems—have emerged. In some of these subdivisions, high- and low-energy aspects of the field interact in a complicated way. These subdivisions, which have emerged because of the discovery of new phenomena and new materials and components, are closely linked. What unifies this vast and multifarious field of engineering, however (and what is also the continuous source of inspiration for new discoveries and applications), is the abstract character and similarity of the mathematical models describing electrical and electronics phenomena and applications.

Electrical and electronics engineering is a field that includes many divisions which are constantly changing and which vary from one country to another. Divisions of the field include the following: (1) electrical engineering, which involves all aspects of electromagnetism and network and systems theory, and the applications of these basic sciences to the development, production, and use of electrical machines and devices; (2) power engineering, which deals with the sources of high-level energy, ways of converting energy from these sources into useful electrical energy, and the means for the transport, connection, protection, and control of electrical energy; (3) electronics, which includes audio, video, and data telecommunications, electroacoustics, and electrooptics; (4) electronic instrumentation, which develops instruments for measurement, control, visualization, and data recording; and (5) applied electronics, which deals with such areas as induction heating, devices for conversion and control of electrical energy, automatic control, computer systems, and bioelectronics. The field also includes the division linked with circuit components, integrated circuits, and complex devices. In the 1960s conceptual models from control and computer science, which have been successfully used in various interdisciplinary fields, have been integrated to form the basis of a new field, known as *system science*.

The field of electrical and electronics engineering has logically related connections with most of the sciences. Natural sciences, especially physics and chemistry, describe the fundamental laws, principles, and phenomena which form the basis for technical solutions. Mathematics offers the abstract models necessary for analysis and interpretations. Computer science is strongly linked with the field because computers are electronic devices for information processing, and they constitute an integral part of most modern electrical and electronics engineering. Practically all fields of engineering have connections with electrical and electronics engineering: chemical engineering and metallurgy through various technologies; and industrial and mechanical engineering through instrumentation, data processing, and automatic control. Transportation, telecommunications, domestic and industrial electrical and electronic equipment, and a major

branch of medical technology are fields of applied electrical and electronics engineering. Finally, such disciplines as linguistics, management, ecology, music, architecture, and the arts have also drawn from the conceptual models and computing techniques common to electrical and electronics engineering.

Electrical and electronics engineering developed from the pursuit of technical applications of phenomena discovered by the natural sciences. Among the natural sciences physics has been the major source of discoveries; and the work of men like Coulomb, Galvani, Volta, Ampère, Gauss, Oersted, Ohm, Maxwell, Faraday, Weber, Kirchhoff, and Joule has resulted in the emergence of electricity as a distinct branch. Electrical engineering developed rapidly after the discovery of the principle of the dynamo (Siemens and Wheatstone, 1866) and the transformation of electrical energy into mechanical energy (Dolivo-Dobrovolski, 1888). The telegraph (Morse, 1843; Edison, 1864), the telephone (Bell, 1876), and radio telegraphy (Hertz, 1887; Popov, 1895; Marconi, 1896) were the first technical applications of electricity to the transmission and processing of information, which forms the basis of communications engineering. The development of electron tubes (Fleming, 1904; De Forest, 1906), the transistor (Bardeen, Brattain, Shockley, 1948), and integrated circuits has changed communications engineering radically through successive generations.

The areas of concern to electrical and electronics engineering first appeared as academic subjects in physics. Among the first schools were *Ecole polytechnique* in Paris (1794), *Ecole supérieure d'électricitée* in Paris (1894), *Eidgenössische technische Hochschule* in Zurich (1855), and *Polytechnische Schule* in Karlsruhe (1825). The first chair of electrical engineering in Germany was founded in 1882 at the *Technische Hochschule* in Darmstadt (1877). In the Soviet Union the first departments of electrical engineering appeared in Moscow and Kiev in 1918. Technical education in Romania began in

1818; the first laboratories and chair of electricity appeared at the University of Bucharest (1891), and the first school of electricity was founded in Iaşi (1910).

Due to the explosive growth of electrical and electronics engineering, education in this field has been constantly changing. New technologies have rapidly emerged in response to discoveries in magneto-hydrodynamics, superconductivity, masers, lasers, and other areas of basic physics. The development of new systems areas (such as satellite communications and computer control of manufacturing processes) and new materials and components has been responsible for the rapid changes in the techniques of engineering practice and in the education of electrical and electronics engineers. Among such changes have been the introduction of new subjects and interdisciplinary studies into the electrical and electronics engineering curriculum. University programs in the field have been upgraded significantly in mathematics and physics; the education of electrical and electronics engineers usually includes such areas as numerical analysis, linear algebra, probability and statistics, operations research, solid-state physics, plasma physics, electromagnetic fields, and abstract network and systems theory. Programs also usually include electrical motors and devices; production, transportation, and conversion of electrical energy; electronic circuits, applied electronics, electrical and electronic instrumentation; and information theory, automatic control, computers and programing, and data transmission and processing. The curriculum for engineers with specialized interests may also include such fields as electroacoustics, optoelectronics, and bioelectronics.

The modern trend in electrical and electronics engineering education is toward flexible and varied programs based on a solid fundamental training. The structure and duration of education may vary from one country to another. For example, in the United States a variety of interdisciplinary programs are available, and the

degrees are offered successively; in some other countries there are terminal degree programs, such as a program for engineers (of four to five years' duration) and a program for technologists (of three years' duration). Apart from these differences, many countries offer educational programs (such as the cooperative education plan in the United States, sandwich courses in the United Kingdom, and evening classes) in conjunction with productive activity. There are also recycling courses for adults and postuniversity programs for bringing specialists up to date in fields where there are rapid developments. Practically all countries award the title of *doctor* (which indicates the superior level of academic standing) to engineers around the age of twenty-six to thirty. Some countries, including the Soviet Union and Romania, award the title of *doctor docent* to worthy recipients around the age of fifty as a recognition of some outstanding activity.

In Romania electrical and electronics engineering education is organized in polytechnic institutes and universities within the faculties of electrical engineering, power engineering, electronics and telecommunication, and automation. A five-year program leads to the diploma of engineer and a three-year program to the diploma of subengineer. The programs for these diplomas are distinct. In all cases the general studies are common and then specialization occurs. In postuniversity education, programs are offered in a large variety of fields.

The internationalization of electrical and electronics engineering education is well illustrated by the exchange of specialists (visiting professors) and students. A large variety of exchanges based on international cultural relations facilitate internationalization. An international organization like UNESCO also contributes to the internationalization of education in the field. Finally, the international character of electrical and electronics education is reflected by the similarity of the educational programs offered in various countries; although different in form, these programs overlap in content.

MARIUS HĂNGĂNUȚ
IOAN ALFRED LETIA

Levels and Programs of Study

Programs in electrical and electronics engineering generally require as a minimum prerequisite a secondary education, with emphasis on science subjects, and lead to the following awards: certificate or diploma, Bachelor of Science or Engineering, Master of Science or Engineering, the doctorate, or their equivalents. Programs deal with the principles and practices of electrical and electronics engineering and consist of classroom and laboratory instruction and, on advanced levels, study, seminar or group discussion, and research in specialized areas of electrical and electronics engineering. The field of activity associated with electrical and electronics engineering is a wide one, ranging from the theory and practice of the generation, transmission, and distribution of electric power through communication systems, aerospace electronic systems, electronic computer design and construction, and the design and construction of biomedical electronic apparatus. These are examples and are not intended to be exhaustive.

Programs that lead to an award not equivalent to a first university degree deal with the principles and practices of electrical and electronics engineering technology. These programs are concerned with the generation, control, distribution, and utilization of electrical energy; with electronic circuit design and analysis; and with the application of electronic equipment to the control of industrial processes and electrical apparatus. Principal course content for both electrical and electronics technology usually includes physics, chemistry, mathematics, applied mechanics, computer programing, electrical measurements, circuit analysis, electronic devices, electronics, communications, introduction to electrical machines, logic circuits, and control systems. Course content for electrical technology includes electrical machines, power systems, pulse circuits, electrical design, instrumentation, and telemetry. Content for electronics technology includes linear electronics, integrated circuits, communications, electronic systems, microwaves and radar, and television systems.

Programs that lead to a first university degree deal with the principles and practices of electrical and electronics engineering. Principal course content usually includes electromagnetic theory, electric networks and systems, electromechanical energy conversions and electric mechanics, power systems, electric measurements, electronic circuits, communication systems, control systems and servomechanisms, and computer technology. Background courses generally include engineering mathematics; basic sciences, such as physics and chemistry; and basic engineering sciences, including engineering materials.

Programs that lead to a postgraduate university degree focus on specialized areas of electrical and electronics engineering. Emphasis is placed on original research work, as substantiated by the presentation and defense of a scholarly thesis or dissertation. Principal subject matter areas for courses and research projects usually include linear and nonlinear electrical and electronics systems, electromagnetic theory, electric power systems, computer methods in power system analysis, microwave theory and techniques, biomedical engineering, theory and design of electronic computer circuitry, power system protection and control, matrix analysis of electrical machines, and solid-state electronics. Usual background studies include appropriate specialties from other engineering programs and appropriate specialties from other related fields such as the natural sciences, the social sciences, mathematics, statistics, and computer science.

[This section was based on UNESCO's *International Standard Classification of Education (ISCED): Three Stage Classification System, 1974* (Paris: UNESCO, 1974).]

Major International and National Organizations

INTERNATIONAL

Commission of Regional Electrical Integration
bulevar Artigas 996
Montevideo, Uruguay

Engineers Joint Council/World Energy
   Conference
345 E. 47th Street
New York, New York 10017 USA

European Committee for Electrotechnical
   Standardization
4 Galérie Revenstein
1000 Brussels, Belgium

Institute of Electrical and Electronics
   Engineers (IEEE)
345 E. 47th Street
New York, New York 10017 USA

International Electronics Association
Internationaler Elektronic-Arbeitskreis e.V.
   (INEA)
Rossmarkt 12
Frankfurt/Main, Federal Republic of Germany

International Electrotechnical Commission
Commission électrotechnique internationale
   (CEI)
1 rue de Varembé
Geneva, Switzerland

International Telecommunication Union
place des Nations 112
Geneva, Switzerland

Union of International Engineering
   Organizations (UIEO)
Union des associations techniques
   internationales (UATI)
62 rue de Courcelles
Paris, France

For a listing of other international organizations interested in electrical engineering see:

Directory of Engineering Societies and Related Organizations. New York: Engineers Joint Council, 1974. A listing of international and United States organizations.
Yearbook of International Organizations. Brussels: Union of International Associations, 1974.

NATIONAL

India:
   Society of Electronic Engineers
   Box 108 High Grounds
   Bangalore

Italy:
   Associazione elettrotecnica ed elettronica
     italiana
   via S. Paolo 10
   Milan

Romania:
   Consiliul national al inginerilor şi
     tehnicienilor
   Calea Victoriei 118
   Bucharest

Soviet Union:
   A. S. Popov Scientific and Engineering
     Society of Radio Engineering and
     Electrical Communications
   ulica Herzena 10
   Moscow

United Kingdom:
   Institution of Electrical Engineers (IEE)
   Savoy Place
   London WC2, England

United States:
   Institute of Electrical and Electronics
     Engineers (IEEE)
   345 East 47th Street
   New York, New York 10017

For a complete list of national organizations consult:

Minerva, Wissenschaftliche Gesellschaften. Berlin, Federal Republic of Germany: de Gruyter, 1972.

Principal Information Sources

GENERAL

General guides to literature in the field of electrical and electronics engineering include:

Burkett, J., and Plumb, P. *How to Find Out in Electrical Engineering.* Elmsford, New York: Pergamon Press, 1967.
Codlin, E. M. *Handlist of Basic Reference Material in Electrical and Electronic Engineering.* (6th ed.) London: Association of Special Libraries and Information Bureaus, ASLIB Electronics Group, 1973.
Funkhouser, R. L. *Guide to Literature on Electrical and Electronics Engineering.* Washington, D.C.: American Society for Engineering Education, 1970. Includes guides to the literature, bibliographies, abstract services, dictionaries, and handbooks.
Moore, C. K., and Spencer, K. J. *Electronics: A Bibliographic Guide.* (2 vols.) London: Macdonald, 1961–1965.
Randle, G. R. *Electronic Industries Information Sources.* Detroit: Gale Research, 1968.
Readers' Guide to Books on Electrical Engineering.

(2nd ed.) London: Library Association, 1964.

Szilard, P. *Electrical Engineering Literature: A Reference Guide.* Honolulu: Thomas H. Hamilton Library, University of Hawaii, 1969.

The following books provide a broad introduction to the field:

Del Toro, V. *Electrical Engineering Fundamentals.* Englewood Cliffs, New Jersey: Prentice-Hall, 1972.

Hayt, W. H., Jr., and Hughes, G. W. *Introduction to Electrical Engineering.* New York: McGraw-Hill, 1968.

Marcus, A. *Basic Electricity.* (3rd ed.) Englewood Cliffs, New Jersey: Prentice-Hall, 1969.

A historical perspective of the field is offered by:

Dunsheath, D. *A History of Electrical Engineering.* London: Faber & Faber, 1962.

Kingsford, W. *Electrical Engineering: A History of the Men and the Ideas.* New York: St. Martin's Press, 1970.

Shiers, G. *Bibliography of the History of Electronics.* Metuchen, New Jersey: Scarecrow Press, 1972.

CURRENT BIBLIOGRAPHIES

The following offer abstracts and references in electronics and electrical engineering:

Bulletin signalétique. Section 140: *Electrotechnique;* Section 145: *Electronique.* Paris: Centre national de la recherche scientifique, 1940–.

Current Papers in Electrical and Electronics Engineering. London: Institution of Electrical Engineers, 1964–.

Electrical and Electronics Abstracts. London: Institution of Electrical Engineers, 1898–. A major abstracting service in the field.

Institut für Dokumentation der deutschen Akademie der Wissenschaften zu Berlin. *Abteilung Elektrotechnik.* Berlin, Federal Republic of Germany: Academie-Verlag, 1951–.

Referativnyĭ zhurnal, Elektrotekhnika i energetika. Moscow: Akademiia nauk, SSSR, Institut nauchnoĭ informatsii, 1956–.

Technical News Bulletin. Manchester, England: Associated Electrical Industries Limited, Power Group Research Laboratories, 1926–.

PERIODICALS

Some of the significant electrical engineering journals are *Acta Electronica* (France), *Archiv für Elektrotechnik* (FRG), *British Journal of Applied Physics, Denki gakkai zasshi* (Japan), *Denshi tsushin gakkai ronbunshi* (Japan), *E.E./Systems Engineering Today* (US), *Electrical Times* (UK), *Electronic Engineering* (UK), *Electronics Weekly* (UK), *Electronics and Power* (UK), *Electrotechnology* (UK), *Electrotehnica* (Romania), *Elektrichestvo/Electric Technology* (USSR), *Engineering Education* (US), *IEEE Spectrum* (US), *Institute of Electrical and Electronics Engineers: Transactions* (US), *Institution of Electrical Engineers Proceedings* (UK), *International Journal of Applied Physics* (FRG), *International Journal of Electrical Engineering Education* (UK), *Journal of Applied Physics* (US), *Radiotekhnika i electronika* (USSR), *Westinghouse Engineer* (US), *Zhurnal tekhnicheskoy fiziki/Soviet Physics.*

Listings of journals may be found in:

Brown, P., and Stratton, G. B. *The World List of Scientific Periodicals Published in the Years 1900–1960.* (3 vols.) London: Butterworth, 1963–1965.

Current Serials and Journals in the M.I.T. Libraries. Cambridge: Massachusetts Institute of Technology, 1957–.

ENCYCLOPEDIAS, DICTIONARIES, HANDBOOKS

Clason, W. E. *Elsevier's Dictionary of Electronics and Wave-Guides.* Amsterdam: Elsevier, 1966. A polyglot dictionary in English, French, Spanish, Italian, Dutch, and German, with Russian supplement.

Concise Encyclopedic Dictionary of Electronics. (3rd ed.) Amsterdam: Elsevier, 1967.

Elsevier's Electrotechnical Dictionary. Amsterdam: Elsevier, 1965.

Fink, D. G. *Electronics Engineers' Handbook.* New York: McGraw-Hill, 1975.

Fink, D. G., and Carroll, J. M. *Standard Handbook for Electrical Engineers.* New York: McGraw-Hill, 1968.

Gödecke, W. *Dictionary of Electrical Engineering, Telecommunications and Electronics/Wörterbuch der Electrotechnik, Fernmeldetechnik, Electronik.* Wiesbaden, Federal Republic of Germany: Brandstetter, 1964–1967.

Hütte. *Des Ingenieurs Taschenbuch.* (5 vols.) Berlin, Federal Republic of Germany: Wilhelm Ernst, 1965. Standard reference handbook for over a century.

International Electrotechnical Vocabulary in Nine Languages. (2nd ed.) Geneva: International Electrotechnical Commission, 1954–. The most extensive polyglot dictionary in the field; issued in twenty-two sections, covering electronics, electroacoustics, machines and transformers, waveguides, and so on.

Liebers, A. *The Electrical Engineer's Handbook.* New York: Key Publishing, 1970.

Say, M. G. *Newnes Concise Encyclopaedia of Electrical Engineering.* London: Newnes, 1962.

Susskind, C. *Encyclopedia of Electronics.* New York: Van Nostrand Reinhold, 1962.

DIRECTORIES

Abbreviations of Associations, Institutions, Research and Trade Associations. London: British Electrical and Allied Manufacturers' Association, 1959.

Cass, J., and Birnbaum, M. *Comparative Guide to Engineering Programs.* New York: Harper & Row, 1971.

Electrical and Electronics Trades Directory: The Blue Book. (86th ed.) London: Benn, 1968.

Engineering College Research and Graduate Study. Washington, D.C.: American Society for Engineering Education, 1972. This directory to the study of engineering lists graduate programs and research projects at institutions in the United States, Puerto Rico, and Canada.

Peterson's Annual Guides to Graduate Study, 1976. Book 5: *Engineering and Applied Sciences.* Princeton, New Jersey: Peterson's Guides, 1975. See section on Electrical and Power Engineering for a listing of United States institutions.

RESEARCH CENTERS, INSTITUTES, INFORMATION CENTERS

Centre national d'études des télécommunications
38-40 rue du Général Leclerc
Issy-les-Moulineaux, Seine, France

Electronics Research Laboratory
Columbia University
632 West 125th Street
New York, New York USA

Institut für Werkstoffe der Elektrotechnik
Aachen, Federal Republic of Germany

Instituto de investigaciones y ensayos eléctricos
University of Chile
Santiago, Chile

Lysteknisk Laboratorium
Electrical Engineering Laboratory
100 Lundtoftevej
DK-2800 Lyngby, Denmark

Philips Laboratories
Eindhoven, Netherlands

Science Research Council
State House, High Holborn
London, England

See the following for additional listings:

Minerva, Wissenschaftliche Gesellschaften. Berlin, Federal Republic of Germany: de Gruyter, 1972. Provides addresses of national and international institutes and centers.

Répertoire des laboratoires européens de recherches électroniques: Universités, écoles d'ingénieurs et centres de recherches/Directory of European Laboratories for Electronics Research: Universities, Schools of Engineering and Research Centers. Paris: Office national des universités et écoles françaises, 1962.

ELECTRICITY, INDUSTRIAL AND DOMESTIC (Field of Study)

The rapid technological advances in modern times have been largely due to man's refinement of his knowledge of electricity. Electricity has become an indispensable component of an industrialized society. Although other forms of energy contributed widely to the world's industrial expansion, electrical energy, because of its versatility, has played an increasingly dominant role. Electricity has the advantages of being easily transmitted over substantial distances and transformed to the special power needs of the individual consumer. It can also be converted to heat, light, and mechanical energy with efficiency and ease to suit a wide variety of needs.

The broad field of electricity embraces the branch of science that is concerned with electrical charges at rest or in motion, electric and electromagnetic fields. Modern science has revealed that there are a number of elemental particles, among them the electron and the proton, both of which have the properties of mass and charge. When these charges are set in motion, they constitute what is known as electric current. When this motion occurs in a material such as copper, the particle involved is the electron. It is the electron that man has harnessed to meet the astronomical power demands of twentieth-century industrial and domestic consumers of electricity.

In order to fulfill the world's electrical needs, a number of occupations requiring various degrees of formal education and experience have evolved. The major professional person in the field of electricity is the electrical engineer, whose education requires a minimum of four years of post-secondary study. Electrical engineers are involved in research, planning, design, testing, installation, and control of electrical systems. As world demand for electric power increased, resulting in larger and more sophisticated power systems, the need for qualified electrical engineers also increased. This need has been somewhat diminished by the emergence of electrical technicians, who are trained for a minimum of two years at a technical institute and can perform many of the tasks previously requiring an engineer. Technicians not only reduce the demand for engineers but also permit engineers to make more efficient use of their time. Technicians are considered semiprofessionals, although many of them advance to professional status by assuming greater responsibility.

In addition to professional and semi-professional personnel, vast numbers of skilled craftsmen—namely electricians and servicemen—are required in the electric power field. The electrician, who installs electrical wiring and apparatus in homes and industrial plants, is required for safety reasons to work for several years under the supervision of a master electrician. After this period of apprenticeship and successful completion of written and/or oral examinations to demonstrate knowledge of the rules and regulations governing proper wiring installation, the electrician is entitled to maintain journeyman status. After another specified period of time in practice, he qualifies for another examination to fulfill the requirements of a master electrician, the second qualifying stage. Each nation has its own criteria for examinations and for the required periods of work experience for electricians to become authorized to install electrical systems and apparatus. Servicemen are normally trained by a specific industry to repair a limited variety of equipment. The amount of time required to train these servicemen is related to the complexity of the equipment that they are to repair; for example, a training period will vary from several weeks for the repair of simple motors to many months for the repair of large computer systems. Of course, service trainees need a foundation in the fundamentals of electricity before they are capable of learning servicing techniques.

The field most closely allied to industrial and domestic electricity is the science of electronics. Although electronics is a branch of electricity, its early development was concentrated in the area of communications; thus, it did not immediately lend itself to direct association with electric power generation and distribution. However, as technology became more sophisticated, electronic devices played a more prominent role in the control of electrical apparatus and the distribution and analysis of electric power. Today giant computers are used not only for control and distribution in power plants but also for maintaining records on electric consumption for each customer.

The occupations of electrical engineer, electrical technician, electrician, and serviceman are the major types required in the field of industrial and domestic electricity. But because of the advanced technology of the 1970s, which has resulted in the construction of complex generating plants and distribution systems, numerous other academic disciplines can be said to be related to the field of electricity. For example, people trained in civil and architectural disciplines are required for the construction of power plants; mechanical disciplines for the installation of equipment; chemical disciplines for fuel control; and environmental disciplines for pollution control. Nuclear engineers and technicians are increasing in demand because of the trend toward nuclear power.

The education of engineers and technicians is becoming increasingly internationalized—mainly because discoveries of electric properties have been made in various countries and because of the recent trend toward a global system of units (metric system). Thus, eventually an engineer or technician trained in one country will be able to provide effective service in another.

The production and consumption of electricity can be classified under three major categories: (1) manufacture; (2) installation; and (3) generation and distribution. The manufacture of electrical components, parts, and appliances involves millions of people, who produce items ranging from 400,000-kilowatt generator units to light bulbs. Increased world demand for electric power has resulted in the installation of many new power plants and the modernization and expansion of existing plants. Electricity is generated and distributed by systems that vary greatly in size and function; such systems may range from simple distribution systems serving a small town to major generating and distribution systems serving the needs of millions of people. The vast majority of generating systems in the world are government owned. In the United States, however, more than 79 percent of the national generating capacity is in investor-owned utilities, which generate, transmit, and distribute to more than 78 percent of the American customers.

The first recorded history of electricity dates back to 600 B.C. in Greece. Thales of Miletus wrote about black stones that were able to attract pieces of iron. Thales also found that he could attract chaff to a piece of amber (the Greek for *amber* is *elektron*) that had been rubbed with fur. William Gilbert in 1600 formally developed these relationships and laid the foundation for the science of electricity. In 1663 the first electromechanical generator was invented by Otto von Guericke. A version of this machine is still used in the classroom to demonstrate electromechanical generation. Knowledge of electricity advanced at an extremely slow pace until 1800, when Allessandro Volta developed the forerunner to the battery. This voltaic pile generated electricity by chemical action using salts and other chemicals. About twenty-five years later, André Marie Ampère found that when a current-carrying wire is formed

into a helix, a concentrated magnetic field appears at each end. This helix-shaped current-carrying wire was the precursor of the solenoid, which is used to form an electromagnet. About 1832, Georg Simon Ohm discovered the relationship between voltage, current, and resistance. His formula for this relationship is known as Ohm's Law: current (amperes) = electromotive force (volts)/resistance (ohms).

During the first half of the nineteenth century the greatest discoveries were made in the field of electricity. Michael Faraday, Hans Christian Oersted, Heinrich Lenz, Pierre Laplace, and Gustav Kirchhoff were but a few of those whose contributions laid the foundation for the development of the incandescent lamp by Thomas Edison in 1879. The invention of the audion tube by Lee DeForest in 1910 made possible the age of electronics, and the invention of the transistor by Walter Brattain, John Bardeen, and William Shockley in 1948 opened up a new era in the field of electronics.

The facilities needed for generating and delivering vital electric power can affect the environment. When the electric industry was relatively small and population was less concentrated in urban areas, the total amount of land, air, and water required for generating plants and distribution systems did not make a heavy impact on public awareness; smokestacks, transmission towers, wooden poles, and power lines were acceptable social costs for the benefits derived from electric power. However, as urban areas became heavily populated and power demands rose astronomically, the burden on land, air, and water also increased. Concern over the decline in natural environmental amenities developed, and laws were passed on the national levels which imposed standards on the electric utility industry. Consequently, the electric utility industry has established new practices to achieve high environmental quality: scrubbers are being installed in smokestacks to remove sulfur oxides from power plant emissions; cooling systems are being improved to avoid thermal discharge into rivers, lakes, and seas; and alternate locations for pole-mounted transformers are being investigated. Demands have been rising for power equipment that will limit pollution—equipment such as municipal waste-treatment facilities, electrically operated rapid transit systems, recycling systems, and electric cars. The improvement to the environment as a result of rigid standards will be costly to the customers of the electric industry, but they generally agree that it is an essential objective.

It has been forecast that world electricity generation will increase from 6.8 trillion kilowatt-hours in 1975 to 22.5 trillion kilowatt-hours in the year 2000. The use of fossil fuel, which is now peaking, will gradually give way to nuclear power. The demand for skilled engineers, technicians, and electricians will continue to increase. This demand will be reflected not only by the industrialized nations but also by such oil-producing nations as Iran, Saudi Arabia, and Algeria, which are now beginning to feel the need to provide higher levels of technology for their people.

ALEXANDER W. AVTGIS

Levels and Programs of Study

Programs in industrial and domestic electricity generally require as a minimum prerequisite a secondary education. In some cases, mature students with relevant work experience may be admitted with lower educational qualifications, especially into programs designed to upgrade the performance of those already employed. A certificate or diploma of industrial electrical technology is the usual award for programs of one year or more, which are typically given in technological or similar institutes. For short courses, many of which are sponsored by employers or employers' associations, a certificate of satisfactory completion is usually awarded.

Programs consist primarily of classroom, laboratory, and workshop study and practice and deal with the applications of electricity and the installation, operation, and maintenance of electrical equipment, machinery, and appliances in factories, buildings, and homes. Principal course content usually includes fundamentals of electricity; industrial electronics; shop practice; electric power and illumination; electrical test equipment; installation, repair, and maintenance of electrical machines; and transmission and distribution of electrical power. Stress is placed on the achievement of practical competence and skill. Programs often consist of periods of study alternating with periods of work in industrial and other enterprises (sandwich courses).

[This section was based on UNESCO's *International Standard Classification of Education (ISCED)*. Paris: UNESCO, 1976.]

Major International and National Organizations

INTERNATIONAL

Commission of Regional Electrical Integration
bulevar Artigas 996
Montevideo, Uruguay

International Association of Electrical
    Contractors
Association internationale des entreprises
    d'équipement électrique
99 rue de la Verrerie
Paris, France

International Commission on Rules for the
    Approval of Electrical Equipment
Utrechtseweg 310
Arnhem, Netherlands

International Conference on Large High
    Tension Electric Systems
Conférence internationale des grands
    réseaux électriques à haute
    tension (CIGRE)
112 boulevard Haussmann
Paris, France

International Federation of Industrial
    Producers of Electricity for Own
    Consumption
Fédération internationale des producteurs
    auto-consommateurs industriels
    d'électricité (FIPACIE)
49 Square-Louise
1040 Brussels, Belgium

International Union of Producers and
Distributors of Electrical Energy
Union internationale des producteurs et
distributeurs d'énergie électrique
(UNIPEDE)
39 avenue de Friedland
Paris, France

Union for Coordinating Production and
Distribution of Electricity
Union pour la coordination de la production
et du transport d l'électricité (UCPTE)
Ziegelhausen Landstrasse 5
Heidelberg, Federal Republic of Germany

For additional international organizations
see:

*Directory of Engineering Societies and Related
Organizations.* New York: Engineers Joint
Council, 1970.
*Scientific and Technical Societies of the U.S. and
Canada.* Washington, D.C.: National Academy of Sciences, National Research Council,
1927–.

NATIONAL

Belgium:
    Société royale belge des électriciens
    1 place du Trône
    Brussels

France:
    Comité électrotechnique français
      et Union technique de l'électricité
    12 place Henri Bergson
    Paris

United States:
    Illuminating Engineering Society
    345 East 47th Street
    New York, New York 10017

    Institute of Electrical and Electronics
      Engineers
    345 East 47th Street
    New York, New York 10017

For a detailed listing of national organizations see:

Minerva, Wissenschaftliche Gesellschaften. Berlin,
Federal Republic of Germany: de Gruyter,
1972.

Principal Information Sources

GENERAL

General guides to the literature in the area
of electricity include:

Kyed, J. M., and Matarazzo, J. M. *Scientific,
Technical and Engineering Societies Publications
in Print, 1974–75.* New York: Bowker, 1974.
Lasworth, E. J. *Reference Sources in Science and
Technology.* Metuchen, New Jersey: Scarecrow Press, 1972.
Mottelay, P. F. *Bibliographic History of Electricity
and Magnetism, Chronologically Arranged.*
London: Griffin, 1922.

Introductory works to the field of industrial
and domestic electricity include:

Adams, J. *Electric Principles and Practices.* New
York: McGraw-Hill, 1973.
Buban, P., and Schmitt, M. *Technical Electricity
and Electronics.* New York: McGraw-Hill,
1972.
Gay, C. M. *Mechanical and Electrical Equipment
for Buildings.* New York: Wiley, 1964.
Hubert, C. *Operational Electricity: Theory, Characteristics, Applications and Mode of Operation
of Circuits and Machines.* New York: Wiley,
1961.
Middleton, R. G. *Practical Electricity.* Indianapolis, Indiana: H. W. Sams, 1969.
Mileaf, H. *Electricity One-Seven Series.* (7 vols.)
New York: Hayden Book Company, 1966.
Rao, B. V. *Operation and Maintenance of Electrical Equipment.* (2 vols.) Bombay: Asia Publishing House, 1968.
Van Valkenburgh, Nooger, and Neville, Inc.
Basic Industrial Electricity. New York: J. F.
Rider, 1962.

A basic history of the field is:

Canby, E. T. *A History of Electricity.* New York:
Hawthorn Books, 1963.

CURRENT BIBLIOGRAPHIES

Useful abstracting and indexing services in
the field of electricity, including vocational
education and training, are:

Applied Science and Technology Index. New York:
Wilson, 1913–.
*BACIE Bibliography of Publications in the Field
of Education and Training in Commerce and
Industry.* London: British Association for
Commercial and Industrial Education,
1963–.
*CIRF Abstracts: Ideas Drawn from the Current
Writings on Vocational Training for Workers,
Supervisors and Technicians.* Geneva: International Vocational Training Information
and Research Center, 1961–.
Electrical and Electronics Abstracts. London:
Institution of Electrical Engineers, 1898–.
Engineering Index. New York: Engineering
Index, Inc., 1884–. The most extensive
abstracting service in engineering and related fields.

Technical Education Abstracts, from British Sources. London: National Federation for Educational Research in England and Wales, Information Service, 1961–.

PERIODICALS

American Vocational Journal, Anales de mecánica y electricidad (Spain), *Anritsu Technical Bulletin* (Japan), *Appliance Service News* (US), *Australian Electrical World, Bulletin d'information des centrales électriques* (France), *Densei Technical Journal* (Japan), *Education and Training* (UK), *Electric Technology USSR, Electro-Technology* (India), *Engineering Education* (US), *Industrial Arts and Vocational Education* (US), *Industrial Education* (US), *Light and Lighting* (UK), *Monde de l'électricité* (Canada), *Mundo elétrico* (Brazil), *New Zealand Electrical Journal, Promyschlennay energetika* (USSR), *School Shop* (US).

For a complete listing of scientific and technical journals see:

Technical Journals for Industry. The Hague: International Federation for Documentation, 1967–.
Union List of Periodicals Held by the Libraries of CEGB Headquarters. London: Central Electricity Generating Board, 1970.
World List of Scientific Periodicals Published in the Years 1900–1960. (3 vols.) London: Butterworth, 1963–1965.

ENCYCLOPEDIAS, DICTIONARIES, HANDBOOKS

Carr, C. E. *American Electricians' Handbook: A Reference Book for Practical Electrical Workers.* (8th ed.) New York: McGraw-Hill, 1961.
Clason, W. E. *Elsevier's Electrotechnical Dictionary in 6 Languages.* Amsterdam: Elsevier, 1965. In English, French, Spanish, Italian, Dutch, and German.
Clements, R., and Parkes, D. *Manual of Maintenance Engineering.* London: Business Publications, 1963.
Day, R. *The Practical Handbook of Electrical Repairs.* New York: Arco, 1969.
Freeman, H. G. *Spezialwörterbuch für das Maschinenwesen.* Essen, Federal Republic of Germany: Girardet, 1958. A comprehensive bilingual (German-English) dictionary covering machine tools, machine elements, and operations useful for workshop practice.
Gerrish, H. *Electricity, Electronics Dictionary.* South Holland, Illinois: Goodheart-Willcox, 1970.
Houston, E. J. *A Dictionary of Electrical Words, Terms and Phrases.* (3rd ed.) New York: W. J. Johnson, 1896.
Hubert, C. *Preventive Maintenance of Electrical*

Equipment. (2nd ed.) New York: McGraw-Hill, 1969.
IEEE Standard Dictionary of Electrical and Electronics Terms. New York: Institute of Electrical and Electronics Engineers, 1972.
James, M. S., and Clark, E. G. *Glossary of Terms Used in Electrical Installation Work.* London: Estates Gazette, 1968.
McPartland, J. *Electrical Equipment Manual.* (3rd ed.) New York: McGraw-Hill, 1965.
Morrow, L. C. *Maintenance Engineering Handbook.* (2nd ed.) New York: McGraw-Hill, 1966.
Polon, D. *Dictionary of Electrical Abbreviations.* Indianapolis, Indiana: Odyssey Press, 1965.
Van Amerongen, C. *The Universal Encyclopedia of Machines or How Things Work.* London: Allen and Unwin, 1967. An encyclopedia dealing with electrical equipment, specifically machines.

DIRECTORIES

Dent, H. C. *The Yearbook of Technical Education and Careers in Industry.* London: Black, 1957–.
Directory to Electronic Industries in the U.S. and Europe. London: Noyes, 1970.
Electrical and Electronics Trades Directory. The Blue Book. (86th ed.) London: Benn, 1968.
Gleazer, E. J. *American Junior Colleges.* (8th ed.) Washington, D.C.: American Council on Education, 1971.
Russell, M. M. *The College Blue Book: Occupational Education.* New York: Macmillan, 1973.
Technical Education Yearbook. Ann Arbor, Michigan: Prakken, 1963–. A United States directory.

ELECTRONIC EQUIPMENT INSTALLATION AND SERVICING (Field of Study)

Although older textbooks define electronics as "the flow of electrons through gases" and electricity as "the flow of electrons through a solid conductor," neither definition is accurate in the mid 1970s. Electronics now involves gases, solids, and vacuums; and electricity no longer needs to be imprisoned in solid conductors; moreover, there is greater intermixing of both fields in modern systems-oriented technology. Electronics, therefore, is concerned primarily with "microflow" of electrons, often through incredibly small devices which are subject to rapid and delicate control; and electricity is concerned with the "macroflow" of electronics, the production and distribution of power subject to gross controls, through larger devices, ranging from relatively small power supplies to the great power generators that harness the water energy flowing over dams. Equipment installation and servicing have of necessity kept pace with the increased sophistication of electronics. A much higher level of training and education is required today than in days before solid-state electronics became commonplace.

The lines separating the divisions of electronics are fuzzy and constantly shifting. However, four main categories can be identified: (1) *Communications* involves mainly radio and television, telephone and telegraph, radar, and telemetry, and includes orbiting satellites as components in a communications system. (2) *Computers*, information-processing machines used in data processing and interpretation in business transactions, are vital components in control systems. The computer processes input data from the system to be controlled, determines the desired reaction of the system, and finally supervises the reaction of the system to its commands. Space vehicles are probably the most dramatic and complex examples of the use of computers in control systems. (3) *Instrumentation* includes electronic instruments in hospitals (electrocardiographs, electroencephalographs, and scanners), in satellites, in military hardware, and in industrial quality-control systems used both as diagnostic and design devices and as input devices to control systems. (4) *Control systems* is a category that embraces the other branches. Control systems range from simple devices with limited functions to complex combinations of all the fields of electronics.

The scope of electronics-dependent technology is so extensive that it defies limitation. Everything tangible involves electronics in one way or another. For example,

electronics is involved in traffic control, production control, avionics, transportation, and medical monitoring and treatment devices. Electronics is also at the heart of market analysis and opinion or political polls. In fact, television networks boast of "electronic prediction" of election results. Jury lists are analyzed by computers to determine which people are most likely to favor the defense or the prosecution. Medical electronic systems permit doctors and hospitals to keep human beings "alive" almost indefinitely.

It is hard for us to imagine, therefore, that in 1900 electronic devices were unknown, even though they were foreshadowed by the first electric bulb. In 1904 Sir John Fleming put the Edison effect—a current crossing a vacuum gap—to use in the first vacuum tube. In 1907 Lee De Forest inserted a grid between the two elements of a vacuum tube—a hot filament and a plate–and demonstrated that weak input signals could be amplified. Vacuum tubes were first used in radio and thus came to be called "radio tubes." (In the United Kingdom they are still known as "valves," Fleming's name for them.)

Radio communication inspired the development of electronics. In the early 1900s, at a naval station in San Jose, California, the United States Navy began classes in radio theory, as well as in installation, maintenance, and servicing of its equipment. In 1909 a college of engineering, started by Charles D. Herrold in San Jose, began broadcasting voice experiments. During World War I civilian development of radio was curtailed, but by the end of the 1920s more than 350,000 people were employed in radio, and 700 broadcasters reached an audience of over 35,000,000. Annual income had mushroomed from two million dollars to six hundred million dollars.

The 1920s also saw increased growth of talking pictures, phonographs, telephone and telegraph using radio signals, remote-control devices, medicine, surgery, mining and oil prospecting, and aviation. Despite this impressive list, installation and servicing were not complicated. Servicing involved mainly testing and replacing relatively simple components, and much of the installation work was mechanical and did not require significant theoretical background.

In the 1930s and early 1940s, home radios and phonographs became very popular. The first radio facsimile transmission was achieved. Other new developments were ship radios and navigational devices, ship-to-shore telephones, auto radios, and public-address systems. The field had become complicated enough to require the establishment of radio correspondence and residence schools, whose graduates, the first true technicians in the field, worked as equipment inspectors, installers, servicemen, and wireless operators.

With the spread of television in the 1940s, trained people were needed in broadcasting, testing, servicing, and installation of antennae. Installation, maintenance, and servicing were still not complex, requiring chiefly mechanical skills.

World War II created an enormous demand for more and better radios and the development of radar. Light-aircraft metals were produced by power supplied by electronic rectifiers. Resistance welding based on electronic rectifiers and timers was used to build military vehicles by the thousands, and the need for fluorescent lighting in the war plants mushroomed. Also during the war, computers were born, and after the war came noncommunications applications: facsimile transmission, oscilloscopes, X rays, induction heating tubes, electrostatic cleaners, arc welding, and circuit breakers.

The level of required education or training still was not significantly affected; a correspondence course or a short training course was sufficient. The turning point occurred in the 1940s, with the renewed interest in crystals as solid-state semiconductors, and culminated in 1947, with the development of the first transistor at Bell

Telephone Laboratories. Thereafter, electronics escalated and with it the need for more schooling, preferably at the post-secondary level, with at least one academic year of electronics or a two-year associate degree that included the equivalent of one year of electronics theory and practice.

In the mid 1970s a person who installs and services electronic equipment is called an electronics technician or, frequently, a field engineer. A field engineer responsible for installation must first determine that the customer has the prerequisites for the equipment—adequate power, cooling, and space. In servicing the equipment, the field engineer must recognize repetitive problems and deal with them as a whole. If the problems are inherent in the equipment, they are reported to the engineering staff of the supplier, so that design changes can be made. If modifications in the original design are called for, the field engineer must know how to adapt the installed equipment to accommodate the modifications. In service work, the field engineer must be able to trouble-shoot the problem and, after diagnosing it, choose the best way to make the repair—either by replacing defective components or by recognizing the side effects of a defective part and making other preventive repairs as well. He must also be able to adjust and fine-tune the equipment. Finally, because of rapid and constant developments, the modern field engineer or electronics technician must keep abreast of the field through continuing education.

In the mid 1970s developments in electron optics, including lasers, near infrared, and far infrared (heat) devices, are being refined. Lasers are being used extensively for communications, measurement, welding, machining, trimming, boring, cutting, bonding, holography, and material impregnation. Also under development, especially in military and space hardware, are heat and remote-sensing devices, a wide variety of instruments, and highly advanced photography. Greater use is being made of microfiche, which allows the field engineer to carry an entire reference library with him to the job site.

Electronics, like basic science, knows no national boundaries, except that the technical capabilities of nations vary tremendously. The technologically advanced countries often sell complete systems to developing countries and send technicians who do the initial installation and short-term servicing. In addition, many of the sales contracts also call for long-term training of natives in servicing.

E. L. FLECKENSTEIN

Levels and Programs of Study

Programs in electronics equipment installation and servicing usually require as a minimum educational prerequisite a secondary education, although mature students with relevant work experience may sometimes be admitted with lower qualifications, especially into programs designed to upgrade the performance of those already employed. The usual award for programs of one or more years, typically given in technological or similar institutes, is a certificate or diploma from the institution or from the examining board of a professional or technical organization. For short courses, many of which are sponsored by employers or employers' associations, a certificate of satisfactory completion is usually given.

Programs consist primarily of classroom, laboratory, and workshop study and practice and deal with applications of electronics and with the installation and servicing of electronic equipment such as radio and television apparatus, electronic controls, electronic computers, and electronic navigation aids. Principal course content usually includes the fundamentals of electricity, principles of electronics, special electronic circuitry, electronic components, electronic test equipment, physics, mathematics, and shop practice. Emphasis is given to the achievement of practical competence and skill. Programs often consist of alternating periods of study and work in industrial and other enterprises (sandwich courses).

[This section was based on UNESCO's *International Standard Classification of Education (ISCED)* Paris: UNESCO, 1976).]

Major International and National Organizations

INTERNATIONAL

European Committee for Electrotechnical
  Standardization
4 Galerie Ravenstein
Brussels, Belgium

European Union of Electrical Wholesalers
Union européenne des grossistes en
  matériel électrique
13 rue Marivaux
Paris, France

Federation of Telecommunications Engineers
  in the European Community
42 rue des Palais
Brussels, Belgium

International Electronics Association
Rossmarkt 12
Frankfurt/Main, Federal Republic of Germany

International Electrotechnical Commission
1 rue de Varembé
Geneva, Switzerland

International Federation of Professional and
  Technical Engineers
1126 16th Street NW
Washington, D.C. 20036 USA

International Radio Consultative Committee
place des Nations
Geneva, Switzerland

Pro Electron
10 avenue Hamoir
Brussels, Belgium

For a more complete listing of international organizations consult:

Directory of Engineering Societies and Related Organizations. New York: Engineers Joint Council, 1970.

Scientific and Technical Societies of the U.S. and Canada. Washington, D.C.: National Academy of Sciences, National Research Council, 1927–.

NATIONAL

France:
  Comité électrotechnique français
    et Union technique de l'électricité
  12 place Henri Bergson
  Paris

United Kingdom:
> British Institute of Radio Engineering
> London, England

United States:
> Institute for the Certification of
> Engineering Technicians
> 2029 K Street NW
> Washington, D.C. 20006

> Institute of Electrical and Electronic
> Engineers (IEEE)
> 345 East 47th Street
> New York, New York 10017

For a complete listing of national organizations and associations consult:

Minerva, Wissenschaftliche Gesellschaften. Berlin, Federal Republic of Germany: de Gruyter, 1972.

Principal Information Sources

GENERAL

Among general guides to the literature in the field are:

The Electronics Books List. London: United Trade Press, 1964.

Kyed, J. M., and Matarazzo, J. M. *Scientific, Technical and Engineering Societies Publications in Print, 1974–75.* New York: Bowker, 1974.

Lasworth, E. J. *Reference Sources in Science and Technology.* Metuchen, New Jersey: Scarecrow Press, 1972.

Moore, C. K., and Spencer, K. J. *Electronics: A Bibliographic Guide.* Vol. 2. New York: Plenum, 1966.

Randle, G. R. *A Guide to Literature and Other Data Sources in Electronic Industries.* Detroit: Gale Research, 1970.

Scientific and Technical Books in Print. New York: Bowker, 1972.

Introductory works to the field of electronics equipment installation and servicing include:

Belt, F. *Practical Electronic Servicing Techniques.* Blue Ridge Summit, Pennsylvania: TAB Books, 1970.

Daly, J., and Greenfield, R. A. *Basic Electronics.* New York: Macmillan, 1959.

Garland, D. J., and Stainer, F. *Modern Electronic Maintenance Principles.* Elmsford, New York: Pergamon Press, 1970.

Mandi, M. *Fundamentals of Electronics.* Englewood Cliffs, New Jersey: Prentice-Hall, 1960.

Shrader, R. L. *Electronic Fundamentals for Technicians.* New York: McGraw-Hill, 1972.

Stanley, J. *Introduction to Electronic Servicing for the Beginner.* Indianapolis, Indiana: H. W. Sams, 1963.

CURRENT BIBLIOGRAPHIES

Among the general bibliographical guides to vocational training and technology are:

Applied Science and Technology Index. New York: Wilson, 1913–.

BACIE Bibliography of Publications in the Field of Education and Training in Commerce and Industry. London: British Association for Commercial and Industrial Education, 1963–.

CIRF Abstracts: Ideas Drawn from the Current Writings on Vocational Training for Workers, Supervisors and Technicians. Geneva: International Vocational Training Information and Research Center/Centre international d'information et de recherche sur la formation professionnelle (CIRF), 1961–.

Abstracting and indexing services providing current information in the field include:

Bibliografia elettrotecnica: Rassegna mensile della stampa tecnica italiana e straniera. Rome: Bibliografia elettrotecnica, 1947–.

Denshi kogyo. Electronician. Tokyo: Komine denshi kogyo kabushiki kaisha, 1952–.

Electronic Technology. London: Iliffe Electrical Publications, 1923–.

Electrotechniek, Literatuuroverzicht. The Hague: Technisch documentatieen informatiecentrum voor de krijgsmacht, 1952–.

Engineering Index. New York: Engineering Index, Inc., 1884–. The most prominent index in engineering and related fields.

Solid State Abstracts. Cambridge, Massachusetts: Communications Corporation, 1960–.

PERIODICALS

Some important journals in the field are *AEG—Telefunken technische Mitteilungen* (FRG), *AEU: Archiv für Elektronik und Übertragungstechnik* (FRG), *American Vocational Journal, Archiv für Elektrotechnik* (FRG), *Electrical Times* (UK), *Electric Technology USSR* (UK), *Electronic Engineering* (UK), *Electronic Technician/Dealer* (US), *Electronics* (US), *Electronics and Power* (US), *Electronics Today International* (Australia), *Electron Technology* (Poland), *Electro-Technology* (US), *ETZ/Elektrotechnische Zeitschrift. Ausgabe B* (FRG), *Industrial Arts and Vocational Education* (US), *Industrial Education* (US), *Journal of Engineering Education* (US), *Mundo electrónico* (Spain), *Occupational Outlook Quarterly* (US), *Popular Electronics* (US), *Practical Electronics* (UK), *Radio and Electronic Engineer* (UK), *Radio Electronics* (UK), *School Shop* (US).

For a listing of additional periodicals in the field see:

Brown, P., and Stratton, G. B. *World List of*

Scientific Periodicals Published in the Years 1900–1960. (3 vols.) London: Butterworth, 1963–1965.

Microelectronics Yearbook. London: Shaw, 1970.

Technical Journals for Industry. The Hague: International Federation for Industry, 1967–.

ENCYCLOPEDIAS, DICTIONARIES, HANDBOOKS

Clason, W. E. *Elsevier's Electrotechnical Dictionary in Six Languages: English/American, French, Spanish, Italian, Dutch, and German.* Amsterdam: Elsevier, 1965.

Electronic and Radio Engineering, International Student Edition. New York: McGraw-Hill, 1964.

Electronic Trouble Shooting: A Manual for Engineers and Technicians. Reston, Virginia: Reston Publishing, 1973.

Elsevier's Dictionary of Amplifications, Modulation, Reception and Transmission in Six Languages: English/American, French, Spanish, Italian, Dutch, and German. Amsterdam: Elsevier, 1960.

Elsevier's Dictionary of Television, Radar and Antennas in Six Languages: English/American, French, Spanish, Italian, Dutch, and German. Amsterdam: Elsevier, 1955.

Gleicher, N. *Dictionary of Electronics.* New York: Funk & Wagnalls, 1969.

Herrington, D., and Meacham, S. *Handbook of Electronic Tables and Formulas.* (2nd ed.) Indianapolis, Indiana: H. W. Sams, 1962. Includes service and installation data, electronic formulas and laws, symbols and codes, and mathematic tables and formulas.

Hope, W. E. *Encyclopedia of Careers and Profession Guidance.* Chicago: Ferguson, 1972. Deals with career possibilities.

Manlet, H. P., and Gorder, L. O. *Drake's Encyclopedia of Radio and Electronics; A Reference and Instruction Book.* (14th ed.) Chicago: Drake, 1958.

Marton, L. *Advances in Electronics.* (15 vols.) New York: Academic Press, 1948–1961.

Neidhardt, P. *Television Engineering and Television Electronics Technical Dictionary.* Elmsford, New York: Pergamon Press, 1964.

DIRECTORIES

Dent, H. C. *The Yearbook of Technical Education and Careers in Industry.* London: Black, 1957–.

Gleazer, E. J. *American Junior Colleges.* (8th ed.) Washington, D.C.: American Council on Education, 1971.

Keefe, J. *Electronics as a Profession: Aim for a Job as an Electrical Technician.* New York: Richards Rosen Press, 1967. A guide to careers in electronics.

Russell, M. M. *The College Blue Book: Occupational Education.* New York: Macmillan, 1973. Includes information on occupational schools, technical programs, courses, and careers in the United States.

Technical Education Yearbook. Ann Arbor, Michigan: Prakken, 1963–. Published annually; a multipurpose directory to United States institutions offering technician training in the engineering sciences; also lists professional organizations concerned with technical training and recent bibliographies.

The World Of Learning. London: Europa, 1947–. Published annually; lists universities, colleges, and institutions throughout the world.

ELECTRONICS ENGINEERING
See Electrical and Electronics Engineering (field of study).

ELITISM IN HIGHER EDUCATION
See Mass Higher Education.

EL SALVADOR, REPUBLIC OF

Population: 3,864,000 (mid 1973 estimate). Student enrollment in primary school: 616,759; secondary school (academic, vocational, technical): 154,770; higher education: 24,498. Language of instruction: Spanish. Academic calendar: February to October. Percentage of gross national product (GNP) expended on all education: 3.26%; higher education: .97%. [Except where otherwise indicated, figures are for 1974.]

On September 15, 1821, the Central American countries declared their independence from Spain. On February 2, 1841, El Salvador left the Central American Federation and became a sovereign independent state. Education has developed slowly in El Salvador. During the first half of the nineteenth century, there were only a few church-related schools, and access to education was limited. When the National University, now the University of El Salvador, was established by legislative decree in the first month of the country's independence, it included in its structure a secondary school, *Colegio de la asunción*, but the educational base was not broadened.

During the early years of the National University, religious influence dominated. The church had almost complete control of the administration; the first presidents were priests; and the curriculum focused on theology and canon law. It was not until 1871, when a decree liberalized teaching, that church influence on the university began to wane; and in 1885, when theological studies were abolished, a more secular and professional pattern became established at the university. Also in 1885 the National Institute, an academic secondary school, was founded. For a number of years, this school was the only public high school in El Salvador, although two others were founded by the end of the century.

In the 1940s there was a strong movement for educational reassessment and reform. The first reforms concentrated on primary education, but steps were also taken to revamp secondary schooling; and the basic pattern of three years of general study followed by academic or vocational programs was initiated at that time. In the 1950s reform attention shifted toward higher education. In 1952 the Higher Normal School for the training of secondary school staff was founded; and in 1965 a private university, José Simeón Cañas, was established after legislation had been passed regulating new universities.

Legal Basis of Educational System

Nine articles in the 1950 constitution of El Salvador pertain to education. According to these articles, it is the responsibility of the state to organize an educational system that will develop a useful and literate citizenry. The articles establish that participation in this system is a right and cannot be denied to anyone for social, racial, or political reasons (Art. 202); that basic education will be free (Art. 199); and that the state will be responsible for educating teachers (Art. 200). The constitution also recognizes the University of El Salvador as an autonomous institution in regard to teaching, administration, and finances and assures that the state will contribute toward maintaining the university (Art. 205).

When the constitution was adopted, the National University was the only university in the country. In March 1965 a law was passed making possible the establishment of private universities, which were given the same freedom and rights as the University of El Salvador (with the exception of the right to validate professional degrees by foreign universities). The new universities have to submit their bylaws for legal approval before opening their doors.

Types of Institutions

El Salvador offers higher education through its two universities, the University of El Salvador and the private José Simeón Cañas University. Both offer education in dentistry, medicine, pharmacy, engineering, law, economics, agronomical sciences, and humanities.

Nonuniversity higher education is available in the Higher Normal School and the School of Social Work. Postsecondary education is also available at the nursing school, the military school, and the agronomical school; and there are also part-time and short courses that lead to diplomas in higher management and banking.

The Central American Technological Institute, which receives technical aid and supervision from the British government, is another higher education institution. Founded in 1969, it is rapidly expanding its facilities and has an enrollment of nearly one thousand students.

Relationship with Secondary Education

There is no compulsory education in the country, but the constitution establishes an obligation that at least primary education, grades 1 through 6, should be made available to all. The primary school age is seven to fourteen, and the chief problem is the number of dropouts. The secondary school graduation age varies between seventeen and twenty, and the program ordinarily takes three years.

At the secondary school level tracking toward specialties allows students to receive specific training in their fields of interest. Academic programs; normal schools; commercial schools; schools of nursing, agriculture, social service, and fine arts; an institute of graphic arts; and technical schools are all available to secondary-level students. The title awarded at the end of secondary level is *bachiller,* followed by the name of the chosen specialty, such as arts, industry, agriculture, accounting, health, academic, or pedagogy. Graduates with the *bachillerato* certificate are eligible for higher education at the university or the other higher education institutions. The University of El Salvador receives nearly 90 percent of the secondary school graduates who continue into higher education.

Administration and Control

Although the University of El Salvador is dependent on the Ministry of Education in budgetary matters, it is otherwise completely autonomous and has full independence in curriculum and administrative affairs. A general university assembly—composed of two professors, two students, and two representatives of each school of the university—elects the rector (the chief administrator of the university), the vice-rector, deans, vice-deans, and the legal officer of the university. The main administrative power is vested in the higher university council, composed of the rector, the legal officer, the secretary general, deans, a representative of the professors of each school, and a representative of the students of each school. Each faculty has an autonomous internal government, which means that there are eight independent bodies loosely held by a central unit. The higher council must have the recommendations of the faculties on curriculum, budget, and student enrollment capacity before acting on such matters. Each faculty names its administrative personnel and teaching staff.

The control of the private university is exercised through a rector and a strong board of directors, which has no student representation. A higher council exists, but there is no student representation on it either. The council is concerned with academic matters and has no authority in administrative affairs; its decisions are liable to veto by the board of directors. The faculties are not autonomous, and their councils serve to advise the dean on faculty matters.

The Higher Normal School and the School of Social Work are under control of the Ministry of Education.

Programs and Degrees

Studies at the two universities vary from three to six years. José Simeón Cañas University offers the title of *licenciado* and professional titles in several fields, including business administration, chemistry, economics, and electrical, industrial, and mechanical engineering. The engineering and business administration degrees require five years of study. The University of El Salvador has eight schools: agriculture, chemistry and pharmacy, dentistry, economics, engineering and architecture, humanities, law, and medicine. In addition, there are departments of biological sciences, physics, and mathematics. There are seventy different programs that offer training in the traditional studies and on a technical level to provide trained personnel for all necessary activities. Thus, there are programs to train technicians in interior decoration, anesthesiology, X-ray technology, and physiotherapy, as well as programs to train teachers for secondary education in the basic sciences.

In general, these careers require three years of study, although training for a dental assistant requires only one and a half years, which is the shortest length of study at the university. The period of study varies between the universities and can be easily modified by a university board; for example, study of economics requires five years in one university and four and a half in another. The university boards have complete control over academic activities, titles, programs, standards, and accreditation of studies. The state university is the only one that can authorize foreign titles through its higher board.

The nonuniversity institutions offer three-year programs.

Financing and Student Financial Aid

With the exception of the military school and private universities, all higher education is financed by the Ministry of Education. Thus, the government finances about 80 percent of the higher education in the country. The rest comes from tuition and some contributions from the governments of other countries. Private contributions exist but are minimal.

Nursing school is free, and approximately 25 percent of the university students also receive free education. In addition, from 8 to 10 percent of the students are aided through small monthly allowances. The academic load is limited to a minimum of three subjects, and passing grades are required to retain a scholarship.

There is no work requirement or any other obligation for this type of aid. A fund called *Educrédito* offers loans at very low interest rates with adequate periods of grace to finance education in El Salvador or abroad. Actually, these loans are offered for a twelve-year period, with payments on capital beginning after the seventh year.

Student Social Background and Access to Higher Education

El Salvador is in a period of educational explosion, and the demand for all types of education is rapidly increasing. Higher education is available to all who have completed secondary education. About twelve thousand students are finishing secondary education yearly, and about 80 to 85 percent of them will continue into higher education. There is no distinction as to social background, age, or sex. El Salvador has no race problems. About 20 percent of university students are women.

Each faculty has a student association that attends to the problems of its students; the associations assist in academic matters, student recreation, management of university cafeterias, and fund raising, and also provide low-cost services. A general student association amalgamates all the different societies of the university and attempts to influence the decisions of the governing bodies through student representatives and other types of pressure. The student association is politically active at the national level and is sometimes aided by national political parties. Traditionally, students have been in opposition to the government and attack it through publications or demonstrations.

Teaching Staff

There are about two thousand persons engaged in teaching in the different areas of higher education. Most are university graduates; some are students in the last two years of study, who work as laboratory assistants and provide other auxiliary functions. The great majority of teaching staff have a doctor's degree in medicine, dentistry, or pharmacy and a *licenciatura* degree in law, economics, or humanities. There are six holders of a Ph.D. and seventy-five master's degree holders on the teaching staff of the University of El Salvador. All have been trained in European or United States universities, since El Salvador offers no master's degree or Ph.D. training programs. Selection of faculty is based mainly on curriculum requirements. Promotions are regulated by the bylaws of the universities in El Salvador.

Research Activities

Research projects are limited, mainly because available funds are used to expand physical facilities and meet the salaries of personnel who service the increasing student body. Some grants are obtained from international organizations such as the Organization of American States, the Food and Agriculture Organization, and UNESCO. Individual professors, backed by the board of directors of their respective schools may apply for a grant from one of these international organizations. Projects are developed by the University of El Salvador, sometimes in collaboration with other institutions. Some basic research, especially in biological or agricultural conditions characteristic to El Salvador, is conducted in collaboration with government institutions. Industries or government institutions may request research on a specific matter, and a team of experts on the subject will then form in order to work on the problem—for instance, tests on building materials, chemical analyses, and quality control. Private industry is charged for the services, paying either in currency or donations of equipment needed for the project; this equipment then becomes permanent property of the university. At present most interest in research has been shown by the schools of agronomical sciences, biology, and chemistry.

Generally, there has been no organized or central direction for the research being conducted. An Institute for Central Research, however, is in the process of being established at the University of El Salvador and should provide the direction that is now lacking.

Current Problems and Trends

Thirty-five percent of the yearly budget of El Salvador is actually dedicated to education, and a broader share will be needed in the future, especially now that the educational reforms started at primary school level some years ago are producing high school graduates in large numbers. Projections indicate an increase in the student body of about 20 percent per year, doubling the number of students going into higher education every five years. A training program aimed at the primary and secondary level, presented by educational television and sponsored by the Ministry of Education, is expected to produce even more secondary school graduates. However, the actual facilities for higher education in El Salvador have reached their limit; and with the great immediate demand, merely expanding the present physical facilities will not solve the problem. Instead, radical changes will have to be made in the current educational system. Learning programs using audiovisual aids or closed-circuit television, computerized training, and other methods of training to handle efficiently the large demand for higher education without lowering its standards are immediate needs in the mid 1970s.

The structure of the University of El Salvador is so flexible that programs and new careers based on demand and needs can easily be incorporated. Orientation programs are carried on by the Ministry of Education through televised programs in the National Educational Television System. These programs try to persuade high school graduates to enter higher education fields that are most important for the nation's needs and that will provide them with employable skills after graduation. Higher education institutions, however, provide absolute freedom of choice and respect the decision of the students. Medicine used to be the subject in greatest demand, but in the mid 1970s more students are entering the field of business administration; engineering, mainly industrial and electrical engineering, is in second place. The trend seems to parallel the demand created by the need for trained personnel in business and industry. Thus, enrollment is stimulated by the law of demand and is influenced by the constant newspaper advertisements calling for trained personnel.

CARLOS ALFARO CASTILLO

Bibliography

Censo universitario latinoamericano, 1971. Mexico City: Secretaría general, 1974.

LaBelle, J. *Education and Development.* Los Angeles: University of California Press, 1972.

Laguardia, J. M. *Legislación universitaria de América latina.* Mexico City: Universidad nacional autónoma de México, 1973.

Parker, F. *The Central American Republics.* London: Oxford University Press, 1964.

Primera conferencia latinoamericana sobre planeamiento universitario. Mexico City: Secretaría general, 1970.

Socio-Economic Progress in Latin America 1967.

Washington, D.C.: Inter-American Development Bank, 1968.

Waggoner, G., and Waggoner, B. A. *Education in Central America.* Lawrence: University Press of Kansas, 1971.

West, R. C., and Augelli, J. P. *Middle America: Its Lands and Peoples.* Englewood Cliffs, New Jersey: Prentice-Hall, 1966.

See also: Archives: Mediterranean, the Vatican, and Latin America, National Archives of; Central America: Regional Analysis.

EMOTIONALLY DISTURBED AND HIGHER EDUCATION

See Handicapped, Higher Education for the Physically.

EMPLOYMENT ABROAD

See Exchange, International: Student Employment Abroad.

ENDOWMENTS

See Financial Affairs: Investments.

ENGINEERING (Field of Study)

The Engineers' Council for Professional Development has defined engineering as "the profession in which a knowledge of the mathematical and natural sciences gained by study, experience, and practice is applied with judgment to develop ways to utilize the materials and forces of nature, economically, for the benefit of mankind." Engineers find useful applications for abstract scientific principles. Originally, engineering served military purposes—constructing war machines and building roads and fortifications. By the middle of the eighteenth century, however, engineering concerned itself with nonmilitary undertakings as well.

The first engineering specialty to develop was civil engineering; its emphasis on the construction of roads, bridges, dams, and water and wastewater treatment systems for nonmilitary (civil) purposes was a natural outgrowth of the earlier military activity. The first professional school to offer formal programs in engineering was the French *Ecole nationale des ponts et chaussées* (1747). By the nineteenth century the United States Military Academy at West Point was established (1802), the Karlsruhe Polytechnic School in Germany opened (1825), and the first civil engineering program was offered in Russia (1832). In time a number of additional branches in the engineering field were recognized. Among these were mechanical engineering, which is concerned with the design and operation of machines and energy conversion devices; and mining engineering, which deals mainly with the production of coal and minerals. Subsequent specialization included electrical engineering, which involves the design of electrical and electronic equipment and devices; chemical engineering, which is concerned primarily with the chemical processes by which materials undergo changes in composition and the related manufacturing processes; and industrial engineering, which deals with the means and methods of production of goods and services.

Within the broad field of engineering, which is related to many aspects of human activities, there are more than two dozen major specializations. The distinctions between them are not always obvious, especially when the differences in the economy or state of development of various countries as well as the differences in universities within a country are taken into account. To those engineering disciplines already mentioned can be added the following programs: agricultural engineering, which deals with the production of food; aeronautical (or aerospace) engineering, which deals with air transportation (and the space program); metallurgical engineering, which relates to metals, alloys, and their production; nuclear engineering, which is involved in the design and construction of nuclear power plants and their fuel-processing systems; biomedical engineering, which concerns the design of medical devices, equipment, and systems; ceramic engineering, which deals with the processing of nonmetallic minerals; ocean engineering, which concerns ocean dynamics and the design of offshore and ocean structures; and petroleum engineering, which deals with the production of oil and its related industry. Many of these programs, and others that are related but have different titles, are basically modifications of the more common and classical mechanical, chemical, electrical, or civil engineering curricula.

Engineering education for these specialties includes instruction and training in engineering design based on mathematics, the sciences, and the engineering sciences, and the application of these disciplines to produce practical solutions for given problems. The university-level programs include courses in mathematics, physics, chemistry, applied mechanics, thermodynamics, electrical science, materials, engineering design, economics, and computer programing. In the United States, study of the social sciences and humanities is included at the university level and is considered important in providing the background necessary to recognize the social implications of engineering solutions to technical problems involving, for example, pollution, housing, transportation, or energy. Outside of the United States the engineering curriculum is more specialized, emphasizing mainly technical areas.

In addition to the professional *engineer,* who usually possesses the minimum of a university degree, and the *technician,* who usually has a two-year certificate or diploma, there has emerged in the United States the *technologist.* As contrasted with engineering, *engineering technology* is defined as that part of the technological field which requires the application of scientific and engineering principles, combined with technical skills, in support of engineering activities. The technologist generally works under the supervision of an engineer, while the technician works under the supervision

of an engineer or a technologist. Engineering technology programs leading to a first university degree (the Bachelor of Science degree) are increasing in number.

The modern trend in engineering and technical education is toward less rigid structuring and greater flexibility in programs. The student is given a greater choice of electives and has more control over his program, so that he can develop his specific interests and career objectives. In some cases programs can be individualized. The fact that interdisciplinary curricula are becoming common is indicative of the growing interaction between the social and the technical sciences.

Engineering education has adapted well to the work-study plan. Although it has different names in different countries (*cooperative education* in the United States, *sandwich plan* in England), the plan consists of alternating periods of study with periods of work in related industries and requires an additional year to obtain a degree. The number of schools offering such programs has increased each year. In addition, refresher courses and adult education programs (continuing education) keep practicing engineers up to date on current developments in their field and prepare them for greater responsibilities or for work in newly developing areas. Such courses may or may not lead to an advanced degree.

Practically all countries have educational programs for training technical personnel. Several countries have university-level programs for their nationals and for students from developing countries or from countries that lack the training facilities and staff necessary for the more advanced programs. The engineering education programs available in the 1970s in Europe, the Soviet Union, and the United States often have students enrolled from many nations. It is not uncommon to find, for example, 25 percent of the engineering students in a large North American university from foreign countries. In this sense, engineering education at the university level is international in character. Another indication of the international character of engineering is the introduction of subject matter from a particular country into programs offered in other parts of the world. This is often brought about as a result of various international exchange plans for students and faculty.

The terms used to designate the various levels of engineering degrees differ from country to country. At the subprofessional or technician level, students usually earn the diploma or certificate at about nineteen or twenty years of age. This first degree is called a *diploma* in Italy and India, a *perito* in Spain, and the *associate degree* in the United States. The first professional degree, usually earned by students of twenty-two or twenty-three years of age, is the bachelor's degree in the United States, Canada, the United Kingdom, Israel, Ireland, and the People's Republic of China. In Austria, Belgium, Finland, Norway, Sweden, Denmark, the Federal Republic of Germany, the Soviet Union, Spain, Switzerland, and South America, the first degree is called *engineer*. The *Diploma engineer* in Austria, Finland, the Federal Republic of Germany, and Switzerland is usually a more advanced degree than the bachelor's degree and is earned at about twenty-three or twenty-four years of age; it is the first professional degree for engineering in France. At the graduate (postbaccalaureate) level, the United States, the United Kingdom, Israel, Canada, Japan, India, and Ireland give the master's degree (similar to the diploma engineer); Denmark grants the *licenciate teknikum ingeniør*, and Italy the *laurea*. Students usually receive these degrees around the age of twenty-four. Most European countries (including the United Kingdom), Japan, India, the USSR, and the United States grant the doctorate and call it that; it is usually earned at the age of twenty-six or twenty-seven. The People's Republic of China has no formal postgraduate program. The estimate of the student's age associated with all of these programs assumes, of course, that the student successfully continues his

technical education uninterrupted through completion of the particular degree program. Whether or not the student has a part-time research or teaching position, a situation quite common in the United States, also influences the age at which the various degrees are received. Interruptions occur in the People's Republic of China, where there is a two-year work period between high school and college; and in Israel, where four years of military service are required after high school graduation. The internationalization of engineering and engineering education is well illustrated by the similarity found in the engineering programs and degrees throughout the world.

MELVIN MARK

Levels and Programs of Study

Programs in engineering generally require as a minimum prerequisite a secondary education, although in some cases mature students with relevant work experience may be admitted with lower educational qualifications, and lead to the following awards: certificate or diploma, Bachelor of Science or Engineering, Master of Science or Engineering, the Ph.D. or Doctor of Engineering, or their equivalents. Programs deal with fundamental and advanced aspects of the theory and application of one or more branches of engineering science and consist of lectures, experimental techniques, laboratory and fieldwork, and, on advanced levels, research methods and experimental techniques.

Programs that lead to an award not equivalent to a first university degree stress the practical and technological aspects of engineering technology, with little time spent on the more general and theoretical principles involved. They are designed to prepare students for careers as relatively high-level technicians in various branches of engineering and include practical demonstrations, fieldwork, and shop work (with periods of employment). Full- or part-time programs are often of relatively short duration (less than one year) and include retraining, refresher, and sandwich courses. They are usually conducted in institutions of technology or technical colleges, but many different kinds of agencies (including professional societies, employers' associations, employers, government agencies, including the armed forces, and research institutes) also sponsor such programs. Principal course content usually includes land surveying (including photogrammetry), engineering drafting and design, chemical engineering technology (including materials technology), industrial engineering technology (including petroleum and gas-extraction technology), metallurgical engineering technology, mining engineering technology, mechanical engineering technology (including technology in the design and development of space vehicles, aeronautical engineering technology, and marine engineering technology), and agricultural and forestry engineering technology.

Programs leading to the first university degree stress the theoretical and scientific principles of engineering subjects as well as the mastery of experimental techniques as a basis for research and investigation. Programs are generally full time, although part-time programs (usually refresher courses) are also available, and are conducted in universities and technical colleges or institutes through regular lectures, seminars, laboratory periods, and fieldwork. Some courses are provided through correspondence or through broadcasts (radio or television). Principal course content includes chemical engineering (for example, physical chemistry, chemical process control, polymer technique, and electrochemistry); civil engineering (for example, structural engineering, highway engineering, and hydraulic engineering); electrical and electronics engineering; industrial engineering (for example, organization and methods engineering and production planning); metallurgical engineering (that is, extractive metallurgy); mining engineering; mechanical engineering (including mechanical, marine, aeronautical, and automotive engineering and

naval architecture); and agricultural and forestry engineering.

In programs that lead to a postgraduate university degree, emphasis is given to the theoretical principles of the subjects included in the programs. Original work, as substantiated by the presentation and defense of a scholarly thesis or dissertation, is usually an important element. Programs at this level are usually restricted to one specialized area within one of the engineering branches. Generally, the research content of the program is paramount. In the main, these programs are full time, although advanced students often teach part time or supervise less advanced students in laboratories or fieldwork. Some examples of part-time programs are refresher courses and special courses designed to introduce new methods and techniques to those already employed in their specialties. Advanced degree programs usually include chemical engineering (the design and operation of industrial chemical processes; the preparation, manipulation, and transformation of materials; and the design, construction, and economic operation of equipment for carrying out industrial chemical processes); civil engineering (the design and construction of public works; includes structural engineering, railway engineering, highway engineering, hydraulic engineering, municipal engineering, and sanitary engineering); electrical and electronics engineering (the theory and practice of the generation, transmission, and utilization of electrical energy as well as the design, manufacture, and assembly of electronic circuitry for many purposes); industrial engineering (the principles and techniques of organizing and conducting industrial processes involving all factors of production); metallurgical engineering (extractive metallurgy); mining engineering (the principles and practices of extracting and mechanically treating ores); mechanical engineering (the principles and practices of designing, constructing, and using apparatus that generates, transmits, and utilizes power;

includes marine, aeronautical, and automotive engineering and naval architecture); and other engineering specialties,
such as engineering science, engineering
mathematics, and engineering physics.

[This section was based on UNESCO's
*International Standard Classification of Edu-
cation (ISCED): Three Stage Classification
System, 1974* (Paris: UNESCO, 1974).]

Major International and National Organizations

INTERNATIONAL

Association for Engineering Education in
  Southeast Asia
College of Engineering
University of the Philippines
Diliman, Quezon City, Philippines

Conference of Engineering Institutes of the
  British Commonwealth
% Institution of Electrical Engineers
Savoy Place
London WC2, England

European Federation of National Associations
  of Engineers
Fédération européenne d'associations
  nationales d'ingénieurs (FEANI)
1 boulevard Malesherbes
Paris, France

European Society for Engineering Education
47 rue de Trèves
1040 Brussels, Belgium

International Federation of Consulting
  Engineers
Fédération internationale des ingénieurs
  conseils
Javastraat 44
The Hague, Netherlands

Pan American Federation of Engineering
  Societies
Unión panamericana de asociaciones de
  ingenieros (UNPADI)
Torre Dorada 11, Piso
Insurjentes Sur 753
Mexico 18, D.F.

United Nations Educational, Scientific and
  Cultural Organization (UNESCO)
Division of Technological Education and
  Research
place de Fontenoy
75 Paris 7e, France

Union of International Engineering
  Organizations
62 rue de Courcelles
Paris, France

World Federation of Engineering
  Organizations
Savoy Place
London WC2, England

For a more complete listing of organizations see:

International Engineering Directory. Washington,
  D.C.: Consulting Engineers Council, 1966.
Yearbook of International Organizations. Brussels:
  Union of International Associations, 1974.

NATIONAL

Australia:
  Institution of Engineering, Australia
  Science House
  Gloucester and Essex Streets
  Sydney, New South Wales

Brazil:
  Federação brasileira de associações de
    engenheiros
  Caixa 1229
  Rio de Janeiro

Canada:
  Engineering Institute of Canada
  2050 Mansfield Street
  Montreal 2, Quebec

Denmark:
  Dansk ingeniorforening
  Ingeniorhuset, Vester Farimagsgade 31
  1606 Copenhagen V

Federal Republic of Germany:
  Verein deutscher Ingenieure
  Graf-Recke-Strasse 84
  4 Düsseldorf

India:
  Indian Society for Technical Education
  % Indian Institute of Technology
  Hauz Khas, New Delhi 29

Israel:
  Association of Engineers and Architects
    in Israel
  200 Dizengoff Road
  Engineers Instítute
  Tel Aviv

Japan:
  Nihon kogakkai
  11, 1-chome, Sakuma-cho, Kanda
  Chiyoda-ku, Tokyo

Mexico:
  Association of Faculties and Schools of
    Engineering
  Director de la Escuela de ingeniería civil
  Universidad iberoamericana
  Cerro de las Torres 395
  Mexico 21, D.F.

Switzerland:
  Schweizerische Ing. und Architekten
    Verein
  Beethovenstrasse 1
  8022 Zurich

United Kingdom:
  Institution of British Engineering
  Windsor House
  46 Victoria Street
  London SW1, England

United States:
  American Society for Engineering
    Education
  1 Dupont Circle
  Washington, D.C. 20036

  Engineers Joint Council
  345 East 47th Street
  New York, New York 10017

See the following for additional listings:

Directory of Engineering Societies and Related Organizations. New York: Engineers Joint Council, 1974. Provides a comprehensive listing of United States and Canadian national organizations as well as fifteen international organizations.

Kyed, J. M., and Matarazzo, J. M. *Scientific, Technical and Engineering Societies Publications in Print 1974–75.* New York: Bowker, 1974. Provides a listing of engineering societies and their publications.

Minerva, Wissenschaftliche Gesellschaften. Berlin, Federal Republic of Germany: de Gruyter, 1972. Provides a complete listing of national organizations throughout the world.

Principal Information Sources

GENERAL

There are many guides to the literature of engineering. A good introductory work which includes bibliographies, guides to bibliographies, encyclopedias, and handbooks is:

Parson, S. A. *How to Find Out About Engineering.* Oxford, England: Pergamon Press, 1972.

Other important reference sources for the fields of engineering and engineering technology include:

Grogan, D. *Science and Technology: An Introduction to the Literature.* (2nd ed.) Hamden, Connecticut: Linnet Books, 1973.

A Guide to the World's Abstracting and Indexing Services in Science and Technology. Washington, D.C.: National Federation of Science Abstracting and Indexing Services, 1963.

Herner, S. *A Brief Guide to Sources of Science and Technology Information.* Washington, D.C.: Information Resources Press, 1970.

Jenkins, F. B. *Science Reference Sources.* (5th ed.) Cambridge, Massachusetts: MIT Press, 1969. Contains a section on engineering sciences, which covers guides to the literature, indexes, dictionaries, encyclopedias, handbooks, and histories.

Lasworth, E. J. *Reference Sources in Science and Technology.* Metuchen, New Jersey: Scarecrow Press, 1972.

Malinowsky, H. R. *Science and Engineering Reference Sources: A Guide for Students and Librarians.* Rochester, New York: Libraries Unlimited, 1967.

Owen, D. B., and Hanchey, M. M. *Abstracts and Indexes in Science and Technology: A Descriptive Guide.* Metuchen, New Jersey: Scarecrow Press, 1974. Includes general science reference sources as well as a section on engineering and technology.

Parke, N. G. *Guide to the Literature of Math and Physics, Including Related Works on Engineering Science.* (2nd ed.) New York: McGraw-Hill, 1958.

Roberts, E. G. *The Literature of Science and Engineering.* (2nd ed.) Atlanta: Georgia Institute of Technology, School of Information Science, 1969.

A Selective Bibliography in Science and Engineering. Boston: Hall, 1964.

Sternberg, V. A. *How to Locate Technical Information.* Englewood Cliffs, New Jersey: Prentice-Hall, 1964.

World Guide to Science Information and Documentation Services. Paris: UNESCO, 1965.

The following are guides to engineering sources in various countries or regions:

A Guide to the Scientific and Technical Literature of Eastern Europe. Washington, D.C.: National Science Foundation, 1962.

Macreary, S. W. *Guide to Science and Technology in the U.K.: A Reference Guide to Science and Technology in Great Britain and Northern Ireland.* Guernsey, Channel Islands: Francis Hodgson, 1971.

Maichel, K. *Guide to Russian Reference Books.* Vol. 5: *Science, Technology, and Medicine.* Stanford, California: Hoover Institution, 1967. Includes a section on engineering fields.

Skevington, D. *Guide to Science and Technology in the U.S.A.: A Reference Guide to Science and Technology in the U.S.A.* Guernsey, Channel Islands: Francis Hodgson, 1971.

White, S. (Ed.) *Guide to Science and Technology in the USSR: A Reference Guide to Science and Technology in the Soviet Union.* Guernsey, Channel Islands: Francis Hodgson, 1971.

Williams, C. H. *Guide to European Sources of Technical Information.* (3rd ed.) Guernsey, Channel Islands: Francis Hodgson, 1970.

For a general introduction to the field of engineering see:

Beakley, G., and Chilton, E. G. *Design, Serving the Needs of Man.* New York: Macmillan, 1974.

Besanko, R., and Jenkins, T. *Engineering Science.* (2nd ed.) London: Oxford University Press, 1970.

Daitch, P. B. *Introduction to College Engineering.* Reading, Massachusetts: Addison-Wesley, 1973.

Glorioso, R. M., and Hill, F. S., Jr. *Introduction to Engineering.* Englewood Cliffs, New Jersey: Prentice-Hall, 1975.

Parsons, C. R. H., and Pick, J. *Engineering Technology: Foundations of Applied Engineering.* London: Sampson Low, Marston, 1966.

Titcomb, G. R. A. *Fundamentals of Engineering Science.* London: Hutchinson, 1970.

General historical overviews are provided by:

Armytage, W. H. G. *A Social History of Engineering.* (3rd ed.) London: Faber & Faber, 1970.

Davenport, W. H., and Rosenthal, D. *Engineering: Its Role and Function in Human Society.* Elmsford, New York: Pergamon Press, 1967.

Finch, J. K. *Engineering and Western Civilization.* New York: McGraw-Hill, 1951.

Kirby, R. S., and others. *Engineering in History.* New York: McGraw-Hill, 1956.

For a discussion of the various aspects of engineering education in different countries and regions see:

Bogomolov, A. I. *Comparability of Engineering Courses and Degrees: A Methodological Study.* Paris: UNESCO, 1974. A study of international equivalences of degrees and comparability of diplomas in engineering.

Christopherson, D. G. *The Engineer in the University.* London: English Universities Press, 1967.

The Continuing Education of Engineers/La formation continuée des ingénieurs. Proceedings of the FEANI-UNESCO Seminar, Helsinki, August 21–24, 1972. Paris: UNESCO, 1974.

Engineering Education and Europe. London: British Council, 1974.

Engineering Education in Russia. New York: McGraw-Hill, 1959.

La enseñanza de las ciencias y de la ingeniería en la América Latina. Washington, D.C.: Pan American Union. A series of national reports on science and engineering in Latin American countries.

Gould, J., and Smith, J. H. (Eds.) *The Teaching of the Social Sciences in Higher Technical Education.* Paris: UNESCO, 1968. An international discussion of programs in engineering and engineering technology.

Hall, N. A. (Ed.) *Brittanica Review of Developments in Engineering Education.* (Vol. 1.) Chicago: Encyclopaedia Brittanica, 1970. A discussion of engineering education developments in the United States.

Hutchings, D. *Engineering Science at the University.* (3rd ed.) Oxford, England: Blackwell, 1969.

International Symposium on the Role of Social Sciences and Humanities in Engineering Education. Paris: UNESCO, 1973.

Standards for Engineering Qualifications: A Comparative Study in Eighteen European Countries. Paris: UNESCO, 1975.

The Training of Professional Engineers. Fifth International Congress of Engineers, September 27–October 1, 1971. London: Institution of Civil Engineers, 1972.

CURRENT BIBLIOGRAPHIES

The oldest and most extensive abstracting service in its field is:

The Engineering Index: Transdisciplinary Index to the World's Engineering Developments. New York: Engineering Index, Inc., 1884–.

Other important bibliographical and abstracting services which provide sources of current information in the areas of engineering are:

Applied Science and Technology Index. New York: Wilson, 1958–.

Bibliography of Scientific Publications of South and Southeast Asia. New Delhi: Insdoc, National Physical Laboratory, 1955–.

British Technical Index. (Vol. 1.) London: Library Association, 1962–.

Bulletin signalétique. Paris: Centre national de la recherche scientifique, 1940–. There are many sections dealing with various aspects of engineering.

Communist China Scientific Abstracts: Engineering and Equipment. Washington, D.C.: U.S. Department of Commerce, 1966–.

Landuyt, M. M. *Bibliography of Engineering Abstracting Services.* New York: Special Libraries Association, 1955–. Covers the United States and Europe.

New Technical Books. New York: New York Public Library, 1915–. Includes bibliographical information and reviews of books in engineering fields.

Referativnyi zhurnal. Moscow: Akademiia nauk, SSSR, Institut nauchnoĭ informatsii, 1963–. Published monthly. There are many sections dealing with various branches of engineering.

USSR and East Europe Scientific Abstracts: Engineering and Equipment. Washington, D.C.: Joint Publications Research, 1973–.

Progress reports and yearbooks also provide useful information. For examples see:

Kempe's Engineering Yearbook. London: Morgan-Grampian, 1894–.

Recent Advances in Engineering Science. New York, London, and Paris: Gordon and Breach, 1967–.

PERIODICALS

Some of the many journals in the field of engineering are *Australasian Engineer* (Australia), *British Engineer, Consulting Engineer* (UK), *Engineering* (UK), *Engineering Education* (US), *Engineers' Digest* (UK), *European Engineering* (US), *Forschung im Ingenieurwesen* (FRG), *Ingénieur* (Canada), *Ingénieur et cadres de France, International Engineering Education News* (US), *International Journal of Engineering Science* (US and UK), *Professional Engineer* (US), *Technion* (Israel), *Technology and Culture* (US), *Technology Review* (US), *Technos* (US).

Guides to periodical literature in engineering include the following:

Abstracts of Selected Articles from Soviet Bloc and Mainland China Technical Journals. Series 4: *Engineering, Machinery, Equipment.* Washington, D.C.: Office of Technical Services, U.S. Department of Commerce, 1961–.

The Engineering Index. New York: Engineering Index, Inc., 1884–. Includes indexes to periodicals in the field.

Fowler, M. J. *Guides to Scientific Periodicals: Annotated Bibliography.* New York: Library Association, 1966.

Himmelsbach, C. J., and Brociner, G. F. *A Guide to Scientific and Technical Journals in Translation.* New York: Special Libraries Association, 1973.

Ulrich's International Periodicals Directory. New York: Bowker, biennial.

World List of Scientific Periodicals Published in the Years 1900–1960. (4th ed.) London: Butterworth, 1963–1965.

DICTIONARIES, ENCYCLOPEDIAS, HANDBOOKS

A comprehensive guide to dictionaries in the field:

Bibliography of Interlingual Scientific and Technical Dictionaries. (5th ed.) Paris: UNESCO, 1969. Lists approximately 2500 dictionaries in seventy-five languages.

The following dictionaries deal with engineering and engineering technology:

Beadle, J. D. *Glossary of Contemporary Engineering.* London: Macmillan, 1972. An English dictionary.

Freiberger, W. F. *The International Dictionary of Applied Mathematics.* New York: Van Nostrand, 1960. A polyglot dictionary.

Pitman's Technical Dictionary of Engineering and Industrial Science. (5 vols.) London: Pitman, 1928–1932. In seven languages.

Scharf, B. *Engineering and Its Language.* London: F. Muller, 1971.

Encyclopedias include:

Jones, F. D., and Schubert, P. B. *Engineering Encyclopedia.* New York: Industrial Press, 1963. A condensed encyclopedia and mechanical dictionary.

Lüger Lexikon der Technik. (17 vols.) Stuttgart, Federal Republic of Germany: Deutsche Verlags-Anstalt, 1960–.

McGraw-Hill Encyclopedia of Science and Technology. New York: McGraw-Hill, 1971. Contains entries on various aspects of engineering, with brief bibliographies.

Handbooks in the field of engineering include:

Eshbach, O. V. *Handbook of Engineering Fundamentals.* (2nd ed.) New York: Wiley, 1952.

Potter, J. H. *Handbook of the Engineering Sciences.* (2 vols.) New York: Van Nostrand, 1967.

Souders, M. *The Engineer's Companion: A Concise Handbook of Engineering Fundamentals.* New York: Wiley, 1966.

DIRECTORIES

Cass, J., and Birnbaum, M. *Comparative Guide to Engineering Programs.* New York: Harper & Row, 1972.

Davis, R. G. *Scientific Engineering and Technical Education in Mexico.* New York: Education and World Affairs (EWA), 1967. Includes graduate programs in engineering.

Deutscher Ingenieurschulführer. Berlin, Federal Republic of Germany: VDE-Verlag, annual. A directory of engineering schools and job opportunities in Germany.

Engineering College Research and Graduate Study. Washington, D.C.: American Society for Engineering Education, annual supplement to *Engineering Education.* Lists research and graduate programs available at institutions in the United States, Puerto Rico, and Canada.

Harvey, A. P. *The Directory of Scientific Directories.* New York: International Publishing Service, 1972. Includes engineering directories to countries throughout the world.

International Handbook of Universities and Other Institutions of Higher Education. (3rd ed.) Paris: UNESCO, 1965.

Peterson's Annual Guides to Graduate Study, 1976. Book 5: *Engineering and Applied Sciences.* Princeton, New Jersey: Peterson's Guides, 1975. Directory to United States institutions.

Reyes-Guerra, D. *Engineering Education in the United States: A Guide to Foreign Students.* New York: Institute of International Education, n.d.

RESEARCH CENTERS, INSTITUTES, INFORMATION CENTERS

Directory of Research Institutions and Laboratories in Japan. Tokyo: Japanese Society for the Promotion of Science, 1962–1964. Includes (3 vols. in 1) information on scientific and technical societies, research institutions and laboratories, and universities and colleges in Japan.

Directory of Selected Research Institutes in Eastern Europe. Prepared by Arthur D. Little, Inc. New York: Columbia University Press, 1967. A comprehensive guide to the scientific research institutes in six Eastern European countries (Bulgaria, Czechoslovakia, Hungary, Poland, Romania, and Yugoslavia).

Directory of Selected Scientific Institutions in Mainland China. Prepared by Surveys and Research Corp. Stanford, California: Hoover Institution, 1970.

Hilton, R. *The Scientific Institutions of Latin America with Special Reference to Their Organization and Information Facilities.* Stanford, California: California Institute of International Studies, 1970. Arranged by country, with additional chapters on international organizations concerned with science and science information in Latin America.

Minerva, Forschungsinstitute. Berlin, Federal Republic of Germany: de Gruyter, 1972. A comprehensive international listing of institutes and centers in the various fields of engineering.

World Guide to Science Information and Documentation Services/Guide mondiale des centres de documentation et d'information scientifique. Paris: UNESCO, 1965. See below for annotation.

World Guide to Technical Information and Documentation Services/Guide mondiale des centres de documentation et d'information technique. Paris: UNESCO, 1969. Companion volumes which list principal centers offering scientific and technical information and documentation services. Names and addresses of various centers and organizations worldwide, as well as descriptions of their activities, purposes, and publications, are included.

See also: Aeronautical and Astronautical Engineering; Agricultural Engineering; Bioengineering; Chemical Engineering; Civil Engineering; Drafting and Design; Electrical and Electronics Engineering; Industrial Engineering; Mechanical Engineering; Metallurgical Engineering and Materials Science; Mining Engineering; Nuclear Engineering; Petroleum Engineering; Surveying.

ENGLISH LANGUAGE CENTERS
See Exchange, International: Campus International Offices.

ENGLISH-SPEAKING UNION OF THE UNITED STATES

The English-Speaking Union of the United States (E-SU), founded in 1920, has a membership of approximately 35,000 in 76 branches throughout the country. E-SU is a nonprofit, tax-exempt organization, supported entirely by membership dues and contributions. The union is nonpartisan, nonpolitical, and nongovernmental.

The purposes of E-SU are to preserve and strengthen the existing friendly relations and respect for common traditions among the peoples of the United States, the United Kingdom, and other nations of the Commonwealth; to further universal understanding, mutual trust, and friendship through communication based on an expanded use of English as a common language; and to develop in the United States and among other English-speaking peoples an informed citizenry.

The program of exchanges, scholarships, and travel grants sponsored and administered by E-SU provides a constant flow of speakers, teachers, students, professional people, books, and information among the English-speaking peoples of the world. E-SU's Books-Across-the-Sea program sends selected American books to the United Kingdom, Australia, Canada, India, and New Zealand, and circulates loan collections of selected Commonwealth books among United States schools, colleges, libraries, and public affairs groups. In addition to the programs administered by the E-SU national headquarters, many E-SU branches sponsor and support their own scholarship and exchange programs for local students and teachers.

Every member receives a copy of the quarterly newsletter, *E-SU News,* as well as the annual report of the organization's activities. *English Around the World,* a twice-yearly survey of the use of the English language in non-English-speaking countries, is mailed to anyone on demand.

16 East 69th Street
New York, New York 10021 USA

ENROLLMENT
See Registrar.

ENROLLMENTS
See Mass Higher Education; Statistics in Higher Education.

ENTOMOLOGY (Field of Study)

Entomology is the study of insects, their interactions with other living organisms and plants, and ways to regulate insect species that affect man and his domestic animals and plants. According to some scientists, the nearly 1 million insect species that have been described may be less than 20 percent of the species actually living on earth today; thus, insects comprise at least 90 percent of all living animal species.

Until the early 1900s entomology was mostly a descriptive (taxonomic) science; but as man and insects began to compete for space and food, the science changed to include various economic practices. For example, in order to understand "pest" problems, the fields of insect physiology, morphology, and ecology became important. Natural control and biological control practices to offset insect losses became firmly established along with other control methods, both chemical and mechanical. Today, major efforts to manipulate insects to man's advantage are carried out through "pest management" or "integrated pest management" to obtain greatest economic control with least loss to the ecosystem under study.

While the basic science of entomology continues to expand in areas of behavior, genetics, physiological ecology, and bio-systematics, the most dramatic changes have been made in pest control procedures and attitudes. Pesticides have been at least partially supplanted by ingenious uses of natural phenomena to control pests; for example, parasitoids, predators, pathogens, pheromones (natural attractants), autocides (sexual sterility), hormones (natural chemicals in insects to keep them as subadults), and sound (both as attractants and repellents).

There are two main divisions of the entomological sciences: basic entomology (both the historical and modern aspects) and applied entomology. In addition, several other disciplinary fields are often, though not always, placed within entomology departments; for example, acarology, the study of mites; parasitology, the study of animal parasites; toxicology, the chemistry of pesticides; and ethology, the study of behavior.

The branches of basic entomology are (1) taxonomy or systematics (the study, description, classification, and evolution of insects), (2) morphology (the study of the form and structure of insects), (3) physiology (the study of insect functions and their relationships to life), (4) ecology (the study of insects in their environment).

The branches of applied entomology are (1) medical and veterinary entomology (the study and control of insects affecting man and higher animals), (2) agricultural entomology (the study and control of insects affecting agricultural crops), (3) urban entomology (the study and control of insects affecting man in the urban environment), (4) forest entomology (the study and control of insects affecting forest trees and the associated biotic ecosystem), (5) plant-insect virus-vector entomology (the study and control of vector insects and their associated plant pathogens), (6) biological and natural control (the study and use of natural organisms to regulate plant and animal pests), (7) insect pathology (the study and use of insect pathogens to regulate insect populations), (8) apiculture (the study of bee biology and honey production), (9) aquatic entomology (the study, control, and use of insects living in aquatic environments), (10) extension entomology (ways and means of communicating entomological science to laymen), (11) pest management or integrated control (the study and use of any and all pest control methods). Other applied fields are insect nutrition, biology of parasitoids, entomogeography, pollination ecology, insect-plant resistance, insect diversity, insect population ecology, numerical taxonomy, phylogenetics and cladistics, and insect genetics.

Sciences closely related to entomology include zoology, the study of all animals; agricultural sciences; botany, particularly in areas such as pollination ecology, plant pathology, biological control of weeds, and coevolutionary studies; medicine, a field related especially to parasitology and insect pathology; chemistry and biochemistry, related through chemical pesticides and through the biochemical aspects of feeding, reproduction, pheromone production, and biochemical coevolution of plants and insects; social biology, since some insects exhibit a very strong social structure; systems ecology; economics; and agronomics. Although entomology reflects many of the natural, social, and physical sciences, it has maintained its integrity since the early 1800s and greatly expanded since 1925.

Entomology began at least as early as 2600 B.C., when honey bees were used, according to a wall relief in an Egyptian temple. The Greek philosopher Aristotle (384–322 B.C.) attempted to classify the insects (which he called *entoma*) and to separate them from other animal groups. It was not until A.D. 1602, however, that the first substantial work on insects, *De Animalibus Insectis,* by the Italian naturalist Ulisse Aldrovandi (1522–1605), was published. The worldwide voyages and explorations between 1600 and 1750 brought European scientists thousands of new insect species, which caused problems of classification.

Carolus Linnaeus (1707–1778) established his system of binomial nomenclature, a classification scheme that has been followed ever since for all animals and plants, when he published his tenth edition of *Systema Naturae* in 1758.

The first handbooks and textbooks on entomology appeared in the early 1800s and included those of Hermann Burmeister, William Curtis, and John Westwood. Entomological societies were also established in England (1833), France (1832), and Germany (1837) during this period. Small informal classes in entomology were also started at this time in Europe. Around 1859, following the publications of Charles Darwin and Alfred Wallace on the theory of evolution, formal classes in entomology were established.

Education in entomology, like research, has changed with the needs of man. For example, although the field of pest management is not yet interdisciplinary, curricula including plant pathology, pathobiology, resource management, systems ecology, agronomy, forestry, parasitology, and biological control—along with the more classical fields of general entomology and insect taxonomy, physiology, and ecology—have been initiated at a number of universities. In some universities a new degree program in pest management at the B.S. and/or M.S. level has been established. A Ph.D. may eventually be awarded in this area. In addition, the field of soil biology (which necessarily includes the study of insects and mites that inhabit soils) is rising in popularity and may be offered as a new degree program. The rapidly expanding field of conservation of natural resources is an example of an interdisciplinary degree program in which entomology plays a significant part. Degrees at the B.S. and M.S. levels are being awarded at several institutions.

International education programs in entomology are few, but recently programs have been developed by the International Organization for Biological Control of Noxious Animals and Plants (headquartered in Switzerland) and by the Office of Assistance for International Development (headquartered in Washington, D.C.). The latter program is set up to train persons from developing nations in pest management. Other international organizations which strongly influence entomology education include the International Congress of Entomology, the World Health Organization, and the Association of Systematic Collections.

Although different countries and regions vary in the range and scope of courses in entomology, most universities attempt to cover the following areas: general entomology, insect classification, insect physiology and morphology, and some aspect of ecology (often only applied ecology); in addition to these more classical areas, most institutions offer one or more courses in applied entomology, such as agricultural entomology, forest entomology, biological control, or medical entomology.

The older and more established nations tend to have programs emphasizing both basic and applied entomology. Because of the urgent need for the newer nations to produce their own food and fiber, most of them emphasize only applied entomology. One serious problem is that, while most insect species are known and described even on a local level in most European countries, parts of North America, and Japan, most of the insect species in the newer nations of Africa and South America are not known well and are mainly undescribed. This dilemma results in both an educational and a research problem which needs the expertise of basic entomology.

Levels and Programs of Study

Programs in entomology generally require as a minimum educational prerequisite a secondary education and lead to the following degrees: bachelor's (B.Sc.), master's (M.Sc.), the doctorate (Ph.D.), or their equivalents. Programs consist of classroom, laboratory, and fieldwork and deal with the principles and practices of entomology.

Principal course content usually in-

cludes some of the following: general entomology, principles of systematics (plant and animal), plant pathology, field entomology (ecology), economic entomology or pest management, insect pathology, and biological control. On advanced levels, the following courses are often included: virology, parasitology, acarology, insect pathology, population ecology, systematic entomology, and evolutionary biology. Programs on advanced levels generally emphasize original research work as substantiated by the presentation and defense of a scholarly thesis or dissertation.

EVERT SCHLINGER

Major International and National Organizations

INTERNATIONAL

Commonwealth Institute of Entomology
58 Queen's Gate
London SW7 5JR, England

International Organization for Biological
Control of Noxious Animals and Plants
% Department of Entomology
Swiss Federal Institute of Technology
Universitätstrasse 2
8006 Zurich, Switzerland

Permanent Committee of the International
Congress of Entomology
% British Museum (Natural History)
Cromwell Road
London SW7, England

NATIONAL

Argentina:
Sociedad entomología argentina
Calle Maipú 267
Buenos Aires

Australia:
Australian Entomological Society
Department of Entomology
University of Queensland
St. Lucia, Brisbane

Austria:
Wiener entomologische Gesellschaft
Getreidemarkt 2
1010 Vienna

Belgium:
Société royale d'entomologie de Belgique
Institut royal des sciences naturelles de
Belgique
rue Rautier 31
1040 Brussels

Brazil:
Sociedade brasileira de entomologia
Caixa Postal 9063
São Paulo

Canada:
Entomological Society of Canada
1320 Carling Avenue
Ottawa, Ontario K1Z 7K9

Chile:
Sociedad chilena de entomología
Huérfanos 669, Casilla 4150
Santiago

Czechoslovakia:
Československé spolecnŏsti
entomologické
Vinitná 7
128 00 Prague

Denmark:
Entomologisk forening
Zoological Museum
2000 Copenhagen

Egypt:
Société entomologique d'Egypte
P.O. Box 340
Cairo

Federal Republic of Germany:
Deutsche entomologische Gesellschaft
Corrensplatz 1
1 Berlin 33

Finland:
Entomological Society of Finland
Pohj. Rautatiek 13
00100 Helsinki 10

France:
Société entomologique de France
45 rue de Buffon
Paris 5

Hungary:
Magyar rovartani társaság
Baross-utca 13
Budapest VIII

India:
Entomological Society of India
Division of Entomology
Indian Agricultural Research Institute
New Delhi 12

Italy:
Società entomologica italiana
via Brigata Liguria 9
16121 Genoa

Japan:
Entomological Society of Japan
Department of Entomology
National Institute of Health
Kamiosaki, Shinagawa-ku
Tokyo

Mexico:
Sociedad mexicana de entomología
Apartado 13312
Mexico, D.F.

Netherlands:
Nederlandse entomologische vereniging
Rijksmuseum van natuurlijke historie
Raamsteeg 2
Leiden

New Zealand:
New Zealand Entomological Society
Box 202
Wellington

Poland:
Polskie towarzystwo entomologiczne
Nowy Swiat 72
Warsaw

South Africa:
Entomological Society of Southern Africa
P.O. Box 103
Pretoria

United Kingdom:
Royal Entomological Society
41 Queen's Gate
London SW7, England

United States:
Entomological Society of America
4603 Calvert Road
College Park, Maryland 20740

For a worldwide listing of national organizations in entomology see:

Sabrosky, C. W. "Entomological Societies." *Bulletin of the Entomological Society of America,* 1956, *2*(4), 1–22.

Principal Information Sources

GENERAL

Bonnet, P. *Bibliographia Araneorum.* (3 vols.) Toulouse, France: The author, 1945–1961.

Bush, E. A. R. *Agriculture: A Bibliographic Guide.* (2 vols.) London: Macdonald, 1974.

Chamberlin, W. J. *Entomological Nomenclature and Literature.* (3rd ed., rev. and enl.) Westport, Connecticut: Greenwood Press, 1970.

Hammock, G. H. *The Serial Literature of Entomology.* College Park, Maryland: Entomological Society of America, 1970.

Horn, W., and Schenkling, S. *Index Literaturae Entomologicae.* (4 vols.) Berlin-Dahlem, Federal Republic of Germany: Dr. Horn, 1928–1929.

Selected List of American Agricultural Books in Print and Current Periodicals. Beltsville, Maryland: National Agricultural Library, 1975. Includes a section on entomology.

Introductions to the field include:

Avidov, Z. *Studies in Agricultural Entomology and Plant Pathology*. Jerusalem: Magnes Press, Hebrew University, 1966. A collection of essays on entomological study.

Borror, D. J., and DeLong, D. M. *An Introduction to the Study of Insects*. (3rd ed.) New York: Holt, Rinehart and Winston, 1971.

Chapman, R. F. *The Insects: Structure and Function*. London: English Universities Press, 1969.

Clausen, C. P. *Entomophagous Insects*. New York: McGraw-Hill, 1940.

DeBauch, P. (Ed.) *Biological Control of Insect Pests and Weeds*. London: Chapman and Hall, 1964. Also available in Spanish and Russian.

Ebeling, W. *Urban Entomology*. Berkeley: University of California, Division of Agricultural Sciences, 1975.

Eidmann, H. *Lehrbuch der Entomologie*. Hamburg, Federal Republic of Germany: Parey, 1970.

Gilmour, D. *The Biochemistry of Insects*. New York: Academic Press, 1961.

Huffaker, C. B. *Biological Control*. New York: Plenum, 1970.

Imms, A. D. *A General Textbook on Entomology Including the Anatomy, Physiology, Development and Classification of Insects*. (9th ed. by O. W. Richards and R. G. Davies.) London: Methuen, 1960.

Linsenmaier, W. *Insects of the World*. New York: McGraw-Hill, 1972.

Little, V. A. *General and Applied Entomology*. (3rd ed.) New York: Harper & Row, 1972.

Metcalf, R. L., and Luckman, W. *Introduction to Insect Pest Management*. New York: Wiley, 1975.

Oldroyd, H. *Elements of Entomology*. London: Weidenfeld and Nicolson, 1968.

Pfadt, R. E. (Ed.) *Fundamentals of Applied Entomology*. New York: Macmillan, 1962.

Pruthi, H. S. *Textbook on Agricultural Entomology*. New Delhi: Indian Council of Agricultural Research, 1969.

Romoser, W. S. *The Science of Entomology*. New York: Macmillan, 1973.

Smith, K. G. V. (Ed.) *Insects and Other Arthropods of Medical Importance*. London: Trustees of the British Museum (Natural History), 1973.

Swan, L. A., and Papp, C. S. *The Common Insects of North America*. New York: Harper & Row, 1972.

Works dealing with the history of the field include:

Essig, E. O. *A History of Entomology*. New York: Hafner, 1965. Facsimile of 1931 edition.

Ordish, G. *John Curtis and the Pioneering of Pest Control*. Reading, Massachusetts: Osprey, 1974.

Osborn, H. *A Brief History of Entomology, Including Time of Demosthenes and Aristotle to Modern Times, with Over Five Hundred Portraits*. Columbus, Ohio: Spahr and Glenn, 1952.

Smith, R. F. (Ed.) *History of Entomology*. Palo Alto, California: Annual Review, Inc., 1973. Supplementary volume to *Annual Review of Entomology*.

Sources dealing with entomological education include:

Barbosa, P. "The Role of Entomology in Science Education." *Bulletin of the Entomological Society of America*, September 1974, *20*(3), 217–220.

Freeborn, S. B. "The Training of a Professional Entomologist." *Bulletin of the Entomological Society of America*, 1956, *2*(4), 23–24.

Giliomee, J. H. *An Investigation into the Training of Entomologists in South Africa*. Pretoria, South Africa: Department of Agricultural Technical Services, 1973.

Quaestiones Entomolgicae: A Periodical Record of Entomological Investigation. Edmonton: University of Alberta, Department of Entomology, 1972. Volume 8, supplement, is devoted to entomological education. Articles include "Entomology and Education: Proceedings of a Symposium Organized by the Department of Entomology, University of Alberta" and "Education and the Professional Entomologist."

Tipton, V. J. *Toward More Effective Teaching: Entomology*. Provo, Utah: Brigham Young University Press, 1973.

Tipton, V. J. *Catalog of Instructional Materials for Entomology*. Provo, Utah: Brigham Young University Press, 1974.

CURRENT BIBLIOGRAPHIES

Abstracts of Entomology: All Abstracts and References Covering Pure and Applied Studies Involving Insects and Arachnids from Biological Abstracts and Biological Research Index. Philadelphia: Biosciences Information Service of Biological Abstracts, 1970–. Covers 97 countries and 35 languages.

Annual Review of Entomology. Palo Alto, California: Annual Review, Inc., 1956–.

Biological Abstracts. Philadelphia: Biosciences Information Service of Biological Abstracts, 1927–.

Biological and Agricultural Index. New York: Wilson, 1916–.

Entomology Abstracts. London: Information Retrieval; New York: CCM Information Corporation, 1969–.

Forestry Abstracts. Farnham Royal, Bucks, England: Commonwealth Agricultural Bureaux, 1939–.

Review of Applied Entomology. Series A: Agricultural. London: Commonwealth Institute of Applied Entomology, 1913–.
Review of Applied Entomology. Series B: Medical and Veterinary. London: Commonwealth Institute of Applied Entomology, 1913–.

PERIODICALS

Acarologia (France), *Acta entomologica Bohemoslovaca* (Czechoslovakia), *Acta Entomologica Sinica* (People's Republic of China), *Advances in Insect Physiology* (UK), *Agricultural Education* (US), *Annales de la Société entomologique de France, Annals of the Entomological Society of America, Anzeiger für Schädlingskunde Pflanzen- und Umweltschutz* (FRG), *Applied Entomology and Zoology* (Japan), *Arbeitsgemeinschaft österreichischer Entomologia Zeitschrift* (Austria), *Australian Entomological Society Journal, Bulletin of Entomological Research* (UK), *Canadian Entomologist, Contributions to Zoology* (US), *Entomologia Experimentalis et Applicata* (Netherlands), *Entomologica Germanica* (FRG), *Entomological Research* (UK), *Entomologica Scandinavia* (Denmark), *Entomologist* (UK), *Entomologists' Monthly Magazine* (UK), *Entomophaga* (France), *Environmental Entomology* (US), *Folia parasitologica* (Czechoslovakia), *Insect Biochemistry* (US), *Insect Morphology and Embryology* (US), *Insect Physiology* (US), *Insecta Matsumurana* (Japan), *International Journal of Insect Morphology and Embryology* (US), *Journal of Economic Entomology* (US), *Journal of Entomology A & B* (UK), *Journal of Experimental Zoology* (US), *Journal of Insect Physiology* (UK), *Journal of Invertebrate Pathology* (US), *Mushi* (Japan), *Revista chilena entomología, Systematic Zoology* (US).

For a more complete listing of periodicals consult:

Liste de périodiques d'entomologie. Brussels: Institut royal des sciences naturelles de Belgique, Service de documentation, 1966.

ENCYCLOPEDIAS, DICTIONARIES, HANDBOOKS

Burton, J. *The Oxford Book of Insects.* London: Oxford University Press, 1968.
Ericson, R. O. *A Glossary of Some Foreign Language Terms in Entomology.* Washington, D.C.: Entomology Research Division, Agricultural Research Service, United States Department of Agriculture, 1961.
Gerrit, F. *Insekten: Taschenlexikon der Entomologie unter besonderer Berücksichtigung der Fauna Mitteleuropas.* Leipzig, German Democratic Republic: Bibliographisches Institut, 1964.
Gray, P. (Ed.) *The Encyclopedia of the Biological Sciences.* New York: Van Nostrand Reinhold, 1961.
International Code of Zoological Nomenclature.

London: International Trust for Zoological Nomenclature, 1961.
Jaeger, E. C. *A Source Book of Biological Names and Terms.* Springfield, Illinois: Thomas, 1950.
Leftwich, A. W. *A Dictionary of Entomology.* New York: Crane, Russak, 1976.
Pest Control: An Assessment of Present and Alternative Technologies. (5 vols.) Vol. 1: *Contemporary Pest Control Practices and Prospects;* Vol. 2: *Corn/Soybeans Pest Control;* Vol. 3: *Cotton Pest Control;* Vol. 4: *Forest Pest Control;* Vol. 5: *Pest Control and Public Health.* Washington, D.C.: National Academy of Sciences, 1976.
Quantanella, R. H. *Glosario de términos entomológicos.* Buenos Aires: Editorial universitaria de Buenos Aires, 1969.
Scortecci, G. *Insetti: Come sono, dove vivono, come cicono.* (2 vols.) Milan: Edizioni Labor, 1960. An encyclopedia.
Séguy, E. *Dictionnaire des termes techniques d'entomologie élémentaire.* Paris: Lechevalier, 1967.
Torre-Bueno, J. R. *A Glossary of Entomology: Smith's "An Explanation of Terms Used in Entomology," Completely Revised and Rewritten.* Brooklyn, New York: Brooklyn Entomological Society, 1973.

DIRECTORIES

Educational directories which include information on agricultural study are:

American Colleges and Universities. Washington, D.C.: American Council on Education, 1928–. Published quadrennially.
Commonwealth Universities Yearbook. London: Association of Commonwealth Universities, 1914–. Published annually.
Gray, P. (Ed.) *AIBS* (American Institute of Biological Sciences) *Directory of Bioscience Departments and Facilities in the United States and Canada.* (2nd ed.) Stroudsburg, Pennsylvania: Dowden, Hutchinson and Ross, 1975.
International Handbook of Universities. Paris: International Association of Universities, 1959–. Published triennially.
The World of Learning. London: Europa, 1947–. Published annually. Lists universities, colleges, institutes, research centers, learned societies, and libraries throughout the world.

RESEARCH CENTERS, INSTITUTES, INFORMATION CENTERS

Guides to research and information in the agricultural sciences include:

Boalch, D. H. *World Directory of Agricultural Libraries and Documentation Centers.* Oxford,

England: International Association of Agricultural Librarians and Documentalists, 1960. Records nearly 2000 libraries in more than 100 countries; a new revised edition is being planned. National Agricultural Library. *Directory of Information Resources in Agriculture and Biology.* Washington, D.C.: U.S. Government Printing Office, 1971.

Museums which house collections of entomological interest are:

Australia:
    Australia Museum
    Sydney

Brazil:
    Museu de zoologia
    Universidade de São Paulo
    avenida Nazareth 481
    Caixa Postal 7172
    0100 São Paulo

Canada:
    Entomology Research Institute
    Canadian Department of Agriculture
    Ottawa, Ontario

France:
    Muséum national d'histoire naturelle
    57 rue Cuvier
    75005 Paris

German Democratic Republic:
    Deutsches entomologisches Institut
    Josef-Nawrocki-Strasse 10
    Berlin-Friedrichshagen

Netherlands:
    Rijksmuseum van natuurlijke historie
    Leiden

Soviet Union:
    Academy of Sciences of U.S.S.R.
    Leninsky prospekt 14
    Moscow B-71

Sweden:
    Zoological Institute
    Radmansgatan 70A
    Stockholm V

United Kingdom:
    British Museum of Natural History
    Cromwell Road
    London SW7, England

United States:
    American Museum of Natural History
    Central Park West at 79th Street
    New York, New York 10024

    Bishop Museum
    1355 Kalihi Street
    P.O. Box 6037
    Honolulu, Hawaii 96817

California Academy of Sciences
Golden Gate Park
San Francisco, California 94118

Museum of Comparative Zoology
Harvard University
Oxford Street
Cambridge, Massachusetts 02138

United States National Museum
Washington, D.C. 20560

[Bibliography prepared with assistance from Evert Schlinger.]

ENVIRONMENTAL CONTROL IN HIGHER EDUCATION
See Health, Safety, and Environmental Control in Higher Education Institutions.

ENVIRONMENTAL STUDIES (Field of Study)

Perceived in different ways in different institutions and nations, environmental studies (or *environmental education,* as the field is sometimes labeled) has not progressed as a distinctive, integrated discipline. Instead, it is an evolving field, developing in response to the growing concern with national and international environmental problems. Educational offerings in this field range from single survey courses to full programs leading to a postgraduate degree.

Environmental studies are usually problem focused rather than discipline centered. They are often organized around broad themes of environmental management and involve the detailed study of one or more of the following topics: land use, pollution abatement and prevention, protection of nature and natural resource use, and human ecology. Programs may include various mixes of the basic disciplines (meteorology, geography, biology, social anthropology, geology, hydrology, mathematics, chemistry), management techniques (engineering sciences, systems analysis, computer science, agriculture, forestry and wildlife management), planning studies (architecture, landscape architecture, urban and regional planning), and policy areas (law, public administration, business, political science). Environmental studies are largely experiential, with an emphasis placed on fieldwork, so that environmental problems can be studied in the systems where they occur. The basic objectives of environmental studies are to provide specialists with a wide understanding of environmental problems, yet with an in-depth knowledge of a particular professional field, and to educate generalists who can coordinate the work of specialists and who understand the environmental systems that are being studied or managed.

The term *environmental studies programs* has been used somewhat loosely to cover any organized program of study or individual course whose purpose or effect is to produce greater awareness or improved understanding of the complex elements of the natural and man-made environments, of man's role in changing the environment, and of the impact of the environment on humans. However, because of the range of experimentation occurring in different educational systems, there is a need for more accurate terms of reference. Some effort has been made in the general area of interdisciplinary studies to develop a precise terminology which can be usefully applied to environmental studies. The following hierarchy of terms was adopted at an OCED seminar held at Nice in September 1970 (Organisation for Economic Co-operation and Development, 1973): (1) *discipline*—a specific body of teachable knowledge with its own background of concepts, procedures, and methods; (2) *multidisciplinary*—juxtaposition of various disciplines, sometimes with no apparent connection among them; (3) *pluridisciplinary*—juxtaposition of disciplines assumed to be more or less related; (4) *interdisciplinary*—an adjective describing the interaction between two or more disciplines; (5) *transdisciplinary*—establishing a common system of axioms for a set of disciplines.

In most countries environmental studies programs are given through existing academic disciplines. As a result, the adjective *environmental* often is attached as a prefix to existing courses without any essential change in the course of study. Whatever the perspective, most institutions in the United States that offer an undergraduate degree provide some type of environmental studies program. Many of these institutions indicate that their environmental programs are the fastest growing of all their academic programs. In other countries environmental studies are increasing, but somewhat less rapidly. Of growing importance at the undergraduate level throughout the world are environmental studies majors. These appear to follow two patterns: the first is primarily organized around existing environmental courses, with some flexibility in the range of disciplines involved; the second has a separate environmental studies core curriculum, with at least some man-and-the-environment courses especially designed for the program. Frequently these courses are integrated interdisciplinary efforts. At some United States institutions—such as the University of Wisconsin at Green Bay and the College of the Atlantic, in Bar Harbor, Maine—the entire undergraduate curriculum is built around an integrated environmental studies core.

At the graduate level, environmental studies programs are much less in evidence. In the United States most of these programs are at the master's level, but a few institutions provide programs leading to the doctorate. For the most part, programs at this level are single-discipline oriented. Graduate programs tend to emphasize engineering and biological sciences, but work in the physical, mathematical, computer, and social sciences may also be required. Mahidol University in Bangkok, Thailand, offers a Master of Science program in the Technology of Environmental Management. According to the university brochure on the program: "The objective is not to produce experts in discrete disciplines but to prepare generalists with the integrative grasp, broad technical base, systems training, and international orientation needed to understand complex transdisciplinary problems which is essential for planning the rational use of the ecosystems resources." Applicants to this program must have already received a bachelor's degree in some field of specialization.

The various academic offerings in environmental studies come in a number of formats: general-awareness or survey courses, discipline-based programs, multidisciplinary or pluridisciplinary approaches, and an integrated approach. General-awareness courses are usually developed to meet the broad educational objectives of undergraduate programs; such courses are usually intended for large numbers of students and provide a background on the interrelationships of humans and environment. Sometimes this kind of course is presented through the regular channels of a single discipline, such as geography or biology; sometimes it is a multidisciplinary course. But whether single disciplinary or multidisciplinary, general-awareness courses usually are not directly related to the disciplines involved and are not aimed at the development of skills.

The discipline-based program is, to a large extent, presented within the framework of a single discipline but often provides a broad multidisciplinary perspective. Understandably, this type of course tends to underline a particular discipline's perception of environmental problems, solutions, and opportunities. It also stresses the acquisition of skills related to the discipline base. Courses of this type are offered at the school of architecture at the University of Auckland in New Zealand; the faculty of law at Hokkaidō University in Sapporo, Japan; and the University of Leeds in England.

The multidisciplinary or pluridisciplinary approach is often an environmental studies major or minor program founded largely or completely on existing courses. In some instances an introductory core course is given as an orientation to the program. The graduate course in environmen-

tal science given at Hokkaidō University is an example of such a program. The range of disciplines included in different programs makes generalization difficult, but most programs of this type include the biological, earth, and social sciences and, in a number of programs, engineering sciences and architecture.

The integrated approach is either interdisciplinary or transdisciplinary. This type of program is often under a separate administrative control. The usual discipline approach is supplanted by a problem orientation, which draws upon the relevant skills from a range of disciplines in order to determine alternative solutions to a problem. Program content varies depending on the background of the faculty involved, career objectives, and, in some instances, student interest and experience. These programs provide for appropriate skill development. Some examples of this type of program include those at Plymouth Polytechnic in England; Huxley College of Environmental Studies at Western Washington State University, Bellingham, Washington; Evergreen State College, Olympia, Washington; the *Programme interdisciplinaire en aménagement du territoire et développement regional* at the *Université Laval* in Quebec, Canada; and the *Fondation universitaire* in Brussels.

The current activity in environmental studies has its antecedents in the earlier conservation movements in the United States and Europe and the intellectual ferment that these movements caused among educators, particularly in the fields of geography, sociology, and public health. Environmentalism had been advocated by some scholars in these fields during the late 1800s and early 1900s. But these various efforts were scattered, both geographically and within academic institutions. Consequently, professional interest and effort declined during the 1920s and 1930s and languished until public and official concern with environmental problems began to develop. Since the late 1960s educators—especially in industrialized nations—have increasingly used the word *environment* to refer to the comprehensive demands of environmental quality and not merely to the necessity for various forms of pollution control. However, the development of environmental studies in higher education has been thwarted because the institutional structure does not foster interdisciplinary communication—a necessary element in any discipline that is problem-focused and needs to draw on a variety of disciplines.

Nonetheless, there is a definite and increasing interest in environmental studies all over the world. This interest has been stimulated and refined by the programs of a number of international organizations, many of which have been active for years in such related areas as the conservation of nature and natural resources. *The World Directory of Environmental Education Programs* describes more than 1100 programs in 750 institutions in 70 countries. Impressive as those figures may seem, there are notable gaps. Even though flexible criteria about the programs to be listed were used, many countries (including the Soviet Union) have only a single entry. More than half of the entries, or 660 programs in 440 schools, are from the United States. This is indicative of the uneven international development of environmental studies programs. It also indicates the difficulties of communication in an evolving academic field that lacks precisely defined terms and accepted frames of reference. The following excerpt is taken from a statement entitled "Framework for Environmental Education," which was drafted and unanimously adopted at the UNESCO-UNEP Environmental Education Workshop held in Belgrade, Yugoslavia, during October 1975:

We need nothing short of a new global ethic. An ethic which espouses attitudes and behaviour for individuals and societies which are consonant with humanity's place within the biosphere—which recognizes and sensitively responds to the complex and ever changing relationships between man and nature and between man and man. Significant changes must occur in all of the world's nations to assure the kind of rational development which will be guided by this new global ideal—changes which will be directed towards an equitable distribution of the world's resources and more fairly satisfying the needs of all peoples. . . . The reform of educational processes and systems is central to the building of this new development ethic and world economic order. Governments and policy-makers can order changes, and new development approaches can begin to improve the world's condition, but all these are no more than short-term solutions unless the youth of the world receives a new kind of education.

In addition to highlighting the political and economic aspects of this area, the statement is significant in that it was agreed to by 120 experts from 65 countries, developed and developing, socialist and capitalist, rich and poor. The workshop was convened to consider the needs and resources for formal and nonformal environmental education, worldwide, for people of all ages. This statement and the other products of the workshop constitute a basis for expanding the scope of environmental studies programs.

The UNESCO-UNEP Environmental Education Programme is an example of a comprehensive effort which is helping to gather additional data, establish a network of individuals and organizations, improve communications, and generally clarify the field in an international context that has important implications for higher education institutions everywhere.

The effective implementation of environmental studies requires rigorous scholarship, as well as examination and possible revision of existing curricula, teaching methods, evaluation techniques, and institutional organization patterns. This demanding process of educational renewal has great promise but has only barely begun.

[*Notes:* Organisation for Economic Cooperation and Development, *Environmental Education at University Level: Trends and Data* (Paris: OECD, Centre for Educational Research and Innovation, 1973), pp. 38–39.]

JAMES L. ALDRICH

Levels and Programs of Study

Programs in environmental studies generally require as a prerequisite a secondary education, though mature students with relevant experience may be admitted with lower educational qualifications. Programs lead to the following awards: certificate or diploma, bachelor's degree (B.A., B.Sc.), master's degree (M.A., M.Sc.), the doctorate (Ph.D.), or their equivalents.

Programs not leading to a first university degree are designed to develop awareness of the environment and the ways in which various factors affect its condition. Attention is given to methods for the protection and rehabilitation of the environment. Programs are usually one to two years in duration and may be part time or full time, day or evening. Through a multidisciplinary approach drawing on courses from the social, biological, and physical sciences and their applications, a background is provided in such subjects as study and control of pollution, protection of the environment, and conservation of natural resources. Programs consist of lectures, seminars, demonstrations, and sometimes study tours and visits to particular locations.

Programs that lead to a first university degree deal with the principles and practices of environmental science; that is, the analysis of environmental problems and environmental protection and rehabilitation. Programs are usually three to four years in duration in a university and consist of lectures, seminars, group discussion, and demonstrations. Through an interdisciplinary approach consisting of a wide variety and combination of courses from the social, behavioral, natural, and physical sciences, a background is provided in such subjects as study and control of environmental pollution, protection of the environment in all its aspects, protection of natural resources, and preservation of the earth's ecology.

Programs that lead to a postgraduate degree deal with specialized aspects of the theory and practice of environmental science, including wildlife protection, and are concentrated in a particular area of environmental studies. Through lectures, seminars, and independent and directed study and research lasting one to three years in a university, these programs provide a thorough coverage of one or more branches of environmental science, such as pollution detection and control, preservation of ecosystems, control and planning of natural resources use, and environmental rehabilitation. On the graduate level, programs consist of a number of prescribed courses, in varying combinations, from the humanities, social sciences, engineering, and medical sciences. In addition, the student must demonstrate competence in one or more foreign languages and prepare a thesis or dissertation based on original research into a particular problem within the major subject.

[This section was based on UNESCO's *International Standard Classification of Education (ISCED): Three Stage Classification System, 1974* (Paris: UNESCO, 1974).]

Major International and National Organizations

INTERNATIONAL

Food and Agriculture Organization of the
    United Nations (FAO)
via delle Terme di Caracalla
00100 Rome, Italy

International Council for Scientific
    Unions (ICSU)
51 boulevard de Montmorency
75016 Paris, France

International Union for the Conservation of
    Nature and Natural Resources (IUCN)
Union internationale pour la conservation de la
    nature et de ses ressources (UICN)
1110 Morges, Switzerland
    The major independent international organization, composed of national governments, governmental agencies, private organizations, and international groups from seventy countries; encourages and sponsors conferences of specialists, studies, and projects; sponsors the Commission on Education, which acts as a clearinghouse for educational materials on the environment.

Organisation for Economic Co-operation and Development (OECD)
Chateau de la Muette
2 rue André Pascal
75775 Paris, France
Concerned with higher education programs in member countries.

United Nations Educational, Scientific and Cultural Organization (UNESCO)
Natural Sciences Sector
place de Fontenoy
75700 Paris, France
This sector, with about eighty national committees, is concerned with professional training through the Man and the Biosphere Program.

United Nations Environment
Programme (UNEP)
Kenyatta Conference Centre
P.O. Box 30552
Nairobi, Kenya
With UNESCO, conducts a major international environmental education program, which deals with the full spectrum of formal and nonformal education.

World Health Organization (WHO)
avenue Appia
1211 Geneva, Switzerland

World Meteorological Organization (WMO)
41 avenue Giuseppe Motta
1211 Geneva, Switzerland

A complete listing of other international intergovernmental and nongovernmental environmental organizations can be found in:

World Directory of Environmental Organizations. San Francisco: Sierra Club, 1973.

For listings of national organizations with environmental programs and concerns see:

Thibeau, C. E. *Directory of Environmental Information Sources.* Boston: National Foundation for Environmental Control, 1972. Lists over 3000 governmental agencies, professional organizations, trade associations, and private groups dealing with ecology and conservation in the United States.
World Directory of Environmental Organizations. San Francisco: Sierra Club, 1973. Includes a country-by-country listing of national and selected regional and local organizations interested in and involved with the environment.

Principal Information Sources

GENERAL

Guides to the literature include:

Bennett, G. F. *Environmental Literature: A Bibliography.* (3rd ed.) Park Ridge, New Jersey: Noyes Data Corp., 1973. Emphasis on American publications, but includes some international titles.
Bibliography, Reference Material and Information Sources on the Environment. Toronto, Ontario: Ministry of the Environment, Information Services Branch, 1973.
Lockard, D. J. *Working International Bibliography on Trends in Environmental Education.* College Park: University of Maryland, 1975.
Morrison, D. E., and others. *Environment: A Bibliography of Social Science and Related Literature.* Washington, D.C.: U.S. Environmental Protection Agency, Office of Research and Monitoring, 1973. An annotated bibliography with mainly United States emphasis, listing 5000 social science items relevant to man and his natural environments.
Winton, H. N. M. *Man and the Environment: A Bibliography of Selected Publications of the United Nations System, 1946–71.* New York: Unipub/Bowker, 1972.
Wolff, G. (Ed.) *Environmental Information Sources Handbook.* New York: Simon & Schuster, 1974. Includes listings of journals, directories, periodicals, bibliographies, and organizations relevant to environmental science.

General studies, reports, and introductions to the field include:

Binder, E. "Teaching of Environmental Sciences at the University Level." *Prospects,* Winter 1972, *2* (4), 467–471.
Continuing Education for Engineers. Helsinki: European Federation of National Associations of Engineers (Fédération d'associations nationales d'ingénieurs: FEANI), UNESCO, 1972.
Cook, R., and Weidner, E. "Environmental Education at the Tertiary Level for General Students." Paper prepared for the UNESCO-UNEP Workshop on Environmental Education, Belgrade. To be published by UNESCO in a book edited by J. L. Aldrich.
Emmelin, L. *Teaching About Environmental Problems at Tertiary Level.* Strasbourg, France: Committee on Higher Education and Research, Council of Europe, in press.
Environmental Conservation Education: Final Report of the European Working Conference of the Commission of Education. Morges, Switzerland: International Union for Conservation of Nature and Natural Resources, 1972.
Environmental Education at Post Secondary Level: The Training of Generalists and Specialists: Paris: Organisation for Economic Co-operation and Development, 1974.
"Environmental Education in the Universities."

OECD Observer, February 1974, *68*, 27–30.

Fanning, O. *Opportunities in Environmental Careers*. New York: Universal Publishing and Distributing, 1971.

Groupe d'experts sur les activités relatives à l'éducation à poursuivre dans le cadre du Programme sur l'Homme et la Biosphère (MAB). Final Report No. 7. December 5–8, 1972. Paris: UNESCO, 1972.

Maldague, M. "International Inquiry on Environmental Education in Universities and Higher Technical Institutes." Unpublished paper, Laval University, Quebec, 1975.

Maldague, M. "Environmental Studies for Specialists in Non-Environmental Fields." Paper prepared for the UNESCO-UNEP Workshop on Environmental Education, Belgrade. To be published by UNESCO in a book edited by J. L. Aldrich.

Meeting of Experts on Environmental Aspects of Engineering Education and Training. Final Report. June 17–21, 1974. Paris: United Nations Environment Programme, 1974.

Organization and Administration of Environmental Programs. Paris: United Nations, 1974. Eight studies, by the Economic and Social Council of the United Nations, with special relevance to the organization and management of environmental programs by governments.

Rogers, A. "Environmental Education: A University Approach." *Bulletin of Environmental Education*, November 1971, 7.

Schmieder, A. A. "The Nature and Philosophy of Environmental Education: Some Fundamental Goals, Concepts, Objectives and Developmental Issues." Paper prepared for the UNESCO-UNEP Workshop on Environmental Education, Belgrade. To be published by UNESCO in a book edited by J. L. Aldrich.

Stapp, W. B., and others. *Environmental Education Needs and Priorities: A Preliminary World Survey*. To be published by UNESCO.

Steinhart, J., and Cherniack, S. *The Universities and Environmental Quality*. Washington, D.C.: U.S. Government Printing Office, 1969.

Comparative education literature in the field includes:

Aldrich, J. L., and Kormondy, E. J. *Environmental Education: Academia's Response*. Washington, D.C.: Commission on Undergraduate Education in the Biological Sciences, 1972. A survey of fifteen United States programs.

Brennan, M. J. "Environmental Conservation Education in the United States of America." *Prospects*, Winter 1972, *2* (4), 472–476.

Eden, R. A. *Higher Education Programs in Environmental Education in Great Britain*. London, Ontario: IUCN, International Workshop, 1972.

Environmental Education at University Level: Trends and Data. Paris: Organisation for Economic Co-operation and Development, 1973. A survey of the state of the art of environmental education in OECD member countries.

Ramachandran, A., and Bhattacharya, R. N. "Environmental Education in India." In UN Environment Programme, Governing Council, *Report . . . on the Work of Its Second Session, 11–22 March 1974*. New York: United Nations, 1974. Pp. 105–110.

Ryabchikov, A. M. "Concept for Study of Environment Changing by Man and Training Specialists in the Soviet Union." In UN Environment Programme, Governing Council, *Report . . . on the Work of Its Second Session, 11–22 March 1974*. New York: United Nations, 1974. Pp. 111–113.

Shaposhnikov, L. K. *Experience in Conservation Education and Propaganda of Nature Conservation in the U.S.S.R. and in the Countries of Eastern Europe*. IUCN Publication New Series, Supplement, Paper No. 7. Morges, Switzerland: IUCN, 1965. Pp. 41–48.

Simms, D. H. *Conservation Education in Universities and Other Institutions of Higher Learning in the United States of America*. IUCN Symposium on Conservation Education at the University Level, Lucerne, Switzerland, June 23–24, 1966.

UN Conference on the Human Environment, Stockholm, 1972. *Report . . . Stockholm, 5–16 June 1972*. New York: United Nations, 1973.

UN Environment Programme, Governing Council. *Report . . . on the Work of Its First Session 12–22 June 1973*. New York: United Nations, 1973.

UN Environment Programme, Governing Council. *Report . . . on the Work of Its Second Session, 11–22 March 1974*. New York: United Nations, 1974.

Historical perspectives on the field include:

Herrscher, W.J., and Cok, R.S. (Eds.) *Environmental Responsibility in higher Education: Processes and Practices*. Madison: Regents of the University of Wisconsin System, 1973.

Ritterbush, P.C. "Environmental Studies: The Search for an Institutional Form." *Minerva*, October 1971, *9* (4), 493–509. Provides excellent historical background and extensive references to the literature.

CURRENT BIBLIOGRAPHIES

Dokumentation für Umweltschutz und Landespflege. Stuttgart, Federal Republic of Germany: Verlag W. Kohlhammer, 1961–.

Environmental Health. Amsterdam: Excerpta Medica Foundation, 1971–.

Environmental Periodicals Bibliography. Santa Barbara, California: Environmental Studies Institute, 1972–. Includes table of contents pages of approximately 300 current journals, from the United States and other countries, dealing with the environment.

Environment Information Access. New York: Environment Information Center, 1971–. Abstracts of books, journal articles, newsletters, and news releases relating to all aspects of the environment.

PERIODICALS

Among the most important periodicals relating to the environment are the following: *Alternatives: Perspectives on Society and Environment* (Canada), *AMBIO* (Norway), *Atmospheric Environment* (UK), *BEE/Bulletin of Environmental Education* (UK), *Clear Air* (Australia), *Connect* (UNESCO newsletter available in French, Spanish, and English), *C.R.C. Critical Reviews in Environmental Control* (US), *Current Sweden, Ecologist* (UK), *Ecology* (US), *Environment* (US), *Environmental Affairs* (US), *Environmental Education* (US); *Environmental Education Report* (US), *Environmental Letters* (US), *Environmental Pollution* (UK), *Environmental Research* (US), *Environmental Resource* (US), *Environmental Science and Technology* (US), *Environment This Month* (UK), *EPI/Environmental Protection and Industry* (Japan), *International Journal of Environmental Studies* (UK), *IUCN Bulletin* (Switzerland), *IYF European Bulletin* (Switzerland), *Journal of Environmental Education* (US); *Journal of Environmental Sciences* (US), *Kankyo eisei* (Japan), *Protectio Vitae Umweltforschung/Research on Environment* (FRG), *Science of the Total Environment* (Netherlands), *Umwelt* (FRG), *Water, Air and Soil Pollution* (Netherlands).

Among directories offering more extensive listings of environmental periodicals are:

Environmental Information Sources Handbook. New York: Simon & Schuster, 1974. Includes extensive list of environmental periodicals, pp. 469–481.

Ulrich's International Periodicals Directory. New York: Bowker, biennial.

ENCYCLOPEDIAS, DICTIONARIES, HANDBOOKS

Durrenberger, R. W. (Comp). *Dictionary of the Environmental Sciences.* Palo Alto, California: National Press Books, 1973.

McGraw-Hill Encyclopedia of Environmental Science. New York: McGraw-Hill, 1974.

Terminology of the Environment. Berlin, Federal Republic of Germany: Erich Schmidt Verlag, 1974. In Italian, German, English, Dutch, and French.

Vocabulaire de l'environnement. (2nd ed.) Paris: Hachette, 1974. Prepared by an international group of specialists working in the main fields of environmental studies in various international institutions. Includes about 800 terms, with their definitions in French and equivalents in English, and is the only work on the subject which is both interdisciplinary and based on environmental ethics and policy.

DIRECTORIES

Environmental Information Sources Handbook. New York: Simon & Schuster, 1974. Includes a list of universities, scientific institutions, independent research organizations and laboratories, and other study centers in the United States.

Environment U.S.A.: A Guide to Agencies, People, and Resources. New York: Bowker, 1974. Lists for each state of the United States educational programs in environmental fields. Also includes a listing of United States environmental libraries.

Quigg, P. W. *World Directory of Environmental Education Programs.* New York: Bowker, 1973. A guide to postsecondary study and training in 70 countries; lists more than 1060 instructional programs in over 700 schools throughout the world. Included is the name and address of the educational institution, name of program or course, cost, eligibility requirements, and available scholarships.

Stapp, W. B. (Ed.) *Environmental Education: A guide to Information Sources.* Vol, 1: *Man and the Environment.* Detroit: Gale Research, 1974.

World Environmental Directory. Silver Springs, Maryland: Business Publishers, 1975. Includes a listing of international organizations, national government agencies, manufacturers, professional organizations, and universities and educational institutions in countries throughout the world.

RESEARCH CENTERS, INSTITUTES, INFORMATION CENTERS

Among the numerous institutes and information centers concerned with the environment on a global scale are:

International Institute for Environmental Affairs
United Nations Plaza
345 East 46th Street
New York, New York 10017 USA

Conducts an annual International Institute for Environmental Affairs in Aspen, Colorado. The institute also includes a Center for International Environment Information.

World Office of Information on Environmental Problems
Office mondial d'information sur les problèmes de l'environnement
115 rue de la Pompe
75116 Paris, France

For guides listing additional organizations see:

Directory of Organizations Concerned with Environmental Research. Fredonia: New York State University, Office of Lake Erie Environmental Studies, 1970.
Environmental Science Centers at Institutions of Higher Education. Washington, D.C.: Environmental Policy Division of the Library of Congress for the United States House Committee on Science and Astronautics, 1969.
Wilson, W. K., and others. *World Directory of Environmental Research Centers.* (2nd ed.) Scottsdale, Arizona: Oryx Press, 1974. Lists organizations doing research on the environment at local, state, and national levels in sixty-eight countries.

EQUALITY OF EDUCATIONAL OPPORTUNITY (Higher Education Report), United States

The report *Equality of Educational Opportunity,* by James Coleman and his associates (Washington, D.C.: U.S. Government Printing Office, 1966), presents the results of a survey, authorized by and carried out by the United States Office of Education, on the inequality of educational opportunity, by reason of race, color, religion, or national origin, in United States public educational institutions. The report addresses four major questions: To what extent are racial and ethnic groups segregated in the public schools? Do the schools offer equal educational opportunities? How much do students learn? What are the relationships between students' achievement and the kinds of schools they attend? The following findings and recommendations are reported.

Considered in the light of the 1954 United States Supreme Court desegregation decision, which held that separate schools for black and white children are inherently unequal, American public education is unequal. The great majority of children attend largely segregated schools: 80 percent of all white pupils are in schools that are from 90 to 100 percent white, 65 percent of all black pupils in the first grade attend schools that are from 90 to 100 percent black. Also, although there are marked regional differences, minority groups generally have less access to facilities and programs that seem most related to academic achievement. The average black pupil attends a school where a greater percentage of the teachers appears to be less able than those in the schools attended by the average white pupil. The average black pupil also has fewer classmates whose parents graduated from high school and is less often enrolled in college preparatory curricula. Finally, the average minority student scores lower on standard achievement tests than the average white student; at higher grade levels the minority scores are even further below the majority scores than at grade 1.

When socioeconomic factors are controlled, schools are very similar in their effect on pupil achievement. However, the achievement of minority pupils is more dependent on the schools they attend than is the achievement of majority pupils. School factors that affect achievement include the existence of science laboratories, teacher quality, and educational background of the peer group. However, pupil attitude factor (the extent to which an individual feels some control over his own destiny) has a stronger relationship to achievement.

In institutions of higher education, about 4.6 percent of all college students are black, and half of them attend the largely segregated institutions in the South. Black students attend colleges with lower faculty salaries, are more likely to enter state colleges than universities, and are more frequently in institutions with high dropout rates. In addition, black students mainly attend institutions with low tuition costs and tend to major in engineering, agriculture, education, social work, social science, and nursing.

The report considers special topics such as Project Head Start, guidance counselors, and vocational education. It also examines future teachers and enrollment rates. Case studies illustrating recurrent problems in school integration also are presented.

EQUAL RIGHTS AND AFFIRMATIVE ACTION

See Affirmative Action; Women and Higher Education: Equal Rights and Affirmative Action.

EQUATORIAL GUINEA, REPUBLIC OF

Equatorial Guinea, an independent republic in West Africa, consists of the island province of Macías Nguema Biyogo (known as Fernando Póo until 1973), located in the Gulf of Guinea, and the mainland province of Río Muni, situated on the west-central coast of Africa between Cameroon and Gabon. In 1974 the population of Equatorial Guinea was estimated at 310,000.

Before independence from Spain in 1968, educational facilities in Equatorial Guinea consisted of 147 elementary schools, 32 primary schools, and 2 secondary schools. The elementary schools provided compulsory education for students through age twelve, while the primary schools provided education for children through age fourteen. The two secondary schools mainly served European children.

Since independence, an increasingly authoritarian government has enacted policies which have significantly altered the social structure of the country. The extent of educational changes is not known at the time of publication; however, it was reported that by 1972 the number of primary schools had tripled and that 60 percent of the school-age children were in

school. In addition, the number of secondary schools had increased to eight. Three postsecondary institutions also were established for administrative training, primary teacher training, and secondary teacher training.

EQUIVALENCES

Free movement of scholars from one university to another was common in the Middle Ages. In the twentieth century, although international cultural exchanges and cooperation have markedly increased, such mobility is hampered by the question of the equivalence of degrees, diplomas, and other qualifications between countries. When transnational exchanges by students became frequent in the 1960s, students found that the qualifications they had acquired, whether at home or abroad, had somehow to be equated with those in the country to which they migrated or to which they returned.

Equivalence, however, is a term that requires further definition. Generically it may include the acceptability, recognition, and validation by the state, by institutions of higher education, or by professional bodies, of any qualifications acquired outside of the home country. Such equivalence does not imply identicality of the courses that lead to qualifications but rather parity, in quality rather than quantity. This parity of esteem, moreover, partly determines the value of a qualification to the individual and also represents the value that society at large is prepared to put on it.

Need for Equivalences

Even at the national level—especially in a federal state—disputes can arise about the comparative worth of qualifications. Predictably, the problems of equivalence are exacerbated between countries. Analysis reveals five cases where mutual recognition of qualifications is important. The first concerns access to higher education— the question of whether the university entrance qualification, usually the full secondary school diploma or leaving certificate, will be acceptable abroad. The second case, which is the most common, arises in moving from one stage to the next in higher education—for example, from undergraduate studies—when the student wishes to continue his work abroad. The third case is closely related; it concerns the recognition at home of periods of study spent abroad. There is, for example, the case of the language student who wishes time spent abroad studying a foreign language to count, perhaps as credit units, when he returns home. The fourth case relates to the degree of recognition accorded by the home authority to qualifications acquired abroad. A graduate with a foreign diploma presenting himself to an employer will hope to receive the same consideration that he would receive if he had obtained his qualification at home. The fifth case, a particular instance of the fourth, is the most important of all; it concerns the granting of a license to a diploma holder to practice a profession, either in his own country or elsewhere, regardless of where his qualification was awarded. For each of these cases, solutions must be found.

Until recently political circumstances often facilitated the necessary recognition. Colonial powers imposed their own systems of higher education on peoples under their tutelage. The orientation and content of courses often merely mirrored practices current in the foreign nation that ruled. Equivalences were thus easier to negotiate. Even today, between Britain and France and their former overseas territories, the evaluation of qualifications is facilitated by this chance of history. Yet, with independence, systems of higher education inevitably began to diverge. Similarly, when requests for recognition were infrequent, they could be treated as exceptions, so that the difficulty was easily resolved. Today, when students migrate to study in remote countries, whose higher education systems are little known elsewhere, the problem is more intractable.

Clearly, a consensus on recognition is easier to achieve where countries share a common linguistic or cultural heritage. Thus, between Britain, the other English-speaking countries of the Commonwealth, Ireland, and the United States, comparatively little difficulty is experienced. The score of Spanish equivalence agreements concluded with the Latin American countries demonstrate the same fact. A useful role is served in this respect by organizations such as the Association of Commonwealth Universities (ACU), the *Association des universités partiellement ou entièrement de langue française* (AUPELF: Association of Partially or Wholly French-Language Universities), the *Oficina de educación ibero-americana* (Bureau of Hispano-American Education), and the Union of Arab Universities. All have been active in promoting multilateral and bilateral agreements founded on cultural or former political ties.

Need for Classification

Recognition is further complicated by the fact that the problem is not confined to universities. It embraces the totality of higher education and is particularly acute in the technical field at a level just below that of institutions of the highest rank. Indeed, the first step toward a solution of the problem might be to grade the institutions most involved. One such classification might include traditional universities, higher-grade technological institutions (usually on a par with universities), higher-grade professional institutions, lower-grade technical institutions, lower-grade semi-professional institutions, higher-grade teacher training institutions, lower-grade teacher training institutions, and other institutions (principally those catering to leisure activities). This approximate hierarchy of institutions would vary considerably, however, from country to country.

Qualifications might also be categorized in a parallel descending order. Unfortunately, save for academic degrees conferred in universities and diplomas awarded in higher-grade technological and professional institutions, comparison of the multiplicity of qualifications that will eventually require equivalence, particularly for occupational purposes, has scarcely begun.

In any case, it might be argued that the concept of levels of qualification has lost some of its validity. It is now increasingly acknowledged that a qualification represents only minimum competence; it is enhanced by experience, whether by research for a higher degree or by practice of the profession or occupation concerned. To represent the idea of continuity, the term *stage* might be more appropriate. Each stage represents the point of competence or maturity reached before moving on to a further gradient of study or experience. In the evaluation of academic qualifications, there are three main ascending stages. In the English-speaking world, these are represented by the bachelor's degree, the master's degree, and the doctorate. In technical education three stages may also be identified: technician, higher-grade technician, and technologist.

Such a categorization becomes more urgent as the necessity for lifelong education increases. The updating, upgrading, or retraining of individual competence must occur more frequently, as knowledge once acquired becomes out of date as promotion is sought, or as an occupation is superseded by automation or the development of new techniques. The refurbishing that these situations imply means that more people will have to seek the courses required abroad. This further emphasizes the provisional nature of all qualifications and vitiates the static view that a qualification, awarded at or near the age of twenty-one, equips its possessor for his entire working life and entitles him to enjoy in perpetuity the status and privileges the qualification formerly carried with it.

Extent of Demand for Equivalences

Global statistics on the numbers of students seeking equivalences are not available, but numbers seem to be increasing exponentially. In the 1960s the overall total of foreign students enrolled in 124 countries grew at an annual rate of 8.1 percent. In 1974 it was surmised that a million students were studying outside their own country (Ballastero, 1974). Information on the nations from which students come and in which they study is also fragmentary. Developing nations probably still head the list of dispatching countries. The most industrialized nations—particularly those possessing a widely understood language, such as English, French, Spanish, or Russian—are the principal host countries, although the Arabic nations are also important.

Thus, some 220,000 foreign students studied in the United States in the 1974–75 academic year. In 1973–74 at least 44 percent of the foreign students in French universities came from the Third World, mainly from former French territories. Some seventy thousand overseas students and nurses (not all in higher education according to the British definition of the term) were in Britain in 1970. Of these, a quarter did not complete their courses or failed their examinations. In technical and teacher training institutions, the failure rate was put as high as 40 percent—a figure that compares very unfavorably with the 90 percent success rate of British students who go abroad to study (Jessel, 1970). Indeed, in France and Britain, foreign students make up 10 percent of the student population (Halls, 1976). In Switzerland, although the number of foreign students involved is much smaller, one student in four comes from outside the country (Halls, 1976). According to *Foreign Students in Higher Education* (UNESCO Office of Statistics, 1975), a document circulated at a UNESCO conference in Helsinki, Finland, in October 1975, Canada attracted 12,425 foreign students in 1972.

Other statistics, however, reveal surprisingly low figures. In 1974, for example, only 1.5 percent of students in the nine countries of the European Economic Community (EEC) were reading for degrees outside their own country, and only .5

percent, despite official pledges of cultural cooperation, were studying in other member states. The uncertain and incomplete nature of the data available is itself a factor that militates against the conclusion of international conventions. Before agreeing to recognition of qualifications, nations will need to know more precisely the extent of their commitment.

Motivation for Study Abroad

No global study has been made of students' reasons for seeking higher education outside their own country. For students in developing nations, the reason most commonly advanced is that facilities for specialist study, usually at postgraduate level, are lacking at home. Prestige is also involved; there is no doubt that some countries and institutions exert a power of attraction. The University of Cairo, for example, enrolls students from throughout the Arab world; universities such as Harvard, Moscow, Oxford, and Paris enjoy an international reputation.

Students are sometimes obliged to study elsewhere because they are not particularly gifted; their qualifications would not give them access to higher education in their own country. Others, although of high intellectual caliber, may find their way barred at home because of the existence of a strict *numerus clausus* (limitation on numbers). Thus, in the 1960s German students excluded by a shortage of places from medical faculties in their own country studied in Austria or Switzerland, where entrance competition was not so severe. North Americans came to Britain to read for a doctorate because studies were less expensive than in their own country.

For a privileged few from all nations, what might be called the "finishing school" syndrome is manifest; the distinction allegedly imparted by certain institutions tempts the rich to study abroad. At the other end of the financial spectrum, some students covertly or openly seek to emigrate permanently from their native land, lured by the prospect of obtaining a qualification that would open up a better career abroad. And there are others who are political refugees seeking asylum overseas. Clearly, the motivation for study abroad is extremely varied.

Treaties and Conventions on Equivalences

Such treaties and conventions on equivalences as exist may be variously classified as multilateral, bilateral and pluricultural, and bilateral and largely unicultural and unilingual. They may be negotiated either between governments or between institutions. In the field of intergovernmental agreements, Spain and the Latin American countries led the way, the first such convention dating from 1840. This convention was followed by a series of accords, which not only recognized academic equivalences but also conferred the right to practice a profession. Early agreements between institutions include those completed between the Universities of Paris and Montreal in 1925 and between the University of Paris and British universities in 1938.

The period after World War II saw the active intervention of UNESCO. This intervention was stimulated by the developing countries, whose own systems of higher education lacked the resources to meet their need for specialized manpower. Demand accelerated as newly independent nations emerged in Africa and Asia. After discussion at its Fourteenth General Conference in 1966, UNESCO instituted several practical measures to aid in the problem of equivalences.

Regional organizations. Regional organizations have also been active in the field. The Council of Europe, comprised of eighteen states of Western Europe, was instrumental in promoting three conventions on equivalences among its member countries. The European Convention on the Equivalence of Diplomas Leading to Admission to Universities was signed in 1953. (An additional protocol, signed in 1964, extended the scope of this agreement to include diplomas awarded in former colonies of the European powers.) The

1953 convention was followed in 1956 by the European Convention on Equivalence of Periods of University Study. This agreement mainly covered modern-language students who spent part of their course abroad and was ratified by fifteen member states of the organization. However, the most general agreement, the European Convention on the Academic Recognition of University Qualifications, was ratified by only a dozen Western European countries in 1959. Indeed, the three treaties contain escape clauses that nullify much of their value. The first convention, for example, merely stipulates that university places for foreigners shall be provided within the limits of availability of places overall.

For the European Economic Community, consisting first of six and now of nine countries of Western Europe, equivalences have become a matter of urgency. The Treaty of Rome (1957), which governs their association, stipulates freedom of establishment within any member state for professional people who are self-employed (Article 57). But this clause of the treaty must await full implementation until agreement is reached on the mutual recognition of the qualifications of doctors, dentists, lawyers, engineers, and others who fall within its scope.

The enlargement of EEC membership has restimulated interest in closer cultural unity. Thus, in June of 1975, the EEC Council of Ministers adopted a draft directive for the mutual recognition of medical qualifications. Preliminary to this agreement, a list of recognized medical qualifications within member countries was drawn up and stipulations made for minimum requirements. The final directive had not been promulgated by the end of 1975. In response to a question in the European Parliament on January 13, 1975, the EEC Commissioner for Research, Science, and Education, Guido Brunner, indicated what he saw as the way forward toward blanket equivalences: "What is needed today is for governments and professional organisa-

tions in Europe to show that they are confident that the doctors, lawyers, architects and engineers trained in their countries are good enough to stand up to 'competitors' from other European countries."

Other intergovernmental groupings have also signed conventions. The Nordic Council, for example, has achieved a high degree of mutual recognition among its four Scandinavian members; members of the council signed a formal Treaty of Cultural Cooperation in 1971. The nine socialist states of Eastern Europe, together with Cuba, signed a Convention on the Mutual Recognition of Qualifications in Prague in 1972. The South East Asia Treaty Organization has also initiated studies with a similar aim in view.

On the bilateral and pluricultural plane, France and the Federal Republic of Germany have achieved a modicum of success. Acting on behalf of their respective national authorities, the French *Conférence des présidents des universités* (Conference of University Presidents) and its German counterpart, the *Westdeutsche Rektorenkonferenz* (West German Rectors Conference), have concluded a number of equivalence agreements on a subject area basis, some of which include dispensations for students spending part of their time in the other country, with provision for reintegrating them on the appropriate rung of the qualifications ladder when they return home. But the kind of detailed examination of courses that this requires is so painstaking that it is probably not suitable for achieving equivalences on a multilateral basis.

Nongovernmental organizations. Among nongovernmental organizations, the International Association of Universities (IAU), with an academic institutional membership in over a hundred countries, has long concerned itself with the question of equivalences. In 1966 it published an invaluable reference collection of the 128 equivalence agreements signed between 1894 and 1961. A second volume, bringing the collection up to date, was in preparation in 1975. The IAU is frequently called on to advise governments and universities as to the level of particular foreign qualifications.

Among specialist bodies, the World Health Organization, as a first step toward equivalences, has initiated studies on the international mobility of health personnel. Increasing movement of school pupils between countries has also brought a demand for a valid worldwide university entrance qualification; hence, the creation of the International Baccalaureate by a private agency, the International Baccalaureate Office in Geneva, Switzerland.

The activities of UNESCO since 1966 are perhaps the most significant. Publications and case studies have been commissioned by UNESCO to survey the problem of equivalences. In 1974 a Regional Convention for the Recognition of Qualifications was signed by the Latin American and Caribbean states. The agreement contained a number of interesting innovations: it allowed for the immediate recognition of stages of higher education already completed, whether for pursuing higher studies or for exercising a profession; it also set up permanent machinery within the region to ensure that the agreement would be fully implemented. UNESCO has also initiated discussions for a regional convention for European and Arab states bordering on the Mediterranean. On the drawing board are plans for similar regional conventions covering all the Arab states, the African states, and the states of Eastern and Western Europe.

The projected pan-European agreement, which may also include the United States and Canada, will undoubtedly be the key convention. Its inspiration derives from declarations on future cooperation made in the Final Act of the Conference on Security and Cooperation in Europe, signed at Helsinki in August 1975 by the major European powers, the United States, and the Soviet Union. The UNESCO vision is indeed ambitious; from a network of overlapping regional agreements, it hopes to arrive at a universal convention on equivalences. This is a long-term goal; reserva-

tions of a political and economic nature about absolute freedom of movement will persist. The equivalences problem is the nub, whether between institutions of higher education or between different national sectors of employment.

Clearly, political considerations constitute the greatest barrier. Where institutions are allowed to negotiate equivalences, they are frequently successful. Universities may draw up, for their own benefit, lists of qualifications that they are prepared to recognize. For example, the Council on Evaluation of Foreign Student Credentials acts as an advisory board for universities and colleges in the United States. Similarly, British universities keep a register of foreign school-leaving certificates that they will accept for university entrance; some also stipulate which first degrees from foreign universities they are prepared to recognize as qualifying for entrance to a higher degree course. In general, institutional provisions appear more liberal than those drawn up by governmental authorities. Yet institutions may be the better judges. By developing a body of formal and informal reports on their foreign counterparts, institutions are able to assess the value of foreign diplomas for their own courses. There is, however, no systematic coordination between institutions that operate on this ad hoc basis.

Equivalences can, however, be granted or withheld by governments as a matter of policy. A country may wish to foster good cultural relations with another, to discourage its own nationals from studying abroad, or to dissuade foreigners from entering its universities, for reasons totally unconnected with academic excellence. Indeed, a touch of chauvinism sometimes enters into national decisions.

Limitation on Numbers and the Establishment of Academic Criteria

The principal political and economic hurdle to the granting of equivalences is that presented by the existence of a *numerus clausus* in university faculties, especially in subjects such as medicine and engineering, where every place offered to a foreigner shuts out a qualified national. Some countries have a fixed quota for foreign students. In the Federal Republic of Germany, the proportion of foreigners admitted in 1975 was set at 8 percent. Furthermore, the heads of German universities have proposed a scheme by which all foreign applicants to universities would be placed in three categories: those from the Third World, whose applications would be considered individually; those from non-EEC countries in Europe and from North America, who would also initially be subject to individual decisions (although an annual review of these would be undertaken by subject of study and country of origin to see if any normative equivalence principles could be derived from practice); and those from EEC countries, who would come under global or blanket equivalence arrangements derived from practice. Thus, one political answer to the problem is the exegesis of a corpus of precedents supplemented by favored-nation clauses. And, even where universities are more autonomous, the influx of foreign students can still be regulated through the immigration laws.

Another political proposal that has found some favor in Western Europe is the establishment of national equivalence centers under the egis of the Council of Europe—a suggestion approved by the 1971 Conference of European Ministers of Education. Three centers—in the Federal Republic of Germany, Sweden, and the United Kingdom—have already been instituted. Such centers, however, are designed to serve merely as information agencies, providing details of postsecondary education and of admission requirements but studiously refraining from evaluating qualifications. A European Equivalences Centre would act as a central clearinghouse. This proposal, although admirable in itself, does not seem to deal fully with the central issues.

Nevertheless, governments are wary of going further. The first efforts of EEC senior officials to establish quantitative criteria for the evaluation of courses leading to professional diplomas encountered opposition. The officials stipulated that a medical degree had to include a specified number of hours of instruction in specific subjects, supplemented by a specified number of hours of practical experience. Scrutiny of such criteria, however, revealed several inconsistencies. There was no unanimity, for example, on what constitutes one hour of instruction or on what form instruction must take (such as lectures, classes, or tutorials). The inclusion of many variables often makes such quantitative criteria imprecise. Moreover, if criteria are laid down in this way as minimum standards, there is a clear risk that they will soon become maximum standards. Such procedures, stemming from an overlegalistic approach, also arouse protest from academics, who see their traditional freedom being threatened.

Another approach, sponsored by the Council of Europe, which attempted to lay down guidelines for the content of subjects taught in universities, proved just as unacceptable to academics. As a model for this approach, the council produced, in 1970, a syllabus of minimum requirements for theoretical mathematics. It was quickly pointed out that such a procedure would stifle all initiative within universities.

In Western Europe, at least, the political and academic will to promote educational harmonization, let alone integration, can only be characterized as weak; cooperation is the most that can be realized at present.

Professional Consequences of Equivalences

The question of what professional consequences may result from recognition of qualifications is not easily resolved. Countries can afford to be generous when a foreign student with a master's degree in philosophy wishes to proceed to a doctorate in the same subject. But it is the *effectus civilis* of recognition of vocational qualifications that is vital. A country that continues to admit large numbers to its engineering schools and to send them out as qualified engineers to seek positions abroad when its own engineers are underemployed may be depriving would-be engineers elsewhere the chance of qualifying or, once qualified, of earning a living. In countries where licenses to practice are not granted by governments but by professional bodies armed with legal powers (such as in the United Kingdom, where over a score of associations regulate entrance requirements and qualifications but entrust the training of their future members to the universities), the outcry against the wholesale granting of equivalences is a warning that no politician can ignore. In contrast, in countries where the state grants degrees conferring the right to exercise a profession, as in France, the problem does not arise so acutely, for matters can be regulated nationally at will.

The high cost of university places—nowhere covered by students' fees alone—is also an economic factor of some importance. In the United Kingdom, for example, higher education is much more expensive than in France, with the result that in the 1973–74 academic year more than ten times as many British students were studying in France as French students in British institutions. Economic reciprocity is difficult to achieve.

A relevant sidelight that has emerged from the recent focus on equivalences is the reassertion of the need for the legal protection of degrees and qualifications. So-called "degree mills," particularly in the United States and Britain, where the practice is not outlawed, still award bogus qualifications—at a price. This procedure may now be stamped out.

Pedagogical Problems of Equivalences

Nomenclature. It might be argued that a political solution to equivalences cannot be satisfactorily achieved unless pedagogical problems are resolved. One difficulty lies in the differences between systems in names of courses, subjects, faculties, departments, and types of institution. "Higher normal school," for example, although an accurate translation, would hardly be a fair description of *Ecole normale supérieure* in Paris, one of the elitist *grandes écoles* at the pinnacle of the French educational system. Originally designed to train secondary teachers, as its name implies, the institution now turns out high-quality scientific researchers and future university lecturers.

Congruence of courses. A second facet of the pedagogical problem concerns the congruence of courses—how the stage of education the student has just completed in his own country fits the higher stage he is seeking to enter abroad. For example, a first-year undergraduate course in mathematics may require knowledge of calculus, but this may not have been required in the secondary course followed by the foreigner in his own country. The mismatch between knowledge previously acquired and knowledge sought is a significant cause of students' dropping out of programs. Similarly, the student armed with a foreign qualification may enter a profession elsewhere without the knowledge of local conditions, laws, and regulations required to practice successfully, despite the fact that, academically, his diploma is of adequate quality. Lack of congruence is a cause of failure not yet sufficiently studied.

There are some remedies available for these deficiencies. Detailed comparisons of courses at all levels is virtually impossible, if only because they are constantly being updated. However, a general outline of the corpus of previous knowledge expected could be made available to the foreigner before he leaves his own country. If the student has gaps, these could then be remedied by special supplementary teaching before departure.

Linguistic and academic competence. Linguistic competence cannot be overstressed, because research has shown this to be the greatest single cause of failure for foreigners who are studying in a language not their own. Again, much might be done before the student arrives in the host country. A university might make its offer of a place dependent on the foreigner's passing, before he arrives, a standard linguistic test, such as TOEFL (Test of English as a Foreign Language); it could even insist on a basic competence in the specialized vocabulary of a subject. Such specific vocabulary lists already exist in French, for example, for the study of biology and for literary criticism. Tests of comprehension to ensure the ability to follow lectures and classes might also be appropriate.

At the same time, more formal requirements might be relaxed. It may not be indispensable, for example, for a foreign student wishing to study a subject in the arts to have reached a pass standard in mathematics (a condition of acceptance often required of indigenous students). In addition, students from developing nations might be exempted from the requirement of competence in a second European language, since their studies are in any case to be carried out in a tongue that is not their own.

Sound equivalence conventions should require the elimination of possible causes of failure. Toward this goal, a diagnosis could be made of the student's academic and linguistic insufficiencies. Further, the foreign student could learn about study methods and modes of evaluation of academic work in the foreign country. Such steps would minimize cultural shock and prevent disorientation during the initial period of the student's stay abroad. If nations offer university places to foreigners, they should ensure that these are not wasted.

Some countries already operate remedial schemes of this nature. To ensure that the foreigner is of sufficient academic caliber and has a requisite command of German, some universities in the Federal Republic of Germany arrange a preparatory course *(Studienkolleg)*. Similarly, the Patrice Lumumba Friendship University in Moscow caters especially to foreigners, who comprise three quarters of the students.

Ideally, candidates for a foreign course not only possess qualifications that would

admit them to a course of comparable difficulty in their own country but arc also of the same intellectual capacity as indigenous students. If, for example, one country admits the top 25 percent of its young people to higher education, then the foreign candidate, if he is to succeed, should clearly not fall below the twenty-fifth percentile of ability in his own country. In short, if the degree of selectivity between two countries wishing to grant mutual recognition of their diplomas is similar, recognition will be a simpler process.

Problems of the returning student. The problem of equivalences does not end with successful completion of the course. The question of what happens when the student, bearing his foreign qualifications, returns home is also of immense importance. Doubts may be raised at home as to whether the diploma he has acquired with so much effort is relevant. For example, a medical degree that does not include some element of tropical medicine would be inappropriate for a future doctor going home to practice in equatorial Africa. Sometimes, therefore, supplementary study may be required after the student has returned home. Such a situation underscores the need for further information about courses on a worldwide basis. Diplomas acquired abroad that go unrecognized represent a waste, which, given the high cost of education, can be tolerated neither by the individual nor by society.

In the last analysis, the sole valid criterion for granting equivalences is whether the person coming from abroad holds a qualification that fits him for the stage of education to which he seeks entrance or enables him to perform the job for which he is theoretically qualified. To apply this criterion, specifications need to be spelled out with some precision. If the foreign student does not have the qualification needed for certain degrees or positions, he could be required to take supplementary courses to fill the gaps in his knowledge or expertise. This is not to denigrate the foreign qualification; in the country where it was awarded, it may well be perfectly adequate. But conditions elsewhere may be different.

New Approaches to Equivalences

If the solution outlined above appears utopian, one must consider the new approach to equivalences within the EEC. For qualifications that relate to the exercise of a vocation, ad hoc committees will examine national lists of qualifications and announce those which they will recognize. While this procedure may facilitate mobility, it will certainly engender other problems. For example, it raises the question of what the effect will be on a profession, as regards status and remuneration, when those qualified but unemployed in one country, where there is an excess of a particular expertise, establish themselves in another country, where there are vacancies to be filled. Much will also depend on the degree of liberality or Malthusianism practiced with regard to entrance to courses of professional training. Only time will show whether the new method will lead to international imbalances within the professions.

Another possible expedient may be recognition ad hominem. Such an approach, however, raises questions about the overall judgment to be made on an individual and whether or not those seeking to move from one country to another should be supplied with a kind of internationally recognized transcript of studies and experience, equivalences passport or profile of ability, which would include brief outlines of all the courses followed. Such a record would resemble the kind of student book already used in German-speaking universities. Assessments of individuals could then at least be made on the basis of functional comparability as opposed to nominal (or paper) comparability.

One might also proceed by way of institutional accreditation, as practiced in the United States. In such a system, institutions in various countries would band together and agree to grant equivalences to students from each other's institutions. They would also inform each other of significant changes in course content. Other institutions would be allowed to join these academic consortia after scrutiny of their standards. Such a move would not entail standardization of programs but rather a real harmonization between academic institutions. Institutional accreditation postulates acceptance of the idea that, within broad parameters, there are many different ways of preparing students for qualifications, coupled with a readiness to admit that one course is as good as another and sufficiently similar to warrant substitution. It implies a slow forging of links between institutions and a growth in mutual trust.

In any case, one must fall back on the fact that formal qualifications are merely end statements that certify that, at a particular moment in time, an individual has reached a certain standard. These qualifications cannot have lifelong validity. Knowledge increases or decreases over time; skills and competences either deteriorate through lack of use or are improved by regular practice. Acknowledgment of this banal truth may inspire institutions (and perhaps governments) to adopt a more liberal policy on equivalences, particularly when the individual concerned has evidence that he has pursued his studies or practiced his skills beyond the level attested to by a formal diploma.

Bibliography

American Association of Collegiate Registrars and Admissions Officers. *Do-It-Yourself Evaluation of Foreign Student Credentials: Guide to the Academic Placement of Students from Foreign Countries in Educational Institutions in the United States of America.* Washington, D.C.: American Association, 1961–1970.

Association des universités partiellement ou entièrement de langue française. *Répertoire des études supérieures et des équivalences de titres, de diplômes et de périodes d'études entre les universités de langue française.* Paris: Association des universités, 1972.

Ballastero, A. T. "From Equivalence to Evaluation: Appraising the Man, Not the Diploma." *UNESCO Chronicle*, 1974, *20*, 146.

Berckx, P. "De integratie van de Belgische
diplomas en getuigschriften in het onderwijs
in Nederland, en omgekeerd." *Tijdschrift
voor bestuurswetenschappen en publiekrecht,*
1974, *29,* 286–334.

Committee of Vice-Chancellors and Principals.
*Compendium of University Entrance Require-
ments, 1976–1977.* London: Association of
Commonwealth Universities, 1975.

Dupuy, R. J., and Tunkin, G. *Comparability of
Degrees and Diplomas in International Law.*
Paris: UNESCO, 1973.

Halls, W. D. (Ed.) *World Guide to Higher Education: A Comparative Survey of Systems, Degrees
and Qualifications.* London: Bower, New
York: UNIPUB, Paris: UNESCO Press,
1976. Compare with *Introduction,* pp. ix–
xxii, by J. Guiton and W. D. Halls.

Halls, W. D. *International Equivalences in Access
to Higher Education.* Paris: UNESCO, 1971.

Institute of International Education. *Handbook
on U.S. Study for Foreign Nationals.* New York:
Institute of International Education, 1975.

International Association of Universities. *Collection of Agreements Concerning the Equivalence
of University Qualifications.* Paris: International Association of Universities, 1966.

International Association of Universities. *Methods of Establishing Equivalence Between Degrees
and Diplomas.* Paris: UNESCO, 1970.

Jessel, S. "Why Many Foreign Students Fail."
(London), September 23, 1970.

Office national des universités et écoles
françaises/Deutscher akademischer Austauschdienst. *Equivalences universitaires
franco-allemandes/Deutsch-französische Studi-
enäquivalenzen.* Paris and Bonn: Office na-
tional/Deutscher akademischer Austauschdienst, 1971.

Sen, A. *Problems of Overseas Students and Nurses.*
Slough, England: National Foundation of
Educational Research, 1970.

UNESCO Office of Statistics. *Foreign Students
in Higher Education: By Country of Origin and
by Host Country, 1972.* Paris: UNESCO, 1975.

W. D. HALLS

See also: Degrees, Diplomas, and Certificates.

ESKIMOS

See Access of Minorities: The North American Indian.

ETHIOPIA

*Population: 26,076,000 (mid 1973 esti-
mate). Student enrollment in primary school:*
*854,000 (1974); secondary school (academic,
vocational, technical): 184,500 (1974); higher
education (university): 10,000 (1973–74). Student enrollment in higher education as percentage of age group (18–22): 0.4%. Language of
instruction: Amharic (primary level); English
(second and third levels). Academic calendar:
September to July. Percentage of gross national
product (GNP) expended on education: 3.4%.*

The system of higher education in Ethiopia should be viewed in the context of the
overall educational system of the country.
Western-style education is a relatively new
phenomenon. It was started in 1907 with
the opening of the first school by Emperor
Menelik II in Addis Ababa. The educational system, which has grown steadily
since then, was interrupted during the
Italian occupation (1936–1941). An accelerated expansion of the school system took
place with the restoration of independence
in 1941, when the government assigned
high priority to education.

It should be noted, however, that prior
to the advent of Western-style education,
Ethiopia had had a long tradition of church
education, going back many centuries.
When the country adopted the Christian
faith in the fourth century A.D., the Ethiopian Orthodox Church began to operate
a rather extensive school system in the
northern and central parts of the country.
Those schools, which were largely religious
and nonsecular, were attached to churches
and monasteries. At times they were single-
room schools run by a local priest, but
often they contained several classes which
not only taught the Ethiopian script but
also offered advanced learning in a variety
of specializations, including church music,
liturgy, poetry, and philosophy (Mulugeta,
1959). The church still operates these
schools, which enroll about 500,000 children. In addition, a large but unknown
number of children attend the Koranic
schools of the large Muslim community.

Although the school system enrolls only
about 20 percent of the school-age population, the growth since 1945 has nonetheless been quite rapid. Table 1, which shows

Table 1. Enrollment Growth Pattern for Selected Years

		1959-60	1973-74
1-6	Primary school	200,000	854,000
7-8	Secondary school	14,600	102,500
9-12		5,200	82,000
Higher Education		827	10,000
Total		220,627	1,048,500

Source: Compiled from Ministry of Education *School Census* publications.

the growth pattern of the education system at the three levels for the period 1959 to 1974, indicates that the school system has grown almost five times in less than fifteen years.

In 1973, the last year for which complete records are available, 20 percent of the primary school age group (seven to twelve), 6 percent of the secondary school age group (twelve to eighteen), and less than .5 percent of the third-level-institution age group were attending school. The literacy rate for the country as a whole is about 15 percent, although it is considerably higher in urban centers.

In 1974 over a million students were enrolled in the school system. Of these approximately 80 percent were in primary schools, 18 percent in second-level institutions, and slightly over 1 percent in third-level institutions. Enrollment in private schools run by religious organizations and nondenominational agencies accounted for 27 percent at the primary level, 12 percent at the secondary level, and about 1 percent at the third level.

In 1974 the government's recurrent expenditure for education, including the university, was slightly over 20 percent of the total government expenditure. This constituted roughly 3.4 percent of the gross national product (GNP).

In 1972 the government undertook a comprehensive study of the educational sector. The main strategy that emerged from that review was that a much larger rate of expansion, 17 percent per annum compared to 10 percent previously, should be effected at the primary school level. In order to achieve this objective, various low-cost educational strategies have been proposed and are being seriously considered by the government.

Types of Institutions

The system of higher education in Ethiopia is quite small. The total enrollment at all third-level institutions was only 10,000 in 1973, of which about 7000 were enrolled at then National University (formerly the Haile Selassie I University, now Addis Ababa University).

The first full-fledged college-level institution was the University College of Addis Ababa, established in 1950 at the initiative of the government. Within the span of a decade, the government established other colleges, the major ones being the Engineering College (1953), the College of Agriculture (1954), the Public Health College (1954), and the College of Building Technology (1955). In addition, the Theological School, which was first started as a second-level institution in 1942, was raised to college status in 1960. The establishment of these colleges made evident the urgent need to coordinate higher education in order to avoid needless duplication. As a consequence, a Commission on Higher Education was formed to advise the government on the future direction of higher education. Largely as a result of the recommendations of this commission, a unified university system—the Haile Selassie I University incorporating the existing colleges—came into being in 1961. Other faculties and colleges established within the university system in the early 1960s were the Faculty of Education (1962), the College of Business Administration (1963), the Law School (1963), and the Medical College (1965). The School of Social Work, which began in 1959 as a second-level institution, became a department of the Faculty of Arts in 1961 and a degree-granting school of the university in 1966.

The university contains eleven faculties and colleges as well as a large and vigorous extension division with an enrollment of nearly three thousand students. Full-time enrollment at the Addis Ababa University is approximately seven thousand. There are about 550 full-time academic staff, of whom about 60 percent are Ethiopian.

In addition to the university, there are several other institutions of higher education. The University of Asmara, a small private university, was chartered in 1968. Established by an Italian Catholic order, it receives assistance from both the Ethiopian and the Italian governments. During the academic year 1973–74, the university had a total enrollment of about 1000 students, half of whom were in a "preparatory college," which is roughly equivalent to the last year of secondary education. Another 20 percent were following an Italian-oriented curriculum leading to degrees granted by the University of Padua. The rest were enrolled in modified Anglo-American curricula leading to degrees in the social sciences, law, and engineering.

The Academy of Pedagogy, located at Bahr Dar on the shores of Lake Tana, is a four-year degree-granting institution that was established by the government in 1972 with the financial assistance of the United Nations Development Programme (UNDP) and with some input from UNESCO. The academy trains instructors for teacher training colleges in a four-year degree program. The students themselves are drawn from former graduates of teacher training colleges with teaching experience. Since the college is new, it is still small, and the approximately three hundred students are all in residence. The institution is operated under the Ministry of Education, but plans are to provide it with an independent charter.

The College of Teacher Education trains junior secondary school teachers of academic subjects in a two-year diploma program. The college is situated in Addis Ababa, but the government has secured the necessary funds to build a new campus in the provinces. Currently it operates under the Ministry of Education.

The Bahr Dar Polytechnic, a two-year postsecondary institution operated under the Ministry of Education, was established in 1962 with assistance from the Soviet Union. It trains middle-level manpower in the technical fields and has an enrollment of about four hundred students.

The Ministry of Agriculture operates the Agricultural Institutes, two small institutions at Ambo and Jima for the training of extension and technician staff in agriculture. They are two-year postsecondary institutions and have a combined enrollment of about four hundred.

The Ministry of Agriculture also operates the Animal Health Institute, located at Debre Zeit, near Addis Ababa. This is also a two-year postsecondary institution. It has an enrollment of approximately 150 students who are being trained as manpower in the fields of animal health and veterinary science.

The training of French-language teachers for the secondary schools is accomplished at the *Ecole normale supérieure*, a small, postsecondary institution of about one hundred students, situated in Addis Ababa.

In addition, two mission secondary schools operate small, two-year postsecondary institutions to train teachers for their schools, the Evangelical College at Debre Zeit, and the Kuyera Adventist College, near Shashemena, in southwestern Ethiopia, which offers programs in teacher training and agromechanics. The combined enrollment of both colleges is approximately two hundred.

Admission Requirements

The minimum admission requirement to degree-granting institutions is the Ethiopian School Leaving Certificate. This certificate is awarded to those who successfully complete the secondary cycle and pass the Ethiopian School Leaving Certificate Examination (ESLCE) administered nationwide by the Ministry of Education through the university. At the minimum, students should pass in at least five subjects and earn a stipulated average. However, in recent years shortage of places at third-level institutions has resulted in keen competition, and only those whose performance is considerably above the minimum average can secure admission to degree programs. The ESLCE is roughly equivalent to the General Certificate of Education (London) at the ordinary level.

Two-year colleges, including the College of Teacher Education, require three papers with a minimum average. However, here again keen competition has meant that only those with higher scores stand a chance for admission to diploma and certificate courses.

Administration and Control

A number of postsecondary institutions are administered and supervised directly by the Ministry of Education. These include the teacher training institutes and to a lesser extent the College of Teacher Education. Similarly, the agricultural institutes are administered by the Ministry of Agriculture.

At the other end of the spectrum, the University of Addis Ababa, in line with the provisions of its charter, enjoys a considerable measure of autonomy, particularly on academic matters. A board of governors, composed mostly of senior government officials, constitutes the highest policymaking body and works closely with the government. Decision making on academic matters is left to the university-wide faculty council, a body composed of elected representatives of the several faculties, colleges, and research centers of the university. At the faculty level, decision making is left to academic commissions, chaired by a dean and composed of five other staff members elected from among the full-time staff members of a faculty. The duties and responsibilities of the board of governors, the university-wide faculty council, and the academic commissions of the faculties are set forth in the charter of the university, promulgated in 1950 for the former University College and revised in 1961 to reflect the new structure and governance that emerged with the incorporation of the various colleges into a single university system. The charter also sets forth in considerable detail the duties and responsibilities of the senior officers of the university, including the president, and the deans of the several colleges and faculties.

The academic rules and regulations of the university—covering such vital areas as admissions, degree requirements, and levels of academic performance—are set forth in the *Consolidated Legislation of the Faculty Council*. As its name signifies, this document contains the decisions of the faculty council as amended and modified over the years. The legislation also contains the provisions governing student unions and publications. In general, this is quite a liberal and forward-looking document which acknowledges the rights of students for self-government. Equally significant is the provision in the legislation which sets forth the principles governing academic freedom, staff employment security (tenure), and freedom of speech and assembly. In 1974 over 60 percent of the staff at then National University were Ethiopian. In addition, a number of prospective staff members are currently undertaking advanced study abroad, under the university's carefully drawn staff development plan. With the return of these staff members, the proportion of Ethiopian staff will increase significantly and is expected to reach 80 percent by 1978. Through the Staff Development and Promotion Committee, one of the standing committees of the faculty council, the university exercises autonomy in the recruitment, training, and promotion of its academic staff.

Programs and Degrees

Addis Ababa University grants undergraduate degrees in all the major disciplines of social and natural sciences and humanities. In addition, the professional schools—education, law, theology, business, engineering, agriculture, and public health—award undergraduate degrees, diplomas, and certificates in their respective areas of specialization. Except for law and engineering, which are five-year courses, all degree courses take four years, plus one year of rural service. The medical school is a special case; it follows basically the British pattern of medical curriculum. Thus far, the university has not started graduate studies. However, in 1973–74 plans were nearing completion to start graduate studies in a few selected areas where manpower requirements justify it and where the university has the requisite strength and capability. The areas that were being seriously considered were agriculture, Ethiopian studies, development studies (applied social science), and applied biological and health sciences.

Several schools and faculties of the university offer nondegree diploma and certificate courses. The university has had a tradition and a commitment to launch specially tailored courses to meet the specific middle-level manpower requirements of the government. In particular, the Faculty of Education and the Public Health College have for many years trained school directors and supervisors, nurses, and medical technicians in one- or two-year courses leading to diplomas or certificates.

Financing

With the exception of the few small private institutions which cater to about 1 percent of the enrollment, third-level institutions are government financed. Addis Ababa University receives its subvention directly from the Ministry of Finance and, within an agreed budgetary framework, enjoys considerable freedom and latitude in the allocation of its funds to its various programs and units. Other institutions, such as the two-year teacher training colleges and the agricultural institutes, receive their funds through their sponsoring government ministry (agriculture, education). The University of Asmara gets its operating funds primarily from the Catholic church

but, in addition, receives an annual government subsidy.

It is difficult to determine accurately the recurrent costs of third-level institutions operated directly by government agencies, because these costs are merged with the total operating costs of the parent ministry. In the case of the university, which receives its funds directly from the treasury and not through another government ministry, the annual government allocation for *recurrent* costs for 1973–74 was about 17 percent of the total government allocation for the education sector, or about 2.5 percent of the total government recurrent expenditure. In addition, the university receives foreign assistance in the form of staff, equipment, and fellowships. Owing to the inflated nature of expatriate salaries, it is difficult to assign dollar equivalents to foreign assistance. However, the university estimates this to be about 18 percent of its total recurrent costs.

Student Financial Aid

Higher education in Ethiopia (tuition, as well as room and board) is entirely free. Government officials have considered instituting a loan system, to cover room and board, and utilizing the savings accrued for the expansion of third-level institutions. No changes in this direction have yet occurred.

The University of Asmara, which is not a residential institution, charges a nominal tuition fee.

Student Social Background and Access to Education

Admission to Addis Ababa University and other third-level institutions is through a nationwide competitive examination, the Ethiopian School Leaving Certificate Examination. As in other African countries, the tendency is for secondary schools to concentrate in urban centers; student enrollment at the university reflects this urban bias. The government has made special efforts to redress the imbalance by promoting higher education opportunities for disadvantaged students, such as those from rural secondary schools or other deprived areas.

Current Problems and Trends

Ethiopia, unlike her sister African countries, was not colonized by European powers; as a result, higher education was not modeled on any one metropolitan system and therefore grew eclectically, benefiting from the experience of a number of foreign models. The system contains several interesting and worthwhile innovations, of which the most significant is the Ethiopian University Service (EUS)—a program that requires every university student to spend one academic year in the provinces doing rural service in his field of training before he can be awarded his degree or diploma.

In Ethiopia, as in many other African countries, higher education is a privilege enjoyed by a tiny minority. The entire educational system, including third-level education, tends to be theoretical and remote from the harsh realities of a poor nation. The excessive dependence on foreign teaching materials and foreign textbooks and the use of foreign languages as the medium of instruction further alienate the youth from their social and cultural milieu. Out of concern for these and related questions, the university launched the Ethiopian University Service. From the beginning, the program was conceived as having both an academic and a service component. The statutes approved by the faculty council on April 17, 1964, state in part: "The Council believes that a program wherein University students spend one academic year using their University training to provide services to local communities will be beneficial, not only to the national welfare but to the students in an educational sense; the program will enable students to understand in a much more significant way the problems and the needs of their country, particularly its less developed areas." A first group (129 students) was sent to the provinces in September 1964. From 1964 to 1974, approximately

3750 students participated in the EUS program. It is the consensus among students, staff, and administrators that the program has been quite successful. The students attest that they return with better insight into the problems of their country. The majority feel that the experience is rewarding and thus worth continuing.

The EUS program has also been adopted by other third-level institutions, including the College of Teacher Education, the Academy of Pedagogy, and the *Ecole normale supérieure*. The Provisional Military Government, which took control in 1974, has widened the scope to include secondary school students above grade 10.

By the spring of 1975 the staff and students of all third-level institutions had been sent, or were being sent, to the provinces to participate in the Rural Development Campaign launched by the Provisional Military Government. Secondary school students in grades 11 and 12 also are participating in this campaign.

The fundamental social and political changes that took place in the country in 1974–75 are bound to affect the future direction and orientation of higher education in Ethiopia. However, it is too early to discern the precise nature and outcome of the change.

International Cooperation

Third-level institutions in Ethiopia have benefited from their close collaboration with international and bilateral agencies. Addis Ababa University is a founding member of the Association of African Universities (AAU); it is also an active member of the International Association of Universities (IAU). In addition, it has received considerable assistance in the form of grants and loans from various bilateral and international agencies, including the United Nations Development Programme (UNDP), the World Bank (IBRD: International Bank for Reconstruction and Development), and the aid agencies of the governments of the United States, the Federal Republic of Germany, Sweden, the

United Kingdom, and others. The Ford Foundation in the United States has also assisted certain programs and units of the university, including the Law School and the main library.

The College of Teacher Education has a number of staff positions funded by UNESCO/UNDP. The French government provides some staff for the *Ecole normale,* and the University of Asmara receives support from the Catholic church and the Italian government.

MULUGETA WODAJO

Educational Associations

Ethiopian University Teachers
  Association (EUTA)
University of Addis Ababa
Addis Ababa, Ethiopia

University Students' Association of
  Addis Ababa
University of Addis Ababa
Addis Ababa, Ethiopia

National Union of Ethiopian University
  Students
University of Addis Ababa
Addis Ababa, Ethiopia

Bibliography

Abir Mordechai. "Education and National Unity in Ethiopia. *African Affairs,* 1970, *69* (274), 511–517.

Akilu Habte, "Brain Drain in the Elementary School, Why Teachers Leave the Profession." *Ethiopian Journal of Education,* 1967, *1* (1).

The Ethiopian University Service. Addis Ababa: Haile Selassie I University, 1973.

First Report of the Advisory Committee on Higher Education to His Imperial Majesty Haile Selassie I, Chancellor of the University. Addis Ababa: Haile Selassie I University, Advisory Committee, 1966.

A Forward Look, A Special Report from the President. Addis Ababa: Haile Selassie I University, 1969.

Germa Amare. "Aims and Purposes of Ethiopian Church Education." *Ethiopian Journal of Education,* 1967, *1* (1), 511–517.

Higher Education in Ethiopia: Survey Report and Recommendation. Salt Lake City: University of Utah Press, 1960.

The Last Decade. Addis Ababa: Haile Selassie I University, 1971.

Maaza Bekele. "Ethiopian Education: Challenge of the 70's." *Educational Leadership,* March 1968, 511–517.

Mulugeta Wodajo. "Post-War Reforms in Ethiopian Education." *Comparative Education Review,* 1959, *1* (2), 24–28.

Mulugeta Wodajo. "Ethiopia: Some Pressing Problems and the Role of Education in Their Resolution." *Journal of Negro Education,* 1961, *30* (3), 232–240.

Mulugeta Wodajo. "Haile Selassie University: A Brief Profile." In T. M. Yesufu (Ed.), *Creating the African University: Emerging Issues of the 1970's.* Ibadan, Nigeria: Oxford University Press, 1973. Pp. 244–250.

Pankhurst, R. "The Foundation of Education, Printing, Newspapers, Libraries and Literacy in Ethiopia." *Ethiopia Observer,* 962, *6* (3), 241–290.

The President's Annual Report. Addis Ababa: Haile Selassie I University, 1968–69, 1969–70, 1970–71, 1972–73.

Report on Investment in Education in Ethiopia. Educational Programming Investment Mission, September to November 1962 (14). Paris: UNESCO, 1963.

Second Report of the Advisory Committee on Higher Education to Haile Selassie I, Chancellor of the University. Addis Ababa: Haile Selassie I University, 1971.

Tadesse Terefe. "Progress, Problems, and Prospects in Ethiopian Education." *Ethiopia Observer,* 1964, *8* (1), 6–18.

Teshome Wagaw. "Access to Haile Selassie I University." *Ethiopia Observer,* 1971, *14* (1), 31–46.

Twentieth Anniversary of Higher Education in Ethiopia. Addis Ababa: Haile Selassie I University, 1971.

See also: Africa, Sub-Saharan: Regional Analysis; Cooperative Education and Off-Campus Experience: Cooperative Education Worldwide.

ETHNIC STUDIES
See Area Studies (field of study).

EUROPEAN ASSOCIATION FOR RESEARCH AND DEVELOPMENT IN HIGHER EDUCATION

The European Association for Research and Development in Higher Education (EARDHE)—an independent, international, nonprofit organization—was founded in May 1972 in Strasbourg, France. The association is the outcome of committee work on research in higher education sponsored by the Council of Europe. The association's aim is to promote educational research and development in European higher education and to aid higher education institutions in decisions concerning purposes, structures, curricula, teaching, and evaluation, taking into account social and cultural changes and demands.

Membership is open to individuals who teach or conduct research on higher education, as well as to national and international agencies, societies, institutes, centers, and other units that support research and development in higher education. Associate membership is open to non-European individuals and bodies engaged in higher education research and development.

The association sponsors congresses, conferences, symposia, and study groups. Cooperating with national and international organizations, the association promotes the establishment of documentation and information centers on research and innovation in higher education and the exchange of researchers in higher education.

A general assembly of the membership is held every two years. The business of the association is conducted by an executive committee. The association is funded by membership dues, publication sales, and contributions.

EARDHE publishes a quarterly newsletter and proceedings of general assemblies.

Eindhoven Technological University
H.G. 87.9, Postbus 513
Eindhoven, Netherlands

EUROPEAN BUREAU OF ADULT EDUCATION

The European Bureau of Adult Education, founded in 1953, provides information for European organizations, centers, and institutes concerned with adult education and acts as a forum for the exchange of ideas and experiences among countries and provides a stimulus for closer European collaboration in the field. The bureau organizes conferences and study tours; disseminates information; and stimulates contact with international bodies such as UNESCO, Council of Europe, European Communities, Food and Agriculture Organization, and International Labour Organisation.

Local, regional, national, or international bodies whose main activity is to train or educate persons above school-leaving age may become associate members. Regional bodies have a set subscription rate, but national associations determine their fees in conjunction with the steering committee.

The earliest activities of the bureau involved a strong element of personal contact and exchange of experiences. Later a need arose to gather, store, and disseminate larger amounts of information; consequently, the bureau began to prepare glossaries, directories, and abstracts. The organization also became involved in adult education legislation, research, and training. A conference on adult education legislation was held in Norway in 1972, and a conference on residential adult education was held in England in 1973. A study tour to France was organized in cooperation with the Dutch Centre of Adult Education.

Publications include *Notes and Studies,* periodical; *Directory of Adult Education;* and abstracts of current articles from European adult education journals.

Nieuweweg 4, P.O. Box 367
Amersfoort, Netherlands

EUROPEAN COUNCIL FOR EDUCATION BY CORRESPONDENCE

The European Council for Education by Correspondence (CEC) is an international nonprofit association of correspondence schools. Founded in 1963 in Brussels, CEC has a registered office in Ghent, Belgium. More than thirty leading correspondence schools from eleven countries belong to the council. The council aims to encourage education by correspondence, promote professional standards, and safeguard the interests of members and students. It cooperates with official bodies and others directly or indirectly interested in education by correspondence, facilitates exchange among its members, and promotes research into the methods of education by correspondence.

The CEC members who meet at the annual meeting elect the executive committee charged with carrying out the council's business. Special responsibilities are delegated to members of the executive committee. The education officer and the external relations officer help CEC members in those countries where assistance is requested. Contacts are established with governmental bodies, national and international correspondence education associations, and organized bodies directly or indirectly connected with the profession.

Since its founding CEC has voluntarily established a code of ethics for correspondence education. Its annual meetings, held since 1963, present opportunities for an active exchange of experiences, ideas, and teaching material on an international basis.

The association gives advice to correspondence institutes on all questions relative to reputable correspondence education, supplies detailed documentation about CEC members and correspondence education in a particular country, and helps to choose and organize courses appropriate to specific educational requirements.

CEC has published several pamphlets on correspondence education and regularly produces a bulletin.

18 rue du Professeur Baekeland
B-9000 Ghent, Belgium

EUROPEAN STUDIES
See Area Studies (field of study).

EVALUATION

Educational evaluation is the process of determining the value of an activity, object, or program. This process can be broken down into three phases: identification of objectives, collection of relevant evidence, and decision making.

Educational research and evaluation are not synonymous terms, although they are often treated as such. Educational research seeks definitive knowledge; evaluation seeks the most effective use of available resources to reach educational and social goals. Moreover, educational research entails careful planning of the experimental design, treatment, and statistical analyses—steps that are seldom possible in the evaluation of an operating program.

The goals or objectives of most educational programs are based on social goals. For example, the educational goal of preparing a specific number of people for various health specialties is designed to fulfill the social goal of improving and extending health care. Social goals may also provide the objectives to be attained by those completing the program. Surveys of social needs are therefore essential in defining the goals underlying the planning of programs and processes. In order to ensure that educational programs successfully fulfill educational and social goals, evaluation must be a part of the selection, planning, and implementation of educational processes and environmental impacts. Evaluation should be both formative (assisting in formulation and reformulation) and summative (assisting in decisions relative to continuance, modification, or termination).

The process of evaluation is continuous and inevitable. Every educational program is initiated and is either continued or discarded because of some form of evaluation by somebody. Yet the process of evaluation, as defined and developed in this essay, is peculiarly a feature of higher education in the United States. It scarcely exists in the United Kingdom, Canada, Australia, France, Federal Republic of Germany, or Japan.

In the United States the impetus for evaluation comes from the general public. Because of its decentralized nature and dependence on elected or appointed lay boards, American higher education is more subject to the public eye and to political processes than most systems. As a result public demand for a justification of university fiscal and academic policies frequently occurs. The different strains of thought and philosophical convictions underlying American higher education have led to a diversity that is widely regarded as a source of strength; at the same time, however, such diverse views about purposes and patterns have provoked a healthy skepticism of tradition and a demand for innovation and reappraisal.

The vast expansion of higher education in the United States—coupled with widespread doubt and dissatisfaction about its efficacy—has led to public insistence on evaluation of accomplishments in relation to resources utilized. As similar developments occur elsewhere in the world, a similar tendency to buttress tradition and authoritative opinion with evaluation becomes apparent.

Few individuals or groups can ever fully agree on the values or value hierarchies to be used in evaluation. As the focus shifts, from the performance of a student or faculty member, to local programs for the disadvantaged, to the national educational system, several elements increase dramatically: the size of the groups concerned, the amounts of money involved, the range of existing interests and values, and, ultimately, the impact of evaluation itself. Moreover, evaluation becomes more difficult to accomplish.

Evaluation of national educational systems proceeds according to the forces and concerns involved. If educated manpower is the prime concern (as it is in many developing countries), evaluation may be directed to the determination of needs and to the expansion or restructuring of the system to meet these needs. If the primary concern is with equal educational opportunity, coupled with individual development and freedom of choice (as it has been in the United States), evaluation may be

directed to the need for new institutions, financial assistance, counseling, or developmental programs. If the primary concern is dissatisfaction with the achievement of students, evaluation may be directed to the construction of measures of achievement and progress, to regional and community analyses, and to factors that explain differential attainment and that can be modified to improve results. If several competing views are operative, both program development and evaluation may be stalled.

An educational institution provides a physical, social, and psychological environment that is designed to facilitate learning. The environment of an urban university may be restricted to instructional facilities and procedures, while the environment of a residential institution may include dormitories, food services, recreational facilities, and social and cultural centers. An educational institution also provides processes or experiences (courses, instruction, social activities, community involvement, recreational and cultural events) that are designed to promote learning. But educational processes in a complex environment may dissipate into unrelated experiences. Departmental isolation and interdepartmental competition, coupled with the myopic concentration of each instructor on his own course, may focus attention on discrete content rather than on pervasive goals and competencies. Where unifying concepts and principles are nonexistent or not apparent, there can be no challenging sequence of steps by which students can rise to new levels of competence and self-confidence.

Evaluation of Students

Selection, classification, and placement of students are preceded by some form of recruitment, usually contacting students in preparatory schools or visiting students in their homes. Prospects sometimes are sought on the basis of exceptional athletic prowess, grades, activities records, or even financial or social status. Recruitment, whether carried out directly by full-time professionals, alumni, athletic coaches, or indirectly by correspondence, may involve blandishment, equivocation, or actual misrepresentation.

Despite widespread recruiting, even by publicly supported institutions, the recruitment process has not been studied in depth. Some private, high-cost institutions recruit merely to exist or to maintain quality. Other institutions recruit to change their image—for instance, by raising the intellectual quality of the student body, upgrading the athletic program, or improving the orchestra or other nonacademic aspects of the program. Still other institutions engage in extensive recruiting simply because their administrators view size, quality, and resources as interrelated. Recruiting can be expensive; costs vary, from a few dollars per student recruited by mail or volunteers, to several hundred dollars per student by full-time recruiters.

Evaluation of recruitment is desirable, if only because recruiters tend to overemphasize their impact. When recruitment costs are high, retention is a major concern, since recruitment costs increase with large student turnover. Recruitment costs can be estimated by dividing total recruiting expenditures by total student years. This calculation is based on a four-year period, but a similar approach can be used for lesser periods. Comparing the effectiveness of individual recruiters can be facilitated by relating each salary (plus expenses) to the years of attendance by those recruited. Such data must be treated cautiously, however, for rigid application would encourage recruiters to concentrate on students already favorable to the institution rather than on new prospects. Students who have been recruited are also a prime source of information in the evaluation of recruitment procedures.

Selection. An institution selects those to be admitted from those who apply or are recruited. At the same time, however, students select the institution to which they will apply. The institutional image, as viewed by students, parents, and high

school teachers, determines in part who will apply. Many initial contacts with the institution are made informally by personal visit or telephone. Lack of enthusiasm at that point may eliminate further contact. Some institutions, which admit almost all applicants, claim selectivity in enrollment on the basis of such informal rejections, even though the institution rather than the inquirer is rejected. The proportion of students who are admitted but do not enroll may run as high as 50 percent; in some institutions, these students may be more able than those who enroll.

Selection continues after the student is admitted and enrolled. Some rather selective institutions eliminate 30 percent of the freshman class by the end of the first year. Public institutions with very coarse admission screens may become selective by elimination within the first year or two.

Most of the emphasis in selection of students is on cognitive evidence: previous grades, high school ranks, test scores, and patterns of courses. High school grades or ranks generally give somewhat higher correlation with college grades than any other types of data. Various types of academic aptitude tests and achievement tests, however, run a close second, and the combination of grades or ranks (which vary with the school) and test scores (which are independent of the variations in schools) yield somewhat better predictions than either taken alone.

The correlation of grades, ranks, or test scores with the first-term grades ranges from .40 to .55; a combination may occasionally reach .70. Using data from a selected group of schools, Bloom and Peters (1961) found that, by employing a progressive adjustment of high school grades for differences in high schools and of college grades for differences in colleges, one could achieve a somewhat higher correlation. Other studies, however, cast doubt on the utility and the generality of that finding; these studies indicate that, regardless of the combination of cognitive evidence used, no more than 50 percent of the variation in first-term college grades will be accounted for. Some students do better than predicted, while others do far worse; some students fail despite the selection process, while those not admitted might have succeeded.

On the whole, secondary school course patterns are not significantly related to success in college, although there are obvious exceptions—the student with no secondary school mathematics, for example, will have difficulty in science or engineering. For transfer students the best evidence is from records at the previous institution. Students frequently suffer a slump in grades their first term after transferring and have a rather higher mortality rate than continuing students at similar levels. Hence, an institution may wish to establish some differential in the prior performance of transfers or to require demonstration of competency equal or superior to that of regular students at the same class level.

For graduate students the undergraduate record plays very much the same role as the high school record does for new freshmen. Again, the disparity in standards among disciplines and among colleges leads many institutions to require the Graduate Record Examination, the Miller Analogies Test, or some other battery of tests as a supplement to grades in making decisions about admission. If only pass-fail grades are available, test results become essential.

Affective factors, such as biographical background, interests, values, and personality, have been studied with a view to improving the selection process. Insofar as grade prediction is concerned, however, the weight of evidence is that affective assessment adds little. Research evidence, for example, thoroughly discredits the interview as a selective procedure. College grades either take little account of affective factors or treat them in a very unsystematic way, depending on the idiosyncrasies of individual instructors. Moreover, extensive use of affective measures raises serious questions about equity. Can imposition of affective requirements ever avoid the appearance of bias or prejudice?

Psychomotor factors, such as athletic prowess, artistic talent, musical skill, and social competency, may also be taken into account in the admissions process, especially if some balances in these factors is considered essential to a stimulating environment. Several American psychologists have argued that colleges depend too much on cognitive qualifications and too little on creative areas.

The cost and effectiveness of recruitment and selection should be critically examined. Such examination might indicate that more effort expended after enrollment would pay greater dividends than increased effort in selection. The most selective institutions graduate 85 to 90 percent of those initially enrolling; less selective ones graduate 30 percent or less.

Classification. Classifying a student into an appropriate major or curriculum may be part of the selection process, especially in complex institutions that have numerous specialized undergraduate programs. At the graduate level classification is almost inevitably part of selection, because applications and admissions are by schools or departments. In many cases, however, classification is separable from admission; the student is qualified for any of several majors or curricula and is himself seeking evidence to assist his choice.

Classification can be conducted on a probabilistic basis, employing objective data. Using the technique of regression analysis, for example, a number of variables can be combined to predict the average grades of a student in each of several fields. A different set of regression weightings would be determined for each field, but the same basic variables (if sufficiently extensive) would be used throughout. Presumably, then, the predicted grade averages would indicate those fields in which the student would be most likely to do the best work. In curricular areas, where grading is relatively generous, satisfactory grades will be predicted for almost all students. Systems of comparative prediction have been worked out in a number of universities; where their use for determination of the field is inappropriate, the results could prove useful in providing individual counseling.

In contrast to comparative prediction, differential prediction involves forecasting differences in performance in fields of study. This type of prediction ideally involves different test batteries for the several fields. The distinctiveness of programs may be limited to a few courses in which success is essential and in which special abilities are required. Thus, differential prediction must include abilities or aptitudes that may not make a major contribution to prediction of the grade point average but that will contribute to successful performance of essential requirements. One difficulty in attempting to set up a differential predictive model is that students seldom, if ever, complete the requirements for a number of different fields. Thus, in practice, no basis exists for predicting the difference in performance of an individual in two or more fields.

The multiple-discriminant function provides another useful tool for classification. Comparative prediction and differential prediction require quantifiable data and use a regression model to predict success in one or more fields. The multiple-discriminant function model takes into account a wide range of information and attempts to isolate subgroups of individuals characterized by a distinctive array of traits. The model then sets up a weighted combination of these traits, so that the spatial separation of the groups is maximized. Information on a given individual can then be utilized to determine his location relative to the various subgroups. The multiple-discriminant function approach may provide usable information where the regression approach does not. Several studies, for example, have indicated that there are indeed differences between students enrolled in the pure and in the applied sciences.

Classification can also be based on a clinical or individual approach. Data developed from analytic procedures may actually be used in counseling. In fact, the multiple-discriminant function analysis corresponds closely to counseling procedures, since it encourages one to consider a wide range of interests, personality traits, and physical competencies, as well as intelligence, and to explore the relationship of these to several possible fields of work. Some counselors utilize a rather directive approach in analyzing aptitudes and interests relative to curricular and vocational possibilities and suggest specific possibilities to an individual. Others urge individuals to engage in self-examination and in an exploration of curricular or vocational possibilities in order to reach their own conclusions.

In the American conception of education as an opportunity for individual development, minimal attention is given to economic and social needs in the classification process. Students may be informed that there are shortages in certain areas and surpluses in others, but they are seldom overtly pressured to choose on this basis.

Placement. Subsequent to selection and classification, a student is placed—a process that may involve several problems. For example, students enter college with and without high school chemistry credits. Furthermore, since chemistry courses in high school vary greatly in quality, a unit of high school chemistry is not in itself an adequate basis for placing the student in a college chemistry course. Testing may indicate that some students should be placed in the second or third quarter of a freshman chemistry sequence or, occasionally, in more advanced courses. Foreign languages and mathematics involve similar problems, because these fields are sometimes pursued for three or four years in the secondary school.

Local placement tests are expensive to develop and often of poor quality. Furthermore, frequent revision is essential in order to maintain a proper relationship between the test and the course. The tests of the Educational Testing Service (Princeton,

New Jersey) may be satisfactory, but their adoption by a faculty is frequently a matter of expediency rather than conviction. The Advanced Placement Tests of the College Entrance Examination Board are useful in placement but are usually taken only by students who have had special programs in secondary school.

In highly sequential disciplines the task of placement may involve comprehensive testing to determine capability for continuation in advanced courses. In noncumulative or nonsequential fields vocabulary level, reading scope, and reading ability may be more significant indicators of the level at which an individual can function. With adults and with transfer students, where the concern in placement is largely that of determining the appropriate class level (freshman or sophomore, for example) rather than placement in particular course sequences, the problem is even more complicated. How does one evaluate the educational level of an intelligent adult who has read widely, traveled extensively, and held responsible positions? Higher education has emphasized knowledge of specifics, despite the transient nature of such knowledge. There are no equivalency examinations that measure whether one has the insight, the power, and the ability to learn—qualities that hopefully remain after specifics have fled. One sensitive issue with respect to this type of placement is the granting of credits; colleges and their faculties are much more willing to grant advanced placement than to give credit for courses waived.

Recognition and reward. The next stage of student evaluation involves continuing appraisal, recognition, and suitable reward for progress. The most prevalent form of continuing appraisal is that of course grades, a form which involves a highly subjective and possibly biased approach by faculty members. In grading factual information is generally overemphasized; the appraisal of application and judgment involves values and therefore is more time consuming and more subjective than testing of knowledge. As a result students are forced to concentrate on memorization and rote recall. The elimination of grades, demanded by many students and some faculty members, is no solution to the problem. Maintenance of quality requires standards, and completely individualized standards are synonymous with no standards. If completion of a course or a degree is to have any significance, judgments must be made about student performance.

The real deficiency in student evaluation lies not so much in the grading system as in the compartmentalization of knowledge and the resultant tendency to lose sight of the major and pervasive goals of a college education. Senior comprehensive examinations—which are still found in some form or another in about a third of American and English universities—constitute one attempt to do this, but comprehensive examinations, like grades, may only assess what the student knows rather than what he is able to do as a result of his education.

Although pass-fail systems of grading are popular, history demonstrates that neither students nor faculty are long satisfied with a mere indication of passing. Studies of pass-fail practices indicate that students, lacking recognition for superior performance, tend to limit their performance to the passing standard and to seek other activities where rewards are forthcoming.

A major weakness of most systems of recognition and reward is that they overemphasize competition, faculty judgments, and public approbation. These emphases are perhaps necessary, given the nature of the human animal, and they may also be essential in demonstrating faculty and institutional commitment to excellence. However, education fails unless it also inculcates in the individual a respect for excellence, a motivation to attain excellence, and some capacity for assessing his own success.

Evaluation of Instruction

Both the evaluation of instruction and the planning of instruction must start from some accepted statement of responsibilities. There are at least six major obligations of instruction. The first obligation is to motivate students to become involved in their courses, in part by being shown the relevance of each course to their ultimate goals. The second obligation is to demonstrate just what is expected of students in the way of new knowledge, behavior, or reactions. This obligation requires some supervision or guidance in helping students to realize these expectations; lecturing is not enough. The third obligation is to provide extensive and meaningful materials upon which students can practice. It is not sufficient to assume that either a demonstration or the actual supervision of a student in one experience will yield mastery. It is hardly much better to suggest that students need more practice and then expect them to select the materials and proceed on their own. The fourth obligation of instruction is to gratify students by indicating that they are making progress, chiefly through pointing out the good as well as the weak and inadequate aspects of their performance. The fifth obligation is to organize the work, so that students can see its sequential cumulative aspect and so that they can relate current learning to past and future study. The learning of isolated facts or skills must be interspersed with activities that give some indication of how these facts and skills fit together. Finally, the sixth obligation of instruction is to provide students with high standards of performance and with means for judging the extent to which their performance meets these standards. If the grading of student performance is to supply an incentive for continued learning and increased mastery, it must go beyond the common testing practices that merely punctuate various phases of learning by the insertion of an A or an F, so that students will be encouraged to strive for high quality performance rather than to settle for satisfactory grades.

If these six functions are accepted as descriptive of the obligations of instruction, one can begin to evaluate instruction either by examining the extent to which these functions are fulfilled or by examining the extent of significant learning or change in the student. The first approach involves an examination or evaluation of the process; the second involves attention to the results. Both are necessary and supplement each other. Systematic evaluation of instruction is essential to the recognition and reward of good instruction, for faculty members, like students, are motivated as much by tangible recognition as by personal satisfaction. Evaluation can provide the knowledge and understanding that will lead to improved instruction and learning.

Student evaluation. The most common approach to the evaluation of instruction is through student evaluation of their professors. Yet programs of student evaluation tend to be sporadic. Student evaluation questionnaires are readily prepared, but—whatever the faculty involvement and the patterns of analysis—most questionnaires have a short life. An objective checklist is most convenient, but finding a set of items that is acceptable to all faculty members is almost impossible. Many contend, too, that a checklist gives no explicit suggestions for improvement. One alternative is a written statement by the student, but such statements are difficult to summarize and are likely to be used solely by the faculty member.

Is student evaluation a valid indication of good teaching? The answer is not a simple yes or no, although no is the unhesitating answer of many professors. Good teaching is basically a facilitation of the learning process; accordingly, every teacher should know what his students think about each course experience. Such an evaluation should include an appraisal of the teaching, the assignments, the examinations, and the textbook used. In addition, students should be able to indicate the objectives of the course and the relationships of the various assigned tasks to the achievement of these purposes; if few students can give such an indication, the instructor is at fault in some manner.

A low rating by one student or an entire class does not prove that teaching is poor, but it does raise questions that deserve the instructor's attention. While grades do not appear to affect student ratings, the issue is of little import. The instructor's obligation is to all students, regardless of their level of performance. The value of student ratings is not to be argued on the grounds that they reveal the truth about the teaching or the course, for truth here is relative. Such ratings are valuable because they reveal the students' judgments of an instructor or a course, and any procedure that accomplishes this is valid in its own right.

Some students respond more frankly to a third person than they do to the instructor or to a rating scale. Thus, systematic interviewing can be a revealing way to evaluate teaching. Moreover, student appraisal may be directed to the course or to the instructor. For obvious reasons teachers may be more receptive to course appraisal than to teacher appraisal. In multiple section courses with uniform policies, comments on the course are especially appropriate. In all procedures, however, student evaluation should be primarily directed to student experiences. No freshman or sophomore can judge the scholarship of a professor, but even a freshman can react to clarity of lectures, individual assistance provided, quality of assignments, content of tests, and fairness of grades.

Peer and administrative evaluations. Peer and administrative evaluations of each instructor are made, whether or not they are formally structured. Departmental associates and deans develop a perception of an instructor's teaching through contacts with the instructor and with his students. These informal appraisals suffer from inadequate evidence, are seldom recorded, and cannot be contested—but they do influence decisions. The complaints of a few students can, in the absence of other information, irretrievably damage the teacher's rating. Peer and administrative evaluation is usually related to decisions on promotion, tenure, and salary, but may also be concerned with improvement of instruction and faculty career development. Administrative evaluation usually depends on the judgments of others closer to the scene.

Self-evaluation. Until an instructor accepts his deficiencies and attempts to correct them, he will resent evaluation. Student ratings, colleague comments, classroom recordings or videotapes—all are clues that the instructor can use for self-improvement. Teaching might be improved by eliminating the incompetent, but the number of really excellent teachers is small. Improvement must be the goal, and encouragement for self-evaluation is essential.

Student achievement. The achievement of students would seem to be the ultimate criterion for evaluating instruction. A demanding and unreasonable teacher, whose students, despite high achievement, refuse further contact with the field of study, is not really a good teacher. In some respects affective outcomes may be more important than cognitive ones. Nevertheless, in multiple-section courses, where student abilities are reasonably matched, if the students of a given teacher regularly excel or regularly fall below the mean performance of the entire group on common examinations, some judgments may be made about teaching capability.

Pitfalls of ratings. All evaluation procedures involve some problems. The first major problem is the question of validity. For example, while the ability of student ratings to identify good teaching may be less significant than finding out what students think, ultimately a judgment must be made about what evidence is valid and on what basis an instructor should be warned that he must improve or face termination. The second problem is the question of reliability. Would the technique used reveal the same results upon repeated use? Would two or more persons viewing the same evidence make the same assessment of it?

While important, problems of reliability and validity are not grounds for eliminating evaluation. Subjectivity and personal bias are constant concerns in appraisal of instruction. Despite faculty objections to systematic evaluation, sporadic and uneven calculations are even more unfair. If one facet of a teacher's instruction or personality is outstanding, judgments about his or her overall teaching may be based on this one factor (halo effect). In the 1960s, for example, an instructor who criticized the administration or sympathized with prevalent student concerns was often regarded by students as a good teacher when he was, at most, a "good guy."

Evaluation of Administration

There is no simple definition of what constitutes the administration of a university. In the United States a governing board is responsible for the operation of the institution. In public institutions there may be several governing boards, with a division of responsibilities. Presidents elected by governing boards are given certain administrative responsibilities, but much of the business of the university, such as instruction and research, is carried on by faculty members organized into disciplinary or departmental groups. Increasingly, the faculty, student body, and even the various classes of nonacademic personnel have, through bargaining associations, demanded a role in policy determination.

Similarly, there are no accepted typologies for discussing governance in higher education. In some institutions the president makes all of the significant decisions. Other institutions operate as bureaucracies and have highly formalized vertical organizational structures, written rules, regulations, policies, and a pattern wherein each unit and individual becomes more interested in preserving personal prerogatives than in advancing the purposes of the university. Another pattern of administration is that of collegiality, in which a group consensus is achieved that is based on discussion, good will, mutual respect, and participatory democracy. Some small institutions may approximate this pattern, and departments in larger institutions may ef-

fectively utilize it. But collegiality easily degenerates into oligarchy. Still another approach, seen by some faculty members as ideal, is a laissez-faire pattern, in which each instructor goes his own way, teaches what he wants when he wants, and in general does as he pleases.

All of these approaches have serious consequences in effective and efficient utilization of resources and suggest alternative approaches to decision making. The ideal must, in some measure, draw upon all of them, preserving some prerogatives for administrators while providing for faculty involvement in decisions and for professional autonomy in pursuing individual assignments and commitments. In addition, most institutions would benefit from improvement in communication, feedback, and deliberations.

The evaluation of administration amounts to the evaluation of the processes utilized in an institution to set goals, develop plans, and work out policies and procedures for their attainment. The quality of the communications system and the mode of involvement by the various university groups in the decision-making process are instrumental to these broad concerns. In turn, the way in which an administrator deals with people, his availability, the clarity of his communications—oral and written—and his sensitivity to the concerns of the individuals and of the various groups with which he must deal are significant aspects of his administrative activity.

Just as a faculty member should know how students react to his teaching, so an administrator should solicit reactions from those with whom he works, perhaps through a questionnaire or checklist filled out anonymously by the faculty. Similarly, many presidents would avoid major difficulties with their boards if they periodically reviewed with the board some of the administrative issues of the preceding several months, discussed their own role in such issues, and then requested the board's evaluation.

An administrator can be sure that his effectiveness is being evaluated. If that evaluation is less laudatory than the administrator believes appropriate, he has a problem and should know about it. The administrator who does not seek and accept evaluation of his own activity is on dubious ground when he insists that his faculty undergo such evaluation.

Evaluation of the Institution

The evaluation of any aspect of an institution, pursued to its fullest ramifications, leads ultimately to an appraisal of the integrity and effectiveness of the institution as a whole. The appraisal of institutions of higher education usually involves an examination of operations rather than results, but efficiency and effectiveness must be judged by the accomplishment of purposes, aims, and objectives. Every institution should engage in continuing appraisal; from time to time it should also undergo a reexamination in depth. An institution can engage a group of educators or a consulting firm to conduct a survey of the total institution or some part of it, or it can itself conduct an institution-wide self-evaluation. A reexamination conducted entirely by outsiders is usually the most expensive and the least effective, although recommendations by outside consultants are especially useful where sensitive problems or major weaknesses in the business or administrative operations exist. Most reexaminations involve a combination of inside and outside evaluators.

Organization for self-evaluation. Whatever the scope of the evaluation, the respective roles of faculty, administration, trustees, students, and alumni must be determined. The difficulty of arranging work sessions will increase as the number of groups involved increases. Moreover, if many groups are involved, the project is likely to move slowly, and the self-evaluation may divide into parts corresponding to the a priori roles of the various groups, with the consequent risk that their report may defend the status quo rather than probe it. If, in addition, a large range of backgrounds is involved in the project, the identification ·

and resolution of specific issues will become more difficult.

Institutional appraisal is most successful when provision for the implementation of recommendations is built into the process. Thus, the best evaluation will include effective and widespread communication, collection and consideration of criticisms and suggestions, preliminary discussion of recommendations, and a final report that carefully analyzes all possibilities and presents a cogent and persuasive argument for the recommendations. An institution that is attempting to reshape its goals and procedures through self-evaluation may reasonably expect to spend as much as 1 percent of its annual budget for such a study, although much of the cost will be hidden in additional time devoted to the study.

Measures of quality. What determines the quality of an institution? The answer will vary, since terms such as *quality, goodness,* and *excellence* have various meanings. Furthermore, almost any college is unlikely to be of equal quality in all respects. Much depends on the point of view and the values of the person making the judgment. The Cartter (1966) and Roose-Andersen (1970) ratings of graduate education emphasize the judgment of department chairmen, senior scholars, and junior scholars in each of the various disciplines, indicating that assessment of quality is based on subjective judgments of the strength of the graduate program and research output of the department. Yet any single measure of quality fails if pushed too far. Regional accrediting associations, for example, which once emphasized quantitative requirements, have generally dropped these in favor of an overall integrative assessment of how well an institution accomplishes the goals it sets for itself.

The degrees, publications, and professional activities of the faculty provide some index of quality, but such activities must be viewed in relation to the nature and purposes of the institution.

The quality of students admitted and

the performance of graduating seniors are two additional indexes of quality. The two are closely related, for the most potent determiner of the performance of graduates is the quality of those admitted.

Library holdings constitute another criterion of excellence. Library utilization is perhaps more significant than either holdings or seating capacity, although deficiencies in holdings or capacity will affect usage. It is commonly suggested that the library appropriation be at least 5 percent of the educational and general budget, but an institution changing its character from a baccalaureate to a postgraduate status will initially require a considerably larger percentage. Large, complex universities with separately funded departmental libraries may manage with a much lower percentage.

The quality and utilization of space and facilities also require attention in evaluating an institution, but the application of any square foot ratio per user is less important than learning how the facilities are utilized and how well they serve the purposes of the institution.

The curriculum can be appraised by reviewing the array of offerings provided in each discipline, but the adequacy of course offerings must be weighed against institutional goals, such as whether the institution currently offers or plans to offer majors in the fields being evaluated.

The quality of maintenance in an institution is sometimes a measure of its operations. Spotless floors may not be a criterion of excellence, but grimy or cluttered science laboratories may well provide evidence not only of inadequate maintenance but also of ineffective instruction and administration.

An appraisal should be based on institutional effectiveness, not on comparisons with other institutions. However, the criteria of institutional effectiveness are many, complex, and fallible; hence, external standards are almost essential in making some judgment. Library appropriation and faculty salary comparisons with other institutions are useful, but comparisons alone cannot determine whether the local situation is satisfactory.

Evaluations of institutions are too often oriented toward the past or present rather than the future. A good institution knows what it is trying to do and where it is going. An evaluation that focuses on current problems without attending to possible changes in the institutional character may impede forward movement. Evaluation should encourage orderly change for anticipated future events but should, at the same time, create flexibility so that adjustments can be made.

Practices and Methods of Evaluation

Evaluation is concerned with the assessment of many diverse areas: student progress; the impact of distinctive environments; various instructional methodologies and learning experiences; costs and effectiveness of alternative programs; attitudes, values, and goals of students, faculty, and the public; student services; effectiveness of research and public service programs; and the tactics, strategy, and politics of effecting desirable change. There is no clear dividing line between institutional research and evaluation, except as assigned roles and responsibilities in an institution clearly delegate certain tasks to one or the other.

Evaluation is not characterized by any particular methodology; instead, it draws upon relevant methodology from several disciplines—sociology, statistics, mathematics, psychology, education, accounting and finance. Evaluation may involve interview techniques; interest, attitude, or value inventories; aptitude and achievement tests; instructional rating scales; analyses of resource sources; allocation and costing methods; experimental or quasi-experimental designs; and the processing, interrelating, and interpretation of these various types of evidence. Indeed, a recurring problem in any evaluation, formative or summative, is to so delimit the scope of the project that it will provide evidence, interpretations, and suggestions in time to influence further developments. Summative evaluations in particular face not only the hazard of denunciation and rejection by those evaluated but the prospect that delay will make the report irrelevant.

The evaluator continually faces a difficult balancing act. If he includes everything that might be relevant, the task becomes endless and useless. If he omits some possibilities, even with the consent of those involved, the omission may later be highlighted to prove inadequacy in design. If he heeds a reiterated faculty proposition that the important results will be evident only five, ten, or twenty years later, he will be led into a lengthy project for which there will be no audience. The evaluator must continually seek to raise the sights and concerns of program personnel beyond the immediate but refuse to be led into a futile search for the ultimate.

The evaluator must advise program personnel about his own role—whether he is responsible and responsive to them, whether he retains independence, or whether his responsibility and loyalty are to an administrator. Outside evaluators, faculty members with evaluative experience, or office of institutional research staff can be used in evaluative efforts; all possible combinations have some strengths and some weaknesses. Most weaknesses can be overcome by an individual evaluator who has achieved a reputation for effective and ethical operation and who carefully defines the precise role he assumes. Even so, extensive evaluative studies should be subjected to external audit by other expert evaluators, who review everything that has been done and render a report on accuracy and adequacy.

End Results

Those who engage in evaluation in higher education are naturally concerned that their efforts show results. Both colleges and universities change slowly. Radical innovations, whether stemming from the

enthusiasm of a small group of faculty or engendered by administrative pressures, tend to regress toward traditional patterns. And, in part, this regression is a result of the antipathy and doubts with which such rapid change is made.

Changes in courses, programs, and instructional, organizational, and administrative patterns must ordinarily be processed through committee and administrative channels, in which politics may weigh more heavily than the evaluation study. An evaluation that is planned to influence these deliberations may be more effective than a summary report that simply asserts that certain changes should be made. Evaluation is seldom conclusive; it raises questions, suggests alternatives, and encourages a continuing search for more effective patterns, both educational and financial. Objectives may be reconsidered and redefined, alternative processes explored, and new and more appropriate evaluation techniques developed.

Some types of evaluation bring immediate action. In the United States, for example, self-evaluation and a site visit by an evaluation team will determine whether or not an institution is accredited. The evaluation of students by grades or by a final comprehensive examination is crucial, because students must be graduated, held for more study, or dismissed. An evaluation that reveals gross errors in student records receives attention immediately.

The effectiveness of evaluation generally rests on its success in encouraging decision making based on evidence sought, analyzed, and probed for future implications prior to reaching a decision. To be successful, evaluation must convince those who want and demand radical change and who are impatient with evaluation; those with a vested interest in the status quo, who neither want nor accept evaluation; those who believe that their expertise and professional judgments are superior to evaluation by others; those who believe that gradual evolution always leads to improvement, and who therefore see a limited role for evaluation; and those who believe that democracy requires that all concerned have equal voice in considering and approving change. In view of these hazards, it is surprising that evaluation is ever effective. But many persons do want evidence and are influenced by it even when it runs against their own values and preconceptions. Ultimately, change results from a political process. The professional evaluator's role is that of affecting and improving this process.

Bibliography

Baird, L. L. "The Practical Utility of Measures of College Environments." *Review of Educational Research,* 1974, *44* (3), 307–329.

Beatty, W. H. (Ed.) *Improving Educational Assessment and an Inventory of Affective Behavior.* Washington, D.C.: Association for Supervision and Curriculum Development, National Education Association, 1969.

Billing, D. E., and Furniss, B. S. *Aims, Methods, and Assessment in Advanced Science Education.* London: Heyden, 1973.

Bloom, B. S., Hastings, J. T., and Madaus, G. F. *Handbook on Formative and Summative Evaluation of Student Learning.* New York: McGraw-Hill, 1971.

Bloom, B. S., and Peters, F. R. *The Use of Academic Prediction Scales for Counseling and Selecting College Entrants.* New York: Free Press, 1961.

Cartter, A. M. *An Assessment of Quality in Graduate Education.* Washington, D.C.: American Council on Education, 1966.

Centra, J. A. *The College Environment Revisited: Current Descriptions and a Comparison of Three Methods of Assessment.* Research Bulletin 70–44. Princeton, New Jersey: Educational Testing Service, 1970.

Eble, K. E. *The Recognition and Evaluation of Teaching.* Washington, D.C.: American Association of University Professors and Association of American Colleges, 1970.

Entwistle, N. J., and Nisbet, J. D. *Educational Research in Action.* London: University of London Press, 1972.

Entwistle, N. J., Percy, K. A., and Nisbet, J. D. *Educational Objectives and Academic Performance in Higher Education.* Lancaster, England: Department of Educational Research, University of Lancaster, 1971.

Falk, B., and Dow, K. L. *The Assessment of University Teaching.* London: Society for Research into Higher Education, 1971.

Freeman, J., and Burne, P. S. *The Assessment of Postgraduate Training in General Practice.* Research into Higher Education Monograph No. 20. London: Society for Research into Higher Education, 1973.

House, E. R. (Ed.) *School Evaluation: The Politics and Process.* Berkeley, California: McCutchan, 1973.

Isaac, S., and Michael, W. B. *Handbook in Research and Evaluation.* San Diego, California: Robert R. Knapp, 1971.

Keller, J. E. *Higher Education Objectives: Measures of Performance and Effectiveness.* Report No. P–7. Berkeley, California: Center for Research in Management Science, University of California, 1970.

Ladd, W. R. *Change in Educational Policy: Self-Studies in Selected Colleges and Universities.* New York: McGraw-Hill, 1970.

McKeachie, W. J., Lin, Y. G., and Mann, W. "Student Ratings of Teacher Effectiveness: Validity Studies." *American Educational Research Journal,* 1971, *8,* 435–445.

Micek, S. S., and Wallhaus, R. A. *An Introduction to the Identification and Uses of Higher Education Outcome Information.* Boulder, Colorado: Western Interstate Commission for Higher Education, 1973.

Miller, R. I. *Developing Programs for Faculty Evaluation: A Sourcebook for Higher Education.* San Francisco: Jossey-Bass, 1974.

Nicholson, E. *Predictors of Graduation from College.* Iowa City, Iowa: American College Testing Program, 1974.

Page, C. F. *Student Evaluation of Teaching: The American Experience.* London: Society for Research into Higher Education, 1974.

Payne, D. A., Rapley, F. E., and Wells, R. A. "Application of a Biographical Data Inventory to Estimate College Academic Achievement." *Measurement and Evaluation in Guidance,* 1973, *6* (3), 152–156.

Phi Delta Kappa National Study Committee on Evaluation. *Educational Evaluation and Decision Making.* Itasca, Illinois: F. T. Peacock, 1971.

Popham, W. J. (Ed.) *Evaluation in Education.* Berkeley, California: McCutchan, 1974.

Provus, M. *Discrepancy Evaluation: For Educational Program Improvement and Assessment.* Berkeley, California: McCutchan, 1971.

Roose, K. D., and Andersen, C. J. *A Rating of Graduate Programs.* Washington, D.C.: American Council on Education, 1970.

School's Council. *Evaluation in Curriculum Development: 12 Case Studies.* London: School's Council, distributed by Macmillan, 1973.

Society for Research into Higher Education. *Register of Research into Higher Education, 1972, Mainly in the United Kingdom.* London:

Society for Research into Higher Education, 1972.

Society for Research into Higher Education. *Register of Research into Higher Education in Western Europe, 1973.* London: Society for Research into Higher Education, 1973.

Stones, E. "Evaluation and the Colleges." In E. Stones (Ed.), *Towards Evaluation.* Birmingham, England: School of Education, University of Birmingham, 1970.

Walberg, H. J. (Ed.) *Evaluating Educational Performance.* Berkeley, California: McCutchan, 1974.

Weiss, J. (Ed.) *Curriculum Evaluation: Potentiality and Reality.* Curriculum Theory Network Monograph Supplement. Toronto, Ontario: Ontario Institute for Studies in Education, 1972.

Williams, B. "University Values and University Organization." *Minerva,* April 1972, *10,* 259–279.

PAUL L. DRESSEL

See also: Academic Standards and Accreditation: International; Academic Standards and Accreditation: United States; Accountability; Evaluation of Administrators; Faculty; Institutional Research; Reform, University; Students, Student Services, and Student Organizations.

EVALUATION OF ADMINISTRATORS

Administrative evaluation refers to the procedures used to assess the performance of noninstructional staff at collegiate institutions. Interest in evaluation of administrative performance grew out of an increasing demand in the middle 1970s for accountability in all sectors of the collegiate community. This interest has been further encouraged by growing concern for professional development programs among members of the instructional staff (faculty development), as well as by a growing interest in the implications of successful business practices for higher education (National Center for Higher Education Management Systems, 1973).

Initiating an Evaluation Program

Several difficult problems confront the collegiate administrator who attempts to initiate an evaluation program. Dressel (1976) has identified four: unclear definition of collegiate administration and of the ways in which it differs from business practices; unclear delineation of collegiate administrative power or severe limitations in its use; unclear statements of institutional purpose; and demands on the collegiate administrator for intentional ambiguity and secrecy.

There are twelve functions that can be provided by an administrative evaluation process, the first nine of which have been identified by Genova and others (1976). (1) This procedure is typically used to determine personnel decisions concerning retention, salary, or promotion; and (2) it can provide the basis for a program of administrative development if it incorporates observation, diagnosis, and training. (3) An institution or department can more readily establish and attain its goals through certain administrative evaluation procedures—notably management-by-objectives (MBO) (Lahti, 1973b). (4) An evaluative procedure can increase the effectiveness and efficiency of an administrative team, if the evaluative data are openly shared in a constructive, problem-solving manner by the team (Sikes, Schlesinger, and Seashore, 1974). (5) Both the strengths and weaknesses of an administrative staff can be assessed. An inventory of personnel resources can aid in referral, consultation, reassignments, or retraining. The sixth, seventh, and eighth functions relate to the issue of accountability. (6) Administrative evaluation can provide information to governing bodies and administrators concerning the degree of congruence between institutional policy and administrative action. (7) External audiences, such as legislators and funding agencies, can keep themselves informed of administrative effectiveness and worth. Administrative evaluation (8) provides a vehicle for all members of the institution to share with administrators in the appraisal of staff performance, and (9) can be used in research projects that focus on factors influencing administrative effectiveness (Dressel, 1976).

In addition to the functions identified by Genova and others, administrative evaluation can (10) help an administrator determine the extent to which he is aware of the perceptions of his colleagues, superiors, or subordinates concerning his performance. (11) An effective administrative evaluation procedure should also help a collegiate administrator and his supervisor define explicitly the role to be played by the administrator in the institution and any expectations concerning the performance of this role. (12) Finally, an administrative evaluation can positively influence other professional improvement programs at the institution. The staff member who engages in a process that is also applied to key administrators is more likely to comply with it.

Evaluation Procedures

Care must be taken in the selection or design of an evaluative procedure; it must be particularly suited to the modes of operation and institutional norms of the college or university. A 1976 survey, taken by the authors, of approximately four hundred colleges and universities in the United States shows at least six different procedures being used in the evaluation of administrators. Each of these six procedures will be briefly described below, with reference to the twelve functions listed above.

Unstructured narration. Unstructured narration is probably among the most commonly used evaluative procedures. The evaluator (in some instances the administrator himself) is asked to prepare a report that summarizes the administrator's activities or accomplishments over a specific period of time, usually one year. The criteria of evaluation are often determined by the evaluator, though they are usually responsive to the superior's expectations concerning administrative activities or accomplishments.

Typically, two or more additional, anonymous unstructured narrations are requested from a superior, a subordinate, a colleague, a member of the instructional staff, or even a student. Dressel recommends that the narrative be based, at least in part, on interviews conducted by "outside, unbiased evaluators or by senior professors or professors emeriti of unimpeachable integrity" (1976, p. 396).

Although the unstructured narration purports to describe activities or accomplishments, it is in fact usually a vehicle for the description of traits or characteristics—leadership, for example. Only in self-evaluations is primary attention given to activities or accomplishments. The unstructured narration is often valuable when performance criteria are unclear and cannot be easily clarified; for example, when an administrator is performing a highly technical, specialized, or creative task. Unfortunately, this mode of evaluation rarely contributes to any of the twelve functions listed above other than personnel decisions (function one).

Unstructured documentation. Unstructured documentation also relies on implicit evaluative criteria and is often based on self-evaluation. An administrator is requested to document his activities or achievements in concrete terms, such as scheduled events, evaluative ratings of program participants, letters of recommendation (often unstructured narrations), interview data, and a log of daily activities. Because the administrator himself is selecting the documents, there will usually be only positive evidence. Consequently, the volume of documentation is often taken into account as a measure of successful performance.

Unstructured documentation is frequently combined with one or more of the five other procedures, especially with unstructured narrations and rating scales. It provides somewhat more substantive data on activities and outcomes than does an unstructured narration and can be effective as a basis for the assessment (function one) and improvement (function two) of professional as well as team (function four) performance. It is also helpful in the identification of personnel needs and resources (function five) and clarification of roles and expectations (function eleven). Several other procedures to be described below, however, generally provide all twelve functions more effectively than does unstructured documentation.

Structured narration. Structured narration involves the use of short-answer questionnaires that require an evaluator to answer a series of general questions concerning administrative performance; for example: "In what areas of administration is this person in need of improvement?" or "Describe the professional practices of this administrator in terms of initiative and vitality." This procedure usually requires the anonymous responses of several different evaluators and is typically coupled with a rating scale that yields more detailed and specific information.

Structured narrations can be designed to provide most of the twelve functions. An inventory of resources and needs, for instance, can be constructed from carefully formulated questions concerning administrative strengths and weaknesses. This evaluative procedure, however, lacks sufficient specificity to be useful as a vehicle for accountability (functions six, seven, and eight); research (function nine); or management-by-objectives (function three).

Rating scales. Rating scales are being used more and more frequently by colleges and universities. In most instances, these scales are used by supervisors or subordinates to assess individual performance. An informal review by the authors of twenty administrative rating scales reveals seven dominant themes. These are (1) Knowledge and capacity—includes job knowledge and skills; knowledge of higher education and modern management techniques; broad intellectual and cultural interests; and physical and mental vigor. (2) Dependability—includes meeting expectations and work schedules; a sense of responsibility; initiative; administrative responsiveness; promptness; integrity; and proper dress and hygiene. (3) Adaptation—includes effective and imaginative planning; aware-

ness; anticipation; judgment; stability; and innovation. (4) Interpersonal relationships—includes conflict management; verbal and nonverbal communication; team management; leadership; tact; working effectively with different kinds of people; working for consensus among subordinates; and judging people perceptively and fairly. (5) Commitment to professional growth—includes commitment to excellence; professional self-improvement; instilling enthusiasm for professional goals; accepting suggestions on professional matters; and encouraging individual professional growth. (6) Resource and personnel management—includes cost awareness; attention to details; saying "no" effectively; concern with basic issues rather than trivia; sound judgment about situation and problems; timely and effective decision making; maintaining efficiency through delegation of responsibility and commensurate authority; processing detailed routine tasks efficiently; and establishing uniform procedures. (7) Institutional loyalty—includes commitment to service; participation in campus activities; working effectively in the community for support of the institution; and inspiring enthusiasm for institutional goals.

In general, rating scales focus on traits, though some assess the quantity (activities) or quality (outcomes) of work performed by the administrator (Miller, 1974; Dressel, 1976). Several scales (for example, Farmer and Mann) assess the quality of relationships between the administrator and his instructors. None of the instruments that were surveyed, however, contain items that deal with the administrator's relationship to students, trustees, alumni, or members of the local community.

As an instrument for developmental purposes, a rating scale usually lacks sufficient specificity, though the Departmental Evaluation of Chairpersons' Activities (DECA) system, which was developed by the Center for Faculty Evaluation and Development at Kansas State University in Manhattan, Kansas, may prove to be an exception. If peer ratings are shared and discussed, or if anticipated ratings by peers, supervisors, or subordinates are compared with actual ratings, the administrative rating scale can be effectively used with administrative teams (function four) or as a vehicle for perception check (function ten). Rating scales can also be excellent research tools (function nine), given their quantitative nature, but they are rarely effective in providing any of the other functions. Rating scales are frequently and inappropriately used, however, to meet the demands for accountability (functions six, seven, and eight).

In several instances (for example, the College and University Environmental Scales, distributed by the Educational Testing Service, Princeton, New Jersey), ratings have been used to assess the characteristics of the institutional environment for which the administrator is held accountable rather than the performance of the administrator directly. This environmental approach to administrative evaluation is based on the questionable assumption that a high-level administrator is ultimately capable of influence and therefore is accountable for all aspects of the campus. These environmental scales do provide a valuable alternative, however, to the highly impressionistic environmental assessments made by a small and biased sample of administrators or trustees during a yearly evaluative tour of the campus. Environmental scale results can be useful if analyzed in conjunction with data specifically focusing on those traits, activities, or outcomes of the administrator that directly influence the campus environment.

Structured documentation (portfolio). Structured documentation has been used for many years in the creative and performing arts. This procedure initially requires that the supervisor and administrator jointly accept a set of categories appropriate to the sphere of activity in which the evaluation is to take place. These categories might relate to job functions, skill areas, or performance objectives. Having established

the categories for documentation, the administrator assumes primary responsibility for documenting success in each of these areas. Other people, such as subordinates, peers, instructors, alumni, or members of the local community, might be included in this process to help establish the categories, to review the documents, or to arbitrate disagreements between the superior and the administrator. More information concerning this subtle and somewhat complex procedure can be obtained from Birmingham Southern College, Birmingham, Alabama; or Empire State College, Saratoga Springs, New York.

The portfolio can be an effective, though often inefficient, procedure for personnel decision (function one), and can be directly tied to many administrative development programs (function two). The portfolio can also be directly linked to institutional goal setting (function three) and role clarification (function eleven), by incorporating the development of categories in the formulation or clarification of the goals or roles.

As a vehicle for team building (function four), portfolios are very effective, especially if the team is involved in the establishment of the portfolio categories or documents. Because portfolios are individualized, and usually quite personal, they are rarely useful in building a personnel inventory (function five) or checking perceptions (function ten). Portfolios are usually not appropriate for research purposes (function nine), unless this research incorporates a flexible, investigatory method such as "illuminative evaluation" (Parlett and Hamilton, 1972) or "action research" (Sanford, 1970). As a vehicle for accountability (functions six, seven, and eight) and for modeling professional development (function twelve), the portfolio is uniquely appropriate. The contracting that occurs between a supervisor or portfolio committee and the administrator clarifies and expands upon accountability, and involves an increasing number of people in a growing experience. In academic institutions, where criteria of administrative success are often vague or even contradictory, a portfolio approach to evaluation may be particularly appropriate.

Management-by-Objectives (MBO). Management-by-objectives is a comprehensive system for personnel management. It minimizes the use of power and maximizes control of administrative processes through a clear specification of goals (Lahti, 1973a). An effective MBO program begins with clear statements of institutional or program mission and goals and the connection of these statements with the identification, clarification, and construction of concrete operational objectives.

MBO programs encounter several significant implementation problems at a collegiate institution. First, as Dressel (1976) has noted, most college and university administrators cannot clearly and consistently state institutional or program mission or goals; nor can operational, quantifiable objectives be easily derived from the educational philosophies or practices of the collegiate institution. Furthermore, to avoid unrealistic or mundane objectives, an MBO program requires a clear consensus concerning the current status of the institution or program. An effective MBO program must be closely linked with an institutional research program that provides data directly related to the goals and objectives of the institution (Bergquist and Shoemaker, 1976). Unfortunately, this interrelationship rarely exists on college campuses. Finally, an MBO program involves highly sophisticated management practices and relies on the competence and self-direction of the participating administrators. Frequently, MBO programs are precipitously introduced without adequate consideration of the extensive professional training and organizational development that must precede or accompany them.

In terms of administrative evaluation, MBO is a valuable goal toward which a collegiate institution might strive. Most collegiate administrators, however, should examine one or more of the other five evaluative procedures and assess the current resources of the institution (research, training, and development) to determine if an MBO program is realistic. Each of the other procedures, if implemented in an appropriate setting, can provide valuable assistance to a collegiate institution as it faces a changing and challenging world.

Bibliography

Anderson, G. L. *The Evaluation of Academic Administrators: Principles, Processes and Outcomes.* University Park: Pennsylvania State University Press, 1975.

Bergquist, W. H., and Shoemaker, W. A. *A Comprehensive Approach to Institutional Development.* San Francisco: Jossey-Bass, 1976.

Dressel, P. L. *Handbook of Academic Evaluation.* Ch. 16. San Francisco: Jossey-Bass, 1976.

Farmer, C. H., and Mann, E. "Administrative Evaluation by Faculty." Paper available from the authors at the Office of Institutional Research, University of Tulsa, Tulsa, Oklahoma 74104.

Genova, W., Madoff, M., Chin, R., and Thomas, G. *Mutual Benefit Education of Faculty and Administration in Higher Education.* Cambridge, Massachusetts: Ballinger, 1976.

Hillway, T. "Evaluating College and University Administration." *Intellect,* 1973, *101*(2349), 426–427.

Lahti, R. E. "Goal-Oriented Evaluation for Educational Managers." *Phi Delta Kappan,* 1973a, *54*(7), 490.

Lahti, R. E. *Innovative College Management.* San Francisco: Jossey-Bass, 1973b.

Miller, R. I. *Developing Programs for Faculty Evaluation.* San Francisco: Jossey-Bass, 1974.

National Center for Higher Education Management Systems. *Reports on Higher Education,* 1973, *19*(3–4), 5.

Parlett, M., and Hamilton, D. *Evaluation as Illumination: A New Approach to the Study of Innovatory Programs.* Edinburgh: Centre for Research in the Educational Sciences, University of Edinburgh, 1972.

Sanford, N. "What Ever Happened to Action Research?" *Journal of Social Issues,* Autumn 1970, *26,* 3–23.

Sikes, W. W., Schlesinger, L. E., and Seashore, C. N. *Renewing Higher Education from Within.* San Francisco: Jossey-Bass, 1974.

Van de Visse, M. "The Evaluation of Administrative Performance in Higher Education: A Survey of Evaluative Practices." Doctoral dissertation, Kent State University, 1974. University microfilms No. 75–7468.

WILLIAM H. BERGQUIST
GERRIT J. TENBRINK

See also: Accountability; General Administration, Organization for; Development of Professional Administrators.

EVALUATION OF FACULTY
See Faculty.

EXAMINATIONS AND TESTS

The use of tests in higher education is often referred to, or implied, in the international literature on higher education, but comprehensive accounts of testing practices are not readily available. Tests have two major purposes in higher education: selection and evaluation. Testing is an important part of the selection procedure for admission to higher education. Tests are also used to guide or evaluate instruction, to promote a student to a higher level, or to certify the completion of all or part of a program. Evaluation testing is often informal and hence not as readily documented as that associated with the more formal selection process.

Basic Concepts

The terms *test* and *examination* often have somewhat different connotations. However, here the terms will be used interchangeably.

Types of tests. It is important to distinguish among different kinds of tests. Most tests used in higher education are designed to measure cognitive skills or knowledge and can be classified as either achievement tests or aptitude tests. Achievement tests are those that provide some measure of what a student has learned or what skills he has acquired in a particular subject area. Aptitude tests, on the other hand, are designed to predict how well a student will do in the future. Scholastic aptitude tests are thus not concerned primarily with current

levels of knowledge or advanced skills. Rather, they attempt to measure how well the student can use common knowledge and skills in new and different ways; this information is then used as a basis for predicting future scholastic performance. The distinction between achievement tests and aptitude tests is particularly important in understanding how testing can best serve different purposes, such as selection or certification.

Other types of tests or measuring instruments less frequently employed are those that assess psychological characteristics such as attitudes, interests, and personality traits. Such tests normally serve to assist in counseling and guidance.

Techniques of testing. The traditional testing technique, still most widely used throughout the world, is the essay test. This type of test requires that the student provide a written response to a question that is often quite broad and general. The generality of the question determines the length of response required, which may vary from several pages to only a few words. The major difficulties with this technique are the subjective and often unreliable nature of evaluation of the responses and the difficulty of covering an adequately representative sample of material in the testing period. The cost of grading and the time required to report results when large numbers of students are involved are often major reasons for using other techniques.

The most widely used alternative to the essay test is the multiple-choice test, in which the student selects a response to a question from among several possibilities. The selected responses can be recorded by a simple mark on a separate answer sheet; the answer sheets can then be scored by machine, and a large number of tests can be graded very quickly and economically. Because very little of the student's time is spent in recording responses, a large number of questions can be asked and a broad sampling of the student's knowledge obtained. Although such questions may require only simple recognition to produce a correct response and do not provide a direct measure of what the individual can produce on his own or how he expresses himself, it is possible to devise multiple-choice questions that call for complex thought processes including the application of knowledge to a new situation, synthesis, and organization. Construction of multiple-choice questions with such qualities is not a simple process; it requires skill, experience, and time, and it is usually not economical when only a few students are involved. However, many ongoing programs are designed to develop pools of questions, or "item banks," so that those concerned with multiple-choice testing can share in test development and use. Computers in a number of central locations are used to store, retrieve, and assemble test items.

Although the multiple-choice question is the most popular of the so-called objective type of test, there are other varieties. These include true-false and matching items. Fill-in or completion questions require the student to produce a response but allow for objective and rapid scoring, although this type of question is somewhat limited in scope. Short-answer questions are often a reasonable compromise between essay tests and objective tests when the number of people to be tested is not too large; in these tests the required response is usually only a sentence, a short paragraph, or perhaps a list of terms.

Oral examinations continue to play a role in assessment, and practical examinations are sometimes required in laboratory or art courses. The defense of a thesis or other project is a form of the oral examination.

Control of testing. An important dimension of testing that is not a characteristic of tests as such is the locus of control—that is, who prepares and who is responsible for administering the test. If the control agent is the institution itself, the control is referred to as "internal." In other cases an agent outside the institution may be responsible and the control is then consid-

ered to be "external." For example, if a secondary school is fully responsible for certifying its students for school-leaving, the control would be internal for school-leaving purposes, but external for a university's purpose of admitting the school's graduates. Conversely, if a university has its own admission test, the control would be internal for its admission purposes but external if the test were used by secondary schools to certify completion of their programs. If a test is the responsibility of a separate board or agency and is used (as in England) by schools and universities for both school-leaving and university admission, it is external for both purposes.

Testing for Admission

In many countries the statement is made, or implied, that there is no formal selective testing for admission to higher education and the satisfactory completion of secondary school is sufficient qualification for college entrance. Quite often, however, the school-leaving certificate is partially or completely dependent on an external examination. Furthermore, in some countries entry to secondary education is limited to those passing a test, and this hurdle can be critical in determining who does and who does not qualify for entry to higher education. A full treatment of these various factors involved in the total process of admission to higher education is available in Bowles (1963).

The school-leaving examination. The school-leaving examination may, in some cases, be entirely internal—that is, the sole responsibility of the secondary school. It more often has some, if not complete, external control. This may be by a governmental unit directly responsible to a ministry or department of education; by a largely autonomous board; or occasionally by a university or group of universities.

Because its major function is to certify satisfactory completion of a program of secondary education, the school-leaving examination is an achievement test. Often, the examination is linked directly to a syllabus, and the two together largely determine the curriculum of the secondary school. The charge is frequently made that when the control of testing is external to the school the whole educational process is geared to preparation for specific questions that can be expected on tests.

At the other extreme, a secondary school may have full responsibility to certify completion of its program under very general guidelines or requirements, and no single test plays a significant role. Under these circumstances, or when the number of qualified secondary school graduates exceeds the number of places available in higher education, additional testing is likely to be required for college or university admission. Each institution of higher education may conduct its own admissions test, several institutions may informally conduct a common test, or an institution may require that candidates take an examination prepared by an outside agency. In some cases formal government procedures may exist. Often this additional test is an achievement test, designed to validate certification.

Scholastic aptitude tests. In many countries, the United States in particular, this admission test is an attempt to assess general scholastic aptitude rather than achievement. Aptitude tests are normally objective multiple-choice tests, scorable by machine and hence particularly appropriate when large numbers of candidates must be tested and results reported in a short time. Because aptitude tests are much less dependent on specific curriculum content than are achievement tests, they put less pressure on students to direct their studies toward answering particular questions. They add a dimension to testing which supplements the achievement test by providing information about the potential of students. A combination of aptitude testing and achievement testing almost always provides a better basis for predicting academic performance than does either type of testing alone.

The two major components of most scholastic aptitude tests are the verbal and the quantitative, or mathematical, sections. These dimensions seem to account for most of the predictable variance in academic achievement as measured by college grades, although more limited and specialized aptitudes are sometimes tested and the results can provide useful information under certain circumstances.

World survey of admissions testing. To obtain a view of the worldwide use of testing as a selective process for admission to higher education, the entries for seventy-four countries in the *World Survey of Education* (1966) were examined for information about admissions testing in each country. The results were tabulated and then summarized. Information was sometimes incomplete, but the summary probably gives a reasonable picture of the worldwide admissions testing situation as of the 1960s. From this information, satisfactory completion of secondary school emerges as the primary and almost universal requirement for admission to higher education. In the majority of countries surveyed a test is involved in certifying that completion. Of the seventy-four countries, 53 percent clearly specified that an examination was required for school-leaving certification and 23 percent implied that examinations were required.

In 57 percent of the countries an additional examination is required for at least some candidates to enter a university, but only 7 percent state that all applicants must take an entrance examination. The remaining 43 percent of the countries give no clear indication that a test is required of any candidate. Only eleven of the seventy-four countries specify the responsibility for administering entrance examinations, but of these eleven only four indicate that the responsibility is external to the universities themselves.

Examples of admissions testing. The following descriptions of admissions testing practices in different countries are based on a series of papers delivered by testing experts at the meeting of the International Association for Educational Assessment held in Paris in May 1976. The association plans to publish a collection of these papers in the mid 1970s.

Among the countries in which the school-leaving certificate, based on an examination, is the primary, if not exclusive, qualification for higher education are England, Wales, Scotland, Austria, and the Netherlands. In England and Wales a number of examining boards issue a General Certificate of Education, which is the usual basis for admission to the university. A certificate may be given either at the ordinary (O) level or at the advanced (A) level. The advanced-level examination syllabi must be approved by the Schools Council (the central board of education for England and Wales), but otherwise the various boards are responsible for their own examinations. The boards place considerably greater emphasis on essay questions than they do on multiple-choice questions. A substantial amount of research on the use of general scholastic aptitude tests has not demonstrated to the boards the desirability of adding aptitude tests to the examination procedure.

In Scotland a Certificate of Education Examination Board provides school-leaving examinations in various subjects, which are required for entrance into most higher education programs, and each college or department specifies its requirements for the purpose of evaluating candidates. Secondary school and higher education representatives are both involved in preparing the examinations, which may be essay, objective, or practical. Oral examinations are used to test achievement in languages.

In Austria the Maturity Examination Certificate is administered by boards chaired by provincial school inspectors and consisting of the administrator and teachers of the regional schools. This certificate is usually sufficient for admission to the university, although some specialized departments require aptitude tests. Complementary examinations may be given if a school does not teach certain subjects.

There is also a professional maturity examination that may be given by the university, particularly by scientific institutions.

The school-leaving examination and certificate are basic for admission to universities in the Netherlands, but there can be some relaxation of this requirement and other methods of admission are allowed.

Israel and Nigeria are examples of countries in which a secondary school certificate is necessary but not sufficient for university admission; an additional examination is almost universally required. In Israel the Ministry of Education and Culture prepares matriculation examinations for secondary school use as achievement tests, but each Israeli university also conducts its own testing, usually involving a scholastic aptitude test as well as an English proficiency test. A national scholastic aptitude test is expected to replace these various university tests, however.

In Nigeria the West African Examinations Council (WAEC) is responsible for the Higher Schools Certificate and the General Certificate of Education. Because the demand for entrance is greater than university capacity, however, individual universities typically add their own entrance examinations, which usually consist of a test of verbal comprehension, an essay test, and advanced achievement tests. The WAEC is developing an aptitude test to supplement these tests, and there is a trend toward the use of a common entrance examination by all Nigerian universities.

In New Zealand most secondary schools are given the responsibility for determining whether or not a student is admissible to the university. For students from schools that may not provide accreditation and for students without school accreditation, a standard university entrance examination is available. This standard examination consists of achievement tests prepared under the direction of a board of representatives from the University Grants Commission, the universities, the secondary schools, and the Department of Education.

Trends in admissions testing. A number of

countries demonstrate interesting new trends. In Australia university admission is largely determined by student performance on examinations at the end of schooling, but a movement exists toward relaxing matriculation requirements and replacing external admission examinations with continuous assessment within the secondary school. In 1976 the state of Queensland was the only Australian state in which the primary basis for university admission was the secondary school's internal assessment. The Australian Scholastic Aptitude Test is used to balance the assessments made among subject areas and by different schools so that a student is not unduly penalized or rewarded because of the ease or difficulty of his subject area or the standards of assessment of his school. Students' test results are not used directly for admission but simply provide a greater degree of equity among assessments.

In Brazil regional groups of higher education institutions produce examinations to be used in common. The pattern of required examinations varies by field of study and a candidate for admission is ranked within his own field. If he applies for admission in several different fields of study, he may receive quite different rankings in each. National legislation recommends that use be made of objective type questions and of standard scores, and that examination questions be prepared in such a way as to avoid emphasis on memorization. Various Brazilian groups have been formed to provide the common examinations, among them the *Fundação Carlos Chagas* and the *Fundação Cesgranrio.*

In the 1970s the Philippines introduced a National College Entrance Examination, which all high school graduates applying to any public or private Philippine university must take. The examination is a general scholastic aptitude test of the multiple-choice type, prepared and administered by the National Education Testing Center. A cutoff score is determined, and no student may be admitted who achieves less than

that score. In addition, some universities require examinations of their own.

An important initiative worth noting is the establishment of the International Baccalaureate Office, located in Geneva. This organization provides a set of internationally prepared syllabi and examinations as a basis for an internationally acceptable school-leaving certificate. The certificate is then a basis for university admission. Although the use of this procedure is not yet widespread, it is gaining increased acceptance and it is probably the only international testing for admission to universities.

Admissions testing in the United States. Most selective four-year higher education institutions in the United States have long employed some form of entrance examination, but the use of these examinations peaked in the early 1960s and has since tapered off as the number of applicants has decreased and as more institutions have moved toward open admission.

Some institutions utilize their own testing programs and some states operate a state program for their state colleges. Most admissions testing, however, is provided by two national organizations: the College Entrance Examination Board (CEEB), utilizing the services of the Educational Testing Service (ETS); and the American College Testing Program. The CEEB is a voluntary association of schools and colleges that controls the policy and determines the nature of its examinations. The Scholastic Aptitude Test (SAT) is the most widely required of the CEEB examinations, and it provides verbal and mathematical scores. In addition, a variety of achievement tests are offered in individual subjects to provide evidence of accomplishment separate from the secondary school record. A higher education institution is free to require whichever achievement test it desires; many institutions do not require achievement tests at all and depend on the SAT exclusively. Neither CEEB nor ETS specifies a passing level, and acceptable scores are left to the determination of the individual institution. Normative information, however, is furnished and assistance is provided in conducting validation studies and other determination of the most appropriate procedure for an individual institution to follow. The SAT is entirely objective, and, with few exceptions, the achievement tests have also been objective.

Tests are also widely used in the United States for admission to graduate and professional schools. The rapid increase of applicants in these areas in the late 1960s and early 1970s led to increased testing at this level. Among the national programs are the Graduate Record Examinations, the Law School Admission Test, the Graduate Management Admission Test, the Miller Analogies, and the Medical College Aptitude Test. Requirement of any of these tests is the choice of each individual institution. Frequently, individual departments in an institution decide whether or not applicants must submit the results of a given examination. The tests are objective in nature and the determination of satisfactory performance levels is up to the individual institution or department.

Testing for Evaluation

Examinations are used throughout the world for promotion from one level of education to the next, for certifying completion of some or all work required, and for awarding degrees. The exact nature and administration of such tests vary tremendously from country to country and from institution to institution. In general, they are an internal rather than an external responsibility, and they are achievement rather than aptitude tests in that they are expected to demonstrate the level of proficiency attained by the student. In some cases they may be focused on group results as part of an overall evaluation of a particular program or institution. In the United States, for example, tests may serve as part of the evidence presented by institutions to accrediting agencies.

Great variation exists in the timing, breadth, and scope of the examinations used for individual evaluation. Some countries and institutions traditionally require a single, final examination covering all the work of several years before certification of completion and the awarding of a degree. In other cases annual, semiannual, and quarterly examinations in specific courses are emphasized for promotion, or permission to proceed, to the next level of work. Most countries that previously depended largely on comprehensive final examinations are increasingly using more frequent testing or other exercises and work performance to supplement their final examinations.

Responsibility for the preparation and grading of examinations also varies. An individual professor may do either or both, particularly for his own courses. A department or faculty may have responsibility, particularly for comprehensive examinations or when sections of the same course are offered by different professors. External examiners or evaluators may also be involved.

Evaluation for crediting achievement. Some academic institutions offer external degrees solely on the basis of examinations. The University of London is an institution that requires no course work at the university but does require the successful completion of appropriate examinations for a degree. The Open University of the United Kingdom also offers degrees on the basis of examinations. Institutions in the United States increasingly offer the possibility of degrees based in full or in part on examinations without course work in the institution. The College-Level Examination Program (CLEP), administered by ETS for the CEEB, is a national program of tests which may be used at the discretion of individual institutions to award credit for either general education in broad subject areas or for individual courses. The Cooperative Assessment of Experiential Learning (CAEL) is a cooperative venture by a number of United States institutions to develop methods of assessing learning achieved outside the classroom in order to award credit. In most cases, the techniques of this assessment process avoid the traditional paper-and-pencil test but instead utilize ways of judging student portfolios or other evidences of accomplishment to determine what sort of institutional credit might be awarded.

Other Tests and Test Uses

In the United States, where educational programs are often not highly structured and some institutions are not highly selective in admissions, tests may be used to place students in groups that are homogeneous in ability and achievement. Aptitude tests are frequently used for guidance as to the level of program appropriate for a student, and achievement tests in individual subjects are used for placement in specific courses. National testing programs provide examinations for these purposes, but institutions also buy published standardized tests which they administer under their own control. A number of institutions have developed their own placement tests to meet their particular needs.

Tests are also used for individual counseling and guidance, although they may be administered on a group basis for convenience. In general, these tests attempt to assess attitudes and interests rather than scholastic aptitude or achievement and are not usually considered appropriate for admission selection or for evaluation of progress.

General intelligence tests, which are very much like scholastic aptitude tests, are sometimes given on an individual basis to verify previous test results or when no previous scores are available.

Interest inventories such as the Strong or Kuder type may be given individually or to entire groups of students to assist in vocational and academic planning, particularly in institutions with a wide range of options and programs. Personality tests are used most often for individual counseling of students who present problems, but

occasionally written personality inventories such as the Minnesota Multiphasic are also used for group screening. Projective techniques such as the Rorschach Ink Blots or the Thematic Apperception Test are normally given individually, but are available for group administration in certain forms.

One test in wide international use is the Test of English as a Foreign Language (TOEFL), administered by ETS throughout the world. This test examines ability to understand, read, and write English, and many English-speaking institutions require applicants whose native language is not English to submit the results of this test.

A variety of testing techniques continue to be tried on an experimental basis in the desire to improve selection, placement, and guidance of students. The two areas toward which most effort has been directed are motivation and creativity. Many procedures have been devised to assess these characteristics (some of which seem to be useful for guidance when administered in a noncompetitive situation), but no tests of either motivation or creativity have yet been produced that are suitable for selection purposes. An intuitive sense of the importance of motivation and creativity keeps research in this area continuing.

Bibliography

Bessa, N. M. *University Entrance Examinations in Brazil: Measurement Procedures.* São Paulo, Brazil: Fundação Carlos Chagas, 1976.

Bowles, F. *Access to Higher Education.* Vol. 1. New York: UNESCO, Columbia University Press, 1963.

D'Oyley, V. R., and Muller-Solger, H. "National Testing for College and University: The Role of the Service for Admission to College and University (SACU) in Canadian Higher Education." *International Review of Higher Education,* 1975, *21,* 91–109.

Halls, W. B. *International Equivalency in Access to Higher Education.* Paris: UNESCO, 1971.

International Association of Universities. *Methods of Establishing Equivalency Between Degrees and Diplomas.* Paris: UNESCO, 1970.

Lippey, G. *Computer-Assisted Test Construction.* Englewood Cliffs, New Jersey: Educational Technology Publications, 1974.

Natarajan, V. "Question Banks, Their Use in

Indian Examinations." *New Frontiers in Education*, 1975, 5, 64–71.

White, M. A. "Sixty Years of Examinations and Matriculation Policy in Western Australia." *Australian Journal of Education*, 1975, *19*, 64–77.

The World Guide to Higher Education: A Comparative Survey of Systems, Degrees and Qualifications. Paris: Unipub/UNESCO Press, 1971.

World Survey of Education. Vol 4: *Higher Education.* Paris: UNESCO, 1966.

JOHN S. HELMICK
SANFORD C. JAMESON

See also: Admissions: An International Perspective; College Entrance Examination Board; Cooperative Education and Off-Campus Experience; Credit, Assessment of Learning for Postsecondary Education; International Baccalaureat; Open University.

EXCHANGE, INTERNATIONAL

1. OVERVIEW

International educational exchange means, broadly, the movement of persons across national boundaries for educational purposes. Involved, typically, are students, scholars, and specialists representing a broad range of interests and expertise. The purposes of such exchanges reflect the diversity of the participants. Nationals of almost every country in the world have been involved in exchange programs, as students, teachers, researchers, or advisers.

History and Growth

Although itinerant students and scholars were common in the great medieval universities of Europe, educational exchange as we know it is very much a product of the twentieth century. At the close of World War I, efforts were made by a number of organizations to promote world peace through increased understanding among peoples, and education was seen as a major vehicle for accomplishing this goal. The Institute of International Education (IIE) was one of the earliest organizations created to promote, facilitate, and administer exchange programs between the United States and other nations. Founded in 1919, it conducted the first of a series of annual censuses of foreign students in the United States in 1921. During that year, 6740 students were reported, a figure that gradually increased during the 1920s, reaching a total of 10,000 in 1930. The period from 1930 through the end of World War II showed a fluctuating pattern of increase and decrease, roughly within the range of 9000 to 5000. After World War II, major efforts were under way in many nations to create a stable world order, and educational exchange programs were massively expanded. In the United States, for example, during the four-year period from 1946 to 1949, the number of foreign students increased from 10,300 to 25,400. Movements of students and scholars in other parts of the world also displayed significant increases.

Two factors are especially important in explaining this period of explosive growth in educational exchange: the establishment of the United Nations Educational, Scientific and Cultural Organization (UNESCO) and the passage, in the United States, of the Fulbright Act. Following a series of meetings between educational leaders in 1944 and 1945, agreement was reached to establish UNESCO, with responsibility to promote cooperation among the nations of the world in the areas specified in its title. In spite of occasional setbacks, there seems little doubt that UNESCO has played a critically important role in educational and cultural interchange. The Fulbright Act, Public Law 584, was passed by the United States Congress in 1946. Under the authority of this act and the Mutual Educational and Cultural Exchange Act of 1961 (the Fulbright-Hays Act), the United States committed itself to a major effort at increasing mutual understanding through the medium of educational exchange. Since its beginnings in 1946, over 118,000 United States and foreign participants have been awarded grants under the Fulbright program to study, teach, research, or lecture in the United States and abroad.

Other countries have contributed substantially to the growth of exchange programs. For example, *Deutscher akademischer Austauschdienst* (DAAD: German Academic Exchange Service) of the Federal Republic of Germany, which was founded in 1925, offers grants, fellowships, and scholarships for foreign academics to study in Germany and for Germans to study abroad. An interesting feature of DAAD is its in-country scholarship program. Through this program, scholarships are granted to African students for study in their own or neighboring countries, both to reduce the impact of culture shock and to speed the process of Africanization of African institutes of higher learning.

There are many organizations whose primary or sole function is the promotion and facilitation of educational exchange. Among the growing number of such organizations are the Japan Foundation, the Association of Southeast Asian Institutions of Higher Learning, the Educational Interchange Council of London, the International Association for the Exchange of Students for Technical Experience in Switzerland, the Council on International

Educational Exchange of New York, and multipurpose organizations such as the Bank of Mexico, which provides scholarships for Mexicans to study outside of their own country.

The Scope of Educational Exchange

Within the myriad of programs that fall within the category of international educational exchange, there are three dominant patterns of activity: academic exchange programs involving students, teachers, and scholars; conferences, seminars, and workshops for the exchange of ideas and experiences; technical assistance programs involving a variety of experts and specialists in the transmission of knowledge and skills in the cause of development.

Academic exchange programs. Academic exchange programs are the most widely known of the exchange activities, largely because of the vast numbers of people involved and the numerous quantitative and qualitative studies of these programs that have been made. The persons involved in these exchanges are engaged in study, teaching, or research abroad in a recognized institution of higher learning. The time span of the experience may be quite short—two or three months—or it may involve a commitment to an academic degree program stretching over four or more years.

UNESCO, among others, has published a wealth of data on exchanges. However, reliable statistics on the numbers of academic personnel who have participated remain elusive, since most of the statistical compilations exclude some of the major countries of the world. According to UNESCO (1975), in 1972 there were 30,423,000 students enrolled in postsecondary education institutions throughout the world. Of this number, 500,593 students, or 1.82 percent of the total, were studying in countries other than their own. The latter figure represents an increase over the twelve-year period from 1960 to 1972 of 132 percent and an average annual increase of 7.3 percent for the same period.

The regional distribution of these students is worth noting; the majority studied in Europe and North America. Significantly lower in the distribution scale in order of numbers were Asia, the Middle East, Africa, Latin America, and Oceania. The UNESCO study further notes that a considerable number of students pursue their academic careers abroad within their own region, reflecting perhaps the constraints imposed by linguistic and economic considerations.

Statistical information on foreign students in the United States is readily available. A major source of these data is the IIE's annual census, the findings of which are reported each year in its publication *Open Doors*. According to the 1975 census, foreign student enrollment in higher education institutions in the United States totaled 219,721, the highest number ever reported since the census was begun, fifty-four years earlier. The majority of these students have come from the developing world—Asia, Latin America, Africa, and the Middle East. Over 25 percent of the students are in the United States on immigrant status. With a total United States college student population exceeding 8,290,000, the percentage of foreign students, approximately 2.6 percent, is small but still significant. Other countries report higher percentages of foreign students. In the Federal Republic of Germany, for example, the number of foreign students in universities and colleges amounted to 35,000 in 1975, or 6.9 percent of the total student population ("Education and Science in the Federal Republic of Germany," 1975, p. 165).

The decrease in the number of students coming to the United States from the nations of Europe and Canada and the increasing numbers of students from Asia, Latin America, and particularly the Near and Middle East are discussed in the 1974 edition of *Open Doors* (p. v):

The countries of the Near and Middle East include the majority of the members of the Organization of Petroleum Exporting Countries (OPEC) and there are early indications of further significant growth in the numbers of foreign students from these nations. In 1973–1974, Saudi Arabia was reported as the home country of more than one thousand students for the first time. Iran, which in 1972–1973 sent the fifth-highest number of foreign students to the United States, in 1973–1974 ranked third, a growth of 22 percent. These increases, although they would seem to reflect the growing wealth of the OPEC countries, preceded the massive shift of funds to the oil-rich nations that occurred during the academic year 1973–1974. The direct effects of the new economic strength of these nations on foreign student enrollment in the United States will be of particular interest in the 1975 *Open Doors* survey now under way and indeed throughout the remainder of the 1970s.

The decline in the number of students from the industrial countries of Europe and the increase in the number from the nations of the developing world suggest a significant shift in goals, motives, and objectives of foreign study. In many (if not most) cases, the goal is clearly that of manpower production on the part of the sponsoring agency, typically a foreign government.

A Venezuelan program provides a possible model for exchanges in the 1970s and 1980s. In 1974 the government of Venezuela announced a new program of scholarships for Venezuelans to study in the United States and several other countries. Known as the program *Gran Mariscal de Ayacucho*, it was deliberately designed to produce the human resources required for the national development objectives of Venezuela. As such, it represents an investment of major proportions in the future growth of that country. The program has several features worthy of note. It was designed to have major impact in terms of numbers, with over ten thousand scholarships projected for the first phase of the program. Approximately 2500 of the students receiving those scholarships were expected to study in the United States by the end of 1975. For most of these students, intensive English-language training precedes their formal academic work.

Selection of fields of study is guided by the findings of a major assessment of manpower needs made in Venezuela in 1975. Planners of the program expect technical, scientific, and vocational fields to predominate. Because of the importance placed on technical education, a wider range of host institutions can be used than in the past. In the United States these would include technical schools and junior and community colleges. Moreover, the program has been designed to widen access to education by offering scholarships to students who come from economically deprived backgrounds and from rural and backward regions of Venezuela.

Some of the oil-producing countries in the Middle East seem likely to follow the Venezuelan pattern in terms of manpower development. The government of Iran has concluded agreements with several American universities for a series of programs involving student exchange and cooperation in research and institutional development. Similar discussions have been held in the United States with Saudi Arabia, Kuwait, and other Middle East nations. At least in the short run, the prospects appear good that a portion of the new wealth generated by increases in oil prices will be allocated to education. Faced with severe shortages of both skilled manpower and local educational institutions, it seems clear that Middle East nations will increase their study abroad programs, if political stability continues.

The operation of academic exchange programs has given rise to a host of issues that demand the attention of professionals in the field. Some of these, such as selection, admissions, orientation, equivalencies of academic curricula, examinations, and degrees, are largely confined to the academy itself. Others bear directly on academic-community relationships, such as hospitality and community relations, immigration policies, and academic-year and summer employment opportunities. These and related issues are likely to increase in scale and importance as study-abroad programs expand.

Exchange of ideas. Conferences, seminars, workshops, and meetings on problems of education are common phenomena. Their objectives vary with the goals of the particular sponsor, which may be a government, an international bank, a private foundation, or a consortium of universities. Many of the international meetings are designed to provide a mechanism of communication for a specific discipline or problem area, such as nuclear physics, development economics, or new methods in language teaching. Others quite deliberately seek to promote communication among scholars and academic leaders for the sake of the dialogue itself.

Many international conferences have opened up new ground in the field of inter-institutional collaboration. For example, formation of the Central American Higher University Council was the result of a series of meetings under multiple sponsorship, including private foundations, Ministries of Education, and regional agencies.

The variety of international meetings in the field of education suggests the richness of this form of communication. Private organizations, such as the International Association of Universities, the International Councils on Higher Education (ICHE), and the several regional groupings of universities (in Latin America, Southeast Asia, Africa, the Arab nations, and the British Commonwealth), meet on a regular basis to consider both substantive issues and ways to strengthen and broaden the dialogue. International organizations such as UNESCO and various regional development banks organize frequent meetings around topics of special interest to international education. In 1975 the annual meeting of the American Council on Education (ACE) was devoted entirely to the theme of higher education in the world community. During the conference, Roger Heyns, ACE's president, noted that the selection of this theme was more than "a gesture to the growing interdependence of peoples and nations. The rationale of the meeting [was] that educational institutions throughout the world confront common issues and common dilemmas transcending parochial barriers of language and culture."

Technical assistance. Programs of technical assistance typically involve the transfer of knowledge, skills, and technology from those who possess such skills to those who need them. Since the essence of this process is educational, all technical assistance across national boundaries can be considered international education. However, few technical assistance projects have any relation to the educational system as such, and an even smaller percentage focus on higher education. Technology transfer projects frequently involve one or more elements in the economic infrastructure of a developing country, ranging from the expansion of a communications system to the planning and design of a heavy industry complex.

There are, however, many examples of technical assistance in the field of education. Most developing countries have been the recipients of expert advice in the planning and design of new universities and other institutions of higher learning. Visiting professors from the developed countries often make it possible for local faculty to be released from academic duties to advance their professional training and careers.

In many cases, local faculties, when so trained, have chosen not to return to their home countries, giving rise to the so-called brain drain. In many developing countries, where trained manpower is a scarce commodity, the brain drain poses serious problems. The conflict that frequently arises between the needs of a developing economy and the freedom of movement of an individual scholar is not easily resolvable.

One of the dramatic efforts at technical assistance since the 1960s has been the United States Peace Corps program. The program has three quite distinct objectives:

to provide skilled manpower for developing countries, largely if not exclusively in the field of education; to provide a visible symbol of the United States as a country willing to share its human resources with others; and to provide the American participants with an international learning experience through a first-hand and lengthy exposure to cultures other than their own. In spite of numerous problems, the record to date clearly indicates that the Peace Corps has been a success.

Political Objectives of Study Abroad

The young men and women who pursue study outside of their own country do so for reasons ranging from whimsy through highly personal career goals to hopes of strengthening the prospects of peace and understanding among peoples of the world. The governments and private business organizations that make their study possible tend, however, to be much more specific and policy oriented. Each of these institutions has an understandable and indeed laudable desire to project as favorable an image as possible to its own constituency, whether that be a cluster of corporations, a particular geographical region, or the world at large.

Some programs have been used quite deliberately to further a nation's political objectives both in courting allies and in undermining adversaries. The 1960s provide many examples of this kind of effort engaged in by most of the leading nations with varying degrees of success. For example, the Soviet Union quite deliberately set out to win the allegiance of students from the developing nations of Africa, Asia, and Latin America through the creation of the Patrice Lumumba Friendship University. This university, located in Moscow, offers facilities for Russian-language training and highly specialized programs in development-related fields, such as agriculture, engineering, and health sciences. A similar experimental program to attract large numbers of African students to the

People's Republic of China fared less well, in part because academic considerations tended to be subordinate to political indoctrination, thus alienating large numbers of the exchange students.

Although involving senior researchers rather than students, the now famous Project Camelot affair did much to undermine the intellectual integrity of United States social science research in Chile and in several other countries in Latin America. This project was designed to measure and forecast the causes of revolutions and insurgency in underdeveloped areas of the world. It was designed and conducted by an affiliate of a United States university as an apparently disinterested piece of social research. When it was later revealed that the project was sponsored and funded by the United States army, it became the target of charges ranging from misrepresentation to espionage (Silvert, 1965).

Issues and Trends

Funding. Many indicators point to a decline in resources available for both international educational exchange and the international component of higher education. Among the complex reasons for this decline, the worldwide financial crisis of the 1970s is clearly crucial. The combination of stagnant economies and inflated currencies has led generally to cutbacks in education, and international education seems to have been hit particularly hard. This cutback has especially affected United States students. Statistics released in 1975 by the World Studies Data Bank indicated a substantial decline in the number of American students studying abroad during both the summer and the full academic year. Increasing costs are a critical factor here, since student fees produce the bulk of the income for these programs.

On the other hand, the number of students from countries other than the United States who study outside their own countries continues to increase. More and more, such students come from the developing world. Since education and education abroad are high priority items in the developing countries, it is reasonable to anticipate additional increases in the years ahead.

Shifts in technical assistance. Projections of technical assistance in the field of education by some of the leading aid agencies—the World Bank, the United States Agency for International Development, the United Nations Development Programme—show a movement away from large-scale assistance to institutions of higher education and greater attention to nonformal education, continuing education, and the problems of the rural poor. The World Bank report notes that past emphasis on higher education tended to be irrelevant to the needs of developing societies, particularly the lower productivity sectors of those societies that make up 60 to 80 percent of the population (International Bank for Reconstruction and Development, 1974). Equity—the need to provide educational assistance to this group of people—will serve as a major guideline for future assistance programs. The impact of these developments on international educational exchange is far from clear.

The impact of exchange. Although proponents of educational exchange are convinced of its value, relatively little research has been conducted on the long-term consequences of a study abroad experience, either for the student himself or for the host institution and country. Without such research, a strong positive case for the value of international exchange programs is difficult to make. The International Committee for the Study of Educational Exchange, under the chairmanship of the chancellor of the University of California at Santa Barbara, is attempting to respond to this need through a major research project.

Exchange and interdependence. Most students of international exchange programs have remarked on the special relevance of such programs in an increasingly interdependent world. The best of these programs, those that emphasize cooperation and two-way communication, are particularly suited to deal with the major challenge of creating a climate for constructive relations between the few wealthy nations of the world and the many poor ones. Zbigniew Brzezinski, director of the Trilateral Commission, has noted:

> In a world much more alive with political demands the greatest single awareness is that of inequity and inequality of the human condition. If I were to generalize broadly, I would say that the nineteenth century was dominated by the passion for liberty while today the demand for equity is the dominant political force in the world and well it should be for the world is truly extraordinarily unequal. The community of one hundred and fifty or so states contains only five (with a population of about two hundred and forty million) where per capita income is over five thousand dollars. . . . Over ninety states, comprising close to 60 percent of the world's populations, have annual per capita incomes under five hundred dollars. . . . The character of the new conflicts in the world scene, the changing position of the advanced world, the new aspirations of the third and fourth worlds united together, seem to me to pose a very major threat to the nature of the international system and ultimately to our own societies. That threat is the threat of *denial of cooperation* [Trilateral Commission, 1975, pp. 11–12].

Cooperation can take many forms, among which programs for the exchange of persons are certainly very prominent and likely to expand. By enlisting the most creative minds in their design, such programs may offer not only mutual understanding but a constructive approach to the problems of the developing nations of this globe.

Bibliography

American Council on Education. *International Directory for Educational Liaison.* Washington, D.C.: American Council on Education, 1973.

Beals, R. L., and Humphrey, N. D. *No Frontier to Learning: The Mexican Student in the United States.* Minneapolis: University of Minnesota Press, 1957.

Board of Foreign Scholarships. *Report on Exchanges: December 1974.* Washington, D.C.: U.S. Government Printing Office, 1973.

Council on International Educational Exchange Annual Report. New York: Council on International Educational Exchange, 1975.

"Education and Science in the Federal Republic of Germany." *Bildung und Wissenschaft,* 1975, *11,* 155–168.

Education and World Affairs. *Intercultural Education.* New York: Education and World Affairs, 1965.

Institute of International Education. *Open Doors.* New York: Institute of International Education, 1974.

International Bank for Reconstruction and Development. *Education Sector Policy: Report No. 561.* Washington, D.C.: International Bank, 1974.

Klineberg, O. *International Educational Exchange: An Assessment of Its Nature and Its Prospects.* Paris: Mouton, 1976.

Kubal, L. A. (Ed.) *International and Intercultural Education in the United States.* New York: Academy for Educational Development, 1975.

Scanlon, D. G., and Shields, J. J., Jr. *Problems and Prospects in International Education.* New York: Teachers College Press, Columbia University, 1968.

Silvert, K. H. "American Academic Ethics and Social Science Research Abroad." *American Universities Field Staff,* 1965, *12,* 1–16.

Spencer, R. E., and Awe, R. *International Educational Exchange: A Bibliography.* New York: Institute of International Education, 1970.

Trilateral Commission. *Trialogue,* 1975, *7,* pages 11–12.

UNESCO. *Educational Development: World and Regional Statistical Trends and Projections Until 1985.* Paris: UNESCO, 1974.

UNESCO. *A Summary Statistical Review of Education in the World.* Paris: UNESCO, 1975.

United States Advisory Commission on International Educational and Cultural Affairs. *International Educational and Cultural Exchange.* Washington, D.C.: U.S. Government Printing Office, 1974.

Von Klemperer, L. *International Education: A Directory of Resource Materials on Comparative Education and Study in Another Country.* Garrett Park, Maryland: Garrett Park Press, 1973.

World Yearbook of Education. *International Understanding.* London: Evans, 1964.

World Yearbook of Education. *Higher Education in a Changing World.* London: Evans, 1971–72.

World Yearbook of Education. *Universities Facing the Future.* London: Evans, 1972–73.

JAMES F. TIERNEY

2. INTERNATIONAL STUDENT

The international student may be defined as a member of that group of students who are pursuing educational programs outside of their home countries. In various countries such a student is also referred to as a foreign or overseas student, *ausländischer* student (Germany), or *étudiant étranger* (in French-speaking nations). Although lacking in grace, the legal definition in the United States of students from other countries encompasses their particular characteristics with legal exactitude. According to the United States Immigration and Naturalization Service, an international student is "an alien having a residence in a foreign country which he has no intention of abandoning, who is a bona-fide student qualified to pursue a full course of study and who seeks to enter the United States temporarily for the purpose of pursuing such a course of study at an established institution of learning or other recognized place of study in the United States." The importance of this definition, which in principle applies to practically every other country with a significant foreign student population, is the fact that it identifies persons who are subject to certain specific conditions of entry into the country and must comply with certain regulations during their stay there. Although the agent and the procedures for such governance may vary in different countries, the requirements for the identification and declaration of purpose of a student entering a country for educational purposes remain constant within contemporary international educational interchange.

As a comprehensive description of many students, from and in many countries, the term *international student* provides a universality that justifies its use. At the same time it must be recognized that this term does not denote a type or category. Each international student is an individual, identified by personality, character, cultural heritage, educational objectives and responsibilities, motivation, and opportunity.

History of the International Student

The international student is not a phenomenon of the twentieth century. Historically, the practice of students seeking sources of knowledge and centers of learning is certainly as old as education itself. In the ancient and medieval academies and universities, the student body was drawn from many different countries. Indeed, in medieval times the newly established universities were composed to a large extent of students from foreign countries. The most significant characteristic of the international student of earlier times was the fact that the student (almost always male) who sought to complete or enhance his education in a foreign country did so on his own initiative and, unless he was a member of some religious order, had to depend on his own or his family's resources. Study in a foreign country, up to the second quarter of the twentieth century, was an individual enterprise restricted almost entirely to the elite. In sharp contrast, the dominant feature of contemporary international educational interchange, apparent especially since the end of World War II, has been the broad dimension of the international student population. According to the *UNESCO Statistical Year Book* (1973), the worldwide international student enrollment in 1971 had reached a total of 528,774 and encompassed a much broader cross section of society than was evident in all the years up to World War II. This dramatic growth in numbers and social outreach reflects the fundamental changes that have taken place in the postwar years as new nations have emerged to take their place in the international arena and multinational economic needs and interests have multiplied the demand for professionally trained manpower. Thus, to individual initiative have been added national interest and institutionalized educational exchange programs—governmental and nongovernmental, national and multinational. Such organized exchanges have by no means supplanted private enterprise in international education; in most countries, and certainly on a global basis, the independent, unsponsored student still constitutes the majority of the international student population. Perhaps the greatest impact of the wider recognition of educational interchange has been to make the concept of study abroad less remote, thus inspiring many more young people to seek an opportunity that an earlier generation considered beyond their reach.

Choice of Host Countries

Many factors influence the choice of host countries made by international students. The greatest movement is toward the developed countries, which, according to the UNESCO statistics, attracted an estimated 412,443 or 78 percent of the total international student population in 1973. Several other factors, such as wealth and power, are influential in students' choices, which may account for the fact that the largest single group of international students (140,126 in 1971) are enrolled in United States colleges and universities. Proximity is also relevant and explains the fact that 76 percent of the international student population in Japan come from Asian countries. International relationships have drawn large numbers of students from the Commonwealth countries to the educational institutions in the United Kingdom, while language brings Latin American students to Spain and French-speaking Africans to France or Belgium. Beyond these reasons, it would appear that certain traditional patterns are responsible for the fact that some countries are hosts to a much greater percentage of international students in proportion to their total student body. Of those countries where there are over 10,000 international students, for example, Lebanon heads the list with 52 percent of its student body drawn from foreign countries; in Switzerland the proportion is 22 percent.

International educational interchange is, almost by definition, a partnership that involves at least two parties, the student applicant and the admitting institution, and often a third, the governmental or private agency or organization that is providing all or part of the funds for the educational program. Each of these partners will have different and sometimes conflicting purposes. The student is primarily concerned with personal education or career preparation; the college or university is typically interested in the international dimension of its educational program, although some institutions may be concerned only with the recruitment of a full complement of students. The sponsor, if governmental, sees the student as an agent in the economic and social development of the home country; if private, it sees the student as an agent in the fulfillment of some clearly defined international philanthropic or educational program. The motivation for educational interchange is thus, if programatic, set forth in some binational or international agreement to which the student is committed by the terms of a grant of scholarship. For the independent, unsponsored student, motivation may come from several sources. Intense competition for limited space in universities at home explains much of the educational interchange among the developed countries, while the availability of particular courses or the prestige and advanced offerings of certain foreign educational institutions will attract students to other countries.

The need for intermediate skills and technology is attracting growing numbers of international students to junior or community colleges in the United States and to the polytechnic institutes in the United Kingdom. The accretion of vast wealth by countries possessing the natural resources needed for global economic development has also begun to affect international educational interchange. By paying for their education abroad, such countries are offering to their young people the opportunity to acquire the knowledge and skills that will enable them to assume responsibility for domestic economic development. Thus, new needs and opportunities are further extending the social outreach and bringing a new dimension to the international student population.

Needs and Problems of
the International Student

For the international students, and for the college or university involved in educational interchange, the success of an educational experience depends on the availability to both parties of adequate information on which to base application and admission decisions. Both parties need to be able to determine whether the student will be in the right institution—that is, one that provides all necessary facilities for his field of study. They also need to know that the student has sufficient academic and financial resources to ensure a reasonable prospect of success in achieving clearly defined academic goals.

One outstanding deficiency in contemporary international educational interchange is the lack of information available to the prospective students in their homelands. Educational institutions are working to develop expertise in the evaluation of foreign educational credentials, in the measurement of language skills, and in the assessment of financial resources—the three factors that generally determine the admission of an international student.

Language. With few exceptions, there are certain easily recognized problems that will face the international student irrespective of country of origin or place of study. The first is the need for adequate knowledge of the language of instruction. Preliminary screening may identify the need for some special attention to this problem. In practice, however, knowledge that may seem adequate in the homeland is often insufficient in the foreign classroom. While many host institutions seek to determine the real language proficiency of the foreign applicant by a variety of tests, the final proof can come only as the student attends lectures and presents the necessary written evidence of understanding. In some countries, for example the United States, it is possible in the initial stages to adjust academic programs to an increasing language facility provided through intensive courses in English as a second language. In the United Kingdom a student, once accepted, is expected to begin studies immediately on arrival. In Norway the *Guide Book for Foreign Students* states categorically that a good command of the language is required before starting regular studies. In other countries, such as Japan, experience has proved that even with some language training in the home country, it usually takes one to one-and-a-half years of intensive language study in Japan before a student is prepared to pursue academic work. Thus, language is not only a problem to be faced but is often a determining factor in the international student's choice of a host country.

Housing. The second problem that has some universality is housing. Although there are variations in the extent of the problem, in many of the countries that attract the largest numbers of international students the search for accommodation presents great difficulties. This problem is particularly acute in large metropolitan areas where many students tend to congregate. Generally, in such areas, dormitory accommodation is in very short supply and alternative housing is scarce and expensive. In addition, in some countries international students are not preferred tenants in the eyes of property owners or managers.

Acculturation. For many international students, the process of orientation to a new cultural environment and adjustment to different educational patterns also presents great difficulties. A general recognition of the significance and diversity of this problem of acculturation has led to the preparation, by national public authorities or private groups, of guidebooks and orientation materials, giving information on living conditions and educational requirements. In some countries there is no orientation except these publications, while others provide orientation courses to assist the international student in adjusting both to the campus and to the community. Such courses may be given at special orientation centers, but most often orientation takes place at the college or university. Experience shows that adjustment to new conditions is a continuing process in which such orientation programs provide only initial guidance. For the international student, adapting personal habits to life and study in a different setting may cause considerable strain, especially when the change is fairly basic—for example, for a student coming from a rural setting in a developing country to a modern metropolis.

Finances. Increasingly, finances are the most acute problem facing the international student in any country, especially as international educational interchange becomes more common and is no longer restricted to the wealthy. Even in those countries where education is free, the rising costs of living often exceed the slender resources of the private student. In those countries, such as the United States, where tuition is charged, the fees over the past few years have not only risen but multiplied to the extent that most students must supplement family resources with grants or scholarships (both of which are very competitive), borrowed funds, or earned income. Earning money is, however, almost impossible for the person studying abroad. A review of the employment regulations in the majority of countries where international students are enrolled reveals that their employment is either forbidden or allowed only with special permission that is often very difficult to obtain. Foreign students enrolled in institutions operating on the cooperative plan of education in the United States, for example, are permitted to work because such experience is a degree requirement at institutions of this type. In many countries, however, the situation has been further complicated by generally high rates of unemployment.

For these reasons, the financial status of the student seeking to enter a foreign country is very carefully examined by both the college or university to which the student has applied and the governmental authority that must eventually authorize entry or continuing residence. Financial problems may be further complicated by restrictions in the transfer of currency from the homeland. In many countries, currency control regulations will prevent the exchange of funds for educational purposes unless special permission has been granted. In this way, control may also be exercised on the student's purpose, as the transfer of funds for study abroad may be limited to certain disciplines that are determined to be in the national interest.

Legal status. Since citizens of most countries require some form of identification, it was inevitable that provisions should be made to establish the legal status of the international student. In practically every case the controlling factor is residence. Persons wishing to remain in any country for more than a brief period (generally from three to six months) must identify themselves and provide a reason for their continued stay. Although the procedures may differ and the controlling authority may be national or local, the student must seek permission to live in a foreign country for purposes of study either at the time of entry or soon thereafter. To obtain such a permit the international student must fulfill at least three conditions: (1) provide evidence of admission to the educational institution; (2) give proof of adequate financial resources; and (3) furnish a medical certificate. Once obtained, the permission, which is generally limited to one year, may be renewed on evidence that the student is continuing to fulfill the purpose for which it was granted. Thus, legal status in the host country is a critical factor in the educational program of the international student. It provides the opportunity and establishes the right of the student to take advantage of the educational resources of the host country, which in many countries are considerable, including free tuition and special privileges for such health and welfare services as medical care and student canteens. At the same time, it involves certain commitments (in the United States, for example, a full course of study for an

international student is defined by government regulations) and determines how
much, if any, of the student's activity may
be devoted to other pursuits, such as part-
time or temporary employment.

Although away from home and subject
to the laws of the host country, international students remain citizens of their
homelands. As such, they may have some
specific liabilities relating to the terms of
scholarships or conditions for the use of
national currency for purposes of education abroad. The international student is
also susceptible to the impact of critical
developments in the home country. Since
the 1950s there has been a series of domestic or international crises that has had a
drastic effect on the personal resources or
the individual serenity of international students across the world. In such circumstances, the solution to temporary problems or the adjustment to permanent
changes has generally been found in the
host country, through short-term loans or
by adjustment of status from that of student
to refugee or immigrant.

It is usually presumed that international
students will be returning home, and it is at
the point of return that the consequences of
an educational experience may be seen. For
those whose educational programs have
required several years of study abroad,
there will be once again a need for adjustment, this time back to an environment and
life patterns that have become somewhat
remote during years of absence. The question of acceptable employment and acceptance into the economic and social system
of the home country may also inhibit the
natural inclination to return home. These
problems of adjustment, along with such
obvious factors as higher standards of
living and greater upward mobility in certain host countries, have caused a number
of international students to choose not to
return home at the end of their academic
programs. For these reasons, international
students are encouraged to relate their
studies as far as possible to needs and opportunities in their homelands. In turn,

educational institutions are working to
ensure that the curriculum offered to the
international student is not inconsistent
with the circumstances and career opportunities he will find on returning home.
In addition, some organizations involved
in the international exchange of persons
are paying increasing attention to keeping
returned international students in touch
with developments in their professions.
Newsletters and subscriptions to professional journals are sent, and periodic meetings are arranged among returned students in the same area.

The International Student
as Educational Resource

In the years since international educational interchange has been given some
universal approval, much has been said
about the international student as an educational resource in international intercultural education. In practice, however, this
resource remains largely unexplored, despite the fact that the rationale for acceptance of international students often includes their potential contribution to the
education of the host country students. In
the United States almost every university
statement referring to international education notes the significance of this new
international dimension in the academic
life of the institution. The official pamphlet, *Admission of University Students to
Canada,* on the admission of university
students to Canada notes that they will
"help broaden the intellectual atmosphere
of Canadian universities." The general
information pamphlet, *General Cultural
Scholarship Scheme* in India, on the cultural
scholarships scheme in India notes that the
participants should "participate in the social and cultural life of the institution" to
which they are admitted. These random
examples emphasize a universal recognition of the potential educational value of
the international student; the next step is
the implementation of this policy in the
various disciplines in the institutional academic program.

Associations for International Student Aid

As the numbers of international students have increased, various services and programs have been designed to take care of their educational programs and personal welfare. One of the earliest evidences of this development was the appointment in some United States colleges and universities of a person designated as the foreign student adviser. In 1948 the National Association of Foreign Student Advisers was established in the United States. The name of this association was changed in 1964 to the National Association for Foreign Students Affairs, acknowledging the additional professional involvement in international education, and thus in the membership of the association, of teachers of English as a second language, admissions officers concerned with the admission of international students, various community organizations providing services and programs to international students, and advisers to United States students on study abroad. Similar organizations or associations were subsequently established in Canada (the Canadian Bureau for International Education), in Japan (the Japanese Association of Foreign Student Advisers), and in the United Kingdom (the United Kingdom Council for Overseas Student Affairs). In several countries, such as France, the Federal Republic of Germany, and India, where no organization or association exists, individual foreign student advisers have been appointed for the international students enrolled in colleges and universities. In other countries, where international educational exchange is essentially a governmental activity, the international student is the responsibility of a designated office of the Ministry of Education.

The description of the international student will change as education changes. Individual aspirations and developments within both the international scene and the community of higher education, such as the establishment of new universities in countries where higher education was previously unavailable, will influence the role, status, interests, and activities of the future international student. Such developments as the creation of the United Nations University, the recognition of an international baccalaureate, the pioneer movement toward the internationalization of education in Sweden, and the proposal for international intercultural curriculum development by the American Association of Community and Junior Colleges all suggest that the international student will become an increasingly important factor in education.

Bibliography

Association of International Education. *Life and Study in Japan.* Tokyo: Association of International Education, 1975.

Bridgers, F. A. *Adviser's Manual of Federal Laws and Federal Agency Regulations Affecting Foreign Students and Faculty.* Part I. Washington, D.C.: National Association for Foreign Student Affairs, 1972.

Deutscher akademischer Austauschdienst. *Academic Studies in the Federal Republic of Germany.* Bonn–Bad Godesberg, Federal Republic of Germany: Deutscher akademischer Austauschdienst, 1975.

Information Service, Embassy of Venezuela. *Venezuela Up-to-Date, XV.* Washington, D.C.: Information Service, 1974.

Jenkins, H. M. *NAFSA and the Student Abroad.* Washington, D.C.: National Association for Foreign Student Affairs, 1972.

Ministry of Education and Social Welfare. *General Cultural Scholarship Scheme.* Faridabad, India: Government of India Press, 1973.

Ministry of Manpower and Immigration. *Admission of University Students to Canada.* Ottawa, Ontario: Information Canada, 1974.

Nordahl-Olsen, G. *University Studies in Norway: A Guide for Foreign Students.* Oslo: Universitetsforlaget, 1974.

Office of the Chancellor of Swedish Universities. *Internationalizing Education: Summary of Reports from the Swedish Committee for Internationalizing University Education.* Stockholm: Office of the Chancellor, 1974.

Perez-Ponce, J. M. *The International Dimension of United States Community, Junior and Technical Colleges.* Washington, D.C.: American Association of Community and Junior Colleges, 1975.

Stecklein, J. E., and Liu, H. C. *Study of Foreign Student Employment and Financial Resources.* Washington, D.C.: National Association for Foreign Student Affairs, 1974.

UNESCO Statistical Year Book. Paris: UNESCO, 1973.

United States Department of Justice, Immigration and Naturalization Service. *Employment of F-1 Nonimmigrant Students in the United States.* Washington, D.C.: U.S. Government Printing Office, 1974.

Wheeler, W. R., King, H. H., and Davidson, A. B. *The Foreign Student in America.* New York: Friendly Relations Committee of the YMCA and YWCA, 1925.

HUGH M. JENKINS

See also: Manpower Planning: Migration of Talent.

3. STUDY ABROAD

It is impossible to make more than a few extremely broad generalizations that apply to study abroad in every country. This article is primarily concerned with United States students' opportunities for higher education in other countries. Some statistical background on foreign students in the United States and on foreign students within some of the member countries of the European Economic Community is also included.

Early Development of United States Study Abroad

The United States was heavily dependent upon foreign study for technological, scientific, medical, and artistic knowledge in the colonial years and in the early years of the republic. Education was a priority for the first settlers. Harvard College was founded in 1636, only a few years after the first New Englanders began to carve a country out of a wilderness. Although, in response to new demands, American education soon began to diverge from the British model, study in Europe remained for many years a prerequisite for education in the professions, the sciences, and the arts.

In the nineteenth century westward expansion, the growth of industry, the building of railroads, and immigration changed the nature of education in the United States. As the society became increasingly multiethnic, education for all became a necessity. In the 1860s the land-grant universities were created and became the basis of the state university systems. Nevertheless, study in Europe, particularly in Germany, was still considered essential for serious scholarship and research, especially in the technical fields. In addition, the intellectual and cultural elites in the United States regarded Europe as the source of refinement and culture. In the same way that wealthy Americans bought European paintings for their homes, American intellectuals drew on European learning.

The American concept of study abroad grew out of this intellectual, social, emotional, and educational mixture. For many years United States students and scholars had been pursuing independent study in Europe, but it was not until the 1920s that a United States college organized and sponsored a year-abroad program. In 1924, Marymount College, in California, established its Junior-Year-in-Paris program. The following year Smith College, in Massachusetts, established a similar Junior-Year-in-Paris program; and Rosary College, in Illinois, started its Rosary-in-Fribourg program in Switzerland. In 1931 Smith College established its Junior-Year-in-Italy program in Florence.

All the earliest study-abroad sponsors were women's colleges, reflecting the notion that women required sheltering and chaperonage and men did not; and the concept that going abroad would extend women's role as guardians of the culture, while undergraduate men remained in the United States to build their careers.

It was not until after World War II that study abroad became relatively commonplace for United States students as a result of accessible transportation costs, relatively low living expenses in Europe in the 1950s and 1960s, and the postwar "education explosion" in general. Ideologically, such programs were motivated in large part by the United States' sudden assumption of the role of a world power, by the end of isolationism, and by the acute awareness of international interdependence. Study abroad became less of a luxury and more of a tool for international understanding.

According to Freeman (1966), there were only six junior-year-abroad programs before 1950. By 1956 the number of study-abroad programs had risen to twenty-two, and they were no longer restricted to junior-year students. For the academic year 1962–63, there were 103 United States college-sponsored programs abroad, and by 1964–65 there were 208. By 1976–77, according to the annual surveys conducted by the Institute of International Education (IIE), there were 669 United States college-sponsored programs, both graduate and undergraduate, scheduled for that academic year. An additional 410 summer-study programs were scheduled to be held in the summer of 1976 (Cohen, 1976b). One out of four United States higher education institutions were planning to sponsor or cosponsor at least one study-abroad program during the academic year (Cohen, 1976a).

Types of United States College-Sponsored Programs Abroad

United States college-sponsored programs abroad, both graduate and undergraduate, tend to fall into one of four categories. IIE has identified the following groups in the 1976 edition of its directory, *U.S. College-Sponsored Programs Abroad: Academic Year* (1976a).

The "combination" program. In this program, students enroll in courses in a foreign institution while they also attend courses arranged for the group by the sponsoring institution. The foreign institution courses may be regular university courses; special foreign university courses for foreigners; courses in specialized institutions, such as teachers colleges or art schools; or courses in private institutions specializing in teaching foreign students. The courses arranged for the group by the sponsoring United States institution may be

taught by faculty members of the home institution or by teachers engaged especially for the program and usually recruited in the host country.

Although statistics are not available, most United States college-sponsored programs abroad appear to be of this type, which satisfies a number of basic and often conflicting requirements for both college and student. The foreign institution courses provide a genuine educational experience in the other culture; the United States institution courses provide academic and linguistic support and interpretation as well as a learning experience that can be measured in United States terms for grading and credit-granting purposes.

The "combination" program probably offers the greatest flexibility for both students and sponsors. In cities with many educational institutions, for example, United States students may be placed in different institutions according to their particular interests and level of language competence. Students proficient in the language can be placed in regular university classes, and those less in command of the language can be placed in special classes for foreign students.

The "fully integrated" program. The "fully integrated" program requires the student to be fully enrolled in regular courses in the foreign institution and to take a full academic program there. The sponsoring United States institution often provides academic support in the form of tutorials or language classes and also assigns the papers or administers the tests by which grades and credits are determined. This is a demanding program, suitable only for students with the requisite linguistic and intellectual abilities.

The "island" or branch-campus program. In the "island" or branch-campus program, all courses are taught by regular faculty members of the sponsoring institution and by foreign and United States faculty members engaged especially for the program. Students live together in housing leased by the sponsor. This form of study-abroad program was common in the 1950s and early 1960s. Its advantages include the ability to reproduce the basic forms of United States courses and instruction in a foreign setting, while taking advantage of the cultural and linguistic opportunities of the foreign country.

Stanford University was one of the leading proponents of the branch-campus program. A. Lee Zeigler of Stanford University, at that time president of the National Association for Foreign Student Affairs, had this to say on the subject in 1972: "Basically it was a very new concept academically in that it provided the opportunity to pick up a castle as a site for a campus, to compose a program that would have no problem of credit transfer, taking its own faculty over to teach, to take the students over in a group and to schedule classes Monday through Thursday, leaving the three-day weekend for students to travel. Expenses for the Stanford student, including one-way transportation, were no greater than staying at the home campus. It all worked out very well and it was a highly selective program. Gradually, other campuses were built up in other countries . . . France, Austria, Italy; the idea being that over one-half the undergraduate student body would be involved in the experience" (Zeigler, 1972, p. 27).

However, in the early 1970s budget cuts on the one hand and increased student careerism on the other led to a phasing out of this type of program. Stanford closed its German branch-campus program in 1976 and made its other programs more academically flexible. This remodeling resulted in an increase in the number of Stanford students who chose overseas study in 1975, after a drop in participation the two previous years.

Other United States colleges with "island" programs had similar experiences. Nevertheless, for many United States students this type of program offers the best opportunity for foreign study, particularly for intensive language instruction.

Independent study. Independent study is not, strictly speaking, a type of institution-sponsored program but rather a means through which United States institutions offer qualified undergraduate or graduate students United States credit for independent study in foreign institutions. Exceptionally well-qualified students prepare study and research programs in advance with advisers on their home campuses. Then they carry out an approved program abroad, involving certain courses, projects, or goals. Such a program may involve formal classroom study in a foreign institution. It usually entails research on specific subjects, frequently in comparative or intercultural studies. Independent study is appropriate for the advanced, gifted, self-reliant student.

Location of United States Programs

Shared cultural heritage and intellectual traditions, relatively accessible languages, and comparatively low transportation costs make Europe the favorite location for study-abroad programs. However, United States institutions are increasing their efforts to establish programs in the Western Hemisphere, Africa, and elsewhere.

Europe. For the academic year 1976–77, 479 out of 699 planned study-abroad programs were scheduled to be held exclusively in Europe. England and France were the two most popular countries, with 114 programs reported for the former and 98 for the latter. The Federal Republic of Germany was host to 54 programs; Spain, 53; and Italy, 33. Of the 410 United States college-sponsored summer programs scheduled for 1976, 313 were in Europe (Cohen, 1976a, b).

The Western Hemisphere. Next to Europe, the Western Hemisphere attracts the most United States college-sponsored programs. For the academic year 1976–77, there were sixty-five programs scheduled to be held in Central and South America, Mexico, the Caribbean, and Canada. Mexico, not surprisingly, attracted the largest number of United States programs in the region;

twenty-six of the Western Hemisphere programs were in Mexico. Costa Rica had seven United States academic-year programs; Colombia, six; and Brazil, five. Other Western Hemisphere countries with United States college programs were Argentina, Canada, Ecuador, Jamaica, Panama Canal Zone, Peru, Puerto Rico, Venezuela, and the Virgin Islands (Cohen, 1976a).

Africa. For 1976 United States colleges and universities planned several academic-year programs in Africa: four in Ghana, four in Kenya, three in Nigeria, one in Cameroon. In addition, the Great Lakes Colleges Association continued the Africa programs it had been conducting since 1962; in 1976 the association offered programs in Sierra Leone, Senegal, and Liberia (Cohen, 1976a).

Programs elsewhere. Forty-seven programs were scheduled in East and South Asia and Oceania for the academic year 1976–77. Japan attracted the largest number in the region—twenty-three, of which ten were in Tokyo. There were also programs planned for Australia, the Republic of China (Taiwan), Hong Kong, India, Nepal, New Zealand, Pakistan, and the Philippines. In the Middle East and North Africa, there were twenty-seven United States college-sponsored programs planned. Nineteen of these were in Israel, and the others in Egypt, Iran, Jordan, Lebanon, and Turkey (Cohen, 1976a).

Fields of Study

Study of the language, culture, and history of the host country has traditionally formed the subject matter of United States college-sponsored study-abroad programs. This remains true; increasingly, however, United States students have been going abroad under United States college sponsorship to study in specific academic disciplines. Host countries are chosen for these programs either because they offer unique opportunities in a field, such as tropical agriculture, or because they offer unique cross-cultural insights.

Art and music are popular subjects for foreign study among United States college students. IIE's survey of academic-year programs for 1976 shows 237 programs offering instruction in art, art history, and studio arts, and 68 programs in music. Political science had 109 academic-year programs in 1976; and there were 76 programs planned in economics, 65 in education, and 70 in sociology. In fact, almost every field of concentration has been offered in study-abroad programs.

Some programs make particularly productive use of host countries' unique resources. For example, the Seattle-based Organization for Tropical Studies—a consortium of twenty-five prestigious public and private United States universities, as well as the Smithsonian Institution, the Inter-American Institute of Agricultural Sciences in Costa Rica, and the University of Costa Rica—offers, year round, two-month graduate courses in tropical biology, botany, forestry, marine sciences, earth sciences, geography, and atmospheric sciences. Students may earn eight credits for each two-month program. New York University's school of education enables graduate students to spend two summers studying in Paris and one at New York University in order to earn a master's degree in French.

Sponsoring Institutions

During the 1975–76 academic year 570 United States colleges and universities were planning to sponsor, either individually or as members of sponsoring consortia, at least one study-abroad program. This figure does not include institutions which sponsor only summer programs, nor institutions which sponsor study-abroad programs only as members of extremely large groups, such as the American Association of State Colleges and Universities (Cohen, 1976a).

Many United States institutions have joined in consortia to cosponsor study-abroad programs. This makes it possible for schools to offer programs in fields of study too remote or too specialized for one school alone to support. An added advantage of consortia is that the administrative work involved in making arrangements with foreign institutions, hiring faculty for the program, and arranging for housing and transportation can be consolidated.

Among the major consortia sponsoring study-abroad programs are the American Association of Colleges for Teacher Education, the American Universities Field Staff, the Association of Colleges and Universities for International-Intercultural Studies, the Center for Arabic Study Abroad, the Central College International Programs, the Coastal Area Teacher Education Service, the Council on International Educational Exchange, the Institute of European Studies, the Kentucky Committee on International Education, the Pennsylvania Consortium for International Education, and the Southern College University Union. In addition, there are many smaller cosponsoring groups, consisting of two or three cosponsoring institutions.

Host Institutions

Foreign universities have always opened their classrooms to United States students, in and out of college-sponsored programs. This remains true in the 1970s, despite increased enrollment pressures on foreign universities.

All over the world, but especially in Europe, student reaction in the 1960s against elitist, traditional university systems led to sweeping modernization of higher education. The democratization of university entrance opportunities was one of the students' demands. As a result, by 1975 European universities faced overwhelming pressures for admission. In the Netherlands, for example, for the 1974–75 academic year, 13,000 candidates for places in key fields of study were rejected because their grade averages fell below 7.5 on a scale of 10. For 1975–76 the Netherlands introduced an admissions lottery (Council of Europe, 1975). In the Federal Republic of Germany there were 80,000 applicants

for spring admission in 1976, and places for only 35,000. The Bonn Ministry of Education predicted that, by 1985, 1,600,000 applicants will compete for 850,000 places (Whitney, 1976). Despite such enrollment, there were twenty-three United States college-sponsored programs planned, in which United States students would attend regular classes in German universities (though not in specific restricted fields) in 1976–77. In addition, many United States students study independently in Germany.

Just as in the United States, there is a general belief in Europe that the presence of foreign students on campus is basically beneficial—a guard against intellectual parochialism and an affirmation of the supranational character of scholarship. Some universities give admissions priority to students from developing countries. Former colonial powers frequently give admissions preference to students from their former colonies. Member countries of the European Economic Community are continuing to work out equivalencies among their higher education programs toward the goal of greater compatibility of systems and therefore greater interchange of students.

Many countries faced with rising admissions pressures have adopted the system of *numerus clausus*—in effect closing enrollment to foreigners in certain high-priority fields. For the most part, these are fields involving scientific and laboratory courses that require more space, equipment, and teaching staff than lecture courses. *Numerus clausus* fields change every year, depending on the pressures. Moreover, some classes of foreign students, such as winners of certain international awards, may be exempt from the restrictions.

Summer-Study Programs and Interim Courses

One form of foreign study that began to flourish in the age of inexpensive air fares was the summer-study program. This program has the advantage, for schools and students alike, of not interrupting the academic year and therefore not interfering with the sequence of prerequisites that undergraduate majors must follow. The program also allows graduate students meeting a language requirement to carry out language study on location.

Most universities in Europe and in much of Africa do not conduct regular classes during the summer months. Some European universities use their facilities to offer special courses for foreigners during these months; others rent them to program sponsors. A number of United States colleges and universities take advantage of foreign university facilities for summer-study programs and engage faculty especially for this time.

For the summer of 1976 United States colleges and universities planned to hold 410 programs in nearly fifty countries (Cohen, 1976b). These flexible programs usually consist of specially arranged classes taught by foreign faculty and supporting classes or tutorials conducted by faculty members of the sponsoring United States institution. The following are examples of interesting, though not necessarily typical, summer-study programs.

New York University's schools of education offered a three-summer graduate-degree program in Asian studies. Students spend the first summer in India, the second in Southeast Asia, the third at the university campus in New York City. Instruction is in English; students earn thirty-six graduate credits if they complete the entire program.

Mississippi University for Women offers a three-week graduate-credit course in England, Ireland, Scotland, and Wales for librarians, with particular emphasis on children's and young adults' literature.

Perhaps more nearly typical is Temple University's Sorbonne study-tour, a program founded in 1950. Participants spend four weeks in Paris studying French language, literature, art, and culture. They may earn from four to six credits.

A number of colleges solve the problem of how to offer study abroad with the least disruption of a student's program by offering short interim courses between semesters, usually in January. Virtually all of these programs offer instruction by faculty members of the home institution, and consist, for the most part, of study-tours of several countries, concentrating on a single subject (Association for Innovation in Higher Education, 1976).

Special Courses for Foreigners

With the exception of medical students, comparatively few United States students study in foreign universities with the intention of earning foreign university degrees. However, many universities, particularly those in Europe, offer special certificate programs in the language, culture, and history of the country. These programs attract substantial numbers of United States students.

As of 1976 twenty-three French universities offer special courses for foreigners during the academic year. The *Cours de civilisation française* of the Sorbonne in Paris is probably the best known of these. Generally, such programs involve two-semester courses running from October to June and leading to various degrees and certificates. The University of Paris III (Sorbonne-Nouvelle) has an advanced Institute for Foreign Teachers of French as well as an advanced Institute of Linguistics and Phonetics. The French Cultural Service (972 Fifth Avenue, New York, New York 10022) provides annual course listings.

In Italy, the Italian University for Foreigners *(Università italiana per stranieri),* in Perugia, offers a wide selection of courses in Italian language, culture, art, and music. The State University of Florence also offers courses in Italian language and culture. The *Istituto italiano di cultura* (686 Park Avenue, New York, New York 10021) provides current information.

Elsewhere, programs are offered at the International Christian University, Sophia University, and Waseda University in Japan; the *Universidad nacional autónoma de México* and the University of the Americas in Mexico; the Universities of Bergen and Oslo in Norway; the University of Lisbon in Portugal; the Universities of Granada, Madrid, Málaga, Navarra (in Pamplona), and Salamanca in Spain; and the Universities of Göteborg, Lund, Stockholm, and Uppsala in Sweden. The University of Lund has an International Swedish University, which offers lectures in English specifically designed for United States sophomores and juniors. The University of Stockholm's Institute for English-Speaking Students offers programs in English for juniors and graduates. In Switzerland, the Universities of Fribourg, Geneva, Lausanne, and Neuchâtel offer programs for foreigners in French, and the University of Bern offers programs in German.

Except for the Swedish programs for English-speaking students and the University of the Americas in Mexico, which is United States accredited, these programs are for all foreign students, not just English-speaking foreigners. Although language classes, for the most part, use audio-lingual methods, lectures are most often given in the language of the country, simplified for a foreign audience. Some offer translations into other major languages, but others do not. United States participants in these programs need a basic familiarity with the language in order to follow lecture courses, even those designed for beginners.

United States Academic Credit

United States students interested in foreign study are almost invariably concerned with earning United States college credit for it. Garraty, von Klemperer, and Taylor (1976) advance the notion that United States academic credit is not absolutely necessary to a rewarding intellectual experience abroad, but relatively few American students appear to agree.

Basically, granting credit is entirely the prerogative of United States institutions. Most institutions will give credit for satisfactory work in reputable programs abroad; usually the United States institution administers a test or assigns a paper or project

as a means of evaluation. However, students are strongly urged to make arrangements with the United States institution from which they want to receive credit before taking the course abroad. Certificates and degrees from special programs for foreigners are not equated with foreign universities' regular degrees.

For students who do earn foreign degrees, or who earn credits from recognized foreign institutions that can be equated with United States credits, United States admissions officers will normally treat these credentials in the same way as if they had been presented by a foreign student.

Nonuniversity Study Programs Abroad

Although there are no reliable figures available on the number of United States students pursuing independent study abroad, it is probably safe to assume that a high proportion of them are studying in privately sponsored programs, both United States and foreign, outside official higher education systems. These courses include special-interest programs in subjects ranging from *haute cuisine* to nuclear research, and most offer audio-lingual classes teaching the language of the country. (For reliable listings of some of these programs, see Institute of International Education, 1976a, 1976b; and Garratty, von Klemperer, and Taylor, 1976.)

Reliable language-study courses are available in many countries through long-established intercultural exchange organizations, including the Goethe Institute in Munich, the Austro-American Society in Vienna, the *Alliance française* in Paris, and the Dante Alighieri Society in Rome. In Mexico there are a number of language schools for foreigners.

United States Higher Education Institutions Abroad

As of 1976 there were only four regionally accredited United States colleges outside of the United States and its territories. In the Western Hemisphere, they are the University of the Americas in Puebla, Mexico, and the Institute of Technology and Higher Education in Monterrey, Mexico, both of which offer instruction in English and Spanish. They are fully accredited by Mexican authorities as well as by the United States Southern Association of Colleges and Schools. As of 1976 the only two United States accredited institutions in Europe were the American College in Paris and Franklin College in Lugano, Switzerland.

There are a number of colleges and universities in the Middle and Far East that are not United States institutions but were originally founded by United States organizations or individuals, frequently missionaries, and have a system of education similar to that found in the United States. The American University of Beirut and the American University in Cairo are two examples. These colleges have attracted many United States students who wish to study abroad while remaining in an academic system similar to the one at home. United States nationals and nationals of other countries frequently enroll in these institutions as foreign students, though some have quotas for United States students.

A number of foreign institutions of particular interest to United States nationals are not readily classifiable. The American School of Classical Studies at Athens is a specialized institution open only to graduates of United States and Canadian universities and colleges who hold bachelor's degrees in classics, archeology, or related subjects. The Institute for American Universities in Aix-en-Provence and Avignon, which is associated with the University of Provence (*Université d'Aix-Marseille I*), offers year-long courses and cooperates with a number of United States institutions in their study-abroad programs.

Medical Study Abroad

Medicine is the one professional field in which significant numbers of United States students receive their professional training in foreign countries. More than six thousand students were believed to be studying medicine abroad at the end of 1975 because of a lack of places in medical schools in the United States. A New York State Regents' Task Force on Medical School Enrollment and Physician Manpower reported at the end of 1975 that about half of the annual state medical licenses were given to physicians with overseas training (Petersen, 1975).

In many cases, the pressure on foreign medical schools has become so great that some countries severely restrict admissions of foreign students. Some will not consider United States nationals at all. This was true of the Netherlands and the Scandinavian countries in 1975 (Marien, 1975).

The foreign medical school that appears to have the largest number of United States students is the *Universidad autónoma de Guadalajara,* in Mexico. It is expensive and has complex admission requirements, but virtually all who meet the requirements are admitted, or have been in the past (Marien, 1975). Until 1973 many hundreds of United States nationals flocked to the Universities of Bologna and Rome to attend medical school. However, in that year Italy tightened the requirements for foreign student admission and reserved the right to assign foreign students to specific schools.

As far as licensing is concerned, United States graduates of foreign medical schools are treated in the same way as other graduates of foreign medical schools. The American Medical Association (AMA) requires that graduates of medical schools outside the United States, Puerto Rico, and Canada must pass the examination of the Educational Commission for Foreign Medical Graduates before they are eligible for appointment to an approved United States internship or residency, which is a prerequisite of licensure in almost all states.

Access to Study Abroad

Prerequisites for foreign study. To admit United States students as regular independent students, most European universities prefer them to have a bachelor's degree, although most will accept students with only two years of study in an accredited United States institution. Entrance examinations vary according to the applicant's field of study, but almost all require foreign applicants to pass a fairly rigorous examination in the language of the country.

Requirements in individual countries throughout Latin America and the Caribbean vary widely. Mexican universities admit United States undergraduates but require, in most cases, at least one year of college in order for the applicant's credentials to be recognized as equivalent to Mexican secondary school credentials. Universities in African countries prefer to give all the available places to students from their own or other African countries. Only a very few United States nationals have the qualifications for study in most of the universities of the Far East.

United States college-sponsored programs abroad, particularly for undergraduates, have an immense range of prerequisites. There are programs for freshmen with no knowledge of the host country and programs which require the student to follow complex university lectures and to take examinations in a foreign language. Most program sponsors require good academic standing and some command of the foreign language.

Costs. In the mid 1970s a year of study abroad cost roughly the same as a year of study at a United States institution, plus the cost of transportation. Higher living costs in many countries are offset by lower tuition costs. Most universities outside the United States are tax supported, and tuition charges are quite low compared to those in the United States. British universities charge foreign students about twice what they charge British students, but the cost remains considerably lower than it would be at a United States private institution. In United States college-sponsored programs abroad, tuition costs are usually the same as they are on the home campus, while other costs are adjusted to those in the country of study. Independent students find predictable variations in living costs according to the country.

It is extremely difficult for United States students to hold jobs while studying abroad. A few United States college-sponsored programs offer work-study opportunities, but these are a small minority. Some resourceful students may earn money by babysitting or giving English lessons, but labor laws in most countries prohibit persons on student visas from working. For the most part, therefore, financial considerations limit study abroad to those who can pay the entire costs without holding a job.

Awards for study abroad. Virtually all awards for United States students to study abroad are for graduate study. However, a number of institutions which sponsor study-abroad programs will permit undergraduates who already hold scholarships to use them in the sponsor's own study-abroad program.

Probably the best-known grant program for United States students is the Mutual Educational Exchange Program, popularly known as the Fulbright program. This program is sponsored cooperatively by participating governments. The Bureau of Educational and Cultural Affairs of the United States Department of State is responsible for United States participation. In the United States, the Board of Foreign Scholarships, appointed by the President, has overall responsibility for the exchange programs, including approval of grant opportunities and the final selection of grantees. Overseas the exchanges are administered either by binational commissions or foundations or by the United States embassies. The Institute of International Education conducts the competition for the grants for United States graduate students and administers the foreign-graduate-student program in the United States. Approximately 130 countries and territories participate in the exchange program.

Comparative Statistics

For the academic year 1973–74, participants in off-campus international programs sponsored by United States colleges and universities numbered 7134 graduate students, 28,726 undergraduate students, and 3940 professionals, for a total of 39,800 (Kubal, 1975).

In the academic year 1974–75 there were 154,580 nonimmigrant foreign students reported enrolled in accredited United States institutions of higher education. Of these, 92,370 came from Asia; 26,290 from Latin America; and 18,400 from Africa. The ten countries with the greatest numbers of students in the United States were, in order, Iran, Hong Kong, Republic of China (Taiwan), Canada, Nigeria, Thailand, Japan, Mexico, and the Republic of Korea (Institute of International Education, 1976e, pp. 11–21).

In France, according to the French Ministry of Education, there were approximately 75,000 foreign students enrolled in French universities in 1974–75. Their number included roughly 33,900 Africans; 15,300 Asians; 14,150 Europeans; 9000 North, South, and Central Americans; and 160 Australians. Of these students, 48 percent studied in Paris.

In the Federal Republic of Germany, in the winter term of 1974–75 there were 35,000 foreign students at universities. Foreign students accounted for 6.9 percent of the total student population. European students made up 47 percent and Asian students 30 percent of foreign student enrollment in West Germany.

In Italy foreign student enrollment in 1973–74 numbered 26,742. Of these students, only 6816 came from the nine countries of the European Economic Community; breakdowns for other areas were not reported.

The University Foundation of Brussels reported that foreign student enrollment in Belgium numbered 9369 in 1974–75. There were approximately 4000 European students, 2000 African, 1700 American, and 1600 Asian students *(Nouvelles universitaires européennes, 1976)*.

Organizations in the Field

There are many organizations involved with foreign-study programs. The three basic ones are:

Institute of International Education (IIE), 809 United Nations Plaza, New York, New York 10017. The institute, founded in 1919, is a private, nonprofit organization which develops and administers programs of educational exchange for foundations, private organizations, governments, colleges, universities, and corporations in the United States and abroad. Approximately 7500 students, teachers, technicians, and specialists from about 110 countries study or train through these programs each year. Through its counseling and information services and its publications, IIE assists thousands of individuals and many organizations in the United States and abroad. Overseas IIE has offices in Hong Kong, Bangkok, Mexico City, Lima, Santiago, and Nairobi and has interviewers in more than twenty countries. In the United States IIE has offices in New York, Washington, Chicago, Atlanta, Denver, Houston, Los Angeles, and San Francisco.

Council on International Educational Exchange (CIEE), 777 United Nations Plaza, New York, New York 10017. Formerly the Council on Student Travel, CIEE administers study-abroad programs for a membership consortium of United States colleges and universities; publishes a number of directories; arranges for certain student jobs abroad; provides information on charter flights and other inexpensive travel for students; and issues an international student identity card, which entitles students to discounts on many services, including transportation, accommodations, museum fees, and concert and theater tickets.

Section on U.S. Students Abroad (SECUSSA) of the National Association for Foreign Student Affairs, 1860 19th Street NW, Washington, D.C. 20009. A professional association of study-abroad advisers and others in the field, SECUSSA conducts workshops and sponsors publications on study abroad.

Study Abroad Publications

Most United States colleges and universities publicize their own study-abroad programs amply in campus publications and on bulletin boards. The two most complete directories of United States college-sponsored programs abroad are IIE's *Summer Study Abroad* (Cohen, 1976b) and *U.S. College-Sponsored Programs Abroad: Academic Year* (Cohen, 1976a).

The *Whole World Handbook,* prepared by the Council on International Educational Exchange (1976), describes study-abroad programs of CIEE member institutions and includes practical information for the student traveler. The *New Guide to Study Abroad* (Garraty, von Klemperer, and Taylor, 1976) gives detailed information and guidance on all kinds of study-abroad programs. IIE's *Handbook on International Study* (1970) series covers foreign university systems, special programs, awards, work and volunteer opportunities, government regulations, and organizations providing services.

Bibliography

Association for Innovation in Higher Education. *Cooperative Listing of Interim Term Courses.* St. Petersburg, Florida: Association for Innovation in Higher Education, 1976.

British Council and Association of Commonwealth Universities. *Higher Education in the United Kingdom, 1974–76: A Handbook for Students from Overseas and Their Advisers.* Essex, England: Longman Group, 1974.

Cohen, G. A., (Ed.) *U.S. College-Sponsored Programs Abroad: Academic Year.* New York: Institute of International Education, 1976a.

Cohen, G. A. (Ed.) *Summer Study Abroad.* New York: Institute of International Education, 1976b.

Council of Europe. *News-Letter.* Strasbourg, France: Council of Europe, 1975.

Council on International Educational Exchange. *Whole World Handbook: A Student Guide to Work, Study, and Travel Abroad.* New York: Council on International Educational Exchange, 1976.

Freeman, S. A. *Introduction to Undergraduate Study Abroad.* New York: Institute of International Education, 1966.

Garraty, J. A., von Klemperer, L., and Taylor, C. *New Guide to Study Abroad, 1976–77.* New York: Harper & Row, 1976.

Hull, F. W., Lemke, W. H., and Houang, R. T. *Students in Sojourn.* Washington, D.C.: National Association for Foreign Student Affairs 1976.

Institute of International Education. *Handbook on International Study for U.S. Nationals.* New York: Institute of International Education, 1970.

Institute of International Education. *Handbook on International Study for U.S. Nationals: Study in Europe.* New York: Institute of International Education, 1976a.

Institute of International Education. *Handbook on International Study for U.S. Nationals: Study in the American Republics Area.* New York: Institute of International Education, 1976b.

Institute of International Education. *Open Doors 1975: Report on International Educational Exchange.* New York: Institute of International Education, 1976c.

Kubal, L. A. (Ed.) *International and Intercultural Education in the United States.* New York: World Studies Data Bank/Academy for International Development, 1975.

Marien, D. *Guide to Foreign Medical Schools.* New York: Institute of International Education in cooperation with Queens College of the City University of New York, 1975.

Nouvelles universitaires européennes, February 1976.

Petersen, I. "Regents Offer Plan to Lure Medical Students to State." *The New York Times,* November 6, 1975.

Study Abroad: International Scholarships and Courses. Paris: UNESCO, 1974.

Whitney, C. R. "Young Germans Worried by Shortage of Colleges." *The New York Times,* March 3, 1976.

Zeigler, A. L. *Study Abroad Programs: A Colloquium.* Los Angeles: Southern California Conference on International Studies, 1972.

MARY LOUISE TAYLOR

4. STUDENT EXCHANGE PROGRAMS

The concept of mobility is as old as the most ancient centers of learning, those of the Islamic world. Even earlier, before such centers were established, scholarly exchanges took place between India and China. Over a century before the first European universities were founded (Bologna, Montpellier, and Paris, in the eleventh and twelfth centuries) the colleges of Cairo, Córdoba (Spain), and Fès (Morocco) received wandering scholars in search of teachers whose fame had encouraged an often perilous journey to be undertaken. The advancement of knowledge through access to the best teaching, wherever it was to be found, was a feature of Islamic universities long before the idea that universities should be international centers of learning found root in Europe. It seems likely that the first "instrument of mobility" was the *ijazah* (license to teach), issued by an Islamic professor to a student who had successfully completed a course of study. The *ijazah* was as much an academic passport as a certificate of competence, for it ensured the academic mobility of the graduate based on his professor's status. The debate on equivalence of diplomas and degrees of the 1970s is bound up with institutional status if not also national pride; the Islamic world had a more reliable instrument, based on an intimate knowledge of the student by a professor whose own status was a guarantee for the qualifications and competence of his graduates.

Of course, there were few students then. Today, if mobility is to continue to characterize institutions of higher learning, so that they may retain the enriching influence of foreign scholars and professors, some more universal instruments of mobility will be needed, for they will have to cover thousands of students in a vast range of academic fields. There are already many instruments of mobility in the form of agreed equivalences, research and study-abroad programs, schemes of academic interchange, bursary and scholarship. There are many opportunities for those wishing to undertake postgraduate studies abroad—there are even examples of generous bursaries going begging for lack of applicants. There appear to be few obstacles in the way of a distinguished scholar bent on advanced study or teaching abroad. The groups for whom access to good academic and training facilities in other countries represents both a major benefit and a major problem are the academics of second rank and the general body of undergraduate students. They who most need to be mobile for personal enrichment or advancement are least well served by exchange and interchange schemes.

The reasons for such difficulties are understandable. Where university teachers of no great distinction are concerned, there is little demand for them from institutions in other countries. Equally, there are no schemes especially designed to suit their need for professional enrichment. In the 1950s and 1960s, but less so in the 1970s, the main opportunities for those in the advanced countries to go abroad arose from the rapid development of higher education institutions in the Third World, particularly in the former colonies of the great nations. Thousands of teaching posts were created. Gradually, the proportion of such posts has diminished, although from the mid 1970s onward for a decade or more, a new wave of university posts in oil-producing countries will be taken up by foreign teachers owing to the lack of university-level teachers there.

Very few arrangements for university or school teaching staff to move from one country to another have a reciprocal element written into them. Yet these migrant teachers do act incidentally as interlocutors, even as representatives, for their home system or university; and the information vital to student mobility is, in consequence, available through them to many interested students. They are thus a useful part of the infrastructure of student exchange.

A committee of the Institute of Education of the European Cultural Foundation, reporting on undergraduate student mobility to the Education Commission of the European Economic Community in 1975, found that fewer than 25,000 of the student population of over 2,500,000 in the nine EEC countries participated in student exchange programs or took advantage of the mobility that, in principle, they possessed (Institut d'éducation de la Fondation européenne de la culture, 1975, p. 22).

There are several instruments of mobility at student level. First, there is the International Baccalaureat (IB), a school-leaving examination developed during the 1960s, which could become a major form of "academic passport." The IB is taken in several countries (including the United States, Canada, Colombia, Singapore, Nigeria, the United Kingdom, Tanzania, and France) and is perhaps the only truly multinational instrument of mobility for the student wishing to attend a university in another country. Taken by only a few thousand pupils up until the mid 1970s, the IB is important mainly in its potential; but its potential may be great.

Second, there is the study course into which a period of study or work abroad has been written as an integral part of the degree program. This is very much a Western European and North American phenomenon, and it has taken two main forms. In the first of these, under arrangements started as long ago as 1905, students of modern languages in nearly half the British universities are obliged to spend an intercalated year (usually after the second university year) in one of the countries of the language they are studying, either as a student attending courses at a university, or as an English-language "assistant." Over 2500 British students take the latter alternative, helping to make up the world's largest scheme of student interchange; for, in all, more than 7000 appointments as foreign-language assistants are made each year of students and recent graduates from the United Kingdom, France, the Federal Republic of Germany, Spain, Austria, Italy, Switzerland, Belgium, and Ireland; the United Kingdom also offers assistantships to nationals of many other countries in Africa and Latin America (Central Bureau for Educational Visits and Exchanges, n.d.).

Another arrangement is found in technological universities and polytechnics in the United Kingdom, their equivalents in some other Western European countries, and an increasing number of universities and colleges in North America, which have adopted a "sandwich course" or cooperative education formula, in which students must spend a period of time outside the institution on course-related work. This period can be as long as eighteen months in a four-year course. A proportion of placements is in firms and offices in other countries. In both types of program, the period spent outside the institution is considered as important as the years spent on formal studies. In the United Kingdom in 1975–76, over 46,000 work placements were arranged; about 10 percent of these were for overseas students, a notable service to student mobility (Daniels, 1976).

Third, there is the academic facility in another country that has been established and is run by a university or consortium of colleges on behalf of their own students. Such arrangements—often known as Junior Year Abroad programs—have been made by many United States universities. They are indeed instruments of mobility, for they enable students to study abroad for a time. However, they have had little impact on exchanges and academic links.

Fourth, there are the equivalences that have been agreed on by individual universities or by Ministries of Education on behalf of all their country's universities, allowing foreign holders of certain schoolleaving or advanced study certificates and degrees to be admitted. In the developed countries it is customary for universities, and sometimes individual departments, to establish their own list of approved certificates, diplomas, and degrees. There also exist advisory bodies with an extensive knowledge of the academic field in other countries, to help universities assess the qualifications of applicants. There may in addition be a central assessment and placement service, as in Britain, though this may not cover all the admission procedures.

Fifth, there is wealth. It is odd that wealth plays a greater role in student mobility in the 1970s than it did in medieval times, when the traveling student was often housed and taught without charge. There is a likelihood, however, that money unsupported by academic qualifications will cease in many countries to afford access to universities, owing to the need to impose limits on the number of student places.

Numerus clausus in one form or another can be expected to be a characteristic feature of many university systems by the mid 1980s. At the department level—in respect to a particular subject or subjects— and at the national level—in respect to the proportion or total number of foreign student places—restrictions on access are certain to increase in many parts of the world where foreign students previously were welcomed in whatever numbers they chose to apply.

Exchange

Student exchange as such results from agreements reached between departments or faculties in universities and other higher education institutions and, in a small number of cases, between countries (France and the Federal Republic of Germany, for instance). Such agreements conform, in the main, to the norms of barter—differing numbers of students may participate for different lengths of time, at different times, and at different costs to the sending and receiving institutions, but overall an approximate and sometimes an exact balance is achieved between sending and receiving institutions. The measuring unit used for this purpose may be "man months," or a more complicated computation of time plus services plus numbers.

However, the term *student exchange* is often used to describe student mobility on a quite different basis from the above. Frequently, it is used as a euphemism for aid programs within cultural agreements, where a special effort is thought to be needed to establish or to build up friendly relations with another country. What has been called "seduction by scholarship" is in no sense student exchange, which is essentially an act of friendly cooperation between two institutions or countries. Education is often used as an instrument of political relations, but this fact does not legitimize the use of an ancient formulation to describe a function that simply uses education as an intermediary for political

ends. However, a university may independently decide to offer more than it can receive from its partner institution; that is in line with university traditions from the earliest days and responds to the international aspirations of most universities. Wherever universities are free, they seek this universal function; student and faculty exchange is a notable expression of that function.

Interchange

Interchange is a term that is correctly used of a more general movement between institutions in different countries, not linked essentially to quotas of time, money, facilities, or services. No detailed study has been undertaken of the full range of international interchange in higher education, but even the most superficial survey would likely reveal an immense intermingling of students and teachers; an intricate network of contacts, study courses, and teaching and research posts taken up in other countries; a constant demand among students and faculty for the facilities or advanced work that can be found only in another country; and an equally constant demand by many universities for high-ranking foreign specialists in certain fields. It is interchange rather than exchange, therefore, that was a feature of the early universities, and it is interchange that dominates educational mobility today.

A thousand years ago universities had special accommodation for students from other countries (Cairo, for example, accommodated students from Iraq, Morocco, and elsewhere in Egypt). The foreign students would be grouped according to their country of origin in so-called "nations" (Sweden retains the term for students from each of the Swedish provinces), each with its own residence. The student body at the University of Paris, for example, included the "English nation" and the "Flemish nation." The medieval university at Timbuktu has long since vanished, but for generations its renown attracted the traveling student, who took back to his own country the new knowledge and understanding he had gained in that then great university, thus enriching the academic life of his own country.

It is a matter of speculation how much more beneficial academically, and how much more profitable in its effect on friendship and understanding between nations, would be a system in which the current modes of overseas aid—which support the greater part of university interchange by giving scholarships—were amended to promote more direct interuniversity cooperation. Certainly many generous scholarship programs exist. The UNESCO publication *Study Abroad* for 1975–76 and 1976–77 lists over 200,000 scholarships, assistantships, and travel grants, as well as international courses, in virtually all fields of study. With these offers are associated more than seventy international organizations and over 2000 national institutions in nearly 130 countries and territories. To ask whether the huge sums of money involved in this nearly worldwide provision of university-level facilities to foreigners are always spent in the most effective ways is not to criticize any particular arrangements. However, were the present schemes the subject of overall review, it is to be doubted whether those concerned with the administration of universities throughout the world would opt for a continuation of all the present types of program. University interchange has so much to offer students, graduates, researchers, and career academics, and so affects nearly every aspect of present-day life, that the time may have come for such a review.

Development of Student Exchange Programs Since 1945

Numbers participating. For brevity's sake the term *exchange* will be used to cover both reciprocal and unilateral programs.

No comprehensive study has been made of the number of students who have participated in exchange programs, although Klineberg (1976) did a detailed study of the situation in seven countries: France, the Federal Republic of Germany, India, Japan, the United Kingdom, the United States, Yugoslavia. However, the percentage of foreign students in universities and other higher education centers in most of the developed countries, based on statistics, varies between 4 and 20 percent of total enrollment. More precisely, in 1975 the ratio of foreign students to the total number of students in the Federal Republic of Germany was 6.4 percent, in France 9.4 percent, in the United Kingdom 11.5 percent, in Belgium 12.7 percent, in Austria 13 percent, and in Switzerland 20.15 percent. (Foreign student statistics are estimated in different ways, depending on the country; in some cases all further and higher education institutions are counted, in other cases only universities.) The majority come from the developing world, and there is very little movement in the opposite direction or between developing countries. The growth in numbers since 1945, despite this geographical limitation, has been great.

Hundreds of links aiming at "one-for-one" exchanges have been negotiated. Worldwide, these links give rise to probably no more than 20,000 undergraduate exchanges; the postgraduate and faculty exchanges that accompany them—though fewer still in number—nonetheless constitute a lively and constructive cooperation, of benefit to each participating university. On the interchange, or unilateral, side the growth has been even more striking. From a few thousand in the 1930s, the number of international scholarships and travel grants for study abroad has risen to over 200,000— and this figure does not include the great number of people who study abroad using their own government's assistance or their own resources. The numbers increased from the early 1950s onward. At first, as Klineberg (1976) points out, there were more undergraduates than graduates, and they preferred courses in engineering, the humanities, natural sciences, social sciences, business, education, medicine, and agriculture, in that order. UNESCO estimates at the time revealed that students from the Far East constituted 36 percent of students abroad, followed by Latin America (19 percent), Europe (14 percent), Middle East (11 percent), North America (10 percent), Africa (6 percent), and Oceania (2 percent). In 1960 238,671 students were enrolled in higher education abroad; by 1971 the number had increased to 528,774. In all, about a million students participated in higher education abroad in the mid 1970s (UNESCO, 1973).

There is no single formula to which this movement is the response. UNESCO had this to say about the reasons for the increase in international mobility: "This need is felt all the more in developing countries because, for some time to come, it will be essential for them to send their future doctors, engineers, teachers, technicians and so forth, to gain their qualifications abroad. . . . It must be acknowledged that mobility, viewed as a whole, has not generally been sufficiently clearly understood, hence the necessity of adapting movements of persons more adequately to the changing conditions of society. Mobility depends on a large number of factors, economic, social, historical and legal. . . . it would thus seem to be a matter of urgent necessity to pave the way for improving such exchanges" (UNESCO, n.d.).

The growth in numbers is indicated by the incoming and outgoing student figures for the United States for the decade 1964–1974 (IIE, 1965 and 1973):

Foreign students in the	1964–65	82,045
United States	1973–74	151,006
United States students	1964–65	3793
studying abroad	1973–74	6522
Foreign scholars, professors, and research scholars in	1964–65	8993
the United States	1973–74	10,084

The 1975 census carried out by the Institute of International Education revealed that the number of foreign students in the United States had risen from 151,006 in 1973–74 to 219,721 in 1974–75, among a student population of about nine million. This figure included 65,129 immigrant students. Of the 219,721, Iran sent the largest contingent, with 13,780. Next in order are Hong Kong with 11,060; the Republic of China with 10,250; India, 9660; Canada, 8430; Nigeria, 7210; Thailand, 6250; Japan, 5930; Mexico, 4000; and South Korea, 3390.

Worldwide, the overall percentage of "international students" in 1975–76 was around 2 percent. If the UNESCO projection of a rise in global enrollment in higher education institutions over the next decade is correct, total numbers will rise from about 54,000,000 in 1975 to about 77,000,000 in 1985. Many institutions in the advanced countries will be subject to demands on their space and facilities well beyond their present capacities. The foreign student incursion will have to be the subject of national and international planning.

Geographical spread. On scholarship programs, students move among almost 130 countries, only a handful of the world's nations being excluded from such exchange. Unassisted interchanges occur between sixty to seventy countries, this number being fewer owing to political situations, difficulty of access to universities in some countries, and the lack of appropriate facilities in others. The Foreign Language Assistant scheme, the world's largest student interchange scheme in numbers and geographical spread, involves about forty countries and makes over 7000 appointments to schools and colleges each year. More than half of these are made by the Central Bureau for Educational Visits and Exchanges, the British government agency that covers virtually the whole spectrum of student and teacher travel, exchange, and interchange in all types of establishments. France, through the *Office des universités*, makes about 2000 appointments, and the Federal Republic of Germany, through its *Pädagogischer Austauschdienst*, about 800.

Finance and other support. International organizations have put substantial sums of money aside for interchange and scholarship schemes since 1945. UNESCO, the Council of Europe, NATO, the Organisation for Economic Co-operation and Development, the European Organisation for Nuclear Research, the European Space Research Organisation, the Food and Agriculture Organization, the Inter-Governmental Maritime Consultative Organisation, the International Atomic Energy Agency, the International Labour Organisation, the United Nations Industrial Development Organisation, the World Health Organization, the International Brain Research Organisation, and, more recently, the European Economic Community, and many other international organizations have contributed handsomely to the advancement of study, research, and teaching abroad. There is room for more coordination, if only in the way information is circulated, but the beneficial results of this widespread activity are incalculable. The statistics are impressive—over 1500 scholars visit the United Kingdom each year under the auspices of the Association of Commonwealth Universities. The British Council, the Commonwealth Scholarship Commission, the Commonwealth Fund for Technical Cooperation, the Royal Society, and the Inter-University Council for Higher Education Overseas are only some of the many other bodies contributing to intra-Commonwealth exchanges. There is an equally massive investment by the French government, rather more centralized than that of the British in the *Services de la coopération culturelle et technique* of the Ministry of Foreign Affairs; though much of this investment is in aid programs, interchange and exchange schemes are also assisted.

Governments have also contributed generously in many cases. Some use interchange programs and scholarships as a means of giving aid; others have an eye to political or cultural indoctrination. A few assist foreign students because of an assumed or formal responsibility for certain poorer countries. One or two schemes that had their origin in a desire to help a country in economic difficulties have become cooperative programs as the recipient country's economy improved. This is the case with the Fulbright-Hays program set up after World War II by the United States government.

The principal purpose governments seem to have had in giving grants to their own students for study abroad is to make up for a lack of facilities at home. Students themselves are attracted by the prestige and marketability of higher degrees gained in certain well-known Western universities. Young graduates in many parts of the world strive to gain admittance to these institutions, and their governments have often been willing to assist them financially. If cynicism seems to accompany academic aspirations in this form of interchange, it is at least understandable. But sending governments would do better to enter into proper agreements with the receiving countries if they seek to make up for their own educational shortcomings. Education is a major industry requiring massive capital expenditure and operating expenses. That interchange has been allowed to develop haphazardly to the levels reached in the mid 1970s is one of the reasons that the foreign student question in many countries is covered in confusion, suspicion, and argument, when it should be an effective and apolitical medium for cooperation and understanding.

Aside from the funding of schemes and projects, the main contribution governments have made to student exchange is in their foundation of, or assistance to, specialized exchange organizations. Among the leading bodies are the Institute of International Education, based in New York City, which administers many of the United States government–supported exchanges; the East-West Center in Hawaii, which oversees comparative study, training, and research in the United States, Asia, and the Pacific area; the *Deutscher akademischer*

Austauschdienst (German Academic Exchange Service) of the Federal Republic of Germany; the *Office national des universités et écoles françaises* (National Office of French Universities and Schools); the Central Bureau for Educational Visits and Exchanges, covering England, Scotland, Wales, and Northern Ireland; the British Council; the Inter-University Council for Higher Education Overseas, based in the United Kingdom. However, in most countries government interest in student exchange tends to fall within the sphere of Ministries of Education, Ministries of Foreign Affairs, or both. There can be no doubt that permanent, specialized agencies of the type mentioned above are essential to the management and development of student and most other forms of educational exchange.

Many higher education institutions, mainly those of university status, offer scholarships to foreign students. However, these scholarships constitute only a small proportion—probably not more than 1 or 2 percent—of the total number of scholarships available through governments, foundations, and industry. There is no set pattern; in the main, scholarships owe their existence to the interests or family backgrounds of individual donors. Because of their special nature, they tend to be directed to a small constituency of potential beneficiaries and thus tend to be well known in that constituency. Private scholarships are, on the whole, a more efficiently used resource than many governmental scholarship schemes.

In several parts of the world, charitable foundations have played an important part in student mobility. In Denmark, for example, the Denmark-American Foundation and the Larssen Legacy offer scholarships to visiting students to add to those offered by the Ministry of Education, the Technical University of Denmark, the Royal Danish School of Pharmacy, the Royal Danish Academy of Fine Arts, and Århus University. The Fine Arts Academy also has foundation grants in addition to its

Danish government travel grants. In North America, foundations such as Ford, Carnegie, Kellogg, and Harkness have given vast sums of money to student exchange, usually at postgraduate and research levels. In the United Kingdom the Winston Churchill Fellowships have introduced an invaluable new dimension into student exchange by giving researchers, teachers, and practitioners in many professions and vocations the opportunity to design and carry out a study of their own special topic in another country for three months. In Sweden, foundations offering grants include the Helge Axelsson Johnson Foundation, the Sweden-America Foundation, Magnus Bergvalls Foundation; Herman Nilsson-Ehle and Henry and Gerda Dunker travel grants (administered by the Royal Physiographic Society); the Swedish National Association Against Heart and Chest Diseases; the Swedish Society of Medical Sciences, the Lars Hierta Memorial Foundation in the social sciences, and many others. Australia has English-Speaking Union grants, the Myer Foundation, and YWCA scholarships. In 1972 the Japan Foundation was established with funds to sponsor student and academic visits and exchanges. Understandably, foundation grants are found most frequently in the industrialized countries, though many of them are open to applicants from developing countries.

Philosophical and religious groups are found in some number among the organizations offering scholarships for study abroad. By directing themselves toward a known and limited constituency, they tend to be taken up in greater proportion than grants made by governments. However, their total number outside the United States and the United Kingdom appears to be small (UNESCO, n.d.).

Industry and commerce provide students with many thousands of grants both for home study and for study abroad. Finland has the Cheese Producers' Foundation, the Walter Ahlström Foundation, and the Stenroth scholarships at the Helsinki

School of Economics. France has hundreds of bursaries offered by chambers of commerce. Guyana has industrial scholarships in engineering, sugar technology, agriculture, and agronomy. Norway has the Oslo City Council scholarships, offering further training in gardening. It is likely that the number of industrial and commercial scholarships will continue to increase, as firms are now trying to establish a lien on future employees not only at the end of their university career but during and even before it. Businesses and armed forces in certain countries now finance students' university courses; in some cases a salary is paid in addition. Some of these grants are tenable abroad or have a study-abroad period included. In a 1976 example, a British-based firm offered to pay the university costs in the United Kingdom of a number of Norwegian students, with a promise to employ them in Norway on completion of their studies.

Establishing and Developing Instruments of Mobility

Efforts are being made in many countries, particularly in the nine member nations of the EEC, to develop or invent instruments of student mobility. The EEC, to meet some of its political unification aims, needs to train many more young people in the ways, languages, and industries of other EEC countries than their own. Already in the mid 1970s, there is a flow of professional workers among the EEC countries, especially in fields such as pharmacology, veterinary science, and medicine; professional associations have responded to the implied need to establish equivalences much quicker than have their academic counterparts, who may take as long as twenty years to reach agreement. The reason is obvious: the professionals must find accommodations, for they must now work across national frontiers, whereas the academics have little occasion for joint projects and can—and probably will—take their time over reaching agreement

on what many of them consider a problem as much philosophical as practical.

Governments will undoubtedly put aside more money for student mobility. Recognition of the interdependence of nations was already well advanced in the early 1970s, and despite some unease about the costs associated with the arrival of large numbers of foreign students in some countries, governments are keen now to give more opportunities for study abroad to their own students and ready to acknowledge the value of receiving reasonable numbers of foreign students—up to about 10 percent in the industrialized countries seems to be considered an acceptable proportion.

Barter arrangements will also be developed. It is impossible for countries with little or no hard currency to purchase student places abroad, and political situations often make it difficult for students to accept offers of bursaries from the richer nations. However, even the poorest countries can offer a few study or training placements, if not in the universities or industry, then in ecology, social work training, geography, construction, medicine, or teaching. Such offers could be put into a common pool from which participating countries would draw opportunities appropriate to their own education and training needs. An exact balance of costs need not be achieved; what is important is that the richer countries understand the educational benefits that may be derived from a period of study or work in a developing country and the advantages of two-way mobility, of cooperation with the developing world in addition to or, wherever possible, in place of the one-way aid that has divided the world into donors and recipients.

It is also likely that student mobility will take on a more vocational slant. In the name of "appropriate technology transfer," much inappropriate technology has been transferred to developing countries. The training of technicians has often been overlooked in favor of scholarship schemes for superior academics. The developing world will demand help that is carefully designed to meet its requirements for qualified workers at all levels.

Exchange programs. Exchange programs are the cheapest of all student mobility arrangements. Departmental and full-institution links will grow in number and variety. They will spread out of their 1970s confines (mainly Western Europe and North America) into many other world areas. "No currency" exchanges will predominate; students will move from country to country on a head-for-head, bed-for-bed basis, and no tuition fees will be paid. Concessions will be available to reduce the cost of accommodation, food, books, and travel. Countries will meet, first bilaterally, then on an increasingly multilateral basis, to agree on exchange programs and quotas. The general conditions surrounding a student's stay in another country will be more standardized. The nine countries of the EEC, for instance, will agree on coordinated, if not standard, arrangements for students from within the EEC, and probably also for students from other regions.

The foreign student will no longer be faced with nine quite different sets of regulations for university entry and attendance, nine different scales of fees, nine different types of lectures and supervision, nine different examination methods, and a degree at the end of it all that has a different status in each of the nine countries.

It is unlikely however, that any great number of students will leave their own countries to take a first degree abroad in the next twenty-five years. The tendency will continue to be to take the first degree at home and then to go abroad for advanced study. There is no indication that the number of first-degree students attending universities abroad on a head-for-head or other direct exchange basis will exceed 100,000 in the year 2000, based on 1971 figures (Table 1), which show that not more than twenty-one thousand students went abroad on a head-for-head exchange program.

Interchange programs. There are many indications that there will be a considerable increase in the number of students traveling abroad for courses of subdegree and

Table 1. Students Studying Abroad in Higher Education, 1971

Country where studying[a]	Country of Origin							
	UK	France	FRG	Canada	USA	Other advanced	Non-advanced[b]	Total in each country
United Kingdom	0	200	300	1,000	2,300	7,300	15,900	27,000
France	800	0	900	600	1,800	15,200	15,600	34,900
Federal Republic of Germany	600	1,800	0	200	2,300	14,200	15,000	34,100
Canada	6,000	900	600	0	6,300	6,500	10,500	30,800
United States	3,500	1,800	2,100	10,400	0	33,200	89,200	140,200
Other	1,600	5,300	2,700	700	8,000	73,600	140,300	232,200
Total from each country	12,500	10,000	6,600	12,900	20,700	150,000	286,500	499,200

[a]The five countries shown separately are the five largest providers for overseas students.

[b]Nonadvanced is, for convenience, defined here as countries in Asia, Africa, and South America. There were 103,800 overseas students studying in these countries, most of them coming from other nonadvanced countries.

Source: UNESCO, *Statistical Yearbook, 1973.*

first-degree level in the next twenty-five years. Regional planning of higher education will supersede the present concentration on planning at single-nation level. It is not possible for all the advanced, much less the poorer countries, to build and maintain the full range of higher education facilities that modern society must have. National centers of excellence, already a feature of national planning in some countries, will be the first step toward regional planning. The example of Sweden, which in 1972 set up a committee to prepare a feasibility study for the internationalization of the Swedish universities, will be followed by other countries. Sweden's action program, decided upon in 1974, is to be introduced during the late 1970s with an initial budget of about 1 percent of the total sum allocated to the Swedish universities. It highlights the importance of contacts and exchanges with universities in other countries and represents the first coordinated attempt by a major university system to adapt itself to the international community, the interdependent society in which it finds itself in the last quarter of the twentieth century.

The increasing dominance of a handful of world languages, especially English, will make for greater mobility and will allow the development of regional facilities in specialist and expensive subjects. From the one million of 1975, the number of students going abroad for a year or longer during their undergraduate years or upon graduation will almost certainly double by the year 2000.

Government policy. The Swedish government has been a leader in establishing the objective of internationalizing not only the universities, but also Swedish society and the schools within it. Student exchange will be funded for the first time as a means of enriching the university system and as a function of the government's social policy. This is a notable advance on the approach adopted by many governments during the 1950s and 1960s, when Ministries of Foreign Affairs seized on educational

and cultural exchange as instruments of political influence. An illustration of this tendency is a statement by Senator Fulbright, a leading proponent of educational exchange: "It is therefore fair to say that the exchange program is an instrument of foreign policy, not just of the United States but of all participating nations—as well as a memorable educational experience for the individual participants" (Fulbright, 1975).

It would be too much to hope, however, that the Swedish model *(Internationalising Education, 1974)* will be readily taken up by those leading nations that are still concerned about their image in the developing world. Cultural imperialism and technical aid have taken the place of conquest by force as a means whereby certain countries seek to exert political influence over others. However, now that the weaknesses of such an approach to the purchase of international goodwill are being recognized, the emphasis is changing. Some of the richer nations are starting to understand the value of international education programs in terms of their own development. The foreign student is seen as an asset to the receiving country and not just an onerous charge upon it. Nonetheless, each country seems to have adopted its own position on foreign students without reference to the broader issue of international cooperation. On the other hand, few—and then only small or totalitarian—countries have devised an overall policy with regard to their own students going abroad.

There are political and economic implications to any international exchange of the size and nature of the student exchange and interchange movement. According to UNESCO, "International action for cooperation among universities and other institutions of higher education requires some serious thinking. The purpose of interinstitutional cooperation particularly in the developing countries, should no longer be to establish new institutions of traditional kinds or to develop those already existing, but rather to assist in the establishment of new types of institutions suited to the needs of the society or the individuals which they are supposed to serve. Twinning or bilateral arrangements among institutions exist already, but they have often resulted in institutions building with 'cooperation,' which can only be a two-way process, being in fact reduced to one-way traffic or 'assistance.' Interuniversity cooperation should be reorientated to take into account the requirements of development and the need for international understanding, mutual appreciation of cultures and international communication" (UNESCO, n.d.).

International Cooperation and the Need for a Global Approach to World Problems

At the Commonwealth Seminar on International Educational Placements, held at the University of Regina, Saskatchewan, Canada, July 1976, Shridath Ramphal, secretary-general of the Commonwealth, said of the need for international cooperation in student exchange:

It is understandable that in the wake of the rapid technological progress which the world has witnessed over the last several decades and the constant need for substantial expansion of the trained manpower in all countries, that countries would emphasise the need to train their own nationals. It would be a pity, however, if the pursuit of the goal was undertaken in so unenlightened a manner as to lead to the exclusion of students from those countries which are only now embarking upon the development of the basic facilities needed to train their people. For such exclusion would not only set back the development process in the developing countries, to which all nations are committed, but would also deny the developed countries of the productive cross-fertilisation of ideas that has been, is, and always will be possible when people at different stages of development bring to bear their collective experience on technological and other problems. It is perhaps not without significance that those countries which have attracted immigrants on a large scale—and through them a transfer of technology—have succeeded in achieving the most sustained growth over the longest period [*Higher Education Exchange*, No. 7].

It is clear that two-way cooperation rather than one-way aid must characterize educational relations between developed and developing nations in the last decades of this century. It is equally clear that there must be more regional cooperation among developing nations; the process began to take root in the early 1970s. This emerging cooperation would be an appropriate subject for massive investment by the richer nations through organizations such as the EEC, the Organisation for Economic Cooperation and Development, and the World Bank for it is unlikely that the single donor nations concept will be acceptable once the developing nations start to cooperate on regional educational resources.

Aid to and cooperation with developing nations. Aid for specific innovations will continue to be given most expertly by single nations and by small groupings such as the Scandinavian countries. The Commonwealth has the advantage of historical connections and ease of communication through the English language. The EEC, with its relatively homogeneous grouping of Western European nations, could become an efficient agency for extensive assistance, provided its educational function is allowed to develop; it seems not to have occurred to the politicians who designed the structure of the EEC in its first years that the educational system is the one vital means of securing prosperity in the long term. Education was not given a separate department (commission) by the EEC until 1973, and even in 1976 there was still no scheme of cooperation or exchange in education that straddled the nine member nations. Cooperation with the Third World, through links that already exist with the forty-plus Associated States of the EEC, could become a major element in the EEC's education portfolio. Unhappily, UNESCO, despite many international conferences and resolutions, has been unable to develop within itself the expertise needed to foster the large-scale student and academic exchange schemes that are required if the full benefits of educational interchange are to be available to developing nations. Nonetheless, UNESCO programs of educational assistance through sending experts and sponsoring thousands of study visits are the basis for education transfer and international cooperation on a global scale. (UNESCO's two-year fellowship schemes offer over 3000 awards to nominees of the governments of its member states.) Its success in this area prompts the hope that the major international bodies will be brought together with the aim of coordinating certain of their educational assistance programs. Just as it is wasteful when individual countries compete to help a poorer nation, so is it when international organizations set up parallel programs.

Foreign policy. If educational assistance and cooperation programs are to be persuaded to move away from their predominantly one-country base, the foreign policy purposes that have determined their size and nature will have to be amended to conform with policies agreed on by the international organizations. It is to be hoped that the international organizations will resist the temptation to use educational exchange as a currency with which the political support of recipient countries may be purchased.

Educational and cultural enrichment. The most brilliant audiovisual teaching system is a poor substitute for personal experience of other countries, peoples, languages, and cultures. The young people of the 1970s constitute the first truly international generation in world history, having an intuitive, if not an electronic, contact with their counterparts throughout the world. Student travel organizations and private initiative give them the chance to congregate on an international basis in many parts of the world during their holiday periods. Voluntary service schemes allow them a privileged insight into life in another country for a while after graduation. Popular music and folk music have become global languages for them. Life styles and fashions of dress have been adopted so widely and rapidly that there is a real danger of the world's youth retreating into a universal anonymity, raceless and cultureless. Face-to-face contact with other peoples helps them to avoid this, by revealing the social and cultural values of other societies, other ways of life, and other attitudes.

Knowledge of just one other land and one other way of life may be a good start to personal enrichment. It is where educational exchange must begin, with a serious and deep study of what constitutes another country and its culture. As young people struggle to establish their own sense of identity, they can benefit educationally and culturally from a personal involvement with their counterparts from another way of life. This is to say nothing of the fact that no country is so rich or so varied as to encompass all the world's riches and all the varieties of human condition. Educational exchange offers the student a challenge, an adventure, a learning opportunity, and, in some cases, also a service opportunity; it responds to his need to equip himself for life in a society that for him will be inescapably international. Indeed, one might say that the young have already decided that they alone constitute the new international society. It is the responsibility of earlier generations to provide the means whereby the implications of this decision may be met in ways that are in keeping with their aspirations, their youth, their energies, and their enthusiasms for international contact. Student exchange is more than a collection of young people attending study courses abroad.

Prestige. National prestige is the overlay for much investment in educational exchange. The overconcentration on postgraduate and academic bursary schemes and the low level of funding for teacher and student exchange schemes reveal how many countries regard exchanges as they regard their national airlines: as flag carriers that enhance their prestige, expensive toys to impress their neighbors and their enemies. The recognition by many developing nations of the real purpose of educational exchange—that is, of its function as an instrument of development, of national identity, and of long-term economic growth—may persuade the donor nations to amend or drop some of the schemes for educational assistance employed in the 1960s and early 1970s. It may also persuade the recipient nations to seek help in building the technician class and the intermediate technology resources that will answer their development needs better than a surplus of highly trained academics. The oil-rich nations are able to buy this expertise and to build the colleges that can preserve and extend their current resources. The poorer nations will have to be helped to acquire a technology appropriate to their circumstances and their present level of development; exchange can play an important role, and it behooves politicians and planners to work out structures of cooperation that have this aim as an intrinsic element in each program.

Profit. The term *student exchange* has been borrowed by many commercial organizations that see it as a useful slogan. Tour operators and travel agents do indeed serve young people well when it comes to international travel opportunities. There are substantial youth and student travel organizations in more than forty countries; those that are designated as national student travel bureaus are brought together in the International Student Travel Conference (ISTC), which is a forum for the discussion of student travel policies, a workshop for interagency contracting, and the basis for certain forms of central servicing, such as joint computer booking facilities. The major student travel bodies also include some that are openly commercial in character, one of their main functions being to earn money for the student unions with which they are affiliated. The heyday of the student travel business was in the 1960s and early 1970s, when it capitalized on the shortsightedness of the scheduled service airlines and set up extensive networks of student charter flights. By the mid 1970s the airlines had caught on, and

they began to introduce their own youth- and student-fare structures, which offered regular flights year-round at little more than the student travel specialists were forced to charge. A number of the leading student travel organizations were unable to compete in this changed market and closed. However, it is likely that the principal members of the ISTC will still be giving a useful service to students worldwide in the 1980s. Students are quick to recognize the merits of utilizing a service especially designed and run for them and subject to a certain amount of control by them. They may have reservations as to how the resulting surpluses are distributed, but, on the whole, they would prefer to see any profits from student travel being "recycled" within the student movement than to watch them disappear into the anonymous vaults of the major airlines and travel agencies.

On the other hand, there are many non-commercial student travel organizations, some comparable in size with medium-sized tour operators. There are also some regional groupings, such as that of the Pacific area student travel agencies, which allow for joint negotiations with airlines and the suppliers of accommodations and other student services. The Eastern European youth and student travel agencies should probably also rank among non-commercial operators, since any profits made are turned over to the sponsoring associations of youth or students or to the sponsoring ministry, a proportion being kept for the development of services. In most cases another share of profits is allocated for exchange visits with countries whose currency has been gained during the transactions.

Very few exchanges, as such, are arranged by the student travel organizations. Nonetheless, these organizations play a valuable part in the development of student opportunities at the international level, and their skills should be kept more in mind when governments debate the prospects and priorities of exchange schemes and educational cooperation with other parts of the world.

Levels and Types of Programs

About one million students were studying abroad by the mid 1970s. During the previous decade there had been a tendency for more students to go abroad for first degrees, for three main reasons.

First, those countries that benefited from increased oil prices were able to purchase places abroad in much greater numbers. There was a lack of further and higher education institutions in those countries and an urgent need to train technicians and technologists abroad until such programs could be completed. In some cases, for example, Venezuela, students in their late teens were sent abroad first to study English to meet the standard required by further and higher education institutions and then to spend up to five years preparing for certificates, diplomas, and degrees. In other cases, for example, Saudi Arabia and other Arab states, deals were made with other countries for the training of large numbers of medical students. In a third case, countries of relative prosperity, such as Norway, still lacked higher education resources, and special grants were given (in Norway through the State Educational Loan Fund) for study abroad. By the mid 1970s nearly 5000 Norwegian students were being financed to take first degrees abroad, mainly in Western Europe and North America (Association of Norwegian Students Abroad, 1975). As time passes the richer developing countries will build their own further and higher education systems—which at least until 1990 will require a constant supply of teachers from the industrialized countries—and the need for first-degree courses abroad will gradually diminish.

Second, more help for study and training placements abroad was available from national ministries concerned with overseas aid and from some of the principal international organizations.

The third reason for the rise in first-

degree study abroad was the problem of finding university places in some of the advanced countries. It had traditionally been difficult to secure entrance into a British university. For example, a high grade of school-leaving certificate was needed, and some universities imposed their own entrance examination on top of that. But, first in France, then in the Federal Republic of Germany, then increasingly in other Western European countries, *numerus clausus* began to be a feature of the university system, and this persuaded some people who were excluded from desired courses in their own country to seek admission to universities elsewhere. The United States and Canada were the prime objectives, but the United Kingdom, France, the Federal Republic of Germany, Austria, and Italy were among a number of other countries that became the subject of searches for first-degree study. There was, however, no noticeable move by any of the European countries to facilitate interchange with neighboring countries other than an agreement between France and the Federal Republic of Germany. However, the EEC sponsored a study of student mobility in 1975 *(Institut d'éducation de la Fondation européenne de la culture, 1975)*, which gave rise to proposals aimed at facilitating access. The French government introduced special facilities for foreign students at each university, but in most cases these did not include access to full degree courses. In fact, admission to full degree courses gradually became more difficult in the mid 1970s. The growth period of mobility was over for students wishing to study abroad on their own initiative. The special cases of oil-rich countries and scholarship schemes for poorer countries aside, the trend would be toward shorter periods of study abroad based largely on institutional links and on contacts between institutions and countries. Negotiations began between governments, with a view to reaching agreement on student exchanges with some control over fees charged, facilities offered, and numbers involved.

Student mobility has long been dominated by those who have just graduated and who seek a second or complementary degree. Inevitably, most of this movement has been toward the relatively small number of countries that have universities of high prestige. Graduates of the *grandes écoles* of France have gone in large numbers to the great engineering universities of the United States (although numbers fell in the mid 1970s, owing to a drop in the number of scholarships offered). French and German universities have generous schemes of employment for graduates who act as assistants in language departments between periods of advanced study. British universities welcome thousands of overseas graduates. The movement is virtually worldwide, and is a credit to university systems everywhere.

At a more advanced level, there are many postgraduate scholarship schemes; these are the dominant feature, for example, of the 200,000 bursaries listed by UNESCO. There is cause to believe that in some parts of the world there are now enough such bursaries, and more emphasis could be placed on assistance for those wishing to take first or second degrees abroad, perhaps especially for those bent on applying themselves to the field of intermediate technology. In some Western European countries a number of postgraduate scholarship schemes have fewer applicants than scholarships, but the inclination almost everywhere is to introduce even more opportunities at this level whenever new funds become available.

The same may be true of opportunities for senior research scholars. The academic world benefits enormously from the international mobility opportunities offered at this level, but the question of balance must be raised. Is it better to concentrate on a relatively small number of costly bursaries for research abroad, or is there an equal justification for broadening the base of student mobility through more investment in undergraduate and graduate scholarship schemes? The answer will probably be different from one country to another. The advanced countries will

continue to seek more opportunities for research abroad and leave undergraduate mobility mainly to university links and exchanges and to private initiative. The poorer countries appear to favor broadening the base of participation in first-degree, diploma, and certificate courses abroad in response to their need for technical personnel rather than new cadres of highly qualified academics.

Links. Exchanges based on institutional links will be the principal characteristic of university interchange in the developed countries in the 1980s. In some countries the exchanges will be assisted financially by government as part of a cultural exchange program, but in the main they will be self-financing. Many schemes based on agreements between linked universities were started in the 1950s and 1960s. By the 1970s the techniques were widely understood and universities were able to conclude "no currency" exchange agreements, which took account of differences in the number of student exchanges, in the length of time they were accommodated in the partner university, in the facilities offered, and in the cost of living of the other country. A start was made to joint courses involving an obligatory period in the other university. If this trend continues, and there are signs that it will despite the misgivings many academics have about equivalences, a more secure foundation will have been found for student mobility.

In the United Kingdom the polytechnics that were founded in the early 1970s became great innovators in student mobility, setting up many links with other Western European institutions; as many as seventeen subjects formed the basis for student interchange with France alone. Increasingly, links between developing countries will be used as a means of overcoming the lack of certain study facilities in the cooperating countries. Regional cooperation of this kind was already active by the end of the 1960s.

Some countries may follow Sweden's example, set forth in a report by the Committee for Internationalising University

Education: "To promote the exchange of university staff and students, we propose that universities and departments strive towards cooperation agreements with counterpart institutions in other countries. What we mostly have in mind here are not general agreements to cooperation but contracts for concrete projects. A more effective exchange program will require documentation, information and service not only for Swedish students and staff members who travel abroad, but also for foreign students and staff members who come to Sweden. We therefore propose forming a network of international secretariats" *(Internationalising Education,* 1974).

In 1975 what is generally known as the Helsinki Agreement—the Final Act of the Conference on Security and Cooperation in Europe—was signed by governments. The Final Act's chapter on "Cooperation in Humanitarian and Other Fields" included sections on human contacts, information, cooperation and exchanges in the field of culture, and cooperation and exchanges in the field of education. The education section is in many ways a summary of many of the resolutions passed by the international conferences previously referred to. What is peculiar to the agreement as a whole is its status as a declaration of intent by each of the signatory governments, and the fact that the agreement called for a further conference to be held (in Belgrade during 1977) "to continue the multilateral process initiated by the Conference." The first joint meeting of European youth and student organizations and European political youth and student organizations was held in Vienna in December 1975, as a direct consequence of the agreement. The meeting became yet another forum for resolutions, rather than a workshop for youth and student exchange project design. However, further meetings of this kind are proposed, and it is likely that the political youth and student organizations will associate themselves more closely with youth and student travel agencies in an attempt to develop more conferences and other international meetings for students.

Whether this process will add much to the opportunities offered by existing organizations, including those in membership of ISTC and the Federation of International Youth Travel Organisations (FIYTO) will depend on whether the political organizations can find enough common ground and whether the signatory nations are serious in their declared intentions to implement the Helsinki Agreement's "Basket III," which incorporates the education section. *Exchange* (1976) carried comments by senior representatives of several Eastern European countries, which suggest that those countries might allocate funds to schemes arising from "Basket III" recommendations. However, it is to be noted that no firm commitments were entered into and that most of the recommendations were weakened by phrases such as "where possible," "where appropriate," and "in the light of national priorities."

Government-assisted programs. The investment by governments in assistance to foreign students and graduates, and, to a lesser extent, to their own students going abroad, is now huge. The total world figure probably exceeded $1,000,000,000 by 1975, including all costs associated with the receiving and sending of students. This is an investment that has been subjected to much critical attention, and by the mid 1970s the economic recession had obliged many governments to review their policies in this matter. Discriminatory (that is, higher) fees for foreign students had been introduced by some countries, but there were political problems associated with such policies, and pressure was exercised to do away with them. However, where special courses needed to be set up, the general tendency was for higher fees to be imposed; but only in rare cases, such as courses in medicine, where there was a great shortage of places, was anything like a true cost figure charged.

It will be a long time before there is unanimity between governments on this matter, because there is no machinery for reaching agreement other than in small groupings of nations, and because each country's interests, needs, and resources are different. It should be possible, however, for groupings such as the EEC and the Council of Europe, the Commonwealth, the Caribbean, East Africa, West Africa, Southeast Asia, and Australasia to find ways of cooperating on the important question of assistance. An example has been given by the excellent work of the Association of Commonwealth Universities, based in London. The future of many nations hangs on their access to higher education facilities abroad. The vitality of higher education systems everywhere depends to a certain extent on a lively interchange of students, graduates, and researchers. Solutions are needed that enable a larger number of students to be moved at a lower cost per student. If the universities cannot invent the resources that an interdependent society needs, governments may feel free to withdraw some of their support in times of economic depression.

United Kingdom universities and polytechnics led the way in writing obligatory periods abroad into study courses for first degrees. The British "sandwich course" (where the student spends at least one year outside his college during a four-year degree course or a three-year diploma course) has its counterpart in North America, and a number of Western European countries began in the mid 1970s to move toward a sandwich course model. Probably not more than 3000 students before that time were obliged to spend six months or a year abroad, but these numbers will certainly grow, and the sandwich mode may well play a large part in the development of course-integrated study and training abroad. In countries where the government pays the tuition fees of many university students, government will have to be persuaded that the advantages of spending part of the degree course abroad outweigh any extra costs involved. This is another challenge for the universities, if

they wish to include an element of international experience in their courses.

Some of the more prosperous countries may again follow Sweden's lead in regarding international exchange as a priority for public funding.

The costs of international exchange can be financed out of the universities' current operating budgets to a very limited extent only. But . . . we also propose a special appropriation to strengthen the universities in their international studies. . . . The appropriation should be distributed among the universities, which are to be vested with discretionary spending powers for the following purposes: group studies in other countries (excursions, field projects, collective study programs at foreign universities); overseas sojourns for Swedish teachers, researchers and educational administrators; costs of seconding foreign teachers and researchers to Swedish universities (temporary employment, travelling expenses, working material and secretarial assistance, etc.).

The total grant-in-aid rise we propose for international exchange amounts to about SKr 20 million, which is roughly equivalent to one percent of the total expenditures on higher education and research (*Internationalising Education*, 1974, pp. 56–57).

The cause of international university exchange would be well served were each country to place at its disposal 1 percent of its higher education budget. It is not too high a proportion, as the Swedish universities have demonstrated, for the world's universities to demand.

Private foundations. The great North American charitable foundations, and some of their Western European counterparts, long acted as the bastions of international education at the undergraduate, graduate, and research scholar levels and for senior academic travel, study, and work abroad. In the early 1970s, however, as the economic recession began to eat away at their income, many of the foundations began to cut their grants to international education programs. There was at first no great change in the funding of research and senior academic travel, but it seemed by mid 1976 that substantial cuts would soon be made in foundation grants for this advanced work, too. The withdrawal of support for university programs quickly has an effect on school programs in countries such as the United States. Cuts in university language programs, for instance, led within two or three years to a significant drop in high school language programs. Foundations and governments have not always been able to predict the serious by-products of even minor cuts in international education programs; short-term reactions rather than long-term planning have characterized their investment policies in this area of education. However, in most parts of the world the foundations have played only a small role in the development of international education programs and student exchange schemes. In many countries they have had no role at all. Nonetheless, where they exist and have influence, they have been a vital partner in innovative work.

Study courses abroad. Until the 1960s the majority of students attending courses abroad had detached themselves temporarily or permanently from their home university. They went abroad as a matter of personal choice, often on the recommendation of a professor, as a supplementary part of their degree program. During the 1960s this situation began to change; more and more students went abroad to study as an integral part of their home university course. They were in many cases supervised by their home tutor while abroad. Some, like the French, would be required to return to their own country during the year to take examinations; others, like the British polytechnic students, would be carefully monitored during their period abroad and visited at least once by their home tutor.

Another major change was the introduction of the United States Junior Year Abroad programs, which took two main forms—first, the establishment of a United States university center in another country, staffed partly or entirely by United States faculty; and second, the implantation within a foreign university of a United States university group led by a member of the home faculty. The United States campus abroad dominated this development until the mid 1970s, when the economic recession began to bite into international education programs, and the high cost of building maintenance and the drop in student populations coincided to bring about a change in the arrangements. The preference was now for a closer integration with universities in the host country, with the advantage of more regular contact with students and teachers in that country, which in turn gave better prospects for student exchange.

So far as students moving from developing to advanced countries for their university education were concerned, by the mid 1970s a large number of schemes supported by governments (both sending and receiving), international organizations, and foundations had been established, and at least a half million students were able to pursue a full university education abroad. By the mid 1980s such schemes may have become part of a more unified program of international assistance and cooperation of crucial importance to the economic development of the Third World.

Conferences and seminars. International conferences and seminars are at once the bane and the envied privilege of the senior academic. A whole industry has grown up around them. The life of many academics is counted in conferences as much as in coffee spoons. A more detailed study of their importance belongs elsewhere, but it is worth noting in this section how little influence the thousands of international conferences and seminars, many of them purposefully designed to encourage more student mobility and exchange, have actually had upon student and teacher mobility and exchange. A count has been made by the writer of over 170 major resolutions on these topics passed between 1948 and 1975 by UNESCO, the International Bureau of Education, the Council of Europe, and other official conferences about educational cooperation and exchange; only a handful have been implemented in any serious way, and only two or three have led to a permanent new scheme of substance. It may therefore be concluded that the negotiation and design of new schemes of exchange and interchange are not, despite all their pretensions to the contrary, the best roles for international conferences and seminars. On the other hand, there is no doubt that the spread of information about new research and trends in education that is assisted by such gatherings, whether in the formal sessions or through informal discussions, is important as a guide to those countries embarking on major changes in their educational systems or seeking advice on modifications to existing structures, methods, and equipment. The friendly contacts that have been established through such meetings have coincidentally become the basis for much student and teacher exchange, and it is to be hoped that means will be found of bringing students and teachers themselves together more frequently in such forums. Students can benefit greatly from acquaintance with the formalities of international negotiations and debate and from close contact with students of their own subject in other countries.

Practical training placements. Course-related work placements, during the degree course, have become a prominent feature of higher education systems in Western Europe and North America. The sandwich courses and cooperative education programs are seen by an increasing number of institutions as a vital component of the course, meriting the same meticulous planning, the same level of supervision, the same evaluation, and the same credits or marks as the periods of traditional study. Most such placements are made in the home country. Of 46,000 placements made by United Kingdom institutions in 1975, only a few hundred were made abroad. But many home-country placements were made far from the student's home or college, and to that degree they acted as an instrument of mobility. One advantage of work placement abroad during the tradi-

tional term or year at a foreign university is that the problem of equivalence is avoided; each placement is—or should be—tailor-made to the student's needs and abilities.

Increasingly, placements are being negotiated in other countries, and a feature of student movement from the developing to the industrialized countries has been the practical training placements made available alongside or on completion of the study courses offered to incoming students. Again, economic recession has made it more difficult to arrange placements, and governments will need to establish clear policies of assistance in this area if one of the most beneficial aspects of student exchange is to increase to the level needed by the Third World.

One answer to the problem may reside in barter agreements between groups of countries, even between developing countries, in which training placements are "exchanged" on a no-fee basis. (This proposal was made at the Commonwealth Seminar on International Educational Placements, University of Regina, Saskatchewan, Canada, July 1976.) That this could be achieved is demonstrated by the success of organizations such as the International Association for the Exchange of Students for Technical Experience (IAESTE), which has arranged over 160,000 international placements since its foundation in 1948, and the *Association internationale des étudiants des sciences économiques et commerciales* (AIESEC: International Association of Students in the Economic and Commercial Sciences). These two bodies each cover about fifty countries, and in only a few cases do their national offices receive government assistance. A very small investment by national governments and international agencies would greatly increase the number of placements made.

Study tours and field trips. Study tours and field trips abroad have been a feature of university courses for more than a century; individual students have undertaken them for a thousand years or more. The problem in the 1970s is not where, why, or for how long; it is mainly, at whose expense? As always, students in the richer countries have the advantage over their fellow students in the developing world. Expeditions; explorations; study tours in music, language, the arts, archeology, and architecture; field trips to investigate cultural, geographical, and scientific phenomena—all these and many more kinds of tours and field trips punctuate the university course of many prosperous countries. Efforts began to be made in the 1970s to link universities in rich and poor countries so that exchanges could be made on the basis of course-related study visits. Short visits may eventually replace the full degree course as the mainstay of assistance to university-level students in the developing world, once higher education structures are fully operational in adequate numbers. Relatively cheap to finance, they respond to the needs of students in many disciplines for a period of orientation and instruction in a country that possesses the highest standard of facilities.

Duration of Programs

The shortest programs of study abroad last one month, as in the United States formula of 4-1-4, where the nine-month academic year is split, with one month in the middle of the year spent abroad. The French and West German authorities have exchanges of students lasting from one month to a year. British and French student teachers of the other country's language have a "bed-for-bed" exchange, involving about 300 exchanges each year. Programs of this length seem to be growing in popularity, perhaps because they are easily arranged (travel agents are frequently used as the intermediary); institutions in at least fifty countries regularly organize programs abroad lasting about one month.

Increasingly popular too is the one-semester program. This can be fitted conveniently into university courses in many countries. Where there are three university terms in a year, a two-term program is seldom found; students tend to go abroad for one term or for the full academic year.

The academic year abroad has been the traditional ground of the language student, who intercalates a year—usually the third—in a course normally lasting four years. The move toward greater student mobility in the EEC countries should offer the same opportunity to students in many other disciplines. As higher education facilities in the developing countries begin to satisfy local requirements at first-degree level, it is likely that many graduates will seek to spend a year, possibly longer, abroad to gain a further qualification.

Full degree courses have hitherto been the principal feature of the education abroad of students from developing countries. Relatively few students in other parts of the world have taken their first degree in another country. In the first place, there has been a lack of homogeneity in school-leaving certificates, although the International Baccalaureat now exists and may serve this purpose on an extensive scale by the mid 1980s. Secondly, most students prefer to take first degrees in their own country, looking abroad for second degrees and doctorates.

Among the few accurate statistics available in this field are those about United States students in the United Kingdom during 1973–74:

Length of stay (in universities and polytechnics):	Number of students
1 term	447
2 terms	36
1 year	950
More than 1 year	506

Source: Higher Education Exchange, No. 2. London: Central Bureau for Educational Visits and Exchanges, Autumn 1974.

Subject Areas

The spread of Buddhism lay behind the first recorded interchanges of scholars 2000 years ago. Today, language study is the basis for much student interchange among Western European countries, and between North America and continental Europe, the two regions where interchange is most intensive. If the visits form part of a degree course, they tend to last a full academic year, but there are also many special language courses of shorter duration that are attended by American students who gain credits for them. Over a million young people go to the United Kingdom each year for English-language courses lasting from ten days to a year; these visits are either linked to school examinations or, for older students, constitute a further qualification in English that is seldom directly related to a course at their home university, though it may improve their performance in the examinations they eventually take. By far the largest group of those studying languages abroad are the students of modern Western European languages in the higher education institutions of France, the United Kingdom, the Federal Republic of Germany, Austria, Spain, Italy, Switzerland, and Scandinavia. Not fewer than 10,000 will be found in any one year enrolled at a university, or as a foreign-language assistant, in one of the other countries.

Nonetheless, the facilities for modern-language students to spend a year abroad are inadequate in terms of studying in a realistic university atmosphere. Opportunities are restricted, owing to lack of financial assistance, even in the richer countries, and are limited to too few countries and languages. Only a small proportion of language students and graduates have the chance of spending a year abroad at a university or of doing practical work, such as that of a language assistant in some of the world's largest and most populous countries. The study of the languages of these nations has been impeded as a result of the lack of opportunities for study and work there.

For hundreds of years European students sought to extend their general education by study and travel abroad; this was considered an essential element in the making of the "full man." Such extension is no longer sought by students aspiring to a career in diplomacy, administration, or politics, although certain countries— notably France—still attract many foreign students to their humanities courses (see Table 1).

Philosophy, theology, mathematics, medicine, and the pure sciences were the cornerstones of student interchange in the eighteenth and nineteenth centuries; this too is no longer the case. Only medicine has held its place, and there is very little movement at either undergraduate or graduate level from developed to developing countries in medicine to compensate for the huge flow of students in the opposite direction. The change has come about because the richer countries have accepted a responsibility to help students from poorer nations, and because study abroad and the interchange and exchange schemes which run parallel with it have become the training grounds for specific professions for which provision is lacking or inadequate in many developing countries.

The various types of engineering courses constitute the largest group of interchange and exchange participants, properly defined, since the medical studies flow is mainly in one direction. Business and economics students are the next largest. The humanities and social sciences are other strong bases for study visits and exchanges. The humanities faculties probably lead the lists of unilateral study abroad programs worldwide; in other respects the interchange and exchange movement shares many of the characteristics of the study-abroad profile.

Teacher training is expected to provide the basis for more student and graduate exchanges in the 1980s. Joint course planning began in 1975 on a four-country model—involving the Federal Republic of Germany, the United Kingdom, France, and the Netherlands—in which to graduate students must attend a semester in at least one of the other three institutions. Early in the 1970s other joint courses were set up between the United Kingdom and France, one of which was connected with Franco-British cooperation on the *Concorde* aircraft. Joint courses in pedagogy and possibly many other subjects could become a prominent feature of many student exchange programs.

Already by the mid 1970s, virtually the whole academic spectrum was represented in greater or lesser degree in student interchange and exchange programs. The movement from one country to another, on a north-south or east-west axis from poor country to rich, rich to rich, and poor to poor, is measured in hundreds of thousands of people. Much of the movement is not organized within formal programs, but the sheer size of the transfer and all the contacts and contributions it gives rise to are slowly influencing governments, institutions, and international organizations in their policies on international educational cooperation. There is an essential interrelationship between the disconnected flow of students seeking courses abroad to compensate for the lack of facilities in their own country and the more organized flow that is sponsored, and sometimes administered directly, by universities and governments. No detailed statistics yet exist; a full statistical analysis would defy any but the most rigorous, extensive, expensive, and continuous survey. It is clear, however, that there has been a shift away from the search for cultural and intellectual enrichment to a pragmatic pursuit of courses that lead directly into the professions.

Bibliography

Association of Norwegian Students Abroad. *Studentstatistik for studiearet 1974/75.* Oslo: Association of Norwegian Students Abroad, 1975.

Bereday, G. Z. F. *Essays on World Education: The Crisis of Supply and Demand.* New York: Columbia University Press, 1969.

British Council and Association of Commonwealth Universities. *Higher Education in the United Kingdom, 1974–76: A Handbook for Students from Overseas and Their Advisers.* Essex, England: Longman Group, 1974.

Camps, M. *The Management of Interdependence: A Preliminary View.* New York: Council on Foreign Relations, 1974.

Cohen, G. A. (Ed.) *U.S. College–Sponsored Programs Abroad: Academic Year.* New York: Institute of International Education, 1976.

Council for Cultural Co-operation, Council of Europe. *Mobility of University Staff.* Strasbourg, France: Council of Europe, 1973.

Council on International Educational Exchange. *Whole World Handbook: A Student Guide to Work, Study, and Travel Abroad.* New York: Council on International Educational Exchange, 1976.

Crabbs, F. F., and Holmquist, F. W. *United States Higher Education and World Affairs.* New York: Praeger, 1967.

Daniels, A. "Review of the Present Scale of Operation and Future Trends." Paper presented to the National Conference on Degree Sandwich Courses, University of Bath, Bath, England, 1976.

Deutsch, S. E. *International Education and Exchange: A Sociological Analysis.* Cleveland, Ohio: Case Western Reserve University Press, 1970.

The Educational Factor for Development: Special Annotated Bibliography. Paris: Organisation for Economic Co-operation and Development, 1966.

Fulbright, J. W. "Creative Power of Exchange." *Exchange,* 1975, *11*(1), 5–43.

Gori, U. *La diplomazia culturale multilaterale dell'Italia.* Rome: Edizioni Bizarri, 1970.

Haigh, A. *Cultural Diplomacy in Europe.* Strasbourg, France: Council of Europe, 1974.

Higher Education Exchange. London: Central Bureau for Educational Visits and Exchanges. Published quarterly.

Institute of International Education. *Handbook on U.S. Study for Foreign Nationals; Summer Study Abroad; Teaching Abroad; U.S. College-Sponsored Programs Abroad;* "Basic Facts on Foreign Study." New York: IIE. All periodically updated.

Institut d'éducation de la Fondation européenne de la culture. *La mobilité intra-européenne des étudiants des premier et deuxième cycles.* Paris: Institut d'éducation de la Fondation européenne de la culture, 1975.

Institute of International Education, *Handbook on International Study for U.S. Nationals.* Vol. 1: *Study in Europe.* New York: IIE, 1976; Vol. 2: *Study in the American Republics.* New York: IIE, 1976; Vol. 3: *Study in Asia, Africa, and Oceania.* New York: IIE, to appear in 1977.

Institute of International Education. *Open Doors, 1964–65* and *1973–74.* New York: IIE, 1965, 1974.

Internationalising Education. Summary of Reports from the Swedish Committee for Internationalising University Education. Stockholm: Office of the Chancellor of the Swedish Universities, 1974.

Klineberg, O. *International Educational Exchange.* The Hague: Mouton, 1976; Paris: Ecole des hautes études en sciences sociales, 1976.

Lesguillions, H. *Objectifs et méthodes du colloque sur la co-opération entre les universités.* Brussels: European Economic Community, 1970.

Marien, D. *Guide to Foreign Medical Schools.* New York: Institute of International Education, in cooperation with Queens College of the City University of New York, 1975.

Perkins, J. A. *International Programs of U.S. Colleges and Universities: Priorities for the Seventies.* New York: International Council for Educational Development, 1971.

Sanders, I. T., and Ward, J. C. *Bridges to Understanding: International Programs of American Colleges and Universities.* New York: McGraw-Hill, 1970.

UNESCO. *Statistical Yearbook, 1973.* Paris: UNESCO, 1973.

UNESCO. *Draft Medium-Term Plan (1977–1982).* Paris: UNESCO, n.d.

UNESCO. *Study Abroad.* Paris: UNESCO, 1976. Published annually.

Voluntary Transnational Cultural Exchange Organizations of the U.S.: A Selected List. Washington, D.C.: Center for a Voluntary Society, 1974.

JAMES PLATT

5. GOVERNMENT REGULATIONS CONCERNING INTERNATIONAL EXCHANGE

International education exchange activities have expanded rapidly since the end of World War II. Government regulations of such activities vary greatly, and students and scholars planning to travel, study, teach, or conduct research abroad should inquire in advance about the immigration laws and regulations of the country or countries they plan to visit. Failure to meet the basic documentary requirements can result in the visitor's being detained, excluded from entrance, and eventually deported.

Every country has its own immigration laws designed to control the number and kinds of persons entering the country, either temporarily or as immigrants. Persons of all nationalities are generally subject to questioning by immigration officials, public health officials, and customs officials before being admitted to each country. Visitors are usually required to present to immigration inspectors a valid passport and visa and evidence of adequate financial resources. Lacking such resources, visitors may be required to post bond or make a cash deposit to ensure that they will not become a public charge. Public health authorities examine the medical records of visitors to ensure that they have received all necessary inoculations and are otherwise admissible on health grounds. Customs officials inspect visitors' belongings to determine whether taxes or tariffs are due on their goods or whether certain goods are illegal for import.

Passport, Visa, and Work Permit Requirements

Passports. A passport is a formal document issued by a country to its citizens for a threefold purpose: (1) it certifies the identity and citizenship of the bearer and is used principally for identification purposes when a person leaves or reenters the country; (2) it enables the bearer to travel within the borders of a foreign country when it has been endorsed with a visa by an authorized official of that country; and (3) it calls upon officials of foreign governments to extend protection to the passport holder when needed. To obtain a passport, a person is generally required to submit proof of citizenship, proper identification, and several recent photographs. Responsibility for issuing passports is generally assigned to the Ministry of Foreign Affairs or its equivalent. All students and scholars going abroad need passports unless their home country and the country to be visited have agreed to waive this requirement.

Visas. A visa is an endorsement made on a passport by authorities of the country the bearer desires to enter. Barring an agreement between countries to the contrary, a visa is generally required before a citizen of one country is admitted to and permitted to travel within the borders of another. Regulations regarding the issuance of visas, as well as their period of validity, vary from country to country. Anyone desiring to go to another country for travel, study, or work should inquire about the specific visa requirements of that country from its nearest consulate or embassy. The embassies of those countries having diplomatic relations with each other are located only in capital cities, but consulates are maintained by most countries in other major cities as well. As a general rule, a person seeking to obtain a visa must present most, if not all, of the following documents to the consular officer: a valid passport; recent photographs; completed visa application forms; photostat of return ticket; proof of inoculations against such diseases as smallpox, yellow fever, and cholera; and a letter from a travel agent or sponsoring organization, stating the purpose of the visit.

Issuance of the wrong type of visa can sometimes have an adverse effect on an individual's educational program and career goals. It is extremely important, therefore, that prospective visitors obtain the appropriate visa to ensure attainment of their educational objectives and conformity with regulations of the host institution or organization and country.

Work permits. Most countries restrict or prohibit the employment of nonresidents. Ministries of Labor and manpower or immigration agencies are generally responsible for issuing and controlling work permits for nonimmigrants.

As a general rule, foreign students are not permitted to work for remuneration during their visits abroad. Similarly, foreign teachers and scholars are not permitted to engage in activities that produce income unless such activities—lectures, for example—are directly related to the purpose and objective of their visit. Each country has its own regulations pertaining to work permits for persons from other countries, and prospective students should check with the embassy or con-

sulate of the country to be visited for specific information.

Nongovernmental requirements. Embassies or consulates can often provide information about requirements. Most have officials who are concerned with public information and educational and cultural affairs, and their advice should be solicited in advance of travel. For example, many schools require proof of language proficiency before admitting a student, and consular officials may be familiar with these and other institutional requirements as well as with such matters as costs of tuition, housing, food, transportation, and books. It is also important to determine the standing of the institution selected for attendance. If a school is not accredited or bona fide, in that it issues widely accepted and recognized degrees or certificates, study abroad can result in bitter disappointment to the visitor.

Students and scholars should also verify such matters as health and accident insurance; baggage insurance; rate of monetary exchange between the country of origin and the country to be visited; restrictions, if any, on amounts of money that may be taken out of the country; feasibility of obtaining in advance credit cards or travelers' checks; availability of charter flights; type of clothing needed; and local customs such as tipping, dating, and holidays.

International organizations. The major international or intergovernmental agencies involved in international educational exchange activities are the United Nations Development Programme (UNDP), 866 United Nations Plaza, New York, New York 10017; the United Nations Educational, Scientific and Cultural Organization (UNESCO), 7 place de Fontenoy, 75700 Paris, France; United Nations Institute for Training and Research (UNITAR), 801 United Nations Plaza, New York, New York 10017; United Nations Research Institute for Social Development (UNRISD), Palais des nations, 1211 Geneva 10, Switzerland; World Health Organization (WHO), 1211 Geneva 27, Switzerland;

Food and Agriculture Organization (FAO), via delle Terme di Caracalla, 00100 Rome, Italy; Organization of American States (OAS), Pan American Union Building, 17th and Constitution Avenue NW, Washington, D.C. 20006; and Pan American Health Organization (PAHO), 23rd and Virginia Avenue NW, Washington, D.C.

The Institute of International Education (IIE), 809 United Nations Plaza, New York, New York 10017, is one of the leading nonprofit organizations in the field of international education. It provides information and counseling services to United States and foreign students, governments, corporations, and academic institutions. It conducts, in the United States and abroad, studies, seminars, workshops, and conferences involving educational exchange. It also publishes a wealth of informational material, such as the *Handbook on International Study for U.S. Nationals, Summer Study Abroad, Teaching Abroad,* and *U.S. College-Sponsored Programs Abroad.* One of IIE's brochures, "Basic Facts on Foreign Study," contains an excellent list of resource and reference material that is useful to all students and scholars interested in study abroad.

Two leading organizations engaged in reciprocal on-the-job practical training opportunities for college and university students from the United States and abroad are the *Association internationale des étudiants en sciences économiques et commerciales* (AISEC), 52 Vanderbilt Avenue, Suite 1110, New York, New York 10017 and the International Association for the Exchange of Students for Technical Experience (IAESTE), American City Building, Columbia, Maryland 21044.

The organizations listed above are a sampling of the many hundreds that are involved in international educational exchange activities. The Bureau of Educational and Cultural Affairs of the United States Department of State periodically publishes a booklet titled *Directory of Contacts for International, Educational, Cultural, and Scientific Exchange Programs.* This direc-

tory gives a listing of the major private and governmental agencies active in international educational exchange programs.

There also exist a number of agencies and commissions that function on a binational basis. The United States, for example, has entered into educational exchange agreements with forty-three other nations to establish binational educational foundations or commissions. These commissions, which are composed of distinguished foreign nationals and resident Americans, are responsible for the administration of the academic exchange programs authorized by the Fulbright-Hays Act. The commissions plan educational exchange projects for students and scholars in cooperation with the local educational institutions, screen local candidates for grants, and assist in the placement and supervision of American students and scholars.

Other binational arrangements function within the Department of State. Information concerning the State Department's involvement in international sports activities may be obtained from the Director, International Athletic Programs, Department of State Bureau of Educational and Cultural Affairs. The bureau's Office of International Arts Affairs can provide information on State Department programs involving performing artists, generally referred to as cultural presentations.

The United States as an Example

As an illustration of the complexity of arrangements to be made by students visiting another country, some regulations required by the United States of both its own students and those coming from other countries are given here.

Passport and visa requirements. The Passport Office of the United States Department of State has the responsibility for issuing passports to United States citizens (Section 104 of the Immigration and Nationality Act—8 U.S.C. 1101). In addition to its main branch in Washington, D.C., the Department of State has passport offices in many other United States cities. Passport applications are also accepted at many federal or state courts as well as at Class 1 post offices. Visa applications should be made to the consulates of countries to be visited.

United States citizens planning to study, travel, work, teach, or conduct research abroad should inquire about the specific visa requirements of the country to be visited by communicating with its embassy or consulates. The addresses and phone numbers of the foreign diplomatic corps in Washington, D.C., can be obtained from the publication *Diplomatic List*, for sale by the Superintendent of Documents, United States Government Printing Office, Washington, D.C. 20402.

Foreign students, trainees, and scholars planning visits to the United States generally have several visa options available to them. Students, for example, can be documented with either an F (student) or J (exchange visitor) visa classification and may sometimes be permitted to enter the United States for a brief period with a B (temporary visitor) visa for the express purpose of visiting several institutions to make a choice. Spouses and children of F and J visa holders are documented with F-2 and J-2 visas. Teachers, lecturers, research scholars, trainees, nurses, doctors, and other persons in the professions are generally documented with either an H (temporary worker-trainee) or J visa if they receive compensation, financial, or otherwise, for services rendered. The L visa classification ("intracompany transferee") is available for executive, managerial, and specialized personnel continuing their employment with international firms or corporations.

In addition, seven other visa classifications exist but seldom involve international educational activities as such. These are: A for foreign diplomats, C for aliens in transit, D for alien crewmen such as seamen or airmen, E for treaty traders, G for government officials assigned to an interna-

tional organization, I for representatives of foreign information media, and K for the fiancé(e) of a United States citizen.

Work permission. Conditions allowing nonimmigrant students, scholars, and trainees to work in the United States illustrate some of the complexities involved in obtaining work permission in another country.

The B (tourist) visa may be used by foreign nationals coming to the United States briefly for the purposes of observation and travel; attending a conference; selecting a school; conducting independent research; or participating in amateur musical, sports, and other events or contests, provided they receive no remuneration. Such visa holders may accept an expense allowance from an American source if they can show that it merely covers their actual living expenses, but they are not permitted to receive a stipend, salary, or honorarium from a United States source.

Students on F visas may be granted permission by school authorities (usually the foreign student adviser) to work on campus, provided they have a good academic record, are enrolled in a full course of study, and will not displace United States resident students from obtaining on-campus jobs. Students on F visas must obtain the prior approval of the Immigration and Naturalization Service (INS) before they are authorized to work off campus. INS grants such authorizations only if students are able to establish that economic necessity unforeseen at the time the visa was issued requires them to work. Students must demonstrate the ability to pursue a full course of study, which means at least twelve hours of instruction per week or its equivalent at the undergraduate level, and are limited in off-campus employment to twenty hours a week during the academic year. After obtaining their degree or certificate from a university or college, students on F visas may be eligible for employment for up to eighteen months in order to obtain practical training in their field of study. An authorized school official must certify to INS officials that the practical training enables the student to round out the academic program and that such training is not available in the student's own country. Approval for the training must then be granted by the INS. Spouses of students on F visas, with F-2 visa classifications, are not permitted to work under any circumstances.

Students on J visas can obtain permission from the responsible officer of the exchange program in which they are participating to work on or off campus. Conditions for their employment are the same as those for students on F visas. Although spouses of students on J visas cannot work to support the student, they are sometimes permitted by INS to work if their employment is necessary to support themselves or their dependent children.

Exchange visitors other than students are not permitted under any circumstances to engage in activities unrelated to their specific program that produce income from United States sources. Any exchange visitors who engage in such work automatically cease to maintain lawful status in the United States and are subject to deportation proceedings. However, teachers, professors, research scholars, specialists, international visitors, business and industrial trainees, doctors, nurses, medical technologists and other medical personnel may be provided a salary, stipend, per diem allowance, and housing by the exchange visitor sponsor under the terms set forth in the Certificate of Eligibility for Exchange Visitor Status (Form DSP-66).

The H (temporary worker-trainee) visa is divided into three categories: H-1 for persons of distinguished merit and ability, H-2 for temporary workers, and H-3 for trainees. A petition for an H visa classification is filed with the Immigration and Naturalization Service by the institution or organization that is to provide the employment or training. The petition is filed on an Immigration Form I-129B, which can be obtained at any regional or district office of the Immigration and Naturalization Service. Labor certification from the Department of Labor is not needed for the approval of an H-1 or H-3 visa but is required before an H-2 visa petition is approved. It indicates that an able, willing, and qualified United States citizen or permanent resident is not available for the job and that employment of the nonimmigrant will not adversely affect the wages and working conditions of the United States workers.

The L (intracompany transferee) visa is available to foreign nationals who, immediately preceding their time of application for admission to the United States, have been employed continuously for at least a year by a firm, corporation, or other legal entity or its affiliate or subsidiary; and who seek to enter the United States temporarily to continue to render service to the same employer in a managerial or executive capacity or one that involves specialized knowledge. The L visa petition should be submitted by the employer to the nearest INS office.

Alien registration and address reports. Upon being admitted to the United States, foreign visitors must be registered for immigration purposes. Arrival-Departure Records (Form I-94), specifying the date up to which they have been authorized to remain in the country, are stapled in their passports. If they wish to remain in the United States beyond that date, visitors must apply to INS for an extension of stay. Each January all aliens, except diplomats with A visas and foreign government officials with G visas, must submit an Alien Address Report (Form I-53) to INS. Form I-53 is available at any United States post office or INS office.

Visits abroad and reentry. Students, scholars, and trainees often leave the United States briefly for the purposes of vacation or travel and then return to the United States to continue their programs. Such persons should be certain that they are in possession of the necessary documents, such as passport, visa, and health certificate, both for entry to the country they are visiting and for reentry to the United States.

Income tax. Foreign students, scholars, and trainees who receive income through employment or other sources are required to file United States tax returns, and nonimmigrants who have earned taxable income must obtain a "sailing permit" or certificate of compliance from the Internal Revenue Service before leaving the United States for destinations other than Canada or Mexico. Information regarding United States income tax obligation of aliens working in the United States can be obtained from the Director of International Operations, Internal Revenue Service (IRS), United States Treasury Department, 1325 K Street NW, Washington, D.C. 20225, or from the nearest local IRS office. Internal Revenue Service publications *Foreign Scholars and Educational and Cultural Exchange Visitors* (No. 518) and *United States Tax Guide for Aliens* (No. 519) can be obtained from the IRS or the Superintendent of Documents, United States Government Printing Office, Washington, D.C. 20402.

Social security coverage. Foreign students, scholars, trainees, and other nonimmigrants often find it necessary to have a social security number to enable them to open bank accounts in the United States, to secure a driver's license, or to complete their college registration. To obtain a number, applicants must furnish evidence of age, identity, citizenship, and alien status to the social security office nearest their place of residence. To obtain a social security number prior to entering the United States, visitors should contact the foreign student adviser or other responsible official of the institution or organization to which they are going. They can also write for details to the Central Office of the Social Security Administration, 6401 Security Boulevard, Baltimore, Maryland 21235. The social security records of nonimmigrants who are not permitted to work are

marked, and if their numbers are ever used for employment, the Immigration and Naturalization Service will be notified and their visa status may be terminated.

The private sector commitment. The success of the United States government's effort in the field of international education is due in no small measure to the cooperation it receives from private individuals, organizations, and institutions. All the major colleges and universities in the country are involved to varying degrees in international educational exchange activities. The activities of nonprofit foundations and associations, school systems, and voluntary organizations facilitate and supplement the government's effort.

Private organizations such as the Danforth, Ford, Hazen, and Rockefeller Foundations are but a few of the many involved in international educational activities. Detailed information on United States foundations can be found in *The Foundation Directory,* published by Columbia University Press. Many of these foundations offer fellowships and scholarships to students and scholars.

The American Council on Education, One Dupont Circle NW, Washington, D.C. 20036, is comprised of the national and regional educational associations and institutions of higher learning. The council's Overseas Liaison Committee published the *International Directory for Educational Liaison* in 1973. The directory gives a comprehensive listing of organizations and institutions, both United States and foreign, involved in international educational activities.

The Educational Council for Foreign Medical Graduates (ECFMG), 3624 Market Street, Philadelphia, Pennsylvania 19104, is a nonprofit organization that assists foreign medical graduates who wish to pursue medical residencies or other types of training projects which involve patient care. ECFMG has two major responsibilities: (1) it administers the ECFMG examination and issues the ECFMG Certification (which certifies that a foreign medical graduate is eligible for an appointment in an American Medical Association approved program for graduate medical training); and (2) it documents all foreign medical graduates who are pursuing clinical training in the United States as exchange visitors (persons on J-1 visas).

From the early 1950s to the mid 1970s, several thousand intern and residency training slots were available in United States hospitals for foreign medical graduates. These vacancies are rapidly diminishing because of the rapid increase in the availability of United States trained medical graduates. The American medical community predicts that the supply-demand curve for United States trained physicians will meet by the end of 1978 and very few, if any, vacancies will then be available for foreign medical graduates.

The National Association for Foreign Student Affairs (NAFSA) is another leading nonprofit organization that publishes a number of papers on international education. NAFSA was founded in 1948 with the cooperation of academic institutions and government and private agencies to develop the knowledge and competence of persons concerned with international education. Its membership includes students, foreign student advisers, admissions officers, teachers of English as a second language, advisers to American students going abroad, university international officers, Fulbright program advisers, and community organizations. In 1976 NAFSA updated and published *The Advisor's Manual of Federal Laws and Regulations Affecting Foreign Students and Scholars.* It can be obtained from NAFSA for a modest fee.

Three additional major organizations involved in overseas travel-study programs for students and teachers are the American Institute for Foreign Study, 102 Greenwich Avenue, Greenwich, Connecticut 06830; the Council on International Educational Exchange, 777 United Nations Plaza, New York, New York 10017; and the Foreign Study League, c/o Reader's Digest Association, Inc., Pleasantville, New York 10570.

Bibliography

The Advisor's Manual of Federal Laws and Regulations Affecting Foreign Students and Scholars. Washington, D.C.: National Association for Foreign Student Affairs, 1976.

The Foundation Center. *Foundation Directory, Edition 5.* New York: Columbia University Press, 1975.

Institute of International Education, *Handbook on International Study for U.S. Nationals,* Vol. 1: *Study in Europe,* New York: 1976; Vol. 2: *Study in the American Republics,* New York: 1976; Vol. 3: *Study in Asia, Africa, and Oceania,* New York: to appear in 1977.

Institute of International Education. *Handbook on U.S. Study for Foreign Nationals; Summer Study Abroad; Teaching Abroad; U.S. College-Sponsored Programs Abroad;* "Basic Facts on Foreign Study." New York: IIE, all periodically updated.

Overseas Liaison Committee. *International Directory for Educational Liaison.* Washington, D.C.: American Council on Education, 1973.

United States Department of State. *Diplomatic List.* Washington, D.C.: U.S. Government Printing Office, periodically updated.

United States Department of State, Bureau of Educational and Cultural Affairs. *Directory of Contacts for International Educational, Cultural, and Scientific Exchange Programs.* Washington, D.C.: U.S. Government Printing Office, periodically updated.

United States Department of the Treasury, Internal Revenue Service Publications. *Foreign Scholars and Educational and Cultural Exchange Visitors* (No. 518); *United States Tax Guide for Aliens* (No. 519). Washington, D.C.: U.S. Government Printing Office, periodically updated.

PAUL A. COOK

6. STUDENT EMPLOYMENT ABROAD

In the world of scholarship the value of travel has been recognized from earliest times. In Biblical, Grecian, Roman, and medieval times, itinerant philosophers, teachers, and students carried the essence of their cultures across the known world and brought back ideas, theories, and inventions that had profound influence on human thought and knowledge. The forces that compelled the early philosophers, teachers, and academics to look beyond their own countries for stimulation are still present. Although few people can indulge in the luxury of the Victorian "grand tour," the opportunity to finance a period abroad through paid employment is taken every year by thousands of people between the ages of eighteen and thirty. Travel by young people, particularly those who are preparing themselves through advanced level courses for vocational careers, is a feature of our times.

Town and Institutional Linkings

The period immediately after World War II saw a great increase in organized travel, both by parties of young people and by individuals. A feature of this period was the establishment, through local governments, of "twin-towns" in different countries. Similar in size and compatible culturally, industrially, or socially, these twin-towns developed cultural, social, and educational links and exchanges. These exchanges continue to be particularly useful at primary and secondary school levels. Each year many thousands of schoolchildren, accompanied by their teachers, travel in groups across Western Europe on reciprocal link or twin-town visits, each lasting about one week. These visits have led to an increase in exchange visits for teachers. Sometimes whole families take part in the exchange, each occupying the other's home for the period of the visit (which may last for several weeks or for an entire academic year). Each teacher's local government or state employer remains responsible for payment of appropriate salary.

In the United Kingdom the principal agency for assisting in setting up links between schools and for assisting in organizing reciprocal teacher exchanges is the Central Bureau for Educational Visits and Exchanges at 43 Dorset Street, London W1H3FN. This bureau is an agency of the Department of Education and Science and is funded by the state.

Since the mid 1960s the concept of twinning, or linking, has expanded to include the higher education sector in Western Europe. This expansion has led to organized study tours of various dura-

tions by parties of advanced-level students in reciprocal arrangements. Such arrangements have proved of great value to students who are required to spend a period abroad as part of their program of studies and for those who simply wish to enlarge their linguistic, cultural, social, industrial, or business horizons by working abroad.

There is also evidence of an extension of the twinning concept between Western Europe and the United States, particularly between academic institutions. Similarly, relatively new universities and colleges in developing countries increasingly approach their more experienced counterparts in the developed world for assistance, guidance, and advice. When contacts and attachments of this kind are made, many of the unknowns that might inhibit travel between countries are removed. Thus, from the two academic bases students frequently move out into temporary employment in the linked foreign country.

Needs and Expectations

Students generally seek employment abroad either to complete requirements for a degree or for cultural and social enrichment. In many cases, the student's academic institution requires a period of employment abroad in order to qualify for a degree or diploma. The minimum duration of the period abroad, its timing within the overall program, and even the content and nature of the experience to be gained may all be stipulated.

Programs of study in foreign languages frequently have such a requirement. In the United Kingdom in particular, under the stimulus of membership in the European Economic Community, there is an increasing awareness of the need and value of foreign-language studies for all undergraduate students. Consequently, foreign-language options now frequently appear in the list of available electives or options in programs of studies. Students who elect to take a foreign language are encouraged to spend a period in the appropriate country during the course. In Western European universities and colleges, the study of English, French, and German has for many years been considered an integral part of the preparation for a professional career.

Students in colleges of education preparing for careers in the teaching of foreign languages frequently find themselves temporarily attached to secondary schools in the country of their chosen language. Usually, such students receive adequate financial assistance through their sponsoring academic institution, if it is state-funded, and therefore are not paid by the employing authority. Privately financed students usually receive a modest salary.

In addition to language studies, many other disciplines include a period of employment experience abroad, either as a requirement for completion of the degree or as a highly desirable element of the overall program of studies. Programs that combine technology with a language, such as chemistry with German or engineering with French or German, may require a period abroad. Programs of study in marketing, particularly at the graduate level, also frequently include a foreign-language element with a period abroad.

Building upon extensive preparation, beginning as early as six or seven years of age in primary school, the professionally qualified European frequently achieves high levels of linguistic competence in at least one and frequently in two languages other than his native tongue. The pressures of geography, culture, and economics which have created this situation are of course absent in the United States, where the extent of linguistic competence among professional people is perhaps lower than that observed in other countries.

The opportunity for students to include a period of employment abroad is limited by the availability of time within a program of studies. Since the summer vacation is the period traditionally used for such employment, the student usually seeks employment for six to ten weeks. Students who seek employment entirely on their own

initiative, even with encouragement from an academic institution, will probably find it extremely difficult. Employment is more likely to be found through cooperative education plans, where academic studies are alternated with periods spent in relevant employment. These systems allow for periods of three, six, or even twelve months to be spent outside the academic institution. A period of employment abroad is thus made more attractive by the prospect of a relatively longer stay with greater benefit and reward in proportion to the practical problems of arrangement.

Many students going abroad seriously underestimate the limitations that lack of linguistic competence can impose. Almost inevitably, a knowledge of the language of the country is required if the student is to derive real benefit from social and cultural situations. If, beyond that, the student wishes to gain experience in the professional application of his chosen field of study, he must attain further competence in the language before he goes abroad. The vocabulary he commands must include at least the usual descriptive words and phrases specific to that profession.

If a student has only marginal competence in a foreign language, however, he will gain only the most superficial impression of social attitudes different from his own. In a work situation the student will be given simple, repetitive, and menial tasks. Students who expect to secure work placement in business offices or functional management areas must possess a competence in reading and writing skills in the language of the country. Many business students fail to find what they want from a work placement, even when the relevant opportunities are there, usually because they lack skills in handling paper work in a foreign language. Students of technology, on the other hand, find that design data and drawings, hardware artifacts, and manufacturing plants are international in form and thus pose no communication problems.

Students looking for experience related to their studies in a work placement abroad need to be especially well prepared. Experience in a similar environment at home is very valuable, as is a threshold of competence in the language. Needed above all are humility, a willingness to learn, and a slowness to criticize or to compare experiences abroad unfavorably with those at home.

Planning Procedures

The student may have little choice among jobs in a foreign country. The demand for paid temporary employment is great and jobs are scarce. There are, however, some aids in locating jobs. Foreign embassies and consulates generally distribute printed information on employment opportunities, regulations, and restrictions. There are also agencies and associations that can be of help. The Council on International Educational Exchange (777 United Nations Plaza, New York, New York 10017), for example, arranges for a wide variety of unskilled summer jobs in France, the Federal Republic of Germany, and Great Britain for United States students. The council also arranges for jobs in Great Britain for longer periods. The *Zentralstelle für Arbeitsvermittlung* (discussed in detail below), the official government labor agency, places United States and Canadian students in summer jobs in Germany. The British Hotel, Restaurant and Caterers Association (20 Upper Brook Street, London W1Y 2B4) accepts a limited number of applications for unskilled work in hotels and restaurants from foreign students. Other organizations place students in agricultural jobs such as grape picking or in camp-counseling jobs. Possibilities also exist for restoration, excavation, and conservation work. Finally, European girls may find *au pair* jobs in other European countries, doing light housework in return for room, board, pocket money, and language practice.

A number of organizations that advertise tempting job placements, however, must be carefully investigated. A helpful booklet titled *A Word of Caution* (prepared by the United States Department of State, Office of Public Information, Bureau of Educational and Cultural Affairs, Washington, D.C. 20502) tells students, teachers, counselors, and parents how to go about evaluating organizations that sponsor private work, study, or travel programs.

Participation in an international work camp provides another type of working holiday. Although no special skills are required, dedication and a general interest in community work are important. Hours are long and conditions can be very spartan. Students may have to pay for room and board. A directory of work camps and lists of work camp projects are published by the Co-ordinating Committee for International Voluntary Work Camps (UNESCO, 1 rue Miollis, 72 Paris, 15). *Invest Yourself*, published by the Commission on Voluntary Service and Action (475 Riverside Drive, New York, New York 10027), is another source of information on volunteer opportunities all over the world.

Most desirable but hardest to obtain are the highly competitive traineeships. The major organization concerned with worldwide reciprocal exchanges of this kind is the International Association for the Exchange of Students for Technical Experience, described in detail below.

The timing of the period to be spent abroad is also important. Apart from the restrictions imposed by the student's own program and his consequent availability, the long summer vacation period of July through September is also a vacation period for many businesses and industries. In some countries manufacturing establishments often close completely for three to four weeks in July and early August. Even if they do not, supervisory and executive management personnel, who would usually supervise a student's program, will be taking vacations at this time. The foreign student will also find himself in competition for work placement with the indigenous student body and with other foreign nationals. Thus, students who are available outside the summer period are at an advantage.

Associated with timing is the factor of accommodation. Vacationers and foreign tourists put great pressure on available accommodations in many places, even in industrial areas, during the summer months. Companies can often assist in finding accommodation, but the standard of amenities often falls short of the student's expectations.

The cost of accommodations is usually related to the level of earnings the student might expect from a work placement. For a foreign student those earnings are likely to be low, perhaps bare subsistence level. In the Federal Republic of Germany, for example, a German student employed in a production situation calling for skills that few students possess may be paid as much as DM 1000 per month. On the other hand, a *praktikant* who is given a carefully designed program of training to follow may receive as little as DM 500 per month, which is below subsistence level. Students going abroad, therefore, may have to subsidize themselves—at least to some extent—from their own resources. The degree to which this is true depends on the value the host company places on the skills or abilities that the student has to offer and on what the student expects to obtain from the situation.

A fact that can cause much distress is that employing organizations do not pay wages in advance. If the student is not to receive his first pay until he has been with a company for a month, he must live on his own resources in the meantime. Most companies will assist in cases of genuine hardship, but it does not help toward mutual confidence if the student asks for an advance of salary after only three or four days with a company. Unfortunately, hoteliers and landlords will often demand payment in advance from young people, which adds to their difficulties.

Students seeking employment abroad should make themselves aware of restrictions imposed by many countries on the entry of foreign nationals for any purpose other than vacation. Passport and visa documentation are obvious requirements, but in addition a residence permit, issued by police authorities, may be required. This requirement is made, for example, between nationals of the United Kingdom and the Federal Republic of Germany, even though both are members of the European Economic Community, in which freedom of movement for any purpose is a declared principle.

Achieving the necessary state of documentation can be frustrating and is certainly time consuming. Health status and clearance also demand attention, which, if not given, can result in the breakdown of an otherwise completed set of arrangements. The student has to be aware that the apparent circumvention of tedious regulations, even with the help of a prospective employer abroad, could place both parties in contravention of the laws of the country, albeit unwittingly. In the Federal Republic of Germany, for example, there are strict regulations concerning the employment of foreign workers, and most companies are well aware of them. The student must be familiar with these regulations too. The United States also imposes very strict regulations in this respect. In fact, it is almost impossible for a foreign student to obtain the necessary work permit to enter the United States and take up employment even for a short period, except under cooperative education schemes. In the United Kingdom the prospective employer must apply for the necessary work permit on behalf of the applicant from abroad and must make a careful submission of the case before it can be considered. The lesson in all this is that a planning period of as long as twelve months ahead of the actual date of expected employment should be allowed. Even then, difficulties can present themselves almost at the last moment.

Once the student has actually arrived at his place of employment, further difficulties, if they arise, can usually be dealt with competently and swiftly by people within the local and national system. At this stage, most students experience the sympathetic, kindly, and helpful understanding that is often extended to the foreign visitor anywhere.

Agencies and Organizations

While there are numerous difficulties likely to be experienced by the student who is attempting to arrange a work placement abroad by his own efforts, there are, fortunately, several experienced organizations active in the field to which students can apply for assistance, some of which have been referred to above. Several of these organizations are discussed below. Although no compendium of references currently exists, factual reports of experiences and information relevant to student employment abroad are available in the journals, annual reports, and informative leaflets published by these organizations.

Since its founding in London in 1948, the International Association for the Exchange of Students for Technical Experience (IAESTE) has placed some 168,000 students from forty-three member countries in practical training positions. The interpretation of the word technical is now very wide and includes most disciplines for which a period abroad might assist in the development of professional competence. The exceptions include those special areas of study for which appropriate arrangements are made by other bodies as, for example, in medicine, teacher training, and language courses. Although strictly an exchange organization, IAESTE interprets the idea of exchange flexibly. If unfilled places are available in member countries, they are placed on open offer without reciprocity.

Students wishing to use the services of IAESTE must be registered for their studies in an affiliated academic institution, which will be in regular communication with the appropriate national secretariat. Placements in such areas as engineering, architecture, mathematics, and the sciences are usually made for eight to twelve weeks during the summer, with some openings up to a full year. The association is concerned with placements both for social and cultural experience and for more specific studies-related experience and training. The number of places available each year in member countries in defined employment fields is limited, although some four thousand placements are made annually. The demand by students for specific placements is growing, as are association attempts through annual international meetings of member countries to effect accurate matches between requests and offers.

The association has close connections with the many national organizations also engaged in the placement of students abroad and is well placed to assist the student in obtaining all necessary documentation. This is a fully professional organization. The address of its international secretariat is IAESTE, Schweizerisches National Komitee, Leonhardstrasse 33, CH-8006 Zurich, Switzerland. Addresses of any of the national offices may be obtained from the international secretariat. In the United States the address is IAESTE/US, American City Building, Suite 217, Columbia, Maryland 21044.

The Standing Conference on Overseas Placement and Exchange (SCOPE) was formed in September 1975, and is located in the offices of the Central Bureau for Educational Visits and Exchanges, 43 Dorset Street, London W1H 3FN, England. This organization is not a placement agency. It acts as a data and information bank on British activity in placing students abroad for experience and training. SCOPE also acts as a forum for exchange of views among those active in the field in universities, polytechnics, colleges, industry, and business, and in the area of training generally. The Central Bureau is an agency of the Department of Education and Science of the British government.

Zentralstelle für Arbeitsvermittlung (ZAV) is the central placement office of the Ministry of Labor and Social Affairs of the government of the Federal Republic of Germany. ZAV places German nationals abroad and foreign nationals in the Federal Republic of Germany, either under special international agreements or under arrangements with particular institutions. ZAV also has an active exchange program for young employees and students. Part of this activity is connected with the federal government's economic aid program to developing countries. The address of ZAV is 6000 Frankfurt/Main, Feuerbachstrasse 42, Federal Republic of Germany.

The *Association internationale des étudiants en sciences économiques et commerciales* (AIESEC) is a student-run, nonpolitical, nonprofit organization financed by participating companies and student fees. The organization has two main objectives: to give students practical business experience during their studies and to promote international understanding through practical programs. Training periods are usually eight to ten weeks and normally occur between June and October. The aim is to provide training related to the student's subject of study in the fields of commerce and business administration. The addresses of national offices change from time to time according to the management location. In the United Kingdom the AIESEC address is % Brevard Press Ltd., % Central Bureau for Educational Visits and Exchanges, 43 Dorset Street, London W1H3FN. The address in the United States is 52 Vanderbilt Avenue, Suite 110, New York, New York 10017.

The Confederation of British Industry (CBI), through its scholarship section, offers training scholarships to enable foreign graduates in engineering to undertake training in British industry. The object is to stimulate trade between England and the countries from which trainees come and to provide technical aid to developing countries. Training periods may last from four months to two years according to purpose. Inquiries should be directed to Scholarships Section, Confederation of British Industry, 21 Tothill Street, London SW1, England.

The Foreign and Commonwealth Office, Overseas Development Administration/ Department of Employment (British Government (ODA/DE) places overseas government-sponsored candidates in British industry for periods from three months to two years for practical training. The purpose is to provide technical assistance to developing countries. For further information on ODA, write to Training Executive FCO ODA, Eland House, Stag Place, London SW1 E5DH, England; or to TA2 Department of Employment, Ebury Bridge House, Ebury Bridge Road, London SW1, England.

The Overseas Students Advisory Bureau (OSAB) assists non-British students already studying in Britain to obtain placement in training in cooperation with their university, polytechnic, or college. The countries from which the students come are almost exclusively the developing countries, mainly Commonwealth nations. For further information, write OSAB, Broadmead House, 21 Panton Street, London SW1Y 4DR, England.

The British Council administers many scholarships and study fellowships in cooperation with the International Labour Organisation (ILO), the Overseas Development Administration (Colombo Plan, Central Treaty Organization [CENTO], Special Commonwealth African Assistance Plan [SCAAP], Technical Assistance for Non-Commonwealth Countries in Africa [TANCA]); and the United Nations (United Nations Conference for Trade and Development [UNCTAD], UNESCO, United Nations Industrial Development Organization [UNIDO]). British Council programs cover observation, on-the-job experience, and formal training, of all types at all levels, in most subjects for any period. For further information, write British Council Science Department, Albion House, 59 New Oxford Street, London WC1A 1BP, England.

The *Deutscher akademischer Austausch-dienst* (DAAD: German Academic Exchange Service) is an academic institution for the advancement of international university relations. As part of a very wide program of exchange activities, DAAD collaborates with IAESTE in the Federal Republic of Germany to enable German and foreign students to attend practical courses in industrial concerns, public service industries, or research institutions, chiefly during their summer vacation. The head office is located at 5300 Bonn–Bad Godesberg 1, Kennedy-Allee 50, Federal Republic of Germany.

The Goethe Institute for the Promotion of the German Language and Culture Abroad (known as the Goethe Institute), with 113 branch institutes in sixty countries, provides information covering every sphere of cultural and social life that is relevant to contemporary Germany. The institute also organizes language courses for young foreigners entering the Federal Republic for studies or vocational training. For further information, write Secretary General, Goethe-Institut, Zentralverwaltung, D-8 Munich 2, Lenbachplatz 3, Federal Republic of Germany.

The *Carl Duisberg-Gesellschaft* (CDG), founded in 1949 by the president of the Federation of German Industry, is now organized in two departments that plan and organize further education programs for persons from industrialized countries in the Federal Republic of Germany and for young Germans in other industrialized countries, as well as programs for persons from developing countries coming to the Federal Republic of Germany. All programs have a common aim—professional experience abroad for the specialists and executives of tomorrow. For further information, write Carl Duisberg-Gesellschaft,

5 Cologne, Kaiser-Friedrich-Ufer 41–45, Federal Republic of Germany.

The aim of the French Language Cultural and Technical Union is to facilitate contacts between peoples and national groups of students who are taught French. Information may be obtained from French Language Cultural and Technical Union, 47 boulevard Lannes, Paris 16e, France.

The *Grandes écoles–Technische Hochschulen* (GETH) conducts industrial traineeship exchange programs. This organization implements educational and cultural programs on the basis of mutual cooperation between corresponding institutions. For further information, write General Secretary, Grandes écoles–Technische Hochschulen, 15 rue Renault, 75017 Paris, France.

The *Association des cercles Europe* is a traineeship exchange program that conducts seminars and study tours abroad, educational projects, and other activities. For information, write Association des cercles Europe, 2 rue Mérimée, 75782 Paris, France.

The United Nations International Development Association (UNIDA) encourages the mobilization of national and international resources of technology, skills, and finance. Its activities include in-plant training, seminars, workshops, studies, and research in a variety of industrial sectors. For information write Executive Director, United Nations International Development Association, Lerchenfelderstrasse 1, PO Box 707, A-1070 Vienna, Austria.

The *Agence pour la cooperation technique industrielle et économique* (ACTIM) organizes industrial training periods in France for highly qualified engineers, managers, and other specialists. The duration of training periods varies between a few weeks and four months. Information may be obtained from Agence pour la coopération technique industrielle et économique, 64 rue Pierre Charrow, Paris 8e, France; or 16 rue des Pyramides, Paris 1er, France.

The Trainees Exchange Office, in cooperation with foreign countries, arranges training placements abroad for young Finnish people and, in cooperation with Finnish organizations and firms, places young people from foreign countries for training in Finland. The office works closely with IAESTE/Finland. A good knowledge of English or German is an essential qualification for assistance by the office. The age bracket is eighteen to thirty, and training periods can be arranged lasting from two months to two years. For further information write Ministry of Communications and Public Works, Trainees Exchange Office, Siltasaarenkatu 3A, Helsinki 53, Finland.

In addition to those listed here, there are many other organizations active in the field of exchanges and placement. Approaches to those given above will usually lead to the particular organization in the appropriate country that might offer advice and assistance.

GERALD SMITH

See also: Cooperative Education and Off-Campus Experience: Cooperative Education Worldwide.

7. TRAVEL ABROAD

It is a truth universally acknowledged that travel abroad extends general education. No teaching program, however sophisticated, can substitute for personal experience of the languages, peoples, and cultures of other countries.

Since the end of World War II, there has been considerable increase in travel abroad, especially as it relates to study. Study-abroad programs in many different forms have become an accepted part of the higher education spectrum. Teaching and research exchange programs have also increased opportunity for travel and residency abroad.

Many members of the higher education community travel informally, unattached to any specific institution or program; it is with this type of independent travel that this article is concerned.

Student Travel Organizations

International travel by students and young people is the concern of youth and student travel organizations in more than forty countries. These include organizations officially designated "national student travel bureaus," as well as those that are purely commercial in character. The national student travel bureaus come under the umbrella of the International Student Travel Conference.

International Student Travel Conference. The International Student Travel Conference (ISTC) was formed in the early 1950s to coordinate the services offered by national student travel offices and other nonprofit organizations active in student travel. The ISTC has its secretariat in Zurich and a membership throughout most of the world. It serves as a platform for the discussion of student travel policies, a base for interagency contracting, and a central body for services such as joint computer booking facilities.

Among its major developments were the introduction in 1975 of a program known as the Budget Accommodations System (BAS), which provides guaranteed low-cost accommodations and eliminates the need for hotel reservations, and the sponsorship in 1969 of the International Student Identity Card (ISIC). The ISIC, which is purchased by over one million students every year, is available to full-time college, university, or vocational school students and is invaluable to the traveling student. It serves as official proof of student status and is recognized internationally.

With the ISIC a student is eligible for many money-saving services and facilities, including reduced or free admission to museums, cinemas, theaters, and historical sites. Some shops also offer discounts to ISIC holders. Student charter flights are available to ISIC holders and often represent a savings of approximately two thirds of the normal commercial fare. In addition, the Student Railpass, which entitles a student to two months of unlimited travel in thirteen European countries, is available to all students under twenty-six years of age on presentation of an ISIC. International student tours, operated by student travel organizations, are also open to ISIC holders.

Council on International Educational Exchange. In the United States the ISIC may be applied for through the offices of the Council on International Educational Exchange (CIEE) in New York. The council was founded in 1947 and was first known as the Council on Student Travel, its main purpose at that time being the reestablishment of student exchange and the facilitation of transatlantic transportation after World War II. Between 1947 and 1969 the council was best known for its chartered ships traveling between the United States and Europe. Since the 1960s the council's main work has been, as its present name suggests, the sponsoring and administering of educational exchange programs; but it still functions in the field of student travel as an information service, answering queries about aspects of work, study, and travel in the United States and in other countries.

The council offers a number of services to help students save money on travel, including arranging for overseas transportation by sea and air at the lowest possible fares. The council works as an agent for the Student Air Travel Association (SATA) and books students onto intra-European student charter flights operated by SATA members.

As a further service to student travelers, the council publishes many guides on all aspects of travel abroad.

Student Air Travel Association. SATA, headquartered in Copenhagen, was set up in 1969 to coordinate student flights. SATA members are national student travel organizations, run by and for students on a nonprofit basis. The activities of SATA include establishing new routes, increasing the flexibility of the student flight program, introducing new booking procedures, and improving standards of service.

Students Overseas Flights for Americans/ European Student Travel Center (SOFA). SOFA is a major international student travel organization for Europe and Israel, with its main office in New York. It operates a network of student charter flights within Europe, similar to those operated by SATA and with similar price reductions. All member organizations of SOFA are also members of SATA and the ISTC. SOFA can arrange for ISIC application; can provide student tours, rail passes, and language courses; and can make available the services of the affiliated student travel bureaus of eleven nations.

Federation of International Youth Travel Organizations. The Federation of International Youth Travel Organizations (FIYTO), which has a secretariat at the Scandinavian Student Travel Service (SSTS) in Copenhagen, has functioned since the mid 1970s as a clearinghouse for student and youth travel agencies. It has a membership of more than one hundred youth, school, and student travel agencies in over thirty countries. In 1976 the federation introduced its own Youth International Educational Exchange Council, which gives benefits similar to those afforded by ISIC, but which can be purchased by all young people, not only by students.

Other European travel organizations. The largest student travel service at the national level is operated by the National Union of Students (NUS) in the United Kingdom. Most Western European countries, including Austria, Belgium, France, Germany, Ireland, Italy, the Netherlands, Norway, Sweden, and Switzerland, have similar national organizations dealing with either youth or student travel, or both. Such organizations concern themselves mainly with providing information on inexpensive accommodation, restaurants, transportation, and other facilities. Some organize activities for visiting students, including educational tours.

Eastern European youth and student travel agencies are closely associated, country to country, and have a joint office known as the *Bureau international pour le tourisme et les échanges de la jeunesse* (BITEJ: International Bureau for Tourism and Youth Exchanges). Almatur, the Polish Students Association Travel and Tourist Office, is very active and arranges tours in Poland with the express purpose of acquainting foreign students with contemporary Poland in all its aspects. Some agencies from other countries also offer tours in Eastern Europe. SSTS, for example, arranges tours of the Soviet Union.

Sponsors of Programs

In addition to organizations that provide information and aid for the independent student traveler, there are several institutions and agencies that sponsor travel-abroad programs for professionals, academics, and students.

Voluntary associations and nongovernmental organizations. Several voluntary associations and nongovernmental organizations organize seminars that are noncredit granting, but which offer a valid educational experience. The Experiment in International Living is a private, nonprofit, educational institution, headquartered in Brattleboro, Vermont. Established in 1932, it conducts summer-abroad programs, designed for high school and college students, which usually include intensive predeparture language courses and always include a three- to four-week stay in the home of a foreign family. The experiment runs both outgoing and incoming programs. Its main aim is to foster mutual understanding and respect among people of all nations, on the premise that "people learn to live together by living together."

The World University Service, which has members in over fifty countries, has also been instrumental in involving thousands of students in a useful travel/learning experience. It holds conferences, workshops, seminars, and studies at the national, regional, and international level to investigate and evaluate current sociopolitical issues.

Travel councils and educational associa-

tions. Travel councils and educational associations offer some financial support for people who wish to travel abroad. However, their support tends to be confined to the areas of coordination, liaison, and information; and their programs are usually related to the professional development of their members. For example, the Canadian Bureau for International Education organized a professional development travel program in Ghana for foreign student advisers at Canadian universities.

Government agencies' travel grants. These grants are usually available in countries where government support for all types of programs is taken for granted. Such grants may, for example, support delegates to an international conference. In Canada travel grants are available through such agencies and departments as External Affairs, the National Research Council, the Canada Council, and the Medical Research Council. Other countries have a similar range of granting agencies.

Other sponsors. Some travel programs are sponsored by institutions of higher education, but many are the result of the endeavors of individual professors. Many travel agencies offer free travel to a professor who can sign up a certain number of students for a trip. Such trips, since they are based institutionally, tend to be closely tied to an academic pursuit. Foundations and private individuals are also active in the field of travel abroad, though groups applying for financial support often have to approach them with an already organized program.

Travel-Abroad Publications

The Council on International Educational Exchange in New York publishes a number of international publications relevant to travel abroad. Among these publications are the *Whole World Handbook,* a resource book for students seeking an overseas experience. Published annually, the handbook contains sections on working abroad, costs, and travel facilities. Its general information sections are followed by chapters on Europe, Asia, Africa, and Latin America. The CIEE also distributes *Let's Go: Europe,* a handbook written by the Harvard Student Agencies, Cambridge, Massachusetts, which includes city-by-city information on sights and events and a list of inexpensive eating places. This publication covers continental Europe, Scandinavia, Turkey, Israel, North Africa, and the Soviet Union. A companion volume, *Let's Go: Great Britain and Ireland,* gives similar information on those countries. Both books are published annually.

Student Travel Services, a cooperative service of CIEE and SOFA, publishes annually the *Student Travel Catalog,* a free booklet that includes advice on travel arrangements as well as descriptions of and order forms for a variety of travel services and publications.

The *SATA—Student Flight Programme,* which is issued three times a year, lists the intra-European student charters that link all the major cities of Europe; it also covers routes to cities in Africa, the Middle East, and Asia.

Many individual student travel agencies throughout the world publish their own handbooks on student travel. Many of these are available through the offices of CIEE in New York. In other countries these books may be obtained from the relevant agencies.

Bibliography

Brett, R. J. *World Study and Travel for Teachers.* Washington, D.C.: American Federation of Teachers, 1975.

Council on International Educational Exchange. *Guidelines on Developing Campus Services for Students Going Abroad.* New York: CIEE, 1975.

Council on International Educational Exchange. *Whole World Handbook: A Student Guide to Work, Study, and Travel Abroad.* New York: CIEE, published annually.

Harvard Student Agencies. *Let's Go: Europe.* New York: Dutton, 1976a.

Harvard Student Agencies. *Let's Go: Great Britain and Ireland.* New York: Dutton, 1976b.

Pearson, J., and McCormack, N. *Study, Work, Travel Overseas: A UTK Handbook.* Knoxville:
University of Tennessee, Division of International Education, 1976.

Student Air Travel Association. *SATA Student Flight Programme.* Copenhagen: SATA, 1976.

Student Travel Services. *The 1976 Student Travel Catalog.* New York: Student Travel Services of CIEE/SOFA, 1976.

United States Department of State. *Youth Travel Abroad: What to Know Before You Go.* Washington, D.C.: U.S. Government Printing Office, 1975.

ALLAN RIX

8. TEACHING AND RESEARCH EXCHANGE

The movement of scholars across national boundaries to teach or share in research with professional colleagues takes many forms. Such exchanges are not a recent phenomenon. However, they have increased tremendously in size and scope since World War II as technological and economic developments have made domestic and international issues increasingly indistinguishable.

This article explores a representative sampling of the many public and private international exchange programs that sponsor organized lectureships or research activities at the university faculty or an equivalent professional level among specific educational or research institutions, among various countries, or on a worldwide scale. The common denominator of a majority of such exchange programs is the achievement of one or more mutual objectives or goals through a shared exchange of persons. Objectives may include learning while teaching; a cooperative research effort; an equality of participation; or an integration of findings, results, or discoveries by scholars from different countries. One purpose of educational exchange, perhaps shared by all such exchanges regardless of sponsor, was described by Senator J. William Fulbright in 1967 as "nothing less than an effort to expand the scope of human moral and intellectual capacity to the extent necessary to close the fateful gap between human needs and human capacity in the nuclear age" (Fulbright, 1967). Teaching and research exchanges, which are widespread, are uniquely suited to this goal. One measure of their volume is the fact that 10,084 foreign scholars were present in the United States alone for 1973–74 in either a teaching or research capacity. In the same period, 6522 American faculty members and administrative staff were working abroad (Institute of International Education, 1975).

Although the number of participants in such exchanges between countries is not as great as that of undergraduate and graduate students and other foreign visitors, their influence at home and abroad on higher education, their impact as advisers to foreign governments, and their contribution to industrial and economic development are significant by any standard. Teaching and research exchanges, while less subject than other programs to short-term political fluctuations among nations, are nonetheless dependent on the continuing confidence and financial vitality of their sponsors, whether public or private. Worldwide inflation is taking its toll in the quantity if not the quality of these senior scholar exchanges. The character of such exchanges—both for teaching and for research—and their sponsorship and motivation are somewhat diversified around the world. However, a representative sampling of international exchange programs can suggest their functions and scope.

Teaching Exchanges

Lecturing or teaching appointments under established exchange arrangements are as varied as the institutions and individuals they serve. One of the largest such exchange programs, conducted on a worldwide basis, is the Fulbright-Hays program, financed by the United States and a number of the participating governments. From 1949 to June of 1974 this program provided lectureship grants abroad, awarded competitively on academic merit, to 8648 American citizens and to 3039 foreign lecturers to come to the United States. Lecturing fields and institutional affiliations for Americans, usually for one academic year abroad, are generally predetermined annually, on consultation with host universities, by binational commissions that plan and administer the exchanges in the forty-five participating countries under bilateral agreements. In the sixty-five countries participating in the program that do not have binational commissions, the American embassy makes the arrangements. Lecturers coming to the United States generally receive Fulbright-Hays travel grants and financial support from participating American universities. Eighty foreign lecturers received grants in 1973–74. American lecturers abroad for the year numbered 366, principally in the social sciences and the humanities.

Similar lectureships are offered by a few other governments. Some are short-term foreign university interchange visits, such as the eighty awards offered annually by the British Council to British scholars and to a similar number of scholars in most of Western Europe, Yugoslavia, and Poland under bilateral agreements with the countries concerned.

No reliable figures are available on the rapidly increasing number of interuniversity international exchange agreements between institutions of two or more countries. However, it is clear that such exchanges have become perhaps the most effective way for faculty and students to exchange information, expertise, and staff; to take part in research or study; or to cooperate generally in fields of mutual interest and benefit over a continuing period. The majority of such linkages provide study and research exchange opportunities rather than exchanges for teaching, but some may combine both.

One example is the teaching fellowships in Latin America and Asia/Pacific at Tufts University in Massachusetts, supported by host institutions, corporations, foundations, and government agencies. Since its inception in 1965 the program has placed over 400 teaching fellows in Latin American institutes and more recently in institutions in the Asia/Pacific area.

A 1975 study of over one thousand academic links between institutions in the United Kingdom and overseas institutions concludes that the majority of really successful links are departmental or are at least faculty links for interdepartmental studies (British Council, 1975). The study notes that unless such links are allowed to grow naturally, without excessive pressure by outside bodies, they are unlikely to last. Additional information about international teaching and research programs of selected universities in the respective countries is available from the United States Office of Education, the American Council on Education, the Education Directorate of the Common Market, the British Council, and embassies and cultural institutes in many capital cities.

Another kind of teaching exchange experience is the special lectureship or chair created for a visiting foreign scholar. While not many universities maintain such professorships, the Pitt and Harmsworth professorships, at Oxford and Cambridge respectively, are illustrative. Both are for American scholars. The Pitt Professor in American History and Institutions, for example, financed by Cambridge University, is a one-year post held by distinguished Americans in succession. In 1973 the Japan Foundation announced a grant of one million dollars in capital funds to each of ten American universities for institutional support of Japanese studies, including the endowment of chairs. Teaching exchanges will undoubtedly play a role in the Japanese effort and in that of other governments, such as that of the Federal Republic of Germany, which are promoting area studies in other countries.

Still another form of exchange carried out by a number of academic organizations and institutions around the world is the invitational guest lectureship. A scholar may be invited for a single lecture, a series at one or more institutions, or for a semester or academic year in residence. An inter-

esting example of such invitational guest lectureships is the cooperative project between the academic communities of the United States and countries of South America. In this program, twelve American universities request specific South American scholars, and the United States government supports the year-long lectureships designed to improve communication between North and South America. Similar invitational guest lectureships by American universities to scholars from other world areas are anticipated.

United States college-sponsored academic programs also offer teaching abroad prospects for American faculty or foreign faculty engaged for that purpose. Such programs have primarily been designed to offer a third or junior year abroad to American students; however, they are expanding dramatically in size and scope. While Europe is still the location for the majority of such programs, Asia and Africa have grown in favor. For 1974–75 the Institute of International Education reports 581 programs, the majority of which combine study in a foreign institution with courses arranged especially for the group (Cohen, 1975). The latter are taught either by American faculty from the home campus or by local and American faculty members engaged by the program sponsors. In cases where the student is fully enrolled in the foreign university, supplemental tutorials may be conducted by American faculty members. For those programs not integrated with an institution in the host country, all courses are taught by faculty members of the sponsoring American institution and by foreign faculty engaged specifically for the program.

Research Exchanges

The international flow of individuals engaged in publicly and privately supported programs of research at the university level is substantially greater than that for lecturing and teaching, although there are no worldwide statistics available. The abundance and diversity of such exchanges, to be briefly examined here, are both cause and effect of the technological age in which we live and a reminder of our global interdependence.

Research exchanges offer many opportunities for international cooperation in areas of mutual interest to mankind, such as space exploration, the environment, food and agriculture, and disarmament. For example, in 1973 some ninety-four countries, including international organizations, cooperated with the United States National Aeronautics and Space Administration (NASA) in research, personnel exchange, surveys, tracking-data acquisition, and other projects. NASA provides to nationals of other countries a number of postdoctoral and senior postdoctoral resident research associateships at its centers in the United States. Regionally, the European Space Research Organization offers research exchange opportunities to nationals of member countries in the space sciences and spacecraft technology. The United States Environmental Protection Agency has had a number of research projects in Egypt, Poland, Tunisia, and Yugoslavia, under special foreign currency programs, with participating foreign nationals as principal investigators in methods of waste disposal and marine pollution. There are also several examples of exchange in the field of agriculture. Between March 1961 and June 1973, the United States Department of Agriculture had completed or terminated 1049 research grants in thirty-one countries, involving animals and animal products, cereals and forage crops, fruits and vegetables, insects, and other fields related to food and agriculture. In addition, a number of bilateral science and technology agreements have been signed between the United States and other countries, providing for cooperative agricultural research, some funded by the National Science Foundation. The Research Service of the Department of Agriculture (ARS) has for many years accepted foreign agricultural researchers who, at their own expense, work on projects in ARS labora-

tories. The United States Agency for International Development (AID) also contracts with ARS to carry out research in various foreign countries. An example is the international winter wheat performance network initiated in 1969; by 1974 it involved collaborative research at fifty-five different locations in thirty-five countries seeking identification of superior winter wheat genotypes and improved nutritional quality in various wheat production areas of the world.

The Antarctica Treaty of 1959 is but one example of long-term international cooperation in the field of disarmament. Under the treaty, twelve countries pledged not only that Antarctica shall be used only for peaceful purposes but also that they would exchange information, personnel, and the scientific observations and results of their explorations and investigations in Antarctica.

The vast majority of research exchanges around the world are university-based. In universities in the United States and elsewhere, one of the fastest-growing fields of specialization since World War II has been language and area studies programs. American experts on foreign areas numbered only a handful in 1940. By 1969 some 3800 language and area specialists in over 200 graduate-level programs were teaching nearly 9000 courses to over 65,000 graduate students, of whom over 3000 were training to be specialists. Over 200,000 undergraduate students were enrolled in foreign-area courses. Although such programs diminished in the economic recession of the mid 1970s, the great expansion in area and language programs represents twenty years of increasing investment by such funding sources as the Rockefeller Foundation, the Carnegie Corporation, the Ford Foundation, and the National Defense Education Act, plus the much larger investment by the American universities involved. The facts about area studies in the United States are set forth in the definitive study by Lambert (1973).

The East-West Center, a national educational institution established in Hawaii by the United States Congress in 1960, is another example of an institution's attracting foreign and American scholars in joint study and research. Through its institutes in communication, cultural learning, food, population, and technology and development, it brings together, in problem-oriented research projects, leaders from education, government, and business, representing more than fifty countries and territories of Asia, the Pacific, and the United States.

Foreign scholars from Eastern European countries, including the Soviet Union, come to some ninety American universities that participate in the academic exchange programs administered by the International Research and Exchanges Board (IREX). The program, supported by the Ford Foundation, the United States Department of State, the National Endowment for the Humanities, and the participating universities, also sends American scholars abroad under reciprocal agreements with the countries concerned (Bulgaria, Czechoslovakia, German Democratic Republic, Hungary, Poland, Romania, and the Soviet Union).

The United Nations and its specialized agencies sponsor a substantial number of fellowships annually, including research exchange opportunities in various fields, such as education, natural science and technology, social sciences, and communication (UNESCO); some opportunities in research institutes in industrial development planning, finance, management, and related subjects (United Nations Industrial Development Organization: UNIDO); and training fellowships to nationals of developing countries in international law and public national and international service (United Nations Institute for Training and Research: UNITAR). The World Health Organization (WHO) also sponsors a number of research fellowships annually to promote the international exchange of scientific knowledge and techniques in the health field.

National governments continue to be a major sponsor of international research exchanges. The German Academic Exchange Service (*Deutscher akademischer Austauschdienst*) offers senior fellowships annually to nationals of all countries for research and observation visits in the Federal Republic of Germany; the Alexander von Humboldt Foundation offers approximately 150 fellowships for postdoctoral research at universities or research institutions in the Federal Republic of Germany for scholars of all countries. In its efforts to encourage the spread of Japanese studies abroad, the Japan Foundation offers research fellowships for work in Japan to faculty and nonfaculty of other countries who have significant experience in Japanese studies; a Japanese science program also offers research and teaching exchange opportunities for scientists of other countries. The Soviet Union, as well as a number of other countries in Eastern Europe, supports a number of research exchanges with other nations under reciprocal agreements. For example, the National Science Foundation (United States) supports a number of cooperative science exchange programs, including those for study and research by American citizens in the Soviet Union, Bulgaria, Czechoslovakia, Hungary, Poland, Romania, and Yugoslavia, under exchange arrangements between the National Academy of Sciences of the United States and the academies of sciences of those countries. The United States, in cooperation with participating countries and universities under the Fulbright-Hays Act, supported 175 American research scholar exchanges in twenty-one countries in 1973–74, as well as 515 foreign research exchanges to the United States from sixty-three countries. An additional thirty-six Americans went to sixteen countries as Fulbright-Hays foreign-area and language research scholars.

Perhaps as significant to international exchange (including teacher and research exchanges) as government support is the support of the philanthropic foundation, whether it be Volkswagen, Olivetti, Toyota, or the Ford Foundation. The Ford Foundation, undoubtedly one of the largest underwriters of such programs over the past twenty years, has supported a range of activities aimed at improving the climate for international peace and well-being of peoples everywhere. An American institution chartered to advance human welfare, the foundation believes that the future of American society is intertwined with a continuing effort to reduce international tensions and human deprivation throughout the world. Through its extensive grants program, including a number open to universities, research institutions, and other organizations in the United States and abroad, the Ford Foundation supports a substantial volume of exchange activities. Support is given in the fields of international agricultural research, population growth, education, the planning and administration of development programs, arms control, international economics, East-West relations, and the preservation of human rights and intellectual freedom.

Scholarship and fellowship programs continue to provide a majority of the support for international teaching and research exchanges. A number of these programs have been mentioned here and elsewhere in the encyclopedia. In addition, *The Grants Register,* published biennially in London and New York, is an invaluable aid in identifying publicly and privately supported study and research fellowship program opportunities offered on a regional, national, or international basis, including those of government ministries in many countries. *The Grants Register* also indicates whether fellowships are limited to nationals of certain countries, lists eligibility criteria, and indicates where to write for further information on each of 2146 programs described in the publication.

Among the other sponsors of research exchange fellowships is the German Marshall Fund of the United States. Its purpose is "to assist individuals and organizations in the United States, Europe and elsewhere to understand and to resolve selected contemporary and emerging problems common to industrial societies, both domestic and international." A second sponsor is the Woodrow Wilson International Center for Scholars in Washington, D.C., which, through its residential fellowship program of advanced research and communication, seeks to commemorate both the scholarly depth and the public concerns of Woodrow Wilson.

With respect to support for faculty research exchanges on the part of the business community, a study of 606 overseas subsidiaries of United States international companies indicated that thirteen supported one or more foreign faculty research exchanges in the United States. More significantly a study, undertaken in 1974 by the Conference Board in cooperation with the United States Department of State, showed that the companies ranked this activity near the bottom of their public service activities, even though their support of educational exchange programs generally is more substantial (Conference Board, 1974). Exchanges in the professions, while not always technically in either the teaching or research area, should nonetheless not be overlooked. Professional associations frequently encourage such exchanges for short-term visits. The International Legal Exchange Program of the American Bar Association, for example, arranges for lawyers from the United States to have several months of training experience abroad in areas of their special legal interest and for lawyers from other countries to have that opportunity in the United States. Similar exchanges take place in the medical and other professions.

No coverage of teaching and research exchanges would be complete without mention of some key organizations, beyond those noted above, which have major roles either in the support and administration of such exchanges or as sources of information about these and other exchanges. In many countries such organizations include the ministries of education (or their

equivalent), cultural offices in many foreign ministries, cultural or educational
attachés of embassies in capital cities, and
cultural institutes or their equivalents.
Among those in the United States are
the American Council of Learned Societies,
the Social Science Research Council, the
National Endowment for the Humanities,
and the Council for International Exchange of Scholars and the American
Council on Education.

Born of idealism in the period after
World War II, teaching and research exchange programs have continued to receive
the public and private support essential
for their measured but steady growth. They
must compete, however, for increasingly
scarce resources from government, the
private foundations, and business during
a time of worldwide inflation. Large grant
contributions, such as those of the government of the Federal Republic of Germany,
Japanese business firms, and others, give
promise of potential new sources of support necessary to sustain these international activities. Beyond financing, these
and other international exchanges need
an atmosphere of trust and confidence on
the part of the participating universities,
governments, business and industry, the
foundations, and people in general. With
these ingredients, these and other exchanges can continue to attract the highly
motivated, exceptionally qualified individual who makes a significant contribution
to effective two-way communication among
the peoples of the world.

Bibliography

Alexander von Humboldt Foundation. *Aims
and Functions of the Alexander von Humboldt
Foundation.* Bonn–Bad Godesberg, Federal
Republic of Germany: Alexander von Humboldt Foundation, 1973.

American Council of Learned Societies. *Aids
to Individual Scholars, 1974–75.* New York:
American Council of Learned Societies,
1974.

Association of Commonwealth Universities.
*Awards for Commonwealth University Staff,
1976–1978.* London: Association of Commonwealth Universities, 1975a.

Association of Commonwealth Universities.
*Scholarship Guide for Commonwealth Post-
Graduate Students.* London: Association of
Commonwealth Universities, 1975b.

Board of Foreign Scholarships. *Report on Exchanges, 1975.* Washington, D.C.: U.S. Department of State, 1975.

British Council. *Survey of Academic Links.* London: British Council, 1975.

Cohen, G. A. (Ed.) *U.S. College-Sponsored Pro
grams Abroad.* New York: Institute of International Education, 1975.

Conference Board. *U.S. Business Support for
International Public Service Activities, Part II:
Support from Overseas Affiliates—An Overview.*
New York: Conference Board, 1974.

Council for European Studies and Western
European Program of the Social Science
Research Council and the American Council
of Learned Societies. *A Guide to Selected
Fellowships and Grants for Research on Western
Europe.* New York: Council for European
Studies and Western European Program,
1975.

Council for International Exchange of Scholars. *University Lecturing, Advanced Research
Under the Fulbright-Hays Act, 1977–1978.*
Washington, D.C.: Council for International Exchange, 1976.

Fellowship Office, Commission on Human Resources, National Research Council. *A
Selected List of Major Fellowship Opportunities
and Aids to Advanced Education for Foreign
Nationals.* Washington, D.C.: National Academy of Sciences, 1974a.

Fellowship Office, Commission on Human Re-
sources, National Research Council. *A
Selected List of Major Fellowship Opportunities
and Aids to Advanced Education for United
States Citizens.* Washington, D.C.: National
Academy of Sciences, 1974b.

Ford Foundation. *Current Interests of the Ford
Foundation, 1976 and 1977.* New York: Ford
Foundation, 1975a.

Ford Foundation. *Ford Foundation Annual Report, 1974.* New York: Ford Foundation,
1975b.

Fulbright, J. W. "Foreword." In A. Michie (Ed.),
*Diversity and Independence Through Interna-
tional Education.* New York: Education and
World Affairs, 1967.

German Marshall Fund. *The German Marshall
Fund of the United States.* Washington, D.C.:
German Marshall Fund, 1975.

Institute of International Education. *Handbook on International Study for U.S. Nationals.*
New York: Institute of International Education, 1971.

Institute of International Education. *Open
Doors, 1974: Report on International Educa-

tional Exchange. New York: Institute of International Education, 1975.

International Association of Universities. *Bulletin.* A quarterly journal, published in Paris.

International Education Project. *Education for Global Interdependence.* Washington, D.C.: American Council on Education, 1975a.

International Education Project. *Transnational Research Collaboration.* Washington, D.C.: American Council on Education, 1975b.

International Research and Exchanges Board. *Exchange Programs with Eastern Europe and the Soviet Union.* New York: International Research, 1974.

Lambert, R. D. *Language and Area Studies Review.* Monograph 17. Philadelphia: American Academy of Political and Social Science, 1973.

Lewis, M. O. (Ed.) *Foundation Directory.* New York: Columbia University Press, 1975.

Reitman, J., and Aroeste, J. (Eds.) *Annual Register of Grant Support 1974–75.* Chicago: Marquis Academic Media, 1974.

Social Science Research Council. *Social Science Research Council Fellowships and Grants to Be Offered in 1975–76.* New York: Social Science Research Council, 1975.

Spencer, R. E., and Awe, R. *International Educational Exchange: A Bibliography.* New York: Institute of International Education, 1968.

Turner, R. *The Grants Register, 1975–1977.* London: St. James Press, 1975.

UNESCO. *Study Abroad, 1975–1977.* Paris: UNESCO, 1974.

United States Office of Education, Department of Health, Education and Welfare. *American Students and Teachers Abroad.* Washington, D.C.: U.S. Office of Education, 1975.

Woodrow Wilson International Center for Scholars. *Fellowship and Guest Scholar Programs.* Washington, D.C.: Woodrow Wilson Center, n.d.

RALPH H. VOGEL

See also: Agriculture in Higher Education: International Cooperation in Agriculture; Manpower Planning: Migration of Talent.

9. INTERNATIONAL HOUSES AND CENTERS

Situated in several countries, firmly grounded in the universities or communities to which they belong, and having much in common though independent of one another, international houses and international centers annually serve thousands of the world's students and post-doctoral scholars. Each house or center, whatever its roots or indigenous characteristics, is dedicated to the advancement of understanding, knowledge, and fellowship among the peoples of all nations.

Houses and *centers* are often interchangeable terms, but common usage emphasizes the major distinction that has developed between them. An international house is a place of residence that provides accommodation during an academic term for both foreign and domestic citizens and typically does so on the basis of an established foreign-to-domestic ratio. An international center focuses on nonresidential activities. Generally accepted criteria for all these institutions include: (1) a nonprofit character; (2) the integration of foreign and domestic students; (3) the operation of a substantial cultural or educational activities program; (4) the absence of religious or political tests in admission or membership policies; and (5) services to persons affiliated with accredited institutions of higher learning. Traditional halls of residence (dormitories), nonresidential clubs, foreign-language facilities, short-term visitor centers, and holiday or vacation retreats, which strive to fulfill similar goals and meet some but not all of the above criteria, are also important to international education but are not included in this discussion.

The First International Houses

Mainly the fruits of persons of vision and generous community spirit, international houses and centers were originally privately inspired and founded. Their roots may be traced to a day in 1909 when Harry Edmonds, a young man employed by the New York Young Men's Christian Association (YMCA) as a leader of its student Christian movement, extended a "good morning" greeting on the steps of the Columbia University library to a passing Chinese student. Astonished, the Chinese student remarked: "I've been in New York three weeks, and you are the first person who has spoken to me."

The chance encounter prompted Edmonds to make inquiries about the numbers and living conditions of foreign students and to consider their loneliness and lack of contact with Americans. Motivated by what he learned, Edmonds and his wife, Florence, invited small groups of foreign students to their home for afternoon tea and then for Sunday supper. Each week the Sunday supper attracted more people until eventually they overflowed the Edmonds' home. In 1911–12, under YMCA auspices, Edmonds and a group of interested friends organized the Intercollegiate Cosmopolitan Club, which was open to students of all nationalities in the colleges, universities, and professional schools of New York City.

By 1919 the members of the club exceeded six hundred from more than sixty-five countries. To the Sunday Suppers, which had become an established tradition, was added a program of home hospitality, social events, nationality evenings, international performances, excursions, discussions of world events, and assistance with housing and part-time employment. The club outgrew rented quarters and Earl Hall of Columbia University. Edmonds, with the assistance of the Cleveland Dodge family, acquired title to a building site and concentrated on the construction of an international house.

International House of New York. John D. Rockefeller, Jr., and his wife became interested in the project, and the Rockefeller gifts, amounting to $3,000,000, led to the realization of Harry and Florence Edmonds' dream. International House of New York, a thirteen-story building overlooking the Hudson River, was formally opened in 1924. The lower floors contained spacious lounges, cafeteria, large auditorium, gymnasium, library, meeting rooms, and game rooms. The ten upper floors provided living accommodations for 525 men and women of foreign and American nationality. The house was privately incorporated with a board of trustees independent of any of the educational institu-

tions attended by the residents. Edmonds served as director and was joined by staff previously associated with the Intercollegiate Cosmopolitan Club. Over the main entrance was chiseled the inscription suggested by John D. Rockefeller, Jr.: "That Brotherhood May Prevail."

The New York International House was an immediate and resounding success, and the building committee was transformed into an "extension committee." Edmonds was commissioned to travel and survey possible locations for other international houses. As a result of Edmonds' journeys, John D. Rockefeller, Jr., again committed funds for the purchases of land and construction of an international house, this time at the University of California in Berkeley. Title was vested in the Board of Regents of the university, which appointed the original governing board for the house, and articles of incorporation were approved that provided for private management on a lease basis and for a self-perpetuating board of directors.

International House Berkeley. International House Berkeley, an eight-story building with residential accommodations for 450 to 550 men and women and extensive social facilities, opened in 1930. Capped by a distinctive dome, Mediterranean in architectural style, and overlooking campus buildings and San Francisco Bay, the land and the structure represented a gift to the University of California of $1,800,000. Allen C. Blaisdell, Edmonds' former assistant in New York, was the first director. Sunday Suppers, already a tradition, formed a pivot around which cultural and social activities, including special interest trips and home hospitality, revolved.

International House of Chicago. Edmonds and the extension committee continued to be active. Two years later, in 1932, John D. Rockefeller 3rd, on behalf of his father, formally dedicated International House at the University of Chicago. A nine-story neo-Gothic building erected at a cost of $3,000,000, the International House of

Chicago provided living and program facilities for 510 men and women. Many first residents were former members of an international students' association that, founded in 1927 by Bruce W. Dickson, the University of Chicago foreign student adviser and former YMCA worker, had developed from Sunday Suppers held in the Dickson home and on the University of Chicago campus. Although the property of the University of Chicago, International House was open to students at other institutions of higher learning in the Chicago area. The principal policymaking body was the board of governors, comprised of community leaders and ex officio university representatives elected or designated by the university board of trustees. Bruce W. Dickson served as the first director.

International House of Paris. The fourth Rockefeller-financed International House, *La maison internationale,* opened at the *Cité universitaire* in Paris in 1936. The *Cité* had been inaugurated in the 1920s, under the egis of a national foundation, to be a residential community for several thousand French and foreign students of the University of Paris. By 1936 it was composed of nineteen "houses," each dedicated to students of a different nationality. Each house had been established either by private gifts or by funds of sponsoring governments, or both; each had its own governing board and management; and each maintained special services and activities. The number of houses grew to thirty-four by 1960, and on fixed ratio bases came to accommodate not only students from the country after which a house was named but also students of French and other nationalities. *La maison internationale* suited ideally the objectives of the principal founder of the *Cité,* André Honnorat, foundation president, French senator, and former minister of public instruction. Supplementing the national houses and without student dormitory rooms, it provided a large social and cultural center patterned after the palace at Fontainebleau, with a restaurant, cafeteria, library, auditorium, gymnasium, swimming pool, lounges, ballroom, music practice room, meeting room, and other facilities where students of all nationalities could engage in organized or informal activities offered by International House or by a bureau of delegates elected from the member houses.

La maison internationale proved to be the last international house financed by John D. Rockefeller, Jr. Land for a fifth building, proposed for students at Harvard University, Massachusetts Institute of Technology, and Boston University, was purchased during the 1930s along the Charles River in Cambridge, Massachusetts, but the persistence of the world's economic depression and declining enrollments of foreign students with war looming on the horizon in Europe and Asia deterred the project's completion. The site was eventually sold (Edmonds, 1971, pp. 92–97, 105–106).

Characteristics of the first houses. The four large international houses—New York, Berkeley, Chicago, Paris—constituted unique efforts in international relations. The bringing together of young people from many countries, cultures, and races represented a great hope for better understanding when the students assumed their public and private responsibilities. Despite their differences in governance, size, and architecture, the fundamental characteristics of the houses were similar: (1) they were built in cosmopolitan urban centers of higher learning with established, sizable foreign student enrollments; (2) they adapted to local precedents and needs; (3) they were founded in coordination with strong local leadership; (4) they were administered by governing boards composed principally of community leaders who became trustees of the international house idea; (5) they were architecturally designed to be indigenous and functional; (6) they were managed by special staff for continuity of purposes and services; (7) they were operated on a self-supporting basis;

and (8) they provided programs to advance institutional objectives and the educational goals of the members.

Smaller International Houses

The first third of the century also witnessed the founding of many smaller international houses. In 1906 in Paris, a "home" for foreign and French women students, the *Foyer international des étudiantes,* was established under independent auspices. The *Foyer* became a project of the University of Paris, with accommodations for 165 students. Its program included planned home visits for both French students and foreign visitors (Jenkins, 1961, pp. 1–2). In 1908 a Presbyterian missionary and his wife launched a home hospitality program for foreign students in their apartment in West Philadelphia, Pennsylvania. The program was adopted by the University of Pennsylvania Christian Association, and in 1918 International Students House, with living accommodations for fifteen, was opened in an old Victorian residence near the University of Pennsylvania campus ("Putting Snowflakes Together," 1965).

The 1930s brought new international houses in Geneva, Switzerland (1936); Washington, D.C. (1936); and Columbus, Ohio (1938). *La maison internationale des étudiants* (International Student House) in Geneva, located near but not affiliated with the University of Geneva, provided accommodation and meals for forty women students (four fifths of whom were foreign), a program of social and recreational events, study and discussion groups, and transient facilities. Under the auspices of a strong local committee with some initial support from the Carnegie Endowment in Europe, and through its founding director, Nellie Tullis, and her successor, Violette E. Balmer, a former resident of the New York House, close ties were maintained with New York and Harry Edmonds (Edmonds, 1971, pp. 120–131; Chrysostom, 1960, p. 24).

International Student House in Washington, D.C., largely the result of a gift of Mrs. Bancroft Davis, was owned and operated for many years by the American Friends Service Committee as part of its international centers program, which included Society of Friends (Quakers) centers in various countries. "Friends believe that, if a simple life, a desire for truth and a belief in the common humanity of all men, become part of our daily living, they provide a basis for a peaceful world" (Chrysostom, 1960, pp. 72–73). The Washington house originally accommodated eighteen; later, in a new location, it was expanded to thirty-five, dining for seventy, and meeting and game rooms for two hundred (Johnston, 1949). Its program was similar to that of the large houses. Eventually, its operation was transferred to a local, independent committee, which built an annex nearly doubling the residential capacity.

In Columbus, Ohio, the George Wells Knight International House was given to a church in Columbus by the wife of a former professor of Ohio State University as a memorial. The house was operated jointly by the church and the university until 1950, when it was deeded to the university. A subsidiary of the campus international student office, the house provided lodging for twenty-one men and served as the center for the university's large foreign student population. Zonta International House, a residence privately owned and operated by the Zonta Club of Columbus for sixteen graduate women students, also opened in 1950 (Young and others, 1953).

Nonresidential Centers

Nonresidential centers developed in the first half of the century in England, Austria, Germany, and the United States. In Russell Square, London, the Student Movement House was established in 1917 by the Student Christian Movement as a memorial to students of all countries killed in World War I. By the late 1930s membership had grown to one thousand, of which one third was British, from several institutions including Oxford and Cambridge Universities. The Student Movement House moved to Gower Street in 1939 and continued to function throughout World War II (Trevelyan, 1942). In 1941 in Bloomsbury, near London University, the Society of Friends and the Friends Service Council opened the Friends International Center, which provided short-term hostel accommodations.

In 1919 a Friends International Center, with both student and nonstudent membership, was opened in Vienna under the auspices of the Philadelphia and London branches of the American Friends Service Council. An international students club was founded in 1926 in the center of Munich and served students from the University of Munich, the technological institutes, and the Munich School of Art. Resumed after World War II, the Munich center had 350 members by 1960, was conducted entirely by students, and sponsored many sports groups in addition to numerous international student activities (Chrysostom, 1960, pp. 16–17).

In the United States there was a proliferation of centers, beginning with the 1904 founding of the Cosmopolitan Club, which built a clubhouse in 1910–1911 at Cornell University, Ithaca, New York. There assembled in 1913 a convention of *Corda Fratres,* an association of cosmopolitan clubs that came to play a role in the development of cultural and social opportunities for foreign students at several American university campuses. Because of financial difficulties, title to the Cornell clubhouse was given in 1932 to the International Association of Ithaca, which operated it for eleven years. In addition to serving several hundred students, the clubhouse included rooms for thirty men. The operation of the building (but not the title) was taken over by the residence halls of the university in 1944 (Bishop, 1962; Haines, 1951; Young and others, 1953).

University-owned centers were opened at New York University, Washington Square (1937); University of Michigan, Ann Arbor (1938); Rollins College, Winter Park, Florida (1942); Michigan State University, East Lansing (1944); and Fisk University, Nashville, Tennessee (1945). A private center, the International Student Association, serving students at thirteen institutions in the greater Boston area, was established in 1940 near Harvard Square, Cambridge, Massachusetts, but was closed in the early 1970s. All the centers, university-owned or private, employed permanent staff substantially assisted by community volunteers.

Formation of International House Association

World War II retarded the growth but not the spirit of the international house movement, which accelerated after the war as increasing numbers of students and postdoctoral scholars crossed international boundaries. Massive influxes into several countries, concurrent with enormous growth in domestic student numbers, severely taxed the capacity of existing accommodation facilities and services. World War II and subsequent regional wars, together with the rise of new nations, the technological and communications revolution, the economic interdependence of the world community, rising expectations of youth, rapidly changing values, and increasing emphasis on advanced professional education all contributed to the growing recognition by individuals, institutions, communities, and governments of the need for increased international and intercultural understanding through the sharing of experiences and problems when individually and collectively confronting cultural and educational change.

Prompted by the leadership in New York of John L. Mott, successor to Harry Edmonds, alumni organizations had developed in New York, Chicago, and Berkeley. November 10, the International House of New York's anniversary date, had become International House Day, an annual occasion for alumni gatherings in points as distant as Stockholm, Oslo, Mexico City, Peking, Port-au-Prince (Haiti), and Copenhagen. In 1937 a cooperative publication, *The International Quarterly* (renamed *The*

International House Quarterly in 1945), was launched with articles about international affairs, often by alumni, and news about individual house activities. In 1947 these pioneering efforts resulted in the organization of the International House Association, Incorporated (IHA) (Sproul, 1937, pp. 13–15; Nohrnberg, 1948, pp. 8–11).

Founded under leadership that included David Rockefeller and Reidar E. Gundersen of New York, Meyer Kestnbaum of Chicago, and Robert Gordon Sproul of Berkeley, the IHA sought to work toward the brotherhood of man by gaining better knowledge and understanding of the life and culture of all peoples and to cooperate with the international houses and other organizations devoted to international understanding and world peace. By 1952 the IHA claimed forty-four chapters in twenty-seven countries, the membership of which was composed chiefly of alumni of the three large American houses. Activities of the IHA included publication of the *Quarterly*, extensive overseas travel by the executive director, promotion of more international houses, the compilation and distribution in 1960 of a directory of international houses and centers, and in 1961 the sponsorship of a five-day World Conference of International Houses and International Student Centers, held at *La maison internationale* in Paris. Delegates from houses, centers, and organizations in eight continental European countries, the United Kingdom, Canada, the United States, Chile, Japan, and India attended the conference in an effort to learn how they might adapt the international house movement to local or national needs.

Although IHA chapters around the world continued to be active, the central organization terminated its activities following the Paris conference in 1961. The *Quarterly* had ceased publication at an earlier date. The effects of the IHA were clear, as were those of Harry Edmonds, whose zeal and efforts to advance the international house movement had not ceased. Many traditions, such as the Sunday Sup-

per, had come to be observed by alumni groups, houses, and centers in many countries. The story of Edmonds meeting the lonely Chinese student in 1909 had become legendary. The motto of John D. Rockefeller, Jr., "That Brotherhood May Prevail," was widely adopted. Ideas for the improvement and growth of the movement had been exchanged and implemented.

Post–World War II Houses

In the Federal Republic of Germany, the postwar reconstruction of cities and universities was accompanied by marked attention to student housing. Affiliated with the *Deutsche Studentenwerk* (German Student Association), the Bonn organization involved in planning or supporting university accommodations, residential and program facilities were built that bore the distinguishing characteristics of international houses. These included *Vereinigung für internationale Studentenarbeit*, Berlin-Charlottenburg (1947), with lodging for 100 non-German and 150 German students; *Christian-Albrecht-Haus*, Kiel (1951), for 85 residents; and *Internationales Haus*, Würzburg (1958), for 151 students. University-affiliated houses included *Vereinigung Studentenwohnheime am Klausenpfad*, Heidelberg (1960), for 200 students; and the *Haus Welt-Club*, Kiel (1952), founded by Professor and Mrs. Fritz Baade, with lodging for 129 students (Edmonds, 1971, pp. 121–122; Chrysostom, 1960, pp. 9–20).

At the University of Hamburg, *Europa-Kolleg* (College of Europe) was founded in 1955 as a special residential college for ninety-two students designed to promote among students of various disciplines a particular interest in European problems. The college's objectives were to overcome nationalism and parochialism through research, study, and discussion and to encourage mutual respect and understanding among the residents (Jenkins, 1961, p. 2; Chrysostom, 1960, pp. 11–12).

At Göttingen, Olva Brennhovd, a Norwegian pastor and a former concentration camp prisoner, founded in 1948 the *Fridtjof*

Nansen Haus. The house was expanded to accommodate 120 students and eventually became a center for all foreign and German students in Göttingen. Partially funded through the central IHA office, its primary sponsor was the *Internationale Studentenfreunde* (International Friends of Students), a private corporation with membership limited to persons who had completed university studies (Brennhovd, 1952; Chrysostom, 1960, pp. 10–11).

New English houses. After World War II, the United Kingdom became a mecca for overseas students. The number of such students jumped from 3000 in 1946 to 55,000 in 1961, with more than half coming from Commonwealth countries. Some were first-degree students with scholarships from their own governments; some undertaking postgraduate studies came under such auspices as the Colombo Plan, the Commonwealth Scholarships Scheme, and the British Council; others were sponsored by international organizations and private benefactors. There were also private students, usually dependent on financial assistance from their families, and "adventurers" with no money and no entrance qualifications (Trevelyan, 1962).

In 1950 the government-affiliated British Council established London hostels for colonial students. With the emergence of new nations from what had been colonial dependencies, the council added three residences, including married students' flats, for students from most of the developing countries at the request of the governments concerned. In addition, a major nonresidential London membership center for all foreign and British students was opened in 1963. Outside London, centers or offices were established in or near all university cities. The Methodist Conference Committee of Overseas Students founded international houses in nine English cities, with each accommodating from 20 to 140 students. In London, as a result of the Lord Mayor's National Thanksgiving Fund, the William Goodenough House was established in 1950 for postgraduate students from the United Kingdom, the Commonwealth and ex-Commonwealth countries, and the United States *(British Council Annual Report,* 1964; Chrysostom, 1960, pp. 25–36).

New houses in the Republic of China, Sweden, and the United States. Elsewhere, the 1940s and 1950s brought small houses to the Republic of China, Sweden, and the United States. The International House of Taipei, established in 1957, consisted of a three-story building with residential accommodations for seventy-seven, a gymnasium-auditorium seating two thousand as a center for cultural and recreational events, visitors' guest rooms, and a sports field. The house attributed its origin to leadership provided by members of the Taipei chapter of the IHA *(International House of Taipei,* n.d.). The International Student House of Lund was founded in Sweden in 1959. Program facilities for students and researchers alike were maintained in four separate but connecting buildings of a contemporary architectural style containing 160 residential rooms. The Lund house functioned during the summer months as a hostel offering an international atmosphere in the tradition of an old university town. The International Student Center of New Haven, Connecticut, was established in 1948 as a private, coeducational residence that accepted married students without children and served as an activities center for several hundred Yale University foreign students and their American friends (Chrysostom, 1960, pp. 58–59).

International centers in North America. International centers sprung up at an even faster pace, especially in North America. They ranged from small student-run organizations, occupying former private dwellings, to institutions employing professional staff, assisted by well-organized volunteer groups, providing extensive on-campus or off-campus activities. A few, such as the large Stephen D. Bechtel International Center of Stanford University, California, founded in 1963, or the International Student Center at the University of Toronto, Canada, established in 1960, included foreign student advising among their numerous services and therefore constituted campus international student offices. Others, such as the Minnesota International Center at the University of Minnesota, Minneapolis, founded in 1953; the Foundation for International Understanding Through Students at the University of Washington, Seattle, founded in 1948; or the International Student Center at the University of California, Los Angeles, founded in 1961, were privately owned but affiliated institutions. Such affiliated relationships could include voluntary contributions of time and funds, university funding, rental of university space, or a special contract for services rendered, together with active, annual fund raising by a center's board of governors. Some centers were entirely independent of any university or college, such as the Foreign Student Service Council of Greater Washington, D.C., founded in 1956, which counseled and presented activities on behalf of students in the District of Columbia as well as those visiting from other cities or countries.

A new Canadian center, the International House at the University of British Columbia in Vancouver, was dedicated on March 4, 1959. Established principally with funds raised by Vancouver Rotary International, it was situated on land provided by the university. Local IHA chapter members and Herrick Young, IHA executive director, gave active encouragement to the project in its formative stages, and an international students' club provided the nucleus for membership. Eleanor Roosevelt, a familiar figure at the New York house events, spoke at the dedication. Modest in size and without residential accommodations, the center developed a substantial program of university and community interaction.

"Villa Jones," Mexico City. Unique among centers was the proprietary institution known as "Villa Jones," founded in Mexico City. Small, nonprofit, and administered by Robert Cuba Jones and Ingeborg H. Jones, the center was devoted to promoting cultural, economic, and social exchange between Latin America and other countries, especially between Mexico and the United States. Although limited accommodations were available for short-term guests, the principal membership included three hundred contributing participants of various countries and fifteen hundred annual visitors. Its program emphasized communication among scholars in the field of Latin American studies; the bringing together of professional people and other visiting specialists with their Mexican counterparts; the operation of a research library; foreign student counseling; workshops, lectures, discussions, and social events; a Spanish-English cultural group; adult education activities; and special programs designed to emphasize the needs of those living in isolated rural areas and underprivileged zones of Mexico (Chrysostom, 1960, pp. 22–23).

New Models of International Houses

By the 1950s and 1960s, several international houses had been established along lines that were quite different from the original models.

The International House of Japan. The International House of Japan, Tokyo, a private, nongovernmental organization, owed its origin to the vision and energy of Shigeharu Matsumoto, founder and managing director; to a preparatory committee of Japanese and American intellectuals, led initially by Aisuke Kabayama; to the encouragement of John D. Rockefeller 3rd; to the Rockefeller Foundation; and to the gifts of five thousand individuals and seven thousand Japanese corporations.

Emphasizing intellectual interchange, especially about the Pacific world, the International House of Japan provided substantial library resources, meeting facilities, and working space for visiting scholars. The house sponsored lectures and discussions on foreign relations, Japanese studies, and current topics; rendered assistance to academic visitors; cooperated with organizations and projects whose aims were similar to those of the house; and provided meeting facilities for conferences. Distinguished visitors and intellectual interchange programs brought to the house renowned scholars and professionals of many countries, and their lectures or the proceedings of meetings were often published. In 1976 the house with its adjacent garden reopened in new, enlarged quarters *(International House of Japan,* 1957; Braisted, 1975, pp. 23–24).

The India International Center. The India International Center, New Delhi, grew out of a conversation in 1958 between Sarvepalli Radhakrishnan, former president of India, and John D. Rockefeller 3rd. With the encouragement of the government of India, the work of a small organizing committee, and the financial help of the Rockefeller Foundation, the cornerstone of the center's buildings was laid on November 30, 1960, by the Crown Prince of Japan. Universities and selected centers of higher learning joined as corporate founding members, making substantial contributions to its establishment. By the 1970s the center had over 1300 individual and corporate members drawn from India and other countries.

Like its Japanese counterpart, The India International Center maintained a reference library, and sponsored seminars, panel discussions, lectures, and question hours on contemporary issues. It maintained a council for cultural studies, undertaking study courses, conferences, exhibitions, bibliographic projects, information services, and research. The center consisted of a complex of closely integrated buildings overlooking Lodi Garden, including an auditorium, meeting and dining rooms, and a residential wing with forty single and twelve double rooms plus two "fellows flats."

International houses in Australia and New Zealand. The 1960s and 1970s brought no diminution of activity in the movement. Six international houses, after evolving

gradually and autonomously out of local committees of planning and organization, appeared in rapid succession at Australian universities: University of Melbourne (1958); University of Queensland (1965); University of Sydney (1967); University of New South Wales (1968); University of Wollongong, New South Wales (1972); and West Australian Institute of Technology, near Perth (1976).

The speed with which the new houses were established paralleled the dramatic development of university and secondary education in Australia. The postwar boom in Australian student numbers, accompanied by the first appreciable influx of overseas students, chiefly Asian but from other countries as well, altered the composition of university populations. The Commonwealth government, active in the field of tertiary education both administratively and financially, made it clear "that the position and expansion of residential colleges at universities should come within the terms of reference of Commonwealth educational activities and instrumentalities. However, Commonwealth assistance for the establishment of additional residential college accommodation was dependent on, and proportionate to, the efforts of State governments (which retained primary constitutional responsibility for education) and private individuals or groups." The latter provided the opportunity for organizations such as Rotary International to perform a significant role in the founding of international houses (Wicks, 1972, p. 192; Harper, 1955, p. 28).

The Melbourne house paved the way for coordinated community and university efforts of considerable breadth. It was initially the idea of students who, in 1948, sought unsuccessfully to open a hostel for overseas and Australian students at several institutions in the city of Melbourne. In 1950 the students concentrated their attention on the University of Melbourne, and the international house resulted from a seven-year campaign involving public figures, business and professional leaders, service clubs, volunteer women's groups, professors, students, and alumni of American international houses. Financing of the project was achieved through fund-raising events, such as large annual international fairs, and contributions from the Commonwealth government, the state of Victoria, corporations, private donors, and from foreign government sources in Singapore, Malaysia, and Sri Lanka. The original wing of the building was named for a principal campaign leader, Ian Clunies Ross (Harper, 1955, pp. 29–31).

Members of local chapters of Rotary International played a prominent role in the development of each of the succeeding houses. Individual Rotarians led efforts to establish the Brisbane house, and were successful in raising $400,000 toward the building of two international houses in Sydney at the Universities of Sydney and New South Wales. Rotarians also were instrumental in obtaining substantial contributions from the state governments and Commonwealth sources.

In keeping with the traditional national pattern, the majority of the Australian international houses were institutions of the collegiate type. A form of the tutorial system was maintained, chiefly as a means whereby undergraduate students were guided and assisted in their studies by senior students. The University of Sydney house, however, was not a college. It alone employed a program director and devoted much attention to programing for community residents (Wicks, 1972, pp. 191–197). Unlike the older church colleges of Australian university campuses, the houses were likely to include both undergraduate and graduate students, but the two Sydney houses were predominantly graduate.

Except for the Perth house, planned initially to accommodate eighty students, house accommodations ranged in size from 120 to 210 persons. All of the houses were coeducational, Melbourne having opened a women's wing to accommodate ninety students in 1972. Programs typical of most of the Australian houses included an an-

nual ball, barbecues, dances, sports, private parties; discussions, lectures, and seminars on current topics; and events to increase the awareness and appreciation of the cultural variety of residents. Philosophies differed somewhat from house to house but generally they were noted for their informality.

Colombo Plan participation and Commonwealth scholarship programs also brought postwar influxes of sponsored and private students, chiefly from Asian and Pacific areas, to New Zealand. Because demand exceeded capacity, specified numbers of spaces were guaranteed for Colombo Plan students at some university and college halls of residence. At Massey University, Manawatu, Colombo Hall was opened in 1964 as part of the Colombo Plan aid program, but accommodation was neither compulsory nor limited to Colombo Plan participants. At Lincoln University College, Christchurch, there was an identically named hall of residence. At the University of Auckland, International House was founded in 1968. The house, which became coeducational in 1971, accommodated 158 undergraduates, half foreign and half from New Zealand, in double rooms. Other halls of residence especially noted for accommodating both overseas and New Zealand students included Warwick House at the University of Canterbury, Christchurch, and Arana Hall at the University of Otago, Dunedin (Kong, 1974).

International houses in Asia. The International Center of the University of the Philippines, Quezon City, opened in May of 1966. A circular building consisting principally of a central lounge, meeting hall, and cafeteria, the center maintained adjacent dormitory accommodations for ninety-six men and women. Planned to include both Filipinos and foreign students, a majority of the residents came from countries of the Pacific and Asia.

Following independence, the government of India participated in international student exchange programs and instituted scholarships under the Colombo and other plans. The Indian Council for Cultural Relations (ICCR) supervised these plans and, in the 1960s, assisted with the opening of international student hostels in Delhi, Bombay, Calcutta, and Madras. Social gatherings and other functions were organized at these hostels to enable foreign students to know Indian students and families. The largest hostel was International Students House, University of Delhi, which opened on July 1, 1964, and was managed by a committee that included the university vice-chancellor and representation from ICCR. The house provided accommodation and dining for ninety-six male students, most of whom came from Fiji, Mauritius, Southeast Asia, East Africa, the Middle East, and Europe *(Indian Council for Cultural Relations*, n.d.; National Council of Y.M.C.A.'s of India, 1963).

International Students House of London. In 1965 International Students House (ISH), soon to become one of the large houses, opened in London, in Park Crescent near Regents Park. Equipped initially with facilities for up to 2000 nonresident members and living accommodation for 134 students, ISH expanded in 1971 to accommodate 305 single men and women and added 42 furnished flats for married couples. Ten of the flats were allotted to students with children, resulting in a total residential accommodation of 412.

International Students House was founded by International Students Trust, a nonprofit private company, registered as an educational charity and with a council of twenty-five governors. The house was the product of leading London residents who developed financing for it from individuals, companies, charitable foundations, and government grants. The total capital investment amounted to just over £1,600,000.

International Students House was the brainchild of Mary Trevelyan, who, prior to serving as the first director, had been assistant warden at Student Movement House, London, in the 1930s. In 1950 she

had become Britain's first university foreign student adviser, and was the founder of the well-known Goats Club. The latter, an institution with immediate and lasting success, had helped to bring together students from all countries studying in the various colleges, schools, and institutes of the University of London.

International Students House opened its membership to all students in London and accepted vacation visitors from elsewhere in the United Kingdom or overseas. An information bureau, student advising, and an extensive program of activities, including the Goats Club, were guided by a professional staff. The house included a large assembly hall, game rooms, library, restaurant, club room, coffee room, television room, and a licensed bar *(International Students House,* n.d.).

New houses in the United States. In the United States, the only other building to match in size the New York, Berkeley, and Chicago houses was the International House of Philadelphia, dedicated on November 22, 1970. This was an $8,500,000 building with residential accommodation for 450 married and single students. It was financed not only by a $5,000,000 grant from the Haas Community Fund of Philadelphia, and $1,000,000 in gifts from private citizens and local business firms, but also by a loan from the United States Department of Housing and Urban Development—a unique feature for an American house.

Although a new structure, International House of Philadelphia could claim as an institution to be an old, if not the oldest, house. It traced its antecedents to the 1908–1910 home hospitality program established in West Philadelphia, to the fifteen-student Victorian residential house maintained near the University of Pennsylvania campus from 1918 to 1959, and to a borrowed former "center city" hotel where, beginning in 1959, more than one hundred residents had been accommodated *(Guide to International House of Philadelphia,* 1974).

Residents at the new Philadelphia house

were principally graduate students, but there were also postdoctoral visiting scholars, postgraduate business and professional trainees (nonuniversity), and a limited number of undergraduates. Students and scholars could be affiliated with any accredited institution in the Delaware Valley, but a majority attended the University of Pennsylvania campus, which was adjacent to the house.

Contemporary in style, the living quarters at Philadelphia were unique in several ways. There was accommodation for married students; above those accommodations the building was divided into eight "houses." Each consisted of four suites of ten single and double bedrooms. Every "house" and every suite contained a community lounge. On the lower floors were an auditorium, dining commons, game and hobby rooms, library, discotheque, coffee house, gift and thrift shops, a large lobby, and other program facilities.

In 1972 a small coeducational international house opened at the University of Arizona, Tucson. The house accommodated fifty students for a limited length of residence (to twelve months). It was directed by a full-time student appointed by the university foreign student adviser and was self-supporting.

International student residences adapted other forms in the United States. At Georgetown University in Washington, D.C., and at the University of North Carolina, Chapel Hill, dormitories under the management of the universities were converted in 1967 into student-run units of ninety and sixty rooms, respectively. At the University of Michigan in Ann Arbor, the Ecumenical Campus Center, a residential "community" of sixty-five students from twenty countries, was formed in 1965 from the merger of several campus ministries. At the State University of New York at Albany, a dormitory built in 1940 was converted in 1972, under the leadership of the campus international student office, into Sayles International House for 114 foreign and American residents.

The 1960s and 1970s brought increasing instances of student-initiated efforts to establish international houses or centers. Competing needs and priorities on campuses, undeveloped funding sources, and the widely held view that such nonacademic facilities must be self-supporting were often powerful deterrents to success. A conspicuous example of student achievement was the international center founded in 1970 at the University of New Mexico, Albuquerque. Student sponsored and student financed through the campus international club and the university's general student organization, and essentially student governed, the international center consisted of a converted university-owned former faculty home with added multipurpose facilities. Community contributions of time, money, and equipment strengthened the center's development as a campus international focal point (Slavin and Carroll, 1972).

Reevaluating the International House Movement

In 1960 Nikitas Chrysostom, editor of the directory of the International House Association, noting that hundreds of thousands of young men and women were pursuing university studies in foreign countries, stated: "This phenomenon is of major historical significance . . . its thrust toward international understanding and raising standards of world civilization is enhanced by the contributions of International Houses and International Student Centers. These institutions provide not only services essential for living but also—and this is their basic *raison d'être*—programs which create conditions and relations conducive to eliciting students' creative potentialities, and to the advancement of meaningful human communication and cooperation; they expose students and the citizens of host countries to the wealth the world's cultures have to offer one another. This is the International House idea" (Chrysostom, 1960, "Introduction").

The statement continues to be valid.

Practical factors of cost and financing, especially in times of marked inflation or deflation, have sometimes caused serious questioning: whether, for example, an international house or center can justify its existence in the face of rising costs of operation; whether, while seeking to maintain reasonable fees for its residents and members, it can remain unique among halls of residence; and whether its role is less meaningful than formerly. Management studies have been undertaken; surveys and inquiries have been made to assess value and relevance. The results of such inquiries have been directed at the reorganization of resources and services and not at the refutation of the idea.

Throughout the course of the movement there has been a distinct sense of reality about results. "The idea . . . is not the sole key to international understanding," wrote Robert Gordon Sproul (1937, p. 3), "nor its contribution so great that the attitude of men will be revolutionized overnight. . . . It rests upon a principle which cannot be controverted, namely, that the similarities between races and nations are always greater than their differences; and through the encouragement of intercourse on some basis other than barter and trade, this fact can be impressed upon individuals and public consciousness." Sproul emphasized that the value of the idea depends on how much participants profit from their opportunities, the degree of their willingness to persevere and strengthen ties that have been established, and to what extent they are successful in developing broader attitudes both in themselves and in their associates.

Bibliography

Bishop, M. *A History of Cornell.* Ithaca, New York: Cornell University Press, 1962.

Blaisdell, A. C. *Foreign Students and the Berkeley International House, 1928–1961.* (Interview conducted by Joann Dietz Ariff.) Berkeley: University of California, Regional Oral History Office, Bancroft Library, 1967.

Braisted, P. J. "Transcultural Cooperation: The Years Ahead." *Exchange,* 1975, *11*(Summer), 20–24, 44–45.

Brennhovd, O. "Fridtjof Nansen House." *International House Quarterly,* 1952, *16*(Spring), 170–172.

British Council Annual Report: 1963–1964. London: British Council, 1964.

Chrysostom, N. (Ed.) *International Houses and Centers: Directory.* New York: International House Association, 1960.

Edmonds, H. *The Founding of the International House Movement.* (Interview conducted by Elizabeth Mezirow.) Berkeley: University of California, Regional Oral History Office, Bancroft Library, 1971.

Guide to International House of Philadelphia. Philadelphia: International House of Philadelphia, 1974.

Haines, R. "Cosmopolitan Clubs." *International House Quarterly,* 1951, *15*, 243–246.

Harper, N. D. "Under One Roof in Melbourne." *International House Quarterly,* 1955, *19*(Spring), 28–31.

Indian Council for Cultural Relations, Proceedings and Reports, 1963–1964. New Delhi: Indian Council, n.d.

International House of Japan: A Center for Cultural Exchange. Tokyo: Kasai, 1957.

International House of Taipei, Annual Reports, 1961–1968. Taipei, Republic of China: International House of Taipei, n.d.

International Students House: The First Ten Years, 1965–1975. London: International Students House, n.d.

Jenkins, H. M. *Report of the First World Conference of International Houses and Centers.* Washington, D.C.: National Association for Foreign Student Affairs, 1961.

Johnston, L. "Washington International Student House." *International House Quarterly,* 1949, *13*(Summer), 153–156.

Kong, N. H. (Ed.) *Overseas Students Handbook.* Wellington: New Zealand University Students' Association, 1974.

National Council of Y.M.C.A.'s of India: Committee on International Student Service. *Consultation on the Welfare of Students from Abroad.* New Delhi: National Council, 1963.

Nohrnberg, A. "Historically Speaking." *International House Quarterly,* 1948, *12*(Winter), 9–12.

"Putting Snowflakes Together: International House Moves Toward Bigger Goals and a New Building." *Today: The Philadelphia Inquirer Magazine,* September 1965, pp. 6–7.

Slavin, G. W., and Carroll, P. W. "The Students Act: New International Center UNM." *Exchange,* 1972, *8*(Fall), 70–74.

Sproul, R. G. "Forward to the International Quarterly." *International Quarterly,* 1937, *1*(Autumn), 13–15.

Trevelyan, M. *From the Ends of the Earth.* London: Faber & Faber, 1942.

Trevelyan, M. "The Welfare of Overseas Commonwealth Students in the United Kingdom." *Journal of the Royal Society of Arts,* April 1962, pp. 333–344.

Wicks, P. "International Houses." In S. Bochner and P. Wicks (Eds.), *Overseas Students in Australia.* Sydney: New South Wales University Press, 1972.

Young, H. B., and others. *International Houses and International Student Centers in the United States.* New York: National Association of Foreign Student Advisers, 1953.

W. SHERIDAN WARRICK

10. CAMPUS INTERNATIONAL OFFICES

A plethora of academic and administrative programs and services operate under the egis of the term *international office.* A directory of such offices on campuses in the United States and Canada reveals a number of variations on this title, including offices of international affairs or international programs, centers or institutes for international education or international studies, foreign student programs, or study abroad (World Studies Data Bank, Academy for Educational Development, Inc., 1971). Determining the functons of such offices from their titles is complicated by the fact that the functions of an office of international affairs on one campus may be those of a foreign student office on another. On still other campuses such offices may be devoted to academic research and have nothing at all to do with the visa status of foreign nationals. Finally, there are also occasions in which an international office is the coordinating agent for a number of internationally oriented campus activities.

Despite variations in titles, eight types of offices appear most common. Four are primarily concerned with students: those responsible for the legal status of foreign nationals on campus; those serving the intensive language needs of foreign students; those whose primary function is the provision of social services for international students; and those concerned with the placement of a college's or university's own students in study-abroad programs, exchange programs, or international work experience.

Two other common types of international offices focus on faculty activities: these include programs of interinstitutional cooperation, technical assistance, and faculty exchange; and international studies or research in international or comparative education curriculum development, area studies, or the internationalization of core curricula subject matter.

The final two most common areas of international office involvement concern international university development and public relations. Development activities include the recruitment of foreign students; the cultivation of foreign alumni (whether a university's own students living or working abroad or foreign nationals who have returned home); or, in those instances in which an institution's overseas involvement is sufficiently extensive to warrant it, the solicitation of funds from international agencies, multinational companies, or foundations having global interests. Finally, in most large universities, there is an office responsible for the arrangement of on-campus appointments for overseas short-term visitors—college presidents, ministers of education, or other government officials—interested in studying a country's educational system.

The professional training of the staff in each of these offices varies in accordance with the nature of the responsibilities. But it is also true that a staff member's professional background and experience often influence the nature of the programs undertaken. International activities, perhaps more than any other segment of university life, are inclined to be shaped by the personal interests, contacts, or experiences of the faculty and staff concerned.

International Student Office

The primary function of an international student office (ISO), the director of which is often called the foreign student adviser, is that of advising aliens on campus of the regulations governing their status in a foreign country and of warning them when their status or actions are in violation of such regulations. These regulations include both those of the host government and those of the institution at which the alien is studying or teaching. Most counseling, therefore, is of a legal nature, having to do with such matters as visas, alien registration, travel permits, employment, extension of stay, taxation, and university regulations governing registration and payment of tuition.

The office has a responsibility to the government immigration, labor, and revenue authorities to maintain accurate records on the status of all aliens on campus and to notify the authorities when an alien fails to honor the obligations under which he was granted his visa. In order to do this, ISO staff mu t be familiar with the terms and conditions governing the numerous types of visas by which aliens may enter or remain in a country. In addition, such offices usually keep a complete list of all aliens on campus, often recorded by college and by country of origin. Most offices maintain a curriculum vitae on each student, research scholar, or exchange teacher, indicating current address; personal background; previous education; financial status; and, for a student, academic record, including any withdrawals or degrees earned while enrolled. In institutions having a limited number of international students, such record keeping and the advising of foreign students may be the responsibility of the university registrar.

On most campuses foreign students and exchange scholars are required to report to the international student office before registering with their school or college to be certain their immigration papers are in order. Initially, a great deal of personal counseling also is necessary. Newly arrived students and faculty often are in need of assistance in finding such things as housing, winter clothing, local transportation, food stores, banks, and medical services. Some students suffer a cultural shock and even severe homesickness, requiring staff counseling on local customs or religious affairs. These early needs for personal counseling often lead many students to feel a strong affinity to the ISO staff, and they may subsequently take all problems, regardless of their nature, to the ISO. In such instances the office must serve as a liaison between the students and other university academic and administrative offices. Academic counseling, for example, is best done by the department or college concerned, but often a student is hesitant to bring his problem to the attention of a dean or a member of the teaching faculty. It then becomes the responsibility of the ISO staff to encourage the student to do so.

To assist other divisions of the university in admitting, counseling, or employing alien students or faculty, the ISO makes a continuous effort to keep all parties apprised of changes in government regulations that may affect a student's or scholar's status and, whenever possible, to provide information regarding foreign universities and degree equivalences.

Since the mid 1960s personal counseling has been extended to a large number of dependents who now accompany foreign students and scholars traveling and studying abroad. The needs of these dependents often are quite different from those they accompany; most require programs designed to improve language skills and social outlets to offset loneliness and to help such persons adjust to a foreign culture. At some universities these needs are met by the foreign student adviser and members of his staff, but at large institutions separate offices or voluntary associations have been created specifically for these purposes.

Office of Intensive Language Instruction

During the 1960s intensive language instruction for aliens and their dependents became a necessity on many campuses. In the United States and Great Britain, for example, the necessity for English language instruction has been greatly increased by the large number of students being sent to these countries by members of the Organization of Petroleum Exporting Countries (OPEC). Many of these OPEC students have had little if any training in the English language, and most have language skills far below the level needed to pursue a full academic program.

In the United States regional centers for English as a second language have been established throughout the country. The services of these centers are available to students at all academic institutions in the immediate area. The first of these English Language Service (ELS) Centers began operations in Washington, D. C., in 1961. In 1976 nineteen such centers were operating on or near colleges or business centers throughout the United States. Programs consist of four-week sessions, which are conducted at several levels of language proficiency. Students may enroll for as many sessions as they find necessary to enable them to undertake collegiate study in the English language. ELS programs also include academic counseling and cultural orientation.

Government sponsors of foreign students often prefer that students receive their academic training at the same school offering an intensive language program. For this reason, in the mid 1970s many colleges and universities began to develop language programs of their own.

College-based programs are usually conducted in one of two ways. In some instances, noncredit remedial English courses are offered under the auspices of an institution's department of English. In addition, there are sometimes intermediate-level English courses for foreign students, for which academic credit is granted. More often than not, however, foreign student language programs are administered by an international student office or a special branch thereof, established for this specific purpose. Some programs supplement formal language instruction with informal conversational practice periods and cultural orientation sessions conducted by

student and faculty volunteers. Some programs limit their services to the university's own students; others open their classes to members of the international community at large. Students enrolled full time in a university normally do not pay an additional stipend for participation in an intensive language program; all others may be charged a fee, but such fees usually entitle the students to additional campus privileges as well.

On those campuses where foreign student enrollments are small, students, faculty, or faculty wives often volunteer to teach language classes for foreign students and their dependents. Many foreign wives have so little proficiency in the language needed that simple tasks such as shopping for food are exceedingly difficult.

Office of Social Services

The academic community has long had an excellent reputation for welcoming foreign scholars into campus social life. International teas or suppers that bring together the students and faculty of all nations have been offered by college fraternities and sororities, religious groups, deans of students, and foreign student advisers for nearly a century. Officially organized "host family" or "brother-sister" programs that seek to draw foreign students into the home life of the host country also are established college traditions; so, too, are the various nationality clubs, which enable students and faculty of a particular geographical region or cultural heritage to socialize together.

On some campuses social functions are the responsibility of the international student office. At other schools such functions are carried out by student service organizations, faculty wives, or community-based agencies. At a few universities having a large international clientele, the coordination of international social services and activities is the responsibility of a separate office created to meet this need. Occasionally, universities have collaborated with private organizations in the establishment of separate social or residential facilities, frequently known as international houses.

The nature and extent of the services provided depend in part on the physical location of the university. At large, urban-based universities, it is not uncommon for these services to include day care centers, furniture pools, clothing pools, charter air flights, sight-seeing trips, home hospitality (especially during holiday seasons), field trips, cooking classes, orientation programs, and the publication of special orientation literature.

Occasionally the work of the campus office is supplemented by community organizations or city-wide student organizations. The Foreign Student Service Council of Greater Washington, located in Washington, D.C., supplements the programs of college campuses by providing special seminars, sight-seeing tours, home hospitality, and other services for foreign students in the Washington area. For nearly thirty years, another organization, the International Student Association in Cambridge, Massachusetts, provided social services to thousands of students in the Greater Boston area. Unfortunately, the association found it economically impossible to continue operations in 1972 and the popular gathering place on Garden Street was closed. Other such organizations include the Minnesota International Center in Minneapolis; the International Center in New York, Inc.; and the International Hospitality Center of the Bay Area, Inc., in San Francisco (National Council for Community Services to International Visitors, 1973).

Another type of social service, travel information, has been provided to students and faculty of all nations since 1947 by the Council on International Educational Exchange (CIEE). Headquartered in New York, the CIEE also maintains offices in San Jose and Los Angeles, California; in Tokyo; and in Paris. Social service offices on CIEE member campuses maintain files of the council's extensive literature, such as *The 1976 Student Travel Catalog* of charter flights and other services provided for United States and foreign students.

Office of Overseas Academic Programs

Study abroad, international exchange, or international work-experience programs are the focus of a fourth type of international office, frequently termed the office of international education or overseas academic programs.

In 1976 the Institute for International Education (IIE), a private organization that administers study-abroad programs for many colleges and universities, published individual listings of nearly 1000 academic-year and summer-study programs sponsored by 570 American colleges and universities (Cohen, 1975a, b). Most such programs are individually operated by the sponsoring academic institution, with the help of agencies such as the IIE, but a growing number of programs are being administered by consortia established specifically for this purpose. Although United States institutions operate the largest number of study-abroad programs, overseas academic study is a global phenomenon of increasing magnitude. During the 1970s contractual agreements for the exchange of students or the operation of special study-abroad programs were being established with institutions in developing nations as well as with the traditional institutions of European culture that dominated academic year–abroad programs for decades.

The administration of overseas programs, though subject to numerous institutional and governmental regulations, is primarily concerned with program restrictions on those who may participate, the nature of instruction, the procurement of faculty, the question of academic credit for overseas study, arrangements for housing of students abroad, overseas transportation and travel within a country as part of a program of study, and scholarship aid for those academically qualified but financially unable to bear the cost of such a program.

Type of program. Many overseas programs are language oriented, and, although they include opportunities for the study of ancillary cultures, their primary intent is to enhance the student's foreign-language skills. In such instances it is not uncommon for the administration of the program to be centered in a university language department rather than in an institution-wide international office. Similarly, single-focus programs of a professional orientation, such as architecture, hotel and restaurant management, marine biology, or international business, also may be administered by an academic department. A second type of program encompasses a broader sphere of interest, such as music and art or area studies. A third program emphasizes a specific segment of time such as a term or semester in a particular country or city. The forerunner of such time-oriented programs was the Junior Year Abroad concept, which once dominated study abroad but is increasingly being replaced by programs of shorter duration. A fourth pattern is that of the extension of the institution itself into a variety of international settings as, for example, programs in some twenty locations sponsored by Georgetown University, Washington, D. C., such as Georgetown-at-Fribourg, or Georgetown-in-Japan.

Academic credit. Academic credit for study abroad under the egis of a student's own institution is commonplace. Administrative problems arise when students of one institution seek to enroll in the study-abroad programs of another institution and then transfer this credit to their own college or university. This is especially true if one institution operates on the quarter plan, the other on the semester plan, and the foreign institution on a third academic calendar. In addition, some institutions require a minimum grade level for the transfer of credit, but grade equivalences at foreign institutions are often difficult to determine. It is always best if the student

and the international office staff explore these problems in advance of the student's departure in order to avoid problems or misunderstandings when the student returns home.

Student housing. Most institutions operating overseas programs assume responsibility for housing students abroad and many lease or buy residences specifically for students enrolled in their overseas programs. A few make contractual arrangements with a cooperating foreign institution for dormitories or other types of student accommodations. Arrangements are often made for students to live with local families, but the word *families* may be loosely interpreted to mean anything from a single household renting out a room for additional income to landladies offering accommodations in the manner of a boarding house. Some students prefer to seek their own accommodations, and this, too, is often permitted.

Transportation and travel. With the exception of short-duration programs, such as semester-abroad or summer-abroad programs, most international offices do not assume responsibility for transporting students to their overseas destinations. Many colleges, however, make use of organizations such as the Council on International Educational Exchange, which offers numerous opportunities for inexpensive student travel. Short-term programs, however, almost always include travel within a country or among several countries as part of the curriculum, and thus travel arrangements become the responsibility of the sponsoring institution. In such instances the cost of the program usually includes the cost of getting there and of touring the area afterward. Such programs are "tours" in the usual sense of the word, but with the enhanced value of having a specific academic focus to their activities and faculty members as tour guides.

Exchange programs. The administration of bilateral student exchange programs between specific institutions is in many ways similar to, but in some ways less complex than the administration of study-abroad programs. More often than not, exchange programs involve a small number of students for whom special courses are not necessary; special faculty needs are confined to matters of academic or cultural counseling. It is perhaps owing to the simplicity of such programs that many institutions interested in international involvement have elected to engage in a limited number of direct exchange programs rather than attempt the more complex aspects of administering a study-abroad program.

Some observers have suggested that the exchange movement could be enhanced if United States colleges operating unilateral summer study-abroad programs would invite overseas host institutions to establish similar programs on United States campuses, with the Americans offering tuition scholarships or waivers for overseas students and the overseas institutions granting academic credit for work at a United States college or university. Two factors have deterred such developments, however: financial aid for foreign students has been declining in the face of inflationary economies; and many foreign institutions remain unwilling to grant academic credit for work outside their country. In addition, European restrictions on foreign student enrollments, housing shortages in academic communities, and inadequate student language skills continue to hamper two-way exchange programs at the undergraduate level.

International work experience. Since World War II international offices have been instrumental in assisting students seeking overseas work experience related to their academic fields of study. For some—students of a foreign language, for example—a period of work abroad is often a degree requirement. For others, who prefer to learn by doing, international work experience, however menial the labor, may be viewed as an alternate form of study abroad.

In the United States, Canada, and Great Britain, the extensive development of cooperative education or "sandwich plan" programs, in which students alternate classroom and work experience, has led in the 1970s to attempts to establish work-exchange opportunities for students enrolled in such programs. Similar bilateral work-exchange programs also have been developed with institutions in France and the Federal Republic of Germany, where practical work experience in technical fields also may be a degree requirement.

The administrative complexities of international labor laws, work permits, income tax, national insurance, and visa restrictions, and the changing pattern of the employment market are such that most campus international offices elect to assist their work-oriented students through the offices of national and international agencies, such as the International Association for the Exchange of Students for Technical Experience, with operations in forty-three member countries. The exceptions are institutions such as Northeastern University in Boston, which, as the world's largest cooperative education institution, operates and administers its own work-exchange programs in England, France, and the Federal Republic of Germany through its College Venture Program, a division of the university's Institute for Off-Campus Experience and Cooperative Education.

Office of Interinstitutional Cooperation and Faculty Exchange

International exchange has had its greatest success at the graduate level and in the area of faculty exchange and technical assistance programs. Such programs are designed to enhance faculty development through teaching and research experiences abroad, to offer technical assistance to new institutions in developing nations, and to promote joint research between teams of international scientists.

Much of the impetus for the development of these programs has come from the financial assistance afforded international scholars by the Fulbright-Hays Act and the subsequent programs of the Fulbright Commission. Further financial impetus has come from national government agencies, private foundations, and international organizations.

Since the 1960s a number of interinstitutional programs of faculty exchange have evolved, based on bilateral or multilateral institutional agreements. Technical assistance contracts between two institutions, such as programs funded by Agency for International Development (AID), are often administered on behalf of the university by the office for interinstitutional cooperation.

The role of a university international office in this context is that of liaison between the university and the various agencies or sister institutions sharing the administration of these programs. In this capacity the international office staff may be asked to help faculty to learn of the various exchange options available and to screen those candidates who then apply for international teaching and research fellowships. The responsibilities of the director may include the handling of negotiations between parties—faculty and representatives of foreign institutions—interested in establishing and subsequently in maintaining bilateral or multilateral exchange agreements. In addition, the director of the office usually is expected to represent the university's international interests on a variety of internal and external policy-making committees. As a result of decisions made in such committees, the director may also assume the responsibility of developing new programs or exchange options in behalf of his institution.

Office of International Studies and Research

International studies, area studies, international education, or comparative education programs, or, on rare occasions, centers for the internationalization of existing curricula constitute a sixth type of campus international office. As such programs are primarily academic, they generally are administered by the office of a provost or other chief academic officer.

Often the director of the program has faculty status and may teach a course in the program. As degree- or research-oriented entities, such offices maintain some liaison with offices for academic programs abroad, exchange programs, technical assistance programs, or international programs conducted by means of interinstitutional cooperation. They may, however, have little cause to interact with international student offices or offices concerned with short-term visitors.

During the 1950s and 1960s, area studies programs throughout the world developed in great numbers, but their impact was minimal. By the 1970s comparative international studies were still a relatively small part of the higher education curriculum. Membership in organizations such as the Comparative and International Education Society in the United States, and its international counterparts in Australia, Canada, Japan, the Republic of Korea, and a few European countries, reflects the limited number of scholars interested in global perspectives. In the United States the decline of financial support for international programs in the wake of pressing domestic needs contributed to the somewhat stunted growth of these programs. Some recent directives should help to spur faculty interest in the development of international studies and research. For example, the 1974 report of the Swedish Committee for Internationalizing University Education, issued under the auspices of the Office of the Chancellor of the Swedish Universities, calls for the internationalization of the Swedish higher education curriculum. The 1975 decree by the American Assembly of Collegiate Schools of Business, urges the internationalization of the undergraduate business curriculum. As interest grows, offices for academic study abroad, faculty exchange programs, and international studies will be forced to a new level of interaction; however, the general lack of funding for such programs will necessitate a high level of creativity and efficiency in programing. Directors of such offices will need to devote considerable time and energy to developing coordinated programs that draw upon and consolidate an institution's fragmented international resources and staff. Interdisciplinary studies and an interdisciplinary appeal for funding may be the only ways in which smaller institutions will be able to afford what some faculty and administrators consider the "luxury" of comparative education programs.

Offices of International Alumni Affairs and Development

The influx of foreign students from developing nations and, in some instances, the availability of petrodollars in support of foreign student enrollments have led an increasing number of colleges and universities to engage in international recruiting. Some institutions undertake such recruiting on their own, disseminating materials abroad through overseas educational information centers and embassies. Others engage in joint recruiting efforts abroad under the auspices of organizations such as the European Council of International Schools or the Caribbean Counselors Association. These organizations, however, recruit only at American dependents' schools in foreign countries and do not recruit foreign students as such. Although student recruitment is the responsibility of admissions offices, assistance can be rendered to admissions recruiters by international office staff knowledgeable about the educational systems, professional teacher associations, and languages of instruction in foreign nations.

The recruitment of overseas students, followed by an institutional commitment to retain such students through selective admissions, orientation programs, intensive language instruction, and special counseling when necessary can result in the development of a large contingent of foreign alumni. The American Alumni Council (which in 1974 merged with the American College Public Relations Association to form the Council for Advancement and

Support of Education—CASE) has developed a number of guidelines for the establishment of international alumni programs. These include alumni clubs sponsoring special programs on behalf of foreign students, sending the alumni magazine to students who have returned home, publishing a special newsletter for international alumni, establishing alumni clubs in foreign cities, organizing alumni meetings in foreign cities when university officials are traveling abroad, sending the college glee club or theater group abroad, and awarding honorary degrees or other special awards to distinguished international alumni (Wichlac, 1974).

There is much that can be done to maintain ties with international alumni through the coordinated efforts of the various university departments and offices involved in international programs. Foreign alumni, in turn, have the potential to serve a college by assisting in the development of study-abroad, travel-abroad, and exchange programs; the recruitment of overseas students; and the hosting of faculty on overseas sabbatical leaves.

When a university has a large commitment to international programs, it may seek financial support for these programs from multinational businesses, foundations, and government agencies. In the United States attempts to secure funding on behalf of an institution are coordinated by a university development office. Within that office, the solicitation of international funding is usually assigned to a particular staff member familiar with the special interests of each business, foundation, or agency. The director of a campus international office generally works closely with the development staff, as he is likely to be among the first to detect shifting international trends or a change of focus within relevant international organizations.

By working closely with admissions, alumni, and university development personnel, the campus international office staff can help to bring about a cogent plan for an institution's international development.

Office of International Visitors

Each year thousands of educators, university officials, government representatives, and professional persons travel abroad to study various aspects of higher education.

The British Council, with headquarters in London and staff in seventy-six countries, assists short-term visitors coming to Britain for study, research, or on-site observation, by arranging their professional appointments and assisting in all travel and accommodation matters.

In the United States such services are provided by a number of agencies, including the Institute of International Education and the Council for International Exchange of Scholars. Many visitors are participants in the International Visitor Program of the Bureau of Educational and Cultural Affairs, United States Department of State. The United States Department of Labor also acts as the programing agent for international visitors traveling under the auspices of the International Labour Office in Geneva, Switzerland.

Some visitors, however, have no agency operating in their behalf and therefore must make their own study-tour itinerary. When such is the case, academic professional societies in the country or countries to be visited are often in a position to give the visitor travel assistance and advice. Often, these societies, through local affiliates, will arrange a complete travel program for the visitor. In the United States such services are provided by groups such as the Committee on Relations with Lawyers of Other Nations of the American Bar Association in Chicago; the American Library Association in Chicago; or the National Council of Teachers of English in Urbana, Illinois.

In the United States there are many organized hospitality programs on college campuses serving the needs of short-term international visitors. Institutions having programs and faculty of international renown frequently find themselves on the itineraries of such guests. In such instances it frequently becomes necessary to establish an office (or at least to assign staff in an existing international office) to serve as program officers responsible for the scheduling of campus appointments on the visitors' behalf.

In large cities community organizations —such as the Center for International Visitors in Greater Boston; the International Visitors Service Council in Washington, D. C.; and the Dallas Committee for Foreign Visitors of the Dallas Council on World Affairs in Texas—serve as a liaison between the Department of State or other agencies and colleges, universities, and businesses. A national organization having a network of such member community agencies, the National Council for Community Services to International Visitors (COSERV) in Washington, D. C., publishes several small pamphlets of benefit to community and campus-based organizations interested in or responsible for professional programing and informal hospitality programs for foreign visitors.

The chief function of the college-based international visitors office is that of planning an efficient schedule of appointments, which enable the visitor to make maximum use of the limited time available to him. Most visitors allow only two or three days in a single locale, despite a list of objectives that would normally require a week to accomplish. Nevertheless, these brief, one-day contacts often provide the impetus for long-term associations and joint international ventures. For this reason their potential can never be underestimated.

Campus-Wide Coordination of International Programing

On many college campuses international programing is a fragmented endeavor in which some offices report to the president, vice-chancellor, or other chief administrative officer, and other offices come under the jurisdiction of the chief academic officer. Often jealousies exist among such offices, with duplication of effort and competition for funding the unfortunate result. It is, therefore, advisable to coordinate all international functions under one administrative head whenever possible. At Michigan State University in East Lansing, for example, international activities are centered in one building under the supervision of a dean of international studies, who reports directly to the president. At Michigan State, these activities include area studies, comparative education, study abroad, educational exchange, visiting professors, and the office of the foreign student adviser. The coordination of all functions under a single administrative unit enables that office to become the campus catalyst for academic planning, institutional linkages, faculty development, and funding, in the area of international education.

In past decades international education has been defined primarily in terms of study abroad or international exchange. In the decades ahead the concept will assume many new dimensions. Ongoing efforts to establish equivalences in degree programs ultimately will lead to reciprocity in the transfer of credits from the institutions of one nation to those of another. Contracts for regional or global research, drawing upon the expertise of faculty from several institutions, will increasingly characterize research programs in social, economic, and environmental problems of international concern. Consequently, there may well emerge large international centers for specific studies to which academics of all nations may have access.

In September 1976 announcement was made of the establishment of a study of international linkages in higher education, sponsored by six major higher education associations representing 3000 higher education institutions in the United States (American Council on Education, 1976). Similar efforts to engage in joint studies are taking place through the Council of Europe, conferences of university rectors, and the embryonic United Nations University. For the campus international office,

the implications are many. The provincialism of past international activities will need to give way to ever broadening horizons of interinstitutional endeavor. Individual campus offices will be responsible for interpreting these new developments to students, faculty, and administrators who do not as yet understand or appreciate the implications of the internationalization of higher education on educational systems and on the professional development of those within them.

Bibliography

American Assembly of Collegiate Schools of Business. *AACSB Accreditation Council Policies, Procedures.* St. Louis, Missouri: American Assembly of Collegiate Schools of Business, 1975.

American Association of State Colleges and Universities. *A Guide: Planning and Funding International Studies.* Washington, D.C.: American Association of State Colleges and Universities, 1976.

American Council on Education. "6 Major Groups Join to Study World Linkages." *International Interaction,* August/September 1976, *4*(1), 5.

Brady, M. W. *Notes for Program Officers in National Agencies.* Washington, D.C.: National Council for Community Services to International Visitors, 1972.

Cohen, G. A. (Ed.) *U.S. College-Sponsored Programs Abroad: Academic Year.* New York: Institute of International Education, 1975a.

Cohen, G. A. (Ed.) *Summer Study Abroad.* New York: Institute of International Education, 1975b.

"COSERV—The First Ten Years of the National Council for Community Services to International Visitors." *International Educational and Cultural EXCHANGE,* 1972, *7*(4), entire issue.

National Council for Community Services to International Visitors. *Handbook for Communities Serving International Visitors.* Washington, D.C.: National Council for Community Services to International Visitors, 1962.

National Council for Community Services to International Visitors. *National Directory of Community Organizations Serving Short-Term International Visitors.* Washington, D.C.: National Council for Community Services to International Visitors, 1973.

The 1976 Student Travel Catalog. New York:

Student Travel Services, Council on International Educational Exchange, 1976.

Perkins, J. A. *International Programs of U.S. Colleges and Universities: Priorities for the Seventies.* New York: International Council for Educational Development, 1971.

Swedish Committee for Internationalizing University Education. *Internationalizing Education.* Stockholm: Office of the Chancellor of the Swedish Universities, 1974.

Wichlac, J. "Thirty-Seven Program Ideas for Foreign Alumni." *Techniques.* American Alumni Council, American College Public Relations Association, October, 1974.

JOY WINKIE VIOLA

EXPANSION AND IMPROVEMENT OF HIGHER EDUCATION (Higher Education Report), Japan

Expansion and Improvement of Higher Education (Tokyo: a report of the Ad Hoc Study Committee for Higher Education) presents recommendations for the expansion and improvement of higher education in Japan. The demand for higher education is expected to expand at least 10 percent by 1985; the committee proposes that planning and policy coordination begin as soon as possible and emphasizes that the expansion should not be concentrated in the big cities, where adequate educational facilities already exist.

The committee envisions an important role for national and public institutions in the proposed expansion. It recommends improvement in vocational education and women's education as well. Large-scale expansion will also be needed in graduate schools. The committee recognizes the importance of private institutions and recommends the formulation of new general institutional and student aid policies in the private sector.

EXPATRIATES' REMUNERATION
See Remuneration: Faculty, Staff, and Chief Executive Officers.

EXPERIENTIAL LEARNING
See Cooperative Education and Off-Campus Experience.

EXPERIMENT IN INTERNATIONAL LIVING, United States

The Experiment in International Living—a private, nonprofit educational institution—began when its founder, Donald Watt, took a group of American students to Switzerland in the summer of 1932. Since that time, the experiment has grown significantly in programs, staff, and alumni. In addition to the United States headquarters (in Brattleboro, Vermont), regional offices are maintained in New York City; Washington, D.C.; Chicago, Illinois; Pensacola, Florida; San Francisco and Los Angeles, California; and Brussels, Belgium. More than fifty autonomous national offices conduct activities in countries throughout the world. About seven thousand persons a year participate in the various programs.

Through these programs the Experiment in International Living tries to develop mutual understanding and respect among people everywhere in the world—regardless of race, creed, or politics—as one means of furthering peace. The association operates on a person-to-person level under the premise that "people learn to live together by living together."

Participants in the programs pay fees, which comprise the largest portion of the institution's income. An annual fund appeal solicits contributions from alumni, parents, host families, and friends. The resulting gift income, totaling a quarter of a million dollars annually, ensures a broad base of participation and keeps a balanced operating budget. The Experiment in International Living receives support from foundations and corporations to initiate and develop new projects until the programs can obtain self-sufficiency.

Summer-abroad programs are designed for students of high school and college age. Each year some 1500 students travel to one of more than thirty countries, 25 percent of them on scholarships sponsored and financed by community and school groups around the nation. Their summer often includes intensive, predeparture language training and always a three- or four-week home stay as a "son" or "daughter" of a family abroad. Academic-study-abroad semesters for high school and college students enroll another four hundred or so Americans, in programs that feature language training, individual research projects, attendance at host country schools or special seminars, and a home stay.

Incoming programs annually bring about three thousand foreign students for home stays in the United States. Some of these students are sponsored by civic and service organizations in about two hundred American communities; others arrive in larger groups organized in their home countries.

Schools' educational excursions are two-week April programs for high school students and their teachers. They are offered in French-, Spanish-, and English-speaking countries and include a week-long home stay and travel.

The School for International Training was founded in 1964 as the formal academic arm of the Experiment in International Living. Located on a 160-acre campus three miles north of Brattleboro, Vermont, the school is recognized by the Vermont State Department of Education as an institution of higher learning and is fully accredited by the New England Association of Schools and Colleges, Inc. The school is eligible for matching gifts programs of some United States corporations.

The school's primary goal is to help students prepare to live, work, travel, or study in another country with high effectiveness and low cross-cultural strain. Close rapport between faculty and students and a low student/faculty ratio take priority over research and outside consultative work. Instructors qualify as specialists in their teaching disciplines yet sometimes have no established professorial ranks. They have direct access to the administration and a strong voice in the creation of programs and policies.

The following programs are noteworthy: (1) A program in international career training offers a Master of International Administration degree to fifty students a year. The students study social relations and development theory, management, cross-cultural issues, and languages for half a year in Vermont, spending the final half in practical internships in the United States or abroad. (2) The world issues program accepts undergraduate juniors and seniors. A Bachelor of International Studies degree is awarded following two years' work in peace studies, environment and ecology, population and family planning, and social and economic development. (3) A Master of Arts in teaching French, Spanish, and/or English as a second language is awarded to about fifty American and foreign graduate students annually. Part of the year's study is done on campus; the remainder is spent in teaching internships in the United States or abroad. (4) About three hundred students a year, representing all continents, take the international students of English curriculum. The curriculum consists of ten weeks of intensive language work and one month with an American family. (5) An international secretaries program prepares students for bilingual secretarial careers. (6) The teacher ambassador and foreign language assistant programs recruit teachers worldwide for one-year assignments in elementary schools, secondary schools, and colleges in about forty American states. (7) The school's department of language education has given instruction in forty-seven languages to more than twelve thousand students in the past decade. Most of these students were participants in the various programs; others were Peace Corps volunteers or adults preparing for business or pleasure trips abroad.

The Experiment in International Living has administered intercultural projects, both domestic and foreign, under contract with various agencies of the United States government. Foreign governments have occasionally provided modest fiscal assistance to organizations of the Experiment in International Living in their respective countries.

Since 1958 the Experiment in International Living has enjoyed consultative status with UNESCO. It is a member of the following organizations: United States National Commission for UNESCO, Society for International Development, Council on International Educational Exchange, National Association for Foreign Student Affairs, National Council for Community Services to International Visitors, Japan Society, American Alumni Council, Association for Innovation in Higher Education, American Council on Education, Association of World Colleges and Universities, and Vermont Higher Education Council.

United States Headquarters
Brattleboro, Vermont 05301 USA

EXTENDED DAY PLAN
See Cooperative Education and Off-Campus Experience: Cooperative Education in the United States.

EXTENSION EDUCATION
See Independent Study.

EXTENSION SERVICES
See Agriculture in Higher Education: Agricultural Research, Extension Services, and Field Stations.

EXTRACURRICULAR ACTIVITIES ON CAMPUS

Extracurricular activities on the campus are generally defined as those out-of-class intellectual, social, cultural, or recreational student activities that are normally given some sort of assistance or recognition short of academic credit by the college or university and are not required for graduation. They are organized around the institution and directed at its students, although other people, such as faculty, staff, families, and townspeople, may participate in them. Together, the activities form the extracurriculum: the range of student pursuits connected with the institution and of institutional programs for students parallel to but separate from the curriculum.

The educational purposes that underlie campus extracurricular activities are accepted in most countries as a significant adjunct to the regularized or required courses of study. Besides education and relaxation, extracurricular activities nurture a sense of collegiality and community participation important to university students. Yet, as long as there has been a curriculum, the extracurriculum has seldom enjoyed the complete confidence of collegiate or any other authorities. The interests and indiscretions of youth, conflicting with the narrow interests of the cleric and the academician, have not always made the campus a completely comfortable home for extracurricular activities. Student activities such as debates, dramatics, music, athletics, politics, and publications often have been in disfavor before eventually becoming incorporated into the curriculum in some form, such as speech, drama, physical education, political science, and journalism. Nonetheless, virtually every new field of knowledge or human interest that is added to the curriculum begins its academic life as an extracurricular activity, and a number of scholars of higher education consider the extracurriculum to be as important an educational program of colleges and universities as the formal curriculum, if not more important.

Measurement of the teaching-learning process, whether in formal academic work or the informal extracurriculum, is far from precise. But among the arguments advanced for the educational value of extracurricular activities are that they develop recreational, intellectual, esthetic, and civic interests; stimulate respect for and ability to work with others; help in establishing friendships; give experience in task completion; provide an opportunity to create and to apply theories studied abstractly in the classroom; and give a healthy balance to curriculum demands as well as an appreciation of the larger community. Issue-oriented groups often gain an international perspective through their work, while service organizations not only aid the community but also broaden student understanding of social problems.

In many countries a significant number of extracurricular activities are discipline-oriented and are essentially an out-of-class extension of the curriculum. As curricula have evolved, they have borrowed extensively from the intellectual and recreational pursuits of students, so that the distinction between curricular and extracurricular interests has sometimes become clouded. In a growing number of universities academic credit is now available for recognized extracurricular activities. This credit is not limited only to quasi-curricular activities, such as playing in the university orchestra or acting in a dramatic production, but may also be extended to volunteer work in the larger community, or to service as a leader in a campus organization or as editor of a student newspaper. Recognition of the educational value of these activities gives substance to the argument that the term *cocurricular* best describes this interrelationship. A later development are the minicourses or courses in free universities in the United States and Canada. These courses provide noncredit instruction in areas of topical interest not available through regular courses of instruction.

It is sometimes asked whether an endeavor can be termed extracurricular if it involves some sort of extrinsic award, such as money, academic credit, scholarship or other grant. Football can scarcely be considered an extracurricular activity for the highly subsidized athlete in the United States. In Britain a student leader may take a paid sabbatical while meeting the demands of office. Students of the performing arts may not consider their performances as extracurricular. It can probably be said that the size of the award may transform an extracurricular activity into a part-time or even full-time vocation, but it remains extracurricular as long as it is neither a required activity for graduation nor a significant source of credit toward graduation.

Similarly, extracurricular activities do not typically refer to the professional management of student service enterprises, as in Scandinavia or other countries where national unions of students provide health insurance (for example, France or Australia), subsidized housing (the Federal Republic of Germany), travel assistance (Great Britain), and other services by paid career professionals. Whether the student newspaper or campus radio station, staffed by students who may be receiving modest stipends or other subvention or academic credit, should be classified as an extracurricular activity, as a service, or as an academic endeavor is a classification to be made locally.

History of Extracurricular Activities

The institutionalization of the medieval university started in both Bologna and Paris with the institutionalization of student housing. In Bologna the student guilds controlled housing and created forms of cooperative housing; in Paris the masters were in charge and solved the housing problem by providing and administering residences.

The clerical background of medieval students freed them from the jurisdiction of civil law, a tradition that extended in some instances for half a millennium. The University of Mexico, for example, was a haven from the police during the troubled 1960s. Thus protected, the medieval student often engaged in brawling, robbery, and worse, and gown and town relations were always strained. Eventually such excesses led to a virtual ban against students in town and fostered the growth of social life in the residential units.

Student life in the 1400s was vigorous. Tavern brawls and burlesques, story telling, feasting, singing, and harlotry as well as disputations and studying occupied much time. Later in Britain bear and bull baiting, card playing, theatricals, and fox hunting preceded the emergence of political clubs. In Germany dueling, fencing, and gymnastics became popular. Student government existed in the student nations and the residence units, which often evolved into colleges. The college movement was particularly strong in England, and both curricular and extracurricular activities at Oxford and Cambridge, for example, developed within the various colleges of the universities.

As higher education became more secular, the student clerics were replaced by aristocrats. In England in the seventeenth century campus life became less barbaric. Clubs emerged, with the political, literary, and debating clubs the most important. Membership was based on congeniality, and the clubs were exclusive. The modern headquarters of many extracurricular activities, the college unions, have their origin in the debate societies of Cambridge, where the union was a coalition of debate organizations that eventually constructed facilities. In the United States the fraternity system evolved from clubs and became an important part of the extracurriculum.

Athletics, the heir of bear baiting, boating, cricket, dueling, and gymnastics became respectable in the early nineteenth century. By mid century in the United States Harvard and Yale had held the first intercollegiate competition—a boat race. The doctrine of a sound mind in a sound body replaced the earlier view that strong muscles and strong intellects were inimical. Out of student interest in sports, physical activities entered the curriculum, just as out of student interest in science, art, literature, and social problems, the experimental sciences, the arts, the modern for-

eign languages, and the social sciences came to receive academic credit. In short, for centuries the extracurriculum has been the forerunner of the curriculum. The clerical heritage of higher education has laid restraints on curriculum makers to which student interests have paid little heed in updating collegiate programs.

Organization of Extracurricular Activities

Extracurricular activities are organized in a variety of ways. Some still follow the independent club or society model, as in middle Europe, while some operate outside the collegiate administrative sphere but with fees collected by the university, as in Scandinavia. The extracurricular activities may be an integral part of the university operation, as in most of the United States, or they may maintain a quasi-independence from the university, as in Canada and the western United States. They may be highly controlled by the institution, as are many musical or dramatic enterprises or intercollegiate athletics, or they may be amorphous, low-key activities that meet the needs of a few students for a few years and which, therefore, require almost no organization. Some pursuits remain popular over the years, while others ebb and flow. A study of these trends can provide valuable insight into the current interests, concerns, and needs of college and university students.

At an annual union conference in Australia in May 1974, six functions of student bodies were delineated. These included: "provision of club-type services, including dining, refreshment, lounge, shower and similar facilities; programming of activities, both social and cultural, either as the prime initiator or by fostering activities of clubs and societies; provision of commercial services, including retail facilities such as shops, or, in some cases, shopping centres; provision of welfare services, sometimes including professional staff, contact services or housing services; provision of sporting facilities; political representation and activity." The first four functions were seen as areas of activity generally regarded as belonging to university unions; the fifth, as more appropriately the concern of sports unions and associations; and the sixth, as the province of student representative councils and staff associations *(Proceedings of Third Annual Conference,* 1974).

The Australian statement not only reflects a common method of organizing the extracurriculum but also suggests how its components can be categorized: club services, social and cultural activities, commercial services, welfare services, sporting facilities, and political activity. The following paragraphs discuss clubs, intramural sports, and political activity. These three categories include an immense range of activities, the extent of which is not always suggested by the title of an activity. Other categories, such as social and cultural activities, including arts and crafts, minicourses, and concerts and lectures, could run to hundreds of subdivisions.

Clubs. Groups and clubs may be devoted to everything from calligraphy, caricature, car rallies, ceramics, equestrianism, fishing and flower arrangement to foreign languages, guitar playing, model railroading, and motorcycling. There are pistol clubs and associations for puppeteering, riflery, science fiction, the tea ceremony, transcendental meditation, wine and ale connoisseurs, and yoga.

Literature, music, and drama are the bases for several associations, as are lectures, debates, and poetry. Musical interests include band, chorus, folk singing, Gilbert and Sullivan, orchestra, pipes and drums, dance, and ballet. There is a wide range of drama activities, such as children's playground theater, dinner theater, experimental drama, koto play, legitimate theater, street theater, and traveling summer drama.

A number of publications are produced on most campuses as an extracurricular group activity. There are poetry annuals, foreign-language newspapers, literary and news magazines, newspapers, and yearbooks. There is also a considerable interest

in film, with film exhibitions and filmmaking groups present in many institutions. Television and radio broadcasting are also done by student groups.

Several extracurricular organizations are issue-oriented, and their work indicates that local issues can reflect international concerns. In South Africa, for example, a student organization works among the "coloured people" of Johannesburg; in Australia there are groups concerned with the rights of the aborigines; in Canada groups work for the indigenous Indians and Eskimo; in the United States the black and Mexican minorities receive much student attention. Other issues addressed on campuses continents removed from each other include imperialism, abortion, prisoners' rights, homosexuality, military conscription, apartheid and racism, amnesty, ecology, and population growth. University groups are often identical in name in many parts of the world: Amnesty International Society, Legalize Marijuana, Whole Earth Society. There is much interest in consumerism, and many minicourses conducted by college unions teach bicycle repair, gardening, cooking, health foods, home building, investments, and similar do-it-yourself subjects. Public Interest Research Groups (PIRG) exist on Australian, Canadian, and United States campuses. Committees, societies, or groups dedicated to local campus issues—academic freedom, civil liberties, more student representation in university governance, curriculum reform, parking—have their counterparts on campus after campus.

Although college students are often characterized as self-centered and career-oriented, the several service enterprises that emerge from the extracurriculum seem to contradict this idea. There is a general concern for the deprived. Tutoring groups are universal. In Britain, SCANUS (Student Community Action National Union of Students) has sponsored volunteer activities that include working with the elderly, vagrants, disadvantaged children, immigrants, drug addicts, the physically disabled, welfare rights staffs, tenant associations, and neighborhood advice centers. In Indonesia the *Kuliah keya nyata* (KKN) volunteers help in rural communities in a number of ways, similar to the United States' VISTA program. A voluntary service builds schools in South Africa. Charity drives or "rags" raise money. Students at Dalhousie University in Nova Scotia sponsor an annual learning disabilities conference. More than two hundred students at Central Michigan University help nearly two thousand handicapped persons to prepare for and compete in the special Olympics for the handicapped. At San Jose State University in California students help the families of prison inmates. In addition, existing peer counseling and hotlines permit students to help each other. Apartment registries assist in overcoming housing shortages. The orientation of new students, including the development of handbooks, is nearly universal, and academic courses and instruction are evaluated by and for students.

Although the involvement of religion and religious organizations in higher education is much diminished, the interest of religious groups in higher education has continued to have an impact on the extracurriculum. The YMCA and YWCA supplanted the prayer bands of the early 1800s and became social organizations with religious overtones. The volunteer movement of Dwight L. Moody recruited students to serve as missionaries. Religious clubs retained an appeal for many students, and religious foundations maintained student headquarters on or near many campuses. In the 1970s a concern for values showed itself in interest in the traditional religions, in values clarification, heightened consciousness, and religious experiences. Transcendental meditation, the interest in Oriental religions in Occidental societies, and such groups as Jews for Jesus suggest the range of such concerns.

Intramural sports. In the category of team sports, extracurricular activities include badminton, baseball, basketball, broomball, cricket, field hockey, football, ice hockey, lacrosse, netball, rugby, soccer, softball, squash, tennis, volleyball, and water polo. Other physical activities include archery, baton twirling, bush walking, canoeing, cross-country, curling, cycling, dancing, diving, fencing, golf, gymnastics, martial arts, mountaineering, orienteering, physical fitness, rowing, skating, skiing, skindiving, skydiving, surfing, swimming, track and field, water skiing, and weight lifting. There are also other outdoor interests, such as aerial navigation, spelunking, and war games, and groups interested in such games as chess and go.

Political activity. Literature and history correctly ascribe a considerable amount of revolutionary zeal to the student movement. This emphasis, however, obscures the fact that students en masse traditionally have not been active. Motonobu Tanaka of Kwansei Gakuin University in Japan notes ruefully that there "only the New Left is active." Participation in student elections is generally low. In the German Democratic Republic most students join the *Freie deutsche Jugend* (Free German Youth) only because such membership is a graduation requirement. Russian students are indifferent to the *Komsomol* (Communist League of Youth). Even in as active an institution as the University of Oslo, only 5 to 10 percent of the students take part in the meetings where representatives are elected. Too often the militant few are taken as the spokesmen for the many.

The term student government is a misnomer. The instances where students really govern themselves—student legislature, student judiciary, student enforcement, and taxation authority—are nearly nonexistent. Student government more usually indicates a measure of student participation in university governance. Some student governments of the 1970s, unhappy with their limited powers, dissolved themselves. However, there is a definite universal thrust, almost always by the unions of students, student councils, senates, or associations, toward greater student participation in the decision-making processes of higher education.

One of the functions of student governments everywhere is the allocation of funds to various extracurricular endeavors. This makes the extracurriculum vulnerable to the manipulations of the few dedicated student politicians, but it also renders the funding process sensitive to the changing needs and desires of the students. The allocation function is hardly ever an exclusive function of student government. Sufficient faculty and/or administrative participation—or veto authority—exists to ensure against political power grabs.

National Student Organizations

A union of students is a common approach to student organization. In some countries national unions of students, an amalgamation of local student unions, represent the concerns of students to government officials and also provide some national and even international services. They are particularly effective in the area of student travel.

National student organizations exist, or have existed, in many countries. There are, for example, the National Union of Students in Great Britain, the *Fédération nationale des étudiants de France* (National Federation of French Students) and the *Union nationale des étudiants de France* (UNEF: National Union of Students in France), the Canadian Union of Students, and the National Union of Australian University Students. In the Federal Republic of Germany the *Verband deutscher Studentschaften* (German National Union of Students) was disbanded in 1975; and a new organization, *Vereinigte deutsche Studentschaften* (United German Student Unions), was formed. There is also another organization, *Arbeitsgemeinschaft deutscher Studentschaften* (Union of German Student Organizations). The student union in the German Democratic Republic is *Freie deutsche Jugend* (Free German Youth). Other student unions include the United States National Student Association, *Sveriges förenade studentkårer* (Swedish National Union of Students), *Zengakuren* (National Federation of Students Self Governing Associations) in Japan, and the *Komsomol* (Communist League of Youth) in the Soviet Union.

The services offered by national student organizations include health and life insurance, health service, inexpensive travel and travel assistance, housing and meals. Fees are often compulsory for all students, as in Great Britain, the Federal Republic of Germany, and Sweden.

In theory these organizations are natural outgrowths of local campus student governments. Their effectiveness varies enormously. In some countries they tend to echo the political philosophy of the state. The strongest national student organizations—in Scandinavia, for example—focus on student services rather than operating as trade or political unions, although recent developments suggest a movement toward more participation in national educational policymaking and in university governance.

Control and Responsibility

The amount of responsibility for extracurricular activities that universities accept varies greatly. In some institutions the provision of a library, classroom space (sometimes widely scattered and in rented quarters), and instructors represents the full extent of the institution's contribution to the student in all matters, curricular or otherwise. At the other extreme is the highly developed residential institution in which residence halls, cafeterias, health services, placement centers, college unions, recreation facilities, performing arts centers, libraries, art galleries, and other facilities are provided and supported by the university. In many instances where the university provides only minimal services, an elaborate network of support for welfare facilities and services has been developed by students. Primary examples are the student towns of Scandinavia, where students, through their unions, operate complexes that include apartment houses, restaurants, bookstores, health centers, music halls, recreation centers, athletic facilities, travel bureaus, ticket offices, barber shops, pharmacies, club rooms, post offices, banks, grocery stores, dry cleaners, shoe repair shops, day care centers, and, at the University of Oslo, even the university press. Students are in the majority on the governing boards of these student towns, and such participation is certainly extracurricular. Students chairing such boards may take sabbatical leaves and receive compensation for their service. However, full-time, well-paid managers are in charge of the actual operations. Student towns generate considerable revenue, some of which comes from summer tourists. The prosperity of such towns is partially due to indulgent socialistic governments, partially to the mandatory student fees, and partially to a society accustomed to cooperative ventures.

Other enterprises that are sometimes part of the university operation, as in the United States, and sometimes operated by unions of students or student governments include advising and counseling, tutoring, insurance, legal aid, orientation of new students, financial aid, and study skills.

With the institutionalization of the university, whether by the Bologna or the Paris pattern, came some institutional control over the activities of students, organized or unorganized. Membership in private clubs or, later, fraternities carried a high degree of freedom. Eventually, however, many educational systems demanded institutional recognition of groups, including the filing of organizational constitutions and lists of offices and adherence to some principles of decorum and fiscal responsibility, in exchange for use of university name, facilities and services, and later, even tax shelters. In the several institutions in which educational possibilities of the extracurriculum were appreciated, student activities offices were established either to enhance these possibilities or to curb excesses, or perhaps both.

Controls are usually shared by the student organizations and the institution and are often more implicit than explicit. Faculty advisers, sometimes required as part of the recognition procedure, exert restraining influences. Often their signatures are required before payment vouchers are honored. It is usually the rule that contracts must be signed by university rather than student officials. In each instance the signatures are usually routine, but nonetheless the controls do exist.

Publications boards, consisting of students, faculty, and administrators, often oversee newspapers and yearbooks, humor magazines, and literary publications. Similar joint trusteeships supervise athletics and student government operations and programs; sometimes these trusteeships are incorporated separately from the institution. Use of the collegiate umbrella, whether it be facilities, funding, collection of fees, or merely the name, is almost certain to involve some institutional control. The larger, more costly, and more visible the activity, the more formal the control is likely to be.

Funding

When higher education meant private education, much of the extracurriculum was also private; that is, it was supported by the participants themselves. In the United States, for example, the citadel of private higher education—the Ivy League— still conducts much of its extracurriculum in this manner. The Harvard Student Agencies, the Yale University newspaper, and many music, drama, and literary groups are independent of their institutions. Some are sizable property owners, and a few are handsomely endowed.

The advent of public higher education brought poorer students to college. The educational and other values of the extracurriculum were generally accepted, and measures were adopted by which the opportunities provided in private institutions by private clubs and societies might be made available to students at the public institutions. Often some modest set of fees was charged to all students. Such fees were often instituted at student request and earmarked to support intercollegiate activities or a student newspaper or yearbook. This did not necessarily eliminate private organizations, as fraternities and sororities in the United States attest.

Students at public colleges thus had access to many activities that earlier had been reserved for the gentry. After World War II the center of activities, the college union, was often among the first buildings constructed on Britain's new university campuses, and it was paid for by appropriated funds.

The contemporary college and university, with some isolated exceptions, is public supported. In some instances funds, particularly capital funds, come directly from the government—municipal, provincial, or national; in other countries (Australia, for example) governmental assistance goes to students, who in turn pay fees to the college or university. In still others, such as Canada, the fees are paid by the students themselves and may be almost the only charge made to them by the college.

The issue of mandatory fees. The collection of mandatory fees to finance a variety of student activities, such as intramural athletics, publications, student government, or lecture programs, bears within it seeds of discord. In the United States in 1971, student lawsuits at the University of Nebraska, claiming that the support of programs and publications by student fees violated both the state and federal rights of students, reached the United States Supreme Court. Sufficient political pressure was exerted on the university regents to lead them to freeze further expenditure of fees (Bennett, 1975, pp. 1 and 11).

Rising costs and new candidates for funding—day care centers, legal assistance, or drug rehabilitation, for example—threaten traditional extracurricular activities supported by mandatory fees. In addition, student foes of the fee are demanding its abolition in favor of a user's

fee paid only by participants. They see the mandatory fee as a surcharge levied on all to support the activities of a few, rather than as a tax that supports a broad spectrum of valuable activities.

Mandatory fees and in some instances, tuition or endowment money, are the base for support of most extracurricular activities, although voluntary dues and membership fees still support some endeavors. A modification, whereby a mandatory fee for a specific activity is charged but may be refunded at the individual student's request, has been adopted in a few places. Another solution to the mandatory fee problem is the checkoff that permits a student at registration to indicate a willingness to be assessed certain fees. Admission charges, particularly in intercollegiate athletics and the performing arts, are important sources of revenue. Service enterprises like cafeterias, pubs, residence halls, bookstores, and travel programs are self-supporting and may even contribute net income for the support of other activities.

Public accountability. Since public higher education has become the only form of higher education in most countries, it hears increasing demands for accountability, not only from the government but also from its students. Accountability transcends fiscal issues and involves such matters as the quality of instruction, granting of tenure, size of teaching load, and freedom of speech.

Extracurricular activities cannot hope to escape the demands for accountability. Students frequently take the position that activity money, particularly fee income, is theirs to do with as they will. Trustees and officials charged with the collection and security of fees, on the other hand, view themselves as legally and morally responsible for their expenditure. Ample historical precedent exists for their concern that such monies not be directed to personal use by student officers, not spent on illegal political or other endeavors, not used for purposes other than those they were intended to serve, and not wasted by

poor procurement policies or by poor accounting procedures.

Accountability tends to follow the source
of funding. Private education has fewer
(but not necessarily less demanding) stew-
ards than tax-supported institutions. Extracurricular activities supported by dues of
members have less accounting to do than
do those supported by mandatory student fees; these, in turn, are less accountable than activities supported from public monies.

It is quite conceivable that activity programs in many democratic nations may be
funded more and more by public monies,
with a consequent loss of freedom and initiative. To counteract such loss, some activities may again be forced into independent, off-campus status, as some segments
of the student press have been. In such
instances these activities, still of vital interest to students as well as to nonstudents,
may no longer receive "recognition or assistance by their parent institutions" and
therefore not qualify by definition as extracurricular activities.

Extracurricular Activities and
Student Activism

As student organizations become more
radical, they tend to become less representative and to receive less recognition
from the parent bodies, whether universities or governments. In France in the
1960s, agitation within UNEF against the
government and particularly against government policies in Algeria tore apart the
organization and cost it government recognition and subsidy. These supports were
transferred to the rival *Fédération nationale
des étudiants de France*. Similarly, in the
Federal Republic of Germany the *Verband
deutscher Studentschaften* lost its governmental support, and the less radical *Arbeitsgemeinschaft deutscher Studentschaften* was
founded.

In Canada, the Canadian Union of
Students dissolved in 1969 after being
wracked by bitter dissension over political

issues, including the Vietnam conflict.
Whatever pretensions toward power the
United States National Student Association
had were dashed by the revelation that it
had received secret financial assistance
from the Central Intelligence Agency. In
the mid 1970s in the United States the
emergence of student lobbies indicated
that legislators might be more accessible
to students than they were to university
officials.

Most nations, authoritarian or democratic, tend to view student activism with
more tolerance than that allotted mature
citizens. Nevertheless, the turbulence of
the 1960s probably destroyed the concept
that the college student as political activist
should receive special protection while on
the campus sanctuary. At the same time,
the extension of the franchise to younger
persons increased the potential for political awareness of the student and has
brought polling booths to some campuses.
Some students have been elected to local
governments.

Opportunities for political activity on
campus vary widely. In Eastern Europe
there is little difference between extracurricular and political activities. In South
Africa political activities are forbidden on
campus. In Australia political discussions
or debates exist, but there is no party alignment. As a rule, where chapters of political parties exist on campus they are privately supported.

Traditional and transgressive groups. Pinner observed that students may join either
"traditional" groups whose role is to prepare their members for future roles in a
conventional society or "transgressive"
groups who aim for social and political
change and whose efforts are directed
against authority structures. Student political groups tend to alienate both officialdom
and their parent political organizations,
thus depriving themselves of continued
support. This deprivation, combined with
the transience of student leadership, militates against the kind of success enjoyed

by the self-reinforcing "traditional" campus organizations (Pinner, 1968, p. 142).

On the other hand, the emergence (or reemergence) of the faculty guild as trade union, combined with existing tenure practices and proliferating campus and system hierarchies, is viewed by many students as a threat. They see the student as consumer with less influence than ever over the components of a college education. Student trade unions, a return to the student guild, are seen by these students as a natural and inevitable reaction to the faculty union. Student lobbies and PIRG units may be harbingers of such a reaction, although the history of "transgressive" movements suggests otherwise.

Discontinuities in the culture and sharp generational divergences in basic social values make for transgressivism and activism. Collegiate activism can be expected in nations with unstable governments, and it is no surprise that emerging nations have political groups on or near campus. The nation of India, where student participation in the civil disobedience movement of the 1930s and the Quit India campaign of the 1940s was most influential, presents a particularly interesting situation. Student involvement in politics in India has been matched elsewhere—in Japan, Latin America, and the People's Republic of China, for example—and should not be underestimated. Nevertheless, the extracurriculum is not often political, although much of it is issue-oriented, with organizations devoted to ecology, women's rights, and abortion, for example, working on campuses around the world. Issues, whether clerical, philosophical, or political, have been the basis for much of what students have done in their spare time for centuries, although these issue-oriented actions may not always fit the definition of extracurricular.

Bibliography

Altbach, P. G., and Uphoff, N. T. *The Student Internationals.* Metuchen, New Jersey: Scarecrow Press, 1973.

Bennett, A. H. "Fees Landmark at Nebraska." *Bulletin of the Association of College Unions–International,* 1975, *43*(2), 1 and 11.

Berry, C. A. "Activities and Citizenship." In *Education for Democratic Citizenship.* Washington, D.C.: National Council for the Social Studies, 1951. Pp. 134–141.

Burn, B. B. *Higher Education in Nine Countries.* New York: McGraw-Hill, 1971.

Butts, P. *State of the College Union Around the World.* Stanford, California: Association of College Unions–International, 1967.

Charles, M. R. "The Development of the Extracurriculum in Higher Education." Unpublished doctoral dissertation, Stanford University, Stanford, California, 1953.

Faid, P. T. "Governance and the Union." In *Proceedings of the 49th Annual Conference of the Association of College Unions–International.* Stanford, California: Association of College Unions, 1972. Section 2, pp. 72–78.

Lipset, S. M. "A Comparative Perspective." *Daedalus,* 1968, *97,* 1–20.

Pinner, F. "Tradition and Transgression: Western European Students in the Postwar World." *Daedalus,* 1968, *97,* 137–155.

Proceedings of the Third Annual Conference of University and College of Advanced Education Union Presidents and Executive Officers. Canberra: Australian National University, 1974.

Sheldon, H. D. *Student Life and Customs.* New York: Appleton-Century-Crofts, 1901.

Williams, A. H., Jr. "International Student Movement." In *Proceedings of the 46th Annual Conference of the Association of College Unions–International.* Stanford, California: Association of College Unions, 1969. Pp. 26–33.

CHESTER A. BERRY

PETER T. FAID

See also: College Unions; Fraternities; Sport, Interuniversity; Students, Student Services, and Student Organizations.

F

FACILITIES, PHYSICAL PLANT

See Business Management of Higher Education: Facilities, Physical Plant.

FACULTY

The most important people in colleges and universities are not the presidents or deans, the students or staff—they are the members of the faculty. The faculty is the essential ingredient in the control of academic programs, and such programs are the basic reason for having colleges and universities. In addition to their role in conducting the educational operations of institutions of higher learning, faculty members are the people in closest and most continuous contact with students. They are the key people who meet with students in classes, laboratories, seminars, and other learning situations. Faculty members are the core of the college or university; they are expected to remain on campus and give continuity to the institution over the years.

Definition of Faculty

There are many meanings attached to the word faculty, the most general being that of teachers. The word derives from the Latin *facultas* and is literally defined as ability, natural aptitude, and power or authority. Over the years its connotation has broadened, and it has been construed as a power or agency of the mind, a branch of learning or instruction in a college or university, a body of persons dispensing instruction in postsecondary institutions, and the members of the academic profession.

In the past, before education became a field of study in itself, persons engaged in teaching were identified by many titles—scribe, rabbi, academician, tutor, lector, and scholar. Although some guilds and professional bodies existed before the formation of academies, schools, colleges, and universities, most early teachers functioned as individuals and not as members of a faculty. As education became institutionalized and teaching became professionalized, teachers banded together first for physical protection and later for professional advancement in a faculty.

Different nations attach somewhat different meanings to the term *faculty*. Generally, in countries other than the United States, *faculty* refers to a scholarly discipline (such as history, mathematics, and biology) or a professional discipline (such as medicine, law, and theology). Thus, we hear of the faculty of education, the faculty of government, and the faculty of humanities. In many European universities, *faculty* refers to a group of related disciplines, such as polytechnics, political science, and health sciences.

In the United States, *faculty* usually refers to the teaching members of an institution of higher education, although other professionals in American postsecondary institutions who are involved in scholarly or scientific research, public service, professional consultation, and institutional administration are sometimes accorded faculty status.

A plethora of titles and ranks are contained within the overall classification of faculty. The title attached to a position generally indicates its rank in the academic or institutional hierarchy. For example, the most common titles, in order of ascending importance, are instructor or lecturer, assistant professor, associate professor, and professor. However, the lower end of the spectrum frequently includes such descriptive titles as reader, tutor, fellow, and innumerable assistants (such as laboratory, research, teaching, and staff assistants). In addition, and usually at the upper levels, are such qualifiers or additions to the professor title as adjunct, research, clinical, distinguished, university, and emeritus professors—each qualifier helping to further define rank as well as to describe the title. All of the above titles, as well as others, can be found in translating the listings of academic ranks in other languages. Examples include *akademischer Rat* (academic counselor) in the Federal Republic of Germany, *assistente straordinario* (special teaching assistant) in Italy, *attaché-chef de clinique* (teaching assistant in clinical subjects with only university duties) in France, *buitengewoon hoogleraar* (part-time university professor) in the Netherlands, *chercheur* (young scientist temporarily employed at a university research institute) in Belgium, *epimélitis klinikis* (teaching assistant in clinical subjects with both hospital and university duties) in Greece, and *hjelpelaerer* (lecturer who is not an established member of the staff) in Norway.

It is highly possible that the definitions of *faculty* will change markedly in the years ahead. As more tutors and technicians, librarians and specialists, mentors and advisers, and coordinators and managers function in teaching capacities, they too probably will be cataloged as faculty, or else a more accurate term will emerge for persons directing educational efforts.

Faculty Responsibilities

The faculty is the professional staff of an institution of higher education—professional in the sense that it is qualified to provide the educational program entrusted to it. Composed of a galaxy of specialists in different ranks, the faculty is supported by many kinds of staff and administrative personnel. Traditionally, the sponsors, governors, or administrators of the university give to the faculty the authority and responsibility to organize and conduct the academic or educational program of the institution.

The faculty consists of a collection of diverse or related subject matter specialists. The great strength of the school, college, or university resides in the collection of scholars or scientists brought together primarily (but not exclusively) for teaching purposes. If the faculty is small in number, but covers a large selection of disciplines, it is considered diverse. The term *a related faculty* is used to describe one which is large in number, but covers a small selection of disciplines. In the faculty at large a high degree of specialization and heterogeneity is represented, from the arts to the sciences; in a related faculty—for example in a faculty of medical sciences—there is less specialization and more homogeneity.

The functions of a faculty are broad and varied, but the common bond is that all of its members are concerned with higher education and most of its members are involved in teaching. Among the other major assignments of faculty members are research (and its publication), public service and consultation. The relative emphases placed on these three major functions of faculty members differ greatly even among institutions of the same type; there are radical differences among institutions in various countries.

In addition to these three major faculty functions, faculty members are nearly always involved in the collegial efforts of institutional governance, student advisement or counseling, and professional advancement and improvement. Service on committees, councils, and senates provides opportunities for collective academic leadership and a democratic approach to decision making that affects the policies and operation of the institution. Student advisement and counseling by faculty personalizes and individualizes the educational program. Professional advancement consists of formal and informal, official and unofficial, individual and group endeavors toward self-improvement in a specialty or a discipline.

As implied above and detailed below, faculty members may be involved in a vast number of relationships that have some bearing on their profession. Obviously, their primary contacts are in their educational institution, their discipline, or their area of specialization. Beyond that, faculty members are involved in social relationships and participate in the cultural life of their society. Many faculty members also make significant contributions as critics of society, their aim being to use their intellectual talents to advance and improve the human condition locally, nationally, and globally.

Faculty Characteristics

Attitudes of faculty members have frequently set them apart from other professionals in society. Many books have been written about the attitudinal characteristics of faculty members (Wilson, 1964; Parsons and Platt, 1973; Ladd and Lipset, 1975). Among the attitudes common, and seemingly natural, to faculty members are a genuine curiosity or inquisitiveness and a desire to investigate phenomena and obtain information. They wish also to share or communicate information and to provoke students and others to seek intellectual involvement. Faculty members are usually knowledgeable, especially in their areas of expertise, but not always sophisticated. They exhibit a wide range of differences in behavior, but it is possible to identify some common patterns. Generally they are thinkers, not doers; they enjoy security, but are not obsessed with it; they often side with the victimized and are concerned for society; they prefer intellectual to physical activities; they are mild, not violent; they are industrious, not profligate. The typical professor has been described as "one who thinks otherwise"; frequently, the behavior of faculty members reflects strong intellectual integrity, commitment, and independence.

The backgrounds of faculty members are as mixed as those of members of other professional groups in society. But, here again, there are some common factors. A significant number come from middle-class families in which there was a genuine concern for learning, an understanding of the importance of education, and a willingness to sacrifice material wealth for intellectual development. As faculty members age, they become somewhat conservative, but are still interested in the pursuit of truth and the defense of liberality. Their modes of life suggest an affinity for quiet, contemplative, individualized approaches. Their responses to physical challenge are usually passive, while the social, cultural, intellectual, or political challenge is welcomed.

Faculty members vary greatly in economic status, but, as in their origins, most are middle class. Society provides some social prestige and reasonable remuneration for educators, but throughout history scholars and teachers have never received generous financial rewards. In fact, in some developing nations it is necessary for professors to have outside sources of income. Even in industrialized nations the economic strains on teachers are severe. The few who escape this financial pressure include the most senior and distinguished professors in specialized fields, such as surgery, nuclear physics, and quantum mechanics.

The militancy of faculty members has concerned societies since the days of Socrates. Militancy, or a strong stand on a problem in a professor's area of expertise, is generally seen as both a right and a responsibility. It is usually assumed that one role of the teacher and researcher is to be a critic (if not a reformer) of society. However, when the faculty member seeks to lead thought or action outside of his discipline or profession, he does so merely as a citizen. Additionally, if the faculty member seeks active participation in the reformation of his institution, his nation, or the world, then he can no longer claim the sanctuary of the objective scholar. Faculty members are traditionally liberal in politics, while their sponsors or supporters in society are frequently conservative.

Faculty morale fluctuates like that of any other institutional, organizational, or professional group. However, since teachers and professors are attracted more to the life of the mind than to the marketplace, wide variations in morale are uncommon. Although the financial rewards are not magnificent, well-qualified faculty members have usually received the kind of societal approbation, prestige, and security that have provided for a reasonably high morale. Faculty morale suffers most when government, the church, or society impresses a particular dogmatic point of view on an institution, a nation, or the world. Such events as the Spanish Inquisition, the rise of the Nazis in Germany, and the United States involvement in the Vietnam War are instances of social pressure that have profoundly affected faculty life and academic culture at large.

Faculty Organization

Just as the systems of higher education are composed of institutions, these institutions are composed of colleges and schools. Colleges and schools in American universities are similar to faculties (a discipline or group of disciplines) in other nations. They are led by a dean, who is usually a former faculty member. In small institu-tions the deans are able to do some limited teaching, but, like institution-wide administrators, their primary assignment is academic administration.

Divisions or departments are the normal subunits of colleges and schools. These units are led by professors who are appointed or elected as directors or chairmen for a particular period to coordinate the programs and personnel in specific units. In all but the largest institutions, such persons carry on (at least part time) as teachers.

Faculty manuals, handbooks, and constitutions provide the formal rules and regulations that structure the relationships of faculty members at all organizational levels. These sets of operating procedures are usually drafted by faculty and administration in consultation and are recommended to the governing board for approval. They are formalized as constitutions or bylaws for the orderly operation of the enterprise, the protection of faculty and other personnel involved, and the conduct of faculty business through representative bodies.

Senates, councils, committees, and other groupings of faculty occur in various combinations in institutions of higher education throughout the world. The enterprise of higher education is creative, scholarly, scientific, and professional, and the intellectuals grouped together in this enterprise have encouraged self-government in universities since their inception. There are innumerable reasons why faculty members should share in decision making, especially since they are the key personnel in the operation of the organization.

Faculty bodies have different names but similar responsibilities. They are composed chiefly of appointed or elected faculty members from throughout the institution. Their functions include introducing, debating, and drafting as operational policy the rules, regulations, and schedules for the institution. Their policies may be advisory, mandatory, or a combination thereof, depending on the constitution and bylaws of the college or university, but most of their powers are delegated by the governing boards.

Many universities (excluding those in the United States) feature subunits, called institutes, which have considerable independence and autonomy. In the socialist universities the institutes have teams or working groups to perform definite educational and scientific duties: these are not static structures, but ad hoc bodies that link research and teaching.

Similarities among university systems in various nations are more common than differences, especially at the classroom level. However, interesting differences in nomenclature and organization warrant mention. For example, in the United States universities are usually divided into colleges, divisions, and departments on disciplinary bases; in other national systems university subdivisions and colleges are chiefly related to residence and tutoring, as at Oxford University in England. The older European universities are divided into faculties, which are subdivided into chairs. In the German Democratic Republic these older units are being replaced by sections. Despite the difference in language or taxonomy, faculty members function similarly (but not identically) at the various levels. For example, a UNESCO study (1974) of higher education in Eastern Europe indicates that in Hungary "there are certain so-called 'central' chairs that do not belong to any of the faculties in respect of organization, yet cover all of them." At major institutions in the United States, the counterpart to the central chair is the university professor.

Associations of individual faculty members occur locally, regionally, nationally, and even internationally. The purpose of these associations is to present a strong, collective, and united front or voice for the membership. There are two kinds of faculty groupings outside the institution: (1) associations that may represent all faculty members, such as the Canadian Association of University Teachers' Organizations, the Association of University Professors and Lecturers in Denmark, and the All India Federation of University and College Teachers' Organizations; and (2) associations in which the faculty member participates for professional improvement in his discipline, such as the Modern Language Association, the Association for Professors of Higher Education, and the American Chemical Society.

Faculty Powers

Internal institutional authority. The degree of internal institutional authority exercised by faculties over the centuries makes their power perhaps greater than that of any other professional group in any other institution of society. Faculties have been given, or have taken, responsibility and authority for the educational programs in nearly every national system of postsecondary education. This central role occurs, and is encouraged, because the professor is the focal point of the entire operation. A neat balance generally obtains between the major components of the university family, however. Usually, the governing authorities establish the financial policies; the faculty establishes the academic policies; the chancellors, presidents, or rectors bring these policies into a viable operational relationship.

Student life and learning is clearly of genuine concern to faculty members, for without students there would be no universities. Furthermore, since teachers have the most direct and constant contact with students, it is only reasonable that the faculty should exert considerable authority over students.

Personnel policies of the faculty are of vital importance to all constituencies within the university. While the faculty itself usually proposes the professional personnel policies, these policies are influenced by students, implemented by administrators, and approved (or disapproved) by the governing board. In the capitalist countries collective bargaining is emerging as a very important aspect of the faculty's reach for additional institutional authority. Promotion, salary, and tenure policies, in many cases, have departed from traditional collegiality and have been merged into the comprehensive or legalistic concepts of collective bargaining. In the socialist countries collective curriculum decisions are made because the faculty is mandated to coordinate with labor leaders to provide the kind, extent, and degree of training that the latter deem vital to agricultural and business needs. In both capitalist and socialist nations, and to a limited extent in the Third World, there is a definite trend toward the involvement of minorities (especially women) in redesigning faculty personnel policies.

Faculty influence on society. The scholarship and expertise of faculty members has much to do with their power. Almost every nation acknowledges that qualified professors occupy a unique position in that they possess knowledge that can be used to advance the national and, perhaps, international well-being of mankind. It is common practice for scholars and scientists in postsecondary institutions to share their skills and ideas for the benefit of the less fortunate in society.

Research and publication, along with teaching, provide the content and form by which such sharing can best occur. All reputable faculty members involve themselves at some time in their careers in the disciplined investigation known as research. Without pure research, teaching would stagnate; without applied research, service to the community would wither. The dissemination of the results of research occurs in the laboratory and the classroom, in publications, and in application to the community.

Consultation and service constitute the third major function of the faculty. Faculty members discover knowledge through research; they disseminate it through teaching; and they apply it through professional consultation and community service. In the industrialized nations faculty members usually provide consultation on a profes-

sional fee basis; in the socialist countries public service is part of the faculty member's assignment; in the developing countries, where many professors are part-time employees, both methods can be found.

Throughout the history of the world, the highly educated, and especially those working in the universities, have inherited unique powers by virtue of their accumulation of knowledge. Faculty members and other intellectuals have been close advisers to persons in power in nearly all nations. This relationship to leaders has given tutors, teachers, and professors opportunities to change the course of history. Aristotle's relationship to Alexander the Great is perhaps the outstanding example. Such power brings serious responsibility. Again the classic example is Greek—Socrates' willingness to accept death rather than to recant responsible teachings of truth. While faculty members still retain considerable prestige and power, many experts agree that in the 1960s their power reached a peak that may not be attained again for a considerable period of time. Power is now shared with many inside the university, such as students and administrators, and it is diffused outside the university among other intellectuals and political power brokers.

Emerging powers and organization. A general centralization of the power of faculty members is occurring for several reasons. Organizational theory has proven that in unity there is strength, and unity is best achieved through concentrating leadership. Within many institutions faculty leadership frequently falls to the articulate academic politician or labor leader.

The change that is taking place in higher education throughout the United States and other parts of the world is a primary reason for the centralization of power. The costs of educating the enormously expanded numbers of students is exceeding the available resources of most individuals and many governments. Thus, to provide needed postsecondary education, greater efficiency of operation becomes essential—and efficiency can be obtained through certain aspects of centralization of power. Critics claim that this development will mean the loss of the truly progressive leadership that is usually generated from the more expensive but more creative decentralization of faculty leadership.

Despite the trend toward centralization in both faculty and administrative affairs, considerable flexibility and resiliency remain in university structures. As old forms disappear, a willingness to experiment with new forms is enhancing the future of higher education. The burgeoning of knowledge in every field is partly responsible for these changes and for the need for flexibility. Professors, for example, are no longer purely dispensers of knowledge; rather, the flexible organization chart depicts them as facilitators of learning. Subject matter specialists are yielding to the generalists; librarians especially must utilize all media and machines in addition to their books. Universities are losing some of their functions to other teaching and learning institutions in the community—such as the museum and the library—and faculties must coordinate and cooperate in these adjuncts to their organizations.

Moreover, a movement to integrate and concentrate all the learning facilities and facilitators—in the university and in the external community—is developing in several countries. The newly developing nations, and even some industrialized nations, have already formulated plans and passed laws to bring about this consolidation, as illustrated by Peru's *Decreto ley* (state law 19326) of 1972 and the nucleus it provides. Another aspect of national alignments of faculty members is the use of professors in the governing bodies of various countries and states. The traditional position of the typical faculty member, in the vanguard of the liberal wing is changing, as witnessed by the numbers of professors attracted to government service.

There is no question about the need in every country to use the intellectually able leaders of the universities in the service of the nation and state. The big question regarding the future powers and organization of faculties is how vigilant faculty members will be about the kind and type of public service that they are willing and able to provide. Faculty members must decide whether they are to be observers, critics, and motivators of society, or actual change agents forcing a particular view, participating in social change as professors, and imposing their will on students. Although faculty members take no Hippocratic Oath as do physicians, teachers in most nations believe that they must stand up and speak out for truth as they see it in the light of their discipline or expertise.

Faculty Evaluation

As desirable as research, publication, and consultation may be, the first function and responsibility of the instructor is to teach students. The primacy of faculty teaching necessitates being able to evaluate this activity. Since faculty research, publication, and consulting services have a relationship to teaching, these functions may also be assessed with some of the criteria, objectives, and measuring tools associated with teaching.

State of the art. The state of the art of faculty evaluation is far from clear. In the United States and other countries the decentralization of higher education and the consequent need to justify its expansion and expenditures has escalated the demand for scientific evaluation and appraisal. While the definition of the term *faculty evaluation* varies among national systems, it may be generally defined as the process of determining the effectiveness of the teaching of faculty members.

At the heart of the evaluation of teaching must be a measure (or measures) of the learning assimilated through the teaching of the faculty. Even within this limited definition of objectives, there is an incredible body of knowledge to be distilled and summarized. The literature in the field of evaluation and higher education abounds with descriptions of systematic approaches to the assessment of faculty quality and contributions (see, for example, Anderson, Ball, and Murphy, 1974; Holmes, 1974; and Page, 1974). Most experts agree that Richard Miller, Associate Director of the Illinois Board of Higher Education, has done the most to encourage postsecondary institutions to assess their faculty in a multidimensional, deliberate, and objective fashion (see Miller, 1972, 1974).

Rationale and principles for evaluation. Different institutions evaluate the faculty for different reasons. In many colleges and universities there is a serious problem of too many older tenured professors blocking the advancement, and sometimes even the employment, of younger teachers. In other institutions the fact that some earlier functions of teaching have been lost to other community institutions and agencies, such as recreation agencies and Sunday schools, has created a need for evaluation. Finally, in some institutions evaluation must address the new thrust toward seeking greater productivity through collective bargaining.

Evaluation attempts to assess the effectiveness of the faculty member and to determine his strengths and weaknesses. The aim of evaluation is for strengths to be shared and weaknesses corrected, so that effectiveness can be rewarded and incompetence eliminated. Even when based on accepted principles and carefully conducted, however, faculty evaluation is often viewed with skepticism. But, as Holmes (1974) predicts, "Teacher effectiveness measurements will be used in many different ways and to an increasing degree until, by 1990, teacher effectiveness measures will be an integral part of a standard professional way of life." As higher education necessarily moves from a labor-intensive to a capital-intensive process, the practice of faculty evaluation will help to preserve the quality of education.

Trends in evaluation. The trend in the United States is toward the development of faculty evaluation programs that are comprehensive and that serve multiple pur-

poses—among them, decisions regarding retention, promotion, salary, and tenure; self-improvement of the person evaluated; student guidance in course selection; faculty enrichment programs; information on accountability and cost-effectiveness factors; research on factors related to faculty performance; and evaluation of core courses, curricula, and sequence. Most institutions, however, concentrate on only one or two of these purposes.

Faculty evaluations, if they are to avoid the charge of discrimination, must spell out in detail the reason for the evaluation, provide for the human rights and professional dignity of the person being evaluated, and share the responsibility of evaluation with that person. An effective evaluation must, in addition show consistency in approaching all aspects of the initial and follow-up processes, an impartial and nonjudgmental attitude by evaluators, and a professional approach by executives in making decisions based on evaluation results.

The variety of evaluation approaches and uses of evaluation results may be suggested by a few examples. An engineering school in the southwestern United States adjusts salary (based on a fixed ratio) to a composite rating of teaching, research, and personal factors, done annually by administrators only. A liberal arts college in the midwestern United States informally asks those who may be interested to submit evaluative comments by letter to the president for decision making; these letters are then kept in a file, which is open to anyone. In many colleges and universities, students conduct their own evaluations of faculty for use in student course selection guides.

Almost all engaged in the process of faculty evaluation hope that it will lead to improved teaching, but few have confidence in this result. Unless formal programs of faculty improvement exist, self-improvement rarely takes place, except in instances where great discrepancies appear between self-ratings and the ratings of others (Massachusetts Advisory Council on Education, 1975).

Methods of evaluation. Traditionally, faculty members have been evaluated by three groups in descending order of frequency and importance: peers, supervisors (administrators), and students. More recently, however, self-evaluation and evaluation by nonacademic professionals have become part of the evaluation process, especially in the socialist nations.

Peer evaluation has long been practiced by inviting colleagues, especially in the same discipline or academic department, to appraise one another's teaching and related professional activities. Certainly this approach has great merit, particularly because teachers in the same field share similar knowledge and therefore can judge its presentation.

Supervisor or administrative evaluation has been used ever since related subjects were grouped into departments and chairmen in the disciplines were elected or appointed. It is a primary responsibility of a department head to assess the professional competence of the persons in his unit. However, the idea of absolute classroom autonomy has militated against this method, since administrators in some institutions and systems are much criticized for visiting classrooms.

Peer and administrative evaluations are usually related to decisions on promotion, tenure, and salary, but may also be concerned with improvement of instruction and with faculty career development.

Although student evaluation is one of the oldest methods of evaluation, it is once again gaining new credence throughout the world (Burns, 1966). Students are the people most exposed to teachers and teaching on a constant basis; as such, they are in the best position to report on the classroom, seminar, or laboratory performance of instructors. However, students are inexperienced in the discipline and emotionally involved because of grade pressures, and they sometimes confuse teaching popularity with productivity. Nearly all the experts in the field of measurement and assessment raise the same

points of caution about student evaluation—that the instrument used in the exercise must be as near foolproof as possible and that student evaluation should be used only in concert with other kinds of evaluation.

Many of the socialist countries have played down the evaluative role of the professor and have brought in outside professional evaluation from government, labor, business, agriculture and the professions. In the United States professional accreditation of specific programs or departments at times replaces the evaluation of individuals.

If done by peers, evaluations are based on more than classroom performance and are presented in individualized, narrative form. If done by administrators, evaluations usually involve perusal of syllabi, in addition to discussion with peers and students. Student evaluations are based chiefly on classroom performance and utilize a standardized questionnaire that can be machine tabulated and used for comparisons. Evaluations by outside professionals can utilize a measure of the student's competence to measure the effectiveness of his teacher. Self-evaluation will use some if not all of the above means.

Faculty in the Future

It is acknowledged that the functions of higher education and its institutions are changing rapidly. Such changes will, of course, affect the role of the faculty. But, in the main, the responsibility of instructors is to instruct, and this will not change. The methods by which these teachers teach will, however, change dramatically. A change in methods is necessary because education is a labor intensive operation and is therefore pricing itself out of existence. Teaching must become capital-intensive; leaders in education must devise ways and means to use less labor (fewer teachers) and more capital (better use of machines, equipment, and facilities).

The problem of expense is occurring at all levels of education throughout the world. It has been conclusively proven that sufficient scientific equipment, materials, and supplies—hardware and software— are now available to revolutionize teaching and learning. These machines and programs will never replace all the teachers and professors. The picture, the book, the teaching machine, and even the computer are directly dependent on the artist, the author, the programmer, and the scientist—all of whom are teachers. But television, the computer, and other communication and informational devices, if properly used, can greatly increase teaching and learning productivity.

High productivity in education, as in all fields of endeavor, is essential if society is to meet the spiraling costs of higher education and maintain its quality. Faculty members need and deserve greater remuneration, but can have it only if they are productive; they will be productive if they make greater use of the scientific devices available to them. The professors of the future will be directors of learning, skillfully diagnosing students' needs and carefully scheduling them into balanced programs, where a combination of live and electronic teaching will maximize learning.

Bibliography

Anderson, S. B., Ball, S., and Murphy, R. T. *Encyclopedia of Educational Evaluation: Concepts and Techniques for Evaluating Education and Training Programs.* San Francisco: Jossey-Bass, 1974.

Arrowsmith, W. "The Future of Teaching." Keynote address delivered to the annual meeting of the American Council on Education, Washington, D.C., October 1966.

Atcon, R. P., and Trucco, H. T. *Teoría sobre administración universitaria: Administración académica.* Guadalajara, Mexico: Universidad autónoma de Guadalajara, 1973.

Bornheimer, D., Burns, G. P., and Dumke, G. S. *The Faculty in Higher Education.* Danville, Illinois: Interstate, 1973.

Burns, G. P. *A Report on University Finance in Europe.* New York: Ford Foundation, 1961.

Burns, G. P. *A Report on University Administration in Asia.* New York: Sloan Foundation, 1963.

Burns, G. P. *Trustees in Higher Education.* New York: Independent College Funds, 1966.

Carnegie Commission on Higher Education. *Priorities for Action: Final Report of The Carnegie Commission On Higher Education.* New York: McGraw-Hill, 1973.

Conant, J. B. *The Education of American Teachers.* New York: McGraw-Hill, 1963.

Dewey, J. *Philosophy of Education.* Ames, Iowa: Littlefield and Adams, 1956.

Dressel, P. L., Johnson, F. C., and Marcus, P. M. *The Confidence Crisis: An Analysis of University Departments.* San Francisco: Jossey-Bass, 1970.

Good, C. V. (Ed.) *Dictionary of Education.* New York: McGraw-Hill, 1945.

Holmes, D. "Evaluating Teacher Effectiveness." In *Assessment of Colleges and Universities.* Iowa City, Iowa: American Testing Program, 1974.

Hook, S., Kurtz, P., and Todorovich, M. *The Idea of a Modern University.* Buffalo, New York: Prometheus, 1974.

Hughs, J. F. (Ed.) *Education and the State.* Washington, D.C.: American Council on Education, 1975.

Jencks, C., and Riesman, D. *The Academic Revolution.* Garden City, New York: Doubleday, 1968.

Knowles, A. S. (Ed.) *Handbook of College and University Administration.* New York: McGraw-Hill, 1970.

Ladd, E. C., Jr., and Lipset, S. M., *The Divided Academy: Professors and Politics.* New York: McGraw-Hill, 1975.

Massachusetts Advisory Council on Education. *MACE Reports,* 1975, 7.

Miller, R. *Evaluating Faculty Performance.* San Francisco: Jossey-Bass, 1972.

Miller, R. *Developing Programs for Faculty Evaluation.* San Francisco: Jossey-Bass, 1974.

Niblett, W. R., and Butts, R. F. (Eds.) *Universities Facing the Future: An International Perspective.* San Francisco: Jossey-Bass, 1972.

Page, C. F. *Student Evaluation of Teaching: The American Experience.* London: Society for Research into Higher Education, 1974.

Parsons, T., and Platt, G. M. *The American University.* Cambridge, Massachusetts: Harvard University Press, 1973.

Pinilla, A. *Educación para el desarrollo nacional.* Lima, Peru: Universidad de Lima, 1966.

UNESCO. *Case Study on the Development of Higher Education in Some East European Countries.* Paris: UNESCO, 1974.

Whitehead, A. N. *The Aims of Education.* New York: New American Library, 1929.

Wilson, L. *The Academic Man.* New York: Octagon Books, 1964.

GERALD P. BURNS

See also: Academic Freedom; Academic Tenure; Due Process and Grievance Procedures; Exchange, International: Teaching and Research Exchange Programs; Faculty Unionism: The United States and Great Britain; Legal Status of Faculty Unionization in the United States; Participatory Democracy; Political Persecution of Academics; Recruitment, Appointment, Promotion, and Termination of Academic Personnel; Remuneration: Faculty, Staff, and Chief Executive Officers; Workloads of Academic Personnel.

FACULTY ASSOCIATIONS
See Faculty Unionism: The United States and Great Britain.

FACULTY FRINGE BENEFITS (LEAVES, SALARY SCALES, FACULTY SALARIES: ACADEMIC STAFF, SALARY INCREMENTS)
See Remuneration: Faculty, Staff, and Chief Executive Officers.

FACULTY REMUNERATION
See Remuneration: Faculty, Staff, and Chief Executive Officers.

FACULTY RESOURCE CENTER,
United States

The Faculty Resource Center was formed in October 1975 at the University of Cincinnati, in Ohio, by a merger of the Institute for Research and Training in Higher Education and the University Media Services Center. Research in higher education, focusing on national and regional problems, is conducted in the following areas: educational planning, university students and faculty, educational technology, curricula and instruction, and reform in higher education.

In addition to research activities, the center consults with faculty and administrators on teaching improvement, evaluation of teaching and administration, academic unit development, and curriculum planning. It develops evaluation tools such as tests and measurements; trains

university teachers, administrators, and researchers; and holds conferences and seminars.

The center's policy is controlled by the university and by the center's director. Funded by the university, the center's staff includes four research professionals, four research assistants and/or graduate students, four technicians, three administrative personnel, and four secretaries. The staff has access to computers.

The center publishes monographs.
University of Cincinnati
446 French Hall
Cincinnati, Ohio 45221 USA

FACULTY UNIONISM: THE UNITED STATES AND GREAT BRITAIN

Although the British and American systems of postsecondary education are fundamentally different, the problems confronting their universities are substantially similar. In both countries rapid expansion in postsecondary education occurred in the 1960s. Existing institutions expanded, new institutions were established, and some existing institutions were converted to university status. Challenges to the traditional university dominance of postsecondary education developed from other types of postsecondary education. With the increase in costs, the explosion of student unrest, and the increasing concern with other pressing social and economic problems, the favored position of the universities deteriorated, and often the relationship of the faculty to the administration changed. With this change new issues came to dominate faculty unions in the 1970s.

Growth of Faculty Unionism in the United States

For many years the American Federation of Teachers (AFT) was the only organization in the United States with aspirations to provide college and university faculty with union representation. The AFT received a national charter from the

American Federation of Labor in 1916 as a union with jurisdiction over teachers at all levels of education. The first college locals were established shortly afterward, but growth of the union among teachers as a whole, and among college faculty in particular, was slow. Although, in contrast to the other major organizations enrolling faculty members, the AFT has always regarded itself as a trade union, until the 1930s it operated mainly in a consultative style through councils of teachers in the schools. As part of the general upsurge in trade union organization in the 1930s, the AFT formally adopted a policy of collective bargaining as its preferred mode of operation. The commitment to collective bargaining, however, did not officially include the assertion of the right of its locals to strike until 1963. Strikes of teachers, of course, had occurred earlier, but their relationship to the existing organizations of teachers had been ambiguous.

Changes in teacher organizations. In the 1950s interest in the unionization of public employees grew rapidly, and by the end of the decade their right to organize and bargain collectively began to be recognized in various jurisdictions, beginning with large municipalities in the highly unionized eastern and midwestern United States. Teachers were among the groups in the vanguard of the new movement. The most important event in the development of teacher unionism was the organization of the New York City schools in 1961. This occurred after a bitter election campaign in which the AFT and the local affiliate of the National Education Association (NEA) competed for the right to represent the instructors in the huge city educational system. Victory in this contest doubled the size of the AFT to about 125,000 members and accelerated a transformation in the character of teacher organizations (Garbarino, 1975).

In terms of size, the National Education Association is the dominant organization of teachers and other professional staff in the educational sector, with about 1,500,000 members (Garbarino, 1975). Until the 1960s it had functioned as a professional association at all levels of education, carefully distinguishing its objectives and practices from the union orientation of the much smaller AFT. But with the spread of public employee unionism and the competition from the AFT for the right to represent teachers in bargaining, the NEA rapidly converted itself into a professional union. By the end of the decade the process was essentially complete.

The American Association of University Professors (AAUP) has been the dominant professional association in higher education since its founding in 1913. In 1976 its membership was 72,000 (AAUP *Bulletin,* 1976). It had functioned primarily as a national, direct membership, professional association concentrating on the protection of academic freedom, promoting the collegial form of university governance, and influencing the salaries and personnel practices of colleges and universities through persuasion and consultation, which were supplemented by occasional, more direct action such as censure and litigation. As the pressure from the competition for representation rights in higher education from the AFT and the NEA increased in the 1960s, the AAUP added collective bargaining for faculty to its range of activities. This decision was taken after considerable debate and discussion within the association. It is one reason for the substantial drop in membership, from about 90,000 to 75,000, that occurred between 1971, when the formal decision was made, and 1974. As of 1975 the AAUP was spending about as much on its collective bargaining activities as on its traditional programs (Garbarino, 1975).

Union merger discussion. These three organizations clearly dominate the organizational pattern of unionism in American higher education, although a few faculties have chosen to be represented by local associations or by other unions. An important question is whether the AFT, the NEA, and the AAUP will continue to compete for membership, or whether some form of merger or alliance will be worked out. A number of combinations between the AFT and the NEA have occurred in various states and localities, and discussions for a national merger have taken place at various times. The largest of these combinations, the AFT-NEA merger in New York State, has, however, been dissolved. The AAUP has also formed alliances with other groups in local organizing campaigns on occasion, and, although no general alliances are in prospect, in the long run some amalgamation may occur.

At the national level it is possible to distinguish among the organizations by their approach to faculty organization. The AFT retains its traditional union orientation, and the AAUP retains, to a large extent, its character as a professional association. The NEA falls in between but clearly lies closer to the AFT end of the organizational spectrum. At the local level, where the competition is direct, the differences in organizational personality are less obvious because the AAUP local chapters adopt a more traditional union stance.

The American Pattern of Organization

Considering both two-year and four-year institutions of higher education, by the beginning of 1976 about 400 separate institutions, including more than 100,000 faculty and professional staff, were unionized in the sense that official recognition had been given to exclusive bargaining representatives (Garbarino, 1975). This means that more than 20 percent of all faculty and staff and about 16 percent of all the institutions were represented by unions. Because individual membership in unions is almost always voluntary, probably not much more than 50,000 were actual union members. (On the other hand, many faculty are members of unions on campuses where the union does not have official recognition.) The movement began in the two-

year institutions in 1963, but it attracted widespread national attention only with the organization of the faculty and staff of the City University of New York in 1969. Although about two thirds of the institutions organized in 1976 were two-year colleges, the four-year colleges are larger and account for two thirds of all the individuals represented (Garbarino, 1975).

Distribution of faculty unions. As of 1976 faculty unionism in the United States was a phenomenon centered in public institutions. Although private institutions employ well over one third of all faculty, they accounted for only one out of every fourteen persons represented by unions (Garbarino, 1975). This low level of organization exists even though, in 1970, the National Labor Relations Board—the federal government agency administering private-sector labor relations—extended its jurisdiction to private higher education throughout the United States.

By contrast, less than half the states have equivalent laws establishing the right of public employees (usually including public higher education employees) to organize and bargain.

The great bulk of faculty unionization has occurred in those few states with favorable laws—states centered in the industrial Northeast in addition to Michigan, Hawaii, and Florida.

The heartland of unionism is New York, where the State University and the City University account for almost one third of all the faculty and staff under collective bargaining contract (Garbarino, 1975). Virtually all public higher education in New York is unionized and this may well be the eventual pattern in other states with strong public employee union movements.

In the nation as a whole there has been no unionization as of 1976 at the more prestigious research universities, including the public institutions. There is, however, some evidence of increasing interest in organization among this group of institutions.

Unions have been most likely to win bargaining rights in state systems of four-year institutions, particularly those that were converted to general-purpose institutions from teacher training colleges during the expansion of the 1960s. The urban two-year colleges are another highly organized sector of higher education. Most of the faculty strikes have taken place in the urban community college districts, but strikes have also occurred in four-year colleges and universities.

Patterns of unionism. The organizational pattern for different types of institutions tends to be related to the identity of the competing employee organizations. The AAUP has been the most successful of all the organizations in the private four-year colleges; it also has substantial representation in public four-year colleges but very little in public two-year colleges. The NEA dominates the organized two-year institutions in general, but the AFT has substantial representation in the large urban districts. The NEA's greatest strength in the four-year sector is in the former teachers colleges. The AFT representation in four-year institutions has been limited, but it has been greatly expanded by its 1976 win in the Florida university system and by the probability that it will retain control of the New York city and state systems since the dissolution of its merger with the NEA in that state.

The relation of faculty unionism to the public employee union movement as a whole suggests that its future rate of growth will depend on the trends in the enactment of laws encouraging public sector unions in those states without favorable laws. There is strong support among unions for proposed federal legislation that would extend organizing rights to public employees in all the states, but as of 1976, the prospects for this legislation are uncertain.

The best prognosis for the future is that faculty unionism will continue to show steady but not spectacular growth. Attitude surveys of faculty reveal that 66 percent indicate general approval of collective bargaining in colleges and universities (Bayer, 1973).

American Issues in Faculty Bargaining

Two major issues lie behind the development of faculty unions in the United States: institutional governance and economics. Of the two, governance issues appear to have dominated the movement's early trend toward bargaining, but as the rate of expansion of higher education slowed in the 1970s and financial pressures increased, economic problems became equally important.

Governance issues. The model of college and university governance is the practice of collegiality, a system of decision making by consultation and, ideally, consensus among those responsible for implementing the decisions—and sometimes including those, for example, students, affected by the decisions. Collegiality is practiced in varying degrees among a variety of institutions but probably exists in its pure form in relatively few of them. Participation in decision making, however, is a goal to which virtually all professionals aspire, and the practices of the leading universities provide a model of what the faculty of other institutions hope to achieve.

The rapid expansion of higher education in the 1960s created conditions in which the aspirations of collegiality were particularly difficult to satisfy. Individual institutions grew in size and complexity, adding new departments, new degree programs, new types of faculty, and new categories of students. Standards for recruitment and promotion of faculty, the administration of salaries, and the requirements for admission and graduation of students became contentious issues. In many institutions a change to an administrative style that faculties felt was more appropriate to the new conditions was slow in coming.

In addition to changes in individual institutions, the expansion in higher education as a whole created a pressure for the rationalization of systems of institutions.

In some states multicampus institutions were created, in others multiinstitutional systems were established, or an increase in the power of centralized administration of existing systems occurred. In other instances "superboards" or supersystems were set up to administer, or at least coordinate, all of public higher education.

One of the best examples of the end product of this process is the State University of New York, which in 1976 included four university centers, thirteen former teachers colleges converted to general colleges, and six two-year agricultural and technical institutes, as well as four other specialized campuses.

These functional and structural changes placed serious strains on the usual administrative machinery and on the traditional methods of reaching decisions. The increase in heterogeneity of both the institutions and the faculty made consensus and coordination more difficult and tended to move the locus of decision making farther from the individual faculty member and his department, and often completely away from the local campus. Divisions within the faculty and between faculty and administrations also arose from the strains caused by the political activism and the student unrest of the 1960s.

The priority of governance issues in explaining unionization is attested to by the increase in faculty organization during the period of rapid growth and financial buoyancy of higher education as a whole. It is also supported by the early and continuing growth of faculty unionism among the community colleges, which continued to enjoy a salubrious economic climate into the mid 1970s.

Economic issues. As financial stringency came to dominate the environment of higher education in the 1970s, faculty unionism became as concerned with economics as with governance. In part, the concern was with a slowing of salary increases, but problems of retrenchment and possible reduction of staff began to govern faculty-administration relations. The con-

ditions under which academic programs could be reduced or eliminated and the methods for selecting staff for retention or termination became subjects of discussion and negotiation along with questions of workload, rank quotas, and other personnel practices. Governance issues remained prominent, but they tended to focus on what has been called the management of decline.

In a "no growth" atmosphere, faculty unions made efforts to protect the tenure principle and at the same time to insist on due process and procedural safeguards for cases of nonretention and denial of reappointment of nontenured faculty. This created fears of inflexibility and professional obsolescence as it became more difficult to add new members to those institutions with increasing proportions of tenured faculty.

A special variety of economic issue explains a substantial part of the growth of faculty unionism in public institutions. As public employee unionism expands, the politics of budgeting decisions puts a premium on organized representation to protect group interests. Education as a whole becomes one of many claimants for public funds. Within education the various levels become competitive, and within higher education there is rivalry among different institutions or systems of institutions. Finally, within individual institutions there is competition between faculty and other employee groups for funds. The failure of any group to be represented in the allocation process appears to put that group's share in jeopardy.

Student participation. One of the unusual developments resulting from the growth of faculty unionism has been a trend toward providing for student participation in the bargaining process. In many colleges and universities during the 1960s, students enjoyed some success in being included in some part of the academic decision-making process. When faculty collective bargaining was introduced, students feared that the institutions of governance they had penetrated were to be superseded by a new form of decision making. Organized students in several states have persistently sought to play an official role in the negotiations for faculty union contracts. Their efforts have enjoyed some success, and in two states, Oregon and Montana, students are by law entitled to participate in negotiations in higher education. This is a unique example of the recognition of the right of a client or public group to have some knowledge of, and perhaps influence in, the course of union negotiations.

In some large universities, unions of graduate students who work as teaching and research assistants have been organized and have secured official recognition. In other instances, employed graduate students have been included with regular faculty members in bargaining units.

In addition to the graduate students, other professional staff, such as librarians, researchers, and lecturers, have been able to acquire some of the traditional perquisites of faculty status as part of the union movement. In many large universities the number of support professionals is substantial; and the bargaining units, as defined by the labor boards, have usually been broader than the traditional regular rank faculty. More inclusive units have contributed to a reduction in the differentials in pay and privilege between regular faculty and other groups.

An Evaluation

There is a theoretical possibility that faculty unionism will come to dominate most academic decision making in the United States because of its legal monopoly of all issues affecting personnel matters. This could result in virtually eliminating the more traditional methods of academic governance, such as academic senates. However, as of 1976, the effect of unions on the governance machinery had not been drastic. There are a number of reasons for this. Firstly, most unions have supported traditional mechanisms for making aca-

demic decisions; secondly, most organized institutions have not had a tradition of effective faculty governance, and faculty unions have often introduced or strengthened senates; and thirdly, even where active senate systems existed, they often had little power in those areas of most interest to unions, such as salary negotiations or individual personnel actions, particularly for nontenured staff.

Effects of outside changes on unionism. Any judgment about the effects of faculty unionism on governance is difficult, not only because the effects will vary depending on the situation but also because faculty organization has coincided with other changes in higher education and society in general. It is, for example, almost certainly true that faculty unions have contributed to a centralization of decision making, particularly in multicampus systems. However, centralization is the product of many other forces, especially in view of financial problems of the system, and it is difficult to measure the effects of unions in isolation. Similarly, unions have introduced due process considerations into personnel actions and have pressed to make personnel decisions more open, more subject to challenge and external review. Again, these kinds of changes are also the result of fundamental shifts in the relations between individuals and institutions in the society at large, and faculty unions are only one of the forces bringing change to academic institutions.

Impacts of unionism. It seems safe to conclude that faculty unions will contribute to the further bureaucratization of American colleges and universities in the sense that they will lead to a growth in numbers of functionaries on both sides, to an expansion of record keeping and report writing, and to a formalization and codification of procedures that had been informal and frequently haphazard.

The results of the spread of faculty organization on economic variables are easier to predict in direction than they are in magnitude. There are substantial direct costs to administering a unionized system associated with the increase in bureaucracy noted above.

Although no definitive studies of the effects of unionism on salaries have been made, there is little doubt that the effect has been positive for unionized faculties as a whole. The unions' effect on salaries is most likely to be greatest in periods of financial stringency. Had there been no faculty unions, it seems likely that salary gains would have been smaller or even negative in some of the states with severe financial crises. The ability of the unions to minimize or altogether prevent the reduction of staff has also been impressive.

The future growth of faculty unions in the private sector of American higher education is likely to be slow and uneven, but the spread of unionism among the larger public sector is likely to be more rapid, paralleling the spread of public employee unionism generally.

Faculty Unionism in Great Britain

The British university system consists of some forty-five separate institutions operating independently but financed largely through a block grant from the national government. The university system expanded rapidly in the post–World War II period with the establishment of several new institutions and the conversion of the former colleges of advanced technology to universities. In the mid 1960s the universities lost their traditional monopoly on degree-level work, and this development is likely to have important consequences for the universities as well as for the faculties and the faculty organizations. New degree-level work has been introduced into the polytechnics, institutions that are regarded as part of the public sector in British terms because they are under the control of local educational authorities. The polytechnics formerly provided a variety of special and technical education, and the introduction of degree work constituted a major and controversial innovation. The colleges of education are another sector of

postsecondary education, but as of 1976 the future of these institutions is unclear because they are being converted or merged into other types of institutions.

The University Grants Committee. The element of the British system of higher education that has probably attracted most attention is the University Grants Committee (UGC). The UGC is regarded as a unique solution to the problem of providing public financing with a minimum of public control of educational policy. It is usually described as a buffer between the Department of Education and Science and the separate university administrations. The only areas in which the department deals directly with the universities is in the collective bargaining structure described below. The members of the UGC are drawn from the civil service and the public, with the latter often chosen from lay members of the governing bodies of universities. Unfortunately, there is a trend in the UGC toward its becoming less of a buffer and more of a transmission belt for pressures from the government. This is similar to the developments affecting the position of lay governing boards of public institutions in the United States. The financial crisis of the early 1970s has accelerated this trend in Britain as it has in the United States.

British faculty associations. The faculty of the universities have been represented by the Association of University Teachers (AUT), a professional association whose transition to a union of professionals is virtually complete. The faculty of the polytechnics were represented by the Association of Teachers in Technical Institutions (ATTI) until 1976. As the polytechnics expanded into degree credit courses, pressures arose to differentiate the faculty, and to some extent the institutions, from other faculty and institutions still engaged in "further" as distinct from "higher" education. This led to the creation of a new organization, the Association of Polytechnic Teachers, basically intended to distinguish the polytechnic staff from that of the other institutions of further education and to stress the potential relation to university staff.

The faculty in the colleges of education and the other teacher training institutions have been represented by the Association of Teachers in Colleges and Departments of Education (ATCDE). As of January 1, 1976, the ATCDE merged with the ATTI to form a new organization, the National Association of Teachers in Further and Higher Education. With about 60,000 members, the new group will be about twice the size of the AUT (Henke, 1976). The importance of the potential competition between the new degree programs in the polytechnics and the traditional universities is illustrated by the fact that polytechnic staff have recently been granted salary parity with comparable grades of university staff, and proposals have been made to introduce research functions and professorial ranks into the polytechnics. These are new developments as of 1976, however, and there is little experience with this pattern.

British Organization of Bargaining

The Association of University Teachers is the British counterpart of the AAUP in the United States in that it was for several decades the professional association of university teaching staff. It began the transition from professional association to professional union earlier and has carried it further than has the AAUP.

The AUT was founded in 1919, almost contemporaneously with the AAUP and the AFT. It began to adopt something of a trade union stance by the early 1950s, and a decade later it was clearly involved in a bargaining relationship with the universities and the ministry responsible for education. It has had over four fifths of the eligible academic staff as members, a proportion more than twice as large as that enjoyed by the AAUP in the United States. In recent years the percentage of British academics belonging to the AUT has risen substantially ("AUT Votes," 1976).

Competition between unions. As noted earlier, the several unions of academic staff in postsecondary education have operated in separate sectors of the system and there has been little direct competition for membership or bargaining rights among them. In recent years there has been increasing conflict between the AUT and the Association of Scientific, Technical, and Managerial Staffs (ASTMS), a white-collar union whose primary jurisdiction is indicated by its name, although most of its membership is in the lower levels of these occupational groups. In the spectrum of union political classification in Britain, the ASTMS is considerably more radical than is the AUT. As a result, it has had considerable attraction for some members of the teaching staff at some of the universities. In addition, ASTMS has organized junior technical, professional, and support staff in the universities, and in some instances their loyalties have remained with ASTMS when they have advanced into positions that fall within the domain of the AUT. The AUT has been flexible in admitting staff in the periphery of the teaching faculty to membership and in adapting its structure to their interest, but as of 1976 some problems in this area still existed. There is little likelihood, however, that competition among the organizations will reach anything similar to the situation existing in the United States.

AUT affiliation with the Trades Union Congress. The best index of the extent of the transformation of the AUT into a union of professionals is the vote of the association in 1976 to affiliate with the national trade union federation, the Trades Union Congress (TUC). In 1971 the AUT had rejected affiliation by a vote of more than two to one, but the 1976 vote reversed that decision by a vote of 13,500 to 7,500 ("AUT Votes," 1976). The change appears to be due to dissatisfaction with the results of salary negotiations over more than a decade and a belief that a link with the main body of trade unions would improve the faculty position vis-à-vis the government through political and direct union support, particularly if economic action were taken. Because both the new teachers association and ASTMS are affiliated unions, the AUT action may also temper the potential competition between these organizations by enforcing more respect for jurisdictional boundaries through the operation of TUC procedures.

University's negotiating structure. The pattern of organization on the universities' side of the bargaining relationship is more complex. The separate universities have had a central coordinating body, the Committee of Vice-Chancellors and Principals of the Universities of the United Kingdom (CVC), since World War I. The powers of the CVC to deal with university-wide policy matters have been carefully limited. In the 1970s its role has shown signs of expanding, particularly on economic matters. The CVC has established a Universities Authorities Panel (UAP) to represent the universities in negotiations with the AUT. Since the 1970 negotiations, bargaining has occurred in a two-tiered structure composed of Committee A and Committee B. In Committee A, negotiations between the UAP and the AUT are conducted under the guidance of a neutral chairman. If the negotiations fail to produce a settlement, the chairman has the power to draw up an agreement that binds the parties. The agreement that comes out of Committee A goes to Committee B as the joint proposal of the universities and the association. In Committee B, the Department of Education and Science represents the government side. The University Grants Committee participates in Committee A's deliberations as a discreet mediator and in Committee B's as the adviser to the department. If no agreement is reached in Committee B, the dispute may be taken to outside arbitration.

In 1975 the parties failed to reach agreement in Committee B and resort was made to arbitration for the first time. A substantial award was proposed, but it was not implemented because the issue became caught up in the national wage agreement to limit pay increases to £6 a week, with a maximum salary above which no increases would be permitted. Dissatisfaction with this incident as well as somewhat similar experiences with earlier versions of governmental pay policy probably influenced the favorable vote on TUC affiliations.

As of 1976 the AUT was asking for changes in the bargaining procedures that would provide a system more like those used for other government-union negotiations.

British Issues in Bargaining

Over the years the primary focus of bargaining has been on economic issues. Since shortly after World War II, the British universities have had a single salary scale. Bargaining has concerned movement of the salary range as a whole and modifications of the structure of salaries, such as adding steps to the range of salaries by rank or varying differentials. In general, faculty have received increments in salary each year, essentially automatically, up to the top of the range for their rank. This creates problems for those persons who reach the top step for their rank, particularly because there has been a maximum ratio of staff permitted at the senior ranks (senior lecturer and professor) at any time. In addition to bargaining to add steps, the AUT has pressed to raise the maximum senior staff ratio.

One major reason for concentration on salary bargaining has been the lack of a well-developed local association system until the 1970s. The AUT was organized to negotiate at the national level, but the universities severely limited the subjects they would consider at that level, retaining control of noneconomic matters in the local university administrations.

The AUT is strengthening its local associations and trying to extend bargaining at the local level, giving particular attention to the development of grievance procedures. Another local issue is the role of the professor in department and university governance. In British universities the title of professor is held by only a relatively small proportion (15–20 percent) of all teaching faculty, and status and pay differentials are substantial (Williams, Blackstone, and Metcalf, 1974, p. 145). Professors often function as department chairmen function in the United States, often for long periods and sometimes for life. The AUT would like to see an increase in multiprofessor departments; a rotation of chairmanships in departments, with other ranks eligible to serve; and an increase in the powers of nonprofessorial staff in all areas of university governance.

As in the United States, relationships in the 1970s have long been dominated by changes in demographic and economic factors that have brought the period of growth and expansion to an end. The result of these changes on the university system, coupled with the changes within the various sectors of the educational system itself, will place the systems of faculty representation under strain. In Britain, the AUT has strengthened its position by moving closer in style and stance to the traditional trade union movement.

The traditional split between educational and economic issues, with the former being left to internal governance mechanisms at the local level while the latter were negotiated at the national level, shows signs of breaking down. Under the pressures of the times, more educational issues are being drawn into the orbit of central administration for settlement, where they are accessible to national negotiations. At the same time, the local associations of the AUT have grown in strength, have gained recognition as representatives of the faculty, and are able to participate more actively in local campus affairs.

British universities have a higher degree of faculty autonomy and a lower level of dominance by professional administrators than do most colleges and universities in the United States. Faculty unionism is likely to be more closely confined to economic matters than is true in North American universities, but the traditional separation

of economic and educational issues that characterized the past will be less pronounced in the future.

Bibliography

American Association of University Professors (AAUP). *Bulletin*, 1976, *62*(1), 69.
"AUT Votes for Affiliation to TUC by 5,556 Majority." *Times (London) Higher Education Supplement*, March 26, 1976.
Bayer, A. E. "Teaching Faculty in Academe." *American Council on Education Research Reports*, 1973, *8*(2).
Carr, R. *Collective Bargaining Comes to the Campus.* Washington, D.C.: American Council on Education, 1973.
Garbarino, J. W. *Faculty Bargaining: Change and Conflict.* New York: McGraw-Hill, 1975.
Henke, D. "New Union's Tough Line Likely." *Times (London) Higher Education Supplement*, March 19, 1976.
Kemerer, R., and Baldridge, V. J. *Unions on Campus.* San Francisco: Jossey-Bass, 1975.
Perkin, H. *Key Profession.* Clifton, New Jersey: Augustus M. Kelley, 1969.
Williams, G., Blackstone, T., and Metcalf, D. *The Academic Labour Market.* Amsterdam: Elsevier, 1974.

JOSEPH W. GARBARINO

See also: Legal Aspects of Higher Education; Legal Status of Faculty Unionization in the United States.

FAEROE ISLANDS

The Faeroe Islands form a self-governing community within the Kingdom of Denmark and follow the mother country's system of primary and secondary education. Further education on the islands is provided by an academy founded in 1965, a teacher training college, two technical schools, a school for marine engineering, a folk high school, and a nursing school. University education is available in Denmark.

See also: Denmark, Kingdom of.

FALKLAND ISLANDS

Population: 2000. Student enrollment in primary school: 196 (100 females); secondary school: 119 (59 females); higher education (abroad): 44 (22 females). Language of instruction: English. [Figures are for 1974.]

The Falkland Islands, a British crown colony in the South Atlantic off the coast of South America, consists of two major islands, East Falkland and West Falkland, and some 200 smaller islands. There are no facilities for postsecondary education on the islands. Students generally attend institutions of higher education in Argentina, the United Kingdom, and Uruguay. In 1974 forty-four students studied abroad, twelve of them receiving government scholarships.

[Information received from Chief Secretary, Stanley, Falkland Islands.]

FASHION DESIGN
(Field of Study)

Fashion design is the application of design principles to wearing apparel for men, women, and children. Designs in clothing are directly affected by fluctuations in taste and indirectly by social, economic, and political changes. A designer, therefore, attempts to impart esthetic values to clothing to satisfy the contemporary taste for adornment, as well as for protection.

The fashion design field has the following subdivisions, each with its own design and manufacturing operation: (1) apparel design, (2) accessory design, and (3) jewelry design. Apparel design is further subdivided into outerwear (dresses, sportswear, coats, and suits) and intimate apparel (loungewear, sleepwear, foundations, and lingerie) for women; and coats and suits, sportswear, and furnishings (shirts, underwear, robes, and sleepwear) for men. The same categories of apparel are designed for children, according to their ages: infants, toddlers, boys and girls. Accessory design includes shoes, handbags, millinery, scarves, belts, and gloves. Jewelry design is self-explanatory.

In the early 1970s fashion was concerned with "life-style," an individual's total environment—housing, apparel, textiles, and foods all became part of a total fashion concept. As people adopted a more casual way of life, they dressed in clothing that was more comfortable and less heavily constructed than in decades past. Because of this emphasis on life-style, the interior designer, jewelry designer, display and exhibit designer, and textile designer directed their efforts toward satisfying the same consumer taste as the apparel designer.

Many other related careers in the fashion industries complement the work of the fashion designer: fashion buying and merchandising; fashion advertising design; fashion illustration; fashion photography; advertising and communications; textile and apparel marketing; and production-oriented careers such as management engineering technology, patternmaking technology, and textile technology.

The first fashion design schools were a part of the medieval guild system of apprenticeship. The earliest actual fashion sketches, however, date to the Italian Renaissance. At the same time, the French were developing fashion dolls which they used as models. During the nineteenth century fashion design expanded, and in 1975 nearly every European country had an established fashion design school. In nineteenth-century America, production of clothing that was not home-sewn was limited to dressmakers, who hired convent-trained apprentices. The industrial revolution and the introduction of the sewing machine, the move westward, and the need for thousands of uniforms during the Civil War spurred the growth of the apparel industry in the United States. Early trade-technical schools limited instruction to such construction skills as sewing and patternmaking. Art schools introduced courses in fashion design but limited these to sketching and developing beautifully finished fashion drawings. More specialized schools began to emerge that combined art and craft skills, but fashion design did not become a recognized discipline in higher education until after World War II.

Apparel production ranges from *haute*

couture—very expensive, limited-edition clothing traditionally associated with Parisian designers—to mass-produced items turned out by the thousands. The practice of fashion as a business is international in scope. Regional preferences and differences exist, but as communications systems grow more sophisticated, the styles of a country may quickly be adopted around the globe; details of ethnic costumes, work clothing, and military surplus of various countries, for example, have been incorporated in the design of apparel.

A consumer appreciation for "natural" things fostered an interesting development in the fashion market in 1975. India has long had a healthy textile industry, but a vogue in the 1970s for pure cotton fabrics and simple traditional Indian clothing designs inspired a tremendous spurt in clothing production in that country. The Indian government wants to establish a school for professional education in the apparel industry. Modern Japan, too, has become heavily involved in apparel production in the 1970s and offers professional-level fashion education at the Bunka College of Fashion in Tokyo. Israel has also entered the world apparel market, and degree programs are available at the Shenkar College of Fashion and Textile Technology in Ramat Gan. Some students at the Fashion Institute of Technology in New York City go to principal European cities—for example, the College for the Distributive Trades in London—to study both comparative fashion marketing and buying and technical aspects of production. Each semester, for example, some FIT students study knitting machinery at an industrial school in Switzerland.

Designers in the 1970s need artistic and technical training, an awareness of alternative life-styles, and a familiarity with modern business management. Accredited degree programs have been developed or are in the process of being developed. Among the most important institutions of higher education teaching fashion design in 1975 were the Fashion Institute of Technology and the Royal College of Art in London.

LINDA OLSHEIM

Levels and Programs of Study

Programs in fashion design usually require as a minimum prerequisite a secondary education and/or demonstrated talent or skill in fashion design and lead to the following awards: a certificate or diploma or a bachelor's degree. Programs are designed to provide professional training in fashion design and consist of lectures, seminars, workshop practice, and demonstrations. Programs stress both the underlying theory of fashion and the practical aspects of design, with the aim of providing a professional and imaginative approach to fashion design. Course content may include some of the following: garment construction and patternmaking, design theory, fashion illustration, design construction, execution of design, history of design and costume, textiles, sketching and drawing techniques, as well as specialized courses in men's, women's, and children's clothing; sportswear; evening attire; fashion accessory design; and jewelry design. Programs prepare students for a variety of careers in the fashion industry.

Major International and National Organizations

INTERNATIONAL

Centro internationale delle arte del costume
Palazzo Grassi
Venice, Italy

EEC Inter-Professional Committee for
   the Clothing Industries
20 avenue des Arts
1040 Brussels, Belgium

European Clothing Manufacturers Association
8 rue de Richelieu
75001 Paris, France

Fashion Group
9 Rockefeller Plaza
New York, New York 10020 USA

International Association of Clothing
  Designers (IACD)
12 South Twelfth Street, Room 512
Philadelphia, Pennsylvania 19107 USA

International Federation Textile and Clothing
Koning Albert-laan, 27
9000 Ghent, Belgium

NATIONAL

Belgium:
  Fédération de la couture de Belgique
  13 rue Brederode
  1000 Brussels

France:
  Chambre syndicale de la mode parisienne
  132 rue du Faubourg Saint-Honoré
  Paris

Italy:
  Camera nazionale della moda italiana
  via Lombardia 44
  00187 Rome

People's Republic of China:
  Fang chich k'o hsueh yen chiu yuan
  Peking, Hopeh

Switzerland:
  Couture-Verband der Schweiz
  Stockerstrasse 44
  8002 Zurich

United Kingdom:
  Associated Fashion Designers of London
  28 Market Place
  London W1, England

United States:
  Council of Fashion Designers of
    America
  32 East 57th Street
  New York, New York 10022

  Educational Foundation for the
    Fashion Industries
  227 West 27th Street
  New York, New York 10001

  National Association of Fashion and
    Accessory Designers
  31 South Yewdall Street
  Philadelphia, Pennsylvania 19139

For additional national and international
organizations consult:

Directory of European Associations. Beckenham,
  Kent, England: CBD Research, 1971.
Yearbook of International Organizations. Brussels:
  Union of International Associations, 1948–.
  Published biennially.

Principal Information Sources

GENERAL

Guides to the literature include:

*Books for Occupational Educational Programs: A
  List for Community Colleges, Technical Institutes,
  and Vocational Schools.* New York: Bowker,
  1971. An unannotated but comprehensive
  basic list of books designed for community
  and junior college programs. Consult pages
  21–30.
Chamberlin. M. W. *Guide to Art Reference
  Books.* Chicago: American Library Association, 1959. A standard guide.
Colas, R. *Bibliographie générale du costume et de
  la mode, description des suites, recueils, séries,
  revues, et livres français et étrangers relatifs au
  costume civil, militaire et religieux aux modes,
  aux coiffures et aux divers accessoires de l'habillement.* (2 vols.) Paris: Colas, 1933. An annotated basic source.
Forrester, G. *Occupational Literature: An Annotated Bibliography.* New York: Wilson, 1964.
  A good source; American in orientation;
  includes a discussion of educational opportunities.
Hiler, H., and Hiler, M. *Bibliography of Costume:
  A Dictionary Catalog of About Eight Thousand
  Books and Periodicals.* (Edited by H. G. Cuch-
  ing, assisted by A. V. Moris.) New York: Wil-
  son, 1939.
Snowden, J. *European Folk Dress: A Guide to 555
  Books and Other Sources of Information for the
  Costume Society.* Bibliography No. 2. London:
  Victoria and Albert Museum, 1973.

Introductions to the field include:

Bigelow, M. S. *Fashion in History: Apparel in the
  Western World.* Minneapolis: Burgess, 1970.
Brockman, H. L. *The Theory of Fashion De-
  sign.* New York: Wiley, 1965. Contains a
  bibliography.
Brogden, J. *Fashion Design.* London: Studio
  Vista, 1971.
Evans, M. *Costume Throughout the Ages.* Phila-
  delphia: Lippincott, 1950. Includes bibliog-
  raphies at the end of chapters as well as a
  general bibliography.
Jarnow, J. A., and Judelle, B. *Inside the Fashion
  Business: Text and Readings.* New York: Wiley,
  1974.
Kolodny, R. *Fashion Design for Moderns.* New
  York: Fairchild, 1966.
Latske, A., and Hostetter, H. P. *The Wide World
  of Clothing, Economics, Social Significance, Selection.* New York: Ronald Press, 1968. Contains a bibliography.

Shelson, M. G. *Design Through Draping.* Minneapolis: Burgess, 1974.

Shultz, G. *How to Be a Fashion Designer.* New York: McBride, 1944.

Sources dealing with education and career opportunities are:

McDermott, I. E., and Norris, J. L. *Opportunities in the Clothing Industry.* Peoria, Illinois: Charles A. Bennett, 1972.

Seigel, M. *Looking Forward to a Career: Fashion.* Minneapolis: Dillon Press, 1970.

"Vocational School's Programs Prepare Students for Clothing Industry." *School Management,* October 1972, *16,* 49–50.

Your Future in Fashion Design. New York: Fashion Group, 1971.

For further educational information consult:

Education Abstracts. Paris: UNESCO, Educational Clearing House, 1963–.

Education Index. New York: Wilson, 1929–. See "Fashion," "Clothing Industry," "Costume."

International Designer. Philadelphia: International Association of Clothing Designers, 1964–.

Histories of the field include:

Daves, J. *Ready-Made Miracle: The American Story of Fashion for the Millions.* New York: Putnam's, 1967.

Evans, M. *Costume Throughout the Ages.* Philadelphia: Lippincott, 1950. Intended as a school text; includes bibliographies, historic dress, and regional costumes.

Köhler, K. *History of Costume.* (Edited and augmented by E. von Sichart; translated by A. K. Dallas.) New York: Watt, 1928. A one-volume history from antiquity to 1870. Emphasis is on the technical side. Includes bibliography and patterns.

Leloir, M. *Histoire du costume de l'antiquité à 1941.* Paris: Ernst, 1933–1949. Each volume of this work covers one period of time and includes bibliographies.

Lester, K. M. *Historic Costume: A Résumé of the Characteristic Types of Costume from the Most Remote Times to the Present Day.* Peoria, Illinois: Manual Arts Press, 1942. A brief survey containing a bibliography.

Planche, J. R. *A Cyclopedia of Costume or Dictionary of Dress Including Notices of Contemporaneous Fashions of the Continent; A General Chronological History of the Principal Countries of Europe from the Commencement of the Christian Era to the Accession of George the Third.* (2 vols.) London: Chatto and Windus, 1876–1879. A standard text; Volume 1 is a dictionary, and Volume 2 is a history.

CURRENT BIBLIOGRAPHIES

Art Index. New York: Wilson, 1933–. Published quarterly.

Bibliography Index. New York: Wilson, 1937–.

Education Index. New York: Wilson, 1929–.

Internationale Bibliographie der Zeitschriftenliteratur aus allen Gebieten des Wissens. Osnabrück, Federal Republic of Germany: Felix Dietrich, 1965–.

PERIODICALS

Clothing Institute Journal (UK), *Confección industrial* (Spain), *Confezione italiana: moda e costume, Couture* (France), *Custom Tailor* (US), *Dressmaking* (Japan), *Fashion Forecast* (UK), *Femme chic* (France), *International Designer* (US), *Officiel de la couture et de la mode de Paris* (France), *Shveinaja promyshlennost* (USSR), *Symcobel* (Belgium), *Tailor and Menswear* (Australia), *Techniques de l'habillement* (France), *Vogue* (US), *Women's Wear Daily* (US), *Women's Wear Manufacturer* (UK).

For a more complete listing of journals in the fashion, clothing, and textile industries consult:

Ulrich's International Periodicals Directory. New York: Bowker, biennial.

ENCYCLOPEDIAS, DICTIONARIES, HANDBOOKS

Fernald, M. *Costume Design and Making: A Practical Handbook.* London: A & C Black, 1969.

Harmuth, L. *Dictionary of Textiles.* (2nd ed.) New York: Fairchild, 1920. Contains 8500 terms and definitions.

Hill, M. H., and Bucknell, P. A. *The Evolution of Fashion: Pattern and Cut from 1066-1930.* New York: Van Nostrand Reinhold, 1968. Handbook of basic patterns, with some history.

Jaffe, H., and Relis, N. *Draping for Fashion Design.* Reston, Virginia: Reston Publishing, 1975.

Leloir, M. *Dictionnaire du costume et de ses accessoires, des armes et des origines à nos jours.* Paris: Grund, 1951. A standard work.

Liton, G. E. *The Modern Textile Dictionary.* New York: Duel, Sloan and Pearce, 1954. A selected list of semitechnical and technical books on textile terms, apparel, color, and fashion.

Liton, G. E. *The Modern Textile and Apparel Dictionary.* Plainfield, New Jersey: Textile Book Service, 1973.

Picken, M. B. *Fashion Dictionary.* New York: Funk and Wagnalls, 1973. Contains more than 10,000 definitions.

DIRECTORIES

American Art Directory. New York: Bowker, 1898–. Published annually. Lists international art schools, entrance requirements, and courses of study in retailing and fashion design.
The World of Learning. London: Europa, 1947–. Published annually. Lists learned societies, associations, research centers, universities, and colleges for every country in the world.

RESEARCH CENTERS, INSTITUTES, INFORMATION CENTERS

Centre d'étude technique des industries
de l'habillement
5 rue Greffuehe
Paris, France

Educational Foundation for the
Fashion Industries
227 West 27th Street
New York, New York 10001 USA
   Works with the Fashion Institute of Technology and provides information on and evaluation of curriculum, course offerings, and placement of graduates.

Fashion Group
9 Rockefeller Plaza
New York, New York 10020 USA
   Publishes *Your Career in Fashion* and has many committees, including Career Course.

Fédération française des industries du
vêtement masculin
8 rue de Richelieu
Paris, France
   An information and research center.

General Association of the Swiss
Clothing Industry
Utoquai 37
8008 Zurich, Switzerland
   Provides information, carries out research in the clothing field, and covers professional examinations for this area.

National Association of Fashion and
Accessory Designers
31 South Yewdall Street
Philadelphia, Pennsylvania 19139 USA
   Fosters development of the black fashion designer, disseminates information on educational and economic opportunities in the field, maintains a library, holds seminars and workshops, offers national scholarships.

Nederlandse economische vereniging voor
de confectie-industrie
Van Eeghenstraat 107
Amsterdam, Netherlands
   Disseminates information; carries on and promotes research and professional examinations in this field.

New York Fashion Designers
1457 Broadway
New York, New York 10036 USA
   Conducts courses for fashion school graduates.

Sveriges konfektionsindustriförbund
Box 16170
103 24 Stockholm 16, Sweden
   Disseminates information and carries on vocational training in the field.

   [Bibliography prepared by Susan Johnson.]

FAURE REPORT
See Learning To Be (Report on Higher Education), Multinational.

FEDERAL MINISTRY FOR EDUCATION AND SCIENCE
(Bundesministerium für Bildung und Wissenschaft), Federal Republic of Germany

   The *Bundesministerium für Bildung und Wissenschaft* (BMBW: Federal Ministry for Education and Science) has federal responsibility in the fields of education and science. These responsibilities are limited in comparison to those of the eleven *Länder* (states); the ministry holds important powers, however—especially in the areas of general educational planning, vocational education, higher education, science promotion, and student aid. BMBW works closely with the state governments in exercising its powers in education and science. In 1974 the budget of BMBW was 3,372,000,000 DM, all derived from federal tax revenue. BMBW and the state governments cooperate in long-range educational planning within the *Bund-Länder-Kommission für Bildungsplanung* (Federal-State Commission for Educational Planning).

   BMBW and the state governments annually set up the *Hochschulrahmenplan* (Higher

Education Outline Plan), which governs construction in the higher education sector. BMBW and the state governments share equally in the cost of these programs. In 1974, BMBW spent roughly 1,890,000,000 DM for this purpose. BMBW also prepared a draft of the *Hochschulrahmengesetz* (Higher Education Sector Law) to establish basic principles to guide the higher education sector.

Federal funds administered by BMBW cover roughly two thirds of all student aid in higher education. In 1974, 49 percent of all students in the higher education sector were supported with up to 500 DM per month on the basis of the *Bundesausbildungsförderungsgesetz* (Federal Education Advancement Law) at a cost of 1,241,500,000 DM for BMBW and 686,500,000 DM for the state governments. Both BMBW and the state governments finance the *Deutsche Forschungsgemeinschaft* (German Research Society). The total budget in 1974 was 593,000,000 DM, which in turn supported the *Sonderforschungsbereiche* (Priority Research Areas) at the universities. On the basis of the *Graduiertenförderungsgesetz* (Graduate Grants Act), both BMBW and the state governments also support the postgraduate studies of future scientists and teachers in higher education. In 1974 the federal government spent 59,600,000 DM and the state governments 16,600,000 DM for this purpose.

In addition to an annual report, BMBW publishes the monthly *Informationen*. BMBW also issues a publication series of educational and scientific studies.

P.O. Box 120124
53 Bonn 12, Federal Republic of
Germany

FEDERAL-STATE COMMISSION FOR EDUCATIONAL PLANNING
(Bund-Länder-Kommission für Bildungsplanung),
Federal Republic of Germany

In June 1970 the governments of the *Bund* (federation) and *Länder* (states) in the Federal Republic of Germany established the *Bund-Länder-Kommission für Bildungsplanung* (BLK: Federal-State Commission for Educational Planning) to serve as the coordinating body between the federal government and the eleven state governments in educational and research matters. The commission has eighteen members, including seven representatives of federal departments and a member from each state government. The federal representatives hold eleven votes, which are cast jointly; each representative of the state governments holds one vote.

Representatives of the German Education Council, Science Council, Local Authorities Central Association, and Federal Committee on Vocational Education participate in the commission's work in an advisory capacity.

The chairmanship of the commission alternates each year between a representative of the federal government and a representative of the *Länder*. The secretary general is appointed by the federal government; his deputy is appointed by the states. The secretariat, incorporated into the budget of the Office of the Federal Republic, has a thirty-member staff.

The commission has four standing committees: Committee for Educational Planning, Committee for the Advancement of Science, Committee for the Educational Budget, and Committee for Educational Innovations. These committees appoint working groups and ad hoc groups or seek the advice of experts when necessary. The commission's recommendations are submitted to the federal and the state governments. Only those governments that have approved a decision are bound by it.

In 1971 a commission agreement for the coordination and joint financing of pilot projects in all sectors of education was approved by the federal and state governments at an annual cost of approximately 120,000,000 DM. In 1972 the federal and state governments approved measures concerning improvements in elementary and vocational education, demands for more teachers, and expansion of higher education.

The commission's *Bildungsgesamtplan* (General Plan for Education) was approved by the federal and state governments in 1973. The plan sets the main goals of educational policy and contains essential data for a national educational budget.

Also in 1973 BLK prepared a draft of the *Rahmenvereinbarung Forschungsförderung* (Federal-State Agreement on Research Promotion), establishing cooperation between the federal and state governments regarding the promotion of scientific research institutions and projects of national importance, such as the *Max-Planck-Gesellschaft* (Max Planck Society) and *Deutsche Forschungsgemeinschaft* (German Research Society).

In 1974 the commission published a study on the demand for teachers. The study presented and recommended the five-year *Kosten- und Finanzierungsplan* (Plan for the Educational System).

The commission publishes the annual *Guide to Higher Education and More University Jobs,* in cooperation with the German Labor Office.

Friedrich-Ebert-Allee 39
D-5300 Bonn 1, Federal Republic of Germany

EBERHARD JOBST

FEDERATION OF ALL-PAKISTAN UNIVERSITIES ACADEMIC STAFF ASSOCIATIONS

In May 1975 the Federation of All-Pakistan Universities Academic Staff Associations (FAPUASA) was founded by representatives of the staff from the University of Sind, Hyderabad; the University of Peshawar; Gomal University, Dera Ismail Khan; Islamia College, Bahawalpur; the University of Agriculture, Lyallpur; the University of Engineering and Technology, Lahore; and University of the Punjab, Lahore. FAPUASA seeks to coordinate activities and safeguard the interests of its members, to further the cause of university education, to improve academic standards, and to seek representation on various policy-forming and decision-making bodies of the government.

The main decision-making body of FAPUASA is the executive council, composed of the presidents and secretaries of the member associations. The president of the council is elected (by the executive council) from the presidents of the member associations and serves for one year; the secretary of the member association from which the council president has been chosen becomes the secretary of the federation. The executive council meets at least twice a year. The constitution of the federation may be amended by a two-thirds' vote of the members present at a meeting of the executive council.

Department of Administrative Science
University of the Punjab, New Campus
Lahore, Pakistan

MUNEER AHMAD

FEDERATION OF PRIVATE UNIVERSITIES OF CENTRAL AMERICA AND PANAMA
(Federación de universidades privadas de América central y Panamá)

The *Federación de universidades privadas de América central y Panamá* (FUPAC: Federation of Private Universities of Central America and Panama, a regional, nongovernmental federation of eight universities, was formed at Managua, Nicaragua, in August 1966. It is concerned primarily with the educational, social, and moral development of the area.

FUPAC devises plans for coordinating curricula and exchange programs, guards the autonomy of member universities, and seeks technical advice and international assistance to improve teaching and research. It also sets reciprocal standards to benefit teachers and students involved in academic exchanges; stimulates the creation of regional institutions in specific fields not covered by other universities; and offers a reciprocal advisory program in administrative and academic areas, including libraries.

The federation is governed by a directive board made up of the rectors of the member universities. The board elects a president and a secretary general at an annual meeting. The secretary general handles administrative and legal details from the permanent headquarters established in Guatemala City, Guatemala, in 1970.

The federation publishes *Boletín informativo* quarterly; and *Informe estadístico*, annual statistical bulletin.

avenida 3-38 Zone 10
Guatemala City, Guatemala

See also: Organization of American States.

FEDERATION OF SOCIALIST UNIONS OF POLISH YOUTH
(Federacja socjalistycznych związków młodzieży polskiej)

The *Federacja socjalistycznych związków młodzieży polskiej* (FSZMP: Federation of Socialist Unions of Polish Youth), established in 1973, consists of five organizations: Union of Socialist Youth, active among working youth; Union of Socialist Rural Youth, active among working rural youth; Socialist Unions of Polish Students, active at universities; Polish Pathfinders Union, active at primary and secondary school levels; and Socialist Union of Military Youth, active among youth on military duty. Membership in the federation numbers around five million. Vice-presidents of the federation are presidents of member organizations.

The main concerns of the federation are the socialist education of Polish youth; participation of youth in the political, economic, and social life of the country; and improvement of educational qualifications of working youth. The federation participates in sports activities, directs two youth travel offices, and maintains contact with other international youth groups.

The federation publishes a daily paper, *Sztandar młodych*. Every member organization publishes its own newspaper, usually weekly.

Nowy Świat 18/20
00-920 Warsaw, Poland

FELLOWSHIPS
See Financial Aid.

FEMALE STUDIES
See Women and Higher Education: Women's Studies and Curricular Modification.

FIELD EXPERIENCE
See Cooperative Education and Off-Campus Experience.

FIELD EXPERIENCE PLAN
See Cooperative Education and Off-Campus Experience: Cooperative Education in the United States.

FIELDS AND PRIORITIES IN ACADEMIC RESEARCH
See Research: Fields and Priorities in Academic Research.

FIELDS OF STUDY

The taxonomy for the fields of studies in the Encyclopedia includes 141 entries. Many of these entries have separate subdivisions. The taxonomy is a composite of classifications contained in the following sources: (1) *International Standard Classification of Education* (ISCED). Paris: UNESCO, 1974 (revised, 1976); (2) Organisation for Economic Co-operation and Development, *Development of Higher Education, 1950–1967. Statistical Survey: Analytical Report.* Paris: OECD, 1970; (3) *School System—A Guide.* Strasbourg: Council of Europe, Council for Cultural Cooperation, 1965; and (4) *A Taxonomy of Instructional Programs in Higher Education.* Washington, D.C.: U.S. Department of Health, Education and Welfare, Office of Education, 1970.

The Encyclopedia taxonomy was based primarily on the *International Standard Classification of Education*. As an international classification scheme it is necessarily abstract in its approach to accommodate the many differences in international education. Therefore, its structure, although based upon existing patterns of education found in many countries, does not reflect the exact educational situation of any one country, nor does its terminology exactly conform to that found in any one country. Therefore, many important fields have been added, some fields of study descriptions have been changed, and other modifications have been made based upon the educational taxonomies consulted and the advice of experts and the professionals in the fields concerned.

Each field of study presentation appearing in this encyclopedia includes an introductory essay describing the nature of the field from an international perspective. Specifically, each essay consists of a brief definition of the field; the branches or divisions of the field; related or allied subjects; history of the field as an academic discipline, recent developments, trends, or innovations; and a brief description of education or training in the field internationally.

Following the introductory essay is a description of the levels and programs of study based on the ISCED classification. Each presentation also has a listing of the national and international organizations in the field, current bibliographies, periodicals, encyclopedias, dictionaries, handbooks, directories, research centers, institutes, and information centers.

Agriculture, Forestry, and Fisheries

Agricultural Economics
Agricultural Engineering
Animal Science
Crop Science
Dairy Science
Entomology
Fisheries Science
Food Science and Technology
Forestry
Horticulture
Plant Pathology
Poultry Science
Soil and Water Science and Technology
Wildlife Ecology and Management

Architecture and Planning

Architecture
City and Regional Planning
Landscape Architecture
Urban Design

Arts, Fine and Applied

Art, History of
Crafts
Dance
Drawing and Painting
Fashion Design
Industrial Design
Interior Design
Music
Photography and Cinematography
Printmaking
Sculpture
Theater Arts

Commerce and Business Administration

Accountancy
Business and Office Technologies
Finance
International Business
Management Education
Marketing
Public Administration

Communications

Mass Communications

Education Science and Teacher Training

Adult Education, Teacher Training for
Counselor Education
Early Childhood Education, Teacher Training for
Educational Administration
Higher Education
Instructional Technology
Physical Education
Special Education

Engineering

Aeronautical and Astronautical
  Engineering
Bioengineering
Chemical Engineering
Civil Engineering
Drafting and Design
Electrical and Electronics Engineering
Industrial Engineering
Mechanical Engineering
Metallurgical Engineering and Materials
  Science
Mining Engineering
Nuclear Engineering
Petroleum Engineering
Surveying

Health Fields

Chiropractic
Dentistry and Dental Specialties
Dental Auxiliaries
Hospital and Health Services
  Administration
Medical Technologies
Medicine and Medical Specialties
Midwifery
Nursing
Occupational Therapy
Optometry
Osteopathic Medicine
Pharmacy
Physical Therapy
Physicians' Assistants, Programs for
Podiatry
Public Health
Radiologic Technologies
Veterinary Medicine

Home Economics

Home Economics

Humanities

Archeology
Classics
Comparative Literature
History
Languages
Linguistics
Literature
Philosophy

Translators' and Interpreters'
  Programs

Law and Jurisprudence

International Law

Mathematics and Computer Sciences

Actuarial Science
Computer Science
Mathematics
Statistics

Military Science

Military Science

Natural Sciences

Astronomy
Biological Sciences
Chemistry
Geological Sciences
Meteorology
Oceanography
Physics

Religion and Theology

Religion and Theology

Service Trades Programs

Cookery
Hotel/Motel Administration
Retailing
Tourist Trades

Social and Behavioral Science

Anthropology
Area Studies
Demography and Population Studies
Economics
Geography
Political Science
Psychology
Sociology

Trade, Craft, and Industrial Programs

Automotice Technologies
Construction and Building Technology
Electricity, Industrial and Domestic
Electronic Equipment Installation and
  Servicing

Metal Trades and Mechanical Repair
    Trades
Optical Lens Making
Textile Technology

Transportation

Transportation

Other

Criminology
Environmental Studies
Interdisciplinary Studies
Library and Information Science
Museum Studies
Nautical Science
Police and Law Enforcement Training
Security, Private or Civil
Social Welfare

15 TO 18: REPORT OF THE CENTRAL ADVISORY COUNCIL FOR EDUCATION (Higher Education Report), England

In its two-volume report *15 to 18* (London: H. M. Stationery Office, 1959, 1960), the Central Advisory Council to the British minister of education, under the chairmanship of G. Crowther, sets forth a twenty-year comprehensive program on the development of education for the fifteen to eighteen age group, considered in light of the country's changing social and economic conditions and the needs of individual citizens. During its investigation, the council focused on the interrelationship of various stages of education, the balance between general and specialized studies, and the role of examinations. The following findings and recommendations are reported.

Both the quality and duration of education for persons in the fifteen to eighteen age group are inadequate. Approximately 50 percent of the student population leave school at age fifteen, the compulsory school-leaving age; 25 percent leave school at age fifteen for employment but participate in some form of part-time further education;

and the remaining 25 percent attend grammar and other selective schools.

The school-leaving age should be raised to sixteen; and county colleges should be developed, so that compulsory part-time education through age eighteen can be provided for those who leave school prior to that age. Part-time education should include provisions for block release for study, smoother transition from full-time to part-time schooling, and greater effort to alleviate high failure rates. An extension of part-time educational opportunities is needed to help meet the growing demand for technicians and craftsmen and to raise the proportion of young people who continue their education after age sixteen. The existing diverse vocational training programs should be gradually transformed into a national system of practical educational training.

The council recommends the retention of the specialization or "education in depth" offered by the grammar and other selective schools; however, it urges greater attention to nonspecialized studies. Moreover, since the demand for higher education far exceeds the supply of places, which creates pressures at the sixth forms, the council recommends a better balance between supply and demand.

If the council's recommendations are put into effect, by 1980 there will be a fourfold increase in full-time education, which will take the form of an expansion of sixth forms, practical courses, and sandwich courses and the creation of new technical schools, comprehensive schools, and perhaps special junior colleges. The expansion should be undertaken to ensure students the freedom to choose among a wide range of fields of study and types of institutions. An increase in the teaching force will be needed to ensure a successful implementation of the proposed reforms. The number of places in the teacher training colleges should be increased and an active campaign conducted to attract university graduates to a teaching career.

Change will require an extensive commitment to an orderly phased program of expansion. Essential to its achievement are public determination and a major research effort to provide the expertise for educational planning.

FIJI

Population: 559,800 (estimate). Student enrollment in primary school: 135,092; secondary school: 26,202; higher education—university: 1031 (1975); higher education—nonuniversity: 2000 (estimate). Student enrollment in higher education as percentage of age group (18–22): 3%. Language of instruction: English (university). Academic calendar: February to November (university). Percentage of national budget expended on all education: 19%; higher education: 2%. [Except where otherwise noted, figures are for 1974.]

Prior to 1965 higher education institutions in the English-language countries of the South Pacific included only a number of postsecondary training facilities and theological colleges. Plans for the creation of a regional university can be traced back to at least 1950, when R. A. Derrick was appointed by the South Pacific Commission (a regional body) to report on vocational schooling in the area. Derrick recommended support for "a complete structure of vocational training within the South Pacific region from primary to university stages" (Beauchamp, 1972. p. 60), but little came of the suggestion.

In 1965 the governments of New Zealand and the United Kingdom, with the cooperation of the Australian government, initiated the Higher Education Mission to the South Pacific to investigate the need for, and feasibility of, creating a regional university for the countries. In 1966 the mission, headed by Sir Charles Morris, recommended establishment of the autonomous University of the South Pacific on the site of the Royal New Zealand Air Force Base in Suva, Fiji. This recommendation was met with criticism from many interests. Subsequently, according to a development

scheme authored by Sir Norman Alexander under the auspices of the British Inter-University Council for Higher Education Overseas, the university was planned to offer preuniversity programs and establish ties with preexisting higher education institutions, among them the Fiji School of Medicine and the South Pacific Regional College of Tropical Agriculture in Western Samoa.

In 1968 the University of the South Pacific began preuniversity programs at the air base facilities, and a year later it started programs for the degree and diploma of education. It received a Royal Charter of the United Kingdom in 1970, and the king of Tonga was appointed its first chancellor. From an enrollment of 160 in 1968, the number of full-time students increased to 1031 in 1975. The students have arrived from American Samoa, the Solomon Islands, the Cook Islands, Fiji, the Gilbert Islands, Tuvalu, Nauru, the New Hebrides, Niue, the Tokelau Islands, Tonga, the Trust Territory of the Pacific Islands, and Western Samoa (*University of the South Pacific Calendar,* 1975, p. 33).

National Educational Policy

The Royal Charter states that the objectives of the regional university are "the maintenance, advancement and dissemination of knowledge by teaching, consultancy and research and otherwise, and the provision at appropriate levels of education and training responsive to the well-being and needs of the communities of the South Pacific" (*University of the South Pacific Calendar,* 1975, p. 34). Admission to the university cannot be contingent upon religious, ethnic, or political background.

In order to implement the goal of providing manpower training to support the public and the private sectors in the countries of the university region (which does not include American Samoa or the United States Trust Territory), the university has instituted a policy of projecting student numbers on the basis, when possible, of national or territorial manpower needs. In addition, the university follows a policy of creating close ties with some of the other third-level institutions in the region; to this end, it has initiated reviews of medical and agricultural education in the region and has established relations with the Derrick Technical Institute, the Fiji School of Agriculture, the South Pacific Regional College of Tropical Agriculture, and the Fiji School of Medicine. The university, in accordance with a policy of supporting general education in the South Pacific, has developed its extension program.

Legal Basis of Educational System and Types of Institutions

The legal basis of the University of the South Pacific is its charter, which describes the powers of the university, the titles and responsibilities of its officers, and its administrative structure; it also contains the university statutes.

Institutions of higher education in Fiji range from a theological school to the regional university. The university is divided into schools of education, natural resources, and social and economic development— each with a specific objective. The school of education prepares secondary teachers and the other school staff for positions in countries served by the university. The school of natural resources promotes the rational use of natural resources and industrial expansion. The school of social and economic development imparts instruction "oriented particularly towards a critical understanding of the development process and its social implications" *(University of the South Pacific Calendar*, 1975, p. 130).

Also located in Fiji are the Fiji School of Agriculture (founded 1954), Derrick Technical Institute (founded 1964), the Central School of Nursing (founded 1944), the Fiji School of Medicine (founded 1886), the Pacific Theological College (founded 1966), the Corpus Christi Teachers' College (founded 1958), and the Pacific Regional Seminary (founded 1972).

Relationship with Secondary Education

Of the students enrolled at the University of the South Pacific by April 1, 1975, 80 percent were Fiji islanders; the remaining 20 percent were residents of the other countries or territories within the university region, and a small number were from countries outside of the region.

The Fiji system of secondary education consists of academic programs leading to the New Zealand School Certificate Examination in the third or fourth year of study and the New Zealand University Entrance Examination in the fourth or fifth year of study; Fiji also offers agriculture, trade, and teacher training programs at the secondary level.

The system of eight years of primary school (classes 1–8) and four years of secondary school (forms 3–6) is gradually being replaced by a system of six years of primary (classes 1–6) and six years of secondary school (forms 1–6). All except 32 of Fiji's 760 primary and secondary schools are run by nongovernment bodies; nearly all the nongovernment schools are heavily subsidized by the government.

Admission Requirements

Admission to the university is possible at several levels of study, from the first preuniversity year to the first year of diploma or degree programs. The minimum requirement for entrance into the university is a pass in the New Zealand School Certificate Examination or the Cambridge Overseas School Certificate Examination. Applicants from outside Fiji are eligible to enter the Preliminary I Program, the first year of preuniversity study, by fulfilling either of these requirements. (The senate, at its discretion, may enroll an applicant who has not met either requirement.) Applicants from Fiji are required to pass the New Zealand University Entrance Examination while still in school (form 6); they are then admitted directly to the university's Preliminary II program. The Preliminary I Program is at the level of form 6 of the organization of secondary school systems in the United Kingdom. Students with different qualifications from those of students entering the Preliminary I Program are subject to other eligibility requirements.

In addition to the above admission requirements for students entering the university, certain restrictions are placed on applicants to particular programs.

Administration and Control

The major officers of the university are the chancellor, the titular head of the institution; the pro-chancellor; the vice-chancellor, who is the chief academic and administrative official; the deputy vice-chancellor; and the registrar, who is secretary of the council and the senate.

University administration consists of three main bodies: the council, the senate, and the court of convocation. The council, headed by the pro-chancellor, is the main executive body of the university. It exercises general control over university affairs and is responsible for the property and revenue of the institution. Any academic affairs coming before the council but not previously discussed by the senate must be referred to the senate by the council. The senate, over which the vice-chancellor presides, is responsible for the academic functions of the institution. Any financial affairs, or any matter which the senate considers "in any way to affect the general well-being of the university" (Charter, Section 21, paragraph 2) or its relationship with outside individuals or bodies, must be submitted to the council by the senate. The court of convocation registers the opinion of alumni on university affairs, addresses queries to the council, and elects certain members of the council. The members of the court of convocation include graduates of tertiary institutions offering at least three years of study beyond the school certificate level within the university region, which, according to the Court of Convocation Ordinance, includes the Solomon Islands, the Cook Islands, Fiji, the Gilbert Islands, Tuvalu, Nauru, the New

Hebrides, Niue, the Tokelau Islands, Tonga, and Western Samoa.

The chancellor is appointed by the council after consultation with the senate, as are the registrar and the deputy vice-chancellor. The vice-chancellor is appointed by the council on the recommendation of the senate and a joint committee of the council and the senate. The pro-chancellor is appointed by the council.

The council consists ex officio of the pro-chancellor, the vice-chancellor, the deputy vice-chancellor, and appointed and elected members. Appointees are persons designated by the governments of the countries and territories within the university region and the British Resident Commission of the New Hebrides, but excluding Niue and the Tokelau Islands; persons designated by the governments of Australia and New Zealand, by the South Pacific Commission, by the Overseas Liaison Committee of the American Council of Education, by the Privy Council, and by the Inter-University Council for Higher Education Overseas of the United Kingdom; persons designated by institutions affiliated to, associated with, or cooperating with the university; and professors designated by the senate. Elected members are persons voted to the council by the court; nonprofessional members of the senate voted to the council by nonprofessional staff in the senate; university students; and coopted members with experience in agriculture, commerce, industry, the professions, or religion.

The senate consists of its ex officio members: the vice-chancellor, the deputy vice-chancellor, the professors, the librarian, and the dean of preliminary studies; it also includes appointees by the council after consultation with, or upon recommendation by, the senate, in addition to members elected by the nonprofessorial staff.

Programs and Degrees

The school of education of the university offers three programs for training secondary teachers, specialist graduate teachers, principals, educational administrators, and advisers in schools of the region: (1) a three-year diploma in education program, (2) a four-year concurrent program for the Bachelor of Arts or Bachelor of Science degree, and (3) a graduate certificate of education for preparing secondary school teachers and graduate specialists.

The school of natural resources prepares students for positions in industry, teaching (in cooperation with the school of education), business and administration, and research. It offers the Bachelor of Science program, which lasts a minimum of five semesters, and the Bachelor of Science with Graduate Certificate in Education program, which is eight semesters in duration. "Acceptance of students for the degree M.Sc. and Ph.D. can only be made in special circumstances and when staff and space permit" *(University of the South Pacific Calendar,* 1975, p. 121).

The school of social and economic development offers a five-semester Bachelor of Arts program in economics, sociology, geography, history, administration, politics, psychology, and accounting. Both the school of education and the school of social and economic development have introduced in-service, short-term diploma and certificate courses in accordance with their objectives.

The university maintains a substantial extension service to conduct external programs. Extension centers in the Solomon Islands, the Cook Islands, and Tonga have been established, and more are planned. Among the activities in extension services are credit courses offered through the university satellite communications network and the external diploma of education program.

The Fiji School of Agriculture (FSA) offers a three-year program to train personnel for the Veterinary, Extension, Research and Fisheries Division of the Fiji Department of Agriculture. Under an arrangement with the university, all students take the Preliminary I (Agriculture) Program as part of their three-year course.

The Derrick Technical Institute (DTI) offers programs in engineering, secretarial skills, and business studies. The business studies are a three-year sandwich (theoretical and practical studies) program or a five-year "release" program, which culminates with the Diploma in Business Studies of the University of the South Pacific. The Central School of Nursing (CNS) offers a program leading to licensing as New Zealand registered nurse. The Fiji School of Medicine conducts five- and four- year programs in medicine and dentistry and shorter programs in related fields. The first year of the program in medicine, dentistry, and dietetics is conducted at the university in the Preliminary II Program.

The two teachers colleges in Fiji offer programs for primary instructors and secondary teachers. The last year of the program offered by the Corpus Christi Teachers' College is parallel to the first year of the degree programs of the university, as is the last year of the DTI business program, the FSA diploma in agriculture program, the CNS nursing program, and the FSM physiotherapy, radiography, laboratory technology, and dietetics programs.

Financing

The governments of the university region have formed a University Grants Committee to counsel them on the amount of funds needed to meet recurring and capital expenditures of the institution. The university's level of recurrent and capital expenditure as recommended by the UGC for the 1975–77 period has been accepted in principle by the financial representatives of the regional governments. "It was apparent, however, that in a period of rapid inflation, the cost of maintaining the University would place heavy strains on the resources of the countries of the region. Having promised the support at the maximum of their abilities the government representatives made it clear that for some years the University would have to depend for part of its recurrent financing on metropolitan governments, in particular those of Australia, Britain, New Zealand" *(University of the South Pacific Calendar,* 1975, p. 35).

The government of New Zealand provided the government of Fiji with the base facilities for the university, and the British government gave £1,250,000 toward establishment and operation of the institution. In 1975 the governments of the university region contributed $610 per student per year, in addition to tuition fees, to meet the financial needs of the university.

Student Financial Aid

Scholarships, bursaries, and awards have been provided to students by regional and international governments, organizations, business interests, and individuals. Public scholarships intended to encourage regional countries to send students to the university have been provided by the governments of Australia, Canada, and New Zealand. Private scholarships for this purpose have been provided by, among others, the Shell Oil Company, the Foundation for the Peoples of the South Pacific, the New Zealand Federation of University Women, and Barclay's Bank in the United Kingdom.

Teaching Staff

The levels of the teaching staff at the University of the South Pacific are professor, reader, senior lecturer, lecturer, and tutor. Appointment committees are set up by the council for the selection of teaching staff. When appointing a professor, the committee is composed of the vice-chancellor as chairman, the head of the appropriate school, a professor, two members of the council, and the registrar as secretary. For the appointment of other ranks, except lecturers in preliminary programs, the committee is similarly composed, except that the professor and two council members are replaced by the head of the appropriate subject, a representative of another discipline, and one or two council members. To appoint a preliminary lecturer, this committee adds the chairman of the preliminary studies committee.

Current Problems and Trends

Three problems have been identified (Beauchamp, 1972) at the University of the South Pacific: (1) The institution, which has shown a trend toward expansion since its beginning, will require increasing funds to continue growth; but there is some doubt that sufficient financing for the programs will be forthcoming from countries in the region as United Kingdom support is phased out. (2) The potential financial problem is hampering the effort to establish regional centers planned to serve areas removed from Fiji; this effort is encumbered further by expensive air transportation and resultant poor communication between countries and territories in the region. (3) The countries and territories are reluctant to merge their tertiary institutions with the university, for fear of loss of the national identity of the institutions.

International Cooperation

International aid to the university has been and is being provided largely by countries of the British Commonwealth, the United States, and the United Nations. The governments of Britain and New Zealand have financed construction of student residences for 368 students. These two countries and Australia and India are contributing significantly to expenses for expatriate staff. Some staff members are teaching at the university under an arrangement with Canberra College of Advanced Education, financed by the Australian government. A fisheries training program is sponsored by the Canadian International Development Agency. The Carnegie Corporation of New York has contributed funds that have enabled the university to establish centers in the Solomon Islands, the Gilbert Islands, and Tonga. Carnegie and the United Nations Development Programme (UNDP), in cooperation with the United States National Aeronautics and Space Administration (NASA), are assisting in an experiment to determine the range of uses of two-way satellite communications to the university.

A university curriculum development project for secondary schools in the region has received substantial support from the United Nations Development Programme and UNESCO.

Students in the countries and territories of the region may have the opportunity for tertiary study under the New Zealand Training Scheme conducted in New Zealand, Fiji, and Western Samoa.

[Prepared with the cooperation of the Assistant Minister for Social Welfare, Fiji.]

Bibliography

Alexander, N. *Report on the University of the South Pacific*. Suva: Government Press, 1967.

Beauchamp, E. R. "A Regional University in the South Pacific." *Intellect*, October 1972, *101*.

First Development Plan. Suva: University of the South Pacific, 1970.

Medical Education in the South Pacific. Suva: University of the South Pacific, 1971.

Openings for Forms 5 and 6 Students—1974. Suva: Ministry of Education, Youth and Sport, 1974.

Report of the Higher Education Mission to the South Pacific. London: H. M. Stationery Office, 1966.

University of the South Pacific Calendar 1975. Suva: University of the South Pacific, 1975.

See also: Cooperative Education and Off-Campus Experience: Cooperative Education Worldwide; Oceania: Regional Analysis.

FILER REPORT

See Giving in America: Toward a Stronger Voluntary Sector (Higher Education Report), United States.

FINANCE
(Field of Study)

The field of finance began with the creation of modern business schools early in the twentieth century. Serious study of finance goes back, however, to the invention of money in prehistoric times. The money changers that Christ threw out of the temple were probably quite conversant with many aspects of foreign exchange and investment. Money changing is an international financial transaction, and, thus, because countries have traded with each other since the invention of governments, throughout the history of financial studies international dimensions have been necessary.

Finance was one of the first courses of study offered in American business schools. The usual topic was investments, and course work dealt largely with analysis of securities to be purchased. This branch, macrofinance, includes materials relating to money and banking, securities analysis, and the structure of financial markets in various countries. Microfinance, on the other hand, which deals with financial analysis in a particular firm, came somewhat more slowly to formal education, although early courses in accounting contained much useful material about budgeting and related financial analysis matters. This business school interest has continued to the mid 1970s, although over the years it has been expanded and refined.

The fields most closely related to finance are mathematics and accounting. In medieval times the scholars most interested in the intricacies of long division were money changers, who struggled with difficult ratio problems of scores of local currencies. Because so much of finance is measurable, the field has been enormously stimulated and expanded by the advent of computers and mathematical analysis, and, thus, modern financial students need extensive training in both areas. Also, since the accounts of any organization are critical to financial analysis, the field of accounting has grown and evolved with finance.

Modern financial analysis (in macrofinance and microfinance) deals essentially with five basic problems: (1) types of financing, (2) sources of capital, (3) major uses of capital, (4) protection of capital, and (5) distribution of earnings. These financial functions are universal and can be applied anywhere—in all political systems, not just capitalistic ones. In the twentieth century, however, as each country evolved its own internal money structure and legal environment governing the use of capital, studies in finance gradually became more provincial. The United States became the leader in financial analysis, and its major activities were internal, as blocked currencies, wars, and expropriations during the 1930s made international financial activities less predictable and often unprofitable. In England the financial picture was much more sophisticated in terms of a global outlook, but as the major money markets became American, students, practitioners, and scholars paid less attention to international financial activities. The slow development in England of graduate schools of business may have assisted this trend as well, since serious students of finance tend to congregate in such institutions. By 1950 most of the textbooks, cases, and other study materials were American. By the mid 1960s the finance field was largely American, and the major texts had only a slim final chapter on international matters—if they covered them at all. Just as the texts were American, so was the environment. The typical American student of finance was expected to know about American laws, rules, agencies, and customs governing major financial markets. Moreover, in discussions of sources of capital and types of financing, the American money market was the only one considered.

But as multinational firms grew rapidly in the 1950s and 1960s, managers and a few scholars gradually began to see that environment can affect the results of financial functions—even though the functions themselves are culture free, in the sense that good analysis can be used anywhere. That is, one can use discounted cash flow concepts in any country, but if interest rates are 10 percent in one country and 4 percent in another, the outcomes will be different. And most important, since rates of inflation vary widely, with the rate in the United States much lower than in many other countries, a good financial decision in a 2 percent inflation situation might be a disaster under 10 percent inflation. More-

over, disparate inflation rates lead to exchange rate fluctuations, which shift capital values between countries.

Considerations of this sort led to the rediscovery of international finance, and by 1970 many major universities were following their multinational firms in studying this field. In 1971 the Western world shifted from a more or less fixed exchange rate to floating rates, determined in part by the supply and demand of various currencies. Even in the 1950s a few firms realized that they could in theory make as much money by forecasting devaluations as they could by making products, since those fixed rates were never quite as fixed as some people believed.

University-level training of financial personnel has gradually evolved along American lines. Where undergraduate training is given, tacticians are trained in accounting, mathematics, and computer science, along with more traditional macrofinancial and microfinancial work. Strategists and high-level staff tend to be trained in graduate schools of business, typically obtaining the Master of Business Administration (M.B.A.) degree. Their work is similar to undergraduate training, but at a much more sophisticated level. Scholars and teachers of finance around the world are usually trained in doctoral programs and receive either a Ph.D. or D.B.A. degree from research-oriented universities. While most university work in finance prior to 1960 was done in American universities, graduate schools of business, particularly at the M.B.A. level, are now found in virtually all developed countries and many Third World countries as well. Doctoral work outside the United States and Canada has expanded rapidly, and serious scholars and research publications are found in Western Europe, Australia, Japan, India, the Middle East, and many other regions and countries.

Gradually in the 1960s and 1970s managers in global corporations began to see the advantages of global, as compared to provincial, financial strategies. Instead of concentrating on national issues, the managers began to see the world as a single unified financial system. Within firms, this meant cash flow planning for the entire company, often in as many as fifty countries, with surplus funds in one country routed to deficit situations in another. It made little sense for a manager to borrow locally at 30 percent when the company could reroute funds from another country where interest rates were 8 percent. Moreover, the global corporation's credit rating was normally so high everywhere that it could take advantage of the best terms. Similarly, it made little sense for an American company to invest at home at an expected return of 15 percent, when it could invest elsewhere at 35 percent. Instead of considering each country as a separate entity, all investments, loans, cash flows, and other financial matters were considered as a whole.

The older domestic financial analysis works well for smaller firms, provincial banks, or other local activities, but because most of the major companies in most Western countries are heavily involved in transnational activities, international finance has become an integral part of strategy planning. To become competent financial executives in major corporations, students must have knowledge of international finance as well as general finance. Thus, finance education in the mid 1970s is in a transition: increasingly, international finance is being taught as part of the older provincial finance.

This new trend has led to increasing complexity for major transnational companies, which must consider exchange risks and fifty or more local environments instead of one. Also, if the rate of inflation is a part of one's problem, companies must consider fifty or more inflation rates, as well as the effects of these fifty rates on the home country currency values. Finally, companies must also know how fifty environments affect internal financial functions in the total firm. Virtually no mathematical work has yet been able to take all

of this into account, and, thus, there remains much more work to make international finance a truly integrated and global field of study and action.

RICHARD N. FARMER

Levels and Programs of Study

Programs in finance generally require as a minimum prerequisite a secondary education, though mature students with relevant experience may be admitted with lower educational qualifications. The following awards are offered: certificate or diploma, bachelor's degree (B.B.A., B.Com., B.Sc.), master's degree (M.B.A.), the doctorate (Ph.D.), or their equivalents. Programs in finance generally build on a broad understanding of the field of management, including accountancy, marketing, production and operations analysis, industrial relations, personnel administration, and business policy and strategy.

Programs that lead to awards not equivalent to a first university degree consist primarily of study and practice in the theory of investment analysis and the operation of the financial markets. Often the programs at this level are specially designed by financial institutions and professional associations for their employees. The principal areas of study include portfolio management, the stock market system, and investment institutions. Principal course content usually includes analysis of company financial reports; analysis of shares, bonds, and other types of securities; procedures for handling securities; market transactions; estate and trust management; portfolio balance; principles of life underwriting; and business law. Background courses often include economic theory, money and banking, corporate finance, and statistics.

Programs that lead to a first university degree consist primarily of instruction and seminar or group discussion dealing with the principles and practices of business management with emphasis on finance and investment. Principal course content includes accountancy, commercial law, corporation finance and administration, mathematics, policy, statistics, and economics. Specialized courses include investment and cash management, appraisal of financial securities, personal investment policies and practices, portfolio management, financial institutions, and credit management. In addition, a broad background in the social sciences and related subjects is often provided.

Advanced degree programs consist basically of two levels. Master of Business Administration (M.B.A.) programs are intended to train top-level managers and senior staff for financial institutions (banks, insurance companies), nonfinancial companies (for example, service industries), and government agencies and other nonprofit organizations. Training involves seminar work, case studies, advanced mathematical model building, advanced computer applications, and financial analysis of firms. The second level is for scholars and teachers, with particular emphasis on research. The Doctor of Business Administration (D.B.A.) or Ph.D. in business is normally awarded. While subjects covered are similar in both programs, the M.B.A. work is focused on decision making and actual management, while the doctoral work focuses on academic research and study of the finance function for public and private investment. Dissertations are not typically required for M.B.A. work but are mandatory for doctoral study. Principal subject matter areas within which study and research projects tend to fall include financial market analysis, financial institutions, appraisal of financial securities, investment portfolio management, special problems of institutional investors, estate management, and public policy and the investment market. In addition, many programs include some study of other business administration subjects, such as commercial law, corporation finance, and accountancy. Background subject areas include economic theory, money and banking, economic fluctuations, mathematics, and statistics.

[This section was based on UNESCO's

International Standard Classification of Education (ISCED) (Paris: UNESCO, 1976), with revisions by Richard N. Farmer.]

Major International and National Organizations

INTERNATIONAL

International Association for the Promotion and Protection of Private Foreign Investments
1299 Commugny
Vaud, Switzerland

International Association of Students of Economics and Commercial Sciences
Association internationale des étudiants en sciences économiques et commerciales (AIESEC)
45 avenue Legrand
B-1050 Brussels, Belgium

International Banker Association (IBA)
422 Washington Building
Washington, D.C. 20005 USA

International Bank for Reconstruction and Development
1818 H Street NW
Washington, D.C. 20433 USA

International Centre of Research and Information on Public and Cooperative Economy
47 quai de Rome
4000 Liège, Belgium

International Economic Association (IEA)
Association internationale des sciences économiques (AISE)
54 boulevard Raspail
75006 Paris, France

International Federation of Stock Exchanges
Fédération internationale des bourses de valeurs (FIBV)
129 rue Montmartre
75002 Paris, France

International Finance Corporation IFC)
Société financière internationale (SFI)
1818 H Street NW
Washington, D.C. 20433 USA

International Fiscal Association (IFA)
% Netherlands School of Economics
Burgemeester Oudlaan 50
3016 Rotterdam, Netherlands

International Institute of Banking Studies
Borsgade 4
Copenhagen, Denmark

International Institute of Public Finance
General Secretary, Saar University
66 Saarbrücken 11, Federal Republic
of Germany

International Monetary Fund
19th and H Streets NW
Washington, D.C. 20431 USA

International Savings Bank Institute (ISBI)
Institut international des caisses
d'épargne (IICE)
1-3 rue Albert Gos
1206 Geneva, Switzerland

World Federation of Investment Clubs
Fédération mondiale des clubs
d'investissement
Brehmplatz 2
4 Düsseldorf 1, Federal Republic of Germany

REGIONAL

Africa:
African Institute for Economic
Development and Planning
P.O. Box 3189
Dakar, Senegal

Asia:
Asian Institute for Economic
Development and Planning
Sri Asyudhya Road
P.O. Box 2-136
Bangkok, Thailand

Europe:
European Federation of Finance House
Associations (EURO FINAS)
Fédération européenne des associations
des instituts de crédit
267 avenue de Tervuren
1150 Brussels, Belgium

European Federation of Financial
Analysts Societies
Fédération européenne des associations
d'analystes financiers (FEAAF)
90 avenue des Champs-Elysées
75008 Paris, France

Latin America:
Latin American Association of Finance
Development Institutions
Asociación latinoamericana de
instituciones financieras de desarrollo
(ALIDE)
Huancavelica 279, 3rd floor
Lima, Peru

Latin American Banking Federation
Federación latinoamericana de bancos
(FELABAN)
Calle 17 N7-35, oficina 809
Apartado Aéreo 13997
Bogotá, Colombia

Centre for Latin American
Monetary Studies
Centro de estudios monetarios
latino-americanos (CEMLA)
Durango 54
Mexico 7, D.F.

Middle East:
Arab Fund for Economic and
Social Development
P.O. Box 21923
Kuwait City, Kuwait

NATIONAL ORGANIZATIONS

Austria:
Österreichische bankwissenschaftliche
Gesellschaft
Franz Kleingasse 1
1190 Vienna

Belgium:
Association belge des analystes financiers
Montagne du Parc 3
1000 Brussels

Federal Republic of Germany:
Gesellschaft für Finanzwirtschaft in der
Unternehmensführung e. V. (GEFIU)
Farbwerke Höchst AG
Postfach 800320
623 Frankfurt/Main 80

France:
Société française des
analystes financiers
125 rue Montmartre
75002 Paris

Ireland:
Irish Association of Investment Clubs
21 Marrion Square
Dublin 2

Italy:
Associazione italiana degli analisti
finanziari (AIAF)
via S. Vittore al Teatro 1
20123 Milan

Netherlands:
Vereniging van beleggingsanalisten
Leidseweg 2, Utrecht

Norway:
Norske finansanalytikeres forening
RS Planton A/S, Dronning Maudsgate 3
Oslo 2

Spain:
> Instituto español de analistas de
> inversiones
> Cedaceros 11-6⁰
> Madrid 14

Sweden:
> Sveriges finansanalytikers förening
> ℅ Direktor Bengt Nyburg, Svenska
> Handelsbanken
> Box 16 341
> 103 26 Stockholm 16

Switzerland:
> Schweizerische Vereinigung für
> Finanzanalyse
> Association suisse des analystes
> financiers (ASAF)
> avenue des Communes-Réunies 66
> 1212 Grand-Lancy

United Kingdom:
> Finance Houses Association Limited
> 14 Queen Anne's Gate
> London SW1, England
>
> National Association of Investment
> Clubs (NAIC)
> 17 Harrington Street
> Liverpool L2 9QF, England
>
> Society of Investment Analysts
> 26-30 Holburn Viaduct
> London EC1A 2BP, England

United States:
> American Finance Association
> Graduate School of Business
> Administration, New York University
> 100 Trinity Place
> New York, New York 10006
>
> Financial Analysts Federation
> 219 East 42nd Street
> New York, New York 10017

Additional national and international organizations may be found in the following directories:

Encyclopedia of Associations. Detroit: Gale Research, annual. Lists United States associations only.
European Financial Almanac, 1974–75. New York: Bowker, 1974. Lists major European organizations in finance; available also in French, Italian, and German.
Yearbook of International Organizations. Brussels: Union of International Associations, biennial.

Principal Information Sources

GENERAL

Guides to the literature include:

A Bibliography for Investment and Economic Analysis: London: Society of Investment Analysts, 1965.
Brealey, R. A. (Comp.) *A Bibliography of Finance and Investment.* Cambridge, Massachusetts: MIT Press, 1973.
Burgess, N. *How to Find Out About Banking and Investment.* Oxford, England: Pergamon Press, 1969.
A Concise Bibliography for Investment Analysis in Europe. Paris: European Federation of Financial Analysts Societies, 1963.
D'Ambrosio, C. A. *A Guide to Successful Investing.* Englewood Cliffs, New Jersey: Prentice-Hall, 1970.
Dean, P. (Ed.) *Bibliography of Income and Wealth 1937–1960.* (8 vols.) New York: Quadrangle Books, 1937–1960.
Donaldson, G., and Stubbs, C. *Corporate and Business Finance: A Classified Bibliography of Recent Literature.* Boston: Harvard University Graduate School of Business Administration, Baker Library, 1964.
Federal Reserve Bank Selected Subjects 1950–1974. Philadelphia: Federal Reserve Bank of Philadelphia, 1975.
Gray, S. J. *Financial Reporting in the EEC and the International Economy: A Selected Bibliography.* Lancaster, England: University of Lancaster, International Centre for Research in Accounting, 1974.
Joint Bank-Fund Library, Washington, D.C. *Economics and Finance: Index to Periodical Articles.* (4 vols.) Boston: Hall, 1972.
Knox, V. H. *Public Finance Information Sources.* Detroit: Gale Research, 1964.
Vargo, R. J. *The Author's Guide to Accounting and Financial Reporting Publications.* (Rev. ed.) Arlington: University of Texas Center for Business and Economic Research of Arlington, 1974.
Woy, J. B. *Investment Information: A Guide to Information Sources.* Detroit: Gale Research, 1970.
Woy, J. B. *Investment Methods: A Bibliographic Guide.* New York: Bowker, 1973.
Zerden, S. *Best Books on the Stock Market: An Analytical Bibliography.* New York: Bowker, 1972.

Overviews and introductions to the field include:

Amling, F. *Investments: An Introduction to Analysis and Management.* (3rd ed.) Englewood Cliffs, New Jersey: Prentice-Hall, 1974.
Bierman, H. *An Introduction to Managerial Finance.* New York: Norton, 1973.
Brigham, E. F. (Ed.) *Readings in Managerial Finance.* New York: Holt, Rinehart and Winston, 1971.

Christy, G. A., and Clendenin, J. C. *Introduction to Investments.* (6th ed.) New York: McGraw-Hill, 1974.
Fama, E., and Miller, M. *Theory of Finance.* New York: Holt, Rinehart and Winston, 1972.
Hunt, P. *Basic Business Finance.* Homewood, Illinois: Irwin, 1974.
Shapiro, E., and others. *Money and Banking.* (5th ed.) New York: Holt, Rinehart and Winston, 1968.
Smith, K. V., and Eiteman, D. K. *Essentials of Investing.* Homewood, Illinois: Irwin, 1974.
Van Horne, J. C. *Fundamentals of Financial Management.* (2nd ed.) Englewood Cliffs, New Jersey: Prentice-Hall, 1974.
Weston, J. F., and Brigham, E. F. *Managerial Finance.* (5th ed.) New York: Holt, Rinehart and Winston, 1975.

Financial histories include:

Adams, T. F. M., and Hoshi, I. *A Financial History of the New Japan.* Palo Alto, California: Kodansha International, 1972.
Dickson, P. G. *The Financial Revolution in England.* New York: St. Martin's, 1967.
Galbraith, J. K. *Money: Whence It Came, Where It Went.* Boston: Houghton Mifflin, 1975.
Kindleberger, C. P. *The Formation of Financial Centers: A Study in Comparative Economic History.* Princeton, New Jersey: International Finance Section, Department of Economics, Princeton University, 1974.
Myers, M. G. *A Financial History of the United States.* New York: Columbia University Press, 1970.
Wyckoff, P. *Wall Street and the Stock Markets: A Chronology (1644–1971).* Radnor, Pennsylvania: Chilton, 1972.

CURRENT BIBLIOGRAPHIES

Anbar Management Services. *Bibliography.* Wembley, England: Anbar, 1961–.
Bibliography of Income and Wealth. Baltimore: Johns Hopkins University Press, 1937/41–.
Business International. New York: Business International Corporation, 1957–.
Business Periodicals Index. New York: Wilson, 1958–.
The Conference Board Index. New York: Conference Board, Inc., 1971–.
Economic Abstracts. The Hague: Martinus Nijhoff, 1963–.
F. & S. Index International. Cleveland, Ohio: Predicasts, 1967–.
F. & S. Index of Corporations and Industries. Cleveland, Ohio: Predicasts, 1960–.
International Bibliography of Economics. Paris: UNESCO, 1952–.
List of Recent Periodical Articles. Washington,

D.C.: International Monetary Fund and International Bank for Reconstruction and Development, 1947–.
Wall Street Journal Index. New York: Dow Jones, 1958–.

PERIODICALS

A selection of periodicals in the field include *Bancaria* (Italy), *Bank and Quotation Record* (US), *Bankers Magazine* (UK), *Bankers Magazine* (US), *Bankers Monthly* (US), *Banking* (US), *Canadian Financial Journal*, *Corporate Financing* (US), *Dun's Review* (US), *Finance* (US), *Finance and Development* (US), *Financial Analysts Journal* (US), *Financial Executive* (US), *Financial Quarterly* (US), *Financial World* (US), *Financiero* (Spain), *Finance studie* (Czechoslovakia), *Finanzarchiv* (FRG), *Forbes* (US), *Fortune* (US), *Fortune française*, *IMF Survey* (US), *International Financial News Survey* (US), *International Financial Statistics* (US), *International Investor* (UK), *International Reports* (US), *Institutional Investor* (US), *Investment Dealers Digest* (US), *Investor's Intelligence* (US), *Journal of Business* (US), *Journal of Finance* (US), *Journal of Financial and Quantitative Analysis* (US), *Journal of International Business Studies* (US), *Magazine of Wall Street* (US), *Public Finance/Finance publiques* (FRG), *United States Investor*, *Wall Street Business Analyst* (US).

Financial newspapers include *American Banker*, *Barrons National Business and Finance Weekly* (US), *Commercial and Financial Chronicle* (US), *Financial Post* (Canada), *Financial Times* (UK), *The MG Financial Weekly* (US), *Money Manager* (US), *Wall Street Journal* (US), *Wall Street Transcript* (US).

For a listing of journals of banking, finance, and investment consult:

Current Periodical Publications in Baker Library. Boston: Graduate School of Business Administration, Harvard University, 1971.

ENCYCLOPEDIAS, DICTIONARIES, HANDBOOKS

The following is a selection of standard works in the field:

Badger, R. E., and Goffman, P. B. (Eds.) *The Complete Guide to Investment Analysis.* New York: McGraw-Hill, 1967.
Baughn, W. H., and Walker, C. E. (Eds.) *The Banker's Handbook.* Homewood, Illinois: Dow Jones–Irwin, 1966.
Bogen, J. I., and others. (Eds.) *Financial Handbook.* (4th rev. ed.) New York: Ronald Press, 1968.
Darst, D. M. *The Complete Bond Book: A Guide to All Types of Fixed Income Securities.* New York: McGraw-Hill, 1975.

Goodman, S. R. *Financial Manager's Manual and Guide.* Englewood Cliffs, New Jersey: Prentice-Hall, 1973.

Goodman, S. R. *Corporate Treasurer's and Controller's Encyclopedia.* (2 vols., rev. ed.) Englewood Cliffs, New Jersey: Prentice-Hall, 1974.

Horn, S. F. *Glossary of Financial Terms in English/American, French, Spanish, German.* New York: American Elsevier, 1965.

Levine, S. N. (Ed.) *Financial Analyst's Handbook.* (2 vols.) Homewood, Illinois: Dow Jones–Irwin, 1975.

List of Definitions. Paris: Study Group on Terminology, European Federation of Financial Analysts Societies, 1966.

Moore, N. D. *Dictionary of Business Finance and Investment.* Dayton, Ohio: Investors Systems, 1975.

Munn, G. G. *Encyclopedia of Banking and Finance.* (7th ed.) Boston: Bankers Publishing, 1973.

Schultz, H. D. *Financial Tactics and Terms for the Sophisticated International Investor.* New York: Harper & Row, 1974.

Servotte, J. V. *Dictionnaire commercial et financier français-néerlandais-anglais-allemand.* (3rd rev. ed.) Brussels: Brepols, 1964.

Thole, B. *Lexicon of Stock Market Terminology.* New York: American Elsevier, 1965.

Vancil, R. F. (Ed.) *Financial Executives Handbook.* Homewood, Illinois: Dow Jones–Irwin, 1970.

Zarb, F. G., and Kerekes, G. T. (Eds.) *the Stock Market Handbook.* Homewood, Illinois: Dow Jones–Irwin, 1970.

DIRECTORIES

McNulty, N. G. *Training Managers: The International Guide.* New York: Harper & Row, 1969. Has a section describing graduate degree programs and courses in finance throughout the world.

Nyhart, J. D., and Janssen, E. F. *A Global Directory of Development Finance Institutions in Developing Countries.* Paris: Development Centre of the Organisation for Economic Co-operation and Development, 1967.

Peterson's Annual Guides to Graduate Study. Book 2: *Humanities and Social Sciences.* Princeton, New Jersey: Peterson's Guides, annual. Lists university finance and banking programs in the United States.

Study Abroad. Paris: UNESCO Press, triennial. Lists programs in banking and finance in several countries.

World Guide to Universities. New York: Bowker; Pullach/Munich, Federal Republic of Germany: Verlag Dokumentation, 1972. Lists universities worldwide with courses of study in finance and banking.

[Bibliography prepared by Paula Kline.]

FINANCIAL AFFAIRS

1. COST ANALYSIS

2. ACCOUNTING AND FINANCIAL REPORTING

3. BUDGETING

4. INVESTMENTS

1. COST ANALYSIS

For the economist "economic costs are benefits lost" (Fisher, 1971, p. 25). A cost estimation on a particular decision is an estimate of the benefits that would have been gained if the resources had been allocated to the best alternative use. Thus, economic costs are often called alternative costs or opportunity costs. Although this definition is theoretically satisfying, many specialists in cost analysis within institutions of higher education are reluctant to use it. In practice, they apply it only in a very limited way (Ziemer, Young, and Topping, 1971, pp. 11–12). There are two main reasons for their reluctance. First, comparing the costs of a program (or a decision) with the benefits that an alternative program would provide implies that such benefits can be evaluated by a monetary unit of measurement as can costs. However, "benefits" or products of activities are difficult to identify, let alone measure in monetary terms, because of their many qualitative aspects. Second, the cost analysis associated with university activities remains very much influenced by traditional accounting practices and rules, which acknowledge expenses and ignore opportunity costs.

Faced with the differing costing approaches of economists and accountants, specialists of institutional analysis have come to the conclusion "that there are no absolute definitions of either the term 'cost' or 'expense'" (Ziemer, Young, and Topping, 1971, p. 10). The term *cost* must be understood in its relationship to the purpose or purposes that it is to serve, which leads Weathersby (1973, p. 2) to state: "costs are opinions, prices are facts."

The difficulty in defining cost stems from the fact that it is used for a variety of purposes. However, a great majority of cost analyses are carried out for purposes of comparison. For this objective, it is possible to define cost as follows: Cost measures the use of institutional resources, or, more comprehensively, "Costs are defined as the measure in dollars of institutional resources used in the process of providing institutional outputs during a given time period" (Ziemer, Young, and Topping, 1971, p. 10).

Based on this definition, it is possible to define cost analysis, in general terms, as the identification and evaluation of resources, used or estimated, which have been used for the implementation of activities, programs, projects, or production of output. However, taking into account the difficulties of defining the product or output of higher education, cost evaluation has tended to concentrate on activities, programs, and projects.

Types of Costs

Of the many types of costs, there are certain ones that are effectively used in the planning and management of higher education institutions. These are, first, positive and normative costs.

Positive and normative costs. All calculated costs are, in practice, positive costs to the extent that they result from the identification and evaluation of resources and input effectively used in the institution during a given period of time. Positive costs therefore represent the consumption of input, evaluated at its real price or average price, without asking whether this consumption corresponds to an optimal combination of production factors (such as labor and capital). In contrast, a normative cost would result from an optimal combination of inputs for the output of a given program or activity. An evaluation of normative costs in education would require studies on the average "quality" of the output of educational activities and on the comparative effectiveness of various pedagogical techniques. Such an evaluation has not yet been done conclusively. Meanwhile, in using

positive costs, the institution has to be aware that these costs are not usually calculated on the basis of systematic research within the institution for an optimal mix of factors. Therefore, positive costs may be used only cautiously for purposes of comparison (Balderston, 1972, pp. 2–10, 20–22).

Fixed and variable costs. Costs that vary directly with the activity or the "rate of production" of an activity are called variable costs, while costs that are relatively independent of a newly created activity or of the "rate of production" are called fixed costs. In higher education the costs of constructing a building and related depreciation are considered fixed costs, as are, to a large extent, salaries of academic staff. On the other hand, maintenance expenses, heating, lighting, and overtime pay for staff are variable costs. The distinction between fixed and variable costs is only relative, as it depends on the importance or scope of the planned decision and on the time involved. In the long term, all costs are variable. In the short term, some costs are fixed.

Total, average, and marginal costs. The distinction among total, average, and marginal costs is no doubt one of the most useful in cost analysis. The total or global cost of an activity or of a program is the sum of the costs—fixed and variable—of the resources used in the achievement of this activity or program.

The average cost or unit cost of an activity is the result of the division of its total cost by the total number of units of activities produced during a given period. This average cost can be total or partial, and may be divided into fixed and variable costs. The problem with the calculation here is the need to find a representative performance indicator for the activities of higher education.

From an economic point of view, knowledge of marginal cost is particularly important in making many decisions. A strict definition of marginal cost is the addition of total cost created by the production of an additional unit of output in a given period of time (for example, the "production" of an additional graduate with a bachelor's degree in economics). In general, higher education institutions are more often confronted with decisions concerning the creation of a new program of studies, the launching of a new research activity, or a substantial increase of student enrollment in a given department or discipline. These are not marginal decisions in the narrow sense of the term. Costs associated with these decisions are called *differential* or *incremental* costs and are equal to the variation of total costs as a result of a shift from one level of output to another, or as a result of the creation of a new activity (such as a course or program), other factors being constant. Relatively few institutions have concentrated their efforts on the evaluation and application of differential costs for decision-making purposes, despite their usefulness in justifying the financing of new programs or activities. However, the implementation of the Program Planning Budgeting System (PPBS) and Management by Objectives (MBO) is increasingly making institutions prepare their budgets as "incremental workload budgets," as well as leading them to introduce information systems that would generate data not available in traditional accounting. The interested reader should consult Ziemer, Young, and Topping (1971) for the mathematical relationships of the various costs and Farmer (1973) for sample values for these costs.

Direct and indirect costs. The distinction between direct and indirect costs is one used by accountants. Direct costs, as defined by Dopuch and Birnberg (1969, p. 19), "are all those product costs traceable either because they are physically visible in the end product or because they act directly on the product." However, as noted earlier, the identification of output in higher education, whether it be in teaching or research, is a rather complex and necessarily incomplete task; therefore, the preceding definition is not directly applicable. In practice, as Farmer (1973, pp. 12, 14) states: "Direct costs are those

which an accountant elects to identify with a specific outcome or product (or program) in order to achieve an average cost." Since there is no universally accepted classification by means of which direct and indirect costs can be classified, analysts propose their own rules. For example, the National Association of College and University Business Officers (1974, p. 43) considers that "the direct costs (for research projects) include the salaries and wages of those working on the project, expenditures for equipment and materials and other expenses specifically identified with the project. Indirect costs are those that cannot be specifically identified with the project but are just as real as direct costs. They include an allotted share of such items as operation and maintenance of the plant, departmental, college and institutional administration; library operations; charges for use of equipment and facilities, and certain more general expenses that are to some degree attributable to sponsored programs." Another organization in higher education in the United States, the National Center for Higher Education Management Systems (NCHEMS), sees direct costs as including instruction/research/public service personnel compensation, administrative/support compensation, other staff compensation, and supplies and services assigned to all activity centers. Capital costs for buildings and land improvements and for equipment, independent operation costs, and scholarships and fellowships are excluded from total direct costs.

Recurring and nonrecurring costs. The distinction between recurring and nonrecurring costs is closely tied to a time concept, to the duration of the activity under cost analysis or to the life span of a program. Within this perspective, it is useful to distinguish between costs that the institution will have to bear only once during the defined time period (usually at the beginning of such a period) and costs that, following an initial decision, will have to be covered regularly (for example, yearly) by the institution during the selected period. The purchase of a large piece of equipment, such as a computer, has a time horizon of four to five years; the construction of a new building has a time horizon of twenty-five to fifty years. These are non-recurring costs. On the other hand, personnel expenses, operating expenses, and maintenance expenses are recurring, to the extent that they have to be covered regularly by the institution over the entire life span of a building or a computer. In the latter case, if the time horizon of the decision is ten years, the cost of purchasing a computer every four to five years then becomes a recurring cost. Thus, one can say that the dividing line between recurring and nonrecurring costs is not absolutely firm and that, in the long run, most costs are recurring.

Internal and external costs. For purposes of management and decision making, it is desirable to determine whether costs are or are not controllable by the decision maker. If a cost is controllable and internally determined by the decision maker, it is an internal cost. Otherwise, it is an external cost.

Whether certain costs are internal or external will vary between institutions within a country and also between countries. For example, in the United States, instructional salary costs are either determined by the department or by the institution. Thus, they are internal costs. In France academic staff are civil servants paid directly by the central public authorities. To the institution in France, therefore, instructional salaries are external costs; to the central government, they are internal costs. Thus, a given cost is internal or external depending on the hierarchical level and domain of the decision maker. The boundary specification of the domain is important, because a decision maker may optimize his subsystem considering his internal cost but not optimize for the system as a whole by ignoring those costs that are external to him but internal to the system. Thus, one function of the higher levels of one hierarchy, such as the funding agen-

cies, is to specify carefully the domain of the decision maker. They also specify the cost analysis done for purposes of planning and the extent of control of the decision maker.

Relevant and irrelevant costs. Relevant costs are those that are pertinent to a specific decision under consideration. Future costs, therefore, are relevant while historical costs are irrelevant. For example, if a new research center occupies an already-built facility, then construction costs are no longer relevant. Costs already borne by the institution result from decisions taken in the past and should have no effect on current or future decisions. Thus, economists speak of sunk costs and refuse to take them into account in cost analyses. The only elements over which a decision maker can exercise a choice are future costs or incremental costs.

Uses of Costs and Cost Analysis

The purposes of cost analysis are to improve managerial capabilities; provide internal and external controls by funding agencies; provide useful information for planning; meet the requirements of accountability made by funding agencies; and justify the need for additional resources.

Higher education institutions that are nonprofit organizations are not subject to the economic laws governing commercial activities. Therefore, the effectiveness of the various activities of these institutions cannot be measured by a comparison of their prices and profits with those of similar institutions. University administrators thus need other signals to tell them where they stand in comparison with their "competitors." They require cost indicators that will allow them to establish useful comparisons with similar institutions. When such cost comparisons show significant discrepancies, they signal the need for detailed analysis to find the cause of the discrepancies and to come to conclusions concerning management and planning within the institution. This process creates a dialog and basic learning in the absence of rules comparable to those of a market economy.

To compare cost information interinstitutionally, it is necessary to have a common set of data elements. Such a set has been developed or is being developed nationally in many countries, including Austria, Belgium, Canada, Sweden, the Federal Republic of Germany, and the United States. In addition, one needs a standard set of procedures, as well as a methodology for cost aggregation, support cost allocation, and unit cost calculation. Also needed is a set of procedures for collecting data and reporting the information to be exchanged. Such procedures have been developed by NCHEMS in the United States (Topping, 1974; Byers, 1975) and are currently being widely used. The cost calculations include unit cost per student for each level of student fields of study and academic degree. These cost calculations are largely a response to pressure from funding agencies for more accountability.

There is, however, some disagreement with the NCHEMS methodology and with its notion of full costs, a subject to be discussed later. Beatty, Gulko, and Sheehan (1974, p. 6) argue that "when the procedures used in cost analysis are so complex that variations in cost differentials are confounded in conventions, allocations and algebraic manipulations, the influence of policy variables is masked." Instead, they propose a set of simplified rules, definitions, and procedures making it possible to establish an instructional cost index. This index is a function of five policy variables: faculty compensation, relative faculty effort, class section size, faculty teaching load, and instructional support expense. It is from a comparison of the values of these five policy variables that the reasons for observed discrepancies in cost indices will emerge.

In Europe unit cost studies are either more theoretical than in the United States (Babeau, Cossu, and Cuenin, 1975) or rather simplified and limited (Pasquier and Sachse, 1975). There are, however,

numerous European studies (both theoretical and empirical) on the use of pricing for internal control for industry (Boiteux, 1960; Drèze, 1964) that have only recently been applied to higher education (Marchand, 1974; Hecquet, Marchand, and Jadot, 1975). There is considerable interest among the developed countries and international organizations like the Organisation for Economic Co-operation and Development in promoting the possibility of exchanging information not only between institutions but also between countries.

In institutions where an important share of university resources comes from tuition and fees paid by students, an increase in real costs constitutes an admissible justification for the increase of fees. From these examples of unit cost studies it is clear that universities need to have information systems adapted to their specific management and planning needs and also need to have available procedures for cost evaluation that meet the justified requirements of all their constituencies (students and their families, professors, public authorities, foundations, donors, alumni, and citizens).

The wide range of applications for cost analysis implies, on the part of the institutions, the ability to determine a wide variety of types of costs. It is evident that users of this information do not all have the same needs. Public authorities would like to have figures available on annual unit costs for each discipline, each level of study, and each category of personnel, to enable it to control the utilization of resources by educational institutions. In the United States institutions are sometimes hesitant to provide cost information because they fear that it will be misused and that sufficient consideration will not be given to necessarily unmeasurable output. (In Europe, where most institutions are federally funded, all information requested by funding agencies must be provided.) Furthermore, cost information may lead to further control of the institution.

Institutions want costs largely for internal management purposes. For this purpose, the costs have to be marginal or incremental costs that correspond to the resources over which they can exercise control in the short term. The cost analyst must, for each of the decisions under study, determine the type and definition of costs to be calculated and make sure that the type and concepts of the selected costs are linked to the characteristic parameters of the decision. In other words, the analysis to be made depends on the objective, timing, scope, and quantitative importance of the decision. It also depends on the use of costs.

There is a variety of techniques and procedures for cost calculation. These fall into two broad categories: economic-accounting methods and econometric methods.

Economic-Accounting Methods

Methods are called economic-accounting because of a number of common characteristics. All such systems use accounting frameworks and procedures that are more detailed and more complex than the traditional accounting frameworks and procedures. By using these, it is possible to record the flow of allocated resources, both by cost centers during a given period and by the various programs and activities of an institution. It is also possible, directly or indirectly, to charge an expense or any effective resource utilization to the ultimate cost objective.

The purpose of economic-accounting systems is to account for all the resources utilized by the institution's programs and activities, even if these do not bring about monetary transactions and flows during the period under consideration (for example, depreciation of buildings and equipment, implicit costs, and opportunity costs). However, they exclude all expenses that do not correspond to a charge on the institution, such as public aid to students and other transfers. These methods tend therefore to trace fairly

closely the economic reality of program and activity costs.

In these systems data used for cost calculations are mainly derived from the institutional expenditures files for a fiscal year. In general, data collection consists of an analysis of each account in order to determine the activities supported by these accounts. It is only when this information is not available that special studies, such as a faculty activity analysis, are carried out to fill existing accounting gaps.

Economic-accounting systems use no highly formalized tools; they do, however, use ratios, allocation techniques, and parameters that are rather similar to the ones used by accountants. Finally, such systems make possible the calculation of total costs by basic cost centers as well as the calculation of average costs of activities and outputs. Only rarely are they used for determining marginal or incremental costs (even though in practice these can be determined from a chronological series of total costs) and even less often to establish cost functions.

Economic-accounting methods are the most widely used methods. In North America work on these methods has been done by NCHEMS (Ziemer, Young, and Topping, 1971; Topping, 1974; Topping, Weldon, and Kirschling, 1974); Beatty, Gulko, and Sheehan (1974); the National Commission on the Financing of Postsecondary Education (1973); the Association of Universities and Colleges in Canada (1970); the Committee of Presidents of Universities of Ontario (1970); Thompson and Lapp (1970); and Segal (1970). Work in Europe includes that done by Carter (1968); Bottomley and others (1972); Appelquist (1974); Babeau, Cossu, and Cuenin (1975); and Pasquier and Sachse (1975).

In order to evaluate desired costs, all of these methods use the same logical scheme of analysis and calculation. The principal steps in their methods may be described on the basis of work carried out in the United States by NCHEMS and in France by Babeau, Cossu, and Cuenin (1975).

When these steps are examined, the major problems and issues that analysts have to face in any methodological approach will appear.

General principles for cost determination: accounting structures. Even though the objective of cost analysis is the calculation of detailed and significant costs, the numerous expenditures and resource utilizations have to be grouped in a classification system "which identifies and categorizes the activities of higher education institutions at a level of detail that results in cost centers that contain relatively homogeneous activities" (Ziemer, Young, and Topping, 1971, p. 24). Activity classification is generally achieved by means of two criteria: first, all basic activities aggregated into one cell have to present a minimum homogeneity; second, it must be possible to identify the costs that these activities generate in order to relate them to a cost center. These homogeneous cells, aggregated in homogeneous activities, are referred to as program elements by NCHEMS and as elementary units of activity (UEA) in the French study. A program element is defined as "a collection of resources, technologies and policies that, through their integrated operation, produce goods or services, i.e., an output that is of value to the organization because it contributes to the achievement of an institutional objective" (Ziemer, Young, and Topping, 1971, p. 25). These elements correspond to "the utilization of the smallest set of resources coordinated in a process designed to produce a final or intermediate output or service of several final or intermediate outputs or services" in Babeau, Cossu, and Cuenin (1975, p. 175).

In some countries (for example, the United States, Canada, Belgium, and the Federal Republic of Germany), there are taxonomies for the program elements. In the United States the taxonomy is called, by Gulko (1971), the Program Classification Structure (PCS). This structure enables the systematic and exhaustive classification of all activities of higher education institutions. When such a classification can be mapped (equated) to the functional classification used by the accounting system in the institution, the PCS becomes the basis for the design of a system that associates each program element to academic programs for analytical and costing purposes.

The PCS developed by NCHEMS classifies all university activities into two major categories: the primary programs (instruction, organized research, and public service) and support programs (academic support, student services, institutional support, and independent operations). In contrast, the French method distinguishes support programs into service-related activities and other administrative services on the basis of a criterion of the measurability and nonmeasurability of outputs.

Cost components: personnel, operational, and capital costs. The main cost components in higher education are personnel costs, operations costs, and capital costs. The identification of these costs and their assignments to cost centers are central concerns of economic-accounting methods.

Personnel or salary costs are the sum of wages and fringe benefits. They form a large part of the total institutional budget, varying from 60 to 90 percent, and typically appear in payroll files. Once identified, they must be assigned to different activity and cost centers. This is very difficult in higher education, where a single instructor has three related products: instruction, research, and administration. In instruction, his contribution may be to more than one level of student and to more than one program and cost center. Therefore, salary costs must be assigned to each program, course level, and cost center.

The most common approach is to assign salaries in proportion to workload. Numerous workload analyses have been conducted largely for this purpose. A survey in the United States in 1971 identified forty-four such studies (Romney, 1971), while a 1974 study listed over one hundred references on this subject (Yuker, 1974). Other workload studies have been conducted in Europe by the Committee of Vice Chancellors and Principals of the Universities of the United Kingdom (1972). However, none of these studies were generally adopted and used in interinstitutional exchange of cost and workload information. Here again, NCHEMS has played a pioneer role by setting up a standardized system (Romney, 1971; Manning and Romney, 1973, 1974) that will make it possible for universities to obtain information on the activities (instructional and administrative) of their staff. This information is used in allocating salaries to programs and cost centers. For primary programs allocation is made as a function both of individual data collected for all personnel subject to a workload analysis and of collective data based on average rates for nonacademic personnel contributing to primary program activities. For personnel engaged in support activities, salaries are directly allocated to the cost center in which they exclusively or principally exercise their functions.

Operational costs are what remains from the operating budget after deducting salaries and special expenses, such as scholarships and fellowships. The ideal method for allocating these operational costs to cost centers would be to identify the real incurred operational expenses by each cost center. However, this procedure would be difficult and costly since much of the necessary data is not typically available in most accounting systems. Moreover, such an allocation would merely create the illusion of being precise, since only a relatively small part of total activity costs would be represented. Therefore, the most commonly used methods consist of identifying the total operating costs from accounting data and selecting allocation parameters that show a correlation between the resources to be allocated and the activities that will receive the allocation. For example, operating costs by discipline will be divided among the courses of each discipline in proportion to the salary costs of instructional staff (at each course level). The total salary costs and operating costs

thus obtained are called the total direct costs of the activity centers. They represent only a portion of full costs because the production of final or intermediate outputs requires capital goods and durable equipment in educational institutions as it does in any other type of public or private enterprise.

Experts are not in agreement concerning the inclusion of capital costs in the evaluation of activity costs. There is also disagreement over the operational usefulness of the concept of full costs (direct costs and capital costs) in the management of higher education institutions. Beatty, Gulko, and Sheehan (1974, p. 6) believe that, to the extent that useful cost comparisons constitute the objective of calculation, the concept of full cost should be avoided. The reason for their belief is that "cost differentials are often due to allocation conventions rather than management decisions as reflected by policy variables. Simply stated, the policy decisions of the institutions are reflected only in direct costs of each program. Indeed, only the direct costs of activities are controllable in a management sense."

This point can be argued, however. In the short term, the utilization of facilities and heavy equipment can give rise to modifications in allocation of resources. Therefore, knowledge of capital cost can help decision makers in better allocation of existing resources. Moreover, to justify long-term decisions, the decision maker has to take capital costs into account. Unless he does so, he cannot obtain a full picture of the resources required for the launching and operation of new projects and programs. Sound management principles also suggest annual forecasts that make it possible to replace capital goods and equipment at the end of their life expectancy. Finally, as much from the institutional decision maker's point of view as from that of the community, immobilization of capital corresponds to giving up the alternative uses of related resources, which, in turn, gives rise to opportunity costs that cannot be neglected in decision making. For all these reasons, it seems important that capital costs be included in the activity costs of higher education institutions.

The identification of annual capital costs includes two elements: the calculation of the annual fixed asset depreciation, and consideration of the fact that these fixed assets deprive the institution of alternative resource uses, particularly investment of the same capital on the financial market. Hence, it is useful to estimate the value of this opportunity cost.

Before calculating fixed asset depreciation, one must calculate the value of fixed assets. This calculation can be done either by using historical purchase costs or, if one wishes to take into account the real value of capital at a given time, by using the replacement value. The first method is recommended by NCHEMS (Topping, 1974), the second by the French group (Babeau, Cossu, and Cuenin, 1975).

Once the annual capital costs are identified, they have to be allocated to the various cost centers. Several techniques and procedures are in use. The allocation method selected by the French group is undoubtedly very precise but difficult to use. The one recommended by NCHEMS (Romney, 1972) is, on the other hand, relatively simple. By the NCHEMS scheme, all annual capital costs corresponding to buildings and land improvements owned by or leased by the institution, are allocated to a fictitious activity center called "capital costs—buildings and land improvements." Related depreciation charges, opportunity costs, and rents are allocated to activity centers as a function of a parameter representative of occupied surfaces called "assignable square feet." Knowledge of these surfaces and assignable square feet is derived from a specific direct-cost study. Procedures and various phases of this study are also recommended by NCHEMS. Annual capital costs corresponding to owned or rented equipment are allocated to another fictitious activity center ("capital costs—equipment") and are then allocated

to activity centers according to rules such as the prorated direct costs.

Allocation of support costs. At this phase of costing, all activity centers have been treated identically regarding the identification of their total costs and have been considered as if they operated independently of each other. In fact, some of them participate directly in the achievement of institutional goals and objectives, while others, although they play a fundamental role in the operation of the institution, do not directly contribute to its missions and objectives. To determine the full costs of the former, it is necessary to allocate or transfer the costs of indirect activity centers (support) to the accounts of the direct activity centers (primary) by means of parameters representative of the services produced by the indirect centers and consumed by the direct. Several rules of allocation have been used. NCHEMS recommends the direct method, by which support activities are assumed to provide services only to the primary activity centers; and the recursive method, which assumes exchanges between support activity centers (Ziemer, Young, and Topping, 1971). A third method, simultaneous allocation, is recommended by Babeau, Cossu, and Cuenin (1975, pp. 73–75). In simultaneous allocation, reciprocal services between support activity centers do take place, but the solution involves simultaneous equations. The method is mathematically elegant but very demanding on detailed input data and difficult to implement. In contrast, while the NCHEMS method may not be theoretically and intellectually appealing, it is the most accessible to a large number of institutions, and it makes relatively good evaluations possible. The approach is based on the premise that absolute exactitude would be costly and difficult. To paraphrase Enthoven, it is better to be roughly right than to be absolutely wrong.

In all methods of allocation the parameters of allocation must be selected. For example, the allocation of library expenses to each academic program may be made in proportion to the number of students, the number of faculty, the level of program, or a weighted relationship of all these factors. The determination is seldom based on economic rationality but rather on what is politically feasible or negotiable. In the case of negotiation, information on the consequences (such as unit cost computation) of each of the rules of allocation is desirable. This information can be attained by a computer program, developed by NCHEMS, that simulates various allocation rules (Beatty, 1972). This simulation helps the decision maker select his allocation parameters. In turn, the allocation of support costs to primary programs or primary cost centers enables the computation of unit costs.

Calculation of unit cost. The problem in calculating unit cost is the determination of the denominator, the units of output or production. For an educational institution, one conspicuous output is students. But the word *student* covers a wide range of very different realities, as much from the educational point of view as from that of the resources required from such education. As a result, the cost per student is only significant if calculated by course, by level of study, and by discipline. However, costs of this type, although they are interesting and often necessary to meet the requirements of funding agencies, are not always adapted to the internal management and planning decisions of an institution. They do not constitute an indicator of student (or faculty) activity or an indicator of progress made by the student toward a certain level of knowledge and academic achievement. Therefore, in practice, a great number of activity indicators are used: staff contact hours, student contact hours, major program of study, course credit hours, student credit course, and annual student credit units. All corresponding unit costs can be, and in general are, calculated by level and by discipline. In the pilot studies made in the United States to test its cost finding principles and procedures, NCHEMS proposed to retain three activity indicators: semester credit, student contact hour, and course enrollment. In Europe the credit hour concept is generally unknown.

Econometric Methods: Cost Functions and Simulation Models

Costing and cost analysis have been rapidly integrated into the procedures for annual and long-range budget negotiations of educational institutions under the pressure of rising costs and the requirements of funding agencies. In these negotiations a variety of factors must be determined; these include the question of the degree to which costs will vary in relation to the variation of the volume of planned activity; the cost arising from an increase in the number of enrollments in a given discipline, or level of students; and the variation of operation cost necessary for a summer session. To make these determinations, it is necessary to have cost functions or simulation models using such functions.

There are numerous cost and resource models currently operational. Almost all these models, however, are concerned with only the nonresearch sectors. But they do differ as to the level of aggregation. The Resource Requirements Prediction Model (RRPM), developed by NCHEMS, used disaggregated cost functions in its first operational version, RRPM 1.3. Thus, in this version there was one cost function for different noninstructional cost centers. In a later version, RRPM 1.6, the user was given the option of an aggregated cost function—one function for all noninstructional cost centers. This option was recognition of the fact that it was very difficult to formulate disaggregated cost functions and determine coefficients for each of these functions. The accounting systems in many universities did not have data at such disaggregated levels, so there was little empirical basis for determining these disaggregated cost coefficients.

Despite this difficulty, some models are using disaggregated cost functions. These include the Comprehensive Analytical

Methods of Planning University Systems (CAMPUS) in North America; Total University Simulation Systems (TUSS) in the Netherlands; and the Hochschule Information System (HIS) in the Federal Republic of Germany (Hussain and Freytag, 1973). The Model of Simulation and Allocation of Resources (MSAR), implemented in Portugal, has the most extensive cost functions, including one for laboratory assistants. The latter is a function of number of students, their contact in the laboratory, and the type of instruction. The question that arises in this case concerns not only the availability of valid coefficients but also the desirability and need of such detailed information for institutional long-range planning.

The problem with cost functions (in a resource model or by itself) is one not only of coefficients but also of the formulation of the function, especially where historical data are scarce or nonexistent. Another related problem is that of the joint product of instruction and research. One solution to the problem is to consider only instruction (Carter, 1968). When research is included, it is done in one of two ways, either as a joint product with instruction or as separate and distinct from instruction (Verry and Layard, 1975).

The relative importance of costing and resource allocation has changed markedly in recent years. In the early release of RRPM in 1971, the unit cost calculations were offered only as a by-product of the resource calculations. However, institutions found the cost calculations more relevant to their planning and control needs. In addition, cost calculations were being demanded by funding agencies. Furthermore, many institutions found the resource model expensive and difficult to run. Consequently, NCHEMS, the designers of RRPM, redesigned their computer system package to provide the unit costs as the main output, with resource calculations as an extension.

In conclusion, it should be pointed out that the development of cost studies and analyses stems from efforts by administrators and institutional research specialists; faculty members have not participated happily in these studies and often have judged them with suspicion, if not disdain. Faculty members have believed that the introduction of such quantitative methods could be a threat to their academic freedom. It is evident, however, that an educational institution can only improve information and decision-making systems if it enjoys the active cooperation of its faculty. This cooperation, which can be attained by overcoming the sometimes justified resistance of the faculty, is a prerequisite for the operational development of quantitative management tools in general and of cost analyses in particular.

As has been emphasized above, for costing to be adapted to various types of decisions, considerable elemental data are needed, of a kind which traditional accounting techniques can provide only with difficulty, if at all. There is therefore a need, more so in Europe than in North America, for institutions to develop information systems adapted to these new informational needs. Such developments would include encouraging universities to adopt common data-element dictionaries, to set up data bases and information systems that meet common objectives, and to adopt standardized procedures to make possible the cost estimation necessary for internal management as well as for funding agencies.

Though the attention of analysts and administrators has concentrated on the instructional and administrative sectors, it is likely that this attention will also turn to the research sector. This sector is an important area for future researchers and practitioners.

Finally, although costing and cost analysis appear to be fundamental for the management of higher education, they still remain imperfect decision tools. Indeed, all good analysts know that costing of an activity or of a program remains an incomplete task if it is not matched with an analysis of related benefits. Cost analysis will render all services expected from it only when outputs of various activities are, if not totally quantified, at least accompanied by numerical and qualitative indicators. Even though interesting studies have been launched in this area (Bowen, 1974), the field is still largely unexplored. Work currently in progress should bring about advances in this area and make management of education more efficient and more effective.

Bibliography

Appelquist, C. G. *Programme Budgets for Graduate Training—Chalmers University of Technology.* Paris: Organisation for Economic Co-operation and Development, 1974.

Association of Universities and Colleges in Canada. *An Exploratory Cost Analysis of Some Canadian Universities.* Ottawa, Ontario: Association of Universities and Colleges in Canada, 1970.

Babeau, A., Cossu, C., and Cuenin, S. *Methods of Calculating Cost in French Universities.* Paris: Organisation for Economic Co-operation and Development, 1975.

Balderston, F. E. *Cost Analysis in Higher Education.* Berkeley: University of California Press, 1972.

Beatty, G., Jr. *Cost Finding Principles Software.* Boulder, Colorado: National Center for Higher Education Management Systems, 1972.

Beatty, G., Jr., Gulko, W. W., and Sheehan, B. S. "The Institutional Cost Index—A Simplified Approach to Interinstitutional Cost Comparison." Paper presented at the ninth annual meeting of the Society for College and University Planning, Berkeley, California, 1974.

Boiteux, M. "Peak Load Pricing." *Journal of Business,* 1960, *33,* 157–179.

Bottomley, J. A., and others. *Costs and Potential Economies—University of Bradford.* Paris: Organisation for Economic Co-operation and Development, 1972.

Bowen, H. R. (Ed.) *New Directions for Institutional Research: Evaluating Institutions for Accountability,* no. 1. San Francisco: Jossey-Bass, 1974.

Byers, M. *Information Exchange Procedures—Outcomes Study Procedures.* Boulder, Colorado: National Center for Higher Education Management Systems, 1975.

Carter, C. F. "The Structure of University Costs." London: Society for Research into Higher Education, 1968.

Committee of Presidents of the Universities of Ontario. *Ring of Iron—A Study of Engineering Education in Ontario.* Toronto, Ontario: Committee of Presidents, 1970.

Committee of Vice Chancellors and Principals of the Universities of the United Kingdom. *Report of an Enquiry into the Uses of Academic Staff Time.* London: CVPU-U.K., 1972.

Dopuch, N., and Birnberg, J. G. *Cost Accounting: Accounting Data for Management Decisions.* New York: Harcourt Brace Jovanovich, 1969.

Drèze, J. "Some Postwar Contributions of French Economists to Theory and Public Policy, with Special Emphasis on Problems of Resource Allocation." *American Economic Review,* 1964, *54,* 1–64.

Farmer, J. *Why Cost Analysis for Higher Education?* Los Angeles: Systems Research, 1973.

Fisher, G. H. *Cost Considerations in Systems Analysis.* New York: American Elsevier, 1971.

Gulko, W. W. *Unit Costs of Instruction: A Methodological Approach in Cost Finding Principles and Procedures.* Boulder, Colorado: National Center for Higher Education Management Systems, 1971.

Gulko, W. W. *Program Classification Structure.* Boulder, Colorado: National Center for Higher Education Management Systems, 1972.

Hecquet, I., Marchand, M., and Jadot, J. *Pricing the Services of the Computer Center at the Catholic University of Louvain.* Paris: Organisation for Economic Co-operation and Development, 1975.

Hussain, K. M., and Freytag, H. *Resource, Costing and Planning Models.* Pullach/Munich, Federal Republic of Germany: Verlag Dokumentation, 1973.

Manning, C. W., and Romney, L. C. *Faculty Activity Analysis: Procedures Manual.* Boulder, Colorado: National Center for Higher Education Management Systems, 1973.

Manning, C. W., and Romney, L. C. *Faculty Activity Analysis: Interpretation and Uses of Data.* Boulder, Colorado: National Center for Higher Education Management Systems, 1974.

Marchand, M. "Priority Pricing." *Management Science,* 1974, *20,* 1131–1140.

National Association of College and University Business Officers. *College and University Business Administration.* Washington, D.C.: NACUBO, 1974.

National Commission on the Financing of Postsecondary Education. *Financing Postsecondary Education in the United States.* Washington, D.C.: U.S. Government Printing Office, 1973.

Pasquier, J., and Sachse, M. *Analysis of Unit Costs in a University: The Example of Fribourg.* Paris: Organisation for Economic Co-operation and Development, 1975.

"Presidential Unit Studies Funding of United States Colleges." *Chronicle of Higher Education,* February 20, 1973, p. 21.

Romney, L. C. *Faculty Activity Analysis: Overview and Major Issues.* Boulder, Colorado: National Center for Higher Education Management Systems, 1971.

Romney, L. C. *Higher Education Facilities Inventory and Classification Manual.* Boulder, Colorado: National Center for Higher Education Management Systems, 1972.

Segal, M. D. *The Political Economy of Resource Distribution in Quebec Universities.* Montreal, Quebec: Regional Commission of the Universities of the Province of Quebec, 1970.

Thompson, I. W., and Lapp, P. A. *A Method for Developing Unit Costs in Educational Programs.* Toronto, Ontario: Committee of Presidents of the Universities of Ontario, 1970.

Topping, J. R. *Cost Analysis Manual.* Boulder, Colorado: National Center for Higher Education Management Systems, 1974.

Topping, J. R., Weldon, K., and Kirschling, W. *Cost Finding Principles: Summary of the Analyses of the Pilot Test Data.* Boulder, Colorado: National Center for Higher Education Management Systems, 1974.

Verry, D. W., and Layard, P. R. G. "Cost Functions for University Teaching and Research." *Economic Journal,* 1975, *85,* 55–74.

Weathersby, G. W. "Prices Are Facts but Costs Are Opinions." *Chronicle of Higher Education,* February 20, 1973.

Weathersby, G. W., and Balderston, F. E. "PPBS in Higher Education Planning and Management. Part II: The University of California Experience." *Higher Education,* 1972, *1,* 299–319.

Yuker, H. E. *Faculty Workload: Facts, Myths and Commentary.* ERIC Higher Educational Research Report No. 6. Washington, D.C.: American Association for Higher Education, 1974.

Ziemer, G., Young, M., and Topping, J. *Cost Finding Principles and Procedures.* Boulder, Colorado: National Center for Higher Education Management Systems, 1971.

GUY TERNY

K. M. HUSSAIN

2. ACCOUNTING AND FINANCIAL REPORTING

An adequate review of any college or university accounting and financial record-keeping system must consider the purposes behind the accumulation of such data. Financial record keeping is designed to aid in the determination of an institution's financial capabilities to conduct its affairs. Such records and reports may also fulfill legal requirements, particularly in state or municipally supported organizations, for public systems are sometimes rigidly regulated. The financial reporting system may also be called on to reveal data necessary to the conduct of government-assisted programs, such as federally financed research, loan, or work-study programs (part-time work financed through federal funds).

Colleges and universities generally separate their financial structures into several identifiable areas, each of which may be thought of as self-balancing, with its own assets, obligations, income, expense, and net worth structure. The various areas flow into a total structure, but each retains separate management and decision-making control. The simple outline on the next page is representative of a typical recording system.

This basic pattern of accumulation of data will be relevant—with individual variations, of course—in most institutions of higher education, whether systems are small or large, manual or highly mechanized. Where funds are restricted, legal permission or approval by a governing board may be required before such funds can be shifted from one area to another. The institution's financial officers, therefore, should be fully familiar with the authority-granting mechanism before contemplating a movement of funds.

Current Fund

The current fund generally represents the largest day-by-day transaction-recording section of the accounting system, for it is here that most of the volume expenditures occur. This fund covers most of an institution's daily operating expenses: faculty and support personnel salaries and fringe benefits, routine plant maintenance and equipment expenses, supplies and

Organization of College or University Recording System

General Ledger Records

Assets
Obligations
Funds
Income
Expense

Current Fund	*Plant Fund*	*Endowment Fund*	*Loan Fund*
Assets	Assets	Assets	Assets
Obligations	Obligations	Obligations	Obligations
Current funds	Funds invested in plant	Fund principal	Fund principal
Income	Unexpended plant funds	Income	Income
Expense	Income	Expense	Expense
	Expense		

printed material purchases, and utility and service costs.

Current fund income accounting. The income-accounting area of the current fund catalogs major sources of revenue for most institutions: tuition and fee payments, miscellaneous fee collections, and a variety of other support service earnings. Endowment income assigned to general operations and student aid funds, as well as government appropriations for operating expenses, are also included, as these revenues are ultimately dispersed through the current fund.

Although the method of income accounting will vary among organizations, a discernible common approach does emerge, its main function being to record the origin of the current fund income. An accepted income-recording system will identify, for example, educational income (tuition and fees, endowments, gifts), auxiliary enterprise income (housing, cafeterias), and student aid income (grants, awards, scholarships). A large institution, such as a complex university of separate colleges, may choose to provide more specific information about sources of income for analytical and decision-making purposes. The accounting system in this case might be expanded to indicate tuition, fees, and miscellaneous income by individual college.

Since the highest volume area in any current fund is the student account section, this area demands some type of detailed subsidiary recording. Records indicating name, address, class, identification number, and, most important, obligation and payment data are usually maintained for each student. Depending on the system, various charges might also be separately recorded or coded for subsequent cumulative purposes. But whatever the system—manual, semimechanized, or highly developed data processing—this important information should be noted.

The effectiveness of detailed record keeping is reflected in the financial reports the records can generate, because in evaluating the income situation one examines not the minutiae of recorded detail but a general cumulative report based on that detail. A typical summary of the recorded information would indicate, by college and administrative division, the cash received, accounts receivable, expected cash receipt, and budget gain or loss to date. Such periodic financial reports may well uncover problems in other areas of a university's affairs; for example, a budget deficiency in admissions might reveal a developing slowdown in enrollment.

Current fund expense accounting. The record keeping for current fund expenditures must similarly be designed to provide the reliable and accurate information basic to sound fiscal management. As with income, accounting systems for current fund expenditures will in part be determined by the peculiarities of the individual institution. Government funding, for instance, may entail regulated expenditure-reporting procedures. Nevertheless, many of the following units are common to the accounting structure of all systems: general administration departments (such as board of trustees, president's office, personnel department, registrar); general expense departments (including alumni association, health services, public relations); instruction and department research (all colleges and departments of the university); extension and public services (continuing education and correspondence courses, among others); physical plant operations (such as superintendent's office, security, ground maintenance); organized research (privately and publicly funded research and contracts); libraries; auxiliary enterprises (dormitories, bookstores); and student aid (scholarships, fellowships, awards).

In addition to examining these larger categories, management must be able to observe the pattern of individual expenditures. Therefore, a current fund's accounting system will also provide a much finer breakdown of expenses, itemizing and detailing expenditures for salaries and fringe benefits (the largest single expenditure in most institutions); office, classroom, and laboratory supplies; equipment purchases; maintenance; utilities; travel; and conferences.

Where a system is large and complex, expenses as well as income may be broken down by college or department, thereby identifying not only the nature but also the location of each expenditure. This detailed accounting can produce periodic reports that allow management to evaluate the institution's current state of finances by relating expenses to original budget projections. It is also often helpful in large institutions to provide college or department heads with current expense and budgeting information drawn from these periodic summary reports.

Certain current fund expenses may require even further subsidiary record keeping. Payroll records, for instance, may accumulate salary data by control unit (college, department, or office) as well as by function (instructional, office, administrative). Government regulations may also demand accounting of individual payroll histories.

Other budgeting areas of the current fund, in addition to income and expenditures, will concern assets and obligations. Assets will involve such sources as cash, checking and savings accounts, accounts receivable, inventories, investments, or prepaid expenses, and obligations entail accounts payable, deposits, or deferred income.

Restricted current funds. Another type of recording often found in the current fund involves restricted funds, which often originate from gifts, bequests, or grants. The current fund will not necessarily dispose of such funds within the fiscal year under consideration since sometimes they must be held until it is possible to satisfy the terms on which the donation was made. Thus for balance sheet purposes, the current fund would be presented as:

Assets	*Liabilities*
Current funds:	Current funds:
General:	General:
Cash	Accounts payable
Investments	Deposits
Accounts receivable	Deferred income
Restricted:	Restricted:
Cash	Restricted funds
Investment	Balances

The restricted portions of the current fund at any fiscal closing will generally find their way into the operating areas of the current fund in the following fiscal year. There are, of course, exceptions—particularly restrictive demands may be placed on funds. However, except in large institutions, restricted funds of this type will be few.

Research. The organized research section of the current fund warrants special mention because of the nature of its support. Sponsors may have funded the research in advance or may plan to reimburse the institution after project completion. In either case, applicable costs must be segregated and classified as are other expenses of the current fund. Sometimes grant funds will be assessed a share of the overhead costs charged to other operating areas; the grant may be charged by a book transfer to, or by drawing checks on, the sponsored research project account and crediting the account of other operating areas. Sponsored research should, in general, be a completely self-balancing function. If the outgo exceeds income, funds must be found or appropriated to cover the project deficit. If funds are in excess, it may be necessary to return the unexpended amount to the sponsoring agency.

Two other research areas merit consideration. The first, and probably more common area, is research supported by the institution itself from its operating or current fund. Often referred to as departmental research, it is a planned, budgeted function whose costs frequently will be subjected to the kinds of record keeping discussed above. The second research area of particular budgetary concern relates to loss of anticipated revenues, either by cancellation or cutbacks in funding for research in progress or by failure to receive expected sponsorship. If such loss occurs, the institution may find itself burdened with personnel, equipment, building space, or other costs that are neither chargeable to outside funds nor covered by departmental resources. Where the research effort is large, management should closely observe and identify such costs so as to be better able to make the necessary adjustments should anticipated funding collapse.

Auxiliary enterprises. Auxiliary enterprises—dormitories, cafeterias, bookstores—entail necessary kinds of current fund or operating expenses; but, unlike the expenses previously examined, they are only indirectly related to the cost structure involved with the operation of the academic programs. Many institutions will aim at self-supporting auxiliary enterprises, while others will provide subsidies from other funds. Some may even prefer to delegate the auxiliary functions to outside management. Where the college or university operates the enterprises itself, it will use accounting systems little different from those used in other areas of the current fund, though a bookstore may involve some additional data accumulation if many kinds of merchandise other than textbooks are sold. In this latter case, the records would classify, in addition to the regular personnel, equipment, and plant facility costs, the sales volume for each type of item handled. Similarly, separate accounts would trace the purchase costs of the merchandise so as to facilitate analysis of profitable and unprofitable lines.

Plant Fund

While the current fund controls day-to-day financial operations of a college or university, the plant fund controls income and expenditures related to construction, land acquisition, and major plant renovation projects. Several sources provide funding for the special projects of this area: gifts and bequests, public appropriations, and loans (either public or private). Expenditures for a typical plant project, such as land acquisition, would entail legal and real estate agent fees, purchase price of the land, and, in certain cases, costs of refacing the property to suit the purpose of the purchase (paving for parking lots, for example).

The accounting structure for the plant fund usually notes the sources of the inflow of the funds as well as the characteristics of the outflow, for these will of necessity be peculiar to the individual undertaking. Separate accounts would identify some of the following: assets (cash in checking accounts, investments, appropriations receivable, equipment); expenditures (construction costs, legal fees, real estate commissions, labor); obligations and reserves (accounts payable, reserves for sinking funds and replacement of assets, loans and mortgages payable); and income (gifts, investment earnings, sales of assets).

The following chart, based on an inflow of $500,000, illustrates the accounting records for a typical plant fund in any fiscal year:

Receipts	$500,000	
Project A (building)		$250,000
Project B (land)		$125,000
Unassigned		$125,000
Expended	$350,000	
Project A		$250,000
Project B		$100,000
Unassigned		$125,000

BALANCE SHEET

Assets

Cash	$125,000
Buildings	$250,000
Land	$125,000
	$500,000

Commitments and Principal

Committed.......................	$ 25,000
Unassigned	$125,000
Funds invested in plant	$350,000
	$500,000

Loan Fund

Another autonomous area of control, and a completely self-balancing one, concerns loan funds for student aid programs. This section of the accounting system will have its own receipts, income, obligations, principal, and possibly even expenditures. However, unlike the current and plant funds, where accounts record a high volume of receipts and expenditures, the loan fund balance sheets primarily reclassify funds; that is, one creates a loan fund by receiving and funding cash. As the cash is loaned, the character of the asset simply is changed from cash to loans receivable.

As an example of typical loan fund record keeping, consider a fund of $1,000,000 from which a total of $250,000 has been loaned. The accounting system would merely substitute the asset, loans receivable, for cash:

$1,000,000 }	Cash ....$ 750,000
	Loans receivable 250,000
	Principal $1,000,000

As with the student accounts section of the current fund, records of individual accounts—containing student's name and address, amount and terms of the loan, and rate of interest—are usually maintained. It is also generally accepted practice to obtain and hold legally binding notes, the format of which is often determined by local laws or the terms on which the funds were granted. In fact, since federal, state, or provincial governments often provide a substantial portion of the fund principal, the institution will probably be required legally to furnish loan fund reports. Management may design the fund's accounting system to generate such information or may opt for periodic analysis of the accounts.

The repayment of loans, usually with interest, provides a simple income feature within the loan fund's structure. In some cases it may be required to accrue this interest to the fund principal; in others it may be possible to consider the interest as income. Expenses may sometimes be charged either directly against the principal or against the income of the fund. Such matters of expenses and earnings will usually be specified in the fund's administrative terms.

Endowment Funds

Endowment funds represent another important fiscal area. Financial activity in these funds usually originates from gifts, grants, or bequests, the principals of which are invested and remain intact with the earnings used for the stipulated purposes of the funds.

Endowed funds will be invested in compliance with local laws and regulations, donor-established restrictions, or the institution's own internal investment policies. Once properly invested, the institution must determine how to handle the earnings as well as the capital appreciation. When a fund earns income for a specified purpose, such as scholarships or faculty salaries, the income revenues may be removed and transferred directly to the other appropriate accounts, or the expenses from other areas (current or plant funds, for example) may be charged against the endowment fund's earnings. The question of capital appreciation is usually decided by one of two basic principles: (1) appreciation accumulates to the principal involved; or (2) appreciation is separately funded and used in a matter legally determined by the institution. Considerable debate surrounds the relative merit of each of these principles; obviously, policies will vary depending on the circumstances of each endowment fund.

Record keeping for endowment funds traces such features as the status and activity of the funds. A typical report may summarize such information under the following headings: name of fund, beginning principal, participation rate, market value, additions, adjusted market value, new participation rates, income distribution, profit and loss distribution, new principal.

Fund Policies

The major funds in a college or university financial structure—current, plant, loan, endowment—must, of course, be managed according to sound fiscal policies. Institutions of higher learning have established practices and procedures by which funds are administered, with authority sometimes retained at the board of trustees level and sometimes delegated to administrative officers of the institution.

Current fund policies. Different issues arise for different types of funds. The board of trustees may have to vote, for example, on some of the following current fund questions: designation of bank depository for institutional funds; designation of disbursing authority; and designation of individuals or positions with

authority to contract on behalf of the institution. On such matters the board would stipulate a particular bank in which to deposit all current fund receipts; it would establish official procedures for the disbursement of funds; and grant, according to the size of a transaction, fund-releasing authority to certain administrative officials; and it would designate, for example, the president or vice-president of finance as contracting officer of the university.

Current fund procedures determined by the institution's administrative officers might involve the collection of tuition and fees or the instigation of legal proceedings against individuals with delinquent accounts. In the first case, it might be established that no student could attend classes after the first week of the term unless his financial obligations were met in full or a satisfactory settlement arranged with the bursar. In the latter case, the university's power to initiate legal action against third parties might be reserved to the president, who would consult with the institution's legal representatives.

Plant fund policies. Because of the large financial commitment involved, decisions concerning capital projects—their nature, size, and financing—are usually reserved to the governing board, although a structure for recommending capital expansion to the board may operate within the institution. An example of a board action affecting the plant fund is authorization of the chief executive to enter into proper agreements for the construction of a library on a specified property at a specified maximum price. Such a decision by the governing board automatically necessitates a host of policy decisions on such matters as the number of bids required from contractors or the retention of outside architects. These questions will normally also be delegated to the chief executive, who may, in turn, decide to retain all authority for policy and procedural decisions or to delegate all or some of that authority.

Loan fund policies. The board of trustees, along with administrative officers, will also decide loan fund policies. A typical board action might be the acceptance of a private gift of $250,000, for example, to be used as a revolving fund for needy engineering students, with loans bearing interest at 5 percent and criteria determined by a committee on financial aid. An administrative unit then would have to decide such issues as limits on an individual's annual borrowing power, criteria for establishing financial need, or percentage allocation of funds by term as well as by class, college, or other distributive categorization. As the gift moves from acceptance to active use in student loans, the various strata of institutional authority, from trustees and president to vice-president of finance and financial aid officers, will become involved in loan fund policy.

Endowment funds policies. Governing board decisions regarding endowment funds are frequently limited to acceptance of the endowment and definition of the endowed program, with authority for specific implementation delegated to the chief executive. The board may decide in some cases, however, to establish institutional policy for the acceptance of such funds. It may demand, for example, that the fund be of a stipulated minimum principal, that it be used for research in areas relevant to the institution, or that its terms not discriminate against potential recipients or contradict any other institutional policies.

Once an endowment has been established, standard procedure is to disseminate basic information about the new fund to all parties involved in its administration. A basic information sheet is commonly distributed, detailing the fund's name, effective date, amount, purpose, donors, restrictions, and sources of information. The sheet also usually outlines screening procedures for applicants and identifies the administrative officer authorized to make final award recommendations.

Annuity and life income fund policies. Most institutions of higher education will, in addition to those funds already mentioned, also establish policy for annuity and life income funds. As with endowments, the governing board will normally define policy for acceptance and perhaps for investment before delegating administrative authority to the chief executive or an appropriate subcommittee. One issue the board may specifically have to resolve, however, concerns capital appreciation, particularly if the institution's investment committee maintains a policy of long-term capital appreciation. The governing board would, in this latter case, either decide to confirm the existing appreciation policy, acknowledging its probable low income yield, or decide to establish a policy of maximum current earnings, recognizing the potential loss in fund principal through inflation.

It should be noted that while the degree of delegation of responsibility will vary from one institution to another, legal policymaking authority for these various funds almost universally resides with the governing board. The trend in higher education in the mid 1970s is, in fact, toward a closer relationship between an institution's internal administration and its board. Perhaps the result of legal decisions affirming the total responsibility of governing boards in institutional matters, these bodies are increasingly involved in policy decisions.

Financial Statements

The complex financial structures and detailed record keeping of modern colleges and universities have created a recognized need for standardized financial statements. There is some disagreement, however, as to the specifics of formalized presentation. If the education community is decidedly different from general business or government, it is argued, it should express itself financially in specially designed financial statements; if not, it should adopt the presentation and terminology of one of the other two sectors. The basic issue, of course, is the ability of the general public to evaluate by means of financial reporting the approaches and relative effectiveness of different institutions.

Although the need for standardized reporting is widely acknowledged, the practice has not, as of the mid 1970s, seen broad international acceptance. It has, however, been adopted, particularly in the private sector, in colleges and universities in the United States, primarily through the efforts of the National Association of College and University Business Officers, the United States Office of Education, and the Committee on College and University Accounting and Auditing of the American Institute of Certified Public Accountants. Because of conflicting state and municipal regulations, acceptance in the public sector has been slower.

Financial statements in United States institutions. In the United States many colleges and universities are required periodically to prepare formal financial statements for presentation to trustees, corporation members, alumni, friends, and the general public. The statements, which are generally presented in terms of the institution's funding structures, involve two basic matters: (1) presentation, in what is commonly referred to as balance sheets, of the financial condition of the organization as of a particular day (often the last day of the fiscal year); and (2) presentation of the revenue-expenditure pattern of the institution's major fund categories in order to identify funding origins and uses.

Balance sheets. In reporting assets, obligations, and equity, balance sheets indicate an institution's financial standing at any one time. The sheets are therefore a vital aid in planning an institution's fiscal affairs. They may be used as a basis for negotiating long- or short-term loans, or they may be used as a guide for fund-raising ventures. For example, if one were organizing a campaign to raise funds for endowment holdings, the balance sheets would provide all the necessary information about the current fund levels.

The balance sheets generally show items at cost, particularly such items as fixed assets like land or buildings. However, in some cases other values may be used if so noted in the balance sheet. When the current market or replacement value for equipment, for example, differs substantially from the original cost, the equipment might be presented according to the current value, which would then be carefully indicated in the statement. A similar distortion might also arise were investments to be presented at cost, for their market values can fluctuate considerably. Therefore, some investments might also be reported on other bases. (It might be noted that during the period of economic growth in the United States in the 1950s and 1960s, some private institutions adopted the practice of reporting endowment investments at market rather than original cost value. The economic slowdown in following years, however, cast some question on the long-term advisability of such procedures, and the question of reporting such funds at market value remains open.)

The sample balance sheets presented in Exhibits A, B, and C illustrate financial statements for an institution of higher learning. These samples are typical in their reporting of financial data in terms of revenues and expenditures in major funding areas. In most cases such basic information would be elaborated on with further schedules and background data.

Financial reporting is moving toward standardization in colleges and universities in the United States, but certain areas of reporting remain problematical. For example, fund flow, or transfers between funds, as illustrated in Exhibits B and C, is difficult to define and indicate in a financial statement. The question of reporting depreciation on fixed assets also remains unresolved. For many years depreciation was essentially unrecognized since budgets were designed to allow for renewal and replacement reserves. As new financial procedures have been adopted, however,

Sample Educational Institution

Balance Sheet
June 30, 19—
With Comparative Figures at June 30, 19—

Assets	Current year	Prior year
Current funds:		
Unrestricted:		
Cash	$ 210,000	110,000
Investments	450,000	360,000
Accounts receivable, less allowance of $18,000 both years	228,000	175,000
Inventories, at lower of cost (first-in first-out basis) or market	90,000	80,000
Prepaid expenses and deferred charges	28,000	20,000
Total unrestricted	1,006,000	745,000
Restricted:		
Cash	145,000	101,000
Investments	175,000	165,000
Accounts receivable, less allowance of $8,000 both years	68,000	160,000
Unbilled charges	72,000	—
Total restricted	460,000	426,000
Total current funds	1,466,000	1,171,000
Loan funds:		
Cash	30,000	20,000
Investments	100,000	100,000
Loans to students, faculty, and staff, less allowance of $10,000 current year—$9,000 prior year	550,000	382,000
Due from unrestricted current funds	3,000	—
Total loan funds	683,000	502,000
Endowment and similar funds:		
Cash	100,000	101,000
Investments	13,900,000	11,800,000
Total endowment and similar funds	14,000,000	11,901,000

Liabilities and Fund Balances	Current year	Prior year
Current funds:		
Unrestricted:		
Accounts payable	$ 125,000	100,000
Accrued liabilities	20,000	15,000
Students' deposits	30,000	35,000
Due to other funds	158,000	120,000
Deferred revenue	30,000	20,000
Fund balance	643,000	455,000
Total unrestricted	1,006,000	745,000
Restricted:		
Accounts payable	14,000	5,000
Fund balances	446,000	421,000
Total restricted	460,000	426,000
Total Current funds	1,466,000	1,171,000
Loan funds:		
Fund balances:		
U.S. Government grants refundable	50,000	33,000
University funds:		
Restricted	483,000	369,000
Unrestricted	150,000	100,000
Total loan funds	683,000	502,000
Endowment and similar funds:		
Fund balances:		
Endowment	7,800,000	6,740,000
Term endowment	3,840,000	3,420,000
Quasi-endowment-unrestricted	2,360,000	1,741,000
Total endowment and similar funds	14,000,000	11,901,000

Assets

Annuity and life income funds:		
Annuity funds:		
Cash	55,000	45,000
Investments	3,260,000	3,010,000
Total annuity funds	3,315,000	3,055,000
Life income funds:		
Cash	15,000	15,000
Investments	2,045,000	1,740,000
Total life income funds	2,060,000	1,755,000
Total annuity and life income funds	5,375,000	4,810,000
Plant funds:		
Unexpended:		
Cash	275,000	410,000
Investments	1,285,000	1,590,000
Due from unrestricted current funds	150,000	120,000
Total unexpended	1,710,000	2,120,000
Renewal and replacement:		
Cash	5,000	4,000
Investments	150,000	286,000
Deposits with trustees	100,000	90,000
Due from unrestricted current funds	5,000	—
Total renewal and replacement	260,000	380,000
Retirement of indebtedness:		
Cash	50,000	40,000
Deposits with trustees	250,000	253,000
Total retirement of indebtedness	300,000	293,000
Investment in plant:		
Land	500,000	500,000
Land improvements	1,000,000	1,110,000
Buildings	25,000,000	24,060,000
Equipment	15,000,000	14,200,000
Library books	100,000	80,000
Total investment in plant	41,600,000	39,950,000
Total plant funds	43,870,000	42,743,000
Agency funds:		
Cash	50,000	70,000
Investments	60,000	20,000
Total agency funds	$ 110,000	90,000

Liabilities and Fund Balances

Annuity and life income funds:		
Annuity funds:		
Annuities payable	2,150,000	2,300,000
Fund balances	1,165,000	755,000
Total annuity funds	3,315,000	3,055,000
Life income funds:		
Income payable	5,000	5,000
Fund balances	2,055,000	1,750,000
Total life income funds	2,060,000	1,755,000
Total annuity and life income funds	5,375,000	4,810,000
Plant funds:		
Unexpended:		
Accounts payable	10,000	—
Notes payable	100,000	—
Bonds payable	400,000	—
Fund balances:		
Restricted	1,000,000	1,860,000
Unrestricted	200,000	260,000
Total unexpended	1,710,000	2,120,000
Renewal and replacement:		
Fund balances:		
Restricted	25,000	180,000
Unrestricted	235,000	200,000
Total renewal and replacement	260,000	380,000
Retirement of indebtedness:		
Fund balances:		
Restricted	185,000	125,000
Unrestricted	115,000	168,000
Total retirement of indebtedness	300,000	293,000
Investment in plant:		
Notes payable	790,000	810,000
Bonds payable	2,200,000	2,400,000
Mortgages payable	400,000	200,000
Net investment in plant	38,210,000	36,540,000
Total investment in plant	41,600,000	39,950,000
Total plant funds	43,870,000	42,743,000
Agency funds:		
Deposits held in custody for others	110,000	90,000
Total agency funds	$ 110,000	90,000

Sample Educational Institution

Statement of Changes in Fund Balances
Year Ended June 30, 19—

	Current Funds		Loans Funds	Endowment and Similar Funds	Annuity and Life Income Funds	Plant Funds			
	Unrestricted	Restricted				Unexpended	Renewal and Replacement	Retirement of Indebtedness	Investment in Plant
Revenues and other additions:									
Educational and general revenues	$ 5,300,000								
Auxiliary enterprises revenues	2,200,000								
Expired term endowment revenues	40,000								
Expired term endowment—restricted									
Gifts and bequests—restricted		370,000	100,000	1,500,000	800,000	50,000			
Grants and contracts—restricted		500,000				115,000		65,000	15,000
Governmental appropriations—restricted						50,000			
Investment income—restricted		224,000	12,000	10,000		5,000	5,000	5,000	
Realized gains on investments—unrestricted				109,000					
Realized gain on investments—restricted			4,000	50,000		10,000	5,000	5,000	
Interest on loans receivable			7,000						
U.S. Government advances			18,000						
Expended for plant facilities (including $100,000 charged to current funds expenditures)									1,550,000
Retirement of indebtedness									220,000
Accrued interest on sale of bonds								3,000	
Matured annuity and life income funds restricted to endowment				10,000					
Total revenues and other additions	7,540,000	1,094,000	141,000	1,679,000	800,000	230,000	10,000	78,000	1,785,000

	(1)	(2)	(3)	(4)	(5)	(6)	(7)	(8)	(9)
Expenditures and other deductions:									
Educational and general expenditures	4,400,000	1,014,000							
Auxiliary enterprises expenditures	1,830,000								
Indirect costs recovered		35,000							
Refunded to grantors		20,000							
Loan cancellations and write-offs			10,000						
Administrative and collection costs			1,000					1,000	
Adjustment of actuarial liability for annuities payable					75,000				
Expended for plant facilities (including noncapitalized expenditures of $50,000)						1,200,000	300,000		
Retirement of indebtedness								220,000	
Interest on indebtedness								190,000	
Disposal of plant facilities									115,000
Expired term endowments ($40,000 unrestricted, $50,000 restricted to plant)				90,000					
Matured annuity and life income funds restricted to endowment					10,000				
Total expenditures and other deductions	6,230,000	1,069,000	12,000	90,000	85,000	1,200,000	300,000	411,000	115,000
Transfers among funds—additions/(deductions):									
Mandatory:									
Principal and interest	(340,000)							340,000	
Renewals and replacements	(170,000)						170,000		
Loan fund matching grant	(2,000)		2,000						
Unrestricted gifts allocated	(650,000)		50,000	550,000	50,000				
Portion of unrestricted quasi-endowment funds investment gains appropriated	40,000			(40,000)					
Total transfers	(1,122,000)		52,000	510,000	50,000		170,000	340,000	
Net increase/(decrease) for the year	188,000	25,000	181,000	2,099,000	(120,000)	715,000	41,000	7,000	1,670,000
Fund balance at beginning of year	455,000	421,000	502,000	11,901,000	2,120,000	2,505,000	380,000	293,000	36,540,000
Fund balance at end of year	$ 643,000	446,000	683,000	14,000,000	2,000,000	3,220,000	421,000	300,000	38,210,000

Exhibit C

Sample Educational Institution

Statement of Current Funds Revenues, Expenditures, and Other Changes
Year Ended June 30,19—
With Comparative Figures for 19—

	Current year			Prior
	Unrestricted	*Restricted*	*Total*	*Year Total*
Revenues:				
Educational and general:				
Student tuition and fees	$2,600,000		2,600,000	2,300,000
Governmental appropriations	1,300,000		1,300,000	1,300,000
Governmental grants and contracts	35,000	425,000	460,000	595,000
Gifts and private grants	850,000	380,000	1,230,000	1,190,000
Endowment income	325,000	209,000	534,000	500,000
Sales and services of educational departments	90,000		90,000	95,000
Organized activities related to educational departments	100,000		100,000	100,000
Other sources (if any)				
Total educational and general	5,300,000	1,014,000	6,314,000	6,080,000
Auxiliary enterprises	2,200,000		2,200,000	2,100,000
Expired term endowment	40,000		40,000	
Total revenues	7,540,000	1,014,000	8,554,000	8,180,000
Expenses and mandatory transfers:				
Educational and general:				
Instruction and departmental research	2,820,000	300,000	3,120,000	2,950,000
Organized activities related to educational departments	140,000	189,000	329,000	350,000
Sponsored research		400,000	400,000	500,000
Other separately budgeted research	100,000		100,000	150,000
Other sponsored programs		25,000	25,000	50,000
Extension and public service	130,000		130,000	125,000
Libraries	250,000		250,000	225,000
Student services	200,000		200,000	195,000
Operation and maintenance of plant	220,000		220,000	200,000
General administration	200,000		200,000	195,000
General institutional expense	250,000		250,000	250,000
Student aid	90,000	100,000	190,000	180,000
Educational and general expenditures	4,400,000	1,014,000	5,414,000	5,370,000
Mandatory transfers for:				
Principal and interest	90,000		90,000	50,000
Renewals and replacements	100,000		100,000	80,000
Loan fund matching grant	2,000		2,000	
Total educational and general	4,592,000	1,014,000	5,606,000	5,500,000
Auxiliary enterprises:				
Expenditures	1,830,000		1,830,000	1,730,000
Mandatory transfers for:				
Principal and interest	250,000		250,000	250,000
Renewals and replacements	70,000		70,000	70,000
Total auxiliary enterprises	2,150,000		2,150,000	2,050,000
Total expenditures and mandatory transfers	6,742,000	1,014,000	7,756,000	7,550,000
Other transfers and additions/(deductions):				
Excess of restricted receipts over transfers to revenues		45,000	45,000	40,000
Refunded to grantors		(20,000)	(20,000)	
Unrestricted gifts allocated to other funds	(650,000)		(650,000)	(510,000)
Portion of quasi-endowment gains appropriated	40,000		40,000	
Net increase in fund balances	$ 188,000	25,000	213,000	160,000

depreciation has been identified as an additional plant fund cost item, although the new practices do not specify its presentation.

At the bottom of these questions of financial statements is the public's right to information about its institutions of higher education. Whatever approach is adopted, be it one of separate or combined fund presentations, the public must have sound and reliable means for evaluating the relative financial status of its colleges and universities. Whether this information will be presented in a manner unique to the education community or in a nonspecialized format familiar in the business and government sectors as well remains an open question.

Bibliography

Audits of Colleges and Universities. New York: American Institute of Certified Public Accountants, 1973.

College and University Business Administration. Washington, D.C.: National Association of College and University Business Officers, 1974.

Collier, D. J. *Higher Education Finance Manual.* Field Review Edition, Technical Report No. 53. Boulder, Colorado: National Center for Higher Education Management Systems at Western Interstate Commission for Higher Education, 1974.

Davidson, E. E., and Scheps, C. *Accounting for Colleges and Universities.* Baton Rouge: Louisiana State University Press, 1971.

DANIEL J. ROBERTS

3. BUDGETING

Most chief executives of institutions of higher learning are directly involved in budget administration, for any plan of operation must eventually be reduced to a numerically expressed document that aims at limiting resource commitments to predictable sources of revenue. Whether the institution's funding originates from private or from public sources, the chief executive must cope with the basic budgetary problem of balancing expenditures with revenues.

The chief executive—the president, chancellor, or rector—usually delegates his role in budgeting to one specialist or to a series of specialists (the number of whom is determined by the size and complexity of the institution) whose responsibility it is to help establish sound budget management. Such titles as vice-chancellor for business operations, vice-president for finance, business manager, or budget officer designate those individuals with delegated authority for budgetary matters. In addition, almost every other officer of the institution will contribute in some fashion to the drafting of the budget document. However, in spite of the many individual contributions, it is the chief executive who bears final responsibility for the presentation and administration of the financial plan.

Development of the Operating Income Budget

The academic community has developed a variety of approaches in budgeting, many of which encompass the social, political, administrative, or academic peculiarities of the institution itself. Yet all institutions of higher education gain their revenue from sources easily cataloged and understood, though the sources, of course, vary from institution to institution. A private university, for example, relies heavily on tuition, fees, and gifts in its revenue structure, along with some additional appropriations from public sources. A public institution, on the other hand, secures the major portion of its revenue from public appropriations, although it, too, may receive part of its revenue from tuition and gifts. In developing an operating income budget, the college or university must anticipate the revenue from these various sources.

Tuition and fees. Tuition and fees represent a major source of income in the operating budgets of many institutions. Anticipated tuition revenue is usually calculated by multiplying the tuition rates by the number of estimated students. However, it is well to modify this figure by a carefully calculated estimate of withdrawals, the objective of such a refinement being the development of a hard revenue figure, for budgets can fail for lack of liquidity in anticipated revenue.

The methods for computing anticipated income from tuition charges vary depending on the size of the institution. A small college enrolling only a few hundred students, for instance, may develop a simple tuition income estimate based on multiplication of anticipated enrollment by tuition rate and modified by experience. But a large university with several colleges and graduate schools may estimate tuition income by individual college or even by department, combining these separate estimates into a final figure for the anticipated university-wide tuition income.

Closely allied to tuition revenues are those revenues derived from fees. In developing an operating income budget, fees are estimated in basically the same manner as are tuition charges. An institution may generate income by assessing a variety of special fees, such as application, athletic, laboratory, late registration, library, or parking charges.

Appropriations. Government appropriations are typically the most important source of funding in the public sector. Usually based on expense analysis of the institution's needs and objectives, the amount of the appropriations may be determined in a variety of ways. One method depends on direct calculation of operating costs: estimated revenues from tuition charges, fees, and other sources are deducted from total anticipated operating costs, thereby arriving at the appropriations figure. Other methods use formulas based, for example, on the numbers of full- or part-time students multiplied by a predetermined allowance per individual. A variation of this formulaic calculation of appropriations is the weighing of full- and part-time students to create full-time equivalencies. Another method, sometimes used in the British system, relies on quinquennial estimates of student enrollments followed by annual determination of appro-

priations. (It might be noted here that while budgetary control procedures vary considerably in the United Kingdom, the United States has moved toward standardized procedures.)

Endowments. Endowments represent another significant source of funding, particularly for private institutions, where they may account for a substantial portion of the operating budget revenue. But the revenue from endowment funds is often restricted, such as when the funds are reserved for underwriting scholarships or for providing grants-in-aid. In spite of such restrictions, however, much of the endowment revenue contributes either directly or indirectly to the tuition and fees income.

Endowment revenues may influence budgeting of expenditures as well as of income. For instance, it is common for endowment funds to support some salaries, research groups, or even departments. The budgeting procedures with such endowment income are not uniform; in some cases, the funds may be restricted to specified expenditures, while in others, where the funds are unrestricted, they may simply be included in the general operating income structure before being budgeted for particular commitments.

The question of restricted versus unrestricted endowment funding has long generated extensive debate among financial administrators. Restricted funds, it is argued, cannot be used to meet current needs or be put to productive use when they are bound to outmoded conditions. Furthermore, freeing such restricted funds often entails long legal entanglements. And, unfortunately, the institution may have little if any voice in the determination of the restrictions, since they are frequently stipulated in the terms of wills, trusts, or other legal documents determined without the institution's awareness.

Auxiliary enterprise revenues. Another source of funding, one budgeted separately, concerns those operations—such as housing, cafeterias, bookstores, or, particularly in North America, some intercollegiate sports—that financially support the institution's main educational and research objectives. There are different philosophies regarding the funding structures for these types of auxiliary operations. One claim is that any auxiliary operation should be at least self-sufficient, balancing its revenues with expenditures without ever placing a drain on the main educational and research budgets. But this argument is by no means totally accepted. Thus, a small, strictly residential institution may choose to consider its housing operation part of its total operation rather than an auxiliary enterprise. Furthermore, many activities, intercollegiate sports among them, may be considered student programs, not auxiliary enterprises at all.

Sponsored research. One major consideration in developing an operating budget is sponsored research. Research is often funded through grants from the government, industry, or private individuals, but it is also sponsored by contracts that usually define the investigation more rigidly than do grants. While there is little problem in predicting revenue when grant support is in hand, it is more difficult to estimate income from research proposals still outstanding. When a proposed project would bear little impact on the operating budget, it might well be omitted and the budget adjusted later if funds are awarded. However, if the proposal represents significant revenue, the probability of funding should be explored: project directors, who can often anticipate the funding decision, might be consulted, and it may even be wise to meet directly with the proposed grantors.

Other miscellaneous revenue. Other sources of revenue that do not appear in the previous categories also bear consideration in drafting a budget. Gifts and grants, for example, can be partially included in the income estimates, particularly when the institution has traditionally received gifts for operating purposes. Certainly, income from short-term investments should be included in the estimates, as should re-
bates and dividends when they are significant enough to be predictable.

Development of the Operating Expense Budget

The development of an operating expense budget, regardless of the type of institution concerned, requires two types of identification: the nature of the expenditure (for instance, salaries and, often, types of salaries, such as faculty, administrative, or staff) and the division, department, or office where the expenditure occurs. The expense budget, usually excluding the auxiliary enterprise or sponsored research budgets, which are compiled independently for control as well as informational purposes, will be drafted, of course, according to the individual institution's control and authorization system. In a large university with decentralized authority, the drafting might start at the department level, incorporating departmental development plans, then move vertically upward through the hierarchy of university authority. As the budget proceeds toward approval, it may undergo stages of compilation, with departments summarized by college or administrative units compiled into service divisions. Throughout the compilation process, however, the nature and location of each expenditure remain identified.

Salaries. Salaries and fringe benefits are among the most vital of items in an operating expense budget, since they represent the largest single expenditure in most institutions. Because these items are so significant to the budget as a whole, it is important to identify their salient features for information, control, and evaluation. Salaries are most commonly identified by one of the following indices: administrative; faculty (teaching, research, sabbatical); faculty support (teaching and research assistants); office support staff (secretaries and administrative assistants); cleaning and custodial services; maintenance services; security services; and other specialist services (coaches, doctors, consultants). While the distribution of salaries among these various categories will vary from institution to institution, all the indices will merit consideration in determination of the budget.

Fringe benefits. Fringe benefits have become an increasingly important part of personnel costs, important enough to require separate cataloging for observational purposes. The nature of many fringe benefits is such that identification by budget unit is possible. Some of these identifying units are medical and life insurance plans, retirement programs, and disability and accident insurance benefits. Where such identification is not possible, the benefits are budgeted in a single pool and considered part of a general administrative expenditure, sometimes disbursed later by formula.

Other expenses. In addition to the major categories of salaries and fringe benefits, any institution will have to consider numerous other expenditures in the development of its operating expense budget. One significant and increasingly expensive item, particularly in cold climates, is utilities, which include electricity, heat, water and sewage, telephone and telegraph. Laboratory, audiovisual, automotive, and other miscellaneous equipment and equipment maintenance costs must be cataloged as well. The operating expense budget also identifies expenditures for travel, conferences, supplies, subscriptions, postage, cleaning, and the many other costs involved in the successful operation of an institution of higher learning. What is important to note is that the budget and control of items must always be designed for the individual institution's particular situation and needs. No two institutions will develop quite the same breakdown of expenditures.

Additional Budget Areas

While the main budget area is operations, there are other areas of budgetary concern. A budget must be developed, for instance, for plant development, an area where budgeting is by project rather than by department and of multiple rather than of single fiscal years. A typical plant budget includes expenditures for acquisition of land, construction of buildings, and renovations of existing facilities.

An early consideration in the implementation of a plant budget is development of the necessary resources for project completion. Funding may be gained from a variety of sources, including the following: (1) direct fund raising; (2) direct government appropriations or grants; (3) designation of unrestricted gifts, grants, or appropriations from either public or private sources; (4) short- or long-term loans authorized under the legal operating mechanism of the institution; (5) direct allocations of funds from the institution's general operating budget (although, with the financial stringency facing higher education in the mid 1970s, it is difficult to write a budget with a calculable margin of revenues); (6) installation of special fees for plant services, perhaps along a partial user philosophy with imposition of, say, a student union or sports fee.

Table 1 illustrates a sample budget plan for a typical development project—land acquisition and construction of a library.

Table 1. Sample Budget

Revenues	*Amount*
Fund raising	$3,500,000
Appropriations (from public source)	3,000,000
Unassigned funds available	500,000
Total	7,000,000
Outlay	
Land acquisition	750,000
Site preparation	100,000
Building construction	4,500,000
Fixed equipment	500,000
Additional book acquisitions	750,000
Architect's fees	300,000
Contingencies	100,000
Total	7,000,000

It should be noted that the nature of a plant development fund dictates the nature of its budgeting process. While the operating budget is geared toward the day-to-day delivery of educational services, the plant budget involves capital items established as permanent budget units.

Loan funds. Funding of student loans is another area of budget consideration. It is sound practice to reduce the annual plan for loan disbursement to a written outline, balancing sources of revenue—such as loan repayments, new government appropriations, university contributions, or private gifts, grants, and endowment income—with commitments to freshmen, upperclassmen, and graduate students. Such a controlled budgetary plan ensures organized distribution of funds according to predetermined needs and priorities.

Endowment funds. A form of budgeting also takes place with endowment funds, for at least a portion of endowment earnings are predictable. Moreover, the commitments and purposes of such funds are clearly established, further facilitating budgetary planning (which is particularly desirable when the funds are numerous). But whether one is contemplating endowments, loans, general operating expenses, or operating income sources, it is vital to view the budget as a document of related areas, with items interdependent of and contributing to one another.

Techniques and Philosophies of Budgeting

A number of techniques and philosophies of college and university budgeting have been developed; some have their roots in the academic community while others have been adapted from the business community. In either case, it is crucial that the best technique for a particular organization at a particular time be selected.

The ZBB theory. In the mid 1970s the newest and perhaps most controversial technique is called zero-base budgeting (ZBB). Adapted from an industrial model, the ZBB technique starts the budgeting process by placing each identifiable activity unit in an organization at base zero, then evaluates each function using the budget as the mechanism by which activities are

sustained or curtailed. The successful implementation of such an extreme budget technique depends on the establishment of an objective mechanism to evaluate the many functions of a complex university.

Total implementation of ZBB in a university setting, however, is probably impractical, if not impossible, since many budgetary commitments are made independent of the evaluative procedures ZBB imposes. Thus, a college may well decide to support student sports or fund other traditional student services regardless of the theoretical elements of ZBB.

It may be that advocates of ZBB in institutions of higher education are not so much seeking total implementation of the technique as they are encouraging periodic review, through budgetary procedures, of established institutional practices; that is, ZBB may force examination of such delicate issues as class size or teaching load—examination which could effect improvement of problematical cost situations. Those departments or services in budgetary trouble that are not subjected to ZBB analysis are likely to be discovered through other basic budgetary approaches.

The PPBS system. Another budgeting technique that seeks wide impact and objectivity is the so-called planning program and budgeting system (PPBS). With this method the budget develops in stages. The first is a multiple-year planning stage, while the second—programing—implements the plans established in the first. This second step may subdivide the total plan into objectives treated separately. The third step—budgeting—translates the programing into economic language consistent with the determined institutional objectives.

This type of budgeting occurs most typically at the beginning of a college or university administration. In theory, at least, a master plan is developed and the methods of implementing devised. But while PPBS functions perfectly in theory, it has, in reality, received only partial adaptation, for it makes the simplistic assumption of constant availability of data bases of accurate and objective material. In fact, the consistent availability of such data bases is questionable. Consequently, PPBS programs need constant updating so that their long-range planning can be subject to alteration and readjustment by day-to-day events. Since a large and complex structure is necessary to keep such a plan current, it is not surprising that PPBS has had limited adaptation as a basic budgeting technique.

The SWGG approach. A budgetary practice, one more widely resorted to than most administrators would like to admit, finds, funds distributed more on a personal than an objectively planned basis. Dubbed the SWGG—"the squeaky wheel gets the grease"—technique, it openly acknowledges the domination of personalities in the field of higher education and, more significantly, the relationship between personality and resource allocation. Often found in universities where the objectives are short run or even nonexistent, the system, quite simply, distributes funds by personality, not planning. Although the SWGG process might be defended on the theory that as the strongest and ablest get the resources, the institution is funding where its strength is, the system allows for no carefully determined long-range funding program.

Budgeting formulas. Formulas are sometimes used, particularly in the public sector, as a budgeting method geared to objectivity in resource allocation. Formulas, which are based in some fashion on the number of persons receiving a particular service, may, in a college or university, concern the total number of students, the number of full- or part-time students, or the number of full-time equivalent students. But institutions of higher learning, unlike large systems in the public domain, have resisted wide acceptance of the formula approach. Although it has been argued that formulas, when used in conjunction with the model approach (a computer-assisted simulation), can produce a reliable budgeting process,

experience with such approaches in the late 1960s and 1970s has not been positive. Higher education in the United States in this period, for example, suffered from some financial constraint. As a result, the formula approach has faced constant criticism, while the model approach still lacks sufficient data control to be relied upon as a means in itself.

Whatever method is used to devise the budget, the final fiscal authority and responsibility probably still reside with an institution's chief executive and governing board. Colleges and universities in the mid 1970s face too much financial uncertainty to risk hazardous overcommitment or further fiscal mismanagement; thus, ultimate budgetary control rests with a central rather than the diversified authority that was the trend from approximately 1965 to 1975. And if higher education faces continued financial stringency, the chief executive will be the focus of increasing competition for limited funds.

Self-financing units. One variation on the central authority approach is the creation within a university of multiple self-financing units. The institution may subdivide into identifiable areas—colleges, for example— that generate their own funding bases while also contributing to university-wide functions. The ability to create fiscally autonomous units is limited, of course, to those institutions large enough to support a significant variety of functions. Such a system also demands a situation in which the subunits are allowed to exercise their delegated authority independently of a central administration. The theory further assumes the existence of a set of circumstances that allows full development of resources along historically patterned lines, which may not coincide with changing times and the future developing role of the institution.

There are, however, some institutions where the self-financing approach is both practical and feasible. A mature university with devoted alumni support, for example, may find the system valid, but the general trend seems to be away from self-financing units. The public sector has never employed them to any significant degree, and increased government funding in the private sector seems to be similarly directing institutions toward central administrative control. The decision to implement the self-financing system must be made according to the same guidelines governing all budgetary process decisions: the system, or combination of systems, under consideration must best serve the specific needs of the institution at that particular moment in its history.

Trends in Budgeting Procedures

During the 1970s there has been in some institutions, particularly in the United States, movement toward standardization of existing budgeting procedures and techniques as well as development of new ones. The National Center for Higher Education Management Systems (NCHEMS) of the Western Interstate Commission for Higher Education (WICHE) in Boulder, Colorado, has introduced one important new concept—program budgeting. This method modifies the more traditional budgeting approach by redirecting some departmental funds into interdisciplinary program budgets.

The NCHEMS approach visualizes four steps, based on the cost per credit hour to the program base, in the development of program budgeting: (1) analysis of student enrollment data; (2) determination of total credit hours in each of the various programs; (3) calculation of direct costs of generating the programs' credit hours; (4) direction of departmental funds to appropriate programs based on credit hour costs established in earlier steps. This program-oriented allocation of funds, it should be stressed, presumes the existence of such specifications as class size, faculty teaching load, salaries, and other factors that can be logically assigned to a direct instructional cost base.

The NCHEMS concept also entails the use of models as a budget tool to examine, revamp, or predict an institution's financial situation. Once the data base is filled, models can be designed to explore options to a degree previously not practical, testing possible enrollment patterns, staffing alternatives, or faculty ratios, as well as many other important facets of an educational program. The relevant features may be adjusted, reapportioned, and analyzed in order to derive a model generating the most suitable budget specifications. Modeling, which is particularly useful in a multiunit educational complex, has impressive analytical possibilities in a public system, serving as a major aid in, though not a substitute for, the decision-making functions in the budgetary process.

The introduction of modeling will by no means invalidate all other techniques and philosophies. Strong personalities will still compete for funding; chief executives will still bear the prime responsibility for decisions; and an institution's traditional patterns will often continue to dominate. But the modeling concept does represent a significant development in budgeting. As the ability to develop new resources stabilizes, the adoption of new tools with which to examine resource allocation and utilization becomes increasingly vital. Indeed, the development of accurate and reliable budget tools is of high priority in the field of higher education.

Bibliography

Bowen, H. "Planning for Higher Education in the Inflationary 1970's." Paper presented at a meeting of the Eastern Association of College and University Business Officers, Montreal, Quebec, 1974.

Clark, D. A., and Huff, R. A. *Instructional Program Budgeting in Higher Education.* Boulder, Colorado: National Center for Higher Education Management Systems at Western Interstate Commission for Higher Education, 1972.

Eustace, R., and Moodie, G. C. *Power and Authority in British Universities.* Montreal, Quebec: Queen's University Press, 1974.

Planning, Budgeting and Accounting. Washington, D.C.: National Association of College and University Business Officers, 1970.

Pyhrr, P. A. *Zero-Base Budgeting*. New York: Wiley, 1973.

DANIEL J. ROBERTS

See also: Evaluation; Financing of Higher Education; Planning, Development and Coordination: Institutional Planning; Remuneration: Faculty, Staff, and Chief Executive Officers.

4. INVESTMENTS

Colleges and universities have two types of funding available for investing. One type demands "short-term investments," available for short periods of time pending the need to pay ongoing expenses. The second type demands "long-term investments," often under control of the governing board for considerable periods of time or in perpetuity. The purpose of these funds is to provide income for the college or university for general or particular purposes. The first may be either operating- or endowment-type funds, and the second is usually associated with endowment funding. They are broadly classified as endowment funds and hereafter will be referred to as "endowments."

Short-Term Investments

These funds come from many different sources, including deposits on tuitions and fees paid on acceptance of admission and deposits paid to hold accommodations in residences; advanced payments on tuition made at the beginning of the term or academic year, but not expended immediately; escrow funds held for specific purposes, to be used at a later date; surplus operating funds resulting from temporary excesses of income over expenditures; capital advances for construction, which must be held until the need to pay contractors arises; research funds received at the beginning of a project, to be expended over a period of months or years; and annual giving funds collected from alumni throughout each year and held until needed to pay operating expenses or other costs.

These short-term investments can be held in non-interest-bearing accounts until needed, or they may be invested on a tem-

porary basis to provide additional income. Good financial management demands that they be invested to earn as much income as possible during the time that they are available. In a large university this income can be very substantial.

Endowment Funds

These long-term investments are funds provided by bequests and gifts or surplus operating funds earmarked by the governing board for endowment purposes. These funds are designated as either unrestricted or restricted.

The income from the investment of unrestricted funds may be used at the discretion of the governing boards. Income from the investment of restricted funds is earmarked for particular purposes, including income to support endowed chairs and professorships; scholarships and fellowships awarded to undergraduates and graduates; prize funds awarded for outstanding achievement; lecture funds used to invite distinguished scholars to the campus; building endowments used to maintain and operate buildings; library book funds expended to purchase books for general library use and special collections; research funds designated for the conduct of particular types of research; and student loan funds established to provide loans for deserving and needy students.

Policies and Guidelines for Investments

The institution's governing board is ultimately responsible for all investments and usually appoints a standing committee to formulate policies and direct investment activities related to both short- and long-term investments. This committee may designate certain persons to carry out the actual investing process, but the committee is ultimately responsible for the results. The policies that are usually established are:

1. Policies for investments for short-term funds. These include the types of investments that might be made, such as savings bank accounts, purchase of cer-

tificates of deposit, short-term treasury notes, short-term municipal notes, and other types of short-term investments.

2. Policies essential for investments best suited for endowment funds. These include limitations on funds that may be invested in different types of stocks, bonds, real estate, or real estate investment trusts; ratios of equity to fixed-income types of securities; limits on foreign versus domestic securities; and the short- and long-term goals of both short- and long-term investments. Such policies might also approve investments in patent rights, oil rights, and similar types of speculative investments, when availability of funds so warrants.

3. The use of advisers. The investment committee of the governing board may decide to handle all investments without external advice; or it may seek the advice of investment counsel or banks or, in some instances, both. Such counsel is costly, but most governing boards feel that it is essential that the best available expertise be employed to aid in maximizing earnings and profits and minimizing losses.

4. Investment of endowment funds for university property. When decisions are made to expand the physical plant and there is need to borrow funds, there may be temptations to use endowment funds for this purpose. A reason frequently given is that the governing board can pay the endowment fund at a lower rate of interest than would be paid to banks. In general, this practice is not considered to be a wise investment for endowment funds.

5. Cash fund in endowments. Investment opportunities arise unexpectedly, and investment committees should have some cash available to take advantage of such opportunities. Therefore, the amount of cash to be held for these purposes requires policy determination.

6. Assigned rate of return on endowment income. The amount of income on endowments will vary from year to year because of variations in the income earned from various types of investments. For a college or university to have a reasonable

certainty as to the amount of income that might be expected from endowments over a period of time, most governing boards adopt what is known as an "assigned rate of return." This means that regardless of fluctuations in earning from year to year, the transfer of income from unrestricted endowments to the operating funds of the university will be a fixed percentage of the total endowment. For example, an assigned rate of return may be fixed at 4 percent of total unrestricted endowment income, although actual earnings may be not over 3 percent in some years and as much as 5 or 6 percent in other years.

7. Depository for securities. It is customary for institutions having substantial endowment funds to designate a bank or banks to be custodian of investment securities. This ensures the safety of the securities and simplifies their transfer to brokers and investment bankers when securities are bought and sold. Such securities are usually held under a special code name.

8. Increments on endowment market value as income. A concept known as the "total return concept in investment accounting" has its origin in decisions made by some governing boards that some of the increased values of securities, as well as dividends and interest, should be made available to meet current operating expenses. This concept has gained some acceptance, but it can be challenged on both legal and philosophical grounds. Approximately half the states in the United States have adopted legislation permitting this practice, but the philosophical arguments have not been resolved.

Another related policy consideration is the use for general purposes of any income derived from a special endowment fund that may be in excess of the income expected at the time the fund was established. For example, a donor might make a gift of $100,000 as endowment to provide income of $5000 to be used as scholarships for students in each successive year. Some colleges have taken the position that the $5000 scholarship was the original amount intended by the donor for use for this purpose; therefore, any income or appreciation tending to increase the amount may, under some circumstances, be available for other purposes. This practice has not been widely adopted and should be viewed with skepticism.

Endowment Fund Performance

Whether endowment funds are managed by an investment committee, professional management investment counsel, trust departments of a bank, or some combinations of these, it is necessary to develop measures of the effectiveness of endowment management in investments. The obvious tests of performance are stock exchange averages pertaining to market values; public statistics of the growth and yields of national and regional funds, including mutual funds; and the growth of other similar portfolios, including published reports of the growth and income of endowments of selected institutions.

As endowment funds grow in amount and new funds are added or withdrawn, the true performance of any endowment fund is difficult to measure. Thus, a widely accepted practice is that of establishing unit values to allow measurement of endowment fund performance.

Accurate measurement requires a comparison of endowments that are composed of the same type and ratio of securities. Thus, to measure equity performance, it is essential that the comparisons of endowment funds be confined to equities; to measure the total endowment fund performance, the comparison must be among endowment funds having the same or similar ratio of stocks to bonds. Even if performance appears negative, it may be necessary to analyze the equity and fixed-income sections of a portfolio to determine where the less than satisfactory performance exists.

If statistics on endowment funds having a mixture of securities and other types of investments are exactly the same as the college or university fund being measured,

the governing board can learn whether or not its own fund is performing similarly to other endowment funds, better than other funds, or more poorly than other funds.

To establish a measure there must be a starting point, and the ideal starting point is when the endowment fund is first established. At that time the book value and market values are the same and provide an opportunity to create the simple performance value of "one." At this point it is necessary to create a performance value as a departure from "one." This will indicate the performance record of the endowment fund, which may be converted to a relative performance figure and matched against the performance of selected similar funds.

In a technical sense, the procedure of assessing a simple balanced fund approach might be followed. A market value is calculated, and then a unit value is assigned. For illustrative purposes, $100 is assigned as an initial value:

Market Value	No. of Units	Unit Value
$500,000	5000	$100
(5 funds of	(5 funds of	
$100,000)	1000 units)	

If, at a later time $50,000 is added to the fund, and if, at this time, the market value has appreciated to $525,000, the condition of the fund at the time of the anticipated addition of funds is:

Market Value	No. of Units	Unit Value
$525,000	5000	$105

The additional fund now adds $50,000, buying units at a value of $105, creating the following results:

Market Value	No. of Units	Unit Value
$575,000	(2) 5476.19	$105
(525,000+50,000)	[(1) 50,000 ÷ 105 = 476.19]	
	[(2) 5000 + (1) 476.19]	

If later the withdrawal of a fund is desired, the same procedure must be used to protect the integrity of the units and the unit value. If it is assumed that Fund A, having 1000 units as one of the five original funds is being withdrawn, and the new market value has reached $600,000, the new unit value will be $109.565 as follows:

Market Value	No. of Units	Unit Value
$600,000	5476.19	$109.565

After removing 1000 units at a value of $109.565 each, the fund will then appear:

Market Value	No. of Units	Unit Value
$490,430	4476.19	$109.565

In elementary fashion, these are the rudiments of the basis of unit measurement and its fundamental effect on the basic endowment fund structure. It is a tool that can aid in the measurement of performance. The previous illustrations show that the unit value has risen from $100 to $109+ over whatever span of time the measurement has taken place. This is obviously 9+ percent and can be compared to the performance of whatever similarly balanced funds may be selected for comparison.

It is probably desirable to keep separate performance statistics on equity and fixed-income performance to provide data for performance comparison. Balanced funds tend to be difficult to compare because of the problem in locating similar balances for comparison.

Management

The most important element in investment fund performance is management. Armed with the institutional policies and objectives, fund managers enter into a marketplace to invest the institution's funds with no guarantee of results. Both novices and skilled professionals operate in the role of investment managers on behalf of institutions.

There is a wealth of professional management service available. No institution should allow itself to succumb to the oversimplified idea that professional management can be justified only if it results in above average performance. An institution can only examine the issue in terms of long-term, stable development in line with its carefully developed purposes and goals. These objectives should be bolstered by the employment of the strongest management structure compatible with the size of the fund. Thus, a heavily endowed institution may use the services of leading banks and investment counselors, together with an internal staff of professionals in varying degrees.

Many banks and private firms offer services ranging from total management to partial or supplemental support for institutional efforts. The development of Teachers Insurance and Annuity Association's Common Fund offers another vehicle, specializing in institutional fund development; it offers the smaller institution the advantage of professional and diverse management not always available by any other means.

Bibliography

The Common Fund: Annual Report, July 1, 1975–June 30, 1976. New York: Common Fund for Non-Profit Organizations, 1976.

The Common Fund for Bond Investments. New York: Common Fund for Non-Profit Organizations, 1976.

Loomis, L. G. "Investment Policies and Procedures." In A. S. Knowles, (Ed.), *Handbook of College and University Administration*. New York: McGraw-Hill, 1970.

Managing Endowment Capital. The transcript of the First Endowment Conference held in New York, April 18, 1969. New York: Donaldson, Lufkin & Jenrette, Inc., 1969.

DANIEL J. ROBERTS

APPENDIX: EXAMPLE OF INVESTMENT POLICIES AND PROCEDURES

Division of Work

The Committee on Funds and Investments divides its work into two categories, one having to do with general plans and policies in regard to the work of the Committee and the other with the supervision of securities; and that matters of policy be the responsibility of the full Committee, but that matters relating to the supervision of investments and approval of the purchase and sale of individual securities be delegated to a subcommittee which shall be known as the Operating Committee.

Chairmanship of the Operating Committee

The Chairmanship of the Operating Committee of the Committee on Funds and Investments may be rotated between the members of such committee and each incumbency of a two-year duration, the appointment of the Chairman to be made by the members of the Operating Committee.

Vice-Chairman of the Committee on Funds and Investments

The Chairman of the Corporation at the Annual Meeting of the Corporation each year shall appoint as Vice-Chairman of the Committee on Funds and Investments the incumbent Chairman of the Operating Committee.

Meetings

Regular meetings of the Operating Committee are to be held on the second Monday of every month, and any intermediate meetings found necessary are to be specifically called.

Common Stocks, Percentage of

Investment in common stocks is to be confined to a participation of from 50 to 75 percent of the market value of the Fund. The Operating Committee is allowed use of discretion in temporarily exceeding the limits if factors seemingly warrant such action. Any long term exceeding the maximum or minimum, however, is to be a matter for consideration by the Committee on Funds and Investments.

Objective of Common Stock Policy

I. Objective is to secure the best long-term return income and appreciation combined. Individual issues should be selected for expected long-term performance so that semipermanent holding is intended. Substantially overpriced issues should be sold, but the primary aim is to secure results from purchase and holding, rather than

trading. Toward this objective the following working guide is suggested:

A. Primary emphasis on companies whose earnings performance can be expected to exceed the average over a full business cycle.

1. Better-than-average trend of industry volume expected over a full business cycle
2. Good or improving competitive position of the economy
3. Adequate financial, management and technical resources

B. Avoid secondary companies in narrowly based industries, and avoid secondary companies in broadly based industries unless fundamentals are strong and price is significantly below front-rank companies.

C. High price earnings ration stocks (over thirty times current earnings) to be acquired only where earnings projection for next three to five years will produce P//E ration comparable with that of Dow-Jones industrials at time of acquisition. This is to be supported by reasonably complete analysis of individual company and industry in which it operates.

D. The Common Stocks portfolio might well include a participation, not to exceed 10 percent of book value, of companies with significantly greater than average possibilities, but where risks may also be higher. Stocks for this purpose can be considered that would not necessarily conform to the above criteria.

II. The advisers will prepare suggested transactions and/or topics for Committee consideration and will distribute same to members of the Committee several days prior to a meeting. The information will include a concise summary of controlling reasons for investment recommendations, including earnings estimates for such periods as can be reasonably projected.

Bond Portfolio Administration Guidelines

1. Maturity shifting within the portfolio can be undertaken at the discretion of the advisers.

2. Investment in any one issue is not to exceed $1,000,000.

3. Investment in any one credit (or issue) is not to exceed $1,000,000 except in certain approved situations where the aggregate investment in parent company and subsidiary issues is not to exceed $2,000,000.

4. Purchase of bonds is limited to a minimum Baa-rated quality.

5. Marketability of bonds is to be an important consideration.

6. The advisers are encouraged to anticipate changes in quality ratings.

7. Notwithstanding any of the above guidelines, turnover of bonds between meetings of the Operating Committee is limited to $1,000,000.

8. The advisers will report to the Operating Committee on a regular basis, and any deviations from the above guidelines will receive prior approval of the Committee.

Guideline on Nondomestic Common Stocks

The investment in nondomestic foreign stocks shall not exceed a maximum of X percent of the equity section valued at market.

Limitation of Investment in Fixed-Income Private Placements

Investment in privately placed, fixed-income obligations shall not exceed 5 percent of the fund valued at market. Monthly appraisal values of Private Placements will be noted at cost. However, on the semi-annual report a footnote will be appended indicating the approximate current market value.

Venture Capital Investments

It was the consensus that venture capital financing is not an appropriate investment medium for the Fund.

Review of Proxies

The general proxy review guidelines established by the Operating Committee are as follows:

1. The Secretary would arrange to have all proxies mailed by the custodian bank to the University.

2. If a proxy is restricted to appointment of auditors and election of directors, it will be executed by the Secretary without further reference.

3. If any other items in addition to the foregoing item 2 are listed, the proxy will be referred to the Operating Committee.

4. If the proxy involves broad social responsibilities or other controversial issues, the items will be referred to Board of Trustees together with the Operating Committee's recommendation via the Secretary.

Execution of Transaction

The Adviser will execute Fund Stock and Bond transactions. It is understood that the Secretary may designate that certain brokers be employed.

FINANCIAL AID

1. FINANCIAL AID TO STUDENTS— A GLOBAL PERSPECTIVE

Use of the term *financial aid* to indicate assistance to students to meet the costs of obtaining an education presupposes that the student or the student's family carry the main burden of educational costs, whereas financial aid—generally public aid—supplements these costs to the individual. Rather than describe the specific procedures for awarding financial aid in different countries, this article attempts to make a worldwide comparison of the goals and methods determining how higher education costs are shared by the individual and society in different nations, the forms and categories into which financial aid can be classified, the sources of aid, and the terms and conditions on which this aid is supplied. Certain facts and statistical data used are based on research of authors contributing to the *International Encyclopedia of Higher Education.*

Goals and Methods of Financial Aid

A review of financial aid systems worldwide reveals that the goals and methods of financial aid are firmly rooted in the social, economic, political, and institutional realities of a nation. Since World War II, financial aid has increased greatly throughout the world and developed into a tool of government to achieve certain goals for the society, either social or economic. Although such goals are not always explicit— as late as 1963 Frank Bowles found that "few countries have decided what their aid systems should achieve" (p. 207)—increasing enrollments and educational costs have forced nations to examine more closely their educational priorities. Educational goals are now often stated in long-range economic plans, and the role of financial aid in those plans is clearly enunciated. For instance, the 1968–1971 development plan in Spain stressed the need for diffusion of education to larger numbers of citizens and stated that "the present system of aid to students will be improved, and will be supplemented by the introduction of personal loans, to be repaid as and when possible out of the student's subsequent earnings." The plan also called for assistance to be awarded so that "access to education will increasingly depend upon the intellectual capacity of the individual, rather than upon his own or his family's financial resources." Turkey similarly stated in its 1968–1972 development plan that "educational facilities beyond the primary level will be secured according to the principle of equality of opportunity. Accordingly, with the aid of scholarships and boarding schools, the capable students will be allowed to obtain the highest levels of education without being hindered by economic difficulties" *(Education in OECD Developing Countries,* 1974, p. 23).

The main goals of financial aid policies are similar throughout the world and usually include the social goal of equalization of access to higher education in terms of social, racial, or religious background; and economic goals, such as the training of manpower needed for the nation's economic development or the redressing of regional imbalances in educational provision.

Equalization of access. Used as a means of equalization of opportunity, government financial aid attempts to redistribute income by opening access to higher income professions for students from social groups that have not previously had access to these professions. Since World War II most of the socialist nations in Eastern Europe, through the provision of liberal financial aid, have followed a deliberate policy of encouraging students from worker and peasant backgrounds to enter higher education. For instance, Czechoslovakia increased the proportion of students from these backgrounds to 55.7 percent of total enrollment in higher education in 1974–75 *(Thirty Years,* 1975, p. 12). In Poland the percentage of students in higher education from worker-peasant backgrounds increased from about 40 percent during the years 1945 to 1950 to 58 percent during the years 1970 to 1973. The German Democratic Republic, in turn, draws about half of its higher education enrollment from a working-class background.

Equalization of access also entails using financial aid to deliberately include specific categories of students in higher education. In India certain castes and tribes, referred to as scheduled castes and scheduled tribes, have been educationally disadvantaged. Special efforts are made to include these groups by reserving 14 percent of the openings in higher education for scheduled castes and 4 percent of places for scheduled tribes as well as by supplying the needed financial assistance. In the United States financial aid has been used since the 1960s to attract to higher education those termed *minority students*—that is, black, Native American, Oriental, and Spanish-speaking students (Chicanos,

Cubans, Puerto Ricans, and persons of Central or South American descent). Between 1968 and 1972 enrollments of these groups more than doubled.

Manpower considerations. Although equal opportunity for education as a goal of government financial aid has become widely accepted since World War II, this goal seems to be more common in the industrialized nations in Europe and North America. Economic considerations, on the other hand, seem to be the basis of financial assistance policy in most of the developing and newly industrializing nations. The training of sufficient numbers of nationals as scientists, technicians, managers, and professionals in the health sciences to effect industrialization and development is prominent in government goals for education in most countries in Africa, Asia, and South America. To achieve diversification of their economies, oil-producing nations such as Iran, Nigeria, Saudi Arabia, and Venezuela expend large funds on wide-ranging financial aid programs for study abroad for nationals as well as for new programs at home.

Regional imbalances in educational provision. In many nations regional differences in the financing and provision of education have impeded equal access to education. Financial aid is often used to equalize educational provision, either through government grants to students or through institutional assistance. Since 1960, for instance, Finland has carried out a deliberate policy of decentralization of higher education by establishing institutions in previously neglected areas of the country—in the 1960s a number of new university-level institutions were established outside the traditional university centers in Helsinki and Turku. Brazil also uses federal financial aid to equalize educational opportunity between the richer and poorer states in the federation.

Many countries, especially industrialized countries such as the United States, France, Sweden, and the nations of Eastern Europe, attempt to strike a balance between the goals of equal access and manpower development. The United States government, for instance, stresses manpower needs in the health sciences through the Health Manpower Financial Aid Programs, while promoting equal access through the Basic Educational Opportunity Grants. In Eastern Europe students are generally guided by strict manpower demands in their choice of field study, but financial aid is available to equalize access for students of varying means.

In general, the extent of financial aid and its provision range throughout the world from those nations that perceive higher education as a public service and a necessary government investment in the production of human resources and so provide education free to those who qualify (as in most socialist and a number of developing countries) to those nations where higher education is mainly supplied privately (as in Brazil, the Philippines, and Japan).

Forms and Categories of Financial Aid

Financial aid can be categorized in two ways, depending on its method of distribution: *indirect,* if it is given collectively to all students; and *direct,* if it is given to students individually.

Indirect financial aid. Indirect financial aid refers to institutional support, that is, aid extended to all students collectively, generally by the government. In addition to capital funds, indirect financial aid includes the provision of free or subsidized education and the availability of subsidies for social services such as room and board, health care, supplies, and travel.

In socialist countries higher education is available free of charge, as are numerous social services such as hostels, reduced rates for meals, and travel. The Soviet Union and the People's Republic of China provide, in addition, a wage to students in certain fields. The payment of a wage is an extension of the concept of education as production, or human development, that should be compensated. Most African countries, the majority of European countries, and Australia also supply free higher education and often provide some, if not all, of the services available in socialist countries.

Most countries, however, do not provide totally free higher education but allocate subsidies of varying magnitude to their higher education institutions. The subsidies, which may be awarded by federal, state, or local authorities, help to reduce tuition substantially for students. European countries that subsidize education while still requiring some tuition are Belgium, France, Ireland, Italy, the Netherlands, Portugal, Switzerland, and the United Kingdom. Among the many other nations that follow similar practices are India, New Zealand, Nigeria, Singapore, Sri Lanka, Tanzania, and the United States.

Some Latin American countries have established indirect support to higher education as a set percentage of their national budgets. This support is delineated in the constitution or in decrees and statutes pertaining to the national universities. The Dominican Republic, for instance, sets aside 5 percent of its national budget for higher education; Costa Rica provides 10 percent of its educational budget to its university (Laguardia, 1973).

Direct financial aid. Direct financial aid is extended to the individual student from private and public sources. Aid for undergraduates (students studying for their first degree) will be described separately from aid to graduate students. The terminology referring to student aid varies. Some terms overlap, so that the same expression is sometimes used for two different kinds of awards, whereas other terms are sometimes interchanged. The following terms, however, are common to most countries: *scholarships, bursaries, grants, grants-in-aid, loans,* and *work-study.* The main differences among these forms of financial aid are in the requirements they place upon the students and the provisions under which they are supplied.

Scholarships often are awarded on the basis of financial need (Australia, for instance, maintains a program of need-based scholarship assistance) but generally are stipends or special recognition given to a student for certain types of proficiency—academic, athletic, or artistic skills—or as encouragement toward high achievement in one of these areas. Scholarships are awarded from private and public sources and do not require repayment.

Scholarships based on academic excellence, in some nations called *merit scholarships,* are generally awarded on the basis of success in secondary school or during study at a higher education institution. Sometimes merit scholarships are awarded according to results of nationwide scholarship examinations. New Zealand arranges a national scholarship examination that qualifies successful candidates for supplementary financial aid for university study. Italy also awards annual scholarships, based on performance on competitive examinations, to students of limited means. In the United States merit scholarships are awarded to students who score highest on the National Merit Scholarship Qualifying Test, an examination organized by the National Merit Scholarship Corporation. In the United Kingdom the Board of Education awards state scholarships based on results of the Higher Certificate Examination.

Many of the newly independent nations and nations in the process of diversifying their industry award scholarships to nationals to train in fields needed for national development or for localization of manpower. For instance, the Venezuelan scholarship plan *Gran Mariscal de Ayacucho* was instituted in 1975 to provide scholarships to some 10,000 Venezuelans yearly to train primarily in technical fields. The bulk of these scholarships go for study abroad, mainly in the United States. In addition, several Venezuelan ministries provide some 2500 scholarships for study in Venezuela or abroad. Similarly, a number of African nations—such as Cameroon, Chad, the Ivory Coast, Liberia, Malawi, and Zambia—also provide scholarships to nationals to train for specific careers in fields where manpower is needed. In many cases, scholarships are also provided by the former colonial power.

Private scholarships, awarded on the basis of financial need or excellence and often disbursed through the university of attendance, are also available in most countries. Private scholarships take many forms; depending on the awarding agency or individual, they are unrestricted or granted on specific conditions.

Grant, a term often interchanged with *scholarship,* generally refers to an appropriation of funds made by a foundation or government agency to an individual or an institution. The amount and purpose of the grant and the period during which the grant is expendable are usually specified at the time of receipt. Grant is the term used by the United States government for most of its direct assistance to students. The United Kingdom has one of the world's most generous grants systems; its government funds higher education costs to 90 percent. In addition to tuition, the need-based grants may cover board and lodging, books, travel, and personal expenses.

In Finland, government grants, the eligibility for which is based on financial need, are allocated to students in secondary and higher education. Some 84,000 students received such government grants in 1974. Financial need is also the criterion for the award of grants in Belgium, as well as the Netherlands, where some 10 percent of students received grants in 1975. From 1977 on, however, the Dutch government plans to supply a minimum grant to all students. In the Federal Republic of Germany, all students are eligible for government grants, and in 1973, 47 percent of all students were assisted. The following year the funding structure of the government's financial aid was changed so that part of the assistance became interest-free loans to be repaid after graduation.

The term *grants-in-aid* refers to a grant of money, often awarded in periodic payments to a financially needy student. Such

a grant does not necessarily depend on academic excellence. The term is also used to denote government or industry assistance for some special purpose, such as improvement of vocational education, research, or teacher training.

Bursary is a term that refers to student assistance or scholarships. It is generally used in Commonwealth or former Commonwealth countries; the term *bourse* is generally used in French-language countries. Bursaries are not awarded uniformly in all countries, however; in Canada and in Great Britain the bursary is generally awarded on the basis of financial need; and in Scotland the bursary exists as an entrance scholarship. In the Republic of Ireland a clear distinction is made between a scholarship and a bursary. The latter is awarded as one sum, is of less value than a scholarship, and is often awarded to a student who fails to win a scholarship. In New Zealand, the Department of Education grants bursaries for the first year of university study to those students who qualify on such examinations as the University Entrance Examination, the Higher School Certificate Examination, or special Bursary Examinations. Receipt of the bursary in following years depends upon the recipient's academic success. In Algeria state *bourses,* or scholarships, are awarded according to financial need and academic accomplishment. The recipients of awards are required to perform social service during vacations and to work for the government after graduation.

Educational loans, another method of financial assistance to students, available from government or other sources, are awarded with the requirement that all or part of the amount advanced be repaid at a future time, generally following graduation or termination of studies. The relative merits of educational loans as a form of financial assistance have been much debated. Proponents argue that loans correctly place the burden of educational costs on the recipients whose earning potential is increased by their education; opponents claim that loans do not contribute to an equalization of educational opportunity and place undue hardship on graduates, who have to enter their working life with a heavy debt.

Provisions for educational loans differ markedly from country to country. Some countries offer loans that carry interest, but other countries provide interest-free loans. Some countries require repayment starting upon graduation; other countries allow a grace period (either for a stipulated time or until the graduate has found employment). It should also be noted that educational loans are most common in those regions with the highest per capita income—specifically, in Western Europe and North America.

The Canada Student Loans Plan offers interest-free loans until six months after graduation, and no repayment of principal is required while the student attends school. The Federal Republic of Germany offers interest-free loans to students with repayment upon graduation. The Scandinavian countries rely upon educational loans as an important form of student assistance. In Finland educational loans, which bear minimum interest while the student attends school, are to be repaid in twice the time the student needed for his or her program of study. In Sweden, financial assistance is awarded partly as grant, partly as repayable loan. The loans are tied to the cost-of-living index but do not carry interest. Their repayment period, starting during the third year after receipt of the last loan assistance, varies from fifteen to twenty-five years, depending on the recipient's age at graduation (*Statligt studiestöd,* 1973). Norway determines the repayment period for its educational loans according to the amount of the loan and the graduate's anticipated income, and Danish graduates pay a higher interest if they start repayment later than the time of graduation. The Netherlands also requires interest on government loans. In Luxembourg, however, educational loans are converted to grants for students who successfully complete their program of study. The Japanese government also has instituted a modest loan program, which in 1970 benefited about 10 percent of college and university students, including graduate students.

Several South American countries in addition to Venezuela have established loan schemes for their students as well. Costa Rica, for instance, has had a National Fund for Loans to Education since 1974. In its first year this fund, through loans repayable upon graduation, assisted 156 students, and it is expected to become an important source of educational assistance. Colombia has a highly regarded assistance program run by the *Instituto colombiano de crédito educativo y estudios técnicos en el exterior* (ICETEX: Colombian Institute for Educational Credit and Technological Studies Abroad). The ICETEX Program is a two-pronged effort, providing loan scholarships (repayable upon graduation) to gifted students of limited means for study both in Colombia and abroad. The repaid funds are then redistributed to new students. Peru has also established student scholarships and loan programs through two specific agencies: *Instituto nacional de becas y crédito educativo* (INABEC: National Institute of Scholarships and Educational Credit) and the private *Instituto peruano de fomento educativo* (IPFE: Peruvian Institute for Educational Development).

A significant form of financial aid to students is *work-study* or *student employment programs.* In the United States, for example, all accredited institutions offer work-study opportunities. One of the most extensive of such programs is College Work Study, a program funded by the federal government under the Economic Opportunity Act of 1965. A number of other programs also provide students with work experience.

Student work programs, known under different names, are offered in many parts of the world. It has been estimated that of all those students in more than thirty nations worldwide who participate in practical work during their period of study, 78.4 percent receive remuneration (Mosbacker, 1975, p. 24). Although financial considerations might not be the main incentive for programs that focus on practical training for students, such as cooperative education or sandwich programs, the salary earned during the period of off-campus experience is of assistance to the student as a source of additional financing. The number of students in practical work is still limited in many countries, but a practical work component in higher education is clearly growing: in Canada some 10,000 students undertake cooperative work assignments (Lancaster, 1974). In the United States more than 200,000 students participate in cooperative education. Practical work is also an integral part of higher education in Eastern European nations as well as in other socialist nations, such as Burma, Cuba, and the Democratic People's Republic of Korea.

Scholarships and loans generally assist undergraduate students, but research fellowships, teaching assistantships, and varying types of grants more commonly assist students at the graduate level. In addition to institutional or government support, nonrepayable graduate financial aid is available from public and private foundations, business and industrial firms, and educational and professional organizations. Although the most common financial aid is academic or research support, the financial aid awarded for graduate study may also consist of travel grants, publication support, or equipment and construction grants. It may also take the form of in-service training possibilities or consist of awards or prizes.

The *Annual Register of Grant Support* lists awards and scholarships available worldwide mainly to scholars from Canada and the United States. The *Grants Register* lists fellowships and grants available in most countries of the world to candidates of any nationality and to candidates of specific nationalities.

Sources and Conditions of Financial Aid

The main source of financial aid to students throughout the world is government assistance. Other financial aid sources for undergraduate students are tuition remission and endowment income (scholarships, grants, loans, and other support awarded or administered by the institution of attendance), and direct or indirect support from industry, community and social service groups, professional associations, regional or international agencies, or individuals.

Although unrestricted scholarships and grants are awarded, much of the support to undergraduates is available according to specific conditions, such as repayment of financial aid in kind. To recover some of the high unit costs of free or highly subsidized education, which in some countries have come to consume a disproportionate amount of government expenditures, some nations have instituted a work requirement. Sometimes termed *bonding*, sometimes *national service*, the requirement stipulates that recipients of aid, upon graduation, serve for a specified period in a position and at a salary determined by the granting agency. In Cameroon, for instance, students enrolled in professional training are bonded for ten years and regarded as civil servants. A government work requirement also exists in France, where graduates of some of the prestigious *grandes écoles*, such as the *Ecole nationale d'administration* and the *Polytechnique*, commit themselves ten years as civil servants in return for their education (French students do, however, sometimes buy themselves out of the service commitment).

Sierra Leone also allows students to repay government loans by entering civil service in which each year of service repays a year of assisted study. Repayment in kind is also possible in the United States for recipients of loans for health-related and law enforcement training, as well as for prospective teachers, who have received a National Direct Student Loan. Among other countries that require similar restitution of government financial aid are Morocco, where in 1974–75 close to 18,000 of the 25,000 students at the Mohammed V University received monthly allowances from the government *(At-ta'leem al'aaly,* 1975). Such students are required to sign a contract for eight years of government service upon graduation. The *Ecole normale supérieure* in the Ivory Coast provides free education to students who agree to ten years of service in public education, and a service requirement also applies in Jordan, where male graduates serve twice the number of years of study while females serve only one year for each year of assistance. Among other nations following this practice are Tanzania, which has instituted a five-year national service period, Cuba, which requires two years of national service for each year of free education, and Nigeria, which requires one year of service upon graduation. In the People's Republic of China, where the higher education system relates directly to economic needs, students who enter higher education are workers in production, and graduates return to production at a higher level of responsibility upon graduation.

In many countries, financial support by industry is also common. Industry sometimes even becomes directly involved in the establishment of institutions of higher education. Although institutions directly funded by industry are not very common, some industry-supported institutions function successfully. Among such institutions are the University of Petroleum and Minerals in Saudi Arabia, supported mainly by oil interests; and the management training institutes, *Centre d'études industrielles* in Geneva and the Management Development Institute in Lausanne, Switzerland, founded by the Alcan Aluminum Corporation of Canada and Nestle Alimentara S. A. of Switzerland, respectively.

Another form of financial aid by industry is sponsorship of a student, usually for study in a specific field of study. These sponsorships, which cover both tuition and maintenance, generally require the student to work for the sponsoring corporation upon graduation. At the University of Technology in Papua New Guinea, al-most all students in their third and fourth years of study are sponsored by industry or government. Sponsorships are also common at the University of Mauritius. A sponsorship arrangement is used as well in some Eastern European countries. For instance, in Hungary students receive a *social scholarship* in return for a contractual agreement to work with an organization or institution for a number of years equal to the period of study. In 1972–73 about 10 percent of all full-time students in Hungary received social scholarships. In Poland a similar arrangement requires a work period of three years; in Czechoslovakia, the period is five years.

In addition to scholarships (which may be awarded to employees, employees' children, or students unrelated to the company through employment), industrial financial aid may take the form of work-study programs, educational loans, employee matching programs, research grants, fellowships, equipment and material assistance to graduate students, and grants-in-aid for research.

Through support of education in specific locations, multinational corporations are developing into a major source of financial aid, while philanthropic foundations such as Ford, Rockefeller, and Carnegie in the United States and European foundations such as Volkswagen in the Federal Republic of Germany and Agnelli in Italy provide support both for research and direct aid to students.

Although regional and international organizations and scholarship programs by virtue of their structure contribute more to international or regional than to national education programs, their impact on any one nation is sometimes considerable. Among such programs are the Colombo Plan for Co-Operative Economic Development in South and Southeast Asia, which provides training programs and financial aid to students in its area of interest, and the Commonwealth Scholarship and Fellowship Plan, which serves the Commonwealth nations, as well as assistance offered by various agencies of the United Nations and the international banks.

Despite substantial growth of financial aid since World War II, enrollment and cost increases have lessened the impact of expanded aid efforts. The need of nations to recover some of the funds expended—for instance, through work requirements or repayable loan schemes—has been briefly commented upon. The financial considerations that determine the direction an aid program will take generally center on the format of the aid package: unrestricted scholarships or repayable loans. These considerations lead back to the even more vital question of who should pay for education: the individual student or the taxpayer. Those who opt to place the financial burden of education on the individual (usually through loan programs) consider education an investment to be made by the individual who will benefit most; those who favor the financing of education from public funds (through grants, subsidies, and scholarships) consider education a societal investment that will benefit the nation as a whole.

Based upon its own educational tradition, goals, and financial resources, each nation arrives at its own mix of private and public support for higher education. The systems adopted can vary from those where education is available free of charge, to the system in the United Kingdom, where 90 percent of the funds for higher education come from the government against a 10 percent funding from the private sector, to the system in the Philippines, where the government contribution amounts to 7 percent. In the middle of this range is the educational system of the United States, where, for example, in 1969–70 an estimated 38.8 percent of educational costs were borne by the individual student (not including foregone income), 52.2 percent by the taxpayers, and 9 percent by philanthropy. A slight change in this distribution has been projected for 1983, when the individual contribution is anticipated at 34.1 percent, the public contribution at 57.5 percent, and the philanthropic contribution at 8.4 percent (Carnegie Commission on Higher Education, 1973). Whatever the system, financial aid policies are generally significantly altered only as a result of sudden increases in revenues, radical political change, or unusually heavy student demands.

Bibliography

Annual Register of Grant Support 1975–76. Chicago: Marquis Academic Media, 1975.

At-ta'leem al'aaly bil Mamlakat-ul-Maghribiya. Rabat, Morocco: Ministry of Higher Education, 1975.

Barnet, R. J., and Muller, R. E. *Global Reach: The Power of the Multinational Corporation.* New York: Simon and Schuster, 1974.

Bowles, F. *Access to Higher Education.* Vol. 1. Paris: UNESCO and the International Association of Universities, 1963.

Carnegie Commission on Higher Education. *Higher Education: Who Pays? Who Benefits? Who Should Pay?* New York: McGraw-Hill, 1973.

Education in OECD Developing Countries: Trends and Perspectives. Paris: Organisation for Economic Co-operation and Development, 1974.

Financing of Education for Economic Growth. Paris: Organisation for Economic Co-operation and Development, 1966.

Golladay, M. A. *The Condition of Education: A Statistical Report on the Condition of Education in the United States.* Washington, D.C.: U.S. Government Printing Office, 1976.

Hall, L. D. (Ed.) *Financial Aids for Graduate Students.* Cincinnati, Ohio: Educational Horizons, 1972.

Hall, L. D. (Ed.) *Financial Aids for Undergraduate Students.* Cincinnati, Ohio: Educational Horizons, 1972.

Handbook of Aid to Higher Education by Corporations. New York: Council for Financial Aid to Education, 1974.

Harrell, W. A. *Educational Reform in Brazil.* Washington, D.C.: U. S. Department of Health, Education and Welfare, 1968.

Harris, S. E. *A Statistical Portrait of Higher Education.* A Report for the Carnegie Commission on Higher Education. New York: McGraw-Hill, 1972.

Harris, S. E. (Ed.) *Higher Education: Resources and Finance.* New York: McGraw-Hill, 1962.

Harris, S. E. (Ed.) *Economic Aspects of Higher Education.* Paris: Organisation for Economic Co-operation and Development, 1964.

Keeslar, O. P. *Financial Aids for Higher Education: 1974–75 Catalog.* Dubuque, Iowa: W. C. Brown, 1974.

Laguardia García, J. M. *Legislación universitaria de América latina.* Mexico City: Universidad nacional autónoma de México, 1973.

Lancaster, G. M. "The Status of Cooperative Education in Canada." Paper presented at the annual conference of the Canadian Association for Cooperative Education, University of Waterloo, Waterloo, Ontario, September 1974.

Mosbacker, W. B. *Growth and Development of Cooperative Education in Countries Outside of the United States.* Cincinnati, Ohio: University of Cincinnati Press, 1975.

National Merit Scholarship Program. *Semifinalists in the Twenty-Second Annual Merit Scholarship Competition.* Evanston, Illinois: National Merit Scholarship Corporation, 1976.

Patrick, K. G., and Eels, R. *Education and the Business Dollar: A Study of Corporate Contributions Policy and American Education.* New York: Macmillan, 1969.

Policies for Higher Education. A report from the Conference on Future Postsecondary Education, Paris, 26th–29th June 1973. Paris: Organisation for Economic Co-operation and Development, 1974.

Scholarships Guide for Commonwealth Postgraduate Students 1975–77. London: Association of Commonwealth Universities, 1974.

Statligt studiestöd. Stockholm: Centrala studiehjälpsnämnden, 1973.

Student Assistance Programs. Washington, D.C.: College Entrance Examination Board, 1975. (Mimeographed.)

Turner, R. (Ed.) *The Grants Register 1975–77.* New York: St. Martin's, 1975.

Wassermann, P., and Wassermann, K. *Awards, Honors, and Prizes.* (2 vols.) Detroit: Gale Research, 1975.

West, E. D. *Financial Aid to the Undergraduate: Issues and Implications.* Washington, D.C.: American Council on Education, 1963.

Windham, D. M. "Social Benefits and the Subsidization of Higher Education: A Critique." *Higher Education,* August 1976, 5(3), 237–252.

SOLVEIG M. TURNER

See also: Aid to Other Nations: Multilateral Corporations and Bilateral Aid; Veterans Education Benefits.

2. FINANCIAL AID TO STUDENTS— UNITED STATES

Without financial aid a substantial number of students and their families would be unable to pay the full costs of higher education. To assist these students in continuing their postsecondary education, most countries have established programs of financial aid. The costs of higher education are rapidly increasing and, fortunately, financial aid resources are also increasing, although often at a slower rate.

In the United States financial aid is perceived as a vehicle to provide students with access and choice in higher education. Access to some form of postsecondary education is a goal served by most grant programs. Choice to attend even the highest cost institution is facilitated by the availability of a combination of scholarships, loans, and work opportunities. Often special grant funds are designed specifically to assist minority students, and a number of agencies in the United States advise low-income students about admission and financial aid.

Types of Financial Aid in the United States

Financial assistance is available in numerous forms for study at United States institutions of higher learning. It may be provided directly to the student by federal or state governments, or it may be funneled through the educational institution itself. Banks, corporations, foundations, and church and civic groups also offer financial aid funds, and many colleges—particularly private ones—have their own financial aid resources.

The largest single source of aid for undergraduate or graduate students is the series of programs administered by the federal government of the United States because most aid to institutions that offsets operating costs comes from states. The federal government estimated that in 1976 its direct aid to students would, in all, equal more than $5,000,000,000, or 80 percent of the total federal aid to higher education (*Student Assistance Programs,* 1975).

Grants. Most of the federal government's direct assistance is in the form of grants that, like scholarships, are outright gifts which require no repayment or immediate service or labor from the recipient. Six agencies administer the major aid programs of the United States government: the Office of Education, the Veterans Administration, the Bureau of Indian Affairs, the Law Enforcement Assistance Administration, and the Bureau of Health Resources Development.

The primary financial assistance programs of the Office of Education are Basic Educational Opportunity Grants, State Student Incentive Grants, Supplemental Educational Opportunity Grants, National Direct Student Loans, and College Work-Study. The most extensive of these programs is the Basic Educational Opportunity Grants (BEOG) program, which was initiated in the fall of 1973.

Any full-, three-quarter-, or half-time student who is a United States citizen or is in the United States for other than a temporary purpose and who is attending an eligible institution of postsecondary education is eligible to apply. Basic grants, which can be used at any of more than five thousand institutions, cannot exceed half of the actual cost of attendance and cannot be more than $1400 per student per year. In the academic year 1978–79, this $1400 ceiling may be raised.

Among the largest federal aid programs is that offered veterans of the armed services by the Veterans Administration (VA). Veterans meeting certain eligibility requirements of length of active service and terms of discharge can take advantage of a variety of education and training benefits, including education loans, grants that match funds saved by the serviceperson while on active duty, and living subsidies for veterans (and their dependents) while in school. For the details of benefits and the terms of current veterans' legislation,

persons should contact their local VA office.

The Bureau of Indian Affairs (of the Department of Interior) administers a special higher education grant program for Native Americans pursuing a regular or graduate degree in an accredited institution of higher learning. In 1968 the bureau's grant program reached 2660 students with $3,000,000 in aid. By 1976 the program had expanded to reach an estimated 17,000 students with $35,000,000 in aid (Galladay, 1976). To be eligible for aid from the Bureau of Indian Affairs, students must show financial need as determined by their college or university. Complete information can be obtained from any Bureau of Indian Affairs office.

The Law Enforcement Education Program (LEEP) of the Law Enforcement Assistance Administration (LEAA) helps law enforcement personnel and students preparing for careers in law enforcement to finance college or university study. The program offers loans up to $2200 per academic year for full-time students and grants up to $250 per academic quarter or $400 per semester for currently employed law enforcement officials studying for degrees full or part time. Recipients of LEEP assistance must agree to remain in or enter into full-time criminal justice employment for stipulated periods. The institutions themselves administer LEEP funds granted to them, and they select the recipients. Additional information on these grants is available from any of the LEAA regional offices or participating institutions.

The Social Security Administration provides financial help to students under the Old-Age Survivors and Disability and Health Insurance Dependents' Benefits. Students seeking aid should contact their nearest social security field office for specific information. In general, eligibility is limited to unmarried dependents of social security beneficiaries between the ages of eighteen and twenty-two who continue their education on a full-time basis. The amount of the aid varies up to a maximum of $230 per month.

The federal government also offers special additional assistance in the form of Supplementary Educational Opportunity Grants to undergraduate students of clearly demonstrated academic promise who without additional aid would be unable to pursue a postsecondary education. These grants, ranging from $200 to $1500 per academic year, can be no more than half of the total amount of financial aid provided the student by or through the institution. No student may receive more than $4000 during a four-year, or $5000 during a five-year, undergraduate course of study. The grant must be reapplied for annually through the postsecondary institution that the student is attending.

State aid programs. Most United States students can turn as well to a number of state aid programs. (All but four of the fifty states offer at least one state aid program.) The federal government, through the Office of Education, offers State Student Incentive Grants, and most states also offer their own educational assistance through loan funds or state scholarships. These programs operate differently from state to state, but they typically are based on need and are limited to state residents. Often state programs are intended to offset differences in tuition rates from one institution to the next, so that actual costs of tuition at public and private colleges in the state are more closely aligned. Each state's department of education can provide full information on available programs and appropriate administering agencies.

State agencies for vocational rehabilitation provide training, personal counseling, and other services to individuals with physical or mental disabilities that are handicaps to employment. Further information can be obtained from local offices of state vocational rehabilitation agencies.

Specialized scholarships. A number of specialized scholarships and grants are also available to many students. Eligibility

for scholarships, as opposed to grants, usually depends on demonstrated academic achievement or special talent. Specialized scholarship funds are, as well, often limited to students in pursuit of a designated academic or vocational course.

A noted program that awards assistance on the basis of academic excellence is the National Merit Scholarship Program. This program, organized by the National Merit Scholarship Corporation, awards its scholarships to those students who score highest on a national qualifying test. The awards are either four-year or nonrenewable one-year scholarships. Of the almost 1,000,000 students who took the examination in 1976, 3850 received awards (National Merit Scholarship Program, 1976).

Competitive scholarships are also offered by the different branches of the armed services under the ROTC (Reserve Officers Training Corps) Vitalization Act of 1964. The navy, for example, sponsors an ROTC College Scholarship Program. Candidates are chosen through a nationwide competition and receive educational and other benefits leading to careers as commissioned officers in the navy or marine corps. Applications are considered according to scores on the Scholastic Aptitude Test or the American College Test.

Students seeking careers in the health professions can take advantage of a particularly large number of specialized aid programs. The federal government, through the Bureau of Health Resources Development, funds such assistance plans as Health Professions Scholarships, National Health Service Corps Scholarships, and Nursing Scholarships. These latter awards are made through approved colleges and schools of nursing and may range as high as $2,000 per year. The major criterion for an award is exceptional financial need.

Specialized fields of medicine and dentistry offer their own scholarships to promising students. The American Dental Hygienists' Association, for instance, offers a Certificate Scholarship Program to students in a dental hygiene program who are entering their final year of training and a Post-Certificate Dental Hygiene Scholarship Program to students who are in their final year of a certificate/associate degree program in dental hygiene or who have graduated from such a program and have been accepted as a full-time bachelor's degree candidate in an accredited four-year college or university. Further information is available from the American Dental Hygienists' Association (211 East Chicago Avenue, Chicago, Illinois 60611).

One-year scholarships of $500 to $650 are available to students entering the field of dental lab technology. Dental Laboratory Technology Teacher Scholarships are also available for students who have completed at least two years in a baccalaureate degree program and who intend to teach. Further information can be obtained from the American Fund for Dental Health (211 East Chicago Avenue, Chicago, Illinois 60611). The American Fund will also provide information about Dental Teacher Training Fellowships, which are offered to students pursuing a two-year master's degree course.

Dental schools themselves offer a number of scholarships. For a summary of these awards and application forms, students should contact the school they have selected to attend or the Association of Dental Schools (1625 Massachusetts Avenue NW, Washington, D.C. 20036).

The American Heart Association sponsors a variety of aid plans for individuals seeking health career opportunities, including work experience, field trips, and educational programs. Further information can be secured from any local office of the Heart Association.

Other specialized scholarships in the health professions are given by the American Optometric Association (7000 Chippewa Street, St. Louis, Missouri 63119) and the American Osteopathic Association, which annually awards National Osteopathic College Scholarships. (For information write American Osteopathic Association, 212 East Ohio Street, Chicago,

Illinois 60611.) The American Podiatry Association annually awards fellowships for graduate study in an area related to podiatry. Additional information can be obtained from the APA Committee on Scholarships and Fellowships (20 Chevy Chase Circle NW, Washington, D.C. 20015). The American Medical Technologists also operates a scholarship program, details of which are available from American Medical Technologists (710 Higgins Road, Park Ridge, Illinois 60068).

Some scholarships in health fields are specially designed for minority students. National Medical Fellowships, for example, are offered to blacks, Native Americans, Chicanos, and mainland Puerto Ricans. (Application information is available from National Medical Fellowships, 3935 Elm Street, Downers Grove, Illinois 60515.) Special five-year fellowships are also available to undergraduate minority students pursuing a career in dentistry. These fellowships cover the final year of predental studies and continue through the four years of dental school. The American Fund for Dental Health has full information on these fellowships.

Special assistance for black students seeking a higher education in any field is available from the National Scholarship Service and Fund for Negro Students (NSSFNS). This service maintains a free college advisory and referral program for black high school juniors and seniors. It also offers a limited number of supplementary renewable three-year scholarships to students who have been counseled by NSSFNS and who have been awarded financial aid insufficient to meet their total college costs. More information is available from NSSFNS (1776 Broadway, New York, New York 10019).

A new scholarship program for students preparing for a career in government has been established by the United States Congress. It is known as Truman Scholarships (in memory of the late President Harry S Truman), these awards will provide up to $5000 a year to cover costs of tuition, fees, books, and room and board and will be given to one student in each state, in the District of Columbia, in Puerto Rico, and in one of the territories. Applicants must be college juniors in September 1977 and must be in an undergraduate field that permits entrance into a graduate program leading to a career in public service. The Harry S Truman Scholarship Foundation (712 Jackson Place NW, Washington, D.C. 20006) can provide complete information on the program.

Education loans. Education loans are another major source of financial aid. The loans furnish students with funds to cover current education costs but, unlike grants and scholarships, require repayment at a later time. The interest charged the student is usually low, however, and repayment terms are typically favorable. For example, the student frequently does not have to begin repayment until after leaving school. Most student loans are guaranteed by the state government, which also provides a subsidy for payment of interest charges while the student is enrolled.

Loans can be obtained through a number of sources, such as government or lending institutions. The federal government has a large education loan program. Through the Office of Education it administers the National Direct Student Loan (NDSL) Program. These need-based loans, available to students through the college or university they are attending, carry a low interest rate (3 percent) and a repayment period of ten years, with a required minimum payment per month of $30. Part of the loan may be repaid, however, through service in public education, and the repayment period does not begin until nine months after the student leaves school. The borrowed funds, which must be used for educational expenses, cannot exceed $2500 per year, while the total of all loans per individual cannot exceed $10,000 for any graduate or professional student, $5000 for any student with two years completed toward a bachelor's degree, and $2500 for any other student. To

be eligible a student must demonstrate financial need and must be accepted for enrollment or enrolled on at least a half-time basis at an eligible postsecondary institution. The educational institution approves and makes the loans and is responsible for collections. It also has to provide one ninth of the total amount it lends to all its students.

The United States federal government also sponsors the Guaranteed Student Loan Program. Loans under this program are available through local banks and savings institutions and are guaranteed directly by the federal government through an agency of the individual state. Some states do not sponsor such a guarantee agency; the loan is then guaranteed directly by the federal government and awarded by an authorized lender, such as a school or fraternal organization with funds available for lending. In order to be eligible, a student must be a citizen of the United States or reside in the United States for other than a temporary purpose, be accepted for enrollment or enrolled in good standing at an eligible institution, and carry at least half of the normal full-time workload. Interest on each loan is 7 percent simple interest per year, and repayment need not start until nine months after graduation. For those students whose family or personal income is below $25,000, the interest is paid to the lender by the federal government while the borrower is in school. During the payout period, the students themselves must pay this interest.

The amount a student may borrow on a Guaranteed Student Loan will be determined by the lender (who bases the determination on the recommendation of the school) with a maximum per academic year of $2500 and an overall maximum per individual of $7500 for undergraduate and $15,000 for graduate students.

Education loans are also awarded in some of the United States manpower training programs. The Law Enforcement Education Program, for instance, provides loans to students with terms that allow service in local law enforcement in lieu of monetary repayment. The Bureau of Health Resources Development administers the Health Professions Loan Program and the Nursing Loan Program. The Health Professions Loans assist students in the fields of medicine, dentistry, veterinary medicine, optometry, pharmacy, podiatry, and osteopathy through long-term, low-interest (3 percent) loans. Loans are repayable over a ten-year period commencing one year after the student ceases full-time study; but up to 60 percent of the loan, plus accrued interest, may be canceled for the practice of medicine, dentistry, optometry, pharmacy, podiatry, or veterinary medicine for at least two years in a designated shortage area. An additional 25 percent will be canceled for a third year of practice in such an area.

Nursing loans are available to students attending approved schools offering a diploma, associate degree, baccalaureate, or equivalent degree in nursing. The amount of the loan may be as much as $2500 per academic year, depending upon need, and a student may borrow a total amount of $10,000. Repayment begins nine months after the borrower ceases to be a full-time student, but it may be deferred during active duty in the armed services or during full-time pursuit of advanced training in nursing. Up to 85 percent of the loan may be canceled if the borrower is employed as a registered nurse under specified circumstances.

Loans for students studying in the health services are also available from the American Fund for Dental Health, the American Dental Hygienists' Association, and the American Optometric Association.

Local awards. Some individuals may also receive financial aid from local awards granted by religious institutions, private firms, clubs, and even individual donors in the student's home community. Such awards are varied and numerous. Representative of them is the Elks Foundation Scholarship award. These scholarships range from $600 to $3000, and American

citizens in their final year of high school or college preparatory school or enrolled as an undergraduate in an accredited college may file an application (available from any Elks lodge or from the secretary of the state Elks association).

Work-study. Work-study programs, offered at all accredited institutions of higher education in the United States, represent another major opportunity for students to alleviate the financial burden of their university education. College Work-Study, a program funded by the federal government (through the Office of Education), is one of the most extensive of student employment efforts. Administered by the individual institution, this program tries to provide part-time work at the sponsoring institution or in the surrounding community to students with financial need. Work-study also provides practical working experience to complement the student's academic studies.

Working hours are generally limited to twenty hours per week while classes are in session and to forty hours per week during regular vacation periods. Up to 80 percent of the student's wages may be paid by the educational institution's federal College Work-Study allocation, with the remaining 20 percent paid by the institution or the off-campus employer. The wages themselves vary, depending on the type of employment and skills required. Students interested in College Work-Study must submit an application and financial statement to the financial aid officer at their college or university.

Cooperative education. Cooperative education programs have developed at continually increasing numbers of institutions of higher education in the United States since the 1960s. Cooperative programs allow students the opportunity to combine periods of academic study with periods of paid employment, usually in their proposed career area. The cooperative work assignments, therefore, represent an important type of financial aid, enabling the student to earn money to help cover education costs while gaining valuable work experience. Students on cooperative work assignments at Northeastern University (in Boston, Massachusetts), the largest cooperative university in the United States, earn an average yearly income of $3000. Although the primary intent of cooperative education is not only financial, such earnings clearly are significant in paying college expenses. Cooperative education plans do differ in terms of how the pattern of work and study is arranged and in the variety of employment opportunities. Full information on these programs is available from the National Commission for Cooperative Education (360 Huntington Avenue, Boston, Massachusetts 02115).

In addition to these many forms and sources, financial aid is available from the institutions of higher education themselves as well as from private industry. Not only do colleges and universities administer programs funded by the federal government, but most institutions (particularly private ones) also have their own funds to help students. When colleges and universities award aid, they usually try to combine the various forms of aid—gifts, loans, and employment.

Private industry in the United States gives a substantial amount of aid to higher education. In 1973–74 American industry provided 15 percent of all voluntary funds, or $354,000,000, in direct aid to colleges and universities (*Handbook of Aid to Higher Education by Corporations,* 1974). Corporations also sometimes sponsor their own scholarship programs.

Determination of Need

To meet the full costs of a higher education, students may well have to combine aid from several of these many sources (in grants and scholarships, loans, and employment) into what is called a financial aid package. Reliance on financial aid packages, or on multiple forms of assistance, developed from the realization that some forms of aid are more desirable than others; therefore, to serve the largest number of

students most effectively, most students are awarded a combination of aid resources.

The eligibility criteria and application procedures for the many forms of aid vary considerably, making the development of a financial aid package a complex, often difficult process. Students should therefore begin their financial planning early to allow themselves plenty of time to learn about the various aid programs, complete the appropriate application forms, and submit the required information well before the announced application deadline.

The majority of aid in the United States is awarded on the basis of a student's financial need, which is defined as the difference between what students and their families can reasonably contribute toward college expenses and the total cost of obtaining higher education. In the United States economists and financial aid experts have developed a national standard—a means test—by which a student's financial need is determined. The standard is based on the principle that parents and students have the primary responsibility to pay as much as they reasonably can toward education costs. Before the need calculation can be made, the family must complete a form about its income, assets, expenses, and debts. The form also asks about family size, the number of family members in college, the number of parents who work, the age of the primary working parent, and other data that affect the family's ability to meet college costs. Once the information is collected, it is possible to calculate the total contribution the family can make and the amount to be met, hopefully, through financial aid. The system ensures that the need of all students is figured in the same way.

Two national United States organizations calculate financial need according to this same national standard: the College Scholarship Service (CSS) of the College Entrance Examination Board and the American College Testing Program. Many students have their need estimated according to the CSS system, as more than three thousand colleges and universities use the services of CSS. The primary document of the CSS is the Parents' Confidential Statements (PCS), which is available from colleges or high schools. The family submits the completed PCS form to the CSS for need analysis. The CSS sends its report, based on the submitted information, along with the PCS form to the institutions from which the student seeks aid. Each college reviews and adjusts the CSS estimates and then figures the student's need. Need differs according to the costs of the college, but each college tries to offer enough to meet a student's full need.

The College Scholarship Service publishes a booklet—*Meeting College Costs*—which explains its need analysis procedures and provides a step-by-step guide which families can use to estimate their need. This booklet is available free of charge from high school counselors, colleges, or the College Board Publication Orders, (Box 2815, Princeton, New Jersey 08540).

Financial Aid to Foreign Students in the United States

Although American students needing financial assistance can turn to many sources of aid, students from other countries who wish to study in the United States can also seek financial help.

For initial information about the aid opportunities, students might contact the foreign student advisers found at many of the larger colleges and universities. In addition, local cultural affairs officers at American embassies and the Institute for International Education (IIE) (809 United Nations Plaza, New York, New York 10017) are valuable sources of information on financial aid for foreign students in the United States. The IIE has overseas offices as well: in Nairobi, Kenya (P.O. Box 5869); in Tsimshatsui, Hong Kong (P.O. Box 6907); and in Lima, Peru (Apartado 300).

Several publications discussing aid opportunities should be consulted. They can be obtained from the sponsoring organization or from American embassies, con-

sulates, or Information Service libraries. *Financial Planning for Study in the United States—A Guide for Students from Other Countries,* a helpful booklet published by the College Entrance Examination Board, discusses college costs, sources of aid, and application procedures. *Fellowships and Loans of the Organization of American States for Study Abroad* provides information for Latin American students interested in graduate study and research outside their home countries. The *Handbook on International Study: For Foreign Nationals,* published by the IIE, is particularly valuable to any foreign student contemplating study in the United States, as is UNESCO's *Study Abroad,* which details fellowships, scholarships, and educational exchange opportunities worldwide and is published in English, French, and Spanish. *A Selected List of Major Fellowship Opportunities and Aids to Advanced Education for Foreign Nationals,* prepared by the Fellowship Office of the National Academy of Sciences, provides specific information on opportunities for graduate study and research.

Foreign students should investigate sources of financial aid in their own countries before approaching international or American sponsors. Possibilities in the student's locale might include the government, private organizations, or, as in a number of Latin American countries, educational credit agencies.

Students wishing to study in the United States might benefit from some of the ongoing contracts between foreign governments and the United States, such as those agreements made with oil-producing nations that lack sufficient educational facilities. Northeastern University, for example, has two such programs—one with Venezuela and another with an organization representing Iran. The IIE in New York handles all these contracts and can provide information on them.

The United States government offers two types of awards, mainly for graduate study, to students from most countries: grants covering tuition and fees, room and board, books and supplies, and incidental expenses, or partial grants covering one or more of these expenses; and grants covering round-trip travel costs only. Awards are for one academic year but are sometimes renewable.

Students must obtain these grants before they leave their home countries. It is not possible to apply for them after they are in the United States. To qualify as a candidate, a student must be between eighteen and thirty-five, have strong academic credentials, and an excellent command of English. Applications are accepted during an annual open competition. For information concerning the dates of competition, eligibility requirements, and current application procedures, students should, if they reside in a capital city, write or visit the cultural affairs officer at the United States embassy or the binational foundation or commission; elsewhere, the United States Information Service or binational center can provide details on the programs. To avoid missing early deadlines, it is best to inquire at least fifteen months in advance of the intended date of study.

Foreign students can also sometimes obtain financial support from United States foundations, corporations, or professional associations. Assistance can be secured as well from international bodies such as the United Nations and its various agencies or the Organization of American States.

Some states also provide financial help to foreign students. New York, for example, appropriates a certain sum for foreign student aid, and Texas offers foreign students a tuition rate lower than that for out-of-state students. Minnesota grants resident status (and hence the lower in-state tuition rate) to foreign students with financial need and has set up an emergency foreign student aid fund. The University of Minnesota, as well, grants resident status to students sponsored by a Minnesota company.

Since financial aid applications are usually required in addition to applications for admission, prospective applicants should indicate in their first inquiry to a college or university that they wish to apply for aid. The proper forms and information can then be sent to them along with the admission application. Because financial aid deadlines are often early (usually between December 1 and February 1 for entrance the following September), students should apply well in advance, usually a year before the intended date of entrance.

On the aid form applicants are required to furnish accurate information about the amount and source of funds they can provide as well as the amount of their need. In order to obtain complete and accurate information, many colleges and universities require a Declaration and Certification of Finances form. Since few financial awards cover all expenses, applicants able to contribute some of the funds themselves often have a better opportunity of winning an award. However, need should not be understated in the expectation of later obtaining additional assistance, for opportunities for receiving aid are severely limited once a foreign student has arrived in the United States. Applicants need not request specific scholarships or fellowships when they do apply, for financial aid candidates are automatically considered for all appropriate awards. It is imperative to note that applicants must not assume an award has been made unless they receive official notification in writing from the institution.

Developments in Financial Aid

As the costs of receiving higher education in the United States continue to rise and as students need increasing amounts of aid to meet those costs, it becomes essential to develop new forms and sources of assistance. Indeed, many American colleges and universities are devising innovative assistance programs. One effort involves the granting of contingency loans in a plan recognizing that some students who borrow funds later earn salaries that make repayment difficult. To reduce financial risks to student borrowers, this program allows students to repay according to their incomes. Contingency loans have been tried on a limited basis, most notably at Yale and Duke Universities.

A "voucher plan"—which has had only limited testing—provides all students with a certain amount of purchasing power to be used at any institution of higher education. Proponents of such a plan claim it offers the student greater choice than does aid channeled through specific institutions. As of 1976, direct student aid usable at any institution of the student's choice is available through the Basic Educational Opportunity Grant program, the Guaranteed Student Loan Program, and a number of state programs.

The rapid growth in cooperative education programs in institutions of higher learning throughout the United States attests to the increased interest in offering students more financial alternatives in meeting the costs of their education. Costs are also being reduced, along with time required for degrees, at the many United States colleges and universities that encourage nontraditional education programs such as granting college credit for prior learning. These efforts illustrate ways in which students' financial burdens can be alleviated through innovative as well as traditional aid programs.

Bibliography

Fellowship Office, National Academy of Sciences. *A Selected List of Major Fellowship Opportunities and Aid to Advanced Education for Foreign Nationals.* Washington, D.C.: National Research Council. Annual.

Fellowships and Loans of the Organization of American States for Study Abroad. Washington, D.C.: Organization of American States. Annual.

Financial Planning for Study in the United States—A Guide for Students from Other Countries. Princeton, New Jersey: College Entrance Examination Board. Annual.

Golladay, M. A. *The Condition of Education: A Statistical Report on the Condition of Education in the United States.* Washington, D.C.: U.S. Government Printing Office, 1976.

Handbook of Aid to Higher Education. New York: Council for Financial Aid to Education, 1974.

Handbook on International Study: For Foreign Nationals. (5th ed.) New York: Institute for International Education, 1973.

Making It: A Guide to Student Finances. Cambridge, Massachusetts: Harvard Student Agencies, 1973.

Meeting College Costs. New York: College Entrance Examination Board.

National Merit Scholarship Program. *Semifinalists in the Twenty-Second Annual Merit Scholarship Competition.* Evanston, Illinois: National Merit Scholarship Corporation, 1976. Annual.

Need a Lift: Educational Opportunities. Indianapolis, Indiana: American Legion. Annual.

The Official College Entrance Examination Board Guide to Financial Aid for Students and Parents. New York: Simon & Schuster, 1975.

Student Assistance Programs. Washington, D.C. College Entrance Examination Board, 1975. (Mimeographed).

Study Abroad. Paris: UNESCO, 1974.

Suchar, E. W., Ivens, S. H., and Jacobson, E. C. *Student Expenses at Postsecondary Institutions, 1975–76.* New York: College Entrance Examination Board, 1976.

Woodhall, M. *Student Loans: A Review of Experience in Scandinavia and Elsewhere.* London: George G. Harrap, 1970.

ELIZABETH W. SUCHAR

See also: Veterans Education Benefits.

3. SCHOLARSHIPS AND FELLOWSHIPS, INTERNATIONAL

Of the many people who study outside their own countries, most do so unaided by any form of financial assistance; those supported by either a fellowship or scholarship offered by a private or governmental agency are a minority. In a study of foreign student employment and financial resources conducted by the National Association for Foreign Student Affairs, the percentage of foreign students studying in the United States with any form of financial assistance was less than those who came unsupported by outside agencies: 12 percent held institutional loans or scholarships, 5.8 percent held scholarships from the United States government, and 7.7 percent held scholarships from foreign governments. According to the study, the most frequently cited support was family resources and personal savings (Stecklin and Lin, 1974, pp. 30–31). In fact, the largest amount of financial assistance given to foreign students in the United States comes from the institutions where they study; for graduate students this assistance usually takes the form of teaching or research assistantships.

Further, in this same study it was found that even those students who did receive some form of financial support still needed additional funds to remain in the United States. For example, of the 7.5 percent of the students receiving a scholarship from a private agency or foundation, it was found that the scholarship amounted to only 62.4 percent of the total support needed by the student (Stecklin and Lin, 1974, p. 85).

Awards and Grants

The facts cited above may be misleading, for in reality more and more students and faculty are studying overseas with partial or total funding from outside sources. At the close of World War II, the awards and grants available numbered only in the hundreds and were actually less than five hundred, but by 1975 they numbered in the thousands. What is known is that an ever increasing number of persons are studying abroad for a period of research. What is not known is that there are many little-publicized grants and awards that are funding these experiences.

There are, however, two major difficulties in applying for fellowships and scholarships. First, there is only a minimal amount of support for undergraduates. Most grants are for pre- or postdoctoral study. An undergraduate might write to the following three organizations for information on fellowships for undergraduate students: Rotary Foundation International, 1600 Ridge Avenue, Evanston, Illinois 60201 (for study in the United States only); Youthgrants in the Humanities, National Endowment for the Humanities, 806 15th Street NW, Washington, D.C. 20506; or Phelps-Stokes Fund, 10 East 87th Street, New York, New York

10028 (for African students only). Second, the competition is extremely keen. For example, for the 1975–76 Fulbright-Hays Grants for Graduate Study Abroad competition, administered by the Institute of International Education (IIE) for United States students who wish to study overseas, there were 3269 applications for 527 awards, giving any applicant only a 20 percent overall chance for acceptance.

Sources of grants. Grants come, essentially, from one of the following three sources: governmental agencies, small and large private foundations, and local bodies. The first two major groups are those most commonly known to persons seeking financial assistance. Almost every government in the world offers some kind of scholarship competition; these competitions are sometimes restricted, allowing only citizens to be recipients or limiting the location of the study. An outstanding example of a governmental program is Venezuela's *Programa de becas Gran Mariscal de Ayacucho* (Scholarship Program "Grand Marshal of Ayacucho"), in which the government fully supports over ten thousand students each year in Venezuela and abroad.

Most often, the private foundations prefer to administer their own grant competitions or to have an organization such as IIE administer them. The last source of funding, that from local bodies, is often the most difficult to locate, but may also be the most lucrative. There are many social and civic organizations, in addition to local philanthropic foundations, willing to assist someone in the funding of a timely project. Finding and utilizing this last source is entirely up to the individual seeking funding; all research can best be done by that individual.

In all cases, the applicant should first discover what sources are already available in his or her home country. These sources will be easier to find, information will be less difficult to obtain, and interviews and personal meetings with the donors can most readily be arranged.

Grant applications. There are certain

similarities in all grant applications, and there are several common rules that should be followed in preparing an application. An applicant should realize that it will take approximately one and a half to two years for the entire procedure to be adequately completed. The applicant will need to spend a large amount of time preparing the application, and once it is submitted, it will usually be one year before the award is actually received. An application or proposal should be mailed well in advance of the deadline date, and the applicant should be certain that he is using current grant applications and information from the granting agency. The purposes of grant awards often change from year to year; unless the applicant is sure of the focus, the application process could be an unprofitable use of his time. The application should be typed, if at all possible, and unless otherwise stated by the granting agency, should be in the language of the country that serves as home to the granting agency. Any additions that an applicant wishes to make to the application are usually acceptable, if these additions or enclosures actually will help the granting agency to make its decision and if this same information could not have been included as part of the application form itself. Useless additions will serve only to detract from the application or proposal.

It is important for the applicant to familiarize himself with the governing purposes of the funding agency. If, for example, a person wishes to study a particular field in a particular country and there is only one body that funds such activity, the applicant should spend his time in preparing one excellent application to that body, rather than preparing applications for other agencies, several of which will be immediately rejected. Further, learning about the actual past policies of the agency and the actual grants recently made by the agency will be of great assistance to an applicant. If the funding agency will agree, it is often quite instructive to study a copy of a grant application that recently has been funded by the particular agency.

In studying the open competitions, it should be noted that there are some fellowships that are very limited in the area of study that they will sponsor or the area of the world for which a student can apply, as well as in the amount of funding that is available. Some grants are for travel only, some for board and lodging only, some for tuition and supply cost only, and some for materials only. Most resource books will make these various differences apparent in their program summaries.

Fellowship and Grant Sources

The following descriptions of several well-known scholarships and fellowships are intended only as examples of the wide variety of funding programs available. Perhaps the best-known fellowship competition is that sponsored broadly under the Fulbright-Hays Acts of 1946 and 1961 (Mutual Educational and Cultural Exchange Act). Under this large program, the United States government and some participating countries sponsor the following programs: (1) predoctoral study or research (for information write Institute of International Education, 809 United Nations Plaza, New York, New York 10017); (2) teaching in elementary and secondary schools and modern language and area studies training and research on both the pre- and postdoctoral levels (for information write Department of Health, Education and Welfare, Office of Education, Division of International Education, Washington, D.C. 20202); (3) postdoctoral research and university lecturing (for information write Council for International Exchange of Scholars, Conference Board of Associated Research Councils, 2101 Constitution Avenue NW, Washington, D.C. 20418).

A non-United States citizen must write to the United States embassy or the Ministry of Education for information on Fulbright awards that are available for nationals of his country. Under most of the programs funded under the Fulbright-

Hays Act, the funding will cover the following areas: travel to and from the place of study, insurance, orientation, board and lodging, tuition or cost of research materials, and, if necessary, a dependent's allowance. Further, the awards are available in many countries, and the area of study allowable under the grant is quite broad.

The American Council of Learned Societies (ACLS: 343 East 46th Street, New York, New York 10017) offers grants-in-aid to support research in the humanities or research projects with a predominantly humanistic emphasis in the social or natural sciences. Available to United States and Canadian citizens and permanent residents holding the Doctor of Philosophy or an equivalent degree, the awards are for short-term research and offer a maximum of $2500. The ACLS also offers research fellowships (award: $12,000) and study fellowships (award: $10,000). The Latin American Scholarship Programs of American Universities (LASPAU: 25 Mount Auburn St., Cambridge, Massachusetts 02138), since its establishment at Harvard University in 1965, has awarded 2100 scholarships to faculty members from Latin American universities for graduate study in the United States. Services have recently been extended to the Caribbean. LASPAU receives funding from sources like USAID, OAS, Fulbright-Hays, and *Banco de México.*

The Carnegie Endowment for International Peace (345 East 46th Street, New York, New York 10017) offers travel and maintenance assistance for scholars with projects relating to changes in the international system resulting in shifts of political authority and allegiance—specifically, transnational relations, elite networks, and impact studies. These awards rarely exceed $5000 and are available to pre- and post-doctoral candidates studying or teaching in the United States or Canada.

The NATO research fellowships, administered through the Committee on International Exchange of Persons (2101 Constitution Avenue, Washington, D.C.

20418), offer funding for advanced research to postdoctoral scholars from NATO member states. These awards are limited to fellows working on projects of direct interest to NATO or to the Atlantic Community as a whole, focusing on historical, political, economic, and social problems. The grants offer twenty-three thousand Belgian francs per month, or an equivalent amount in the currency of any other NATO member country. In addition, NATO pays for air travel for approved journeys in connection with the research project.

The fellowships listed above are well known, both for the number of grants awarded per year and for the relatively broad fields of study allowed under the terms of the grant. Other scholarships are more narrow in their focus. For example, the Wenner-Gren Foundation for Anthropological Research (14 East 71st Street, New York, New York 10021) offers awards in anthropology that are available to nationals of all countries and tenable in any country. Under the terms of the predoctoral fellowships program, the recipient of the award is given approximately $4000. Under the Richard Carley Hunt Memorial Fellowships, which are open to candidates with a doctoral degree and are usually intended to aid completion of specific studies or the preparation of field materials by younger scholars, the maximum amount available per grant is $2500.

The International Federation of University Women (IFUW: 17a King's Road, Sloane Square, London SW3, England) offers awards to members of national associations of university women affiliated with the IFUW for study in any other country than that of the recipient. Candidates must have completed at least one year of graduate work and be well advanced on a research program. The award is for approximately one thousand pounds maximum, for one academic year. Persons interested in this particular award should write to the headquarters of the national association of their home country in time for their application to be forwarded and received at IFUW by December 1.

For specific countries, a potential applicant is encouraged to write to his own embassy to find if there are organizations that are specifically designed to encourage academic exchange between his own and other countries. The African-American Institute (833 United Nations Plaza, New York, New York 10017), the American Friends of the Middle East (1717 Massachusetts Avenue NW, Washington, D.C. 20036), the American-Kor-Asian Foundation Inc. (345 East 46th Street, New York, New York 10017), the Belgian-American Educational Foundation (420 Lexington Avenue, New York, New York 10017), and the *Fondation des Etats-unis* (15 boulevard Jourdan, 75690 Paris Cedex 14) are examples of agencies that can be of great assistance to applicants. Many of them sponsor scholarship competitions; all of them can direct persons to other organizations that may be of help.

Information Sources

Perhaps one of the more useful sources for addresses and a brief description of grant opportunities around the world is the UNESCO publication entitled *Study Abroad (Etudes à l'étranger; Estudios en el extranjero)*. Over 2000 different awards are described in this trilingual (English, French, and Spanish) publication. Many of the awards listed are not found in any other publication, and information on them is difficult to obtain from other sources. *Study Abroad* may be ordered from the Editor, Division of Free Flow Information and International Exchanges, UNESCO, 7 place de Fontenoy, 75700 Paris.

There are several other resource books on grants and fellowships for study abroad. The Association of Commonwealth Universities in London published, in 1974, a *Scholarships Guide for Commonwealth Postgraduate Students: 75–77*. This book describes awards open to graduates of Commonwealth universities wishing to study at a Commonwealth university outside their own countries. *Aids to the Humanities and the Social Sciences*, published by the Canada Council in Ottawa, Ontario, describes fellowships for Canadian citizens.

For students from other countries wishing to study in the United States, *Entering Higher Education in the United States* lists addresses for several United States Information Services offices where helpful counseling may be found. This pamphlet may be ordered from the College Entrance Examination Board (888 Seventh Avenue, New York, New York 10019).

There are two other useful sources for students coming to the United States. *Fields of Study in United States Colleges and Universities* is available from the Institute of International Education (address above). *Financial Planning for Study in the United States: A Guide for Students from Other Countries* lists several educational credit agencies that can be of assistance. This booklet is available from the College Entrance Examination Board.

For United States students planning to study abroad, *Grants for Graduate Study Abroad* is very useful as an initial source for those seeking financial aid. It describes awards available to United States citizens offered under the Fulbright-Hays Act and those administered by IIE. *American Students and Teachers Abroad,* by P. K. McIntyre, is available from the Division of International Education, Office of Education, Department of Health, Education and Welfare. Also available from the Office of Education are the *Catalog of Educational Assistance Programs* and *Opportunities Abroad for Teachers*. An additional very helpful source on financial aid is the *SECUSSA Sourcebook: A Guide for Advisors of United States Students Planning an Overseas Experience,* published by the National Association for Foreign Student Affairs (1860 19th Street NW, Washington, D.C. 20009).

Finally, for students from all countries who wish to study abroad, an excellent and highly recommended source is *Scholarships and Fellowships for Foreign Study: A Selected Bibliography,* published by IIE.

If *Study Abroad* or any of the other suggested resources are not available in a library, current prices and editions are usually available from several publishing clearinghouses, such as Europa Publications (18 Bedford Square, London WC1B 8JN, England), Unipub (Box 433, New York, New York 10016), and North American Association of Venezuela (Edificio Blandin, Plaza Chacaito, Caracas, Venezuela).

Bibliography

Angeli, F. (Ed.) *Guide to European Foundations.* New York: Columbia University Press, 1972.

Annual Register of Grant Support. Chicago: Marquis Academic Media, 1974.

Council for European Studies. *Fellowship Guide for Western Europe.* Pittsburgh: Council for European Studies, 1974.

Institute of International Education. *Evaluating Foreign Students' Credentials.* New York: IIE, 1975.

Lewis, M. O. *Foundation Directory.* New York: Columbia University Press, 1971.

Mathies, L., and Thomas, W. R. *Overseas Opportunities for American Educators and Students.* New York: Macmillan, 1973.

McCormack, N. M., and Pearson, J. *Fellowships, Scholarships and Related Opportunities in International Education.* Knoxville: University of Tennessee, annual.

National Research Council. *A Selected List of Major Fellowship Opportunities and Aids to Advanced Education for U.S. Citizens.* Washington, D.C.: National Research Council, annual.

National Science Foundation. *National Science Foundation Grants and Awards for Fiscal Year 1974.* Washington, D.C.: National Science Foundation, 1975.

Stecklin, J. E., and Lin, H. C. *Study of Foreign Student Employment and Financial Resources.* Washington, D.C.: National Association for Foreign Student Affairs, 1974.

Taylor, M. L. (Ed.) *Handbook on International Study for United States Nationals.* New York: Institute of International Education, 1973.

Taylor, M.L. *Handbook on United States Study for Foreign Nationals.* New York: Institute of International Education, 1973.

Turner, R. (Ed.) *The Grants Register.* New York: St. Martin's, 1973.

NANCY MCCORMACK

See also: Exchange, International: Student Employment Abroad, Teaching and Research Exchange Programs; Students, Student Services, and Student Organizations.

FINANCIAL REPORTING
See Financial Affairs.

FINANCING AND CONTROL OF RESEARCH
See Research: Financing and Control of Research.

FINANCING CONSTRUCTION
See Financing of Higher Education: Financing of Institutions and Systems.

FINANCING OF HIGHER EDUCATION

1. FINANCING OF INSTITUTIONS AND SYSTEMS

2. UNIVERSITY GRANTS COMMITTEES

1. FINANCING OF INSTITUTIONS AND SYSTEMS

The financing of higher education includes the means of providing financial resources to a variety of claimants, both organizational and individual. It has often become the focal point of debates about national priorities, distributional equities among classes of society, and the nature and composition of economic and social growth within a nation.

Although higher education is a huge worldwide enterprise involving several hundred billions of dollars (as in the United States) its financing amounts to but a relatively small fraction of the gross national product (GNP) of most countries. This portion of the GNP ranges from a fraction of 1 percent in many countries (.5 percent, for example, in the Federal Republic of Germany) to a high of about 3 percent in the United States and some of the wealthy, developing countries, such as Iran. Therefore, a relatively small portion of the world's wealth goes to higher education.

Forms of Financing

General institutional assistance comes from a variety of sources in a variety of forms. Each of these forms is discussed below.

Budget appropriations. Budgetary appropriations from federal, state, and local governments constitute the major sources of financing for higher education throughout the world. Institutions of higher education usually estimate their financial needs for a period of time and then present their budget requests to state or federal agencies of education and social services. On review and approval, these agencies usually present aggregate budget requests for higher education to the legislative bodies that, upon further review and approval, allocate public funds to higher education. General fund revenues are the usual source for meeting public budget appropriations, but a variety of specialized fund sources have been used. Jordan allocates higher education a fixed percentage of revenues derived from import taxes. Brazil and other South American countries allocate a fixed percentage of total federal or state revenues for education. Nigeria and Iran have chosen to allocate a portion of oil revenues to education. In general, however, income, property, and corporate taxes are the major sources of support for higher education. Governmental funds constitute 70 to 100 percent of total higher educational expenditures (depending on local circumstances) for public institutions.

The United States is unusual in that it has a high proportion of privately financed colleges and universities that receive only a small proportion of their total revenues from public sources. In socialist countries, developing nations, much of Western Europe, and some public colleges in the United States, virtually all institutional support is provided by public sources made available through government appropriations, and students attain higher education without fee.

The appropriations process causes the periodic review of the functioning of educational institutions as well as the goals or objectives that public funders have for those institutions. The budgetary system is a major accountability and governance process that, during each budgetary cycle, permits public funders to reconsider their willingness to support higher education. The 1970s has brought on a period of increasingly stringent reviews, often precipitated by the financial crises of governments in a period of worldwide recession. These reviews reflect a fundamental reconsideration of the purposes, objectives, and impacts of higher education.

Budget appropriations impose varying degrees of constraint in terms of institutional usage of funds that are provided. A strict line-item budgetary control restricts institutions to fund usages that are specified in great detail by the appropriating body. This method is often used to segregate capital and operating funds. It also can be used to segregate different items of a budget, such as faculty salaries, staff salaries, student assistance, supplies and consumables, and the purchase of services. Partly in reaction to the high level of specificity implied by line-item budgets and partly because of the effects of legislative involvement on governance, a number of legislative bodies have taken to providing lump-sum grants to higher education.

Lump-sum grants. Grants are usually provided through a University Grants Committee, as is the case in Great Britain and New Zealand. Such intermediate bodies present a multiyear request for the total funding of national higher education to the appropriate government agencies and legislative bodies. On review, they receive a lump sum, and they then typically provide a lump-sum award to each institution in the form of multiyear support. This process is intended to insulate institutions from intimate involvement in the political process and to ensure some medium-term stability in their financing. The general international experience has been that in times of increasing financial capacities of nations, lump-sum financing has achieved its purpose, but during economically stringent periods the multiyear awards have not necessarily been honored, and some faculty and staff retrenchment has become necessary. Also, while this method affords maximum flexibility in terms of the use of finances, it provides the least amount of accountability to its funders.

Tuition and fees. The fees derived from students constitute a major source of support for privately financed institutions. In the United States, where a large private-university system exists, student fees play a major financial role. In many other countries such fees provide 10 to 15 percent of the operating capital of public institutions.

The question of what part of the cost of education should be borne by students is complex and has both political and economic overtones. It is clear that the cost of higher education is a barrier that deters the participation of many young people from low-income families. For this reason, it has been suggested that student fees should be adjusted relative to the students' ability to pay, their academic ability, or their chosen field of study. Arrangements of this sort are prevalent in many countries.

There are strong arguments in favor of the student tuition and fee system. As a nation becomes highly developed, the benefits of higher education become more of an advantage to the individual than to the society as a whole. On this basis, it becomes reasonable to expect the student to assume the major cost of his education.

Capitation grants. Capitation grants are provided to an institution in proportion to the number of students enrolled who are residents of a given political area. This is the method used by a number of the states of the United States to provide support to private institutions that enroll state residents in their undergraduate programs. It is also the means used by a number of the developing nations to provide support to institutions or governments in other countries that permit the registration of stu-

dents from the developing nation. For example, several Middle Eastern nations have negotiated contracts with major universities in the United States for the enrollment of students from their countries.

The basic principle of capitation grants is that the sponsoring agency pays only for students actually enrolled. From the institution's perspective, the attractiveness of sponsored students is due to the associated financial support.

Workload grants. Workload grants are basically similar to lump-sum or capitation grants except that the amount of the award varies with the workload of the institution. For example, external degree programs and nontraditional programs, such as those of the Open University in England, are funded on quite a different workload basis than are traditional institutions of higher education. The Open University is funded at a faculty/student ratio of 1:63 as opposed to a more traditional ratio of 1:15 to 1:20. France and a number of American state governments differentiate their grants for enrolled students by providing higher funding for students in technical and certain professional areas as well as for students at the graduate level. The rationale behind these funding formulas is that it is more costly for institutions to conduct specialized than unspecialized programs.

Employment subsidies. Subsidies are sometimes provided by governments to institutions for the employment of certain types of students. In the United States many millions of dollars are provided each year to institutions of higher education on a matching basis to employ financially needy students on campus. Employment subsidy programs recognize that many students work in addition to attending higher education. Subsidies not only provide them with income but also provide employment opportunities on campus less deleterious to a student's academic undertaking than off-campus work. These employment subsidies are different from cooperative work-study programs that a number of institutions have undertaken to provide a substantively different education-work experience for students. The primary purpose of employment subsidies is to create an incentive for institutions to employ students in place of nonstudents and thereby increase student incomes.

Unrestricted gifts. Unrestricted gifts from private and corporate sectors to institutions of higher education can be used for any legitimate purpose of the institution. The total amount of funds available to institutions of higher education in the form of unrestricted gifts is very small. But such funds often can be used by administrators to fund activities not included in their budgets or to provide matching funds when it is to the institution's advantage to do so.

Unrestricted earnings. Unrestricted earnings are funds derived annually from the investment of unrestricted gifts. The private endowment of a college or university is an old tradition derived from the days of private church sponsorship, but most of the more recently formed colleges and universities have very limited endowments. Most institutions in the United States and throughout the world, however, have very small, if any, endowments. Therefore endowments are of very little financial significance to most institutions of higher education.

Program support. Occasionally, funds are provided to support a particular activity or objective of an institution. For example, Sweden awards funds to institutions to pursue particular objectives or activities. Some countries provide massive program support for agricultural extension and research in which the institution retains substantial discretion over the actual use of funds within broad programmatic objectives. Thus, program support is typically more limited than general budget appropriations but not as specific in regard to individual tasks, activities, or individual staff requirements. In this sense, program support has an intermediate level of specificity and categorical control between

general institutional assistance and narrowly defined project, grant, or contract support.

Project, grant, and contract support. These are funds provided to institutions to support particular activities of specifically identified individuals over relatively short periods of time. Most research and development activities in higher education are supported by grants or contracts. This support provides the funders with the largest degree of control over the individual, the task, the time schedule, the intended outcomes, and the extensive accountability requirements. From the institutional perspective, grants and contracts are the most restrictive form of categorical assistance, but they also frequently carry a large administrative overhead stipend that can be used as unrestricted income by the institution. For this reason, many institutions find such grants and contracts highly desirable.

Service contracts. Arrangements between institutions and funders or third-party clientele to provide a service that would otherwise not be available are termed service contracts. Rural development programs, educational programs, health care programs, specialized occupational and professional training, and a host of other such programs are examples of such services. There have been various attempts to make the fees associated with service contracts contingent on the magnitude or quality of service delivered. Called "performance contracting," this plan is intuitively appealing but in practice has developed numerous problems, most of which are related to an inherent inability to measure the quantity and quality of academic services.

Restricted gifts. Private and corporate funds are sometimes provided to an institution for particular purposes specified by the donors. To the extent that these restricted gifts are used for purposes that would otherwise have to be financed by unrestricted funds, these gifts become, in effect, additional general institutional support. On the other hand, if restricted gifts require the institution to spend substantial funds to match or maintain the specified activities, they can be a drain on institutional resources.

Construction assistance. In addition to operating assistance of a general or categorical nature, funders provide construction assistance to institutions of higher education in various forms.

Project grants or loans are funds for the purposes of capital construction provided directly by a funder to an institution with or without the requirement of repayment. Most of the construction costs of public institutions of higher education are provided directly by government and are often financed by long-term bond issues. In some cases, governments provide loans instead of grants, with the requirement that the recipient institution repay the loan over a period of time.

Direct and indirect interest subsidies are methods of stimulating capital investment by higher education. Private lenders may be unwilling to provide capital funds for higher education due to the poor market for used educational buildings. Lenders would have some difficulty in recovering their investment should an institution default on a mortgage. In this regard, public action can stimulate the investment of private funds by guaranteeing the repayment of loans.

User charges are a frequent form of providing revenues by charging students for the use of dormitory facilities, parking facilities, recreation facilities, and other noninstructional facilities. To the extent that educational facilities are also used by the general public, user charges enable the institution to defray some of the capital costs of their original construction.

Tax Benefits

Another form of financing for higher education is that provided by the alleviation of taxation. Most countries impose substantial taxes on property and on the net revenues of organizations except for those officially designated as tax exempt. Also, many countries have provisions in their tax codes that allow individuals to deduct contributions to educational institutions from their income or taxes. These tax law conditions are peculiar to each country and often to state, regional, or local governments within each country, but they generally provide important financial benefits to higher education.

Tax exemptions. Exempt institutions are able to avoid paying taxes for which they would otherwise be liable, such as property, sales, and income taxes. Foregoing a general cost has the same dollar impact as receiving an unrestricted revenue and, in this regard, the costs avoided by tax exemption accrue both to public and private institutions. Tax exemptions may be the major form of public assistance to private higher education. It is also a very important form of public assistance to public higher education. Local taxes, especially property taxes, are often used to provide local services, some of which are consumed by institutions of higher education. In recognition of this fact, many institutions provide payments to local communities in lieu of taxes and to pay their fair share for the fire, police, and other community services that they receive. However, institutions of higher education serve to stimulate local economic activity and consequently tend to increase the revenues and tax base of a community.

Tax deductions for donors. By allowing individuals to deduct donations to institutions of higher education from their income or their taxes, governments provide an important incentive for individuals to contribute to higher education. While gift giving is intrinsically satisfying to a number of people, the financial incentive for private support of higher education is a result of the tax system of a particular nation. Allowing donors to deduct the market value of their gift from their pretax earnings creates a strong incentive for people of means to support tax-deductible causes, including higher education.

Tax credits for donors. Tax credits are a new and still somewhat experimental form of tax deduction that enable people to deduct from their taxes, rather than from their pretax income, some proportion of what they contribute to tax-deductible causes. Several states in the United States provide tax credits for donations to charitable causes, including higher education. What evidence exists suggests that tax credits create a stimulus for donations to higher education.

Aid to Students

Although funds provided to institutions have been the major mechanism of financing higher education, assistance provided to students is growing in magnitude and in general policy concern to funders. Charging anything less than the full price that students would otherwise be willing to pay for higher education is financial assistance. Except for the proprietary institutions in the United States and a few other countries, virtually all of higher education is subsidized in that students pay less than the maximum price which they would otherwise be willing to pay for higher education. At all public institutions students pay less than the cost of their education.

Many countries charge low or minimal tuition for attendance at public institutions of higher education. Informally, this is undoubtedly the major means of providing assistance to students. However, providing low-price higher education is a form of financial subsidy that does not show up in the accounting records of institutions or governments. It would be inappropriate to charge to student subsidies the full cost of public appropriations to institutions of higher education because there is no evidence that, if a free market prevailed, students would be willing to pay a price for higher education that reflects the full cost borne by the public. The usual argument that economists make is that the social benefits of higher education are supplementary to its private benefits. They hold that, without public investment, individuals

would not choose to invest in higher education to the full extent appropriate for public purpose.

Direct grants and fellowships. The most prevalent form of providing direct financial assistance to students is through grants, scholarships, and fellowships. In the socialist and developing countries, it is common practice to provide stipends for their support. In addition to the income subsidy provisions of some countries, there are highly differentiated grants and fellowship programs provided to students either directly or indirectly through institutions of higher education.

Grants made directly to students are usually differentiated according to some criterion, the most frequently used being financial need as evidenced by the income and assets of the student's parents. If the student is not financially dependent on others, then the criterion becomes the financial need of the student. "Financial need" is a complicated index that supposedly represents the ability of parents or students to meet educational costs and does not directly reflect their financial "willingness to pay." An individual's or a family's willingness to pay is a function of how greatly they value higher education and of what other alternatives exist for individual advancement in a society. In most countries higher education is an enterprise that involves a small proportion of youth and virtually no adults; even in the United States, only one fourth of those between the ages of eighteen and twenty-four attend postsecondary education. Therefore, a willingness to pay for higher education is not evinced by most families or most individuals. Having no way to measure willingness to pay, most scholarship agencies have developed some indicator of financial capacity as a basis for the award of grants or scholarships. Many institutions, as well as the federal and state governments of the United States, operate need-based scholarship programs. A similar system exists in Great Britain.

Academic ability as demonstrated on

standardized test instruments has long been a prime criterion for the award of public grants and scholarships, particularly in Western Europe, where access to post-secondary education has been regulated by performance tests in a number of countries. With academic performance determining access, it is very understandable that the same measures would be used for the distribution of financial assistance. However, as funds become increasingly limited, the willingness of governments to provide resources to high ability but financially able students has begun to be reduced.

Grants and scholarships are also provided to students to accomplish a variety of special purposes, including the encouragement of individuals to train for particular professions, the encouragement of disadvantaged or traditionally nonparticipating groups to enroll in higher education, and the encouragement of individuals who would otherwise be likely not to complete their college programs. In some countries direct grants and scholarships are a form of income subsidy to individuals and their families based solely on the student's attendance in higher education. Ironically, this same effect occurs with the need-based scholarship programs, because there is evidence that a substantial number of scholarship participants would attend higher education without funding. In this sense, many scholarship programs are in fact income subsidy programs even though their sponsors may believe they are access-oriented financing programs.

Grants and scholarships provided through institutions. In addition to their own grant and scholarship programs, a number of governments fund institutional scholarship programs. The institutions operate their own scholarship agencies that determine student eligibility and award levels. This decentralization of scholarship determination and awards is particularly common in the United States, where the complex pattern of public and private institutions with enormously different re-

sources makes it difficult to administer a single federal or state program that can treat all students' needs fairly. Providing scholarship funds to institutions leaves open the question of the needs determination or the criteria on which scholarship awards will be made. Institutions have traditionally used criteria similar to those favored by governmental agencies. These include financial need, academic ability, and a variety of special criteria ranging from athletic and musical ability to family heritage. In the United States, where this practice is more prevalent, institutionally distributed public funds for financial assistance make up approximately 10 percent of the total public funds used for student financial aid. The vast majority of these funds are provided directly to students.

The consequence of grants and scholarship programs for students, provided either directly or indirectly through institutions, is that the price of education is differentiated by the characteristics of the consumer rather than by the characteristics of the educational service provided. In this regard, higher education is a very unusual service. For most goods and services, the price is differentiated according to the kind and quality of the goods or service instead of according to the purchaser. In higher education a group of students may all receive the identical service, and each may pay a substantially different price, depending on the amount of financial assistance each has received. The purpose of such discriminatory pricing is usually to produce a nondiscriminatory result and, in this sense, is one of the most unusual aspects of higher education finance.

Student loans. In addition to providing grants and scholarships, and in recognition of the severely limited resources of higher education, some governments also provide funds in the form of student loans, with the restriction that some or all of the funds be repaid at a later date. The rationale of student loans is twofold.

The first argument is that individuals are willing to pay the cost of higher education because they anticipate earning a higher income in the future and so are willing to pledge future income to the repayment of the cost of their education. It is only the absence of a capital market—that is, the availability of educational loans—that prevents individuals from exercising, to the fullest extent, their willingness to attend higher education. Publicly provided loan programs enable individuals to borrow this special kind of capital that is secured only by the promise of future earnings.

A second argument is based on the concept that the major beneficiaries of higher education are the individuals themselves, as they enroll in, and successfully complete, programs in higher education. Therefore, the cost of education should be borne by these individuals while they are receiving the benefits of their education.

Both of these arguments are relatively recent and reflect the financial condition of the funders of higher education much more than any basic principles of higher education finance. Repayments received from loans reduce the cost of the loan program from the equivalent cost of a grant or scholarship program.

Loans can be provided directly to students from public or private sources, as is the custom in the United States, Norway, Japan, and other nations. Alternatively, public funders can guarantee loans made by private lenders and, especially if the government is a guarantor, the willingness of private lenders to provide unsecured funds to students will be drastically increased. Guaranteeing loans is a common practice in the housing market and other areas of individual finance that are deemed to be socially useful. The cost of the guarantee is usually added as an additional interest rate to the loan, but the faith in the credit of the sponsoring government is the major guarantee to the private lenders. Finally, in the United States, where tuition in private institutions is substantial, a few experimental programs have been designed to provide tuition deferral, by which unpaid tuition becomes a loan to be repaid out of future earnings. In a sense, these institutions are willing to invest some of their unrestricted capital in student loans rather than use other alternative financial instruments. If their students have a high likelihood of substantial lifetime earnings, student loans may be a good investment for these institutions.

Tax benefits to students. A form of student assistance that is as indirect as low tuition is the tax benefit programs sponsored by some governments. These programs provide for the deduction of certain educational expenses from either pretax income or from actual taxes. These tax deduction or tax credit programs are a way of providing assistance independent of financial need, academic ability, or other criteria. In cases where income tax programs are progressive, tax benefit programs distribute a greater return to high-income families or individuals than they do to low-income families or individuals. This regressiveness of tax reduction programs has limited their appeal.

Overview

There is a wide variety of means available to finance higher education. They vary from providing resources to institutions to providing resources to individuals. Each form has different implications in terms of cost to the funders, expected effectiveness in terms of individual and institutional behavior, the degree of congruity between funding objectives and resulting behaviors of individuals and institutions, and the perceived needs of the economy and the society of the sponsoring nation. What is often overlooked is that financing is a means of creating incentives for institutional and individual behavior. Each financing system becomes a system that rewards certain kinds of behavior and not others.

Financing systems often lead to very unintended consequences, such as rapidly expanding facilities to provide education in the sciences during a time when additional scientists are not needed in a society. Rational individual and institutional behavior may not be socially rational or constructive for society at large. The major challenge to funders is to provide financial assistance to higher education in such a way that the incentives created by the financing program are consistent with the objectives of the funders and the consequences of the individual and institutional programs. The purposes and objectives of funders differ widely among states and nations. Therefore, the forms of finance should differ from funder to funder and should reflect their best estimate of the most appropriate and efficacious means of accomplishing their objectives.

Note: Detailed discussion of the financing of higher education in each nation will be found in the articles describing these national systems of higher education. Facts and statistical data pertaining to the nations cited herein are based on research of contributing authors and other research conducted under the auspices of the *International Encyclopedia of Higher Education.* These materials are now on file at the Center for International Higher Education Documentation at Northeastern University, Boston, Massachusetts.

Bibliography

Carnegie Commission on Higher Education. *Higher Education: Who Pays? Who Benefits? Who Should Pay?* New York: McGraw-Hill, 1973.

National Commission on the Financing of Postsecondary Education. *Financing Postsecondary Education in the United States.* Washington, D.C.: U.S. Government Printing Office, 1973.

Whitehead, J. S. *The Separation of College and State.* New Haven, Connecticut: Yale University Press, 1973.

Zymelman, M. *Financing and Efficiency in Education.* Boston: Nimrod Press, 1973.

GEORGE B. WEATHERSBY

See also: Financial Affairs; Financial Aid.

2. UNIVERSITY GRANTS COMMITTEES

The University Grants Committee (UGC) in Great Britain, established by the issue of a Treasury Minute in July 1919, served as the model for similar organizations—established for basically the same reason but with local variations in purpose and organization—in Australia, New Zealand, India, Pakistan, Bangladesh, and Israel. The UGC in Great Britain was given the task of advising the government on the financial needs of the universities. Its terms of reference were extended in 1946, and today they read: "To enquire into the financial needs of university education in Great Britain; to advise the government as to the application of any grants made by parliament toward meeting them; to collect, examine, and make available information relating to university education throughout the United Kingdom; and to assist, in consultation with the universities and other bodies concerned, the preparation and execution of such plans for the development of the universities as may from time to time be required in order to ensure that they are fully adequate to national needs."

In Australia the grants committee has been known as the Australian Universities Commission. In 1975, however, plans were submitted to the Australian parliament for legislation designed to create a new Tertiary Education Commission, which would combine the functions of the Universities Commission and the Commission on Advanced Education. Details of the proposed merger have been set forth in an unpublished "Report of the Panel to Advise on Arrangements for Amalgamating the Universities Commission and the Commission on Advanced Education"; action on the matter was "tabled" by parliament in 1976.

In New Zealand the University Grants Committee is an independent statutory body, which advises the government on the universities' current spending and capital works. The sum the government votes for expenditure on university education is apportioned to each of the six universities by the UGC. The universities receive quinquennial (five-year) grants for current operating costs; they then deploy the funds as they see fit. Salary scales for academic staff, however, are determined by the UGC and apply to all universities, while the individual university determines the academic status appropriate for each staff member.

The five-year planning period seems to lessen the risk of political control and, despite disadvantages, has for a decade of expansion been an acceptable system of financing and control.

The University Grants Committee in India at present is an academic, administrative, and grant-giving body consisting of a chairman, a vice-chairman, and twelve members. In consultation with the universities and other bodies concerned, the committee can take all steps it thinks proper for the promotion and coordination of university education and for the determination and maintenance of standards of teaching, examination, and research in universities. Thus, the UGC can inspect any department to ascertain financial needs and to recommend action to be taken; it can recommend measures necessary for improvement of education in any university and has the power to withhold funds if any university fails to comply with its recommendations in a reasonable time; it can also refuse grants to any university that is established without its previous approval and the approval of the central government.

In Pakistan the University Grants Commission assists the federal Ministry of Education in planning and executing educational policies. The UGC, as envisioned under the Education Policy, is designed to guide and control overall university development and, as a body distinct from the national government, to protect universities from undue political interference. The committee distributes government grants to the universities, advises authorities on the establishment of new institutions or the expansion of older ones, inspects faculties and financial records, and can withdraw funds.

The University Grants Commission in Bangladesh was constituted after the country had become a sovereign state. Its activities are conducted within the framework of economic development, and it is responsible for the fundamental planning of all higher education. Eventually, the UGC will determine higher education's financial needs and allocate grants to the universities of Bangladesh. The UGC consists of a chairman, two permanent members, and two vice-chancellors, who are replaced biannually by vote of the combined university chancellors.

In Israel the Planning and Grants Committee (PGC), in consultation with the institutions, prepares budget estimates, both recurrent and developmental, on a triennial basis; allocates the approved total budget; presents plans for the development of higher education and its financing; encourages coordination, cooperation, efficiency, and economy among institutions; and collects statistics on higher education and manpower requirements. The PGC is not involved in negotiations on conditions of service or tuition fees.

The PGC has six members, including a chairman, and at least four of those members must be full professors, individually appointed. The chairman is employed full time, while the others devote one day a week to committee work. The chairman takes part in all discussions on higher education budgets at government and other relevant levels.

The composition of the PGC is a guarantee against the erosion of academic freedom, and its creation has meant greater accountability by the universities of Israel. These universities may negotiate on their budgets only with the PGC; above all, those budgets must be balanced.

The minister and the Council for Higher Education have agreed that there will be no new universities for the decade from 1974 to 1984 in Israel, so that the PGC will devote its attention to the consolidation of the existing ones.

The British Model

The British University Grants Committee, the model for others in the Commonwealth nations, is not a statutory body, and there is no legislation governing its existence. UGC members are appointed by the secretary of state for education and science, after consultation with the secretaries of state for Scotland and Wales. All members serve in an individual capacity; none is representative of any particular university, organization, or interest, although collectively their knowledge and experience cover a wide field. Only the chairman is full time. Members devote about one fifth of their time to the committee's business; otherwise they are actively engaged in their professions. At present, apart from the chairman, there are twenty full members, fourteen of whom are drawn from the universities, two from industry, and four from other sectors of education. Assessors from education departments, research councils, and other government departments, while they are represented on the committee, have no responsibility for committee decisions. Committee reports to the secretary of state for education and science are confidential.

The UGC is supported by a system of advisory subcommittees, which meet under the chairmanship of a member of the committee. Subcommittees are composed of experts, drawn largely from the universities, in the field concerned; members are appointed by the UGC. From time to time working parties are set up for a limited period to consider particular problems.

The committee and its subcommittees and working parties are served by a secretariat, which performs administrative, executive, and technical functions. The secretariat staff is provided by the Department of Education and Science but is responsible solely to the committee. The office of the committee is located at 14 Park Crescent, London W1N 4DH.

The UGC meets once a month throughout the year, except in August, and special meetings are arranged when necessary. In addition, the UGC holds a weekend conference once a year and has periodic meetings with the Committee of Vice-Chancellors and Principals and with the Association of University Teachers.

Vice-chancellors and other university officers are in constant contact with the chairman and officers of the UGC about the day-to-day problems of individual universities. The UGC, as a committee, visits each university at least once in each quinquennium. During these visits the UGC has discussions with groups of staff, students, university officials, and members of the governing bodies. No subject of interest to the university is barred from discussion, but the UGC finds it most helpful to concentrate on such matters as plans for academic development, the balance between teaching and research, teaching methods, library services, interfaculty and interdepartmental cooperation, channels of communication, relations between staff and students, and student welfare.

When on visits the UGC is sometimes asked to help secure more money for a particular purpose or to endorse a particular proposal. The committee endeavors to avoid intervening in matters that are best decided by the university itself, though the committee may draw appropriate cases to the attention of the university's governing body.

Visits are not operational, since no decisions are based on them, nor are they in any sense inspections. Visits provide an opportunity for the UGC to acquaint itself with individual university policies and problems and to exchange views in an informal atmosphere. Visits and conferences are also arranged by the UGC's advisory subcommittees, so that committee members may become better informed of developments in their particular field and thereby better advise the UGC.

UGC Grants to Universities of Great Britain

The universities of Great Britain are independent, self-governing institutions, usually established by charter. Free to conduct their own affairs, they are not subject to legislative control or ministerial directive. On the other hand, they depend on the government for the greater part of their funds. Since the normal methods of controlling government expenditure are not appropriate to university funding, some machinery had to be devised that would enable public funds to flow into the universities without direct governmental intervention and that would also reconcile the interests of the state as paymaster and the requirements of national policy with the proper academic freedom and autonomy of the universities. The machinery adopted for this purpose, and endorsed by successive governments of all parties, was the University Grants Committee.

The grant system. In 1975 the UGC grant list covered forty-three universities (thirty-four in England, one in Wales, and eight in Scotland) and two business schools. The list includes the Universities of Oxford and Cambridge, but their individual colleges are not supported by UGC grants.

After examining the universities' own estimates and proposals, the UGC periodically prepares a statement to the government of the overall financial needs of the universities. The total sums to be made available are fixed by the government, but the UGC decides how these sums are to be allocated among the individual universities. The financial assistance provided by the government to the universities through the UGC covers three broad categories of expenditure: recurrent, nonrecurrent, and equipment. The UGC is not concerned with grants to individual students or with students' union subscriptions.

Recurrent grants. Expenditures for staff salaries, departmental budgets, laboratories, libraries, and maintenance of premises are covered by recurrent grants. The total amounts are determined by the government and appropriated for periods of five years. These funds are allocated among individual universities by the UGC as annual sums (covering the academic year, from August 1 to July 31) for each year of the five-year period. The present five-year period runs from August 1, 1972, to July 31, 1977. The total amount of the five-year grant, announced in December 1972, rose through additional increments from

£295,500,000 in 1972–73 to £367,000,000 in 1976–77.

The total amount of a five-year grant is not normally increased during the period of the quinquennium, except to help meet increases in three types of costs: (1) costs resulting from major changes in government policy (for example, changes in the desired rate of expansion in student numbers); (2) costs resulting from government-approved increases in academic salary scales; (3) costs resulting from rises in prices that, on the basis of an index of university costs, are accepted by the government after considering representations submitted periodically by the UGC. Special grants are made by the government (outside of the recurrent grant settlement) to cover universities' liability for rates (tax obligations), which total about £13,500,000 annually.

Nonrecurrent grants. Nonrecurrent grants exist for four specific purposes: the financing of approved building work, the purchase of sites and properties, the payment of professional fees, and the furnishing of buildings not covered by the new furniture/equipment grant. The financing of building work receives by far the greatest annual expenditure and also largely determines the requirements of the other three grant purposes. The government fixes the total value of grant-aided building work that may be started within a given financial year (beginning on April 1). The distribution of university building programs within the total is decided by the UGC, which is also responsible for controlling standards and costs.

Furniture/equipment grants. A new system for awarding grants for the purchase of equipment for teaching and research came into operation on April 1, 1968. Previously, grants had been available only for the initial equipping of new accommodations; universities were required to provide for the replacement and renewal of equipment from their recurrent income. Under the new system each university was provided with a fixed annual sum for a specific period of years—a sum based primarily on the number of students in the university—to cover both the initial equipping of new buildings and the replacement of existing equipment. From the beginning of the 1973–74 academic year, these grants were combined with a new system of furniture grants. Universities are free to accumulate the money in a furniture/equipment fund and to deploy it as they think best, both on the replacement of furniture and equipment in existing buildings and on the initial provision for new buildings.

Planning of University Development in Great Britain

In assessing the financial needs of the universities, the UGC takes into account the plans put forward by the individual universities themselves, the demand from students for university places, national needs for qualified graduates, and the likely availability of resources. The UGC therefore must pay close attention to the pattern of the future size and balance of the universities, both in terms of student numbers and in terms of available resources. It is the UGC's responsibility to formulate a broad central strategy of development for the universities as a whole and for each university within that whole. Planning university development involves the UGC in close and continuing dialogues with the government and with the universities, both individually and collectively (through the Committee of Vice-Chancellors and Principals), in the collection and analysis of a wide range of statistics about university numbers and costs.

Such collaboration is also designed to give the universities as clear and positive an indication as possible about the pattern of development envisaged. In allocating recurrent grants for the 1972–1977 quinquennium, for example, the UGC gave each university (1) a statement of the student numbers (distinguished between undergraduates and postgraduates and between arts-based and science-based students) on which the grant for 1972–1977 had been calculated; (2) a memorandum

of general guidance on university development in the five-year period, and (3) comments on proposals put forward by the individual university that the UGC wished particularly to encourage or discourage.

University budgetary autonomy. Recurrent grants are given, in the main, as annual block grants without strings. Each university determines the internal disposition of its grant as a matter of its own budgetary autonomy. This block grant principle is regarded as necessary to ensure a proper degree of freedom to universities in the conduct of their academic affairs and to avoid the management of the universities by the UGC. No attempt is made to lay down in detail how much of a university's grant should be spent on teaching or research or on a particular department or activity. Grants earmarked for special purposes are occasionally made in order to stimulate a particular development, but such grants are incorporated in the block grants as soon as possible.

The freedom of discretion afforded to universities by the block grant principle is qualified, in practice, by convention. Universities understand that it is the UGC's business to set the general strategy and that, while they are free to plan their own development in the light of their own particular circumstances, they have a responsibility to exercise this freedom within the framework of national needs and priorities and in the light of the guidance given to them by the UGC. This is a well-established convention and an essential part of the UGC system.

Some nonrecurrent grants are designated for specific capital projects and cannot be used for a different project without the consent of the UGC. Equipment grants, however, are block grants, and universities have full discretion to use them as they wish.

Publications. At the end of each five-year period the UGC publishes a report on university development. In addition, it publishes annually: an annual survey; a volume of statistics on university staff, students, income, and expenditures; and a volume of information about the employment or training chosen by students on attaining a first or higher degree. The UGC also issues a handbook of guidance on the procedure under which building grants are approved, entitled *Capital Grants—Notes on Procedure 1971.* Other handbooks include a 1966 volume on residential catering (the spaces and equipment required for catering facilities in residential accommodations); a 1967 volume on student residence (the planning and construction of halls of residence); and a 1972 volume on kitchen planning.

Bibliography

Atkins, M. "Why the UGC Is Failing in Its Bounden Duty." *Times (London) Higher Education Supplement,* September 20, 1974.

Australian Commission on Advanced Education. Third Report 1973–1975. Canberra, Australia: Government Printing Service, 1975.

Chaudhuri, M. A. "The Universities of Bangladesh." In *Commonwealth Universities Yearbook.* London: Association of Commonwealth Universities, 1973.

Education Policy 1972–80. Islamabad, Pakistan: Ministry of Education, 1972.

Guy, S. "Educational Credits: The Answer to the Grants Problem?" *Times (London) Higher Education Supplement,* April 26, 1974.

Misra, A. *Financing of Indian Education.* Bombay, India: Asia Publishing House, 1967.

Ormian, H. (Ed.) *Education in Israel.* Jerusalem: Ministry of Education and Culture, 1973. (In Hebrew).

Report of the University Grants Committee and University Institutions. Wellington, New Zealand: Government Printer, 1974.

Stanner, R. *The Legal Basis of Education in Israel.* Jerusalem: Ministry of Education and Culture, 1963.

Tertiary Education in Australia. 2 vols. Melbourne: Government Printer, 1964–1965.

UNESCO. *Financing of Education.* Geneva: International Bureau of Education, 1955.

United Kingdom University Grants Committee. *Second Report from the Expenditure Committee.* Session 1970–71, No. 545. London: H. M. Stationery Office, 1971.

University Grants Committee. *University Development 1962–67.* Cmnd. 3820. Quinquennial Report. London: H. M. Stationery Office, 1967.

FREDERICK DAINTON

See also: Financial Affairs; Financial Aid.

FINANCING OF HIGHER EDUCATION IN CANADA
(Higher Education Report)

Financing of Higher Education in Canada (Toronto, Ontario: University of Toronto Press, 1965) is a report of the special commission appointed by the Association of Universities and Colleges of Canada, under the chairmanship of V. Bladen. The report examines financing of Canadian higher education for the period 1965–1975 — specifically, the organization of financing, prospective financial requirements, proportion of funds contributed by various sources, policies of allocation, and criteria of eligibility for aid. The following findings and recommendations are reported.

Federal and provincial governments should provide for the expansion of higher learning and meet the immediate financial needs of the universities. The federal government and the provincial governments should annually assess federal support for higher education, and a federal minister should be designated to coordinate aid to universities with the assistance of an advisory committee representative of university faculty in all regions of the country.

Specifically, the federal government should increase per capita grants to the universities, establish a new capital grants fund, and significantly increase university research grant funds. The federal government also should improve medical education and increase tax advantages for parents of students and private corporate donors. Provincial governments should establish grants commissions, if they have not done so, and make provision for adequate research facilities. Provincial governments should resist popular pressure for abolition of fees and establish financial aid systems for undergraduate and graduate students.

Greater cooperation among the universities also is urged. Universities should explore methods of reducing costs and should appoint special student aid counseling officers. Private donors are asked to support experimental ventures designed to improve tertiary programs. Graduates, in particular, are requested to contribute 1 percent of their incomes to the universities.

FINANCING POSTSECONDARY EDUCATION IN THE UNITED STATES (Higher Education Report)

Financing Postsecondary Education in the United States (Washington, D.C.: U.S. Government Printing Office, 1973)—a report of the National Commission on the Financing of Postsecondary Education, under the chairmanship of D. Leonard—presents a framework for analyzing alternative methods of financing postsecondary education in the United States and suggests financing policies that would serve the national interest. For the purposes of this study, the commission considered postsecondary education to include all collegiate and noncollegiate institutions eligible to participate in federal programs. The report notes that the financing of these institutions will be significantly affected by social changes such as enrollment decreases in the 1980s and greater participation in postsecondary education by minorities, women, older persons, and less affluent persons. The following findings and recommendations are reported.

Policies for financing postsecondary education should be formulated to reflect the following national objectives: (1) access to an effective form of postsecondary education for each individual, (2) right of a student to select an institution regardless of personal finances, (3) fulfillment of the educational needs of all students, (4) institutional diversity sufficient to serve the needs of students and society, (5) adequate means of measuring institutional excellence, (6) institutional independence, (7) institutional accountability, and (8) adequate public and private funding for the achievement of national objectives for postsecondary education.

The commission developed a systematic approach for studying the interrelating objectives, variables, and data of postsecondary education. This analytical framework employs ten major elements: (1) objectives of postsecondary education, (2) criteria to measure objectives, (3) assumptions about society and institutions, (4) policies to accomplish the objectives, (5) financing mechanisms to carry out the policies, (6) specific financing programs, (7) data base for postsecondary education, (8) a model for estimating student and institutional responses to changes in financing, (9) measurements to describe the achievement of objectives, and (10) a review of the financing mechanisms and programs in relation to the objectives.

The commission applied its framework to study over fifty alternative financing plans, eight of which are included in the report. While the commission chose to demonstrate the usefulness of the framework rather than indicate any preference among alternative plans, it does suggest that some findings are of special significance. For example, to increase student access, aid to students is more effective than aid to institutions. Increased student aid also would result in proportionately higher enrollments in private institutions than in public, and expanded access would require increased financial assistance to institutions.

The commission recommends further development of similar frameworks and collection of significant data. The federal government is urged to develop national standard procedures for calculating costs per student and to support a national center for educational information.

FINANCING, STUDENT AID
See Financing of Higher Education: Financing of Institutions and Systems.

FINE AND APPLIED ARTS
See Arts, Fine and Applied (field of study).

FINE ARTS GALLERIES
See Art Collections, College and University.

FINLAND, NATIONAL ARCHIVES OF
See Archives: Northern Europe, National Archives of.

FINLAND, REPUBLIC OF

Population: 4,727,111. Student enrollment in primary school: 393,242; secondary school: 516,979; higher education: 67,881 (university: 65,823; nonuniversity: 2,058). Language of instruction: Finnish/Swedish. Academic calendar: September to May, two semesters. Percentage of gross national product (GNP) expended on all education: 2.5%; higher education: .68%. Percentage of national budget expended on all education: 19%; higher education: 3.5%. [Figures are for 1975-76.]

Åbo University, now the University of Helsinki, was the first institution of higher education in Finland. It was founded in 1640 on the model of the great European universities. Although literacy was quite widespread in the country—probably because the Lutheran church required a reading knowledge of the basic Christian doctrine before confirmation and marriage—no further extension of the school system or higher education took place during the next two centuries.

While Finland was under Swedish rule (1155–1809), the official language of the country was Swedish and remained so during the major portion of the period when it was a grand duchy of Russia (1809–1917). In the mid nineteenth century European Romanticism influenced a "national awakening," a period of nationalism focused on the question of a national language; and the Finnish language, which until then had existed in written form only in a Bible translation and some religious books, became well established. By 1863 a Language Edict ensured Finnish equal status with Swedish as an official language, thus offering most of the population greater educational and employment opportunities. By the 1880s the number of Finnish students equaled the number of Swedish-speaking students at the University of Helsinki. Finnish is now the language of some 95 percent of the population, while Swedish has the status of a second national language.

The "national awakening" eventually led to a vigorous expansion of the educational system, including higher education. During the first two decades of the twentieth century, while Finland was still ruled by the Russian czar, one full university, a technological university, and two schools of economics and business administration were founded. By 1920, 3600 students were enrolled in higher education institutions, but after independence the numbers increased relatively slowly. By 1940, 9200 students were enrolled in higher education institutions. In the next two decades enrollments increased by about five thousand per decade. In the 1960s, however, a second expansion of higher education occurred, and the number of students began to increase by some five thousand per year.

To accommodate the growing enrollment, an expansion of facilities and better geographical distribution of students became necessary. Thus, during the 1960s a regionalization of facilities, which would permit better student distribution, was begun. Until the 1950s some 90 percent of all students had been enrolled in Helsinki, the capital in the southern part of the country; but by the end of the 1970s it is expected that less than 60 percent of students will study there. During the period 1960 to 1970 seven new institutions were opened—four new universities, one school of economics, and two technological universities—all located in areas that previously had lacked institutions of higher education.

Changes were also occurring at the lower levels of the educational system. A new nine-year comprehensive school was developed, which would profoundly affect the development of higher education; at the same time, there was a great increase in student population at the secondary level. Both of these factors necessitated careful long-term planning. Based on forecasts of the demand for labor in various fields, an overall plan, Act on the Development of the System of Higher Education, was passed by parliament for the period 1967–1981. It provided a framework for the development of higher education within which more precise plans could be drawn up. Thus, the Finnish system of higher education has begun to develop in a direction carefully charted according to national manpower demands.

National Educational Policy

Education in Finland is structured to develop a harmonious individual valuing democracy and humanism. All citizens are to be given education commensurate with their ability, while the system is expected to fulfill the need of society for educated manpower.

Legal Basis of Educational System

Laws promulgated in the 1970s, which provide the current legal basis of higher education, can be divided into four categories: (1) decrees relevant to the nationalization of higher education institutions; (2) decrees pertaining to the reorganization of teacher training; (3) decrees reorganizing the National Council for Higher Education; (4) decrees regulating law and medical degrees, and cabinet decisions (which are equivalent to decrees) on the reform of degrees in higher education.

Laws relevant to nationalization of higher education institutions include the decree of July 31, 1974, which provided for a temporary administration at the nationalized universities of Tampere and Turku and at the Helsinki School of Economics. Teacher training reform is based on the law of 1971. According to this law, teacher training is the province of the Ministry of Education's Department for Higher Education and Research. The reform considers other organizational

changes in teacher training and also the educational content of training. The National Council for Higher Education was reformed by a decree of September 20, 1974. A decree on law degrees was issued in 1974 and a decree on medical degrees in 1975. The cabinet's decision covering the reform of basic degrees in higher education was issued on December 19, 1974.

Types of Institutions

In Finland the term *higher education institution* refers to institutions where higher scientific and professional education is provided, where both teaching and research are undertaken, and where studies extend to the doctorate. Thus, the seventeen Finnish institutions of higher education can be grouped as follows: (1) eight full universities: those of Helsinki (1640), Joensuu (1969), Jyväskylä (1966), Kuopio (1966), Oulu (1959), Tampere (1966), Turku (1920), and *Åbo akademi* (1917); (2) three universities of technology: Helsinki (1908), Lappeenranta (1969), and Tampere (1965); (3) five schools of economics and business administration: the Helsinki School of Economics and Business Administration (1911), the Swedish School of Economics and Business Administration in Helsinki (1909), the Swedish University School of Economics and Business Administration of *Åbo akademi* (1927), the Turku School of Economics and Business Administration (1949), and the Vaasa School of Economics and Business Administration (1968); and (4) the College of Veterinary Medicine in Helsinki (1945). Of these seventeen institutions thirteen are state owned; the remainder are private but receive state subsidies amounting to 70 to 90 percent of operating costs.

Also, there are a number of institutions that can be classified as higher education institutions because they generally require a completed secondary school program for admission, although they do not offer degrees and thus are not at the university level. Among these institutions are the technical institutes, which train nondiploma engineers in a program lasting three to four years; the military, naval, and air force academies; the schools for health personnel such as nurses, physiotherapists, and medical technicians; the Sibelius Academy for musical training; the four language institutes for interpreters and translators; the Helsinki College of Advanced Secretarial Training; the Swedish School of Social Sciences and Local Administration in Helsinki; the School of Theatrical Arts; and the Institute of Pictorial Art and Industrial Design.

Since 1974 all teacher training has been undertaken at the university level. Adult education is an important aspect of education in Finland and has been a part of university activities since the 1930s. Training for adult education instructors was started in 1927 at the School of Social Sciences, now the University of Tampere, where a professorship in adult education was established in 1945. The university's Institute of Adult Education carries out research and teaching. Special programs are conducted in summer universities (there are no formal university programs in the summer) and provide numerous courses and seminars to all adults, regardless of educational background, who wish to attend. Adult education, as part of the lifelong process of education, has been assuming a new dimension in recent educational planning.

Relationship with Secondary Education

A thorough reform of the lower levels of the educational system has been under way for some time. The reform would create an "open" system, whereby students would no longer be segregated, at the age of eleven, into academic and vocational programs. The system, which will be operational throughout the country by 1980, consists of nine-year compulsory comprehensive schooling for students age seven to sixteen. An important aspect of the new system is the inclusion of two obligatory foreign languages in the curriculum. Depending on the parents' choice, students may attend either Swedish- or Finnish-language schools but must study the other national language and English.

The upper secondary school *(lukio/gymnasium)* lasts three years and culminates in the matriculation examination, which has generally been the prerequisite for admission to higher study. Students in some secondary schools, which are not yet administered by municipalities, are required to pay a modest fee and supply their own equipment and transportation. However, a number of "free places" are available to students with limited means. Students at this level are also eligible for study loans and grants.

In 1972 the right to participate in the matriculation examination was extended to students who had not attended the upper secondary school but had graduated from technical or commercial institutes.

Admission Requirements

The matriculation certificate (passing levels in a comprehensive school-leaving examination in four obligatory and one or two optional subjects) and a leaving certificate from the upper secondary school have been the usual entrance requirements to university-level institutions. However, a *numerus clausus* (closed number), or restricted admission, has been instituted in practically all faculties. With the exception of those students with the highest marks on the matriculation examination, who are guaranteed admission without an entrance examination to some faculties, all applicants are required to pass an entrance examination.

More open access was called for in the 1971 Act on Matriculation, which advocated admitting candidates without the matriculation certificate but with a diploma from a lower technical, commercial, or nursing institute. A quota of 5-15 percent of admissions is set aside for such students. Admission standards for university-level entry are part of the current debate on educational reform.

Some of the nonuniversity institutions

of higher education—such as the higher technical institutes, the Swedish School of Social Sciences and Local Administration, and the institutes for health personnel—require various periods of practical experience for admission in addition to the matriculation examination.

Administration and Control

The system of higher education in Finland is highly centralized. The Ministry of Education is in charge of overall planning and development of education and prepares budget proposals and laws for consideration by the cabinet and the parliament. The central organ responsible for administration of higher education at the ministry is the Department of Higher Education and Research, which since 1974 has had six sections: administration, higher education, scientific affairs, teacher training, construction, and planning of higher education and research. By virtue of its funding powers, parliament may make amendments and recommendations to proposals. The statutes for the state universities are given by a presidential decree, while those for private universities are confirmed by the cabinet. The president also appoints the professors for the state institutions and the chairmen of important educational bodies. The state exercises supervision over private institutions through budget appropriations. No direct influence can be exerted on matters such as course contents and research; the state grants, however, ensure that the general principles and the standards of the state institutions prevail.

Permanent bodies and ad hoc committees advise the Ministry of Education. Among these, the National Council for Higher Education, established in 1966, considers the problems of planning and development and the overall long-term needs of the nation and makes proposals accordingly. The council consists of ten members acquainted with problems of higher education who are appointed by the cabinet for a three-year period. Each

of the members has a personal alternate. The cabinet also appoints the chairman and the vice-chairman from among the council members. A Science Policy Council advises the cabinet and the ministries in matters concerning scientific research and education.

The highest administrative authority at the University of Helsinki is the chancellor. He approves the annual curriculum, is generally responsible for the well-being of the university, and appoints administrators and teachers. The chancellor of the University of Helsinki is appointed by the president of the republic from three candidates nominated by the professors and associate professors, while in the private institutions the chancellor is elected by a special collegiate body or the university council. The chief executive of all the universities is the rector, who is assisted in administrative matters by one or two vice-rectors or by an administrative director. The rector is elected from among the professors. The highest governing body, the university council, is composed of all ordinary professors and considers all university matters of major importance. The administrative council is the main administrative body. It consists of the rector, vice-rectors, and deans and vice-deans of faculties or, when applicable, department heads. In addition to university councils, the private universities have administrative bodies which include non-university members and which make decisions in fiscal matters.

The full universities are further divided into faculties and subdivided into institutions, while the universities of technology are divided into departments. The faculty, which consists of all professors within the faculty, is the main unit of administration. It is relatively independent in areas such as appointments, examination structure, and the assessment of work submitted for approval. The authority of the institutes extends to matters of teaching and research content and to the recruitment of junior teaching staff. The external relations of these units are largely unregulated: institutes make their own decisions, more or less independently, on research collaboration with units outside the higher education establishment.

The universities established in the 1960s and the newly nationalized institutions have a different type of administration. The cabinet nominates the highest administrative body, the university council. One third of the council's members are professors and associate professors; one third are other university personnel; and one third are students. The university council nominates the rector and the faculty and department councils. These councils are structured according to the same principle as the university council.

The private schools of economics and business administration are headed by a board of trustees and a governing council, composed of members of the business community and the rector and vice-rector, ex officio.

Programs and Degrees

The universities offer programs in faculties, the numbers of which vary among the eight universities. The University of Helsinki has seven faculties: agriculture and forestry, law, medicine, humanities, mathematics and natural sciences, social sciences, and theology. The University of Tampere has four faculties offering professionally oriented courses in social sciences, humanities, economics and business administration, and medicine, with special sections in social work and public administration. The programs offered at the eight universities cover the range of study generally available in other industrialized nations and lead to two kinds of degrees: first degrees and postgraduate degrees.

The first degree is the *kandidaatti/kandidat,* generally preceded by the name of the faculty; for example, *fil. kand.* (candidate of philosophy). This degree can be achieved at one of two levels: at the lower level it requires two and a half to four years of study and can be considered roughly equivalent to a Bachelor of Arts degree; at the higher level it requires four to six years of study and is comparable to a Master of Arts. The honorary title *maisteri/magister* is granted to persons who receive the higher first degree.

The university programs are structured in a three-stage system: the *approbatur, cum laude,* and *laudatur* stages. *Approbatur* requires general knowledge of a group of subjects, as evidenced by successful completion of a comprehensive final examination; the *cum laude* stage requires a more extensive knowledge of the subject, again culminating in a comprehensive final examination, written and oral; while *laudatur* indicates mastery of the subjects. Candidates for the lower first degree must study three subjects and achieve *cum laude* in two of them and *approbatur* in one; for the higher first degree, the *laudatur* and a thesis in the major subject as well as *cum laude* in two minor subjects are required.

The postgraduate degree, *lisensiaatti/licensiat,* takes another two to four years of study and requires a *lisensiaatti* examination, as well as a thesis, in the major subject and a *laudatur* thesis in the minor subject. A thesis, but no course work, is required for the doctorate, which is awarded with a mention of faculty; *metsätieteen tohtori* (Doctor of Forestry) is an example.

The universities of technology, the schools of economics and business administration, and the College of Veterinary Medicine offer professional education leading to degrees such as a Master of Science in Engineering and Bachelor of Economic Sciences. Graduates from the other schools of higher education receive titles which differ from the higher titles awarded at the universities and technical universities.

Financing

In the 1970s, approximately 18 percent of the Finnish national budget has been allocated to education and culture. The share of the total educational budget allocated to higher education has approximated 16 percent (*Educational Development,* 1975, p. 66). The state budget is the largest single source of revenue for all higher education institutions; in the private universities the state support ranges between 70 and 90 percent of their budgets.

Government investment in higher education increased rapidly during the early 1970s: from 274,000,000 marks in 1970 to 898,000,000 in 1976 (1976 state budget proposal). During the remainder of the 1970s, increase in expenditure for higher education is expected to average 12 to 13 percent per year, because of the transferral of all teacher training facilities to the universities and the transfer of some private institutions to state ownership.

Student Financial Aid

According to the Education Act of July 1972, there are two forms of financial support for students: grants and low-interest loans with a state guarantee. Part of the interest is paid by the student, part by the government. In 1974–75 nearly 84,000 students received grants, and 124,000 had low-interest loans (these figures also include students in vocational institutions). Qualifications for grants are based on the income and property of the applicant and the applicant's spouse or, if the student is supported by parents, the income and property of the parents. For state-guaranteed loans the financial means of the student's parents are not considered. The trend is toward more grants, particularly in the secondary-level vocational sector.

In addition to financial supports, students enjoy indirect support in the form of housing, health care, and other social services. Most of these services are financed by the student organizations with government assistance.

Student Social Background and Access to Education

Since World War II attempts have been made to remove economic, social, and regional barriers to study opportunities by improving the economic aid extended by society to students. Planning and research in this area have been directed by the State Centre for Aid to Education, which in 1973 published a new program of development. These efforts have led to an estimated student enrollment of about one third of students from the highest social groups, another third from the middle-income strata, and a final third from families where the father is a skilled or unskilled worker or a farmer.

The percentage of female enrollment at the universities is one of the highest in the world, fluctuating between some 49 and 51 percent of each entering group. As in most other countries, a preponderance of female students can be found in the humanities, while only some 5 percent attend technical universities.

The Finnish student unions are active in politics and participate in many ways in the planning of new government educational policy. As in the other Nordic countries, student organizations have assumed a large part of the responsibility for many social services, such as housing and health care. The student organizations are financially independent of the universities, and dues are paid by every student on registering. Housing for students is built by student organizations or by foundations established by the organizations. Since the mid 1960s the government has supported this activity financially through the National Board of Housing, which grants loans to the student organizations for the construction of housing. The Foundation of Student Housing in the Greater Helsinki Area, established in 1969, has set a goal of one thousand new housing units per year for students during the period 1972–1981.

Medical care has been provided through the Foundation for the Medical Care of University Students; but, because of financial restrictions, problems have been encountered. Following the recommendations of a 1971 study group on student health, the government is assuming greater responsibility for student health and, in accordance with the National Health Act of 1972, will integrate student health facilities into the national health service. A special Students Health Service Council will be appointed to assist the National Medical Board.

Teaching Staff

Members of the teaching staff in the institutions of higher learning are ranked as professors, associate professors, *dosentit,* (special professors), lecturers and instructors, and assistants and special teachers. Professors at the state institutions are generally appointed by the president of the republic after being nominated by the faculty. The other ranks of teaching staff are nominated by the faculty or department and appointed by the rector's office or equivalent administrative organ. In the private institutions, professors are nominated and appointed by the head of the institution. Professors and associate professors receive permanent appointment, while lecturers and instructors usually are appointed for terms of three or five years.

The general prerequisite for appointment as professor or associate professor is the doctoral degree (except at the technical universities); if the appointment includes teaching duties, proof of teaching skill also is required but is generally not a significant criterion. The major criteria are previous experience, competence, and published research. Lecturers and instructors must have the licentiate degree or must have taken a qualifying examination for appointment to public office. When the appointment calls for teaching duties, teaching experience is required. The special professors *(dosentit)* have a special status. Their appointment is honorary and calls for only part-time teaching.

Research Activities

The major bodies carrying out research in Finland are the institutions of higher education, the forty state research institutes, and private enterprise. The state research institutes concentrate on applied research, product development, and control and testing; their tasks are specified by law. Business enterprises spend most of their funding on applied and developmental research.

General science policy planning is the responsibility of the Science Policy Council; it evaluates the ministries' proposals for research development and then submits the proposals to the government for action. Members of the council are ministers, the chairmen of the National Council on Higher Education and the Central Board of Research Councils (Academy of Finland), and five additional persons appointed by the government. The prime minister serves as chairman of the council.

The cabinet makes decisions on research by its power to allocate resources. It determines the amount of funds to be given to the Academy of Finland and the distribution of research posts.

The Academy of Finland is the central body for research administration and operates under the authority of the Ministry of Education. The academy consists of a central board, six research councils, and an administrative office. Its research activities are pursued in institutions of higher education, which in Finland are the major centers for conducting basic research. Responsibility for basic research thus falls to the Ministry of Education, to which all institutions of higher education are subordinated, while the administration of applied research belongs to the appropriate ministries. The main organization in the field of educational research is the Institute for Educational Research at the University of Jyväskylä.

A total of 1 percent of the gross national product is spent on all research in Finland; 45 percent is spent by private enterprise, 49 percent by the government, and various other sources contribute the remaining 6 percent.

Current Problems and Trends

By government plans, a minimum of 60,000 student places should be available in Finland by the end of 1981. However, enrollments had already increased to 65,000 students by 1975, so that projections for the 1980s had to be increased to 75,000, although a subsequent leveling off based on population trends is anticipated. The major issues confronting the planners in the mid 1970s are (1) reform of the internal administration of the institutions of higher education; (2) changes in admission procedures; (3) a reform of the system of degree examinations, to be implemented in all major fields of higher education; and (4) university-level teacher training.

The basis of the reform plans for internal administration is democratization of education, which means implementing the principle of equality of opportunity for all by diminishing the social disparities in access to education and allowing teachers, students, and nonteaching staff members to participate in defining the goals and planning the activities of the institution. In 1968 the cabinet appointed a committee to reform the internal administration of the institutions of higher education. The ideas presented by the committee in 1969 were elaborated by the Ministry of Education, and a proposal for a law was submitted to parliament in December 1969. The proposal was rejected—largely because of the "one individual–one vote" principle, which was to be applied in all institutions of higher education and which would allow all members of an institution to participate in decision making. After several revisions and additional preparation, a new version of the bill—leaving the main principles untouched—was submitted to parliament in June 1972. This bill was also rejected, but by 1976 negotiations were continuing.

A change in admission procedures has focused on a centralized system of admissions, which would mean standardizing admission criteria and unifying selection procedures in the various fields of study and in different institutions of higher education. In February 1972 an Examina-

tion Planning Committee was appointed by the Ministry of Education to consider the transfer from the secondary to the postsecondary level and to redefine the role of the secondary school-leaving certificate and entrance examinations as admission criteria.

The effort to reform degree examinations reflects the change in thinking of the 1970s. In the 1960s the quantitative and organizational aspects of higher education were the central issues, but in the mid 1970s the quality of education is demanding attention. The proposed changes in degree examinations have generated considerable discussion in terms of their level, content, and relationship to the ultimate goals of education, while a suggested reform of the structure of studies and examinations—adopting a credit-point system—also has met with resistance. In 1969 the Ministry of Education appointed a committee to prepare a reform of examinations in the faculties of philosophy and social sciences. The committee report (FYTT report) was issued in 1972. For the present, it is the most comprehensive study on the development of higher education. As a result of the report's recommendations, plans are under way to change examination structures at the Finnish institutions of higher education. Thus far, new decrees have been issued on the degree examinations in law (October 18, 1974) and in medicine (September 26, 1975). The decrees will enter into force in 1977 and 1978.

In the FYTT report, a degree program is defined as an educational program of goal-oriented learning processes within one or several educational units (a discipline or similar cluster of subjects). Reforms would change the educational programs, which consist of fairly rigid course combinations and examinations, to educational degree programs consisting of a set of learning periods, or modules, devoted to goal-oriented learning, study, research, and similar activities. The educational programs or their subunits would be categorized on the basis of time required to complete the program; a week or a year may be used as a unit.

The FYTT report favors the idea of one basic degree in all subjects. This could be achieved after four years of full-time studies in a proper learning environment and in circumstances where the quantity and quality of the teaching staff and the necessary equipment are of a required standard. The basic degree program would implement a polytechnic education model, which combines scientific and theoretical studies with employment-oriented training and promotes a critical and multidisciplinary approach toward educational content and the problems of society in general.

Educational content has been classified in three main categories: general education, subject-centered studies, and specialization. The proposed reform is extensive and interrelated with other problems of the development of the system of higher education. For the time being, the reform of degree examinations is based on the decision passed by the cabinet on December 19, 1974; the decision was based on the FYTT report. According to the decision, the new degree examinations will be gradually introduced in the late 1970s, so that in 1978 all new university students will pursue studies that reflect the new educational programs. The faculty of social sciences at the University of Jyväskylä was the first faculty to implement the reform of degree examinations. Students who enrolled in the autumn of 1975 are following the new system.

According to the Teacher Training Act of 1971, the basic education of teachers consists of the studies that are necessary to qualify for a teaching position; further training increases the teacher's qualifications to perform the various tasks in the school system. The new system calls for teacher training units to be established in seven universities or institutions of higher education. Further training for teachers will also be provided by the central state offices subordinated to the Ministry of Education. This reform makes teacher training more homogeneous. In addition, teachers of the lower level and teachers of vocational subjects will receive a diploma based on a four-year program of study at an institution of higher education. The program of study may be pursued intermittently. Emphasis has been put on further training, and new forms of further training for teachers are being developed largely because of the change to a comprehensive school system.

TAPIO RAJAVUORI

Educational Associations

Korkeakoulujen ja opetusalan henkilökuntaliitto
Union of University Teachers and Personnel
Fabianinkatu 28E
SF-00100 Helsinki 10, Finland

Suomen ylioppilaskuntien liitto
National Union of Finnish Students
Opastinsilta 10B
SF-00520 Helsinki 52, Finland

Bibliography

The Admission and Academic Placement of Students from Nordic Countries. A Workshop Report. Washington, D.C.: National Association for Foreign Student Affairs and American Association of College Registrars and Admissions Officers, 1974.

Comprehensive School in Finland: Goals and an Outline for Curriculum. Reference Publications 5. Helsinki: Ministry of Education, 1971.

Educational Development in Finland 1973–1975. Reference Publications 7. Helsinki: Ministry of Education, 1975.

Educational Reform in Finland in the 1970's. Reference Publications 4. Helsinki: Ministry of Education, 1970.

Higher Education and Research in Finland. Reference Publications 6. Helsinki: Ministry of Education, 1973.

See also: Academic Dress and Insignia; Adult Education: Role of Labor and Industry; Archives: Northern Europe, National Archives of; Research: Financing and Control of Research; Science Policies: Highly Industrialized Nations: Western Europe.

FINNISH COUNCIL OF UNIVERSITY RECTORS
(Suomen korkeakoulujen rehtorien neuvosto/Finlands högskolerektorers råd)

The Finnish Council of University Rectors is an association for cooperation among rectors of Finnish universities and equivalent institutions. The council makes recommendations and renders opinions on topics and issues concerning university government, research, and academic life in Finland. Membership is open to rectors of Finnish universities or equivalent institutions approved by the council. In 1975 seventeen rectors were council members. Vice-rectors are normally deputy members. If a university has more than ten thousand students, however, its vice-rector serves as an ordinary, but nonvoting, member. Every member of the council or his deputy has one vote. Decisions are taken by a majority vote. A member who does not participate in a decision is not bound by it.

The council meets in September to elect a president, a vice-president, an executive committee, and two auditors. The executive committee consists of the president, the vice-president, and three other members elected by the council among its members. The executive committee prepares the questions to be discussed at the meetings of the council, implements council decisions, represents the council when necessary, and supervises the work of the bureau. The bureau consists of a secretary general and staff members. The secretary general, appointed by the council, is secretary of the council and the executive committee and directs the bureau.

The expenses of the council are covered by contributions paid by each university according to size. The executive committee and the secretary general are responsible for implementing the budget.

University of Helsinki

Fabianinkatu 33

Helsinki 17, Finland

FISHERIES SCIENCE
(Field of Study)

Fisheries science, in the broad sense, is the study of exploited aquatic animal resources for the purpose of generating an increased benefit to man. The science concerns itself with the nature of the resource (generally a population of fin fish but also other aquatic vertebrates and invertebrates) and the nature of the exploitation process. Historically, fisheries, the occupation of catching fish, has taken two distinct and contrasting forms, determined principally by the ownership of the resource: exploitation of wild stocks, in cases of common property resources; and harvest of cultured, privately owned captive stocks. The former represents a specialized form of hunting; the latter, a form of production agriculture. Fisheries science has also diverged into distinct areas of commercial and recreational (sport) fisheries. Emphasis on these areas varies greatly around the world, with recreational fisheries playing a more significant role in the developed nations. Nevertheless, local interest in sport fisheries and the economic impact of tourism have led to the development of recreational fisheries in numerous developing countries.

Fisheries and aquaculture, fields traditionally based on biology, were among the earliest-known agricultural activities of man. During the nineteenth century, however, ichthyology—the study of fishes—emerged as a field recognizably distinct from biology. Because fishes constitute the largest and most diverse group of vertebrates, ichthyologists faced the enormous task of classifying fishes into taxonomic groups. Consequently, early ichthyologists concentrated mostly on systematics and natural history of fishes. The applied field of fisheries biology emerged in the early twentieth century, and ichthyologists were called upon for answers to management questions. Simultaneous development of the closely allied fields of limnology and oceanography, often at the same facilities or institutions having fisheries biologists, contributed substantially to the understanding of the biological, chemical, and physical aspects of aquatic ecosystems needed to approach management scientifically.

Although fisheries biologists were scattered in a variety of university departments, university programs in fisheries biology began in North America with the establishment of a College of Fisheries at the University of Washington, in Seattle, in 1919 and the Ontario Fisheries Research Laboratory at the University of Toronto in 1920. Aquaculture developed as an academic discipline at Auburn University, in Alabama, in the 1930s and led to the establishment of the Department of Fisheries and Allied Aquacultures at that institution. Simultaneously, programs developed in the Soviet Union, where several universities and some of the institutes of the Academy of Science became involved in studies of fisheries science and concentrated on the biological aspects of fisheries as well.

As qualitative knowledge became available, the science turned toward quantitative analyses, particularly those descriptive of populations and their responses to fishing. By the mid twentieth century, mathematical models of fish populations and particularly yield models were formulated to predict the effects of fishing and of variations in fish population parameters on yield to the fishery. Modeling eventually moved in two separate directions: ecosystem models were developed to predict, analyze, and evaluate effects of environmental changes; and yield models were expanded from the concept of maximum sustainable yield, based on biology, to that of optimum sustained yield, based on economics and overall quality of the yield measured in benefits to man.

Because requirements and responses of the individul organism, as well as those of the population, needed to be understood, the sciences of physiology and ecology be-

came important in fisheries science. Knowledge of the physiological requirements of organisms throughout their entire life cycles allowed fish to be maintained in confinement. Consequently, fish of known genetic and ecological history became available for experimentation and culture. Selective breeding then led to development of standardized strains of certain species. Emphasis on ecological requirements also became important in the evaluation of effects of environmental degradations. Changes in aquatic biota had long been recognized as indicators of pollution, and fish developed as major test organisms in laboratory studies.

Because of the interactions between studies of the resource and of the overall harvest process, interdisciplinary approaches have become fundamental to fisheries science. Fisheries agencies and educational institutions have developed staffs which integrate biology, environmental sciences, seafood technology, economics, marketing, sociology, and law. The international nature of exploitative fisheries has produced similar impetus. As nearly all marine fishery resources have become overexploited by multinational fisheries, analyses of management alternatives based on international and interdisciplinary studies have become imperative, in spite of the complexity of the system. Recent Law of the Sea Conference negotiations have emphasized the interactions of fisheries management with coastal energy developments, marine commerce, and other seemingly unrelated activities. Unilateral extension of territorial limits (coastal economic zones) by several nations may eventually lead to decreased complexity in the overall system, and consequently less international and interdisciplinary concern for fisheries science. However, in the mid 1970s the novelty and nonuniformity of the territorial extensions are requiring greater sociological, political, and economic inputs than ever before.

In the area of aquaculture similar interdisciplinary approaches occur. For example, in the developed nations emphasis on high-value fishes, generally those in relatively short natural supply, causes the industry to be subject to effects of variations in consumer demands, related to the state of the economy. In contrast, developing nations have promoted intensive production of easily cultured, high-protein fishes, which often have little value on the worldwide food market. Consequently, major concerns in such nations have been efficient production, product technology, shipping, and marketing.

Educational programs in fisheries science have taken various forms, depending upon the nations and the institutions involved. Throughout most of the world, formal education in universities is combined with education of the public through extension programs.

In the United States and Canada, established university curricula are available in most states and provinces. The programs generally are offered in departments of fisheries, fish and wildlife, natural resources, or biology. Undergraduate education, most often based on a strong biology foundation, usually must be supplemented with postbaccalaureate training for employment as a professional. Education of the general public, particularly in the United States, is carried out through county agricultural extension programs, which are part of the land-grant university system. Significant impetus to interdisciplinary efforts in research, teaching, and extension in the United States has been provided by the Sea Grant Program, another cooperative federal-state-university effort.

In the United Kingdom strong fisheries education programs have developed at several universities. Emphasis in these programs is primarily biologically oriented. Similar programs have developed in Australia and New Zealand and in most Western and Northern European countries, where emphasis has included aquatic biology and limnology.

In the Soviet Union and other Eastern European nations, biological information

has been complemented by a strong emphasis on food technology. Major contributions to the development of principles of fisheries science have been made possible through programs in universities of the Soviet Union.

In the Middle East dependence upon intensive fish culture in Israel has led to the establishment of strong university programs in aquaculture. Emphasis on nutrition, genetics, selective breeding, disease prevention and control, and polyculture (multispecies aquaculture) has led to highly efficient production systems. In the rest of Asia fisheries education programs are somewhat less developed, in spite of the major contribution to aquacultural production by Southeast Asia and the Far East. In Africa limited educational systems have developed to meet the local emphasis on fisheries. Private fish farm operations have been built in West Africa, whereas exploitative fisheries play a relatively greater role on the remainder of the continent. In Latin America little aquacultural development has occurred, despite well-developed exploitative fisheries in both freshwater and marine environments in some countries. Fisheries scientists and educational programs in any of the disciplines of fisheries science are seldom encountered in Latin American institutions.

To meet the need for expertise in training and fisheries management, many nations in Asia, Africa, and Latin America have provided means for their students to participate in educational programs in the United States, Canada, the Soviet Union, and Western Europe. Much additional educational aid has been provided through the services of the Food and Agricultural Organization of the United Nations, which has assisted worldwide in education in both exploitative fisheries and aquaculture.

RICHARD L. NOBLE

Levels and Programs of Study

Programs in fisheries usually require as a minimum educational prerequisite a secondary education and lead to the following awards: certificate or diploma, bachelor's degree (B.Sc.), master's degree (M.Sc.), the doctorate (Ph.D), or their equivalents. Programs deal with principles and practices of fisheries science and consist of classroom, field, and laboratory instruction.

Programs that lead to an award not equivalent to a first university degree deal with fishery technology. Principal course content usually includes some of the following: elements of fishery technology, fish culture, fish propagation, fishing gear technology, fish detection, and fishery aspects of water pollution. Background courses usually include marine biology, oceanography, ichthyology, seamanship, marine law, fish processing, and fishery law and regulation.

Programs that lead to a first university degree deal with fisheries science. Principal course content usually includes specialized fisheries science subjects, such as ichthyology, fisheries management, fishery economics, fish culture, fish propagation, nets and other gear, international fish distribution, and fishery aspects of water pollution. Background courses often included are invertebrate zoology, fundamentals of limnology, ecology, principles of physiology, general chemistry, general physics, mathematics, economics, and statistical analysis.

Programs that lead to a postgraduate university degree consist of seminars and research in fisheries science. Emphasis is given to original research work as substantiated by the presentation of a scholarly thesis or dissertation. Principal subject matter areas within which courses and research projects tend to fall include ichthyology, limnology, fish and marine life culture, fishery resource management, fishery economics, commercial fishery exploitation, sport fishery management, and fish pathology. Subject areas within which background studies tend to fall include specialties in biology, chemistry, biochemistry, aquatic ecology, fisheries products technology, mathematics, and statistical analysis.

[This section was based on UNESCO's *International Standard Classification of Education (ISCED)* (Paris: UNESCO, 1976).]

Major International and National Organizations

INTERNATIONAL

American Fisheries Society
5410 Grosvenor Lane
Bethesda, Maryland 20014 USA

East African Fisheries Research Organization
P.O. Box 343
Jinja, Uganda

Food and Agriculture Organization of the
  United Nations (FAO)
Organisation des Nations unies pour
  l'alimentation et l'agriculture
via delle Terme di Caracalla
00100 Rome, Italy

General Fisheries Council for the
  Mediterranean (GFCM)
Conseil général des pêches pour la
  Méditerranée
FAO
via delle Terme di Caracalla
00100 Rome, Italy

Great Lakes Fisheries Commission
5104 I.S.T. Building
2200 Bonisteel Boulevard
Ann Arbor, Michigan 48105 USA

Gulf and Caribbean Fisheries Institute
10 Rickenbacker Causeway
Miami, Florida 33149 USA

Inter-American Tropical Tuna Commission
  (IATTC)
% National Marine Fisheries Service
Department of Commerce
Washington, D.C. 20002 USA

International Association of Game, Fish and
  Conservation Commissions
1709 New York Avenue NW
Washington, D.C. 20006 USA

International Commission for Northwest
  Atlantic Fisheries (ICNAF)
P.O. Box 638
Dartmouth, Nova Scotia, Canada

International Commission for the Southeast
  Atlantic Fisheries
65 Paseo de la Habana
Madrid 16, Spain

International Council for the Exploration
  of the Sea
Conseil international pour l'exploration
  de la mer
Charlottenlund Slot 2920
Charlottenlund, Copenhagen, Denmark

International North Pacific Fisheries
  Commission
6640 Northwest Marine Drive
Vancouver 8, British Columbia, Canada

International Whaling Commission (IWC)
Commission internationale baleinière
Great Westminster House
Horseferry Road
London SW1 ZAE, England

North-East Atlantic Fisheries Commission
Room 275, Great Westminster House
Horseferry Road
London SW1 ZAE, England

NATIONAL

France:
    Société centrale d'agriculture et
      de pêche
    14 avenue de St. Mandé
    Paris

Japan:
    Nihon suisan gakkai
    % Tokyo suisan daigaku
    4-5-7 Minami, Minato-ku
    Tokyo 108

Mexico:
    Instituto nacional de pesca
    José Azueta 9
    Mexico, D.F.

United Kingdom:
    British Ichthyological Society
    60 Newfields
    Welwyn Garden City, England

    Fisheries Society of the British Isles
    Huntington Reserve Centre
    Huntington, England

United States:
    National Fisheries Institute
    1730 Pennsylvania Avenue NW
    Washington, D.C. 20006

    Sport Fishing Institute
    608 13th Street NW
    Washington, D.C. 20006

Principal Information Sources

GENERAL

Guides to the literature of fisheries science
include:

*Bibliography of Theses on Fisheries Biology, First
  Supplement, 1959–1971: A Compilation of Graduate Theses on Fisheries Biology and Related
  Subjects.* Washington, D.C.: Sport Fishing
  Institute, 1972.
Blanchard, J. R., and Ostvold, H. *Literature
  of Agricultural Research.* Berkeley: University
  of California Press, 1958. Somewhat dated,
  but a classic guide to reference materials.
Bush, E. A. R. *Agriculture: A Bibliographic Guide.*
  (2 vols.) London: Macdonald, 1974. Includes
  sources on fisheries.
*Fisheries Index of FAO Publications and Documents
  (1945–1969).* (2 vols.) Rome: FAO, 1969.
Ocean Research Index. Guernsey, Channel Is-
  lands: Francis Hodgson, 1970. Includes in-
  formation on fisheries research.
Potter, D. R., Sharpe, K. M., and Hendee, J. C.
  *Human Behavior Aspects of Fish and Wild-
  life Conservation—An Annotated Bibliography.*
  USDA Forest Service General Technical
  Report PNW-4. Portland, Oregon: Pacific
  Northwest Forest and Range Experiment
  Station, 1973.
Winston, H. N. M. *Man and the Environment:
  A Bibliography of Selected Publications of the
  United Nations System 1946–1971.* New York:
  Bowker, 1972.

Introductions to the field include:

Bardach, J. E., Ryther, J. H., and McLarney,
  W. O. *Aquaculture.* New York: Wiley-Inter-
  science, 1972.
Bennett, G. W. *Management of Lakes and Ponds.*
  (2nd ed.) New York: Van Nostrand Rein-
  hold, 1971.
Beverton, R. J. H., and Holt, S. J. *On the Dy-
  namics of Exploited Fish Populations, Fishery
  Investigations.* Series II, Vol. 19. London:
  H. M. Stationery Office, 1957.
Carlander, K. D. *Handbook of Freshwater Fishery
  Biology.* (3rd ed.) Ames: Iowa State Univer-
  sity Press, 1969.
Christy, F. T. *Alternative Arrangements for Marine
  Fisheries: An Overview.* Baltimore: Johns
  Hopkins University Press, 1973.
Cushing, D. H. *Fisheries Biology—A Study in Pop-
  ulation Dynamics.* Madison: University of
  Wisconsin Press, 1968.
Everhart, W. H, and others. *Principles of Fishery
  Science.* Ithaca, New York: Comstock Pub-
  lishing Associates, 1975.
Gerking, S. D. (Ed.) *The Biological Basis of Fresh-
  water Fish Production.* New York: Wiley, 1967.
Gulland, J. A. *The Management of Marine Fish-
  eries.* Seattle: University of Washington Press,
  1974.
Hall, G. E. (Ed.) *Reservoir Fisheries and Limnol-
  ogy.* Special Publication 8. Washington, D.C.:
  American Fisheries Society, 1971.

Hickling, C. F. *Fish Culture.* London: Faber & Faber, 1971.

Huet, M. *Traité de pisciculture.* (4th ed.) Brussels: Editions Ch. de Wyngaert, 1970.

Lackey, R. *Introductory Fisheries Science.* Blacksburg, Virginia: VPI & SU Sea Grant Program, 1974.

Reichenbach-Klinke, H. H. *Grundzüge der Fischkunde.* Stuttgart, Federal Republic of Germany: Gustav Fischer, 1970.

Ricker, W. E. *Methods of Assessment of Fish Production in Fresh Waters.* Oxford, England: Blackwell Scientific Publications, 1968.

Rothschild, B. J. (Ed.) *World Fisheries Policy.* Seattle: University of Washington Press, 1972.

Royce, W. F. *Introduction to the Fishery Sciences.* New York: Academic Press, 1972.

Weatherly, A. H. *Growth and Ecology of Fish Populations.* New York: Academic Press, 1972.

A history of the field is:

Benson, N. G. *A Century of Fisheries in North America.* Washington, D.C.: American Fisheries Society, 1970.

A source for educational and career guidance is:

Myers, G. S. *How to Become an Ichthyologist.* Neptune City, New Jersey: T.F.H. Publications, 1970.

CURRENT BIBLIOGRAPHIES

Agrindex. Rome: FAO, 1975–. Includes information on fisheries, natural resource protection, and agricultural education.

Aquatic Sciences and Fisheries Abstracts. Rome: FAO, 1971–. Supersedes *Aquatic Biology Abstracts* and *Current Bibliography for Aquatic Sciences and Fisheries.*

Biological Abstracts. Philadelphia: Biosciences Information Service of Biological Abstracts, 1927–.

Commercial Fisheries Abstracts. Washington, D.C.: U.S. Department of the Interior, Bureau of Commercial Fisheries, Fish and Wildlife Service, 1947–. Covers fish industries.

Sport Fishery Abstracts: An Abstract Service for Fishery Research and Management. Washington, D.C.: U.S. Department of the Interior, Bureau of Sport Fisheries and Wildlife, Fish and Wildlife Service, 1955–.

World Fisheries Abstracts: A Bi-monthly Review of Technical Literature on Fisheries and Related Industries. Rome: FAO, 1950–.

PERIODICALS

American Fisheries Society Transactions, Australian Journal of Marine and Freshwater Research, *Archiv für Fischereiwissenschaft* (FRG), *Bamidgeh* (Israel), *Boletim de estudos de pesca* (Brazil), *Bulletin français de pisciculture* (France), *Bulletin of the Faculty of Fisheries, Hokkaido University* (Japan), *Bulletin of the Japanese Society of Scientific Fisheries, Canadian Fisheries Research Board Journal, FAO Fisheries Synopsis* (Italy), *Finnish Fisheries Research, Fishery Bulletin* (US), *Fishery Technology* (India), *Ichthyologica: An International Journal of Ichthyology and Hydrobiology* (India), *Indian Journal of Fisheries, Japanese Journal of Ichthyology, Journal of the Faculty of Fisheries and Animal Husbandry, Hiroshima University* (Japan), *Journal of Fish Biology* (UK), *Journal of the Marine Biological Association* (UK), *Journal of the Tokyo University of Fisheries* (Japan), *Marine Fisheries Review* (US), *Netherlands Journal of Sea Research, New Zealand Journal of Marine and Freshwater Research, Polish Agriculture Annual, Proceedings of the World Mariculture Society* (US), *Reports of the Institute for Freshwater Research* (Sweden), *Rivista italiana di pisciculture e ittiopatologia, Rybnoe khozyaistvo* (USSR), *Suomen kalatalous* (Finland), *Voprosy ikhtiologii* (USSR).

For a more extensive listing see:

Aquatic Biology Serials: A Worldwide List of Titles (Both Current and Ceased), with Selected Descriptive Information. Washington, D.C.: Biological Sciences Communication Project, George Washington University, 1963.

1000 Selected Journals in Agricultural and Related Subjects. Beltsville, Maryland: National Agricultural Library, 1973. An international listing covering all aspects of agriculture and related fields.

Ulrich's International Periodicals Directory. New York: Bowker, biennial.

World List of Periodicals for Aquatic Sciences and Fisheries. Rome: FAO, Fisheries Division, Biology Branch, 1962.

ENCYCLOPEDIAS, DICTIONARIES, HANDBOOKS

Ben-Yomi, M. (Ed.) *Russian-English Glossary of Fishing and Related Marine Terms.* Beaverton, Oregon: International Scholarly Books Service, 1975.

Haneko, H. (Ed.) *Suisan yogo jiten/Dictionary of Fisheries Technical Terms.* Tokyo: Koseisha Koseikaku, 1971. English-Japanese, Japanese-English.

Holt, S. J. *Multilingual Vocabulary and Notation for Fishery Dynamics.* Rome: FAO, 1960.

Lindberg, G. U. *Fishes of the World: A Key to Families and a Checklist.* New York: Wiley, 1974.

La protection de la nature et les parcs nationaux dans le monde. Notes et études documentaires, No. 3224. Paris: Documentation française (Secrétariat général du gouvernement, Direction de la documentation), 1965. Gives location and brief descriptions of national parks throughout the world.

DIRECTORIES

Directories to educational and research institutions are:

Conservation Directory, 1975. (20th ed.) Washington, D.C.: National Wildlife Federation, 1975.

Fisheries Industry Index International. London: Haymarket Press, 1970–. Published annually; formerly *Fisheries Year-Book and Directory,* 1952–1970.

Fishery Research and Educational Institutions in North and South America. Washington, D.C.: FAO, Fisheries Division, 1950. Includes government organizations and educational institutions.

International Handbook of Universities. Paris: International Association of Universities, 1950–. Published triennially.

Ocean Research Index: A Guide to Ocean and Freshwater Research Including Fisheries Research. Guernsey, Channel Islands: Francis Hodgson, 1970. International and national.

Underseas Technology Handbook Directory. Arlington, Virginia: Compass Publications, 1971–72. Includes fishery organizations.

World Directory of Environmental Education Programs. New York: Bowker, 1973. Postsecondary study and training in seventy countries.

World Directory of Hydrobiological and Fisheries Institutions. Washington, D.C.: American Institute of Biological Sciences, 1963.

FLEXNER REPORT
See Medical Education in the United States and Canada (Higher Education Report).

FOOD AND AGRICULTURE ORGANIZATION OF THE UNITED NATIONS

The Food and Agriculture Organization of the United Nations (FAO), one of the specialized agencies of the United Nations, is involved in technical education and training in food and agriculture at all levels, from university education and intermediate levels to farmer training. Included in this broad field of agricultural education

are various specialized subject matter fields, for which the different divisions of FAO take responsibility: plant production and protection, animal production and health, land and water development (including farm management and agricultural engineering), forestry, fisheries, agricultural economics (including commodities and statistics), nutrition (including home economics), and rural institutions (including agricultural education, agrarian reform, cooperatives, credit, agricultural extension, marketing and organization of agricultural services and research, and integrated rural development).

The educational interests and activities of FAO are coordinated through an Inter-Divisional Working Group on Education and Training, of which the director of the Human Resources, Institutions and Agrarian Reform Division is chairman. It also collaborates with UNESCO and the International Labour Organisation through an Inter-Secretariat Working Group and a Joint Advisory Committee, which meet at regular intervals.

FAO helps member countries plan and develop agricultural education and training in accordance with national development plans and the need for trained manpower. This assistance takes the form of technical advice and help in the development of university faculties and departments. Funding is commonly sought through the United Nations Development Programme, the World Bank, foundations, and bilateral aid.

FAO is one of the agencies that administer United Nations Special Fund projects and therefore is involved in recruiting university teachers and in arranging fellowships for local counterpart staff. Regular international seminars on higher agricultural education are organized in various regions of the world to provide an opportunity for deans of faculties, senior university officials, and representatives of aid-giving bodies to exchange ideas and experiences on the development of agricultural education at university level to serve the needs of developing countries. Increased emphasis is now being placed on intermediate-level agricultural education and training, in accordance with the recommendations of the 1970 World Conference on Agricultural Education and Training held in Copenhagen. FAO has established advisory panels on forestry education, dairy education, and veterinary education.

The Agricultural Education and Extension Service in the Human Resources, Institutions and Agrarian Reform Division coordinates the agricultural education interests and activities of FAO.

via delle Terme di Caracalla
00100 Rome, Italy

See also: Aid to Other Nations; International Bank for Reconstruction and Development.

FOOD PROCESSING
See Food Science and Technology (field of study).

FOOD SCIENCE AND TECHNOLOGY (Field of Study)

Food science and technology is the application of science and engineering to the production, processing, packaging, distribution, preparation, storage, evaluation, and utilization of food. In carrying out the study of food and food ingredients, the food scientist (also called a food technologist) utilizes many disciplines, such as chemistry, microbiology, physics, biology, engineering, nutrition, and toxicology.

Food science and technology encompasses a number of branches: food chemistry (the structure of properties of food and the chemistry of changes occurring during processing and utilization), food analysis (principles and techniques used in the quantitative physical and chemical analysis of food and food properties), food microbiology (roles of microorganisms in the preservation and spoilage of food), food engineering (fundamentals of engineering as they apply to food processing), nutrition (analysis of nutrients in food, their role in metabolism, and their function in maintaining health), food processing (methods of preservation, automation, packaging, and pollution control), food distribution, and food marketing.

Food science and technology dates back to early history, when edible materials had to be preserved during times of plenty for survival during times of shortage. Early preservation methods were limited to sun drying, smoking, salting, and fermentation. In addition, freezing was used in northern climates because of the suitable atmospheric environment. Far-ranging wars, disasters of nature, migration, and other social and economic factors have hastened the evolution of food science. Food science as a formal science emerged in the nineteenth century as a result of basic discoveries by Louis Pasteur and Nicolas François Appert. Toward the end of the century, scientific investigation relating to the importance of bacterial types in the canning process was carried out in the United States by S. C. Prescott of the Massachusetts Institute of Technology and by William Underwood. Their work is considered to be the first attempt to apply scientific principles to the canning process. Food science formally emerged as a profession during and immediately following World War II, when universities began to establish departments and grant degrees in this discipline.

Improvements and refinements in the control and methodology of food processing, preservation, packaging, and quality assurance are constantly occurring. One example of an important new development in food science is the creation of methodologies for isolating the protein fraction from soybeans. This development offers the potential for increasing the availability of essential protein. Another important development in food science is the creation of the Codex Alimentarius Commission under the auspices of the World Health Organization and the Food and Agriculture Organization. The purpose of the commission is to establish international standards of identity for foods. Such standardization by food scientists may alleviate the confusion caused by the different names given to food marketed in various countries.

The typical professional food scientist or food technologist holds a first university or college degree and is trained in chemistry and biology. A food scientist or technologist generally studies food science only after successfully achieving a basic scientific knowledge. Graduate food scientists with postgraduate university degrees may specialize in such major fields as food chemistry, food microbiology, food packaging, food engineering, or nutrition. Throughout the world major universities stressing technical training have food science courses or have departments which confer degrees in food science and/or technology. Students in such institutions study basic disciplines such as chemistry or microbiology and work toward advanced degrees in food science and technology. The names of many existing food science units often include the term *nutrition*. In other instances, food science may be coupled with related programs or departments, such as dairy science, horticulture, or animal science. However, the trend is away from a commodity-oriented name and toward more general terminology such as *food science* and *nutrition*.

In the United States and Canada there are approximately seventy-five university or college programs in food science and technology. First (bachelor's), second (master's), and third (doctoral) degrees may be conferred upon students who successfully achieve the individual school requirements. In other countries food science is taught in a variety of educational institutions. In Latin America, for example, food science is generally taught in agricultural universities or colleges. The entire region has about fifty such facilities; Brazil is among the leaders in the field, with several universities providing courses or having depart-

ments in food science. The food industry in Mexico is growing rapidly; as a result, a number of universities are offering first university degree and advanced programs in food science and technology.

Food science in the United Kingdom has long been recognized as a science, and several colleges and universities provide programs on all levels. In Australia the University of New South Wales and the Royal Melbourne Institute of Technology both grant degrees in food science. In India the Central Food Technological Research Institute in Mysore and several other institutes and universities offer first university degrees and master's degrees in food science.

In Central Europe, Scandinavia, Italy, France, Switzerland, and the Federal Republic of Germany principal universities provide programs and, in some instances, confer degrees in food technology. In various Eastern European countries (for example, Bulgaria, Czechoslovakia, the German Democratic Republic, Hungary, Poland, and Yugoslavia) food technologists, nutritionists, and food engineers are trained both on university (or equivalent) and below university levels. In almost all these countries education in food science and technology has become more specialized than in the Western world. In some places particular branch specialization starts immediately after grammar school or after the first preparatory university year. Another characteristic of food science education in Eastern European countries is that not only central research institutes but also very specialized regional research organizations educate specialized food technologists and grant the highest degrees.

A number of food science programs are carried out in Egypt within agricultural institutions. The American University in Beirut, Lebanon, offers food science degrees up to the Master of Science degree level. In Turkey food technologists are trained in the food technology departments of several of the agricultural universities. These departments offer courses in basic agricultural sciences, biochemistry, analytical chemistry, microbiology, statistics, food control, food machinery, and agricultural economics. Plans are also underway to open a food engineering department in the Middle East Technical University at Ankara. Israel has several principal universities offering degrees in food science and technology, both at first university degree and advanced levels. The educational approach in Israel is based on unit operations (that is, technical processes) rather than commodities (the finished products). The department of food technology in the Technion (Israel Institute of Technology, Haifa) has been training engineers and scientists since the early 1960s to meet the specialized needs of the local food industry. The department has also been active in training students from abroad on various levels.

Japan has been very active in the training of food scientists, and a number of universities and agricultural colleges grant first university and advanced degrees. In the Philippines, a few universities offer first university degrees in food science or technology. At the University of the Philippines (Quezon City), for example, the bachelor's degree program is structured so that in the first two years the students enroll in liberal education courses; in their third and fourth years they take basic and applied science courses; and in their fifth year they intern in the University Pilot Food Plan to better appreciate the problems they are likely to meet in industry. A Master of Science in Food Technology (later revised and renamed M.S. of Food Science) degree course was instituted in 1962 at the University of the Philippines.

The growing population rate in many developing countries has necessitated the expansion of training in the field of food science and technology. Departments of food science have been created in the universities, colleges, and institutions of several countries, including Nigeria and Ghana. Generally, education in food science is dependent on the pressures of local needs within any given country and the occupational opportunities available for food science students.

Food scientists, upon successful completion of their academic studies, may become instructors or carry out research in colleges and universities, or they may choose an industrial career. In the food industry the food scientists may carry out basic and applied research on the physical, chemical, flavor, and texture characteristics of food and food ingredients in a food manufacturer's laboratory, or they may supervise the commercial processing, manufacturing, and packaging of foods. Quality control laboratories responsible for maintaining the standards for the food being produced are staffed by food scientists. State and federal regulatory agencies responsible for upholding the laws regarding the manufacture and distribution of food also employ food scientists. The food scientist may also pursue his profession in an international agency such as the Food and Agricultural Organization of the United Nations.

JOHN H. MORIARTY

Levels and Programs of Study

Programs in food science and technology usually require as a minimum prerequisite a secondary education, although mature students with relevant work experience may be admitted with lower qualifications, especially into programs designed to upgrade the performance of those already employed. Programs lead to the following awards: certificate or diploma, Bachelor of Science or *licence,* Master of Science, Ph.D., or their equivalents. Programs primarily consist of classroom, laboratory, and workshop study and practice.

Programs that lead to awards not equivalent to a first university degree deal with the industrial, commercial, and similar processing of food. Programs of one year or more are usually given in technological or similar institutes and often consist of alternating periods of study and work in industrial and other enterprises (sandwich courses). For short courses, many of which are sponsored by employers or employers' associations, a certificate of satisfactory completion is usually given. Principal course content for work at this level usually includes biology, chemistry, theory and principles of food processing, food handling, food purchasing, test cooking, food preservation, business management, human relations, merchandising, and the technology of industrial cooking equipment. Emphasis is placed on the achievement of practical competence and skill.

Programs leading to the first university degree are designed for the study of the applications of chemistry, bacteriology, engineering, and other sciences to food processing and preservation. Programs at this level usually include specialized food-related subjects, such as the principles of food technology, food chemistry, food preservation, food-processing systems, dairy technology, meat technology, poultry technology, milk and water sanitation, and nutrition.

In programs that lead to a postgraduate university degree, students specialize in a particular apsect of food science, such as food microbiology, food packing, food engineering, or nutrition. Advanced topics are studied and an emphasis is placed on original research as substantiated by a thesis or dissertation.

[This section was based on UNESCO's *International Standard Classification of Education (ISCED): Three Stage Classification System, 1974* (Paris: UNESCO, 1974).

Major International and National Organizations

INTERNATIONAL

Food and Agriculture Organization of the
    United Nations (FAO)
via delle Terme di Caracalla
Rome, Italy

League for International Food Education
1155 16th Street NW, Room 705
Washington, D.C. 20036 USA

Institute of Food Technologists
221 North LaSalle Street
Chicago, Illinois 60601 USA

International Union of Food Science and
    Technology (IUFoST)
Swedish Institute for Food
    Preservation Research
Fack, s-40021
Göteborg 16, Sweden

NATIONAL

Argentina:
    Argentine Association of Food
        Technology
    Corrientes 1485-3° G.
    Buenos Aires

Australia:
    Australian Institute of Food Science
        and Technology
    % Halycon Proteins Pty. Ltd.
    25 George Street
    Sandringham, Victoria 3191

Austria:
    Verein österreichischer Lebensmittel
        und Garungstechnologen
    % Institut für Lebensmitteltechnologie
    Gregor-Mendel-Strasse 33
    1180 Vienna

Canada:
    Canadian Institute of Food Science
        and Technology
    Suite 10
    46 Elgin Street
    Ottawa, Ontario K1P 5K6

Chile:
    Chilean Society of Food Technology
    Casilla 3968
    Santiago

Denmark:
    Danish Society of Food Technology
        and Hygiene
    V. Farimagsgade 31
    1606 Copenhagen V

Federal Republic of Germany:
    Bundesforschungsanstalt für
        Lebensmittelfrischhaltung
    National Committee of IUFoST of the
        Federal Republic of Germany
    Engesserstrasse 20
    75 Karlsruhe 1

Finland:
    Finnish Society of Food Science
        and Technology
    Helsinki University
    SF00710 EKT Helsinki 71

France:
> Comité français de science, technologie
> et économie des industries
> alimentaires (STEIA)
> 156 boulevard de Magenta
> Paris 10e

Hungary:
> Hungarian Scientific Society for
> Food Industry
> V. Academia u. 1-3, Budapest

India:
> Association of Food Scientists and
> Technologists
> Central Food Technological Research
> Institute
> V.V. Mohalla P.O, Mysore 2A

Israel:
> Israel Society for Food and Nutrition
> Sciences
> Institute for Technology & Storage of
> Agricultural Products
> Agricultural Research Organization,
> Volcani Center
> P.O. Box 6, Bet Dagan

Italy:
> Istituto de tecnologie alimentari
> via Celoria 2
> 20133 Milan

Japan:
> International Union of Food Science
> and Technology of Japan
> Department of Agriculture
> 1-1 Sakuragaoka 1-chome
> Setagayaku, Tokyo

Lebanon:
> Professional Association of Food
> Technology and Nutrition
> American University
> Beirut

Mexico:
> Asociación de técnicos en alimentos de
> México
> Indianapolis 63-2
> Col. Napoles
> Mexico 18, D.F.

Netherlands:
> Nederlandse vereniging voor
> voedingsleer en
> levensmiddelentechnologie
> Unilever Research Laboratorium, Duiven
> Postbus 7, Zevenaar

New Zealand:
> New Zealand Institute of Food Science
> and Technology
> % Biotechnology Department
> Massey University
> Palmerston North

Norway:
> Norwegian National Committee of Food
> Science and Technology
> % Food Research Institute
> Postboks 8146, Oslo Dep.

Philippines:
> Philippine Association of Food
> Technologists
> Food Research Laboratory
> FNRC, NIST, Herran St.
> Manila

Poland:
> Polish Academy of Science
> Palac Kultury i Nauki
> Warsaw

Republic of Korea:
> Korean Society of Food Science and
> Technology
> % National Industrial Research Institute
> 199, Tongsoong-Dong
> Chongro-Koo, Seoul

South Africa:
> South African Association of Food
> Science and Technology
> % Fishing Industry Research Institute
> Private Bag
> Rondebosch CP

Spain:
> Instituto nacional de ciencia y tecnología
> de alimentos
> Instituto de agroquímica y tecnología
> de alimentos
> % Jaime Roig
> Valencia 10

Sweden:
> Swedish National Committee of Food
> Science and Technology
> % Swedish Institute for Food
> Preservation Research
> Fack s-40021
> Göteborg 16

Switzerland:
> Swiss Committee of IUFoST
> % Eidgenössische technische Hochschule
> Universitätstrasse 2
> 8006 Zurich

Thailand:
>   Institute of Food Research and Product
>   Development
>   P.O. Box 4
>   170 Bangkok 4

United Kingdom:
>   Institute of Food Science and Technology
>   3a Hoskins Road
>   Oxted, Surrey, England

United States:
>   Institute of Food Technologists
>   Suite 2120
>   221 North La Salle Street
>   Chicago, Illinois 60601

Principal Information Sources

GENERAL

Bibliographical guides to the literature in the field of food science and technology include:

Baker, E. A., and Foskett, D. J. *Bibliography of Food: A Select International Bibliography of Nutrition, Food, and Beverage Technology and Distribution, 1936–1956.* London: Butterworth, 1958.

Food Technology: A Select Bibliography. London: Lambeth Public Libraries, 1967.

Mann, E. J. *Evaluation of the World Food Literature: Results of an International Survey.* Farnham Royal, Bucks, England: Commonwealth Agricultural Bureaux, 1967. A survey of the world's literature pertaining to food science and technology, focusing primarily on periodicals.

Noling, A. W. *Beverage Literature: A Bibliography.* Metuchen, New Jersey: Scarecrow Press, 1971.

A Select List of Books of Food Science and Technology. Reading, England: National College of Food Technology, University of Reading, 1970.

Winston, H. N. M. *Man and the Environment: A Bibliography of Selected Publications of the United Nations System 1946–71.* New York: Bowker, 1972. Includes sources on food production, supply, food processing, nutrition, and food and population.

Wu Leung, W.-T., Butrum, R. R., and Huang Chang, F. *A Select Bibliography of East Asian Foods and Nutrition Arranged According to Subject Matter and Area.* Rome: Food and Agriculture Organization, 1972.

For a comparative introduction to the field see:

Peterson, M. S., and Tressler, D. K. *Food Technology the World Over.* (2 vols.) Westport,

Connecticut: AVI Publishing, 1963–1965. Volume 1 contains information on Europe, Canada, the United States, and Australia (1963); Volume 2, South America, Africa, and the Middle East (1965).

Other introductory works include:

Birch, G. G. *Food Science.* Oxford, England: Pergamon Press, 1972.

Borgstrom, G. *Principles of Food Science.* (2 vols.) New York: Macmillan, 1968.

Charley, C. H. *Food Science.* New York: Ronald Press, 1970.

Potter, N. N. *Food Science.* (2nd ed.) Westport, Connecticut: AVI Publishing, 1973. An important work that has been translated into Japanese and Spanish.

Pye, M. *Food Science and Technology.* (3rd ed.) London: Murray, 1970.

CURRENT BIBLIOGRAPHIES

Some important abstracting and indexing services which include sources on food science and technology are:

Abstracts from Current Scientific and Technical Literature. Leatherhead, Surrey, England: British Food Manufacturing Industries Research Association, 1948–. Published monthly.

"Bulletin analytique du Centre de documentation de la Commission internationale des industries agricoles." In *Industries alimentaires et agricoles.* Paris: Commission internationale des industries agricoles, 1884–.

Food Technology. Chicago: Institute of Food Technologists, 1974–. Published monthly.

Journal of Food Science. Chicago: Institute of Food Technologists, 1936–. Published bimonthly.

Journal of the Science of Food and Agriculture. London: Society of Chemical Industry, 1954–. Provides monthly abstracts on food, agriculture, and sanitation.

Mann, E. J. (Ed.) *Food Science and Technology Abstracts.* Reading, England: International Food Information Service, 1969–. Published monthly. A major abstracting service in the field.

Nutrition Abstracts and Reviews. Farnham Royal, Bucks, England: Commonwealth Agricultural Bureaux, 1931–. Published quarterly.

Referativnyĭ zhurnal. 36: *Oborudovanie pishchevoi promyshlennosti.* Moscow: Akademiia nauk, SSSR, Institut nauchnoĭ informatsii, VINITI, 1964–. Published monthly.

Research Index. London: Institute of Food Industries, annual.

"Zeitschriftenreferate." In *Zeitschrift für Lebensmittel Untersuchung und Forschung,* Munich,

Federal Republic of Germany: Bergamm, 1890–. Provides abstracts on the preparation and preservation of foodstuffs.

Progress reports are also useful sources of current information in the field. See:

Advances in Food Research. New York and London: Academic Press, 1948–.
Recent Advances in Food Science. London: Butterworth, 1962–.

PERIODICALS

The following are selected periodicals in the field: *Alimenta* (Switzerland), *Alimentaires* (Belgium), *Alimentaria: Revista de tecnología e higiene de los alimentos* (Spain), *Archivos latino americanos de nutrición* (Venezuela), *British Food Journal, Canadian Institute of Food Science and Technology Journal, Die Lebensmittel Industrie* (GDR), *Egyptian Journal of Food Science, Food Industries* (Bulgaria), *Food Processing* (US), *Food Technology* (US), *Food Technology in Australia, Gordian* (GDR), *Grasa y aceites* (Spain), *Indian Journal of Nutrition and Dietetics, Industria alimentara* (Romania), *Industrie agrarie* (Italy), *Industrie alimentari* (Italy), *Industries alimentaires* (France), *Journal of Agriculture and Food Chemistry* (US), *Journal of Food Science* (US), *Journal of Food Science and Technology* (US), *Journal of Food Technology* (UK), *Journal of Milk and Food Technology* (US), *Journal of the Science of Food and Agriculture* (US), *Lebensmittel-Wissenschaft und Technologie* (Switzerland), *Livsmedelteknik* (Sweden), *Myasnaya industriya SSSR* (USSR), *Naeringsmiddel industrien* (Norway), *Przemysl spozywczy* (Poland), *Revista alimentaria* (Spain), *Revista de agroquímica y tecnología de alimentos* (Spain), *Revue des fermentations et des industries* (France), *Revue technique de l'industrie alimentaire* (France), *Scienza e tecnologia degli alimenti* (Italy), *Zpravodaj masneho prumyslu CSSR* (USSR).

For a more complete listing of journals see:

Ulrich's International Periodicals Directory. New York: Bowker, biennial.

ENCYCLOPEDIAS, DICTIONARIES, HANDBOOKS

Encyclopedias in the field include:

Hall, C. W., and others. *Encyclopedia of Food Engineering.* Westport, Connecticut: AVI Publishing, 1971.
Johnson, A. H., and Peterson, M. S. *Encyclopedia of Food Technology.* Westport, Connecticut: AVI Publishing, 1974.

Some useful handbooks and manuals covering aspects of food science and technology are:

Blanck, F. C. *Handbook for Food and Agriculture.* New York: Van Nostrand Reinhold, 1955.
Furia, T. E. *Handbook of Food Additives.* Cleveland, Ohio: Chemical Rubber Co., 1968.
Handbook of Food Chemistry/Handbuch der Lebensmittel Chemie. Vol. 1: *Analysis of Foods/Analytik der Lebensmittel;* Vol. 2: *Analysis of Foods, Detection and Determination of Food Components/ Analytik der Lebensmittel, Nachweis und Bestimmung von Lebensmittelinhatsstoffen.* Berlin, Federal Republic of Germany: Springer-Verlag, 1967.
Joslyn, M. A., and Heid, J. L. *Food Processing Operations: Their Management, Machines, Materials, and Methods.* (3 vols.) Westport, Connecticut: AVI Publishing, 1963–1964.
Woolen, A. *Food Industries Manual.* (20th ed.) London: Hill, 1969.

For dictionaries in the field consult:

Bender, A. *A Dictionary of Nutrition and Food Technology.* (3rd ed.) London: Butterworth, 1968.
Luck, E. *English-Deutsch Fachwörterbuch des Lebensmittelsessens.* Wiesbaden, Federal Republic of Germany: Brandstetter, 1963
Norton, E. *Dictionary of Food.* London: Mills and Boon, 1969.

DIRECTORIES

Food Science and Related Fields. Chicago: Education Committee, Institute of Food technologists, n.d. A directory to study and scholarships in the field of food science and technology in the United States and Canada.
Food Science and Technology Scholarships in the U.S. and Canada. Chicago: Career Guidance Committee, Institute of Food Technologists, 1973.
Worldwide List of Food Technology Institutions. (3rd ed.) Rome: Food and Agriculture Organization, 1971. The most comprehensive international listing of institutions (excluding those in the United States).

RESEARCH CENTERS, INSTITUTES, INFORMATION CENTERS

Central Food Technological Research Institute
Mysore-2A India
(Experimental stations at Trichur, Ludhiana, Nagpur, Bombay, Mangalore, and Lucknow.)

Central Institute for Nutrition and Food Research
Utrechtsweg 48
Zeist, Netherlands

Central Scientific Research Laboratory of the
  Food Industry
Leningrad, Soviet Union

Centre d'études et de recherches des industries
  agricoles et alimentaires (CERDIA)
Le Noyer-Lambert
Massy (Essonne), France

Commonwealth Scientific and Industrial
  Research Organization (CSIRO)
Division of Food Preservation
P.O. Box 43
Ryde, New South Wales 2112 Australia

Food Research Institute
Ministry of Agriculture and Forestry
2 Hamazono-cho
Fukagawa, Koto, Tokyo, Japan

Food Research Laboratories
Polytechnical Institute
Buenos Aires, Argentina

Food Technology Laboratory
Bygning 221
Lyngby, Denmark

International Food Information Service
% Commonwealth Agricultural Bureaux
Central Sales Branch
Farnham House
Farnham Royal, Bucks, England

National Food Research Institute
CSIRO
P.O. Box 395
Pretoria, South Africa

Research Institute of Food Technology
Vyskumny ustav potravinayskeho prumyalu
Na Belidle 21
Prague, Czechoslovakia

In the United States the Department of Agriculture and the land-grant universities operate laboratories that conduct research relating to various aspects of food technology and science.

See the following for listings of research centers and institutes in the field:

Index of Agriculture Research Institutes of Europe.
  Rome: Food and Agriculture Organization, 1963.
Worldwide List of Food Technology Institutions.
  (3rd ed.) Rome: Food and Agriculture Organization, 1971. A useful source that provides a complete listing of institutes and research centers in food science and technology.

FOREIGN SCHOLARS
See Exchange, International; Legal Aspects of Higher Education.

FOREIGN STUDENT OFFICE
See Exchange, International: Campus International Offices.

FOREIGN STUDENT SERVICE COUNCIL, United States

The Foreign Student Service Council, founded in 1956, is a private, nonprofit organization seeking to promote international education and understanding by offering services for foreign students living or visiting in Washington, D.C. Acting as a bridge between campus and community, the council provides a way for foreign students to get to know America and Americans. Hospitality programs and seminars sponsored by the council are designed to give the university-level international student an understanding of the United States government and an introduction to people in the nation's capital.

For students visiting the area, the hospitality program provides three-day home stays with American families or young adults, as well as dinners and holiday visits in private homes, sightseeing, and information on inexpensive accommodations. In addition, the council sponsors International Student Day, an annual event proclaimed by the mayor of Washington, D.C., in honor of the international students in the area.

The seminar program includes two types of seminars. The International Leadership Seminars are week-long experiences in Washington, D.C., for international graduate students from universities all over America. Seminar participants are house guests of local families and meet with top-level leaders in government, labor, journalism, and international agencies. Participants are selected by foreign student advisers and department heads at their universities. The Today in Washington seminars are day-long programs for international students attending area colleges and universities. Each seminar focuses on a particular area of activity in the nation's capital, such as the city government, United States Congress, and the arts.

There are over 150,000 foreign students in the United States. Of these, 9000 live in the Washington, D.C., area, and a majority of the rest visit the United States capital during their stay. During 1974 the council helped nearly 5000 students from more than 80 countries gain a better understanding of the United States through personal contact with local citizens and officials. The council tenders all its services to foreign students without charge.

The council's business is conducted by a small professional staff, a large group of volunteers, and a board of directors. The council receives grants from the United States Department of State and from foundations, corporations, and educational institutions. Other funds are obtained through annual membership drives and benefits.

1860-19th Street NW
Washington, D.C. 20009 USA

FOREIGN STUDENT
See Exchange, International: International Student in Postsecondary Education.

FORESTRY (Field of Study)

Forestry is the science, art, and practice of managing and using forestlands and related natural resources for human benefit. It encompasses a wide range of activity designed to satisfy not only the material needs of man from the forest (timber, paper, and other wood products; high-quality water for domestic, agricultural, and industrial uses; and forage for livestock) but also some of his spiritual, psychological, or leisure-time needs (wilderness, urban greenbelts, and recreational opportunity). The forester must decide how to attain particular multiple-use (rarely single-use) goals—for instance, how a particular land area in a developed country can be used simultaneously for timber, water, and recreation. The integration of these goals in a society where various organizations make exclusive demands upon the resource and those who manage it provides one of the greatest challenges to the profession.

In early stages of national forestry development, when timber production is usually the predominant goal, management is somewhat less complex.

In earliest times man used wood for fuel and for the construction of shelters, tool handles, and rafts. By the dawn of history his use of wood had become increasingly sophisticated. As a result of the great demand for wood products, timber shortages occurred in China and Egypt, causing rulers to regulate cutting. In other countries as well, overcutting contributed significantly to shortages; overgrazing and fire were also major causes of timber shortages. Removal of the forest, particularly in mountainous regions, often resulted in the destruction of settlements by floods and mud flows. Because of the undesirable effects of forest mismanagement, between the twelfth and eighteenth centuries many European countries adopted laws regulating cutting, and some encouraged planting. During the early nineteenth century concepts of forest management developed in central and northern Europe. State regulation was instituted, and technical aid and tax inducements were offered to owners who practiced sustained yield, a system of management in which removals plus mortality equals growth.

Formal education and research in forestry began in Europe about 1820, at Tharandt in Germany and at Nancy in France. Both education and research in forestry are now found on all forested continents of the world.

Forestry may be subdivided according to the principal human benefits derived from the forest. Wood is one product having great contemporary and historical importance. Forest engineering is concerned with effective removal of wood crops; it includes such activities as road location and construction, harvesting methods, watershed and soil protection, and related matters—all aimed at minimizing costs to the consumer and maintaining productivity of the soil. With worldwide concern about energy, resources, and the environment, wood is being recognized as a low-energy-using, renewable, biodegradable raw material of increasing potential.

Water has long been recognized as a major product of the forest. Management can affect the annual yield, the quality, and the timing of waterflow from forested land. The science of forested watershed management or forest hydrology has developed significantly.

Because many forested areas, particularly in the mountainous regions, are interspersed with grasslands, the forester may find it necessary to manage rangelands for forage for domestic livestock and wildlife species. Although range management is somewhat peripheral to forest management as such, the forester's education often includes at least some exposure to this activity.

The forest is one of the major habitats for wildlife, providing food and cover and affecting the available water supply. Management of the forest may be directed toward the provision of appropriate habitat for birds and mammals as well as for other forms of animals. Freshwater fish can be affected significantly by the influence of forest management practices upon sediment yield, stream temperature, or chemicals in the water.

In areas of the world where the standard of living provides an affluent society with substantial leisure time that can be used in a variety of outdoor recreational activities, the value of forests for skiing, hunting, bird watching, fishing, hiking, camping, backpacking, or canoeing is recognized.

Finally, forests and tree plantings have many amenity values as urban greenbelts, sound barriers, windbreaks and shelterbelts, landscape components, oxygen producers, temperature modifiers, or habitats for endangered species. They also act as effective "living filters," since liquid sewage effluent spread on the forest floor will benefit vegetation without detriment to the groundwater supply. In recent years these human benefits, aside from wood, water and forage, have been given increased recognition, particularly in developed countries.

The field of forestry is sometimes subdivided according to the discipline involved. Examples of such specialties are forest tree physiology, forest ecology, forest soils, forest hydrology, forestry economics, forestry administration and policy, forest entomology, forest mensuration, forest fire management, forest pathology, tree improvement and genetics, silviculture, and wood science. Particularly at the level of graduate or postbaccalaureate education, institutions may build strong programs in certain disciplines within forestry but not in others.

Innovations and recent trends in forestry and forest engineering include such developments as increased sophistication of logging equipment and methods (for example, balloon logging, rubber-tired skidders, complete tree harvest, and whole tree transport); remote sensing for inventory purposes; a substantial broadening of the definition of forestry to include all of the human benefits to be derived from the forest; and greater concern with the effects of management upon water and air quality. At various institutions of higher education certain aspects may be emphasized. The need for diversity in forestry education is being recognized, particularly in developed countries with many universities which offer forestry programs.

The education required of employees in forestry, forest products, forest engineering, and related fields occurs at four levels: vocational, technician, professional, and graduate specialization. Most workers with vocational (skill) training backgrounds in the industrialized countries are employed in the wood-using industries. At the technician (postsecondary) level, European and African countries have educated many more, proportionate to professionals, than North America, where professionally educated foresters substantially outnumber technicians. Europe has about sixty professional programs in forestry, but nearly three times that many at the nonuniversity level. Sweden, Romania, Finland, and France have twenty or more nonuniversity programs in forestry and fewer than five professional programs per country. However, since the mid 1960s the number of nonuniversity programs in the United States has grown substantially and is approaching the number (fifty-one) of professional programs. In Asia professional programs outnumber nonuniversity programs. At the graduate level, foresters are prepared primarily for research and teaching, though some enter management. Most strong graduate programs are found in North America and in Europe. Developing countries are appropriately concentrating their efforts at the vocational, technical, and professional levels.

In 1975 some 230 professional educational programs in forestry existed in about sixty countries. About half of these programs were found in six countries: the United States, Japan, the People's Republic of China, the Soviet Union, Indonesia, and the Republic of Korea. Nearly two thirds of the sixty countries required only a single educational program to meet the needs for professional foresters. Some nations with forestland had no professional forestry education program at all.

In professional forestry education, the subject matter varies from country to country. Amenity values in forestry are important in highly developed countries, where many of the basic human needs have been met. Consequently, forestry education in North America, and to some degree in Europe, is diverse (and probably will become more so) and emphasizes not only timber production but, in a rather substantial way, recreational and amenity values as well. On the other hand, many developing countries in Asia, Africa, and Latin America place primary emphasis upon inventory and utilization of the timber resource but very little emphasis upon amenity values. Concentration upon timber exploitation and management is typical of early developmental stages of forestry education in all countries.

International cooperation in forestry education has been promoted by the Food and Agriculture Organization (FAO) of the United Nations and by several countries working through nationally sponsored programs for international educational development, through bilateral agreements, or in other ways. During the last few years several international programs and conferences in forestry education have been sponsored by FAO and its cooperating governments, and by other international bodies such as the International Union of Societies of Foresters.

DONALD P. DUNCAN

Levels and Programs of Study

Programs in forestry generally require as a minimum prerequisite a secondary education and lead to the following awards: certificate or diploma, bachelor's degree (B.Sc. or B.S.F.), master's degree (M.F. or M.Sc.), the doctorate (Ph.D.), or their equivalents. Programs deal with the principles and practices of forestry, forest management, and/or forest products and consist primarily of classroom and field instruction.

Programs that lead to an award not equivalent to a first university degree deal with the principles and practices of forestry and forest product technology. Principal course content usually includes some of the following: general forestry, silviculture, wood technology, forest scaling, forest entomology, fire control, forest improvement, forest cropping, and woodlot management. Background courses usually include general botany, surveying, photogrammetry, lumber grading, forest road technology, bookkeeping, and marketing of forest products.

Programs that lead to a first university degree deal with the principles of forest resource management and/or forest products. Principal course content usually includes specialized forest-related subjects, such as forest biology, forest soils, forest management, silviculture, forest pathology, dendrology, forest entomology, forest photogrammetry, silvics, wood science, nontimber resources, forest economics, and forest policy. Background courses often included are communications, mathematics, biology, chemistry, physics, geology, plant physiology, economics and other social sciences, and humanities.

Programs that lead to a postgraduate university degree consist primarily of seminar and research work dealing with the principles and practices of forest management but may include additional advanced-level course work. Emphasis may be given to the production, protection, and harvesting of wood crops and products, as well as to the effective management of forestland for water, forage, wildlife, recreation, and other amenity values. Original research terminating in the presentation and defense of a scholarly thesis or dissertation is often required. Principal subject matter areas within which courses and research projects tend to fall include forest management, forest resource utilization, forest mensuration and photogrammetry, wood science, forest policy, forest biology, forest protection, forest economics, reforestation, wildlife management, forest watershed management, development and protection of forest recreational areas, and forestland use. Subject areas within which background studies tend to fall include botany, zoology, chemistry, physics, economics, sociology, photogrammetry, hydrology, soils, law, mathematics, computer science, and statistical analysis.

Programs in forestry engineering also require as a minimum prerequisite a secondary education and lead to the following degrees: bachelor's degree (B.Sc. [Eng.], B.Eng., B.For.Eng.), master's degree (M.Sc. [Eng.], M.For.Eng.), the doctorate (D.Eng., Ph.D.), or their equivalents. Programs deal with the principles and practices of forestry engineering; that is, the application of engineering principles to forestry programs, with emphasis on logging operations.

Principal course content for university-level programs includes some of the following: dendrology, wood technology and utilization, forest management operations, forest mensuration, hydrology, logging production planning and control in logging, logging transportation, and forest econom-ics. Elective courses from other engineering disciplines make up part of the program. Background courses usually include mathematics, natural sciences such as chemistry and biology, and social sciences such as economics and sociology.

On advanced levels, principal subject matter areas within which courses and research projects tend to fall include forestry engineering methods, forest hydrology, water quality and forestland use, forest ecology, forest mensuration, forestland management, production planning and cost control in logging, logging methods, logging engineering, and transport of logs and related forest products. Subject areas within which background studies tend to fall include appropriate specialties from other engineering programs and appropriate specialties from related fields such as physical sciences, biological sciences, social sciences, commercial and business administration, forestry, mathematics, statistics, and computer science.

[This section was based on UNESCO's *International Standard Classification of Education (ISCED): Three Stage Classification System, 1974* (Paris: UNESCO, 1974).]

Major International and National Organizations

INTERNATIONAL

Asia-Pacific Forestry Commission
% FAO Regional Office
Maliwan Mansion
Phra Atit Road
Bangkok, Thailand

Commonwealth Forestry Bureau
Bureau forestier du Commonwealth
Commonwealth Forestry Institute
South Parks Road
Oxford OX1 3RD, England

East African Agriculture and Forestry Research
     Organization (EAAFRO)
Organisation de recherches forestières et
     agricoles de l'Afrique orientale
P.O. Box 30148
Nairobi, Kenya

Food and Agriculture Organization of the
     United Nations (FAO)
Department of Forestry
Rome, Italy

International Centre of Information in Agriculture and Forestry
Centre international d'information agricole et forestière
Slezsko 7, Prague 2, Czechoslovakia

International Union of Forestry Research Organizations (IUFRO)
Union internationale des instituts de recherches forestières
Norwegian Forest Research Institute
1432 As-NLH, Norway

International Union of Societies of Foresters
% Society of Finnish Foresters
Salomonkatu 17 B
00010 Helsinki 10, Finland

For a complete listing of national and international organizations see:

World Directory of Professional Forestry Societies. Helsinki: International Union of Societies of Foresters, n.d.

NATIONAL

Austria:
Österreichische Gesellschaft für Holzforschung
A-1030 Vienna

Canada:
Canadian Forestry Association
3285 Cavendish Boulevard
Suite 655
Montreal, Quebec

Denmark:
Dansk skoforening
Danish Forestry Society
Vester Voldgade 86
1552 Copenhagen V.

Federal Republic of Germany:
Deutscher Forstwirtschaftsrat
Schützenhaus
5308 Rheinbach b., Bonn

Italy:
Associazione forestale italiana
via Salaria 30
Rome

Japan:
Nippon ringakkai
Japanese Forestry Society
% Government Forest Station
Meguro-ku, Tokyo

Mexico:
Sociedad forestal mexicana
Calle de Jesús Terán 11
Mexico 1, D.F.

People's Republic of China:
Chung-kuo lin hsueh hui
Chinese Society of Forestry
Peking, Hopeh

United Kingdom:
Royal Forestry Society of England Wales and Northern Ireland
49 Russell Square
London WC1, England

Society of Foresters of Great Britain
51 Colcokes Road
Banstead, Surrey, England

United States:
American Forestry Association
919 17th Street NW
Washington, D.C. 20006

Society of American Foresters
5400 Grosvenor Lane
Washington, D.C. 20014

For additional national organizations see:

Minerva, Wissenschaftliche Gesellschaften. Berlin, Federal Republic of Germany: de Gruyter, 1972.

Principal Information Sources

GENERAL

Guides to the literature include:

Bush, E. A. R. *Agriculture: An Annotated Bibliography.* London: Macdonald, 1974. A comprehensive bibliography which covers forestry; includes bibliographies, dictionaries, periodicals, and general references.

Forestry (1967–1973): Annotated Bibliography; Author and Subject Index. (2 vols.) Rome: Food and Agriculture Organization, 1974. List of publications and documents produced by FAO, covering many aspects of forestry. Previous FAO forestry bibliography, covering the years 1945–1966, was published in 1967.

Hemmings, E. F. (Ed.) *Basic Library List for Forestry.* (4th ed.) Oxford, England: Commonwealth Forestry Institute Library, University of Oxford, 1967. Lists predominantly English sources.

Library Catalogue of Books. London: Forestry Commission, 1971. Revised to October 1970.

Selected List of American Agricultural Books in Print and Current Periodicals. Beltsville, Maryland: National Agricultural Library, U.S. Department of Agriculture, 1975. Includes a section on forestry.

Subject Catalogue of Forestry Literature, 1951–1964. Oxford, England: Commonwealth Forestry Institute Library, Oxford University, 1965.

Introductions and overviews include:

Sartorius, P., and Henle, H. *Forestry and Economic Development.* New York: Praeger, 1968.

Waters, D. *Forestry.* Elmsford, New York: Pergamon Press, 1966.

For a historical discussion of the literature, training, and research in the field see:

Mantel, K. "History of the International Science of Forestry with Special Consideration of Central Europe." *International Review of Forestry Research,* 1964, *1,* 1–37.

For a discussion of forestry education in the United States see:

Dana, S. T., and Johnson, E. W. *Forestry Education in America Today and Tomorrow.* Washington, D.C.: Society of American Foresters, 1963.

For a discussion of career opportunities and vocational guidance in forestry see:

Shirley, H. L. *Forestry and Its Career Opportunities.* (3rd ed.) New York: McGraw-Hill, 1973.

Sidney, H. (Ed.) *Agricultural, Forestry, and Oceanographic Technicians.* Chicago: Ferguson, 1969.

CURRENT BIBLIOGRAPHIES

Bibliography of Agriculture. Beltsville, Maryland: National Agricultural Library, U.S. Department of Agriculture, 1942–. International source; covers forestry.

Biological and Agricultural Index: Cumulative Subject Index to Periodicals in the Fields of Biology, Agriculture and Related Sciences (formerly *Agricultural Index).* New York: Wilson, 1916–. Lists English-language sources.

Forestry Abstracts. Oxford, England: Commonwealth Forestry Bureau, Commonwealth Agricultural Bureaux, 1939–. Published quarterly. International in scope; covers all aspects of forestry.

Referativnyĭ zhurnal. 56: Lesovedenie i lesovodstvo. Moscow: Akademiia nauk, SSSR, Institut nauchnoĭ informatsii, 1964–. Published monthly. Abstracts on forestry.

Yale Forestry Library. *Dictionary Catalogue of the Yale Forestry Library, Henry S. Graves Memorial Library.* Boston: Hall, 1962–.

A progress report is:

International Review of Forestry Research. New York: Academic Press, 1964–.

PERIODICALS

Australian Forestry, Canadian Journal of Forest Research, Commonwealth Forestry Review (UK), *Forest Conservation* (Canada), *Forest History* (US),

Forestry (UK), *Forestry Chronicle* (Canada), *Forest Science: A Journal of Research and Technical Progress* (US), *Forstwissenschaftliches Zentralblatt/ Forestry Research Journal* (FRG), *International Review of Forestry Research* (US), *Japanese Forestry Society Journal/Nippon ringaku kaishi, Journal of Forestry: A Journal Reporting on the Science, Practice, and Profession of Forestry* (US), *New Zealand Journal of Forestry, Norsk skogbruk, Quarterly Journal of Forestry* (UK), *Revista padurilor* (Romania), *Schweizerische Zeitschrift für Forstwesen/Journal forestier suisse, Skogen* (Sweden), *Unasylva: An International Journal of Forestry and Forest Products* (FAO, Italy).

For complete listings of journals in the field see:

Howse, J. S. *List of Periodicals and Serials in the Forestry Library.* (3rd ed.) Oxford, England: Commonwealth Forestry Institute Library, Oxford University, 1968.

Ulrich's International Periodicals Directory. New York: Bowker, biennial.

World List of Periodicals and Serials of Interest to Forestry, 1960–1964. Rome: Food and Agriculture Organization, 1965.

ENCYCLOPEDIAS, DICTIONARIES, HANDBOOKS

Forbes, R. D., and Meyer, A. B. (Eds.) *Forestry Handbook.* New York: Ronald Press, 1955. An important reference tool.

Forestry Terminology: A Glossary of Technical Terms Used in Forestry. (3rd ed.) Washington, D.C.: Society of American Foresters, 1958. An English dictionary.

List of Bilingual and Multilingual Dictionaries and Glossaries of Interest to Forestry. Rome: Food and Agriculture Organization, 1969.

Titmuss, F. H. *A Concise Encyclopedia of World Timbers.* (2nd ed.) London: Technical Press, 1959.

Weck, J., and others. (Comps.) *Dictionary of Forestry in Five Languages: German-English-French-Spanish-Russian.* Amsterdam: Elsevier, 1966.

DIRECTORIES

The Commonwealth Forestry Handbook. (8th ed.) London: Empire Forestry Association, 1962. A directory listing member associations and societies, forest research and educational institutions, forest services, and periodicals.

Directory of Institutions Educating Professional Foresters. (Rev. ed.) Washington, D.C.: International Union of Societies of Foresters, 1974. A listing of institutions, colleges, and universities throughout the world that offer professional training in forestry.

Forestry Research: A World Directory of Forest and Forest Products Research Institutions. Rome:

Food and Agriculture Organization, 1963. An extensive international listing of institutions.

Forestry Schools in the United States. Washington, D.C.: U.S. Government Printing Office, U.S. Department of Agriculture, 1970.

Institutions in the United States Offering Professional Education in Forestry. Washington, D.C.: Society of American Foresters, 1971.

World List of Forestry Schools. Rome: Food and Agriculture Organization, Forestry Department, 1974.

FORT PIERCE BUREAU
See Smithsonian Institution.

FOUNDATIONS
See Philanthropy and Foundations.

FOUNDATIONS IN RESEARCH
See Research: Foundations in Academic Research.

FOURTH REVOLUTION, THE
(Higher Education Report),
United States

The Fourth Revolution: Instructional Technology in Higher Education (New York: McGraw-Hill, June 1972), a report of the Carnegie Commission on Higher Education, contains the following findings and recommendations.

Higher education in the United States will be revolutionized by the use in the instructional process of new electronic technology such as the computer, closed-circuit television, and the video cassette. By the year 2000, 10 to 20 percent of all instruction on college and university campuses may be carried out through informational technology, and informational technology may be the dominant form of off-campus instruction. The use of electronic technology for instructional purposes will increase access to education for persons isolated from the campus, expand independent study opportunities and courses and methods of instruction, reduce

the routine instructional responsibilities of faculty, and eventually reduce instructional costs by increasing student and faculty productivity.

The lack of instructional material designed for existing equipment has limited the use of the new technology in the instructional process. Therefore, financial support is needed for developing quality instructional programs and materials and for compensating faculty who participate in the formation of instructional units for use with the expanding technologies. A staff of technologists and specialists will be required to assist faculty in the development of such units. Libraries should receive comparable financial support to enable them to utilize the new technologies for miniaturization purposes and for the automation of operations and services.

Extramural educational systems are suited to the expanded use of the new technologies for several reasons: (1) They provide education for those who are unable or unwilling to attend regular university or college classes and therefore are able to utilize self-instructional learning materials. (2) They are mass oriented. (3) They have no physical boundaries and do not require student attendance at a central location. (4) They do not follow the structured academic calendar of traditional universities. The commission recommends that the federal and state governments provide financial support to expand the use of informational technology for nontraditional forms of study and that the federal government continue to provide substantial financial assistance for research and development and for the expansion of the new technologies to college and university campuses. Funds for the production and utilization of learning materials and instructional media for use with the technologies should be increased. By 1980 federal expenditures for these purposes should equal 1 percent of the total national expenditures on higher education. To minimize the costs of establishing the new technologies, the commission proposes a movement toward interinstitutional cooperation and recommends the formation of seven regional cooperative learning-technology centers by 1992.

Finally, to oversee the progress and results of the expansion of instructional technology in higher education, the commission proposes the creation of an independent commission under the auspices of the United States Department of Health, Education and Welfare or a private foundation.

FOUR-YEAR COLLEGE ADMINISTRATION
See General Administration, Organization for.

FRANCE
See French Republic.

FRANCE, NATIONAL ARCHIVES OF
See Archives: France, National Archives of.

FRANCE, NATIONAL LIBRARY OF
See Libraries: National Library of France (Bibliothèque Nationale), France.

FRATERNITIES

The college fraternity is a secret society of students whose members are initiated by invitation. The men's groups are known simply as fraternities, while the women's groups, popularly called sororities, are more correctly known as women's fraternities. Although rooted in the traditions of medieval European and English residential colleges, modern fraternities are predominantly an American phenomenon. The fraternities that do exist in Europe and England today reflect each country's par-

ticular culture and traditions. Student societies in the residential colleges of English universities, for example, reflect the British tradition of masters' imposing discipline on students; the force of tradition is similarly apparent in the *Verbindungen* (clubs) of German universities. Although World War II halted the activities of the German *Korporationen* (fraternities with a predominantly conservative outlook), they unexpectedly revived. Dueling societies have existed for centuries at such universities as Heidelberg, Hamburg, Bremen, Munich, Freiburg, and Mannheim; at Heidelberg thirteen of the thirty-two fraternities, which bear such Latin names as *Allemagna, Danubia, Normania,* and *Rheno-Nicaria,* still engage in the *Mensur* (duel), though the end of this custom may be in sight. Membership in these societies is lifelong and is reputed to assure social status and useful connections in professional life.

Similarly, in the United States cultural influences—among them what Alexis de Tocqueville (1956) described as a predilection to "constantly form associations"—have resulted in the development of seven distinct types of Greek-letter societies: men's social, women's social, men's professional, women's professional, honor, service, and recognition societies. The social fraternity, which overshadows the other types and gives the Greek-letter system its public image, is a society established by students for purposes of fellowship. Characteristic features include secret initiation rites and a name composed usually of two or three Greek letters that represent the society's motto.

A fraternity may be local in scope, existing on a single campus; it may be national in scope if branches, called chapters, exist on campuses throughout the United States; or it may be international, as in the case of American fraternities with chapters at Canadian universities. Each fraternity has its own ritual, motto, badge and other insignia, laws, journal of information, songs, flag, and traditions.

History of Student Societies

The earliest European student societies, called nations, developed in the late eleventh century at the University of Bologna, Italy. Students at that time exercised complete control of university affairs under the office of a student-elected rector. The object of these societies was the cultivation of "fraternity, charity, mutual association and amity, the consolation of the sick and support of the needy, the conduct of funerals and the extirpation of rancor and quarrels," and "the spiritual advantage of members" (Rashdall, 1895, pp. 159–60). The Bologna pattern of student control was adopted in other universities, ranging from Modena, Italy, in 1182 to Valencia, Spain, in 1500. The form is still apparent at Sweden's oldest university, Uppsala, founded in 1477, where student groups arrange member housing, administer scholarships, and provide other services. At the Royal University of Mexico, founded in 1551, the practice of students' electing their professors continued until 1780. Student influence was also dominant at the University of San Marcos de Lima, Peru, established in 1551, the oldest continuing university in the Western Hemisphere.

The first residential college was founded in 1180 at the University of Paris by Jocius, a Londoner. Previously, the university had avoided involvement in the private lives of students and had ignored their most basic needs, such as lodging. Provided with a *hospicum* (communal house), the students chose their own leadership, made their own rules, shared expenses, and enjoyed unregimented fellowship. In establishing the first Oxford residential college in 1263, Walter de Merton at first provided for its government by senior students; in 1264, however, he deprived students of most of their power and set regulations almost monastic in nature. Founders of subsequent residential colleges continued the strict discipline.

In the United States the earliest struggles for student independence took place in reaction to the rigors of the English style of discipline. In their quest for a freer scholarly environment, students moved their colleges toward liberal and intellectual ideas and a more worldly curriculum through their literary societies. The debating or literary society, a forerunner of the fraternity, appeared at Yale University in 1753 and soon after at Princeton and Harvard. Phi Beta Kappa, founded December 5, 1776, at the College of William and Mary, Williamsburg, Virginia, was the first student society to adopt a Greek-letter name and the first to be concerned with social life, though it retained much of the character of the literary society. (It has been suggested, though never historically authenticated, that Phi Beta Kappa was an outgrowth of the Flat Hat Club, formed in 1750 for the purpose of collecting a library for its members.)

The formation of Phi Beta Kappa, like that of the literary societies, is best understood as a protest against traditional English discipline: it was a revolt against the authority of the college and a student assertion of the rights of assembly, free speech, independent decision, and the pursuit of freedom—issues of concern throughout the newly independent United States. The group introduced what are now considered the essential characteristics of such societies: a secret oath, a badge (the key), a code of laws, an initiation ceremony, a seal, a grip, and mottoes in Greek and Latin. "Love of wisdom the guide of life" is the translation of the Greek motto of the key, which is supplemented by the Latin motto on the seal: *Per aspera ad astra*. The first members of Phi Beta Kappa debated such subjects as "The cause and origin of Society"; "Whether a wise state hath any interest nearer at Heart than the Education of the Youth"; and "Whether anything is more dangerous to Civil Liberty in a Free State than a standing Army in time of Peace" (Robson, 1968, p. 665). In 1779 the mother chapter granted charters to

Harvard and Yale Universities, but two years later became inactive when invasion of Tidewater, Virginia, by British troops disrupted the life of the college; not until 1851 was the chapter revived.

The Greek-letter societies of the 1820s were the first to provide a sustaining fellowship of kindred souls, to bring a spiritual quality into daily life, and to create a meaningful and conspicuously vital extracurriculum. The rituals of fraternities reflect their continuing evolution. Thus, those established prior to 1850 emphasized comradeship, recreation, relief from university discipline, and a carefree campus life. By the late 1880s a new type of ritual had developed, which enjoined members to live "lives of useful, law-abiding, God-fearing citizens, trained in mind and body, loyal to their colleges and appreciative of their peculiar obligation to serve and help the less fortunate" (Robson, 1968, p. 9). After World War I fraternities and sororities began to function with a social responsibility far above that of the campus at large. In the 1920s chapters began to house students from abroad; thousands of refugee children were helped; humanitarian appeals turned chapter houses into collection centers. Charities benefited enormously from annual fraternity drives. For both women's and men's groups, paint-up, fix-up, and clean-up projects became traditional.

The idea of establishing branches of fraternities is believed to have been a Masonic inspiration. The Phi Beta Kappa requirement of secrecy was removed in the 1820s. In 1875 two women were admitted as members of Phi Beta Kappa by the University of Vermont chapter; this act signaled the end of Phi Beta Kappa as a social entity and the beginning of its career as a prestigious honor society for men and women. Kappa Alpha, the oldest continuing social fraternity, was founded in 1825 at Union College, Schenectady, New York, as an answer to the establishment of the fifth chapter of Phi Beta Kappa on that campus in 1817. Kappa Alpha also adopted

a key for its emblem, the only other national social fraternity to do so. It was followed at Union by Sigma Phi and Delta Phi in 1827. Pi Beta Phi was established at Union in 1813 with a "hope to equal the learned societies of this country, both in fame and utility" (Robson, 1968, p. 6), but it remained local, as did Chi Delta Theta (Yale, 1821) and Chi Phi (Princeton, 1824); none of these societies had a continuing influence or left substantial impress on American college life.

Dissatisfaction with practices of established fraternities contributed to the diversification of the Greek system and led to the founding of three fraternities at Miami University, Oxford, Ohio: Beta Theta Pi was founded in 1839 as a dissident offshoot of Alpha Delta Phi (Hamilton College, Clinton, New York, 1832), Phi Delta Theta was founded in 1848 in objection to policies of Alpha Delta Phi and Beta Theta Pi, and Sigma Chi was founded in 1855 over dissatisfaction with the principles of Delta Kappa Epsilon (Yale, 1844). Delta Upsilon was founded in 1839 at Williams College, Williamstown, Massachusetts, as an anti-secret Greek-letter fraternity.

Zeta Psi (New York University, 1847) became the first international fraternity on a continuing basis when it installed a chapter at the University of Toronto in 1879; it was also the first to establish a chapter on the Pacific Coast (University of California, 1870). Many fraternities referred to as national are in fact international; there are nearly a hundred chapters of American fraternities at Canadian schools. The export of American fraternities to Canada gave rise to the founding, in 1913, of Phi Kappa Pi, which remains the only truly Canadian national fraternity. Lambda Phi Mu was formed at the University of Bologna, Italy, in 1920 as a brotherhood of American medical students of Italian ancestry. Rho Psi, a fraternity for students and alumni of Chinese background, was founded at Cornell University, Ithaca, New York, in 1916; chapters were subsequently established in the United

States, including Hawaii, and in the Republic of China and Hong Kong. In the Philippines, societies bearing Greek-letter names were established in imitation of American university practices. Efforts to extend national Greek-letter societies beyond American borders to Scotland, Liberia, and Australia have failed.

Modern Fraternal Organizations

By 1880 there was one chapter of a men's national fraternity for every 107 male students enrolled in an American college. Relaxation of paternalistic control on American campuses and growth of the nation geographically and with respect to population hastened the spread of the modern Greek-letter society. New groups were organized and old ones took on fresh functions. As pioneers moved west and founded new colleges, extension of the Greek-letter system followed as a natural course. Yet national collegiate societies for women were still in their infancy. Wesleyan Female College, Macon, Georgia, opened its doors in 1839, and in 1851 the first women's collegiate society, Adelphean, was formed there as a forerunner of the Greek-letter sorority. I. C. Sorosis, now called Pi Beta Phi, was founded at Monmouth College, Monmouth, Illinois, in 1867 as the first women's national fraternity. Kappa Alpha Theta, founded in 1870 at Indiana Asbury University, Greencastle, Indiana (now DePauw University), is the oldest Greek-letter society for women.

The oldest and largest of the social fraternities for black male students, Alpha Phi Alpha, originated at Yale University in 1906 and became international by charterings at Hamilton, Bermuda, and London, England. Alpha Kappa Alpha, the first sorority for black college women, was founded at Howard University, Washington, D.C., in 1908. Three additional fraternities for black male students and three for black female students came into being early in the century.

The first professional fraternity, Phi Delta Phi, was formed in 1869 by a group of male law students at the University of Michigan, Ann Arbor, Michigan. Delta Sigma Delta, founded at the same university in 1882 as the first dental fraternity, is unique in that it maintains several graduate chapters in Europe and Australia. The first professional sorority, Zeta Phi Eta, serving the speech arts, was founded in 1893 at Northwestern University, Evanston, Illinois. Tau Beta Pi, the first Greek-letter organization to be formed as an honor society, was founded by engineering students at Lehigh University, Bethlehem, Pennsylvania, in 1885; the honor societies are now unofficially coordinated by the Association of College Honor Societies. The first of the recognition societies, Alpha Zeta, which is devoted to agriculture, was founded in 1897 at Ohio State University, Columbus, Ohio. The first service fraternity, Alpha Phi Omega, which is recognized by the National Council of the Boy Scouts of America as the college service organization for scout-trained men, was founded at Lafayette College, Easton, Pennsylvania, in 1925.

The professional fraternities closely resemble the social in purpose and in method of operation: congeniality is an essential goal, chapters are organized along similar lines, and both types of societies maintain a chapter house. For their part, the honor and recognition societies make no pretense of organizing a group social life, while the professional groups make no pretense of conferring honor. The recognition societies, which serve the spectrum from advertising to theology, have no intergroup association as do the others and tend to be less formal in method of operation.

Membership criteria, housing, and activities. Membership in a Greek-letter society is simultaneously selective and voluntary. In social fraternities and sororities the chapter sets out to attract new students who are interested in fraternity life; these persons, known as rushees, are introduced to all members and entertained at various types of parties that acquaint them with the social and physical atmosphere of the chapter. If found acceptable, the rushee receives a bid or invitation; if the rushee finds the group acceptable, he or she accepts pledgeship. As a pledge, the potential member is instructed in fraternity history and traditions for six to twelve weeks in preparation for initiation into membership. During the week prior to initiation, the pledge is required to perform duties aimed at placing him or her in the proper psychological, spiritual, and physical condition for initiation. Until the 1950s this week, known as Hell Week, was characterized by hazing practices that were frequently harmful; as these practices were gradually replaced by a program of constructive activities, the preinitiation period was renamed Help Week.

In 1864, when Kappa Alpha at Williams College occupied the first chapter house, fraternities supplied the only living quarters for men on most campuses. Later, more colleges and universities constructed their own living quarters for students, and by the mid-twentieth century many institutions were providing housing space for men's and women's fraternities. Most chapter houses accommodate about thirty-five members, but the largest may accommodate as many as eighty or more.

The fraternity chapter is governed by an executive committee composed of the president, controller, secretary, recorder, and, in many chapters, a chaplain. A faculty brother customarily serves as counselor. Many chapters employ a housemother, who oversees general house management and helps to provide social training. Clubs for mothers, fathers, brothers, and sisters of fraternity members are auxiliary organizations. Fraternities assume that the men and women they initiate will maintain a lifetime bond; rushees are told this, and it is emphasized in pledge training. Stabilization of chapter operation depends to a great extent on alumni loyalty: chapters hold alumni reunions once or twice each year and often publish newsletters for their alumni; career opportunities are opened for young men by alumni brothers of influence.

National administration. Prior to the Civil War each fraternity chapter acted independently of its sister chapters. Central administration of social fraternities began with conventions organized by delegates from the undergraduate and alumni membership. The convention, or grand chapter, functions today as the supreme governing body of the fraternity; meetings are held annually in some fraternities but biennially in most. The convention helps to draw all chapters into a cohesive unit and in many instances affords the sole contact of chapter with chapter. Between conventions a board of directors exercises full authority.

The central office serves as a base for the national coordination of fraternity records, activities, and communications, as well as for the publication of the national fraternity journal. The national office also organizes national or regional leadership workshops, where experienced alumni members instruct chapter leaders in fraternity practices. Financial operations of the fraternity are supported by pledge and initiation fees and alumni contributions; most fraternities also have an endowment fund and special-purpose funds built up mainly through undergraduate assessments, alumni contributions, and bequests. An educational foundation makes possible the annual award of collegiate scholarships.

Interfraternity organizations. Campus organizations of Greek-letter societies include the Interfraternity Council (IFC) for men and the Campus Panhellenic for women. Made up of representatives from member fraternities and sororities, these organizations regulate rushing programs and procedures, promote amity among their constituents, and inspire good public relations through the conduct of Greek Week and other inter-Greek functions. At many schools a dean of fraternities and a dean of sororities coordinate these programs and counsel IFC and Panhellenic leaders.

In addition to campus organizations,

several national interfraternity bodies hold annual or biennial conferences, where issues vital to their members are discussed, better performance is inspired, standards are agreed on, and a collective national fraternal consciousness is generated. The National Panhellenic Conference (NPC) was formed in 1902 in Chicago, at a meeting called by Alpha Phi; representatives from seven sororities were present. The NPC meets biennially and includes as affiliates more than two hundred Campus Panhellenics and an even larger number of City Panhellenics throughout the United States, Canada, and Europe, which carry on meetings, social activities, and philanthropic projects, and provide loyal service to nearby collegiate chapters. Through committee work at its conferences, the NPC has concerned itself with the practical problems of fair play in rushing, standards of social conduct, scholarship, and housing.

The National Interfraternity Conference (NIC) was established in 1909 in New York City, at a meeting held at the invitation of President W. H. P. Faunce of Brown University, Providence, Rhode Island, who felt that the fraternities needed a regulatory agency. Alumni from twenty-six men's national fraternities were present. From the beginning, the NIC has enjoyed a constructive partnership at its annual meetings between fraternity alumni and college administrators. It is the only interfraternity association to maintain a permanent central office (located in Indianapolis, Indiana) and to conduct a national Undergraduate Interfraternity Conference within its framework. Through its committees and its three subsidiary associations of fraternity executive directors, editors, and scholarship officers, much valuable research has been accomplished in areas of fraternity operation.

The Professional Panhellenic Association was founded in 1925, when a number of women's professional fraternities joined to promote common interests. The purpose of the organization is to broaden the educational advantage of the individual member through programs of professional guidance. Meetings are biennial. The Association of College Honor Societies, also founded in 1925, was organized by a group of college and university teachers, administrators, and representatives of several honor societies. In its supervision of the character, function, and standards of membership, and in its concern for the multiplicity and undesirable duplication of honor societies, it serves unofficially as an accrediting agency. The Professional Interfraternity Conference was organized in 1928 by representatives of the leading men's professional fraternities. Its functions are to promote high ideals and ethics among fraternity members and to maintain high standards in the chapters. Meetings are biennial. The National Panhellenic Council was organized and incorporated in 1929 by the eight existing black fraternities and sororities to consider questions and problems of mutual interest. Meetings are held annually. The National Interfraternity Foundation was incorporated in 1945 by officers of the NIC. Its chief contribution has been to help the NIC maintain its scholarship improvement program and to aid the fraternity system financially. The Interfraternity Research and Advisory Council, established in 1946 by representatives of men's and women's social and professional fraternity conferences, coordinates interfraternity public relations and conducts research. A monthly newsletter, the *IRAC Bulletin,* is widely circulated.

Perspectives

By the 1970s American and Canadian universities and colleges sheltered approximately 300 separate intercollegiate societies with more than 21,000 operating chapters that had initiated nearly 10,000,000 male and female students. These societies included 75 men's social fraternities, with 2,783,215 initiates; 35 women's social fraternities, with 1,519,145 initiates; 65 men's professional fraternities, with 1,230,000 initiates; 23 women's professional fraternities, with 290,000 initiates; and approximately 4,000,000 members of honor, service, and recognition societies (Robson, 1968). In 1970 the system received a modest impetus for further growth when, by amendment of NIC laws, accredited junior colleges became eligible for the installation of chapters.

Throughout their two-hundred-year history in the United States, fraternities have advanced steadily in an atmosphere of free and open association, student initiative and enterprise, adaptation to changing needs and conditions, and citizenship development, but that atmosphere has been threatened on occasion. Antifraternity legislation resulted in the suspension of fraternities in South Carolina from 1897 to 1929 and in Mississippi from 1912 to 1926; similar legislation introduced in Arkansas and Indiana failed of enactment. A New York State law denationalized chapters at the University of Buffalo in 1962, when that school became a part of the University of the State of New York system. In 1964 and 1972 fraternity membership selection processes were briefly threatened by antidiscrimination laws (later amended to exclude fraternities). Some women's and men's groups opposed the Equal Rights Amendment, introduced in 1971, which forbids bias on the basis of sex: the fraternities feared that strict enforcement of antidiscrimination laws could conceivably lead to charges of illegal cohabitation in the chapter houses.

Wars and economic depressions have handicapped fraternity life, since they cause declines in male higher education enrollment, thus drastically reducing the number of men qualifying for fraternity membership. Administrative strictures, such as the insistence on 100 percent membership opportunity by Amherst, Hamilton, and Williams Colleges in 1953, have actually destroyed the system on certain campuses. In the 1960s a trend began toward coeducational chapters, which has

resulted in some erosion of traditional fraternity spirit. In addition, antireligious trends and campus organizations antagonistic to spiritual ideals have, at times, impeded the progress of fraternities. Finally, bureaucratic techniques, such as stringent regulations of rushing and pledging, have cramped selection methods for both fraternities and rushees.

During the campus upheavals of the 1960s, when the questioning of traditional values by youth became a universal pastime, fraternity membership declined seriously; in the early 1970s, however, the Greeks again came into focus as perhaps the most stable campus force to which administrators could turn for aid in monitoring campus order. Thoughtful members, realizing that the curriculum failed to profess a sustaining system of values, and recognizing these values in their own lives of brotherhood and sisterhood, began to encourage more discussions with faculty in the chapter house. Faculty elders adjured their young fraternity mates that the philosophy of learning to live together as brothers merited a broader and more complete understanding; one national fraternity librarian was inspired by that sentiment to write a book urging chapters to establish libraries of "reading ladders for brotherhood." As the decade of the 1970s progressed, this idea posed a heightened challenge to fraternities.

Bibliography

Burn, B. *Higher Education in Nine Countries.* New York: McGraw-Hill, 1971.

Eberly, C. G. *Building and Maintaining a Chapter Library.* Menasha, Wisconsin: Banta, 1970.

Johnson, C. S. "An American Fraternity Abroad." *Banta's Greek Exchange*, 1957, 45 (4), 246–249.

Johnson, C. S. *Fraternities in Our Colleges.* New York: National Interfraternity Foundation, 1972.

Lerner, M. *America as a Civilization.* New York: Simon & Schuster, 1957.

Rashdall, H. *The Universities of Europe in the Middle Ages. Vol. I. Salerno, Bologna, Paris.* London: Oxford University Press, 1895, pp. 159–160.

Robson, J. *The College Fraternity and Its Modern Role.* Menasha, Wisconsin: Banta, 1966.

Robson, J. (Ed.) *Baird's Manual of American College Fraternities.* (18th ed.) Menasha, Wisconsin: Banta: 1968.

Rudolph, F. *The American College and University.* New York: Knopf, 1962.

Tocqueville, A. de. *Democracy in America.* New York: New American Library, 1956.

JOHN ROBSON

See also: College Unions; Extracurricular Activities on Campus; Sport, Interuniversity.

FRAUDULENT INSTITUTIONS
See Diploma Mills.

FREE SPEECH MOVEMENT
See Unrest, Campus.

FREEDOM OF STUDENT PRESS
See Courts and Higher Education; Student Publications.

FREER GALLERY OF ART
See Smithsonian Institution.

FRENCH ALLIANCE
(Alliance française)

Founded in Paris by a group of eminent Frenchmen in 1883, the *Alliance française* has aimed, since its inception, to preserve and spread knowledge of the French language and culture at home and abroad. In 1975 there were 1300 *Alliances françaises*—independent, nonpolitical societies of friends of France. The principal activity of the society in Paris is educational. Officially affiliated with the University of Paris, it operates the *Ecole internationale de langue et de civilisation françaises* (International School of French Language and Civilization). Since 1945 some 800,000 students, ranging in age from ten to eighty, have attended this school—everyone from the beginner to the professor of French. Operating year around, it offers courses at all levels of competency: audiovisual courses for beginners; intensive and accelerated French courses; conversation courses; commercial translation courses in French, English, and German; correspondence courses; and teacher training courses, including an advanced course. Some 300 persons yearly take the Paris school's instruction for teachers of French in foreign countries; this program includes sessions on literature, linguistics, and phonetics; group seminars on topics such as audiovisual techniques; and teaching demonstrations in class. In addition, some 400 professors take a special training course.

The principal task of the societies abroad is also educational. They help to spread the knowledge of France and French culture through conferences, films, meetings, libraries, and reading rooms. Three hundred alliances have schools: high school, college, or French teaching centers. These schools are located in apartments or houses rented or owned by the local committee. During the past thirty years more than fifty society houses have been built abroad.

The schools of the *Alliance française* employ 2500 professors, of whom 400 are delegated and paid by the French Ministry of Foreign Affairs.

Alliance publications include *Bulletin pédagogique*, a monthly; *Cours de langue et de civilisation françaises* (four volumes); *Grammaire pratique du français d'aujourdhui; Le français élémentaire* (two booklets).

101 boulevard Raspail
75270 Paris, France

FRENCH GUIANA

Population: 55,125. Student enrollment in primary school (public and private): 10,736; secondary school (public and private): 5628; higher education (Centre universitaire Antilles-Guyane): *154. Language of instruction: French. Academic calendar: November to May. [All figures are for 1974–75.]*

Located on the northeast coast of South America, French Guiana is the largest and the most sparsely populated of the four overseas departments of the French Republic. The educational system of Guiana is identical to that of France. Education is compulsory through age sixteen and is provided by a five-year primary cycle followed by a four-year program of either general, technical, or professional study at the lower secondary level. Upon completion of the nine-year compulsory cycle, students may elect to follow a short or a long upper secondary program. The short program involves one to three years of technical or professional training, leading to employment. Students enrolled in the long program, which lasts three years, prepare for the *baccalauréat* or the *baccalauréat de technicien;* either of these certificates entitles the student to pursue higher education at home or abroad.

The majority of secondary school graduates who pursue higher education enter either the *Centre universitaire Antilles-Guyane* (CUAG: Antilles-Guiana University Center) or higher education institutions in France. The CUAG mainly serves the three overseas departments of French Guiana, Guadeloupe, and Martinique. Admission is determined by the *baccalauréat* or equivalent diploma or by a special entrance examination.

The CUAG consists of five education and research units *(unités d'enseignement et de recherche:* UER). Four of the UERs are in Pointe-à-Pitre, Guadeloupe: *lettres et sciences humaines* (letters and humanities), *sciences juridiques et économiques* (legal and economic sciences), *sciences exactes et naturelles* (exact and natural sciences), and *sciences de la santé* (health sciences). The fifth, *sciences juridiques et économiques* (legal and economic sciences), is in Fort-de-France, Martinique. A law institute, *Institut Henri Vizióz de Cayenne,* located in Cayenne, French Guiana, is also part of the CUAG.

Degree programs at the CUAG are carried out in three cycles. All three cycles are offered only in law, and students in other fields usually complete their second and/or third cycles in France. The first cycle, sanctioned by the *diplôme d'études universitaires générales* (DUEG: Diploma of General University Study), is available in law, economic sciences, letters, and sciences. The second cycle, offered only in law and economic sciences, requires an additional two years of study and leads to the *licence.* Students in law may study an additional year and earn the *diplôme d'études supérieures spécialisées* (DESS: Diploma of Specialized Higher Study) in the third cycle. The CUAG also offers a below-degree-level program in law, which leads to the *certificat de capacité en droit* (Certificate of Capacity in Law). Holders of this certificate have access to certain legal and paralegal professions and are able to compete for civil service positions. Others may qualify for entrance to the *licence* program in law.

Students enrolled in the sciences and humanities either attend facilities in Guadeloupe or complete their studies by correspondence. Students following medical studies register with the CUAG but, by agreement, undertake the first cycle and the first year of the second cycle of study in the French Universities of Bordeaux, Montpellier, or Toulouse and then return to the CUAG for the completion of their program.

[Assistance provided by Jean-Pierre Lassale, Recteur de l'Académie des Antilles et de la Guyane, Fort-de-France, Martinique.]

Bibliography

Le bac ... et après? ... Les études au Centre universitaire Antilles-Guyane. Pointe-à-Pitre, Guadeloupe: Centre universitaire Antilles-Guyane, Cellule d'information et d'orientation, 1976.

"Les étudiants. Effectifs des étudiants dans les universités. Année scolaire 1973–1974." In *Statistiques des enseignements.* Vanves, France: Service central des statistiques et sondages, 1975.

Tableaux de l'éducation nationale. Paris: Ministère de l'éducation nationale, Service d'informations économiques et statistiques, 1975.

See also: Caribbean: Regional Analysis.

FRENCH INSTITUTE
(Institut de France)

Founded in 1795, the *Institut de France* (French Institute) held its first meeting at the Louvre in Paris on April 4, 1796, before an array of scholars, writers, artists, and diplomats. In 1803 Bonaparte divided the institute into four categories: physical and mathematical sciences, French language and literature, ancient history and literature, and fine arts. He abolished a former category—moral and political sciences. Bonaparte offered free membership to associates and foreign associates; associates living in France but away from Paris were called correspondents.

In 1804 Bonaparte issued a decree establishing a decennial prize for works of science, literature, or art. The following year he moved the four sections from the Louvre to the College of the Four Nations, in Paris. In 1816, during the Restoration, the four categories were given the names of former academies: French Academy, Academy of Inscriptions and Letters, Academy of Sciences, and Academy of Arts. In 1832 the Academy of Moral and Political Sciences was reestablished.

The Second Empire kept a watchful eye over the institute. A decree of April 14, 1855, gave the government the right to regulate the institute's annual public meetings and to name a part of the Commission of Prizes. Later, government control was imposed by a decree which created a sixth section—politics, administration, and finance—named by the Emperor. This was a serious departure from a fundamental principle of the academies—that members are elected by their peers. The sixth section was abolished in 1866. In 1872, on the eve of the Third Republic, President Louis Adolphe Thiers, who was a member of the French Academy, did away with the decree of 1855.

The contemporary French Institute has five academies: the French Academy, with forty ordinary members; the Academy of Inscriptions and Letters, with forty-five members, ten free members, twenty for-eign associates, thirty French correspondents, and forty foreign correspondents; the Academy of Sciences, with sixty-six ordinary members, fourteen free members, twelve nonresident members, six members for the application of science to industry, twenty-eight foreign associates, and one hundred twenty correspondents; the Academy of Arts, with fifty ordinary members, fifteen foreign associates, and fifty correspondents; and the Academy of Moral and Political Sciences, with fifty members, twelve foreign associates, and sixty correspondents.

The institute celebrates its birthday each year by a public meeting where each section sends a delegate to read a speech, thus manifesting the moral and administrative unity of the institute.

Publications of the institute's academies include *Comptes rendus, Mémoires, Notices et extraits des MSS., Savants étrangers, Annuaire de l'Académie des beaux-arts, Revue des travaux de l'Académie et comptes rendus de ses séances, Ordonnances des rois de France*, and *Notices biographiques et bibliographiques.*

23 quai de Conti
Paris 6e, France

FRENCH POLYNESIA

Population: 120,000 (1973 estimate). Student enrollment in primary school: 35,868 (17,304 females); secondary school: 7046 (4006 females). Language of instruction: French and Polynesian. [Unless otherwise indicated, figures are for 1974.]

French Polynesia, which is composed of 120 scattered islands in the South Central Pacific Ocean, has been a French overseas territory since 1958, having been a French colony since the late nineteenth century.

Primary and secondary education on the islands follow the French system and lead to the *baccalauréat*. Higher education is not available on the islands.

The French government and various social organizations, such as Rotary, assist students in achieving higher education abroad. The exact number of students abroad is not available.

[Information received from the Vice-Rector of the Academy of French Polynesia, Papeete, Tahiti.]

FRENCH REPUBLIC

Population: 52,655,000 (1975). Student enrollment in primary school: 4,570,405; secondary school (academic, technical): 4,791,875; higher education: 850,000 (public institutions, (1975). Student enrollment as percentage of age group (18–22): 15%. Language of instruction: French. Academic calendar: October to May. Percentage of gross national product (GNP) expended on all education: approximately 3.2%; higher education: .8%. Percentage of national budget expended on education: 18%. [Enrollment figures are for 1973–74; budget figures are for 1975. Source: Tableaux de l'éducation nationale, *1974.]*

The French system of higher education is one of the oldest in the world. The University of Paris, founded as *Universitas Magistrorum* in 1150 and confirmed by papal bull in 1215—together with the universities in Bologna, Italy; Oxford, England; and Salamanca, Spain—decisively influenced the development of higher education, first in Europe and later in the former European colonies in Africa, the Americas, and Asia. From the founding of the University of Paris until the middle of the seventeenth century, universities were established in all the important cities of France. For instance, in the thirteenth century universities opened in Montpellier (1220), Toulouse (1229), and Lyon (1245); in the fourteenth century at Orléans (1306); and in the fifteenth century at Poitiers (1431), Bordeaux (1441), and Nantes (1460) as well as in other cities. The sixteenth century saw the inception of universities at Reims (1548), Lille (1560), and Nancy (1572). These universities were founded by the church and recognized by papal bull, although a few were established by the sovereign: Charles V established the

University of Angers in 1364 and Henry VI of England the University of Caen in 1432. Each of these universities was later confirmed by the pope. The universities were under the jurisdiction of the church and existed independently of the laws of the government. The original fields of study were canon law and medicine, but eventually law, letters, and science were also added. The programs led to diplomas and degrees: *baccalauréat, licence, maîtrise.* The French universities provided a model of teaching and research for the rest of Europe until the National Convention in 1793 abolished all universities in France.

In 1806 Napoleon I recreated higher education but in a new and reorganized form. The faculties of the former universities were accorded legal status and financial autonomy as professional schools of medicine, law, and pharmacy and as faculties of science and letters, but were placed under the jurisdiction of a Grand Master and a council in Paris. Also included in this single university system was all primary and secondary education. This highly centralized system of education, known as the Napoleonic university, remained in force for most of the nineteenth century and came to influence a number of the South and Central American universities founded after the independence of the American republics in the early nineteenth century. This system was unique in the uniformity of its curricula, teaching methods, and degree requirements.

In the late 1800s French higher education underwent another period of reorganization. Among changes introduced by Jules Ferry, the minister of education, was the separation of church and state in education, codified in the law of March 28, 1882. This law granted individuals and associations the right to establish private institutions, but only within the framework and standards of the National Ministry of Education. In 1896 Ferry regrouped the individual schools and faculties into separate universities and divided France into twenty-three educational districts, *acad-*

émies, each with its own university.

At the same time as the re-creation of the universities, many institutions of higher education for professional training in engineering and administration, the *grandes écoles,* were established. Thus was born a dual system of higher education which has lasted until today. On one hand, this system consisted of the *grandes écoles,* which concentrated on teaching rather than research and produced executive personnel for government and industry; on the other hand, there were the universities, which trained doctors, lawyers, pharmacists, and secondary school teachers. The *grandes écoles* were elite institutions with highly competitive entrance standards and a high graduation rate. At the universities access was open to all holders of the *baccalauréat* (secondary school-leaving certificate); and failure rates, especially in the humanities, were sometimes 50 percent in the first year. The university became the center of cultural transmission and research, while the *grandes écoles* offered practical training. There was no transfer of students between the two types of institutions and little interaction between teaching staff and administrations.

Despite the nineteenth-century reorganization of the university system into twenty-three individual universities, French university education remained highly centralized under the minister of national education. Each university consisted of the same five faculties: law, medicine, pharmacy, letters, and science. Teaching methods, examinations, and degree requirements were identical, and any changes or innovations had to be approved by the minister. Thus, in practice, the universities still comprised one university system—the National French University. Little change was undertaken until the 1960s, and then change came in response to pressures of enrollments.

Student numbers expanded as the number of secondary school graduates increased; from 5517 graduates in 1900, or 1 percent of the generation, it grew to 31,691 in 1949, or approximately 5 percent of the generation, and to 196,000 in 1974, or 23 percent of the generation (Le Bris, 1975, p. 89). As university enrollments increased from some 134,000 in 1950 to about 500,000 in 1967, the university proved increasingly unable to offer sufficient services to the students, and the number of failures and dropouts increased. While the university sector continued to expand as a result of its open admissions policy, the *grandes écoles* (because of their strict admission requirements) were less affected by the enrollment increases. A number of new *grandes écoles* were also created.

In 1966 the first important change since the end of the nineteenth century occurred in the system. Two-year *instituts universitaires de technologie* (IUT: university institutes of technology) were introduced to offer training to higher technicians. This attempt at diversifying educational offerings to reflect the technological orientation of the latter part of the twentieth century, did not, however, affect large numbers of students. By 1975, 70 of these institutions had been founded, enrolling 50,000 students.

The problems of the university system—the overcrowding, the high failure rates during the first year of study, the lack of student and faculty input into administrative structures that had remained unchanged since before the turn of the century—were brought to national attention in the student unrest of May 1968. The French government was quick to respond to student demands. By November 12 of the same year, it promulgated the *Loi d'orientation de l'enseignement supérieur* (Orientation of Higher Education Act), designed to reorient the whole French university system. The act, as conceived by the then minister of education, Edgar Faure, was designed to include the participation of students and faculty in decision making and to introduce greater university autonomy by creating new interdisciplinary units of study with more autonomy in administration, financing, and teaching methods. The faculties of all the universities were reorganized into some seven hundred and eighty interdisciplinary units, *unités d'enseignement et de recherche* (UER: units of teaching and research), which were later regrouped into universities and assimilated institutions. By 1975 there were seventy-four universities, one university in each major French city, thirteen in the Paris area alone.

Since 1968 a number of further reforms have been recommended by the government. Some have been implemented, such as the creation of a Secretariat of State for Higher Education to supervise the whole system of higher education; others are in varying stages of implementation, having met with resistance from the groups affected or having been the victim of budget cuts. Among recommended changes is a restructuring of the teaching staff to include only two ranks, *professeurs* and *maîtres-assistants.* Such a change might prove costly because of the upgrading that would become necessary for large numbers of staff of lower ranks.

Legal Basis of Educational System

The legal basis of French higher education is the *Loi d'orientation de l'enseignement supérieur* of November 12, 1968 (with additions in 1971), which restructured the system of university education in accordance with principles of autonomy, provided for student and faculty participation in decision making, and introduced the concept of interdisciplinary programs. The law also established the *Conseil national de l'enseignement supérieur et de la recherche* (National Council of Higher Education and Research) to advise the minister of education in matters of higher education. Further changes in the university structure have been made by decree.

The *Conférence des présidents d'universités* (Conference of University Presidents), established by decree in 1971, although purely advisory, offers university presidents an opportunity to influence university planning and development.

Types of Institutions

French higher education, which in 1975 enrolled about 850,000 students in public institutions, can be divided into two sectors: universities and nonuniversity institutions of higher education. The universities, including the *instituts universitaires de technologie,* enroll more than 80 percent of all students in higher education. The nonuniversity institutions include the university-level *grandes écoles,* the preparatory classes for the *grandes écoles (classes préparatoires aux grandes écoles),* the *sections de techniciens supérieurs* (sections for higher technical training) and the *écoles normales* (teacher training schools).

Only the state universities are entitled to award national degrees. There are seven private, denominational universities—five Catholic and two Protestant; their students generally are enrolled simultaneously in a state university to receive national degrees. Since the 1968 Orientation of Higher Education Act, the universities have been divided into units of teaching and research (UERs). Seven hundred and eighty such units were in operation in 1975–76; their combined enrollment was approximately 765,000. Introduced in 1966, the university institutes of technology (IUTs) have since been attached to the universities as UERs, although they are allowed to retain their autonomy and distinct structure. The IUTs offer two-year programs leading to a diploma of technology, which qualifies graduates for positions as higher technicians. Graduates may enter the universities in the second cycle of study. Unlike the universities, the IUTs include a large number of practicing professionals in their teaching staff. Almost 50,000 students were enrolled in these programs in 1975–76 (their numbers are included in university statistics).

The *grandes écoles*—composed of engineering schools, normal schools, higher schools of commerce, and various other specialized schools—are training high-level personnel for government and industry. The *grandes écoles* enrolled some 80,000 students in 1972–73. About half of the *grandes écoles* are under the jurisdiction of the secretary of state for universities; some 25 percent are responsible to ministries such as industry, agriculture, defense; and about 25 percent are privately organized. The older *grandes écoles* possess a large measure of autonomy; in contrast, some of the newest have been attached to universities. Among the most famous *grandes écoles* are the *Ecole polytechnique,* the *Ecole centrale des arts et manufactures,* the *Ecole des hautes études commerciales,* and the four *écoles normales supérieures.* Although the higher normal schools were founded to train secondary school teachers, their level of training is such that most of their graduates prefer to enter university teaching or research. Preparatory classes for the *grandes écoles,* generally lasting two years, are considered higher education, since only holders of the *baccalauréat* are admitted. The schools enrolled over 30,000 students in 1975–76, the majority in public institutions.

The *sections de techniciens supérieurs* provide training at an intermediate level in three major areas of specialization: agricultural, industrial, and clerical and business-oriented vocational training. The latter area comprises secretarial and bookkeeping training, distribution, communications, and hotel work. In 1975–76 about 25,000 students were enrolled in the public sector of these programs.

The *écoles normales* offer two-year primary school teacher training to holders of the *baccalauréat.*

In the 1970s a new concept of education was introduced in France: the *éducation permanente* (recurrent education), designed for working adults. Within the framework of *éducation permanente* can be found the *formation professionelle continue* (continual professional training), established by a law of July 16, 1971. This law stipulates that professionals have a right to a period of additional training, to be financed by employers to the amount of 1 percent of the payroll of a company. The portion of this educational contribution not spent by the company for the training of its employees has to be remitted to the state, which distributes the available funds and controls every part of the training.

The advanced classes of the *Centre national de téléenseignement* (National Center for Multi-Media Teaching) have a large part-time audience. With education imparted through radio, television, and booklets, this home-study program awards its own certificates up to degree level.

Relationship with Secondary Education

In accordance with the decree of January 6, 1959, there are ten years of compulsory education, from age six to sixteen. Primary education has been free since 1882; secondary education, since 1933. The primary cycle lasts five years. The secondary program is divided into two cycles: a compulsory first cycle of four years, offered in *collèges d'enseignement général* or *collèges d'enseignement secondaire;* and a second cycle, which lasts two years (short program) or three years (long program). The three-year program, offered in academic or technical *lycées,* prepares students for the *baccalauréat* diploma in a number of specialties: literature and philosophy, economics and social sciences, mathematics and physical sciences, natural sciences, and technical specialties. In 1975, 202,000 students were successful in the *baccalauréat* examination; most of them continued into higher education.

The two-year secondary program is available in *collèges d'enseignement technique.* Graduates enter the labor force.

There are private schools in both cycles. Since 1959 private schools have been eligible for financial assistance from the state.

Admission Requirements

The general requirement for admission to the universities is the *baccalauréat* or equivalent qualifications. Students enroll directly in the respective UER they wish to attend. Those lacking the *baccalauréat* are eligible for admission by special examination if they are twenty years old by October 1 of the year of the examination and have two years of experience in salaried employment or if they are at least twenty-five years old by October 1 of the year of the examination. Two examinations are given depending on the desired area of study: humanities or sciences.

Entry to the preparatory classes for the *grandes écoles* is highly selective and based upon the results in the *baccalauréat* with a specialty in mathematics and physics. After two years of study, students are required to pass a competitive examination to be admitted to a *grande école*. The failure rate for the examination is about 70 percent, but those students who fail have the option of entering directly into the second cycle of a degree program at a university.

Although the *baccalauréat* is not required for entry to the IUTs, most students have this qualification.

Administration and Control

Since July 1974 authority for the French university system has been vested in the secretary of state for universities. The secretary has direct authority over the *chanceliers* (chancellors) of the universities, who are appointed by the government and also function as rectors of the academies. The *chanceliers* are responsible for primary and secondary education and serve as a link between the universities and the secretary of state; the secretary also has authority over the *Conseil national de l'enseignement supérieur et de la recherche* (National Council for Higher Education and Research), over which the secretary presides. The function of the council is to advise the secretary on financial and administrative matters. About half of its ninety members are elected by the individual university councils from a national list presented by staff and student unions or associations. The remaining members are appointed

from outside the university by the secretary. The secretary also supervises the *Conférence des présidents d'universités*, (Conference of University Presidents), which in meetings with the secretary discusses questions of common interest to its members.

According to the 1968 law, the universities have administrative autonomy. The administrative head of the university is the president, who is elected by the university council for five years. The university council is the highest administrative body. Members include teachers, elected from all ranks; students; administrative and technical personnel; and persons from outside the university chosen by the secretary. The council establishes rules and regulations for the whole university, elects the president, and prepares the budget, allocating the funds for each UER. It also elects members to the National Council for Higher Education and Research (Patterson, 1972, pp. 286–289).

Each UER is headed by a director, usually a professor elected for three years by the UER council. The UER council is composed of members elected by and from the teaching and research staff, students (half of the council members), and non-teaching personnel. The function of the UER council is to determine the internal structure of the UER and the extent of its cooperation with other units in programs of study, teaching methods, research activities, and examinations.

Those *grandes écoles* under the direct authority of the secretary of state for universities generally follow the same pattern. However, their directors are not elected but are appointed by the secretary of state. The *grandes écoles* under the authority of other ministries are controlled directly by the concerned ministry. Private *grandes écoles* are administered by a board of trustees and have the status of a nonprofit organization.

The IUTs are headed by a director, who is also appointed by the secretary of state and has administrative duties similar to those of the director of a UER.

Programs and Degrees

The programs at French universities are organized into three cycles, each lasting two years. According to a decree of March 3, 1973, the first cycle of study leads to the *diplôme d'études universitaires générales* (DEUG: diploma of general university studies) in one of the following fields of study: arts and letters, economics, humanities and social sciences, law, sciences, economic and social administration, applied mathematics, and social sciences. In addition to courses stipulated by the government, the curriculum includes courses set by the individual university and elective courses. This cycle is designed to provide students with a broad enough training to allow them to start a professional career. Most students, however, prefer to continue into the second cycle, which leads to the *licence* in arts or sciences at the end of the first year and to the *maîtrise* at the end of the second. The full two years of the second cycle are required for the *licence* in law and economics. Both the *licence* and the *maîtrise* are necessary for those who wish to take the examinations to qualify as secondary school teachers: the *certificat d'aptitude au professorat de l'enseignement secondaire* (CAPES) and the *agrégation*.

The third cycle of study is one of specialization and research leading to postgraduate degrees. A *diplôme d'études supérieures specialisées* (DESS) is awarded after one year of a highly specialized program, which includes practical training to prepare the student for work in his field.

The program for the *doctorat du troisième cycle* primarily involves research. A one-year introduction to research techniques through seminars and laboratory training leads to a *diplôme d'études approfondies* (DEA). One or two additional years of study are then required for the doctorate. The *doctorat d'état*, awarded after proven ability to undertake original research, is the most prestigious degree. The program does not require attendance at the university during the period of the thesis preparation; however, the candidate must register to defend his thesis under the guidance of a research director at the university and defend the thesis before a jury. In science the work for the state doctorate may last five years, and in the humanities it may last ten. A *doctorat d'université* (university doctorate) is less prestigious than the *doctorat d'état* and does not qualify for university teaching.

The *doctorat du troisième cycle* and the *doctorat d'état* are national diplomas signed by the secretary of state for universities; the *doctorat d'université* is awarded by the university and signed by the president of the university.

Studies in medicine are divided into two cycles. The first cycle lasts two years and includes both theory and practice. At the end of the first year, students sit for a competitive examination. Only the best students are permitted to continue, because the places available in hospital facilities are limited. The second cycle lasts four years. During the first year students establish their first contact with the hospital; the following years are devoted to pathology and therapeutic studies. On achieving a diploma of Doctor in Medicine, students can prepare for advanced certificates in various specialties. The three cycles in pharmacy and dentistry are respectively one year (preparatory year), three years for general training, and one year for specialization.

The *grande école* offers three years of experimental and theoretical training leading to a diploma of engineer or a business school diploma. Usually the third year is used for specialization.

The *diplôme universitaire de technologie* (DUT), which is awarded at the end of the program of study at an IUT, allows students to enter the second cycle of some programs for the *maîtrise* in sciences or certain *grandes écoles*.

The *sections de techniciens supérieurs* in a program of two years award the *brevet de technicien supérieur* (BTS: higher technician diploma), which is similar to the DUT diploma.

Financing and Student Financial Aid

Public expenditure on higher education as a proportion of the gross national product (GNP) increased from .2 percent in 1958 to .5 percent in 1965 and about .8 percent in 1975 (*Tableaux de l'éducation nationale,* 1975). This increase was due partly to the rapidly increasing student numbers.

Through the secretary of state for universities, the state provides financing to the public universities, the IUTs, and half of the *grandes écoles*. Other *grandes écoles* are supported by their respective sponsoring ministries. Private institutions are financed mainly by student fees but also receive state subsidies.

Prior to the 1968 reform, funds for the universities were allotted by the then Ministry of Education in accordance with enrollments, size of the physical plant, and the fields of study offered. Since 1968 state funds have been allotted to the universities as block grants, allowing the university internal fiscal autonomy.

All students pay a student fee (in 1974, about US$40, including health insurance) and can apply for scholarships and waivers of fees. In the academic year 1974–75, 120,000 students received some assistance from the government. Retention of the scholarship depends on the students' records, which have to be submitted each year to a government commission for validation. Students also may apply for public or private loans, but this still constitutes a small portion of student assistance. Other forms of student assistance include subsidized meals in student cafeterias, low-cost housing, health insurance, low-cost travel, and tax deductions for those supporting a student.

Student Social Background and Access to Education

Under the French constitution, the nation guarantees all students equal access to education and training. The establishment of a free, secular, public education system is the duty of the state. Despite some progress, however, access to education is not yet equal. Although blue-collar workers constitute some 38 percent of the population, only 11.6 percent of students in IUTs and universities belonged to this group in 1973–74. On the other hand, children of professionals, who constitute only about 5 percent of the economically active population, constituted 30.2 percent of enrollment (*Journal officiel,* August 10, 1974).

Socioeconomic background is often also reflected in the choice of field of study. Children of professionals are likely to be enrolled in the *grandes écoles* and in medical study, while children of blue-collar workers are found in the IUTs or technical training.

Women were relative latecomers in French education. They were admitted to universities in 1885; but due to the lack of secondary school facilities for women, few women were able to attend the universities. By 1937 complete equality of programs for male and female students was achieved in secondary schools. In the mid 1970s, more than half of the student body in institutions of higher education are females. Women also constitute close to 50 percent of university enrollments but tend to congregate in traditionally female-dominated specialties such as humanities (65.84 percent of enrollment). Women constitute only 16 percent of enrollments at IUTs and 30 percent in medicine and sciences. The famous *Ecole polytechnique* was finally opened to women in 1972.

There has been a continuous increase in the number of foreign students in France. About 75,000 foreign students attended French universities in 1975, mainly from Africa and the mideast.

Despite the role of the students in the 1968 reforms, French student associations are weak and mainly organized according to political parties. The former *Union nationale des étudiants de France* (UNEF: National French Student Union) has split into two factions: *UNEF—ex-Renouveau* (renewal), with a traditional communist ideology; and *UNEF—Unité syndicale* (federative unity), which is influenced by Trotskyism. A third student organization is the moderate *Fédération nationale des étudiants français* (FNEF: National Federation of French Students).

Teaching Staff

Teachers and research workers in French institutions of higher education and research establishments are ranked as professors, *maîtres de conférences* (senior lecturers), *maîtres-assistants* (lecturers), and assistants. There are also temporary assistants and other special staff such as *chargés de cours, chargés d'enseignement,* and *moniteurs,* who are usually employed on contract for a specific time.

Professors are appointed by the president of the republic on recommendation of the university council and the Consultative Committee of Universities. Their teaching duties generally do not exceed three hours a week; their main responsibility is supervision of teaching and research within a UER (which entails substantial administrative duties).

Professors are assisted in their teaching duties by the *maîtres de conférences,* while smaller classes and laboratory sessions are supervised by the *maîtres-assistants* and assistants.

The *maîtres de conférences* are appointed by the secretary of state for universities. Professors and *maîtres de conférences* are required to have the *doctorat d'état* degree and to be included on a national list of eligible candidates. They are considered senior staff and are eligible for election to the highest administrative positions within the university.

Maîtres-assistants are employed as trainees and later permanently appointed by the secretary of state for universities from an aptitude list on the recommendation of the Consultative Committee of Universities. Appointment procedures are different in the fields of law, economics, and medicine, in which a competitive examination—the *agrégation de l'enseignement supérieur*—is required in lieu of the *doctorat.*

All permanent staff are civil servants; their salaries are determined by the government.

Research Activities

Research is an integral part of the modern French universities. Most of the nation's basic research is undertaken at the universities, the *grandes écoles,* the so-called *grands établissements (Collège de France, Observatoire de Paris, Muséum national d'histoire naturelle,* and others), and the *Centre national de la recherche scientifique* (CNRS: National Center for Scientific Research). These institutions receive their funding from the state.

Most other public research involves applied research. The *Commissariat à l'énergie atomique* (CEA: Atomic Energy Commission), the *Institut national de la santé et de la recherche médicale* (INSERM: National Institute for Health and Medical Research), the *Institut national de recherche agronomique* (INRA: National Institute for Agronomic Research), and the *Centre national d'études spatiales* (CNES: National Center for Space Studies) form the applied sector of the government research establishments. Some 45,000 research workers are employed in the public research organizations.

CNRS was founded in 1939 to promote basic research and research training in the universities. In the 1970s more emphasis is being accorded applied research. The *Agence nationale pour la valorisation de la recherche* (ANVAR: National Agency for the Promotion of Research) was created in 1966 to bridge the gap between government-sponsored basic research and the needs of industry.

Over 60 percent of all research in France (including military research) is funded by the state. Research planning is coordinated through the Committee of Ministers for Scientific and Technical Research. The prime minister presides over the committee, which is assisted by an Advisory Committee for Scientific and Technical Research, composed of twelve noted scientists. Both committees are served by the same secretariat: *Délégation générale à la recherche scientifique et technique* (DGRST: General Delegation for Scientific and Technical Research). Funding for public research has declined since the late 1960s. Government appropriations for public research amounted to 2.2 percent of the gross national product in 1967 and had decreased to 1.5 percent in 1975.

Current Problems and Trends

The problems leading to the 1968 student unrest—the overcrowding in the universities; the high failure rates; the lack of student and faculty participation in decision making; the centralization of the whole higher education system under the Ministry of National Education in Paris, with little attention paid to regional diversity and problems—were symptoms of the inability of the traditional French university system to cope with mass education. The 1968 reforms emphasized autonomy of the individual universities, participation of faculty and students in decision making, and interdisciplinary study. Decentralization efforts have given each university and the UERs greater internal autonomy; fiscal autonomy has also increased as a result of the allocation of bulk grants to universities rather than grants to individual faculties. Although student participation in the administration bodies of the universities and the UERs has not been as successful as expected, some progress has been made. However, the concept of interdisciplinary programs has fared less well. Going against the whole French university tradition, the breakup of the faculties into UERs at first seemed to afford opportunities for interdisciplinary study, but later the UERs again grouped themselves into universities much in the style of the former faculties.

In the mid 1970s many of the problems encountered in 1968 are still plaguing the French higher education system. University enrollments continue to increase: from 734,000 in 1972 to 765,000 in 1975. Furthermore, enrollments continue to favor the humanities, which in 1975 enrolled 409,000 students against 323,000 students in sciences. Employment opportunities in science-related fields are good, but enrollments have been declining: in 1974, only 23,000 students entered science study. The IUTs also have not yet reached capacity. On the other hand, teaching positions (major source of employment for humanities graduates) have decreased for a number of years. In 1975, only sixteen hundred positions were open for graduates with the *agrégation* and five thousand for graduates of the CAPES, the two national competitive teacher recruitment examinations. The enrollment increases have been coupled with government financial austerity, and thus a number of expansions and new programs previously envisioned have not been implemented.

Government efforts to introduce some form of guidance to orient students to areas of study offering employment opportunities have met with great resistance from French students, who treasure their academic freedom; other government changes that have also met with great resistance are a change in the second cycle of study that would place greater emphasis on cooperation with industry; a reorganization of the teacher training program to better reflect employment realities; a simplification of the professional ranks at the universities to include only two ranks: *professeur* and *maître-assistant*.

The new degree programs were slated to go into effect in 1977; however, serious student protests and strikes in the spring of 1976 may effect their implementation.

Relationship with Industry

The *grandes écoles,* which supply industry with high-level engineers, researchers, and administrators, have always had a close working relationship with industry. The universities, on the other hand, which have emphasized cultural transmission and the training of medical doctors, pharmacists, lawyers, and secondary school teachers, have had little contact with industry. Mass higher education and the oversupply of arts graduates, with attendant unemployment, is expected to change the emphasis in university education from humanities to technological training. In many universities new technological training programs have been created, which can lead to the *diplôme d'ingénieur*. Introduction of work-study programs *(enseignement alterné)* as a component of the program for the *maîtrise* is promoted by the government. Another example of the new emphasis is the *Université technologique de Compiègne*, which is closely integrated with industrial demands; it includes experts from industry on its council and on its teaching staff; its curriculum is geared to national manpower needs. A second such university is being planned at Metz. An additional area of cooperation with industry is the IUT, where practicing professionals make up much of the teaching staff.

Cuts in the government's research grants to universities have led to closer cooperation between universities and industry in the form of research contracts. In the mid 1970s there is thus a move away from the traditional distance between the French university and industry.

International Cooperation

France is providing extensive educational assistance to other countries, especially North African Arabic nations and the former French colonies in Africa. The assistance is generally based upon bilateral agreements and takes many forms: funding for operating expenses, capital expenditure, teaching staff, and student scholarships. A major cooperative effort is the research assistance extended by the *Office de la recherche scientifique et technique outre-mer* (ORSTOM: Overseas Office of Scientific and Technical Research), which extends research assistance to French-speaking tropical nations. In 1974–75 France also hosted 75,000 foreign students, who comprised 10 percent of total university enrollments that year.

The Department of Cooperation within the Ministry of Education is in charge of relations with international organizations, student and staff exchanges, and recruitment of personnel to be seconded abroad as technical assistants. In 1974 some 32,000 teachers and 11,000 technical assistants were assigned to foreign countries at a cost of two and a half billion francs *(France,* December 1974, p. 8).

France is cooperating in all major European organizations concerned with education, especially the Council of Europe and the Organisation for Economic Cooperation and Development (OECD), in matters of educational research and planning and the mobility of academic staff. Greater cooperation in the area of employment of academic staff has been under way since the 1968 Orientation of Higher Education Act and the passage of an order of April 28, 1972, allowing the appointment in France of foreign teachers as professors and *maîtres de conférences (Mobility of University Staff,* 1973, p. 66).

France has been and still is making a major effort to promote the French language and French culture abroad. In addition to university cooperation through technical and other assistance, France also contributes to other levels of education: primary and secondary school teachers are seconded by the government, and extensive adult education services are prompted.

Overseas institutes for the dissemination of the French language and culture are operated by French organizations such as the *Alliance française* or are run in cooperation with the host country. Over 1200 such centers are operating in ninety countries enrolling close to 300,000 foreigners in the study of French *(France,* December 1974, p. 8). Some of these centers contribute important services to the host nation's higher education system. An example is Haiti, where the French institute has contributed greatly to higher education.

As a result of the French cultural effort, foreign assistance is extended and students are invited to France. Reverse cooperation is less active; while 3500 students from the United States studied in France in 1973, only 1700 French students attended higher education institutions in the United States, and lesser numbers attended higher education institutions in other foreign countries.

[Assistance received from Frédéric Gaussen, Editor-in-Chief, *Le monde de l'éducation,* Paris.]

BERNARD VEYRET

Educational Associations

Syndicat national de l'enseignement supérieur (SNE-Sup.)
78 rue du Faubourg Saint-Denis
75010 Paris, France

Fédération nationale des syndicats autonomes de l'enseignement supérieur
18 rue du docteur Roux
75015 Paris, France

Syndicat général de l'éducation nationale (SGEN-CFDT)
5, rue Mayran
75009 Paris, France

Union nationale des étudiants de France (UNEF—ex-Renouveau)
1 rue de Provence
75009 Paris, France

Union nationale des étudiants de France (UNEF—Unité syndicale)
8 rue de Hanovre
75002 Paris, France

Bibliography

de l'Ain, G. B., and others. *L'enseignement supérieur en alternance. Actes du Colloque national de Rennes.* Paris: La documentation française, 1974.

Burn, B. *Higher Education in Nine Countries.* New York: McGraw-Hill, 1971.

Chevallier, J. *L'enseignement supérieur.* Paris: Presses universitaires de France, 1971.

"Les étudiants. Effectifs des étudiants dans les universités. Année scolaire 1973–1974." In *Statistiques des enseignements.* Vanves: Service central des statistiques et sondages, 1975.

France. New York: Press and Information Division, French Embassy, published monthly or semimonthly.

French Universities. New York: Cultural Services of the French Embassy, January 1975.

Higher Education in France. New York: Cultural Services of the French Embassy, 1975.

Le Bris, R. F. "Egalitarisme ou élitisme dans la système française d'éducation supérieure." In P. G. Altbach (Ed.), *The University's Response to Societal Demands.* New York: Inter-

national Council for Educational Development, 1975.

Mobility of University Staff. Strasbourg: Council for Cultural Co-operation, 1973.

Patterson, M. "French University Reform: Renaissance or Restoration?" *Comparative Education Review,* June 1972, 281–302.

La recherche scientifique et technique en France. Paris: La documentation française, June-July 1967.

Reviews of National Policies for Education: France. Paris: Organisation for Economic Co-operation and Development, 1971.

Tableaux de l'éducation nationale. Paris: Ministère de l'éducation nationale, Service d'informations économiques et statistiques, 1975.

See also: Academies; Adult Education: Elderly, Programs for the, Role of Labor and Industry; Agriculture in Higher Education: Early History of Agricultural Education; Aid to Other Nations: Colonial Policies and Practices; Archives: France, National Archives of; Cooperative Education and Off-Campus Experience: Cooperative Education Worldwide; Courts and Higher Education; Equivalences; Graduate and Professional Education: General History and Contemporary Survey; History of Higher Education; Independent Study; Internationalization of Higher Education; Libraries: Bibliothèque Nationale; Library Administration Outside the United States; Research: History, Purpose, and Organization of Academic Research; Financing and Control of Research; Short-Cycle Education; Science Policies: Highly Industrialized Nations: Western Europe; Structures in Postsecondary Education; Towns, University; Unrest, Campus; Western Europe and the United Kingdom: Regional Analysis.

FRINGE BENEFITS

See Remuneration: Faculty, Staff, and Chief Executive Officers.

FROM ISOLATION TO MAINSTREAM: PROBLEMS OF THE COLLEGES FOUNDED FOR NEGROES (Higher Education Report), United States

From Isolation to Mainstream: Problems of the Colleges Founded for Negroes (New York: McGraw-Hill, February 1971), a report of the Carnegie Commission on Higher Education, examines the changing role of black colleges in the United States and the problems they face as they compete with other higher education institutions for students, faculty, and financial assistance. The following findings and recommendations are reported.

Historically, the 105 black colleges provided the only education available to the nation's black minority. Since the desegregation legislation of the mid 1950s, opportunities for black students and faculty have increased in more colleges throughout the country. While black colleges will serve a decreasing proportion of the total black student enrollment in higher education, their total enrollment may double as early as 1980. To be competitive, black colleges must increase their enrollment capacities and expand educational programs. The commission recommends a comprehensive undergraduate curriculum that emphasizes preprofessional fields, preparation for advanced education, and training for high-demand occupations. Adult education programs should be expanded, and Afro-American studies programs at selected black colleges should be strengthened.

Black colleges should also improve their compensatory education programs to better serve those students subject to prior educational deprivation. The commission recommends that the federal government establish regional centers for research and teacher training in compensatory education. Efforts should also be made to increase the salary of faculty in black colleges and to enlarge the pool of black faculty available to all institutions of higher education.

Inadequate financial resources have restricted the development of black colleges. In addition to subsidizing a large number of students from low-income families, black colleges have had to meet the high costs of compensatory education programs while receiving proportionately lower amounts of public monies. The states must rectify this imbalance. The financial status of black colleges will also improve if several programs recommended by the commission in other reports are adopted. The programs

call for increased federal spending for construction grants, library expansion, educational opportunity grants, and work-study programs. The commission recommends the development of a federal agency, within the proposed National Foundation for the Development of Higher Education, to oversee the development of black colleges.

Black colleges are national assets whose emergence into fully competitive institutions of higher education should be encouraged by public and private support.

FROOMKIN REPORT
See Post-Secondary Education, A Study To Identify the Trends in the Sources of Support for (Higher Education Report), United States.

FUND RAISING
See Alumni Affairs; Developmental, College and University

FURTHER EDUCATION

Further education is a term used predominantly in England and Wales which usually refers to all postsecondary school education except higher education. It is, however an administrative term as some colleges of further education offer programs at a degree level considered higher education. In the mid-1970s some 7200 establishments were offering further education; the number and type of schools can be broken down as follows: (1) thirty polytechnics providing a comprehensive but mainly higher-level education, including first and higher degrees; (2) about 110 colleges of art, some of which were merging with colleges of commerce and technology to form polytechnics; (3) over forty agricultural colleges and institutes; (4) about 470 technical colleges, colleges of commerce, and further education colleges, which often overlap with secondary schools for the sixteen-to-eighteen-year age group but also offer advanced courses below the degree and higher diploma level; (5) national colleges for particular skills in certain industries such as leather technology, agricultural engineering, and food technology (six of the eight schools in this category have merged with universities or polytechnics or attained independent status); (6) about 6500 evening institutes offering educational and recreational courses.

Since the early 1970s further education has been undergoing much change and realignment. A white paper *(Education: A Framework for Expansion,* 1972) sketched a growth program for all education over the 1971–1981 decade. During this period polytechnics are expected to double their full-time and part-time aggregate from 90,000 to 180,000 students, but in 1972–73 low increase figures suggested that the aggregate in 1981–82 may produce less than half the increase projected.

Polytechnics were set up after a government white paper *(A Plan for Polytechnics and Other Colleges,* 1966) that announced their inauguration as "the main centers of full-time and higher education within the further education system." However, they were to retain a comprehensive function in that they could provide for subdegree work leading to a high-level national diploma, and students could attend part time or full time. They were not to be new custom-built institutions but existing colleges upgraded, extended, and linked together under one governing body to form one academic institution. Thus, colleges of art, commerce, and technology could form a new polytechnic, and four, five, or more establishments, often miles apart in the same city or in neighboring towns, could be grouped into a putatively unitary administrative structure.

Since the polytechnics are essentially regional institutions, with local authorities forming the governing committees and with a vocational or applied emphasis allied to career outlets in industry and commerce, they are regarded as primarily teaching institutions, with research of smaller importance. The pull to be like universities in style, government, financing, and educational purpose is there, however; and the master's degree courses offered by some point up the way many of the polytechnics would like to go.

In 1970 nearly 200,000 students were taking full-time and part-time qualifications of all kinds in all institutions of further education; of these nearly 36,000 or 18 percent were taking degrees, and of these degree students 28,000 were in polytechnics. About 5 percent were studying for higher degrees. Of all full-time courses in further education, over 70 percent are given in polytechnics; and the proportion continues to grow. The number of nonadvanced courses in polytechnics, despite the comprehensive function, has dropped by over 50 percent since 1969. High-level nondegree courses like the Higher National Diplomas, whether in technology or business studies, are fairly evenly split between the polytechnics and other colleges of further education.

Students in the polytechnics, even more than those in the universities, have been neglecting courses in applied science and technology. Social sciences, business studies, law, art, and the humanities are the new lifesavers for the polytechnics, which were originally intended to build on what technical education had achieved.

In 1964 a nonuniversity body called the Council for National Academic Awards (CNAA) was set up by Royal Charter and given the power to award recognized degrees and diplomas of any kind, up to and including higher doctorates, subject to academic scrutiny and approval of courses, staff, and equipment by expert boards. Up to 1964 only universities could confer degrees, and in Great Britain degrees are jealously guarded; diplomas or certificates are considered lower awards. Regional advisory committees coordinate the arrangements for courses in further education. Thus, at one end of the broad spectrum, one sees further education in the process of edging into the university sector of higher education through the polytechnics, while the colleges of education are being edged out of higher education into further education; at the other end, colleges of further education are overlapping with the secondary schools.

Another branch of further education, called adult education, is usually liberal/vocational and postexperience (Corresponding to extension studies in the United States, it usually operates through university extramural departments, bodies like the Workers Educational Association, and evening institutes. Nearly all these extension courses are part time *(Adult Education: A Plan for Development,* 1973). Increasing emphasis on lifelong education, permanent education, or continuing education is raising new possibilities of educational life patterns for adults that could be of high significance for further education.

The fluidity of further education in England and Wales reflects a concern for the broad mass of the people from age sixteen onward, after full-time schooling. Higher education at degree, postgraduate, and research levels is taken care of in universities: full-time, high-level specialist education from diploma up to degree level is handled in polytechnics and colleges of education. The need for both full-time and part-time study at lower levels and for courses not aimed at specific qualifications is increasingly being found in other establishments of further education. In capital planning and recurrent expenditure, the universities use national funds filtered through the University Grants Committee. The polytechnics, differently financed, have their eye on this liberal planning organization as a model for themselves.

Bibliography

Adult Education: A Plan for Development (the Russell Report). London: H. M. Stationery Office, 1973.

A Plan for Polytechnics and Other Colleges. Cmnd. 3006. London: H. M. Stationery Office, 1966.

Education: A Framework for Expansion. Cmnd. 5174. London: H. M. Stationery Office, 1972.

W. A. CAMPBELL STEWART

See also: United Kingdom.